WHERE
TO
FISH
1994-1995

84th EDITION

EDITED BY
D. A. ORTON

THOMAS HARMSWORTH PUBLISHING
COMPANY

84th Edition published 1994 by
Thomas Harmsworth Publishing Company
Old Rectory Offices
Stoke Abbott
Beaminster
Dorset DT8 3JT
United Kingdom

© 1994 Thomas Harmsworth Publishing Company
ISBN 0-948807-18-0

British Cataloguing in Publication Data
Where to fish.1994-1995
1. Fishing-Great Britain-Directories
799.1'025'41   SH605
ISBN 0 948807-18-0

Printed in Great Britain by
Bookcraft (Bath) Ltd.

5 PALL MALL, LONDON, S.W.1.
Telephone: 071-839 2423

Open till 6 p.m. weekdays and 4 p.m. Saturdays

Only 3 minutes walk from Piccadilly Circus & Trafalgar Square

Until you can visit us, our full colour catalogue will give you a glimpse of what is in store
Free on request

CONTENTS

Abbreviations: The following abbreviations are used throughout the book: S, salmon; T, trout; MT, migratory trout, NT, non-migratory trout; C, char; FF or FW, freshwater (ie coarse fish); RD, River Division (or its equivalent); s, season; m, month (National Rivers Authority list only); f, fortnight; w, week; d, day; t, ticket; ns, nearest railway station. In the list of fishing stations the abbreviation m means mile or miles, except when it is used in conjunction with t, ie, mt, when it means monthly ticket. Likewise, st means season ticket, wt weekly ticket, dt daily ticket, and so on.

BACK TOWARDS SQUARE ONE?

The salient fact reflected in the text of the previous edition of **Where to Fish** - 1992-1993 - was the newly-established uniformity of fishing licences for fishing in England and Wales.
£12.50 throughout the entire area, covering all species of freshwater fish, salmon and sea trout included. There was a discounted rate for pensioners, registered disabled and juveniles of £6.50.

There were grave doubts among the wiser and more experienced among us as to whether the National Rivers Authority had done its financial forecasting with sufficient sobriety; a feeling that the arithmetic had been done during a day trip to Cloud Cuckoo Land.

That feeling was embodied in the 1992-1993 leading article. Sometimes the natural pleasure in saying 'I told you so' is a wry one. It is now. Nevertheless, the news now to be given could have been less palatable and very nearly was so. Those who fish for salmon and sea trout could have been faced, in addition to their other very considerable expenses, by a £75 licence fee wherever they fished in England or Wales, and came within a whisker of that fate as the debate surged to and fro.

But the outcome was less drastic: £45 for a full season's licence, moderated by sense and reason for those who fish infrequently to £13.50 for an 8-day licence or £4.50 for a single day. On the full season's licence there is a reduced rate for pensioners, registered disabled and young people in the 12-16 year old age bracket of £22.50. As before, children under 12 years of age do not require a licence to fish.

For adults and adolescents fishing for non-migratory trout, coarse fish and eels, the full season's licence is now priced at £15, with concessional licence at £7.50 for the three already-named categories of beneficiary. There are also 8-day and 24-hour licences at £4.50 and £1.50 respectively. The rise in price of trout and coarse fish licences is - give or take the odd percentage point - in line with inflation.

The item of real value which remains undisturbed is the universality of the arrangements throughout England and Wales. With most of the dust raised by the radicality of the changes introduced in 1992 now settled, there should not be any serious difficulty in obtaining licences from the traditional sources, fishing tackle shops included.

Anglers must remember, though, that to fish without an appropriate licence is an offence against the law; also that the licence alone does not confer the right to fish. It merely authorises the holder to be present with fishing tackle in use or ready for use beside or on a water where permission to fish has been granted by the riparian owner or some other person lawfully entitled to give such permission on the owner's behalf.

Licences remain a national matter throughout the regions administered by the National Rivers Authority, but not seasons, size and bag limits, methods, restrictions, etc. For details of these, **Where to Fish** continues to serve its traditional and unique purpose. Turn to pages 14-19 for details.

FISHERY AGENTS

ENGLAND

Harris & Stokes, 125 Eign Street, Hereford HR4 0AJ (0432-354455). Some 500 rods to let each season on the Wye, Usk and other rivers.

Hatton Fishing Tackle, 64 St Owen Street, Hereford (0432 272317). Up-to-the-minute information on fishing on Wye and Lugg.

Sale & Partners, 18-20 Glendale Road, Wooler, Northumberland (Tel: 0668 81611, Fax: 0668 81113).

Knight Frank & Rutley, 20 Hanover Square, London W1R 0AH (071-629 8171).

Rod Box, London Road, Kingsworthy, Winchester, Hants (0962 883600). Day or season lettings on some of finest dry fly, chalk stream fishing. Salmon, sea trout fishing in Scotland, Norway, and Alaska.

Savills, 20 Grosvenor Hill, Berkeley Square, London, W1X 0HQ (071-499 8644).

Strutt & Parker, 13 Hill Street, Berkeley Square, London, W1X 8DL (Tel: 071-629 7282, fax 071 499 1657, telex: 8955508 STRUTT G).

WALES

Knight Frank & Rutley, 14 Broad Street, Hereford, HR4 9AL (0432-273087).

Woosnam and Tyler, Dolgarreg, North Road, Builth Wells, Powys, LD2 3DD. Salmon fishing on Wye, Usk and tributaries. By the day or week (0982-553248).

SCOTLAND

Bell-Ingram, Durn, Isla Rd, Perth PH2 7HF (0738-21121). Deveron, Cassley, Dee, etc.

Forrest & Son, 35 The Square, Kelso (Tel: 224687, Fax: 224687). For Tweed and Teviot (Kelso AA trout fisheries), and Makerstoun, trout only.

Knight, Frank & Rutley, 2 North Charlotte Street, Edinburgh EH2 4HR (031 225 7105).

J H Leeming, Stichill House, Kelso, Roxburghshire TD5 7TB (Tel: 0573 470280, Fax: 0573 470259, fax inf serv: 0573 470322). River Tweed.

Lovat Estate, Beauly, Inverness (782205).

Mrs J Atkinson, 8 Sinclair Street, Thurso (0847 62824). Halladale and Naver Rivers; trout fishing on lochs in Caithness and Sutherland.

Thurso Fisheries Ltd, Thurso East, Thurso, Caithness (Thurso 63134). River Thurso.

FISHING HOLIDAY AGENTS

Anglers Abroad, 14 High Street, Wombwell, Barnsley, S Yorks S73 0AA, Tel: 0226 751704.

Arthur Oglesby, 4 Barker Lane, York YO1 1JR, Tel: 0904 627234, Fax: 0904 613101. Host to parties on such rivers as the Beauly in Scotland, Orkla in Norway, Alagnak in Alaska and the Ranga in Iceland.

Cast Away, Irish Angling Holidays, Irish Travel Bureau, 49 Old Hall Road, Sale, Manchester, M33 2HY, Tel: 061 976 3887.

Clifford Smart's Angling Holidays, 29 Bridle Road, Burton Latimer, Northants NN15 5QP, Tel: 0536 725453/724226. Fax: 0536 726481. Holidays in Northern and Southern Ireland, Denmark, Holland. Coarse, game and sea.

Kings Angling Holidays, 27 Minster Way, Hornchurch, Essex RM11 3TH, Tel: 0708 453043.

OVERSEAS TOUR PROMOTERS

Hunt Travel Ltd., Worth Corner, Turners Hill Road, Pound Hill, Crawley, West Sussex RH10 4SL. Tel: 0293 882609. Fax: 0293 886982.

Nimrod Safaris Ltd., Water Eaton, Cricklade, Wiltshire SN6 6JU. Tel: 0285 810132. Fax: 0285 810693.

Pemba Channel Fishing Club, P O Box 34, Shimoni via Msambweni, Kenya.

Tasmania, Tasmanian Travel Centre, 80 Elizabeth St, Hobart, Tasmania 7000, Australia.

BRITISH FISH FARMS

Anna Valley Trout Farm Ltd, Andover, Hants (0264 710382).
Berkshire Trout Farm, Hungerford, Berkshire, RG17 0UN. (Tel: 0488-682520, Fax: 0488 685002) *(see advt).*
Bibury Trout Farm, Bibury, near Cirencester, Gloucestershire. Rainbow and brown trout bred on Coln. (Tel: 028574 0212/215, Fax: 0285 740392). Catch Your Own fishery on R Coln. *(see advt).*
Chirk Fishery Co Ltd, Chirk, Wrexham, Clwyd LL14 5BL. Brown, brook and rainbow trout; ova, fry, yearlings and two-year-olds. (069 186 2420).
Clearwater Fish Farm, East Hendred, Wantage, Oxon (Tel: 0235 833732, Fax: 0235 835586).
Exe Valley Fishery Ltd, Exbridge, Dulverton, Somerset, TA22 9AY. Rainbow trout available. (Tel: 0398 23328, Fax: 0398 24079).
Glenaray Fish Farm, Low Balantyre, Inveraray PA32 8XJ. Brown and rainbow trout. Separate bait and fly lochans. (0499 2233).
Hooke Springs Trout Farm, The Mill House, Hooke, Beaminster, Dorset. Brown and rainbow trout. (0308 862553).
Howietoun Fishery, Sauchieburn, Bannockburn, Stirling. Brown trout. Salmon and Sea Trout - Eggs, Ova, Fry and Smolts. (Bannockburn 0786 812473).
Kilnsey Park Trout Farm, Kilnsey, Skipton, North Yorkshire (0756 752150).
Loch Levern Fishery, Kinross Estates Office, Kinross. Trout. (Kinross 863407).
Ludworth Trout Farm, Marple Bridge, Cheshire SK6 5NS (061 449 9520).
Nettesheim Fish Farm, Lake Mochdre, Newtown, Powys (0686 25623).
The Solway Fishery, New Abbey, Dumfries. Brown and brook trout. (038785 235).
Stambridge Starr Fisheries, Stambridge Road, Great Stambridge, near Rochford, Essex. King carp, grass carp and tench; rainbow trout. (Canewdon 274).
Trent Fish Culture Co Ltd, Mercaston, Ashbourne, Derbyshire DE6 3BL. Brown, Rainbow and American brook trout. Ova, fry, yearlings and two-year-olds to 13in; larger fish on application. (0335-60318).
Upper Mills Trout Farm, Glyn Ceiriog, Llangollen, Clwyd (0691 718225).
Watermill Trout Farms Ltd, Welton Springs, Louth, Lincs LN11 0QT. Brown and rainbow trout. (Tel: 0507 602524, Fax: 0507 600592, Telex: 56528).
Welham Park Trout Farms Ltd, Malton, Yorkshire YO19 9DU. Brown and Loch Leven trout. (Tel & Fax: 0751 474200)*(see advt).*
Weir House Trout Farms Ltd, Latimer Road, Chesham, Bucks (0494 775954).
Westacre Trout Farm, King's Lynn, Norfolk. Brown and rainbow trout for immediate delivery. (0760 755 240).
Wye Valley Fisheries, Tyn-y-Cwm Trout Farm, Beulah, Llanwrtyd Wells, Powys. Rainbow trout. (Langammarch Wells 244).

Further information about **British Fish Farms** can be had from **British Trout Farmers' Restocking Association,** Secretary, A Darbyshire, Sinnington Trout, York YO6 6RB, tel & Fax: 0751 31948; **British Trout Association Ltd,** P O Box 2, Clitheroe BB7 3ED or from **British Trout Information Bureau,** P O Box 189, London SW6 7UT, Tel: 071 385 1158, Fax: 071 381 9620.

FISHING SCHOOLS AND COURSES

A.P.G.A.I. (Association of Professional Game Angling Instructors), Little Saxby's Farm, Cowden, Kent TN8 7DN Tel: 0342 850765, Fax: 0342 850926. The Association has approximately 80 members both in the UK and abroad offering a range of tuition from simple casting lessons to full residential courses. Members can be contacted through the Association.

Charles Bingham, West Down, Whitchurch, Tavistock, Devon PL19 9LD. Wild brown trout, sea trout and salmon on Dartmoor rivers. Also stillwater trout.

Elite School of Game Angling, New Farm Cottage, Mansell Gamage, Hereford. Trout and salmon on Rivers Wye and Monnow.

Fishing Breaks Ltd, Simon Cooper, 16 Bickerton Rd, Upper Holloway, London N19 5JR. Stillwater and chalkstream trout (R Test).

Half Stone Sporting Agency, Roddy Rae, 6 Hescane Park, Cheriton Bishop, Exeter EX6 6JP. Brown trout, sea trout and salmon on Teign and Exe.

J.M.M. Killorglin Ltd, J Pembroke and P O'Reilly, Ardlahas, Killorglin, Co Kerry, Eire. Sea trout and salmon on Rivers Laune and Caragh, and Caragh Lake. Also Lough Currane.

Parkburn Guest House, High Street, Grantown on Spey, Scotland. Sea trout and salmon on River Spey.

Wessex Fly Fishing School, Southover, Tolpuddle, Dorchester, Dorset DT2 7HF. Tel: 0305 848460. Chalk-stream fishing for trout on Rivers Piddle and Frome.

West Wales School of Fly Fishing, Pat O'Reilly, Ffoshelyg, Lancych, Boncath, Dyfed SA37 0LJ. Sea trout and salmon on Rivers Teifi, Cych and Gwili.

(All the above are REFFIS Approved Fly Fishing Schools, and may be contacted through Wessex Fly Fishing School.)

Arthur Oglesby, 4 Barker Lane, York YO1 1JR, Tel: 0904 627234, Fax: 0904 613101.

The Arundell Arms, Lifton, Devon PL16 0AA. Tel: 0566 784666, Fax: 0566 784494. A full range of residential courses from beginners' to advanced. Private tuition also offered.

School of Casting, Salmon & Trout Fishing, Michael and Margaret Waller, Station House, Clovenfords, Galashiels, Selkirkshire TD1 3LU. Tel: 089685 293. Brown trout, sea trout and salmon on River Tweed and other waters in area; also Rivers Glass and Farrar in Inverness-shire, together with lochs in area.

Seafield Lodge Hotel, Alasdair Buchanan, Grantown on Spey, Moray PH26 3JN. Tel: 0479 872152. Fax: 0479 872340. Access to seven miles of Association water.

A sport for the young.

NY   Northumbria and Yorkshire Region NRA
NW   North West Region NRA
S-T   Severn-Trent Region NRA
Wales   Welsh Region NRA
A   Anglian Region NRA
T   Thames Region NRA
S   Southern Region NRA
SW   South Western Region NRA

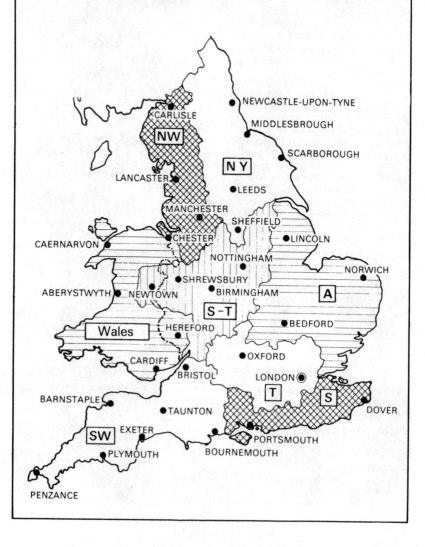

FISHING IN ENGLAND and WALES

NRA structure, close seasons, licence duties etc.

In England and Wales one requires not only a permit issued by the proprietor of a particular fishery, but also a licence issued by the State. The issue of these licences is a duty undertaken by the National Rivers Authority. They use the revenue to help them perform their duties in the general interest of fisheries and fishings in their areas. It is an offence to fish in freshwater without a licence. The burden is on the angler to be correctly informed as to that, and to be sure to comply with the Law. Charges are as follows:

Salmon and Migratory Trout - Full season £45 (concessionary rate £22.50), 8 consecutive days £13.50, Single day £4.50.

Non-migratory Trout, Grayling, Freshwater (coarse) fish and eels - Full season £15 (concessionary rate £7.50), 8 consecutive days £4.50, Single day £1.50.

Concessionary rates are available for retired persons in receipt of State Pension, registered disabled, persons of 12 to 16 years of age (inclusive). There are no concessionary rates for short-term licences.

Anglers are reminded that the expression 'immature' in relation to salmon means that the fish is less than 12in long; taking immature salmon is prohibited throughout England and Wales. In relation to other fish the expression 'immature' means that the fish is of a length less than that prescribed by bye-law. Unless otherwise stated, it may be assumed that the length is measured from the tip of the snout to the fork of the tail.

The word 'salmon' means all fish of the salmon species. The word 'trout' means all fish of the salmon species commonly known as trout. The expression 'migratory trout' means trout that migrate to and from the sea. The expression 'freshwater (ie coarse) fish' means any fish living in fresh water except salmon, trout, all kinds of fish which migrate to and from tidal water, eels and their fry.

NOTE: In the following lists the telephone numbers are given to enable anglers to contact officers outside office hours. This facility is included specifically to enable prompt advice to be given in cases of serious pollution. Anglers are asked to use these numbers with discretion and not to disturb officers in their off-duty hours unnecessarily.

Abbreviations: The following abbreviations are used throughout the book: S, salmon; T, trout; MT, migratory trout, NT, non-migratory trout; C, char; FF or FW, freshwater (ie coarse fish); s, season; m, month (Following list only); f, fortnight; w, week; d, day; t, ticket, ns, nearest railway station. In the lists of fishing stations the abbreviation m means mile or miles, except when it is used in conjunction with t, ie, mt, when it means monthly ticket. Likewise, st means season ticket, wt weekly ticket, dt daily ticket, and so on.

Regions of the National Rivers Authority

SOUTHERN REGION, Guildbourne House, Chatsworth Road, Worthing, Sussex BN11 1LD. (Tel: 0903 820692).
Regional Fisheries Officer: Dr T Owen.

Rivers controlled: Medway, Stour, Rother, RM Canal, Adur, Arun, Ouse, Cuckmere, all rivers in Pevensey Levels, Test, Itchen, Hamble, Meon, Beaulieu, Lymington, Fletch, Keyhaven, Eastern Yar, Medina, and the tributaries of all these rivers.

Divisional offices.
Kent: Kent Fisheries Officer, Medway House, Powder Mill Lane, Leigh, Tonbridge, Kent TN11 9AS. Tel: 0732 838858.
Sussex: Sussex Fisheries Officer, Rivers House, 3 Liverpool Gardens, Worthing BN11 1TF. Tel: 0323 762691.

Pollution reporting: Brighton 606766.

Hampshire/Isle of Wight. Hampshire Fisheries Officer, Sarum Court, Sarum Road, Winchester, Hampshire SO22 5DP. Tel: 0962 713267.

Pollution reporting, outside office hours: Winchester and Isle of Wight, Tel: 0962 713267; Chichester, Tel: 0243 786431; Pevensey, Tel: 0323 762691; Rye, Tel: 0797 223256; Leigh 0732 838858; Canterbury, Tel: 0634 830655. 24 hour emergencies - Freephone: 0800 252676.

Close Seasons: Salmon 3 October-16 January. Sea trout 1 November-1 30 April. Brown trout 1 November-2 April. Coarse fish 15 March-15 June. No close season for rainbow trout in enclosed waters. All close seasons are 'periods between' dates quoted.

SOUTH WESTERN REGION, Headquarters: Manley House, Kestrel Way, Exeter, Devon, EX2 7LQ. (Tel: 0392 444000).
Regional Headquarters: Fisheries, Recreation Conservation and Navigation Manager: E S Bray.

Cornwall Area: Victoria Square, Bodmin, Cornwall. (Tel: 0208 78301).
Fisheries, Recreation and Conservation Manager: B R Letts.
Rivers controlled: Camel, Fowey, Looe, Lynher, Plym, Tamar, Tavy, Yealm and tributaries, including Bude Canal.

Devon Area: Manley House, Kestrel Way, Exeter. (Tel: 0392 444000).
Fisheries, Recreation and Conservation Manager: N A Reader.
Rivers controlled: Avon, Axe, Dart, Erme, Exe, Lyn, Otter, Taw, Teign, Torridge and tributaries, including Exeter and Tiverton Canal.

North Wessex Area: Rivers House, East Quay, Bridgwater, Somerset TA6 4YS. Tel: 0278 457333. Fax: 0278 452985.
Fisheries, Recreation and Conservation Manager: E R Merry.
Rivers controlled: Axe, Bristol Avon, Brue, Parrett and their tributaries, including Tone, Huntspill, King's Sedgemoor Drain and Bridgwater and Taunton Canal.

South Wessex Area: Rivers House, Sunrise Business Park, Higher Shaftsbury Road, Blandford Forum, Dorset DT11 8ST (Tel: 0258 456080).
Rivers controlled: Hampshire Avon and Stour, Frome, Piddle, Brit and Char. (All rivers entering the sea between Lyme Regis and Christchurch).

Rod Seasons:

Devon and Cornwall Areas

Salmon: Avon - 15 April to 30 November (E). Erme - 15 March to 31 October. Axe, Otter, Sid - 15 March to 31 October. Camel - 1 April to 15 December. Dart - 1 February to 30 September. Exe - 14 February to 30 September. Fowey, Looe - 1 April to 15 December. Tamar, Tavy, Lynher - 1 March to 14 October. Plym - 1 April to 15 December. Yealm - 1 April to 15 December. Taw, Torridge - 1 March to 30 September. Lyn - 1 February to 31 October. Teign - 1 February to 30 September. Lim - 1 March to 30 September. Migratory trout: Avon - 15 April to 30 September. Erme - 15 March to 30 September. Axe, Otter, Sid - 15 April to 31 October. Camel, Gannel, Menalhyl, Valency - 1 April to 30 September. Dart - 15 March to 30 September. Exe - 15 March to 30 September. Fowey, Looe, Seaton, Tresillian - 1 April to 30 September. Tamar, Lynher, Plym, Tavy, Yealm - 3 March to 30 September. Taw, Torridge, Lyn - 15 March to 30 September. Teign, Bovey - 15 March to 12 October. Lim - 16 April to 31 October. Brown trout: Camel, Fowey - 1 April to 30 September. Other rivers and streams - 15 March to 30 September. All other waters - 15 March to 12 October. Rainbow Trout and Coarse Fish - entire region - NO CLOSE SEASON.

North and South Wessex Areas

S, Frome and Piddle - 1 March to 31 August. Other rivers - 1 February to 31 August. MT, 15 April to 31 October, NT. Rivers 1 April to 15 October. Reservoirs, lakes and ponds 17 March to 15 October. Rainbow trout - still waters only - no closed season. FF all waters. 16 June to 14 March following year.

NORTH WEST REGION, Richard Fairclough House, Knutsford Road, Warrington WA4 1HG. (Tel: 0925 53999. Fax: 0925 415961).
Principal Fisheries, Recreation, Conservation and Biology Manager: Dr M Diamond
Pollution reporting: Tel: 0925 53999.

North Area
Area Fisheries, Ecology and Recreation Manager: N C Durie, Chertsey Hill, London Road, Carlisle CA1 2QX, Tel: 0228 25151.
Rivers controlled: Esk, Liddel, Lyne, Irthing, Petteril, Wampool, Caldew, Ellen, Derwent, Eamont, Eden, Cocker, Ehen, Irt, Esk, Brathay, Duddon, Crake, Rawthey, Leven, Kent, Keer, Greta, Wenning, and their tributaries. The lakes Derwentwater, Thirlmere, Ullswater, Haweswater, Bassenthwaite, Windermere, Pendlewater, Coniston Water, Esthwaite Water, Grasmere, Rydal Water.

Central Area
Area Fisheries, Ecology and Recreation Manager: Viscount Mills, Lostock House, Holme Road, Bamber Bridge, PR5 6RE, Tel: 0772 39882.
Rivers controlled: Ribble, Hodder, Lune, Wyre, Calder, Crossens, Yarrow, Douglas, Alt and their tributaries.

South Area
Area Fisheries, Ecology and Recreation Manager: A R Lee, Carrington Lane, Sale M33 5NL, 061 973 2237.
Rivers controlled: Roch, Irwell, Tame, Etherow, Mersey, Goyt, Bollin, Dean, Weaver, Dane, Gowey, and their tributaries.

Close seasons: Salmon, 1 November to 31 January, except R. Eden system - 15 October to 14 January. Migratory trout, 16 October to 30 April, except rivers Annas, Bleng, Esk, Mite, Irt, Calder, Ehen and all tributaries - 1 November to 30 April. Trout, 1 October to 14 March. Coarse Fish, 15 March to 15 June (no close season for coarse fish in enclosed waters).

NORTHUMBRIA AND YORKSHIRE REGION, Rivers House, 21 Park Square South, Leeds LS1 2QG.
Northumbria Area
Ecology and Recreation Manager: Godfrey Williams, Tel: 091 213066.

Dales Area
Ecology and Recreation Manager: Dr John Shillcock, Tel: 0904 692296.

South Yorkshire Area
Ecology and Recreation Manager: Dr John Pygott, Tel: 0532 440191.
Rivers controlled: Aln, Coquet, Wansbeck, Blyth, Tyne, Wear, Tees, Swale, Ure, Esk, Derwent, Wharfe, Nidd, Ouse, Aire, Calder, Rother, Don, Dearne and Hull system.

Close seasons: S - 1 November to 31 January. MT - 1 November to 2 April. NT - 1 October to 21 March. FF - statutory for rivers and streams. Stillwaters - no close season.

ANGLIAN REGION, Kingfisher House, Goldhay Way, Orton Goldhay, Peterborough PE2 0ZR. (Tel: 0733 371811).
Regional Fisheries Manager: Andrew Wood.
Regional Recreation, Conservation and Navigation Manager: Peter Barham.

Northern Area: Acqua Harvey Street Lincoln LN1 1TF. (Tel: 0522 513100).
Fisheries, Recreation, Conservation and Navigation Manager: Irven Forbes.

Central Area: Bromholme Lane, Brampton, Huntingdon PE18 8NE. (Tel: 0480 414581).
Fisheries, Recreation, Conservation and Navigation Manager: John Adams.

Eastern Area: Cobham Road, Ipswich, Suffolk IP3 9JE (Tel: 0473 727712).
Fisheries, Recreation, Conservation and Navigation Manager: Dr Jonathan Wortley.

Close Seasons: S and MT 29 September-last day of February. T 30 October-31 March. Rainbow T; no close season on enclosed waters, otherwise 30 October-31 March. FF 15 March-15 June.

Emergencies: A 24 hour service is provided at Regional Headquarters, Tel: 0733 371811.

SEVERN-TRENT REGION, Sapphire East, 550 Streetsbrook Road, Solihull B91 1QT. Tel: 021 711 2324. Fax: 021 711 5824.
Regional Manager, Fisheries, Conservation and Recreation: Dr P Hickley

Severn Area
Area Fisheries, Conservation and Recreation Manager: A S Churchward, Lower Severn Area NRA, Riversmeet House, Newtown Industrial Estate, Northway Lane, Tewkesbury, Glos GL20 7JG. Tel: 0684 850951.
Rivers controlled: Severn, Warwickshire Avon, Teme, and all other tributary streams in the Severn south of Worcester and all other canals and pools. The Authority also owns or rents water on the Avon and Severn.
Area Fisheries, Conservation and Recreation Manager: Dr J V Wooland, Upper Severn Area NRA, Hafren House, Welshpool Road, Shelton, Shrewsbury SY3 8BB. Tel: 0743 272828.
Rivers controlled: Severn and tributaries north of Worcester, Teme, Vyrnwy, Tanet, Banwy, Tern, Roden, Mease, Perry and all other canals and pools.

Trent Area
Area Fisheries, Conservation and Recreation Manager: L M Stark, Lower Trent Area NRA. Trentside Offices, Scarrington Road, West Bridgford, Nottingham NG2 5FA. Tel: 0602 455722.
Rivers controlled: Trent, east of Dove confluence, Soar, Derbyshire Derwent and their tributaries, all canals and pools.
Principal Fisheries Officer: M J Cooper, Upper Trent Area NRA, Sentinel House, Wellington Crescent, Fradley Park, Lichfield, Staffs WS13 8RR. Tel: 0543 444141.
Rivers controlled: Trent west of Dove confluence, Tame, Dove, Manifold, Churnet, Derbyshire Wye and their tributaries, all canals and pools.
Close seasons: Brown trout: 8 October to 17 March inclusive. Rainbow trout: no close season except for Rivers Derwent and Amber, check locally. Salmon: 8 October to 31 January inclusive. Freshwater fish: 15 March to 15 June inclusive.
Pollution reports: Please report any pollution or dead fish to the following Freephone number: 0800 888833.

THAMES REGION, Kings Meadow House, Kings Meadow Road, Reading, RG1 8DQ. Tel: Reading 535000.
Fisheries Manager: Dr J W Banks, Tel: Reading 535502.
Area Fisheries and Conservation Manager (West): Denton House, Iffley Turn, Oxford OX4 4HJ, Tel: 749400. River Thames (source to Hurley); Rivers Churn, Coln, Windrush, Evenlode, Cherwell, Ray, Cole, Ock, Thame, Wye, Oxford Canal; Kennet, Kennet and Avon Canal, Lambourne, Pang, Leach, Enborme.
Area Fisheries and Conservation Manager (North East): J Reeves, The Grange, Cedar House, Crossbrook Street, Waltham Cross, Herts, EN8 8HE. Tel: Waltham Cross 35566. Rivers Lee, Stort, Rib, Ash (Herts), Mimram, Beane and tributaries, Roding, Rom, Beam, Ingrebourne and tributaries, Colne, Colnebrook, Ver, Misbourne, Gade Chess and tributaries. Grand Union Canal. Slough Arm, Paddington Arm.
Area Fisheries and Conservation Manager(South East): Rivers Thames (Wargrave to Yantlet), Loddon, Blackwater, Wey, Mole, Wandle and 5 London tributaries. Canals: Basingstoke and parts of Grand Union and Regents.
River Pollution, Fish Mortality and Disease: Reports by Members of the Public: phone FREEFONE RIVER POLLUTION. This number covers the whole of the Thames Water catchment 24 hours a day, 7 days a week; or phone 0800 252768.

Seasons: Salmon and Trout (excluding rainbow trout): 1 April to 30 September; enclosed waters: 1 April to 29 October. Rainbow trout: 1 April to 30 September (does not apply to enclosed waters). Freshwater fish: 16 June to 14 March.

WELSH REGION, St Mellons Business Park, Cardiff CF3 0LT. (Tel: 0222 770088. Fax 0222 798555).
Regional Fisheries, Conservation and Recreation Officer: W J Ayton.

OPEN SEASONS
Special junior licence, for all species of fish, periods and areas, available to children under

10 years of age, at a cost of £1.

DIVISIONS OF THE AUTHORITY

Dee and Clwyd Area: Shire Hall, Mold, Clwyd. (Tel: 0352 700176).
Fisheries Officer: Dr B P Hodgson.
Rivers controlled: Dee (Welsh) Clwyd, Elwy, Alwen, Alyn, Ceiriog, Ceirw, Lliw, Tryweryn, Twrch, Bala Lake and their feeders.

Gower Area: Glan Tawe, 154 St Helens Road, Swansea, West Glamorgan. (Tel: 0792 645300).
Fisheries Officer: J Lambert.
Rivers controlled: Neath, Afan, Kenfig, Ogmore, Ewenny, Llynfi, Tawe, Afan, Kenfig, Gwendraeth Fawr, Gwendraeth Fach and Loughor.

Gwynedd Area: Highfield House, Priestley Road, Caernarfon, Gwynedd. (Tel: 0286 672247).
Divisional Fisheries Officer: M F Harcup.
Area Fisheries Officer: R A Brassington.
Rivers controlled: Waters in an area bounded by watersheds of rivers (including their tributaries and all lakes) running into the sea between the eastern boundary of the Division's area at Old Gwyrch, Denbighshire, and the southern extremity at Upper Borth, Cardiganshire. The principal rivers are: Dulas, Conway, Lledr, Llugwy (with Lakes Elsi, Crafnant, Cowlyd, Eigiau, Conway, Melynllyn, Dulyn), Aber, Ogwen (with Lakes Anafon, Ogwen, Idwal, Ffynnon, Loer), all waters in Anglesey, Seiont, Gwyrfai, Llyfni (with Lakes Padarn, Cwellyn, Gader, Nantlle), Erch, Soch, Rhydhir, Afon Wen, Dwyfawr, Dwyfach (with Lake Cwmystradlyn), Glaslyn, Dwyryd, Prysor (with Lakes Dinas, Gwynant, Llagi Adar, Trawsfynydd, Gamallt, Morwynion, Cwmorthin), Glyn, Eisingrug (with Lakes Techwyn Isaf, Techwyn Uchaf, Artro, Mawddach, Eden, Wnion (with Lakes Cwm Bychan, Bodlyn, Gwernan, Gregennen), Dysynny, Dovey, Dulas, Twmyn (with Lake Tal-y-Llyn).

Taff/Usk Area: Rivers House, St Mellons Business Park, Cardiff CF3 0LT. (Tel: 0222 770088).
Area Fisheries Officer: D A Bunt.

Rivers controlled: Thaw, Ely, Taff, Rhymney, Usk and tributaries, including Cilienni, Honddu, Yscir, Bran, Cray, Senni, Tarrell, Cynrig, Crawnon, Rhiangoll, Gwryne-fawr, Grwynefechan, Olway, Afon Lwyd and Ebbw and tributary Sirhowy.

West Wales Area: National Rivers Authority, Llys Afon, Hawthorne Rise, Haverfordwest, Dyfed SA61 2BQ. (Tel: 0437 760081).
Divisional Fisheries Officer: A G Harvey.
Area Fisheries, Recreation, Conservation and Navigation Manager: P V Varallo.
District Fisheries, Recreation, Conservation and Navigation Manager: D C Gardner.
Rivers controlled: Towy, Teifi, Taf, Eastern and Western Cleddau, Gwaun, Nevern, Aeron, Clarach, Rheidol, Ystwyth, Wyre, and the tributaries of these rivers.

Wye Area: National Rivers Authority, Hadnock Road, Monmouth, Gwent. (Tel: 0600 772245).
Area Fisheries Officer: P G Hilder.
Rivers controlled: Wye and all rivers and brooks of the Wye watershed including Monnow, Trothy, Lugg, Arrow, Ithon and Irfon.

Seasons. At the time of going to press changes in the seasons were being discussed in the Welsh Region. Please refer to any NRA office in the Region for a free copy of their bye-laws.

A sport for the mature.

ENGLISH FISHING STATIONS

Main catchments are given in alphabetical order, fishing stations listed in mouth to source order, first main river, then tributaries. Where national borders are crossed - e.g. Wye and Border Esk - allocation has been arbitrary. Some small streams have been grouped in counties rather than catchments.

National Rivers Authority rod licences are now required almost everywhere in England and Wales for all freshwater fishing. Details appear on pages 14-19. A list of fishing clubs appears at the end of each national section. 'Free fishing' means only that a riparian owner is reputed to allow fishing without making a charge. It does not imply a right and such information should be checked locally before an attempt to fish is made. All charges shown are exclusive of VAT unless otherwise stated. Reduced charges to juniors, the disabled, pensioners, and in some instances to ladies, are now quite commonplace. In many instances, they are specified. Where they are not, they may nevertheless be in force. If in doubt, ask when booking.

ADUR

(For close seasons, licences, etc, see Southern Region NRA, p15).

Rises SW of Horsham and flows into the English Channel at Shoreham. A coarse fish river of no great reputation, but occasionally provides good sport.

Shoreham (Sussex). Bass, codling, flats, eels, mullet from harbour and shore.

Bramber and **Steyning** (Sussex). Bream, roach, chub, dace, pike and carp. Pulborough AS has 3m from Bramber Bridge upstream to Streatham Old Railway Bridge. On tidal water, low water best. Dt £4 (£2.50, conc). River also has run of sea trout. Dt available from Hyde Square News, Hyde Square, Upper Beeding, or Prime Angling, Brighton Rd, Worthing.

Henfield (Sussex). Roach, bream, perch, chub, dace (mullet good Sept). Henfield AS and Comrades AC have fishing rights on about 8m. No dt. Henfield AS membership £37. Apply hon sec Henfield AS for annual membership.

Shermanbury Place. Stocked coarse fishing lakes, also 1½m of river, with trout. Carp run to 22lb, tench to 6lb, roach over 1lb. St, dt. Lake fishing Summer only. Parking facilities, no night fishing. Phone Partridge Green 710280 for details.

ALDE

(For licences, etc, see Anglian Region NRA, p17)

A small Suffolk stream, rising near Saxmundham and flowing into the North Sea at Orford Haven, 6½m NE of Felixstowe. Coarse fish.

Aldeburgh (Suffolk). Bass, codling, flatfish, etc, can be taken in estuary from jetty and boat; cod and whiting from beach; October and November best months. Hotels: Brudenell, White Lion, Wentworth, East Suffolk *(see also Suffolk, Sea Fishing Stations).*

Snape (Suffolk). River tidal. Roach, dace,

eels above sluice. Fishing free. Other free fishing at Thorpness Mere, nr Leiston. Tackle shop: Saxmundham Angling Centre, Market Place, Saxmundham, tel: 0728 603443: licences; details of local lake fishing for carp, tench, rudd and pike. Hotels: White Hart, Bell.

ALN

(For close seasons, etc, see Northumbrian and Yorkshire Region NRA, p17)

Short Northumberland river, flowing into North Sea at Alnmouth. Trout and sea trout, occasional salmon; usually a late run river.

Alnwick (Northumberland). Aln AA water (owned by the Duke of Northumberland) includes most reaches between Denwick Bridge and Alnmouth Bridge (4 to 5m).

Stocked twice yearly with brown trout. Portion running through grounds at Lesbury House private. Visitors (excl Sundays) mt £40, wt £25, from Murraysport,

Narrowgate, Alnwick, and Leslie Jobson, Tower Showrooms during business hours. Coquet and Till within easy reach.

Hotels: White Swan and Hotspur, Alnwick; Schooner, Alnmouth.

ANCHOLME

(For close seasons, etc, see Anglian Region NRA, p17)

This river, in South Humberside and Lincolnshire, with its tributaries drains about 240 square miles of country. Falls into the Humber at **South Ferriby,** where there is a sluice and tidal lock. The lower part is embanked for about 19 miles and is owned by Anglian Water. The fishing rights are leased to Scunthorpe and District Angling Association. Temporary membership day permits are available from their bailiffs on the bankside or local tackle shop; Dan's, tel: 0724 281877. Match bookings to Mr J R Walker, 24 High St, Messingham, Scunthorpe DN17 3RS. The river is abundantly stocked with coarse fish, especially roach and bream. Winter shoals found mainly at **Brigg** and **Snitterby - Brandy Wharf** areas. Fishing accesses: South Ferriby Sluice, 4m from Barton upon Humber: **Saxby Bridge,** 6m from Barton upon Humber: Broughton, Castlethorpe, **Cadney** and **Hibaldstow Bridges** near Brigg through which town river passes; Brandy Wharf, Snitterby, **Bishop Bridge,** 6m from **Market Rasen.** NRA have constructed disabled fishing stands in Brigg and at Hibaldstow Bridge. At Barton upon Humber are **Barton Broads** (10 acres), dt £3, owner Ainsworth and Fox, Barton Broads, Maltkiln Rd, Barton upon Humber; **Westfield Lakes:** two 15 acre lakes, mixed coarse fish, dt £2 from Westfield Lakes Hotel, Barton upon Humber DN18 5RG, tel: 32315; Hoe Hill Pond, 10 acres, and **Pasture House Fishery,** 20 acres, dt £2 from Mrs K Smith, Barton upon Humber 635119; North Lincolnshire Sailing Club (59 acres), has st £12 from bailiff Mr C C Haddock, Queens Avenue, Barton upon Humber. **Winter Brothers Pond,** East Halton, 21 acre coarse lake, dt £1. Mr Winter, Marsh Lane, East Halton, tel: 0469 40238.

ARUN

(For close seasons, etc, see Southern Region NRA, p15)

Rises on NW border of Sussex, flows past Horsham and enters English Channel at Littlehampton. Noted coarse-fish river, largely controlled by clubs. Some sea trout; May to October.

Littlehampton (Sussex). *See under Sea Fishing Stations.* HQ of Littlehampton and Dist AC is at Arun View Hotel, right by river.

Arundel (Sussex). River tidal and mainly mud-bottomed. Roach and dace run large; bream, perch, pike, chub and occasional sea trout. Bass and mullet taken in fair numbers June, July, August between Ford railway bridge and Arundel, where fishing is free. Leger best method when tide running; trotting down successful in slack water. Victoria AC has 5m of bank north of Arundel town, with roach, dace, bream to 6lb, mullet and bass in summer months. Dt £2 from Black Rabbit, Offham; George and Dragon, Burpham; or Tropicana, 6 Pier Rd, Littlehampton.

Castle Trout Pond, Mill Rd, Arundel, open June to Sept, tel: 0903 8837427. Hotels: Norfolk Arms; Swan; Howards.

Chalk Springs Fishery, Park Bottom, Arundel, West Sussex (BN1 0AA). Four lakes, clear water, stocked with brown and rainbow trout of 2lb and above. Dt £24.50. Part-day £14.50, £14, £19.50. Refreshments, tackle for hire and sale. Tel: 0903 883742.

Amberley (Sussex). Bream, roach, dace, perch, pike, occasional sea trout. Worthing Piscatorial Society, Rother AC and Bognor Freshwater AC (member of Hants and Sussex Anglers Alliance, 24 still water and river fisheries available, some dt) have stretches on the Arun at **Greatham** and **Bury Ferry.** The Central

---

Keep the banks clean

Several clubs have stopped issuing tickets to visitors because of the state of the banks after they have left. Spend a few moments clearing up.

Association of London and Provincial Angling Clubs hold both banks downstream of Houghton Bridge to Stoke Bridge. This area to Stopham involved in Sussex RD improvement scheme. **Pulborough** (Sussex). Pike, bream, roach, chub, dace, sea trout (May 1 - Oct 29, sport improving). Central Association of London and Provincial ACs leases stretch on south bank from railway bridge downstream and course fishing pond at **Epsom,** Surrey: dt from bailiffs. River above Greatham Manor *(see Amberley).* Pulborough and District AS has fishing on the tidal Arun from Pulborough to Greatham Bridge, approx 3m, 1m on **Rother,** 3m on **Adur, Duncans Lake,** Pulborough (good for young anglers) and

6 small lakes near **Ashington,** coarse fish. St £39, conc, from sec S Marshall, 17 Mill Way, Billinghurst. Dt £4 (£2.50 conc) for Adur only, see Bramber and Steyning. At **Wisborough Green** Crawley AS has water; Dt available. At **Horsham** is **Newells Lake,** carp fishery, dt in advance from 040376 424. 4m north of Horsham at Kingsfold is **Wattlehurst Lake** trout fishery. Dt £18 or £12, 4 or 2 fish limit, from G Nye, tel: 030 679341. For **Rudgewick** fishing, contact Hon Sec, Rudgewick AS. Tackle shops: Tropicana, Pier Rd; Prime Angling, 74 Brighton Rd, Worthing; Cowfold Angling Centre, Cowfold. Hotel: Arun Hotel, Lower street.

Tributaries of the Arun.

WESTERN ROTHER:
Petworth (Sussex). Pike, perch, roach, dace, chub, few trout and sea trout. Mostly preserved by Leconfield Estate, which grants permits only to estate workers. Hants and Sussex AA has 5½m in all, limited dt; also stretch downstream from Coultershaw Mill to Shopham Bridge, and 1m (N bank only) from Shopham Bridge. Then both banks for 1m from Fittleworth Bridge. St £21 + £10 joining fee, dt £2.50, from sec. Contact Richard Etherington, South Dean, Petworth GU28 0RE, for 1½m stocked fly fishing on Rother for browns and rainbows, 3 miles from Petworth. **Burton Mill Pond** holds good pike, perch, roach, rudd, carp, tench. **Duncton Mill,** Petworth, GU28 0LF. 9 acres, brown and rainbow trout, average bags 3 fish, 7½lb total; st £640, ft £336, wt £176. Cottage with mill pond fishing to let. Tel: 0798 42294 or 42048.
Selham (Sussex). Pitshill Fly Fishing Waters: 1½m double bank downstream from Lods Bridge; also ½m of tributary. R Etherbridge, South Dean, Tillington, Petworth, tel: 07985 222. Rotherbridge Fly

Fishing Assn has 3m downstream of Pitshill beat; agents, King & Chasemore. Both these beats are stocked with b and r trout.
Midhurst (Sussex). Rother AC has river and three lakes; coarse fish incl dace, roach, bream, tench, carp and pike, eels. Tickets for Rother only, £3, conc, from 'Logo', West Street, Midhurst, for part of river only. Match Secretary: C Boxall, Innisfree, Ashfield Rd, Midhurst.
Chithurst (Sussex). Petersfield & Dist AC is affiliated to the Hants and Sussex Anglers Alliance who have fishing on the Arun, **Rother,** and eleven stillwaters. Fishing is predominately coarse with all species available. Coombe Pond, Rake, has tench to 4lb. Joining fee £10, st £19, dt £3. Dt £1.75 adult, £1 junior are available for Heath lake (with carp to 27lb), Petersfield, from local tackle shop. Enquiries to hon sec. Tel: 0730 66793. Southern Anglers have trout and coarse fishing on Rother at Habin Bridge, Rogate; tickets from Wyndham Arms, Rogate.

AVON (Bristol)
(For close seasons, licences, etc, see South Western Region NRA, p16)

Coarse fishing now excellent in places. Large chub, barbel, pike, bream, good roach, dace and grayling. Trout in weir pools, including exceptional specimens occasionally, and in some tributaries. Much of Avon and tributaries controlled by Bristol, Bath and Wiltshire Anglers, a merger of clubs which makes all their waters available on one subscription, though each club retains its identity. Members have choice of more than 100m of fishing. Cards (concessions for ladies, juniors and pensioners) are available from tackle shops in the main Avon centres or hon sec. Dt available. BB&WA is among clubs affiliated to Bristol & West of

England Federation, which itself has good water on Avon, Kennet and Avon Canal, Frome and Ham Green Lake.

Bristol. On Avon and Frome and in Somerset. Some free fishing on NRA licence from Netham Weir u/s to Hanham, towpath only. BB&WA full members may fish at **Tockenham Lake**, tel: 0272-672977. Good sport with trout on **Blagdon Lake, Chew Valley** and **Barrow Reservoirs** *(See Somerset streams, lakes and reservoirs).* Among coarse fishing lakes in area are **Bowood** (2m W of Calne, dt at waterside); **Longleat** apply Nick Robbins, Bailiff, Swancombe Cottage, Crockerton, Warminster (Tel. 844496); dt £4 bottom and middle lake, £5 top (carp). B & B from Mrs Crossman, Stalls Farm, Corsley, 0985 844323. **Bitterwell Lake** (N of Bristol) excellent bream, roach, rudd, a few common, mirror and crucian carp, perch. Tuck shop and tackle sold. Dt on bank, £2, £1 conc, from Mrs M Reid, The Chalet, Bitterwell Lake, Coalpit Heath, Bristol BS17 2UF, tel: 0454 778960. **Henleaze Lake** (north of Bristol, dt June-Sep from R W Steel, 63 Hill View, Henleaze, Bristol). City Council runs **Abbots Pool**, Abbots Leigh. Tackle shops: Fish and Field, 60 Broad St, Chipping Sodbury; Scotts, 42 Soundwell Road; Staple Hill; S Shipp, 7 Victoria St, Staple Hill; Avon Angling Centre, 348 Whitewell Road, St George; Bristol Angling Centre, 12 Doncaster Road, Southmead.

Keynsham (Avon). Chub, perch, eels, roach and dace. Free fishing on NRA licence at R **Chew** confluence, end of recreation ground, left bank; also R Chew in Keynsham Park. Keynsham AA has water extending from Compton Dando to Woolland (trout), Chewton Place, Durley Lane, and Willsbury to Swinford. St £8 (jun £4), from J Nix, 5 Bathhill. No dt. Special facilities for young anglers. Bristol & West of England Federation has water here. BB&WA has six stretches of river here and one at **Willsbridge**. Tackle shop: John Nix, Keynsham; J R Sports, Brislington.

Saltford (Avon). BB&WA has stretch at Avon Farm and one field at Swineford. Bathampton AA has 2½m; most coarse fish, including carp and tench, few large trout. Tickets £2 from bailiffs, local tackle shops and hon sec. Tackle shop in Saltford: J D Roberts, 18 High St.

Bath (Avon). Coarse fish; barbel present from here to Limpley Stoke; few large trout. Some free fishing at Pulteney Weir d/s to Newbridge, along towpath; Bathampton Weir u/s to car park, most of footpath. Bath AA are part of Bristol, Bath and Wiltshire A. and have water at Kensington meadows and from Bathampton to city weirs. Good trout fishing in tributary streams, all preserved. **Kennet and Avon Canal** to Limpley Stoke aqueduct preserved by Bathampton AA. Assn also fishes on Newton Park, Hunstrete and Woodborough Lakes. Bye Brook at Shockerwhick and Middlehill, fly only, are permit waters. Contact K Rippin, The Grove, Langridge, Bath. Knowle AA has **Emborough Pond**, Ston Easton; carp, tench, roach, perch, pike; dt from keeper. Tackle shops: I M Crudgington, 37 Broad Street; (information and tickets for Bath AA and Bathampton AA waters).

Batheaston (Avon). BB&WA has two fields here.

Bathampton (Avon). All-round fishing. BB&WA and Bathampton AA have water; dt available. Bathampton AA also has water at **Kelston, Newton St Loe, Newbridge, Salford**, and on **Kennet and Avon Canal, Hunstrete, Newton Park** and **Woodborough Lakes** (good carp, tench), and **Bye Brook**, some ponds near Bridgwater. St £13.50, dt £1.50 for some waters, from hon sec. and local tackle shops.

Claverton (Avon). Bathampton AA has 2m; very good chub, few trout. BB&WA also has water.

Warleigh (Avon). Bathampton AA has four meadows here: (as Claverton above). BB&WA has five meadows.

Limpley Stoke (Wilts). Good all-round fishing; large carp, with tench, chub, roach bream and trout; fly-fishing on **River Frome**, Freshford to Farleigh Hungerford, and **Midford Brook** from Avon to Midford village; stocked with trout every year; preserved by Avon and Tributaries AA; visitors accompanied by member only. Bathampton AA holds **Kennet and Avon Canal** from Limpley Stoke to confluence with Avon at Bath (5½m): dt from hon sec, tackle shops and bailiffs. BB&WA controls 3m from Limpley Stoke down to Kensington, coarse fish and trout; tickets from hon sec, two stretches.

Midford (Avon). **Midford Brook;** trout only; preserved and stocked by the Avon and Tributaries AA. Dt to members' guests only.

Freshford (Avon). BB&WA has water on Avon here; dt issued. **Frome:** trout, coarse fish, stocked and preserved by Avon and Tributaries AA (annual sub £90); from Avon up to Farleigh Hungerford. Limited dt for members' guests. Association also has part of Avon, Freshford to Avoncliffe, fly only water on **Midford, Wellow** and **Cam Brooks.**

Bradford-on-Avon (Wilts). Coarse fish, including pike, few trout. **Kennet and Avon Canal;** coarse fish. Some miles of Avon and canal preserved by Bradford-on-Avon and Dist AA. Dt from hon sec or tackle shops Wests, Roundstone Street; Roses, Fore Street; Smith and Ford, Fore St (all Trowbridge) and Top Gun and Rod, Treenwood Trading Estate, Bradford-on-Avon. Accom. with fishing facilities, Avonvilla, Avoncliff, tel: 0225 863867.

Melksham (Wilts). Coarse fish, few trout. BB&WA has Lacock stretch 1m from Melksham: excellent barbel. Avon AC has waters at **Waddon.** St £6, dt £1 from hon sec or tackle shops. RD licences from hon sec and Avon Angling & Sports Centre (tackle shop), 13 Bath Road, or St Margarets News, St Margaret's St. Baits from Gogoozler, Marina. Lavington AC has water on **Semington Brook** at Lavington Mill and Baldham Mill. Leech Pool Farm has coarse fishing at **Broughton Gifford.** Barge Inn, 17 Frome Rd, accommodates anglers.

Lacock (Wilts). BB&W AA have water here. Tickets from Coles, Market Place, Chippenham. Dt on site for **Silverlands Lake.** Carp and tench. Isis AC has water at **Pewsham;** apply hon sec for permit

details.

Chippenham (Wilts). Chub, barbel, bream, perch, roach. Chippenham AA has water; st £9, wt £3, dt £1.50 from Coles, who also have dt for **Sword Lake,** trout, and **Sabre Lake,** coarse with carp. BB&WA has about 1½m between here and **Lacock.** Isis AC has water on Avon and **Marden;** members only. Licences, tackle and bait from Robs Tackle, 22 Marshfield Road. Mill Farm Trout Lakes, Gt Cheverill: apply to B Coleman, tel: Lavington 3325. **Devizes,** as centre for Devizes AA waters, 15m of **Kennet and Avon Canal,** 1m of Avon at Beanacre, Melksham, various coarse, dt £2.50, conc, from tackle shop Rod & Reel, 11 Sidmouth Street.

Christian Malford (Wilts). Several fields controlled by BB&WA here, and at **Sutton Benger** Isis AC has 4m including 2 weirs and backwater; further water near **Seagry Mill.** Somerfords FA has water upstream from Seagry to Kingsmead Mill (part of it, from Dauntsey road bridge, is trout water) and 2m above Kingsmead Mill on left bank and 1m on right bank. Good chub and perch. Assn also has water on **Frome.** Dt for trout and coarse fishing issued. Golden Valley FC has water at Seagry.

Malmesbury (Wilts). Bristol, Bath and Wiltshire Anglers has fishing here, members only; trout and coarse fish. RD licences from Sports and Leisure, 36 High Street.

Lower Moor Fishery, Oaksey Malmesbury, Wiltshire SN16 9TW. Tel: 0666 860232. Forty-five acres of trout fishing on three lakes, stocked weekly with r and b. Two confined to nymph and dry fly on floating line. Dt £16 or £9. Junior £8 (4 and 2 fish limits). Fine fly hatch, exceptional mayfly and damsel. Open end of Mar to early Jan.

Tributaries of the Avon (Bristol)

FROME (Bristol). Rises near Chipping Sodbury and joins Avon estuary near Bristol. Small tributaries upstream provide ideal conditions for trout. Fishing on **Mells River, Whatley** and **Nunney Brooks.** Coarse species are barbel, bream, carp, eel, perch, roach, tench, chub and grayling.

Frampton Cotterell (Glos). Most of lower Frome controlled by Bristol, Bath and Wiltshire Anglers.

Yate (Glos). Frome Vale AC has water

from Moorend Weir to viaduct. Dodington Park Lake, 6m; carp, perch; preserved. **Badminton Park Lake,** 8m; carp; preserved by the Duke of Beaufort; apply Estate Office, Badminton, Glos. Tanhouse Farm, Yate Rocks, has coarse fishing lake available.

CHEW: From Confluence to Compton Dando, coarse fish; thereafter, trout.

Keynsham (Avon). BB&WA has two fields. Keynsham AA has fishing (see *Avon*).

Malmesbury (Wilts). Free fishing on NRA licence at Sherston Avon u/s of Cascade at Silk Mills; Tetbury Avon u/s Station Yard Weir, Fire Station, left bank. Five fields right bank downstream held by BB&WA. Club also has long stretch of **Woodbridge Brook.**

Chewton Keynsham (Avon). Water held by BB&WA. Keynsham AA also has water; dt issued for fly and coarse fishing. Stretch in Keynsham Park free to licence holders.

Compton Dando (Avon). Mainly trout, grayling and dace. Keynsham AA has water here from above Woollard Weir some way downstream; no dt. BB&WA has water between here and Burnett; dt from hon sec, Golden Carp AA.

Pensford (Avon). Trout and coarse fish. Lakes: **Hunstrete Park Lake;** carp, tench, bream, roach, perch; Bathampton AA; members only.

Stanton Drew, Chew Magna, Chew Stoke (Avon). Trout dominant; some roach and dace. No spinning. Dt from local inns and Bristol tackle shops from June 15 to Sept 30 (Mon-Fri only). Stretches of 2m at Compton Dando and ½m at Chew Magna held by BB&WA; trout; bait or fly. **Emborough Pond;** carp, tench, roach, perch; dt (limited) from bailiff. *(For Chew Reservoirs, see Somerset (lakes and streams)).*

BOYD BROOK: Trout in upper reaches, coarse fish, BB&WA has water at **Doynton** (Glos); dt issued (see Lacock). Golden Valley FC has stretch above and below Bitton.

CAM BROOK: Trout, Avon and tributaries AA has water (members' guests only). BB&WA has stretch at **Dunkerton** (Som), and at **Midford;** dt issued. Cameley Trout Lakes are at Temple Cloud. St and dt, apply to J Harris, tel: Temple Cloud 52790/52423.

BY (BOX) BROOK: Trout, coarse fish. Bathampton AA has water at **Shocker-wick** (Som) and **Box** (Wilts); st £12, dt £1.50. By Brook Fly FC and Two Mills Flyfishers have water for members. Manor House Hotel, Castle Combe, has ½m of good trout fishing in grounds.

SEMINGTON BROOK: Trout, coarse fish. Lavington AC has Bulkington Brook. St £15 and st £3. Concessions for juniors. Members only. Tel: 0380 830425. Baldham Mill fishery now rented by St George's AC, Trowbridge. For **Erlestoke Lake,** D Hampton, Longwater, Erlestoke, Devizes, Wilts. 7 acres, coarse fish. Carp to 22lb. St £65, wt £25, dt £6. Juv £12.50, £2.50. Ban on nut baits and keepnets.

FROME: Coarse fish, trout.

Frome (Som). Frome and Dist AA has several miles between Marston and Beckington plus coarse fish lakes at Berkley and Marston, both 3m from Frome. Regular matches. St £10, conc. Information from R Lee, tel: Frome 461433. Dt £2 from Frome Angling Centre, 11 Church St, Frome; tel: 467143. Witham Friary Lake coarse fishing, tel: Nunney 239. Other tackle shop: Haines Tackle, Christchurch St West. Hotel: George, Market Place.

Wolverton (Avon). Trout, coarse fish.

MARDEN: Coarse fish, trout.

Calne (Wilts). Trout, barbel, chub, rudd, carp, tench, pike, perch, roach, dace, bream; 6m held by Calne AA: at Christian Malford, dt available; at Spye Park, members only. Isis AC has stretch at Newleaze Farm; members only. Above Calne is preserved dry fly water. **Bowood Lake,** large pike (to 26lb), perch, carp, tench, roach; from Bowood Estate, Calne, Wilts SN11 0LZ, tel: 0249 812102, who issue st £95, jun conc. Waiting list. North end of lake private. *Note: access to lake only at Pillars Lodge entrance on Calne - Melksham road.* Tackle shop: TK Tackle 123a London Road; Pet & Tackle, 1A Newcroft Rd.

Check before you go

While every effort has been made to ensure that the information given in **Where to Fish** *is correct, the position is continually changing, and anglers are urged, in their own interests, to make enquiries before travelling to selected venues. This is especially important with reference to prices quoted. Anglers attention is also drawn to the fact that hotels mentioned under the various fishing stations do not necessarily have water of their own. Any amendments or further data for inclusion in subsequent editions, and any criticism, will be welcome.*

AVON (Wiltshire)

(For close seasons, licences, etc, see South Western Region NRA p16)

In years gone by the most famous mixed fishery in England. In its upper reaches, the Avon is a typical chalk stream, populated by free-rising trout and grayling. A decline in the coarse fishing which set in thirty years ago has been the subject of investigation and there are now signs of improvement.

Christchurch (Dorset). Avon and Stour. Excellent sea and coarse fishing in Christchurch Harbour, which is leased to Christchurch AC. Bass, mullet, flounders and (higher up) dace, roach, bream and eels. Other Club waters include several stretches of Dorset Stour from Christchurch Harbour to Wimborne, lakes and gravel pits with large carp and pike. Membership £62. Dt for these waters and the Royalty Fishery on the Avon (excluding Parlour and Bridge Pool) can be obtained from Mr G K Pepler, Davis Tackle Shop, 75 Bargates, Christchurch (Tel: 0202 485169). June 16 to Mar 14 inclusive. The Royalty Fishery price structure ranges between £28 per day for salmon, sea trout and coarse fishing, double rod £66-£48 and £6 single rod for coarse fishing. Concessions. Davis will supply brochure on receipt of request and SAE. Top Weir Compound, Parlour and Bridge Pool permits from Fishery Manager: advance bookings only, except 1 Nov-31 Jan. No advance bookings on Upper and Lower Main River. Limit 2 salmon except Parlour Pool, one per day. Permits for fishings on Stour and in Christchurch Harbour also obtainable from Davis Tackle Shop *(see also Stour (Dorset))*. For other salmon and sea trout fishing apply early in writing to the Royalty Fishery Manager, West Hants Water Co, Mill Road, Christchurch. **Hordle Lakes;** mixed fishery on 5 lakes near **New Milton**. Tickets from Smiths Sports Shop, Lymington and Davis Tackle, dt £5-£3. Good sea fishing at Mudeford; boats available. Tackle shops: Davis, 75 Bargates (open from 7.45 am, Sundays incl); Pro Fishing Tackle, 258 Barrack Rd. Hotels: Kings Arms; Fishermans Haunt, Winkton.

Winkton (Dorset). Davis Fishing Tackle, 75 Bargates, Christchurch now sole agents for coarse fishing on this fishery. Season is June 16 to Mar 14; good roach, large chub and barbel, pike; also dace, perch. Dt £5. Salmon fishing is occasionally available. Details from Davis Tackle, tel: 0202 485169. Hotel: Fishermans Haunt.

Sopley (Hants). Sopley Mill Avon Fishery is near Sopley Village on B3347. Comprises 1m of millstream and approx 350 yds R Avon. Barbel over 13lb, good chub and dace. Dt from Davis Tackle, Christchurch.

Ringwood (Hants). Ringwood & Dist AA has fishing on rivers as follows: **Avon;** Breamore, 1½m (barbel, chub), Fordingbridge (trout), Ibsley, 2m (S and specimen coarse fish), side streams at Ibsley, Ringwood, 2m (coarse fish), East Mills, 1½m (coarse fish), Fordingbridge Park, ¼m (coarse fish); **Stour;** twelve stretches totalling more than 12m (coarse fish); **Test;** over 2m at Broadlands Est. (members only); also nine still waters totalling over 120 acres. St £26 + £4 entry; Junior £12; OAP, dis, ladies £13, Dt for much of the water from tackle shops. N Ward, Avon Dairy Farm, The Bridges, Ringwood, issue dt on behalf of riparian owners, £1.50, also wt and st. Dt £5 from Ringwood Tackle for ¾m both banks above Ringwood; 1¼m E. bank below and several coarse fishing lakes, dt £4. **Beeches Brook,** Forest Rd, Burley (tel: 2373) is dt coarse lake off A31 to Southampton. **High Town,** Ringwood; 23 acre pit containing most coarse species. Tickets from Ringwood and Christchurch tackle shops. Other dt waters: river at Lifelands Fishery; Martins Farm Carp Lake, Woodlands, tel: 0202 822335; Hurst Pond. Tackle shops: Ringwood Tackle, 5 The Bridges, West Street, Ringwood BH24 1EA. Tel: 0425 475155; Hales Tackle; Davis, Christchurch. Hotels: Crown, Star Inn, Fish Inn, Nag's Head, White Hart.

Fordingbridge (Hants). Trout, grayling, perch, pike and roach. Park Recreation Ground has fishing, dt from Council grounds staff, Sept to Mar. Dt for Burgate water from Burgate Manor Farm *(see Salisbury)*. Albany Hotel has short river frontage (licences obtainable). Few dt for Bickton Estate water from river bailiff, 2 New Cottages, **Bickton;** St (trout streams) £300, st (coarse) £35, st (salmon) £60, dt (trout streams) £12. No licence needed as block licence purchased. Tackle shop on premises. East Mills Manor, Shepherds Spring Restaurant has 1½m of river and lake. Dt available. Two excellent stillwater fisheries in the vicinity. **Damerham** and **Lapsley's Fishery** (ex Allens Farm). Hotel: Ashburn.

Breamore (Hants). Bat and Ball Hotel has 2m of salmon, trout and coarse fish on dt basis, from £2.50. Phone Breamore 252.

Downton (Wilts). Trout, roach, grayling, dace. Downtown AA have water. St £18.50, from Reids Tackle, Warminster Rd, Wilton. Hotels: Bull, Bat & BAll, Breamore.

Salisbury (Wilts). Avon, Wylye and Bourne; trout, grayling, coarse fish; preserved. Salisbury and Dist AC has water on Avon as follows: 3m within city boundary; 3m at **Durnford**, 2m at **West Amesbury**, **Countess Fishery** on Upper Avon; plus **R Wylye** at **Stapleford**, dry fly fishing, grayling in late Autumn and winter, **R Bourne** at **Hurdcott**, the same; **Burgate Mill Stream**. Excellent trout, grayling, roach, etc, in all waters. Dt for some waters from Brabans Newsagents, Wilton Rd, Salisbury. Membership £92

game, £62 course. The Piscatorial Society has Avon fishing nr **Amesbury**, members only. Other local clubs: Tisbury AC, Downton AA. Langford Fisheries, 22 acre trout lakes at Duck St, **Steeple Langford**. Good dry fly fishing. Dt £24-£17, 5 fish limit. Boat for 2 rods, £60. ½ day terms and conc. available. Tel: 0722 790770. London AA has **Britford Fishery**; excellent coarse fishing, good sport with trout, some salmon. Members only; no dt. Fishing on short stretch of Avon at Fisherton Recreation Ground for small charge; apply Town Clerk, Salisbury City Council. Humberts, 8 Rollestone Street, may know of annual rods to let. For **Avon Springs Fisheries**, Salisbury, tel: 0980 53557. Hotels: County, White Hart and Red Lion. Tackle shops: John Eadie, 20 Catherine Street; Reids Tackle, Kingsway House, Wilton, Salisbury (NRA licences). Hotels: Grasmere; Old Mill, Harnham; Lamb, Hinton; Bell, South Newton.

Netheravon (Wilts). Trout, grayling; preserved. The 6m from **Enford** to **Bulford** is The Services Dry Fly FA (Salisbury Plain) water; strictly members only, no tickets available.

Fishing the dry fly on the River Nadder. *Photo: Eric Chalker.*

AVON (Hampshire) tributaries

BOURNE: Enters near Salisbury. Trout, grayling, coarse fish. Fishing stations: **Porton** and **Salisbury** (Wilts).
EBBLE: Joins Avon below Salisbury; good trout fishing, but mostly private.
WYLYE: Trout, grayling. **Wishford** (Wilts).Preserved by Wilton Fly Fishing Club, closed membership of 45. **Stapleford** (Wilts). Salisbury AC has fishing here; members only. (*See Salisbury.*) **Warminster** (Wilts). Warminster AC has water on Wylye, and coarse fishing on lakes and ponds; members only (membership restricted to rural area). Hunters Moon Lodge, Henford Marsh BA12 9PA has fishing for guests and club members. Tel: 0985 219977 or 212481. **Longleat** Estate owns just over 2m of upper river. Excellent coarse fishing in three lakes in Longleat Park, carp included. Tickets are issued by Bailiff, Parkhill Cottage, Longleat Estate or directly from Estate (Maiden Bradley 551). St £50, dt £2.50-£4. The Sutton Veny Estate, Pound Barton (Tel Warminster 40682), lets rods, part rods and quarter-rods on 4½m of Wylye, dry fly trout fishing only. Not less than £395 per season. Occasional dt, £25. Enquiries to Estate Office for precise terms or Roxtons Sporting Agency, Hungerford. Tackle shops: The Rod Box; Silver Tackle, 6 Silver St; B & S Tackle, Pound St.
NADDER: Tributary of Wylye. Trout, grayling, roach, dace. Mostly preserved by landowners. Fishing stations: **Wilton, Tisbury.** Tisbury AC has about 4m; dt and wt from Arundell Arms, Beckford Arms and hon sec; exchanges with Warminster and Salisbury clubs. Club also has lake at Old Wardens Castle; carp, tench, etc.

AXE

(For close seasons, licences, etc, see S W Region NRA, p16)

Rises in Dorset and flows south to the English Channel at Seaton. Trout, sea trout and salmon. Fishing difficult to come by, but one or two hotels can provide facilities.

Seaton (Devon). Trout, salmon. Some sea trout fishing available on ticket from Abbeygate Farm, near Axminster, and from Ackermans. Axe estuary fishable (for bass, mullet, flounders, etc), on £2 dt from harbour filling station or Axe Farm camp site, Axemouth. Tackle and licences: F Ackerman & Co Ltd, Fore Street (*see Sea Fishing Stations*). Hotel: Pole Arms. R and b trout fishing available at **Colyton,** dt £3; Mrs E Pady, Higher Cownhayne Farm, Colyton, tel: 0297 52267.
Axminster (Devon). Axe, Yarty; trout and salmon. Trouting good especially in April and May. Taunton Fly Fishing Club has beats on the Axe at Chard, Tytherleigh, Musbury. Hotels: Cavalier, Bear Inn, Colyton.
Crewkerne (Som). Axe (3m off); trout. Parret (1m off); trout, roach, dace. Stoke-sub-Hamdon AA has trout fishing from Bow Mills to Creedy Bridge on **Parret;** members only. Fees, £5, £2.50. Wt available, Yeovil AA has trout and coarse fishing on **Yeo** and tributaries; st £3, dt £1 from hon sec and That Tackle Shop, Yeovil. Trout fishing in **Sutton Bingham Reservoir,** near Yeovil. Tackle shops: That Tackle Shop, 29 Princes Street; Yeovil Angling Centre, Forrest Hill.

BLACKWATER

(For close seasons, licences, etc, see Anglian Region NRA, p17)

Rises in NW of county, flows by Braintree to Maldon and empties into North Sea through large estuary. Coarse fish include pike, chub, rudd and some carp.

Maldon (Essex). Maldon AS has approx 32 acres of stillwaters, one in **Colchester,** one in **Southminster,** the rest in Maldon area; Four stretches totalling 2m, of **R Blackwater,** 5m of **Chelmer** and **Blackwater Canal.** All coarse, carp over 45lb. Membership available. Permits for Beeleigh Lock to Heybridge Basin Lock from bailiffs on bank; Leisure sport **Chigborough** gravel pits of 8½ acres at **Drapers Farm.** Coarse fish, tench, bream, crucian, etc. St £20, conc. £10. Dt £1.50, jun conc, from bailiff on bank. Phone Chertsey 564872. Tackle shop: Maldon Bait & Tackle, 146 High St. Hotels: Swan, White Hart, King's Head.

Chigboro' Fisheries, Maldon, Essex CM9 7RE. Sixteen acre lake with brown and rainbow trout of average weight 2 lbs. 4 boats available. St from £170. Dt £18.50 (4 fish), or £13.50 (2 fish), from bailiff on water or office. Tel: 0621 57368. Braxted Water trout fishery is also under this management.

Witham (Essex). Blackwater and **Brain.** Coarse fish. Kelvedon and Dist AA has 7½m from here to **Braintree;** members only. **Witham Lake,** 5½ acres; **Bovingdon Mere, Hatfield Peverel;** 4 acre lake coarse fishery, Colchester APS waters. Tackle shop: E & J Tackle, 16 Church St.

Kelvedon (Essex). Kelvedon and Dist AA has various stretches as well as water on Suffolk **Stour,** reservoir and threepits at Tiptree, **Silver End Pits,** 6 acres each, and two 2 acre pits at **Layer Marney.** St £30, conc, dt £3.50 from M Murton, 189 High Street, Kelvedon. Tench, crucian carp, rudd, roach. Club organises sea-fishing boat trips. Maldon AS has water here and at **Feering** and **Braxted;** members only *(see Witham, Coggeshall and Maldon).* Tackle shop: E & J Tackle, Church St, Witham.

Coggeshall (Essex). Coarse fish. Kelvedon and Dist AA has water here; members only *(see Witham and Kelvedon).*

Braintree (Essex). Braintree and Bocking AS owns most of water on main river, banks, from Shalford to Bradwell Village and on **Pant.** Well stocked with roach, perch, rudd, dace, and chub. St £17, Juv £6, OAP £2 from local tackle shop *(see below)* and subscription sec D Clack, tel: 0376 44201. *For Gosfield and Sparrows Lakes see Essex (Streams and Lakes).* Tackle: The Right Angle Tackle Shop, 18 New Street. Hotels: Horne, White Horse, Nag's Head.

CHELMER AND **CAN:** Coarse fish:

Chelmsford (Essex). River stocked: roach, dace, bream, tench, carp, pike, perch. Public fishing in town parks. Dt £3 for towpath between Brown's Wharf and Ricketts Lock, and for **Heybridge Canal** from Beeleigh to Hall Bridge from bailiff on bank. Chelmsford AA, has 14m of river, from Browns Wharf, Chelmsford, to Heybridge Basin, plus 18 lakes, two carp only, the rest mixed coarse fishing. Membership £30, concessions for ladies, OAP, jun). Leisure sport gravel pit at **Boreham** offers good carp fishing. St £20, conc. £10. Phone Chertsey 564872 for details. Tackle shops: Edwards Tackle, 16 Broomfield Rd; Brians Sport & Tackle, 50B Moulsham St; Ronnie Crowe, Maldon Road, Gt. Baddow. Hotels: County, South Lodge.

BLYTH (Northumberland)

(For close seasons, licences, etc, see Northumbria and Yorkshire Region NRA, p17)

Rises near Throckington and flows 20m to North Sea at Blyth. Trout and grayling with coarse fish (especially roach) in lower reaches. Bedlington and Blagdon AA have members only fishing at Bedlington. No tickets.

Stannington (Northumberland). Brown trout and grayling, gudgeon, roach. Occasional dt available from Mr S Symons, tel: 0670 822011, for **Plessey Woods** fishing. Nr Belsay, Bolam Lake Country Park fishing, coarse, incl golden rudd. Tel: 0661 881234.

BRUE

(For close seasons, licences, etc, see South Western Region NRA, p16).

Rises in Mendips and flows to Bristol Channel at Burnham. Coarse fish, except in higher reaches, where trout fishing is preserved. From West Lydford to Glastonbury, a number of weirs provide deep water in which coarse fish predominate. A good late season river, too much weed growth earlier, contains large carp and bream.

Highbridge (Som). Roach, bream, etc. North Somerset AA has some of best waters. Club also has Rivers **Kenn,** Axe, **Apex Pit,** between Highbridge and Burnham, (match record 35lb 11oz), Newtown Pond, Highbridge (carp to 20lb), South and North Drains. St £14, dt £2.50 from tackle shop P & J Thyer, 1A Church Street, Highbridge TA9 3AE, or Richards Tackle Shop, Cross St, Burnham on Sea. Highbridge AA is part of N. Somerset AA, and holds junior matches, and other events. Further information from hon sec. Huntspill River is 2m; Bridgwater AA water *(see Bridgwater - Parret)*. BB&WA has water at **East Huntspill, Burtle, Tealham Moor, Westhay** and **Lydford-on-Fosse.** St. £8 *(see Bristol).* Hotels: Highbridge; The George (clubs accommodated). Lamb Guest House, Church St, is recommended locally, for visiting anglers.

Bason Bridge (Som). Area around milk factory noted for carp; fish run up to 16lb or so. Also roach, chub, tench, perch and pike. BB&WA holds extensive stretches here and Highbridge AA also has water.

Mark (Som). Carp, pike, perch, roach, chub, tench. N Somerset AA has 2¹/₂m on river and 3 to 4m on North Drain; dt and wt from hon sec. Highbridge AA also has water on North Drain. Inn: Pack Horse.

Westhay (Som). Glaston Manor AA has stretch from Lydford to below Westhay. BB&WA has water from below Westhay to North Drain.

Glastonbury (Som). Roach, bream, chub, etc, in lower stretches of River Brue. Glaston Manor, BB&WA and N Somerset AA clubs have water. Dt from hon secs. Trout from **Baltonsborough** to **West Lydford.** Fishing extends from White House, Westhay, to Fosseway Bridge, West Lydford (trout av ¹/₂lb). No dt. Windmill AC has coarse ponds at Butleigh Rd, nr Street, members only, £12 per annum. Apply to Sec. Tackle shops: G F Miller, 22 Benedict St; Street Angling Centre, 160 High Street, Street.

BUDE RIVER AND CANAL

(For close seasons, licences, etc, see South Western Region NRA, p16)

Two branches of River Neet from Week St Mary and Stratton (latter often referred to as the Strat) converge at Hele Bridge, flow into the Bude Canal and out again towards Bude. Neet has small brown trout in good seasons. Visitors should apply to F J Proudfoot, Whales Borough Farmhouse, Marhamchurch, for Hele Bridges system. Bude Canal has 1¹/₄ miles of wider than average canal with good banks and full variety of coarse fish. Apply to hon sec, Bude AA.

Bude (Cornwall). Bass from beaches, breakwater and rocks; bass and mullet in estuary of Bude River. Details from hon sec Bude & Dist SAC, or Bude Stratton Town Council, The Castle. Bude Angling Association has fishing on a total of 6¹/₂m of banks of **Tamar** and **Claw** from near Bude to half way to Launceston. Wild brown trout plus some dace in downstream beats. Membership £5, wt £5, dt £3; from Bude Sports Shop, Queens St, Bude, North Cornwall Pet Shop, Princes St, Bude, or the DIY Centre, Holsworthy,

Devon. Membership enquiries (with 50p if map req.) to hon sec, Bude AA. **Tamar Lake** and **Crowdy** (trout reservoir) controlled by SW Water *(see Cornwall lakes, etc).* **Bude Canal** (roach, bream, eels, dace, perch, carp to 25lb and tench) 1m from town centre towards Marhamchurch leased by Bude Canal AA; wt £10, dt £2, £1 jun and OAP, on bank or from Pet Shop, Princes St, Bude. 3 acre rainbow trout lake, Ash Fishery; fly only, tel: 0288 84317/84326. Hotel: Globe, The Strand, Bude.

BURE

(see Norfolk and Suffolk Broads)

CAMEL

(For close seasons, licences etc, see South Western Region NRA, p16)

A spate river, rising on the moors near Davidstow, flowing about 30m to enter the Atlantic between Pentire and Steppar Points. Salmon, sea trout and small brown trout. Salmon enter from April; grilse from June, with the main runs in October, November and December. Sea trout from June to August. Best brown trout fishing in tributaries Allen, De Lank, Lanivet and Ruthern and in the topmost reaches of the main river. Rainfall influences salmon fishing to an exceptional extent. Fishing on upper reaches dependent on heavy rainfall. There is a voluntary restriction in place covering the whole river. No fishing in April and a limit of 2 salmon per day and 4 per week, and 4 sea trout per day; also no selling of fish and no maggots.

Wadebridge (Cornwall). Trout, sea trout, salmon; good mullet fishing in tidal

reaches, with bass and pollack in estuary. Good stretches held by Wadebridge and Dist AA at Pencarrow, Grogley, Wenford, Key Bridge, 4½m. Membership of Wadebridge & Dist, via a short waiting list, is £25. Dt for visitors £15, wt £45 from Country Wise, Molesworth St, Wadebridge. Hotels: Molesworth Arms, Bridge-on-Wool, Swan Lanarth Hotel and Country Club, St Kew. *(For sea fishing see Padstow)*
Bodmin (Cornwall). A few miles from the Camel and Fowey, where Bodmin AA issues permits (ten per day) on some 10 miles of the best water. Details from hon sec Wt £30, dt £10 from May 1-Sept 30. Dt £18, Oct-Nov. No permits in Dec. St, wt and dt from hon sec. Concessions for jun and OAP. Free maps and NRA li-

cences also available from hon sec R Burrows, 26 Meadow Place, Bodmin, on receipt of sae. Telephone 0208 75513.Mr D Rodgers, Gwendreath, Dunmere, Bodmin, has permits for 1½m R Camel. Mr T Jackson, Butterwell, Nanstallon, Bodmin, PL30 5LQ has 1½m salmon and sea trout fishing, occasional day permits with preference given to residents. Self-catering cottage and limited b and b. Tel: 0208 831515. For Fenwick Trout Fishery, phone 0208 78296. Lakeview Country Club, **Lanivet**, has 3 lakes, 6 acres, stocked; specimen carp, etc. Dt £3.50. Tel: 0208 831808. Tackle shop: Roger, Stan Mays Garage, Higher Bore St., Bodmin. 0208 72659 (closed Wednesday). They also issue tickets for Fowey and Lostwithiel.

CHESHIRE (Lakes/Reservoirs)

APPLETON RESERVOIR, nr Warrington. Trout fishery controlled by Warrington AA. Members only, membership is available, £20 per annum plus £20 joining fee, with generous concessions. This is one of the larger fishing clubs of Great Britain, controlling approximately sixty fisheries on rivers, lakes, reservoirs, canals and pools. The club keeps a coarse fishing close season between 15 Mar-15 Jun. It may be contacted through PO Box 71, Warrington WA1 1LR, tel: 0928 716238.
BLACKSHAW FARM LAKES, Leek. 4 acre coarse fishery; carp, tench, bream, roach. Prince Albert AS water, members only, £55 subscription plus £55 entrance fee.
BOSLEY RESERVOIR. Fishing station: **Bosley.** Roach (good), bream, pike, perch, carp, few trout. Prince Albert AS water, members only.
CAPESTHORNE POOLS. Fishing station: **Siddington.** Large carp, tench, bream, roach, rudd and pike. Stock pond has excellent carp and tench. Dt £6, ½ day £4 from A Bradley, East Lodge Capesthorne (Tel: Chelford 861584). Park and Garden pools controlled by

Stoke-on-Trent AS. No tickets.
DOVE MERE, SAND MERE, WOODLANDS LAKE. Allostock, Knutsford. Prince Albert AS waters, members only. Heavily stocked, including large carp. St £55; waiting list.
GREAT BUDWORTH MERE. Nr. **Northwich,** 50-acre lake holding good bream, pike, etc. Northwich AA; tickets from hon sec, st only, £20 plus £20 joining fee, conc. **Pickmere** and **Petty Pool** are assn waters nearby.
LAKE REDESMERE. Fishing station: **Siddington.** Excellent roach and pike, with bream, carp and tench. Stoke-on-Trent AS water, members only, no day tickets. for prospective membership, £39 + £19, contact club hon. sec.
LANGLEY BOTTOMS and **LAMALOAD RESERVOIRS. Nr Macclesfield.** Good fly fishing for trout. Prince Albert AS. Limited dt £8 from Barlows Tackle, Macclesfield.
LYMM DAM, 15 acre lake, good all year round fishing with big carp and pike. Lymm AC water, 50 pegs available, £20 booking fee plus peg fee £2 or £2.50. Contact hon. sec. for this and seven other dt waters.

POLLUTION

Anglers are united in deploring pollution. To combat it, urgent action may be called for at any time from any one of us. If numbers of fish are found dead, dying, or seriously distressed, take samples of both fish and water and contact the officer responsible for pollution at the appropriate National Rivers Authority.

MANCHESTER RESERVOIRS:
Tintwistle (A628). Trout, perch. Vale House: fly fishing, for trout. Bottoms: bait fishing. Cote Lodge (Glossop): bait fishing. These NWW reservoirs are now leased to various clubs. Enquiries to Fisheries Section, Richard Fairclough House, Knutsford Rd, Warrington WA4 1HG, tel: 53999.

MILL LODGE, BOLLINGTON. 3 acres. Large carp. Prince Albert AS, members only.

OULTON MILL POOL. Fishing station: Tarporley. Well stocked with good carp, bream, tench and pike. Dt from Mill Office.

ROMAN LAKES. Fishing station: **Marple.** Roach, perch, carp (up to 20lb) and brown trout. Dt from Lakeside Cafe.

ROSSMERE LAKE. 6 acres. Fishing station: **Wilmslow.** Heavily stocked. 80 match pegs. Prince Albert AS, members only.

THORNEYCROFT HALL LAKES, Gawsworth. Prince Albert AS water, members only. Carp, tench, roach, pike.

COLNE (Essex)

(For close seasons, licences, etc, see Anglian Region NRA, p17)

Rises in north of county and flows to North Sea via Colchester. Improving as coarse fishery.

Colchester (Essex). Colchester APS controls 2½m, roach, chub, perch, pike, bream, dace; no tickets. The society has also **Layer Pit;** pike, perch, bream, roach, rudd, tench, carp. Society also has water on **Stour,** Hatfield Peverell Lakes, Witham Lake, Olivers Lake at Witham and Bovingdon Pits. St £31.71 + £10 entry. Concessions to jun, OAP, disabled. Colchester Piscatorial Society has water on Langham Ponds, Stour and Colne; members only. ½m of Colne fished by Kelvedon AA. Tackle shops: Wass, Long Wyre Street; Trofish, Miltary Rd; E J Porter, Barrack St. Hotels: George, Red Lion.

Aldham (Essex). Colnes AS has water at Fordham and Aldham, Stour near Bures, two reservoirs and lake. Most fish may be caught. Improved access for disabled. Members only, £16, conc, from P Emson, Tackle Shop, 16 Station Rd, Colne Engaine. Colchester.

Halstead (Essex). Coarse fish, including tench. **Gosfield Hall Lake** (45 acres), Church Rd, Gosfield, well stocked carp, with perch, roach, tench, pike, rudd; dt £4, evening £2.75. Also **Sparrows Pond,** Gosfield; coarse fish including carp and tench; Halstead and Hedingham AC members only (st £12) has several miles of Pant, stretch of Colne, from Yeldham to Halstead, 2 reservoirs and pits. Tackle shop: E McDowell, High Street.

COQUET

(For close seasons, licences, etc, see Northumbria and Yorkshire Region NRA, p17)

Rises in Cheviots and enters North Sea near Warkworth. Salmon, sea trout and trout. Sport still very good. Facilities for visitors. Good run of spring salmon.

Warkworth (Northumberland). Trout, sea trout; salmon from Feb onwards to late summer and autumn. Duke of Northumberland leases large part of his water to Northumbrian Anglers Federation. St £42 salmon, £25 trout. Concessions for OAP. Applications to Head Bailiff, Thirston Mill, Felton, Northumberland, or tackle dealers for trout permits only. Additional £37 permit for tidal section.

Acklington (Northumberland). Trout, sea trout and salmon. Northumbrian AF water on Coquet and tributary, Thirston Burn.

Felton (Northumberland).Salmon, sea trout (spring and autumn), trout. Northumbrian A Fedn; permits from Post Office (*see Warkworth*).

Weldon Bridge (Northumberland).Nearest station: Morpeth, 9½m. Trout (sea trout and salmon, late summer and autumn). Anglers Arms Hotel has fishing available, tel: 0665 570655/570271.

Rothbury (Northumberland). A late salmon run and excellent sea trout fishing in June and Oct. Brown trout, including fish to 3lb. Northumbrian AF has 4m of Coquet (*see Warkworth*). Tickets for 6m stretch from Whitton Farm House Hotel. Thropton & Rothbury AC has water on Coquet, Alwyn and Wreigh Burn. Main runs of salmon and sea trout, Sept and

Oct. Non members welcome, tickets, £5, conc, from Thropton P O, Morpeth and tackle shop. Reservoir**Fontburn Reservoir,** Ewesley, nr Rothbury, trout fishery of 87 acres with b and r trout, fly or worm permitted. Dt £6, 6 fish. conc. Tel: 0669 20465. Hotel: Whitton Farm House. **Holystone** (Northumberland). Salmon (late), trout; mostly private. Holystone Burn, trout; Grasslees Burn, trout. Inn: Salmon, where particulars can be had. **Harbottle** (Northumberland). Good trout and some late salmon fishing on Coquet and Alwin. Upper Coquetdale AC has extensive parts of upper river; members only.

CORNWALL (streams, lakes, etc)

(For close seasons, licences, etc, see South Western Region NRA p16)

The seven reservoirs mentioned below are all South Western Water PLC waters. Fishing on all of them is by dt from self-service units on site.

ARGAL and COLLEGE RESERVOIRS. (3m W of Falmouth.) **Argal:** 65 acres, fly only for rainbow trout. Season: Mar 24-Oct 31 incl. Dt £10.50, evening £6.50, 6 fish limit, concessions for OAP etc. Boats £5 per day, bookable in advance. **College:** 38 acres coarse fishing with carp over 30lb, large perch, bream, tench. St £73.50, £49; dt £3.25; 12-month season: all fish to be returned. **STITHIANS RESERVOIR.** (3m S of Redruth.) 247 acres. Brown and rainbow trout; fly, spinning, bait fishing zoned. Season Mar 15-Oct 12. St £80, dt £5.50, concessions for jun, OAP, dis. 4 fish limit. No boats. Permits from Londis Shop, Stithians; Peninsula Watersports Centre, Stithians.
PORTH RESERVOIR. (4m E of Newquay.) 40 acres, bream, rudd, tench and carp.
CROWDY RESERVOIR. (2m E of Camelford.) 115 acres. Brown and rainbow trout; fly, spinning and bait fishing zoned. Season Mar 15-Oct 12. St £65, dt £5, concessions for jun, OAP, dis. 4 fish limit.
SIBLYBACK LAKE. (5m N of Liskeard). 140 acres. Fly only for stocked rainbow trout. Season Mar 24-Oct 31. Contact Peninsular Water Sports Centre, Siblyback, Common Moor, Liskeard, tel: 0579 346522.
COLLIFORD LAKE. (Nr. Liskeard; 900 acres.) Fly fishing for naturally-bred brown trout. St £85, dt £6.50 (4 fish),

concessions for jun, OAP, dis. Self service tickets in Simon's Stone car park. No boats.
BREAM. Fishing station: **Par.** Heavily polluted, but tributary **Redmoor River** has good head of trout. Sand-eels at Par Sands, mackerel from the bay, pollack by Gribben Head and near harbour, and bass between harbour and Shorthorne Beach. Boats for hire at Par and Polkerris. Hotels: Royal, Par; Carlyon Bay, St Austell.
CONSTANTINE BROOK. Fishing station; **Constantine,** ns Penryn WR, 6m. Trout; free on permission of farmers. Constantine joins estuary of **Helford River** (few trout, permission of farmers). Sea fishing off Helford Mouth *(see Falmouth).* Ashton, near **Helston, Wheal Grey Pool;** stocked coarse fishery with large carp. **Boscathnoe Reservoir,** Heamore, near Penzance; stocked coarse fishery. Both Marazion AC waters. Contact hon sec.
DRIFT RESERVOIR. Near **Penzance** (3m) sixty-five acres in quiet valley. Wild brown and stocked rainbow trout (fly only). Limit, six fish per day. St, wt and dt (half price junior) and evening, from Chyandour Estate Office, Penzance (Penzance 3021) or Mr Terry Shorland, Driftways, Drift Dam, Penzance (0736 63869). Also near Penzance are 3 carp pools at **Tindeen Fishery,** dt £1.50, tel: Germoe 3486; **St Buryan Lake** carp pool, tel: St Buryan 220.
GWITHIAN BROOK. Fishing station:

Fishing available?

*If you own, manage, or know of first-class fishing available to the public which should be considered for inclusion in **Where to Fish** please apply to the publishers (address in the front of the book) for a form for submission, on completion, to the Editor. (Inclusion is at the sole discretion of the Editor).*

A good fish. A triumph shared at Drift Reservoir, Penzance.

Camborne. No longer recommended for trout fishing. Several course lakes in area, also very good beach and rock fishing. Camborne AA is sea fishing club. Tackle shops: The County Angler, 39 Cross Street. Hotels: Golden Lion, Regal, Tyack's.

HAYLE. Fishing stations: **Relubbus, Hayle Causeway** and **Gwinear.** Trout and sea trout; improving. Good beach fishing near Hayle, and estuary fishing very good, particularly for bass, mullet and flats; plenty of natural bait. Tackle shop: Angoves Sports, Copperhouse, Hayle.

LOOE. East and West Looe Rivers both approx 7 miles in length. East Looe runs to Moorswater Liskeard. West Looe to Herodsfoot. Both carry runs of sea trout, occasional Salmon. Liskeard & District AC has water on both. Shark fishing annual festival: details from sec, The Quay, East Looe. Permits from Looe Tropical and Pet Supplies, East Looe, tel: 05036 3535. **Shilla Mill Lakes,** 4 lakes, 6m west of Looe on B3359. Carp, tench, roach. Club house facilities. J Facey, tel: 0503 20271. Hotels: Punch Bowl, Jubilee. Good sea fishing.

LYNHER. Short spate river holds trout, with runs of sea trout and salmon. Grilse run in summer. Liskeard and District AC have fishing rights on all stretches of river. Permits for all Liskeard AC water on **Fowey, Camel, Seaton** and **Looe, Inny** and **Lynher** Rivers; 26 miles single/double bank fishing. Weekly/day tickets from tackle shops in local towns. Membership application to T Sobey, Trevartha Farm, Liskeard. Waiting list. Siblyback Lake is near. SWW have carp pool at **Crafthole,** near Saltash; carp, tench; dt £3, ½ for OAP, jun, from Post Office, St Germans. Royal Albert Bridge AC have 2 acre coarse fishing lake at **St Germans.**

MENALHYL. Newquay. Brown trout. Contact. sec, Mawgan AC or The Merrymoor, Mawgan Porth for tickets, wt £5.

PETHERICK WATER. Fishing station: Padstow. Small trout. Boats available for estuary fishing, which can be excellent for bass, plaice, turbot, ray.

RETALLACK WATERS. St Columb. 3 lakes, with over 200 pegs, coarse fishing; carp to 27lb, roach, rudd, tench, eels. Dt £3.50, 24 hr £7. OAP jun £2.50. All tackle and bait available from 'The Bait Bunker' on site. Open seven days a week.

Meadowside Coarse Fishery, Winnards Perch, St Columb; three lakes with carp and mixed coarse fish. Dt £3.50, £4.50 2 rods, conc. Mrs Holmes, tel: 0637 880544. Rosewater Lakes, 3 acres, carp, and mixed coarse. Dt £3, conc. Holiday cottages soon to be available. Nr Perranporth, tel: 0872 573040, or 573992.

ST ALLEN RIVER. Fishing Station: **Truro.** St Allen and **Kenwyn** Rivers at Truro; **Tresillian** River (3m from Truro on St Austell road); **Kennel** or **Perranarworthal** River (5m from Truro); free on farmer's permission; trout six to the pound; a few sea trout run into **Lower Tresillian** River. Gwarnick Mill Fly Fishing Lake, 1½ acres, is at St Allen. R trout, tel: 087254 487. At **Perranporth,** nr Redruth, Bolingey Coarse Fishing Lake, coarse fish. Dt £5. Contact John and Maddy, tel: Truro 572388. Hotel: The Morgans, Perranporth *(see also Sea Fishing Stations)*

ST AUSTELL. Roche (St Austell) AC has club waters in area at St Dennis, Rosevean, St Blazey, Bugle and Glynn. Coarse fishing for perch, roach, rudd, carp, tench and eels. Temporary membership available at tackle shops: Angling Centre, Victoria Place, St Austell; Rogers Tackle Shop, c/o Stan Mayes Garage, Bodmin.

SEATON RIVER. Seaton rises N of Liskeard, runs 1m E of the town and to the sea in 9m. Good trout stream, though bushed over. Liskeard and Dist AC has considerable stretch.

TAMAR LAKE (LOWER). Fishing station: **Kilkhampton** (Bude 5m). 40 acres. Coarse fishing for carp, tench, rudd, bream and dace. A South Western Water fishery. No close season. St £73.50 to £49, dt (from self-service unit at reservoir) £3.25. Concessions. No boats. Tackle shops: Weys of Bude, Queen Street.

TAMAR LAKE (UPPER). 81 acres. Rainbow trout best; fly only. Season Mar 24-Oct 15. SWW water (from self-service unit at reservoir dam). St £70, £42 conc, dt £5, 4 fish limit, £3 conc. Bank fishing only. Picnic area and refreshment kiosk. Tackle shop: Fishing Tackle Shop, 13 Lower Lux Street.

TIDDY. Fishing station: **St Germans.** Sea trout to Tideford, trout elsewhere.

VALENCY. Fishing station: **Boscastle.** Valency is 4m long; holds small trout and few sea trout. Hotels: Wellington, in Boscastle (NRA licences); Eliot Arms, Tregadillet 15m. Sea fishing good for bass, mackerel, pollack, etc. **WHITEACRES COUNTRY PARK,** White Cross, **Newquay,** TR8 4LW. Four stocked coarse fishing lakes in 28 acres. Carp to 25lb, tench 7lb, large bream and roach. Night fishing, matches and competitions. Tel: 0726 860220.

CUCKMERE

(For close seasons, licences, etc, see Southern Region NRA p15)

Formed by two tributaries, which join at Hellingly, and enters sea at Cuckmere Haven, west of Beachy Head. Mainly coarse fish, good roach and bream, the later to 6lb. Also chub, carp , dace and specimen pike.

Alfriston (Sussex). St £25, concessions, for both banks up and downstream of Shermans Bridge on A27 West of Wilmington, from the Compleat Angler FC, The Polegate Angling Centre or any Eastbourne tackle shop. Dt available for several club fisheries, including Pevensey Haven and Wallers Haven. Below Alfriston Lock the river is salt and tidal, being open to mouth at Cuckmere Haven. In summer grey mullet are plentiful near Exceat Bridge (Eastbourne-Seaford road); also bass and occasionally sea trout. Cuckmere is tidal to ¹/₂m upstream from Alfriston.

Hailsham (Sussex). Cuckmere 2m. Hailsham AA has 2m of **Wallers Haven,** 2m on **Pevensey Haven; Abbotts Wood,** lake 3¹/₂ acres. Members only on Cuckmere, dt £2 or £3 for other water from hon sec or tackle shops: Polegate Angling Centre; Tony's Tackle, both Eastbourne; Anglers Den, Pevensey Bay.

CUMBRIA (lakes)

(See English Lake District)

CUMBRIA (streams)

(For close seasons, licences, etc, see NW Region NRA, p17, unless otherwise stated).

ANNAS. Fishing station: **Bootle.** Small trout; good sea trout and salmon; late. Millom AA has fishing. Also water on **Esk, Lickle, Irt** and **Lazy.** St £60 + £10 entrance from hon sec Millom & Dist AA. Dt £15 from Duddon Sports. NRA licences from Bootle Stores, 4 Main Street, Bootle; Haverigg P O.

BLACK BECK. Fishing station: **Green Road.** This stream rises on Thwaites Fell, and in 7¹/₂m reaches Duddon Estuary. Millom AA has water.

CALDER. Empties into Irish Sea some 150 yards from mouth of Ehen. Salmon, sea trout, a few brown trout. Sea trout run large; 10lb and more. Best June onwards: good salmon fishing, July-Oct.

Calderbridge (Cumbria). Calder AA owns most of the river from the upper reaches to **Sellafield,** approx 5m in all. Visitor's st £47, dt £10, accompanied by member. Thirty only issued pa; apply to hon sec Calder AA. Tackle shop: W Holmes, Egremont.

EHEN. Outflow of Ennerdale Water. Flows into Irish Sea on west coast of Cumberland. Salmon, sea trout (June to Oct) and brown trout. At **Egremont** the local anglers' assn has about 8m of good salmon and sea trout fishing; st £30, wt £30; May 1-Oct 31 apply hon sec or tackle shop. Hotels: Black Beck, Egremont and Sea Cote (St Bees); Scawfell, Seascale. Good fishing in upper reaches held by Wath Brow and Ennerdale AA; st and wt. Tackle shop: W Holmes, 45 Main Street, Egremont, has permits for Ehen, Ennerdale Lake and all local fishing.

ELLEN. Rises on Great Lingy Hill and flows into the Solway Firth at Maryport. Salmon and sea trout runs increasing; best late July onwards. Good brown trout fishing (Mar-June best).

Maryport (Cumbria). Trout; sea trout, salmon. Local club: Ellen AA, which has water. Tickets and licences (st £7.50, dt £4.50) from Solway Leisure, 66 Senhouse Street. Boats from Maryport Angling Centre, 0900 817926. Hotels: Golden Lion; Waverley.

Aspatria (Cumbria). Trout; sea trout, and salmon from July. Club: Aspatria AC; weekly permits £22 to £3, trout only, from R & J Holt, The Colour Shop. Hotels: Grapes, Sun.

ESK. Rises near Scawfell and flows into Irish Sea near Ravenglass. Good runs of salmon, sea trout, July onwards.

Ravenglass (Cumbria). Salmon, sea trout. Rivers Mite and Irt here join Esk estuary *(see also Irt)*. Ravenglass; Millom AA has 620 yds south bank on Esk. St £60. Wt and dt from sec. Outward Bound School, Eskdale Green, has brown and rainbow trout fishing in private tarn (also perch). Limited to specific days. Enquiries to Bursar (Eskdale 281). May and June are best for trout; June, July, Aug for sea trout; Sept, Oct for salmon. Hotel: Pennington Arms where licences are sold and help given in arranging fishing locally.

Eskdale (Cumbria); trout; sea trout, salmon; various private owners. Inexpensive fishing on **Wastwater** and **Burnmoor Tarn.** Good sea fishing for bass within five miles.

IRT. Outflow of Wastwater, joining Esk in tidal water. **Bleng** is main tributary. Runs of salmon and sea trout July onwards, some heavy fish taken.

Gosforth. Gosforth AC has apprx 6m, single and double bank; tickets available for two visitors Mon-Fri, £70, from sec. No dt. Tackle shop: W N Holmes, Egremont. Hotel: Horse and Groom.

Holmrook (Cumbria). Salmon, sea trout, brown trout. Short free stretch in village. Enquire at hotel. Lutwidge Arms Hotel is sole agent for supply of permits for 1½m of Sporting Tribune water, limit of 6 rods. Wt £50, dt £11. Tel: 094672 4230. Millom AA holds two stretches, Holme Bridge and Drigg Village; tickets available. *(see River Duddon).* Carleton Green

Guest House issue dt for Millom anglers. Tackle shop: E W Mitchell & Son. Licences also from Duddon Sports and Leisure, Millom.

Netherwastdale (Cumbria). On **Wastwater Lake;** trout, permits *(see English Lake District).* Greendale Tarn and Low Tarn feed Wastwater. Sport is good in May and June.

MITE. Flows south for short course from slopes near Eskdale to join estuary of Irt and Esk at **Ravenglass.** A late river. Sea trout, good brown trout but small, occasional salmon later on, but few opportunities for visitors.

WAMPOOL. Fishing stations: **Wigton** and **Curthwaite.** Wampool, under the name of Chalk Beck, rises on Broad Moor. Sea trout in lower reaches mostly free.

WAVER. Trout stream, flowing into the Solway Firth. Some water free, but most subject to agreement by farmers and landowners. NRA licences may be obtained from Saundersons (Ironmongers), 11-13 King Street, **Wigton** CA7 9EB. Waver has run of sea trout and herling, Particularly in its lower reaches.

Wigton (Cumbria). Wiza Beck, Wampool, 2m N. Waver, 2m W. Ellen, 8m SW. Lakes: Moorhouse Tarn, 2m N (private). Tackle shop: Saunderson (Ironmongers), 11-13 King Street. Hotels: Royal Oak and Kildare.

CRUMMOCK BECK (tributary of Waver). Flows into Holm Dub, tributary of Waver. Free, but difficult to fish. *(For licences see Waver).*

Leegate (Cumbria). Waver, 1m E.

WHICHAM BECK. Fishing Station: **Sile Croft.** After a course of 6m runs into Haverigg Pool, which joins Duddon estuary at Haverigg (NWW).

DARENT

(For close seasons, licences, etc, see Southern Region NRA p15)

Rises by Westerham and enters Thames estuary at Dartford. Small Kentish stream which runs dry in Summer. Modest trout fishing in upper reaches, coarse fishing downstream, roach, dace, chub.

Dartford (Kent). Dartford and Dist A & PS have lakes along river valley which hold coarse fish, including carp and tench, plus stretches of Medway, Beult and L Tiesse. Long waiting list for membership. Tackle shops: Bob Morris, 1 Lincolnshire

Terrace, Lane End; Angling Centre, 84 Lowfield St; Horner's, Hawley Rd.
Otford (Kent). Trout, perch, roach, dace. Holmesdale AS has junior water. For Otford Trout Fishers, John Wickens, 23, Broughton Rd, Otford, Kent TN14 5LY. Tel: 09592 3793.
Shoreham (Kent). Trout, chub, roach, dace. Darent Valley Trout Fishers have good 2½m stretch of water between Shoreham and Eynsford; strictly private and members only (waiting list). Sepham Trout Fishery is nearby, at Sepham Farm, Filstone Lane, Shoreham, TN14 5JT. Tel: 09592 2774.
Sevenoaks (Kent). River preserved. For

Chipstead Lakes contact S Banks, 58 Chevening Rd, Chipstead, Sevenoaks Tel: 0732 458216. Tickets for friends from tackle shop: Manklows Kit & Tackle, 44 Seal Road. Manklows will supply useful information about local fishing. Bromley AS has fishing in area.
Longford Lake: private water of Holmesdale AS. Day Tickets issued only to members' guests. Coltsfoot Mill trout fishery, Oxted, 2½ acres: tel: 0883 715666. Bromley (Kent) and Dist AS has Kent Sand Pits, Sevenoaks, and trout water on Darent; members only.

Tributary of the Darent

CRAY: Coarse fish.
Crayford (Kent). Free fishing at Five Arches. Thameside Works AS has Cray; bream, roach, perch, rudd, pike; members only. They also have a lake at Northfleet and Shorne Country Park lakes. Coarse fish. Dt for Shorne only, £2.50, £1.50 jun. from bailiff. Membership from R Gra-

ham, 186 Waterdales, Northfleet. SAE, please. **Ruxley Pits, Orpington,** coarse fish; Orpington AA has lakes in a Nature Reserve. No dt. Waiting list for membership. Tackle shop: Orpington Angling Suppliers, 304 High Street, St Mary Cray; A & I Fishing Tackle, 33 High St, Green St Green.

DART

(For close seasons, licences, etc, see, South Western Region NRA p16)

Rises in centre of Dartmoor and at once divides into two, the East and the West Dart. East Dart runs to Postbridge and thence to Dartmeet, where it unites with West Dart which flows through Two Bridges. The West Dart above Dartmeet and the East Dart above Walla Brook, including tributaries, belong to Duchy of Cornwall. The river has runs of salmon and peal (sea trout). Best months for salmon are April and May in the lower reaches and May to September higher up. For peal July to September are favoured.

Dartmouth (Devon). Sea fishing from boats and rocks; thornback ray to 15lb (best bait prawn) pollack, dabs, pouting, mullet in tidal water. Baits, squid, rag, lug, peeler crab. Wrasse, bass and garfish off castle rocks. Late Sept best (and quietest) time for river angling: conger record 60lb. Boats effective in river and sea: many for hire. Skerrie banks and wrecks popular venues. Flatfish off sand. Club: Dartmouth & Dist AA, clubroom open at weekends. Salmon, peal and trout fishing in Dart on Dart AA water *(see Totnes, Buckfastleigh)* and a trout reservoir. Lake; Slapton Ley; pike, rudd, etc, 8m *(see Devonshire, small streams and lakes)*. Also, **Old Mill,** SWW carp pool, dt. Tackle and frozen baits from Sport 'n' Tackle; Sea Haven, Newcomen Road. Hotel: Victoria, Victoria Rd.
Totnes (Devon). Salmon, peal, trout. Dart AA controls Dart from Staverton Weir to

Austins Bridge, left bank only; Totnes Weir. Permits, Totnes Angling Centre; Newton Abbot Angling Centre. Wt (S) £30, dt £10. (T) £15, £5. Weir only, dt (S) £12, (ST) £9. Salmon av 10lb; peal 2lb in May-June and about 1lb thereafter. 4lb and 5lb peal not rare. School peal run from late June to mid-Aug. Nearly all peal caught after dark in normal conditions; Aug usually best. Fly only for peal and trout. Newhouse Fishery, Moreleigh, Totnes TQ9 7JS, tel: 054882 426, has 3 acre trout lake open all year. Dt £15, 3 fish. New Barn Angling Centre, Totnes Rd, Paignton, has coarse and trout ponds, plus accom. Tel Paignton 553602. Hotels: Seymour, Royal Seven Stars and Cott Inn (at Darlington). At Staverton, near Totnes, is the Sea Trout Inn, close to the river. Old Mill, Harberton, has ½m trout fishing on **River Harbourne.**
Buckfastleigh (Devon). Salmon, peal,

trout. SWW Plc has fishery, ¼m Dart, Austins Bridge to Nursery Pool; salmon, sea trout. St £45, 16 rods. Tel: 0392 219666. Holne Chase Hotel, near Ashburton, has about 1m right bank upstream from bridge free to residents. Limited st, £75, and dt £12, to non-residents. Fishing on Duchy of Cornwall waters arranged for guests, with tuition if adequate notice given. Fly only. Five holding pools. Permits also from Black Rock Guest House; Bossell Guest House (tuition available); Dart Bridge farm.

Princetown (Devon). Permits for salmon and trout fishing on main river, **East** and **West Dart, Wallabrook, Swincombe** and **Cherrybrook** from The Land Steward, Duchy of Cornwall Office, Liskeard, Cornwall PL14 4EE and most tackle shops in S Devon, also the Prince Hall Hotel, Two Bridges Hotel, both Princetown, Mabin's News, Fore St, Poundsgate and Princetown Post Office. Salmon best May-Sept. Charges: S and MT, st £80, wt £40, dt £12, T, st £35, wt £8, dt £1.50. Accommodation: Two Bridges Hotel and Prince Hall Hotel, Princetown.

Hexworthy (Devon); Salmon, sea trout (peal), brown trout. Hotel: Forest Inn, Hexworthy PL20 6SD, tel: 03642 211; dt, wt or st, at hotel, for Duchy of Cornwall water. Ghillie, instruction available; inn buys catch. Good centre for E and W Dart and Cherrybrook.

DEBEN

(For close seasons, licences, etc see Anglian Region NRA, p17)

Short Suffolk river (about 30 miles long) rising near Debenham and flowing to North Sea near Felixstowe. Coarse fishing.

Woodbridge (Suffolk). Tidal. Roach, pike, tench, perch above town. Club: Woodbridge and Dist AC, who also have Loam Pond, Sutton, and Holton Pit; st £12, dt £2, from tackle shop or Saxmundham Angling Centre or Anglia Photographics, Halesworth. Other club with Deben fishing, Framlington & Dist AC, tel: 0728 860123. Tackle shop: Rod & Gun Shop, 18 Church St. Hotels: Bull, Crown.

Wickham Market (Suffolk). Roach, perch, pike. Woodbridge AC has river and Wickham Market Reservoir; dt. St only for stretch between Glevering Bridge and Wickham Market Bridge from Rod & Gun Shop, Woodbridge.

DERWENT (Cumbria)

(For close seasons, licences, etc, see South Western Region NRA p16)

Rises on north side of Scawfell and flows through Borrowdale, Derwentwater and Bassenthwaite Lakes to the Solway Firth at Workington. Salmon and trout practically throughout length. A late river. Best months for salmon, July to October. Trout fishing on some stretches excellent. River also holds pike and perch.

Cockermouth to **Workington** (Cumbria). Salmon, sea trout, brown trout. Trout and salmon fishing may occasionally be permitted on dt. Enquiries to fishery Manager, Cockermouth Castle. Permit charges under review. Permits for **Cocker** also (limited). Waters through town can be fished on permit from Tourist Information Office by residents and visitors staying locally on weekly basis. Cockermouth AA has water on Cocker (members only) but issues dt £5.50 for **Cogra Moss. Mockerkin Tarn,** stocked with carp. Fishing within reach on Bassenthwaite, Loweswater, Crummock and Buttermere. Tackle shops: D Lothian, 35 Main St and N H Temple, 11 Station Street, Keswick; both issue licences and permits, and will give information. Workington tackle shop: Graham's Guns Sports Services, 17 Fisher Street. Hotels: Trout, Globe, Cockermouth Pheasant, Bassenthwaite Lake, Sun, Bassenthwaite.

Brigham (Cumbria). Trout, sea trout, salmon. Broughton Working Men's AA has about 1m from here to Broughton Cross. Permits to local working men only.

Bassenthwaite (Cumbria). Derwent, 1m N; trout, salmon; private. Lakes: Bassenthwaite; pike, perch, trout, occasional salmon *(see English Lake District - Bassenthwaite)*. Hotels: Swan, Pheasant, Armathwaite Hall.

Keswick (Cumbria). For rivers Derwent and Greta. Salmon, trout (average ¼lb), pike, perch, eels; mid August onwards for salmon. Permits for Keswick AA water (Portinscale to ½ mile above Bassenthwaite Lake). Visitors Salmon wt £75, dt £20. Trout permit includes Derwentwater, wt £25, dt £5 (reductions for juniors all fishing) from Field and Stream, 79 Main Street, Keswick. Visitors st by application to sec, £110. Tickets issued for Derwent cover Greta also. Hotels: Hazeldene, Queen's Royal Oak,

Lake, George, County King's Arms. The Derwentwater Hotel. Permit charges subject to annual review.

Borrowdale (Cumbria). Trout, salmon; gin-clear as a rule and best fished after dark. Lakes: Derwentwater; trout, perch, pike; small charge for fishing. Watendlath Tarn 2m S; Blea Tarn, 4m S; trout. Hotels: Scawfell; Borrowdale; Lodore Swiss.

Tributaries of the Derwent (Cumbria)

COCKER: Salmon, sea trout, trout. July to October best for migratory fish. Mostly private, but dt for Cockermouth AA water (and for **Loweswater, Buttermere** and **Crummock Water**) from D Lothian, Tackle Shop, Cockermouth.

Scalehill (Cumbria). Cockermouth. 7m Cocker: Salmon, sea trout, trout. Private. National Trust lakes. Hotel: Scale Hill.

Cogra Moss. 40 acre trout reservoir 8m S of Cockermouth. Browns and rainbows. St £60, wt £15, dt £5.50. Season April 1-Sept 30. From The Gun Shop, Lorton Street, D W Lothian, Main Street, Cock-

ermouth; Inglenook Caravan Park, Lamplugh.

NEWLANDS BECK: Trout.

Braithwaite (Cumbria); ns Keswick, 2m. Beck; fishable above Braithwaite, ruined by dredging below.

GRETA: Trout (av ¼lb); salmon.

Threlkeld (Cumbria). Keswick AA have fishing here *(tickets see Keswick)*. Best months for salmon Sept and Oct; mostly spinning and worm fishing. Glenderamackin Beck; trout; fishable throughout length, but very narrow and fish few and far between.

DEVONSHIRE (streams and lakes)

(For close seasons, licences, etc, see SW Region NRA, p16)

AVON. Rises on Dartmoor and flows 22m SE, entering English Channel near Thurlestone via long, twisting estuary. Tide flows to Aveton Gifford. Trout (3 or 4lb), sea trout, salmon.

Thurlestone (Devon). Near mouth of Avon estuary. Capital bass fishing off Bantham Sands at mouth.

Aveton Gifford (Devon). About 6¹/₄m of left bank and 8¹/₄m of right bank, 1m both banks above Gara Bridge, ¹/₂m left bank only below Gara Bridge controlled by Avon FA. Sea trout (end of May onwards), some salmon; good dry-fly trout water (3 to the lb). Banks heavily wooded; good wading. Mt, ft, wt, from post office at Loddiswell; P O'Neil, 55 Church Street, Kingsbridge.

Kingsbridge (Devon). Avon, 2½m N at **Loddiswell;** trout, salmon, sea trout. Further information from hon sec Avon FA *(see also Aveton Gifford)*. Capital bass and pollack in Kingsbridge estuary. Tackle shop: Perrott Bros, 26 Fore Street. Hotels: King's Arms; Buttville; Torcross (for Slapton Ley).

Brent (Devon). Salmon, trout, sea trout.

Avon FA water below *(See Aveton Gifford)*. Mrs J Theobald, Little Aish Riding Stables, South Brent, issues dt for stretch of Aish Woods. Red Brook, 2m N; trout. Black Brook, 2m S; trout. Hotel: Anchor.

AVON DAM (8m NE of Totnes). Brown trout, zoned worm, spinning and fly fishing free to NRA licence holders. No boats. Season March 15-Oct 12. Reservoir is about 1½m beyond **Shipley Bridge,** car park available.

BELLBROOK VALLEY TROUT FISHERY, Oakford, Tiverton EX16 9EX. Three specimen lakes, min stock 3lb, and three normal fishing lakes; dt £33 and £18.50, specimen fishing, or dt £9.50 plus £1.60/lb fish caught. ½ day £6.50 plus same. Limits 8 and 5 fish. Record 1993, 18lb 4oz. Tuition available. Accommodation at fishery farmhouse.

BLAKEWELL FISHERY. 1m N. Barnstaple. Brown and rb. trout av. 2¼ lb. Dt £15, 3 fish, £13, evening £10, from fishery. 4 fish and 2 fish limits. This establishment also runs a commercial fish farm. Tel: 0271 44533.

BURRATOR RESERVOIR, Yelverton.

Burrator Reservoir, near Plymouth. *Photo: Mike Weaver.*

150 acres. Zoned fly fishing and spinning for brown and rainbow trout. Open Mar 15-Sept 30. Dt £5, st £70 (concessions), 4 fish limit, from D K Sports, The Barbican, Plymouth, or Burrator Inn, Dousland, Yelverton.

ERME. Rises on Dartmoor and flows 14m S to Bigbury Bay. Trout. **Ivybridge.** Fishing now restricted to local young people only.

FERNWORTHY RESERVOIR, near Chagford. South Western Water Plc. 76 acres, b trout, largest 4lb 2oz; May 1-Oct 12. Dt £13 (evenings £8). Boat £6 (evenings £4). 4 fish limit; concessions. Self-service unit by hut on S side of reservoir. Advisable to book boat 24 hr in advance.

GAMMATON, DARRACOTT and **JENNETS RESERVOIRS, Bideford** *(see Torridge).*

MELDON RESERVOIR (3m SE of Okehampton). 54 acres, natural brown and stocked rainbow trout. Spinning, bait and fly fishing, free to NRA licence holders. Season Mar 15-Oct 30. K Spalding, SWW Ranger, tel: 083787 535.

LYN, near **Lynmouth** (Devon). This beautiful river has good run of salmon, July onwards. Also sea trout and brown trout; latter small. NRA **Watersmeet** and **Glenthorne** fisheries. Limits, 2 S, 6 ST, 8 T. S & MT: wt £20, dt £6.50. T: st £16, wt £5, dt £1.50, from C F Kingston, 1 Lee Rd, Lynton; Williams, Lower Bourne House, High Street Porlock; The Pet Shop, Lynton; Price, East Lyn House, Watersmeet Rd, Lynmouth. Season March 1-Sept 30. Mrs Lester, Glebe House, Brendon, issues dt for 3m (both banks) of East Lyn. Other contacts for East Lyn fishing are Simpkins, Rockford Inn, Brendon; Rising Sun Hotel Lynmouth; Doone Valley Riding Stables, Brendon. Tackle shops: D & M Woolgrove, 13 The Parade, Minehead. *(See also Sea Fishing Stations).*

PLYM. Devon trout stream which enters English Channel at Plymouth.

Plymouth (Devon). Good runs of sea trout on Plym and Tavy. Salmon run late on Plym, Oct to 15 Dec. Plymouth and Dist freshwater AA has R Plym from Plymbridge upstream for about 3m, and Tavy, north of Tavistock. Annual subscription £65, from hon sec D L Owen, tel: 0752 705033. Dt for first mile from D K Sports. Length above Bickleigh Bridge,

controlled by Tavy, Walkham and Plym FC Club issues tickets (salmon, sea trout, brown trout) for its water *(see Tamar - Tavy)*. Sea fishing excellent. Tackle shops: D K Sports, 88 Vauxhall St; Osborne & Cragg, 37 Bretonside.
MEAVY (tributary of the Plym). Fishing stations: **Shaugh** and **Clearbrook.**
OAREWATER, Brendon. Trout, Dt and wt from W Burge, Oaremead.
SID, Sidmouth. Trout.
SLADE RESERVOIRS, Ilfracombe. In **Upper Slade** and **Lower Slade,** coarse fishing for carp, tench, bream, roach and perch. St £60-£41; dt £2.75 from Lee Road Post Office, Slade.
SLAPTON LEY, Dartmouth 7m. Pike, rudd, roach, eel and perch. Part of nature reserve, bank fishing prohibited. For day tickets only, £6-£10, £9-£15, £12-£20, for one, two or three anglers, apply Field Centre, Slapton, Kingsbridge, TQ7 2QP (Kingsbridge 580466). Life-jackets available, compulsory for anglers under 18 years of age. Excellent sea fishing for bass, turbot, plaice, brill and large whiting. Tackle shops: Sport and Fish, 16 Fairfax Place, Dartmouth; Anchor Sports Cabin, Bridge St, Kingsbridge. Hotels: The Torcross and (in Slapton) the Tower Inn. Many guest houses.
SQUABMOOR RESERVOIR. E Budleigh. Bait fishing for coarse fish. St £60-£41, dt £2.75, conc, contact Dell Mills, Peninsula Fisheries, tel: 0752 766897. Permits from Knowle Garage, Knowle, or Tackle Shop, 20 The Strand, Exmouth. **Hogsbrook Lake,** 2½ acres, at Woodbury Salterton is dt coarse fishery nearby. Contact F W S Carter, Greenshill

Barton, Woodbury Salterton, tel: 0395 33340/68183.
STAFFORD MOOR FISHERY, Winkleigh EX19 8PW. Two lakes of fourteen acres and eight acres; regularly stocked with rainbow trout, av. weight over 2lb. Tackle, over 400 patterns of flies, on sale. Dt £15, 5 fish, £12, 3 fish. Beginners pond. Tel: 08054 360.
KENNICK, TOTTIFORD and **TRENCHFORD RESERVOIRS** (8m NE of Newton Abbot). Kennick 45 and Tottiford 35 acres. Rainbow trout. Fly only. £10.50, evenings £6.50. 5/6 fish limit. Season: April 1-Oct 31. Boats available. Tickets from self-service unit on site. Trenchford is coarse fishing, pike to 24lb. Open Oct 1-Mar 14. Dt £2.50, conc, from self service unit.
VENFORD RESERVOIR. Ns **Hexworthy.** Brown, and rainbow trout. Spinning and bubble-float fishing, free to NRA licence-holders. Season: March 15-Oct 12.
WISTLANDPOUND RESERVOIR, Arlington. Brown trout. Fly only, Apr 1-Oct 31. Dt £5. Concessions to OAP and Jun, from Sports Centre, South Molton.
YEALM. Rises on southern heights of Dartmoor and flows 12m south and west to English Channel, which it enters by a long estuary. Trout, sea trout (about 6-8lb) occasional late salmon. Fishing private. Good bass and pollack in estuary (Cornwall NRA).
Newton Ferrers (Devon). On estuary. One of finest deep-sea fishing stations in south-west. Hotel: River Yealm, tel: 0752 872419, has its own harbour frontage and jetty.

DORSET (streams)

(For close seasons licences, etc, see South Western Region NRA, p16)

BRIT AND **ASKER.** Fishing station: **Bridport.** Trout. Rivers mostly private or over-grown, but Civil Service Sports

Council has stretch of Brit for members only. Also **Radipole Lakes;** dt for latter; coarse fish. Tickets from Weymouth

---

Check before you go

While every effort has been made to ensure that the information given in **Where to Fish** *is correct, the position is continually changing, and anglers are urged, in their own interests, to make preliminary enquiries before travelling to selected venues. This is especially important with reference to prices quoted. Inevitably the rate of inflation is affecting stability in this quarter. Anglers' attention is also drawn to the fact that the hotels mentioned under the various fishing stations do not necessarily have water of their own. Any amendments or further data for inclusion in subsequent editions, and any criticism, will be welcome.*

tackle shops. Dt for **Osmington Mills Lake** (carp and tench) available on site only. Trout fishing at **Watermill Lake**, well stocked with rainbows. Mangerton Mill, Mangerton, Bridport, tel: 030885 224.

CHAR. Fishing station: **Charmouth.** Char is some 7m long; trout, private, but leave may sometimes be obtained. General sea fishing. Hotels: Coach and Horses, Queen's Arms, Hammons Mead.

CORFE. Rises 1m W of Corfe Castle and runs into Poole Harbour 5m down. Coarse fishing sometimes available from landowners. Dt can be obtained for Arfleet Lake at Corfe Castle.

DURHAM (reservoirs)

DERWENT. Edmundbyers. May 1-Oct 14, 1,000 acre trout water run by Sunderland & South Shields Water Co, 29 John Street, Sunderland. Well stocked with 2-year-old brown rainbow trout (av $3/4$lb); fly only. St (from company) £145. Dt £5, obtainable on site. Motor boats £13, rowing boats £6.50, NRA licence required. Tel: Edmundbyers 55250 for boat bookings. Hotel: Lord Crewe Arms. **Note:**

Reservoir also partly in Northumberland.

SMIDDY SHAW, and **WASKERLEY.** Good trouting, preserved by North-West Durham AA. Dt £3, Waskerley only, in the hut by the reservoir. Season April 1-Sept 30. Nearest towns: **Wolsingham, Consett** and **Stanhope.** Hotel: Royal Derwent at Allensford.

EDEN

(For close season licences, etc, see North West Region NRA p17)

Rises south of Kirkby Stephen and empties into Solway Firth 5m NW of Carlisle. Salmon, sea trout, brown trout. Still some spring fish, but now more a back-end river. Sea trout in lower and middle reaches and tributaries from June onwards. Trouting best in middle and upper reaches, fish run to good average size for north. Chub and grayling in parts.

Carlisle (Cumbria). Salmon in spring and autumn, sea trout and herling in July and August, brown trout fair, some chub and dace. Carlisle AA has 7m on Eden, dt before Aug 31 from McHardy or Wilson (see below). **Lough Trout Fishery,** Thurstonfield CA5 6HB; 25 acres, dt £15, 4 fish limit, tel: 0228 76 552. For Warwick Hall, **Warwick-on-Eden,** salmon and trout fishing, inquire Maj Murphy, Carlisle 61018, or Mr Haughin, 60545. Hotels: Crown and Mitre, Central, Hilltop. There are two lakes of 25 acres with trout and coarse fishing, and salmon and sea trout in adjacent rivers, at Border Game Fishers Ltd, Longtown, CA6 5NA, tel: 0228 791108. Tackle shops: Murrays, Lowther Arcade; Wilsons', 36 Portland Place; McHardy's, South Henry Street.

Wetheral (Cumbria). Salmon and sea trout preserved for 3m, both banks from Warwick Bridge upstream, by the Yorkshire Fly-fishers' Club here and at Great Corby; Cairn Beck, 2m, Irthing, 3m N. Scotby Beck, 2m W at Scotby. Hotel: Crown.

Armathwaite (Cumbria). Salmon, trout, grayling. Croglin Waters, 3m E.

Lazonby (Cumbria). Salmon, trout and grayling. Bracken Bank Lodge (Tel: 0768 898241), has three good salmon and trout stretches on Eden for its guests at Great Salkeld, Little Salkeld and Syke Foot, with some fine pools. Trout average $1/2$lb. Details sent on application to the Secretary. St £300-350; dt(S) £23 to £25.50; (T) £10. Accommodation at the lodge with reduced fishing terms. Mixed fishery at Crossfield Farm, Kirkoswald, Penrith. Record ide caught, 1993, 3lbs $4^{1}/2$ ozs. Special match tickets available. Trout limit 2 fish. Disabled facilities. Holiday accom. on site. Tel: 0768 896275.

Great Salkeld (Cumbria). Fetherston Arms Hotel, Kirkoswald, has $2^{1}/2$m (Lazonby 284). High Drove Inn has salmon and trout fishing; salmon 75p day, trout 50p.

Langwathby (Cumbria). Salmon, trout; preserved by Yorkshire FFC.

Culgaith (Cumbria). Trout; preserved by Yorkshire FFC from Culgaith to below Langwathby apart from vicinity of Watersmeet. Winderwath, left bank. Hotels: Black Swan, Culgaith, King's Arms, Temple Sowerby.

Temple Sowerby (Cumbria). Salmon, trout, grayling; preserved (with some miles of Eamont) by Yorkshire FFC; members only. Penrith AA (with 45m of fishing in all) has Powis House Water above Bolton Village; water upstream of Oustenstand Island. Wt and st issued at various prices for different stretches. King's Arms Hotel has trout fishing for guests on 1½m of Eden; licences and tickets available at hotel; trout average 1lb.

Kirkby Thore (Cumbria). Salmon, trout and grayling. Penrith AA preserves 2m on main river and Kirkby Thore Beck from road bridge 1m upstream.

Appleby (Cumbria). Eden trout are very free risers, averaging about three to pound with better fish to 3 and even 4lb. Tufton Arms can arrange Eden fishing and instruction for guests. Tel: 07683 51593/52761. Sandford Arms, Sandford CA16 6NR, has private fly fishing for guests. Tel: 07683 51121. Tickets £10 for Upper Appleby fishings from John Pape *(see below)*. Brown trout, fly only. Sedge fishing in evenings good May to August.

Grayling provide good winter sport. Licences and local flies from John Pape, Appleby Shoe & Sports Supplies, Market Place; Appleby Sports, The Cloisters, Boroughgate.

Kirkby Stephen (Cumbria). Kirkby Stephen and Dist AA has about 15m on main river and becks, fly only. *(See Belah and Scandal Tributaries)*. Visitors' st £65, joining fee £15, from hon sec. Dt £15 from Robinson, Silver Street (waiting list for membership). Fly fishing ponds at Bessy Beck Trout, 05396; Eden Valley Trout Lake, 07683 71489. Redenol House, 56 South Rd, has private trout fishing for guests. Tel: 07683 71489. H Parr, 11 Nateby Rd, runs local fishing courses and holidays, tel: 07683 72223. Licences from Mounsey, Newsagent, 46 Market St. Tackle and tickets from H S Robinson, 2 Market St. Hotels: Kings Arms; Pennine; Black Bull, White Lion.

Tributaries of the Eden

PETTERIL joins Eden at Carlisle. Good trout fishing, but lower half mostly private. Penrith AA has 10m of water on upper reaches.

Plumpton (Cumbria). Trout. Penrith AA preserves from Kettleside Farm to Petteril Bank.

IRTHING. Rises on Grey Fell Common and joins Eden east of Carlisle. Salmon, trout, grayling and few sea trout.

Brampton (Cumbria). Irthing; 1m N; Gelt, 1m S; trout, grayling, chub. Brampton AS preserves; st (£16), wt (£12), dt (£4) and NRA licence from Sports Haus, Front St. Trout average ½ to ¾lb, early months best. Hotels: White Lion, Scotch Arms, Sand House, Howard Arms. Tackle shops: Sporting Guns and Fishing Tackle, 2 Market Place; W Warwick, Front Street.

EAMONT flows from Ullswater Lake. Penrith AA has most of this water. Lake Ullswater good trout fishing; free, but NRA licence required.

Penrith (Cumbria). Eamont, 1m S; salmon, trout. Upper portion (trout only) preserved by Penrith AA (fly fishing only for visitors) from Pooley Bridge on left bank to Yanwath Viaduct, and on right bank from Pooley Bridge to Yanwath Wood. Also on **Eden, Lowther** and on becks. Wt covers a variety of fishings, available from C R Sykes only *(see below)*. Trout

fishing at **Blencarn Lake** from Mr and Mrs Stampter, Blencarn Hall, Culgaith 076888 284. Yorkshire Flyfishers preserve left bank of Eamont from Broughton Castle down to Barrack Bank and then on left bank only to below Udford; members only. Other water on Eamont private. Coarse fish at Whins Pond, **Edenhall;** Mrs Siddle, tel 62671. Sockbridge Mill Trout Farm, tel 0768 65338, off B5320, is suitable family venue, fishing dt £1.50 + £1.65 per lb caught. **Haweswater,** 10m SE; rights in hands of North West Water, and guests at Haweswater Hotel, Mardale, Bampton, near Penrith, may obtain permits at hotel *(see Westmorland lakes)*. Crown & Mitre Hotel, Bampton Grange, has 8m of salmon and trout fishing on Eden and tributaries available to residents. Other hotels: Crown, George, Gloucester Arms, Kings Arms, Edenhall, near Langwathby. Licences from tackle shops: S Norris of Penrith, London Rd, or C R Sykes, 4 Great Dockray, both Penrith; or Langwathby PO.

Pooley Bridge (Cumbria). Eamont; salmon, trout. Penrith AA water.

Patterdale (Cumbria). The becks Goldrill, Grisedale, Deepdale and Hartsop; free. Aira Force below NT property (3m) free. N Hawes and Riggindale Becks, permits N West Water. Blea Tarn and Smallwater, N West Water. **Ullswater.** Trout numerous, average three to pound. Evening rise during May and June yields heavy baskets; six brace of trout in evening quite common. Day fishing also good; and heavier fish begin to move about middle of May. Numerous boats available. Angle Tarn, permits. Greenside Reservoir, Red Tarn, Grisdale Tarn, free. Hotels: Ullswater, Patterdale; White Lion, Brotherswater; Glenridding (boats).

LOWTHER (tributary of Eamont). Salmon and trout. Abstraction affecting salmon sport -- autumn run now very late. Sport with trout remains good (av ¾lb). Crown and Mitre Hotel, **Bampton** (via Penrith), has more than 3m fishing for guests (trout and late salmon) including Haweswater

Beck; a good centre, only 100 yds from river. Penrith AA holds substantial stretches of good fly water on river; other assn water on Eden, Eamont and Petteril; £5. NRA licences from hotel or Penrith tackle shops.

LYVENNET. Good trout stream; runs in a few miles below Temple Sowerby. Leave from farmers in some parts. 1m preserved for Yorkshire Flyfishers' Club.

BELAH. Flows from Pennine fells to join Eden 2m below Kirkby Stephen. Lower reaches, from Brough Sowerby, rented by Kirkby Stephen and Dist AA; members only.

SCANDAL BECK, Smardale (Cumbria) and **Crosby Garrett** (Cumbria). Kirkby Stephen & Dist AA has water. *(See Kirkby Stephen under Eden.)*

ENGLISH LAKE DISTRICT

(For close seasons, licences, etc, see North West Region NRA, p17)

BASSENTHWAITE, 5m Cockermouth; 8m Keswick. Long famous for its pike, also perch and some brown trout. Hotels: Pheasant Inn, Swan, Armathwaite Hall.

BLEA TARN. About 2m above Watendlath Tarn; perch; some trout. Contact Mrs My-

ers, Blea Tarn Farmhouse, Langdale.

BLELHAM TARN. Ns Windermere. Pike, perch, some trout, tickets from Mr F Hilton, Hawkshead AC, Co-op, Main St, Hawkshead.

BROTHERSWATER. Good trout and

Coniston Water.

pike. National Trust; fishing free.
BUTTERMERE. National Trust lake.
Char, trout, pike, perch. Permits (wt £8,
dt £2) which cover Crummock and
Loweswater, too, from Mr & Mrs Parker,
Dalegarth.
CODALE TARN, 4m from **Grasmere.**
Perch, some trout; free. Hotels: *(see
Grasmere).*
CONISTON. Trout, char, perch, pike. free;
NRA licence needed. Boats from Conis-
ton Power Boat Co, Bridge End Café, and
café at boat-house. Tackle and licences
from David Wilson, Tackle and Gift
Shop, Tilberthwaite Ave, or Sun Hotel,
both Coniston. Local club: Coniston and
Torver AA, which has fishing on Yew
Tree Tarn. Hotels: Sun, Black Bull,
Crown, Ship Inn.
CRUMMOCKWATER. National Trust
lake. Pike, trout, char, a lot of perch;
salmon and sea trout from Cocker sometimes caught by trolling. Fishes best June
and July. St £35, wt £8 and dt £2 (covering also Buttermere and Loweswater)
from Mrs Beard, Rannerdale Farm, Buttermere CA13 9UY, tel: 07687 70232
(rowing boats for hire). Best periods for
Crummock, Buttermere and Loweswater
are: Trout, late May and early June (good
mayfly hatch); char, July and August
(special technique required -- trolling 60
to 90 feet down). *(For hotels see Buttermere).*
DERWENTWATER. Keswick. Trout very
good size are best fished for from a boat
in mayfly season. Good sized perch and
pike, salmon present but rarely taken.
Fishing rights leased to Keswick AA. Wt
£25, dt £5 (which includes all KAA waters) from Field and Stream, Keswick.
Boats may be hired from Nicoll End, and
Keswick landings. Hotels: too numerous
for detailed reference.
DEVOKE WATER near **Ravenglass** (5m
E). Moorland tarn offering sport with fair
sized trout. Millom AA holds rights. Dt
£10 from Duddon Sports, Millom or Carleton Green Guest House, Salcoats,
Holmrook; Waberthwaite PO.
DRUNKEN DUCK TARNS, Ambleside.
Brown trout to 4½lb, rainbow to 6lb. Wt
£60, dt £12 (reductions for ½ day and
evenings), from Drunken Duck Hotel;
early booking necessary. Six rods, incl
two for Grizedale AC. Guided days on
Windemere May/June; boat, food incl.
Tackle shop: Ambleside Angling, 3 Old
Post Office Buildings, Millans Park Rd,

Ambleside.
EASEDALE TARN, 3m from **Grasmere.**
Good perch, few trout. Free fishing. Managed by National Trust, The Hollens,
Grasmere, Cumbria LA22 9QZ.
ELTERWATER, ns Windermere. Pike
and perch, few trout.
ENNERDALE, ns Whitehaven. Trout,
char; controlled by Ennerdale Lake fisheries formed by Egremont Anglers, Wath
Brow and Ennerdale Anglers; St £10 and
wt £5 from Wath Brow Post Office, Cleator Moor, or W N Holmes, Main St, Egremont. Enquiries to D Crellin (hon. sec.)
0946 823 337.
ESTHWAITE WATER (nr **Hawkshead,**
Lancashire). ns Windermere, 3m. Good
pike, perch and trout (av ¾lb). Fishing by
permit only (St £145, wt £32, dt £8.50)
from Collins & Butterworth, Post Office,
Hawkshead, near Ambleside (also daily
boat permits, tackle and licences). Nearest accommodation is in Hawkshead,
Sawrey and Windermere. Trout fishing
by any method at Hawkshead Trout
Farm, The Boathouse, Ridding Wood,
tel: 05394 36541.
FISHER TARN, ns Kendal, 3m. Kendal's
water supply. Few trout of good average
size; privately leased.
GRASMERE, ns Windermere. Large
pike, perch, brown trout; Windermere,
Ambleside and Dist AA water, boats
available from Allonby's Boat Yard,
Grasmere. For **Rydal Water** and **River
Rothay** apply Windermere, Ambleside
and Dist AA, c/o Musgroves Ltd, Lake
Rd, Windermere. Hotels: Swan, Red
Lion, Rothay, Prince of Wales, Dale
Lodge, Ben Place (private), Moss Grove
(private).
**GREAT RUNDALE TARN, ns Long
Marton,** 5m. Seamore Tarn and Little
Rundale Tarn are in the vicinity. Small
trout.
GRIZEDALE LEA RESERVOIR. Trout;
hon sec, Kirkham and Dist FFC issues dt
(limited), boat extra; fly only.
HAWESWATER, ns Penrith or **Shap.** A
good head of wild brown trout, char,
gwyniad and perch. Bank fishing, fly
only, free to all holders of NRA licence.
HAYES WATER, ns Penrith. Trout (3 to
lb) and perch. Penrith AA; members only.
**KILLINGTON RESERVOIR, ns Oxen-
holme,** 3m. Trout, pike, perch. Leased to
Kent AA. St £11, wt £4.50, dt £2 from
Kendal tackle shops or Keeper at reservoir. Concession st to jun. Parties should

book in advance through Kent AA sec.

KNOTT END TARN: Birkby, Ravenglass. Regular stocking of brown and rb trout to 6lb. Dry fly and nymph (barbless hook) only. fly casting instruction, also suitable for handicapped anglers. Day tickets, 0800-1700 hrs, £10. Evenings: £10. Bookings to W Arnold, tel: 0229 717255. Tackle and information from Esso Garage, Holmrook.

LOUGHRIGG TARN, nr **Ambleside.** Pike, perch, roach and eels; apply to Mrs Murphy, Tarn Foot Farm, Loughrigg, Nr Ambleside.

LONGLANDS LAKE. Cleator, West Cumbria. Wath Brow and Ennerdale Anglers. Tickets from Farrens Family Store, Cleator, or Wath Brow GPO.

LOWESWATER. National Trust lake. Pike, perch, trout (av 1½-2lb but hard to catch; fly only up to June 16); For wt £8 and dt £2 (covering also Buttermere and Crummockwater) apply to Mr and Mrs Leck, Water End Farm, Loweswater, tel: 0946 861465.

MEADLEY RESERVOIR. Cleator Moor, West Cumbria. Brown trout up to 3lb, and rainbow up to 10lb. St £130, dt £10, from Wath Brow P O, or contact R H Moyle and W Morley 13 Clayton Ave, Cleator Moor.

MOCKERKIN, near Loweswater. Tarn stocked with carp by Haigh AA, Whitehaven.

RYDAL WATER and **HIGH ARNSIDE TARN,** ns **Windermere.** Pike, perch and fair-sized trout; trout only, H Arnside. Preserved by Windermere, Ambleside and Dist AA. Tickets from Tourist IC and Allonby's, Grasmere.

SKELSMERGH, ns **Kendal,** 3m. Swarms with small roach and rudd, fishing free; bank treacherous.

SPRINKLING TARN. Right up Stye Head Pass. Trout. Good on a favourable day until July.

STYE HEAD TARN. Same information as Sprinkling Tarn.

THIRLMERE. Perch, pike, trout. Preserved by N West Water, who issue privilege tickets only to employees.

ULLSWATER, ns **Penrith.** Covers 2,200 acres. Free, with NRA license. Noted trout fishery. Also perch, and gwyniad. Trout average 3 to 1b but fish up to 8lb taken. Hotels: Ullswater, Patterdale, White Lion, Glenridding, Waterfoot, Waternook, Sharrow Bay, Rampsbeck, Brackenrigg, Howtown, Crown, Sun (last two Pooley Bridge). Boats available.

WATENDLATH TARN. Keswick 3m. Brown and rainbow trout fishery, fly only, stocked weekly; boats available. Apply to Mrs Richardson, Fold Head Farm, Watendlath. Charges on request.

WINDERMERE, nr **Windermere.** Largest lake. 10½m long and nearly 1m wide. Good pike and perch, also eels, char and trout (trout best March-June). Fishing free, apart from NRA licence. Big fish taken by trolling. Boats from Bowness Bay, Waterhead Bay and Fell Foot NT Caravan park. Local club: Windermere, Ambleside Dist AA, which issues dt and wt for fishing on **Grasmere, Rydal Water,** Rivers **Rothay, Brathay,** three tarns, **Ghyll head Reservoir,** 11 acres, r trout to 8lb, and Dudds Reservoir, 7 acres. Assc trout fishing on **High Newton Reservoir,** Grange-over-Sands, fly only, dt available, two fish limit. **Ratherhead** and **Cleabarrow** Tarns are now coarse fisheries, dt £3, from local tackle shops: Allsports Ltd, Victoria Buildings, Royal Square, Bowness-on-Windermere, Carlson Tackle Shop, Kendal; Lakes Tackle Shop, 3 Belsfield Terrace, Bowness, arrange fishing trips by boat, and have all local day tickets, plus rods for hire. Tel: 05394 45978. Hotels: Lonsdale, Lake Rd; Cragwood Country House; Applegarth; Oakthorpe. Ambleside: Skelwith Bridge; Langdale Chase; Fisherbeck. All these offer free fishing on

---

Check before you go

While every effort has been made to ensure that the information given in **Where to Fish** *is correct, the position is continually changing, and anglers are urged, in their own interests, to make preliminary enquiries before travelling to selected venues. This is especially important with reference to prices quoted. Inevitably the rate of inflation is affecting stability in this quarter. Anglers' attention is also drawn to the fact that the hotels mentioned under the various fishing stations do not necessarily have water of their own. Any amendments or further data for inclusion in subsequent editions, and any criticism, will be welcome.*

WADAA waters. Boat fishing trips on Lake Windermere with all bait and tackle supplied, may be had from tel: Windermere 88027/45780 daytime, 88348 evenings. Fishing trips also operate from Low Wood Watersports Centre, tel: 05394 34004/47113.

YEW TREE TARN, near **Coniston**. Rainbow and brown trout; day tickets £6, conc, from David Wilson, Tackle and Gift Shop, Tilberthwaite Ave, or Sun Hotel, both Coniston.

ESK (Border)

(Esk in England is under North West Region NRA; close seasons, licences, etc, see p17. Statutory close times apply to rivers in Scotland; no licence needed).

Rises in Dumfriesshire and flows into the Solway firth but is classed as an English river. Upper reaches of Esk and main tributary, Liddle, good for brown trout but rivers are primarily sea trout and salmon waters from Langholm and Newcastleton to the mouth. Heavy run of sea trout and herling from July to September. Salmon in spring and autumn, September and October being best months. Chub and dace in lower reaches provide good sport in winter.

Canonbie (Dumfries and Galloway). Salmon, sea trout, herling, trout; Esk and Liddle Fisheries issue permits: St £300 to £40, wt £8 to £52, dt £6 to £30. (Jun ½ price.) From Secretary's office, Bank of Scotland, Langholm; G Graham, riverwatcher, Hagg on Esk, Canonbie. Liddle tickets from J D Ewart, Douglas Square, and Mrs B Elliott, Thistlesyke, both Newcastleton. Also contact Stevenson and Johnson, Bank of Scotland Buildings, Langholm, Dumfriesshire DG13 0AD. No NRA licence needed. Hotels: Cross Keys.

Langholm (Dumfries and Galloway).

Salmon, sea trout, herling, brown trout. Certain stretches of Esk and its tributary the Liddle, are under the control of Esk and Liddle Fisheries *(see above)*. Netherby Estate Offices, Longtown, issue permits for salmon and sea trout fishing at **Netherby**. No Sunday fishing and restricted night fishing. There are also restrictions on spinning and worm fishing. Full particulars from secretary. Tackle shops: Border Guns & Tackle, 40 High Street; Patties of Dumfries. Hotels: Eskdale, Douglas or Cross Keys (Canonbie).

Westerkirk (Dumfries and Galloway). Salmon, sea trout, herling, trout.

Tributaries of the Border Esk

LIDDLE: Salmon, sea trout, herling, brown trout.

Newcastleton (Roxburgh). Salmon, sea trout, herling, brown trout. Esk and Liddle Fisheries have much water. Tickets for 5m stretch. *(See Canonbie)*. Bailey Mill Farm Holidays, Bailey TO9 0TR, offer fishing holidays on 7m of Liddle, with accommodation, also 12m of Esk nr **Longton**. Hotels: Liddlesdale, Grapes (fishing arranged on Esk, Liddle and local waters) *(see also Esk, Langholm)*.

LYNE: Lyne rises on Bewcastle Fells and joins Esk ½m above Metal Bridge. Salmon, sea trout, herling, trout. Riparian owners sometimes give permission.

SARK: Trout stream about 10m long, form-

ing for a short distance boundary between England and Scotland, and emptying into Solway at **Gretna**; has run of sea trout and herling (best July onwards).

KIRTLE WATER: Stream which empties into the Solway at Kirtlefoot. Sea trout, herling, trout. Humbers Lodge Hotel, Rigg and Kirtleside farm, Rigg.

Kirtlebridge (Dumfries and Galloway). Sea trout and trout; short free length. Winterhope Burn. Penoben Burn. Annan, 3m SW. Well-stocked reservoir 3m off, **Middlebie Dam**, fishable by permit; trouting very good.

Kirkpatrick (Dumfries and Galloway). Trout.

ESK (Yorkshire)

(For close seasons, licences, etc, see Northumbria and Yorkshire Region NRA, p17)

Rises on Westerdale Moor and runs into sea at Whitby. Salmon, trout and grayling. This stream, from which salmon had disappeared, was artificially restocked, and now holds good head of fish. Represents most successful effort at restocking with salmon. Good runs of sea trout; brown trout plentiful but small . River largely controlled by Esk Fishery Association.

Whitby (Yorks). Salmon, sea trout, trout, grayling, eels; largely preserved by the Esk FA from Whitby to beyond Glaisdale. Applications for vacancies in association should be addressed to the hon sec. Visitors' tickets available only for water between Ruswarp and Sleights. No maggot fishing is allowed. fishing from Iburndale Beck down to Ruswarp Dam. St, dt. Salmon, sea trout and brown trout. Tickets from boat-landing at Ruswarp.

RUSWARP (Yorks). Salmon, sea trout, trout, grayling, eels; preserved for 2m by Esk Fishery Association. Tickets from Boatyard, Ruswarp.

Sleights (Yorks). Salmon, sea trout, trout, grayling, eels; preserved by Esk fishery Association. Tickets from Boatyard, Ruswarp.

Goathland (Yorks). Salmon, sea trout, trout, grayling. Murk Esk; trout. Goathland AC water; members only.

Grosmont (Yorks). Trout, salmon; preserved by the Esk FA above to Glaisdale, and below to Whitby.

Egton Bridge (Yorks). Salmon, trout; some water preserved by the Esk FA. Other water (1½m both banks) owned by Egton Estates Co. Tickets sometimes issued. Trout fishing in **Randymere Reservoir,** between here and Goathland and **Scaling Dam** (worm and fly). Hotels: Horse Shoe; Wheatsheaf Inn; Station.

Glaisdale (N Yorks). Salmon, sea trout, trout; preserved below by the Esk FA *(see Whitby).* Hotel: Angler's Rest. Esk FA bailiff, D J Swales, Rosedene, Priory Park, Grosmont, Whitby. Dt from Yorkshire Water.

Danby (N Yorks). Salmon, sea trout, brown trout, grayling, preserved by landowners and Danby AC. Danby AC has about 8m of water stocked each year with approx 800 11. brown trout, also between Castleton and Leaholm; st (limited) £12, dt £3 from Duke of Wellington (Danby); Post Offices, Castleton and Danby; John Simpson Gun Shop, Stokesley, N Yorks, and F Farrow, 11 Dale End, Danby, (Club bailiff). Restrictions on method according to date. Accommodation, licences, tickets, available at Duke of Wellington.

Westerdale (N Yorks). Trout, grayling. Stokesley AC has about 3m above and below village. Members only.

Tributaries of the Esk (Yorkshire)

MURK ESK: Salmon and trout. Tributaries are: Little Beck, Brocka Beck, Eller Beck, Little Eller Beck. Fishing station: Grosmont.

COMMONDALE BROOK: **Commondale** (Yorks). Trout: preserved by the owners.

ESSEX (streams, lakes and reservoirs)

(For close seasons, licences, etc, see Anglian Region NRA, p17)

ARDLEIGH RESERVOIR, nr Colchester. Of the A 137, stocked with brown and rainbow trout. Small pond winter rainbow fishery available. Fly only reservoir season: last Sat in March to Oct 29. Any legal method trout and coarse season, Oct 1-Feb 28. Coarse fishing allowed on restricted areas, Mar 16-30 Sept. New 7 acre carp and tench fishery open during coarse fishing season. Barclaycard Visa payments accepted. Concessions to anglers under 19 years. Discount permit scheme operates and private tuition available. Free childrens' classes. Fly tying classes, Nov-Mar. Enq to fisheries & Estate Officer, Ardleigh Reservoir, Nr Colchester, Essex CO7 7PT, with sae, Tel: 0206 230642.

AVELEY LAKES, Romford Road, Aveley. 25 acre coarse fishery, st only. Carp, av 10lb, chub, rudd, tench, crucian to be stocked. A few tickets, £125 to £65, conc, apply to fishing lodge.

BERWICK PONDS, Rainham. Operated by Berwick Ponds, 105 Suttons Avenue, Hornchurch RM12 4LZ. Tench, roach, bream, pike, carp. Dt £3; OAP £1.50, jun £2 from bailiff on bank.

CONNAUGHT WATERS, Chingford. Roach, bream, carp; free.

COBBLERS MEAD LAKE, Corringham. Excellent coarse fishing; large bream and carp, good tench and roach. Monthly competitions. Members only, st £25; night fishing, extra £20. G Hyde, Box 18, Canvey Island, Essex SS8 0AZ, tel: 0268 683946; or Stanford Tackle Centre, Wharfe Rd, Stanford-le-Hope, Essex. Basildon Angling Centre, 422 Whitmore Way, **Basildon,** tel: 0268 520144 has day tickets for several local small coarse fisheries, including Pipps Hill, Slough House, and Range Water.

EPPING FOREST PONDS. Most notable is Wake Valley Pond, near Wake Arms on A11; roach, bream, tench and small carp. Ponds usually free except for Ornamental Water: dt £2.50. Perch Pond: £2, Hollow Pond, Connaught Water: £2.50, from bailiff on site. The office of Superintendent of Epping forest is at The Warren, Loughton, IG10 4RW.

FISHERS GREEN, Waltham Abbey. Pike, tench, bream, roach, barbel, chub, perch, eels. A Leisure Sport restricted permit fishery of 68 and 65 acre gravel pits, 3900m of R Lea, 3160 of Lea Relief Channel. St £32 + £4 key deposit, no dt. Concessions for jun, OAP, dis. Applications to LSA, Thorpe Park, Staines Road, Chertsey KT16 8PN. Tel: 0932 564872.

GOSFIELD LAKE, Halstead (Essex). 45 acres; well-stocked with carp, perch, roach, tench, pike. Inquire C W Turp, Gosfield Lake Ltd, Church Road, Gosfield. Dt (7.30 am - 7.30 pm) £4, concessions to jun, obtainable from the shop.

HANNINGFIELD RESERVOIR. Near **Chelmsford.** Excellent trout fishery. Regular stocking. Bank and boat fishing. Season: Apr 1-Oct 31. Full St: £375; Mon-Fri: £295; named week-day: £225; Sat and Sun £300, weekend one named day £250. Dt at £13.50 per day. Motor Boats £17 per day, rowing boats £10.50. Part day and evening boats also available. All prices include VAT. Limit 6 fish. Car parks and fishing lodge. Total catch around 50,000, average weight 2lb, Enquiries telephone Basildon 710101. Fisheries Officer, Essex Water Company, Hall Street, Chelmsford, CM2 0HH.

HATFIELD FOREST LAKE. Near Hatfield Broad Oak and Bishop's Stortford. National Trust property; good pike and tench, carp and bream; some roach and rudd. Full st £70, night £50, day £40 and dt £3.50, OAP and juv conc. For tickets apply Lake Warden, Bob Adams, The Shell House, Takeley, Bishop's Stortford CM22 6NH (Tel: 0279 870477). Restric-

tions on use of groundbait.

HOOKS MARSH. 40 acre Leisure Sport gravel pit nr **Waltham Abbey.** Bream, tench, roach, perch and pike. Dt £2.50, conc. £1.25, from P & B Hall, 44 Highbridge St, Waltham Abbey, or on bank.

LAYER PITS. 6m S of **Colchester;** controlled by Colchester APS; coarse fish; members only. Colchester Piscatorial Society has **Langham Ponds;** no tickets.

NAZEING MEADS, Meadgate Lane, Nazeing, Essex. Fours gravel pits totalling 125 acres. Pike are main species, with large carp, bream, roach, eels, chub. By written application only, to Lee Valley Regional Park Authority, Myddelton House, Bulls Cross, Enfield, EN2 9HG, tel: 0992 717711.

STAMBRIDGE STARR FISHERIES, Great Stambridge, Essex, one stocked trout lake, one coarse lake. Dt £3. per 3 hours plus £2.25 per lb fish caught. Coarse dt £5, night fishing. Casting instruction and rod hire. Barbless hooks only. Tel: 0702 258274.

STANFORD-LE-HOPE. Two Leisure Sport gravel pits, 13 acres. Large carp, crucian, perch, pike, tench. St £24, concessions to Jun, OAP, Dis. No dt. Applications to LSA, Thorpe Park, Staines Road, Chertsey KT16 8PN. Tel: 0932 564872.

MARDYKE: Fishing stations: **Purfleet** and **Ockendon.** Rises by East Horndon and flows 12m to Thames at Purfleet. There are some club lengths. Moor Hall & Belhus AS have two members only coarse fisheries at South Ockendon, st on application to Sec.

PANT. Bocking. Upper part of R Blackwater *(see Blackwater in main list).*

ONGAR. Coarse fish; good chub, roach, dace and perch. Practically whole of fishable Roding controlled by clubs, principally Ongar and Dist AS (members only; river and pit), Collier Row AS (st available from hon sec). Fishing showing considerable improvement. Tackle shop: Morris, Kings Road and Roblin, 114 High Street, **Brentwood.**

POLLUTION

Anglers are united in deploring pollution. To combat it, urgent action may be called for at any time from any one of us. If numbers of fish are found dead, dying, or seriously distressed, take samples of both fish and water and contact the officer responsible for pollution at the appropriate National Rivers Authority.

PASSINGFORD BRIDGE. Roach, chub, pike; bream, carp, tench. Barkingside and Dist AS has 1½m downstream; bailiff on water. Dt from bailiffs on bank for ¾m upstream of bridge. Woodford AS has 1½m north of bridge; members only (st for associates from hon sec), Elm Park AS has water; dt from bailiff. Tackle shop: Edko Sports, 136 North Street, **Romford**.

SCRUBBS LAKE, Hadleigh (Essex). Good perch, roach, rudd, etc; dt.

SHOEBURY PARK LAKE, Shoeburyness (Essex). Coarse fish; dt issued.

SOUTH WEALD LAKES. Weald, Thorndon, Belhus Woods and Danbury Country Parks all have fishing run by Essex County Council. Usual freshwater fish, esp. carp. St £50, dt £250, £1.30 jun, OAP; on lakeside or from Weald Office, Weald Country Park, South Weald, Brentwood, Essex CM14 5QS; tel:0277 216297.

THE CHASE, Dagenham (Essex). White Hart Anglers' water; gravel pit; roach, bream, tench (excellent), carp (common, mirror and crucian), rudd, pike, perch; no night fishing; hempseed banned; dt from bailiff; NRA licences needed. Tackle shops: Ridge & Co, 277 Oxlow Lane; Edko Sports, 136 North Street, Romford.

WANSTEAD & WOODFORD LAKES AND PONDS. Eagle Pond, Snaresbrook (roach, perch, carp); **Knighton Wood Pond, Woodford; Hollow Pond, Whipps Cross**; all free.

OTHER TICKET WATERS. Priory Lakes, Priory Park, **Southend;** Eastwood Pit, **Rayleigh;** Essex Carp Fishery (crucian carp, bream) at Mollands Lane, **South Ockendon;** Old Hall Lake, **Herongate;** Moor Hall Farm Fishery, **Aveley;** Raphael Park Lake, **Romford;** Danbury Park Lakes, near **Chelmsford;** Harwood Hall at Corbets Tey, and Parklands Lake, both near **Upminster;** Warren Pond, **Chingford;** carp, bream. Tickets mostly available from bailiffs on site. Some Essex tackle shops: Essex Angling & Sport, 5 Broadway Parade, Elm Park; Avenue Angling, 22A Woodford Avenue, Ilford; Angling Centre, 226 Hornchurch Rd, Hornchurch.

For Walthamstow reservoirs, see under London.

EXE

(For close seasons, licences, etc, see South Western Region NRA p16)

Rises on Exmoor and runs south through Devon to Exmouth. Salmon and trout, with grayling and coarse fish in lower reaches. At several points on upper reaches trout fishing (moorland) and occasional salmon fishing may be had by hotel guests.

Exeter (Devon). Bream, carp, dace, gudgeon, pike, perch, roach, rudd, tench and eels. **Exeter Ship** and **Tiverton Grand Western** Canals contain bream, carp, pike, perch, rudd, roach, tench, eels and odd dace. Better part of Exeter canal from Broadwater (lime Kilns) to Turf (where canal enters Exe estuary). Hotels on canal banks: Double Locks, Turf. Exeter & Dist AA (amalgamation of local clubs) has coarse fishing rights on R Exe (eleven fishings) on **Culm** and **Creedy**, from City Basin to Turf Locks on Exeter Ship Canal, and on ponds at Kingsteignton, Cowley, Sampford Peveril, Ottery St Mary and Mamhead. St, visitors wt, dt. For fishing on Tiverton Canal contact Tiverton AC, tel: 0884 256721 or tackle shops. At Exwick right bank visitors may fish for ½m, and from Exwick Mills d/s 400 yds below Exwick Rd Bridge. NRA has 3m of salmon fishing on lower Exe in Cowley and Countess Wear areas. Dt £4, st £60, fly or spinning, from Feb 14 to Sept 30, available from tackle shops in Exeter, Taunton, Tiverton. Apply Exeter AC, Smythen Street. Dt £2.50, wt £7 for Exeter & Dist AA waters from tackle shops. South View Fishery, Shillingford St George, 6 acres coarse, with carp to 20lb; dt £3.50. Tel: 0392 832278. 2m W of city, **Haldon Ponds** trout fishery, stocked with rainbows to 10lb, b to 7lb. Wt £35, dt £6, evening £3. Rods limited. Boats. Phone Exeter 32967. One permit a day available for salmon fishing (weekdays only) from Exeter Angling Centre, Smythen Street; Brailey's Field Sports Centre, Market St; Tony Gould, 47 Longbrook Street.

Brampford Speke (Devon). Salmon, trout, dace; preserved. Pynes Water, from here down to Cowley Weir (2½m) fished by local syndicate. Exeter & Dist AA water towards Stoke Canon (see Culm). Kingfisher Youth AC are a sponsored club, offering every advantage and incentive to young anglers, incl. disabled. Annual membership £12.50. See club list for address.

Thorverton (Devon). For fly only brown trout dt, 4 fish limit, contact T Mortimer, High Banks, Latchmore, Thorveton EX50 51Z; tel: 0392 860241.

Silverton (Devon). Trout, roach, dace, pike, perch; preserved. Exeter & Dist AA has coarse fishing on Culm here *(see Exeter and Culm)*.

Bickleigh (Devon). Trout, salmon. Fisherman's Cot Hotel has ³/₄m both banks adjoining hotel for salmon and/or trout. Mainly for residents, but a few £12 dt available.

Tiverton (Devon). Exe, Lowman and Little Dart; trout, salmon. **Tiverton Canal;** pike, perch, roach, tench. Exe preserved for 2m both above and below town (trout and grayling) by Tiverton FFC, fly only. St £7.50 for residents only. Dt £2, ½m above Tiverton; fly only, for visitors. River walk in Tiverton, ½m, free trout fishing to jun. Salmon, st £33, dt £3.30. Hotels: Bark House at Oakford Bridge; Fisherman's Cot, Bickleigh (beat on Exe). At Tiverton Junction is Railway Hotel, where accommodation can be had by anglers fishing **Tiverton Canal;** tickets. Tackle shop: Country Sports, 9 William St.

Dulverton (Som). Salmon, trout, grayling. Usually good run of salmon (May onwards and autumn) to Dulverton and beyond, depending on water conditions. Trout fishing good on Exe and **Barle** (four to lb). For 540m single bank, contact Lance Nicholson *(see below)*. Grayling less plentiful. Guests at Carnarvon Arms may fish on 6m of Exe and Barle; individual beats and gillie. Wt £100-£130 (S). Dt (S) £12-£25. Trout dt £7-£12. A few day tickets sometimes available for non-residents. Some free fishing for guests at Lion Hotel. Royal Oak, Winsford, issues permits. **Exe Valley Fishery,** Exebridge, Dulverton TA22 9AY. One large lake and two small onees stocked with browns and rainbows averaging 2lb+. Dt £5.50 (£1.40 per lb caught extra) available at tackle shop on site throughout year. Limit: 2½ brace. For two miles of Exe and Hadoe trout fishing, 15 Mar-30 Sept, dt £8, half day £5, also Exe salmon fishing nr Cove, dt £20, contact John Sharpe, Parlour Cottage, Higher Grants, Exebridge, Dulverton, tel: 0398 23104. Coarse fishing and tuition also available. Tackle shop: Lance Nicholson, High St. Accom. at Anchor Inn, Exebridge, Dulverton.

Exford (Som). Trout. Crown Hotel can arrange fishing on Exe and instruction on stocked trout ponds. Trout fishing also available on Nutscale, Clatworthy and Wimbleball Reservoirs (rainbow and brown) and Badgeworthy Water and Oarewater (both banks) in Doone Valley on Exmoor, Salmon is available in the area, especially in the Lyn.

Winsford (Som). Exe; trout. Royal Oak Inn, Winsford TA24 7JE, has 5m of water on Exe and Haddeo stocked with b trout, plus limited water on middle Exe for salmon. Also small lake for quality rainbow. Dt £17 lake, £12 river, from J S Sporting, Parlour Cottage, Higher Grants, Exebridge, Dulverton. Tarr Steps Hotel has 6m of salmon and trout fishing, fly only, on the Barle.

Tributaries of the Exe

CREEDY: Trout, coarse fish.

Cowley Bridge (Exeter). Coarse fish. Exeter and Dist AA has rights (see Exeter).

Crediton (Devon). Trout; preserved by owners. Yeo 3m; trout; leave from farmers. Crediton FFC has over 5m, mainly double bank, on Creedy and Yeo, also 1½m on R Taw at Tawbridge. Limited dt £8 (Mon-Fri) Fly only. Contact Sec Crediton FFC. Fly only. Tackle shop: Ladd's Sports. Hotels: Ship, White Hart.

CULM: Trout, coarse fish, few grayling. Stock dwindled through pollution.

Stoke Canon, Rewe and **Silverton** (Devon). Dace, roach, perch and occasional grayling. Exeter and Dist AA has water.

Cullompton (Devon). Trout. River mostly preserved. Stout Trout Fishery: 2 acre lake, r and b trout, fly only. Billingsmoor Farm, Butterleigh, tel: 08845 248. Licences from Country Sports, 3 Station Rd. Hotels: Railway and Collumpton.

Uffculme. Permits for stretch from ³/₄m above bridge to Five Fords (about ³/₄m) issued by J E Metters, 11 Alleyn Rd, London SE21 8AB, tel: 081-670 4208; st £20, mt £15, wt £5, dt £1.50. M Dixon, Culmside, Uffculme has ³/₄m at Uffculme.

Hemyock (Devon). Trout, small and few. Lower water preserved and stocked by

---

TARR STEPS HOTEL
Devon/Somerset Border
HAWKRIDGE, nr. DULVERTON, SOMERSET, TA22 9PY

An informal, sporting country house hotel, providing excellent food and wines and an atmosphere which combines quiet luxury, privacy and friendliness. Overlooks the beautiful Barle Valley and set in heavily-wooded moorland scenery.

FISHING (free) for salmon and trout, fly only, on three miles of River Barle.

CLAY PIGEON and ROUGH SHOOTING in 500 acres of privately owned land surrounding the hotel.
HUNTING with six well-known packs. Hunting weekends arranged.
RIDING AND TREKKING from nearby stables. The hotel has excellent loose boxes for guests own horses. Hay and straw can be provided.
Brochure on request   MID-WEEK SPECIAL BREAKS   *Telephone Winsford (064 385) 293*

Hemyock-Culmstock syndicate
Clayhidon (Devon). Upper Culm FA preserves about 4m in this district (see Hemyock). No Sunday fishing. Hotel: Half Moon.

Killerton (Devon). National Trust controls coarse fishing on Killerton Estate; tickets from tackle shops for Exeter AA water.

BARLE. Runs through beautifully wooded valley and holds salmon (av 7-10lb) and trout (av 8-10 in).

Tarr Steps (Som). Salmon, trout. Tarr Steps Hotel Hawkridge TA22 9PY, has 3m of salmon and trout fishing, fly only, free for guests. Non-guests dt S £15, T £5. Tel: 064385 293 *(see advt)*.

Withypool (Som). Trout; some salmon. Crown Hotel, Exford, can arrange fishing. Inn: Royal Oak.

Simonsbath (Som). Exmoor Forest Hotel has rights on 8m of Barle, free to hotel guests. St £50 to dt £3.50, for non-residents. NRA licences at hotel. Spinning for salmon allowed. Convenient for **Wimbleball Reservoir.**

FAL
(For close seasons, licences, etc, see South Western Region NRA, p16)

Rises near Roche and flows about 23 miles, due south, past Grampound and Tregony to the English Channel at Falmouth. Fair trouting.

Falmouth (Cornwall). Excellent trout fishing in reservoirs. Trout in many of the small streams flowing into creeks around Falmouth free in most on permission of farmers. Coarse fish at stocked pond at Tory Farm, Ponsanooth; permission from farmer. Tackle shops: A B Harvey, Market Strand (NRA licences; reservoir permits); Berks, Arwenack St; Cunningham's, 10 Lower Market St, Penryn.

Tregony (Cornwall). Trout, 2m off runs Polglaze Brook, 4m long; trout.

FOWEY
(For close seasons, licences, etc, see South Western Region NRA p16)

Rises on Bodmin Moor and enters English Channel by estuary at Fowey. Noted sea trout and salmon river. Sea trout best time mid-June to August. A spate river with middle and upper reaches fishing best after heavy rain.

Fowey (Cornwall). Capital sea fishing *(see Sea Fishing section).* Tackle shops: Leisure Time, 10 The Esplanade; Marine Services, 21/27 Station Rd. Hotels: Fowey, Riverside, Ship, Fowey Hall, Marina.

Lostwithiel (Cornwall). Sea trout, salmon. Fishing for rod and line below Lostwithiel Bridge free. Lostwithiel AC has 2m fishing mainly double bank upsteam of town roadbridge. Permits from J.H. Hooper, 4 Reed's Park, Lostwithiel. 0208 872937 Dt £10, wt £20 st £30. Dt and wk permits also available from Roger, Stan May's Garage, Bodmin. 0208 72659.

Respryn Bridge (Cornwall). Most water upstream is in the hands of Lanhydrock AA, NT Cornwall Regional Office, **Lanhydrock** Park, PL30 4DE. St £40 (waiting list), wt £25, dt £10. No live bait. Hotels: Royal Talbot, King's Arms, Earl of Chatham, Royal Oak, Globe, Trevone Guest House and Restormel Lodge

Bodmin Parkway (Cornwall). Trout, sea trout, salmon. Liskeard and Dist AC has rights on some 25m of single and double bank of **Fowey, Lynher, Camel,** and on minor rivers, East and West Looe, Seaton and Inny. Restricted full membership, open season varies details, dt and wt from T Sobey, Trevartha Farm or Tremar Tropical of Liskeard. M.Barker (0208 82464) 1m single bank seatrout and salmon fishing available with self-catering cottages.

FROME AND PIDDLE (Dorset)

(For close seasons, licences, etc, see South Western Region NRA, p16)

Frome rises above Hooke in West Dorset and flows into the English Channel at Poole Harbour near Wareham. Piddle rises in a mill pond 1 mile north of Piddletrenthide and enters Poole Harbour near mouth of Frome near Wareham. Both are chalk streams and closely preserved but sport may sometimes be had. Some very good sea trout have been caught in the Frome, which also receives a run of heavy salmon. Trout in both rivers plentiful and good. Bass run up to where the river enters Poole Harbour. Piddle carries small stock of heavy salmon. There is free coarse fishing on Frome on right hand bank downstream to mouth at Poole Harbour.

Wareham (Dorset). On Frome and Piddle; salmon, sea trout, trout, grayling, pike, roach and dace. Salmon and trout preserved, but leave sometimes from owners of waters. Morden Estate Office, Charborough Park, Wareham, sometimes has rods available for entire season (never for day or week) as follows: salmon, Frome and Piddle; trout, Piddle and Bere, and River Stour, coarse fishing. NRA lets 14 rods for the season (on the basis of two per day) for fishery on Piddle; salmon, sea trout (details from Area Fisheries and Recreations Officer). South Drain nr Poole Harbour is Wareham & Dist AS water. Club has 22 local waters, membership £24, £5 jun. Hotels: Red Lion and Black Bear. Tackle shop and bait: G Elmes & Son, St John's Hill; Guns & Sports, 24 South Street.

Wool (Dorset). Frome: Salmon, sea trout.

Woolbridge Manor (100 yards from river) has 1¼m; fly and spinning. Salmon run large, fish over 30lb not rare. Summer run of grilse 6 to 10lb. Season 1 Mar to 30 Sept. St £200, dt £25. NRA licence required. Nr **Puddletown, Pallington Lakes, Tincleton,** one trout, one coarse, one carp and tench only. Daily stocking. Trout dt £19; four fish limit. Coarse fishing £4, conc. Records include salmon 19lb, r trout 11lb 12oz and carp 22½lb. Tel: 0305 848141. At Tolpuddle, **Wessex Fly Fishing,** Lawrences Farm, tel: 0305 848460. Rivers, lakes and pools, accom. and tuition. Rivers are chalk streams in a natural state, with a good head of wild-bred brown trout. Improving from over-abstraction. Spring salmon scarce, summer and autumn fish plentiful in Frome. Dt £20, ½ day £16.

Dorchester (Dorset). Frome: trout; pre-

Check before you go

While every effort has been made to ensure that the information given in **Where to Fish** *is correct, the position is continually changing, and anglers are urged, in their own interests, to make preliminary enquiries before travelling to selected venues. This is especially important with reference to prices quoted. Inevitably the rate of inflation is affecting stability in this quarter. Anglers' attention is also drawn to the fact that the hotels mentioned under the various fishing stations do not necessarily have water of their own. Any amendments or further data for inclusion in subsequent editions, and any criticism, will be welcome.*

Pallington Lakes Trout Fishery, Tincleton, Dorchester. *Photo: Eric Chalker.*

served from Bockhampton to Gascoyne Bridge nr Bradford Peverell by Dorchester FC dry fly only. Rest of river strictly preserved by land owners. Dt and licences from tackle shop. Other society: Dorchester and Dist AS (coarse fishing only) who issue dt for short stretch of **Stour**. At **Kingcombe**, Higher Kingcombe Farm. 8 ponds - coarse fishing; Paul Crocker 0300 320537, St £75, £3 full day, £2 evenings, £5 night. **Hooke**, Knights in the Bottom Lake, fly only trout fishing; Jill Haynes, 0308 862157. Trout fishery on 5 lakes, brown and rainbow. Dt £17, £13, £10. Limit, full day, 4 fish. **Rawlsbury Waters**, 4 small trout lakes, tel: 0258 817446. Luckfield Lake, 1½ acre coarse fishery at Watergates Lane, Broadmayne. Carp to 25lb, Dt £3.50 from tackle shop. John Aplin also has dt for good carp and tench fishing at Luckfield Lake, **Broadmayne**. Hotels: King's Arms. **Flowers Farm Lakes**, Hilfield; trout fishery of 5 lakes, brown and rainbow. Dt £17, £13, £10. Limit, full day 4 fish. Dorchester, Dorset DT2 7BA; tel: 0300 341351. Tackle shop: Specialist Angling Supplies, 1 Athelstan Road.

GIPPING (Orwell)

(For close seasons, licences, etc, see Anglian Region NRA, p17)

Rises between Stowmarket and Bury St Edmunds, and flows into the North Sea by an estuary near Ipswich. Coarse fish.

Ipswich (Suffolk). Most coarse fish. From Yarmouth Rd Bridge to Norwich Railway Bridge, 1m, dt on bank. 2m stretch from Railway Bridge to Sproughton Bridge, dt from tackle shops. Gipping APS controls 10m between Stowmarket and Ipswich. Soc. issues special st £6.60, dt £1.30 for small section of river from Sproughton to Ipswich, from Ipswich tackle shops; members only on other fishings. **Alton Water**, 350 acre coarse fish reservoir at Stutton Holbrook, under control of AW, with bream to 4lb and pike to 25lb. St £25, dt £2.50, conc. Holbrook Rd, Stutton, Ipswich, IP9 2RY. Tel: 0473 327398. Leisure Sport stretch on river is at **Bramford**. St £18, conc, no dt. Details from LSA, Thorpe Park, Chertsey, Surrey; tel: 0932 564872. Good codling, skate, whiting and flounder fishing below town. Tackle shops: Viscount Tackle, Clapgate Lane; R Markham, Woodbridge Road East; Bosmere Tackle, 57 High Street, Needham Market.

Stowmarket (Suffolk). Permits to fish Green Meadow stretch from Bosmere Tackle, see below. Stowmarket and Dist AA has short stretch of **Rattle;** members only. Needham Lake, 10 acres: most coarse fish. Water users permit £6 required, from District Council, plus Gipping Valley AC permit from Bosmere Tackle, 57 High St, Needham Market.

GLOUCESTERSHIRE (streams)

BIDEFORD BROOK. Fishing station: **Awre.** Rises in Abbot's Wood and flows 7m to Severn estuary; coarse fish; preserved. **Blackpool Brook** enters at Awre; Forest of Dean AC; members only.

CONE. fishing station: **Woolaston.** Cone rises by Hewelsfield, and is 5m long. Eels and flounders.

FROME. Rises near Cheltenham and flows into Severn estuary. Coarse fish; a few trout higher up. Fishing stations: **Stonehouse** (Glos), coarse fish, and **Stroud** (Glos), a few trout and coarse fish. Several brooks in vicinity. Stroud AA controls 2m Thames at Lechlade and 1m at Newbridge. Enquire Batemans *(see below)*. Pike and coarse fishing in Stroudwater Canal. Stroud tackle shop: Batemans Sports, Kendrick Street, GL5 1AB, tel: 0453 764320, who issue st £8, £4 juv for local club waters, including Frome at **Eastington** and **Whitminster** and Severn at **Wainlode**, and tickets for small carp lakes. Tackle shop: Lobby's, 48A High St, Stonehouse.

NAILSWORTH BROOK (tributary of Frome). Fishing stations: **Nailsworth** (Glos) and **Woodchester** (Glos). Brook reported polluted in parts. Lakes: Long-

fords Lake, pike, carp. Woodchester Park lakes: pike, perch, roach, tench, brown and rainbow trout; now preserved.

Coombe Lakes, Wotton-under-Edge GL12 ZNE. Trout (fly only) and coarse fishing. Invitation only. Tel: 0453 843136. At Nailsworth is The Midland Fishery trout farm *(see p11)*

HOPE BROOK. Fishing station: **Westbury-on-Severn**, ns Grange Court, 1½m. Hope Brook rises 2m above Longhope, runs 5m to Westbury and Severn estuary (1m). Coarse fish, mostly preserved. Inn: Red Lion.

LITTLE AVON: Small Gloucestershire stream flowing into Severn estuary.

Berkeley (Glos). Coarse fish, trout, Waterley Brook. Fishing below Charfield preserved. Close by station rises Billow Brook, which runs thence 3m to estuary. Clubs have water on **Gloucester and Berkeley Canal;** 16m Sharpness to Gloucester.

LYD. Chub, roach, perch. Fishing station: **Lydney.** Lydney AA holds stretch from railway station to Tufts Junction. Club also has **Lydney Lake** (carp, roach and perch). **Lydney Canal** and a dam.

HAMPSHIRE (Streams, lakes and canal)

(For close seasons, licences, etc, see Southern Region NRA, p15)

BASINGSTOKE CANAL. Fishing stations: **Greywell, North Warnborough, Odiham, Winchfield, Crookham, Fleet, Farnborough, Aldershot, Ash Vale.** Pike, carp, roach, good tench, perch; fishing from towpath only; dt for 17m of Hampshire section from Greywell Tunnel to Ash Lock from tackle shops Noels Tackle, 314 Fernhill Rd, Cove; Young World, 4 Grand Parade, Hook. Andover AC has fishing. Further enquiries about Basingstoke Canal to P R Andrews, 121

South Ham Road, Basingstoke RG22 6AB. Farnborough AS also has rights on **Whitewater** at **Heckfield, Loddon** at **Winnersh, Ash Vale Lake,** 5 acres, **Shawfields Lake,** 3 acres, mixed, and gravel pits. St £13 from Raisons, tackle shops, Park Road, Farnborough for **Willow Park Fisheries,** Ash Vale, three lakes stocked with carp, tench and other coarse fish. Bait and refreshments on site. Dt on site £1 and £1.50, concession for jun. Four Leisure Sport gravel pits at

Frimley. Carp, crucian carp, bream, perch, tench, perch, rudd, eel and pike. Large specimens recorded. No night fishing, no dt. St £21, ½ price conc, from LSA, Thorpe Park, Chertsey. Tel: 564872. Tackle shops: Two Guys, 27 Burnby Close, Basingstoke; Raison's, 2 Park Road, Farnborough; Tackle Up, 151 Fleet Road, Fleet: The Creel, 36 Station Road, Aldershot. **Ewhurst Lake** (6m N); pike, perch, roach, strictly limited st £30; inquire of Estate Office.

BEAULIEU. The Beaulieu River is approx 14 miles long. Tickets for tidal stretch, Beaulieu to Needs Ore (bass, mullet) st £12, dt £1. Access from Bailey's Hard and Buckler's Hard. Tickets from Harbour Master, Buckler's Hard (tel: 616200) or Resident Land Agent, John Montagu Building, Beaulieu (tel: 0590 612345). Coarse fishing on **Hatchett Pond** and **Cadmans Pool** (Forestry Commission); bream, carp, tench and pike; tickets from Forestry Commission, Queen's House, Lyndhurst SO43 7NH, campsite offices during camping season and local tackle shops (st £56.00, mt £17.50, wt £8, dt £3.50, VAT incl, jun conc, barbless hooks only). NRA rod licences are not required for Forestry Com. waters within New Forest. Hotels: Montagu Arms; The Beaulieu, nr Lyndhurst. Accommodation at Newhouse Farm, 0590 612297.

DAMERHAM TROUT LAKES, Fordingbridge (3m). Six lakes, and river for St holders. R and b trout. Open March 15 until October 31. Advance bookings only. St £1050, half £525, quarter £350. Corporate rates on application. Bed and breakast available in annex to 16th C. thatched cottage. Tel: Rockbourne 446 (07253 446).

FLEET POND. Fishing station: **Fleet.** Cove AS water. No tickets. Tackle shop: Fleet S C, 182 Fleet Road.

HAMBLE. Sea trout and trout. **Bishop's Waltham.** Fishing mostly private.

LADYWELL LAKES. Alresford, Hants. 3 lakes totalling about 2½ acres and providing 900 yds of fishable bank, stocked with brown and rainbow trout averaging approx 2lbs. One lake brown trout only. Also short length of chalk stream with wild brown trout. St £468, ½ st £234, dt £20, ½ dt £12. Enquiries and bookings to Mr and Mrs Ng, 55 West Hill Avenue, Epsom, Surrey. Special arrangement for day hire of fishery. Bag limits, and restriction to single fly no larger than hook size 8.

LYMINGTON RIVER. Fishing station: Lymington. Sea trout (2-11lb), brown trout (¾ to 1lb). Sea trout best June to Sept. Fishing improved by Brockenhurst Manor FFC; private. Mixed fishery at Sway Lakes, Barrows Lane, Sway Lymington, tel: 0590 682010. Tackle from Smith's Sports Shop, 24/5 Queen St, Lymington.

MEON. Trout; sea trout in lower reaches. Fishing station: **East Meon;** Hants and Sussex Alliance has water; inquire hon sec. NRA licence required. Portsmouth Services FFA has 5 miles on Meon and 1¾ miles on Itchen below Winchester. Membership is immediately available for serving personnel, those retired may have to wait 2 years. Serving members £70, retired £140, guests £14 per day. Portsmouth and Dist AS hold some eight coarse fisheries in and around **Portsmouth,** plus river trout fishing on Arun and Rother. Enquiries to hon sec. Chiphall Lake Trout Fishery, 5 acres: Northfields Farm, Wickham. Wintershill Lake, trout fishing on 6 acres: Durley Street, Bishops Waltham. Tackle shops: Rover's, 178B West St, Fareham; Coombs Tackle Centre, 165 New Rd, Coptnor, Portsmouth.

SANDLEHEATH. Six lakes and three chalk stream beats at **Rockbourne Trout Fishery, Rockbourne,** Fordingbridge, Hampshire SP6 1QG. Excellent fishing for rainbow trout in lakes and brown trout and grayling in streams, fly only, various period terms from dt £24, limit 5 fish, ½ day £20.50. Blocks of tickets at discount. Concessions for Jun. Tuition, tackle hire, licenced cafeteria. B & B at fishery house. Tel: 07253 603 or 0425 52479 for

---

Keep the banks clean

Several clubs have stopped issuing tickets to visitors because of the state of the banks after they have left. Spend a few moments clearing up.

TRING RESERVOIRS, HERTFORDSHIRE

Reputation	PERCH	3 lbs 15 oz	
for	TENCH	12 lbs 8 oz	(National Record 1988)
Specimen	ROACH	13 lbs 13 oz	
and	BREAM	13 lbs 14 oz	
National	PIKE	35 lbs 8 oz	
Record Fish	CATFISH	43 lbs 8 oz	(National Record 1974)

Day and Season tickets available on the bank – Trout Fishing available by Season ticket only
Contact: Bailiff, B. Double – Tel: (044282) 2379

full details.

TWO LAKES, near **Romsey.** Very large trout on dry fly (average over 2lb). St only, £611 incl VAT. Apply Mr Alex Behrendt, Two Lakes, Crampmoor, nr Romsey, Hants.

WAGGONERS' WELLS, near **Haslemere.** Three lakes; National Trust waters, now managed by Greyshott AC. Coarse fishing; carp, roach, tench, gudgeon, a few trout. Dt available from Greyshott Tackle, Crossway Road, Greyshott, Hindhead, or bailiff on bank. Hotel: Punchbowl Hotel, Hindhead.

WARBURN. Dace, trout, salmon; preserved; leave sometimes from landowners; joins sea at **Key Haven.**

HERTS AND GREATER LONDON (reservoirs and lakes)

(see also London Reservoirs)

ALDENHAM (Herts). **Aldenham Country Park Reservoir.** Managed by Herts CC. Coarse fishing, incl. tench, pike to 37lb, carp to 39lb, plus very good roach and bream. No night fishing. Dt £3 (jun, OAP £1.50), punt £6-£4. Dis free. From bailiff on site or from Park Manager, Park Office, Dagger Lane, Elstree, Herts WD6 3AT. Tel: 081-953 1259; or 0831 837446, bailiff's mobile phone.

Shepperton (Middx); **Ashmere Fisheries,** Felix Lane, Shepperton TW17 8NN. Four lakes, total 20 acres, stocked with rainbow trout. Boats available. Annual membership only, £350-£585. Self-catering accommodation. Apply Mrs Jean Howman, Ashmere Fisheries, Felix Lane, Shepperton (Tel: 0932 225445, fax: 0932 253793).

STANSTEAD ABBOTS. Leisure Sport coarse fisheries consisting of 5 gravel pits with carp over 40lb, mill stream and part of main river. Other species include roach, tench, dace, pike, barbel. Season tickets £24. Concessions to jun, OAP, dis. No dt. Applications to LSA, Thorpe Park, Staines Road, Chertsey, Surrey. Tel: Chertsey 564872.

TRING (Herts). Four large reservoirs: **Marsworth, Startops End** and **Wilstone** (2m from Tring) main feeders for Grand Union Canal. Good fishing for specimen hunters. Bream over 10lb, former British record tench 12½lb, pike to 26lb, many large roach, British record catfish, 43½lb. Sunday fishing now available. St £55 (including night fishing), dt £3, con £2, evening £2. Tickets obtainable on bank from bailiff, B C Double, Watery Lane, Marsworth or tel: 822379. The fourth reservoir is a private trout fishery; Applications may be made to go on waiting list. The Tring Anglers have extensive fishing on Grand Union Canal and Arms, Thame, Thames at Eynsham, Ouzel nr Newport Pagnell and Stoke

Hammond, plus lakes and ponds. Club also fishes Oxford & Dist AA waters on Thames and elsewhere. Membership £28 plus £10 joining fee. Contact PR Officer

Dennis Welling, tel: 0494 772728. Tackle shop: Chiltern Tackle, 33 Western Rd, Tring. Hotels: Anglers' Retreat, Startops End, Rose and Crown.

HULL

(For close seasons, licences, etc, see Northumbria and Yorkshire Region NRA, p17)

Tidal river from North Frodingham to Hull is free fishing to anyone holding current NRA licence, but hit by pollution. From Beverley first-class sport may be had with roach, dace, pike, chub, bream, etc. Higher up still, on West Beck, there is excellent but preserved trout fishing of chalk-stream character.

Hull (North Humberside). River polluted. Drains giving good coarse fishing. Free fishing on NRA license from North Frodingham to Hull. Hull & Dist AA has water on **Derwent** at **Breighton, Wressle** and **Newton;** on the **Rye** at **Butterwick** and **Swinton;** and on the **Trent** at **Carlton.** Also the **Brandsburton Ponds** (open all the year), Tilery Lake, the Broomfleet and other ponds, 4½m of **Market Weighton Canal,** 17m from Hull, mixed coarse fishery held jointly with Goole AA, and **Melton Pond,** 99 acres, mixed coarse fish. Membership is unrestricted, st £15. Stone Creek and Patrington Haven hold flounders. Good sea fishing. Burstwick Watersports have coarse fishing nr **Burstwick;** dt £2 or £1.50. Contact P Hall, tel: 0482 26455. Rush Lyvars Lake, coarse fishery at **Hedon,** dt £1.20. Tel: 0482 898970. **Pickering Park Lake** owned by City Council, fine pike. Coarse dt £1.10. Tel: 0482 222693. Tackle shops: Fishing Basket, 470 Beverley Road; Everetts Fishing Tackle, 691 Holderness Rd; G W Hutchinson & Co, 27 Anlaby Rd; B B Fishing Tackle, 567 Holderness Rd.

Beverley (N Humberside). Tidal River Hull and drains give good coarse fishing; from Hull Bridge upstream through **Arram, Aike Wilfholme, Baswicke** and **Hempholme** to Frodingham Beck: Northumbria and Yorkshire Region NRA, for

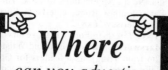

Where

can you advertise for so many months at a price many would charge for one month?

in

Where to Fish

Get in touch!

(The Publishers' address is at the front of the book)

Specimen roach are not caught as freely in rivers these days as they were in years gone by. There are exceptions though, such as the one in this picture, which came from Hempholme Lock on the River Hull. *Photo: Bruno Broughton.*

enquiries; weedy June to Nov. Free fishing in Beverley Beck, a canalised stream running from Foresters Arms to R Hull, owned by Borough Council. Small course fish. Dt £2 for 2 coarse ponds in Lakeminster Park, tel: 0482 882655. **Leven Canal** (6m): course fish, Hull AA water except for 250 yds to right of bridge, Trailer and Marina Ltd, tel: 0482 896879. Fine tench. Dt from Minster Tackle, 3 Flemingate, Everett's Fishing Tackle, Beverley, Leven Marina, and 11 The Meadows, Leven. Hotel: Beverley Arms.

Brandesburton (N Humberside). River Hull 3m W, excellent coarse fishing in gravel pits *(see Hull).*

Wansford (N Humberside). Free left bank below Lock Dow to Brigham. **Driffield Canal Fishery**, from Town Lock, Driffield along B1249 to Snake Holme Lock, ½m west of Wansford. Trout, both bait and fly. Controlled by Tony Harrison on behalf of E Yorkshire CA. Dt £4, 3 fish, conc. Tel: 0377 44152. **West Beck** preserved by Golden Hill AS and West Beck PS; members only. Fishponds Farm and Fishery, Woldgate, Nr **Bridlington** YO16 4XE, has 3 ponds coarse fish and one trout pond. Dt £2.50, 2 rods. ½ day £1. Tel: 0262 605873.

Tributaries of the Hull

FOSTON BECK (or **KELK** or **FRODINGHAM BECK**):
North Frodingham, Foston-on-the-Wolds and **Lowthorpe** (N Humberside). Rises in Yorkshire wolds; true chalk stream containing brown trout averaging well over the pound. Preserved from Bracey Bridge to Foston Mill by Foston FC (members only). for ¾m below Foston

Mill water stocked with trout by Millhouse Beck AC; private.

Driffield Beck:
Driffield (N Humberside). Provides chalk stream fishing for trout and grayling of high order; preserved. Controlled by Driffield AC, Golden Hill Club and West Beck PS.

ISLE OF MAN

The geographical nature of the Isle of Man tends to dictate the type of river, fish and hence fishing one may encounter when angling in the Island. Being a relatively mountainous place, rivers and streams are small, swift flowing and very clear. There are no coarse fish on the Isle of Man but nevertheless excellent sport can be had in the numerous trout streams where the art of approach to the river bank and the gentle and accurate cast of the true angler becomes vital.

There are very few preserved stretches of river in the Island and a well chosen word with the land owner is often all that is required to enable an angler to fish in peace. Approximately a half mile of the River Douglas through the Nunnery Estate is exclusively reserved for the Manx Game FC. Small sections of the rivers Dhoo and Glass can only be fished under permit from the Douglas and District Angling Club. Applications for membership should be sent to Mr A Ashton, 58 Laurel Ave, Birchill, Onchan. Subscriptions are now £9, £3 junior. Natural baits (worms, bread, cheese) and artificials are allowed on the Island's rivers, ponds and streams but anglers are reminded that only artificials are allowed when reservoir fishing (except Eairy Dam). Further details of all freshwater angling can be obtained from the Freshwater Fishery Inspector, Cornaa, Maughold. Anglers must abide by the regulations wherever they fish. (1) Not to use or carry a gaff or tailer. (2) Not to use a line the diameter of which exceeds 0.033 cm, excepting that a fly line used solely for fly fishing may exceed 0.033 cm diameter, provided the leader exceeds five feet in length and does at no point exceed 0.033 cm in diameter. (0.033 cm diameter is approximately equivalent to 10lb breaking strain). (3) Not use more than one hook on a line unless (a) Pennel or Stewart tackles are being used for bait fishing; (b) a 'point with two droppers' is being used for fly fishing only; (c) a spinner is being used for spinning only. (4) Not to use a hook larger than No 6 Redditch scale, unless the hook is comprised in an artificial fly. (5) Return to the water all fish foul hooked. (6) Return to the water unharmed any freshwater fish hooked which is less than 18 cm in length overall. (7) Chest waders prohibited.

The river fishing season commences on the Thursday preceding Good Friday, and finishes on the 30 September for trout and 31 October for salmon. The reservoir season begins on the same date and continues until 31 October. A freshwater fishing licence is required to fish any river, pond or reservoir.

Salmon fishing takes place mainly in the Autumn as the Island does not enjoy a spring run of any size. Salmon and sea trout are usually taken during or after spate conditions. There is a bag limit for the rivers of 6 T and 2 S in any one day. Fish are small and rarely if ever exceed 20lb -- a more reasonable average would be 5-10lb.

The Department of Agriculture, Fisheries and Forestry pursues a continual stocking programme of rivers, ponds and reservoirs throughout the spring and early summer, with trout (brown and rainbow) of a takeable size, i.e. in excess of 7" and in the 1lb to 2lb range.

At present there are seven reservoirs open for fishing. They are: (a) The West Baldwin Reservoir (300 mg) is near the centre of the Island. A main road goes past the end of the dam. There is an infrequent bus service to West Baldwin village 1⅓ miles from the reservoir. (b) Clypse and Kerrowdhoo Reservoirs lie, one beyond the other, about 1½ miles north of Onchan Village. A private road runs, off the road to Grange Farm, to the Attendants house where there is room to park cars. (c) Ballure Reservoir is just south of Ramsey. Access is by a private road branching off the main road to Douglas, on the Douglas side of the MER crossing near the town boundary. (d) Cringle Reservoir is just north of the road from Ronague to Foxdale and is on the south slopes of South Barrule. Cars can be parked on the reservoir land. (e) Sulby Reservoir is close to the A14 Sulby-Snaefell road. (f) Eairy Dam is alongside the A24 Douglas to Foxdale road. It is not a water supply and restrictions on the use of live bait do not apply.

Fishing Licences

Freshwater fishing licences - needed before *any* fishing commences - cost: St (rivers) £15, reservoirs £45. (Jun £5 and £15 respectively.) Wt (available to Sep 30) rivers: £5, reservoirs: £15, jun £2 and £5 respectively.) Jun: under 16 years of age. Dt for reservoirs, £5. Only st available after 30 Sept.

They are obtained from: I.O.M. Department of Agriculture, Fisheries and Forestry, Bucks Road, Douglas; from Department of Tourism, Information Bureau, Victoria Street and Harris Promenade, Douglas, from local Commissioners offices in Onchan and Laxey, and from any Post Office.

No licence required for sea fishing, which from pier, rocks or boat is excellent, especially for pollack - locally called 'calig' - mackerel, cod and codling, whiting and plaice. Chief bait for ground fish is herring, but lugworm, sand-eels and shellfish also found. Jigging with white and coloured feathers and artificial sand-eel for pollack, mackerel and cod is successful. Good centres for most species are Peel, Port Erin, Port St Mary and Ramsey. Department of Tourism, Douglas, issues useful booklet on sea and river fishing. Principal rivers as follows:

COLBY RIVER. Trout. This stream is 4m long; preserved in lower reaches.

DOUGLAS RIVER. Salmon, sea trout, trout. Douglas formed by junction of Dhoo and Glass, half a mile above the town of **Douglas.** Fishing on Glass River and lower part of Dhoo preserved, but free above **Union Mills.** Glass largely rented by Douglas AC.

GLEN MOOR BURN, 3m long. Trout; fishing free, but not very good. Fishing station: **Kirk Michael.**

LAXEY RIVER. Trout; free but poor. This stream is 5m long. 1m above junction with sea at Laxey, Glen River (trout), 3m long, joins on right bank. Fishing station: **Laxey.**

NEB. Trout; mostly free and good; salmon from Aug. Neb (sometimes called Peel River) rises above **Little London** and Blabae and runs 3m to **Glen Helen** (Hotel: Glen Helen). It then runs 4m to **St John's.** Here **Foxdale River,** 6m long, joins on left bank. Hence to **Peel** is 3m. 3m S is **Glen Maye River** 4m long; sea

trout below waterfall, trout above.

SANTON BURN. 6m long; trout; mostly preserved, but poor; salmon from Aug. Fishing station: **Santon.**

SILVER BURN. Trout, sea trout; free. This stream rises on the slopes of South Barrule, runs 5m to **Ballasalla,** where Awin Ruy, 4m long, joins on left bank. Silver Burn runs 3m to the sea at **Castletown.** Best sport downstream for about 1m to Castletown.

SULBY. Salmon (from Aug), sea trout; free; moderate in lower reaches only, upstream from Claddaghs, poor. Five miles S is **Cornaa River,** 5m long, which runs into sea at Port Cornaa, the site of the Fishery Department's hatchery. Good for salmon and sea trout in lower portion (Sept, Oct).

WYLLIN BURN. 4m long; trout; free; fishing poor. Near **Kirk Michael.**

(For further information about sea fishing on the Island, see under Sea Fishing Stations)

ISLE OF WIGHT

(For close seasons, licences, etc, see Southern Region NRA p 15)

Freshwater fishing on the Island is better than is generally appreciated. The **Yar** from St Helens, Bembridge, to Alverstone holds fair numbers of roach, dace and rudd, with perch, carp and bream to 7lb in some stretches. Tickets are available from IWFAA or tackle shops. Assc has coarse fishing for dace, roach, carp, bream, perch, tench, pike and others at Yarbridge and Alverstone on Yar, dt £4, conc, on bank for latter, **Gunville Pond,** Newport (members only), **Somerton Reservoir,** Cowes, dt available from bailiff. NRA licence required. At Morton Farm, Brading, tel 0983 740941, is coarse fishing on small lake and R Yar. Hale Manor Lakes are both 1 acre, carp and mixed coarse. Hale Manor, Arreton, tel: 0983 865204. Mixed fishery at Meadow Lakes, Brighstone, tel: 0983 740941. Ideal junior coarse ponds at Jolliffes Farm, Whitewell, 0983 730783. **Yafford Fish Farm** ponds are near Brighstone. Tackle shops: Doug Stephens Tackle, Union Street, Newport; G C Young, The Sports Shop, 74 Regent Street, Shanklin; W Bates & Son, 5 Springhill, Ventnor; The Sports & Model Shop, Ryde; David's Food Market, Lane End Court, Bembridge; 'Scotties', 11 Lugley Street, Street, Newport. Light sea fishing, for which freshwater tackle may be employed, available at Whippingham (River Medina), Fishbourne (Wootton Creek) and in Bembridge Harbour; mullet, bass, flatfish, etc.

ITCHEN

(For close seasons licences, etc, see Southern Region NRA p15)

Rises some miles north-west of Petersfield and flows via Winchester into Southampton Water at Southampton. Famous Hampshire chalk stream. Trout fishing excellent, but strictly preserved for most part. Some salmon and sea trout lower down, but also preserved. Principal tributaries are **Alre** and **Candover Brook;** both strictly preserved.

Southampton (Hants). Itchen and Test es-   tuaries. Pout, whiting and eels in

Southampton Water; and whiting, bass, grey mullet from the piers and quays. Free coarse fishing from public footpath between Woodmill and Mansbridge. **Leominstead Trout Fishery,** Emery Down, **Lyndhurst** SO43 7GA has 8 acres of trout and coarse fishing, trout dt £25, 5 fish limit. Coarse dt £5, jun £2.50. Tel: 0703 282610. Mopley Farm Trout Fishery, Blackfield, 3 acres, fly only, open 3 Apr to 31 Oct. Tel: South. 891616. Holbury Manor Pond, Gang Warily Rec. Cen, tel: Fawley 893603.

Eastleigh (Hants) Trout, salmon and grayling; preserved. Eastleigh & Dist AC has various game and coarse fishing, incl 3 stretches of river and 12 lakes, dt on two waters: Stoneham Lakes and Lakeside

Enjoy a day's flyfishing in the tranquil setting of the South East's most celebrated water

*T*he season at Bewl Water starts on Sunday 3rd April (prior booking only). 640 acres of first class fishing. Day and season tickets - 54 motor boats for hire - tackle hire and sales - clothing hire service - boat and bank day courses - anglers ferry. Great fishing in some of the most attractive surroundings you can find.

Bewl Water
Lamberhurst
Tunbridge Wells
Kent TN3 8JH
Tel: (0892) 890661

Bewl Water is owned and operated by Southern Water Services

Bewl Water

Park, both Eastleigh. Bishopstoke FC has water, which affords excellent sport. Water holds large trout. Salmon run right up to Brambridge. Some sea trout also come up; private. Junior st from Borough Council for Bishopstoke Riverside Rd stretch. Tackle shop: Eastleigh Angling Centre, 325 Market Street. Accom. at Park Farm, Stoneham Lane.

Bishopstoke (Hants), ns Eastleigh. Salmon, trout and grayling; preserved by Bishopstoke FC and other owners.

Winchester (Hants). Trout above city; trout and grayling below. Free fishing on NRA licence between the city weirs, and the left bank of the **Itchen Navigation,** between Blackbridge and St Catherine's Lock. Portsmouth Services FFA has 1¾ miles below town; terms of club membership are described under R Meon entry. The Rod Box, London Road, King's Worthy, S023 7QN. Tel: 0962 883600 offers dry fly fishing on st and dt basis and other rods on celebrated private stretches of the **Test** and on the **Itchen, Nadder, Anton, Bourne** and **Whitewater,** and on lakes. Charges on request. Marwell Manor Farm has trout fishing on 2½ acre lake. Tel: 0962 74280. Fishers Pond is coarse fishery at Colden Common. Tel: Southampton 694412. Tackle shops: The Rod Box, Kings Worthy; Aries Angling Centre, 11 The Precinct, Chandlers Ford.

Itchen Abbas (Hants). Trout; preserved by riparian owners. **Avington Trout Fishery,** three lakes plus stretch of R Itchen, provide excellent trout fishing. Open all year, stocked daily. Limit 2 brace. St and dt. British rainbow record broken there several times. (Tel: 0962 779 312.) Tackle Shop: The Rod Box, Kingsworthy, Winchester. Many hotels.

Arlesford (Hants). **Candover Brook, Alre, Itchen;** trout; preserved by riparian owners. Grange Lakes, Alresford Pond; coarse fish; preserved.

KENT (lakes and streams)

BAYHAM LAKE nr **Lamberhurst.** 16 acre lake stocked with rb trout, average size large and mile of River **Teise.** Variety of st offerings £150-£500. Dt £20 (4 fish); ½ day £15 (3 fish). Boats from £3-£5. Course fishing 16 June-15 Mar. For further details phone John Parkman, 0892 890276.

BEWL WATER: *(see advt)* 770 acre SW

fly-only trout fishery nr. **Lamberhurst.** St (full) £390, 6 fish daily. (Mon-Fri) £290. Dt £10.50. Evenings, £8.10, 4 fish. Concessions for beginners and jun, with reduced limits. Motor and pulling boats, £15 and £9.40; evenings: £10.50 and £6.20. Season: April 4-Oct 26. Enquiries: 0892 890352 (out of season) 890661.

BROOKLANDS LAKES. Dartford. Dart-

A 7$^1/_2$ lb Bewl rainbow - a fine example of the productivity of Southern waters.

ford and Dist APS, variety of coarse fish;
dt £3 available from bailiffs on bank.
CHIDDINGSTONE CASTLE LAKE
Good coarse fishing, especially carp. No
night fishing. Prepaid booking advisable
at weekends. Dt £8 from Custodian. One
onlooker only, per fisherman, £3. Apply
to the Administrator, Chiddingstone Castle, near **Edenbridge**. TN8 7AD. Tel:
0892 870347.
LARKFIELD LAKES. Three pits of 47,
20, 27 acres. Carp, tench, pike, bream,
eels, roach, perch. St £22. Concessions
on all for jun, OAP, dis. No dt. Applications to LSA, Thorpe Park, Staines Lane,
Chertsey, Surrey. Tel: 0932 564872.
HAWKHURST. Small stillwater fishery
for rainbow trout to 3lb. Phone 3457.
LONGFORD LAKE. Sevenoaks. Private
water of Holmesdale AS, who also have
junior water Montreal Park Lake; st £10,
£50. Dt £2.50 for guests of members
only, from S Banks, 57 Chevening Rd,
Chipstead, Kent.
LULLINGSTONE LAKE, near **Eynsford.**
Trout. Kingfisher APS; no tickets.
MID KENT FISHERIES, Chilham Water
Mill, **Chilham** CT4 8EE, tel: 0227
730668. Coarse fishing is available on 13
lakes, from 26 to 3 acres, well stocked
with all species. Catches include large
bream, perch, rudd, tench, and pike to
27lb. St £80, half price concessions for
OAP, juv, dis. A £5 dt is available on one
lake, with same conc.
MOTE PARK LAKE. Maidstone *(see
Medway).* Coarse fish (including speci-
men bream, tench and pike); no day tickets, all permits are dealt with by Medway
Victory Angling and Medway Preservation Society, 33 Hackney Rd, Maidstone,
Kent ME16 8LN.
BROOMBANKS PITS, at **Murston,** 1¼m
N of Sittingbourne. Sittingbourne AC has
three pits; coarse fish; membership
£37.50 + £12.50, enquiries to member-
ship sec. Tackle shop, Kent Angling, 2
Chapel House, Shakespeare Rd.
OARE PITS. At Oare, 1½m N of **Faver-**

sham. Faversham AC has large pool containing carp (30lb plus), tench, bream,
roach and pike. Also other pits holding
coarse fish. St £17 + £17 entrance fee. Dt
£1.50 from waterside or hon sec.
PETT POOLS. Fishing stations: **Winchelsea,** 2m; Rye, 4m. 25 acres, coarse fish;
dt £4 (limited) from T G King, Market
Stores, Pett Level, Nr Hastings TN35
4EH. St from Hastings and Bexhill AC,
tel: 0424 52678.
ROMNEY MARSH. Much good fishing on
marsh, especially in main drains to
Rother; best in summer (large bream
shoals); water on low side in winter.
Clubs with water here are: Ashford and
Dist APS; Cinque Ports AS; Clive Vale
AC (who fish Jury's Gap Sewer; Clive
Vale reservoirs (carp), Ecclesbourne
Reservoir, Hastings), Bexhill and Dist
AA (members only); Rye and Dist AS;
Tenterden and Dist APS; Linesmen AC
(also waters on **Medway, Beult** and
Stour; details: hon sec). Tackle shops:
Romney Tackle, The Avenue, New Rom-
ney; Point Tackle Shop, Dungeness.
ROYAL MILITARY CANAL. Summer
fishing only; level partially lowered in
winter for drainage. Stations: **Hythe** and
Ashford. Cinque Ports AS has 7m from
Seabrook outfall to Giggers Green; carp,
bream, roach, rudd, tench, eels, tench,
perch, pike; most sections have dt from
bailiff or tackle shops. West Hythe Bal-
last Pit is members only. Ashford and
Dist A & PS has about 16m from West
Hythe Dam to Iden Lock (south bank
only from dam to Appledore Bridge) and
quarry stocked with large carp. Tickets
available from inns near canal at West
Hythe, Ruckinge, Warehorne, Appledore, and from cottage at canal bridge.
Hon sec Ashford and Dist APS will give
further information. Spurringbrook
Sewer, nr Appledore, is CALPAC water,
and may be fished from Mock Hill Farm
to Arrow Head Bridge. Tackle shops:
Ashford Angling Centre, 3B Stanhope
Sq; Hythe Angling, Dymchurch Rd.

LANCASHIRE AND CUMBRIA (Westmorland) streams

*(For close seasons, licences, etc, see North West Region NRA, p17 unless otherwise
stated)*

BELA. Cumbrian trout stream, flowing
from Lily Mere to estuary of Kent at
Milnthorpe. Much of its course is through
low-lying country with heavy water. Size
of fish better than in some northern

streams; many dry-fly reaches. Salmon
and sea trout below Beetham Mills private. One of the earliest of northern
streams; fishing starts March 3.
Milnthorpe (Cumbria). Trout. Preserved

by Milnthorpe AA and confined to members and guests. Association also preserves St Sunday's Beck from Deepthwaite Bridge and Peasey Beck from Farleton Beck downwards and thence, from confluence of these streams, to Beetham Mills, which is as far as salmon run. Fishing below mills private. Sport very good in March, April, May and Aug. NRA licences and tackle from Kendal Sports, Stramongate, Kendal (also Kent AA tickets) *(see River Kent)*. Hotels at Milnthorpe: Cross Keys, Bull's Head, Coach and Horses; Wheatsheaf at Beetham.

Oxenholme (Cumbria). Bela, 2m E. Beehive Beck, 1m E. Old Hutton Beck, 3m SE. **Killington Reservoir;** large area of water, 3m E. Pike, perch and some big trout. Now privately fished. *(See Kendal).*

CONDOR. Fishing station: Galgate. Brown trout and sea trout. Galgate AA water, members only.

DUDDON. Fishing station: **Broughton-in-Furness.** Sea trout, salmon. Dt from E A Clark, solicitor, for river from Duddon Bridge to Greety Gate, both banks. Millom & Dist AA has rights to 366 yds of north bank from Duddon Bridge, and permission on Mr Hagel's Hall Bridge stretch, reviewed annually; dt £15 available. Assn also has water on **Esk, Lickle, Annas, Irt, Lazy, Devoke Water** (salmon, sea trout, trout) and **Baystone Bank Reservoir** (fly only); dt £10. Close to Broughton-in-Furness, **River Lickle** joins Duddon on left bank. River rented by Millom AA. Day tickets. Applications for membership to hon sec.

Ulpha (Cumbria). Good sea trout and salmon, few brown trout. All river below down to Ulpha Bridge private. **Devoke Water** (large trout) may also be fished from here. Millom AA has rights, wt and dt available. Applications for membership to hon sec. Below this point Duddon runs into estuary. Hotel: Old King's Head.

KENT. Fast-flowing salmon and trout stream running into Morecambe Bay. Fishing reported much improved following pollution and drainage schemes. Salmon, sea trout, trout.

Kendal (Cumbria). Salmon, sea trout, trout. A few spring salmon with main run and sea trout moving up about June; fairly plentiful Aug onwards. Fishing for the public is available at Lower Levens

Farm. Permits from Olde Peat Cotes, Sampool Lane, Levens, Near Kendal. South of the town to Basinghyll Bridge (both banks) held by Kent AA, membership subject to waiting list, wt £20 to May 31, £40 thereafter; dt £7 to May 31, £15 thereafter. NRA licence necessary. Tickets and licences from Kendal Sports (see below). Stainton Beck 2m; trout. Kendal Corporation owns Fisher Tarn; now privately leased. **Killington Reservoir** (ns Oxenholme), is property of British Waterways; pike, perch and trout. Fishing rights leased to Kent AA, wt £4.50, dt £2. Tackle shops: Carlsons Fishing Tackle, 64 Kirkland, Kendal; Lakes Tackle Shop, 3 Belsfield Terrace; Kendal Sports, 28-30, Stramondgate, who issue Kent AA tickets and licences. Hotels: County, Woolpack, Globe.

Burneside (Cumbria). Burneside AA water from a little below junction of Sprint up to Beckmickleing Wood near Staveley, including mill dams at Burneside, Bowston, and Cowan Head, which hold large trout (up to 1½lb); salmon and sea trout from July. *(See Sprint below).* Permits and accommodation at Jolly Anglers Inn, st £25, wt £12, dt £5. Burneside Lakes (not assn): Skelsmergh Tarn, 2m NE; Gurnal Dubs, private fishing administered by Ellergreen Estates, 3m north.

Staveley (Cumbria). Trout, salmon and sea trout in Sept and Oct. Staveley and Dist AA has 4m of local Kent and Gowan fishing. Tickets from D & H Woof, 22 Main Street, Staveley. **Kentmere Fishery:** 4 acre lake with rainbow trout to 12lbs, browns to 5lbs, also 30 acre lake through which river runs with natural browns. Fly only, dt £15, 4 fish, half day £8, evening £6. Tel: 0768 63123. Hotels: Eagle and Child, Duke William, Railway.

MINT (tributary of Kent). Best fished from Kendal. Joins Kent about 1m above town; holds good head of small trout. Kent AA has lowest water *(see Kendal).*

SPRINT (tributary of Kent). Joins Kent at Burneside. Burneside AA (see Burneside) has about 1m of fishing from junction with Kent. Kent AA has ½m (L bank only). Salmon and sea trout from Aug; brown trout small; banks much wooded.

KEER. Rises 4m above Borwick, runs into Morecambe Bay 3m below **Carnforth.** Good sea trout and brown trout (no coarse fish). Carnforth AA has water; wt and dt on application to hon sec. Whorleys Moss Fishery, Nether Kellet, Carn-

forth, has small pond with b and r trout from 3lb. Dt £13.50, 3 fish. ½ day and evening tickets also. Tel: 0524 420300.

LEVEN: Drains Windermere, and is joined by River Crake (from Coniston Water) at Greenodd, near Ulverston, before flowing into Morecambe Bay. Salmon, sea trout, trout. Ulverston AA has members only fishing on R Crake.

Ulverston (Cumbria). Salmon, sea trout, trout. Ulverston AA has fishing on **Ulverston Canal,** 1¼m long, specimen tench, carp, etc; restocked; day (£2-£1) and season tickets (£20-£10) from Canal Tavern Inn, Angling and Hiking Centre, 62 Forshaw Street, Barrow-in-Furness, E Sharp, Sports shop. St £18, dt £1.75, concessions to OAP and jun. Match permits from AA sec. Lakes: **Knottallow Tarn,** (brown trout fishing, available on associate membership to visitors). Hotels: Armadale, Sun, Queen's, King's, Bay Horse, Lonsdale House.

Newby Bridge (Cumbria).Salmon, trout; preserved by Leven AA down to Greenodd railway bridge; members only. Swan Hotel issues dt £3.50, from hotel, 9am to 6pm. Lakes: Windermere, 1m N; Bawtry Tarn, 2m NE. **Bigland Hall** Country Sports Ltd, Backbarrow LA12 8PB. 13 acre coarse fish lake and 16 acre fly only trout fishery (barbless hooks only, catch and release). Dt £15, 4 fish, coarse £4, conc, must be booked in advance. Contact Ken Dawes, tel: 05395 31361.

Lake Side (Cumbria). Salmon, trout, pike, perch, trout. Some free fishing; other sections of the shore private; inquire locally.

TORVER BECK (tributary of Coniston lake), Torver (Cumbria). Lakes: Coniston, 1m E; pike, perch and trout, Goat's Water, 3m NE. Beacon Tarn, 5m S. Hotel: Church House Inn.

CRAKE (tributary of Leven):

Greenodd (Cumbria). Crake; salmon, sea trout, trout. From Sparks Bridge to Little Dicks Bridge, Ulveston AA, members only. Assc. offers £2 dt on bank for **Ulverston Canal** fishing: coarse fish. **Rusland Pool River,** tributary of Leven. Forestry Commission, Satterthwaite issues tickets. Tackle from Angling & Hiking Centre, Forshaw St, Barrow-in-Furnace.

Coniston (Cumbria). Yewdale Beck, Torver Beck, 2½m S. Crake; salmon, sea trout. Duddon, 8m; salmon, sea trout, (Millom & Dist AA water). Lakes: Con-

iston; pike, perch, char, trout and eels. Goat's Water, 2m W; Low Tarn, 3m NE. Esthwaite Lake, 4m; pike and perch *(see Hawkshead).* Char fishing in Coniston Lake very good from May to October. Lake free to holders of NRA licence. St £17.25, wt £6.90, dt £3.45 from Gift and Sports, Yewdale Road, Coniston LA21 8DU. Tel: 05394 41412.

GRIZEDALE BECK (tributary of Leven): **Hawkshead** (Cumbria). Forestry Commission, small brown trout, low population at present, let to Grizedale AA. Wt £7.50, dt £2, jun ½ at Forest Shop. Esthwaite Water; trout, pike, perch; preserved, but visitors can obtain tickets *(see English Lake District).*

TROUTBECK (trib of L Windermere):

WINDERMERE (Cumbria). Water on river given up by Windermere, Ambleside & Dist AA but fly fishing for trout on three tarns in the area (**School Knot, Moss Eccles,** and **High Arnside,** all stocked regularly) available to visitors. St £17.25, wt £6.40, dt £3.45 from Gift and Sports, Coniston. Tel: 05394- 41412. Hotels: Old England, Windermere, Stag's Head. Boats at Lakeside, Bowness, Millerground, Waterhead. Lake free to licence-holders.

AMBLESIDE (Cumbria) ns Windermere, 5m Windermere, Ambleside and Dist AA has trout fishing on **Rothay** and **Brathay,** streams running into the lake from the N, on **Rydal Water,** (chiefly pike and perch) and on tarns. St £12, wt £6, dt £3. Jun & OAP ½ price. Other waters near Ambleside: Scandal Beck; trout; preserved. Rydale Rock, 2m N Windermere; pike, perch and trout; free. Belham Tarn, 3m S. Yew Tree Tarn; Coniston AA. Hotels: Salutation, White Lion, Waterhead (boats).

Grasmere (Cumbria). Rothay; trout, Easdale Beck; trout. Lakes: Grasmere (now Winderemere, Ambleside & D. AA water); pike, perch and few trout. Rydal Water, 3m SE; perch, pike and few trout. Stream joining Grasmere with Rydal gives fair trouting. Easdale Tarn, 3m NW; good perch, trout. Codale Tarn, 4m NW; trout, perch. Hotels: Rothay, Prince of Wales (boats), Dale Lodge, Swan, Allonby (boats).

WINSTER. Parallel with Windermere for 6m. Joins the sea by **Grange-over-Sands.** Salmon, sea trout, brown trout, coarse fish. Brown trout and sea trout (late) may be taken in **River Eea.** Dt and wt from Commodore Hotel, Grange-over-Sands.

LANCASHIRE (lakes and reservoirs)

(see North West Region NRA, p17, unless otherwise stated)

BARROW-IN-FURNESS RESERVOIRS
Barrow AA has trout fishing in five reservoirs. No tickets. Furness FA (Game section) issues day tickets for stocked waters. Coarse section fishes 5 waters, 3m from Barrow-in-Furnace, and Ormsgill Reservoir. Dt £4, conc, not sold on bank. Contact G H Grainger, 0229 832129. Details from Angling and Hiking Centre, 62 Forshaw Street, Barrow-in-Furness. *(See also Sea Fishing Stations).*
BARNSFOLD WATERS. 7m NE of Preston. Two trout lakes, 22 acres, fly only. St and dt £15 to £5. Boats £5 to £10. F J Casson, Barnsfold Waters, Barns Lane, Goosnargh, Preston PR3 2NJ. Tel: 0995 61583. Tackle shop: Ted Carter, Church St, Preston.
BUCKLEY WOOD RESERVOIR, Rochdale. Leased by NWW to Rochdale Walton AS. Inquire hon sec *(see also Mersey and Rochdale).*
BROWNHILL RESERVOIR. Between **Colne** and **Foulridge**. Feeder for Leeds and Liverpool Canal. Holds brown trout; preserved by Colne AA, tickets for members' guests only.
DEAN CLOUGH RESERVOIR. Great Harwood. Brown and Rainbow trout, fly only, Lancashire FFA, who issue season tickets; dt £9 from Hyndburn Angling Centre, 71 Abbey Street, Accrington (tel: Acc. 397612).
EARNSDALE RESERVOIR, Darwen. NWW (S Rivers Div). Brown and rainbow trout. Darwen AA has rights on reservoir; good fly water, limit 4; limited st £50, dt £8; information from County Sports, Duckworth St, Darwen. Tel: 0254 702187 or hon. sec, 0254 775501.
HEAPY LODGES. Chorley. 28 acres. Four Reservoirs stocked with indigenous trout, and course fish of most suitable species, including a well established population of carp. Wigan and Dist AA water. St £14.75, juv £4. Map books £1.25 + SAE from K Hogg, 95 Holme Terrace, Wigan. Tackle shop: The Fishery Tackle Shop, 32 Steeley Lane, Chorley PR6 0RD.
NORTH WEST WATER RESERVOIRS. Rivington. These reservoirs which include **Upper** and **Lower Rivington, Anglezarke, Upper Roddlesworth** are about 35m northeast of Liverpool.
UPPER RODDLESWORTH RESERVOIR. This water now club managed by Horwich Fly Fishers Club. Club members and day ticket only, concessions for OAP, juniors, disabled. Available from Andrew Leach, Sports Outfitters, Leigh Lane, Horwich, Bolton. Lower Roddlesworth and Rakebrook reservoirs are managed by Withnell AC. Members only. Dt from Brinscall Tackle Shop.
UPPER RIVINGTON RESERVOIR. Mixed fishery. This water is now managed by Bolton AA.
LOWER RIVINGTON RESERVOIR. Mixed fishery. This water is now managed by Greater Manchester Youth Assc. Dt only, (conc for OAP, dis, jun), on the bank from bailiff.
MITCHELS HOUSE RESERVOIRS, Higher Baxenden. Accrington & Dist FC waters; stocked monthly with 14" rainbows. Dt £6, 2 fish limit. Membership is open. Heaviest fish 1992, 7¼lb.
OLDHAM RESERVOIRS. Oldham United AS leases six reservoirs from NWW. **Lower Strinesdale, Castleshaw** and **Kitcliffe** (trout); **Upper Strinesdale, Ogden Reservoirs,** pike, perch, bream, roach, carp, tench, chub; some trout. Tickets by post from sec or A Dyson, 7 Raven Avenue, Chadderton. Tackle shop: Grundy's Tackle and Guns, 292 Manchester Street, Werneth, Oldham.
ORMSGILL LOWER RESERVOIR. Barrow. Trout, tench, carp. Furness FA water. Inquiries to Hannays, 50 Crellin St, Barrow-in-furness.
PENNINGTON FLASH. Leigh. Good coarse fishing. Pennington Flash AA issues st £2.50 and dt 50p. Inquiries to G Unsworth, 142 Chestnut Drive S, Leigh, Lancs.
SABDEN RESERVOIR. Whalley. Trout (av 10in), carp. Accrington and Dist FC water. Members only. Heaviest fish 1992, 7½lb.
STOCKS RESERVOIR. Slaidburn. 300 acre trout fishery, brown, and rainbow up to 11lb. Fly only, there is a close season. 1992 bag av, 2.5. Boats and tackle available, outboard an optional extra. St £150-£130, wt £40, dt £12-£8. 3 and 2 fish limit. Boat, £7-£5, o/b £7. Enquiries to

Bentham Trout Farm, Low Mill, Bentham LA2 7DA. Tel: 05242 61305.
WEYOH RESERVOIR, nr **Edgeworth.** 100 acres, Northern Anglers water, with most species of coarse fish, and trout. Closed from Mar 15 to Jun 15. Dt £1.25 on bank.
WITHNELL RESERVOIRS. Withnell Fisheries Ltd, 11 Kearsley Drive, Bolton BL3 2PG manage three reservoirs fishable with season ticket, £32. Waiting list, which restricts fishing to local anglers.

WORTHINGTON RESERVOIRS. Wigan. 39 Acres, 3 reservoirs, one trout, two coarse fish. Wigan & Dist AA water. Assn. also controls several miles of **Ribble** and **Wyre.** enquiries to K Hogg, Card Secretary, 95 Holme Terrace, Wigan. Wigan tackle shops: T & K Tackle, 85 Ormskirk Rd, Newton; George's Fishing Tackle, 15 Frog Lane, Wigan; North West Angling Centre, 160 Market St, Hindley.

LEE or LEA

(For close seasons, licences, etc, see Thames Region NRA, p18)

Walton's river; flows through Bedfordshire and Hertfordshire then along boundary between Essex and Middlesex to join Thames near Blackwall; 46m long. Building and canalization have largely removed its charm, but still holds good qualtities of roach, bream, perch, and in places, barbel, dace and chub. Very little free fishing, but permits are available from bailiffs on most stretches.

Tottenham (London). Fishing controlled by Lee Valley Anglers Consultative Assc, T Mansbridge, 7 Warren Rd, Chingford E4 6QR, tel: 081 524 0869. Good access points are at Lea Bridge Rd, Hackney Marshes, Carpenters Rd, Dace Rd. Dt available from tackle shops and bailiffs. Picketts Lock and Stonebridge Lock are popular fisheries, used for matches, with good roach and bream. TW reservoirs close to Tottenham Hale (roach, perch,bream, pike; or stocked with brown and rainbow trout) *(see under London).* D/s of Enfield Lock, **Ponders End** is a good venue with large shoals of bream and roach. Tackle shop: Don's, 239 Fore Street, Edmonton.

Enfield Lock (Middx). Plenty of roach, perch, bream, tench and pike. Tickets available. Controlled by Lee valley ACA, T Mansbridge, tel: 081 524 0869.

Waltham Abbey (Herts): **Lee Relief Channel** from Hooks Marsh to Highbridge St, Waltham Abbey: 1½m of bank, mixed coarse fishing, with large barbel, chub, tench, bream and carp. This fishery is run by LVRPA *(see Hoddesdon, below).* A 4½ acre lake stocked with r and b trout is available at Waltham Abbey. Limited rods available, no dt. Contact Hon Sec,

Civil Service FS. Tackle shops: P & B Hall, 44 Highbridge Rd; A1 Angling, 176 High Rd, Woodford Green.

Cheshunt (Herts). Good chub, roach, bream fishing, controlled by Lee Valley ACA. *(See Tottenham).* Red Spinner AS has Cheshunt South Reservoir; carp and roach. Members only. Cheshunt AC has Friday Lake; members only. Kings Arms AC and Cheshunt Carp Club have Cheshunt North Reservoir. Bowyers Water, Windmill Lane: 35 acre gravel pit with carp, tench, bream, pike; Northmet Pit, gravel pit of 58 acres, various coarse species incl large carp and eels (dt available); both fisheries run by LVRPA *(see Hoddesdon).* Tackle shops: Angling Centre, 77 High St, Waltham Cross, Simpsons, Turnford.

Wormley (Herts). The famous **King's Weir Fishery** (½m R Lee, ½m of Flood Relief Channel and ½m of bank at Langridge Lake), available on st £30 + £4 key payment, £15 conc. Large carp (30lb) and pike. Dt £7 for 9 swims on Wier Pool. Contact Kings Weir House. Tel: Hoddesdon 468394 for bookings.

Broxbourne (Herts). Leased by BT Committee from King's Weir Fishery boundary below Broxbourne bridge up to

POLLUTION

Anglers are united in deploring pollution. To combat it, urgent action may be called for at any time from any one of us. If numbers of fish are found dead, dying, or seriously distressed, take samples of both fish and water and contact the officer responsible for pollution at the appropriate National Rivers Authority.

Dobbs' Lock above, including the **Crown Fisheries** and **Redlands Carthagena Fishery;** 2 lakes in 15 acres, stocked with coarse fish; ⅓m of Old R Lee, 1m of Lee Navigation. St £20, juv, OAP £10. Dt for towpath only, £1.50, 80p, from P Brill, Carthagena Lock. Tel: 0992 463656. Broxbourne Meadows fishery, Mill Lane, sections of R Lynch, Lee Navigation cut off, Mill Pool, with roach, chub, pike, bream, perch, carp, run by LVRPA (*see* Hoddesdon, below).

Hoddesdon (Herts), ns Rye House or Broxbourne. On Lee, Stort and New River Lee: Dobbs' Weir Fishery, Essex Rd; bream, roach, pike, chub and perch, carp, tench, barbel. Dt from bailiffs. Admirals Walk Lake, 25 acre gravel pit at Conker lane, pike, tench, bream, roach, carp; run by Lee Valley Regional Park Authority, Middleton House, Bulls Cross, Enfield EN2 9HG, tel: 0992 717711. By written application only. Tackle shop: C J Ross, 2 Amwell Street. Hotel: Fish and Eels.

Rye House (Herts). Roach, chub, dace, bream, pike, perch, tench. Rye House Bridge to October Hole is London AA water; West Ham AC controls east bank and Lee Valley ACA, west bank, at Fieldes Weir. Dt from bailiff. Hotel: Ye Olde Rye House.

St Margaret's (Herts). Old River Lee. River fishing from towing-path. Lee Valley ACA, Mr T Mansbridge, tel: 081 524 0869.

Ware (Herts). Old River Lee. Fishing in Lee Navigation controlled by Lee Valley ACA. Contact 081 524 0869. Ware AC have members only carp ponds. Membership £14, consessions.

Hertford (Herts). For **Lee, Mimram, Beane, Rib** and **New River.** Lee Valley ACA (*see Tottenham*) controls the Lee angling from Hertford to Stort Confluence at Feildes Weir. Very good course fishing. Access points at Folly Bridge, Mill Rd, Marshgate Drive. London AA has stretch from Town Mill gate to junction with Lee Navigation (¾m); members only. For Hertford AC contact C Bite, tel: 0992 467585. for Ware AC contact D Bridgeman, tel: 0920 461054; both clubs have local fishing. Tackle shop: Hertford Tackle, 6a The Maltings, Railway Place, Hertford, who have £5 st and £1 dt available. Hotels: Salisbury Arms, Dimsdale Arms, White Hart, Station.

Hatfield (Herts). Hatfield and Dist AS has rights on river from Mill Green to Essendon (about 2½m); including seven-acre broadwater (large carp and bream). Members only.

Luton (Beds). Tring Reservoirs (10m); Grand Union Canal (10m); Great Ouse (20m). Clubs: Milton Keynes AC (0908 270723), Leighton Buzzard AC (0582 28114), Ampthill & Dist AC (0525 715457), Vauxhall AC (0582 571738). Tackle shops: Anglers & Pets Cabin, 61 High Town Rd; Lesiles, 89 Park Square.

Tributaries of the Lee

STORT: Preserved from source to Bishops Stortford.

Roydon (Essex). Roach, dace, perch, pike, chub, bream. Water between road bridge and railway bridge is Two Bridges AS fishing; hon sec B Bird, 8 Ducketts Mead, Roydon. Global Enterprises Ltd, Roydon Mill Park, Roydon, Essex (tel: 0279 792777) have 2m fishing available to guests camping or caravanning. This includes well stocked weir pool. No Dt, residents only. Lychnobite AS leases Temple Farm Fishery, (about 2m of fishing). Dt from bailiff on water. Two Leisure Sport gravel pits of 16 acres plus 160 mtrs R Stort at **Ryemeads,** offering large pike, chub, dace, tench, bream and roach. No day tickets, St £20, concessions for jun, OAP, dis. Applications to LSA, Thorpe Park, Staines Road, Chertsey, Surrey. Tel: 0932 564872.

Harlow (Essex). Coarse fish. Harlow DC has town nine waters including Rye Mead and Harlow Town Park. Inquiries to Leisure Services, Town Hall. London AA has water here and at Spellbrook and **Thorley;** (available to associates). LAA grants facilities for Harlow residents on its water. Inquiries to hon sec. Tackle shop: Harlow Angling Centre, 5 Long House, Bush Fair.

Sawbridgeworth (Herts). Good head of all coarse fish with many large roach; fishes best Sept onwards. Sawbridgeworth AS has from confluence at Spellbrook to confluence of Little Hallingbury Brook, left hand bank; pike fishing (after Oct 1), limited number of st. Dt and tackle from The Pet Shop, Knight Street. Hotel: Queens Head (club HQ). Visiting parties welcome; apply hon sec for reservation.

Bishop's Stortford (Herts). Navigational

stretch opened by British Waterways. Bishop's Stortford and Dist AS has coarse fishing to Spellbrook Lock (tickets), a length at Harlow, Cam at Clayhithe, lakes, 10 acre gravel pit. Tackle shop: Anglers Corner, 40A Hockerill St. Hotels: Foxley, George.

ASH. Fishing stations: **Widford** (Herts) and **Hadham** (Essex); a few trout, pike, etc; preserved.

RIB: Trout, coarse fish. Abbey Cross AS has a stretch from Hertford to Watton Rd, nr Ware; members only.

BEANE: This once-excellent trout stream has been largely ruined by abstraction. Some stretches still hold good fish, however. No public fishing except at Hartham Common, Herts.

MIMRAM: Trout, preserved.

LINCOLNSHIRE (small streams)

(For close seasons, licences, etc, see Anglian Region NRA, p17)

GREAT EAU or **WITHERN.** Rises above Aby and flows some 12m to sea at Saltfleet; coarse fish; much free water; fishes best in autumn.

Saltfleet (Lincs), ns Saltfleet, 3m. Grayfleet, South Eau, and Mar Dyke; coarse fish; some free water. At Saltfleetby St Peters is pond on which fishing is available; dt, at shop near pond; no Sunday fishing. Sea trout in Haven in Sept; also flounders.

Louth (Lincs). Great Eau private above bridge on main Louth-**Mablethorpe** road, including Calceby Brook, Aby and South Ormesby Park; free below to licence holders as far as Gayton lugs, thence ½m private to members of Mablethorpe, Sutton-on-Sea Dist AC (also another ¾m stretch), thence free to Cloves Bridge. Louth Crown & Woolpack AC has 2 acre coarse pond at Charles St, membership £10. **Theddlethorpe** (Mablethorpe Dist AC), and free below Cloves Bridge. Altogether 10m free fishing to licence holders; coarse fish, including good roach, bream, perch. pike, rainbow trout (few and mostly small) and grayling. **Lud** generally free below Louth to outfall at Tetney. Coarse fishing in ponds at **Louth, Grainthorpe, North** and **South Somercotes, Fulstow, Saltfleetby, Legbourne, West Ashby,** Hogsthorpe, Chapel St Leonards, Skegness, Wainfleet, Authorpe, Addlethorpe, Alford, Farlesthorpe, Spilsby, all available on dt from local tackle shops. Sutton Brick Pits, Alfred Rd, **Sutton-on-Sea;** dt at adjacent houses. Hatton Lake, trout, tel: Wragby 858682. Parts of **Louth Canal** free to licence-holders from Louth to sea outlet at **Tetney;** part controlled by Witham and Dist. JAF; coarse fish; some private access; permission from farmers. Tackle shops: Castaline, 18/20 Upgate; Tackle Box, 323 Somercotes Hill, Somercotes; Belas, 54-56 High Street, Mablethorpe. Hotels: Kings Head, Lincolnshire Poacher, both Louth.

STEEPING. Rises 5m above **Spilsby** (1m off on left bank), runs thence to **Wainfleet** and joins the sea 4m below near **Skegness;** coarse fish; Croft AC has stretch at Haven House; tickets. Witham and Dist. JAF controls 20m from Wainfleet upstream, and **Wainfleet Relief Channel.** £1.30 temporary members ticket from Storr's Shop, Market Place, Wainfleet. Spilsby AA has **Ereby Canal;** good bream, tench, Perch, etc; members only; confined to 13m radius; st and dt from hon sec or Higgs Bros Tackle Shop. Spilsby, who also issue licences.

LINCOLNSHIRE (small lakes and ponds)

Ashby Park Fisheries, Horncastle LN9 5PP, tel: 0507 527966. 5 lakes, mixed coarse fishing, dt £3.50 on site.

Brickyard Fishery, South Rd, **South Somercoates,** Louth LN11 7PY. 4 acre coarse fishing water, dt £3 on site.

Belleau Bridge Farm Lake, Alford. 6 acre coarse fishery. Dt from Mr Harrop, tel: 0507 480226.

Culverthorpe Lakes, Culverthorpe Hall, tel: 05295 249. 16½ acre lake with pike to 30lb, carp to 27lb, tench, 8½lb. Contact G A D Emerson.

Fish Pond Farm, Usselby, **Market Raison.** tel: 0673 828219. 2 lakes, mixed coarse fishing, dt on site, £3, B&B & meals available.

Goltho Lake, Goltho Wragby LN3 5JD, tel: 0673 858358. 2 acre mixed coarse fishery, dt £2 on site.

A fine male tench from a gravel pit day ticket water. Lincolnshire is renowned for its tench fishing. The sex of this specimen is identified by its paddle-shaped pelvic fins. *Photo: Bruno Broughton.*

Grimsthorpe Lake, Grimsthorpe and Drummond Castle Trust, tel: 0778 32205. 36 acres, mixed coarse fishing.

Hartsholme Country Park Lake, Skellingthorpe Rd, LN6 0EY, tel: 0522 534174; 27 acre lake, mixed coarse fishery, permits on site, st £16.50, dt £2.

Hill View Lakes, Skegness Rd, **Hogsthorpe**, tel: 0754 72979. One fly only trout lake, one coarse lake, dt on site, from £6.50, trout (27 Mar 16 Oct), £2.50 coarse.

Hollands Park, Wedland Lane, **Thorpe St Peter**, tel: 0754 880576. Coarse fishing lake, dt £2 on site.

Hatton Trout Lake, Hatton, Nr Wragby, tel: 0673 858682. Dt on site, £7.50-£5.

Lakeside Leisure Ltd, **Chapel St Leonards**, PE24 5TU, tel: 0754 72631. 3 acre mixed coarse lake, dt on site, £2.90, £4 double.

North Kelsey Park, North Kelsey LN7 6QH, tel: 0831 132819. Large lake, mixed coarse fishery, dt £2.50 on site.

North Thoresby Fisheries, Fen Lane, North Thoresby. 3 lakes, 2 available on dt. 1 acre trout, 4½ acre coarse, mostly carp. Contact J Casswell, 0472 812518.

Olsten Fishery, Mill Lane, **Legbourne**, Louth LN11 8LT, tel: 0507 607432; coarse fishing in lake, trout in chalk stream. Dt £12-£5, coarse £3, on site.

Pelican Pond, **Barton-on-Humber**, tel: 0652 33600. 80 acre coarse fishery with large stocks of roach, tench, pike, eels, bream. St only, available on bank. Contact North Lincs Sailing Club, Pasture Rd.

Rossways Water, 189 London Rd, **Wyberton** PE21 7HG. Two lakes mixed coarse fishing, dt £3, subject to availability. Cafe, bait and tackle on site.

Starmers Pit, Tritton Rd, **Lincoln**, tel: 0522 534174. 7 acre lake, mixed coarse fishery. Dt £2 on site.

Sycamore Lakes, Skegness Rd, **Burgh-le-Marsh**, tel: 0754 810749. 4 acre mixed coarse lakes, dt £3 on site. Tackle and bait shop, snacks, caravan and camping.

Tattershall Leisure Park, Sleaford Rd, tel: 0526 343315. 7 lakes, mixed coarse fishing, dt on site, £2.

Toft Newton Trout Reservoir, **Market Raison** LN8 3NE. 40 acres, bank and boat fly fishing, rainbow and brown, fly only. Dt £11, 6 fish, £5.50, 2 fish. Boat

(must be booked in advance) £8.
Thorpe Le Vale Fishery, Louth. 5 acre trout fishery, brown and rainbow. Fly only. Dt from G Wildsmith, Thorpe le Vale, Ludford, Louth. Season, Mar-Dec.
Willow Lakes, Ashby Hill Top Farm, **Ashby-cum-Fenby** DN37 0RY, tel: 0472 220777. 3 lakes, 1 trout, 1 mixed coarse,

1 carp and tench, dt on site by prior arrangement only. Luxury accomodation on site.
Woodlands Fishery, Ashby Rd, **Spilsby,** tel: 0709 54252. 1 trout and two coarse lakes, dt £6.50, trout, £2 coarse. Tackle and refreshments on site.

LONDON (Thames Water reservoirs, etc)

Most of the waters referred to below are in the area termed Greater London. All are easily accessible from Central London. A number are rented by angling clubs and reserved for members, but at others fishing is available to the general public at modest charges on season or day ticket basis.

It seems appropriate to mention here two important angling bodies:- first, the **London Anglers' Association,** which has water on one reservoir as well as scores of miles on rivers, streams and lakes (125 fisheries in all). The Association now has about 5,000 full members through 160 affiliated clubs. It has offices at Izaac Walton House, 2A Hervey Park Road, Walthamstow, London E17 6LJ (telephone number: 081-520 7477). For a brochure and application form please send a stamped addressed envelope to the above address. Annual membership (associate) £21.50. Jun, OAP, regd disabled £8.50.

The **Central Association of London and Provincial Angling Clubs** (HQ The Lord Raglan, St Martins Le Grand EC2) has about 120 affiliated clubs and fisheries on rivers, canals and lakes in the South of England. Day tickets issued for many fisheries. Full details from hon sec.

Among tackle shops in Central London are: Hardy Bros, of 61 Pall Mall; C Farlow & Co Ltd, 5b Pall Mall *(see advt)*. Tackle dealers in the suburbs are too numerous to list. The Angling Trades Association is at 7 Swallow Street, Piccadilly (Tel: 071-437 7281). Tackle shops in Metropolitan area listed under individual centres.

Thames Water Reservoirs where fishing rights are let to clubs include the following:
Lambeth (No 4) to London AA.
Banbury, Walthamstow to Civil Service Sports Council.
Cheshunt (South) to Red Spinner AS.

Reservoirs open to the public for game fishing (stocked with rainbow or brown trout).

Walthamstow Nos 4 & 5. Barn Elms 5 & 6 are all stocked with trout. Two are reserved for fly fishing only, in two others bait fishing and spinning, with certain restrictions, are permitted. Boat on Barn Elms 5.
East Warwick, rainbow trout, limited stocking, fly and spinner. Ferry Lane,

Tottenham. Tel: 01-808 1527. **Wroughton,** r and b trout, stocked. fly only. Comprehensive leaflet issued by TW, supplied on request, by the Information Officer, Thames Water, Nugent House, Vastern Road, Reading. Tel: Reading 593538.

Reservoirs open to the public for coarse fishing.
King George North & South, Chingford: coarse fishing, st only, from gatehouse, Ferry Lane, opp. Ferry Boat Inn.
Northmet Pit, Cheshunt, has pike to 35lb; dt £1.50, juv, OAP 75p. Contact Lee Valley Leisure Park.

Walthamstow Nos 1, 2 & 3, High and **Low Maynard, Coppermill Stream, New Cut, Lee Navigation** (¼m at Walthamstow). Coarse fisheries, st. Comprehensive leaflet issued by TW, supplied on request. See above.

Keep the banks clean

Several clubs have stopped issuing tickets to visitors because of the state of the banks after they have left. Spend a few moments clearing up.

IF YOU HAVE A NAGGING FEELING THAT YOU COULD DO MORE TO PROTECT GAME FISH AND THEIR ENVIRONMENT – YOU ARE RIGHT!

You could join the 100,000 or so trout and salmon anglers who already support The Salmon & Trout Association. You would be in good company alongside Members of Parliament and thousands and thousands of anglers just like yourself. We don't just monitor and report on the many threats to the wonderful sport that brings us all together . . . **WE ACT!**

Phone for a brochure and enrolment form now!
Telephone: 071-283 5838

The Salmon & Trout Association
Guardians of the Game Fishing Environment
Patron: HM Queen Elizabeth the Queen Mother
President: HRH The Prince of Wales

The Salmon & Trout Association

SPONSORED BY **LAPHROAIG**

WHO'S LOOKING AFTER YOUR INTERESTS?

S&TA Fishmongers' Hall, London Bridge, London EC4R 9EL Telephone: 071-283 5838 Fax: 071-929 1389

LUNE

(For close seasons, licences, etc, see North West Region NRA, p17)

Rises on Ravenstonedale Common (Westmorland) and flows through beautiful valley into Irish Sea near Lancaster. Excellent sport with salmon, sea trout and brown Lower reaches also well-stocked with coarse fish. August and September best for s and sea trout.

Lancaster (Lancs). Salmon, sea trout, trout. NRA has Skerton and Halton fisheries. Salmon, Feb 1 to Oct 31, mt, May 1 to Oct 15. Bt Mar 15 to Sept 30. FF June 16 to Mar 14. Lansil Sports and Social Club has $1\frac{1}{2}$m both banks just above tidal stretch, with additional coarse fishing for usual species plus specimen bream (12lb+). Salmon st £50 + £25 joining fee, other fishing, £20, conc. Tackle shops: Gunsmiths & Fishing Tackle, 7 Great John Street, who supply licences; Gerry's of Morecombe, 108 Heysham Rd, Morecombe.

Halton (Lancs). Lune; salmon, sea trout, trout, coarse fish. Permits for Halton top and bottom beats and limited amount of tackle from Halton Stores, 9 St Wilfreds Park, St Wilfreds Park, Halton, tel: 0524 811507.

Caton (Lancs). Lancaster and Dist AA has fishing over 6 bank miles divided into three sections. Waiting list for membership. Permits £10 to £18 depending on season, weekdays only, from Mrs Curwen, Greenup Cottage, Caton. No dt Saturdays and Sundays, though Sunday fishing is allowed to members. Fly only when water level 1ft 6in or below, Worm prohibited in October, except at water level of 3 ft. No maggot, shrimp, prawn or grub fishing. No boat fishing. Prince Albert AS also have water, and at **Killington.** For Bank House Fly Fishery, Caton, contact Mr D Dobson, tel: 0524 770412.

Hornby (Lancs). Salmon, sea trout, trout. Lancaster AA has Claughton stretch *(see Caton)*. No dt. From Wenning Foot (North) for $\frac{3}{4}$m, Southport Fly Fishers, members only.

Whittington (Lancs). Salmon, sea trout and brown trout. Apply to H G Mackereth &

Son, Whittington Farm, tel: Kirkby Lonsdale 71286/72375.

Kirkby Lonsdale (Cumbria). Salmon, sea trout, trout. Trout and sea trout fishing are very good; average $1\frac{1}{2}$lb; sea trout up to 8lb. Kirby Lonsdale AA has about $4\frac{1}{2}$m of water. Limited wt £35-50 to persons staying locally only (not caravanners or campers), from Tourist Information Office. Below Kirkby Lonsdale & Dist AA water, Lancaster & Dist AA has water. Lancashire FFA has water here and at Tebay. Hotels: Royal, (can arrange salmon and trout fishing), Red Dragon, King's Arms, Sun, Fleece Inn. Casterton Hotel at Casterton, 1m upstream, is convenient for association waters. Salmon (best August, September); sea trout (June onwards), trout.

Barbon (Cumbria). Lune, 1m W Barbon Beck. Barbon is good centre for Kirkby Lonsdale AA water. Hotel: Barbon Inn.

Sedbergh (Cumbria). Sedbergh AA has about 20m on Lune and tributaries **Rawthey, Dee** and **Clough.** Brown trout; salmon and sea trout from July. Visitors st from visitors hon sec; wt and 3 day (weekdays) from Lowis' Sports Shop, Main Street. Manchester AA has stretch at **Firbank;** members only. Tickets for 9m on **Clough** from Lowis's, 23-5 Main Street, Sedbergh. Hotels: The Bull, The Dalesman.

Low Gill (Cumbria). Trout, sea trout and salmon (salmon and sea trout best at backend); about $2\frac{1}{2}$m both banks preserved by A Barnes, Gunsell Lodge, Wood Lane, Tugby, Leics. Local representative, A Hogg, Tarn Close, Beckfoot, Low Gill, Sedbergh, tel: 0539 846580. Dt £10 or £15. Blackburn AA also has water.

Tebay (Cumbria). Salmon and sea trout (August onwards best), trout (average 3

Fishing available?

If you own, manage, or know of first-class fishing available to the public which should be considered for inclusion in **Where to Fish** *please apply to the publishers (address in the front of the book) for a form for submission, on completion, to the Editor. (Inclusion is at the sole discretion of the Editor).*

to lb). Telbay and Dist has 15m of good water; wt £30, OAP £20, but not in Oct. Juv £5. Tickets from Cross Keys Hotel. Other club, Lancashire FFA has water. Hotel: Cross Keys.

Orton (Cumbria). Trout (all season),

salmon, sea trout. Pinfold Lake, **Raisbeck**; r trout, dt £14 (4 fish) from tackle shop J Pape, Market Place, Appleby. Accommodation at George Hotel. NRA licences: Davies, 8 North Terrace, Tebay.

Tributaries of the Lune

RAWTHEY. Trout, with sea trout and occasional salmon late in season. Sedbergh AA has good stretch on river and tributary Dee; visitor's st £100, wt £50.

WENNING. Sea trout (good), brown trout, few salmon (late). Best latter part of season. Fishing station: **Bentham** (Yorks). Bentham AA has about 3½m of water; fast stream, good sport; visitors' tickets: st £30 + £10 entrance fee, wt £20, dt £5 (jun ½) from hon sec, or Churchills, Station Rd, Bentham. Ingleborough Estate holds 5m. St £15, wt £4.50 (limited); apply Estate Office, Clapham; trout run 3 to 1lb. Accrington FC has Hazel Hall Farm fishing, near Clapham. Barnoldswick AC have two stretches of Wenning, upstream from Farrars Viaduct, downstream from

Clintsfield Viaduct. Hotels: The Coach House, Black Bull. Punch Bowl Hotel also has ¾m private trout and sea trout fishing and issues dt £5.

GRETA. Trout (4 to 1b) and late run of salmon and sea trout. Fishing stations: **Ingleton** and **Burton-in-Lonsdale** (Yorks). Trout. Ingleton AA controls 6m of unbroken water on Greta, **Twiss** and **Doe**; st £30, wt £20, dt £7 (½ price jun) from Village Pet Supplies, High Bentham, and hon sec. Sunday fishing on approx 3m, maps issued with permits. Accrington FC has 2m, Burton-in-Lonsdale, members only. Hotel: Punch Bowl, Burton-in-Lonsdale (NRA licences).

MEDWAY

(For close seasons, licences, etc, see Southern Region NRA, p15)

Kentish river joining estuary of Thames at Sheerness through estuary of its own. Coarse fish (abundant bream, record barbel, 1993) with few trout in upper reaches.

Maidstone (Kent). Free on NRA licence from Maidstone to East Farleigh, North Bank, except new mooring area. Medway Victory Angling and Medway PS have water at Barming, Teston, Wateringbury and Yalding. Permits from hon sec and local tackle shops. Free fishing on Brookland Lake, Snodland Council, 0634 240228. **Lambden Trout Fishery** is at **Gillingham;** tel: 023384 674. **Johnsons Lakes,** Larkfield; large bream, carp and pike. Temporary membership from bailiff on bank. Mallaras Way Lake, details from Len Valley A & PS. **Abbeycourt Lake,** Sandling; coarse fishing, dt. Tel: 0622 690318 after 6 pm. Information from A Sanders, 85 Bank Street (tickets and licences). Other tackle shops: Maidstone Angling Centre, 63 Sandling Road; Medway Bait and Tackle, 64B St Johns Road, Gillingham. Inns: Medway; West Kent; Rose and Crown; Queen's Head.

East Farleigh (Kent). Free fishing as described under Maidstone; thence mostly Maidstone Victory Angling and Medway Pres Soc water; tickets. Inn: Victory.

Barming (Kent). CALPAC has water upstream and downstream of bridge. Contact J C Watts, 9 Kemble Road, West Croydon.

Wateringbury (Kent). Maidstone Victory Angling and Medway Pres Soc has most of towpath bank here and at **Teston,** incl. Teston Bridge Picnic site, dt. Medway Wharf Marina, Bow Bridge, has fishing for boat and caravan owners using their services. Dt £4. Tel: Maidstone 813927. Barking AS has a meadow; members only but open to visiting clubs. Inn: King's Head.

Yalding (Kent). Free fishing on NRA licence u/s from Yalding Sluice 200m, South Bank. Maidstone Victory Angling and Medway Pres Soc has towpath bank downstream of Railway Inn; tickets. Yalding AS has water; dt (weekdays only). New Studio AS has short length. Central Assoc of London and Prov AC has one meadow at junction of Medway and **Beult;** members only. Dt £3 per rod available (from bailiff or cafe) for their other Yalding fishery, 1200yd of towpath, commencing above the large oak tree. Inns: Railway (tackle, but no accommodation); George; Anchor (boats).

Tonbridge (Kent). Tonbridge and Dist A & FPS has 9m of Medway, 1½m of Eden and gravel pits of 4 to 8 acres. Dt for parts of Medway and one pit, only. Contact sec for details. Vacancies for membership; £20 + £5 joining fee, concessions for OAP. Paddock Wood AC offer dt for **Gedges Lake,** coarse fishing. Tel: 0892 832730. Sherwood Park AC has local fishing. Contact C Willard, 20 Pinewood Rd. **Mousehole Lake,** 3 acre fly only trout fishery, on B2015 at Nettleshead Green. Dt on site all year. **East Peckham Lakes,** 5½ acres are Maidstone Ex Services AC water. Good mixed coarse fishery. Tel: 0622 8424353. Tackle shops: Tonbridge Rod and Line, 17a Priory Road; Medway Tackle, 103 Shipbourne Road.

Tunbridge Wells (Kent). Royal Tunbridge Wells AS has coarse fishery at **Ashurst** and **Fordcombe,** trout waters on Medway from Forest Row to Hartfield, Withyham to Ashurst, and coarse fishing from Ashurst to Poundsbridge (4m), also on **Teise** below Finchlock's Bridge to Hope Mill, **Goudhurst.** Grayling and barbel in places. Fishing on three ponds also. Membership limited. Annual subscription £46, joining fee £15, concessions for ladies and jun. Coarse fishing dt for Court Lodge Down, Neville Golf Course. Pembury 2388. Tackle shops: Bob's Tackle, 21-23 Quarry Road; Crowborough Tackle, White Hill Rd, Crowborough; MA Wickham, 4 Middle Row, E Grinstead; Wadhurst Rod & Line, Highbury Place, Wadhurst.

Ashurst (Kent). Coarse fish, some trout, grayling, barbel to 12lb. Tunbridge Wells AS has water *(see above).* Limited tickets for members' guests only.

Fordcombe (Kent). Trout, coarse fish, barbel 15½lb. Tunbridge Wells AS has water, limited tickets for members' guests.

Tributaries of the Medway

BEULT: Excellent coarse fishing; lower reaches noted for chub, bream and tench; trout higher. Gravesend Kingfisher A & PA (stretches at **Smarden, Hunton, Headcorn** and **Staplehurst;** members only); London AA has water at **Hunton** and **Linton;** members only. Lewisham Piscatorials and Dartford AA has fishing. CALPAC has water at Headcorn for members only. ACT Fisheries Ltd issue tickets for fishing between Linton and **Yalding.** 170 Sydenham Road, London SE26. **Biddenden Trout Fishery** issues dt £15.50, 4 fish limit, on lake at Pond Farm, Headcorn Rd, Biddenden. Tel: 0580 291576. Coarse fishing dt for Brogues Wood, Biddenden from 05806 4851.

EDEN: Coarse fish.

Penshurst (Kent). On Eden and Medway; coarse fish. Penshurst AS has rights from Ensfield Bridge to Pounds Bridge and from The Point on Medway to weir on Eden; members only. No dt.

Edenbridge (Kent). Coarse fish. 8m controlled by Edenbridge AS (members only) also a mile at Penshurst. Short stretches rented by Holland AS, also Crawley AS.

TEISE: Joins Medway at Yalding. Trout, coarse fish.

Laddingford (Kent). London AA has water for members only at Mileham Farm and Hunton Bridge right bank.

Goudhurst (Kent). Teise Anglers and Owners' Association holds water from Goudhurst to Marden; brown and rainbow trout; mainly fly only, and winter grayling fishing. Members only (£155 sub, joining fee £50). Ass. also has stocked farm reservoir for trout fishing at Marden. Apply to B Wait, 101 Stanhope Grove, Beckenham, Kent. Season, April 3 to Sept 30. Tunbridge Wells AS has stretch, listed under Tunbridge Wells.

Lamberhurst (Kent). Tunbridge Wells AS has trout and course fishing water d/s of the Chequers Hotel for approx 4½m; members and guests only. **Hoathley** Fishery (2m of Teise plus ¾m on **Bartley Mill Stream**) has natural stock of trout, chub, roach, dace, etc, supplemented by b and rb trout from Bayham Lake. Fly, spinning and bait. Dt £3 from Hoathley Farm, Clay Hill Rd, Lamberhurst TN3 8LS or Bassetts Garage, opp. Bayham Abbey. Tel: Lamberhurst 890201 for advance bookings. For **Bartley Mill Trout Fishery,** tel: 0892 890372. Childrens catch'n'keep trout pools available. Rod hire £1 plus £2.50 per trout. **Bayham Lake** trout fishery near here. Tackle shop: Glyn Hopper Angling, High St. Fishing accommodation: Maj Allen

Austin, Goudhurst, 0580 891471.

MERSEY

(For close seasons, licences, etc, see North West Region NRA, p17)

Forms Liverpool Channel and seaport. Main river polluted and of no account for fishing except in higher reaches. Some tributaries contain trout.

Liverpool (Merseyside). Liverpool and Dist AA has stretch on **Leeds & Liverpool Canal.** Northern AA has stretches on **R Dee** at **Worthenbury, Ribble** at Balderstone, Worthenbury and Emeral Brooks; and also fishes Bridgewater and Macclesfield Canals and **R Weaver** at **Vale Royal.** Dt £1.50 on all waters. 50m section of **Shropshire Union Canal,** starting from Ellesmere Port, directly controlled by BW. Liverpool AA st £9, dt £1 to £2. Tackle shops: Johnsons', 469 Rice Lane; Matchmans, 183 Breckfield Rd North; Taskers Tackle, 25 Utting Avenue, Liverpool 4; Hoppys, 14 Sefton Street, Litherland 21; Garston Angling, 8 St Marys Rd, Liverpool 19.

Wirral (Cheshire). **Burton Mere Carp Fishery, Burton Wirral:** dt £3.50 from Rod & Reel, Enfield Rd, Ellesmere Port. Free coarse fishing in ponds at Wirral Country Park. Contact Head Ranger, tel: 051 648 4371. Local club, Irby AC. Tackle shops: Gary Bonner Angling, 119 Duke St; Wirral Angling Centre, 207 Church Road, Tranmere, both Birken-

head; Ken Hopkins, Moreton, Wirral.

Stockport (Cheshire). Stockport County Anglers have private water at Davenport; four pools; carp up to 10lb. Stockport Waltonians AA also has private waters; coarse fish and trout. Tackle shops: Gresty's Tackle, 220-222 Shaw Heath; Edgeley Sports & Fishing, 145/7 Castle St.

Whaley Bridge (Derbyshire). River here known as Goyt; polluted. Dt (not Sundays), for one bank only. **Todd Brook Reservoir,** Whaley Bridge, stocked with trout and coarse fish. Dt 25p for **Bosley Reservoir,** near Macclesfield, from Harrington Arms on Macclesfield-Leek Road, and Mr J Arnold at 1 Lakeside Estate, Bosley. Both waters hold roach, perch, bream, carp, pike, gudgeon *(see also Weaver).* **Peak Forest Canal** starts here; coarse, sport patchy. Lock pools at **Marple** stocked with carp and tench. Canal to Ashton Junction being opened and dredged. County Palatine AA has water on canal.

Tributaries of the Mersey

NEWTON BROOK (tributary of Sankey Brook):

St Helens (Merseyside). All brooks polluted. Lakes: **Eccleston Mill Dam, Eccleston Mere** and other local dams preserved by two works' clubs; members only. **Carr Mill Dam;** perch, pike, bream, roach. St Helens AA has waters in dams and canals and on the **Calder.** St £10, conc, from tackle shops. Good carp, roach, chub, tench and dace in **St Helen's Canal** (Church Street length) and in Blackbrook stretch. Lymm AC offer dt on Sankey/St Helens Canal. St Helens

Tackle shops: A & L Bailey, 237 Boundary Rd; Angling Centre, 196 Islands Brow.

BOLLIN:

Heatley (Cheshire). Occasional trout, roach, dace, pike. **Arden Brook,** 1m SE; Mersey, 1m N. Warrington AA has stretch of Bollin at **Bowden.**

Ashley (Cheshire). Bollin, 1m N; trout, roach, dace, pike; Bollin and Birkin AA; private.

BIRKIN (tributary of Bollin):

Knutsford (Cheshire). Birkin, 4m; Bollin and Birkin AA has water; private. **Tabley**

POLLUTION

Anglers are united in deploring pollution. To combat it, urgent action may be called for at any time from any one of us. If numbers of fish are found dead, dying, or seriously distressed, take samples of both fish and water and contact the officer responsible for pollution at the appropriate National Rivers Authority.

Mere, 3m, is let to Lymm AC; no permits available. Toft Hall Pool, 1½m S; occasional permits. Tatton Park, Knutsford, coarse fishing; details from Head Ranger, tel: 0565 654822. **Redesmere** and **Capesthorne Lakes** (6m S of Wilmslow on A34 road); Stoke AS waters; tench, king carp dt for Capesthorne stock pond only, £5 from A Bradley, Bailiff, East Lodge, Capesthorne (Tel. Chelford 861584). Tackle shop: Naylor's Sports, 2 Minshall Street; Trevor Allen, 16 Altringham Rd, Wilmslow.

IRWELL:

Manchester. River polluted, but some waters have been leased to clubs. At **Poynton,** 10m out, Stockport & Dist FA has pool. St only. 18m from Manchester, at Northwich, is coarse fishing in Weaver *(see Weaver).* Bolton & Dist AA has **Manchester, Bolton & Bury Canal,** from Hall Lane to Blue Wall length, 6 reservoirs, R Wyre, R Ribble nr Longridge, and other fisheries. No day tickets, but st available from tackle shops in district. Warrington AA has a twenty mile stretch of **Bridgewater Canal** as well as water on Dee, **Ribble, Severn** and tributaries and **Dane,** reservoirs, meres, etc. Apply hon sec. St £20 plus £20 joining fee, concessions for ladies, juniors etc. Macclesfield Prince Albert AS has rights on canal from Buxton road bridge to Bosley Aqueduct (about 6m). Tickets from hon sec or Balows Tackle, Macclesfield. Macclesfield Victoria AC controls **Turks Head Reservoir,** members only. Moss Side AS has water *(see Whaley Bridge).* Tackle shops: Arrowsmiths, 1a Gorton Lane, West Gorton; Gorton Angling Centre, 804 Hyde Rd, Gorton; David Marsh Tackle, 79 Long Street, Middleton; Trafford Angling Supplies, 34 Moss Rd, Stretford; Kear's, 1 Market St, Droylsden; Seedley Angling, 489 Liverpool St, Salford. **Bolton** tackle shops; V Smith, Highfield Road, Farnworth; Anglers Corner, Haliwell Road.

ROCH:

Bury (G. Manchester). Brooks polluted. Accrington and Dist AA has water on **Ribble, Lune, Wenning** and **Hodder.**

Oldham and Dist AA have ¾m length upstream from Fairfield General Hospital. Dt available. Bury and Dist AS and has stretches of R Irwell, several small ponds and reservoirs including **Elton;** mostly coarse fishing. Bury AS mem £15 + £5 joining fee, concessions. Trout fishing at Entwistle (Entwistle FFC) and Dingle (Dingle FFC). Tackle shop: Angling Centre, 195 Rochdale Road; Bury. Also Fishing Tackle, 12-14 Southworth Street, **Blackburn;** Fishermans Haunt, 161 Blackburn Road, **Accrington.**

Rochdale (G. Manchester). Rochdale Walton AS. **Buckley Wood,** 1m N (coarse and trout), also Healey Dell Lodge, dt only on application to hon sec. Visitors must be accompanied by a member. Rochdale and Dist AS has trout and coarse fishing at Castleton (dt 50p; visitors must be accompanied by member), and coarse fishing on **Rochdale Canal,** 3m from town; st, dt from tackle shops. Length of canal also held by Dunlop Cotton Mill Social Club; tickets from local tackle shops. Olham AA has **Coronation Lodge,** course fishing, members only. **Hollingsworth Lakes,** Littleborough; coarse fish; dt from tackle shops: Towers of Rochdale, 52 Whitworth Road; Kay's, 18 St Marys Gate; Dave's Tackle Shop, Yorkshire St; W Pennine Angling Supplies, 204 Yorkshire Street, who issues tickets for fly-only trout fishery (fish to 12lb) and for coarse fishing in **Calderbrook Dam.** *For Rochdale Canal see also Calder (Yorks) - Hebden.*

TAME:

Ashton-under-Lyne (G. Manchester). River polluted. Oldham AA have short length at **Greenfield** (dt available), from Canal Aquaduct, Royal George Greenfield downstream to Scout Mill, **Mossley.** NWW reservoir **Walker Wood,** 2m NE; trout; st £180, dt £8, 10d £70. Tackle shop Pet Man, 142 Stamford Street; Harry's Tackle, 213 Old Road, Ashton-in-Makerfield.

COMBS RESERVOIR:

Chapel-en-le-Frith (Derby). **Combs Reservoir,** 2m W; 57 acres, a variety of coarse fish including pike to 27lb, carp to

---

Keep the banks clean

Several clubs have stopped issuing tickets to visitors because of the state of the banks after they have left. Spend a few moments clearing up.

20lb, roach, bream, tench, perch; dt £3.50; Bailiff collects on bank; enquiries to C N Farley, Lakeside, Combs Rd, Chapel-en-le-Frith, tel: 0298 812186.

MIDLANDS (reservoirs and lakes)

BLENHEIM LAKE. Woodstock, Oxon; excellent tench, perch, roach in summer; pike winter. Boat fishing only for visitors. Apply by letter to Estate Office, Blenheim Palace, Woodstock, Oxon OX20 1PS for details of current charges. Tel: (during normal office hours) 0993 811432.

BODDINGTON RESERVOIR. Byfield (Northants); **Banbury,** 7m. 65 acres. Pike to 32 lbs, bream, perch, roach, carp to 27 lbs, tench; st £24 one rod, £29 two, jun £13, and mid-week 3-day ticket £10 from BW Principal Fisheries Officer (South). Address is listed in Canal section.

CASTLE ASHBY LAKES. Northampton 7m. Coarse fishing in three lakes, two carp and one mixed coarse, leased to Mr M Hewlett, 176 Birchfield Rd East, Abington, NN3 2HG, 0604 712346. Dt available. **Menagerie Pond** (specimen carp fishery). St £130; Details from Estate Office, Castle Ashby, Northampton NN7 1LJ, tel: 0604 696232. NRA licence required.

CLAYDON LAKES. Buckingham, 6m. Upper and Middle Lakes at Middle Claydon, near Winslow, are Leighton Buzzard AC water; Danubian catfish, pike-perch, big carp. Members only.

CARSINGTON WATER, nr **Ashbourne,** Derbyshire. Owned by Severn Trent Water Ltd. Opens as brown trout fishery in 1994. Season 14 Apr-16 Oct. Day and evening tickets for bank and boats, plus concessionary for bank only; dt £10.00, Evenings £7.50. Boats £8.00 - day, £5.50 - evenings. Disabled facilities and catering available. Enquiries to the Fishery Office, Carsington Water, Ashbourne, Derbys DE6 1ST. Tel: 0629 85695.

CLUMBER PARK LAKE. National Trust property, 4½m from **Worksop;** coarse fish (including pike); st £40, dt £2.50 (jun and dis £1.25) from bailiff on bank. **COSGROVE PITS. Milton Keynes,** 2m (Bucks). Coarse fishing on 8 lakes from 2 to 25 acres, and Rivers Tove and Great Ouse. 2 lakes members only, otherwise dt £2 at waterside from Manager, Cosgrove Leisure Park, Milton Keynes MK19 7JP, tel: 0908 563360 Tackle and bait shop on site, camping, caravan site available.

CORNBURY PARK. Charlbury, Nr Oxford. Brown and rainbow trout fishing over three beautiful marl lakes set in an historic deer park. Day tickets available over two lakes, membership only on remaining water. For further details and day ticket prices contact Cornbury Park Fishery, Southill Lodge, Cornbury Park, Charlbury, Oxon OX7 3EH. Tel: 0608 811509.

CRANFLEET CANAL. Roach, perch, gudgeon. Trent Lock held by Long Eaton Victoria AS, also Erewash Canal, Long Eaton Lock to Trent Loch. Membership £12, concessions.

CRANSLEY RESERVOIR. Kettering (Northants) 2½m; Northampton 13m. Roach, perch, pike, large tench. Controlled by Derek Jones Commercials Ltd, Kettering Rd, Islip.

DENTON RESERVOIR. Denton (Lincs). Excellent coarse fishing; held by Grantham AA; st £11, conc, from hon sec (tel: 0476 75628), bailiffs and tackle shops. No day tickets.

DRAYCOTE WATER, near **Rugby** (Warks) 600 acre reservoir, brown and rainbow trout. Owned by Severn Trent Water Ltd, 2297 Coventry Rd, B'ham B26 3PU. Season April 1-Oct 23. Dt £11.40, 8 fish limit; Evenings £8.10, 5 fish limit. OAP, jun, dis, £6.70. Boats £10.40, engine £8.30 extra. After 4pm £6.200, engine £6.20. Bank anglers limited to 300. Disabled facilities, catering and courses. Optional catch and release. Information from Fishing Lodge (tel: 0788 811107). Advance bookings, from Kites Hardwick Filling Station, 300 yards from entrance on Banbury side. (Tel: 0788 812018).

DRAYTON RESERVOIR, Daventry. 18 acres, principally carp to 4 lbs, also roach, perch and tench. Average catches, 15lb. Permits £4 per day from patrolling bailiff, £2 concessions. Match bookings welcome. Contact British Waterways, Southern Region.

DUKERIES LAKES. Worksop Welbeck and Clumber Lakes are fishable on a restricted issue of permits from the Estate Offices to members of the Worksop & District AAA and to other approved applicants. Applications to Mr G Rollinson, Lincoln St, Worksop. The Association has rights on **Sandhills Lake** and **Harthill Reservoir**, also.

EYEBROOK RESERVOIR. Caldecott (Leicestershire), off A6003 Uppingham Caldecott Road. 400 acres good trout fishing. 25,000 caught each year. Fly only. Boats must be paid for in advance. Season 1 Apr-30 Oct. Prices are as follows: dt £9, evening £7, juv OAP £6, st £255, £185 juv OAP, mid week st £190, wt £45, boats £9.50, £7.50, £5.50. Fishing tickets and NRA licences at reservoir office (Rockingham 770264). Inquiries out of season to Corby (Northants) and District Water Co, Geddington Road, Corby, Northants NN18 8ES, tel: 0536 404298.

FOREMARK RESERVOIR. Nr Repton, Derbys. 230 acres, owned by Severn Trent Water Ltd. 1994 season 1 Apr-15 Oct. Dt £9.70, 8 fish, evening £7.70, 4 fish. Conc, £6.00, 4 fish. Rowing boats £8.20 to £5.70. Disabled facilities, catering and courses. Permits available on site. Tel: 0283 703202.

GRAFHAM WATER. St Neots (Hunts). 1,560-acre reservoir stocked with brown and rainbow trout. Now managed by Anglian Water Services from the lodge at Mander car park, West Perry PE18 0BX.

Records include b trout 12lb 6oz, r 13lb 13oz. Full st £399, mid-week £359. Dt £11, 8 fish limit, evening £8, 4 fish. Beginners dt £3, 1 fish. Motor boats £17 to £12. It is advisable to book these in advance. Tel: 0480 810531; Fax 0480 812488.

GRIMSBURY RESERVOIR. Banbury (Oxon). Coarse fishery leased to Banbury AA. Dt £1.50. Contact tel: 268047.

HARLESTHORPE DAM. Clowne, Derbys. Trout, coarse fish. St £70, dt £4 on site; night fishing £7 by arrangement, also tackle and bait. Tel; 0246 810231.

LADYBOWER RESERVOIR, Bamford, (Derbyshire). Severn-Trent Water Plc, 2297 Coventry Road, B'ham B26 3PU. 1994 season 10 Mar-15 Oct. St £204, weekday £154. Dt £8.90, evening £5.70, concessionary £5.20. Limit, 4 fish up to May 31, thereafter 6 fish. Evening 3 and 4. Boats £7.80 to £5.70. Disabled facilities. Limited permits from warden for fly fishing on R Derwent below Ladybower Dam. All prices include VAT. Enquiries to fishing office, tel: 0433 651254.

LINACRE RESERVOIRS, near Chesterfield. 43 acres in well wooded valley, 3 reservoirs, 2 stocked r trout, one wild b. St £95, from G Nixon, Netherthorpe,

When hope runs at its highest. A day begins on the Eyebrook Reservoir.

Staveley, Chesterfield. Dt £6.50 (4 fish) from The Angling Centre, Chester St, Chesterfield; Peacock Hotel, Cutthorpe, or at water.

NASEBY RESERVOIR, Northants. 85 acres. Carp to 19lb, tench to 5lb, rudd. Leased by BW to Naseby Water AC, sec I A McNeil, Bufton, Walcote, Nr Leicester LE17 4JS.

NANPANTAN RESERVOIR. 2m S of **Loughborough.** 8-acre coarse fishery. Stocked with carp. Dt £1.50 (concessionary 75p) from W H Wortley & Son, 45 Baxter Gate, Loughborough.

OGSTON RESERVOIR, near Chesterfield, Derbyshire. 203-acre water owned by Severn-Trent Water Plc. Large trout. Dt £7.40, conc £3 (limited), from STW, 2297 Coventry Road, Sheldon, B'ham B26 3PU and New Napoleon Inn, Woolley Moor, opposite reservoir. (Tel: 0246 590413).

PACKINGTON FISHERIES, Meriden (Warks). Excellent trout fishing on 100 acres of pool, 2½m of river. Dt £16, boats £6.50. Dt for 2 in a boat, £38.50. Flexi 5 hour ticket £11. Fishing on **Somers** fishery for carp, tench, roach, perch, pike, bream and rudd. St £140-£70, dt £6.50-£3. Concessions for juniors and OAP. Reduced rates for evenings. Details from Packington Fisheries, Broadwater, Maxstoke Lane, Meriden, nr Coventry CV7 7HR (0676 22754).

PATSHULL PARK FISHERIES, Burnhill Green, Wolverhampton WV6 7HY. 75 acre lake, well stocked with b and r trout; fly only. St £260, dt £13 inc 2 fish catch and release (other fish £2.40 each.) Ticket from 2pm £9, inc 1 fish. Boats £5, £3. Conc. Regular fly fishing contests held. Small stocked coarse pool. Tel: 0902 700774.

PITSFORD RESERVOIR, Northampton 5m. 750 acres, owned and managed by Anglian Water. Rainbow and brown trout, fly only. Good fly hatches all season. Best brown 8lb 9oz, best r 13lb 8oz. St £299, mid week st £269, 8 fish, dt (8 fish) £10. Evening £2 (4 fish). Beginners £3. 50% reduction for juniors. Boats £17 to £9. Permits from Pitsford Lodge, Brixworth Rd, Holcot NN6 9SJ, tel: 0604 781350.

RAVENSTHORPE RESERVOIR, Northampton 8m. 100 acres, owned and managed by Anglian Water. Brown and rainbow trout, fly only. Best rainbow, 12lb.5oz. Dt £10 (6 fish limit), evenings:

£7 (3 fish). Beginners £3. Boats £10, £7-£5 eve, motor £5. Pike fishing in December. Open 1 Mar to 31 Dec. Brown trout 1 Apr-29 Oct. Apply to Pitsford Fishing Lodge, Brixworth Rd, Holcot NN6 9SJ, tel: 0604 781350. Accom, White Swan Inn, Holcot; Poplars Hotel, Moulton.

RINGSTEAD ISLAND, Ringstead, 25 acre stocked with carp to 20lb, bream to 6lb, good pike in winter. Wellingborough Nene AC water, membership £8, conc. £3.

RUTLAND WATER, Leics. Stamford & A1 5m, **Oakham** 3m; managed by Anglian Water Services; Normanton Fishing Lodge, Rutland Water South Shore, Edith Weston, Oakham, LE15 8HD, tel: 0780 86770. 3,000 acres, 17m of fishing bank, largest stocked trout fishery in Britain. Browns to 15 lbs and rainbows to 13 lbs. Pike fishing in late Oct-early Nov. 65 motor boats. Competition facilities available, accommodation list. St £379 full, mid week £329, 8 fish limit, conc £206. Dt £11 (8 fish), £8 (4 fish). Package hol. with motor boat, £99. Juv 50%. Open 1 April to 29 October.

SHELSWELL LAKE, Buckingham 7m. Tench, perch, roach and pike, winter best; st £8, conc £3, from hon sec, Bicester AS and Allmonds Sports, Market Square, Bicester; boat available at no extra charge. Bicester AS also has two stretches on **River Ray;** coarse fish; no tickets.

SHUSTOKE RESERVOIR. Shustoke; Coleshill 3m. Leased to Shustoke fly fishers by STW. St £255 to £305, dt £12, 5 fish limit, £7 for 4 hours, 2 fish, boat £3; t on site from 12 Apr. Tel: 0675 81702.

SULBY RESERVOIR. 1m **Welford,** 14m **Northampton.** Coarse fishing; specimen carp, all fish between 10-39 lbs. Limited st only, £150. Applications to BW Principal Fisheries Officer (South). Address is listed in Canal section.

STAUNTON HAROLD RESERVOIR, near **Melbourne,** Derbys. Severn-Trent W coarse fishery, 209 acres, leased to Swadlincote AC. Tackle shop, Melbourne Tackle and Gun, 52/54 High St, Melbourne. Tel: Derby 862091

SYWELL RESERVOIR. Northampton 6m. Now a County Park. Large tench (6lb or over), pike (over 20lb), perch, roach and carp; members of Wellingborough and Dist Nene AC only. St £8, conc £3; apply hon sec, warden or tackle shops for details.

THORNTON RESERVOIR. Leicester 3m S of junction 22 on the M1. 76 acres. Trout, annual stocking of 15,000, fly only, Mar to Nov. Leased to Cambrian fisheries by STW. St £300 and £160, dt £12, ½ day £8. Boats £6.50 and £4.50. Bag limits, 6 and 2. Tickets on site. Tel: 0530 230807.

TITTESWORTH RESERVOIR, near **Leek,** (Staffs). 184-acre trout water now leased by STW to Tittesworth Fly Fishers Ltd. St, long waiting list. Dt and boats available, 6 fish limit, advance bookings from fishing lodge at reservoir. Tel: Blackshaw 389. Concessions to jun, OAP and regd disabled.

TRIMPLEY RESERVOIR, near **Bewdley,** Worcs. Trout, fly only, from early March-July 31. Aug 1-Oct 15, mixed fishery; then coarse fishing until Feb 28. St £110 weekday, £75 weekend; mixed £40; coarse £15. There is a £15 joining fee. Dt for guests of members only. Write for details to sec, Trimpley AA.

WELFORD RESERVOIR, near **Welford,** Leics, 20-acre coarse fishery. Many specimen bream, pike, carp, tench, rudd and roach. St only £13 (Jun half price) from BW or bailiff W Williams, Welford Grange Farm. Waiting list.

NENE

(For close seasons, licences, etc, see Anglian Region NRA, p17)

Rises in West Northamptonshire and flows to Wash. Good, all-round coarse fishery slow-running for most part. Roach and bream predominate, the bream in particular running to a good average size. Excellent sport with carp in Peterborough and Northampton areas. Trout Fishery in upper reaches,

Wisbech (Cambs). Centre of intricate system of rivers and drains, including the Nene-Ouse Navigation Link; all waters well stocked with pike, bream, roach, perch and some good tench. Fenland Assn of Anglers is centred in Wisbech. Wisbech and Dist AA sub hires some waters. NRA licence and Assn wt required. Concession price for locals. **Great Ouse Relief Channel** provides 11m of good fishing from Downham to King's Lynn. Algethi Guest House, 136 Lynn Rd, caters for anglers. Tel: 0945 582278. Tackle shops: Brian Lakey, 12 Hill St; Mark One Tackle, 32 Norwich Rd. Hotels: Queens, Rose and Crown, Marmion House.

Peterborough. Excellent centre for roach, bream, chub, tench, carp, dace, eels and pike. Peterborough AA now controls most of the N bank of the Nene from **Wansford** to the Dog in a Doublet and some fishings on the S bank in the same area. The Association also has water on the **Welland** from **Spalding** to u/s of Crowland. St £15, dt £2.50, conc. Dt **Ferry Meadows Lakes,** £2.50, from bailiffs. Wansford AC waters now members only. At **Wansford** A1 road bridge, Stamford Welland AAA have ½m of south bank, downstream. Brotherhoods Sports Centre issue dt for their water on the Nene at **Warmington,** where Warmington AC also has stretch for members only (membership restricted). Grantham AA now too have water at Warmington. Apply John Bradshaw, New Lane, Stibbington, for dt on Nene and 4 acre coarse lake newly available 8m from **Stamford.** First-class sport in fen drains and brick pits, but many pits being filled in. Licences, st, wt and dt from tackle shops: Webbs, 196 Newark Avenue, Dogsthorpe, for North Bank Trout Fishery (£12, 6 fish), and local coarse fisheries **Thrapston Pits, Gerards Pit** at **Maxey, Werrington Lakes, Tallington Lakes. Orton Water** trout fishery, 25 acres, is near Peterborough. Best rainbow 16lb, best brown 7.5lb. Dt £12 with boat £5 extra (5 fish limit), 10% discount conc. Tel: 0733 239995. Tackle shops: C Shelton & Sons , tel: 65287; K. Wade, 65159; Peterborough. Nobby's, 57

Fishing available?

If you own, manage, or know of first-class fishing available to the public which should be considered for inclusion in **Where to Fish** *please apply to the publishers (address in the front of the book) for a form for submission, on completion, to the Editor. (Inclusion is at the sole discretion of the Editor).*

Manor Way, Deeping St James.

Cotterstock (Northants). Excellent fishing for roach, chub, bream, perch, tench, dace and pike held by Cotterstock AA here and at **Tansor**. St £5, conc, and dt £1.50 from B Wing, Manor Farm and hon sec. Jun, OAP, clubs welcome.

Elton (Northants). Leicester and Dist Amal Soc of Anglers has extensive stretches here and at **Nassington** and **Fotheringhay**. Dt £1.50 from hon sec or bailiffs. Coventry AA has 55 pegs at Fotheringhay. Good head of tench, roach and bream. Dt £2.50.

Oundle (Northants). Roach, bream, carp, tench, dace, etc. Oundle AA has water on both banks; limited st £10, dt £2. OAP free. Coventry AA has 70 peg stretch with good head of tench and bream and roach. St £13.50, conc £5, dt £2.50. Wellingborough Nene AC has 3m at Barnwell, just upstream of Oundle and 2 acre gravel pit (tench, pike, perch and rudd). Members only. **Elinor Trout Fishery**, Aldwincle, 36 acre lake stocked b, r and salmon. Dt £8.50 (6 fish), evening £6, same limit, boats £5 or £7. Conc. Inquiries to E Foster, Lowick Rd, Aldwincle, Kettering. Tel: 08015 786. Perio Mill, tel: 08326 241/376, has trout stream stretch of 1 km, fly only, £30, 4 fish limit. Wadenhoe Mill Stream Trout Fishery: river fishing on backwater of Nene, 900 yds well stocked, dt £9.50, 4 fish, evening £5.50 2 fish. Permits from Aldwincle PO, or Kings Head, Wadenhoe. Tackle shop: Stuarts, Corby. Hotels: Talbot, caters for anglers, 0832 273621; Ship; Chequered Skipper, Ashton(Oundle HQ).

Thrapston (Northants). Roach, dace, perch. Kettering, Thrapston & Dist AA no longer issue guest tickets; membership: £8 pa. Northampton Castle AA fish Thorpe lakes, Thrapston, 40 acres, coarse with bream, roach, crucian carp. Assc has several other lakes in county. Dt £3-£5 from Northampton tackle shops or on bank.

Rushden, Higham Ferrers and **Irchester** (Northants). Coarse fish. With new sewage works completed, fishing now showing marked improvement. Rushden, Higham Ferrers AC have water at **Bletsoe** and **Turvey** on Ouse: barbel and chub. Information, tackle and Rushden club cards (membership £10 pa) from Dave Walker, 26 Church St, Rushden and Webster, Corn merchant, Irthlingborough.

Ditchford Lakes in the vicinity, well stocked and with improved banks; excellent trout and salmon fishery at **Ringstead Grange**, 36 acres, well-stocked with large fish. Dt £11, boat for two £9 extra, evening, OAP and junior tickets. Limit 6 fish, full day. Tel: 0933 622960. Irthlingborough AC has several gravel pits. St £12. No dt. Tackle shops: J Leach, 26 Church St; Rawlings Tackle, 63 Newton Rd, both Rushden. Hotels: Rilton; Westward, both Rushden.

Wellingborough (Northants). Wellingborough Nene AC from Ditchford Weir to one meadow below Hardwater Crossing. Other club waters: **Great Ouse** at Harrold, small section of R **Ise, Ditchford, Sywell, Ringstead** and **Barnwell Lakes,** and backwaters at Barnwell, Ringstead, Denford and Ditchford, all off **Nene.** These fisheries contain many large carp, chub, bream, pike, etc. Membership £8, £3 conc. from hon sec. Northampton Nene AC has from Doddington up to paper mills, excluding Earls Barton AC water (1m) and water at **Billing** *(see Castle Asby, Billing and Northampton).* Tackle shops: Ron's Tackle, 18 Park Rd; J C Angling Supplies, 13 Eastfield Rd, Wollaston. Hotels: Hind; Columbia; Fairfield.

Castle Ashby (Northants). Pike, perch, bream, tench, roach; preserved for most part by Northampton Nene AC, which issues dt. Lakes on **CA Estate** (1¼m S); pike, bream, tench, perch, roach; dt from bailiff at waterside or estate office. *(See also Midlands Reservoirs).* Hotel: Falcon.

Billing (Northants). Pike, roach, perch, bream, tench, chub: preserved by Northampton Nene AC, which issues dt for 1½m on both banks of river. Good coarse fishing at Billing Aquadrome. Seven lakes open from June 16 to Oct 16. St £15, wt £4, dt £1. All available on site. Tel: Northampton 408181 or 0933 679985.

Northampton (Northants). Pike, perch, bream, chub, roach, carp, etc; Nene AC controls north bank from Weston Mill to Clifford Hill Lock. Northampton good centre for lake and reservoir fishing. **Heyford Fishery**, Nether Heyford, is a purpose-built match fishery, with annual stocking of 800lbs of carp, roach, bream, and other coarse species. Dt £5 on bank or from Trinders, address below. Northampton Britannia AC controls much local canal fishing, members only. Affiliated with Leicester & Dist ASA. Tackle shops: Gilders, 250/2 Wellingborough Road; Angling Centre, 85 St Leonards Rd, Trinders, 221 Birchfield Rd East.

Weedon (Northants). Pike, perch, bream, roach. **Grand Union Canal.** Northampton Nene AC has rights from Weedon to Yardley Gobion (16m); dt. Lakes: **Fawsley Park** (two lakes); pike, roach, rudd, etc; dt from Nene AC. Nene and Ouse licences needed for canal. Welland and Nene RD has stocked **Bugbrooke** reaches with trout (3½m in all between Heyford Mill and Harpole Mill); limited dt from Fisheries Officer. **Hollowell Reservoir**, 140 acres, pike to 35lb, large roach and rudd. St £55, dt £5, conc. The Fishery Warden, c/o Pitsford Water, Holcot, NN6 9SJ, tel: 0604 781350.

Tributaries of the Nene

OLD RIVER NENE:

March (Cambs). Pike, perch, bream, rudd, roach, tench. Fen drains. **Old River Nene** mostly free to licence-holders. **Reed Fen** (south bank) is now private fishing. **Twenty Foot** controlled by March and Dis AA (tickets). **Popham's Eau,** and **Middle Level** are Wisbech AA waters. **Forty Foot** is now leased by Chatteris WMC. Dt £1 are available on bank. **Mortens Leam,** 5m from March, 7m of river fishing from Rings End to Whittlesey. Wide variety of coarse fish. Dt available on bank. Tackle shop: Mill View fishing Tackle, 3 Nene Parade, March. Hotels: Griffen, Wades, Temperance.

Ramsey (Hunts). Pike, perch, bream, etc, Holme Brook. Wiston Brook. Lake: Ramsey Mere, 3m NE. Ramsey AS has fishing on both banks. Contact Mr P E Aldred, 9 Blackmill Road, Chatteris, tel: 0354 32232. To the east and north of **Sawtry**, Holme and Dist AA have fishing on both banks of **Kings Dyke, Yaxley Lode, New Dyke, Monks Lode** and **Great Ravely Drain**. Contact Mr K Burt, 55 Windsor Rd, Yaxley, Peterborough, tel: 0733 241119.

WILLOW BROOK: Trout, coarse fish; preserved.

King's Cliffe (Northants). Willow Brook. Welland, 3m NW.

ISE:

Kettering (Northants). **Cransley Reservoir;** roach, perch and tench *(see Midlands Reservoirs and Lakes).* For st and dt on **Wicksteed Lake,** also preserved water on Nene at **Trapston,** apply Kettering AA. Tackle and licences from Stuarts Tackle, 86 Rockingham Rd, Corby, Kettering, tel: Corby 202900.

Geddington (Northants). Preserved to Warkton.

STRECK:

Crick (Northants). Streck, 2m S. Dunsland Reservoirs (pike, perch, etc) 3m SW; private.

Daventry (Northants). **Daventry Reservoir** coarse fishery, pike, perch, etc; Daventry Dist Council water. **Drayton Reservoir,** see Midlands reservoirs and lakes. Hellidon Lakes Hotel, Hellidon NN11 6LN has fishing, tel: Daventry 62550. Tackle shop, Trinders Tackle, Station Close, Vicar Lane.

NORFOLK AND SUFFOLK BROADS

(Rivers Bure, Waveney and Yare)

(For close seasons, licences, etc, see Anglian Region NRA, p17)

Rivers Bure, Waveney and Yare, their tributaries and Broads are among the finest coarse fisheries in England. They contain pike, perch, roach, dace and large chub. Some banks of tidal water which can be fished free. For details, contact regional NRA. Some Broads are preserved and can be fished on payment. Rivers and most Broads very busy with boating traffic in summer, so early morning and late evening fishing advised. Best sport in autumn and winter. Boats essential for Broads

BURE

Strong current from Yarmouth to little above Acle; upper reaches gentle and ideal for float fishing. The river contains a good head of coarse fish. Excellent roach, bream and pike etc, at Thurne Mouth, St Benets, Horning, Wroxham. Several Broads are connected and can be fished as well as tributaries Thurne and Ant.

Stokesby (Norfolk). Bream, roach, pike, perch. Strong tides and sometimes brackish; legering best; free. St £2 for Muckfleet Dyke from Greensteads Tackle Gorleston, or Boultons, Norwich.

Acle (Norfolk). Bream, roach, pike, perch. Tides often strong. River traffic heavy in summer. Acle and Burgh Marshes free fishing on NRA licence. Inns: East Norwich Inn, Old Rd, Acle; Travel Lodge, A47 By Pass, Acle.

S Walsham and Upton. 3¾m R bank below Ant mouth, and 1m right bank from S Walsham Broad to Bure confluence free to licence-holders.

St Benets Abbey, bream and roach. North bank from Ant d/s, Norwich & Dist AA. Dt from Ludham PO. Accommodation at Holly Farm, Old Hall Farm and Olde Post Office.

Horning (Norfolk); ns Wroxham, 3½m. Good coarse fishing; free to licence holders; boat almost essential; roach, rudd, bream, perch, pike, tench; river very busy in summer, hence early morning and late evening fishing gives best results. At **Woodbastwick** NRA has ¾m of right bank, tidal; free to licence-holders. Broads: **Ranworth** (tickets for Inner Ranworth from store on Staithe); **Decoy** (club water), **Salhouse** (dt issued); and **Wroxham,** small charge, upstream. Tackle shop: Granary Stores, The Staithe, Ranworth. Several boat yards. Hotels: Swan, Kepplegate and Petersfield House Hotel.

Wroxham (Norfolk). Roach, rudd, bream, pike, perch, tench; good pike and bream in winter; boats only. Much river traffic, summer. Broads: **Bridge Broad,** boats only. **Salhouse Broad,** right bank, dt issued. **Alderfen Broad,** specimen tench. Boats £5 per day from Wroxham Angling Centre Station Rd, Hoveton. Hotels: Broads; Hotel Wroxham.

Coltishall (Norfolk). Boats available. Hotels: King's Head; Risings; Norfolk Mead.

Buxton Lamas (Norfolk). All banks now private.

Abbots Hall (Norfolk). Ingworth. Brown trout, stocked 4 times during season. 1m both banks, dry fly, or upstream nymph only, available to Salmon and Trout Assc members. Applications to R J S Bramall at Hockley's, 36 Prince of Wales Rd, Norwich NR1 1LH, tel: 620551.

Bure Valley Lakes, nr **Aylsham** NR1 16NW, 10 acres with rainbow trout up to 12lb, browns up to 6lb. Dt £8.50 plus £1.50/lb trout caught. Fishing for coarse with large carp, also. Free casting instruction for beginners. Tel: 026387 666.

Blickling (Norfolk). Trout upstream from Ingworth Bridge. Abbots Hall, R Bure at Ingworth, 1m both banks, Salmon and Trout Assn members fishing. Tel: 0603 620551. Dt for Blickling Lake (20 acres), from bailiff at 1 Park Gates, Blickling NR11 6NJ; £3, jun £1. No night fishing. Tickets on bank in summer. Pike season Oct 1 to Mar 14.

Tributaries of the Bure

THURNE: Slow-flowing, typical Broadland river; tidal below Potter Heigham. Coarse fish, good bream and roach. NRA water at **Potter Heigham, Martham, Thurne Marshes.**

Thurne Mouth (Norfolk). Good roach, bream, perch and eels. Only NRA licence required, available from Lion Inn, public house. Accom. at self catering chalets, Hedera House, tel: 0692 670242.

Potter Heigham (Norfolk). Popular centre; good roach and bream; fair-sized eels. Bure. 3m, S. Broads: **Womack,** 1½m; **Hickling Broad** and **Heigham Sound** (tench, bream, roach, perch). Approx 3½m left bank, Martham to Repps and 4½m right bank Martham to Coldharbour free to licence-holders. Access points at Ferry Rd, Martham; Potter Heigham Bridge and Repp's Staithe. Hotels: Broads Haven, Cringles, Broadland House. Boats from C George, Ferry Dyke, tel: Great Yarmouth 850394; Whispering Reeds Boatyard, Hickling, tel: Hickling 314; Arthur Walch, Nurses House, Martham. Licences, tackle, etc. from Ken Latham, Bridge Road, Potter Heigham (Tel 388).

Martham (Norfolk). Rudd, tench, bream, roach, perch, pike; good bank fishing; **Heigham Sound** 1m free on NRA licence. Dt £2 for 24 hours on **Martham Pits,** 3½ acres good coarse fishing, from Mollys Sweet Shop, Martham. Local club is Martham and Dist. AC. Boats: Beale, The Staithe, Hickling; and Whispering Reeds Boatyard, Hickling. Accommodation at Mustard Hyrn Farm.

ANT:

Ludham. Roach, bream. 2¼m of the river, upstream and downstream of Ludham Bridge, free to licence-holders.

Irstead and **Neatishead** (Norfolk). Good bream, perch, rudd, pike; also tench and roach. Fishing free.

Stalham (Norfolk). River clear, slow-running and weedy in summer; roach, rudd, bream, perch, pike and few tench. Broads: **Barton,** 1m; rudd, bream and big pike; free fishing. Boats from Barton Angler Country Inn, Neatishead NR12 8XP, or Cox, Barton Turf Staithe. **Hickling,** 3m by road; good pike, bream, etc. Sutton Broad overgrown. Tackle shop: Broadland Angling and Pet Centre, High Street. Hotel: Sutton Staithe Hotel and Kingfisher. Inns: The Thatched Cottage, Sutton.

Wayford Bridge (Norfolk). Upper Ant; head of navigation; fishing free to licence-holders; roach, rudd, perch, pike, tench, bream; boat advisable; river is narrow and fairly busy at times in summer; weedy and clear. Boats from George Mixer & Co Ltd, Catfield, Gt Yarmouth, tel: Stalham 580355, who reserve ½m downstream. Bait and tackle from Stalham. Good fishing also above the head of Ant Navigation in Dilham and North Walsham Canal, navigable to rowing boats as far as Honing Lock. Caravan site and food at Wood Farm Inn. Houseboat accom. from tel: 0692 650491.

North Walsham (Norfolk). **East Tuddenham,** 3½ acres b and r trout. Tel: 0692 402162. **Hevingham Lakes:** group of small pits, coarse fish. Dt £2. Tel: 060548 368. Tackle shop: Tatters Tackle, 49 Market Place. Tel: 0692 403162. Inns; Ockley House; Toll Barn.

SAW MILL LAKE: Fishing station: **Gunton** (Norfolk) near Cromer. 16 acre lake in Gunton Park, 3m; coarse fish; dt £3, from bailiff, on bank. Jun, OAP £1.50.

Horning (Norfolk). **Salhouse Broad;** too much traffic in summer, but good fishing in early mornings and from Oct to March. Dt issued. **Ranworth Broad** (tickets for Inner Ranworth from store on Staithe). **Malthouse Broad;** free. **Decoy Broad;** now open only to clubs. Tackle, licences, bait at Post Office.

Ormesby, Rollesby and **Filby.** Fishing by boat only, available from: Eels Foot Inn, tel: 0493 730217 (Ormesby); Mr Millstead, tel: 0493 748232 (Rollesby); Mr Thompson, tel: 049377 250; J & J Barnes, Filby Bridge Restaurant, Filby NR29 3AA (Filby). These Broads are connected and undisturbed by motor cruisers and yachts; fishing good everywhere. Excellent pike in winter. Wt £27.50. **Little Ormesby Broad,** free fishing by boat only, available from Mr French, tel: 0493 732173.

Salhouse (Norfolk). Salhouse Broad, 1m NE; few pike in winter.

Broads connected with the Bure

Wroxham Broad, 1m N; *(see Wroxham);* Information and boat-hire from Wroxham Angling Centre, tel: Norwich '782453. **Decoy** or **Woodbastwick Broad,** 2m NE; fishing on payment. **Little Ranworth Broad,** 3m E; good for bream. These three are controlled by Norwich & Dist AA. **South Walsham Broad,** 5m E; private; good bream and pike fishing; leave from owner.

Wroxham (Norfolk). **Wroxham Broad,** boat fishing only. Dt from Tom Boulton, 175 Drayton Rd, Norwich, 0603 426834. **Bridge Broad,** boat fishing only. **Salhouse Broad,** right bank, 2m SE. **Alderfen Broad,** has specimen tench and bream; dt £5 from Wroxham Angling Centre, tel Norwich 782453.

Check before you go

While every effort has been made to ensure that the information given in **Where to Fish** *is correct, the position is continually changing, and anglers are urged, in their own interests, to make preliminary enquiries before travelling to selected venues. This is especially important with reference to prices quoted. Inevitably the rate of inflation is affecting stability in this quarter. Anglers' attention is also drawn to the fact that the hotels mentioned under the various fishing stations do not necessarily have water of their own. Any amendments or further data for inclusion in subsequent editions, and any criticism, will be welcome.*

Broads connected with the Thurne and Ant

Potter Heigham (Norfolk). **Heigham Sounds;** fine fishing in summer; pike fishing, roach and bream in winter (free). Pike fishing on Horsey (no live-baiting). Womack Water dredged and cleared of weed, and may be fished from quay below. *(For hotels, boats, etc, see entry under Thurne.)*

Hickling (Norfolk). **Horsey, Barton** and **Hickling Broads,** bream, roach, pike, perch. All free except Horsey: dt from keepers. Licences from Post Office and stores; boats available. Accommodation: St Austell.

Martham (Norfolk). R Thurne. Bream.

WAVENEY

Flows along Norfolk-Suffolk border. Beccles is noted centre for roach and bream fishing, and reach between Geldeston Lock and St Olaves gives some wonderful sport with bream in most seasons.

Lowestoft (Suffolk). Oulton Broad and Waveney, which connects with Broad; bream, perch, roach, pike, etc; boats at Broad. Flounders and smelts in harbour. Good sea fishing in Oct, Nov and Dec from boats and beach for whiting, cod and flatfish. Several Broads within easy reach. Much of **River Hundred** is Kessingland AC water. **Oulton Broad** (Suffolk). Broad gives good sport with eels to 5lb, bream, roach, etc, but crowded with boats in summer. Bank fishing from Nicholas Everitt Park. Waveney near; 2m of free fishing at Puddingmoor Lane, **Barsham;** 170 yds at **Worlingham;** best from boat. Good perch and pike (best Oct-March); roach (good all season, best Jan, Feb, Mar), bream (moderate, best June-Nov); dace. **North Cove;** 400 yards with bream to 7lb, big pike, st from Post Office. **Oulton Dyke** (north side only); bream (excellent Aug, Sept, Oct); perch, roach, eels. Club: Oulton Broad Piscatorial Society. Tackle shops: Oulton Broad Angling Centre, Commodore Road; Ted Bean, 175 London Rd; P & J Fishing Tackle, 52 High St, Kessingland. Hotels: Wherry; George Borrow; Broadlands.

Haddiscoe (Norfolk). **New Cut:** good coarse fishing; free. **Fritton Lake;** 163 acres, perch, pike, roach, rudd, tench. Accommodation at Fritton Old Hall, NR15 2QR. Other hotels: Crown, Queen's Head.

Worlingham (Suffolk). 170yds of Suffolk bank free fishing via Marsh Lane.

Beccles (Suffolk). Good roach, bream, pike, etc; best early or late in summer but especially good Oct onwards, when river traffic eases off. Free fishing from Beccles Quay. Beccles AC has 31 pegs at Barsham Drain, half mile out of Beccles off Bungay Rd, and Haddiscoe Lake, 5m

away. Various coarse species. St £15 from tackle shop. 400 yds stretch at **Aldeby** is George Prior AC water. **Aldeby Pits** coarse fishery is 5m from Beccles, on Waveney. Tackle shop *(see below)* is helpful, and issue st and dt for waters belonging to Beccles, Bungay Cherry Tree, and Harleston and Wortwell clubs, on river and lakes. Charges range from st £17 to £5; dt from £1.50 to 50p. Tackle shop: Beccles Angling Centre, 27 Blyburgate. Hotels: King's Head; Waveney House; Ship House.

Geldeston (Norfolk). Good pike, roach, perch, bream, etc; free. Inns: Wherry (NRA licences) and Geldeston Lock. Tackle shop in Beccles (3m).

Barsham (Suffolk). 2m free fishing on Suffolk bank from Puddingmoor Lane.

Bungay (Suffolk). Good roach, chub, bream, perch, pike and tench; fishes best at back end. Bungay Cherry Tree AC has from Earsham to Geldeston, 2m between Wainford and Ellingham, mostly roach, and **Ditchingham Pits,** dt, Tel Mr Gosling, 0986 892982. Suffolk Co Council AAA has Bungay Common stretch, dt from Angling Centre. Bungay Chery Tree AC also has **Broome Pits,** tel: 0986 894711. **Halycon Lake,** 5 acres b and r trout, tel: Homersfield 517. Accommodation at White Lion, Earsham St, Bungay.

Homersfield (Suffolk). Pike, perch, roach (large), dace, tench. Licences from Black Swan Hotel, Harleston IP20 0ET for 300 yds of free fishing. There is also excellent specimen carp fishing locally here and at **Wortwell** Leisure Sport gravel pit.

Harleston (Norfolk). Waveney, 1m S; coarse fish. Harleston, Wortwell and Dist AC has about 7m on Waveney and 5 lakes, including Thorpe Abbots. Dt

£2.50, £1 conc. available from Waveney Angling, 5 London Road, Harleston IP20 9BH. Tel: 0379 853034 for details. Dt on site at Waveney Valley Lakes. Mendham Mill Trout Fishery, Harleston; fly fishing on R Waveney and lakes. 1 Mar to 31 Dec. Tel: 0379 852328, Mr Watts.

Eye (Suffolk). **Dove Brook;** large dace. Fishing in Waveney at Hoxne, 3m. **Weybread Pits,** permits from Mr Bowman,

tel: 0379 852248.

Diss (Norfolk). **Waveney** and **Dove.** Diss & Dist AC has good quality stocked water on Waveney at Billingford, Hoyne, Brockdish; Dove at Oakley, d/s of Bridge, roach, bream, pike, tench; **Diss Mere,** 5 acres, mirror carp, roach and crucian carp. St £14, jun £6, for all fisheries from Platt's Fishing Tackle, Denmark St, Diss.

Broads connected with the Waveney

Lowestoft (Suffolk). **Flixton Decoy,** 3m W. Large bream stocks (to 7lb); also roach, rudd, tench, perch, pike and large eels. No bank fishing. Boats available from South Lodge, Flixton. Dt prices range

from £2-£1. Enquiries to Mr Green, tel: 0502 703568.

Belton (Suffolk). **Breydon Water;** salt estuary; no fishing.

YARE

Rises few miles from East Dereham and flows through Norwich to Yarmouth. Still one of the best Broads rivers for roach and bream; specially good for roach in middle reaches bream in lower.

Great Yarmouth (Norfolk). Broads and rivers. Rivers Yare, Bure and Waveney fall into **Breydon Water** (Bure joined in upper reaches by Thurne and Ant). In all, some 200 miles of rivers well suited to boat and bank angling are within easy reach; some Broads are landlocked, strictly reserved for angling and free from river traffic; others connected to rivers, but mostly best fished from boat. Many Broads easily accessible; also rivers **Bure, Thurne, Ant** and **Waveney.** Trout in Bure. Also good sea fishing. Tackle shops: Dave Docwra, 79 Churchill Rd; Pownell and Son, 74 Regent Rd.

Reedham (Norfolk). Strong tide; legering best; roach, perch, bream, eels; free at Langley on NRA licence. Hotel: Ship.

Cantley (Norfolk). Roach, bream, perch; bream and perch plentiful; fishing free to licence-holders; mostly by leger. Inn: Red House.

Buckenham (Norfolk). Bream, roach, perch; pike; boats at Beauchamp Arms; fishing free to licence-holders here and at Claxton, Rockland and Langley, 2900 yds left bank and 5200 right bank. Mouth of Hassingham Dyke is good spot. Lakes Strumpshaw Broad, 1m NW. Buckenham Broad and Hassingham Broad, 1m SE;

preserved. Rockland Broad, 1½m SW on other bank of river; free.

Brundall (Norfolk). Roach, bream, perch in Yare. Several reaches between Coldham Hall and Surlingham Ferry can be fished by boat. Surlingham Broad belongs to National Trust; fishing only fair in summer; water shallow and weedy; pike in winter.

Norwich (Norfolk). Free fishing at Earlham Bridge to Cringleford Bridge, 2m of left bank, with dace, roach, chub, bream, pike. **Wensum** above city holds fine roach, perch, dace, chub and pike. Good roach and bream fishing at **Rockland Broad;** 7m from Norwich; but poor access to banks. Boats, Dye, tel: Surlingham 640. Haveringland Lake coarse fishery is available on wt. Tel: 0603 871302 for details. Norwich AA has water on **Bure, Thurne, Ant** and **Yare, Ranworth Inner Broad** and **Woodbastwick Decoy** (fishing by boat only on last two waters); dt from hon sec and tackle shops. Tackle shops: from Gallyons Country Clothing and Fishing Tackle, 7 Bedford St NR2 1AN; Dave Plummer, 476 Sprowston Rd; John's Tackle Den, 16 Bridewell Alley; Tom Boulton, 173 Drayton Rd. Hotel: Maid's Head.

Keep the banks clean

Several clubs have stopped issuing tickets to visitors because of the state of the banks after they have left. Spend a few moments clearing up.

The Broadland Conservation Centre at Ranworth, Norfolk. Conserving stocks for future pleasure has long been central to the angler's thinking. Today, the term has taken on wider implications.

Tributaries of the Yare

CHET:

Loddon (Norfolk). Free coarse fishing in Chet at Loddon Staithe: roach, bream. This water now navigable and fishes best in autumn and winter when traffic finishes. Hardley Marshes, coarse dt £1. Licences, river and sea bait and tackle from C Nicholls, 14, The Market Place and P Clemence, 22 High St, Loddon. Hotels: Swan, and Angel Inn, Loddon; White Horse, Chedgrave.

WENSUM: Coarse fish (good chub and barbel).

Norwich (Norfolk). Tidal. Riverside Rd, Oak St and Hellesdon Mill controlled by City Amenities Dept. Free fishing at Fye Bridge Steps, Cow Tower, Bishop Bridge, Yacht Station and d/s of Foundry Bridge to apprx 100yds d/s of Carrow Bridge..

Costessey (Norfolk). Chub, roach, dace, bream and pike. Dt from Harford Engineering, tel: 0603 743211. Norwich & Dist AA have 600 yds u/s of Costessey Mill. Membership from local tackle shops. At **Taverham,** 5 gravel pits known as the Ringland Pits, large carp, pike, roach, bream, and 480m R Wensum. St £24, conc. ½ price, from Leisure Sport, tel: Chertsey 564872, dt £2, £1, from bailiff at lakes. Costessey Pits, 100 acres: coarse fish, dt from Norwich tackle shops, or tel: 0603 43625. Shallowbrook Lake, 2¼ acres, coarse fish, st water, tel: 0603 742822.

Drayton (Norfolk). Free fishing at Drayton Green Lane for half mile, with roach, chub, bream, dace and pike. **Attlebridge** (Norfolk). Good trout fishing here, some miles of water being preserved. Tud, 4m S; private. Lakes: Haveringland, 3½m N; private. Hopground Lake, Honingham, 4m S; private. At **Reepham Beck Farm,** Norwich Road, has 4 acre carp fishery, with carp to 26lb, tench to 6lb. Dt £3 from B W Daws.

Lenwade (Norfolk). For 1m at Sparham Hall, with pike, chub, roach and bream, contact Norfolk Anglers Conservation Assc, Mr J Nunn, Heronfield, West

Somerton NR29 4DJ. Fishing in three old gravel pits set in 25 acres, administered by the trustees of two Great Witchingham charities. There is a lake with carp to 20 lbs. plus mixed coarse fishing. Permits £3 day, £7 night (conc. jun, OAP) from bailiff. Enquiries to Mrs D M Carvin, Blessings, The Street, Lenwade, Norwich NR9 5QH, tel: 0603 872399.

Swanton Morley (Norfolk). Four lakes totalling 65 acres. Local permits and information from B Todd, Gun and Tackle Shop, E Dereham. **Whinburgh Trout Lakes,** East Dereham, 4 acres of stocked b and r trout fishing. Tel: 0362 850201, Mr Potter.

Hellesdon (Norfolk). Roach, chub, dace, carp, pike. Free fishing from Mill Pool to New Mills.

Lyng (Norfolk). Fine roach, dace and some trout. Dereham and Dist AC has water; **Lyng Pit,** tench, bream, pike, roach; **Worthing Pits,** carp etc, and stretches of **Blackwater** and **Wensum,** coarse fish. Membership £10, £4 conc. from Dereham Gun and Tackle, 24 Norwich St, Dereham NR19 1BX; Myhills pet Shop, Church St, Dereham; Wilson's, or Boulton's, both Norwich. London AA has water for members only. Accom, Park Farm, Swanton Morley, 0362 637457.

Elsing (Norfolk). NRA has 1,270 yards of right bank.

North Elmham (Norfolk). Fishing in Wensum for pike, roach, perch, dace and few trout. Permission from riparian owners. **Roosting Hills,** 6 acre lake at Beetley. For details of fishing contact P Green,

Two Oaks, Fakenham Rd, Beetley, tel: 0362 860219.

Fakenham (Norfolk). Trout and dace, some roach. Fakenham AC has 2m. Dt £3 from Davies Fishing Tackle, 1 Rear Norwich Street. For 2m of Salmon and Trout Assc, members only, on Wensum at **Bintry Mill,** fly only stocked trout fishing; contact A H Chapman, Dolphin House, Vicarage Meadow, Dereham, tel: 698287. Several coarse lakes in area: **Willsmore Lake,** 0328 863054; **Railway Lakes,** 0328 863054. Hotel: Limes.

TASS or TAES:

Swainsthorpe (Norfolk). Yare, 3m N. Lakes: Bracon Hall and Carlton Lodge, 2m W. All private. **Taswood Lakes,** good carp and other coarse fish. Dt £4, night £4.50, conc. Tel: 0508 470919.

BASS:

Wymondham (Norfolk). Yare, 4m N at Barford and 6m N at Marlingford; roach. Club: Wymondham AC. Season tickets £5 from sec, or Myhills Tackle, Queens Square, Attleborough. Lakes: Ketteringham Hall lake, 4m E; private. Shropham, 8m S; bream, tench. Tackle shop: F W Myhill & Son, Fairland St (branches at Swaftham, Dereham and Thetford). Hotel: Abbey.

BLACKWATER: Trout; preserved.

Booton (Norfolk). Booton Clay Pit, with carp to 30lb, bream to 10lb and large roach, tench, etc; stocked by Cawston Angling Club. 24 hour dt £2 from bailiff on bank. Under 16, 50p. For further details contact S Brownsell, tel: 0692 406824.

Broads connected with the Yare

Buckenham. Rockland Broad, 1½m SW; good roach fishing and pike fishing in winter. R Dye, The Kilns Boatyard or tel: 05088 251/301, has some boats available.

Bed & breakfast nr Broad.

Brundall. Belongs to National Trust; shallow water grown up in summer, but good for pike in winter.

NORFOLK (small streams)

(For close seasons, licences, etc, see Anglian Regional NRA, p17, unless otherwise stated.)

BABINGLEY RIVER. Fishing station: **Castle Rising,** ns North Wootton, 2m.

Rises in the lake at Hillington Hall, and is 9m long. King's Lynn AA has water; no

---

Fishing available?

*If you own, manage, or know of first-class fishing available to the public which should be considered for inclusion in **Where to Fish** please apply to the publishers (address in the front of the book) for a form for submission, on completion, to the Editor. (Inclusion is at the sole discretion of the Editor).*

tickets. *See King's Lynn - Ouse (Great)*.
GLAVEN. Rises 3m E of **Holt** and joins sea at **Cley**, 6m down. 1m at Cley. Fishing now held privately. No permits. At Holt, Edgefield Hall, 5 acre trout fishery, brown and rainbow. Dt £8, 4 fish. Tel: 0263 712437. There are several small coarse lakes in this area. **Letheringsett, Booton** at **Cawston, Selbrigg** at **Hemstead;** dt on bank, £2.50. **Felbrigg Park Lake,** NT fishery, dt £2.50 in advance, tel: 026375 444. Tackle: Sheringham. Tel: 0263 822033.

NAR. Rises above **Narborough** to enter the Wash at **King's Lynn.** 2m both banks below Narborough Mill, dry fly and upstream nymph only, stocked trout fishing. Salmon and Trout Assc members only. Contact Mr Burrows, Appletree Lodge, Squires Hill, Marham. Tel: 0760 337222. At Narborough, five trout lakes. £2 per ½ day session plus charge for trout taken. Enq to Narborough Mill, tel 0760 338005.
TASS. Rises N of **Wacton,** 11m S of **Norwich,** to enter Yare on outskirts of city.

OTTER

(For close seasons, licences, etc, see South Western Region NRA, p16)

Noted Devonshire trout stream flowing into English Channel immediately east of Exe. Mullet in estuary and some sea trout, with brown trout of good average size for West Country higher up, where hotels have some excellent dry-fly water.

Budleigh Salterton (Devon). Tidal. Free fishing from river mouth to Clamour Bridge (about 1½m, both banks) to visitors staying in East Budleigh or Budleigh Salterton. NRA licence necessary. Sea trout, brown trout, grey mullet plentiful but difficult to catch. Fishing on both banks from Clamour Bridge to Newton Poppleford. Sea fishing; bass, flatfish, etc, from extensive beach. *(see Sea Fishing Stations under Sidmouth).*
Ottery St Mary (Devon). Some good trout water in vicinity.

Honiton (Devon). Deer Park Hotel has 3m (both banks) of first-class trout fishing; trout up to 2lb, average 1lb; rods limited to six daily. St £400, wt £100, dt £30 at hotel. Hotel also has Coly at Colyford, and 2 acre lake with r trout. Otter Inn, **Warton,** has trout fishing on 100 yds of Otter, tel: 0404 2594. Coarse fishing on 3 acre lake at Fishponds House, Dunkeswell. Carp, rudd, tench.

OUSE (Great)

(For close seasons, licences, etc, see Anglian Region NRA, p17)

Rises in Buckinghamshire and flows north-east through Northamptonshire, Bedfordshire, Cambridgeshire, Huntingdonshire and Norfolk, entering the North Sea by The Wash. Coarse fishing throughout. Slow, winding river for most part. Roach and dace are to be found in quantity, and barbel towards Newport Pagnell. Between Newport Pagnell and Bedford there are large raoch and chub.

King's Lynn (Norfolk). Coarse fish of all kinds except barbel. King's Lynn AA has water on the Ouse from Modney Court to Denver Sluice east bank; Denver Sluice to Danby's Drove, west bank; on the Wissey, From Dereham Belt to R Ouse; on the **Relief Channel Drain,** King's Lynn to Denver Sluice; on the **Middle Level Drain** from St Germans to aquaduct, 8m; the Nar, Engine Drain, Ten Mile Bank, and pits. St £14, wt £6.50, dt £2.30, conc.; from bailiffs. Valley Fisheries, Walpole, 2½ acre lake with large trout. Tel: 071 790 8932 or 098684 488. Catton Water, Hillington, 8 acre lake well stocked with r trout. Tel: 0485 600643, Mr Donaldson. Willow Lakes Trout Fishery, Chediston, Halesworth. 4 acres stocked trout fishing, 1 Apr to 15 Oct. tel Mr P Gregory on 098 685 392. Woodlakes, 8m south of King's Lynn, coarse and trout fishing at Caravan Park, Holme Rd, Stow Bridge, PE34 3PX, tel: 0553 810414. Swaffham AC has Bradmoor lakes, Narborough, stocked with carp, bream, etc. St £16.50, conc. Tackle shops: Anglers Corner, 55 London Rd; Geoff's Tackle Box, 38 Tower St, King's Lynn. Hotel: Park View.
Downham Market (Norfolk). Coarse fish, sea trout; tidal.
Hilgay (Norfolk). King's Lynn AA water on Ouse and **Wissey** *(see King's Lynn).* London AA has water on Ouse; dt from

bailiffs.

Littleport (Cambs). Ouse and **Lark;** coarse fish, except barbel, good pike and bream, with roach, perch, zander. Littleport AC has fishing on Ouse; permits from bailiff on bank or Tackle shop. London AA controls 14m of water from Littleport Bridge to Southery (Norfolk), both banks. Dt from bailiffs. Ely Beet Sports and Social Club has fishing on both banks of Ouse and Lark, at confluence. Contact Mr R J Oakman, tel: 0353 649451. Tackle shop: Coleby's Tackle, Granby St.

Ely (Cambs). Free fishing from Lincoln Boatyard upstream to Newmarket Railway Bridge. Ely Highflyers have about 5m downstream from this and last mile of River Lark (Queen Adelaide stretch); dt and club-cards from Ely Trophy Shop, 21A High Street. Rosewell pits hired by Ely Beet Sugar Factory FC; dt (limited), Dt for Borrow Pit from Cambridge FPS. Hotel: Lamb. Tackle shops: Ely Trophy Shop; Thornton's, Broad Street.

Earith (Hunts). **Old West River.** Earith Bridge to Pope's Corner (Cambs); partly hired by Cambridge Albion AS; good coarse fishing. **Old Bedford River** from Earith to Welches Dam and **New Bedford Level** or **Hundred Foot** (tidal) from Sutton Gault to Ox Willow Lode controlled by Cambridge Albion AS and Shefford AS; members only but dt issued by hon sec for Ivel. Ploughman's Pit (good carp, bream, pike; dt also from Airman public house) and lake at Oldfield Farm. St obtainable at local inns near the waters and Cambridge tackle shops. The Hundred Foot (Earith to Sutton Gault), rented by Cambridge FPS, tidal; practically all coarse fish, except barbel; **Borrow Pit** nr Ely, coarse fish, dt £1.50, in advance, from hon sec or local inns for Cambridge FPS water. Cambridge Albion AS has stretch on **Delph** from Welches Dam to Chequers, Purls bridge. Hitchin AC and Letchworth AC share stretch of Old Bedford from Purls Bridge to Welches Dam, both banks; dt on water. Great Ouse Fishery Consultative Association rents water on **Counterwash Drain, Old Bedford River, Pingles Pit** (Mepal) and the **Hundred Foot.** Affiliated clubs have rights. Members of Sheffield AAS may fish these waters, the **Delph** at Manea (Manea AC water) and the **Bedford River** from Purls Bridge to **Welches Dam** (Letchworth AA).

Over and **Swavesey** (Cambs). Bream, perch, chub, rudd, tench, pike, dace and zander. Sea trout runs up to the locks; fish over 12lb taken. Occasional salmon. Over and Swavesey Dist AS has water. St £10, conc, from all Cambridge tackle shops.

Holywell Ferry (Hunts). Hotel: Ferry Boat. Pike, bream, roach, rudd, chub, etc; free; boats available; good fishing, especially roach. Over and Swavesey Dist AS has water downstream on Cambridgeshire bank *(see Over and Swavesey).*

St Ives (Hunts). All coarse fish, bream, dace, perch, chub, gudgeon in quantity; also carp, barbel, rudd and tench. Ample bank fishing, but boats available. St Ives FP & AS has 2½m water; st £12, dt £1.50, conc. Adjoining water held by LAA, Houghton and Wyton and Hemingfords AS. Histon & DIst AS has Holywell stretch. Tackle shop: St Ives Angling Centre, 5 Crown St PE17 4EB. Hotels: Golden Lion, Slepe Hall, Firs.

Godmanchester (Hunts). Good bream, roach, chub and chance of carp. Godmanchester A & FPS has about 10m. Tickets from hon sec or tackle shop. St £6, dt £1. London AA has Portholme Meadow, Berry Lane Meadows and 1¼m Old West River at Stretham (members only). Boats from Huntingdon; no free fishing. Tackle shop: Stanjay Sports, who manage **Woolpack Fishery,** Cow Lane, 60 acres of well stocked coarse fishing. St £35, £20 jun, OAP. Dt £2.50. Hotels: Black Bull, Exhibition, Bridge and George.

Huntingdon (Hunts). Chub, bream, roach and tench; good when boat traffic declines. Huntingdon AS has water below town. St £5, dt £1.50 from tackle shop. London AA *(see Clubs)* has 4½m of Ouse, stretch of **Alconbury Brook, Brampton Mill Pool** and millstream, and other water at **Brampton;** members only. Tickets issued for some waters; inquire Stanjay Fishing Tackle, 7 Old Court Wall, Godmanchester.

Offord Cluny (Hunts). Stocked by NRA. Chub, roach, bream, tench, carp. Offord and Buckden AS has 4m of Great Ouse between Offord and Brampton; dt £2 from bank by car park. 50p for OAP, juniors, junior competitions run each season. Several sections are free of boat traffic at all times. Coach-party enquiries (40p per peg) from E Blowfield, 4 Monks Cottages, Huntingdon. 0480-810166.

St Neots (Hunts). St Neots and Dist AS has extensive fishing from Barford Power

Station with some gaps down to Wray House, Great Paxton and Paxton Lake; good tench, chub, bream, roach and carp to 30lb. St £9.50, wt £3.75. dt 75p (concessions for OAP, juniors and disabled) from hon sec and bailiffs. London AA has water at **Tempsford** and **Blunham** *(see Ivel)*. 30 acres of lake and ¼m of Ouse at **Little Paxton** available from OWR/Redland. 3 pits open. St £15, wt £8, dt £2. Permits from Fishery Manager, Mrs M R May, 5 Hayling Avenue, Little Paxton. Tel: Huntingdon 212059.

Biggleswade (Beds). Ouse, Ivel, Biggleswade, Hitchin & Dis. AC AA has 7m on mid Ouse at Wyboston, and 15 acre lake at Eaton Socon with large carp, tench, rudd, bream. St £18.00, conc, from sec of local tackle shops. **Arlesey Lake** (4m S); syndicate water, members only. Tackle shop: Thompson Tackle, 2B Hitchin Rd, Arlesey.

Bedford (Beds). Some 4m water in town centre and above, free to NRA rod licence-holders. Bedford AC controls most other fishing and issues limited dt at £2.50, st £15, concessions for OAP and juniors, from Dixon Bros. Sunday fishing allowed; sport excellent. Ampthill FPS fishes Ampthill Reservoir, and Marston Pits, membership £18. Hotels: Embankment, Swan, Lion. Tackle shops: Dixon Bros. 95 Tavistock Street.

Felmersham (7m N of Bedford) Ampthill FPS stretch here, at Pavenham and at Goldington Storm Drain. Membership available, £18. Concessions.

Sharnbrook (Beds). Wellingborough and Dist. Nene AC has ¾m upstream of **Harrold** and one field at **Pavenham.** Leighton Buzzard AC has water on left bank here. Ampthill AC has 1½m stretch on river at Dairy Farm, **Renhold,** with Gadsey Brook and Westminster Pool, and Stafford Bridge stretch. St £18, (½ price conc.) for Leisure Sport **Harrold Fishery** (1500m Ouse, 1200m Ivel and Lower Caldecott), with carp, chub, roach, dace, pike, catfish, barbel. No dt. Apply LSA, Thorpe Park, Staines Lane, Chertsey, Surrey. Tel: 0932 564872.

Newton Blossomville (Bucks). Coarse fish. Northampton Nene AC has water; strictly limited dt £2 from hon sec.

Olney (Bucks), Coarse fish, good bream. Leighton Buzzard AC has ¾m stretch at **Stoke Goldington,** from Gayhurst Spinney to brook, st £14.50; jun, OAP £4.

Newport Pagnell (Bucks). Good barbel, roach, bream, etc. Stretch fishes well in winter. Newport Pagnell FA has about 10m of river and six gravel pits. Membership £15, £5 jun. At **Great Linford** there is a complex of gravel pits holding bream, roach, tench and pike on which the fishing rights are now held by ARC. Luton & Dist AA has 8m of main river and a gravel pit. Inquire hon sec. Club has vacancies. St £2. **Vicarage Spinney** is 8 acre trout fishery at **Little Linford,** stocked with large r, 11lb to 18lb. St £200, dt £10, 4 fish, and boats £5. 6 acre b trout lake, large fish. Tel: 0908 614969. Tackle shop: Tackle Box, 3 Oliver Rd, Milton Keynes.Hotel:Bull Inn (club HQ).

Stony Stratford (Bucks). Deanshanger and Stony Stratford AA has 6m of Ouse, bream, roach, perch, chub and pike, plus Grand Union Canal at **Castlethorpe,** st £14, dt £3 on bank, or £2 from Lake Bros, Church St, Wolverton, Milton Keynes. Milton Keynes AC also has fishing here, and between Wolverton and Haversham. **Cosgrove Lodge** lakes at Cosgrove (Northants): noted for roach, tench, bream, pike; dt on water. Kingfisher Sporting Club, Deanshanger, has lakes of 36 acres. Trout, fly only. Dt £25.60 or £17.40 (non members), £18.40 to £10.25 (members), 4 fish and 2 fish. Tel; 0908 562332. Hotels: Cock; Bull.

Buckingham (Bucks). Coarse fish, some trout. Buckingham and Dist AA has water. Members may now fish on ODAA Water on Thames by Oxford. Joining fee £10, st £15, dt £3, from tackle shop, Fish and Field, 62 Nelson St. Claydon Lakes, 6m; Leighton Buzzard AA; no dt. At **Mursley** Church Hill Farm, MK17 0RS has 2 lakes of 10 acres stocked daily with r and b trout. Dt £20.50, evening £11, 4 and 2 fish. Tel: 029672 524.

Keep the banks clean

Several clubs have stopped issuing tickets to visitors because of the state of the banks after they have left. Spend a few moments clearing up.

Tributaries of the Ouse (Great)

WISSEY:

Hilgay (Norfolk). King's Lynn AA have 2m of both banks down to Ouse. St £14, wt £5, dt £2.50. London AA issues dt for Five Mile House Farm.

LITTLE OUSE: Good bream and roach.

Brandon (Suffolk). The above species, plus dace, perch, pike (good), a few chub and zander. Brandon and Dist AC has 2 ponds and ¾m river at Recreation Park, and 1½m L Ouse at Weeting, Norfolk. No dt, membership £8 annually, from Recreation Centre. Kempston AC has three fisheries around Hilgay; Thetford and Breckland AC has water above bridge, and London AA has a fishery here; members only. Hotel: The Ram.

Thetford (Norfolk). Little Ouse and Thet. Roach, rudd, tench, chub and pike; and dace to specimen size. Fishing free for 7 miles through town centre out to Santon Downham. Thetford Breckland AC (Chairman J Reeves, 0842 753895) have stretch at Cloverfields to Kilverstone and **Barnham Pit.** Tackle shop: Rod and Line, 15 White Hart St, who have tickets available for several local club waters, for £2-£3.

LARK: Trout and coarse fish.

Mildenhall (Suffolk). Trout, carp, rudd, roach, perch, tench, bream, pike, dace, gudgeon, eels, chub, bream. Mildenhall AC has several stretches of very good coarse fishing on Lark and West Row Drains, around village and to Isleham Lock. Memmbership available, contact sec, 0638 718205. From Bury St Edmunds to Lackford controlled by Bury St Edmund's AA; trout water; no permits. Lark APS has 12 miles of good water here, with 5 mile trout section. Trout membership £100, coarse £10, conc. Tackle shops: Stebbing Sports, 6 Mill Street, Mildenhall; John's Tackle, Newmarket. Hotels: White Hart; Riverside.

Bury St Edmunds (Suffolk). Coarse fish. Club: Bury St Edmunds AA, who have L Ouse, Blackbourne and Stour stretches, and lakes at Rougham and West Stow Country Park, mainly carp. St £15, jun £6, OAP £1, from sec N Bruton, tel: Bury 766074, or tackle shop: R Nunn, Tackle Up, 49a St John's Street, IP33 1SP. Other tackle shop: Anglia Arms, Risbygate St. **CAM:** Excellent fishery, with good roach and pike. Best catches between Baitsbite Lock and Clayhithe Bridge.

Waterbeach (Cambs). Waterbeach AC has fishing on both banks here, and on Bottisham and Swaffham Bulbeck Lodes. Contact H Reynolds, tel: 0223 351696. Cambridge FP & AS has Reach, Burwell and Wicken Lodes.

Cambridge. Cambridge FP & AS leases west bank of Cam from Pike & Eel, Chesterton to Clayhithe; st £13, dt £4 on bank or £2 from hon sec or local tackle shops. Concessions to OAP, juniors and disabled. Society also has about 4m of the **Hundred Foot River** from Earith Bridge to Sutton Gault and sole rights on whole of **Burwell Lode** and **Reach Lode,** plus 1m of **Great Ouse** at Barway, 1m of **Lark** below **Prickwillow Bridge;** and pits; inquire hon sec for permits. London AA has water for members only at **Swaffham Prior.** Cambridge Albion AS has two stretches at Wicken Fen, and Dimmocks Cote, also **Barnwell Lake,** Barnwell Bridge. **Cam** and **Granta** offer some free fishing to licence-holders. Cambridge Izaac Walton Society has R Granta fishing at **Shelford,** (very good head of chub, dace and roach, plus other species)and **R Rhee,** another small tributary, at **Barrington** (specimen chub, roach and pike). Tackle shops: Cast, 143 Milton Rd; Cooper & Son, 12 Milton Rd; Farrington, 2/4 Ferry Lane, Royston Angling Centre, Corn Exchange Market Hill, Royston.

OLD WEST RIVER: Good stock of coarse fish. **Milton Lake.** Large carp and other coarse fish.

Cottenham (Cambs). Hermitage Lock, Earith to Cottenham, Counter Wash Drain, Earith to Manea, controlled by Histon and Dist AS.

IVEL: Dace, roach and perch.

Tempsford (Beds). Ouse and Ivel. Biggleswade AC, now merged with Hitchin and District AA, has water on both rivers. London AA has several miles on Ouse here and at Blunham; members only.

Blunham (Beds). Ouse (1m W). Tickets from hon sec, Blunham FC for Ivel. Below Blunham Bridge to Ouse held by Biggleswade and District AC. Club also has right bank of Ivel from Langford Mill to Broom Mill; no dt. Shefford AC has left bank. **Lower Caldecote** (Beds). Leisure sport has ¾m stretch, with trout, dace, chub, mirror carp and barbel to 3lb.

HIZ (tributary of Ivel). Controlled by Big-

gleswade, Hitchin and District AA who have 15 acre coarse fishery nearby, and 7m increase of water on Middle Ouse. Membership £16 pa, specimen perch, etc. Club also has water on **Ouse,** River **Oughton** (trout, few chub, restocking under consideration; members only), and fishes waters of Great Ouse FCA and Ivel Protection Assn. St £16. Tackle shop: Alan Brown, Nightingale Road, **Hitchin.**
OUZEL: Coarse fish.
Leighton Buzzard (Beds). Leighton Buzzard AC preserves various stretches above Leighton Buzzard and at Stoke Hammond, Water Eaton, Bletchley and Newport Pagnell. Club also has several stretches on **Gt Ouse** (three at **Emberton** and others at **Stoke Goldington),** five on **Thame Shabbington,** 3m of **Oxford Canal** and 3m of **Grand Union Canal.** Also **Claydon Lakes, Tiddenfoot** and other

pits. Annual membership £14.50. Concessions to jun & OAP. Leisure Sport has two gravel pits stocked with large pike, carp and catfish. St £21 (conc. ½ price). Phone Chertsey 564872 for details. Tackle shop: Leighton Tackle Centre, 18 Peacock Market LU7 8JH.
RELIEF CHANNEL: not strictly a tributary but included here because of the status traditionally enjoyed as an excellent coarse fishery in its own right, now re-established as such, after a difficult period with zander, by an intensive programme of investigation and re-stocking by AWA. Now rented to Wisbech & Dist AA which issues dt.
TOVE: Coarse fish.
Towcester (Northants). **Towcester** and Dist AA has water on river and three ponds; members only.

OUSE (Sussex)

(For close seasons, licences, etc, see Southern Region NRA, p15)

Rises few miles south-east of Horsham and flows for 33 miles to enter English Channel at Newhaven. Tidal for 12 miles from mouth to point 4m upstream of Lewes. Coarse fish and trout, but notable for run of big sea trout.

Lewes and **Barcombe Mills** (Sussex). Sea trout (good), barbel, perch, bream, roach, dace, chub, carp and pike. Ouse APS has west bank from Hamsey to Barcombe Mills (about 4m) and certain stretches of non tidal water above the mills. Limited st only at £30, jun £10. Sea trout from May to Oct, but June to August best, given rain. Barcombe Mills Pool and side streams reserved for sea-trout fishing and available to st holders at £3 a day (two rods daily) bookable in advance from hon sec. Old Mill Farm, Barcombe, has Ouse fishing. Dt available at farm. Trout fishing available on 40 acre **Barcombe Reservoir** to st holders on payment of £7 day, 4 fish limit. Limited dt after July 1st. Full details from hon. sec, Ouse APS; The Old Barn Cottage, Peak Lane, East Preston. Tackle shop: Percy's, 9 Cliffe High Street. Hotels: Shelleys; White Hart; Crown (all Lewes). for Barcombe Mills: Angler's Rest, Anchor Inn.
Isfield (Sussex). Coarse fish, trout and sea trout. Isfield and Dist AC has sections of Ouse at Isfield Club also has stretches of **Cuckmere** at Upper Dicker, **Uck** at **Uckfield.** and lakes around **E Grinstead, Uckfield, Horsted Keynes** and elsewhere, twenty four fisheries in all. Large

carp, tench, bream, perch, eels and pike. St £40 plus £10 joining fee, conc, from memb. sec (sae). No dt. Exchange ticket system with other clubs. Hotels: Laughing Fish, Isfield (club HQ); Maiden's Head, Uckfield. *(Tackle see Lewes).*
Haywards Heath (Sussex). Coarse fish and trout. Haywards Heath & Dist AS has 11½m bank of **Ouse** from **Linfield** down to **Newick,** and several lakes, including Balcombe Lake, **Slaugham Mill Pond, Valebridge Mill Pond.** Fishing coarse mainly, trout in river, and is for members only. Membership open to approved applicants, with concessions. Tackle shops: Sporting Chance, 29 Boltro Rd; Angling Centre, 143 Church Rd, Burgess Hill.
UCK: mainly coarse fishing below Uckfield with occasional sea trout. Joins Ouse at Isfield.
Isfield (Sussex). Coarse fish and trout. Isfield and Dist AC has water from here to **Uckfield** (members only), with excellent course fishing and trout to 3lb. **Colin Godman's Trouting,** 3 lakes, 7 acres: tel: 0825 74 322. **Yew Tree Trout Fishery,** three fly fishing lakes in 6 acres, is at **Rotherfield** TN6 3QP; dt £16, four fish, or £8.50 plus cost of fish Tel: 089285 2529.

OUSE (Yorkshire)

(For close seasons, licences, etc, see Nothumbria and Yorkshire Region NRA, p17)

Forms with Trent the estuary of the Humber. Coarse fish, with some trout. Dunsforth. Beningbrough and Poppleton reaches noted for barbel and chub. Large bream present but difficult to catch. Most water held by Leeds and York clubs. Tributaries give excellent trout and coarse fishing.

Goole (N Humberside). Don enters Ouse here. Goole AA has stretch of **Derwent** from Wressle to Breighton; good roach, chub, pike, dace, few trout. No dt. Club also has water on **Selby Canal, Market Weighton Canal,** and local ponds. Memberships (£13.50, concessionary £5 pa) from Barry's of Goole Ltd, Westfield Avenue. Carlton AC has dt £1.25 for several fishings around Selby and Goole, including R Derwent at Bubwith, West Haddlesey Lake, and Selby Canal, from local tackle shops. Selby Miners Welfare AC offers dt £2.50 on bank at Selby Canal between Brayton and Burn Bridges, with roach, chub, carp, dace and other species. Selby tackle shops: Selby Angling Centre, 69 Brook St; Field Sports, 24/26 New St, Selby.

Acaster (N Yorks). Coarse fishing. Controlled by the Leeds Amalgamation. Tickets at Blacksmith's Arms, Naburn, and Manor Guest House, Acaster Maibis. Castleford Anglers fish on 150 yds below old salmon hut. Dt £1. Fish include barbel; above dam, trout and coarse fish.

Accommodation: Manor Guest House.

Naburn (N Yorks). Below dam, right bank to old salmon hut, York Amalgamated. Left bank, tickets £3 from lock keeper. or tackle dealer G E Hill, of York.

York (N Yorks). Coarse fish; some free fishing on public waters. On left bank nearly all free except 8m from Rawcliffe Ings and Clifton Ings up to Aldwark. York Amalgamation has fishing on 80m of **Ouse, Derwent, Nidd, Rye, Seven,** and several still waters. St £25, conc. £3 from local tackle shop for lower Nidd. 4m on Rivers Rye and Seven; very good grayling and trout; ½m on Derwent. all three fisheries members only. York Tradesmen's AA has rights on several becks, members only. Tackle shops: G E Hill, 40 Clarence Street; Anglers Corner, 41 Huby Court, Walgate.

Poppleton and **Newton** (N Yorks). Good barbel, pike, etc. York and Leeds Amalgamations have extensive stretches. Dt from Fox Inn, Nether Poppleton, and Post Office.

Aldwark (N Yorks). Coarse fish. York

Amal have 2½m above and ½m below Aldwark Bridge with exception of short stretch. Hotels: Three Horseshoes and Crown, Great Ouseburn; Bay Horse, Aldwark.

Low Dunsforth. from Low Dunsforth to Aldwark Bridge (about 4m right bank) fishing is in hands of Leeds Amal. Dt from Angler Inn, Low Dunsforth. Leeds Amal also has good length at **Hunterslodge** on opposite side below Aldwark bridge (left bank). Tickets as above.

Tributaries of the Ouse (Yorkshire)

DON (tributary of Ouse). Rises on Wike Head and flows through Sheffield and Doncaster to the estuary of the Ouse; now less polluted in its lower reaches but efforts of NRA beginning to bear fruit. Elsewhere holds coarse fish. Some tributaries hold trout,

Doncaster (S Yorks). River now fishable. **Thrybergh Reservoir,** 34 acres, near **Rotherham;** Rotherham MBC trout fishery. Permits on site. Rotherham MBC also has **Fitzwilliam Canal,** Rotherham 1m, dt. Doncaster & Dist AA has water on the **Idle** at Misson (10m) the **Torne** at Candy Farm pump to Pilfrey Bridge (12m) the **Trent** at Marton and Littleborough, the **Sheffield & S Yorkshire Navigation Canal,** 6m of **New Junction Canal** from Barnaby Dun to the **Aire & Calder** junction, 7m **Warping Drain,** Sheffield and South Yorks Navigation Canal (Sprotborough to Long Sandall). £2 dt available on the banks. Tinsley & dist AA offer £2 dt for canal fishing in the area. Tel 0709 366142. BW Castleford Anglers have **Woodnook Reservoir.** St from Assn HQ and tackle shops. Barnby Dun Social AC have dt £1 on bank at S Yorkshire Navigation Canal between **Barnby Dun** and Kirk Sandall, with chub, roach, perch, bream, gudgeon. Tel: 0302 886024 for match bookings. Tackle shops: Tom Pickering Angling, 207 Carrhouse Rd; R & R Sports, 40 High St, Bawtry; Pete's Tackle Shop, 65 Main Street, Mexborough; Pauls Tackle Centre, Denaby Main, nr Doncaster.

Sheffield (S Yorks). Don polluted. **Damflask,** YW reservoir, 5m W; trout. **Underbank,** corporation reservoir, coarse fishing and q few large trout. Tickets from attendant's office. Further information under '*Yorkshire Lakes*'. Sheffield Amal AS (membership books from Lord Nelson, Arundel Street) has three waters on Trent, at Besthorpe, Girton and North and South Clifton. Dt from bailiff on bank. Sheffield and Dist AA has water on Rivers **Trent,**

DEARNE (tributary of Don):

Barnsley (S Yorks). Dearne; Free fishing on length within Hoyle Mill Country Park. Mainly free, between here and **Darfield,** and through common near Wombwell. Stocked at **Haigh,** where Wakefield AC has water. Club also has lakes near **Wakefield,** fishing on R Calder, and Calder & Hebble Navigation. Membership £12, conc, from Wakefield tackle shops. Barnsley MBC control six lakes and ponds, dt available from 50p to £3. Barnsley Trout Canal fishes **Scout Dike Reservoir;** trout av ¾lb; bait restrictions, dt on site. **Wintersett Reservoir;** coarse fish; dt from bailiff. Barnley AA fishes for all species of coarse at Fiskerton on Trent, R Torne at Finningley, **Worsbrough Reservoir;** dt £2 on bank. Tackle shops: Barnsley Angling Centre, 48/50 Sheffield Road; Tackle Box, 7, Doncaster Rd, Wombwell Angling Centre, 25 Barnsley Rd.

Claycross (Derby). Lakes: Williamthorpe Ponds, 2m NE. Wingerworth Hall Lakes (two), 2½m NW. Great Dam, 3½m NW.

ROTHER (tributary of Don):

Killamarsh (Derby). Short Brook. Lakes: Woodhall Moor Dams, 2m E. Barlborough Hall Lake, 3m SE. Pebley Dam, 3m SE. Harthill Reservoir, 3m E. Woodhall Pond, 3m E.

AIRE: Issues from ground at Aire Head, half a mile south of Malham village. Its upper reaches contain quality trout and grayling, which give place to coarse fish between Steeton and Keighley. Marsden Star AS has 800 yds at Crossflats, nr Bingley and 500 yds at Stockbridge, Keighley, plus other fishing on ponds and Leeds & Liverpool Canal; st £14, dt £1.50, conc,. Tackle shop in Keighley. Lower reaches and others near large towns polluted. *(For Malham Tarn-see Ribble-Settle).*

Leeds (W Yorks). Polluted. Adel Beck and Dam (private). **Roundhay Park Lakes,** 4m NE. Leeds and Dist ASA have fishing; dt from local tackle shops. Larger lake (Waterloo) contains pike, perch, roach. tench, carp, etc; small lake stocked with carp, bream and roach. Leeds Amal has extensive fishing on Ouse and tributaries, canals and lakes, dt for many waters; full details from hon sec. Also trout at Pool and Arthington *(see Ouse (Yorks)-Wharfe)*. Castleford & Dist SA fish Fairburn Ings and Fairburn Cut. Dt £1 on site. At **Swinsty** and **Fewston**, 7m from **Otley**, are YWS reservoirs, containing trout; visitors' dt can be had at Reservoir Lodge, Fewston. Minnow and fly only. Tackle shops: Abbey Match Anglers, 38 Commercial Rd; Kirkgate Anglers, 95 Kirkgate; Lewis & Wardman, 5 Grand Arcade; Bob's Tackle Shop, 1A Chapel Lane, Garforth; Headingly Angling Centre, 58 North Lane.

Bradford (W Yorks). Aire, 7m N. Bradford City AA has extensive rights here and on water on the canals at **Apperley Bridge** and near Skipton; on **Wharfe, Ure** and **Swale,** reservoirs and lakes. Bradford No 1 AA has water on Wharfe, **Aire, Swale, Ure, Nidd, Derwent, Leeds and Liverpool Canal,** and reservoirs. Addingham AA have water on **Wharfe** (Addingham, 1½m; Denton and Ben Rhydding, 2½m; trout and grayling) and three reservoirs holding trout and perch; members only £85. Waiting list. Tackle shops: Carter's, 15 Bridge Street; Fly Box, 45 Pine Street; Wibsey Angling Centre, 208 High Street, Wibsey, Bradford; D Richmond, 110 Morley Street.

Bingley, Saltaire (W Yorks). Trout, coarse fish; Bingley AC has good coarse fishery; restocked annually. St £13 and dt £2. Club has good trout fishing on **Sunnydale Reservoir,** Eastmorton; 2 fish limit, no bait restrictions, dt £2.50 from hon sec or Cullimores of Bingley; also two dams and beck. Trout waters are for members only. Saltaire AA has stretch of Aire from Baildon Bridge upstream to Bankfield Hotel, mixed fishery, dt £1.50 available. Marsden Star AS has stretch at Crossflats nr Bingley. Members only. Excellent trout preserve in **Myrtle Park;** water restocked; dt 75p. Dt £1 for **Leeds & Liverpool Canal** from tackleist Cullimore. Saltaire AA (HQ Ring of Bells, Bradford Rd, Shipley) has water on **Aire** at Shipley and Saltaire, Leeds & Liverpool Canal (large carp) and at **Tong Park Dam;** wt £3, dt £1.50. From Bankfield Hotel downstream to Baildon Bridge (both banks, except Roberts Park) is Bradford No 1 water. Tackle shops: G A Cullimore, 29a Park Road BD16 4BQ.

Keighley (W Yorks). Trout, grayling, coarse fish, chub plentiful. Sport improved after restocking. Keighley AC has 14m; st £17 (concessions to ladies, juniors, OAP) dt £2 for R Aire only. Trout to 5 lbs; best May-June and Sept. Club also has fishing on the **Leeds-Liverpool Canal, Whitefields Reservoir,** stocked with carp, tench, roach and perch, and, for members only, **Roberts Pond** (large tench, carp, pike), **Sugden End Reservoir,** Crossroads, (large trout, roach, perch, and tench, dt £3.50) and the **R Worth,** trout. *(See also Yorkshire lakes, reservoirs, etc)*. Club also has water at Stockbridge and at Riddlesden, dt £2. Tackle shops: Willis Walker, 109 Cavendish Street, K & L Tackle, Keighley.

Cononley (W Yorks). Trout, perch, chub, roach, dace, bream, grayling; dt after June 1, for Bradford City AA water, dt £2 from Post Office or tackle shops from 16 June. Bradford No 1 AA also has water. Dt from tackle shops.

Skipton (N Yorks). Trout, grayling, pike, chub, roach, perch, dace and bream. At Skipton, Skipton AA has three miles of fishing, both banks; st £40 (entrance fee £15), dt £3.50 (£2.50 Winter fishing), from hon sec. or tackle shops. Association also has rights on **Embsay Reservoir** (trout), **Whinnygill Reservoirs** (trout and coarse fish) dt and wt, and beck fishing on Eller Beck at Skipton. Bradford City AA water begins on both banks below Skipton water; about 7m in all. Near Skipton at **Kilnsey Park,** are two trout lakes of 3 acres. Tel: 0756 752150. Dt £13, £9.50. Tackle shop: K Tackle, 9 Water Street, issues st £13.50 for Aire below Skipton and dt £1 for **Leeds & Liverpool Canal.** Bradford No 1 AA has **Bradley Fishery;** roach, pike, chub, trout. St from hon sec. Hotels: Devonshire Arms, Herriots.

Bellbusk (N Yorks). Trout; preserved by owners. Lakes: **Conniston House;** trout. **Eshton Tarn,** 2m NE; pike. **Malham Tarn,** 8m N; trout and perch; tickets *(see Ribble-Settle)*

CALDER (tributary of Aire): Good coarse fishing from Brighouse to Sowerby Bridge.

Halifax (W Yorks). Calder 2m S. Clubs: Halifax and Dist AC (dams); Dean Clough AC (canal at Copley); Brighouse AA, Friendly AC, The Friendly Inn, Ovenden. Ripponden Flyfishers have good trout fishing in **Ryburn Reservoir,** Ripponden. Brighouse AA and Bradford No 1 AA control 14m on Calder above and below **Brighouse;** heavily restocked and now provides sport with good-quality roach. St £16.10 + £13.80 joining fee from D B Arnett, 49 Templars Way, Bradford, but one year waiting list. No dt. Brighouse AA also has water on canal and gravel pits. Tackle shop: A J Jewson, Westgate; Pond Works Warehouse, 364 Bradford Road, Brighouse HD6 4DJ. Hotels: Imperial Crown; Calder & Hebble Inn; Black Horse Inn, Brighouse.

Hebden (W Yorks). Hebden Bridge AS has 7½m water on **Calder and Rochdale Canal.** Roach, bream, carp, chub, perch, pike, tench. Dt £2. At **Todmorden** (Yorks, postal address Lancs). The Todmorden AS has mixed coarse fishing on the **Rochdale Canal,** from Todmorden to Littleborough, **New Mill Dam, Grove Lodge, R Calder;** all waters members only, except Cliviger Fishponds, dt £3 from Clivinger petrol station; annual membership, £16, plus £10 joining fee (conc.½), from Tackle dealers (*below*), or those in Burnley and Rochdale. Dt £1.50 for **Calderbrook Bottom Dam, Littleborough,** Daves Tackle Shop or Summit Store, Summit, Littleborough. **Calder and Hebble Navigation.** From Salterhebble Top Lock, through Brighouse, Lower Hopton Bridge, Thornhill, to upstream of Ganny Lock, the following clubs have water: Dean Clough AS, Mackintosh AC, Brighouse AA, Bradford No. 1, Slaithwaite AA, Thornhill C & BC, Unity AC. Unity AC also have fishing on R Aire, R Calder and R Ure, members only on most waters, but dt available for Leeds and Liverpool Canal, £1.50. Tackle shops: Hebden Bridge Angling, Hebden Bridge; Arches Tackle, 1 Halifax Rd, Littleborough. Hotel: Queen.

COLNE (tributary of Calder):

Huddersfield (W Yorks). **Longwood Compensation Reservoir** preserved and stocked by Huddersfield AA. Good head of pike, perch, roach and gudgeon. Members plus 50 special permit holders only. Other local clubs: Holme Valley Piscatorials; Cleckheaton, Spenborough & Dist AC. Heathwalk Trout Fishery has 2 acre lake, tel: 0274 877498. Tackle shops: Chris Roberts, 98 Northgate; Angling Centre, 22 Chapel Hill; Watercraft Products, 51 Warrenside, Deighton. Hotel: Huddersfield and many others.

Slaithwaite (W Yorks). Slaithwaite and Dist AC (st £15 + £5 joining,) has rights on **Trent** at Sutton, tidal, trout fishery on **Colne,** coarse on R Swale at Helperby, as well as **Narrow Canal,** Longroyd Bridge to Sparth, reservoirs, dams and ponds; trout, coarse fish; enquiries to D Rushforth, 122 Longwood Gate, Longwood, Hudds.

HOLME (tributary of Colne);

Holmfirth (W Yorks). Lakes: **Holmstyes Reservoir;** trout (Huddersfield 8m) preserved by Huddersfield AA. St £38. **Boshaw Reservoir** (Huddersfield 8m); preserved as above. Holme Valley Piscatorials have water on the Sir John Ramsden Canal, R Calder, Fenay Beck (both 2½m from Huddersfield) and Magdale Dam. St £10 from Membership Sec, dt £2 from tackle shops.

DERWENT: Rises in high moors and flows almost to coast near Scarborough where it turns south and enters estuary of Ouse. Its upper reaches, most easily reached from Scarborough, are trout and grayling waters (*see Ayton*). Lower down coarse fish predominate, barbel included.

Wressle (N Humberside). Coarse fish free, some access.

Breighton (N Humberside); ns Wressle 1m. Bubwith 1m. Chub, dace, pike, etc; fishing free.

Bubwith (N Humberside). Coarse fish;

Howden and Dist AC: 4m controlled by Mike Redman, 2 Meadowfield, Breighton Rd, Bubwith YO8 7DZ, 0757 288891.

Ellerton; roach, perch, dace, bream, chub, eels and pike; flatfish lower down. For Ellerton Landing, 2m, Aughton, 1m, Bubwith, 1m, dt from White Swan Inn; V G Shop; Mike Redman, 2 Meadowfield, all bubwith, or Boot and Shoe, Ellerton.

Wheldrake (N Yorks). Tidal. Coarse fish. York AA has 1½m right bank; dt from the Alice Hawthorne Inn, Nun Monkton.

East Cottingwith (N Yorks); ns High Field, 4m. Coarse fish (pike and chub very good). York AA controls East Cotting-with Water (2m) and 10m of good coarse fishing on **Pocklington Canal.** Dt from secretary or Blue Bell Inn. At **Thor-ganby,** on other side of Derwent, Ferry Boat Inn has day tickets £1.50 for approximately 1½m of river. Very good pike fishing.

Pocklington (N Yorks). **Pocklington Canal;** Well stocked with bream, roach, perch, pike, etc. York AA water. Dt from Canal Head; College Arms, Beilby; Melbourne Arms, Melbourne; and The Cottage at Coats Bridge.

Ellerton Landing (N Yorks). Mixed fishing Hotel: White Swan, Bubwith.

Kexby (N Yorks). Pike, chub, etc. York and Leeds Amalgamated Societies have water; members only.

Low Catton (N Yorks). Coarse fish. Leeds and Dist AS has good length of water on left bank; members only.

Stamford Bridge (N Yorks). Excellent for roach, pike, chub, dace. York and Dist Amal has fishing on good length down to Kexby Brickworks and length at Stamford Bridge Bottom, acquired from Leeds ASA; also pits. Dt at cafes in Stamford Bridge.

Howsham (N Yorks). Coarse fishing. York and Dist AA has water on Derwent and Barton Hill Beck; Bradford No 1 AA has water; members only.

Kirkham Abbey (N Yorks). Coarse fish, some trout. Leeds and York Amalgamations have water; members only. Scarborough Mere AC has approx 1,300 yds north bank u/s from bridge. Members only.

Castle Howard (N Yorks). **Castle Howard Great Lake** contains specimen coarse fish, including pike, perch, tench, bream, roach and bank fishing only. For further details, see *'Yorkshire Lakes.'*

Huttons Ambo (Yorks). Roach, pike, dace,

barbel, grayling, perch and few trout. South bank, 1m down and 1m up, held by Malton and Norton AC, no dt. North bank held by Huttons Ambo AC for 2m down and 2m up; membership, for people resident within 10m Malton, £3 pa.

Malton (Yorks). Coarse fish, mainly roach. Malton and Norton AC. Waters extend to 1m below Huttons Ambo. Membership discretionary, st £10, wt £3.50, dt 75p issued by hon sec M Foggins, 123 Well-ram Rd, Norton Malton, and N & C Swift, Castlegate, Malton. York and Dist AA has 5½ at Old Malton to Ryemouth; st £18, dt £1.80. D S Johnson, 45 Mayfield Grove, Dring Houses, York. Tel: 704464. Castleford & Dist SA fish R Costa Ryton, with Slaithwaite AC. Good deal of free water on Derwent and Rye. Tackle shops: J Anderson & Son, Market Place (tickets for Malton AC waters); and C Swift, Castlegate. Hotel: Green Man.

Rillington (Yorks). Derwent, 1m N. Coarse fish; Leeds Amal water, st £21, dt £1.50. Scampston Beck, 1m E, private. Rye, 2m N. Costa Beck, 3m N.

Yedingham (Yorks). Coarse fish. Dt at Providence Inn for Leeds Amal waters. Inn also has private stretch. Foul Bridge Farm issue dt.

Ganton (Yorks). Chub, pike, dace, grayling; dt for 1m each way from Hay Bridge, from Mr and Mrs Seller, Bogg Hall Farm, at first house across railway crossing at Ganton. Ruston Beck, 2m W. Dt waters at **Seamer** (Malton Rd), from house by stream. Tackle from Grettons, 10 North St, Scarborough.

Ayton (Yorks). Some good trout water, Scarborough Mere AC has **Scarborough Mere,** just outside town; coarse fish; dt £2; mere restocked regularly. About 2m trout fishing from Ayton towards Ganton controlled by Leeds Amal; no tickets. Dt from farm at East Ayton.

Hackness (Yorks). Derwent AC, controls 10m of trout (brown and rainbow) and grayling fishing down to **East Ayton,** for part of which dt at £15 are available from July 1 to Sept 30. Farther up, above Lang-dale End Bridge (3m both banks), dt available at £6 from April 1 to Sept 30. Fishing one fly only, wet or dry, is club rule on all water. Tickets from Grange Hotel (rods for residents on 8m of Der-went). Sunday fishing reserved for members and guests on lower club water, and all fishing between Hilla Green bridge and Langdale End bridge exclusively reserved to members and guests. Size limit for trout 10 in; limited two brace per day. Wading allowed.

FOSS BECK (tributary of Derwent). Fishing station: **Fangfoss** (Yorks); fishing private.

SPITTLE BECK (tributary of Derwent)

Barton Hill (Yorks). Derwent, 2m E. Whitecarr Beck, 4m SE. Loppington Beck, 4m SE. Swallowpits Beck, 5m SE at Scrayingham. York and Dist AA have trout water **Barton Hill Beck.**

RYE (tributary of Derwent): Trout, grayling, other coarse fish.

Ryton (Yorks). Scarborough Mere AC has 5 fields at Ryton Bridge: trout, grayling and coarse fish, including barbel. Members only.

Butterwick (Yorks). Trout, coarse fish. Scarborough Mere AC has stretch, members only.

Hawnby (Yorks). Hawnby Hotel has 8m private fishing in Rye and **Seph;** trout; fly only on Rye; thigh waders and shortish rods advised; dt for non-residents £5, weekend £6, from hotel, tel: 04396 202.

PICKERING BECK (tributary of Rye) and Costa Beck (chalk stream). Trout, grayling.

Pickering (Yorks). About 1m of free fishing in town; private above, preserved below (3m) by Pickering FA; fly only; membership limited to 120; st £60, entrance fee 1.5 times annual subscription. Junior conc. Water also on **Costa Beck** and **Oxfold Becks,** trout and grayling, and **Duchy of Lancaster Water, Newbridge.** Two trout lakes. Dt for members' guests only. Club HQ: Bay Horse Hotel. Trout fishing at Newgate Foot Farm Saltersgate Estate, Lockton. Tel: 0751 60215 or 60205. Moorland Trout Lake, Newbridge YO18 8JJ, tel: 0751 73101. Scarborough Mere AC has 6m on **Rye** near Pickering and Bradford No 1 have **Newsham Bridge** fishing on Rye, near Great Habton. Hotels: White Swan, Black Swan, Forest and Vale, Crossways.

SEVEN (tributary of Rye): Trout, grayling; some coarse fish.

Newsham Bridge (Yorks). York and Dist AA has water on Seven and Rye; no dt.

Marton (Yorks). Private from mill to Marton; below Marton some free water; grayling, pike, chub, dace and a few trout. Tackle shop in Malton, 12m.

Sinnington (Yorks). Seven AC has 2½m downstream; trout and grayling; mem-

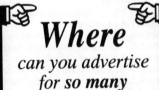

bers only, long waiting list. Coarse fishing mainly below large weir and bottom farm.

WATH BECK (tributary of Rye):

Slingsby (Yorks). Trout; preserved. Rye, NE.

DOVE-IN-FARNDALE (tributary of Rye):

Kirby Moorside (N Yorks). Dove-in-Farndale, 1m E; trout; private. Dt for stretches downstream of Kirby Moorside available from some of the farms. Hodge Beck, in Sleightholme Dale, 1m W, trout only. Hotel: King's Head.

THORNTON BECK (tributary of Derwent):

Thornton-le-Dale (N Yorks). Trout and grayling; preserved. Pickering Beck, 3m W. Derwent, 3m S. Hotels: The Hall; The Buck; all Thornton-le-Dale.

WHARFE: Rises on Cam Fell and flows 60m south-east to join Ouse near Cawood. Trout in upper reaches, with coarse fish downstream.

Ryther (N Yorks); ns Ulleskelf, 3m. Castleford and Dis ASA has water; mainly coarse fish. Hotel: Ryther Arms.

Ulleskelf (N Yorks). Coarse fish; preserved by Leeds Amal; dt £1.50 from Golden Swan. Other hotel, The Ship.

Tadcaster (N Yorks). Trout, chub and dace, good head of barbel perch and bream; preserved by Tadcaster Angling and Preservation Association on both banks downstream from road bridge to Sewage Farm (1m) and from road bridge to Grimston Park (2m); st £15; dt £1.50, OAP, jun 50%. Tickets from hon sec, The Bay Horse; Newsagent and Chris's Tackle Shop, Wharfe Bank.

Boston Spa (W Yorks). Trout, grayling other coarse fish (chub, barbel and pike good; bream introduced) Most rights held by Boston Spa AC. Dt £1 from Lower Wharfe Anglers, Boston Spa. Spa Baths issue dt £1.50 for stretch from river bridge to Wharfedale Hall, S bank. Club members (who must live within 3m of Boston Spa Post Office) allowed 12 guests a year at current cost of dt and guest must fish with member on non-ticket waters. Club stocks water with trout and grayling of 12 in or over. Limit two trout, one grayling, or vice-versa; trout 12 in. May best month for trout and August for barbel and chub.

Wetherby (W Yorks). Wetherby and Dist AC water (stocked with trout and coarse fish) extends from Collingham Beck to Wetherby Weir, south bank (about 350 yards in Collingham Wood, south bank is private). Club also has four fields between golf course and playing fields, north bank. This water is open for visitors on st (above weir), and dt. Members only below and on weir, but visitors may fish if accompanied by a member. Same charge as above. Dt from: The Paper Shop, Market Place, Wetherby; Star Garage, Collingham Bridge. No legitimate bait or lure barred. Trout limit 11 in. Tackle shops: J R Country & Pet Supplies, & Horsefair; Lower Wharfe Angling Centre, 236 High St, Boston Spa.

Collingham (W Yorks). Wetherby AC has water here; trout and coarse fish including barbel, grayling and good dace.

Pool (W Yorks). Trout, few chub; preserved by the Leeds and Dist ASA which has 5m of fishing from River **Washburn** to Castley Beck on left bank. Dt £1.50 from Leeds tackle shops. Members of Leeds AA, small private club, may fish Harewood Estate preserves, 3m right bank, 2m left bank.

Otley (W Yorks). Otley AC hold 2m left bank and 2½m right bank below Otley Bridge. Fishing for members only, no dt. Dt £1.50 available for Leeds & Dist ASA **Knotford Lagoon**, near Otley; large carp and other coarse fish; stocked. Also some r trout. Bradford No 1 AA has three stretches here. At Yeadon (6m) Airboro' and Dist AA has **Yeadon Tarn,** Cemetery Rd; Good catches of roach, perch, carp, tench. Dt £1.50 from newsagent in same road. Tackle shop in Otley: Angling and Country Sports, 36 Cross Green, Pool Road, Otley, tel: Otley 462770.

Burley and **Askwith** (W Yorks). Trout, grayling, chub, dace. Bradford clubs have rights for members only.

Addingham (W Yorks). Trout, grayling; Bradford City AA has water here; also Bradford No 1 AA, no dt obtainable. Bradford Waltonians have water at **Denton** and **Ben Rhydding;** also 4 resrvoirs including **Chelker Reservoir** near here. Tickets £7 to members' guests, only. Membership £200, subscription £200. Bradford No 1 AA has some left bank at Denton and right bank at Ben Rhydding. Keighley AC has water; dt from hon sec.

Ilkley (W Yorks). Ilkley and Dist AC have water from Old Bridge to Stepping Stones and both banks at Ben Rhydding, with trout, grayling and chub. Dt £6. Membership restricted by waiting list. St £39 + £39 joining, jun, OAP ½, (April

15-Sept 30 inc) from Tourist Office, Ilkley Centre, or Runnymead News Agency, Ben Rhydding, Ilkley. Club also has coarse ponds. Good trout, grayling and dace fishing (restocked annually) from Brook Street Bridge to Stepping Stones, both banks (abt 1m); worm and fly only; no Sunday fishing. Tackle from Tack and Turnout, Valley Drive, Ilkley. Hotels: Riverside (Ilkley AA HQ), Ilkley Moor, Troutbeck, Craiglands.

Bolton Abbey (N Yorks). Trout. Dt from Estate Office, Bolton Abbey for 5 miles stretch (both banks) from Barden Bridge to Kex Beck below Bolton Bridge. Fly only. Trout April 1-September 30. Grayling if caught to be released. St £200, wt £50, dt £12.50, Conc. Limit 4 fish of not less than 10 ins. Fishing not recommended on Sundays and Bank Holidays. Apply Estate Office, Bolton Abbey, Skipton, BD23 6EX, tel: 0756 710227. Hotel, Devonshire Arms,

Burnsall (N Yorks). Trout (av ½lb-1lb; many large fish), grayling; preserved by Appletreewick, Barden and Burnsall AC from Linton Stepping Stones, below Grassington, to Barden Bridge, 7m. Dt for trout, June-Sept (excluding June and Sept week-ends) £16.50; wt £80, fly only during trout season; limit three brace; grayling dt £5 Nov to Jan (fly only). Waters re-stocked regularly with trout from ½ to 1lb and over. Waiting list. Tickets from Red Lion Hotel and Fell Hotel, Burnsall. River watcher, Bob Mason, Conistone House, Main Street, Burnsall, Skipton BD23 6BU (Tel: Burnsall 650). Bradford City AA has water at **Appletreewick**; members only. Dt for stretch at Appletreewick from New Inn (left bank only).

Grassington (N Yorks). Trout (av ¾lb), grayling (av ¾lb); preserved by Linton,

Threshfield and Grassington AC for 2½m both banks (also in Captain Beck and Linton and Threshfield Becks until August 31); wt £50, dt £12 for fly-fishing only. Long waiting list for membership. No night or Sunday fishing. No canoeing. Trout season: April 1 to Sept 30 inclusive. Grayling only from Oct 1 to Feb 28; st £20, dt £5; fly only during Oct. Tickets from Post Office, or Black Horse Hotel, Grassington. Saltaire AA also has left bank at **Linton**, no dt. Fishing best in May. **Eller Beck, Hebden Beck,** 2m E. Lakes: **Blea Beck** dams 4m NE. Hotels: Black Horse (Saltaire AA HQ), and others.

Kilnsey (N Yorks). Trout. Preserved by Kilnsey AC of 65 members, from Beckamonds to Yockenthwaite and from 1m above Starbotton down to Netherside 2m below Kilnsey; st £400 from hon sec, wt £100, dt £20 from Keeper, C S Nesbitt at the Tennant Arms daily, between 9am and 10am (number limited, and none on Sundays or Bank Holidays). **Skirfare**; trout; preserved as Wharfe up to 1m below Arncliffe. Hotels: Tennant Arms, Falcon.

Buckden (N Yorks). Trout. Bradford City AA has 2m; dt £3.45 from Dalesgarth Holiday Cott. Other fishing for guests at Buck Inn; dt issued.

SKIRFARE (tributary of Wharfe); well stocked with trout av. 1lb.

Arncliffe (N Yorks). 2½m on Skirfare and 1½m on **Cowside Beck** available to guests at Falcon Inn *(see advt)*. Dt £7, no Sunday fishing. Dt Fishing on Wharfe held by Kilnsey AC *(see Kilnsey)*.

FOSS (tributary of Ouse): Trout.

Earswick (N Yorks). Free fishing on right bank. Owners are Joseph Rowntree Trust.

Strensall (N Yorks). Foss Navigation Cut, 1m NE. **Whitecar Beck,** 1m NE. York and Dist Amal has coarse fishing here and at **Towthorpe;** members only.

NIDD: Trout and grayling, with coarse fish from Birstwith downstream in increasing numbers.

Nun Monkton (N Yorks). Coarse fish. Bradford No 1 has 1½m reserved here, at **Ramsgill** and at **Summerbridge,** for members only.

Moor Monkton (N Yorks). Leeds ASA has 1m mixed fishery, members only.

Kirk Hammerton (N Yorks). Coarse fish. Following on Harrogate AA water *(see Goldsborough)* almost all fishing downstream to where Nidd joins the Ouse controlled by Leeds and York Amalgamations. York Amal holds York side of river from Skip Bridge on Boroughbridge Road upstream for about 2m and also for about 1m above Hammerton Mill dam. Tickets from York tackle shops; York Road Service Station, Mrs Abel, Crown Inn, Kirk Hammerton and Myers, Skip Bridge Filling Station.

Cowthorpe (N Yorks). Coarse fish. Stretch of 1m, one bank, belongs to Old Oak Inn, tickets issued; Sunday fishing. Licences and tackle available in Wetherby.

Goldsborough (N Yorks). Trout, grayling and mixed coarse fishing, including pike and barbel. Left hand bank at Goldsborough, Knaresborough Piscatorials. From Little Ribston downstream through Walshford Bridge to first meadow below Cattall Bridge belongs to Harrogate AA. Association also has both banks of **Crimple Beck** from confluence with Nidd above Walshford Bridge up to Spofforth. Waiting list for membership. Dt issued by hon sec to members' guests only. Water otherwise strictly preserved.

Knaresborough (N Yorks). Trout, grayling and coarse fish, including barbel. Practically all fishing in vicinity controlled by Knaresborough AC and Knaresborough Piscatorials. Former issues at £25 and dt £2 for good stretch upstream from Little Ribston village. Club also owns fly only trout lake in Knaresborough area, members only. Full membership £110. Knaresborough Piscatorials provides st, wt and dt for visitors. York Amal has good stretches here. Tickets from PH & JR Smith, Tackle Dealers, 28 High Street and M & C Johnson, 2 Briggate; also from C J Fishing Tackle *(see Harrogate).*

Farmire Lake, Farnham, has b and r trout fishing; tel: 0423 866417.

Ripley, Nidd Bridge (N Yorks). Trout,

grayling and coarse fish. On right bank from about 300 yds below Harrogate-Ripon road bridge to Killinghall and downstream to Sewerage Works, about 2½m, held by Harrogate and Claro Anglers, who have full membership and long waiting list. Downstream for 2m river privately owned. Knaresborough AC holds stretch of Nidd between Hampsthwaite and Ripley, fly only, members only. Waiting list.

Birstwith (N Yorks). Trout and grayling above Birstwith Dam upstream to upper reaches of Nidd. Below Dam there are also coarse fish. Knaresborough AC has recently acquired about 1000 yd of right bank downstream from Hampsthwaite Bridge. Members and their guests only.

Darley (N Yorks). Trout and grayling water, preserved by Harrogate Fly Fishers. No tickets.

Pateley Bridge (N Yorks). Trout and grayling. From 1½m above Pateley Bridge down to **Summerbridge,** owned and rented by Nidderdale AC, who hold nearly all water, both banks, except short pieces here and there which are private; also Scar House Reservoir. Wt and dt (concessions to juniors) at local post offices and Stebbings Gift Shop, Pateley Bridge. Anglers must obtain tickets before fishing.

Gouthwaite (N Yorks). River enters **Gouthwaite Reservoir,** privately owned and fished; no permits. Below reservoir Nidd private.

CRIMPLE (tributary of Nidd). This river is about 12m long, very narrow and joins Nidd near Walshford Bridge, where for short distance there is reasonably good fishing. **Plumpton Lake:** mixed coarse and trout fishery, Plumpton.

Harrogate (N Yorks). Trout and coarse fishing, within easy reach of town in Nidd, Wharfe and Ure. Details from Information Bureau, Royal Baths. Harrogate Flyfishers preserve excellent trout and grayling water at Darley. Membership details from hon sec. Newby Hall coarse fishing, **Skelton-on-Ure,** st £23, dt £2. Tel: 322583. Hotels: Crown, Majestic, Old Swan, St George, Cairn, Prospect. Tackle shops: C J Fishing Tackle, 182 Kings Road; Linsley Bros, 4/6 Cheltenham Parade.

KYLE: Coarse fish.

Tollerton (N Yorks). Coarse fishing free down to Alne. Ouse at Aldwark, 4m W, and Linton Lock, 3m S and 7m NE, at

Fly-fishing historian, Don Overfield, on a small Yorkshire beck. *Photo: Roy Shaw.*

Stillington.
URE (or YORE): Noted for grayling, but also holds good trout. Coarse fish from Middleham downstream.
Boroughbridge (N Yorks). Fine coarse fishing (especially chub and roach, bream increasing); few trout and grayling; Boroughbridge and Dist AC, issues dt £2 (weekdays only, from June 1-Feb 27) available from Post Office and Horsefair Grocers. At **Aldborough** Bradford City AA has 6m (roach, perch, dace, pike, chub); no dt, limited privilege tickets for members only. Bradford No 1 AA also has Langthorpe stretch, left bank. Harrogate and Claro CAC have Ure water at Boroughbridge, with chub, dace and pike. Dt available £3, from tackle shops in Boroughbridge, Harrogate and Knaresborough. Other club with water here, Unity AC. Tickets from Three Horseshoes. Other hotel: Boroughbridge Social Club.
Ripon (N Yorks). Trout, grayling, pike, perch, chub, barbel, roach; preserved for 5m both banks by Ripon Piscatorial Assn: waiting list. Association also has Racecourse Lake and 6m on **R Laver.** Visitors weekly ticket, £8. Ripon AC has **R Skell** at Ripon, 1m on Ure and 7m fly only on **Laver.** Limited dt £5. These and Piscatorial Assn tickets from tackle dealers. **Lumley Moor Reservoir;** trout fly only; no dt. Lakes: Queen Mary's Ponds; coarse fish; Bradford No 1 AA. Dt for **Swinton Estate** trout fishery, Ripon, 100 acres, tel: 0765 89224 or 89713. Hotels: Spa, Unicorn, Studley Royal, Station, South Lodge. Tackle shop: Ripon Angling Centre, 64 North Street.
Tanfield (N Yorks). Trout, grayling; preserved for about 5m, mostly both banks, by Tanfield AC. Guests must be accompanied by member. Full time bailiff employed. Long waiting list.
Masham (N Yorks). Trout (stocked), grayling. 6½m west bank belongs to Swinton Estate. Limited st £175 + VAT. Details from Estate Office, Swinton, Masham. Well stocked 2½m stretch of Swinton water fished by Masham AC; brown trout and grayling; waiting list. St £130 + £40 Joining. Jun conc. Apply to Mr B Wynn, River Keeper, Wellgarth, Masham; tel: 0765 689734. Yorkshire Flyfishers hold Clifton Castle water (about 2m left bank) above Masham. No tickets. Tackle from A Plumpton, Hairdresser, Silver St. Hotel: King's Head. **Leighton Reservoir** near here. *See Yorkshire Lakes.*

Cover Bridge (N Yorks). Trout, grayling. East Witton Estate issue dt on **R Cover** from Hullo Bridge to Cover Bridge. Mostly both banks, fly only, £2. Tickets from Cover Bridge Inn, Middleham.
Middleham (N Yorks). Bradford No 1 AA has stretch, members only. Fishing may be had in Leeds ASA waters at Middleham Deeps and 1m upstream from Middleham Bridge both banks by dt from Old Horn Inn, Spennithorne. Excellent barbel, chub and grayling; few large trout; odd salmon. Dt £1 from Cover Bridge Inn for trout and grayling fishing on Cover.
Leyburn (N Yorks). Grayling, trout, coarse fish. Two dt available from Blue Lion, E Witton, for E Witton Estate water on Ure from Ulshaw Bridge to Harker Beck, 1¾m S bank, fly only. Thornaby AA have members only water here. Hotels: Bolton Arms, Golden Lion. Tackle shops: Wray Bros, Town Hall (also licences).
Redmire (N Yorks). Trout, grayling; preserved. Restocked; fly only. All fishing now by st only (£120); numbers limited; apply Bolton Estate Office, Wensley, Leyburn. Trout best April, May and June; grayling Oct and Nov. Hotels: King's Arms, Redmire; White Swan, Middleham; Rose and Crown, Bainbridge; Wensleydale Heifer, Westwittom.
Aysgarth (N Yorks). Trout, grayling. Bradford AA has approx 2m from footbridge, both banks, 3¾m both banks at **Worton Bridge;** Palmer Flatt Hotel has short stretch. Wensleydale AA water begins at **Worton Bottom.** Richmond & Dis AS has 1m west of Aysgarth.
Askrigg (N Yorks). Trout, grayling; preserved by Wensleydale AA. Tickets from King's Arms or Victoria Arms, Worton. Hotel: King's Arms.
Bainbridge (N Yorks); ns Askrigg. Hotel: Rose and Crown (HQ of Wensleydale AA). Wensleydale AA water includes 6m on Yore, 2m of Bain, flowing from **Lake Semerwater,** and 2m trout water above lake. Tickets from: Village Shop, Bainbridge; also from King's Arms, Askrigg; Victoria Arms, Worton. Other accommodation at Greenways Guest House; Victoria Arms, Worton.
Hawes (N Yorks). Trout, grayling; preserved with tributaries, from headwaters to 2m downstream of Hawes, by Hawes and High Abbotside AA. The fishing is pleasant, peaceful and not crowded. No Sunday fishing, no ground bait. Tickets from Visitors st £40, wt £20, dt £8, conc,

from hon sec or Lowis Country Wear, Hawes, The Gift Shop; or Board Hotel Main St. Assc also has rights on Cotterdale, Hardraw, Duerley and Snaizeholme Becks, all both banks, trout and grayling. Below Hawes Wensleydale AA has several miles of excellent water. Disabled anglers may fish Widdale Beck at Apperset, near Hawes. Hotel: White Hart.

SWALE: Good chub and barbel water. Trouting best in upper reaches.

Helperby (N Yorks). Coarse fish; right bank from Swing Bridge to Myton Plantation controlled by Leeds Amal; dt from Golden Lion, Helperby. Dun Royal Hotel also issues tickets. Helperby & Brafferton AC have left bank from footbridge to ¾m d/s. Dt £2 from Plowman-Render Groceries, Main St. Club also has **Fawdington Fishery,** from above Thornton Bridge to apprx 1½m u/s to Fawdington Beck mouth. Chub, barbel, dace, pike, etc. Dt from 16 Jun-30 Sept. Hotel: Farmers Inn.

Topcliffe (N Yorks). Noted coarse fishing centre; especially good for chub and barbel. Thirsk AC has Skipton and Baldersby fishing, dt from Thirsk Anglers Centre, Town End, Thirsk; Bradford clubs have much water in this area; inquire hon secs. Black Bull Hotel, Topcliffe YO7 3PB has water. Assn of Teeside and Dist ACs has 1½m at **Sand Hutton;** members only. **Cod Beck;** trout; preserved by Bradford City AA; apply hon sec for permits.

Pickhill (N Yorks). Coarse fish; trout. Thornaby AA has two fields (about 500 yds); members only. Leeds Amalgamation has a ¾m stretch at **Ainderby.**

Morton-on-Swale (N Yorks). Roach, roach, chub, dace, barbel; fishing good. Northallerton AC has 2½m left bank downstream from A684 road bridge, for which dt £3 can be had from Mrs Grainger, Morton-on-Swale; tackle dealers Pratt, Arcade, Northallerton.

Great Langton (N Yorks). Trout, grayling, coarse fish; Kirkby Fleetham AC has both banks for 2m downstream from Langton Bridge, linking up with Northallerton AC's water at Bramper Farm; fly only; no tickets. Membership limited, with preference given to local residents.

Catterick (N Yorks). Good mixed fishing; trout, grayling, dace, chub, barbel, few roach and pike. Trout from 8oz to 1lb; fast takers. Richmond & Dist AS has 14m of water on both banks, Richmond being the centre. Thornaby AA has Thornbrough Farm 1m upstream from railway bridge above Catterick Bridge; noted grayling, trout and barbel stretch; members only. Also other fishings on **Swale, Ure, Tees** and **Eden.** Hotels: Farmers' Arms; Angel Inn. Tackle, licences and permits: E & B Langstaff, Parkgate, Darlington.

Richmond (N Yorks). Above town, trout; below, trout, grayling, chub, dace and barbel. Richmond and Dist AS preserves 14 miles above and below town centre, stocked with trout, plus most coarse species. St £24.50, wt £12, dt £3. Jun ½ price. From tackle shop, 5 Market Place or Richmond Angling Centre, 8 Temple Square, Graven Gate, Richmond.

Grinton (N Yorks). Trout. Thornaby AA has whole south bank and part of north bank, from Isles Bridge to Grinton Bridge (about 5½m); trout three to the lb. No tickets, but help given by hon sec to visiting anglers who write with SAE. Tackle shops: F Fynn, 12 Varo Terrace, Stockton; or J W Wright & Son, 107 Park Gate, Darlington.

Reeth (N Yorks). Swale; trout. Black Bull Hotel has water for residents £1 day.

Muker (N Yorks). Trout; strictly preserved. Muker Beck; trout; Thwaite Beck, 1m W; trout; free. Summer Lodge Beck, 5m E; trout; preserved.

Keld (N Yorks). Trout; plentiful but small; preserved.

Check before you go

While every effort has been made to ensure that the information given in **Where to Fish** *is correct, the position is continually changing, and anglers are urged, in their own interests, to make preliminary enquiries before travelling to selected venues. This is especially important with reference to prices quoted. Inevitably the rate of inflation is affecting stability in this quarter. Anglers' attention is also drawn to the fact that the hotels mentioned under the various fishing stations do not necessarily have water of their own. Any amendments or further data for inclusion in subsequent editions, and any criticism, will be welcome.*

GUN BECK (tributary of Swale):

Husthwaite (N Yorks). Centre for good trouting on **Husthwaite Beck;** dt from York tackle shops.

Coxwold (N Yorks). Pond Head Reservoirs (two), 3m SE; perch and pike. Hole Beck and Gun Beck preserved.

BEDALE BECK (tributary of Swale):

Leeming (N Yorks). Swale, 2m NE; preserved by Black Ox AC from A1 road to confluence with Swale, excepting only two small fields above Leeming Bridge. Trout and coarse fish. St £5 from R M Wright, 5 Lascelles Lane, Northallerton.

COD BECK (tributary of Swale); good trout water, but recent pollution of lower reaches has affected sport.

Thirsk (N Yorks). Thirsk AC has water on Swale; dt from tackle dealer. York and Dist AA have 5½ acre lake at **Sand Hutton,** Park View. Hotels: Royal Oak,

Three Tuns. Tackle shop: Thirsk Anglers Centre, Sowerby Rd.

Sessay (N Yorks). Cod Beck, 2m W; Thirsk AC, Swale, 2m SW; Bradford club now has fishing on P J Till's farm (The Heights). Inn: Railway, Dalton.

Brawith (N Yorks). Trout; preserved. For Cod Beck Reservoir see Northallerton.

Topcliffe (N Yorks). Bradford AA has water here, and on **Swale.**

WISKE (tributary of Swale): River still troubled by pollution.

Otterington (N Yorks). Cod Beck, 2m E. Broad Beck. Sorrow Beck, 4m E.

Northallerton (N Yorks). Roach, dace, chub pike; preserved: fishing good. Northallerton AC has fishing on Wiske (members only) and on several miles of water on the Swale at Morton Bridge. Clubs tickets are listed under Morton-on-Swale.

PARRETT

(For close seasons, licences, etc, see South Western Region NRA, p16)

Rises in hills on border of Somerset and Dorset, and flows into Bristol Channel near Bridgwater. Roach, bream and dace predominate. Thorney-Middle Chinnock stretch and some of tributaries hold trout. Occasional salmon and sea trout run through into Tone.

Bridgwater (Som). River tidal here. Now a Marina. **King's Sedgemoor Drain** is also preserved by Bridgwater AA which has fishing ¾m above Greylake Bridge, where 18ft Rhyne enters Cary River to A38 Road bridge at Dunball. Good roach, rudd, pike, tench, bream, carp and perch. St, wt, dt, from tackle shops in area or L Williams, 7 Webbers Way, Puriton. Other Bridgwater AA fisheries: Rivers **Parrett, Isle, Hunstspill** and **Cripps** Rivers, **North Drain** (jointly held with North Somerset AA), **South Drain** (jointly held with Glaston Manor AA), **18ft Rhyne, Langacre Rhyne, Bridgwater and Taunton Canal, Dunwear, Screech Owl, Taunton Road, Combwich** and **Walrow** Lakes (carp, bream, roach, rudd, tench, perch). Season, weekly and day tickets, with concessions for jun, OAP. Permits cover all waters. Pocket maps from hon sec. **South Drain,** lower part, is held by North Somerset AA. Bathampton AA has ponds near

here; details from hon sec. Day/night coarse fishing on Westhay Lake, 3½ acres, large tench and carp. Tel: 0278 456429. Tackle shops: John's Tackle, 35 St John Street; Angling Centre, Unit 1, Wye Avenue; Waynes Tackle, 66 Eastover. Accommodation with special facilities for anglers: Admiral Blake Guest House, 58/60 Monmouth St; Brickyard Farmhouse, River Rd, Pawlett; Whites Farm, N Newton. Hotels: Brookland; Friarn Court.

Langport (Som). Parret; pike, perch, carp, bream, roach, dace, tench, chub, rudd. Wessex Fed holds long section from **Oath Lock** to **Monks Lease Clyse,** and from **Huish Bridge** to **Thorney,** also water on Isle; open to affiliated clubs. Langport AA issues st £5.50, wt £2.50 and dt £2, obtainable from Langport Angling Centre, North Street. Stoke-sub-Hamdon AA has stretches at **West Chinnock** and **Thorney.** Thorney Lakes, tel: 0458 25011, has trout and course

---

Keep the banks clean

Several clubs have stopped issuing tickets to visitors because of the state of the banks after they have left. Spend a few moments clearing up.

fishing, dt £5 and £3 respectively. Accommodation at Gothic House, Muchelney, tel: 0458 250626, who have Thorney Lakes adjacent.

Crewkerne (Som). Trout, coarse fish. Stoke-sub-Hamdon AA has trout fishing (with restocking) from Bow Mills to Hurdle Pool (trout av ¾lb); members only; coarse fishing, 12 different species including 3 types of carp, from Hurdle Pool to Thorney Mill. St £4, concessions to jun & OAP, from local tackle shops and committee members.

TONE: Trout above Taunton, coarse fish. Weedy in summer below **Taunton** but provides first-class coarse fishing in winter.

Taunton (Som). Fishing free at French weir and through Taunton. Taunton Fly Fishing Club has water on the Tone, trout and grayling, fly only. St £50 and dt for restricted areas of Tone from Topp Tackle, 63 Station Rd. (Taunton AA bona fide members have been granted access to FFC's Rough Moor water. See below, for list of AA waters.) Other tackle shop: Viaduct Fishery, Cary Valley, Somerton, TA11 6LJ, tel: 0458 74022, has trout fly fishing in 25 acre site, dt £19, 5 fish. Additional coarse fishing, dt £3. Enterprise Angling, East Reach, has tickets for 4 venues in locality, fishable in close season. Hotels: Castle (which advises angling visitors on local facilities); County.

Hillfarrance Brook (a Tone tributary, from Hillfarrance to confluence with Tone). Trout, grayling, fly only, Taunton FFC water, members only. Axe (Chard Junction) ¾m single bank fishing below the village, fly only, Taunton FFC, members only. Axe (Axminster) ½m single bank fishing both sides of Cloakham Bridge, fly only, Taunton FFC members only. Annual subscription £50. Tickets for restricted areas available from Topp Tackle. Taunton AA has water on **Bridgwater Canal** at Taunton; **West Sedgemoor Drain** from Pincombe Bridge, Stathe; **R Tone** fast stretch at Taunton, Rushton, Creech and Ham; Ponds at Walton, Norton and Wych

Lodge. St £14, wt £7.50, dt £3.

Wellington (Som). Trout, roach, dace; trout average ½lb. Wellington AA has water from Fox Bros' works 2m up stream; mt and dt from hon sec. Thereafter preserved by owners through Bradford to Taunton FFC water. Tackle and licences from Wellington Country Sports, Brooks Place, High Street TA21 8RA.

Wiveliscombe (Som). Tone, Milverton Brook and Norton Brook; trout; leave from owners, banks bushed.

NORTON BROOK (tributary of Tone):

Bishops Lydeard (Som). Trout; banks overgrown.

MILVERTON BROOK (tributary of Tone).

Milverton (Som). Trout; private; leave from owners; banks bushed.

YEO: Coarse fish, some trout.

Long Lode (Som). Good coarse fishing; permission from farmers.

Ilchester (Som). Mainly roach, dace, eels and some trout. Dt and st from A D Coles, greengrocer. Club: Ilchester AC, who have fishing on **Yeo** and **Cam** above Ilchester. Viaduct Fishery, Somerton, 2 lakes, 4 acres, trout. Tel: 0458 74022. Tackle shop: Ilchester Angling Centre, Ilchester Garage, Northover. Hotel: Ivelchester.

Yeovil (Som). Trout (av 12in), roach, chub, dace. Yeovil and Sherborne AA have water downstream of **Sherborne Lake, Sutton Bingham Stream** from Filter Station to Yeovil Junction and R Wriggle from Yetminster to R Yeo; trout. Tackle shops: Marney's, 20 Bond Street; A D Goddard, 27/29 Forest Hill. Hotels: Mermaid; Manor; The Choughs.

ISLE: Prolific chub water; also roach, dace, etc. First ½ mile from junction with Parrett held by Wessex Federation of Anglers.

Isle Brewers (Som). Roach, chub, dace, some trout from Fivehead Road to Hambridge; Newton Abbott FA water at Hambridge, plus twelve lakes and ponds at Rackerhayes, Kingsteignton and Bovey Tracy. Dt £4.

Ilminster (Som). Roach, chub, dace. Chard

Fishing available?

If you own, manage, or know of first-class fishing available to the public which should be considered for inclusion in **Where to Fish** *please apply to the publishers (address in the front of the book) for a form for submission, on completion, to the Editor. (Inclusion is at the sole discretion of the Editor).*

& Dist AA water, members only, £10 membership from Chard Angling Centre. From below Ilminster to just above Five-head River, Ilminster AA water; dt £2.50 from hon sec or Chard Angling Centre, 2

Holyrood St, Chard. Bathampton AA obtain fishing through exchange tickets. Contact hon sec or tackle shop: T Clapp, West Street.

RIBBLE

(For close seasons, licences, etc, see North West Region NRA, p17)

Rises in the Pennines and flows 56 miles into the Irish Sea between St Anne's and Southport. Good coarse fishing lower down, between Great Mitton and Preston. Also coarse fishing in Long Preston Deeps. Best salmon, sea trout, brown trout and grayling fishing is between Settle and Great Mitton. Above Settle there are only brown trout. Tributary Hodder has good salmon, sea trout and brown trout fishing throughout length but much affected by water abstraction. Upper waters impounded in Stocks Reservoirs. Its main tributary, the Loud, also provides good trout and sea trout fishing.

Preston (Lancs). Coarse fish, few salmon and sea trout. 2m Preston Federated Anglers water through town; st £5.25, dt £1, including other waters on **Ribble** and **Wyre**, and **Rufford Canal. Twin Lakes Trout Fishery, Croston**, 6 acres, stocked r and b trout, best r 15¼lb. Dt £15.30 (4 fish), ½ day £9.15 (2 fish). Tel: 0772 601093. Further information from tackle shops in Preston; C & R Calderbank, 33 Moor Lane; Ted Carter, 87/88 Church Street. R Crossens, 1m from Southport, fished by Southport & Dist AA. Dt from Robinsons Tackle Shop, 71 Sussex Road, Southport.

Samlesbury (Lancs). Coarse fish, few salmon and sea trout. Several miles preserved by Ribble and Wyre FA, dt from hon sec. Members only. Assc also has stretch of R Wyre at St Michaels on Wyre, and dt £1.50 on Anglezarke Reservoir.

Balderstone (Lancs). Northern AA have 2¼m at Balderstone Hall Farm to Lower House Farm. Fishing 4 am to 11 pm. Coarse, with game fish (Mar 15-Jun 15). Dt £1.20 on bank, conc. 30p, OAP, juv.

Longridge (Lancs). Ribble, 3m SE. Hodder, 5m NE. Salmon, sea trout and trout. Loud 2m N. Most of right bank preserved by Loud and Hodder AA. Visitors' tickets issued if accompanied by member. Bolton & Dist AA have two stretches near here. No dt, but st £12, conc. £4, from any tackle shop in district. Prince Albert AS, Macclesfield, own several miles above M6 bridge. Warrington AA has short stretch at **Hurst Green.**

Mitton (Yorks); ns Whalley, 2m. Salmon, sea trout, trout and coarse fish. NRA controls left bank d/s from Mitton Bridge. Four trout permits per day, ten salmon.

Enquiries, Mrs Haynes, Mitton Hall Farm, 0254 826281.

Clitheroe (Lancs). Trout, salmon, sea trout. Clitheroe AA Ltd fishes 3m of Ribble and 1m of **Lune.** Members only, no dt. Townson Bros, Charbury Trading Estate, Clitheroe, have 6m double and single bank of Ribble and Hodder; st £176.25. The Inn at Whitewell, in the Forest of Bowland, offers fishing to guests. By the A59 between Clitheroe and Accrington, **Whalley Abbey** trout fishery. St and dt. Phone 025 4822211 for details. **Churn Clough Reservoir**, 16 acres, 4 miles from Clitheroe, has trout to 10lb, fly only, tel 0254 62071, weekends and evenings. Disabled facilities. Lancashire FFA have 4m; tickets only members' guests. Blackburn and Dist AA have several miles on Ribble and other fisheries on **Lune, Wenning, Aire, Gilpin** and reservoirs. Some dt; apply hon sec. Ribble Valley Borough Council issues st £16.20 to residents for water at Brungerley and below Edisford Bridge. Wt £8.50 available for visitors, also dt £3.50 for Edisford alone, from T I Centre, Edisford caravan site or tackle shop. 120 yds right bank above Edisford Bridge, Roefield Nursing and Rest Home. Tickets available, tel: 0200 22010. Two rods on Hodder for residents of Red Pump Hotel, Bashall Eaves; dt issued. Some permits from Rectory, Stoneyhurst College. Tackle shops: Ken Varey, 4 Newmarket, Clitheroe; Fishing Tackle, 12-14 Southworth Street, Blackburn. Hotels: Inn at Whitewell, Old Post House; Calf's Head, Swan and Royal; Victoria.

Chatburn (Lancs). **Ribble,** 1m W; good trout, occasional salmon and sea trout. Several miles of river preserved by Clitheroe AA; limited visitors' tickets

Anglers afloat on Malham Tarn. *Photo: Arthur Oglesby.*

through members only. Hotels: Pendle; Manor House Cottage.

Sawley (N Yorks). On Ribble. Salmon, sea trout, trout and grayling. Trout and salmon fishing good. Several miles preserved by Yorkshire FFC (visitors' tickets through members only). Inn: Spread Eagle.

Gisburn (N Yorks). Trout, salmon. Lancashire FFA have water at Ribchester and Gisburn. Fly fishing for members only. Hotels: Park House; Stirk House.

Long Preston (N Yorks). Ribble, 1m W. Trout, grayling, odd salmon, coarse fish. Left bank is preserve of Padiham & Dist AS. Members only. Staincliffe AC also have water, members plus 5 tickets for their guests. Hotels: Boar's Head; Maypole.

Settle (N Yorks). Settle AA has 7½m of good trout and grayling fishing in Ribble between Langcliffe, Settle and vicinity of Long Preston. Wt £45, dt £12 at Royal Oak Hotel during licensing hours. Fly only; limit 1½ brace. Water stocked yearly. **Malham Tarn** is 6m from Settle and holds large trout. Dt available *(see Yorkshire lakes, reservoirs, etc).* Further north are Manchester AA's waters. Licences from C M & G L Ball, The Sports Shop, Cheapside, Settle. Other hotels at Settle: Falcon Manor and Golden Lion.

Horton in Ribblesdale (N Yorks). Trout; preserved from source to Helwith Bridge, including all tributaries, by Manchester AA. Assn also has **Newhouses Tarn** (fly only); stocked b and r trout. No tickets. Annual membership: £155, plus £100 entrance fee.

Tributaries of the Ribble

HODDER: Good salmon and trout water.

Higher Hodder Bridge (Lancs and Yorks). Salmon, sea trout, trout, grayling and coarse fish.

Chipping (Lancs). Hodder, 1½m E. Salmon, sea trout and grayling. Loud, 1m SE. Trout and sea trout. About ½m of Hodder below Doeford Bridge on right bank and several miles of **River Loud** are preserved by Loud and Hodder AA; tickets if accompanied by member. Hotel: Derby Arms.

Whitewell (Lancs). Salmon, sea trout, trout, grayling. The Inn at Whitewell, Forest of Bowland BB7 3AT, has four rods for residents on 6m of the Whitewell FA water. Wt from £50, dt from £11. Tel: 02008 222 for details. The Red Pump Hotel, Bashall Eaves, has two rods 8m further down the river.

Newton (Lancs); Lancashire FFA have water downstream from Newton to Dunsop Bridge. At **Chaigley,** Southport FF have water, and Edisford Hall Estate; contact Townson Bros, Pendle Trading Estate, Chatburn, Clitheroe BB7 3LJ. Also at Chaigley, Hodder Bridge Hotel has 100 yds right bank u/s of Hodder Higher Bridge.

Slaidburn (Lancs); ns Clitheroe, 8½m. Hodder; salmon, sea trout and trout; all preserved. Hotel: Bounty.

CALDER: Coarse fishing. Some club water.

Whalley (Lancs). West Calder. Ribble, 2m W; salmon, sea trout and coarse fish. Hodder, 2m W; salmon, sea trout and trout. At Billington, Accrington FC have fishing, members only. Contact A Balderstone, 42 Townley Ave, Huncoat, Accrington, tel: 0254 233517.

Barrowford (Lancs). Pendle Water; trout. Marsden Star AS has from Quaker Bridge to Barden Lane Bridge. Colne Water (polluted) and Pendle join near Barrowford to form Calder (polluted). **Leeds and Liverpool Canal** from Bank Newton to Long Ings at Barnoldswick (10m), and

3½m at Keighley leased to Marsden Star AS. Dt £1 available.

Burnley (Lancs). Local waters mostly polluted. Burnley AS leases **Lea Green Reservoir,** at Hapton but tickets available only to local ratepayers; trout. **Hapton Lodges Reservoir** at Hapton stocked with rainbow trout; contact Blythe Angling Club. Marsden Star AS fishes Gawthorpe Hall Pool at Padiham, members only. Tackle shops: Littlewoods, Parker Lane; H McLoughlan, 33a Parliament Street.

COLNE (tributary of Calder). Much pollution but holds some trout and coarse fish.

Colne (Lancs). Colne; trout. Water held by Colne Water AS. **Leeds and Liverpool Canal** held by Marsden Star AS (10m from Barnoldswick to Bank Newton, and 3½m Howden to Morton); pike, trout, tench, bream, roach, rudd, carp and perch; st and dt for waters held by both clubs. Marsden Star AS also fishes Knotts Lane Ponds at Colne, coarse fish, members only. Tackle shops: D W & D Foden, Post Office Buildings, Barnoldswick; Colne Angling Centre, Windsor Street; Jackson's Tackle Shop, Albion Street, Earby; Boyces, 44 Manchester Road, and Fly and Tackle, 59 Cross Street, both Nelson.

Foulridge (Lancs). Four British Waterways reservoirs: **Lower** (or **Burwains**), **Upper, Slipperhill, White Moor.** Let to clubs: members only.

ROTHER

(For close seasons, licences, etc, see Southern Region NRA, p15)

Rises near Rotherfield and reaches the sea at Rye Bay. Mostly coarse fish, with trout in upper reaches and tributaries but runs of sea trout increasing. Mullet and bass in estuary.

Rye (Sussex). Near mouth of Rother; coarse fish. Clive Vale AS has 1m of **Tillingham River** above Rye and **Rother** at Wittersham to Iden Bridge, south bank footpath for 2 fields on **Royal Military Canal** at Winchelsea. Romney Marsh is close by. Several clubs have water, including Hastings, Bexhill and Dist (Freshwater) AA; st £29, dt £3, conc. Tackle shop: Shoot A Line, 46 Ferry Road.

Wittersham (Sussex). Clive Vale AC have 2 good stretches at Blackwall Bridge and Otter Channel junction. Dt £3, only in advance, from hon sec or Hastings tackle shops. Rother Fishery Assn has fishing;

tickets available either on a club basis or by prior booking. Contact Mr Hodd, tel: 0580 850597.

Newenden (Sussex). Large bream, chub and roach; Rother Fishery Assn has fishing rights, terms described under Wittersham.

Bodiam (Sussex). Trout (small), coarse fish. Sussex Rother AC and Edenbridge AC. Hotels: Castle, Justins.

Etchingham (Sussex). Hastings, Bexhill and Dist AA has 4 stretches on the **Rother,** many miles of dykes and drains noted for pike, bream, tench and rudd on **Romney Marsh** between **Gulderford** and **Appledore,** Wishingtree, **Buckshole**

and **Harmers Reservoirs,** ponds, **Pett Pools,** 20 acres nr **Hastings;** st £33, dt £5, conc, from hon sec or local tackle shops. CALPAC controls **Spurringbrook Sewer,** nr **Appledore,** 2 stretches available. Tel: 081 642 7586 (strictly after 6 pm), Mr Henry. At **Burwash** is **Lakedown Trout Fishery,** 4 lakes, 5 acres each, b and r trout from 1½lb to 16lb. Dt £22, 5 fish, ½ day £16, 3 fish. Contact A Bristow, Lakedown Fishery, Broad Oak, Heathfield TN21 8UX; tel: 0435 883449.

Stonegate (Sussex). Wadhurst AS has trout water; dt to members' guests only. Hotel: Bridge.

Tenterden (Kent). Tenterden and Dist AA has many miles on Rother and tributaries; no day or period tickets. Club HQ at The Vine, Station Rd. Tackle shop: Tackle & Gun Shop, 1 East Cross.

BREDE: Rother tributary. Coarse fish, a few small trout; 6 fisheries controlled by Clive Vale AC. No dt. St £16 from hon sec or local tackle shops. Fishing station **Rye, Winchelsea.**

SEVERN

(For close seasons, licences, etc, see Severn-Trent Region NRA, p18)

Longest river in England. Rises in Wales (N Powys) and flows 180m into Bristol Channel. Fair salmon river, with commercial fisheries near mouth; spring salmon in January/April and May. Average size good. Some trout and grayling in upper reaches, but river notable chiefly for coarse fishing, especially for chub in the upper reaches and barbel in the middle river. Shad runs up river in May and are taken on rod and line, principally at Tewkesbury Weir.

Sharpness (Glos). Coarse fishing in the **Gloucester and Berkeley Canal** from Severn Bridge to Hempstead Bridge, Gloucester (about 16m); bank licence from any bridge house.

Gloucester (Glos). Gloucester United AA controls several miles of Severn from Hawbridge u/s and d/s, and Stank Lane. Dt £2, from bailiffs. (Assn also has water from **Lower Lode** to **Deerhurst,** on gravel pit at **Saul** and on **Gloucester Sharpness Canal**). Red Lion Inn, Wainlode Hill, has Severn fishing with facilities for disabled. Tel: 0452 730251. At Little Witcombe, nr Birdlip, **Witcombe Reservoirs** managed by Cambrian Fisheries. Fly only; brown and rainbow trout. St £184 and £92, tickets for guests of members. Tel: 0452 864413. Tackle shops: Allsports, 126/128 Eastgate Street (dt for Wye salmon fishing); Rod & Gun, 67 Alvin St; Essex Tackle, 42 Goldsmith Road; Tredworth Tackle, High St, Tredworth; D & J Sports, 75 Cricklade Street, Cirencester; Coronation Tackle, 42 Goldsmith Rd; Ian Coley 442/444 High St, both Cheltenham. Hotels: New County, Fleece, New Inn.

Tewkesbury (Glos). Salmon, twait and coarse fish. Avon: coarse fish. Below weir shoals of big bream. Birmingham AA has 38 stretches on Severn including those at Bushley, Ripple, Uckinghall, Severn Stoke, Deerhurst, Chaceley, Apperley (2 pools at Apperley, also) and Maisemore; also Church End Trout Fishery. Tewkesbury Popular AA has water on **Severn, and Mill Avon;** full membership limited to 3m radius of Tewkesbury Cross, otherwise limited membership; st £13, ft £5, conc, from R Danter. Gloucester United AA have water at Drirhurst and Lower Lode. Dt from bailiff, tackle shops and Hon Sec. Trout fly fishing at Witcombe Waters, Great Witcombe, tel: 0452 863591. Tackle shop: R Danter, Tackle Shop, 31 Barton Street GL20 5PR. Hotels: Abbey; Malvern View; many others.

Ripple (Worcs). Bream, pike, perch, chub, dace, roach. NRA fishery, free to licence holders, is on 1m east bank, at M50 viaduct. Birmingham AA has 2 meadows and Uckingham pool, Ripple.

Upton-on-Severn (Worcs). Chub, barbel, bream, roach, dace, perch and pike. R bank for 1500 yds west bank above old railway embankment free to NRA licence holders. Upton-upon-Severn AA has 15 pegs at Hanley Rd, 42 pegs at Upper Ham. Free parking. Dt £1 in advance or £2 from G Shinn, tackle shop, 21 Old Street. Birmingham AA has 7 meadows, members only. Hotels: King's Head, Swan, Star.

Worcester (Worcs). Pike, barbel, chub, dace, bream, roach, salmon, trout, etc. Free stretch behind cricket ground. Worcester & Dist United AA has more than 5m in seven stretches, including the salmon fishery below **Diglis Weir.** St for Salmon £100 and £32, dt £2.50 issued.

Honorary members' books issued by hon sec or through tackle shops (below); society also has stretch of **Worcester-Birmingham Canal,** from Blackpole Bridge to Commandery, 1½m on **Avon** and three stretches on Teme at Knightwick, Broadwas, Cotheridge. **Teme,** 2m S; coarse fish, trout, salmon. Birmingham AA has stretches at Severn Stoke, Hallow, Kempsey, Grimley and Holt Fleet, rights on Worcester and Birmingham Canal from King's Norton to Blackpole (near Worcester); bream, roach, perch, pike. Hotels: Star, Great Western, Commis, Pack Horse. Tackle shops: Alans Tackle, 26 Malvern Road, Worcester; I M Richardson, 28 St John's; Vicking Afloat, Lowesmoor Wharf.

Lincombe and **Holt** (Worcs). Holt, Fleet and Wharf Hotels issue dt for water below bridge. Good perch at Lincombe. Whitmore Reans CAA has **Seed Green** and **Larford** fishing. High Chaperal, 0905 620289, ownes Old Wharf stretch, dt available.

Stourport-on-Severn (Worcs). At confluence of Severn and Stour: barbel, chub and large roach; but **Staffordshire and Worcestershire Canal:** coarse fish. Lyttelton AA has 80 pegs right bank u/s of Stourport. Tickets from Mark Lewis only. Birmingham AA has ½m both banks. Hampstall Cider House, Astley Burf, issues dt. Tackle shop: Mark Lewis, Raven Street, where Lyttelton AA tickets are sold during opening hours. 1¼m both banks downstream of **Cilcewydd Bridge** is NRA fishery, free to licence holders.

Bewdley (Worcs). Salmon, trout, excellent head of coarse fish in general, barbel exceptional. Kidderminster AA has six stretches, 2m ¾m of water above and below town, and 1m below Stourport at **Winnalls.** St £13.50, conc, from local tackle shops: no day permits, card holders only. Harbour Inn, Arley, has two meadows. Dt from bailiff. Birmingham AA has six stretches in vicinity. Cards for both clubs from Stan Lewis, tackle shop, 1-4 Senside South, who runs own riverside guest-house and clubroom and issues tickets for 1½m Severn at Bewdley and 4 local pools under his own supervision. Various coarse fish, dt £2. Tackle shops; Whites, Stourport; Lewis, Bewley; Stevens, Cradley Heath; Storey, Kidderminster; Hingley, Stourbridge; Leavsley Fishing Tackle, Severnside North, Bewdley.

Upper Arley (Worcs). Salmon, trout, grayling, chub, dace, pike, etc. Dowles Brook, 3m S. Birmingham AA has stretches at **Arley Stanley, Arley Kinlet, Arley, Aveley** and **Rhea Hall.** Hotels: Valentia, Harbour and Unicorn (last two issue dt).

Hampton Loade (Salop). Pike, perch, chub, dace, trout, salmon. Birmingham AA has extensive fishing here, on both banks, and at **Alveley.**

Bridgnorth (Salop). Salmon, trout, barbel (good), chub, pike, etc. Whitmore Reans AA rents a stretch here of about 1m. Bridgnorth AS has water (st £6, wt £5, dt - excluding Sundays - £1) and Birmingham AA has stretches at **Knowle Sands, Danery, Quatford** and **Eardington.** **Willey Park Pools** at **Broseley** (5m) and pools at **Ticklerton** are also on club card; rainbow, brown and some American brook trout. Membership limited. Approx 6m and 8m S, on Kidderminster Road, **Pool Hall** (tel: 02997 458) and **Koi Lakes** (formerly Shatterford) (tel: 0562 851129), dt trout fisheries, including carp pools. Two trout pools at **Quatt, Kingsnordley Fly Fisheries;** dt £6, 6 fish. Tel: 0746 780247. For details of **Underton Trout Lakes,** fly fishing, tel: 074635 254. Astbury Falls Fish Farm, tel: 0746 766797, has £3 dt plus £1.80 per lb caught, also coarse dt £3, large carp. Tackle and licences from Stuart Williams, 5 Underhill Street. Fishing holidays available at Bandon Arms, Mill St, 0746 763135. Accommodation with facilities for anglers at The Woodberry Down, Victoria Rd, tel: 0746 76236. Kidderminster tackle shops: Siviter Sports, 2 Tower Building, Blackwell St; Storey's Angling Centre, 129 Sutton Rd. Hotels: Severn Arms; Falcon; Croft; Kings Head.

Coalport (Salop). Chub, barbel, pike, etc, fewer roach and dace than are found farther downstream. Some free water. Rowley Regis and Dist AS has stretch on right bank. No tickets.

Iron Bridge (Salop). Same fish species as Coalport; Birmingham AA has ¼m. 600 yds of fishing on left bank free to NRA licence-holders. Dawley AS has right bank d/s from power station fence to Free Bridge. Dt £2, conc, on site. Hazeldine Anglers have 1½m fishing at Buidwas Park, west of Iron Bridge. Queens Arms AC has 35 pegs u/s and d/s of Free Bridge. Dt from bailiff on bank. Hotel: Tontine.

Berrington (Salop). Severn, 1m N; chub;

dace, pike, trout, salmon. Cound Brook, 1½ SW; trout; private. Tern, 2½m N; two pools; private. Hotel: Cound Lodge, Cound.

Atcham (Salop). NRA issues dt for 800 yds above bridge (both banks) and 3½m on R bank below, single bank, obtainable at Atcham Service Station. Macclesfield Prince Albert AS has members only fisheries here, at **Bicton, Melverley, Longnor, Royal Hill, The Isle, Welshpool** and **Newton.** Also fishings on the rivers **Gam, Vyrnwy** and **Banwy.**

Shrewsbury (Salop). Chub, pike, perch, roach, barbel, dace, a few trout; fishing free or by ticket. Spring salmon fishing; best months Mar, Apr and May. **Monkmoor** and **Weir** fisheries controlled by council, tel: 0743 231456 for fisheries; 356046 for bailiff. St £29.60 to £26.64, salmon; £14.30 to £6.60 course. Old LMS SC has fine stretches at **Emstry,** with fords and runs. Dt from all local tackle shops. Wingfield Arms Inn, Montford Bridge SY4 1EB, has fishing. Tel: 0743 850750. Birmingham AA has stretches at **Underdale, Pool Quay** and **Buttington Bridge.** Warrington AA has **Severn** at **Loton Park,** Alberbury, **Mytton,** near **Montford Bridge.** Lymm AC has dt water here with very large chub and barbel. Tackle shops: Ebrall Bros, Smithfield Road; Chris Partington's Vintage Tackle Shop, 103 Longden Coleham; Kingfisher Angling Centre, 8 New St; Sundorne Fishing Tackle, 1 Sundorne Avenue.

Melverley (Salop). Two meadows on left bank, about 500 yds, free to NRA licence-holders. Chester AA has 800yds immediately d/s of NRA stretch.

Llandrinio (Montgomery). Chub, dace, trout, salmon; leave from farmers. Lymm AC has dt water in this area. Montgomery AA has 2,290 yds left bank, upstream from bridge to Lower Farm. Cheshire AA has Haughton Farm and Pentre stretches. St £10. Canal; coarse fish, tickets (*see Welshpool).* **Maerdy Brook,** 2m SW. Arddleen Brook, excellent trout, dace and chub. Hotel: Golden Lion.

Welshpool (Powys). Salmon, trout, coarse fish (inc grayling). Trout small in streams, few but big in river. Welshpool and Dist AC now in Montgomeryshire AA which has 60m of coarse and game fishing in **Severn, Camlad, Vyrnwy, Banwy.** Also **Shropshire Union Canal** (coarse fishing). Their 2 Welshpool

stretches are at **Coed-y-Dinas** and **Lower Leighton.** St £14, dt £2. Black Pools trout fishery, fly only, is 1m from Welshpool on Llanfair Rd; Montgomery AA water, dt £10, 4 fish, from A E Bond. Some permits are available for **Maesmawr Pool** (5m NW). Bank and boat fishing (dt £9 and £4) on Marton Pool, Marton, 5m SE. Good coarse fishing. Apply to Site Manager, Marton Pool Caravan Park. Warrington AA has Hope Farm stretch, Welshpool. Tackle permits and NRA licences from A E Bond, 9 Hall Street. Hotels: Westwood Park, Salop Rd, Welshpool, who have Montgomery AA tickets; Bear, Newton; Black Lion, Llanfair Caereinion.

Forden (Powys). Montgomery, 3m. Trout, salmon, chub, dace, etc. Birmingham AA has 3m. Camlad; trout, grayling. Montgomeryshire AA and Cheshire AA have water on river; tickets.

Montgomery (Powys). Severn, 2m; trout, salmon, grayling, chub, pike and perch. Lion Hotel, Caerhowell has 400 yards of Severn; st £25 dt £1.50. **Camlad,** 2m N; good trout, grayling, chub. Montgomeryshire AA has water; tickets. Warrington AA has waters at Caerhowell Hall, **Dolwen, Fron** and **Llanidloes.** Also **Vyrnwy, Dee,** canals and pools. Herbert Arms, Cherbury, has 1½m; dt. Tackle shops in Welshpool and Newtown.

Abermule (Powys). **Severn** and **Mule;** salmon, trout, grayling, coarse fish; mostly private but dt for some lengths. Water not always fishable in summer. Montgomeryshire AA has 1¼m of Severn and water at Mule junction; dt from hon sec. Warrington AA has stretch.

Newtown (Powys). Salmon, trout, grayling, pike, chub, dace. Newtown and Dist FC, Llanfair Caerinion FC and Welshpool AC form Montgomeryshire AA, who have waters here as follows: the old free stretch from above Halfpenny Bridge, both banks; Newtown recreation ground; **Vaynor Estate; Glanhafren Hall; Penstrowed** and **Dolwerw;** also **Fachwen Pool,** fly only r trout fishing. St and dt from Mikes Tackle, and M Cakebread's Garage, Pool Rd, Newtown. Caersws AA has fishing, dt from Postmans Shop, Short Bridge St. Prince Albert AS has stretch here. Penllwyn Lodges (tel: 0686 640269) offers self-catering log cabins with fishing in 1m of canal plus small lake; tench, chub, carp. Tackle shop has dt £1.50 for canal at **Abermule** and **Net-**

tershiem **Trout Lake,** $4\frac{1}{2}$ acres, £10. Tackle shops: Mikes Tackle Centre, 15 Shortbridge Street; Mid Wales Angling, Unit 2E6, Lion Works, Pool Rd. Hotels: Elephant and Castle, Maesmawr Hall, Dolforwyn Hall.

Caersws (Powys). Maesmawr Hall Hotel has $3\frac{1}{2}$m on Severn free to guests. Trout, coarse fish, some salmon. Caersws AC has water here and at Red House. ST £50, wt £20, dt £4 for good trout and grayling from Post Office or Bucks Hotel, Caersws. St £45, dt £4, for Caersws stretch from Bill Pritchard, tel: 0686 625814.

Llandinam (Powys). 4m of trout and grayling fishing on both banks. Dt £4, OAP, jun £2 from Lion Hotel, Llandinam. Warrington AA has stretch from Llandinam to Dolwen Bridge. Licences from Post Office Stores.

Llanidloes (Montgomery). Trout, salmon, pike, chub, dace, grayling. Llanidloes AA has about 20m fishing on upper **Severn, Afon Clywedog** and other tributaries. St and dt from hon sec. Warrington AA has Dolwen Bridge to Llanidloes. NRA has $\frac{1}{2}$m on R bank which is free fishing to licence holders. O S Evans, Dol Llys Farm, SY18 6JA has 300 yds right bank, tel 05512 2694. Warrington AA, has water downstream. At **Trefeglwys** (4m N) is caravan park with of fishing (trout and coarse) on **Trannon.** Best months for trout April-July. Hotels: Lloyds, Unicorn, Queen's Head, Angel, Temperance, Royal Oak, Red Lion.

Tributaries of the Severn.

LEADON: Trout, coarse fish (some barbel introduced).

Ledbury (Hereford). Ledbury AA has trout water, no dt. Castlemorton Lake; coarse fishing; free, but NRA licence necessary.

AVON: The principal tributary of the lower Severn. Roach, chub, dace and perch dominate higher reaches; bream and pike, the latter patchily distributed, below Evesham. Barbel beginning to appear.

Tewkesbury (Glos). Confluence of Avon and Severn, connected also by 'Mill Avon'. Weirs and weir-pool fishing, including twaite shad during the spawning run. Cheltenham AC controls 2m of Avon at Corpus Christi by **Strensham** village. Good coarse fishing, chub, roach, bream, perch, pike included. Membership £11, dt £2, conc, (Mon to Sun only) from hon sec, Chetltenham tackle shops or the Bell Inn, Eckington. Hazeldine AA controls 4 meadows at **Chaceley.**

Twyning (Glos). Chub, dace, roach, pike, perch, bream. White Swan Piscatorials preserve left bank of river from near Bredon Church to four meadows below Twyning lane. Birmingham AA has $\frac{1}{2}$m stretch.

Pershore (Worcs). Pike, perch, roach, dace, chub, bream. NRA licence-holders may boat-fish free from mouth of **Piddle Brook** to **Pomona Works Meadows,** and at **Wyre Mill.** Worcester & Dist United AA has 5 stretches near Pershore, st £15.30, dt £2.50. Cheltenham AC has stretches at **Birlingham** and **Corpus Christi;** dt from Gloucester and Tewkes-bury tackle shops. Fox Inn AC has water $1\frac{1}{2}$m below Pershore, tel: 021 458 2797 or 021 327 3113. Stratford-on-Avon AA and Redditch FA have water nearby at Wick. Birmingham AA has water here, both banks and at Pensham, Birlingham, **Nafford, Eckington, Bredon, Twyning, Bredons Hardwick** and **Mythe Farm.** Hazeldine AA has 30 pegs at **Defford.** Some free water in recreation ground. Jacksons Farm Fishery has £3 dt, coarse fish. Throckmorton Rd, Nr Pershore. Tackle shop: Rochelle Country Sports, 32 Bridge St; Hotel: Angel.

Evesham (Worcs). Pike, perch, bream, roach, dace, chub. Evesham AA has water in town, wt £3.50, dt £1 from bailiff on bank. Two stretches at **Hampton Ferry:** S M Raphael has 124 pegs, with fishing for disabled; tel: 0386 442458. E W Huxley has stretch for 160 anglers; Dt £2 from cafe or bailiffs office on bank; matches booked at £2 per peg. Birmingham AA has fisheries here and at **Swifts, Wood Norton, Chadbury, Charlton, Cropthorne, Fladbury, Lower Moor** and **Wick.** Manor Farm Leisure (caravan holidays), Anchor Lane, Harvington, 0386 870039, has coarse fishing on Avon. **Hampton Playing Field, Waterside** and **Workman Gardens** (overnight only), reserved for local anglers; permits from Council and tackle shop: J Heritage, 17 Boat Lane; Mug of Maggots, 92A High St, Bideford-on-Avon. Alcester tackle shop: Sports and Tackle, 3A High St, Alcester. Dt £2 river, £3 carp pool at

Twyford Farm fishing, Evesham. Contact May Vince, tel: 0386 446108, day, 0789 778365 evening.

Stratford-upon-Avon (Warwick). A stretch of the Avon preserved by Corporation. Royal Leamington Spa AA has Lido and Recreation Ground fishing; dt. Local club, Stratford-on-Avon AA has waters on R Avon at Luddington, Stratford, Wick nr Pershore, and R Stour from Wimpstone to Preston-on-Stour, with good variety of coarse fish in both; also fishing in South Stratford Canal, Stratford to Wilmcote, and Grand Union Canal; membership £13.50, conc, dt £2 for Seven Meadows, Stratford, from Tony's Fishing Tackle. Hazeldine AA has fishing at **Welford** on Avon. Birmingham AA has stretches at **Avon Meadows, Milcote, Welford, Barton, Bidford, Marlcliff, Cleeve Prior** and **Salford Priors.** Good chub and dace and also water on **Stour** (2m S).

Stratford Canal provides good coarse fishing. Dene, 5m NE. Alveston Village AC has 20 pegs at Alveston. Tackle shops: Tony's Fishing Tackle, 28 East Green Drive; Dave Jones Angling Centre, 17 Evesham Rd; Alcester Sports & Tackle, 3A High St, Alcester. Permits for a number of waters in the district; NRA licences. Hotels: Welcombe, Falcon, Arden and many others.

Leamington (Warwick). Bream, chub, dace, roach, pike, perch. Avon at **Barford, Wasperton** and **Stratford** Lido and Recreation Ground preserved by Royal Leamington Spa AA. Assn, annual membership £14, conc, has 12½m in Grand Union Canal, Warwick to Napton, Rowington, coarse fish (good carp and tench in June, July, Aug); R **Itchen** at Long Itchington, R **Leam, Offchurch** to outfall of Avon, several ponds. Dt £2, conc, for most of these at Stratford from Frosts or Nickards, tackle shops. At Bishops Itchington are **Bishop's Bowl Lakes.** 40 acres of trout and course fishing in flooded limestone quarries. Fish of high average size. Trout dt £20 (6 fish) to £13 (3 fish). Season 1 Mar to 31 Oct. Coarse dt £6 or £3.50. Matches, 18 pegs, £98 or £54. Tel: 0926 613344. **Chesterton Mill Pool** Trout Fishery, Harbury Heath, **Harbury** CU33 9NL, has dts £18.15 to £10 on site. Tel: 0926 613235. Tackle shops: Frosts, Bath St; Nickards Tackle Cellar, Russell Terrace; Baileys, 30 Emscote Rd, Warwick.

Rugby (Warwick). Rugby Fed of Anglers has water on Oxford Canal, Hillmorton to Barby Lane, and **Newbold Quarry,** 25 acres, 1½m from town centre; large tench and carp, with pike. St £10 (£2 juv), dt £1.50 canal, £3.50 quarry, from Banks & Burr *(see below)* or bailiffs. Coventry AA has water on **Oxford Canal** and **Coventry Canal.** Details from tackle shops. Details of **Foxholes Fishery** at **Crick** (three lakes stocked with carp, tench etc) apply R Chaplin, Gt Arbour Close, Kenilworth. For **Stemborough Mill,** 4 acre trout fishery at **Lutterworth,** tel: 0455 209264. Tackle shops: Banks & Burr, 27 Claremont Road; Donalds, 155 Bilton Rd. Hotels: Three Horseshoes, Rugby; Albany, Crick.

ARROW joined by the **Alne** at Alcester; flows into Avon at Salford Priors: Coarse fish, some trout.

Salford Priors (Worcs). Arrow and Avon; coarse fish. Birmingham AA has ¾m.

Wixford (Warwick). Pike, perch, roach, dace, chub and bream; dt for about 1m of water from Fish Inn. Dt £2.50 for water L bank above bridge from public house. Lakes: Ragley Park, 1m NW.

Redditch (Worcs). Redditch & Dist FA are local federation, who fish **Arrow Valley Lake,** with carp to 25lb, large roach and other coarse fish. Dt £2.80 on site, Avon at Wick nr **Pershore** and **Birmingham - Stratford Canal.** Contact S Mousey, tel: 0527 854160. 3m SW of town, Powell's Fishery on 3½ acre **Norgrove Pool.** R trout to 6lb, av 1½lb. Dt £8 + £2 per fish, 5 fish limit. Barbless hooks, no tandem lures. 12 rods per day. Contact Powell's *(see below).* Good fishing in **Lodge Pool,** tench and carp. Tackle shops: Powells, 28 Mount Pleasant, tel: 62669; Corn Stores, Headless Cross. Hotels: Royal, Southcrest.

Alvechurch (Worcs). Barnt Green FC has rights on **Upper and Lower Bittell Reservoirs, Arrow Pools** and **Canal feeder. Lower Bittell** and **Mill Shrub** trout (fly only) remainder coarse fish. Guest tickets issued by members.

STOUR (tributary of Avon): Coarse fish, trout, mostly preserved.

Shipston (Warwick). Shipston-on-Stour AC has water; members only. Knee Brook (2½m S); landowner issues ticket. Hotel: George. Birmingham AA has Stour fishing at Milcote.

LEAM (tributary of Avon): Coarse fish.

Eathorpe (Warwick). Coventry Godiva AS

has fishery here; coarse fish. Good winter fishing; st. Dt for fishing at Newbold Common, Avon confluence, from Frosts, Bath St, Leamington. Red Lion waters, **Hunningham**, from Red Lion, 0926 632715.

HAM BROOK (tributary of Leam): Coarse fish.

Fenny Compton (Warwick): Good pike, bream, tench, roach in **Oxford Canal** (no longer London AA water). **Claydon.** Stoneton House Lake, 2½m NE.

SOWE (tributary of Avon): few fish.

Coventry (W Midlands). Excellent trout and coarse fishing on **Packington Estate. Meriden.** More than five miles of river fishing and 160 acres of lakes. Rainbow and brown trout; also coarse fishery 2m off. *(For details see Midlands (reservoirs and lakes)).* Coventry AA has extensive fishing on rivers, canals and reservoirs and coarse fishing in **Trent, Nene, Thames** and **R Anker.** Day tickets for some of these may be had from tackle shops in Coventry area or hon sec. Canal waters include stretches on **Coventry Canal** and **Oxford Canal.** Dt £4 from bailiffs for Assn's **Napton Reservoirs,** noted bream, carp, tench and roach water, also pike to 22lb. Tackle shops: W H Lane & Son Ltd, 31/33 London Road, Coventry CV1 2JP (licences and assn cards); Harrisons Fishing Tackle, 467 Holyhead Rd; Bennett's, 153 Station Rd East; Tusses Fishing Tackle, 360 Aldermans Green Rd; Angling Centre, 55 Mill St, Bedworth.

BRAUNSTON CANAL: Coarse fish; sport only fair.

TEME: Trout and coarse fish, with a few salmon; grayling returning slowly. Very large barbel, strong tackle recommended. Trout in upper reaches.

Worcester (Worcs). Worcester St John's AS has some water. Worcester and Dist UAS has Knightwick, Broadwas, Cotheridge.

Broadwas (Worcs). Trout, grayling, chub, dace. Birmingham AA has stretch of left bank here and at Eardiston, 1¼m.

Leigh Court (Worcs). Trout, chub, dace, grayling, pike, perch, salmon. Bransford AS and local clubs rent Leigh to Powick; members only.

Tenbury (Worcs). Good trout, grayling, coarse fish. Salmon run from Feb to end of season, following removal of obstructions at Worcester (April, May, June best). Peacock Inn has ½m one bank

(mainly bottom and spinning water). Dt for 300 yds right bank, Burgage Recreation Ground from attendant. Tenbury FA has 1m stretch of south bank a little to the west of town, and 2m stretch to west of Knighton. Limited dt £7, fly only; bottom fishing available. Tickets from Mr Bill Drew, 42 Teme St, Tenbury Wells. Dt for ¾m at **Ashford Bowdler** (near Ludlow) from Mrs Wall. For **Kyre** carp pool, apply S Lewis, 2 Severnside, Bewdley. Hotels: Royal Oak, Swan, Crow.

Ludlow (Salop). Trout, grayling, chub, dace, roach, perch, pike. Ludlow AC has 400 yds right bank d/s of Dinham Bridge, 1m right bank u/s of Dinham Weir; dt from C W A *(below)* or C Jones, Mitre House, Lower Corve St, Ludlow. Tickets for Little Hereford, right bank d/s of bridge, A Jones, Westbrook Farm, 0584 711280. Birmingham AA has 1m here, Ashford Carbonnel, Eastham and Lindridge. **Ledwyche Brook,** 1½m E; trout, grayling, chub, etc; landowners sometimes give permission on this water. Birchfield Pools, the Birchfields, Upper Rochford, WR15 8SR, tel: 0584 79 236: trout fishing, dt £6, 2 fish limit, extra charge per lb caught. Delbury Hall Trout Fishery, Diddlebury SY7 9DH, tel: 058 476 267: dt £18, 2 fish limit. Tackle shops: C W A, Upper Galdeford; leisure Needs, Broomfield Rd. Hotels: The Feathers, Angel, Bull, Bull Ring Tavern, Charlton Arms, and Exchange.

Bromfield (Salop). Trout, grayling, chub, pike, all water strictly preserved by Earl of Plymouth Estates, who also own some 5m of **Corve.**

Bucknell (Salop). Trout, grayling, chub; preserved by landowners. Redlake Brook; trout and eels.

Knighton (Powys). Trout; strictly preserved except for 1m free to licence-holders. Accom. with fishing, Mr Habersham, tel: Craven Arms 3314 (office hours), also at Red Lion, Llanfair Waterdine, on Teme (tel: 528214). For brown trout, fly fishing pool nr **Llangunllo**, G Morgan, tel: 054781 219. Farmhouse accom available. Permits for **Elan Valley** fishing from Mr R Potts, 19 Station Rd. Licences from Prince & Pugh, 23 Broad St. Hotels: Swan, Norton Arms.

ONNY: Good trout, grayling, chub, etc.

Plowden (Salop). Trout, chub; strictly private. Plowden Club has 4m running through Plowden Estate.

Craven Arms (Salop). Grove Estate water,

N of Craven Arms, 1½m. Onny, 3½m. Quinney and Byne Brooks, preserved and strictly keepered by Midland Flyfishers; trout, grayling; members only; no tickets; club also has water from Stokesay Castle Bridge to Bromfield. Stokesay Pool; pike, chub. Bache Pool, Bache Farm; carp; dt from farm. Dt for trout and grayling fishing on 150 yards of Onny from Mrs Maund, 1 Onny Cottage, The Grove.

SALWARPE: Trout, coarse fish. Birmingham AA has 1,300 yds at **Claines.**

Droitwich (Worcs). Trout above, coarse fish below; leave from landowners. Severn 6m W. Droitwich and District AS has water at **Holt Fleet;** dt from hon sec to members' guests only. Noted chub waters. Society also has **Heriotts Pool** (large carp). Dt 80p on site. Some coarse fishing in Droitwich Canal, £1 tickets on site. Some local clubs are: Barley Mow, 0905 771388; Red Lion, 0905 774749; Working Mens, 0905 774683, Railway, 0905 770965. Tackle shop: Droitwich Fishing Tackle, 27 High St.

Bromsgrove (Worcs). Tardebigge Reservoir rented to Bourneville Club (messrs Cadburys) for many years. Limited st for local anglers. Upper and Lower Bittel Reservoirs owned by Barnt Green FC; members only *(see also Arrow-Alvechurch).* Hewell Grange Lake; permits for local clubs. (See also Worcester and Birmingham Canal). Tackle shops; Bromsgrove Angling, 54 Broad St, Sidemoor; Roy Huin, 138 Worcester Rd.

STOUR: Once heavily polluted, but fish now returning in some areas, principally lower Stour.

Stourbridge (Worcs). **Staffordshire and Worcestershire Canal;** coarse fish. Tackle shop: Riley's, Lower High Street (see also canal).

Brierley Hill (W Midlands). Stour, 3m S, polluted. **Himley Park Lake;** coarse fish; Dudley Corpn issues dt. Clubs: Brierley Hill AC (no water) and various works clubs. Tackle shop: Black Country Tackle, 51 High St.

Dudley (W Midlands). Lakes: Pensnett Grove Pool, Middle Pool, Fenns Pool, 3m SW *(see Brierley Hill).* **Netherton Reservoir;** Himley Park Lakes and Common Pool, 4m W. Plenty of fishing in canals within 6m radius. Lodge Farm Reservoir; Dudley Corporation. At Parkes Hall, **Coseley,** 2½m away, is good pool for which dt can be had; coarse fish (Dudley Corporation). Some local clubs are:

Dudley AS (0384 831924); Dudley AF (0384 294016); Cross Keys AC, 0384 259147. NRA licences from Val's Pets, 100 Childs Avenue, Sedgley. Tackle from Hingley's, 46 Wolverhampton St, Dudley.

SMESTOW (tributary of Stour): Polluted.

Wolverhampton (W Midlands). Smestow, 2m W; polluted. Some fishing in **Penk** at Penkridge. Whitmore Reans AS preserves water on Severn at Womborne, 3m canals. Most local water on Severn held by Birmingham AA; permits from tackle shops, Patshull Pool, Pool Hall (2m away). Lakes at Himley Park have dt £2.50. Further information from local tackle shops: Fenwicks, Pitt Street; Catchers Angling, 386 Bilston Rd; Fenwick's, Pitt St; A & B Tackle, 29 Lower St, Wednesbury.

TERN: Coarse fish, some trout.

Telford (Salop). St Georges & Dist Assn have water at Walcot, Wellington. Tickets from Telford Tackle, St Georges. Airfluid Hydraulic AC have Little Bolas stretch, dt from Paint & Tool Stores, Wellington, Telford. Tackle shop: Telford Tackle, Church St, St Georges, Telford.

Crudgington (Salop). A few trout and coarse fish. White Swan Piscatorials *(see Twyning-Avon, Severn)* have a fishery here. Cheshire AA have ¾m.

Hodnet (Salop). Tern. 1m E; a few trout and coarse fish. Strine Brook, 2m E. Lakes: Rose Hill Ponds, 4m NE. **Hawkstone Park Lake,** 3½m; excellent tench and carp water (40lb bags not uncommon) and large roach, rudd, pike and eels; private preserve of Wem AC, membership closed.

Market Drayton (Shrops/Staffs). Trout. Approx. 2m of river stocked weekly with r and b trout. Tern Fisheries Ltd, Broomhall Grange, M Drayton TF9 2PA, tel: 0630 653222; fax 657444. St £175, dt £12, ½ day £9. eve £6. At **Great Sowdley,** 7m SE, are canal reservoirs; Stoke AS; perch, pike, roach, tench, carp. Stoke AA has Tyrley Pool. Market Drayton AC fishes Shropshire Union Canal at Knighton, Bridges 45-47 dt £1.50 on bank. Warrington AA controls 2⅓m of **Roden** at **Shawbury.** Licences from Coopers Sports, Queen Street. Hotels: Lamb; Corbett Arms.

MEESE (tributary of Tern); Trout, coarse fish.

Newport (Salop). Meese, 1m N; trout; private. Lakes: Chetwynd Park Pond, 1m N.

A good day on Blagdon draws to a close. *Photo: J. Wilshaw.*

Minton's, Limekiln and Wildmoor Pools, 3m S. Moss Pool, 1½m NE. Whitmore Reans CAA has 2m of right bank at Wood Farm, **Caynton.** Park AC has good coarse fishing water on Grand Union Canal, with carp to 20lb, bream to 5lb, perch to 4lb: dt £2 on bank. Tackle shop, Newport Tackle, 91A High St. Hotels: Bridge Inn; Fox & Duck.

REA: Trout, grayling; preserved but leave sometimes given.

Minsterley (Salop). Trout, grayling, Minsterley Brook. Habberley Brook, 3m SE. Lake: Marton Pool, 7m SW. **Lea Cross;** Warrington AA fishes on 1,000 yds stretch.

SHELL BROOK (tributary of Roden):

Ellesmere (Salop). Shell Brook, 2m NW; preserved. Halghton Brook, 4m N. Roden, 6m SE. Lakes: **Ellesmere Meres,** noted for bream (12lb plus). Ellesmere AC (st £10), issues wt £5, dt £1.50 for **Whitemere** and **Blakemere** (bank fishing only). Sunday fishing is allowed. Boats available on most assn waters for members only. Ellesmere AC members may fish 4m stretch of **Shropshire Union Canal;** coarse fish. Tickets from tackle shops: Clay & Sons, 5a Scotland Street; Steve's Tackle, High St, Ellesmere. Hotels: Black Lion, Bridgewater, Red Lion (Ellesmere AC HQ); tickets *(see also Shropshire lakes).*

PERRY: Trout, preserved.

Baschurch (Salop). Perry, 1m W; trout; some leave from landowners. Lakes: Birch Grove, 1½m NE. Berth Pool, 1m NE. Fennymere Pool, 2m E. Marton Pool, 2m NE.

Ruyton Eleven Towns (Salop). Warrington AA fishes on Platt Mill Farm stretch.

VYRNWY; Provides sport with trout, grayling, coarse fish and salmon.

Llanymynech (Salop). Trout, salmon, grayling, roach, perch, pike, eels, chub, barbel, etc. Oswestry AC has water here, members only, £10 st, conc. For Lord Bradford's water at Lower House Farm inquire of agent, Llanymynech. Phoenix AC has ¾m at Domgay Farm, and **R Lugg** at Moreton, dt £2. Contact Hon Sec. Tackle shop: Brian's Tackle, North Rd, Canalside, tel: 0691 830027, which supplies Montgomery AA tickets. Other hotels: Bradford Arms, Cross Keys, Dolphin. Good trout fishing at **Lake Vrynwy** *(see lakes in Welsh section).*

Llansantffraid (Powys). Warrington AA has water here on Vyrnwy and **R Cain,** on

Vrynwy at **Four Crosses,** and **Cross Keys.** Cheshire AA has Myliniog Farm stretch.

Meiford (Powys). Montgomeryshire AA has water; here and at **Maesbrook;** restricted to 12 rods; dt 60p from hon sec.

MORDA (tributary of Vyrnwy): mostly trout, but some coarse fish in lower reaches.

Oswestry (Salop). Most river fishing preserved. Lloran Ganol Farm, **Llansilin** (tel: 0691 70286) offers accommodation with fishing; also Woran Isaf, **Wansilin** SY10 7QX, with trout lake (tel: 0691 70253). Oswestry AS has coarse fishing pools, st £10. Fawnog Fishing Lake, **Porthywaen,** well stocked with r and b trout. Tel: 0691 828474. Turfmoor Fishery, mixed, **Edgerley;** tel: 074381 512. West Lake, 2½ acres, stocked r and b trout fishing, fly only. Dt £14, ½ day terms. Domgay Rd, Four Crosses, **Llandrinio** SY22 6SJ, tel: 0691 831475. Tackle shops: Custom Rods, 65 Church St; Guns & Ammo, 95 Beatrice St; Brians Angling Supplies, North Rd, Wanymynech. Accom. with fishing: lloran Ganol Farm, Llanisil, 0691 70287: private lake. Hand Hotel, Llanarmon D C. 0691 76666.

TANAT (tributary of Vyrnwy): Trout (good average size), chub and grayling, but fewer than there used to be.

Llan-y-Blodwel (Salop). Horseshoe Inn has 1½m (dt £3), 3 rods per day, fly only, and Green Inn, Llangedwyn, has short stretch; dt issued (3 rods only); fly only.

Llanrhaiadr-y-Mochnant (Powys); trout; free. Tanat, 1m; trout, grayling, chub, etc; 6m from Llangedwyn to Llangynog strictly preserved. No dt.

CAIN (tributary of Vyrnwy): Trout, coarse fish.

Llanfyllin (Powys). Trout. Hotel: Bodfach Hall, which caters for fishermen and has 200 yds. Guests may fish adjoining ¼m free of extra charge. Warrington AA has two stretches near **Llansantffraid.**

BANWY (tributary of Vyrnwy): Trout, grayling, chub, pike, dace and chance of salmon here and there.

Llanfair-Caereinion (Powys). Montgomeryshire AA has right bank downstream from town bridge to boundary fence; mainly trout, some chub and dace. At **Cyffronydd** Warrington AA has 610 yds. 700 yds right bank at **Neuadd Bridge;** dt from Mr Edwards, Neuadd Bridge Farm, Caereinion. **Maesmawr Hall Lake** lies at

Guilsfield, Welshpool. Course fishing for pike, bream, roach, etc. Limited permits £2.50 from Maesmawr Hall. Hotel: Wynnstay Arms.

Llangadfan (Powys). Trout; Montgomeryshire AA has good stretch; dt from hon sec.

SHROPSHIRE LAKES

ELLESMERE LAKES. Fishing station: **Ellesmere.** Excellent coarse fishing in Ellesmere (noted for bream), **Crosemere, Newton Mere, Blakemere, Whitemere** (bream of 12lb 4oz taken). Controlled by Ellesmere AC who issue dt £1, bank fishing only, on **Blakemere.** Dt also for **Hardwick Pool** (1m) noted tench water

from Clay, 5a Scotland Street.
WALCOT LAKES. Lydbury North, 3m NE of Clun. Two extensive lakes, one controlled by Birmingham Anglers' Assn. Tench, pike and other coarse fish. *For membership details see Birmingham, under Rea (tributary of Trent).*

SOMERSET (streams, lakes and reservoirs)
(For close seasons, licences, etc, see South Western Region NRA, p16)

AXE. Rises on Mendips and flows 25m NW to Bristol Channel near Weston-super-Mare. A few trout in upper reaches and tributaries, but essentially a coarse fish river, containing a mixture of the usual species, with roach now predominating.
Weston-super-Mare and Bleadon (Som). North Somerset AA (which includes Weston-super-Mare) has water on Axe from below Clewer to Bean Cross, excluding just u/s of Crab Hole; **Brue** at Mark, near **Highbridge, South Drain** from Gold Corner to Edington Bridge, several ponds, stretches of **Old Glastonbury Canal, Old Bridge River, New Blind Yeo, Cheddar Yeo, Congresbury Yeo, Kenn, South Drain** and **North Drain,** Newtown Lake, Apex and Walrow Ponds, together with some smaller rivers. Cheddar AC has 6m stretch upstream of **Clewer** to Westbury Moor, and **Hixham Rhyne.** Inquire hon sec. Wessex Federation have **Parrett** from Thorney to Yeo, and below Langport. Tackle shops: Colings Angling Centre, 11 Nightingale Court, Mead Vale, Worle, Weston-super-Mare; Weston Angling Centre, Locking Road. Many hotels *(see Sea Fishing Stations).* BB&WA has water below **Clewer.**
BRICKYARD PONDS: Pawlett. BB&WA tench fishery. St from hon sec or tackle shops *(see Bristol).*
BRISTOL RESERVOIRS:
Chew Valley, Blagdon and **Barrow** reservoirs provide some of the best lake trout fishing in Europe, with a total annual catch of 46,000 fish of high average size. Season and day tickets available. All fishing is fly only. Limits are four brace

per day, two brace per evening bank permit at Chew. NRA licence required for all waters. Details as follows:
Barrow Reservoirs - Barrow Gurney. Open April to Oct 15; brown and rainbow trout; from Bristol Water *(see Chew Valley Lake),* fly only.
Blagdon Lake - Blagdon. Open April to Oct 15; noted brown and rainbow trout water.
Chew Valley Lake - Chew Stoke. Open April to Oct 15; noted brown and rainbow trout water where fish run large. For all waters apply to: Bristol Waterworks Company, Recreations Department, Woodford Lodge, Chew Stoke, Bristol BS18 8XH (Chew Magna 332339). Bank dt from self-service kiosks at all waters. Reduced charges for boats after 3.00 pm. Concessions for jun (under 17), OAP and registered disabled. Prices, incl VAT, are as follows: Blagdon, Chew and the Barrows, st £450 (concessionary £270), junior, £198; dt £11, conc £9, jun £5.50. Chew and the Barrows, st £360 (£215 conc, £160 Jun), dt (bank), £9, £7 conc, £4.50 junior. Barrows only, st £245, conc £147, jun £110; dt (bank), £7.50, £6, £4. Dt (boat), Blagdon (rowing), £21.50 to £14; Chew (motor), £27 to £17.
Cheddar Reservoir - Cheddar. Coarse fishery managed by Cheddar AC. St £15, £7.50 conc, dt £5, £3, from Broadway House Caravan Park, opposite reservoir.
WESSEX WATER RESERVOIRS, North Division managed by the Production Manager (West), Quay House, The Ambury, Bath BA1 2YP. South Division, by Production Manager (South), 2 Nuffield Road, Poole, Dorset BH17 7RL. The

North Division, Sutton Bingham by South Division. Licence-fee included in permit charge: concessions for jun and OAP. St from above addresses; dt from dispensing units at reservoirs. There is a season ticket covering Clatworthy, Sutton Bingham, Hawkridge: £300, £240 conc. Dt £10, conc £8. Boat £8 (2 anglers max), outboard £15. Limits: 4 fish on st, 5 fish on dt, 2 fish on evening ticket.

Clatworthy Reservoir. 12m from **Taunton** in Brendon Hills; 130 acres brown and rainbow trout; fly only; 2¼m bank fishing. Season March 18-Oct 14. Tel: 0984 23549.

Durleigh Reservoir. 2m W of **Bridgwater.** 77 acres; coarse fishing. Tel: 0935 873087 for information.

Hawkridge Reservoir. 7m W of Bridgwater. 32 acres. Brown and rainbow trout; fly only. Season March 17-Oct 14. No boats. Tel: 0278 671840.

Otterhead Lakes. About 1m from **Churchingford** nr Taunton. Two lakes of 2¾ and 2 acres; brown and rainbow trout; fly only; no boats. St £147, dt £7. Season March 18-Oct 14.

Sutton Bingham Reservoir. 3m S of Ye-

ovil. 142 acres. Brown and rainbow trout; average 1¼lb; fly only; season March 17-Oct 14. Tel: 0935 872389.

CHARGOT WATER, Luxborough. 3 ponds. Trout; fly only.

DONIFORD STREAM (Swill River at Doniford) and **WASHFORD RIVER, Taunton.** Trout; strictly preserved.

HORNER WATER. On National Trust Holnicote Estate, Selworthy TA24 8TJ; upstream from Packhorse Bridge, Horner, to Pool Bridge, approx 2½m; fly fishing, small wild trout. Dt £1 from Horner Tea Garden.

WIMBLEBALL RESERVOIR. 4m NE of Dulverton. Rainbow and brown trout largest 10¼lb. 374 acres. Fly only. Season May 1-Oct 31. SWW water. Dt £8.50 evening £5, boats £5.50. Allenard boat for disabled. Concessions jun and OAP. 5 fish limit. Tackle shop: L Nicholson, High St, Dulverton. Hotel: Carnarvon Arms.

YEO. Fishing station: **Congresbury.** Tidal, good fly water for trout; a few coarse fish. BB&WA and N Somerset AA have various short stretches in area.

STOUR (Dorset)

(For close seasons, licences, etc, see South Western Region NRA, p16)

Rises in Wiltshire Downs and flows through Dorset, joining Hampshire Avon at its mouth at Christchurch. Noted coarse fishery (large barbel, chub, roach, dace and pike are common), salmon up to Wimborne, trout and grayling patchily distributed. Salmon not numerous, but large. River best for coarse fish in winter.

Christchurch (Dorset). Avon and Stour. Salmon, pike, perch, chub, roach, tench, dace. Christchurch AC has many miles of Stour, Avon, plus numerous gravel pits, lakes and ponds. Limited dt available for lower Stour and harbour, and Lifelands stretch of Hants Avon, Ringwood, from Davis (address below). Club membership, £66 pa, juv and OAP, half. **Hordle Lakes,** 1m from New Milton; 5 lakes of total 5 acres, coarse fishing. Dt £3 from Davis (below). Coarse fishing can be had on Royalty Fishery waters *(see Avon).* Sea fishing from Mudeford in Christ-

church Bay is fair. Tackle shops: Pro Fishing Tackle, 258 Barrack Road; Davis Fishing Tackle, 75 Bargates; Yesterday Tackle, 42 Clingan. Hotel: King's Arms, Christchurch.

Throop (Dorset). Throop fisheries; 5½m of top quality coarse fishing; preserved. Carp to 18¼lb, pike to 27lb, barbel to 11½lb, chub to 6½lb, roach to 3lb in 1990. Also a mill pool stocked with roach, bream, carp and tench. Coarse fishing: st £71, ft £33.25, wt £19, dt £4.75 (reduced rates for OAP and jun; special rates for clubs: booking essential).

Fishing available?

If you own, manage, or know of first-class fishing available to the public which should be considered for inclusion in **Where to Fish** *please apply to the publishers (address in the front of the book) for a form for submission, on completion, to the Editor. (Inclusion is at the sole discretion of the Editor).*

Throop Fisheries own holiday cottage for family summer lets, overlooking river. Disabled facilities. Tackle and bait shop open throughout season. For tickets, licences and all inquiries apply to Glen Sutcliffe, Manager, South Lodge, Hold-enhurst Village, Bournemouth. Tel 0202 35532, fax 0202 395532.

Hurn Bridge (Dorset). Stour and Moors; no angling. Preserved now as a bird sanctuary.

STOUR (Dorset) - Tributaries

Wimborne (Dorset). Good chub, roach, dace and pike. Some trout, small runs of salmon and sea trout. Red Spinner AS has water at Barford and Eyebridge; about 9m in all; members only. Wimborne & Dist AC has about 10m of Stour in Wimborne, Longham and Charlton Marshall areas; nine coarse fish and two trout lakes plus 2m of trout stream. Membership £30 pa, from treasurer Mr B Heap, 76 Higher Blandford Rd, Broadstone, Dorset. Wt £20, dt £5, conc, from hon sec (tel: 0202 658703), who will answer all queries about club. Tackle shop: Wessex Angling Centre 321 Wimborne Rd, Oakdale, Poole. Hotels: Griffen, King's Head, Three Lions, Greyhound.

Sturminster Marshall (Dorset). Southampton PS has about 2m here. Coarse, a few trout; dt £3 from Minster Sports, Wimborn Minster; ten venues available. The Old Mill Guest House, Corfe Mullen, now lets to Wimborne AC, day tickets £5 from local tackle shops. Dt on site available for Dorset Springs, Sturminster Marshall, 0258 857653, 3 acre stocked coarse fishery.

Shapwick (Dorset). Coarse fish. Southampton PS has several miles of fishing here; dt £3, conc, from Minster Sports, Wimborne Minster.

Blandford Forum (Dorset). Fine roach, chub, dace, perch, bream, carp and pike; good all year. Durweston AS has fishing. St £20, dt £5, from C Light, 4 Water Lane, Durweston, Blandford. Dt from Durweston Stores. Blandford and Dist AC have most fishing from **Durweston** Bridge to **Crawford** Bridge (tickets for Bryanston school stretch £3, £1 conc) and 2 coarse lakes at **Buckland Newton**. St £19, dt £2 (lakes) from hon sec or A Conyers (tackle shop), West Street. Also club membership forms and NRA licences (Tel: 02584 2307). Other clubs with fishing in area: Durweston AC, Ringwood AC.

Sturminster Newton (Dorset). Chub, roach, dace, pike, perch, tench, bream; fishing good. Sturminster and Hinton AA has 7m above and below town and 2 lakes at Stoke Wake, with tench. St £10. For wt £10 and dt £3 apply to Harts Garden Centre, or Roses Garage, both Sturminster Newton. Hotel: White Hart.

Stalbridge (Dorset). Stalbridge AS (membership £10 pa) has 2m of Stour, 2m on **Lydden** and 2 lakes for members only at **Buckland Newton**. Wt £15, dt £2 (jun ½ price) from Corner Cottage Tackle Shop.

Gillingham (Dorset). Trout and coarse fish; Gillingham and Dist AA has fishing, with dt £2 available from tackle shops or Suttle, Chemist. Assn membership £22, ½ conc. Coarse fishing in **Turner's Paddock Lake** is for members only. Hotels: Royal, Red Lion.

Stourton (Wilts). **Stourhead New Lake** on Stourhead (western) Estate at Stourton, near Mere. Now a fly fishing syndicate water, no day tickets available.

MOORS: As Allen.

Verwood (Dorset). Allen and Moors. Moors trout in parts, otherwise mainly roach; Ringwood club has water.

STOUR (Kent)

(For close seasons, licences etc, see Thames Region NRA, p18)

Rises in two arms north-west and south-east of Ashford, where they join. From junction river flows about 30m north-east and east to sea beyond Sandwich. Below Canterbury, good roach fishing with fish to 2lb common, bream to 6lb and pike over 20lb. Trout fishing restricted to club members in upper reaches.

Sandwich (Kent). River fast-flowing from Minster to Sandwich (Vigo Sluice); good fishing for bream and roach; few perch and tench; sea trout and grey mullet. Free fishing from quay and from Ropewalk. Private fishing from Richborough Road, upstream. Sandwich and Dist AA has Reed Pond (now private), **Stonar Lake**

(stocked, carp and roach) and North and South Streams, **Lydden.** Tackle shops: Pretts, The Chain. Hotel: Bell.

Grove Ferry. Stour and Little Stour. Betteshanger Colliery Welfare AS has 6m on Stour from **Plucks' Gutter** to **Stonar.** Roach, bream and mullet (Red Lion stretch, June-Aug). Society also has stretch at **Minster.** Tickets from hon sec, Red Lion or bailiff on bank.

Canterbury (Kent). Trout, coarse fish. Free within city boundary, except for municipal gardens stretch. River from city boundary to **Grove Ferry** private for members of Canterbury & Dist AA. St £33, ½ price conc, dt £3 for stretch from Grove Ferry Bridge to Plucks' Gutter, from bailiff on bank. Mid Kent Fisheries, Chilham CT4 8EE, tel: 0227 730668 have Stour coarse fishing here (St £80, conc), and brown trout fly fishing at **Chilham.** Dt for fly fishing is £35-£18, strictly in advance. Stour and Trenchley Lakes, fine coarse fishing, and **Fordwich Lake,** members only. **Chilham Lake,** 27 acre coarse fishery, dt from Odsal House, tel: 0227 455999. **Honeycroft Fisheries,** 7 acre coarse lake, large carp. Tel 0732 851544. Tackle shops: Greenfield's Rod and Gun Store, 4/5 Upper Bridge Street; Kent Angling, St Georges Place. Hotels: County; Falstaff; George and Dragon.

Wye (Kent). Pike, roach, etc; private but some permission from owners. Hotel: King's Head.

Ashford (Kent). Ashford AS holds **River Stour** between **Ashford** and **Wye** (members only) and **Royal Military Canal;** 16m between **Iden Lock** and **West Hythe Dam.** Coarse fish; wt and dt. Water level fluctuates during winter due to land drainage, thus making fishing at times difficult. Cinque Ports AS controls 4½m of Royal Military Canal from Seabrook Outfall, Hythe, to Giggers Green, Ashford. St £15 (+ entrance fee £7.50, conc), dt £2, conc 50p, from bailiff. Ashford Working Men's Club has a pit; good tench, carp, rudd; members only; no dt. Chequer Tree Trout Fishery is at **Bethersden,** tel: 0233 820383. Dt £15 to £6.50. Licences, tuition, tackle hire and camping facilities on site. Coarse dt £2. Tackle shops: Ashford Angling Centre, 36 Stanhope Square; Denn's Tackle, Dymchurch Rd, Hythe. Hotels: County, Kent Arms.

LITTLE STOUR: Same fish as main river but overgrown in places. Most fishing now private.

WANTSUM. Coarse fish. Wantsum AC has water from sea wall between Reculver and Minnis Bay to Chambers Wall Farm at St Nicholas-at-Wade, and on Stour at Minster. Left of car park at R Wantsum members only, otherwise dt £2, conc £1, on bank. Membership £20, conc £5. Tackle shop: Kingfisheries, 34 King Street, Margate.

STOUR (Suffolk)

(For close seasons, licences etc, see Thames Region NRA, p18)

Coarse fish river forming border between Suffolk and Essex. Some sea trout in semi-tidal waters below Flatford.

Manningtree (Essex). Tidal; roach, dace, perch, pike and occasional sea trout (fish of 9lb caught). Lawford AC has stretch at **Cattewade** (A137 bridge). Tickets available. Dt from bailiff for Elm Park, Hornchurch and Dist AS stretch between club notices at **Flatford Mill.** Hotel: White Hart.

Nayland (Suffolk). Bream, chub, dace, perch, pike, roach, tench. Colchester APS has water here and at **Wormingford, Boxted, Langham** and **Stratford St Mary.** New membership £41.71 incl £10 entry, to Box 1286, Colchester CO2 8PG. No dt. Colchester APS has rights at Boxted; no tickets. Colnes AS has stretches at **Little Horkesley.** Dt from P Emsom,

Tackle Shop, Earls Colne.

Bures (Essex). Colnes AC has stretch. Dt from Emson, Tackle Shop, Earls Colne. London AA controls a good deal of water here and in **Clare, Cavendish** and **Sudbury** areas. Also **Bures Lake;** members only, but some waters available to associates at Bures. Moor Hall and Belhus AS has 2 excellent lakes of 5 and 7 acres at **South Ockenden.** Members only.

Henny Bridge (Essex). Great Cornard AC fishes from Henny Bridge to Henny Weir: hon sec P Franklin, 48 Queensway, Gt Cornard, Suffolk.

Sudbury (Suffolk). 7 miles of fishing at Sudbury and Gt Cornard controlled by Sudbury & Dist AA. Bream, roach, chub, dace, tench, carp, perch, pike, barbel. Membership £25, conc. Tickets from bailiff or tackle shops: The Tackle Box, North St; Stour Valley Tackle, East St, both Sudbury. Hadleigh & Dist AS have

various stretches on Stour, R Brett and stillwaters. Membership on application, concessions. D R Warner, 5 Churchill Ave, Hadleigh, IP7 6BT.

SURREY (lakes)

BURY HILL FISHERIES. Nr. Dorking. 12½ acres, well known coarse fishery of three lakes, with tench, roach, carp, bream, pike and zander. Also good stocks of rudd, perch and crucian carp. Open all year, bank and boat fishing, toilet and refreshments, incl disabled facilities. Dt £8, one rod, second rod £4 extra. Boat: £3 extra. Evening £4. Concessions to jun, OAP. From Fishery Manager, Estate Office, tel: Dorking 883621.

ENTON LAKES. Witley. Trout fishery of two lakes, 16 acres of water, average trout weight 2½lb. Dt £25 (4 fish), boat £5 per person extra, advance booking only. Malcolm Clark, Enton Lakes, Petworth Rd, Witley, GU8 5LZ, tel: 042868 2620.

EVERSLEY, nr Sandhurst. 30 acre gravel pit with excellent fishing for tench, bream, crucian and grass carp, pike. Season ticket only, £30, conc £15, from Parade Pets & Angling, 80 High St, Sandhurst; tel; 0252 871452. A Leisure Sports fishery.

FRENSHAM PONDS. Farnham (4m). Farnham AS has rights on Great Pond leased from N T, and Little Pond, leased from Waverley Borough Council; coarse fishing; permits from hon sec and bailiff. Leisure Sport gravel pits at Yateley. Coarse fish. Tel: Chertsey 564872.

RIPLEY. Papercourt fishery, Sendmarsh. Pike, bream, tench, chub, perch, eels, roach. A Leisure Sport restricted permit fishery. St £24, ½ price conc. £4 key deposit. No day ticket. Applications to LSA, Thorpe Park, Staines Road, Chertsey, Surrey. Tel: Chertsey 564872.

SWAN LANE, Yateley. 10 acre gravel pit with general coarse fishing. A Leisure Sports fishery; dt £3, £1.50 conc, from

Parade Pets & Sports, 80 High St, Sandhurst; tel: 0252 871452.

TRILAKES. Sandhurst. Mixed fishery; well stocked with tench, carp (common and crucian, ghost), bream, rudd, roach, perch, pike, eels, trout. Open 7am to sunset Apr-Oct, 8am to sunset, Nov-Mar. Purchase dt on entry. Car park, toilets, licensed cafe: (Tel 0252 873191).

VIRGINIA WATER. Virginia Water, Johnson Pond and Obelisk Pond, Windsor Great Park fishable by season ticket only; coarse fish; st £21 (incl VAT). Early application advised in writing, to Crown Estate Office, Windsor Great Park (sae).

WILLOW PARK, Ash Vale, nr Aldershot. Three lakes of 15 acres, mixed fishery stocked with a variety of species. Dt £6, £12 double rod, from bailiff. Night t £15 from fishery, Youngs Drive, Shawfields Rd; tel: 0252 25867.

WINKWORTH LAKES. Winkworth, nr Godalming. National Trust property. Trout fishery (fly fishing and boats only) managed by Winkworth Fly Fishers. St £146, waiting list. Details from hon sec. (see Club list).

WIREMILL POOL. Nr Lingfield. Coarse fish include tench up to 6lb, bream up to 7lb, roach up to 3lb, carp up to 6lb.

YATELEY. Nr Camberley. Thirteen Leisure Sport lakes totalling 73 acres stocked with pike, carp, tench, roach and perch, bream, rudd, catfish, crucian carp. Large specimens recorded, carp to 46lb. A restricted permit fishery. St £30, day and night £60. Key deposit £4. No dt. Concessions to jun, OAP, dis. Applications to LSA, Thorpe Park, Staines Road, Chertsey, Surrey KT16 8PN. Tel: 564872.

SUSSEX (lakes and streams)

ARDINGLY RESERVOIR. Ardingly, nr Haywards Heath. 198 acre coarse fishery, open 16 Jun to 14 Mar, pike from 1 Oct dt, 1 Sept st. (only very experienced specialist pike anglers allowed, 18+.) Restocked this season with over 30,000

roach and bream, excellent coarse fishing. Enq to Nigel Roberts, The Lodge, Ardingly Reservoir, Ardingly, W Sussex RH17 6SQ. Tel: 0444 892549.

ARLINGTON RESERVOIR, Berwick, Polegate, BN26 6TF, tel: 0323 870810.

A brace of 20 pdrs. caught at Ardingly Reservoir during the winter of 1993. *Photo: N. Roberts.*

Fly fishing for rainbow trout. Information from Fishing Lodge. Dt in advance only.

BUXTED. Uckfield. Three fisheries: Buxted Park, trout and coarse, tel: 2710; Buxted Oast Farm, coarse, Mr Greenland, tel: 0835 733446; Howbourne Lake, contact Mr Cottenham, tel: 3455

CHICHESTER LAKES. Chichester (Sussex). Chichester and Dist AS has four gravel pits; roach, rudd, carp, tench, bream, chub, perch, pike. No dt, only weekly or full membership, from Hon Sec. Chichester Canal AA has 2½m of **Chichester Canal** from Chichester to Birdham/Donnington area, excluding Canal Basin. Roach, rudd, perch, carp, tench, bream, pike, eels, chub and dace. Dt £2.40, conc, from bailiffs on bank. Mixed fishery at Lakeside Village, tel: 0243 787715. Tackle shops: Southern Leisure Centre, Vinnestrow Rd; Southern Angling Specialists, 2 Stockbridge Place; Fisherman's Den, 110 London Rd, Bognor.

DARWELL WATER. At Mountfield, **Robertsbridge** (Tel: Robertsbridge 880 407); brown and rainbow trout to 6lb; 180 acres; leased from Southern Water by Hastings Flyfishers Club Ltd; st £200, dt £12.50, self vending service at fishing lodge; boats £10 day extra, to be booked 48 hrs in advance from bailiff. Fly only; limit 6 fish; season Apr 3-Oct 31. Take precise care over approach route down small lanes.

FRAMFIELD PARK FISHERY, Brookhouse Rd, Framfield, Nr Uckfield TN22 5QJ, tel: 0825 890948. Three coarse fishing lakes of 3, 1.5 and 1.5 acres, two for matches of 36 pegs each, one specimen lake with 10 pegs. Good match weights, with large tench, bream and carp. Shop on site. Bailiff will give instruction, free to juniors. Dt £6, £4 OAP, juv.

FURNACE BROOK TROUT FISHERY Nr. Herstmonceux. Brown and rainbow trout from 2lbs up. Dt £10. St available. Phone 0435 830298 or 830151 for details.

FEN PLACE MILL. Turners Hill, **East Grinstead** RH10 4QQ. 14 acres of stillwater trout fishing on three spring fed lakes nr source of R Medway. Brown and rainbow trout av 2½lb, top weight 15lb. Season Mar 6-Oct 31. All amenities. St £675 and dt £25, £15 and £10. Tel 0342 715466.

POWDERMILL WATER. Sedlescombe. 54 acres, brown and rainbow trout up to 6lb. Hastings Flyfishers Club Ltd. Bookings 0580 88407, between 8.30 and 9.30 am. For prices, see Darwell Water.

MILTON MOUNT LAKE. Three Bridges (Sussex). Crawley AS water (st £20); mostly carp; dt, Crawley AS also has Tittermus Lake (pike, tench, carp, roach, perch) and **Sandford Brook** (trout; fly only) in Tilgate Forest; Roffey Park Lake, near Colgate (carp, roach, tench, perch, gudgeon); New Pond, Pease Pottage (carp and crucian carp, tench), the Mill Pond, Gossops Green, and Furnace Lake, Felbridge (carp and crucian carp). These are for members and guests only. At **Buchan Park** nr Crawley, Crawley AS has lakes; dt £2 from hon sec; carp pike, etc.

CLIVE VALE RESERVOIRS. Harold Road: ECCLESBOURNE RESERVOIR. Hastings. Good carp, tench, roach, bream pike and rudd. Tickets issued by Hastings Clive Vale AC. St £18 from hon sec. Dt £3, jun £1.50, from all local tackle shops.

PEVENSEY LEVELS. Marshland drained by various streams into **Pevensey Haven** and **Wallers Haven;** good coarse fishing on large streams (pike, roach, rudd, perch, bream, carp and tench), most of best waters rented by clubs. Fishing stations: **Eastbourne, Hailsham, Pevensey.** Compleat Angler FC has substantial stretches on one bank of Wallers Haven, good fisheries on both banks of Pevensey Haven and water on **Langney Haven** and **R Cuckmere.** Tickets, st £25, dt £2 from hon sec or Compleat Angler, 22 Pevensey Road, Eastbourne. Good coarse fishing on Old Haven (3½m) controlled by Hailsham AA *(see also Cuckmere);* dt from hon sec. Lydd AC also has water; dt from bailiff on bank.

SCARLETTS LAKE. 3 acres, between E Grinstead and **Tunbridge Wells.** Good coarse fishing, carp incl (Free st offered to any angler beating record carp, 23lb 4oz). Dt £5 at lakeside. St £50 from lakeside or Jackson, Scarletts Lake, Furnace Lane, Cowden, Edenbridge, Kent TN8 7JJ. (Tel: 0342 850414). F/t students, OAP, jun, dis, unemployed, 50%.

WEIR WOOD RESERVOIR. Forest Row (Sussex), 1½m; **East Grinstead,** 4m; 280 acres. Re-stocked with trout for 1986 season, after some years as a coarse fishery. Fly only April 2-Oct 31, thereafter any legal rod & line method. St £275, mt £80, wt £30, dt £2 to £8. 2, 4 and 6-fish limits. Enq in writing to The Lodge, Weir

Wood Reservoir, Forest Row, Sussex. Tel: 08833 715242 (evenings). Tackle shop: Mike Wickams Fishing Tackle, 4 Middle Row, E Grinstead.

TAMAR

(For close seasons, licences etc, see South Western Region NRA, p16)

Rises in Cornwall and follows boundary between Devon and Cornwall for good part of course, emptying finally into Plymouth Sound. Holds salmon, sea trout, brown trout of fair size - pounders not uncommon - and grayling.

Milton Abbot (Devon). Endsleigh FC has 9m. Limited wt and dt (£140-£315 and £20-£45) for guests at historic Endsleigh House PL19 0PQ, tel: 0822 87248. Average salmon catch 217; 90% taken on fly. Good car access to pools. Tuition available. Apply to Manager for more details.

Lifton (Devon). Tamar, **Lyd, Thrushel, Carey, Wolf** and **Ottery;** trout, sea trout (late June to end Sept), salmon (May, to mid-October). Hotel: Arundell Arms, Lifton, Devon PL16 0AA, which has 20m of excellent water in lovely surroundings; 23 individual beats, also 3-acre trout lake, brown and rainbow trout to 9lb. Licences and tackle at hotel, fly fishing courses (beginners and semi-advanced) by two resident instructors. Dt (when there are vacancies) for S & ST £15.50-£22, according to date; lake trout £15, brown trout £13.50. Tel: 0566 784666

Fax: 0566 784494 *(see advt)*.

Launceston (Cornwall). Salmon, sea trout, trout. Permits can be obtained for seven miles of Tamar, also **Ottery, Kensey, Inney** and **Carey** from Launceston AA, which has about 16m of fishing in all. Lakes and ponds: **Stone Lake,** $4\frac{1}{2}$ acres coarse fishing, dt £1.30, tel: 083786 253. **Tredidon Barton Lake,** dt £2, tel: 056686 288. **Alder Quarry Pond,** $4\frac{1}{2}$ acres, coarse, dt, tel: 056683 444. **Dutson Water,** coarse fishing, tel: 0566 2607. Hotels: White Hart (NRA licences), Eagle House, Race Horse Inn, North Hill. Launceston Publicity Committee issue booklet listing accommodation.

Bridgerule (Devon). Farmers may give permission. **Tamar Lakes** here: SWW waters for which tickets are issued, *(See Cornwall lakes)*. Hotel: Court Barn, Clawton, Holsworthy.

ne of the most famous sporting hotels in England, the Arundell Arms has 20 miles of its own fishing on the Tamar, Lyd, Carey, Wolf and Thrushel. Delicate dry fly fishing for wild brown trout, exciting mid-summer, night seatrout fishing, salmon from mid-May and a beat of your own on some of the most beautiful moorland-fed rivers in Devon.

We also run courses for beginners and give advanced tuition on river and lake fishing.

An all-round sporting hotel that is warm and comfortable and noted for friendliness, good food and good wine.

- *AA 2 rosetted restaurant.*
- *Skilled instruction and advice.*
- *3 and 4 day beginners' courses.*
- *Stocked 3 acre lake.*
- *Shooting, hunting, riding, golf.*

Details from Anne Voss-Bark

THE ARUNDELL ARMS

Lifton, Devon
Telephone: Lifton (0566) 784666
Fax: 0566 784494

Tributaries of the Tamar

TAVY: Rises in Cranmere Pool on Dartmoor and flows about 17m before forming estuary below Buckland Abbey. Excellent salmon and sea-trout river.

Tavistock (Devon). Tavy, Walkham and Plym FC; limited membership. Salmon, sea trout and brown trout permits for visitors on main river, **Meavy**, **Plym** and **Walkham**. Spinning allowed but no natural baits. St £50, wt £25, dt £10. Brown trout only; st £30, mt £15, wt £10, dt £3. Available from Barkells, 15 Duke Street, Tavistock PL19 0BB, Moorland Greengrocery, Yelverton; DK Sports, The Barbican, Plymouth; The Keep, Tavistock. Hotels: Bedford (salmon and trout fishing on Tamar and Tavy); Endsleigh.

Mary Tavy (Devon). Brown trout; late run of salmon and sea trout. Fishing mostly privately owned; riparian owners some times give permission. Plymouth & Dist Freshwater AA has rights at **Peter Tavy** (members only, st £65 from D L Owen, tel: 0752 705033).

Yelverton (Devon). Good centre for Tavy, Walkham and Plym FC waters. Salmon, sea trout. Ticket suppliers listed under Tavistock. Hotels: Moorland Links; Rock.

WALKHAM (tributary of Tavy): Upper reaches rocky and overhung, but downstream from Horrabridge there are many nice pools. Peal run from July onwards.

INNEY: Trout.

LYD: Trout, sea trout, some salmon.

Lifton (Devon). Arundell Arms *(see advt)* has fishing for salmon, sea trout and brown trout, also on main river and other tributaries.

TAW

(For close seasons, licences etc, see South Western Region NRA, p16)

Rises on Dartmoor and flows 50m to Barnstaple Bay, where it joins estuary of Torridge. Salmon (best March-May) with sea trout (peal) from July onwards. Brown trout and good coarse fishing in places.

Barnstaple (Devon). Bass and mullet in estuary. Salmon, trout, peal, roach and dace. Salmon best March, April, May; peal July, August. Barnstaple and Dist AA has water immediately below New Bridge (some free water below this), on **Yeo** (trout and sea trout), and on pond at **Lake Venn** (carp, tench, bream, rudd, perch). Visitors' tickets for salmon, trout and coarse fisheries from local tackle shops or hon sec. Coarse fishing in ponds: visitors may become assn members which entitles them to fish ponds (Mon-Fri only). Tickets limited and not weekends or Bank Holidays. Riverton House, EX32 0QX, tel: 0271 830009, have coarse fishing open all year, large carp and other species. Dt £3. C L and Mrs Hartnell, Little Bray House, **Brayford**, have about 1m (both banks) of Bray; small trout only; dt £2. For other trout fishing see tributary Yeo. East and West Lyns, Badgeworthy Water and Heddon are accessible, as well as fishing on Wistlandpound and Slade Reservoirs. Tackle shops: The Kingfisher, 22 Castle St.

Chapelton (Devon). Salmon, peal, trout, dace. Taw mostly private down to New Bridge. Barnstaple and Dist AC water below *(see Barnstaple)*.

Umberleigh (Devon). Salmon, peal, trout; preserved. Rising Sun has almost 4m of water (eight beats) for which dt are issued when not required for residents; fly only after April 30. Sunday fishing is allowed; salmon best March, April, May, August and September; sea trout June, July, August and September. Brochure, giving charges, etc, on request. Dt £25 non-residents, £21.50 residents only *(see advt)*. Other hotel: Northcote Manor, Burrington.

South Molton (Devon). Oaktree Carp Farm and Fishery, Bottreaux Mill, EX36 3PU, tel: 03984 568, large carp, tench, rudd, roach, dt £5.

Eggesford, Chulmleigh (Devon). Fox and Hounds Hotel has 7m of private salmon, sea trout and brown trout fishing on Taw. Spinning March to May. Fly only from May 1. No fishing in Feb. St £600-£350, wt £100, dt £18.50 and £10. Salmon fishing available March-April. Full details from Hotel *(see advt)*.

Coldridge (Devon). Taw Fishing Club has water from Brushford Bridge to Hawkridge Bridge; very good trout fishing; complimentary for member guests only. St £40 + joining fee £40. Limited to 30.

Lapford (Devon). Salmon, sea trout, trout. St only, £110. Contact J O Yates, Gemini, Lanham Lane, Winchester; or R Drayton, 46 Godfrey Gardens, Bow, Crediton.

North Tawton (Devon). Trout. Burton Hall Hotel has about 4m of water here; trout; occasional sea trout and salmon. Free to guests; dt issued subject to hotel bookings. K Dunn, The Barton, also issues dt for about 1m.

Sticklepath (Devon). Trout. Dt £1 from Mr & Mrs P A Herriman, Davencourt, Taw Green, S Tawton for ½m downstream. Accommodation: Taw River Inn.

YEO (Barnstaple): Sea and brown trout. Barnstaple and Dist AA has water on Yeo, wt and dt from Barnstaple tackle shop. *(See Barnstaple).*

MOLE:

South Molton (Devon). South Molton AC has water with salmon, trout and peal on **Bray** and **Mole, Gt Rapscote**, fly only; £5 dt issued, from Mr Ducker, 2 South St, South Molton, or hon sec.

BRAY (tributary of Mole):

North Molton (Devon). Trout, sea trout, few salmon; ns South Molton, 2m. Poltimore Arms Hotel has 2m of fishing on Bray; fishing good. Cdr R H Dean, Little Bray House, Brayford, issues dt for about 1m of river.

TEES

(For close seasons, licences etc, see Northumbria and Yorkshire Region NRA, p17)

Rises below Cross Fell in Pennines, flows eastwards between Durham and Yorkshire and empties into North Sea near Middlesbrough. River suffers from pollution in the lower tidal reaches, but from Yarm upstream offers some excellent coarse fishing. Well stocked from Middleton-on-Tees down to Croft. The Tees Barrage is under construction, due for completion in 1995, and should create a much cleaner river, upstream. River tidal to Worsall.

Middlesbrough (Cleveland). River polluted. NW reservoirs **Lockwood** and **Scaling Dam** in vicinity. Stocked with trout; dt on site. Middlesbrough AA have R Tees at Over Dinsdale, trout and usual coarse fish, R Leven, R Swale nr Thirsk, Marske Reservoir and ponds. Local tackle shop: Anglers Choice, Clive Rd, who has st £16, dt £3, conc, for Middlesb. AA waters.

Stockton (Cleveland). Trout; grayling, coarse fish on one of best stretches of river. Stockton AA has over 10m at **Gainford, Winston, Dinsdale, Middleton-on-Row**, nr Darlington, **Aislaby**, nr Yarm, and on **Swale**, nr **Ainderby** (Moreton-on-Swale) and above Great Langton; membership £40, access to all waters; £20, lower reaches of Tees and Swale fishings. Juv £5.50. **Hartlepool Reservoir** is coarse fishery run by Hartlepool & Dist AC. Contact Mr J Hartland, 7 Chillingham Ct, Billingham, Teeside. Tackle shop: F Flynn, 12 Varo Terrace, Stockton; Tackle Box, Station Rd, Billingham, Stockton..

Thornaby (Cleveland). Trout, grayling and coarse fish. Thornaby AA has 1½m below Leven Beck mouth at **Ingleby Barwick** (coarse fish; tidal), 4½m at Croft (trout, grayling, dace, chub, roach, perch, pike, gudgeon), and stretches on **Leven, Wear, Eden, Swale** and **Ure**. Annual membership: £14. Concessions. No tickets but applications to secretary will be sympathetically considered. Thornaby AA are allied with Teeside & Dist AC. Tackle shops: Cleveland Angling Centre, 22a Westbury St; Walker & Ingram, 107 Parkgate, Darlington.

Eaglescliff, (Cleveland). Yorkshire bank in Yarm free fishing. **Leven** joins just below Yarm. Trout and coarse fish. Middlesbrough AA to falls; Thornaby and Yarm AA together up to Hutton Rudby. Excellent brown trout fishing; occasional sea trout.

Yarm (Cleveland). Tidal good coarse fishing; chub, dace, roach, occasional trout. Some free fishing on Yorkshire bank on NRA licence. Yarm AA, strong team club with 5½-6m tidal water, are members of Assc. of Teeside & Dist Angling Clubs, with 10m water; st £29, dt £1.50; limited dt from Yarm AA headquarters, 4 Blenavon Court, Yarm, tel: 064278 6444.

Croft (Durham). Fair head of trout, grayling and coarse fish. Free fishing for 200 yds upstream of road bridge. Thornaby AA has downstream; 7m both banks.

Darlington (Durham). Trout, grayling, coarse fish. Council water permits free to residents. Darlington Brown Trout AA has water between Middleton and Croft, also on **Swale**. Dt for members' guests only. Stockton AA has water at **Winston**.

At **Whorlton,** T J Richardson, Whorlton Farm, issues limited permits for stretch. Tackle shops (and licences): Walker & Ingram, 107 Parkgate; W P Adams Fishing Tackle & Guns, 42 Duke Street; tel: 0325 468069.

Piercebridge (Durham). Trout, grayling, dace, chub, gudgeon. Tickets available for Raby Estates water, £25 trout, £20 coarse; Estate Office, Staindrop, Darlington DL2 3NF. Otherwise preserved. Clow Beck, 3m S of Darlington; part is Darlington AC water; otherwise preserved. Forcett Park Lake, 8m SW; pike, perch; private, occasional winter Permits. Hotel: George.

Gainford (Durham). Trout, grayling, coarse fish. Up to Winston, most of the water held by Stockton AA. No tickets. Alwent Beck, 1m W; trout; private. Langton Beck, 2m N.

Barnard Castle (Durham). Trout, grayling. Free fishing on south bank d/s from stone bridge to Thorngate footbridge. Taking of salmon prohibited. M Hutchinson, Thorngate Mill, has fishing available. Barnard Castle FFC has from Tees Viaduct to Baxton Gill, near **Cotherstone;** private club water. Barnard Castle AS has from a point above Abbey Bridge to Tees Viaduct; private club water, but some dt to visitors staying locally. Darlington FFC has 2½m above and below Abbey Bridge, 1m below Barnard Castle. Water holds some big grayling; members only. Other fishing on permission from riparian owners. Grassholme, Selset, Balderhead, Blackton and Hury reservoirs, 5m NW; dt obtainable *(see Tees Valley Reservoirs).* Licences; T R & E Oliver, 40 Horsemarket. Hotel: King's Head, Market Place.

Mickleton (Durham). Trout. St £15, wt £6, dt £3 for S bank between Cronkley Bridge and Lune Fort from Cleveland Arms; J Raine & Son, Horsemarket; both Middleton-in-Teesdale.

Middleton-in-Teesdale (Durham). Trout (plentiful but small). Several miles open to dt on Raby Estate water, tel: 0833 40209 (office hours). Ferryhill AC has water, tel: 091 388 3557. Teesdale Hotel (0833 40264) offers dt on several miles of south bank. Free fishing on NRA licence at **Neasham,** Durham bank. Licences: S W Mitchell, 25 Market Place.

GRETA: Trout.

Bowes (Durham). All private fishing.

TEIGN

(For close seasons, licences etc, see South Western Region NRA, p16)

Rises on Dartmoor, 5m south-west of Chagford, and flows 30m south-east to the sea through an estuary beginning below Newton Abbot. Best known as sea trout river; salmon incidental bonus. Principal tributary is Bovey. Salmon, sea trout (peal) and brown trout. A spring river. Teign usually fishes best for salmon from late March to early June.

Newton Abbot (Devon). Salmon, sea trout, trout; preserved by Lower Teign FA from Sowton Weir to Teignbridge (excluding stretch from New Bridge to Preston Footbridge). Three separate beats. Dt (3 per beat) £10, valid for 24 hrs from sunrise. Spinning by day, at night fly only. Assn also has 3m on Bovey, members only *(see Bovey).* Tickets £10, conc, for three beats from Drum Sports *(see below).* Newton Abbot FA has six lakes at **Rackerhayes,** five at **Preston,** Bradley Ponds **Bovey Tracey** and **R Isle** at **Hambridge.** Dt for most of these waters from tackle shops. Coarse fish, including carp. **Watercress Farm,** 4 acres trout fishing, tel: 0626 852168. **Trago Mills** has 600 yds coarse fishing, dt £3, OAP, jun £2. G Mole, tel: 0626 821111. Decoy Lake, small coarse lake open all year, stocked. Tackle shops: Drum Sports, 47a Courtenay Street; Newton Angling Centre, Rydon Industrial Estate, Kingsteignton.

Chudleigh (Devon). Salmon, sea trout, trout; Lower Teign FA has water (see Newton Abbot). Dt £17 for 1m of Teign

---

Fishing available?

If you own, manage, or know of first-class fishing available to the public which should be considered for inclusion in **Where to Fish** *please apply to the publishers (address in the front of the book) for a form for submission, on completion, to the Editor. (Inclusion is at the sole discretion of the Editor).*

from Mrs C Thatcher, Ryecroft, Chris-tow, tel: 0647 52805. 2½ acre coarse lake at Finlake Woodland Village. Open 31 Mar to 31 Oct.

Chagford (Devon). Trout, sea trout, Upper Teign FA preserves about 14m in all, fly only before June 1 on some parts and whole season elsewhere; size limit 7in. Tickets: Drum Sports, 47a Courtenay Street, Newton Abbot, or Bowdens, The Square, Chagford. Salmon and sea trout tickets from Anglers Rest only, Fingle Bridge, Drewsteignton, £12. Halfstone Sporting Agency offers salmon and sea trout fishing and instruction; 6 Hescane Park, Cheriton Bishop EX6 6SP, tel: 0647 24643. Fernworthy Reservoir, 3½m.

Tributary of the Teign.

BOVEY: Salmon, sea trout, trout.

Bovey (Devon). On Bovey and Teign. Fishing above Bovey preserved by land-owners and below by Lower Teign FA. No tickets. Lakes: Tottiford and Kennick Reservoirs; trout *(see Devon lakes, streams, etc).* Borkley Leisure Caravan Park has Bluewater Pool, coarse fishing, 3 acres, dt. Bradley Small Pond open to visitors. Hotels: Manor House, one mile from North Bovey (water on Bovey and Bowden, and salmon and trout fisheries on Teign); Glebe House, North Bovey.

TEST

(For close seasons, licences etc, see Southern Region NRA, p15)

Rises from springs in the chalk near Overton, above Whitchurch and flows via Stockbridge and Romsey to enter Southampton Water. Brown and rainbow trout, salmon run as far as Romsey. The Test and Itchen Association represents virtually all riperian owners and many who wish to fish these rivers and their tributaries. The secretary maintains a register of rods to let. *(See clubs list.)* Roxton Bailey Robinson let beats on a daily, weekly and seasonal basis. 25 High St, Hungerford, RG17 0NF, tel: 0488 683222, fax: 0488 682977.

Romsey (Hants). Trout and grayling fishing good; salmon fishing good below the town, all preserved by the different land-owners. **Broadlands Estates** lets salmon rods and ½ rods, a named day per week for two for £800 and a named day for two per fortnight for £405. Trout fishing st for one rod (1 day per week) is £995 and £545 (1 day per fortnight), 2 brace, dry fly only. Trout fishing in carrier stream 1 May to 15 Oct, st £845 There is also an excellent stillwater coarse fishery of two lakes. 24 hr dt £11-£8, dt £6, evening £2.50. Golden orfe a special feature. En-quiries: Fisheries Manager, Estate Of-fice, Broadlands, Romsey S05 9ZE. Tel: 0703 739438 game fishing, or 869881/733167, coarse fishing. Dt for residents from Council Offices, Duttons Road, for Romsey Memorial Park; lim-ited to two rods daily. Salmon, few small trout, grayling, coarse fish. Good trout fishing at **Two Lakes,** near Romsey *(see Hampshire, streams, lakes, etc).* Kim-bridge Lake, 4 acres, trout fishing, boat or bank, tel: 0794 40428.

Stockbridge (Hants). Greyhound Hotel has water stocked with brown and rainbow trout; Dry fly and nymph only. Fish aver-age 3lb. St (2 rods) (one day per month) £425. Dt £50 May/June, £40 otherwise; 4 fish limit. Instruction, £30 per day. Early booking advisable as limited rods avail-able. Special fishing/accomodation pack-age can be arranged. Roy Gumbrell, tel: 0264 810833.

Awbridge (Hants). The Parsonage, Aw-bridge: St £1295 (30 day), £695 (15 day), dt £100-£90 for trout, grayling and occa-sional salmon, from Fishing Breaks Ltd, 16 Bickerton Rd, Upper Holloway, Lon-don N19 5JR, tel 071 281 6737, fax: 071 281 8151.

Houghton (Hants). Bossington Estate, Stockbridge SO20 6LT lets rods by sea-son. (Tel 0794-388265; waiting list.)

Fullerton Bridge (Hants). Trout (av 2lb 8oz). Season mid-April to end of Sept.

Tributaries of the Test

ANTON: Trout, grayling.

Andover (Hants). Anton joins Test at Test-combe Bridge. Trout and grayling; all preserved. At **Rooksbury Mill,** Rooksbury Road, a first-class trout fish-ery offering a choice of st terms, from

Presenting a dry fly with care on a 'carrier' of the River Test. Southern trout streams derive much of their character from the flow-management methods developed initially many years ago for deliberate winter-time inundation in the interests of livestock management. *Photo: Eric Chalker.*

£115 to £620, a £25 (5 fish) dt and boats available, £7 or £4 ½ day. Tel: 0264 52921 for full details. Andover AC owns Foxcotte Lake at **Charlton,** 50 to 60 pegs approx. Usual coarse species; also has access to Broadlands at **Romsey** and **Basingstoke Canal.** Dt from tackle shop John Eadies, 5b Union St or Charlton PO. **Dever Springs Trout Fishery,** 2 lakes, 7 acres and river: contact tel: 026472 592. Other Tackle shops: Cole & Son, 67 High Street, who also supply st £18, which includes Broadlands Lake fishing; Andover Angling Centre, 1 Swan Court. Hotels: Star and Garter, White Hart, Junction, George, Anton Arms, Globe Central.

PILL HILL BROOK: Trout, grayling.

Amport and Monxton (Hants). Trout and grayling. Nearly as long as Anton, but pure chalk-stream. Monxton Mill reach greatly improved and contains full head of locally bred brown trout averaging 14oz, with occasional heavier fish. Fishing preserved by landowners, who occasionally give permits. Dry-fly only.

DEVER: Trout, grayling.
Dever joins Test at Newton Stacey.

Bullington (Hants). Trout and grayling fishing. St £1295 (30 day), £695 (15 day), dt £100-£90 for trout, grayling and occasional salmon, from Fishing Breaks Ltd, 16 Bickerton Rd, Upper Holloway, London N19 5JR, tel 071 281 6737/4932, fax: 071 281 8151.

BOURNE:

St Mary Bourne (Hants). Strictly preserved. Bourne joins Test above Longparish.

THAMES

(For close seasons, licences, etc, see Thames Region NRA, p18)

Second longest river in England. Tidal reaches much recovered from pollution and fish returning in considerable numbers. Salmon are running again in modest numbers together with a few sea-trout, dace, roach, flounder and common, bream, perch, carp and smelt; rainbow trout are caught quite regularly in the freshwater tideway. River worth fishing from Southwark Bridge upstream. Downstream of this point, estuarine species such as eel, flounder, bass and even whiting may be caught. Above Teddington Lock boat traffic largely spoils sport in summer, except in weir pools, but fishing can be good early and late. River fishes well from October to March. Holds good stock of coarse fish, with excellent bream and barbel in some stretches. Perch seem to be making a welcome return toi the river throughout its length. However, the tremendous dace fishing of recent years has declined. Bream, roach and perch now dominate the lower river, above Teddington, with chub becoming more numerous the further up the river one goes. Among famous tributaries are Kennet, which comes in at Reading and is one of best mixed fisheries in England. Trout and coarse fish run large. Higher up, Coln, Evenlode and Windrush are noted trout streams, but for most part are very strictly preserved and fishing difficult to obtain. Fishing on Thames open up to City Stone at Staines. Above, permission often necessary and lock-keepers and local tackle shops should be consulted. Weir permits issued by Thames NRA. The Thames Angling Preservation Society, (membership fee £2) founded in 1838, has restocked seven tributaries - now keeps close watch on water quality and fish stocks in whole Thames basin. It is not a fishing club, but a fishery preservation society supported by anglers, membership details from secretary, A E Hodges, The Pines, 32 Tile Kiln Lane, Bexley, Kent DA5 2BB. London Anglers Association (LAA) HQ, Izaac Walton House, 2A Hervey Park Road, London E17 6LJ, has numerous fishings on Thames and elsewhere. St £21, dt £1.50 (concession to OAP and juniors), issued for some waters. Several reservoirs in which fishing is allowed (coarse fish and trout). *(See London - Reservoirs, etc).*

London Docklands. Redevelopment has led to increased angling facilities at **Shadwell, Millwall, Royal Docks** and **Southwark,** each locality with it's own angling society. Details available from London Docklands Watersports, tel: 081 515 3000 or 222 8000.

Isleworth to **London Bridge** (G London). Tidal. Dace, flounder, eel, roach, perch, with some carp and bream. Juvenile bass common at seaward end of this stretch; free from towpath or boats and foreshore throughout Central London 2 hrs each side of low tide. Fly-fishing for dace in shallows when tide is down. Reach down past Chiswick Eyot can be good for roach, dace; towpath only; free. Tackle shops: Hounslow Angling Centre, Bath Road also Colne-Wraysbury).

Richmond (G London). Half-tidal. Down to Isleworth is fishing for roach, dace, bream, perch, eel, the odd chub; free from towpath or boats (boatmen on towpath). Barnes and Mortlake AS are local club, with members only coarse lake at Barnes, st £15. In Richmond Park **Pen Ponds** hold perch, carp, bream, roach and pike. St £9.50, jun £5, under 10s free with permit holder. Apply to Park Superintendent at his office in Richmond Park, Richmond, TW10 5HS (enclose sae). Tackle shops: Hounslow Angling Centre, 267 Bath Rd, Hounslow; Ron's Tackle, 465 Upper Richmond Rd West.

Twickenham (G London). Coarse fishing;

free from boats and towpath. Deeps hold barbel, roach, bream, eel, carp. Corporation allow fishing from Radnor, Orleans and Terrace Gardens. Tackle shop: T & S Angling, 150 Heath Rd; Guns and Tackle, 81 High Street, Whitton. Hotels: Bird's Nest, White Swan.

Teddington (G London). Thames holds dace, roach, bream, eel, perch; fishable from boats but none available on spot; free fishing from towpath. Molesley Lock on NRA permit, tel: 081 979 4482. Hotels: Anglers', Clarence, Railway.

Kingston (G London). Canbury Gardens is very popular stretch and has yielded large carp, bream, perch and roach.

Hampton Court (G London). Thames, Mole; coarse fish. Good roach, dace, perch, barbel, pike, carp, chub, etc, in Molesey Weir. Barge Walk, left bank, requires a Royal Parks permit. **Bushey Park Ponds;** roach, tench, pike. **Home Park Ponds** and **Long Water,** Hampton Court, hold eels and tench; large carp in all three; permission from Park Superintendent (send sae if by post). St £9.50, £5 for OAP and young people 10-17. No night fishing. Tackle shops: E C Cheeseman, 11 Bridge Road, East Molesey.

Hampton (G London). Hampton Deeps hold bream, pike, perch and sometimes a good trout; free fishing from towpath and boats. Inns: Ye Old Red Lion, Bell.

Sunbury (Surrey). Excellent for all-round angling; free. Fine weir and weir shallows fishable on NRA permit, tel: 09327 82089; barbel, chub, dace, bream and occasional trout may be taken. Tackle shop: Tackle Up, 363 Staines Rd West, Ashford Common, sells tickets for local fisheries, trout and coarse. Hotel: Magpie.

Walton-on-Thames (Surrey). Bream, perch, dace, chub, carp and pike; perch and pike in backwater. Club: Walton AS (water on Mole, Cobham).

Shepperton (Surrey). Pike, barbel, perch, bream and carp; free; boats available. Shepperton Lock NRA fishery, tel: 09322 21840. Ashmere Fisheries, contact Mrs J B Howman, Felix Lane, tel: 0932 225445. Two Leisure Sport gravel pits, 16 acres, coarse fishing for carp, rach, chub, pike, eels, etc. No night fishing. St £20, ½ price conc. No dt. For full details phone Chertsey 564872. Hotel: Anchor.

Weybridge (Surrey). Members of Byfleet AA and five other clubs have fishing on 9 sections of **Wey Navigation** Canal from Thames Lock to Walsham Lock and have formed Wey Navigation Angling Amalgamation; dt £1.50 from bailiff. Hotels: Ship, Thames St; Lincoln Arms, Thames Street; Oatlands Parks; Blue Anchor.

Chertsey (Surrey). Pike, perch, chub, roach, bream, occasional trout; free fishing from boats and towpath. LSA, Thorpe Park, Staines Road, Chertsey KT16 8NP. Tel: 0932 564872 have 4½ acre gravel pit and 1,000m of River Bourne. Excellent tench, bream, carp, roach and pike in pit, chub, roach, dace and perch in river. St £20, ½ price jun, OAP, dis. Club: Addlestone AA, which has water at **New Haw, Wey** and **Bourne** and a gravel pit at Laleham; dt to members' guests only. Leisure Sport have two stretches of Wey at **Addlestone**, 600m total, with pike, barbel, chub, carp, roach, bream, dace, perch. St only, £18. Several boat yards. Hotels: Cricketers, Bridge.

Staines (Surrey). Good coarse fishing; free

A happy angler with a pike in the upper teens. From Lechlade to the tidewater, the Thames has always, water quality permitting, been a fine habitat for this splendid sporting species. *Photo: Bruno Broughton.*

from boats and towpath. NRA fishery at Penton Hook Lock, tel: 0784 452657, good for barbel and chub. Club: Staines AS, stretch opposite Runnymede; members only. Tackle shop: Davies Angling, 47/9 Church St.

Wraysbury (Bucks). Two Leisure Sport gravel pits, 260 acres, tench to 14lb, carp to 50lb, bream, perch, eels, large pike. St £24 and dt £2, concessions to jun, OAP, dis. LSA **Kingsmead Fishery**, 2 lakes of 80 and 6 acres with pike to 38lbs, and other coarse species. St £24. LSA also has fishery at **Horton** nr Wraysbury; syndicate membership. Specimen carp, bream, tench. Applications to LSA, Thorpe Park, Staines Road, Chertsey, Surrey KT16 8PN. Tel: 564872. **Queen Mother Trout Fishery**, Horton Rd, Horton, **Slough**. 475 acre trout fishery, st on application, dt. Tel: 0753 683605. Berkshire Fisheries Assoc. has Slough Arm of G Union Canal from **Cowley** to Slough Basin, approx 5m, excellent fishery in summer, very little boat traffic. Specimen tench and other species, and good pike fishing in winter; dt from bailiff. Tackle shop: Stows Tackle, Wexford Rd, Slough.

Windsor (Berks). Chub, barbel, bream, roach, dace, perch, pike. Fishing from south bank below Windsor Bridge and north bank to Eton-Windsor road bridge, by NRA license only. Dt issued for club waters near Maidenhead; enq tackle shops. Salt Hill AC has Clewer Meadow, Windsor, dt on bank. Old Windsor AC has Romney Island fishing to east of Windsor, Albert Bridge and Old Windsor Lock Cut. Tickets £2.50 for all three fisheries on bank or from Windsor Angling Centre. Free public fishing on right bank from Victoria Bridge u/s to railway bridge. Royal Berkshire Fishery, North St, Winkfield, tel: 0344 891101: 3 small lakes with coarse fish. Dt on bank. Marlow AC has Bray Lake, off A308. Large bream and other species. Contact Mr G Hoing, tel: 0628 522405. Fishing can be had in Windsor Great Park ponds and Virginia Water (*see Surrey lakes*). Tackle shops: Windsor Angling Centre, 153 St Leonard's Rd.

Boveney (Bucks). Coarse fish. Backwater good for pike, and weir pool for trout and barbel. Towpath free. LAA Eton Wick fishery here. Hotels: Clarence, Royal Windsor.

Bray (Berks). Weir pool good for trout, and free from boat or punt. Bray Mill tail from 1m above lock to lock cut private. Towpath free. Monkey Island Hotel caters for anglers. Tel: 0628 23400.

Maidenhead (Berks). Roach, pike, perch, barbel, dace, chance of trout. Some free fishing right bank, Maidenhead Bridge to Boulter's Lock. Hurley Lock, NRA fishery, tel: 062882 4334. Maidenhead and District AS has Left bank u/s from Boveney Lock to gardens at Dorney Reach. Permits from hon sec. Dt for clubs stretch from My Lady Ferry to gardens at Maidenhead from bailiff. Boats: Andrew Bros; Bushnell Ltd. Tackle shops: Kings, 18 Ray St; Jack Smith, 4 High Street; Burnham Angling Centre, 71A High St, Burnham.

Cookham (Berks). Cookham & Dist AC has right bank u/s of Cookham Bridge to Railway Bridge. London AA has water at Spade Oak Ferry, members only. Hotels: Ferry, Royal Exchange, King's Arms, Bell and Dragon, Crown.

Bourne End (Bucks). Wide, open water with some shallow stretches, good for fly fishing. London AA has water here. Stretch also available to associates.

Marlow (Bucks). Usual coarse fish, including barbel; good spot for Thames trout. NRA fishery at Marlow Lock, tel: 06284 2867. Marlow AC has water from Riverswood Drive to opp. first islands and left bank u/s from Marlow Bridge opp. Temple Island, and pits; tickets from Kings Tackle, 1 Ray St, Maidenhead. Free fishing d/s from Marlowe Lock to end of Riverside Drive. The Compleat Angler Hotel has fishing from grounds, free for residents, non-residents at hotel's discretion.

Hurley (Berks). London AA has fisheries at Frogmill Farm and Hurley Flats. Dt issued for 1½m. Members and associates only. Hurley Lock NRA fishery, tel: 062882 4334.

Henley (Oxon). Pike, roach, perch, tench, bream, eels. Free fishing u/s from Promenade to Cold Bath Ditch. NRA fisheries at Hambledon Lock, tel: 0491 571269, and Marsh Lock, tel: 0491 572992. Barbel and trout at Hambledon Weir. Chub fly-fishing below weir and at Marsh Lock (upstream). Remenham AS has fishing on both banks incl from Henley Bridge downstream on Berks bank to within ¾m of Hambledon Lock. Tickets from bailiff for Berkshire bank fishing only. Weir fishing controlled by Thames Conservancy, Nugent House, Vastern Rd, Reading. Oxon and Bucks bank water controlled by society for members only. Also from end of Henley Promenade upstream to Marsh Lock, bridges and meadows upstream from Marsh Lock. London AA has stretches for members. Tackle shops: Alf Parrot, 15 Thameside; Sports Centre, Greys Rd. Boats: Hobbs, Parrott. Good accommodation for anglers at Flower Pot Hotel, Aston, RG9 3DG.

Wargrave (Berks). Thames and Loddon; good coarse fishing.

Sonning (Berks); ns Twyford. Bank and boat fishing. Good stretch for Thames trout, especially Shiplake Hole. Much fishing from **Shiplake** to Sonning Bridge on Oxfordshire bank controlled by Shiplake and Binfield Heath AS; members only. Mill Tails preserved by Lord Phillimore. Guests at White Hart can fish private stretch of ½m on Berkshire bank towards Shiplake. London AA has water for members only at Shiplake, Lowfield and Mapledurham. Reading & Dist AA has Sonning Eye fishery (lake and river); dt from bailiff, Lake View. NRA fishery at Shiplake Lock, tel: 073522 3350.

Reading (Berks). Most coarse fish. Reading Borough Council controls length from opposite Caversham Court Gazebo to 1½m u/s of Caversham Bridge. The fishing from Thames-Side Promenade to Scours Lane is controlled by Thames Water. There is some free water on the **Kennet** from Horseshoe Bridge to County Weir (adjacent to Inner Distribution Road). Reading and District AA, comprising thirty eight miles of river and canal, plus thirteen lakes in Berkshire and Oxfordshire. Subscription £20.50, with concessions. Dt available on site for two Assc. waters. Farnborough AS has good trout and coarse fishing on **Whitewater** at Heckfield (8m), also 2m fly only stretch. St £30, joining fee £10. dt £4, conc. Countryside Club, 109 Upper Woodcote Road, Caversham Heights, Reading, has trout and carp fishing let on a family st basis; At Bradfield, **Pang Val-**

ley trout lake, approx 6 acres, stocked with rainbow trout. Dt £12.50, 4 fish limit, from tackle shop Turner *(see below)*. Leisure Sport has coarse fisheries available on permit at **St Patrick's Stream, Twyford** and **Theale** (52 acres), apply LSA, Thorpe Park, Chertsey, tel: 0932 564872. Tackle shops: Reading Angling Centre, 69 Tadley Angling, Padworth Rd; Thameside Fishing, 147 Caversham Rd; North'land Avenue; T Turner & Son Ltd, 21 Whitley Street. Hotels: Thameside; Thames House; Pennyfarthings, Swallowfield.

Tilehurst (Berks). Elthorne Alliance and Reading and District AA control the fishing on the Oxfordshire bank. Free fishing from towpath to Caversham *(see restrictions under Reading)*. Roebuck Hotel has private stretch on south bank. Tackle shop: Thames Valley Angling, 258 Kentwood Hill, Tilehurst.

Goring (Oxon). Pike, bream, roach, chub, perch and (in weir pool especially) barbel and a few trout; weir pool NRA fishery, tel: 0491 872687. Other fishing can be had from towpath above and below lock. London AA has R bank from Beetle & Wedge Hotel to Cleeve Lock; Gatehampton Farm fishery. Members only, but ¾m available to associates. Hotel: Leathern Bottle.

Pangbourne and **Whitchurch** (Berks). Thames and **Pang.** Trout, perch, pike, roach, bream, chub, dace. River fishes well in winter; free fishing 1½m above and below Whitchurch Bridge; good coarse fishing; boats available. Weir pool private. Pang holds trout, especially near Tidmarsh, but is strictly preserved; trout at its mouth. Pangbourne and Whitchurch AS is affiliated with Reading AA, and fishes in a number of localities, including 3m of R Kennet with good chub, barbel, roach and dace. St £23 from hon sec.

Moulsford (Berks). All coarse fish. London AA has water here; members only. Hotel: Beetle.

South Stoke (Oxon). London AA controls the water from footbridge above railway bridge down to Beetle and Wedge ferry

---

Keep the banks clean

Several clubs have stopped issuing tickets to visitors because of the state of the banks after they have left. Spend a few moments clearing up.

and second meadow below the ferry down to Runsford Hole; members only.

Wallingford (Oxon). Usual coarse fish. Local club: Jolly Anglers, who have four stretches (good bream in summer. chub in winter); st £10, wt £5, dt £2 (concessions for juniors), from Castle's, 45 St Mary's Street and Wallingford Sports Shop, 71 High Street; C & D Fishing Tackle, 12 Mill St, Wantage.

Cleeve (Oxon). Usual coarse fish. Landlord of Leathern Bottle issues dt for 1m upstream of Cleeve Lock, including ferry.

Benson (Oxon). Usual coarse fish. Club: Benson AS. Wt £5, dt £2 from E Bond, 5 Sands Way, Benson 0X10 6NG, from Benson Marina or from Hon Sec. Sundays reserved for matches. Benson Lock is NRA fishery, tel: 0491 35255.

Shillingford (Oxon). Wallingford AA has water upstream; dt from hon sec. Shillingford Bridge Hotel nr Wallingford OX10 8LZ has good pike fishing with trout, tench, dace, etc, on ¼m (both banks) reserved for guests and High Wycombe AC. Tel: 086732 8567; Fax: 086732 8636.

Little Wittesham (Berks). Thame comes in here.

Clifton Hampden (Berks). Abingdon & Oxford AA has water here, at Eynsham, Radley and Sandford; Hon Sec M J Ponting, tel: 0865 67008. The Tring Anglers have water here (*See Tring*). Clifton Lock is NRA fishery, tel: 086 730 7821. Inn: The Barley Mow.

Appleford (Berks). London AA controls from just above the railway bridge down to beginning of Clifton Hampden cutting; both banks, then a short stretch on R bank only; members only.

Culham (Oxon). All water except weir pools controlled by Abingdon & Dist ARA. Other clubs: Culham AC and Sutton Courtenay AC has pits. No day tickets.

Abingdon (Oxon). Bream, chub, pike and barbel good. Free fishing for residents. Tickets from Town Clerk's office for the 1½m controlled by Council, from Nuneham railway bridge to noticeboard 200 yds u/s from Culham footbridge. Details from Stratton Lodge, 52 Bath Street, Abingdon. Fishery includes weir, but must be fished from bank. Abingdon & Oxford Anglers Alliance has much local fishing. The Alliance trout section has lake at **Standlake**, Oxon, st £50, entrance fee £15. Members and their guests only:

R H Williams, 2 Holyoake Rd, Oxford, 0X3 8AE. Millets Farm Fishery at **Fyfield** has 2 lakes in 7 acres, stocked with b and r trout. St, dt, conc for OAP, dis: Orchard Way, Fyfield, Oxon, tel: 0865 391394. Tackle shops: Hayden Tackle, 15/17 Lombard St; Mick's Tackle, 47 Ock St; The Right Angle, Wootton Rd. Hotels: Crown and Thistle; Knowl.

Sandford-on-Thames (Oxon). Pike, bream, roach, perch, etc. Oxford and Dist AA has water here; members only. Abingdon A & RA have water; R Pitson, tel: 0235 25140. NRA fishery at Sandford Lock, tel: 0865 775889.

Iffley (Oxon). Thames (or Isis). From here to Folly Bridge is Oxford and Dist AS water; no tickets. Inn: Isis Tavern.

Oxford (Oxon). Thames (Isis), **Cherwell** and **Oxford Canal**. All coarse fish. N Oxford AS has water on Thames, at **Gostow** and **Carrot's Ham,** Cherwell, canal, and carp and tench fishing in **Dukes Lake, Hinksey Lake** and **Pickford Lake.** Their best water is **Seacourt Stream** at Carrot's Ham, with many species. N Oxford AS and Oxford AA form Oxford Alliance, controlling 70m of river-bank, plus gravel pits. Club offers dt on water between Godstow and Seacourt Overspill, and Seacourt Stream from Overspill to A420. Rose Revived Hotel, Newbridge, tel: 086 731 221 has tickets for 2 fields d/s on left bank at Newbridge and from road bridge to confluence with left hand bank R Windrush. The Tring Anglers fish at **Eynsham** and **Donnington**, and also fish Oxford AA waters. (*See Tring.*) 4½m W of Oxford, **Farmoor Reservoir** no.1 leased by Farmoor Flyfishers. Members only. Reservoir no. 2 is trout fishery. Phone Oxford 863033 for advance bookings. Tickets for **Adderbury Lakes** coarse fishing from Lynes Stores, Adderbury. Tackle shops: North Oxford Tackle, 95 Islip Rd; Dells of Oxford, 136 Oxford Rd. Hotels: Cherwell, Oxford; Swan, Islip; Prince of Wales, Cowley Rd (APS HQ).

Eynsham (Oxon). Good coarse fishing; large bream. Oxford Angling and Pres Soc has water (*see Oxford*). Eynsham Weir fishing available to holders of NRA weir permits (tel: 0865 881324). Hotels: Ye Talbot Inn, Railway, Red Lion.

Bablock Hythe (Oxon). Ferryman Inn issues dt for 1½m on north bank downstream. Special fishing mini-break for two persons, any two nights, £70. Tel:

0865 880028. Water upstream on north bank (and some on south bank) is Appleton and Tubney AS as far as Oxford APS water.

Newbridge (Oxon). Near Witney. Good coarse fishing (bream increasing), few trout in the **Windrush.** Shifford Lock is one of NRA's fisheries, tel: 036787 247. Newland AC has water from **Shifford** to within 600 yds of Newbridge, Steadies Lane, Stanton Harcourt and Heyford Lakes, Standlake, with specimen fish. St, dt for lakes only. Non-locals membership by approval of committee, only. Hotels: Rose Revived (¾m water on Thames and Windrush; good coarse fish, some trout) and May Bush (½m water on Thames). Witney AS have Thames fishing here, R Windrush, trout only, and coarse pits; members only, £20 per annum, conc. Stroud AA have 1m of Thames (dt Batemans Sports, Stroud. Tel: 4320). Tackle shop: State Fishing Tackle, 19 Fettiplace Rd, Witney, tel: 0993 702587, who can give further information.

Tadpole Bridge, Buckland (Berks). Coventry & Dist AA has Rushey Wier fishery. Good chub and barbel; pike in weir-pool, NRA fishery, tel: 036787 218. Trout Inn issues dt for own stretch. Ac-

commodation at Trout Inn (caravans, camp sites). At **Pyreford,** Walton-on-Thames AS has a mile of river and a lake. Dt for members' guests only.

Radcot (Berks). Thames trout; bream, chub barbel and roach. Radcot AC has 5m. St £7, mt £4, wt £3, dt £1.50. Apply hon sec or Swan Hotel. Clanfield AC also has left bank, Old Man's Bridge to Rushey Lock. Clubs catered for. Radcot Lock is NRA fishery, tel: 0367 20676. Also Grafton Lock, tel: 036781 251, and Buscot Lock, tel: 0367 52434. Permits for stretch from **Buscot** to Grafton Loch, Turner's Tackle, Faringdon, tel: 0367 21044. Anchor Inn, **Eaton,** Hastings has 3m of fishing. Dt and st. Clubs welcome.

Lechlade (Glos). For Thames, Coln and Leach. Stroud AA controls 2m of Thames at Lechlade upstream from Trout Inn to Murdoch Ditch. Permits from Trout Inn or from Batemans, Sports, Stroud. St £7.50. For Highworth AC water between Lechlade and Buscot, contact M Mills, 58 Croft Rd, Swindon.

Cricklade (Wilts). Thames known here a Isis. Isis AC has water on main river, tributaries **Ray** and **Churn** and 12 acre gravel pit at **South Cerney** (Glos), carp to 30lb.

Tributaries of the Thames

MOLE: Coarse fish.

Esher (Surrey). Pike, roach, perch the odd big chub. CALPAC has fishing at Norwood Farm. Feltham Piscatorials has 'The Ledges'. Epsom AS has ½m at Wayne Flete and ½m on Wey at **Weybridge.** St £10, conc £4, from sec or Winslo Tackle, Gilders Rd, Chessington. Tackle shop: Weybridge Guns & Tackle.

Cobham (Surrey). Walton-on-Thames AS has 1¾m of Mole (good chub water); and one lake holding pike and carp, roach, tench and bream. Tickets to members guests only. Cobham Court AC have water adjacent and above: large chub, pike, very big perch and eels. Some rainbows stocked.

Leatherhead (Surrey). Dace, chub, pike, roach and perch. Hotel: New Bull. Leatherhead & Dist AS have waters above A246 road bridge, Sunmead AS below.

Dorking (Surrey). Coarse fish. Dorking AS has about 4½m; chub, barbel, pike, dace; members only. Dt £3, £1 jun for Fourwents Pond, South Holmswood, available on bank. Tackle shop: S C Fuller, South

Street. Leisure Sport Angling has two gravel pits at **Newdigate** heavily stocked with carp, pike, roach, rudd, crucian carp; St £22, ½ price conc. Full details from LSA, Thorpe Park. Tel: Chertsey 564872. Hotels: White Horse, Bell, Arundel.

Brockham (Surrey). Chub, roach, carp and bream. Brockham AS water.

Betchworth (Surrey). Chub dominate below weir, anything can, and does appear above weir. Carshalton and Dist AS has water; members only.

Sidlow (Surrey). The stretch from Sidlow to Horley has shown great improvement over the past five years, with match weights exceeding 30lb being taken. Roach dominate, together with perch, carp, chub. Horley P S fish much of this water.

WEY: Coarse fish, trout higher up.

Weybridge (Surrey). Wey Amalgamation have water here *(see Thames),* St £12.50, dt £1.50, jun, OAP, 50%; from bailiff. **Woking** (Surrey). Roach, chub, pike, etc. Woking and Dist AS has rights on 23 miles of river bank and two ponds (perch, carp and tench) at Send; dt for members' guests only. New members welcome; details from hon sec. At **Old Woking** Walton-on-Thames AS has 1m of Hoe Stream plus small lake holding tench and carp.

Wisley (Surrey); ns Ripley. Ponds: Wisley Mere, Hut Pond, and several other ponds on Ripley and Ockham Commons; carp, pike, perch, roach.

Guildford (Surrey). Guildford AS has about 9½m. At Clandon Park are some lakes, also on Broad Street and Whitmoor Common (carp to 19lb in Britton Pond). At Shamley Green **Willinghurst Trout Fishery,** 7 lakes totalling about 12 acres. St £450, dt £23, ½ dt £16.50 + VAT. 6 fish per week, 1 Apr to 30 Oct. 3 lakes coarse fishing also; dt £5. Apply J M G Syms, Willinghurst, Shamley Green. Tel: 0483 275048. **Albury Estate Fisheries** are at Albury. 9 acres, 3 dt waters: Powdermills, Weston and Belmont; one st/corporate: Park Fishery. B and r trout. St £475, dt £20. Limits 4 or 6 fish. Instruction by arrangement. Tel: 048641 2323. Tackle shops: S R Jeffrey & Son, 134 High St; Guildford; P Cockwill, 32 Meadrow, Farncombe. Hotels: Angel, Guildford; Drummond Arms, Albury.

Shalford (Surrey). Wey; bream, roach, pike, etc. **Tillingbourne;** trout; strictly preserved. Inns: Parrot, Victoria, Sea Horse, Percy Arms, Chilworth.

Godalming (Surrey). Godalming AS has Wey from Eashing Bridge (Stag Inn) to Broadfield Bridge (about 8m); grayling, coarse fish and trout; society also has Broadwater Lake (11 acres) which holds good carp, tench and perch; (no boats or camping) and limited fishing on Busbridge Lake. St £15 (long waiting list). Dt for accompanied guests £2 from tackle shop Allchorne. At Milford, Enton Flyfishers' Club has four trout lakes *(see Surrey lakes).* Peper Harow Flyfishers have about 2m of Wey and three ponds (brown and rainbow trout); rods limited;

st £205, no dt. **Wintershall Waters,** Bramley, is 3 acre trout fishery. St only. Tel: 0483 275019. Tackle shops in **Farncombe:** Patrick's, St John Street; F J Goodman & Sons, Silo Road. Tackle shops in Godalming: A & G Allchorne, 10 Bridge Street; Atkinson, New Road, Milford. Hotels: Broadwater, Farncombe Manor, Lake, King's Arms (Godalming AS HQ).

Frensham (Surrey). Farnham AS has trout water below Frensham Mill, **Frensham, Great and Little Ponds,** roach, perch, carp, etc; open membership for coarse fishing. St £39 (joining fee £20), conc, Dt £5, conc, from The Creel, Station Rd, Aldershot.

Haslemere (Surrey). Coarse fish. Surrey Trout Farm is here. At St Patricks Lane, **Liss,** is coarse fishing on 2 lakes, plus 5 ponds at **Rake** for matches only. Dt £4 from MBK Leisure, Marken, Kingsley, Bordon GU35 9JS; tel: 0420 474969.

Farnham (Surrey). Farnham AS provides sport for trout and coarse angler. Trout at **Frensham;** stocked, but only open to members and their guests. Coarse fishing at Farnham, Frensham, **Elstead, Badshot Lea Ponds, Lodge Pond, Stockbridge Pond** at **Tilford,** and **Loddon** at **Aborfield,** lakes at **Yateley, R Blackwater,** Farnborough (excellent roach), R Wey, Elstead. Tickets for some; apply hon sec for details. Note: All waters heavily fished early in season.

COLNE: Coarse fish, some trout. Information about the river is obtainable from the Colne Valley Anglers Consultative, Mr R McNab, 136 Braybourne Close, Uxbridge UB8 1UL.

Wraysbury (Bucks). Blenheim AS has **Colne Brook** from Wraysbury Rd to Hythe End Bridge; coarse fish and occasional trout. Also Cargill and Silver Wings Lake, members only. Civil Service AS has Poyle Park Fishery, **Colnbrook.** Twickenham PS and Staines AC have

---

Check before you go

While every effort has been made to ensure that the information given in **Where to Fish** *is correct, the position is continually changing, and anglers are urged, in their own interests, to make preliminary enquiries before travelling to selected venues. This is especially important with reference to prices quoted. Inevitably the rate of inflation is affecting stability in this quarter. Anglers' attention is also drawn to the fact that the hotels mentioned under the various fishing stations do not necessarily have water of their own. Any amendments or further data for inclusion in subsequent editions, and any criticism, will be welcome.*

gravel pits; no tickets.

West Drayton (G London). Trout, pike, perch, bream, dace, roach, tench, chub. Grand Union Canal is near.

Uxbridge (G London). Pike, perch, roach, dace and bream. Fishing free on Uxbridge Moor. London AA holds long stretches of **Grand Union Canal,** on which dt £1.50 are issued. **Osterley Park Lake** holds bream, tench, etc; now a National Trust property. St £15. No night fishing. Enquiries to Head Gardener, Osterley Park, Jersey Rd, Isleworth, Middx TW7 4RB. **Farlows Pit, Iver,** holds roach, tench, carp, bream, pike; limited number of st.

Denham (Bucks). Colne; coarse fish. Blenheim AS has 3m of **Grand Union Canal;** members only. Dt on Rickmansworth stretch.

Harefield (G London). **Savay Lake,** Moorhall Road. A 52 acre gravel pit stocked with specimen coarse fish. St £35, conc, from P Broxup, Fishery Manager, 309 Shirland Road, W9; dt £3, £1.50 conc, from newsagents, Peverills, Harefield, or Balfours, Denham. Concessions for junior and OAP. Tackle shop: Harefield Tackle, 9 Park Lane.

Rickmansworth (Herts). Trout, chub, dace, roach, pike, perch. Leisure Sport stretch of 600m and two gravel pits, 80 acres total, with large carp, pike, bream, dace, roach, tench and others. Restricted venue. Inquiries to LSA, Thorpe Park, Staines Road, Chertsey, Surrey. Tel: 564872. Blenheim AS has 1½m of **Grand Union Canal;** good roach and bream; dt from bailiff on water. Limited st from Harefield Tackle. Watford Piscators have 1½m canal and 2 lakes at Aquadrome, good carp and other species, dt from bailiff. **Batchworth Lake** and **Bury Lake;** dt on site. Club has 12 to 16 jun. section. **Croxley Hall** Trout Fishery, Rickmansworth WD3 3BQ; four lakes in 20 acres: trout, fly only. Expected catch 1991 10,000, av 2lb. St £250, dt £20.50. Tel: 0923 778290. **Gade;** trout; preserved. **Chess;** trout; strictly preserved. North Harrow Waltonians have water in river and lake; members only. Tackle shops: Tudor Tackle, Money Hill Parade; Tackle Corner, 157 St Albans Rd, Watford.

Watford (Herts). **Gade** at Cassiobury is free fishing for approx 1m. Ticket waters: Elstree and Tring reservoirs and Grand Union Canal. London AA issues dt for canal from Hunton Bridge to Tring. Free fishing in Gade in Cassiobury Park. Further information from tackle shop: The Tackle Carrier, St Alban's Road; and from Watford Piscators. Hotels: Maldon, Clarendon, Rose and Crown.

CHESS: Brown and rainbow trout - one of few British streams where rainbows spawn naturally. There is free public fishing at Scotts Bridge Playing Fields, Rickmansworth.

Chorleywood (Bucks). Chess; trout.

Chesham (Bucks). Brown and rainbow trout. Private. Tackle shop: Cox the Saddler, 23, High Street. Hotel: George and Dragon.

Latimer (Bucks). Upper river and two lakes (12 acres in all) available for trout fishing; brown and rainbow; average 2lb 6oz; daily restocking; boat available. Fly only. Season: Mar to Oct. St £540, ½ st £285. Dt £23, short day £18, evenings £13. Advance booking essential. Details from Latimer Park Lakes Chesham, Bucks HP5 1TT, tel: 0494 762396.

GADE: coarse fish.

Boxmoor (Herts). Boxmoor and Dist AS has private water at Westbrook and Berkhamstead AS now controls Pixies Meres; members only; no tickets. Boxmoor Trout Fishery, 3 acres of converted water cress farm. St £350 to £15 on flexible basis. Inquiries to R Hands, 23 Sebright Rd, Boxmoor, Hemel Hempstead, tel: 0442 64893 or to Fishery, 81 Marlowes, Hemel Hempstead.

Berkhamsted (Herts). Visitors can fish London AA water on Grand Union Canal; coarse fish, dt £1.50 from bailiff. No free water. Hotels: King's Arms (Trust House), Crown, Swan.

LODDON: coarse fish, barbel improving, trout scarce.

Twyford (Berks). Three pits, 100 acres, with carp, bream, tench, pike, chub, dace, eels at Twyford, plus Charvil and St Patrick's stream (fine barbel), held by Leisure Sport Angling. St £21, concessions to jun, OAP, dis. Applications to LSA, Thorpe Park, Staines Road, Chertsey, Surrey. Tel: 564872.

Arborfield Cross (Berks). Farnham AS has a stretch here, and 1½m at Stanford End; coarse fish, barbel in faster stretches *(see Wey - Farnham).* Cove AS also has water near here at **Shinfield** and on **Hart** and **Whitewater;** members only *(see also Fleet).* Farnborough AS has 2½m R Loddon at **Winnersh,** 4m R Whitewater at

BERKSHIRE TROUT FARM

The largest restocking farm in UK
(Established 1907)

BROWN, RAINBOW, TROUT

Hand selected pink fleshed for restocking rivers, lakes, reservoirs, etc.

Delivered by lorry or land-rover to waterside

Hungerford, Berks RG17 0UN

Tel: 0488 682520　　　　　　　　　　　　　Fax: 0488 685002

Heckfield, Basingstoke Canal and Shaw-fields Lake and Hollybush Pits. Fine mixed coarse fishing, fly fishing available, membership £30 + £10 joining fee. At **Binfield** is Felix Farm Trout Fishery, Howe lane RG12 5QL; tel: 0734 345527; dt £25, 5 fish, ½ day £17, 3 fish, evening £13, 2 fish. Contact Martin Suddards at fishery for more details.

KENNET: One of England's finest mixed coarse fisheries; upper reaches noted for trout and grayling.

Theale (Berks), Water west of point 1m upstream of Bridge House (Wide Mead Lock) strictly preserved; few trout and coarse fish. Englefield Lake, 2m. Pike, and fine tench and carp (private). Reading and Dist AA has water on lower Kennet, Holybrooke and backwaters, for about 10m in all; association controls from Wide Mead Lock east through Theale to Fobney. No dt. Leisure Sport gravel pits at Theale, 52 acres, and **Burghfield**, 101 acres plus 1300m R Kennet. Roach, bream, tench and pike. St £20, Theale, and £24, Burghfield. ½ price conc.

Aldermaston (Berks). Coarse fish and few trout. Old Mill issues permits for about 1m of water; dt £4, club bookings £70 inc. Nr Reading. London AA has 2m on **Fisherman's Brook;** coarse fish; members only. Off Aldermaston - Tadley Road, a chain of seven Leisure Sport gravel pits, heavily stocked, fishable by permit. Carp, tench, perch, rudd, bream, crucian carp. St £26, dt £3 on bank. Conc, jun, etc. No night fishing. Applications to LSA Thorpe Park, Chertsey. Tel: Chertsey 564872. Korda Fisheries offer fishing on **R Enborne** for trout and coarse. See Thatcham, below.

Thatcham (Berks). Fishing between Reading and Thatcham controlled chiefly by

Reading & Dist AA. Members only on river, but dt on sight for Assc. water Whylie's Lake, Thatcham. Details from hon sec *(see club list)*. Thatcham AA has water on canal, R Kennet plus lakes. Members only, £52.50 per annum. Korda Fisheries have opened a new carp fishery here, carp to 20lb. 10/11 Pleasant Place, West Hyde, Rickmansworth, WD3 2XZ, tel: 0895 824455. Korda Fisheries also offer fishing on R Colne and R Enborne nr Aldermaston. Tackle shops: Thatcham Angling Centre, 156 Sagecroft Rd; Berkshire Angling Centre, Turnpike Garden Centre.

Newbury (Berks). On Rivers Kennet and **Lambourn** and **Kennet and Avon Canal;** trout and coarse fishing. Newbury & Dist AA, Thatcham AA and Reading & Dist AA hold water in this area. St for Newbury AA £33, £10 conc. Tackle shops: Field and Stream, 109 Bartholomew Street and Nobby's, Kingsbridge Road. Foley Lodge Hotel (0635 528770) and Millwaters (0635 528838) both cater for anglers.

Hungerford (Berks). Kennet and **Dunn;** trout, grayling; strictly preserved. **Hungerford Canal** fishing in hands of Hungerford Canal AA (3m). Frequently restocked with rainbow trout and coarse fish from local rivers. Excellent fishing. Recent captures: tench 7½lb, roach 3lb 2oz, bream 5lb 6oz, trout 6lb 14oz; st and dt from hon sec or Lamb Inn. Accommodation at Home Cafe, Red Lion, Three Swans, Bear, Lamb Hotel (Canal AA HQ).

Lockinge (Oxon). 2m E of Wantage, **Lockinge Trout Fishery.** Av brown 1¾lb, brown, 2½lb. St £468. Enq. to Lockinge Trust, Ardington, Wantage. Tel 0235 833200.

Marlborough (Wilts). Trout at Axford,

Marlborough and District AA has fishing rights in **Kennet and Avon Canal** from Milkhouse Water to Burbage Wharf and Bruce Tunnel to Little Bedwyn. St £12 + £2 entry, conc. **Wroughton Reservoir,** near **Swindon,** stocked with brown and rainbow trout, eight dt per day, £6. £1.20 extra for punt. Booking with Thames Water, 17 Bath Rd. Swindon. Tel: 24331. No Saturday fishing. Bristol AA has **Tockenham Reservoir,** near Swindon, members only. Tackle shops: H Duck and Leathercraft, both High Street. Tackle shops in Swindon: Cotswold Angling, Hyde Road, Kingsdown; Angling Centre, 5 Sheppard Street; House of Angling, 60 Commercial Road. Hotels: Aylesbury Arms, Savernake, Castle and Ball, Crown (Marlborough AA HQ).

THAME: Coarse fish.

Dorchester (Oxon). Thames and Thame. Coarse fish; good chub and dace, and carp quite numerous. Dorchester AA has water; dt from hon sec or Fleur-de-Lys.

Thame (Oxon). Roach, bream, perch, chub. Leighton Buzzard AC has stretches at **Shabbington, Worminghall, Ickford** and **Waterperry.** Tackle shop: Seal Seam (Thame) Ltd, Chestnuts Yard, tel: 084 421 2129.

Eythrope (Bucks). Roach, bream, perch, chub, good dace. Aylesbury Dist and Izaak Walton AA has water (4m from Aylesbury), members and friends only. Blenheim AS has water at Shabbington, members only. Tackle shops: S G Waters, Cambridge Street, and H Cobbold, Britannia Street (both Aylesbury).

CHERWELL: Coarse fish.

Islip (Oxon). Cherwell and Ray; good chub, roach, perch and pike fishing may be had in the Cherwell. Preserved by Oxford Angling and Preservation Society, st £8.50, dt £1.50. The Bicester AS has 1½m on Cherwell Northbrook, and ½ acre carp pool, 2m Bicester. St £12 from tackle shops. Bicester AS members may fish Oxford AA waters. Abingdon & Oxford AA has water at Kidlington; wt from tackle shops. Bicester AA has Kirdington water. Ft from Allmond Tackle Shop. Other Bicester tackle shop: J & K Tackle, 8/9 Wesley Precinct. Inns: Red Lion, Swan.

Heyford (Oxon). Preserved by Banbury and Dist AA; members only.

Banbury (Oxon). Banbury AA (HQ Reindeer Inn, Parsons Street) has fishing at Cropedy, Nell Bridge, Clifton, Somerton, Heyford and Bletchington, also **Clattercote** and **Grimsbury Reservoirs.** Dt available for Clattercote. Coventry AA hold stretch 8m of **Oxford Canal,** with large carp, amongst other species. Dt on bank, £2. Farnborough Hall Lake is leased to Banbury AA. Coarse fishing at Butler Hill Farm, Gt Rollright, tel: Long Compton 243. Cheyney Manor Fishery, **Barford St Michael;** 5 acres, trout and carp stocked in separate pools. Tel: 0869 38207. Tackle shops: Banbury Angling Centre, 76a East St; Castaway, 86 Warwick Rd OX16 7AJ; Tight Lines, 55/6 George St.

EVENLODE: Trout, coarse fish (roach and dace especially).

Hanborough (Oxon). Red Spinner AS rents 10 to 12m of the Evenlode; trout (restocked annually), dace, roach, chub, pike; members only. Glyme Valley Fly Fishers have 1½m of the **Glyme** nr Wooton restocked yearly with trout. St £185; ½ rod £95. Members only. Good fishing on **Blenheim Park Lakes,** property of Duke of Marlborough. Excellent tench, perch and roach, with pike in winter. Boat fishing only. *(See Midlands lakes, reservoirs, etc).* At Rectory Farm, Salford, Nr Chipping Norton, **Salford Trout Lakes;** 5 and 3½ acres stocked with r and b trout. St £200 (55 fish per season), dt £15 (4 fish limit), ½ dt £10. E A Colston, Rectory Farm, Salford, Chipping Norton. Tel: 0608 643209.

WINDRUSH: Trout, grayling, coarse fish (dace up to 1lb and 2lb roach not rare).

Witney (Oxon). Large trout; preserved below; leave must be obtained from the Proprietors; good hatch of mayfly. Witney AS (HQ Eagle Vaults) has water. No dt and membership £15 pa restricted to county as a rule, but outside applications considered; apply hon sec. Club now has water on gravel pits at **Stanton Harcourt** (carp, tench, etc). Newland AC have stretch of backstream from Hardwick Village downstream, and Heyford Lakes Fishery, dt £2.50. Tackle shop: Derek State, Tackle, 19 Fettiplace Rd.

Minster Lovell (Oxon). Cotswold Flyfishers have 10m at **Swinbrook** and **Stanton Harcourt;** trout (restocked yearly), fly only; membership limited; no dt. Whitney AA has water on Windrush at **Worsham** (1m above village; trout re-stocked yearly) and Thames at **Newbridge** and **Standlake;** trout, grayling, coarse fish; fishing much improved. **Linch Hill Lei-**

sure Park, Stanton Harcourt; Willow Pool stocked with specialist carp; Stoneacres Lake mixed trout and coarse fishing. 10 acre Christchurch lake, carp. St £25, dt £2.50 to £5.50, depending on which pool fished. Concessions. Boats for hire. Tel: 0865 882215. Hotel: Old Swan Inn.

Burford (Oxon). Burford AC holds water in vicinity; trout and coarse fish. St £10 from J Swallow, 8 Meadow End, Fulbrook, Burford, Oxon. Dt £4 from Carpenters Arms, Fulbrook. Hotels: Cotswold Gateway, Lamb, Bay Tree, Bull, Winters Tale.

COLN: notable dry fly fishing for trout of good average size; grayling.

Fairford (Glos). Trout; excellent; April 1 to sept 30. Grayling Oct-Mar. Dry fly only upstream. Well stocked. Tickets can be had for 1½m from Bull Hotel, Market Place. Catch/return; trout of 1-1½lb plentiful. Dt £15, half day 39 (reduction for residents). Nearest tackle shop at Lechdale, 4m.

Bibury (Glos). Coln: trout. Swan Hotel GL7 5NW, tel: 0285 740495 has 300 yds facing hotel free to residents: dry fly only, 3 rods available. Hotel sells tickets.

TORRIDGE

(For close seasons, licences, etc, see South Western Region NRA p16)

Rises near Cornish border of Devonshire and joins the Taw estuary at Appledore, to flow into Bideford (also termed Barnstaple) Bay. Salmon, sea trout (peal) and brown trout (small).

Bideford (Devon). River for 2m on east side, and two reservoirs, at **Gammaton,** stocked with brown and rainbow trout, leased by Torridge Fly Fishing Club; st £100 from hon sec, written application only; dt £7 from Torridge Angling Centre, 7 Allhalland St, Bideford. **Weare Gifford,** salmon, sea trout, brown trout; dt from A Hooper, Post Office. At **Jennetts Reservoir,** 8 acre SWW coarse fishery, open 24 hr day, carp and tench. Dt £3.25 from Torridge Angling Centre, 7 Allhalland St, Bideford. Hotels: Royal, New Inn, Tanton's, Ring o'Bells, Market.

Torrington (Devon). Salmon, sea trout, brown trout. Torridge, Taw, Bray. Lower Torridge Fishery has 7 beats on 5m of water from Torrington to Blinsham, 5 beats fly only. From May 1, apply C R Rowe, Oak Tree Cottage, Stafford Way, Dolton, Winkleigh, Devon. Tel: Dolton 389. Best months for salmon, March, April, May; for sea trout, July, Aug, Sept. Fishing lodge and occasional day rods on **Beaford** stretch; contact Group Capt P Norton-Smith, Little Warham, Beaford, Winkleigh; tel: 08053 317. Coarse fishing at **Darracott Reservoir,** Torrington; 3 acres, open all the year, 24 hr day. Dt £2.50 from Sports, 9 High St, The

Square, Torrington, or The Kingfisher, 22 Castle St, Barnstaple.

Woodford Bridge (Devon). Brown trout (av 8-9 in). Woodford Bridge Hotel, Milton Damerel has 7m of brown trout fishing and 2m of salmon and sea trout water free to residents at hotel. Dt for non-residents as available: S & MT, £12, brown trout £8. Tel 040 926481.

Shebbear (Devon). Devil's Stone Inn has 2½m of salmon, sea trout and brown trout fishing on Torridge; fly and spinning; excellent dry-fly trout water. Nearest beat 2m. NRA licences and tackle, and angling instruction available. Dt sometimes issued to non-residents.

Sheepwash (Devon). Half Moon Inn has 12m of salmon, sea trout and brown trout fishing on Torridge. Banks cleared to facilitate fly fishing on all beats. Spinning allowed to April 30. Five upper beats stocked regularly with 1lb brown trout; fly only. Season opens March 1. Dt £11, salmon, £9, b trout. Brochure on request from Charles Inniss.

Hatherleigh (Devon). Torridge, Lew, Okement; salmon, sea trout, brown trout. Highhampton Trout Lakes, 6 acres, fly only, r trout. Mr S Thomas, Greenacres, Highhampton, tel; 040923 216. Coarse lakes at **Halwill**, 'Anglers Paradise Holidays'. Specimen fish: Z Gregorek, The Gables, Winsford, Beauworthy, 0409 221559. Tackle shops: D.I.Y. Centre, 25

The Square. Holsworthy. Hotel: New Inn, Meeth (½m on Torridge; dts for salmon and trout).

Tributaries of the Torridge

LEW: Sea trout, trout.
OKEMENT:
Okehampton (Devon). Torridge and Dartmoor streams accessible. Trout fishing, st £10, from Hill Barton Farm, tel: 0837

52454. **Mill Leat Fishery,** Thornbury, Holsworthy and **Highampton Trout Fishery** are accessible from Oakhampton.

TRENT

(For close seasons, licences, etc, see Severn-Trent Region NRA p18)

Largest river system in England. Rising in Staffordshire, Trent drains much of Derbyshire, Nottinghamshire and Lincolnshire, and empties into Humber. A hundred years ago, one of England's principal fisheries; now recovering its status following massive effort at water quality improvement. The tide-water, in particular, now fishing excellently. Some famous trout-holding tributaries, notably Dove, Wye and Derwent.

Gainsborough (Lincoln). Pike, perch, roach, chub. There are a few fish to 3m below Gainsborough. Tidal. Lincoln & Dist AA has stretch at Marton. Tickets from bailiff, Mr P Robinson, 37 Lincoln Rd, Fenton LN1 2EP. Goole AA has fishing at **Church Laneham,** right bank. No dt, st £11 from hon sec of tackle shops. Scunthorpe AA has ¾m, Coates to N. Leverton. Dt on bank. Tackle shop: Tackle shop, Kings Court, Bridge Rd.

Torksey (Lincoln). Pike, roach, chub. Sheffield & Dist AA has left bank at Cottam as shown by notice boards, dt from Dunham Garage.

Dunham (Notts). Sheffield and Dist AA have a lake and left bank of Trent. Dt £2 from Bridge Garage, Dunham.

High Marnham (Notts). Nottingham Fedn has stretch above power station; dt and matches; tidal. Mansfield & Dist AA has 50 pegs here and 35 pegs at **Normanton-on-Trent.** Dt on bank.

Sutton-on-Trent (Notts). Tidal water. Pike, roach, dace, chub. Slaithwaite & Dist AC has fishing here; Sheffield AA has Sutton left bank. Dt from Lord Nelson, Sutton-on-Trent. Sheffield Amalgamated AS has sole right of Newcastle Fishery, about 6m. Heavily match-fished. Lincoln & Dist AA has fishing at **North Clifton** and **Laughterton.** Tickets from tackle shops in Lincoln and Gainsborough.

Carlton-on-Trent (Notts). Sheffield & Dist AA has left bank here and at **Fledborough,** right bank at **Girton.** Dt from Bridge Garage, Dunham.

Collingham (Notts). Club water. Trent 2m W; pike, carp, barbel, roach, dace, chub, perch, bream. Collingham AA has 4m from Cromwell Weir to Besthorpe parish boundary; dt £2.50 from bailiff on bank. All round coarse fishing. Between Holme and **Winthorpe** are several waters of Worksop AAA. At Besthorpe Wharf is Newcastle Fishery; dt 50p. Sheffield AAA. Hotels: Royal Oak, King's Head, Grey Horse.

Muskham (Notts). Nottingham PS preserves from Fir Tree Corner (Kelham boundary) to Crankley Point, both sides, including gravel pits; members only.

Averham, Kelham (Notts). Very good coarse fishing; preserved by Nottingham PS for members only - roach, dace, chub (excellent fly water) - from railway bridge at Averham to South Muskham boundary on both sides of the river.

Newark-on-Trent (Notts). Roach, dace, pike, chub, bream, barbel, gudgeon, perch, eels. Newark and Dist Piscatorial Federation has water on Trent Dyke, Trent at **Winthrope,** and **Newark Dyke,** east bank, Weir Field to Devon Mouth and west bank, Crowtrees and Red Bridge, dt on bank. Sheffield Amal AS 6m at **Besthorpe, Girton** and **South Clifton,** dt on bank or from HQ Lord Nelson, Arundel St, Sheffield. Mansfield & Dist AA have Besthorpe and High Marnham fishing, dt for latter on bank. Sheffield & Dist AA has left bank at **Cromwell,** right bank and lake at **Winthrope.** Dt from Level Crossing Cottage, Winthrope. Nottingham AA fishes from

Farndon Ferry to Newark Dyke. Dt from bailiff on bank. Other dt stretches: **Holme, Winthrope Crossing, Footits Marsh, North Muskham,** Worksop & Dist AA; **Hazelford Ferry, Bleasby,** Mrs Mitchell, tel: 0636 813014; Trent Lane, **Collingham,** Collingham AA. Tickets on bank. Tackle shop: Angling Centre, 29 Albert Rd, Newark.

Farndon (Notts). Nottingham Piscatorial Society has north bank (tickets as Rolleston), south bank let to Nottingham AA; dt issued.

Rolleston (Notts). Nottingham Piscatorial Society water from Greet mouth to Staythorpe power station (excluding members field and car park); good roach, barbel and chub; dt £2 from tackle shops and Pa Li Chuang, Fiskerton Rd, Rolleston, Newark. No permits on bank. Greet, trout; preserved. Nottingham AA has water at **Farndon Ferry** (opp Rolleston); dt from bailiff; matches can be arranged in advance. Sheffield & Dist AA has left bank at **Normanton,** dt.

Fiskerton (Notts). Good roach and chub fishing. Barnsley Anglers have 9m, south of Newark-on-Trent. Dt £2 from bailiffs. The Greet enters Trent at Fiskerton; trout; preserved.

Hazleford (Nott). Hazleford Ferry water, Fiskerton, now rented by Star and Garter Hotel; dt for about 1m water from Hotel, fishing free from hotel grounds for guests.

Hoveringham (Notts). Coarse fish. Nottingham PS has stretch to Willow Holt; members only. Dt £2 for Nottingham AA stretch from Star and Garter 1¾m u/s. Midland AS has stretch to Caythorpe, barbel, roach, chub, bream, gudgeon, etc. 134 pegs, dt £2.20 on bank. Dt £2 for Nottingham AA stretch from Hazelford

Ferry hotel.

Gunthorpe (Notts). Good coarse fishing; roach, dace, chub.

Burton Joyce (Notts). Chub, roach (mainly), dace. Nottingham and Dist Fedn has good stretch for which dt issued (matches arranged, booked in advance after Nov 1 for following season); tickets from bailiff, hon sec, Stoke Ferry Boat Inn, Lord Nelson. Nottingham AA has from **Colwick** Viaduct downstream for one field.

Shelford (Notts). Stoke Weir to Cherry Orchard and Gunthorpe Bridge to Boatyard, Nottingham AA water. Dt on bank.

Radcliffe-on-Trent (Notts). Roach, chub, dace and gudgeon, with perch, pike and tench in Lily Ponds. From Stoke Weir down to **Gunthorpe,** Nottingham AA; dt. From Stoke Weir up to Radcliffe Ferry, including Lily Ponds, Nottingham Fedn; dt. Fedn also holds from Radcliffe Ferry upstream (members only) and water below Radcliffe railway bridge *(see Burton Joyce).* Accommodation at Chestnuts Club.

Nottingham (Notts). Good mixed fishing. Several miles in city free. Nottingham AA has **Clifton,** south bank; **Holme Pit Frontage; Colwick,** viaduct d/s 600 yds; **East Bridgford,** 180 yds below weir, d/s for 1,350 yds. Dt £2 from bailiff, st £15. Nottingham Piscatorial Society has fishing at **Rolleston, Fiskerton** and **Farndon;** dt from tackle shops only. Long Eaton Victoria AS has **Thrumpton Fishery,** and 30 pegs below Colwick sluices, left bank; dt £1.50. Midland AS has Dover Beck Mount d/s to **Hoveringham;** Eastwood Anglers; Lady Bay bridge, football ground. Parkside FC; **Long Higgin.** Earl Manvers AC; Long Higgin. Dt on bank for all these waters. Nottingham and District Federation of Angling Societies comprises upwards of 68 clubs; water at **Burton Joyce** and **Stoke Bardolph.** West Bridgford British Legion AC has some water on Trent; st and dt from hon sec. Lake in **Wollaton Park** may be fished by dt from Parks Superintendent, Wollaton Park. Bream, tench, roach, pike, perch at **Colwick Park,** a coarse fishery operated by STW and Nottingham City Council. St £18.50, dt 80p, concession for OAP, juniors. Tickets from the Lodge. Council also runs Newstead Abbey Park fishing. Long Eaton Victoria AS has left bank below sluice at Colwick; dt £1.50 on bank. Holme Pierrepont tel: 0602 821212, offer angling holidays on 1½m of Trent and coarse lake. Tackle shops: Junction Tackle, 210 Tamworth Rd; Gerry's, 96/100 Radford Boulevard, and many others.

Ilkeston (Notts). Cotmanhay AC has Manor Floods Fishery: roach, tench, chub, carp, bream; dt £1.75, conc, on bank or from Taylor's Tackle. Tackle shops: Tom C Saville Ltd (mail order specialists) Unit 7, Salisbury Square, off Ilkeston Road *(see advt).* Walkers, 9-15 Nottingham Road, Trowell; T Watson, 1 Oak Street, Carrington; Toni Bridge, 25 Clayfield Close NG6 8DG; Taylors Tackle, 136 Cotmanhay Rd, Ilkeston. Hotels: Not-

tingham Moat House; Queens; St George.

Wilford (Notts). Rivermead to Wilford footbridge, Nottingham AA; dt on bank. Club also has Iron Mongers Pond, dt on bank. Clifton Grove is Nottingham FA water.

Beeston (Notts). Chub, roach, dace, bleak, gudgeon; preserved by Nottingham AA. Dt for stretch from N Bank Lock from bailiff. Assn also has water on **Beeston Canal.** Nine Leisure Sport gravel pits in **Attenborough Nature Reserve** total 315 acres. Bream, tench, roach, pike, carp, perch, eels, barbel, chub, crucian carp. Fishery includes 2,500m R Trent. Northern part permit only, southern part permit and dt. No night fishing. St £21, dt £1.50. ½ price conc, from LSA, Thorpe Park, Chertsey. Tel: 564872. Tackle shop: Beeston Angling Centre, 33 Humber Rd; Supertackle, 192 Station Rd. Hotels: Brackley House; Hylands.

Thrumpton and Long Eaton (Notts). Roach, bream, dace, chub, perch, barbel. Long Eaton Victoria AS has Thrumpton Ferry field. Full membership £10, or £4.50 and £2. Coventry & Dist AA also has water here, dt for Ferry Farm on bank. **Erewash.** Roach, gudgeon, bream, carp, perch, chub. Dt at Sandiacre, £1 on bank, or from West End AC. Long Eaton Victoria AS has **Soar,** at Kegworth, Rad-

Trotting the redworm for grayling in Derbyshire. Some say they feed more freely when snow is on the ground. *Photo: Bruno Broughton.*

cliffe, dt £1.50; canal fishing, on Cranfleet Canal (Trent Lock), Erewash Canal, (Long Eaton Loch to Trent Lock), also ponds in Long Eaton, members only. Long Eaton and Dist AF has water on Trent at Trent Lock, Soar, and canal fishing. Tackle shops: Wainwrights; Horseshoe Fishing Tackle, 1 Station Rd; Bridge Tackle, 30 Derby Rd; Junction Tackle, 210 Tamworth Rd, Sawley. Hotels; Elms; Europa; Sleep Inn.

Chellaston (Derby). Trent, 1m SW, at Swarkestone. Derby AA has water below, and upstream, through **Ingleby** and **Twyford,** to above **Willington.** Stretches are held on both banks, with few breaks. Most species of coarse fish present. Club also has 14m on **Trent and Mersey Canal,** lakes and Kingstanding Pools. St £24, wt £5; concessions for OAP, juniors. From hon sec and Derby tackle dealers.

Burton-on-Trent (Staffs). Good free fishing for roach and chub at **Newton** and **Willington.** Burton Mutual AA fishes **Dove** at **Tutbury** to confluence with Trent, and Branstone gravel pit; members only. Good pools at Barton and Walton. Warrington AA has **Claymills** river fishery. **Hartshorne Dams,** 2 coarse lakes, are 2 min off A50 at Woodville. Dt from Rooney Inn or Manor Farm, both Hartshorne. Ripley & Dist AC has 1m left bank of Dove at **Scropton;** mixed fishery, members only. Tickets for canals, various stretches on the R Trent and a variety of other waters from tackle shops Mullarkey, 184 Waterloo Street; Burton Angling Supplies, 30 Borough Rd. Hotels: Queen's, Station and Midland.

Alrewas (Staffs). Perch, dace, roach. Birmingham AA has water here, **Wychnor, Kings Bromley** and at **Yoxall. Trent and Mersey Canal,** dt from keeper. Tackle shop: Country Lines, 115 Main St.

Rugeley (Staffs). Usual species. Rugeley and Brereton AS has about 1m on Trent and water on **Trent and Mersey Canal** from Armitage to Wolseley Bridge. From here to Colwich held by British Waterways (dt from them); roach, pike, perch. Tickets available from Manton, Bow Street (tackle shops). **Blithfield Reservoir,** 4m NE; trout; South Staffs. Water Company allows fishing on season permit only. Inquiries to: Recreations Office, Blithfield Reservoir, Abbots Bromley, Staffs.

Colwich (Staffs). Not the best part of the river, but some coarse fish. **Sow,** 4m W; controlled by Stafford Anglers. Blyth 5m E; preserved. Sherbrook and Oakedge Pools preserved by Lord Lichfield. Rugeley and Brereton AS has water on canal; roach, pike, chub, perch; dt and st at small fee *(see also Rugeley).* Hotel: Lamb and Flag.

Great Haywood (Staffs). Usual species. Trent and Mersey Canal; roach, pike, chub, perch; length held by Shugborough Park FC (no tickets). Hotel: Clifford Arms.

Stone (Staffs). Stone & Dist AS fishes Trent here, and Ellenhall Pools, **Eccleshall.** Tickets available from Dales Tackle Shop, Albert St, Stone. Crown AC has pools at Eccleshall and Market Drayton, as well as Shropshire Union Canal. Dt £1.50 from tackle shops: Dales Tackle, Albert St, Stone; Cooper Sports, Queen St, Market Drayton.

Stoke-on-Trent (Staffs). Stoke City & Dist AA has Longwaste fishing on **R Tern, R Roden** at Poynton Bridge, **R Meece** at Norton Bridge, **Trent & Mersey Canal,** from Aston Lock to Burston and in city between Wieldon and Etruria Road Bridges; **Shropshire Union Canal** (200-peg match venue, enq invited) and **Knighton Reservoir, Cheswardine.** Also pools at Stoke, Market Drayton and Eccleshall. Coarse fish, members only on all waters. Subscription £20, conc. £9, for ladies, jun, OAP, from mem sec D Deaville, 1 Churston Place, Sneyd Green. Tel: 267081. Club also has 6 and 4 acre trout lakes, 36 rod syndicate, extra cost. apply to hon sec. Fenton AS has canal fishing and pools in area, membership £15, conc, from Stoke tackle shops. Tackle shops: Abbey Pet Stores, 1493 Leek Road, Abbey Hulton; Dolphin Discount, Old Whieldon Road, Stoke; Tackle Box, 37 Hartshill Road, Stoke; Mellors Tackle, Hanley. Horsley's 63/7 Church St, Audley; Anchors Away, 294 High St, Tunstall and many others.

Trentham (Staffs). Lake in Trentham Gardens; area about 70 acres. Village about 3m from Stoke-on-Trent on main road London to Manchester. Fishing tickets at Lodge Gate. Trentham Hotel 1m. Catering available in Trentham Gardens, caravan site.

Weston-on-Trent (Staffs). Coarse fishing in **Trent and Mersey Canal;** chub, roach, bream, perch.

Tributaries of the Trent

IDLE: Excellent coarse fishing in parts. NRA fishery at **Bawtry**, free to licence holders.

Misterton (Lincs). Coarse fish. Worksop AA have Haxey fishing, dt on bank, £2.

Misson (Notts). Doncaster and Dist AA has from Newington to Idlestop, about 10m on the Misson side. Good roach, bream, perch, pike; st and dt from tackle dealers. Assn also has Warping Drain and ponds at Idle Stop, with carp, pike, tench, roach, eels.

Retford (Notts). Poulter, 4m S. Meden, 4m S. Maun, 4m S. Idle above Retford private. Derbyshire County AC has 2½m, Lound to East Retford, with chub, roach, dace, bream, pike. Apply to secretary. Worksop AA controls a stretch of the **Chesterfield Canal** from Drakeholes Basin to West Retford bridge, 10½m, famous for chub, match weights up to 50lb. Limited membership. Tackle Shops at Doncaster.

TORNE and NEW IDLE. Doncaster and Dist AA has 12m from Candy Farm to Pilfrey Bridges and water on **Stainforth and Keadby Canal;** dt from E Drury, Candy Corner Pumping Station, Finningly, nr Doncaster.

Althorpe (S Humberside). **Stainforth & Keadby Canal;** coarse fish; about 14m of water above and down to Trent; good fishing; rights held by Sheffield, Rotherham, Doncaster, Scunthorpe and British Rail associations. Other fishing stations for canal are **Thorne** and **Crowle. Lindholme Lakes, Sandtoft,** mixed fishery on 3 lakes, 1 trout, 1 carp and a general coarse lake. Dt available, tel: 0427 872015/872905.

Crowle (S Humberside). Excellent centre for coarse fishing. **Stainforth and Keadby Canal, Torne** and **Ring Drain,** are ½m from Crowle Central Station; Doncaster AA; roach, tench, bream, perch, carp, pike. Three Drains on A18; Sheffield and Dist AA; roach, perch, tench, carp. Licences, association books and dt from hotels or hon sec (enclose s/a envelope). Tackle shop: Thorne Pet & Angling, 5 The Green; also many in Doncaster and Scunthorpe. Hotels: South Yorkshire, Crowle; Friendship Inn, Keadby. Tackle shops in Doncaster (17m) or Scunthorpe (10m).

RYTON (tributary of Idle); Coarse fish.

Scrooby (Notts). Ryton. From Bramshall's farm to junction with Idle, 2m; dt from Pilgrim Fathers and the garage, Scrooby.

Worksop (Notts). On Ryton and **Chesterfield Canal;** coarse fish. Worksop and Dist AA has 11m of canal from W Retford Bridge to Drakeholes Basin. Dt £2 from bailiffs on bank, or tackle shops. Lakes: **Dukeries Lakes, Clumber Park Lake** (National Trust), where dt and st can be had; and **Sandhill Lake;** trout, coarse fish. For **Langold Lake,** north of Worksop, D A Emmerson, Regal Centre, Carlton Rd, tel: 0909 475531 ext 234. Tackle shops: B Tomlinson, 84 Gateford Rd; Angling Supplies, 49 Retford Rd; Ken Ward Sports, Carlton Rd.

MAUN (tributary of Idle): Polluted, but fish returning in some parts.

Mansfield (Notts). Field Mill Dam; coarse fish, dt. Vicar Water, Clipstone; coarse fish, dt. Mansfield & Dist AA has water at Newark and High Marnham on **Trent,** gravel pits at Newark; Dt available for some of these from hon sec and tackle shops: Forest Town Angling, 113 Clipstone Road; Angling & Game Centre, 20 Byron Street; MPS Products, 296 Chesterfield Rd.

Sutton-in-Ashfield (Notts). Lakes: Lawn, Dam. King's Mill Reservoir, 1m NE; tickets on bank. Hardwick Lakes, Hardwick Hall, are 6m W. Tackle shop: H Burrows, 91 Outram Street NG17 4AQ. Hotels: Nag's Head, Denman's Head.

DEVON: Coarse fish.

Bottesford (Notts). Smite, 3m NW at Orston. Car Dyke, 5m NW. Bottesford AA preserves 5m of **Grantham Canal** at Bottesford, Muston and Woolsthorpe-by-Belvoir; st and dt from Bull Inn and Rutland Arms, Woolsthorpe-by-Belvoir (on canal bank), and from hon sec and from bailiffs on bank. Good coarse fishing, with pike over 20lb.

Belvoir Castle (Leics). Between Melton Mowbray and Grantham. Belvoir Lakes, 1m SE, and Knipton Reservoir, 2m S (coarse fish); st £45, ½ st £28, dt £4, conc £3, from Estate Office, or keeper, Belvoir Castle, Grantham Tel: 0476 870262, fax: 0476 870443. Also a chain of carp lakes, st only. **Nottingham and Grantham Canal:** Bottesford and District AA has water. Other stations on canal are **Long Clawson, Harby, Hose** and **Stathern.**

GREET: Trout; coarse fish; preserved.

Southwell (Notts). River private. Trent, 3m

SE at Fiskerton. At Oxton, 5m SW, Nottingham Fly Fishers' Club has a trout lake at Gibsmere; strictly members only, long waiting list. Greet FC, too, has trout fishing. Cromwell Fly Fishers, 20 Norwood Gardens, Southwell, has a lake north of Cromwell.

NUT BROOK no longer a fishery.

West Hallam (Derby). Lakes: **Mapperley Reservoir,** 2m N, **Shipley Park Lakes, Lescoe Dam** and stretch of Erewash Canal all NCB waters. St £12. jun, dis, £3 from D Allsop, 27 Hardy Barn, Shipley, Derbys. Dt £1 from park rangers. Other Shipley tackle shop: Shipley Angling Centre, 23 Westgate.

SOAR: Very popular coarse fishery with anglers in the Leicester area. NRA fishery at **Thurmaston**, free to licence holders.

Radcliffe (Derby); Good coarse fishing. Long Eaton & Dist AF administrate between Kegworth and Radcliffe Flood Locks, and 1m Trent, Trent Lock, south bank. Dt £2 from tackle dealers.

Kegworth (Derby). Roach, dace, bream, tench, chub, perch. Confluence with R Trent upstream approx 75 pegs, Zingari AC. Dt from bailiff on bank. From Kegworth Bridge up to Kegworth Lock held by Long Eaton Victoria AS. Dt and st. Nottingham AA has from notice board below Kegworth Bridge to Kingston Dyke (members only). Long Eaton AF has good 2m stretch down to Radcliffe; £2 dt from bailiff Mike Weaver, 4 Redhill Rd, Kegworth. Soar AS has water here. Kegworth AS has approx 400 mtrs.

Normanton-on-Soar (Leics), Good coarse fishing. Loughborough Soar AS water.

Loughborough (Leics). Loughborough Soar AS has fishing near here and Barrow on Soar with large carp, chub, bream, roach, perch, plus dace and barbel on two stretches. Dt £2 in advance from tackle shop: Soar Valley Tackle, 7 Woodbrook Rd. **Proctor's Lake and River Fishing,** The Park, Barrow-on-Soar (5m SE). Dt issued *(see Barrow)*. Hotels: King's Head and Central.

Quorn (Leics). Roach, bream. Quorn AS has rights on stretches of river and 1m of canal; they now have joint ticket with Leicester & Dist AS, st £6, jun £2.50; inquire hon sec. River fishes best in autumn and winter.

Barrow-upon-Soar (Leics). About 3m river and canal fishing; good roach and bream; recently restocked. Fishes best autumn and winter. Loughborough Soar AS has water. (*See Loughborough*), also Quorn AC. Proctor's Lake and River Fishing, The Park (Quorn 2323). Caravanning and camping and fishing facilities. Dt from machine at entrance. Tackle shop: Webster and Barnes, 68 High Street.

Leicester (Leics). Coarse fish. Canal Northgate Bridge to Swan's Nest Weir, Holden Street to Birstall, Birstall to Johnsons Bridge, Thurmaston, Wreake Junction, Cossington, Rothley, Mountsorrel, Barrow-on-Soar, Thackholme Deeps, held by Leicester and Dist Amal Soc of Anglers; also several stretches on **Wreake**, three on **Nene**, and canals. Membership £7. St and dt from bailiffs or Lakeside Marina, 0533 640222. Leicester AC: Soar and canal; dt and st; and Wigston AS: canal; tickets from C Burnham, Blaby Road, S Wigston. **Leicester Canal;** some good coarse fish but boat traffic ruins summer sport. Exceptionally high quality coarse fishing in five lakes totalling 22 acres in **Mallory Park**. St £150 (covering all five lakes) from Marks and Marlow, address below. The Pool, Groby, 5m NW; bream, tench, roach, pike; dt from house at pool. Broome AS fishes Birstall Park Lakes, 50 acres, **Birstall**; mixed coarse fishing. Membership , £28 per annum, conc, available from Mr G Taylor, 100 New Romnet Cres, Leicester, tel: 0533 417018. (Two year waiting list). Hotels: Grand, Royal, Hermitage (Oadby). Tackle shops: Marks & Marlow, 39 Tudor Road; The Angling Man, 228 Melton Road; J C Townsend, 394 Humberstone Road; Wigston Angling, 51 Leicester Rd; Cooper's 225 Saffron Rd; Match Catch, Syston; Bob Berry, 8 Dunton St, S Wigston;.

Narborough (Leics). Hinckley and Dist AA has water here containing trout and grayling; permits from permits sec. Broome AS has a stretch here and at **Wanlip**, roach, perch, chub, barbel. For membership, see Leicester, above.

WREAKE (tributary of Soar): An attractive coarse fishery on which Leicester and Dist ASA has extensive coarse fishing rights between Thrussington and Melton Mowbray; dt.

Ashfordby (Leics). Roach, perch, dace, pike, chub. Mostly Leicester ASA water; dt £1.50 from E Edwards, G Rainbow, bailiffs. Ashfordby SOA has water on Wreake and pits at **Frisby** (1m). Mem-

bers only, no dt. Dt for **Holwell Works Reservoir** from E Madden, The Limes, Ashford-by-Valley.

Melton Mowbray (Leics). Leicester and Dist AS has water at Brokesby, Hoby, Frisby on the Wreake, Pig Sties. Dt from bailiff. **Knipton Reservoir,** 8m N, at Branston. Tackle shop: Hook Line & Sinker, 52 King St.

DERWENT: Noted trout and grayling water in upper reaches; downstream coarse fish come into their own.

Sawley (Derby). Coarse fish. Pride of Derby AC has from Wilne Weir to mouth of Derwent (south bank), 750 yd stretch on north bank, and both banks of **Trent** above confluence to Red House on one bank and Sutton's Eaves on other. Also canal from Derwent Lock to Trent and Trent to Sawley Lock. Further water on Trent below Sawley Weir towards lock house and including the island and several ponds. Members only (st £22 are issued to anglers living in 16m radius of Derby only; long waiting list, applications to hon sec). Long Eaton & Dist AF has 1m south bank at Sawley, dt £1.50. Inn: Harrington Arms, Old Sawley, Long Eaton (permits for local waters).

Borrowash (Derby). Coarse fish. Earl of Harrington AC waters (*see Derby*). Derbyshire County AC has 5m from Borrowash to Sawley, mainly double bank, with barbel, chub, roach, bream, carp, tench, perch and pike. Apply to secretary.

Spondon (Derby). Coarse fish; preserved by Earl of Harrington AC. Chaddesden Brook, 1m NW, and Locko Park, 2m N. Private.

Derby (Derby). Coarse fish, Earl of Harrington AC has Derwent from Borrowash Bridge through to Midland Station. St £10, £2 jun, dt £1.50, conc, from hon sec and tackle shops. Derby City Council issues dt £1.60, ½ conc, for Derwent from Darley Abbey to Derby railway station. Council also issues tickets for coarse fishing at **Alvaston Lake, Markeaton Park Lake, Allestree Park Lake** and **Derwent** in **Darley Abbey Park** (dts from keeper). DCC, Leisure Services Dept, Council House, Corporation St DE1 2XJ. Locko Park Lake and Chaddesden Brook private, Other clubs: Pride of Derby AA (*see Sawley);* Derby RIFC (water on Derwent, **Trent, Dove, Ecclesbourne;** canals). Earl of Harrington AC (Derwent, 1m of **Big Shrine** at Borrowash, canal, dt). Derby Federation has

A nice bag of fine winter grayling taken on trotted redworm, caught from a small tributary of the Derbyshire Derwent. But grayling are found in fast-flowing clean rivers in most parts of Great Britain south of the Scottish Highlands. *Photo: Bruno Broughton*, who also caught the fish.

water at **Duffield,** from Milford Bridge to Little Eaton. Trout and coarse fish. Tackle shops: Anglers Corner, 344 Osmaston Rd; Artisan Angling, 141 London Road; Nathan's, 1 Ward St; Angling Centre, 29/33 Nightingale Rd; Roach Pole 82, 246 St Thomas Rd.

Duffield (Derby). Coarse fish, trout and grayling. Derbyshire AF water. Dt for trout and grayling from Bridge Inn, Duffield.

Belper (Derby). Grayling, pike, trout, coarse fish; 8m held by Belper AC. Club also has Wyver Lane Pond, coarse fish. Dt £2 from Hendersons Quality Tackle, 37 Bridge Street. Earl of Harrington AC has ¾m of trout fishing on Ecclesbourne at **Turnditch** (3m W); fly only; members only (see Derby). Black Brook, Holbrook Road, 2m SE.

Ambergate (Derby). Few trout, pike, coarse fish. Alderwasley Ponds, 2m NW. **Butterley Reservoir** and **Codnor Park Reservoir;** roach, bream, tench, carp, pike; Ripley and Dist AA waters, st £18, dt £2 from hon sec, bailiffs and tackle shops. Loscoe Dam; dt from keeper. Hotel: Hurt Arms.

Whatstandwell (Derby). Mostly grayling and trout, with former predominant and some large chub. Dt £2 from Derwent Hotel, Derby Rd, Whatstandwell, which has ¼m fishing; rather overhung with trees, but plenty of fish and good wading in low water. Free fishing to hotel guests.

Cromford (Derby). Trout; fly only; preserved below road bridge (both banks), as far as and including Homesford Meadows, by Cromford Fly Fishers; members only, no tickets. St £100 + £200 entrance fee; 4 year waiting list. Above bridge, Derbyshire CC AC water. No tickets. Hotel: Greyhound.

Matlock (Derby). Trout (some rainbows), grayling and coarse fish. Matlock AC issue wt and dt; dt from Midland Hotel (Matlock Bath); water at Matlock and Matlock Bath; trout and coarse; about 1m.

Rowsley (Derby). Trout, brown and rainbow; grayling. Warrington AA has fishing at Darley Abbey. Two dt available to guests at Peacock Hotel, Rowsley: £20.50. Two dt on similar terms for guests at Grouse and Claret Hotel for ½m north of Rowsley Bridge. Haddon Estate has rights on **River Wye** from Rowsley to just north of Bakewell, together with Rivers Lathkill and **Bradford** for most of their length. Wye has pure wild rainbows and fine head of natural browns and grayling. Dt £20.50, 12 rod limit, available from Peacock Hotel, Rowsley. Lathkill and Bradford are booked well in advance. For information contact Head River Keeper P M White, tel: 0629 636255.

Baslow (Derby); nr Bakewell, 4m. The Cavendish Hotel, originally the famous Peacock, has 6 rods on the Chatsworth and Monsal Dale fisheries, by courtesy of Chatsworth Estate. 4½m of the **Derwent,** brown and rainbow trout and grayling. 4½m of the Wye, brown and rainbow trout. Priority booking for residents. For full details, phone 0246 582311. For membership of Chatsworth Fishery apply to Estate Office, Edensor, Bakewell DE4 1PH.

Hathersage (Derby). Trout, grayling; preserved by the Derwent FFC; also at Bamford and Grindleford (members only).

Bamford (Derby). Trout, grayling. Derwent FFC has water below Bamford Mill; and from Bamford Mill to Yorkshire Bridge; members only. Peak Forest AC has **River Noe** upstream from Derwent confluence to Jaggers Clough in Edale;

fly fishing. Members only; subscriptions £350 + £100 entrance fee. Tel: 0742 369224.

Ladybower. Centre for **Ladybower and Derwent Reservoirs;** trout; fly only *(see Midlands reservoirs and lakes).* Hotels: Ladybower Inn, Yorkshire Bridge Inn, Ye Derwent Hotel, Bamford (1m), Anglers' Rest (1m), Marquis of Granby, Bamford (2m), Rising Sun, Bamford (2m).

AMBER (tributary of Derwent): trout, coarse fish.

Alfreton (Derby). St £18. dt £2 from Ripley AC for reservoirs at **Butterley** and **Codnor Park:** pike, perch, roach, tench, bream, and carp; dt also from keepers. Sheffield Trout Anglers have water on Amber at Wingfield. Tackle shop: Alfreton Angling, 77 Mansfield Rd. Hotels: George, Castle. Also fair fishing in Derwent at Ambergate, 5m SW.

WYE (tributary of Derwent): One of few rivers in which rainbow trout breed. Also holds good brown trout.

Bakewell (Derby). Trout. Fishing preserved by Haddon Hall Estate. Details are to be found under **Rowsley,** above. Tackle shop: Piscatoria, 3A Hebden Court, sells large selection of local flies, plus fly tying materials and tools.

Monsal Dale (Derby). The Chatsworth Estate has excellent trout fishing on ¾m double bank. 4 rods per day only. Apply for day tickets at £18 to River Keeper on 0629 640484.

Buxton (Derby). River private. Brown and rainbow trout fishing in **Lightwood** and **Stanley Moor reservoirs;** Buxton FFC: dt £8, conc, from Buckingham Hotel, Buxton, tel: 0298 70481. Errwood Reservoir, Goyt Valley, leases to Errwood FFC. Dt from Pete Aquatics & Tackle, 4 Fairfield Rd, Buxton. Tackle shop: Peak Aquatics, 4 Fairfield Rd, Buxton.

DOVE. Dovedale waters, where Izaak Walton and Chas Cotton fished, are preserved, no tickets available. Good sport with trout and grayling elsewhere. In lower reaches, where polluted Churnet enters Dove, angling is improving.

Stretches below Uttoxeter, Doveridge, Marchington, Sudbury, etc, also improving: barbel, chub, grayling, pike present. Very limited opportunities for day tickets.

Uttoxeter (Staffs). Trout, grayling. Uttoxer AA preserves good deal of water between Rocester and Uttoxeter; no permits. Tackle shop: Uttoxeter Sports, 9A Market Place.

Rocester (Staffs). Trout, grayling above town; grayling, few trout below. Churnet; fishing spoilt by pollution, but improving; Private.

Ashbourne (Derby). Several miles of **R Henmore** and **Bentley Brook,** both tributaries stocked with trout and grayling, and two small lakes controlled by Ashbourne Fly Fishers' Club. St only; no dt. In **Dovedale** 3m of good trout and grayling fishing can be had by guests at Izaak Walton Hotel. Tackle shop: Fosters Sporting Services, Compton Bridge. Hotel in Ashbourne; Green Man; hotel at Mayfield, 2m SW (Staffs); Royal Oak.

Hartington (Derby). Trout. Charles Cotton Hotel has about 250 yds of the River Dove; residents only. Proprietor will give data about stretches available from farmers.

CHURNET (tributary of Dove): Mixed fishery spoilt by pollution for some years, but improving.

Cheddleton (Staffs). Endon Brook, 1m NW. West Brook, 1m SE. Pond by Wetley, 3m S. Basford Coarse Fishery, Turners Croft, **Basford** ST13 7ER; carp and other coarse fish, dt £3, £1 jun acc by adult. Tel Mr Smith, 0538 360616.

Leek (Staffs). Trout, coarse fish; preserved above Leek town by landowners. Fishing improving as pollution decreases. Leek and Morland's FC has local fishing, tickets from John Morgan, see below. **Turners Pool,** Swythamley, nr Rushton Spencer; coarse fish, dt £4. Mr Wilshaw, tel: 0260 227225. Springfield Fishery, Onecote: r and b trout, 4 fish dt £7.50. Tel: 0538 300 223/452. Freshwater Trout Farm, Macclesfield Rd, tel: 0538 33684. Dt £1.41 plus charge for fish caught.

POLLUTION

Anglers are united in deploring pollution. To combat it, urgent action may be called for at any time from any one of us. If numbers of fish are found dead, dying, or seriously distressed, take samples of both fish and water and contact the officer responsible for pollution at the appropriate National Rivers Authority.

Cast your line towards Northumbria

NORTHUMBRIAN WATER LIMITED manages fifteen fisheries in the North East of England, offering everything for the stillwater angler.

Each of our waters provides excellent fishing in stunning surroundings, giving the angler a wide variety of sport at highly competitive prices. For example, a 1994 Permit to fish one of our stocked waters, offering a six fish bag limit, costs as little as £9.00 for a full daily session. An unstocked water costs only £5.00. Concessionary, season and evening permits are also available.

For your FREE copy of our 1994 Fisherman's Handbook, a full-colour, 32 page fishing guide, packed with useful information to help the fisherman get the most from our waters, or for any further information please contact:

The Recreation Department, Northumbrian Water Limited, Abbey Road, Pity Me, County Durham DH1 5FJ. Telephone (091) 383 2222

A Member of the Association of Stillwater Game Fishery Managers.

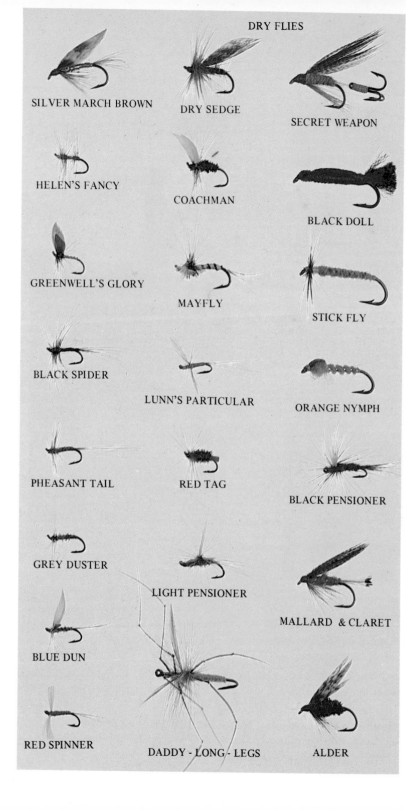

DRY FLIES

SILVER MARCH BROWN

DRY SEDGE

SECRET WEAPON

HELEN'S FANCY

COACHMAN

BLACK DOLL

GREENWELL'S GLORY

MAYFLY

STICK FLY

BLACK SPIDER

LUNN'S PARTICULAR

ORANGE NYMPH

PHEASANT TAIL

RED TAG

BLACK PENSIONER

GREY DUSTER

LIGHT PENSIONER

MALLARD & CLARET

BLUE DUN

RED SPINNER

DADDY - LONG - LEGS

ALDER

Rudyard Lake is 3m NW, 170 acre reservoir; very good bream, with roach, perch, and pike to 30lb; dt £2.50-£1.50, depending on season. Punts on half and full day from water bailiff Lake House, Rudyard, near Leek or from BW. Match lengths pegged. **Tittesworth Reservoir:** 189-acre Severn-Trent W trout fishery. *(See Midlands reservoirs and lakes).* Tackle shops: John Morgans, Albion Mill, Albion St; Leek Pet and Fishing Centre, 36 St Edward St.

MANIFOLD (tributary of Dove): Offers visitors few opportunities.

Longnor (Staffs). Buxton, 7m; trout. Dove, 1m E; trout, grayling. Crewe and Harpur Arms stretch now acquired by Derbyshire County AC; members only. Part of Hoo Brook and Manifold is National Trust property; trout restocked.

MEASE. Coarse fish. Fishing stations are: **Measham** (Leics); **Snarestone** (Leics); and **Ashby-de-la-Zouch** (Leics); **Netherseal** (Derby); **Edingale** and **Harlaston** (Staffs); Birmingham AA has water at last three. Hazeldine AA has Clifton Campville fishing. Hotels: Queen's Head, Royal.

SEAL BROOK (tributary of Mease): a small watercourse with few fish.

Over Seal (Leics). Lakes: Ashby Wolds Reservoir, 1m N.

TAME: After a long history of pollution, much recovered under the care of the Severn-Trent W. Fish now present in many stretches. Further improvement scheduled.

Tamworth (Staffs). Tributary Anker holds roach, pike and perch. Town waters are all let to clubs, tickets available from Tamworth Tackle. Birmingham AA has approx 1,300 yds here. Hazeldine AA also has stretch. Dt issued for Castle Pleasure Grounds from bailiff or tackle shop; other dt from Warren Farm, **Amington.** Mease; roach, chub, dace; Haunton, **Harleston;** dt from W T Ward and Harleston Mill. Local clubs: Lamb AC; Fazeley Victory AC; Birch Coppice AC; Tamworth WMC; which fishes Coventry and Birmingham Canals; some tickets available. Tackle shops: Tamworth Fishing Tackle, 23 Lichfield St; Fazeley Pet & Angling, 9 Coleshill St, Fazeley.

Kingsbury (Warwicks). Kingsbury Water Park, 600 acres, including specialist pike and carp fisheries, plus lakes stocked with a variety of coarse fish. Carp dt £3, Coarse fish dt £1.30, conc. Information from Country Park Managers Office, Kingsbury Water Park, Bodymoor Heath Lane, Sutton Coldfield, B76 0DY, tel: 0827 872660.

Sutton Coldfield (W Midlands). Lakes:

Not just a sport for men. Miss Tricia King prepares to return a 24 lb. common carp alive and well to the water. *Photo: Bruno Broughton.*

Bracebridge Pool, 2m NW; Blackroot Pool, 1m NW; Powell's Pool; all in Sutton Park; dt £1.25 (50p jun) from keepers. St £16. Local club: Sutton Coldfield AS has fishing on rivers and lakes. Membership applications to hon sec. Permits for members' guests only.

ANKER (tributary of Tame): coarse fish; best sport in winter. Dt on bank at Tamworth Castle Pleasure Grounds, also Pretty Pigs Public House, Amington.

Polesworth (Warwick). Coventry AA has 2m plus 20 acre lake; good head of tench and chub in river, large carp and bream in lake. Dt on bank. St from hon sec. Assn also has 7m on canal; dt from Association, bailiffs and tackle shops.

SENCE (tributary of Anker); small stream, but good trout and grayling in places, as well as chub, roach and dace.

BOSWORTH BROOK (tributary of Sence): Trout; preserved.

Market Bosworth (Leics). Bosworth Brook, 1m North; trout; preserved by owner of Bosworth Hall. Sence, 3m W. Tweed, 3m SW., Lakes: The Duckery, Bosworth Park, 1m S; pike, etc. Gabriel Pool, 3m NE.

BOURNE BROOK (tributary of Bourne). Fishing station: Plough Inn, **Shustoke,** Warwicks. Trout fishing in Avon Division STW Shustoke Reservoir.

BLYTH (tributary of Tame): Coarse fish. Centres: **Coleshill** (Warwicks), Chub, perch, pike, roach. **Hampton-in-Arden** (Warwicks). Chub, dace, roach. **Solihull** (Warwicks). Earlswood Lakes, 6m SW; ticket for three coarse lakes on bank from bailiff. **Olton Mere** coarse fishing; apply to sec, Olton Mere Club.

REA (tributary of Tame): Polluted and fishless.

Birmingham (W Midlands). Birmingham AA, formed from a number of local clubs, controls extensive water on river, canal and lake throughout the Midlands and into Wales. St £15. Ladies, juniors, OAP, regd disabled £5, covering salmon, trout and coarse fish. The club-card gives details of all fishing rights, which include numerous fisheries on **Severn and tributaries, Trent and tributaries, Wye and tributaries,** canals, lakes and ponds. A detailed guide with excellent maps is issued price 30p from Assn HQ, 100 Icknield Port Road, Rotton Park, Birmingham B16 0AP. White Swan Piscatorials own or rent waters on the **Severn, Avon, Teme, Mease, Tern, Rea, Lugg,**

Ithon, Herefordshire Arrow and numerous pools. St £32 + £32 entrance fee; limited. Game Fishers' Club has water on **Lugg, Rea, Monnow** and several brooks. Trout and grayling. Both clubs restrict day permits to members' guests only. St £50. Reservoir at **Edgbaston** fishable on permit. **Park Lakes:** coarse fishing on 14 lakes and pools in city. Dt from park keepers. Special st for pensioners available. Tackle shops: William Powell, 35 Carrs Lane; Anglers Corner, 1246 Pershore Rd, Stirchley; Triplex Angling, 213 Monyhullhall Rd, Kings Norton; Barry's, 4 School Rd, Hall Green; West Heath Tackle, 36 The Fordrough, W Heath; John's, 42 Kitsland Rd, Shard End; Curdworth Angling, Kingsbury Rd, Curdworth; Jim's Tackle, 11 Hollyfield Rd South, Sutton Coldfield; Allmarks, 429 Hagley Rd, Quinton, and many others. Many hotels.

Lifford (Birmingham). Bourne Brook, 2m N. Cole, 2m E. British Waterways reservoir. Good coarse fishing. Dt from park keeper.

FORD BROOK (tributary of Tame). Fishing stations : **Pelsall** and **Walsall** (W Midlands). Brook polluted. Lake: Hatherton Lake; pike. Swan AC leases **Sneyd Pool,** Essington Wyrley and Shropshire Union Canals, coarse fishing. Dt on bank. Match booking available. Walsall and Dist AS has **Hatherton Canal. Park Lime Pits;** carp, bream, roach, perch, pike; dt and st for small charge. **Aboretum Lake;** bream, tench, roach, perch, pike; dt.

SOWE: Coarse fish, some trout.

Stafford (Staffs). Upstream of town; perch, pike, dace, roach, chub. Downstream; perch, roach, bream, chub, occasional trout. Free for about $\frac{1}{4}$m upstream of town on left bank only; remainder preserved by Izaak Walton (Stafford) AA. This association has fisheries on the Sowe, the **Penk, Trent & Mersey Canal, Shropshire Union Canal** and **Hopton Pools,** carp, tench and other coarse fish. Apply hon sec for annual membership, wt and dt. Hotels: Swan, Station, Vine, Royal Oak, Garth, Tillington Hall.

Great Bridgford (Staffs). Sowe, Whitmore Reans AA has water. Izaak Walton (Stafford) AA has about $1\frac{1}{2}$m (see Stafford).

Eccleshall (Staffs); Trout; preserved. Stoke City & Dist AA fishes Garmelow Pool, 4 rods per day; bookings to E Gardner, tel: Stoke-on-Trent 818380. Stone & Dist AS

fishes Ellenhall Pools. Dt available.
PENK (tributary of Sowe):
Penkridge (Staffs). Coarse fish. Whitmore Reans AA has fishing here. **Staffordshire and Worcestershire Canal.** Stafford AA has water *(see Stafford).* Radford Bridge (Staffs). Izaak Walton

(Stafford) AA has water here. **Gailey Upper Reservoir,** Cannock, trout fishery. Apply to Club Office, Gailey Lea Lane, Penkridge, Staffs, tel: 0785 715848. Tackle shop: Tight Lines, Market Place, Penkridge.

TYNE

(For close seasons, licences, etc, see Northumbria and Yorkshire Region NRA p17)

Formed by junction of North and South Tyne at Hexham, and empties into North Sea at Tynemouth (Northumberland). Since recovery from pollution this river is considered by some to be the best salmon river in England; trout fishing fair. Pike are increasing in lower reaches (below Hexham) and dace in the North and South Tyne.

Newcastle upon Tyne (North'land). **Whittle Dene Reservoirs, Stamfordham,** trout fishery of 26 acres, leased to Westwater Angling. Dt from fishing hut at reservoir, 6 fish limit, self service. Tel: 0434 681 405. George Hotel has fishing at **Chollerford.** Throckley Reigh coarse fishery; C Woulhave, tel: 091 413 4603. Free fishing at Killingworth Pond, N Tyneside. **Killingworth Lake** is dt coarse fishery, tel: 091 266 8673. Westwater AC has 67 acre trout fishery on 4 lakes. Tel: 0434 681 405. Tackle shops: Angling Centre, 123/5 Clayton St West; J Robertson, 101 Percy Street; Bagnall & Kirkwood, 52 Grey Street.

Ryton (Tyne and Wear). Occasional salmon; trout, coarse fish. Federation water.

Wylam (North'land). Federation water. Salmon; trout, coarse fish.

Prudhoe (North'land). Trout, coarse fish; occasional salmon; water here and at **Ovingham** and **Wylam** preserved by the Northumbrian Anglers' Federation; also Coquet at Warkworth, Felton and Rothbury. St £42 salmon from Head Bailiff, Thirston Mill, Felton, tel: 0670 787663; £25 trout, from most Newcastle tackle shops and Music Box, 8 Front St, Prudhoe.

Mickley (North'land). Trout, coarse fish; occasional salmon; Federation water *(See Prudhoe).* Lakes: Whittle Dene Reservoirs, 5m N.

Bywell (North'land). Salmon, sea trout, coarse fish. Permits for 3m double bank from Reeltime Fishing Services, Roe House Farmyard, Stocksfield, tel: 0661 843799.

Corbridge (North'land). Trout and dace; trout plentiful but small with runs of sea trout and salmon. Corbridge Riverside Sports Club has 3m on south bank; membership restricted to persons living locally; dt to members' guests only. Newcastle's **Hallington Reservoirs** (8m N), Westwater Angling, J J Todd, The Club House, Hallington Reservoir. Licences; The Fly Box, 23a Princes St.

Hexham (North'land). Trout (av ¾lb), coarse fish; salmon improving. Tynedale Council has ½m on south bank off Tyne Green from Hexham bridge upstream. St £23, dt £4.20, conc for residents, OAP, etc, from Hexham House, Gilesgate, Hexham, or Tourist I.C. All other salmon water preserved. Langley Dam, 8m west of Hexham: 14 acre lake stocked weekly with r trout. Fly only. Dt £14, 7 fish; £12, 5 fish. Club: Hexham AA has water; no tickets. 4 miles south, Linnelwood Lake, fly only trout lake of 4½ acres. Dt £10, 3 fish. Tel: 0434 673262. Licences from Blair, Post Office, Allendale; Cresswell, 40 Priestpopple, Hexham. Hotels: Bowes, Bardon Mill.

Tributaries of the Tyne

DERWENT: Few trout. Trout average about ¼lb, but hard to catch owing to plentiful feed; early months best. Grayling Sept to 31 Dec.

Swalwell (Durham). Some pollution. Derwent Haugh to Lintzford, held by Axwell Park and Derwent Valley AA; dt for b and r trout, fly only until June 1, then limited worm. Membership restricted; PO Box 12, Blaydon NE1 25TQ.

Shotley Bridge (Durham). Derwent, 1m W; trout and grayling. Derwent AA preserves about 14m of river from Lintzford to **Derwent Reservoir** trout, *(see Dur-*

ham reservoirs) and one bank above reservoir to Baybridge; fly only. Membership restricted to Derwentside residents. Licences from Post Office, Shotley Bridge. Hotels: Crown; Cross Swords.

NORTH TYNE: trout water, with one or two salmon.

Chollerford (North'land). Trout, coarse fish. The George Hotel, Chollerford has ³⁄₄m bank fishing upstream of bridge. Trout average ¹⁄₂lb. St £27 S, £7 T; dt £8 S, £1.55 T, free to guests.

Bellingham (North'land). Trout, salmon sea trout; runs have improved since 1965; best July-Oct. Bellingham AC has 5m water above and below town. Membership limited. Ferryhill AC has water, tel: 091 388 3557. Riverdale Hall Hotel has 3m salmon and trout fishing at no additional cost to residents, on Tyne and Rede. Tel: 0434 220254. Licences; Bellingham Hardware, Park Side Place. Hotels: Rose and Crown, Cheviot, Black Bull, Riverdale Hall.

Falstone (North'land). Forestry Commission offers dt £2, wt £12 for stretch between **Butteryhaugh** and **Deadwater.** The permit also covers Akenshaw, Lewis, Kielder and Ridge End Burns. Available at Kielder Castle Forest Centre.

Kielder (North'land). Major NW reservoir of 2,700 acres. Natural brown trout fishery. Dt £4 and £3, motor boats £14 or £12, 6 fish. Fly only both here and at **Bakethin Reservoir** (stocked); dt £8. Boats £8 per day. Concessions for both waters to OAP, juniors and regd disabled. Tickets on site. Hotels: Riverdale Hall, Bellingham; Percy Arms, Otterburn.

REDE: Trout and pike, with few autumn salmon.

Otterburn (North'land). Otterburn Tower Hotel, NE19 1NS, has 3¹⁄₂m on Rede, south of Mill Bridge. Trout dt £5. **Sweethope Lake, Kirkwhelpington,**

trout fishing for natural b, stocked r; mt £42, dt £7, 6 fish, boat £3 extra. Contact Ray Demesne, Tweedwood Enterprises, Kirkwhelpington, Northumberland NE19 2RG; tel: 0830 40349. Northumbrian AF has water on Rede and Durtrees Burn; also 2m (both banks) **River Font.** Dt for **Fontburn Reservoir,** with stocked rainbows, on site. Linn Heads Lake, r trout fishing 4m w of Kirkwhelpington: tel: 0830 40349. Otterburn Towers Hotel distributes licences. Other hotel, Percy Arms.

SOUTH TYNE: A spate river, usually fishes well by September. One or two clubs issue tickets for trout and salmon fishing.

Fourstones (North'land). Trout and occasional salmon. Newbrough and Fourstones AA has 2¹⁄₂m of north bank only; no visitors' tickets.

Haydon Bridge (North'land). Trout and occasional late salmon. South Tyne AA preserves 5m of water. No spinning before June 1. Wt for visitors staying in parish £50, from J O Moore, 24 Struther Close, Haydon Bridge. Licences; Hindshield Fisheries, North Rd. Hotel: Anchor, adjoins river.

Haltwhistle (North'land), Brown trout, sea trout, salmon. Haltwhistle and Dist AA has visitors st £200, wt £80, conc, for 6m from Featherstone to Barton Mill. Available at Greggs Sports Shop, Main St. Hotels: Railway, Vallum Lodge, Manor House, Wallace Arms.

Alston (Cumbria). Salmon, sea trout, trout. Alston AA has 12m with wt £20 to £60 and dt £5 to £15, ¹⁄₂ price conc, available from A & P Struthers, Newsagents, Front Street, 0434 381462.

EAST ALLEN: Allendale AA stocks river with brown trout, and issues wt £5, dt £1 for 6m stretch. Jun ¹⁄₂ price. From Allendale Post Office, tel: 0434 683201.

Check before you go

While every effort has been made to ensure that the information given in **Where to Fish** *is correct, the position is continually changing, and anglers are urged, in their own interests, to make preliminary enquiries before travelling to selected venues. This is especially important with reference to prices quoted. Inevitably the rate of inflation is affecting stability in this quarter. Anglers' attention is also drawn to the fact that the hotels mentioned under the various fishing stations do not necessarily have water of their own. Any amendments or further data for inclusion in subsequent editions, and any criticism, will be welcome.*

WANSBECK

(For close seasons, licences, etc, see Northumbria and Yorkshire Region NRA p17)

Northumberland trout stream which fishes well under favourable conditions of water, but opportunities for visitors are few.

Morpeth (North'land). Brown trout; preserved by Wansbeck AA for 5m; members only, st £10 + joining £10. Water in town free to NRA licence holders. Licences obtainable from D Bell, 9 Biltons Court, Morpeth. Tackle shops: McDermotts Fishing Tackle, Station Rd, Ashington; Tackle and Game Supplies, Black Rigg, Morpeth; Chevy Sports, PO Box 1. Hotels: Waterford Lodge, Queen's Head, Angler's Arms, Weldon Bridge.

Tributary of the Wansbeck

BROOKER BURN:
Longhirst (North'land). Wansbeck, 2m S; trout. Lyne, 2m N.

WAVENEY

(see Norfolk and Suffolk Broads)

WEAR

(For close seasons, licences, etc, see Northumbria and Yorkshire Region NRA p17)

Rises on Kilhope Moors in extreme west of Co Durham and enters North Sea at Wearmouth. After history of pollution, river now contains salmon, sea trout, brown trout, dace, chub, roach and barbel, perch and bream. Tributaries Browney and Rookhope are improving. Bedburn preserved.

Chester-le-Street (Durham). Sea trout, brown trout (stocked by club) excellent coarse fish. AC (annual membership £29 + £4 joining fee) has 12m good water with the above species plus salmon, dace, chub, barbel, eels, roach. St £15, dt £1.25, from O'Briens, North Burns. Tackle shops: Angling Centre, 21 North Burns; Sports and Photographs, 139 Front Street. Dunelm AA fishes Chester Moor and Frankland stretches. Contact G Hedley tel: 091 386 4603.

Durham (Durham). Trout, sea trout. Free fishing on NRA licence from Milburngate Bridge to Sewage Works, also Ice Rink to Kepier Farm. Durham City AC has 1½m on river, and stillwater fisheries stocked with coarse fish. St £28 + £10 joining fee. Concessions to jun + OAP. Dt for guests of members only. Enquiries to Mr R K Ellesen, 32 St Monica Grove Crossgate Moor, Durham DH1 4AT. Grange AC has Kepier Viaduct area, tel: 091 584236. Dt for syndicate stretch at Kepier from Anglers Services, tel: 091 384 7584, or I & D Tackle, 091 276 3401. Bear Park, Cornsay and New Branspeth Assns all have water on **Browney**, 4m W of Durham; limited dt; restocking. North-West Durham AA has trout water on three reservoirs: **Waskerley, Smiddy**

Shaw and **Hisehope. Durham Beck** is fished by Ferryhill & Dist AC, tel: 091 388 3557. Tackle shop: Anglers Services, 45 Claypath.

Willington (Durham). Willington & Dist AC has fishing at Sunnybrow to Page Bank. Dt from Bonds Tackle Shop, High St, or Anglers Services, Claypath, Durham City.

Bishop Auckland (Durham). Sea trout, brown trout, grayling, salmon. Bishop Auckland & Dist AC controls some 20m of water on Wear, between Witton le Wear and Croxdale. Also Witton Castle Lakes, trout stillwater. Dt at lakes or tackle shop. Membership £93.50 + 25% joining fee, conc. Dt £5-£20, according to date from Windrow Sports, Fore Bondgate; hotels, post offices and other tackle shops in the area. Further details from hon sec. Ferryhill & Dist AC has fishing at **Croxdale, Tudhoe, Witworth Estate; Byers Green** and **Old Durham** fisheries, also **Newfield** and **Hunwick.** Hotel: Manor House, West Auckland.

Witton le Wear (Durham). For Witton Castle and considerable other stretches, including Croxdale, contact Mr J Winter, 7 Royal Grove, Crook DL15 9ER.

Wolsingham (Durham). Trout, sea trout (good). Wolsingham AA has water;

members only (limited st £29 + £10 joining, for visitors). Long waiting list. No dt. At Hagbridge, **Eastgate** (about 8m W), Northumbrian NRA has stretch; dt available. North-West Durham AA has **Waskerley** and **Smiddy Shaw Reservoirs. Tunstall** an NW fishery.

Frosterley (Durham). Trout, sea trout. About 1½m water belongs to Frosterley AC; members only, who must reside in area.

Stanhope (Durham). Trout, sea trout and salmon. About 2m water (both banks) belongs to Stanhope AA; limited st for visitors, £15. local st £6, conc, from hon sec. Sea trout June onwards. Northumbrian

Water has 2m. Dt (limited) from West End Filling Station. Tackle from Ian Fisher, Market Place. Hotels: King's Arms, Phoenix. For **Eastgate** fishing: Miss Bell, tel: 0388 528414.

Upper Weardale (Durham). Trout, sea trout (Sept and Oct). Upper Weardale AA has about 8m of Wear and tributaries from Westgate to Cowshill; st £18, wt £10, dt £3, jun 50%, from Post Office or Golden Lion at St John's Chapel. Water re-stocked annually with fish up to 12in. For **Burnhope** reservoir r trout fishing tel: F Graham, 0498 81263. Dt from lodge.

Tributary of the Wear

BROWNEY: now free of pollution; trout and sea trout.

Langley Park (Durham). Langley Park AA lease river here. Trout only. St £24, conc. 3m radius, waiting list. Assc. also has R Wear at Durham, trout and coarse, and coarse ponds. Tackle from P Arrowsmith,

Claypath. Hotel, Blue Star.

Burn Hill (Durham). Waskerley, Tunstall Hisehope and Smiddy Shaw Reservoir close together on moors between Stanhope and Consett. *(See above and under Durham Reservoirs).*

WEAVER

(For close seasons, licences, etc, see North West Region NRA p17)

Rises south-west of Cheshire and flows into Mersey estuary. Most species of coarse fish, trout in the upper reaches. **Northwich** (Cheshire). Good coarse fishing held by Northwich AA. Water on **Weaver, Dane, Trent and Mersey Canal** (about 17m); **Billinge Green Pools; Great Budworth Mere; Petty Pool Mere** (limited access); **Pickmere Lake.** Comprehensive st (all waters); St £15, wt £5. Exceptional concessions to OAP and regd disabled, from Box 18, Northwich. No tickets sold on bank. Tackle shops: Scotts Tackle, 84 Station Road; Firthfield, 66 Witton Street. Hotels: Moulton Crow Inn, Moulton; Mayfield Guest House, London Rd.

Winsford (Cheshire). Roach, bream, carp. Winsford & Dist AA have stretch from New Bridge upstream to Church Minshull, several pools around Winsford and R Dane at **Middlewich,** Croxton Lane to King St. St £13, conc, from sec, dt £2 on bank for Dane, Mon-Fri, and Weaver, Newbridge to Bottom Flash. Tackle shop: Deans Tackle, Delamere St. Hotel: Red Lion.

Minshull Vernon (Cheshire). Weaver 1m W. Wheelock, 1m E. Ash Brook, 3m. Stockport & Dist AF has water on Rochdale Canal, Weaver and the lake in Drinkwater Park. Dt on bank. Crewe LMR Sports AS has Sandhole Pool (coarse fish) and good tench water at **Warmingham** (½m); some permits *(see Crewe).*

Worleston (Cheshire). Coarse fish. Weaver. Pool Brook (of little account)

and Wistaston Brook.

Crewe (Cheshire). Weaver 2½m W. No fishing in Crewe, but Crewe LMR Sports AS has 3m of Weaver near Nantwich (4m away) on Batherton Estate. **Sandhole Pool** (1m), and **Doddington Hall Pool** (5m), rights on **Shropshire Union Canal** and stretches of **Severn, Weaver** and **Dane,** as well as good bream, tench and pike fishing on **Hortons Flash.** Guest tickets are not issued for any of these waters. Dt for Macclesfield Canal; coarse fish *(see also Congleton).* Tackle shops: Tilleys Tackle Shop, 10 Edleston Road.

Nantwich (Cheshire). Trout, grayling, dace, roach, chub, Nantwich AS controls nearly all Weaver near Nantwich; st only; water starts on Reaseheath Estate and stretches SE of town for 7m mainly on both banks, broken at Batherton Mill. Society also has stretch on **Severn** at Trewern. Other clubs with water near Nantwich are Pioneer AA, Amalgamated Anglers and LMR Sports (all Crewe), Wyche Anglers and Winsford and District AA; **Dane,** (Croxton Lane to King Street), **Weaver;** flashes; pools; st, dt from hon sec. These 4 clubs are members of Cheshire AA. Winsford Club's pools contain fine tench, carp, bream and pike. Weaver is chalk stream here; well stocked with roach, dace and chub. Middlewich AS are amalgamated with 2 other clubs to form Middlewich Joint Anglers. They control 6m of **R Dane,** course fish, trout on **Bostock** lengths only, 2m Trent & Mersey Canal, Sandbach side of M'wich, lakes and pools. St £20, dt £2, £1 canal, from sec of Dave's Tackle Shop,

Middlewich. **Shropshire Union Canal** controlled by BW: dt from bank ranger; st from tackle shop. Other waters within 10m of Nantwich are: Big Mere, Quoisley Mere (boats), Osmere, Blakemere (boats), Combermere (boats). Tackle shop: J & A Tackle, 35 Pepper Street, Nantwich. Hotels: Lamb, Crown, Three Pigeons.

Audlem (Cheshire). Adderley Brook. Birchall Brook, 2m NE. Lake: Woolfall Pool, 2m NE. Hotels: Lamb, Crown. *(for club water see Nantwich).*

Wrenbury (Cheshire). Nantwich AS has water in area; no tickets. Marbury Brook. Sale Brook, 2m S. Baddiley Brook, 2m N. Hotel: Combermere Arms, Burleydam, Whitchurch.

Tributaries of the Weaver

DANE: Good trouting in upper reaches, but difficult to come by. Coarse fishing, with odd trout and grayling lower down.

Northwich (Cheshire). Chub, dace and roach. Northwich AA have fishing, dt available.

Davenham (Cheshire). Trout, barbel, roach. Davenham AC have fishing, members only, Davenham to Leftwich.

Middlewich (Cheshire).Trout, dace, roach, chub. Winsford and Dist AA have fishing from Croxton Lane to King St, dt available.

Congleton (Cheshire). Dace, roach, chub, gudgeon and occasional grayling and perch. 6m of prolific water in and around Congleton controlled by Congleton AS, plus 2m Macclesfiled Canal. Dt £2 from bailiff or Sec, or tackle shop. From Radnor Bridge towards Holmes Chapel partly controlled by Prince Albert AS, Cheshire AA, Grove and Whitnall AA and Warrington AA. St for Cheshire AA stretch at **Somerfordbooths** from secretary or Crewe tackle shops. Assn also has water on Severn. Buglawton Trout Club have fly only water from Eaton to Congleton Park, and at Holmes Chapel, Saltersford. Dt available, mainly coarse fish. Moreton Trout Lake, Newcastle Rd, 0260 299496. Westlow Mere Trout Fisheries, Giantswood Lane, 0260 270012. **Macclesfield Canal:** Corbridge AS; roach, perch, tench, bream, pike; recently dredged; st and dt at small charge from bailiff; Congleton AS (*see above*). Winsford AA and Lymm AC also have stretches of Dane. Tackle shop: Terry's

of Congleton, 47 Lawton St.

Bosley nr **Macclesfield** (Cheshire). Roach, chub, carp, bream, pike; private. Lake: **Bosley Reservoir;** Prince Albert AS water, members only.

Macclesfield (Cheshire). **Langley Bottoms and Lamaload Reservoirs** (trout; fly only) controlled by Prince Albert AS, a nationally famous club with many fisheries in the NW of England and in Wales. These include stretches on the R Dane, the **Severn,** the **Ribble, Wye, Towy, Teifi, Cothi, Banwy, Twymyn, Trent, Dove, Winster, Vyrnwy, Lledr, Dulas, Dysinni, Dee, Dovey, Mawddach** and **Lune; Marbury Mere,** Whitchurch, **Isle Lake,** Shrewsbury, **Langley Bottoms and Lamaload Reservoirs,** Macclesfield and others. St £55 + £55, long waiting list. Dt issued for a few of their waters. Danebridge Fisheries has small trout lake at Wincle, fish to 16lb, dt £8; tel: 0260 227293. Tackle shop: Barlows Tackle, Bond St, Macclesfield.

Teggsnose Reservoir (various coarse fish) is Macclesfield Waltonian AS water; dt £3 Barlows of Bond St, Macclesfield. Other clubs: Macclesfield Fly-fishers' Club (12m on Dane and **Clough,** strictly preserved; no tickets), and Macclesfield and District Amalgamated Society of Anglers. **Macclesfield Canal:** good carp, pike, roach, etc. Prince Albert AS has approx 6m. Dt from Barlows Tackle, Macclesfield. Macclesfield Waltonians also fish stretch, at Buglawton, dt from Maccl. Tile Centre, Windmill St. **Redesmere** and **Capesthorne;** roach, bream, tench, perch, pike, mirror and crucian carp; dt from bailiff. East Lodge, Capesthorne *(see Cheshire lakes, meres, etc)*. Other waters in area: **South Park Pool;** carp, roach, perch, pike; dt. **Knypersley Reservoir** controlled by Cheshire AA; dt from bailiff. No night fishing.

WHEELOCK (tributary of Dane):

Sandbach (Cheshire). Wheelock and brooks polluted. Clubs with fishing in vicinity are Northwich AA, Winsford &

Dist AA, Middlewich AS.

ARTLE BROOK:

Keele (Cheshire). Artle, 1m W. Lake: Madeley Manor, 1m W. Doddington Pool (permits only); coarse fish.

MARBURY BROOK:

Malpas (Cheshire). Holywell Brook, 2m NE. Weaver, 3m NE. Marbury Brook, 3m SE. Moss Meres, Capel Mere (Cholmondeley Park), 3m NE and Barmere, 3m SE.

WELLAND

(For close seasons, licences, etc, see Anglian Region NRA p17)

Rises near Market Harborough and flows through Lincolnshire Fens to The Wash. Coarse fishing very good, much of it controlled by clubs. Bream and roach plentiful and run to good size in most areas and pike, perch, dace, chub, with some carp and tench, also taken. River stocked with trout in upper reaches. Fen Drains hold roach, bream, tench and pike, but few fish in North and South Drove Drains.

Spalding (Lincs). Welland, from Spalding to The Deepings, provides 12m of good fishing for pike, perch, chub, roach, dace, bream and tench; controlled by Peterborough AA to Crowland. Dt £2 from D T Ball. **Lincolnshire Drains;** good coarse fishing. Spalding FC preserves Counter, North, South and Vernatts Drains; pike, perch, roach, carp, rudd, bream, tench; also **River Glen** from Guthram Gowt to Surfleet village bridge and **New River** from Spalding to Crowland. **Coronation Channel** also fishable (east bank reserved for matches). Worksop and Dist AAA now lease 2½m, both banks, at Spalding. Tickets from D T Ball, Fishing Tackle Shop, 3 Hawthorne Bank, Spalding PE11 1JJ; or M Tidwells, Fen Lane. Two caravan parks with fishing available: Foreman's Bridge, Sutton St James, 0945 85346; Lake Ross, West Pinchbeck, 0775 761690.

Cowbit (Lincs). Pike, perch, dace. Spalding FC water *(see Spalding)*.

Crowland (Lincs). Pike, perch, dace. Nene, 2m SE at Black Horse Mills. New River from Spalding to Crowland preserved by Spalding FC; pike, roach, perch, dace, rudd, bream, tench; tickets from D T Ball, or M Tidwells *(see Spalding)*.

Deeping St James (Lincs). Chub, dace,

roach, bream, rudd, catfish, pike; preserved. Deeping St James AC controls Greatford Cut (Tallington), also Welland at Market Deeping. Dt available. Tackle shop: Nobby's Tackle. Hotels: Three Tuns (HQ).

Market Deeping (Lincs). Several Fishery controlled by Deeping St James AC. It extends 6½m from Market Deeping to Kennulph's Stone, on Deeping high bank, also on **Welland,** at **Maxey** and **Tallington, Greatford Cut, Folly River,** Peakirk and **Maxey Cut.** Notice boards erected. Dt £2.50 on most club waters, from bailiffs or tackle shop Nobby's Tackle, Deeping St James. Fishing opens June 16 to Mar 14. Glen, 4m N, at Kates Bridge. Hotel: Bull.

Stamford (Lincs). Chub, dace, roach, pike, perch; fishing free to NRA licence holders on N bank between Town and Broadeng Bridges; approx 1¼m. Elsewhere preserved by Stamford Welland AAA. Approx 18m of water, stretching from Barrowden to confluence of R Gwash and w bank of **Gwash** to Newstead road bridge, eight stretches in all. St £12, jun £3, OAP free, from hon sec or tackle shop. Other local assn, Stamford & Dist AA. **Burghley Park Lake,** 1m SE (bream an tench, some rudd), Monday to

POLLUTION

Anglers are united in deploring pollution. To combat it, urgent action may be called for at any time from any one of us. If numbers of fish are found dead, dying, or seriously distressed, take samples of both fish and water and contact the officer responsible for pollution at the appropriate National Rivers Authority.

Saturdays; dt £5 to fish island side of Burghley Lake from Burghley Estate Office, St Martins, Stamford, tel: 0780 52075. Tackle shop: Bob's Tackle, 13A Foundry Road.

Ketton (Leics). Oakham AS has water here and on **River Chater;** members only; coarse fish. Broome AS has 1m at **Duddington,** with roach, chub, perch, bream, dace. St £28, half price for juv, OAP, etc, from Mem sec Mr G Taylor, 100 New Romney Cres, Leicester, tel: 0533 417018. 2 year waiting list.

Rockingham (Northants). Eye Brook Reservoir; good trout fishing *(see Midlands reservoirs and lakes).* Hotels: Falcon, tel:

0572 823535; Central, both Uppingham, 5m N; Castle Inn, Caldecott.

Market Harborough (Leics). **Saddington Reservoir** is Saddington AA water. Enquiries to hon sec. Market Harborough and District Society of Anglers has about 1½m of **Grand Union Canal,** good for tench, bream, carp early in season; roach Nov-March. Membership cards £10, dt £2, conc, from Sports & Leisure, 7 St Mary's Road; or bailiffs on bank. Hotels: Angel, Grove. At Leire, near Lutterworth is **Stemborough Mill Trout Farm,** well stocked with r trout. Dt £12 6 fish, £10 4 fish. Open all year. Tel: Leir 209624.

Tributaries of the Welland

GLEN: River free from Surfleet village to reservoir, coarse fish; trout above Bourne.

Surfleet (Lincs). Glen free below village. Preserved above by Spalding FC.

Pinchbeck (Lincs). Permits issued by Welland and Nene RD. River Welland, 2m SE at Spalding; also Coronation Channel.

Counter Drain (Lincs). Counter Drain; coarse fish; Spalding FC.

Bourne (Lincs). Glen holds trout upstream landowners sometimes give permission.

GWASH: Fair trout and grayling stream.

Private fishing. Stamford Welland AA have confluence with Welland to Newstead road bridge, W bank.

CHATER:

Ketton (Leics). Roach and dace. Stamford Welland AA has stretch from junction with Welland to Ketton road bridge, both banks.

EYE BROOK: Good head of roach, dace and chub; trout upstream.

Uppingham (Leics). Welland, 3m SE, at Seaton. Chater, 3m N. Gwash, 4m N at Manton.

WITHAM

(For close seasons, licences, etc, see Anglian Region NRA p17)

Rises south of Grantham and flows northward to Lincoln, then south-eastwards to Boston, where it enters the Wash. Above Grantham noted mainly for trout, mainly private. Between Grantham and Lincoln it is a good mixed coarse fishery, with chub dace and roach, mainly private clubs. From Lincoln to Boston it is entirely embanked with excellent roach and bream fishing. The fishing rights for the majority of this length are leased to the Witham and District Joint Anglers' Federation. Members of affiliated associations have free fishing. Otherwise, temporary members, day-permits price £1.75 are available from their bailiffs on the bankside or local tackle shops. Match bookings to Secretary, R Hobley, 30 Gunby Avenue, Lincoln. Main fishing accesses are **Washingborough, Bardney, Southrey, Stixwold, Kirkstead Bridge** to **Tattershall Bridge** (road alongside), **Chapel Hill, Langrick Bridge** and **Boston. Woodhall Spa** is another good centre for Witham angling, with tackle shop 1 Church Rd, Martin Dales, and several hotels catering for anglers, including Kings Arms, 0526 52633; Railway, 0526 352580; Dunns, 0526 52969.

Boston (Lincs). Angling facilities exceptionally good; at least 100 miles of good coarse fishing (pike, perch, dace, tench, roach and bream) in Witham; Witham and Dist JAF holds 30m between Lincoln and Boston, also tributaries. **R Bain, South Forty Foot Drain, Sibsey Trader, Bargate Drain** (Horncastle Rd) and **East and West Fen Catchwaters** are Boston & Dist AA waters within easy reach. Dt

£1.50, disabled facilities on some waters. Lincoln & Dist AA have sole rights on Upper Witham between Lincoln and **Hykeham** to confluence with **R Brant,** approx 8m, plus **Upper Witham,** Norton Disney to Bassingham, Dt £2. Tackle shops: Burdens, Northend, Swineshead; Gon' Fishing, Main Ridge; Don Whites, 122/4 West Street; Vanguard Fishing Tackle, 25 Wide Bargate, Don White,

West St. Match bookings for Witham JAF to Fed secretary; for Boston AA waters to hon sec. Accom. with fishing at Moon Cottage, Cowbridge PE22 7BA, tel: 0205 350478.

Lincoln (Lincs). Good coarse fishing. Witham fishes best from Aug-Oct with bream predominant. Lincoln is HQ for Lincolnshire Anglers Fedn and Lincolnshire Rivers Anglers Consultative Assn. Witham and Dist JAF has Witham from Stamp End Lock to Boston West on right bank, with exception of a few short stretches, Witham left bank, Lincoln 1500 yds d/s of Stamp End Lock to Bardney, with exception of 1200 yds in Willingh Fen, Witham at Stixwould to Kirkstead Bridge; **Sincil Drain/South Delph** between Stamp End Lock and point 630 yds u/s of Bardney Lock; **North Delph, Branston Delph, Sandhill Beck, Timberland Delph, Billinghay Skerth, Kyme Eau.** Dt £1.75 available from bailiffs, local inns or Secretary. Lincoln AA has excellent coarse fishing on **Trent, Till,** drains, dykes and **Hartsholme Lake** (good bream and carp). Membership books £16.50 from tackle shops, concessions to jun, OAP. Dt £2. 11m **Fossdyke Canal** between Torksey and Lincoln now BW managed: address in Canal section. **North Hykeham; Richmond Lakes,** 40 acres, coarse; dt £1.50, on bank. Tel: Lincoln 681329. St £24, ½ conc. for Leisure Sports **Hykeham** fishery, 200 acre lake with roach, bream, rudd, tench, pike to 30lb. No day tickets. LSA, Thorpe Park, Staines Road, Chertsey, Surrey. Tel: 0932 564872. **Butterley Aggregates Lake;** 200 acre coarse; dt 80p on site. Lincoln tackle shops: South End Pet Stores, 447 High Street; G Harrison, 55 Croft Street; Boundary Pet Stores, 6 Bunkers Hill; J Wheater, Tentecroft Street; Boundary Pet Stores, 6 Bunkers Hill. Newport Tackle Shop, 85 Newport, Lincoln.

Grantham (Lincs). Grantham AA has good coarse fishing on Witham, **Grantham Canal** and **Denton Reservoir;** dt £1.50 for canal from local tackle shops. (Note: Grantham AA is a member of the federation of Midlands clubs. This federation, which includes Peterborough, Wreake, Boston, Oakham, Newark, Asfordby and Deeping St James Clubs, has been established to protect fisheries in area and leases waters on **Bourne Eau** and the **Glen**). Tackle shops: Arbon & Watts; Gun Shop, both Westgate, Grantham.

Long Bennington (Lincs). Chub, roach, perch, grayling, etc. No dt. Trout lakes at Syston Park (tel: 0400 50000); Lakeside Farm, Caythorpe (0400 72758). Pickworth Hall, Folkingham, has fishery, tel: 05297 257.

Tributaries of the Witham

SOUTH FORTY FOOT DRAIN: Good coarse fishing. Between Hubbert's Bridge and Swineshead Bridge, Boston and Dist AA, wt £6, dt £1.50. Matches booked through D G Wootton, Myyorn, Hall Lane, West Keal, Spilsby, Lincs. Centres are **Boston, Wyberton, Hubberts Bridge, Swineshead, Donington.**

RIVER BAIN: Trout above Horncastle; chub and dace below. Private fishing.

Horncastle (Lincs). Rivers Bain and Waring; trout, roach; preserved. Some good chub water, free fishing. Tupholme Brook 7m NW. Horncastle AA has an old brick pit in Hemingby Lane and about 1½m on canal from Bath House to lock pit; no dt for canal but st covers canal and brick pit (from hon sec). **Revesby Reservoir;** 2 lakes, 42 acres, coarse fish; contains big pike; apply at estate; tel: 065886 395, dt limited and not granted Sundays. Tickets for local fishing from tackle shop: F & D Grantham, Synchro Sports, Market Place. Hotels: Bull, Red Lion, Rodney.

FOSSDYKE NAVIGATION: Fossdyke held by BW. Centres: **Lincoln, Saxilby** and **Torksey.** Good coarse fishing.

HOBHOLE DRAIN, EAST AND WEST FEN DRAINS: All canalised lengths of river forming part of fen drainage system. Hold good stock of coarse fish (bream, roach, perch, pike, tench), and include following waters: **Maud Foster, Sibsey Trader, East Fen Catchwater drains, West Fen, Kelsey** and **Bellwater drains.** St £5 and dt £1 from Boston tackle shops and D G Wootton, Myyorn, Hall Lane, Spilsby, Lincs PE23 4BJ. Match pegs 80p. Hobhole and West Fen drains may be fished on NRA licence only. St covers also fishing on **Witham, Steeping, Steeping Relief Channel, Glen, Bourne Eau** and **South Forty Foot.**

SLEA: Rises west of Sleaford and enters Witham at Chapel Hill. Trout in upper reaches. Coarse fish, particularly roach, elsewhere. Private fishing throughout length. Tackle shop: Slingsby. Hotel: Carr Arms.

WYE

(For close seasons, licences, etc, see Welsh Region NRA p18)

Most famous of English salmon rivers. Rises on south side of Plynlimmon near source of Severn and enters estuary of Severn 2m south of Chepstow. Most of rod fishing in private hands, but there are several hotels and one or two associations with rights on river. Richard Harris & Stokes have more than 30m under management. Sea trout fishing of no account, but coarse fishing in lower reaches exceptionally good. No free fishing. Licences may be obtained from distributors in most villages and have usually to be produced when obtaining tickets or other permits to fish. Good brown trout fishing in Upper Wye and tributaries. The River Wye Preservation Trust may be contacted through it's secretary, Mrs Y Wylie J.P, The Cottage, Yarleton Lane, Mayhill, Longhope, Glos, tel: 0452 830989. There is also a Wye Salmon Fishery Owners Association: Baron von Mayland, 30 St Mary St, Monmouth, Gwent NP5 3DB, tel: 0600 715295.

Tintern (Gwent). Tidal; mostly eels and flatfish, though salmon sometimes taken. Contact J Jones, The Rock, Tintern, Gwent. Rose and Crown Inn.

Redbrook (Gwent). Chub, dace, pike, perch, salmon. Contact the Post Office, Redbrook. For Whitebrook fishing, V Cullimore, Tump Farm, Whitebrook, Gwent. For Fairoak Fishery, The Cot, St Arvans, Chepstow, Gwent, tel: 0291 689711, trout.

Monmouth (Gwent). Wye holds salmon, pike, trout, grayling, chub, dace; preserved. Monmouth Dist AS has 1½m of Winter fishing on both banks from Wye Bridge downstream to Trothy mouth, also ½m from Mally Brook upstream to Wyastone Leys. Glamorgan AC fishing lies between these stretches. **Monnow;** trout, grayling, chub, dace; Monmouth Dist AS has 1½m from Monnow Bridge upstream to Osbaston. Stocked annually with trout. Skenfrith AS also has water: Bob Fforest-Webb, 1 Trelesdee Cottages, St Weonards, HR2 8PU, tel: 09818 497. Trothy, trout; preserved. Brockweir to Livox Quarries, trout and coarse fish; St £20, dt £6 from Tackle shop: Tackle Centre, St James Street.

Symonds Yat (Hereford). Salmon, trout and coarse fishing all preserved. 1½m both banks between **Goodrich** and Symonds Yat controlled by Newport AA. Good S water; members only. Enquiries to hon sec. For Lower Lydbrook, contact G H Crouch, Greenway Cottage, Stowefield Rd, Lower Lydbrook, Glos,. Tel: 0594 60048.

Kerne Bridge (Hereford). Chub, dace, pike, perch, salmon, trout; preserved. Castle Brook, Garron, 2m; trout. Luke

Brook, 2m. Lammerch Brook, 5m.

Ross (Hereford). Salmon, trout, barbel, bleak, carp, bream, roach, large pike, chub and good dace. Ross-on-Wye AC has coarse fishing; st £20 + £15 joining fee, wt £12, dt £3. Permits may be obtained at G & B Sports, 19 Broad Street. Enq to T Gibson, tel: 0989 67775. Town water available to visitors at above rates. Garron, Gamber, 6m, and Monnow, 9m, are very good trout streams; landowners sometimes give permission. Salmon fishing available through Ross-on-Wye AC. Ebbw Vale Welfare AC has 2½m at **Foy**, with chub, dace, roach, barbel. Members only, membership available. Hotels: Royal, Radcliffe Guest House. Ross-on-Wye AC will be pleased to help visitors; send sae if writing. Foy Bridge Fishery, Lyndor has 250 mtrs double bank, spinning and fly fishing. Boats available. Tel: 0989 63833. **Wye Lea Fishery**, **Bridstow**, 1m single bank from Backney to Wye Lea. Salmon, end Jan - mid Oct, coarse mid Jun - mid Mar. 40 pegs. Tel: 0989 62880. Hartleton Trout Lake, 14 acres, tel: 0989 63723. Licences from G B Sports, Broad St.

Hereford (Hereford). Salmon, trout, grayling, other coarse fish. Hereford and Dist AA holds 11½m water on Wye and 8½m **Lugg**. Tickets; dt and wt for salmon, trout and coarse fish. Special membership may be granted to visitors for salmon, trout and coarse fish, or for trout and coarse fish only. St £45 to £20, coarse dt £3. Membership applications to Hereford & Dist AA, PO Box 35, Hereford. Tickets from tackle shops. 40 pegs at Monte Bishop, 12 Old Eign Hill, HR1 1TU, tel: 0432 342665. Permits from Mordiford

PO. Other Wye fishing in area: Letton Court, 05446 294, day, 04973 665, evening, R F Pennington. Birmingham AA also has water on Lugg at Dinmore and Moreton. Longworth Hall Hotel, **Lugwardine,** has trout and coarse fishing on Wye (outside salmon season) and a short stretch on the Lugg. For other fishing inquire Garnons Estate Office, Bridge Sollars, who sometimes have salmon dt available, in advance only, also coarse dt; phone bailiff on 09812 2270. W Jones, Carrier Cottage, Whitney-on-Wye; and Red Lion, Bredwardine. Local tackle shops: Hattons (also fishery agent, pleased to give information), 73 St Owen Street (2317); Perkins, 23 Commercial Road, tel: 274152, dt available for local pools. Hotels: City Arms, Green Dragon, Kerry Arms, Booth Hall. Red House Farm, Eaton Bishop, caters for anglers.

Bredwardine (Hereford). 4m salmon, trout and coarse fishing available at Moccas Fishery, Red Lion Hotel HR3 6BU, 500 yds from river. 16 Jun-31 Mar, 100 pegs. Tel: 0981 7303.

Hay-on-Wye (Hereford). Salmon, trout, pike, perch, chub. Hay-on-Wye Fishermens Assn is local club, Mr B Wigington, The Flat, 4 High Town, Hay-on-Wye. Tackle, NRA licences and permits (£25 to £3) for Hay Town Council water from H R Grant & Son, 6 Castle Street. Hotel: Swan, has fishing on Wye. For R Llynfi and Ford Fawr, Wye confluence, contact Mrs Lloyd, Bridgend Cottage, Glasbury-on-Wye, tel: 0497 847227. **Llangorse Lake** can be fished from here. Other fishing in area belongs to Sportsmail Ltd, Cardiff.

Glasbury-on-Wye (Hereford). Salmon, trout, chub, dace, grayling, pike. Fishing in Wye and Llynfi preserved. Llangorse lake is accessible.

Builth Wells (Powys). Salmon (best April, May, June and Oct); wild brown trout

declining. Groe Park & Irfon AC has $2\frac{3}{4}$m on Wye, $\frac{3}{4}$m on Irfon including some double bank, with 8 salmon catches on Wye and 4 late season catches on **Irfon.** Best S $38\frac{1}{2}$lb, b trout $5\frac{1}{2}$lb. Club stocks heavily with 14oz rainbows. Wt (S) £25, (T) £15, 3-dt (S) £15, (T) £10, coarse dt £3, jun 50%. No keep nets for grayling on club waters, prawn and shrimp for salmon banned. **Elan Estate Reservoirs** accessible *(see Rhayader).* Cueiddon, Duhonw, Baili and Edw preserved. Tackle and permits: M Morgan, Glanbran, 23 Garth Road. Hotels: Park Hotel; Lion; Caer Beris Manor Hotel.

Newbridge-on-Wye (Powys). Salmon, trout, grayling, chub, dace, pike, roach; preserved, Ithon; trout; preserved. Accommodation with fishing at Disserth Farm, tel: 277; Mr Philips, Laundry Cottage, tel: 237/208.

Rhayader (Powys). Wye; trout (av $\frac{1}{2}$lb; Wye record, $10\frac{1}{2}$lb, caught at Rhayader Bridge), salmon. Rhayader AA has 4m on Wye, 3m on Marteg to St Harmon and 16-acre Llyngyn at Nant Glas, trout; fly only; wt £10, dt £3. Jun $\frac{1}{2}$ price. Rhayader AA is partner in Elan Valley Fisheries, which controls b trout fishing in **Elan Valley,** (Caban Coch, Garreg Ddu, Peny Garreg and Craig Goch), st £15, dt £1.50, from Ranger at Visitors' Centre below Caban Coch dam, and Mrs Powell, Newsagent, West St. Rhayader. H Roberts, Bellmullet, Rhayader, tel: 0597 810368, has dt £4 for local Wye stretch and **Llngwyn Fishery.** Tickets also available from newsagents, Main St. Spinning on Craig Goch; other waters fly only. Elan Valley AC fish **Dolymynach Reservoir,** brown trout, members only, £11 per annum. (3-6m W) **Claerwen Reservoir** (650 acres) and streams controlled by WW. Dt £3.50, concessions. Accom. with fishing: Glanrhos Fishing Cottages, on Wye, tel: Rhayader 810277; Gigrin

---

Check before you go

While every effort has been made to ensure that the information given in **Where to Fish** *is correct, the position is continually changing, and anglers are urged, in their own interests, to make preliminary enquiries before travelling to selected venues. This is especially important with reference to prices quoted. Inevitably the rate of inflation is affecting stability in this quarter. Anglers' attention is also drawn to the fact that the hotels mentioned under the various fishing stations do not necessarily have water of their own. Any amendments or further data for inclusion in subsequent editions, and any criticism, will be welcome.*

Farm, tel: 810243; Mrs P H Hills, Kingsville, tel: 810334. Hotels which ca-

ter for anglers: Elan; Elan Valley; Castle; Lion Royal.

Tributaries of the Wye

TROTHY: Trout, some assn water.

Dingestow (Gwent). Trout; preserved. Glamorgan AC, Cardiff, has 6m fishing. Inquiries to the hon sec. Monmouth and Dist AS has 4m, mostly double bank. Trout and eels, excellent mayfly. St £20, dt £6 from Tackle Centre, St James St, Monmouth.

MONNOW: Good trout and grayling stream. 1m north of Monmouth, **Osbaston Fishery**, leased by Cwmbran AA. Trout, coarse fish. St £18 and dt £2, conc, from Pontnewydd, Pontypool, Cwmbran and Newport tackle shops.

Skenfrith (Hereford). Trout, chub, dace. Birmingham AA has fly fishing here. The Priory Hotel has 300 yards; free to guests.

Pontrilas (Hereford). Trout, grayling; preserved by owner of Kentchurch to 3m below here, thence by private owners to within 1m of Monmouth.

Pandy (Gwent). Trout, grayling; preserved. Honddu: trout; preserved. Hotel: Pandy Inn.

HONDDU (tributary of Monnow): Trout.

Llanfihangel Crucorney (Gwent). Trout only, preserved. No tickets issued.

Llanthony. Fishing for trout in unstocked water can sometimes be arranged at Abbey Hotel; variable charge, not expensive.

LUGG: Trout and grayling, with coarse fish in some stretches.

Mordiford (Hereford). Trout, grayling, etc; Birmingham AA has good stretch here, also water at Tidnor, Lugg Mill, Bodenham, Dinmore, Marden and Moreton. Inn: The Moon.

Longworth (Hereford). Longworth Hall Hotel has trout and coarse fishing, and on **Wye**, outside salmon season. Mt £34, wt £9, dt £1.50. Advance booking recommended.

Lugwardine (Hereford). 8½m preserved by Hereford and District AA. Dt available for right bank d/s starting some 150 yds below the Worcester Rd.

Leominster (Hereford). Trout, grayling, pike, perch, dace. Above town Lugg preserved by landowners. White Swan Piscatorials also have water; otherwise preserved by landowners. **Pinsley Brook;** trout, grayling; landowners sometimes give permission. Coarse pools

at Docklow: Mrs Brooke, tel: 056882 269, dt £3; Mr Bozwood, tel: 056882 256, dt £3.50. Hotels: Royal Oak (where fishing can be arranged for guests); Talbot.

Kingsland (Hereford). Lugg. Arrow, and Pinsley Brook; trout, grayling. Fishing generally preserved by landowners. 2m from Kingsland is River Arrow at Eardisland. Accommodation: Angel and Mortimer Cross.

Presteigne (Powys). Lugg, Arrow and Teme afford excellent trout and grayling fishing, generally dry fly; preserved but landowners may give permission. The Gamefishers Club has Lugg here, as well as Monnow and Honduu, Rea and Cound Brook, Salop, 13m in all. Subscription £70 + £60 entrance: J H Andrews, Meadow View, Dinedore, Hereford, HR2 6LQ, tel: 0432 870 202. At **Walton,** fly fishing for trout in 4-acre lake reserved for tenants of holiday cottages, boat available. Wt £20, children usually fish free of charge. Details from Mrs A Goodwin, Hindwell Farm, Walton, Presteigne. Tel: 054421 252.

FROME (tributary of Lugg). Trout, preserved.

Ashperton (Hereford). Frome, 2½m Leddon, 2½m. Lakes: Devereux Park Lakes, 4m.

ARROW (tributary of Lugg): Trout, grayling, dace; but few opportunities for visitors.

Pembridge (Hereford). Trout, grayling, dace; preserved by landowners. White Swan Piscatorials have a stretch at Ivington. No tickets. Inn: New Inn.

Kington (Hereford). Trout; preserved. Inns: Swan, Royal Oak.

LLYNFI: Trout, grayling, etc; preserved.

Glasbury-on-Wye (Hereford). Lynfi enters Wye here. Trout, grayling, chub. Fishing good, but mostly preserved. Hotel: Maesllwch Arms.

Talgarth (Powys). Llynfi. Dulais brook. Rhiangoll; trout. Treffrwd, 2m. **Llangorse Lake** (pike, perch) can be fished from here (4m); boats available. Hotel: Castle. Visitors' tickets from local association.

IRFON: limited salmon, trout few unless stocked; good grayling.

Llangammarch Wells (Powys). Lake

Country House Hotel (tel: 05912 202) has about 5m of Irfon and nearby streams (**Garth Dulas, Chwefri,** etc), and some rods for salmon fishing on Wye negotiated each year and charged accordingly. Also 2½ acre trout lake (brown and rainbow; fish to 3½lb) in grounds. Lake and rivers restocked annually. Fly only on some beats. Wt and dt available. Salmon dt £20, trout £12. Neuadd Farm has accom. with fishing on Ithon, tel: 2571. Cammarch Hotel (05912 205) has 7½m of trout and salmon fishing on **Irfon,** 3¼m fly only, stocked with r trout 4 times a year; excellent grayling fishing. 1m of Wye and about 3½m of **Cammarch** and Upper **Dulais.** Dt £12 trout, £18 salmon. **Wye,** Salmon £20-£25. Licences and tackle at both hotels.

Llanwrtyd Wells (Powys). Trout. 3m of Association water. Lakes. Riverside Guest house has accom. with fishing, tel: 429. Victoria Wells Mountain Centre has accom. with fishing, tel: 334. Hotel: Neuadd Arms has 1½m of fishing.

ITHON: Trout, chub, few salmon. Good hotel and assn water.

Llandrindod Wells (Powys). Trout, grayling, chub, some eels and salmon. Llandrindod Wells AA controls 5m of trout fishing close to town, mainly between Disserth and Llanyre Bridges. Available to visitors on st £21, wt £13, dt £4.50. Concessions for OAP, jun. Limit five brace per day. Sunday fishing; no spinning for trout allowed, 9" size limit; waders essential. Accom, Corven Hall, Howey, tel: 82 3368; Greenway Manor, Crossgates, tel: Penybont 230; Dolberthog Farm, tel: 82 2255. Tackle shops: A Selwyn & Sons, Park Crescent (Tel: 82 2397), NRA licences and association tickets. Hotel: The Bell, Llanyre.

Penybont (Powys). Trout, chub, grayling, autumn salmon. Hotel: Severn Arms, which has 6m of trout fishing (on Ithon) free to residents. Dt £3 for non residents. Fish run 3 to lb average. Licences at tackle shops in Llandrindod.

Llanbadarn Fynydd (Powys). Upper Ithon. New Inn has 3½m trout fishing; free to guests (fly only); also rough shooting.

WYRE

(For close seasons, licences, etc, see North West Region NRA p17)

From Churchtown downstream coarse fish and brown trout. Above Churchtown limited amount of salmon fishing and good sea trout and brown trout fishing. Ribble and Wyre FA, an amalgamation of Wigan, Bolton and Preston Assns, controls good deal of water. No dt, information regarding membership from hon sec.

Fleetwood (Lancs). Sport in estuary improving as pollution lessens; flatfish mostly. Bolton AA have water, st £12, £4 conc, from tackle shops. Licences and sea baits from Langhornes, 80 Poulton Road, tel: 0253 872653.

St Michael's (Lancs). Mainly brown trout and coarse fish. Ribble and Wyre FA have fishing at St Michaels, some sea trout. Hotel: Grapes.

Churchtown (Lancs). Salmon, sea trout, trout and coarse fish. Warrington AA has fishing here.

Garstang (Lancs). Salmon, sea trout, trout and coarse fish. Garstang AA preserves 3m both banks. Fly only. No dt, members only. wt for temporary residents in area from tackle shop. Lonsdale AC has two stretches here. Dt available. Tackle shop: Garstang Fishing and Shooting, 6 Pringle Court. Hotels: Royal Oak, Eagle and Child, Crown.

Scorton (Lancs). Salmon, sea trout, trout, coarse fish. Wyresdale Anglers have 7m water; no tickets.

Fishing available?

If you own, manage, or know of first-class fishing available to the public which should be considered for inclusion in **Where to Fish** *please apply to the publishers (address in the front of the book) for a form for submission, on completion, to the Editor. (Inclusion is at the sole discretion of the Editor).*

YARE

(See Norfolk and Suffolk Broads)

YORKSHIRE (lakes, reservoirs, canals and streams)

(For close seasons, licences, etc, see Northumbria and Yorkshire Region NRA p17)

BRANDESBURTON PONDS. Several ponds offering varied sport to leisure anglers and specialists. Hull and District AAA, membership available from local tackle shop or Secretary. No dt.

BURTON CONSTABLE LAKES. At caravan park in grounds of Burton Constable Hall; excellent coarse fishing for roach, bream, perch, tench, carp and pike. St £25, mt £12, wt £6 from Warden, Old Lodge, Sproatley, nr Hull. 25 acres of fishing. Season 1 Mar-31 Oct.

CASTLE HOWARD GREAT LAKE. Near **Malton.** 74 acres, noted for specimen pike over 40lb, perch, tench, bream to 14lb, roach, and eels to 8lb+. Fishing 6am to sunset. Ground bait allowed in moderation. Peat and leam banned. Maggots, groundbait and tackle on sale from bailiff. Dt £3, OAP and children £1.50 from Richard Callan, Head Bailiff, North Lodge, Castle Howard, York YO6 7DH, tel: 065384 331. Close season 15 Mar-15 Jun. Sunday fishing.

CHELKER, SILSDEN, LEESHAW and WINTERBURN RESERVOIRS. Trout; let to Bradford Waltonians; no tickets. Waiting list. Near Silsden and Ilkley.

DAMFLASK and UNDERBANK RESERVOIRS. YW Services Ltd. Damflask, 5m from Sheffield. Underbank 10m. Stocked with trout (2 fish limit) Damflask with coarse fish, pike to 34lb. Season: March 25 to following Feb 28. Dt £3 sold from machines at reservoirs. Concessions.

DOE PARK RESERVOIR, Denholme. 20 acres. Trout, coarse fish; let to Bradford City AA; dt £5, Mon-Fri incl, 7 am (8.30 weekends) until 1 hour after sunset.

EMBSAY, and WHINNYGILL RESERVOIRS. Let by YW to Skipton AA, jointly with Addingham AA. St £40 + £15 entrance fee. Dt £5 (Embsay, trout), £3.95 (Whinnygill, Trout, roach and perch). £2 Winter coarse fishing. Assn also has fishing on R Aire, dt £3.50. Tickets obtainable from Paper Shop, Embsay, and Skipton and Earby tackle shops.

FEWSTON and SWINSTY RESERVOIRS. YW trout fishery, 153 acres each, fly only, barbless hooks. Regular stocking, 11lb 6oz av, 3lb rainbows. Dt (limit 4/2 fish), from machine at Fishing Office at Swinsty Moor Plantation. Area for disabled only, at Swinsty Lagoon where worm or fly may be used. Av catches for 1990 3 fish per rod. Near **Harrogate** and **Otley.**

HEWENDEN RESERVOIR. Between **Keighley** and **Bradford.** Trout, pike, roach, bream. Central Division AC. St £3.50 + £2.50 entrance fee from hon sec, A R Healey, 49 Green End Road, E Morton, nr Keighley, W Yorks. Waiting list.

HORNSEA MERE. Hornsea HU18 1AX. Yorkshire's largest inland water (350 acres). Very good pike, carp, bream, rudd, perch, roach, tench. Hornsea Mere Marine Co (Tel: 0964 533277). Dt £1.50, evening and junior 75p, punts £5 day (limited boat and bank fishing).

LEEMING RESERVOIR. Fishing station: **Oxenhope.** 20 acres; good trout fishing, brown and rainbow. Bradford City AA; dt £3, Mon-Fri.

LEIGHTON RESERVOIR. Masham, N Yorks. 105 acre water-supply reservoir on the Swinton Estate stocked with large rainbow trout (some very large) for season and day ticket fishing. Barbless hooks. St £300 (4 fish), £200 (2 fish) available, dt £10, (4 fish), evening £5, (2 fish). Catch and return allowed after limit reached. Concessions. Estate Office, Swinton, N Yorks HG4 4JH. Phone 0765 689224 for further details.

LEVEN CANAL. Beverley 6m. 3m of good coarse fishing.

LINDHOLME LAKE. 12m E of **Doncaster.** 18 acre fly only trout fishery. St (35 visits) £75. Extra visits by arrangement. Bag limit. Severn-Trent licence required. Inquiries to Epworth 872015.

MALHAM TARN. 6m from **Settle.** A Nature Reserve leased from National Trust by the Malham Tarn Field Centre, BD24 9PU. Boat fishing only, for trout with fly, and for perch with worm. Fish may run large. Dt £7 boat, £5 rod. Weekends, £12 boat, £5 rod. ½ price conc. No outboard motors allowed. Bookings and detailed information from Warden or Secretary (Tel Airton 331). Phone bookings recommended. Seasons May 1 to Sept 30 for trout. Accommodation available at Centre or in locality.

MARKET WEIGHTON CANAL. Fishing stations: **Newport** and **Broomfleet.** 6m long; bream, perch, roach, pike. Match fishing leased from NRA. Dt available locally.

MOREHALL RESERVOIR. Sheffield 7m. YW Services Ltd. Trout, fly only; dt £4 from machine at reservoir (limit 4 fish).

NOSTELL PRIORY LAKES. Foulby, nr Wakefield. Well-stocked with perch, pike, eels, carp, bream, tench and roach. St £50, dt £3.50, ½ day £2.25. Various concessions. Details from Fisheries Shop, Foulby Lodge. Tel 0924 863562. Open from 6.00 daily.

SCOUT DIKE, Penistone. 16m from Sheffield. YW (Southern Division). Trout, 2 fish limit; st £17.50. Dt £3.50 sold from machine at reservoir.

SEMERWATER LAKE. Fishing station: **Bainbridge.** Trout, perch, bream and rudd. Water ski-ing at weekends. Dt £2.50 for Wensleydale AA waters (west side and 2m of River Bain near lake) from Rose & Crown, Bainbridge *(see Yore - Bainbridge).*

SHIPTON LAKE. Shipton-by-Beningbrough. Tench, perch, roach, trout, pike. Bradford City AA, members only.

STAINFORTH AND KEADBY CANAL. Controlled by joint committee including following clubs: Rotherham, Doncaster, Sheffield Amal, Scunthorpe AA and British Railways. Usual Coarse fish.

TEES VALLEY AND CLEVELAND RESERVOIRS. These groups of reservoirs, managed by the Northumbrian Water, includes both stocked and wild waters. **Grassholme, Cow Green, Balderhead, Selset, Scaling, Blackton, Hury, Lockwood Beck, Kielder.** Fly only on Lockwood Beck, **Bakethin** and **Tunstall.** Prices are as follows: Elite Per-

mit, covering all waters, £340, £260 conc; Select Permit, excluding fly only waters, £300, £230 conc. Dt from £11 to £5, conc £8 to £4. Rowing boats where available £9-£7; motor boat (Kielder) £15-£13. For information: Bakethin and Kielder, 0430 240398; Fontburn, 0669 21368; Burnhope, 091 383 2222; Tunstall, 0388 527293; Cow Green, Grassholme, Balderhead, Hury and Selset, 0833 50204; Lockwood Beck and Scaling Dam, 0287 640214. **Waskerley** is controlled privately, with dt on site. Fly, worm, spinning, limit 6 fish. Tel: 091 383 2222 (NW Rec. Dept.) or Sec, 0207 501237.

THORNTON STEWARD RESERVOIR, Bedale. 35 acre YW trout fishery, fly only, barbless hooks. Regularly stocked, 1lb 6oz av, together with many 3lb rainbows. Season: Mar 25 to Oct 31. 4/2 fish limit, dt from Finghall Sub-PO, tel: 0677 50245.

TILERY LAKE, Faxfleet, nr Goole. 60 acres of water with carp to 30lb, bream, pike and roach. Controlled by Hull AA, st from hon sec or tackle shops in Hull and Goole locality. No night fishing without special permit, available from night permit sec.

ULLEY COUNTRY PARK. Sheffield; 7m. Rotherham MBC. 33 acre coarse fishery. Disabled access available. Season: June 1 to Feb 27. Dt £3 from ticket machine at fishery. Enquiries to Ulley C P, Pleasley Road, Ulley S31 0YL. Tel: 0709 365332.

WORSBROUGH RESERVOIR, Barnsley. Coarse fish, all species, open all year. Barnsley AS has rights and on ½m of canal. St £15, ladies, juniors, disabled £8. Dt £2 from bailiffs walking the bank. Sunday fishing to assn members only; hempseed and bloodworm barred, no keep nets.

POLLUTION

Anglers are united in deploring pollution. To combat it, urgent action may be called for at any time from any one of us. If numbers of fish are found dead, dying, or seriously distressed, take samples of both fish and water and contact the officer responsible for pollution at the appropriate National Rivers Authority.

Carp specialist John Aplin with a 40 lb. 6 oz. common carp caught in December 1992.

ENGLISH CANAL FISHING

British Waterways own 1100 miles of canal, and 92 operational supply reservoirs. The large majority of these fisheries are leased to fishing clubs, but the Board retains 125 miles of directly controlled fishing on canals and several reservoirs (shown below) or in the appropriate geographical section of the book, with season or day tickets easily available.

Stocking levels are extremely good and surpass the E.E.C. designated standard. The fishing is governed, as elsewhere, by water quality and natural food supply. Facilities for anglers in wheelchairs have been introduced in places; competitions can be arranged on directly controlled waters on application to the Fisheries Manager. Canal and lock cottages are let for holidays on some stretches. 770,000 anglers over the age of 12 fish British Waterways Fisheries regularly. They form an important part of the coarse fishing on offer in England and Wales. Roach, perch, bream, gudgeon, eels, pike and other coarse fish are to be found. On some canals there is moderate trout fishing. Carp to 28lb have been reported from Middlewich Branch Canal, and in some Grand Union stretches, a good head of tench, larger bream and crucian carp. **Anglers should take special care to avoid overhead power lines above rural canals.**

There are now three administrative areas of British Waterways Fisheries: North West Region, Navigation Road, Northwich, Cheshire SW8 1BH (tel: 0606 74321); North East and Midlands Regions, Peel's Wharf, Watling Street, Fazeley, Staffordshire (tel: 0827 252000); South East and South West Regions, Brindley House, Lawn Lane, Hemel Hempstead, Hertfordshire HP3 9YT (tel: 0442 235400, fax 0442 234932). Some of the fishing clubs mentioned below are, for reasons of space, are not in the club lists of this edition. The Regional Fisheries Manager at the appropriate office will supply addresses and other information.

SOUTH REGION:

Grand Union Canal; Osterley Lock to Hayes leased by London AA. Hayes to West Drayton, Central Assc of London & Prov AC. West Drayton to Denham, London AA. Denham to Batchworth, Blenheim AS. Sabeys Pool and part of R Chess, West Hampstead AS. Batchworth to Lot Mead Lock, Sceptre AC. Lot Mead to Cassionbury Park, Watford Piscators, and to Hunton Bridge plus R Gade stretch, Kings Langley AS. Hunton Bridge to Tring, plus small R Gade length at Kings Langley, London AA. Tring to Cheddington, Tring Anglers. Cheddington to Stoke Hammond. Luton AC. R Ouzel at Three Locks, Chiltern Tackle AC. ¼m from Stoke Hammond, plus Great Ouse, Milton Keynes AA. To Simpson, Coventry & Dist AA. Simpson to Great Linford, Milton Keynes AA. Milton Keynes Marina, Milton Keynes Marina Ltd. Great Linford to Wolverton Bridge, North Bucks Div. SE Midlands, CIU Ltd. Old Wolverton to R Ouse Aqueduct, Galleon AC. 400m Canal and Broadwater at Cosgrove, Mr & Mrs M Palmer, Lock House, Cosgrove. Cosgrove to Castlethorpe, Deanshanger & Old Stratford AA. Castlethorpe to Yardley Gobion, Britannia AC. Yardley Gobion to Dodford, Northampton Nene AC. Brockhall to Watling Street Bridge, Daventry & Dist AA. Norton Junction to southern end of Braunston Tunnel, AM-PRO UK Ltd AC.

Grand Union: Arms and Branches:

Paddington Arm; Bulls Bridge Junction to Lock Bridge at Paddington, London AA. **Paddington Basin;** Westminster AC.

Regents Canal; Little Venice to Islington, Raven AC. Islington to Mile End, London AA. Mile End Lock to Commercial Road, Brunswick Brothers AS. **Hertford Union Canal;** Junction with Regents Canal nr Victoria Park to Lee Navigation at Old Ford, London AA. **Slough Arm;** Whole of Arm from junction with Main Line at

---

POLLUTION

Anglers are united in deploring pollution. To combat it, urgent action may be called for at any time from any one of us. If numbers of fish are found dead, dying, or seriously distressed, take samples of both fish and water and contact the officer responsible for pollution at the appropriate National Rivers Authority.

Cowley to Slough, Berkshire FA. **Wendover Arm;** Main Line to Tringford Pumping Station, Tring Anglers. **Aylesbury Arm;** Main Line to Red House Lock, Tring A. Red House Lock nr Aston Clinton to u/s of Aylesbury Basin, Aylesbury & Dist AF. To the Basin Terminus, Aylesbury Canal Society. **Northampton Arm;** Main Line to Milton Malsor, Northampton Britannia AC. Milton Malsor, Northampton Castle AA. Milton Malsor to Hardingstone, Northampton Conservative WMC. Hardingstone to Duston Mill Lane, Northampton Castle AA. Bridges 13 to 14, Glebe AC, Bridges 14 to 18, Northampton Castle AA. Gayton Marina, Gayton AC. **Leicester Branch;** Norton Junction to Crick Tunnel, Towcester & Dist AA. North end of Crick Tunnel to Bridge 20, Knightley AC. Bridges 20 to 22 at Yelverton, Eldon Sports and SC. Bridges 31 to 33, Lutterworth AC. Bridges 34 to 37, and 39 to 41, White Hart Match Group. Bridges 37 to 39, Bostrom AC. Bridges 41 to 45, Brixworth AC. North Kilworth to southern end of Bosworth Tunnel, White Hart Match Group. To Bridge 47, Broughton & Dunton AC. Bridges 47 to 51, Friendlies AC. Bridges 51 to 54, Broughton & Dunton AC. Bridge 54 to Foxton Locks, Britannia WMC. Whole of Welford Arm, Bostrom Europe AC.

River Lee Navigation; Limehouse Basin to Blackwell Tunnel, Bruswick Brothers AS. Bow Lock strectch, Lee Anglers Consortium. Cheshunt, off-side bank plus Cadmore Lane Gravel Pit, Metrop Police AS. West bank Old R Lee, Kings Weir, W E Newton, Slipe Lane, Wormley. Carthegena Lock, Mr P Brill, Carthagena Lock, Broxbourne, Herts. Above Kings Weir to below Aqueduct Lock, London AA. Dodds Wier, L.V.R.P.A. Wier Pool at Feildes Weir, and Feildes Weir Lock to Rye House Station Bridge, plus stretch ½m u/s of Ryehouse Bridge, Lee Anglers Consortium. Ryehouse Bridge for 1020 metres, London AA. Offside Bank between Hardemeade and Stansted Locks, Ware AC.

Oxford Canal (South); Dukes Cut, Wolvercote Pool, Hythe Bridge Street to Kidlington Green Lock, North Oxford AS. Kidlington Green Lock to Bullers Bridge, N. Oxford AS. Bullers Bridge to Langford Lane, Kidlington AS. Langford Lane to Bridge 221, Reading AA. Bridge 221 to end of moorings at Thrupp,

Thrupp Canal Cruising Club. Thrupp to Bridge 216, Reading AA. Bridges 216 to Lower Heyford, plus River Cherwell at Enslow, Kirtlington, and Northbrook, Oxford & Dist AA. Lower Heyford to Aynho, Banbury & Dist AA. Aynho to Banbury, Coventry & Dist AA. Banbury to Cropredy, Banbury & Dist AA. Cropredy Lock to Bridge 148, Standard-Triumph Recreation C. Bridge 148 to Claydon, Sphinx C. Claydon to Fenny Compton, Ford (Leamington) AC. Fenny Compton Marina to Bridge 136, Cowroast Marina AC. Folly Bridge to Napton Junction, Leamington Liberal AC. Napton Junction to Bridge 103, and Bridges 101 to 102, Coventry & Dist AA.

River Stort; From junction with Lee Navigation to Lower Lock, Lee Anglers Cosortium. From Road Bridge 6 to Railway Bridge 7, Roydon, Two Bridges AS. To Hunsdon Mill Lock, Globe AS. Stort and Stort Navigation at Burnt Mill, Harlow FA. Burnt Mill Lock to Parndon Lock, Stort Valley AA. Spellbrook Backwater, O J Smith, Spellbrook Lane East, Bishops Stortford. Bishops Stortford and to Spellbrook Lock, Bishops Stortford & Dist AS. Further stretch to Sawbridgeworth AS.

Oxford Canal (North); Bridges 101 to 97, Warwick & Dist AA. Bridges 97 to 85, Willoughby, Braunston Turn and Braunston Tunnel, Braunston AC. Willoughby Wharf Bridge to Bridge 83, Goerge AC. Bridges 80 to 77, Avon Ho AC. Bridge 76 to Hillmorton Top Lock, Rugby Federation of Anglers. Hillmorton Bottom Lock to Bridge 66, Banks and Burr AC. Clifton Bridge to Boughton Road Bridge, Hi-Shear Fasteners Europe Ltd. Boughton Road Bridge to Bridge 43, Aces AC. Bridges 43 to 41, Peugeot Talbot AC. Bridges 41 to 9, Aces AC.

Oxford Canal, Branches; Stretton Arm, B. Wilson, The Railway Inn, Stretton-under-Fosse. **Rugby Arm,** BW directly managed. **Newbold Arm,** BW directly managed.

SOUTH WEST REGION:

Bridgwater and Taunton Canal; Bridgwater to Durston, Bridgwater AA. Durston to Taunton, Taunton AA.

Gloucester and Sharpness & Stroudwater Canals; Hempsted Bridge, Gloucester, to Sharpness, leased to Gloucester Canal Angling. Frontage of Borrow Silos (150 yds), Babcock AC. Tanker Bay Area, MEB AC. Offside bank at Two Mile

Bend, nr Gloucester, and Rea Bridge to north of Sellars Bridge, Gloucester United AA. Stroudwater Canal; Walk Bridge to 'Feeders', Frampton & Dist AA, also from Ryalls Farm to 'Stone' near Frampton. Walk Bridge to Whitminster, Whitbread AC.

Kennet and Avon Canal; Eight stretches from Bear Wharf, Reading, to Kennet Junction, Reading & Dist AA, with the exception of stretch near Sulhampstead Lock, Central Assc of London & Prov AC. Woolhampton Lock to Heales Lock and stretch near Oxlease Swing Bridge to Heales Lock, Glendale AC. Heales Lock to Midgham Bridge, Reading & Dist AA. Junction with Kennet at Northcroft, Two stretches at Midgham Lock, Reed Thatcham AA. Thatcham to Widmead Lock, Thatcham AA. Bulls Lock to Ham Lock, Newbury AA. Ham Mill (offside bank) I Fidler, Ham Mill, London Road, Newbury. Whitehouse Turnover Bridge to Greenham Lock, Twickenham PS. Greenham Lock to Greenham Island, Newbury, and Northcroft to Guyers Bridge, Newbury AA. Two sections at Kintbury (560 yds), Civil Service AS. Ladies Bridge near Wilcote to Milkhouse Water Bridge, Pewsey and District AA. Ladies Bridge to Semington Bridge, Devizes AA. Semington Bridge to Avoncliffe Aqueduct, and Bradford Lock to Winsley Bridge, Bradford on Avon Dist AA. Winsley Bridge tp Limpley Stoke Bridge, Kingswood Disabled AC. Limpley Stoke Bridge to R Avon confluence, Bathampton AA.

Monmouthshire and Brecon Canal; from Pontypool to Brecon, BW directly controlled fishery. Goytre Marina, Red Line Boats. Cattle Upper Bridge to Llanfoist Bridge, Cwmcelyn AC. Stretch nr Llanfoist, Mr R Tod, Boat House, Llanfoist, Abergavenny. Auckland Bridge to Haunted House Bridge, Gilwern & Dist AC. Haunted House Bridge to Penpedair Heal Bridge, Gwent Avengers. Workhouse Bridge to Fro Bridge, Ebbw Vale Welfare AC. Brynich Lock to Canal Terminus at Brecon, B Wilcocks, Llanfaes, Brecon. River Usk; at Llanfrynach, J Howell, Fernbank, Hartlepool, Kidderminster. At Brynich, Llangynidr Service Station AC, Llangynidr, Crickhowell.

River Severn Navigation; Island bank at Upper Lode Lock, D G Jones, 2 Upper Lode Lock, Forthampton, Glos. Diglis (350 yds), BW directly controlled.

Belvere Lock, G H Drake, 30 Dunstans Close, Worcester. East bank at Diglis, Punchbowl AC. Bevere Lock, Mrs M E Smith, Bevere Lock, Grimley. Holt Lock u/s and d/s, A S Portman, Holt Lock, Holt Heath, near Worcester. Salmon rights, Lincomb Lock, P Gough, Courtnay House, Feiashill Road, Trysull, WV5 7HT. Coarse rights, B Turner, Lincomb Lock, Stourport. West bank, Lincomb Lock, Carter Jones, 20 St Owen St, Hereford. (Severn Valley Sand & Gravel Ltd).

MIDLAND REGION:

Ashby Canal; Stretches leased by B & D Morris AC, Wykin AC, Ferry Pickering AC, Birchmoor AC, Shackerstone & Dist AC, Measham AC.

Birmingham and Fazeley Canal; Tyburn to Curdworth Tunnel, Fosters of Birmingham, Dams and Lock AC, BRS (Midlands) AC, Stirrup Cup AC. Curdworth Tunnel to Whittington is Birmingham AA, Fazeley Victory AC, Lamb AC and Hope and Anchor AC. Whittington Bridge to Huddlesford Junction, Whittington Social AC, 'Above All' AC.

Birmingham Canal Navigation (BCN), Wyreley and Essington Canal; Cannock Extension; Yates AC, Chase Social AC. **BCN Rushall and Daw End Branch Canal;** Rushall Junction to Chasewater Reservoir, developed as BW direct management scheme. BCN Soho Loop, Fisherman of England AC.

Coventry Canal; Coventry to Polesworth, Coventry & Dist AA. The remaining sections leased by Birchmoor AC, Amington AC, Tamworth Progressive AC, Weddington Social Club AS, Dordon AC. Huddlesford Junction to Fradley Junction, Lamb AC, Lichfield Marina AC, Pirelli AC.

Grand Union Canal, Main Line; North Napton Junction, through Calcutt Bottom Lock to Junction Bridge, Warwick, Royal Leamington Spa AA. Junction Bridge to Ugly Bridge, Warwick & Dist AA. **Saltisford Arm;** Saltisford Canal (Trading) Ltd. Hatton Top Lock to south end of Shrewley Tunnel, Stratford upon Avon AA. Shrewley Tunnel to Rowington, Charterhouse WMC. Rowington to Chessets Wood and Small Arm at Kingswood Junction, Massey Ferguson Recreation C. Knowle, Civil Service AC. Knowle Top Lock to Birmingham, Tavern AC, Crown Leisure AC, Wild Manufacturing AC, Hay Mills AC.

Staffordshire and Worcester Canal,

South; York Street Stourport to Botterham Lock, Birmingham AA. Botterham Lock to Dimmingsdale Lock, Wolverhampton AA. **Stratford-upon-Avon Canal;** leased by Square AC, Raven AC, Redditch FA, Solihull AC. **South Stratford Canal;** Avon to Kingswood Junction, Birmingham AA. **Worcester and Birmingham Canal;** Diglis Basin to Blackpole Bridge, Worcester UA. Blackpole Bridge to Kings Norton Tunnel, Birmingham AA.

Staffordshire and Worcester Canal, Northern Section; stretches held by Lilleshall & Dist AS, Marston Palmer AS, Goodyear AS, New Invertion WMC, Littleton & Mid-Cannock AC, Union Locks Anglers, Staffs Co Council AC, Four Ashes FC, Whitmore Reans CAA. Roseford Bridge to Milford Aqueduct, Izaac Walton (Staffs) AA. Milford Aqueduct to Great Haywood Junction, Potteries AS.

Trent and Mersey Canal; Derwent Mouth to Weston-upon-Trent, Derby AC. Weston-upon-Trent, Derby Railway AC. Weston-on-Trent to Clay Mills, Derby AA. Clay Mills Bridge to Wychnor Lock, Burton Mutual AA. Findern Crossing Pond, Derby RAC. Wychnor Lock - south west, Alrewas AC. Section to Woodend Turn, Woodside Caravan Park AC. Handsacre Bridge to Wolseley Bridge, Rugeley & Brereton AS. Wolseley Bridge to Colwich Lock, Norton Lido AC. Three stretches between Great Haywood Lock and Ingestre Bridge, Evode AC. Ingestre Bridge to Weston Lock, White Eagle Anglers. Next beat, Fenton & Dist AC. RAF Stafford AC to Salt Bridge. Salt Bridge to Sandon Lock, Universal Sports C. Sandon Lock to Flute Meadow Bridge, Olditch AC. Flute Meadow Bridge to Long Meadow Bridge, Stone AS. Section to Aston Lock, Stoke City & Dist AA. Aston Lock to Meaford Lock, Stone & Dist AS. Meaford to

Stoke-on-Trent, Fenton & Dist AC.

Shropshire Union Canal; in Wolverhampton area Whitmore Reans CAA have section, also Post Office AC, Cleveland Rd WMC, then Tettenhall Club & Inst, George Carter Ltd AC. Further sections leased by Codsall Legionaires AC, Penkridge Anglers; section to Stretton Aqueduct, Swan AC. Stretton, Brewood AC. Next two sections are leased by Hazeldine AA and Royal Exchange AS. Section to Cowley Tunnel, Izaac Walton (Stafford) AA. To Gnossal, Marston Palmer AS. The leased sections to Tyreley are held by the following clubs, Market Drayton AC, Eaton Lodge AC, Park AC, Stafford Hospital AC, Hodnet WMC AC, Palesthorpes AS, Crown AC. Tyreley Locks to Audlem, Crewe Pioneers AC. Audlem Bottom Lock to Ellesmere Port is BW managed.

NORTH EAST REGION:

Chesterfield Canal; Stockwith to Drakeholes Low Wharf, Sheffield & Dist AA, Clayworth Church Lane Bridge to Retsford Bridge, Worksop & Dist. AAA. West Retford Bridge to Chequer House Bridge, Retford & Dist AA. Chequer House to Bracebridge Lock, Worksop United AA. Bracebridge Lock to High Grounds Farm Bridge, Grafton AA.

Erewash Canal; Trent Lock to Long Eaton Lock, Long Eaton Victoria AS, also **Cranfleet Canal.** Long Eaton Lock to Sandiacre Lock, Long Eaton & Dist FA. Sandiacre Lock to B5010 Bridge, West End AC. B5010 to Pasture Lock, Lace Webb Spring Co Sports & SC. Pasture Lock to Stanton Lock, Draycott AC. Stanton Lock to Greens Lock, and on to A6096, Middleton WMC. A6096 to Common Bottom Lock, Durham Ox FC. Common Bottom Lock to Shipley Lock, Cotmanhay AC. Shipley Lock to Langley Mill Lock, NCB No 5 Area FC. **Grantham Canal;** Grantham to Woolsthorpe-by-Belvoir, Grantham AA. Lady Day

---

Check before you go

*While every effort has been made to ensure that the information given in **Where to Fish** is correct, the position is continually changing, and anglers are urged, in their own interests, to make enquiries before travelling to selected venues. This is especially important with reference to prices quoted. Anglers attention is also drawn to the fact that hotels mentioned under the various fishing stations do not necessarily have water of their own. Any amendments or further data for inclusion in subsequent editions, and any criticism, will be welcome.*

Bridge to Gamston Bridge, Matchman Supplies AC. Other sections, Nottingham AA. Very little of this canal is fishable. **River Stoar Navigation;** Sections at Thurmaston and Wreake Junction, Leicester & Dist ASA. Barrow Shallow to Kegworth Old Lock, Loughborough Soar AS. 400 metres at Lock Island, Kegworth AS. Kegworth Flood Lock to Ratcliffe Lock, Long Eaton & Dist AF. **River Trent;** Hazelford Island, BW directly managed. Lenton, Raleigh FC. Beeston Canal, Nottingham AA. Trent at Gunthorpe, Nottingham & Dist FAS. These are small fisheries.

Grand Union Canal: Arms and Branches; Market Harborough Arm; Junction, Foxton Boats Ltd. Foxton to Mkt Harborough, Tungstone FC, Desborough and Rothwell AC, Mkt Harborough AC. Foxton to Leicester, Wigston AS.

Huddersfield Broad Canal; section from Apsley Basin entrance, Holme Valley PA. Red Doles Lock to Deighton Mill, Huddersfield Broad Canal Alliance. **Pocklington Canal;** Pocklington to Derwent junction, East Cottingwith, York & Dist AA. **Ripon Canal;** terminal to R Ure junction, Ripon Canal Fisheries (T Welbourne, 116 Stonebridgegate, Ripon). **Selby Canal;** wide commercial waterway. Selby Basin to Bawtry Road bridge, Wheatsheaf AC. Bawtry Bridge to Brayton Bridge, Knottingley Conservative Club AS. Brayton Bridge to Burn Bridge, Selby AA. Burn Bridge to Paperhouse Bridge, Goole & Dist AA. Paperhouse Bridge to Tankards bridge, Carlton AC.

Sheffield and South Yorkshire Navigation (Stainforth and Keadby Canal); Keadby Lock to Mauds Bridge, Stainforth & Keadby Joint AC. M18 to Dunston Hill Bridge, Hatfield Colliery AC. Dunston Hill to Stainforth High Bridge, Stainforth AA. Bramwith Lock to Barnby Dun Swing Bridge, Northfield to aqueduct on New Junction Canal, and on past Sykehouse Lock, Doncaster & Dist AA.

Sheffield and South Yorkshire Navigation; wide commercial section. Barnby Dun to Kirk Sandal, Barnby Dun SAC. Kirk Sandal to Railway Bridge, Pilkington (Kirk Sandal) Rec C. Rotherham to Sprotborough (9 miles) all Rotherham AA, except short lengths controlled by Group 35 AC, Conisborough AC, E Hemingthorpe S & SC, and Guest & Chrimes Ltd AS. Sprotborough to Kirk Sandall (6 miles) all Doncaster AA.

Remainder Length; Tinsley & Dist ACA have two sections; Tinsley Canal junction with R Don, and R Don to Holmes Lock. Tinsley Wire Sports & SC have two basins, as do Firth-Derihon (Tinsley) FC. Broughton Lane to Tinsley, BSC (Tinsley) Sports & SC. To Coleridge Road, Tuffnells AC. Between bridges at Coleridge Road and Darnall Road, Fox House Social Club AS. Darnall Road to Shirland Road, Sheffield Works Dept AC. Shirland Rd to Staniforth Rd, Firth Park WMC. Staniforth Road to Bacon Lane, Horse & Jockey AC. Bacon Lane to Bernard Road, Arundel AC. Bernard Road to Cadman Street, Woodseats WMC. **River Ure;** Ure and Milby Cut at Boroughbridge, Plus Milby Lock to Tinkers Lane; Harrogate & Claro Conservative AA. Also on Ure and Milby Cut at Boroughbridge, Unity AC.

NORTH WEST REGION:

Caldon Canal; very good water quality. Bedford St Double Lock to Planet Lock no 3, Adderley Green AC. Planet Lock no 3 to Lichfield St Bridge, Fenton & Dist AS. Lichfield St Bridge to Ivy House Bridge, Lewis's AC. Ivy House Bridge to Keelings Bridge, Cookson Ceramics AC. Keelings Bridge to Abbey Rd Bridge, Abbey Hulton Suburban AS. To Foxley, Corbridge Coronation CIUC. Foxley Lift Bridge to Downfield Bridge, Birchshead Gardeners AC. Downfield Bridge to Heakley Hall Bridge, Burslem Suburban AC. Stanley Rd Bridge to Doles Bridge 27, Abbey Hulton Suburban A. Basford Bridge to Bridge 47, Stoke Telephone AC. Bridges 47 to 48, JCB AC. 53 to 54, TBJ AC. Froghall Tunnel Bridge to Bridge 55, Stoke on Trent Disabled AC. To terminus, Wharf AC. Horse Bridge to Leek Wharf, Leek & Moorlands FC.

Llangollen Canal; Hurleston Locks to Bache House Bridge, Crewe LMR AS. Bache House Bridge to Wrexham Road Bridge, Caldy AC. Wrexham Toad Bridge to Butchers Bridge, Wyche AC. Halls Lane to Wrenbury Heath, Crewe Post Office AS. Poveys Lock to Dansons Farm Bridge, Rubery Owen AC. Bridge 44 to 46, Wem AC. 300 yds west of Bridge 46 to Cornhill Bridge, Rubery Owen AC. Hampton Bank Bridge to Bridge 51, Old LMS AC. 51 to 53, Perkins AC. Ellesmere to Tetchill, Oswestry Dist AC.

Macclesfield Canal; Hardingswood Junction to Hall Green Stop Lock, Kidsgrove & Dist AA. Five sections to Watery Lane Aqueduct, Burslem Surburban AC, Mow Cop AC, Radway Green Sports & Social C, Royal Doulton AC, Victoria AC. Bridges 72 to 77, Congleton AS. From Henshalls Bridge to Lamberts Lane Bridge, Victoria and Biddulph AS. Porters Farm Bridge to Buxton Road Bridge, Congleton, Macclesfield Waltonian AS.

Montgomery Canal; Bridges 131 to 134, Montgomery AA. To Tan-y-Fron, Penllwyn Lodges AC. Bridge 142 to Glanhafren Bridge, Lymm AC. 143 to 144, Montgomery AA. 144 to 145, Pant Piscatorials. Brynderwen Lock to Bridge 148, Severnside AC. Severn at Penarth Weir, Potteries AS. Penllwyn AC have stretch at Tan-y-fron. R Severn at Penarth Weir, Potteries AS. **Peak Forest Canal;** Dukinfield Junction to Whaley Bridge Terminus, Stockport & Dist AF.

Trent and Mersey Canal; Trentham Lock to Stoke Basin, Fenton & Dist AS. Eturia to Whieldon Road Bridge, Stoke, Stoke City & Dist AA. Lloyd St Bridge to Longport, Middleport WMC. N end of Harecastle Tunnel to Bridge 134, Kidsgrove AA. Kidsgrove to Lawton Lock, Rolls Royce AC. Lawton Lock to Rode Heath Bridge, Victoria AC. Rode Heath to Rookery Bridge and Booth Lane Top Lock, Cheshire AA. Rookery Bridge to Booth Lane Top Lock, Middlewich Joint A. St Anne's Bridge, Middlewich to Preston Brook, Trent & Mersey Canal AA.

River Weaver; various sections between Winsford and Newbridge, Winsford & Dist AA. Between Newbridge and Bostock Works, Meadowbank Sports and Social C AS. Newbridge to Saltersford leased by Northwich AA.

Ashton Canal; Ashton New Road Bridge to Clayton Lane Bridge, Clayton Aniline AS. Fairfield Bottom Lock to Top Lock, Water Sports Adventure Centre. Fairfield Road Bridge to Ashton Hill Bridge, Hollinwood Inst. AS. Ashton Hill Lane Bridge to Guide Bridge 26, Stockport & Dist AF. Guide Bridge 26 to Bridge 28, Tootal AC. Bridge 28 to to Whitelands Rd, Glossop AAS.

Huddersfield Narrow Canal; water tends to acidity, but contains trout. Bayley St, Stalybridge to Lock no 1, Stalybridge Fox AS. Scout Tunnel to Mottram Rd, Stalybridge, Digge AC. Mossley to Scout Tunnel, Micklehurst Liberal Club Ltd. Greenfield to Mossley, Medlock Bridge AC. Saddleworth to Greenfield, Diggle AC. Diggle to Saddleworth, Saddleworth & Dist AS. Three stretches from Saddleworth to Milnsbridge, Slaithwaite & Dist AC.

Lancaster Canal; whole of canal from Stocks Bridge, Preston, to Stainton, Northern AA.

Leeds and Liverpool Canal (East); Thorley to Niffany Swing Bridge, Skipton AA. Niffany Swing Bridge to Snaygill Stone Bridge, Craven AA. Snaygill Stone Bridge to Hamblethorpe Swing Bridge, Magnet AC. Hamblethorpe to Lodge Hill Bridge, Keighley AC. Lodge Hill to Swine Lane Bridge, Marsden Star AS. Swine Lane to Dowley Gap Top Lock, Bingley AC. Bridges 198 to Dowley Top Lock, Bingley AC. To Bridge 207A, Saltaire AC. 07A to 210, Dovesdale AC. 11 to Field Lock, Thackley, Sefton Hall Piscatorial AC. Thackley to Idle Swing Bridge, Unity AC. Idle Swing Bridge to Thornhill Bridge, Idle and Thackley AA. 215 to 216A Listerhill Old Boys AA. Horseforth Rd Bridge to Rodley Swing Bridge, Rodley Boats AC. 222 to 225, Leeds & Dist ASA. Johnsona Hill Btm Lock to Barnoldswick, Northern AA

Leeds and Liverpool Canal (West); Johnson's Hillock Bottom Lock to Barnoldswick Long Ing Bridge, Northern AA. Leigh Branch; Dover Lock to Plank Lane Bridge, Ashton & Dist Centre Northern AA. To Leigh Wharf, Leigh & Dist AA.

Manchester, Bolton and Bury Canal; Withins Bridge to School St, Radcliffe, Manchester, Bolton & Bury Canal AC. Hall Lane to Nob End, Bolton & Dist AA. **St Helens Canal;** Section leased by St Helens AA; Blackbrook Branch, Carr Mill End to Old Double Locks.

RESERVOIRS AND LAKES in **English Canal System:**

Keep the banks clean

Several clubs have stopped issuing tickets to visitors because of the state of the banks after they have left. Spend a few moments clearing up.

Halton Reservoir, Wendover. Coarse fishery leased from BW by Prestwood & Dist AC. Enquiries to hon sec.

Wormleighton Reservoir, near **Banbury.** Coarse fishery leased from BW by Wormleighton FC. Enquiries to hon sec.

Gayton Pool, Gayton, near Northampton. Carp fishery; Gayton AC members only.

Tardebigge Reservoir, Bromsgrove, leased by Newton Works AC. Selectively open to public membership at moderate charge.

Upper and **Lower Bittell Reservoirs** (near **Bromsgrove**). Rights owned by Barnt Green FC, who stock Lower Bittell and adjacent Arrow Pools with trout; other pools hold coarse fish, including pike and bream. Tickets for coarse fishing to members' personal guests only *(see also Arrow tributary of Warwickshire Avon).*

Lifford Reservoir. Birmingham Parks. Dt from park keeper.

Earlswood Lakes. BW direct managed fishery. Three Lakes totalling 85 acres stocked with roach, perch, bream, pike; carp and tench in two. Large eels. Dt on bank from bailiff. Match booking enquiries to Mr J Howells, tel: 021 783 4233.

Stockton Reservoir. Excellent coarse fishery, tickets available from Blue Lias public house, near site.

Sneyd Pool, Walsall. Coarse fishing leased by Swan AC.

Harthill, near **Worksop.** Coarse fishing leased by Worksop & Dist AA.

Gailey Lower Reservoir, near **Wolverhampton.** 64 acre coarse fishery, intensively stocked. BW managed, dt £2.50. Match booking enquiries to tel: 0827 252 000.

Calf Heath Reservoir, nr **Wolverhampton.** Good coarse fishery with carp, tench, big bream. Leased to Blackford Progressive AS.

Lodge Farm Reservoir, Dudley. Coarse fishery. Enquiries to Dudley Corporation.

Himley Hall Lake, Himley. Trout, coarse fish. Enquiries to Dudley Corporation.

Trench Pool, Telford. 16 acres, coarse fishing. Leased to Telford AA.

Elton Reservoir, Greater Manchester. Leased to Bury AA.

Wern Clay Pits, Montgomery. Leased by Mid-Wales Glass AC.

Stanley Lake, Stoke-on-Trent. Coarse fishery leased by Stoke-on-Trent AS.

Huddersfield Narrow Canal Reservoirs. Brunclough, Saddleworth & Dist AS water; **Tunnel End, Slaithwaite, Red Brook, March Haigh, Black Moss, Swellands** and **Sparth,** Slaithwaite & Dist AS waters.

Check before you go

While every effort has been made to ensure that the information given in **Where to Fish** *is correct, the position is continually changing, and anglers are urged, in their own interests, to make preliminary enquiries before travelling to selected venues. This is especially important with reference to prices quoted. Inevitably the rate of inflation is affecting stability in this quarter. Anglers' attention is also drawn to the fact that the hotels mentioned under the various fishing stations do not necessarily have water of their own. Any amendments or further data for inclusion in subsequent editions, and any criticism, will be welcome.*

ENGLISH SEA FISHING STATIONS

In the following list the principal stations are arranged in order from north-east to south-west and then to north-west. Sea fishing can, of course, be had at many other places, but most of those mentioned cater especially for the sea angler. Names and addresses of club secretaries will be found in the list of angling clubs; secretaries and tackle shops are usually willing to help visiting anglers either personally or by post on receipt of a stamped and addressed envelope. Details of accommodation, etc, can generally be had from the local authority amenities officer or information bureau of the town concerned.

Seaham (Co Durham). Cod (Oct-April all beaches especially Blast), codling, whiting (all in winter), mackerel (June-Aug), coalfish, flounders, plaice (mainly from boats), skate (Seaham Hall beach, June-Sept, night fishing, early flood), pouting, gurnard, etc. Excellent fishing from two piers. Dt £1.50 from Harbour Gatehouse. Seaham SAC, Clifford House, is local sea angling club. Details and boat information from J Franklin, 14 Conningham Terrace, Houghton-le-Spring (Tel 842271). Tackle shops: R Wright, 20 Green Street; K B Fox, North Terrace. Further information from R M Shenton, 54 Fern Crescent, Parkside.

Sunderland (Co Durham). Cod and codling (best Oct-April), whiting (best Sept-Oct), mackerel (June-Aug), coalfish, flounders, dabs, plaice, throughout year. Roker Pier provides good sport with cod and flatfish. North Pier is free of charge to anglers. Several small-boat owners at North Dock will arrange fishing parties, but there are also good beaches. R Wear banks at entrance good for flounders throughout year. Bait can be dug in Whitburn Bay and bought from tackle shops. Clubs: Sunderland Sea AA. Ryhope Sea AA (both affiliated to Assn of Wearside Angling Clubs). Tackle shops: Coast & Country Sports, 3 Derwent St; East Coast Tackle, 18 Roker Ave; P J Flies, 40 Windsor Terrace; Rutherfords, 125 Roker Ave; Waltons, 21A Derwent St. Hotels: Parkside, 2 park Ave; Parkview, 25 Park Ave.

Saltburn (Cleveland). Flatfish, coalfish, codling, whiting, mackerel, gurnard, some bass in summer and haddock late autumn. Float-fishing from pier in summer gives good sport; good codling fishing Oct to March. Club: Saltburn and Dist AA.

Redcar (Cleveland). Five miles of fishing off rock and sand. Principal fish caught: Jan-April, codling; April-June, flatfish; summer months, coalfish (billet), whiting, mackerel, gurnard. Larger codling arrive latter part of August and remain all winter. South Gare breakwater (4m away); good fishing, but hard on tackle, spinning for mackerel successful. Good fishing from beach two hours before and after low tide. Competitions every month. Tackle shops: Catch Tackle, 129 Lord St; Redcar Angling Centre, 159 High St, Redcar TS10 3AH; Anglers Services, 27 Park Rd, Hartlepool.

Whitby (N Yorks). Increasingly popular centre for boat, pier and beach fishing. Cod up to 42lb taken from boats, as well as large catches of haddock, whiting, flatfish, black bream, wolf fish, ling, etc. West Pier: fishing only from lower part of pier extension. Mainly sandy bottom, but weeds and rock towards end. Billet, codling, flatfish, mackerel and whiting in season. East Pier: mainly on rocky bottom, weed off pier extension. More and bigger codling off this pier. Beach fishing from the sands either to Sandsend or Saltwick: billet, codling, flatfish, whiting, mackerel, a few bass. Small area at end of New Quay Rd for children only. No fishing allowed in harbour entrance. Best baits are lugworm, mussel, peeler crab. Boat Fishing: boats to accommodate 8 to 12 persons on hire at quays: Cyanita, tel: 810448; Gannet, tel: 601501; Guide Me, tel: 820320, and others. For local association contact Mr Johnson, 14 Runswick Ave, 0947 604025. Tackle shops: E Wilson, 65 Haggersgate, tel 0947 603855; Blue Star Angling, Langborne Rd.

Scarborough (N Yorks). Sea fishing good from boat or harbour piers most of year. Autumn whiting very good in bay. West Pier fishes on sandy bottom, East Pier on rock, with better chances of bigger codling. Marine Drive good all year round cod fishing. Codling most plentiful Aug onwards. Winter codling fishing from First or Second Points to south of Scarborough and the Marine Drive. Mackerel, June-Sept, float or spinning. Various boats take out parties; bags of 3-4,000lb of cod in 12hr sessions at times taken. Many over 40lb. Festival in Sept. Clubs: Scarborough Rock AC; South Cliff AC; Scarborough Boat AC. Tackle shops: at 56 Eastborough, and Buckley's Angling Supplies; 6 Leading Post Street (who issue dt for the Mere; coarse fish). Sixteen charter boats available, taking 8-12 anglers. Charge: approx £2.50 per person for 4 hrs but longer trips to fish reefs and wrecks now popular. Phone (0723) 890134, 72791, 362083, 374885 or 71775.

Filey (N Humberside). Famous Filey Brigg, ridge of rocks from which baits can be cast into deep water, is best mark. From June to Sept very good float fishing with sliding float for mackerel, coalfish (billet) and pollack. Good flatfish from shore and boats in summer. Best mackerel mid-July to end of Sept; for cod Sept to March. Local bait digging prohibited. Boats may be hired from beach from May to Sept. Advanced booking advisable in winter. Filey Brigg AS (st £3) organises fishing festival every year (first week of Sept). Good flyfishing for coalfish (billet) from Brigg. Tackle and bait from Filey Tackle, Hope St. Hotel: White Lodge.

Bridlington (N Humberside). South Pier may be fished free all year and North Pier in winter only. Sport in summer only fair - small whiting, billet, flatfish mainly - but good codling from Dec-March. Launches and cobles sail daily from Harbour at 0630, 0930, 1330, 1800 during summer. They operate round **Flamborough Head**, or wrecks. Catches include cod, haddock, plaice, ling and skate. Rock fishing from shore at Thornwick Bay. Bait: lugworm may be dug in South Bay and small sandeels caught by raking and digging on edge of tide. Sea angling festival Sept 21-25. Boats: I Taylor, 679434; J Jarvis, 604750; D Brown, 676949. Cobles: R Emerson, 850575. Tackle shops: Linford's, 12 Hilderthorpe Road; Field, 22 West St. Hotels: Windsor, Lonsborough and others.

Hornsea (N Humberside). Tope, skate, flounders, occasional bass from shore; cod, haddock, plaice, dabs, tope, skate from boats. May to Oct. Whiting, dabs, codling, Oct to May.

Grimsby (S Humberside). Sea fishing along Humber bank free, and along foreshore to Tetney Lock; plaice, codling,

dabs, flounders, eels. West Pier: st from Dock Office. Boat fishing: 12 hour trips, mainly around oil rigs. Tel: 0472 885649 or 72422. All boats and persons in charge of boats must be licensed by Great Grimsby Council. Enquiries to Municipal Officers, Town Hall Square; or Port Health Offices, Fish Dock Road. Good centre for fens and broads. Clubs: Humber SAC, Cromwell Social Club (SA section). Tackle shops: Padgett's Pets & Tackle, 114 Cromwell Rd; Fred's Fishing Tackle, 413 Weelsby St; Pets & Tackle, 206 Lord St.

Mablethorpe (Lincs). Good sea fishing from Mablethorpe to Sutton-on-Sea. Beach all sand; mainly flatfish, but some bass, skate, mackerel, tope from boats. Cod in winter. Sept-Dec best. Boat fishing limited by surf and open beach. Good flounders in Saltfleet Haven; also sea trout in Sept. Local club: Mablethorpe, Sutton-on-Sea and Dist AC (water on Great Eau for members only). Tackle shop: Bela's, 54-56 High Street. Hotels at Mablethorpe, Trusthorpe, Sutton-on-Sea.

Skegness (Lincs). Beach fishing for cod, dab and whiting in winter; silver eels and dabs in summer; whiting and dab in Sept and Oct. Chapel Point, Huttoft Bank and Ingoldmells the best beaches in winter, 3 hrs before high tide until 2 hours after. Lugworm best bait. No charter boats operate in Lincolnshire. Club: Skegness SAC. Tackle and bait from Skegness Fishing Tackle, 155 Roman Bank.

Salthouse, near **Sheringham** (Norfolk). Sea here is deep quite close in shore, and fishing considered good. Good flatfish, Oct-Jan. Occasional bass and mackerel in summer. Guest house: Salthouse Hall.

Sheringham (Norfolk). Flatfish all year; cod autumn and winter, mackerel June-Sept. Beaches good all year, best months April and May. Best sport west of lifeboat shed towards Weybourne or extreme east towards Cromer. Centre beaches too crowded in season. Bait can be ordered from tackle shops. Boat fishing best well off shore. Tope to 40lb and thornbacks to 20lb; plenty of mackerel. Tackle shop: Fiddy's Fishing Tackle, 28 Beeston Road. Club: Sheringham Sea AC. Blakeney: good launching ramps, boat hire from R Bishop, 0263 740200.

Cromer (Norfolk). Good all-year fishing; mainly cod (Sept-April), whiting and dabs, with odd tope (summer); skate and bass (summer) from pier (50p) and beaches. Around the third breakwater east of the pier the water is deeper, last three hours of flood tide best time. Occasional mackerel from end of pier. Boat fishing in calm weather (beach-launching). Fresh lugworm available from Marine Sports Shop, New St, Cromer (open Sundays), High St. Hotels: Cliftonville, Red Lion, Hotel de Paris, Cliff House.

Great Yarmouth, (Norfolk). All styles of sea fishing catered for, including two piers, several miles of perfect shore line for beach angler, two miles of well-wharved river from harbour's mouth to Haven Bridge, and boat angling. To north are Caister, Hemsby, Winterton, Horsey, Palling, Weybourne etc, and to south, Gorleston-on-Sea and Corton. The riverside at Gorlestone from the lifeboat shed leading to the harbour entrance, and Gorleston Pier are popular venues. Sport very similar in all these places; Sept to Jan, whiting, dabs, flounders, eels, cod from latter end of October. Most successful baits are lugworm, herring or mackerel. Boats: Dyble, tel: 0493 731305/369582; Read, tel: 0493 859653; Bishops, tel: 0493 664739. Tackle shops: Dave Docwra, 79 Churchill Rd; Gorleston Tackle Centre, 7/8 Pier Walk; Dyble's, Hemsby Rd, Scratby (rod hire).

Gorleston-on-Sea (Norfolk). Whiting, cod, dabs and flounders from beaches and in estuary (best Oct to March); good skate Aug and Sept. Sport good in these periods from boats, pier or at Harbour Bend in river and on beaches. Baits: lugworm, crab and ragworm. Freshwater fishing (coarse fish) within easy reach on rivers and broads. Boats: Bishop Boat Services, 48 Warren Rd, tel: 664739. Tackle shops: Gorleston Tackle Centre, 7/8 Pier Walk; Greenstead Tackle Centre, 72 High St.

Lowestoft (Suffolk). Noted centre for cod, autumn-May. Also whiting, flatfish, pollack and coalfish, with bass, tope, ray from charter boats and mullet in warmer months. Lugworm best bait. Good sloping beaches to north and south. Hopton, Pakefield, Kessingland are best. North best on flood, south on ebb. Baits from Ted Bean and other tackle shops. Boats from Bob Williams, tel: 566183; K Howells, 0502 517296. East Anglian beach championships; inquire hon sec, Assn of E Anglian Sea Anglers. Tackle shops: Ted Bean, 175 London Road N; Other club: Lowestoft SA. Further information from Tourist IC, The Esplanade; tel:

523000.

Southwold (Suffolk); ns Halesworth. Good codling, whiting, bass, plaice, flounder, dab, pollack, mackerel, mullet fishing from beach, October to March. Bass main species in summer from harbour or shore; soles and silver eels also provide sport May to Sept. Reydon Lakes are local freshwater fishery. Licences from Purdy's Newsagents, High St. Hotels: Swan, Crown, Red Lion, Avondale.

Felixstowe (Suffolk). Best in autumn and winter, when cod are about. Good sport in summer with bass, garfish from the pier by day and sole at night, and with eels in the estuaries. Skate fishing good in May, June and July, especially in harbour. Best sport from boats and pier. Good fishing in evenings from Manor Terrace to Landguard Point, Sept onwards. Wrecking trips arranged. Tackle shops: Casaway, 20 Undercliff Rd; Carries Corner, 107 High Rd. Clubs: Felixstowe SAS and Felixstowe Dock.

Harwich and **Dovercourt** (Essex). Bass, mullet, eels, garfish, flatfish, sting-ray, thornback, skate, soles (all May to Sept), whiting, pouting, codling (Sept to March). Best fishing from boats, but Stone Breakwater, Dovercourt, is good. Several good boat marks in estuary of Stour and Orwell and in harbour approaches. Best baits: lug, king rag, soft and peeler crabs. Boats: Bartons Marina, 8 West St, 0255 503552, or V Caunter, 0255 552855. Club: Harwich AC (freshwater). Devonshire Arms Sea Angling Club. Tackle shop: Barton Marine, 8 West Street, Harwich. Copy of Borough Guide supplied by Town Clerk on request.

Walton (Essex). Cod, skate, mullet and dab are species most commonly caught, best fishing is from pier, Frinton Wall and Frinton Sea Front. Cod fishing begins about second week in Sept and runs to end of March. Club: Walton-on-Naze Sea AC. Boats may be chartered in Walton: S Murphy, tel: 0255 674274. Tackle shop: J Metcalfe, 15 Newgate St. Hotels: Elmos; Queens.

Clacton (Essex). Mainly autumn and winter fishing for whiting and cod. Summer fishing from beach, pier and boats - bass, eels, thornback, dogfish, tope, flatfish, sting ray to 50lb (Walton-on-Naze). Annual festivals arranged by Clacton Sea AC. Charter boats from Mr Fossett, 0702 462221, A Richards, 0702 206488.

Tackle shop: Brian Dean, 43 Pallister Road; bait supplied and boats available: 0255 425992. Hotels: Carlton View, Melrose, many others.

Southend-on-Sea (Essex). Mullet, bass, mackerel, scad, garfish, plaice and flounders are the main catches from the pier during the summer, with cod, codling and large flounders in the winter. A fleet of registered charter boats operate daily from the Pierhead, but prior booking is recommended. Thornback, stingray, smoothhound, bass, tope, plaice and cod can be expected. Pier: st £14, dt £1.25. Application form from Southend Council, Pier Hill, Southend. Off season shore fishing available, with all year round facilities at the Thorpe Bay and Westcliff bastions, also the river Crouch. Numerous open, pier, shore and boat events organised, including the Borough two-day festival. Tackle shops: (Southend) Goings, (A Report Station), 20 Market Place, Alexandra Street; Jetty Anglers. Essex Angling Centre (Westcliff).

Whitstable and **Tankerton** (Kent). Good fishing in spring and summer on shore between Swale and Whitstable. Dabs, plaice, bass, skate, flounders, eels, etc. Lugworm and white ragworm are to be found in shallow areas. Peeler crabs are plentiful in Swale estuary. Cod in winter from Tankerton beach. Boats available. Freshwater fishing on Seasalter Marshes, near Whitstable; roach, rudd, tench, pike, eels. T I Centre: Horsebridge, Whitstable. Tackle dealers in Sheerness: Island Bait & Tackle Shop, Neptune Terrace, Marine Parade; other branch at Oxford House, Russell St.

Herne Bay (Kent). Shore fishing for flounders, bass and eels, with whiting and codling in autumn and winter. A few bass in spring and summer. A few sting ray off Bishopstone and thornbacks from Woolpack area. Sea defence wall open for fishing. Excellent facilities for anglers with own dinghies to launch and recover from new harbour areas. Clubs: Herne Bay AA, HQ 59 Central Parade; Heron AS, Red Shelter, Spa Esplanade. Tackle and licences: Ron Edwards, 50 High Street; Herne Bay Angling, 224 High St. Hotels: Victoria, Adelaide and Beauville Guest Houses, all Central Parade.

Margate (Kent). Noted for mixed catches. Fine bass often taken from shore on paternoster, and boat by spinning. Stone pier good for cod and whiting in winter.

Bass and cod from rocks at low water. Cod best Nov to May; fish up to 20lb. April and May mixed bags of bass and eels. Most popular rock marks are at Foreness, Botany Bay, Kingsgate, Dumpton Gap. Skate at Minnis Bay, Birchington. Tope fishing from boat from June on through summer. Also dogfish and conger. Clubs: Margate Fishing Club; Old Centrals AC (130 Grosvenor Place). Tackle shop: Kingfisheries, 34 King Street.

Broadstairs (Kent). Bass, plaice, flounders eels, from beaches or stone jetty. Best in winter months. Lugworm usual bait, dug in Pegwell Bay. T I Centre: Pierremont Hall, High St. Tackle shop: Broadstairs Fishing Tackle, 8 Nelson Place.

Ramsgate (Kent). Good sport along 2m of shore, harbour piers (free fishing), and Eastern and Western Chines. East Pier gives ample scope, best in winter. Beaches crowded in summer, so night fishing best. In spring and summer good bass fishing (from shore), also soles, flounders, dabs and thornbacks. In autumn and winter; cod in large quantities, whiting. Pegwell Bay Foreness and Dumpton Gap are good boat marks for mackerel, bass and pollack. Upwards of twenty boats operate at Harbour. Goodwin Sands produce skate, bass, dogfish, spurdog, tope and plaice. The Elbow and Hole in the Wall, also marks for boat fishing. Lugworm may be dug in Pegwell Bay. Licences, baits, fishing trips and freshwater angling information from tackle shop: Fisherman's Corner, 6 Kent Place. Hotels in Thanet too many to list.

Sandwich (Kent). Bass at the mouth of the haven; sea trout and mullet run up the river; flounders, grey mullet, plaice, dabs, codling and pouting more seaward. Entry to Sandwich Bay by toll road, 9am to 5pm. For winter cod fishing, deep water off yacht club end of bay is best. Local club: Sandwich and Dist AS. Hotels: Bell, Haven Guest House. *For freshwater fishing see Stour (Kent).*

Deal and **Walmer** (Kent). Excellent sea fishing throughout the year from beaches and pier, open 8 am to 10 pm, all night Saturday, dt 90p to £2.20. Winter cod fishing, from Sandown Castle, Deal Castle, Walmer Castle. Charter boats take anglers to the Goodwin Sands and Kingsdown. Cod and whiting in winter, plaice, dabs, sole, mackerel, eels, flounders, mullet and garfish. Strong tidal currents. Tables from Harbour House, Dover. Deal & Walmer Inshore Fishermen's Assn supplies list of boats: R Tucker, tel: Deal 372962. T I Centre: Town Hall, Deal. Clubs: Deal and Walmer AA. Deal 1919 AC. Tackle shops: Channel Angling, North Toll House, Deal Pier; The Foc'sle 33 Beach St; The Downs Tackle Centre, 29 The Strand, Walmer. B & B: Admiral Penn; Dunkerleys. Hotel: Royal.

Dover (Kent). Excellent boat and beach fishing in the area; cod taken from wrecks and sand banks; good fishing for bass, codling, whiting and flatfish. Good beach fishing from Shakespeare Beach. Prince of Wales Pier suitable for all anglers, incl junior and handicapped. First half of Admiralty Pier controlled by Dover Sea AA: open 8 am to 4 pm, and 6 am to 6 pm Fri and Sat. £2.50 dt, conc. Access to Sandwich Bay is by toll road, £2.50. Boat trip (Dover Motor Boat Co, 0304 206809) to fish Southern Breakwater departs 8 am, £2 + £2.75, from Prince of Wales Pier. Tackle shops: Channel Angling (Dover), 146 Snargate Street, tel: 0304 203742; Bills Bait & Tackle, 121 Snargate St. Hotels: Ardmore, Beaufort; many others.

Folkestone (Kent). Good boat, beach and pier fishing. Conger, cod, bass, bream, flatfish, whiting, pouting and pollack, with mackerel in mid-summer. Pier open to anglers, £2 per day. Cod caught from boats on the Varne Bank all through the year, but from the shore, Oct-Feb only. Beach fishing best dusk onwards for bass and conger. The Warren produces good catches of cod in winter and bass in summer. Good sport from pier (fly). Some good offshore marks. Popular rock spots are Rotunda Beach, Mermaid Point, Sandgate Riviera. For tickets, boats and bait apply: Garry's Tackle Shop, 12 Tontine Street. Other tackle shops: Angler's Den, 2 Denmark St; Folkestone Tackle Centre, 57 The Old High Street. T I Centre, Harbour St. Hotels: Burlington, Windsor and others; Beachborough Park Hotel has course fishing.

Sandgate (Kent). Very good fishing from beach and boats. There is a ridge of rock extending for over a mile 20 yds out from low-water mark. Bass good July-October; codling, whiting, pouting, conger March-May, August-Nov; good plaice taken May-June, especially from boats. Best months for boat fishing, Sept-Nov. The hon sec, Sandgate AS, will be glad to give information. Hotel: Channel View Guest House, 4 Wellington Terrace.

Hythe (Kent). Fishing from boat and shore for bass, codling, pouting, whiting, conger and flats. Princes Parade, Seabrook, is popular for cod fishing, between Sept and Jan, lugworm is the best bait. Open storm beach, giving pouting, whiting, mackerel, sole, dab and flounder in summer and cod (up to 25lb), whiting and pouting in winter. Few bass. Clubs: Seabrook Sea AS; Sandgate Sea AS; Castaways Sea AS. Tackle shops: Hythe Angling, 1 Thirstane Terrace; Romney Tackle, 19 Littlestone Rd, Littlestone. Hotels: Nyanza Lodge, 87 Seabrook Rd; Romney Bay House, New Romney.

Dungeness (Kent). Cod fishing around the lighthouse, with whiting, and dab in winter, pout, bass, dab, eels and sole in summer. Best baits in winter are black or yellowtail lugworm. Denge Marsh is a top venue for sole, marks are at Diamond and towards Galloways, ragworm and lugworm for bait. Best months: May to Oct for boat fishing; Oct to Feb for shore fishing. Club: Brett Marine AC.

Hastings (Sussex). Sea fishing from pier and boats. Tope, bass, conger, plaice, codling, whiting, etc. Boats available from local fishermen. Hastings and St Leonards SAA has its own boats on beach opposite headquarters. Association also has clubroom on Hastings Pier. East Hastings Sea AA has clubhouse and own boats on foreshore. Annual International Sea Angling Festival in October. Bait, tackle: Tony's Tackle Shop; Redfearn's, 8 Castle Street, who have good knowledge of local course fishing, and have dt. International boat and pier festivals held in the autumn.

St Leonards (Sussex). Good sea fishing all the year round from boats and beach for flatfish, bass, mackerel, conger, tope, whiting, cod, bull huss, turbot. Boats and boatmen from Warrior Square slipway. St Leonards Sea Anglers' club house at 16 Grand Parade. Competitions run throughout the year, boats and beach. Annual subscription £9 + £2 joining fee. Concessionary £4.

Bexhill (Sussex). Boat and shore fishing. Cod, conger, whiting (Sept to end Dec). Dabs, plaice, mackerel, tope (July-Sept). Bass, best months May, June and July. Club: Bexhill AC (hon sec will help visitors, enclose sae). Freshwater fishing in Pevensey Sluice, Pevensey Haven and dykes; coarse fish. Tackle shop: Reenies Tackle Shop. Hotel: Granville.

Eastbourne (Sussex). Boat, pier and shore fishing. Dabs, huss, pouting and conger (all year), cod in winter and skate (May to Dec). Best for plaice and bream from June to Nov. Also soles, whiting, flounders, mullet. Good bass and mullet in warmer months. Notable tope centre, many around 40lb; June and July best. Some of the best beach fishing for bass around Beachy Head (up to 17lb). Pollack from rocks. Flatfish off Langney Point and from landing stages of pier. Best marks for beach fishing are on east side of pier. West side can be rocky in places. Club: Eastbourne AA, Club House, Royal Parade, tel: 23442. Boats available to members. Tackle shops: Compleat Angler, 22 Pevensey Road; Tony's, 211 Seaside.

Seaford (Sussex). Beach and boat fishing. Bass, cod, codling, conger, flats, huss, mackerel and few ling and pollack. Good catches of tope few miles offshore. Seaford AC has freshwater fishing on five local waters, st only. Tel: 0273 516849. Tackle shop: Peacehaven Angler, Coast Rd, Peacehaven.

Newhaven (Sussex). Centre for deep sea fishing. Beach fishing for bass excellent May-Oct. Flounders from Tide Mills Beach. Good cod fishing from beaches between Seaford Head and Newhaven's East Pier, late Oct to early March. Breakwater gives good all-round sport, with bass, and cod all running large. Boat fishing excellent for cod in winter, large Channel whiting also give good sport. Monkfish off Beachy Head late August and Sept. Boats from Harbour Tackle Shop, Fort Rd (tel 514441). Other tackle shops: Dennis's, 107 Fort Road; Book & Bacca, 8 Bridge Street. Hotel: Sheffield.

Brighton and Hove (Sussex). Charter boats are available from Shoreham, Newhaven and Brighton Marina. Deep sea and wreck fishing are available. In spring and summer boat fishing produces bream, bass, conger, tope, plaice and dabs; shore fishing: mackerel off marina wall, bass at night or l/w surf, mullet. Winter boat fishing for large cod, whiting, bull huss; shore for for whiting, flounders and cod. Tackle shops: Brighton Angler, Madeira Drive; Jack Ball, Edward St. Most dealers supply bait. Brighton Deep Sea Anglers offer membership £117.50 which gives access to 14 club boats moored in Brighton Marina: free fishing. Hove Deep Sea AC members launch boats from beach, and generally fish inshore marks. Marina arms for mackerel, garfish, pollack, occasional bass, fishing free of charge.

Shoreham and **Southwick** (Sussex). Boat and harbour fishing. Bass (July and August); grey mullet, skate and huss (June to Sept); cod and whiting (Sept to Dec); dabs, plaice, pouting, black bream, conger, mackerel and flounders (May onwards). Mullet fishing in River Adur near Lancing College very good July-August; light paternoster tackle and red ragworm recommended. Baits: white rag, red rag and lugworms may be dug from beach and mudbanks of river. Mussels and other baits can also be obtained.

Worthing (Sussex). Boat, beach and pier fishing. Garfish, small bass, eels. Mullet and flatfish fewer owing to netting. Mixed catches from boats. River Adur, east of Worthing, noted for flounders, mullet and eels. Bait digging in Adur restricted to between toll bridge and harbour. Local association: Worthing Sea AA (HQ, Worthing Pier), annual membership £7 + £1 entrance fee. Tackle shops: Ken Denman Ltd, 2 Marine Place (opp Pier entrance); Prime Angling, 74 Brighton Rd, Worthing, tel: 0903 821594. Boats from harbours at Shoreham and Littlehampton. Popular one day pier festival held in early September. Reduced fee to OAP and juniors.

Littlehampton (Sussex). Noted for black bream, which are taken in large numbers during May and early June, but wide variety, including skate (all year), bass (June-Oct), cod (winter best) and plaice. Club: Licensed Victuallers Deep Sea AC (HQ Arun View Inn, The Bridge; membership open to publicans). Littlehampton and Dist AC, annual membership £4.50. Best sport from boats. A large fleet of boats caters for sea anglers, and there is good fishing from beaches and in Harbour, silver eels caught. Well known marks are kingsmere Rocks and West Ditch. Boats also travel to Hooe Bank in high summer for specimen conger. Boats from: J Rapnick, tel: 0903 731430; C Bagshaw, 725652; M Pratt, 0798 42370; D Leggett, 0243 554113; Marina Cafe, 722154; Bait & Tackle Shop, Ferry Rd, Marina, 721211 and others. Tackle shops: J D Moore, 45 Beaconsfield Rd; Tropicana, 5 Pier Rd. Hotels: Fairview,

Tudor, Lodge, Regency.

Bognor Regis (Sussex). Good sea fishing at several marks off Bognor. Tope, bass, pollack, mackerel, whiting, wrasse. From May to July bream are plentiful. The conger, skate and sole fishing is very good. Grey mullet abound in the shallow water between Felpham and Littlehampton Harbour. Good cod fishing between September and November. Bass weighing 5-10lb and more caught from pier and shore. Boat hire: Fred Durrant, tel: 262616; Dickie Legget, 554113. Club: Bognor Regis Surfcasters AC. Tackle shops: Fisherman's Den, 110 London Rd; Suttons, 7 Shore Rd, East Wittering; Raycrafts Angling Centre, 119 high St, Selsey.

Hayling Island (Hants). From the South Beach of Hayling Island good fishing can be had with a rod and line for bass, plaice, flounders, dabs, whiting, etc, according to season. Fishing from boats in Hayling Bay for tope, skate, bass, mackerel, etc, is popular and a much favoured area is in the vicinity of the Church Rocks and in Chichester Harbour. Portsmouth AS has coarse lake in area. Dt available. Tackle shop: D J Baker, 2A Nutbourne Rd, Hayling Island.

Southsea (Hants). Over 4m of beach from Eastney to Portsmouth Harbour provide good sport all year. Bass fishing especially good from spring to September. Flatfish and rays numerous, large mackerel shoals in midsummer. Best sport from boats. Boom defence line from Southsea to IoW, although navigational hazard, is probably one of the best bass fishing marks on the South Coast. Vicinity of forts yields good bags of pollack, bass, black bream, skate, etc. Tope fishing good during summer. Portsmouth, Langstone and Chichester within easy reach and provide good sheltered water in rough weather. Boats can be hired from Portsmouth boatmen. Tackle shops: A & S Fishing Tackle, 147 Winter Rd, Southsea; Alan's Marine, 143 Twyford Ave; Coombs Tackle Centre, 165/167 New Rd, both Portsmouth.

Southampton (Hants). Fishing in Southampton Water really estuary fishing; thus not so varied as at some coastal stations. However, flounders abound (float and/or baited spoon fishing recommended), and whiting, pouting, silver eels, conger, bass, grey mullet, soles, dogfish, thornback, skate, stingray, plaice, dabs, scad, shad, mackerel have all been caught. At the entrance to Southampton Water, in Stokes Bay and the Solent generally, excellent tope fishing may be had. Angling from Hythe Pier, and from Netley and Hamble shores, but best fishing from boats. Southampton Water is rarely unfishable. Good sport in power station outflow. Tackle shops: Patstone & Cox, 25 High St; Sea Anglers Suppliers, 425A Millbrook Rd, Millbrook; John Conning Sports & Tackle, Woolston; Rovers, 135A High St, Lee on Solent.

Lymington (Hants). Tope, sting-ray in Lymington and Beaulieu rivers. Facilities through Lymington & Dist Sea AC. Hurst Castle area good beach spot for cod and large bass. Hurst and Pennington-Lymington Marshes, boat and shore. Mackerel and bass are caught, spinning in Solent from small boats. Flatfish on all beaches from Hurst Castle westwards to Mudeford. Boat fishing from Keyhaven around Needles area: tel 0590 622923 and 0831 460977; 'Lady M' and 'Star Bird'. Tackle shops: Smiths Sports, 25 Queen Street; Sea Angling Centre, Quay St, Lymington; Spreadbury's, 28 High St, Milford on Sea.

Mudeford (Dorset). Christchurch Harbour at Stanpit is good for bass and grey mullet. All-round sea fishing in Christchurch and Poole Bay, the vicinity of the Ledge Rocks and farther afield on the Dolphin Banks. Fishing is free below Royalty Fishery boundary (a line of yellow buoys across harbour). Tope, dogfish, conger, bream, pout, pollack, whiting and good sport spinning for mackerel and bass. Plaice off Southbourne; flounders, dabs, skate and sole off beaches at Highcliffe, Barton and Southbourne; flatfish, bass, whiting, etc, from quay, beach, groyne or shore at Hengistbury Head; large tope, stingray, skate and occasional thresher shark off The Dolphins. Fairly good cod fishing in winter, Needles-Christchurch Ledge, Pout Hole and Avon Beach (off Hengistbury Head). Whole squid favourite bait, but large baited spoons and jigs also successful. Good sole from Taddiford and Highcliffe Castle (best after dark). Groyne at Hengistbury good for bass in summer; sand eels by day and squid by night. Best months for general sport, mid-June to mid- or late Sept. Most local fishermen now take parties out mackerel fishing in summer. Flounders, eels, bass and mullet taken inside the harbour. Boats from R A Stride, The Watch House, Coastguards Way, Mudeford, and R Keynes, The Quay, Christchurch. Hotels: Avonmouth, Waterford Lodge, The Pines Guest House. For tackle shops and freshwater fishing, see Christchurch under Avon (Wiltshire) and Stour (Dorset).

Bournemouth (Dorset). Fishing good at times from the pier yielding bass, grey mullet, plaice, dabs, etc. Excellent catches of plaice, dabs, codling, silver whiting, mackerel (spinning), tope up to 40lb, conger, skate, from boats. Merlin Boat Hire, tel: 0202 474145, has 18 foot boats which fish up to four rods, from £35 per day. Shore fishing, when sea is suitable, for bass and other usual sea fish. Bait supplies fairly good. Clubs: Boscombe and Southbourne SFC; Bay AS; Christchurch & Dist FC. Tackle shops: Christchurch Angling Centre, 7 Castle Parade, Iford Bridge, Bournemouth; Bournemouth Marine, 79 Green Rd. Good accommodation for anglers at Edelweiss Guest House, 32 Drummon Rd, and Malvern Guest House, 7 Hamilton Rd, Boscombe (angling proprietor); Bournemouth Fishing Lodge, 904 Wimborne Rd, Moordown. For freshwater fishing, *see Avon (Wiltshire) and Stour (Dorset)*.

Poole (Dorset). Boat, beach and quay fishing in vast natural harbour. Great variety of fish, but now noted for deep-sea boat angling and bass fishing. Conger, tope, bream, etc, are caught within three miles of the shore. Bass, plaice, flounders, etc, caught inside the harbour at Sandbanks and Hamworthy Park in their seasons. Local tackle shops should be consulted for up-to-the-minute information. Boat fishing facilities largely controlled by Southern Angling (tel 676597), who has over thirty boats available. Sea Fishing (Poole) Ltd also cater for bass and deep-sea angling (tel 679666). Baits favoured locally: mackerel, squid, sand eel and ragworm. Tackle shops: Southern Angling Supplies, 5 High Street; Poole Angling Centre, 19 High Street; Dicks Fishing Tackle, 66a High Street; Sea Fishing Poole, Fisherman's Dock, The Quay.

Swanage (Dorset). Four tides a day in area. Many species taken from pier during summer incl bass, mullet, pollack, mackerel, flounder and pouting. Beach here and at **Studland Bay** produces good bass,

flounder and dabs at night; too crowded for daytime fishing. skate, conger, black bream and brill taken from boats outside bay. In colder months, cod may be caught in waters close to Swanage, and boats are available daily from Swanage Angling Centre: three hour trips at 10.30 am, 2.30 pm, or all day at 10.30 am. Around Peveril Ledge and Durlston Head there is good pollack fishing to St Alban's Head; also bass and mackerel. Mackerel fishing trips available from The Quay. Chapman's Pool: pollack, codling, bass, pout. Old Harry Rocks: bass, prawns. Durlston Bay good for mullet. Two sea angling festivals held annually, usually in August, one is the RNLI, the other sponsored by Town Council and local association, Swanage and Dist AC (annual membership: £4), Peveril Point, Swanage. Purbeck T I Centre, Town Hall, East St, Wareham. Tackle and boat hire from Swanage Angling & Chandlery Shop, 6 High St. Many hotels.

Weymouth (Dorset). Centre for the famous Chesil Beach, Shambles Bank, Portland and Lulworth Ledges. The steeply sloping Chesil Beach provides year-round sport for many species, but autumn and winter best for mackerel, codling, whiting, bream and dogfish; beach fishes best at night; fairly heavy tackle required. Good conger fishing at the Chesil Cove end, Ringstead Bay, Redcliffe and round the piers. Piers yield good sport with grey mullet. Good bass from Greenhill beach in heavy surf, with variety of flatfish at most times. Ferrybridge and the Fleet noted for bass, mullet and flounders. Boat fishing: In the area around Portland Bill some big skate and stingray give good sport, while the notable Shambles Bank continues to yield turbot and skate, etc. Lulworth Ledges have a large variety of fish including tope, blue shark, conger, skate, dogfish, black bream, pollack, whiting, etc. Best baits are lugworm, ragworm, soft crab, mackerel and squid. No boats from Chesil Bank, but 16 boatmen operate from Weymouth throughout year. Angling Society booklet from Weymouth Publicity Office, Weymouth Corporation and hon sec. Tackle shops: Anglers' Tackle Store, 56 Park Street; Hayman's 13 Trinity St; Denning Tackle & Guns, 114 Portland Road, Wyke Regis.

Portland (Dorset). Good bass fishing in harbour; live prawns for bait. Mullet, mackerel, whiting and conger are plenti-

ESSENTIAL READING . . .

BROWN MARABOU

SHREDGE

MACLAREN

MURDOCH'S BUTCHER

DOG NOBBLERS.

ful. Boats from fishermen at Castletown (for the harbour), Church Ope, The Bill and on the beach. Near the breakwater is a good spot, where refuse from the warships drifts up.

Bridport (Dorset). Beach fishing yields bass, pouting, flatfish, thornback rays and conger, with whiting and cod in winter and large numbers of mackerel in summer. From boats: black bream, conger, pollock, whiting, pout, dogfish, bull huss, rays, cod and wrasse. West Bay the angling centre. Burton Bradstock, Cogden, West Bexington and Abbotsbury are popular venues on Chesil Beach. Eype and Seatown favoured to west. Bait: lugworn, ragworm, squid, mackerel favoured. Boat hire from West Bay: Grey Goose, 24134; Tia Maria, 23475; Leo One, 074934 3902; Channel Warrior, 0395 822011. Club: West Bay Sea AC, has thriving junior section with special competitions, etc. Tackle shops: West Bay Water Sports, George St, West Bay; The Tackle Shop, Clarence House, West Bay, who arranges boat-fishing (Tel: 0308-23475). Hotel: The George, West Bay.

Lyme Regis (Dorset). Bass may be caught from the shore (bait with fresh mackerel obtained from motorboats in harbour or lugworm dug in harbour at low tide). Mackerel may be caught from May to October. Pollack plentiful in spring months. Conger and skate can be caught from boats about 2m from shore. Motor boats can be hired at harbour.

Seaton (Devon). Boat fishing. Pollack, pouting, conger, wrasse (March to Sept), bass (virtually all year, but best Sept-Nov), bream, mackerel, dabs, skate, plaice, dogfish. Axe estuary good for bass, mullet and sea trout: dt from Harbour Services Filling Station, Seaton. Tackle shop: Royal Clarence Sports, Harbour Rd, Seaton EX12 2LX; tel: 0297 22276. Hotels: Seaton Heights; Swallows Eaves, Colyford.

Sidmouth (Devon). Sea fishing in Sidmouth Bay. Mackerel (May to Oct), pollack (excellent sport spring and summer east and west of town), bass (to 13lb in surf at Jacob's Ladder beach during summer), wrasse, large winter whiting (July-Oct on rocky bottom), skate to 105lb and conger to 44lb have been taken; bull huss to 19lb, and tope. Also plaice, dabs, flounders and occasional turbot. At **Budleigh Salterton,** a few wrasse and

bass at Otter mouth; beach best at night for flat-fish.

Exmouth (Devon). Main species caught here in summer are pollack, wrasse, pout whiting, garfish and Mackerel. Favourite baits are lugworm, ragworm, peeler crab and sandeel. Pollack are caught on artificial sandeels. Popular places are: car park near Beach Hotel, docks area, estuary beaches, where flounders are caught, mid Sept to Jan. Deep Sea fishing trips can be booked, with chances of big conger eel, or small cuckoo wrasse, from W Means, skipper of Cormorant. Details from tackle shop: Exmouth Tackle & Sport, 20 The Strand. Other charter boats: Foxey Lady, 0404 822181; Trinitas, 0626 865768, Pioneer, 0404 822183.

Dawlish (Devon). Dabs and whiting in bay off Parson and Clerk Rock and between Smugglers' Gap and Sprey Point. Mackerel good in summer. Conger eels and dogfish about $^3/_4$m from shore between Parson and Clerk Rock and Shell Cove. Good fishing sometimes off breakwater by station and from wall of Boat Cove. Boats from Boat Cove. Good trout fishing at Chagford and Moretonhampstead. Tackle Shop: Black Swan Angling Centre, 1A Piermont Place, tel: 867078.

Teignmouth (Devon). Sea fishing ideal (especially for light spool casting with sandeels for bass). Bass, pollack, flounders in estuary. Mackerel, dabs and whiting in the bay. Good flounder fishing from the shore. Deep sea, wreck and offshore trips available. The town has an annual sea fishing festival. Club: Teignmouth SAS (HQ, River Beach). Tackle shop: The Sea Chest, 8 Northumberland Place (licences, permits for Newton Abbot waters, coarse fishing; bait for sea angling; information). Boats and bait from Peter Stenner, Sid Back, and John Harvey. Bait from Jim Joyce. Details of accommodation from Town Enquiry Bureau, The Den. It should be noted that the estuary is a bass nursery area between May and October.

Torcross; nr Kingsbridge (Devon). Hotel: Torcross Apartment Hotel, offering both self-catering facilities and high-class catering beside the Slapton Ley nature reserve and coarse fishery. Slapton Sands; ns Kingsbridge. The sea fishing is very good, especially the bass fishing. Hotel can make arrangements. For coarse fishing see 'Slapton Ley'.

Torquay (Devon). Base for famous Skerries Bank and Torbay wrecks; conger, cod, pollack, turbot, flatfish, whiting, etc. Hope's Nose peninsula provides best venue for shore angler, with bass and plaice mainly sought. Other species caught are dabs, wrasse, mullet, flounder, gurnard. Babbacombe Pier good for mackerel. Bass and pollack off the rocks. Natural bait hard to come by except for mussels from harbour walls, but tackle dealers can supply: Plainmoor Angling Centre, 141 St Marychurch Road, Plainmoor, who have tickets and information on several clubs and freshwater fisheries; Fletcher Sports, 9 Fleet St; Kiddy D, 28 Barton Rd; The Sea Chest, 11 Torwood Rd. Local associations: Sea AA, Torbay ASA, Babbacombe SA (HQ, Babbacombe Beach Cafe, membership £5, jun £1.50). Details of accommodation from Local Authority Publicity Dept, 9 Vaughan Parade. *For freshwater fishing, including Torquay Corporation reservoirs, see Teign and Dart.*

Paignton (Devon). Summer and autumn best. Bass, mackerel and garfish can be taken from beaches between Preston and Broadsands and from harbour, promenade and pier respectively. Mullet also present, but very shy. Fishing from rock marks, too. Club: Paignton Sea AA, who have information service and social centre for anglers at HQ at Ravenswood, 26 Cliff Road, The Harbour (open 7.30 pm onwards); annual membership £5, and £10 joining fee. Tackle shops: H Cove Clark, 45-47 Torbay Road; The Sports Room, 7a Dartmouth Road; Venture Sports, 371 Torquay Rd, Preston. Details of accommodation from Tourist IC, Festival Theatre, Esplanade. Trout fishing 2½m away at New Barn Angling Centre, a series of lakes and pools, £3 per day, fish caught extra, tel: 553602.

Brixham (Devon). Boat fishing in bay for plaice, dabs, mackerel. Good pollack off East and West Cod rocks of Berry Head. Neap tides best; baits: worms or prawn. Farther out is Mudstone Ridge, a deep area, strong tide run, but good general fishing with big conger. Local boats take visitors out to deep water marks (wreck fishing) or to Skerries Bank, off Dartmouth, for turbot, plaice, etc; advance bookings (at harbour) advisable. Charter boats: Tight Lines, 0308 851185; 'Sea Spray II', Vic Evans, 851328. Shore fishing: bass, pollack, wrasse, conger, mackerel from Fishcombe Point, Shoalstone and the long Breakwater. Grey mullet

abound in the harbour area (bait, bread or whiting flesh). Bass from St Mary's Beach (best after dark) and south side of Berry Head (bottom of cliffs) for flat fishing. Sharkham Point good for mackerel and bass (float with mackerel, strip bait or prawn for bass). Mansands Point good for bass and pollack (float). Night fishing from Elbury or Broadsands beach for bass, flatfish or conger (use thigh boots). Club: Brixham SAA. Annual membership: £9. Quayside Hotel has boats. Tackle shops: Tackle Box, 22 The Quay; Fletcher, 9 Fleet St.

Dartmouth (Devon). River holds large conger, record around 60lb; thornback ray to 15lb: best bait, prawn; also dabs, flounder, mullet, pollack, pouting. Baits, squid, ragworm, peeler crab. Shore angling is best from late Sept. Good marks are rocks at castle and compass: wrasse, bass, garfish; Eastern Black Stone: conger, wrasse, pollack, bull huss; plaice, gurnard, bass off sand. Charter boats: Barry Lingham 0803 833485; Steve Parker, 0803 329414; Chris Turner, 0803 833485. Association Club House is at 5 Oxford St. Tackle shops: Sport 'n' Fish, 16 Fairfax Place, Dartmouth TQ6 9AB; Sea Haven, Newcomen Road. Hotels: Castle, Victoria, Dart Marina. *For freshwater fishing, see Dart.*

Salcombe (Devon). Entire estuary is a bass nursery area, and it is illegal to land boat caught bass between April-December. Mackerel June to Sept and turbot, dabs, flounders, plaice, skate and rays rest of year. Plenty of natural bait. Beaches crowded in summer, but fishable in winter. Wreck fishing for conger, bream, etc. June-Oct. Turbot numerous. Boats: White Strand Boat Hire; Tuckers Boat Hire, Victoria Quay. Both sell tackle, Tuckers sells bait. Club: Salcombe and Dist SAA (HQ: Fortesque Inn, Union St.); annual membership £6 (jun £3); annual festival, four weeks from mid August; special prizes and trophies for visitors throughout season.

Newton Ferrers (Devon). Noted station on Yealm Estuary. All-year bottom fishing; bass, flounders, pollack (from rocks), with mullet, conger, mackerel and flat fish from boats; shark June-Oct. Good base for trips to Eddystone. Boats from D Hockaday (Tel: 359); L Carter (Tel: 210). Abundant bait in estuary. Hotels: River Yealm, Family, Anglers, Yachtsmen.

Plymouth (Devon). One of finest stations in country for off-shore deep water fishing at such marks as East & West Rutts, Hands Deep and, of course, famous Eddystone Reef. Specimen pollack, conger, ling, whiting, pouting, cod, bream and mackerel plentiful. Fishing vessels available for charter are Decca and Sounder equipped - fast exploring numerous wrecks within easy steaming of port; outstanding specimens taken. Inshore fishing for same species off Stoke Point, The Mewstone, Penlee, Rame and The Ledges. Sheltered boat and shore fishing in deep water harbour and extensive estuary network - at its best in autumn for bass, pollack, flounders, thornback and mullet. Shore fishing from rocks at Hilsea, Stoke, Gara Point, Rame Head, Penlee and Queeners for bass, pollack and wrasse, etc. Beach (surf) fishing at Whitsands and sand bar estuaries of Yealm, Erme and Avon rivers for bass, flounder and ray. All angling associations in city - British Conger Club, Plymouth Federation Sea AC and Plymouth SAC - now under one roof, on waterfront, at Plymouth Sea Angling Centre, Vauxhall Quay. Visiting anglers cordially welcomed. Tackle shops: D K Sports Ltd, 88 Vauxhall Street; Osborne & Cragg, 37 Bretonside; The Tackle Box, 85 Exeter Street; Clive's Tackle and Bait, 182 Exeter St. Charter boats are all moored on Sea Angling Centre Marina, Vauxhall Quay, and ownership is as follows: J Folland, tel: 668322; D Brett, 551548; F Goudge, 338545; G Hannaford, 500531; B Hoskins, 404603; Mac, 666141; B Warner, 262470; R Street, 768892; D Northmore, 786821; D Booker, 666576; R Strevens, 812871. Plymouth Angling Boatman's Assc, 0752 565010.

Looe (Cornwall). Excellent centre for all-round sport. Bass, pollack and mullet from 'Banjo Pier' breakwater Mar to end Sept. Good rock fishing from White Rock, Hannafore, westwards to Talland Bay and Llansallos, where pollack, bass, conger and wrasse can be taken. Eastwards, flatfish and bass from beaches at Millendreath, Downderry and Whitsand Bay. Bass, flounders, eels, pollack and mullet from river at quayside and upriver. Excellent sport from boats on deep-sea marks; porbeagle, mako, blue and some thresher shark taken, and wide variety of other fish. Deep sea boats from Cottons Tackle Shop, Fish Quay, East Looe, 0503

262189, whose boat charges are as follows: shark, £20 per head; bottom fishing, £20 per head. Inshore, £6 for 3 hours, £8 for 4 hours. Bait from tackle shops or may be dug in river estuary. Clubs: HQ of Shark AC of Gt Britain is at Cottons, above; Looe is official weighing-in station for British Conger Club; Looe Sea AA (information from hon sec, Dave Snell). Information also from Looe Information Bureau. Useful booklets from tackle shops.

Polperro (Cornwall). Few boats, shore fishing weedy. Bass, whiting, pollack, mackerel are most likely catches. Hotels: Claremont, Noughts & Crosses, Ship, Three Pilchards; also farm accommodation.

Fowey (Cornwall). Excellent sport with bass (June to Oct) in estuary and local bays from Udder to Cannis. Pollack numerous and heavy (20lb and more). Good bream, cod, conger, dogfish, ling, mullet, mackerel, wrasse, whiting and flatfish (big flounders and turbot). Bass, mullet and flounders taken from river. Par Beach to west also good for bass. Rock fishing at Polruan, Gribben Head and Pencarrow. Sand-eel, rag and lugworm obtainable. Clubs: Polruan Sea AC, 9 Greenbank, Polruan; Foye Tightliners SAC, 20 Polvillion Rd, Fowey. Boats: Fowey Town Quay, Troy Chandlers, 072 683 3265. Tackle shops: Leisure Time, 10 Esplanade; Fowey Marine Services, 21/27 Station Rd.

Mevagissey (Cornwall). Excellent sea fishing, boat and shore, especially in summer. Shark boats are based here (local club affiliated to the Shark AC of Great Britain). Shark Centre & Tackle Shop will make arrangements for shark and deep-sea trips. £15 per day, £7 half day. Shore fishing quite productive, especially bass from beach. Good pollack off Dodman Point and from marks out to sea. Bass in large numbers were at one time taken at the Gwinges, but few have been caught in recent years. Excellent sport with large mackerel at Gwinges and close to Dodman from late Aug. Sport from the pier can be very good at times, especially with mullet. Boatmen can be contacted through The Tackle Shop, Fore St, 0726 843513. Club: Mevagissey SAC (HQ, The Ship Inn, Pentewan; visitors welcome). Annual sub £3.

Gorran Haven (Cornwall). Same marks fished as at Mevagissey. Rock fishing available. Bass from sand beach. The Gorran Haven fishermen offer some facilities for visitors wishing a day's fishing. Excellent pollack fishing from boat with rubber sand-eel off Dodman Point. Limited accommodation at the Barley Sheaf (1½m); also Llawnroc Country Club and houses.

Falmouth (Cornwall). Excellent estuary, harbour (pier, shore and boat) and offshore fishing, especially over Manacles Rocks. Noted for big bass and pollack, latter taken off wreck and rock marks. Pendennis Point for wrasse and pollack; St Anthonys Head for wrasse, black bream at night in autumn. Porthallow for coalfish and conger; Lizard for wrasse, mackerel, and conger at night. Bait in estuary or from tackle shops. For boat fishing towards the Manacles, G Hill, Falmouth Boat Owners Assc, Custom House Quay, tel: 0326 311434. Boats in St Mawes: M E Balcombe, 0860 745351. Club Falmouth and Penryn AA (festival each autumn). Tackle shops: AB Harvey, Market Strand; Goodwins, Church Street. For wreck and shark fishing apply: Frank Vinnicombe, West Winds, Mylor Bridge, near Falmouth (Falmouth 372775). Charter-rates per rod £18, Per boat £140. Details of hotel accommodation from Town Information Bureau, Killigrew Street. *For freshwater fishing, see River Fal.*

Porthleven (Cornwall). Bass are to be taken from the rocks in Mount's Bay. Best bass fishing from Loe Bar, 1½m E. Good pollack and mackerel fishing outside the rocks. Nearly all fishing is done from the Mount's Bay type of boat in deep water. For charter boats, contact Harbourmaster. Hotel: Tye Rock.

Penzance (Cornwall). Excellent boat, pier, rock and shore fishing for pollack, mackerel, mullet and bass. Marazion beaches offer flatfish and ray. Pier at Lamorna, turbot, gurnard and dogfish. Breakwater at Sennen, the same. Boat trips can be arranged with The Shell Shop, tel: 68565 or Ken's Tackle Shop, tel: 61969. Shark fishing also available. Best months: June-Nov. Club: Mount's Bay AS (headquarters: Dolphin Inn, Newlyn). Annual fishing festival, five weeks, Aug-Sept. Tackle shops: Ken's Tackle, 9 Beachfield Court; Newtown Angling Centre, Newton Germoe.

Mousehole, via **Penzance** (Cornwall). Good station for fishing Mount's Bay. Excellent mackerel, bream, pollack, conger, whiting, bass close to harbour according to season. Sheltered from west. Rock fishing available in rough weather. Bell Rock between Newlyn and Mousehole has produced record catches. Between Mousehole and Lamorna, Penza Point, Kemyell Point and Carn Dhu are marks. Charter boat: Talisman, contact S Farley, tel: 0736 731895/731154. Best grounds: Longships and Runnel Stone. Good results with sharks. Hotels: The Ship; Old Coastguards; The Lobster Pot.

Isles of Scilly. From shores and small boats around islands, wrasse, pollack, mackerel, conger and plaice; farther off in deep sea, particularly on The Powl, south-west of St Agnes, big catches made of cod, ling, conger, pollack, etc. Mullet pay periodical visits inshore, but usually caught by net; bass rare in these waters. Some shark fishing, but visitors advised to take own tackle. Peninnis Head and Deep Point on St Mary's are good rock marks for pollack, wrasse and mackerel; Pelistry Bay likely beach venue. Boating can be dangerous, so experience essential. Accommodation limited, early bookings advisable between May and Sept. Full information from Tourist IC, Porthcressa, St Mary's. For boats inquire of St Mary's Boating Assn, High Street, St Mary's. Several shops stock tackle.

St Ives (Cornwall). Surf fishing for bass principal sport. Mullet, mackerel, pollack, flatfish (plaice, flounders, occasional turbot) can all be caught from shore, especially from island, Aire Point, Cape Cornwall, Portheras, Besigrau, Man's Head, Clodgy Point; Godrevy Point offers mackerel, pollack and wrasse, which are also found at Navax Point. Chapel Porth good for ray and turbot. Boat fishing gives sport with mackerel (summer months) and large pollack (off reef from Godrevy Island). For boats contact Harbourmaster, tel: 0736 795081. Bass, tope, mullet, flatfish and occasional sea trout taken in Hayle river estuary. Trout fishing on Drift Reservoir, Penzance and St Erth Stream (4m). No tackle shop now, but Symons of Market Place sells rods and bait. Hotels: Dunmar; Demelza; St Margarets, and many others.

Newquay (Cornwall). Boat, beach; rock and estuary fishing. Mackerel (April to Oct); school bass (June-Sept); larger fish July onwards, including winter; pollack (May-Nov); flatfish, wrasse (May-Sept); whiting in winter. Mullet good from

June-Sept. Beach fishing at Perranporth, Holywell Bay, Crantock and Watergate Bay: ray, turbot and plaice. Off-peak times only. Shark and deep sea fishing possible. Club: Treninnick Tavern AC, HQ the Tavern, holds monthly competitions. Tackle hire, F Bickers, Fore St; Fishing Centre, 2 Beach St. For boats, contact Boatmans Assc. 876352/871886; Anchor Sea Angling Centre, 0636 877613/874570, or Harbourmaster, 06373 2809. Trout fishing in Porth Reservoir. Sea trout and brown trout in Gannel estuary. Tackle Shop: Beach Rd; Goin Fishin, 32 Fore St. Numerous hotels.

Padstow (Cornwall). Trevose Head, Park Head and Stepper Point are good marks in summer for float fishing and spinning for mackerel, pollack, garfish, bass, wrasse, rays, dog fish, plaice, turbot, occ. tope, and in winter for whiting, codling, dogfish, conger. The beaches at Trevone, Harlyn, Mother Ivys, Boobys, Constantine, Treyarnon, Porthcothan, Mawgan Porth, provide surf casting for bass, plaice, turbot, rays. The estuary has good flounder fishing in winter. Clubs are Padstow AC, Social Club, Padstow, St Columb Club, The Red Lion, St Columb, Glenville Fishing Club, Social Club, St Dennis. Tackle shop: Treyarnon Angling Centre, provides shore fishing guide. Hotel: Treyarnon Bay.

Bude (Cornwall). Codling, flatfish, mackerel, whiting and dogfish from breakwater and Crackington Haven. Northcott Mouth Crooklets, Maer, good for skate and flatfish. Widemouth Bay is good venue. Rays may be taken from shore in late summer and autumn. Good rock fishing is to be had from Upton, Wanson and Millock. Boats may be booked for parties: Ken Cave, Ashton Cottage, Stibb, Bude EX23 9HL. Several boats work from Port Isaac in summer. Tackle shop, N Cornwall Pet & Garden Centre, Princess Street; Vennings, Fore St, Tintagel. Club: Bude and Dist SAC.

Hartland (Devon); ns Barnstaple, 24m. Good all-round sea fishing, especially for bass at times with india-rubber sand-eel, prawn or limpet from beach or rocks according to tide (bass up to $11\frac{1}{2}$lb have been caught); whiting, mullet, conger and pouting also taken. Hotels: Hartland Quay, New Inn, King's Arms.

Lundy (Bristol Channel). Good mackerel, conger, pollack and wrasse inshore. Ray, plaice, dabs, tope and bass at East Bank.

$1\frac{1}{4}$ to $2\frac{1}{2}$m E. Good anchorage at Lundy, but no harbour. Boats occasionally on hire for 8 persons fishing. For accommodation write to The Agent, Lundy, Bristol Channel, N Devon EX39 2LY.

Clovelly (Devon); W of Bideford. Whiting, cod, conger, bull huss, dogfish and the occasional plaice caught all the year round; ray in spring, bass and mackerel in summer. Few inshore boats; fishing from the breakwater forbidden from 9 am to 6 pm in summer. Tackle shops: see Bideford. Hotels: New Inn; Red Lion.

Appledore. N of Bideford in Torridge estuary. In summer, good bass fishing from rocks. Greysands and boats. Cod, some over 20lb, and whiting in winter. Lugworm beds at Appledore and Instow. Few boats. Tackle shop: B & K Angling Supplies, 14 The Quay.

Bideford (Devon). Bass (from the bridge, in summer) flounders, mullet higher up the river. 2m miles away at Westward Ho, extensive beach and rocks from which bass, dogfish, smooth-hounds, bull huss, tope and mackerel may be taken in summer; cod in winter. Tackle shop: The Tackle Box, Kings Shopping Centre, Bideford, who supply dt for several local coarse fisheries. Tel: 0237 470043.

Ilfracombe (Devon). From shore pollack, coalfish, wrasse, bass, a few flatfish. From boat, conger, skate, ray. Mackerel Jun to Sept. Bait: mackerel, squid, sandeel, rag and lugworm, peeler crab. Boat hire, tel: Ilfracombe 863460, 864957 or 867308. Pier is favourite spot for conger and pollack; Capstone Point for bass. Club: Ilfracombe and District AA. Reservoir trout fishing available *(see freshwater section)*. Hotel: Longwood, Montpelier Terrace, Royal Britannia. Details of other accommodation from Publicity Officer, Tourist Information Centre, The Promenade. Tackle and bait from Tackle Box, 2b Portland St, or Variety Sports, 23 Broad St.

Lynmouth (Devon). Good harbour and boat fishing. Grey mullet and bass from harbour arm. Trolling for pollack and mackerel. Tope, skate and conger in Lynmouth Bay and off Sand Ridge, 1m. Motor boats with skipper available. Contact 0598 53207 or 0598 53684. Best months: June to Oct. Several hotels in Lynton and Lynmouth; details from Visitor Centre, The Esplanade, Lynmouth. *(For freshwater fishing see Lyn).*

Minehead (Som). Beach, boat and rock

fishing, principally for tope, skate, ling, thornback ray, conger, cod, bass and flatfish (Dunster to Porlock good for bass from beaches). Dogfish in bay. Mackerel in summer. Harbour and promenade walls provide sport with mullet, codling and some bass. Boats: through the tackle shop named below, all year round. Bait from sands at low water. Club: Minehead and Dist SAC. Tackle shop: Minehead Sports, 55 The Avenue. For further information and for boats contact Information Centre, Market House, The Parade.

Watchet (Som). Watchet and Dist Sea Angling Society fishes all the year round, covering coast from St Audries Bay to Porlock Wier. Monthly competitions from piers and shore. Codling, bass, whiting, conger and skate, according to season. Good boat fishing. New members welcomed by AS.

Weston-super-Mare (Avon). Record list of the Weston-super-Mare Sea AA includes conger at 25lb, sole at 2lb 8oz, bass, 13lb, skate 16lb 8oz, cod at 22lb, silver eel at 4lb, whiting and flounder at 2lb. Best venues 2 hours either side of low tide are Brean Down, conger, skate; Weston Beach, flatfish; Knightstone, the same. Woodspring is fishable throughout year, best at autumn. Boats for parties of up to 12 persons: P Holder, tel: 0934 631527; D Payne, 626238; 24 persons, F Watts, 624497. For baits, beds of lugworms are to be found along the low water mark of the town beach and off Kewstoke Rocks. Also from Tackle shops: Weston Angling Centre, Locking Rd, Weston-s-Mare; Burnham Tackle Box, 10 Regent Street, Burnham; Burnham Tackle Centre, 29 Victoria Street, Burnham.

Southport (Merseyside). Dabs and flounders, with whiting and codling in winter, chief fish caught here; also skate, mullet, dogfish, sole, plaice, conger, gurnard and some bass. Shore flat and sandy, and fishing mainly from pier. Local clubs: Southport SAS. Good coarse fishing on River Crossens run by Southport AS; dt. Tackle shops: Robinsons, 71 Sussex Road.

Blackpool (Lancs). Seven miles of beach fishing for plaice, bass, mackerel and dabs in summer, whiting and cod in winter. Fishing from North Pier for codling, whiting and dabs. Oct to March best, night fishing allowed Nov-May. Boat trips from Fleetwood Charter Boats, P Atkinson, Chairman, tel: 0253 778295; Star Fishing Co, 0253 875339. Tidal parts of R Wyre may be fished without a licence. Tickets for certain parts of Wyre from tackle shops. Coarse fishing in Stanley Park Lake. Dt. Tackle shops: S Waterhouse & Son, 66 Norbreck Rd; B Ogden, 254 Church Street; Howarth, 128 Watson Rd; Anglers Den, 41 Warley Rd. Many hotels.

Morecambe and **Heysham** (Lancs). Beach and pier fishing throughout year. Beaches yield plaice, flounders, dabs, bass and eels from June to October, and dabs, codling, whiting and flounders in winter. Estuary catches up to 100 flounders to 2lb weight at Arnside. Central Pier open for angling; plaice, bass, flounder, eels. From Stone Jetty angling free; good catches of plaice, flounders, codling, whiting. At Heysham Harbour day permits. Flounders, dabs, pouting, conger and mullet can be taken. Storm Groynes is producing good flatfish. Club: Heysham AC. Tackle shops: Gerry's Fishing Tackle, 108 Heysham Road; Morecombe Angling Centre, Thornton Rd; Charlton & Bagnall, 3/5 Damside St, Lancaster.

Fleetwood (Lancs). Plaice, whiting, skate, codling, tope, etc, from boats and shore. Club: Fleetwood and District AC. Sea baits from tackle shop: Langhorne's, 80 Poulton Road, tel: 0253 872653. Boats: C B Bird, 25 Upper Lune Street, Tel: 0253 873494; Viking Princess, 0253 873045, Harvester, 0253 778295.

Barrow-in-Furness (Cumbria). Boat and shore fishing for tope, bass, cod, plaice, whiting, skate. Good marks include Foulney Island, Roa Island, Piel Island, Scarth Hole and Black Tower (Walney Island) and Roanhead. Frozen bait and tackle from Angling and Hiking Centre, 62 Forshaw Street; A Parker, 185 Rawlinson St.

POLLUTION

Anglers are united in deploring pollution. To combat it, urgent action may be called for at any time from any one of us. If numbers of fish are found dead, dying, or seriously distressed, take samples of both fish and water and contact the officer responsible for pollution at the appropriate National Rivers Authority.

ISLE OF WIGHT

The Island provides a wealth of shore and boat fishing, and sheltered conditions can always be found, Bass are the main quarry for beach anglers, but pollack, conger, mackerel, pouting, thornback rays, flatfish and wrasse, with occasional tope, are also taken. Black bream, skate and shark are caught by boat anglers as well as the species already mentioned. Cod run regularly to 20lb in autumn. Due to strong tides on the north coast and lack of harbours on the south coast, the visiting angler would be best advised to arrange boat trips with one of the local charter skippers working out of Yarmouth or Bembridge. Strong tides also mean heavy leads and sometimes, wire line. There are a large number of fishing clubs on the island. T I centres provide information about them.

Alum Bay. This necessitates a steep descent from the car park down the steps provided. From March to October there is a chair lift in operation. Fishes well after dark for large conger, bass, rays and sole, especially when rough. From the old pier remains to the white cliffs is the main area, although the rocks to the east, towards Totland, make a good station from which to spin for bass in the tide race, or to light leger with squid or mackerel. Deep water at all states of tide.

Atherfield. A number of record fish have been taken from this stretch. The beach is of shingle with scattered rock, easily reached via path alongside holiday camp. Bass, rays, pout, etc after dark, to mackerel, squid and cuttle baits. Crab bait produces smooth hounds. Ragworm fished over the drying ledge to the left of this mark produces large wrasse and bass, day or night. Large cod in late autumn.

Bembridge. The shore from Whitecliff to Bembridge is mainly rock formation with stretches of shingle and is good ground for bass and conger although not fished a great deal. Bass, mullet, eels, among the rocks. Here, the beach turns to fine flat sand and flatfish and bass are taken. Bembridge Harbour is a wide inlet with St Helens on the opposite bank. Shark fishing, July-August, drifting from St Catherines Light to Nab Tower. Boats and bait obtainable on shore. A sand gully near the 'Crab and Lobster' can be fished from the rocks. Fine bream may be taken from boats on Bembridge Ledge, early May to June, plenty of mackerel, also. A good number of fish are taken in the harbour: flounders, eels, bass. Many large mullet can be seen but are seldom fished for. Very strong tide in narrowest part of entrance. Kingrag and lugworm are good baits for ledgering and small mud ragworm on light float tackle is successful. Baited spoon or wander tackle works well for flounder and plaice. Sea wall at St Helens is a convenient place to park and fish over the top of the tide. Club: Bembridge AC, holds 12 competitions p.a. Membership £12 annually.

Bonchurch. Bass, conger, wrasse and pout from beach. Good fishing in gulleys between the extensive rocks at flood tide, after dark, especially after a south westerly gale.

Brooke. A shallow water mark that fishes well when the sea is coloured. Expect conger, bass, pout, plus cod in late autumn. One good spot is to be found in front of easy cliff path, 200 yds to left of point.

Chale. Best beach for rays on island, reached by steep cliff path. Specimen small eyed rays are taken on frozen sand eel, day or night, from Mar-Sept, when sea is coloured after a storm. Some bass and conger, plus mackerel in summer.

Colwell Bay. A shallow sandy beach with easy access. Bass, sole, wrasse after dark, when crowds have gone home.

Totland Bay. Next to Colwell Bay, deeper water. More chance of bass, especially when rough. It's possible to fish straight from a car on the sea wall. Fishing is good beside the disused pier.

Compton Bay. 1m west of Brooke. Long flat sandy beach with patches of flat rock. Occasional bass when the sea is rough. Avoid the rocks under the cliff at the west end, where there is a danger of major cliff falls.

Cowes. The River Medina runs from Newport to Cowes Harbour and offers flounder fishing throughout the year with the best sport from the late summer to autumn. The shoals move about the river with the tide and location is often a matter of local knowledge. As a general guide the fish may be expected further upstream on the stronger spring tides. Weights average up to a pound. Bass also move into the river and have been taken to 4lbs, often on flounder tackle. Rowing boats may be launched from the Folly Inn on the East bank, reached by turning off the main Newport to East Cowes road. Kingston power station about a mile down from Folly is a good boat mark for school bass, plaice, sole. Mullet and silver eels may be caught anywhere. Ragworm is usually used in preference to lugworm..

Cowes Harbour. Bass, flounder, plaice and sole may be taken by the boat angler from either side of the fairway above and below the floating bridge and during the summer there are many large mullet within the harbour. Inside the breakwater to the east, flounder and plaice are taken on the bottom from along the edge of the hovercraft channel to inshore towards the East Cowes Esplanade. Flounder and plaice are also taken from the mud-flats outside the East Cowes breakwater.

West Cowes Esplanade to **Gurnard.** Float fishing and spinning from the slipways and jetties for bass and mullet. Along the Princes Green to Egypt Light, bass and conger can be found and in late summer bass often venture close in under the walls in search of prawns and may be taken by trailing a worm over the balustrade and walking it quietly along. At Egypt Light, the shingle slopes steeply so long casting is unnecessary, and tope have occasionally been landed here as well as bass to 8lb, and cod to 20lb in late autumn. The sandy patches among the rocks may yield sole and plaice in season. Free car parking here.

Freshwater Bay. Pouting, bass, small pollack and few conger. Fish from middle of beach when rough. Survey at low tide, then fish after dark. Very easy access.

Newport. Nearest sea fishing in River Medina; flounders, school bass, mullet, plaice, eels. Tackle/ boat hire from Scotties, branch at 11 Lugley St, tel 522115.

Newtown. Bass and flounders in Newtown River. Clamerkin reach is best, using light gear and ragworm. Limited access, as large area is nature reserve.

Ventnor to **St Catherines.** Sseries of rocky ledges and gullies, best surveyed at low water. Bass, conger, pout, wrass etc after dark and some mullet during calm days.

Yarmouth. Flounder and mullet and school bass in harbour. Bass, rays and mackerel from pier in summer. Notable cod venue in late autumn but strong tides prevail.

Ryde. A very shallow, sandy beech, popular with holiday makers. Bass, small pollock, plaice, flounders, eels, bream and grey mullet from pier. Conger, dogfish,

dabs, skate, mackerel from deep water marks, and plaice, flounder, bass and sole fishing inshore. Cod up to 24lb taken in autumn. Sheltered resort giving ideal fishing conditions all year. All beaches fishable. King rag and lugworm plentiful. Vectis Boating and Fishing Club offers annual membership. Details from hon sec (enclose sae). Boats can be hired along shore.

Sandown. Fishing from end of pier (daytime only) produces plaice, rays, bass and bream on sandy ground. Float fishing produces mackerel, scad, small pollack and mullet. Local club: Sandown and Lake AS, organising frequent open competitions. Visitors welcome. Boat hire and tackle, Scotties, 22 Fitzroy Street.

Seaview. From St Helens to Seaview the coast is a mixture of rocks and sand and shingle. Priory Bay is reached by boat and provides very good mackerel and bass fishing. Plaice may be taken to 3lb from early April, with lugworm. During the summer months bream can also be taken from this spot. From June onwards, bass and mackerel are shoaling and large catches from boats are common. Cod are also taken late in the year.

Shanklin. Pier has been demolished. Various other venues exist which fish well for specific species, such as sting ray, but require very detailed directions re access, times to fish, etc. Contact Scotties of Newport for such details, and to obtain a wide variety of suitable baits. Norfolk House Hotel, The Esplanade, PO37 6BN, offers fishing holidays of two or three nights, for experienced angler and novice, with two full days at sea with all bait and tackle supplied. Contact Alan Davis, tel: 0983 863023.

Totland. Bass off shingle bank from boat. Bass, conger from shore. Fishing also from pier. Boats from Fair Deal Amusements, The Pier. Hotels: Chalet, Sentry Mead.

Ventnor. The western end of the beach is good for bass, skate, pout and conger and the sea wall in front of the canoe lake is a good bass spot. Boat (from Blakes) for pollack and mackerel. Club: Ventnor AC (associate members welcome). Tackle and bait: Bates & Son, 5 Spring Hill; J Chiverton 70 High St. Beach fishing *(see also Bonchurch).*

Wootton. School bass and flounders.

Yarmouth. Bass, small pollack; pier fishing.

CHANNEL ISLANDS

Wide variety of sport from beaches, rocky headlands and boats. Many specimen fish landed from deep-sea marks. Shark fishing growing in popularity. Boats easy to come by.

Guernsey. No fewer than 52 different species are recorded in Bailiwick of Guernsey rod-caught record list. Guernsey is 15 minutes from the Hurd Deep, near major shipping lanes, and hundreds of wrecks yield high catches. Inshore, many headlands offer first-class spinning, and a flat, sandy, west coast gives good surf-casting for bass and a few flatfish. Several Guernsey fish accepted as new British records. The most common species are bass, bream, conger, dogfish, garfish, mackerel, mullet, plaice, pollack and wrasse. Anglers may fish anywhere from the shore except for marinas, the fishermans quay, and the land reclamation to the south of St Sampson's Harbour. Bottom fishing is productive in spring, late autumn and winter; spinning in summer. Long casting is no advantage, on westerly rocks. Baits: ragworm is found in the rocky bays on west coast, Grand Havre, Bordeaux North, to Beaucette Marina, Bellgreve Bay; lugworm in sandy bays, especially, Grand Havre, Cobo and Vazon. Crabs, prawns and catbait can also be obtained. In north east, Fort Doyle is one of the best marks; south east, Soldiers Bay. South west cliffs are fishable but dangerous. There are nine different fishing competitions between June and December. Boat charter; A Brehaut, tel: 63730; D Lane, 45444; P Holland, 56341; R Taylor, 37959. Tackle shops: Tackle & Accessories Centre, The Market, tel: 723225; Marquand Bros, North Quay, St Peter Port, tel: 0481 720962. Baits, rod hire. For further information about Guernsey fisheries contact States Sea Fisheries Committee, Burnt Lane, St Martins.

Jersey. Winter fishing yields pollack, cod, ray and other flatfish, conger, a few bass. Spring: garfish, early mackerel off such points as Sorel and La Moye; grey mullet, porbeagle, blue shark and other species. Summer fishing is good for all forms of fishing except lobster potting, especially at night, by boat on offshore reefs. In autumn, whitebait concentrates at places such as Belle Hougue bring in large mackerel and bass. Flatfish move into shallow waters in the Islands bays. Venues: St Helier's harbour heads; Noirmont Point; St Brelade's Bay; La Corbiere; L'Etacq; Plemont; Greve de Lecq; Bonne Nuit Bay harbour; Bouley Bay harbour; Rozel Bay harbour; St Catherine's breakwater; St Aubin's Bay. Clubs: Jerset Sea Fishing Club, hon sec Mr Tom Jones, 9 Valley Close, St Saviour, tel: 53689; Jersey Specimen Hunters Group, hon sec, Frank Casado, Flat 2, 89 St Saviour's Rd, St Helier, tel: 26842; Norman's Fishing & Social Club, hon sec P J Bourgourd, Le Carrefour Cottage, Bouley Bay, tel: 621136. Charter boats: A Heart, tel: 888552 (pm), 'Portrush', Bob Wood, tel 51181; 'Theseus', D Nuth, tel 861620. Tackle shops: PJN Fishing Tackle, 7 Beresford St. Tel: 0534 74875; Hunt Stewart, 71 King St, and 28 Broad St; I S Marine, 15/16 Commercial Buildings; J F S Sport, Green St; all St Helier. Hotel catering for anglers is Cornucopia, Mont Pinel, St Helier JE2 4RS, tel: 0534 32646.

ISLE OF MAN

The Island's coastline is extremely varied. The long, flat, surf beaches of the North contrast sharply with the sheer faces of the South. Similarly, its fishing methods and species of fish are equally diverse. Despite the Island's location, coastline and clean waters, saltwater angling from both shore and boat remains unexploited and largely undiscovered. Information is available from Isle of Man Tourist and Leisure Department, Sea Terminal, Douglas, tel: 0624 686766.

Castletown. Conger, pollack, cod, wrasse, tope, flatfish from beach and boat; best months, June to Oct. Big skate from boats 600 yds off Langness; best Aug-Sept Boats available locally.

Douglas. Plaice, sole (British record lemon sole), coalfish, pollack, flounder from Victoria Pier; best months, May to Oct, coalfish, wrasse, cod, plaice, dabs, sole from boats in Douglas Bay. Rock fishing off Douglas Head; float or spinner (good for pollack). Cod, wrasse, red gurnard, plaice, Little Ness Head to Douglas Head; skate from boats 2m out, and large tope, conger, cod, etc. Club: Douglas (IOM) and District AC, annual membership fee £12 (£4 discount before 28 Feb), jun £3 (membership includes trout fishing rights in **R Glass**). Club sec/treasurer, Mrs Sue McCoubrey, 47 Hildesley Rd, Douglas, takes applications for membership. Tackle shops: Hobbytime, Castle St; Intersport, 58 Duke St. Also, Tackle Bow, at Foxdale.

Kirk Michael. Beach fishing from here to Point of Ayre is excellent for bass, flatfish, dogfish.

Laxey. Plaice, dabs and bass from March to Oct from beach. Cod, mackerel, flat-fish, offshore from boats at Garwick Bay. Clubs: Garwick Sailing and Fishing Club.

Peel. Breakwater: cod, coalfish, dogfish plentiful all year round; mackerel, dogfish, coalfish, plaice, flounder, dabs (July to Oct). Beach: similar. Rock fishing: from Castle rocks and headlands plenty of pollack. Sand eel best bait all season. Limited lugworm on beach. Boat fishing, but hire limited: cod and haddock in winter. In spring and summer spur dogfish common. Rock fishing off St Patrick's Isle for mackerel, wrasse, coalfish; float and spinner. Local club; Peel Angling Club.

Port Erin. Good sport from pier and break-

water for pollack, mackerel, wrasse, grey mullet, coalfish, angler fish and conger. The bay yields flatfish and mackerel, with cod in the colder months. Tackle shop: Henry Crellin, IOM Sea Sports Ltd, Strand Road. Hotels: Balmoral; Falcons Nest.

Port St Mary. Probably best centre on island. Pollack, coalfish, wrasse from rocks, pier, boats (most of year). Flatfish and mackerel offshore and pier during herring season. Tope, skate, cod, conger, ling from boats. Boats from J Williams, Beach Cliff, Bay View Rd and W Halsall, Lime Street PSM. Several competitions. Inquiries to hon sec, Southern AC. Visitors welcome. Tackle shop: The Tackle Box, Foxdale. Hotels: Station; Albert.

Ramsey. Plaice and cod from pier. Dogfish, flatfish, conger and (in Sept) bass from Ramsey beach to Point of Ayre. Coalfish, pollack and wrasse may be caught float fishing from rocks, using lugworm for bait. Pollack also taken by spinning with artificial sand-eel. For help with bait and boats, contact officials of Ramsey SAC, annual membership fee: £2.50. Tackle shop: The Ramsey Warehouse, 37 Parliament Street.

Check before you go

While every effort has been made to ensure that the information given in **Where to Fish** *is correct, the position is continually changing, and anglers are urged, in their own interests, to make preliminary enquiries before travelling to selected venues. This is especially important with reference to prices quoted. Inevitably the rate of inflation is affecting stability in this quarter. Anglers' attention is also drawn to the fact that the hotels mentioned under the various fishing stations do not necessarily have water of their own. Any amendments or further data for inclusion in subsequent editions, and any criticism, will be welcome.*

FISHING CLUBS & ASSOCIATIONS IN ENGLAND

These have once again been expanded and now total well over 1000, covering freshwater and sea angling. Further information can be had from the Secretaries. A stamped addressed envelope should be enclosed with postal enquiries. Some clubs have had to be omitted because of lack of space. **Note:** *Where information has been supplied, waters held by the club are usually noted, and availability of tickets, at end of each entry. Further details under individual centres.* Please advise the publishers (address at the front of the book) of any changed details for the next edition.

NATIONAL BODIES

Anglers' Co-operative Association
Allen Edwards, Director
23 Castlegate,
Grantham,
Lincs NG31 6SW
Tel: 0476 61008, Fax: 0476 60900

Angling Foundation
23 Brighton Road,
South Croydon CR2 6EA

Angling Trade Association
23 Brighton Road,
South Croydon CR2 6EA

Atlantic Salmon Trust
Moulin, Pitlochry
Perthshire PH16 5JQ
Director: Rear Admiral D J Mackenzie

Association of Professional Game
  Angling Instructors
Michael Evans, Secretary
Little Saxbys Farm
Cowden, Kent TN8 7DX
Tel: 0342 850765. Fax: 0342 850926.

Association of Stillwater Game Fishery
  Managers
Packington Fisheries
Meriden, Coventry
West Midlands

British Conger Club
Tom Matchett
112 Bearsdown Road
Eggbuckland
Plymouth, Devon PL6 5TT
Tel: 0752 769262
HQ: Sea Angling Centre,
Vauxhall Quay, Sutton Harbour,
Plymouth,

Devon
British Field Sports Society
Peter Smith
59 Kennington Road
London SEI 7PZ
Tel: 071-928 4742.
Fax: 071-620 1401

British Record (rod-caught) Fish
  Committee
David Rowe, Acting Secretary
c/o National Federation of Sea Anglers
51A Queen Street
Newton Abbot
Devon TQ12 2QJ
Tel & Fax: 0626 331330

British Trout Association
10 Barley Mow Passage
Chiswick
London W4 4PH
Tel: 081 994 6477. Fax: 081 742 3080

British Trout Farmers' Restocking
  Association
A Darbyshire
Sinnington Trout
York YO6 6RB
Tel & Fax: 0751 31948

British Trout Information Bureau
P O Box 189
London SW6 7UT
Tel: 071 385 1158
Fax: 01 381 9620

British Waterways Board
Melbury House, Melbury Terrace
London NWI 6JX
Tel: 071-723 8486
All Fishery enquiries to

Fishing Clubs

When you appoint a new secretary, do not forget to give us details of the change. Write to the publishers (address at front of the book). Thank you!

Fisheries Manager:
Brindley House, Corner Hall
Lawn Lane, Hemel Hempstead
Hertfordshire HP3 9YT
Tel: 0442 235400.
Fax: 0442 234932

Flyfishers' Club
Commander N T Fuller RN
24a Old Burlington Street
London Wl
Private members club, no fishery.
Publishers of The Flyfishers Journal-
editor Kenneth Robson
Tel: 071-734 9229

Freshwater Biological Association
The Director
The Ferry House
Far Sawrey, Ambleside
Cumbria LA22 OLP
Tel: 05394 42468

Grayling Society
Dr R B Broughton
10 Park Road
Salford M6 8HL

International Fly Fishing Association
R W Newport, Secretary and Treasurer
Nairn
Glenvar Park
Blackrock, Co Dublin
Ireland

**Marine Biological Association of the
United Kingdom**
The Secretary
The Laboratory
Citadel Hill
Plymouth PLI 2PB
Tel: 222772

**National Association of Specialist
Anglers**
B Crawford
Waters Edge
6 Holmer Lane
Stirchley, Telford
Shropshire
Tel: 0952 591131

National Federation of Anglers
Secretary General

2 Wilson Street
Derby DEI IPG
Tel: 0332 362000

National Federation of Anglers
Southern Region
I Epps, Secretary
62 Longmynd Drive,
Fareham
Hants PO14 1SS

National Federation of Anglers
Chief Administration Officer
Halliday House
2 Wilson Street
Derby, DE1 1PG
Tel: 0332 362000

National Federation of Sea Anglers
D Rowe
NFSA Development Officer
NFSA Office,
51A Queen Street
Newton Abbot,
Devon TQl2 2QJ
Tel & Fax: 0626 331330

Salmon and Trout Association
C W Poupard, Director
Fishmongers' Hall
London Bridge
London EC4R 9EL
Tel: 071-283 5838
Fax: 071 9291389
(List of local organisers at end of book)

Sea Anglers Match Federation
The Secretary
Mr A Yates
1 Great Pincham Farm Cottages
Pincham
Dover, Kent

Shark Angling Club of Great Britain
Karan Sayer
The Quay, East Looe
Cornwall PLl3 IDX
Tel: Looe 262642

Sports Council
16 Upper Woburn Place
London WCIH OQP
Tel: 071-388 1277

CLUBS

Abbey Hulton Suburban Angling Society
Steve Nicholson
1379 Leek Road
Abbey Hulton
Stoke on Trent, Staffs
ST2 8BW

**Abingdon and District Angling and
Restocking Association**

R Pitson
Tel: 0235 25140
Thames at Sandford and Duxford

Abingdon and Oxford Anglers Alliance
R Bateman
16 The Gap
Marcham
Abingdon, Berkshire

Accrington and District Fishing Club
A Balderstone
42 Townley Avenue
Huncoat, Lancashire
Greta. Tickets

Addingham Angling Association
Fleece Inn
Addingham
West Yorkshire

Aln Angling Association
L Johnson
Tower Showrooms
Alnwick, Northumberland
Aln. Tickets

Alrewas Angling Club
A R Booth
3 Ivanhoe Road
Lichfield
Staffs WS14 9AV

Alcester Angling Club
D Stain
Alcester Trades and Labour Club
St Faiths Road
Alcester, Warks

Alston and District Angling Association
C J Sayer
The Grove
Alston, Cumbria CA9 3DA
S Tyne. Tickets

Alveston Village Association Angling Club
M Pitcher
6 Ferry Lane, Alveston
Stratford upon Avon CN37 7QX

Ampthill and District Angling and Fish Preservation Society
R Dempsey
34 Falcon Crescent
Flitwick
Beds MK45 1LZ
Tel: 0525 714743
River, pits, season ticket

Anchor Angling Association
F James
54 Hilliat Fields
Drayton,
near Abingdon, Berkshire

Andover Angling Club
Martin Hopper
4 Loveridge Close
Andover SP10 5ND

Appleby Angling Association
J A Henderson
c/o Barclays Bank,
Appleby, Westmorland
Eden. Tickets

Appletreewick Barden and Burnsall Angling Club
J G H Mackrell
Mouldgreave
Oxenhope
N Keighley, West Yorks BD22 9RT
Wharfe. Tickets

Apuldram Fishing and Boat Club
P G Foster
5 St George's Drive
Donnington
Chichester

Arundel Victoria AC
R Cranham
Crabtree House
Bilsham Road, Yapton
Arundel BN18 0JN

Asfordby Society of Anglers
Mr & Mrs H Birch
Riverside Cottage, Mill Lane
Asfordby, Melton Mowbray
Leicestershire

Ashbourne Fly-Fishers' Club
C Woolliscroft
10 Hillside Avenue
Ashbourne, Derbyshire
Dove. Members only

Ashby Angling Club
A S Lyndon
45 Station Road, Woodville
Burton-on-Trent
Staffs DE11 7DX

Ashfield Angling
J K Taylor
74 Edward Street
Kirkby-in-Ash
Notts

Ashmere Fisheries
Mr & Mrs K Howman
Felix Lane
Shepperton, Middlesex
Trout lake. Season tickets only

Ashton and District Centre Northern Anglers Association
A Brown
10 Dale Road, Golbourne
Warrington, Lancs WA3 3PN

Aspatria Angling Club
R Baxter
25 Outgang Road,
Aspatria, Cumberland
Ellen. Members only

Association of East Anglian Sea Anglers
F Culshaw
84 Westwood Avenue
Lowestoft, Suffolk

Association of Teesside and District Angling Clubs
A Allan
1 Scalby Grove, Fairfield
Stockton-on-Tees, Teesside
Reservoir. Tickets

Avon Angling Club (Melksham)
R Edwards
56 Addisar Road
Melksham

Avon Fishing Association (Devon)
J E Coombes
19 Stella Road, Preston
Paignton, South Devon
Devonshire Avon. Tickets

Avon Fly Fishers Club
S Filton
39 Fouracres Close
Withywood, Bristol

Avon Ho Angling Club
B Wilkinson
31 Kings Newnham Lane
Church Lawford
Rugby, Warks

**Avon and Tributaries Angling
Association**
J G L Lewis
Chapel Cottage
Clarendon Road
Widcombe Hill
Bath BA2 4NJ

**Avon Preservation and Restocking
Society**
W D Hunter
2 Fairy Hill, Compton Dando
Bristol BS18 4LJ

Avondale Angling Club
M Clark
71 Lister Road
Atherstone, Warwickshire CV9 BX

Axminster Sea Angling Club
Miss K Hawkes
208 Henson Park
Chard, Somerset

**Aylesbury District and Izaak Walton
Angling Association**
W Cheney
14 Yardley Green, Elmhurst Estate
Aylesbury,
Buckinghamshire

**Aylesbury and District Angling
Federation**
G E Bateman
The Malton
8 Burcott Lane, Bierton
Aylesbury HP22 5AU

Aylsham and District Angling Club
K Sutton
17 Town Lane
Aylsham,
Norfolk

Babbacombe Sea Angling Association
Mrs A Hern
29 Westhill Road
Torquay

Babcock Angling Club
R G Evans
5 Andrew's Close
Brookthorpe, Gloucester GL4 0UR

**Banbury and District Angling
Association**
G V Bradbeer
7 Bentley Close
Banbury, Oxon
Cherwell and Oxford Canal. Tickets

Barnard Castle Angling Society
C Henshaw
10 Sherwood Close
Barnard Castle, Co Durham
Tees

Barnard Castle Fly-Fishing Club
J F Cooke Hurle
Startforth Hall
Barnard Castle, Co Durham
DL12 9RA

Barnby Dun Social Angling Club
W Salter
1 Greengates
High Street
Barnby Dun
Doncaster DB3 1DU

Barnes and Mortlake Angling Society
K Dellard
23 Cleveland Gardens
Barnes SW13 0AE

Barnley and District Anglers Association
M Riley
Church Lane
Gawber HG3 2HB

**Barnsley and District Amalgamated
Anglers' Society**
T Eaton
60 Walton Street
Gawber, Barnsley
Yorkshire S75 2PD

**Barnstaple and District Angling
Association**
A J Penny
Endswell House,
Raleigh Road
Barnstaple, North Devon
Taw. Visitors' Tickets only from local
tackleists

Barnt Green Fishing Club
Reservoir Cottage
Upper Bittell
Barnt Green
Birmingham B45 8BH

Barrow Angling Association
J R Jones
69 Prince Street
Dalton-in-Furness,
Lancashire
Reservoirs. No Tickets

Basingstoke Angling Club
M C Elie
10 Verdi Close,
Brighton Hill
Basingstoke, Hampshire

Bath Anglers' Association
A J Smith
68 Bloomfield Rise
Odd Down, Bath
Avon, brooks. Tickets

Bathampton Angling Associstion
D Crookes
25 Otago Terrace
Larkhall
Bath, Avon
Trout and coarse fishing
Avon, canal, brooks. Tickets

Beachcasters (Brighton) Angling Club
D H Shead
53 Scotland Street
Brighton

Beccles Angling Club
A W J Crane
27 Rigbourne Hill
Beccles, Suffolk
NR34 JG

Bedford Angling Club (1)
Mrs M E Appleton
18 Moriston Road
Bedford

Bedford Angling Centre Match Group
G P McFiggins
35 High Street
Riseley, Beds MK44 10X

Bedlington and Blagdon Angling Association
S Symons
8 Moorland Drive
Bedlington, Northumberland
NE22 7HB
Blyth. Tickets

Belper and District Angling Club
J Nelson
4 Wilmot Road
Belper, Derbyshire

Bembridge (IOW) Angling Club
P Knight
Berrylands
Heathfield Road
Bembridge
IOW

Benson Angling Society
J Billington
28 Old London Road
Benson, Oxford OX10 6RR

Bentham Angling Association
7 Mayfield Road
High Bentham
Lancaster LA2 7LP

Wenning. Tickets

Berkshire Fisheries Association
E G Mears, see Raven A C

Betteshanger Colliery Welfare Angling Society
A Herbert
58 Celtic Road
Deal, Kent
Medway. Tickets

Bexhill Sea Angling Club
J Boston
17 St James Street
Bexhill-on-Sea, Sussex

Bicester Angling Society
W H Bunce
Tel: Bicester 44653

Bideford and District Angling Club
V B Eveleigh
21 Capern Road
Bideford
Sea and coarse fishing

Bideford and District Sea Angling Club
Harry Bottomley
Glen View, Raleigh Hill
Bideford, Devon

Biggleswade, Hitchin and District Angling Association
P Currell
10 Poplar Close
Sandy, Beds SG19 1HH

Bike Bitz Anglers
M Warnecke
165 Lon Pontyllyn
Maesydail, Newton
Powys

Bingley Angling Club
A Greenwood
Press Officer
17 Park Top Cottages
Eldwick, Bingley
W Yorks
Aire, lakes. Members only

Birchmoor Angling Club
P Mason
19 Beyer Close
Glascote Heath
Tamworth, Staffs

Birmingham Anglers' Association Ltd
F A Jennings
100 Icknield Port Road
Rotton Park, Birmingham B16 0AP
Severn and tributaries,
Avon, and tributaries,
Wye and tributaries, canals and lakes.
Members only

Birstwith Private Angling Club
P W Lowndes
Prospect House
Kirkby Overblow

Near Harrogate, N Yorks HG3 1HQ
Nidd. Members only

**Bishop Auckland and District Angling
Club**
J Winter
7 Royal Grove
Crook, Co Durham DLl5 9ER
Wear. Tickets

**Bishop's Stortford and District Angling
Society**
C Costema
31 Thornbera Road
Bishop's Stortford, Hertfordshire
Stort. Tickets

**Blackburn and District Sea Anglers'
Association**
Harold Walton
55 Redlam
Blackburn, Lancashire

Black Ox Angling Club
R M Wright
5 Lascelles Lane
Northallerton, N Yorks
Bedale Beck and Swale. No tickets

Blackfords Progressive Angling Society
T W Ponder
4 Long Croft
Huntingdon
Cannock, Staffs

Blackpool and Layton Angling Society
E Wadeson
24 Elgin Place
Blackpool,
Lancashire

Blandford and District Angling Club
Mrs J Leslie
20 Fields Oak
Blandford Forum
Dorset DT11 7PP
Dorset Stour. Tickets

Blenheim Angling Society
F W Lancaster
Brairwood, Burtons Lane
Chalfont St Giles
Buckinghamshire

Blunham Angling Club
Hon Sec
c/o Horse Shoes Inn
Blunham,
Bedfordshire
Ivel. No tickets

Blyth Angling Club
G A Blake
45 Woodhorn Drive
Stakeford, Choppington
Northumberland

Blyth Valley Freshwater Angling Club
19 Gresham Close
Southfield Green, Cramlington

Northumberland

Bodmin Anglers' Association
R Burrows
26 Meadow Place
Bodmin, Cornwall PL31 1JD
Camel. Tickets

**Bognor Regis and District Freshwater
Angling Club**
R Huskisson
Tel: 024 36539

Bolton and District Angling Club
Terence A McKee
1 Lever Edge Lane
Great Lever
Bolton, Lancs BL3 3BU

Bolton Fishing Association
J H Siddall
Fairfields
The Shawl
Leyburn, Yorkshire
Ure. Restricted tickets

Boroughbridge and District Angling Club
G Whitaker
9 Manor Drive
Kirby Hill
Boroughbridge, Yorkshire
Ure. Tickets

**Boscombe and Southbourne Sea-Fishing
Club**
E White
14 Clifton Road
Boscombe, Bournemouth

Boston and District Angling Association
Mrs Jill Sawyer
Hatfield,
 Wyberton West Road
Boston
Lincolnshire PE21 7LQ

Boston Spa Angling Club
A Waddington
The Cottage
17 The Village
Thorp Arch
Wetherby, Yorkshire
Wharfe. Tickets

Bostrom Europe Angling Club
M J Reynolds
37 Weggs Farm Road
St Giles Park Estate
Duston,
Northampton

**Bottesford and District Angling
Association**
G C Baker
8 Meadow End
Gotham,
Notts
Grantham Canal (dated)
River Devon (summer time only)

Boxmoor and District Angling Society
K Charge
11 Catsdell
Hemel Hempstead

Bradford City Angling Association
H Briggs
4 Brown Hill Close
Birkenshaw
Bradford, W Yorks
Ure, Wharfe, Aire, Swale, canals, lakes.
Tickets

Bradford No 1 Angling Association
C W Smith
44 Fleet Lane
Queenbury
Bradford, West Yorks
Wharfe, Ure, canal, lake. Tickets

Bradford-on-Avon and District Angling Association
M Harding
9 Grosvenor Villas
Claremont Road
Larkhall, Bath
Avon, Biss, Frome, canal, brook. Tickets

Bradford Waltonians' Angling Club
H J B Swarbrick
43 Hawksworth Drive
Menston, Ilkley
West Yorkshire LS29 6HP

Braintree and Bocking Angling Society
S Giovanni
32 Drake Gardens,
Braintree, Essex

Brampton Angling Society
T Donockley
1 Denton Crescent
Low Row
Brampton, Cumberland
Irthing and tributaries, Gelt, King, Cambeck. Tickets

Brandon and District Angling Club
P Cooper
16 High Street
Feltwell, Thetford
Norfolk
Little Ouse. Tickets

Brett Marine Angling Club
Galloways Road
Lydd, Kent

Brewood Angling Club
F W Hodgkins
290 Wolverhampton Road
Sedgley
Dudley, Staffs

Brewood and District Royal British Legion (Fishing Club)
M A Brown
3 Richmond Drive, Perton
Wolverhampton, W Mids

Bridges Angling Society
B G Beckwith
2 Ducketts Mead
Roydon, Essex CM19 5EG

Bridgnorth Angling Society
R J Ball
23 Haughton Close
Tasley
Bridgnorth, Shropshire

Bridgwater Angling Association
Chairman
L Osbourne
1 Grange Drive
Bridgwater

Bridlington Angling Association
W Farr
53 Milner Road
Bridlington, Yorkshire

Brighouse Angling Association
M Riley
30 Ravenstone Drive
Greetland
Halifax

Brighton Cruising Club Angling Section
J G Pennell
79 King's Road Arches
Brighton, Sussex

Brighton Deep Sea Anglers
F Bean
139 King's Road Arches
Brighton, Sussex

Brighton Palace Pier Angling Association
L R Lawrence
1 Hamblin House, Broadway
Southall,
Middlesex

Bristol, Bath and Wiltshire Anglers
J S Parker
16 Lansdown View
Kingswood,
Bristol BS15 4AW

Bristol and West of England Federation of Anglers
B Williams
157 Whiteway Road
Bristol BS5 7RH
Avon, Kennet and Avon Canal, Frome, lake. Affiliated clubs share rights

Bristol Avon and District Anglers Consultative Association
J S Parker, see Bristol, Bath & Wiltshire Anglers

Bristol Channel Federation of Sea Anglers
R Rogers
1 Willow Cottage
East Bower, Bridgwater

Bristol Golden Carp Angling Association
C Golding

24 Queens Street
Two Mile Hill
Kingswood, Bristol BS15 2AZ
Bristol Reservoir Flyfishers' Association
Derek Stenner
103 Beach Road
Sand Bay, Weston-super-Mare
Avon
Brixham Sea Anglers' Association
G Walton
85 New Road
Brixham, Devon
Clubhouse at 16a Castor Road, Brixham
Brockenhurst Manor Fly-Fishing Club
Mrs Chessell
The Laurels,
Dibden Purlieu
near Southampton, Hampshire
Brockham Angling Society
W J Momk
Riseholm, Cliftonville
Dorking
Surrey RH4 2JF
Bromsgrove and District Association of Angling Clubs
D Pennells
5 Burcot Lane
Bromsgrove, Worcestershire
Bromley and District Angling Society
N A long
40 Hackington Crescent
Beckenham BR3 1RZ
Broome Angling Society
A Smith
73 Farrier Lane
Leicester LE4 0WB
Broughton and Dunton Angling Club
M Startin
5 Ashby Rise
Great Glen, Leicester
Brunswick Brothers Angling Club
T E Taylor
40 St Andrews Road
Cranbrook
Ilford IG1 3PF
Buchan Park Angling Association
D W Newnham
The Bungalow
Coombe House Lane
Bolney,
Sussex
Lakes. Permits

Buckingham and District Angling Association
B Lewis
38 Queen Catherine Road
Steeple Claydon, Bucks
Hyde Lane Pits, Great Ouse Tickets (limited) from local tackle shop only
Bude Angling Association
Mrs P Casson
29 West Park Road
Bude, Cornwall EX23 0NA Tamar. Tickets
Bude and District Sea Angling Club
Don Harris
3 Quarry Close
Bude, Cornwall
EX23 8JG
Bude Canal Angling Association
M J Colwill
Hele Grove, Hele Road
Marhamchurch
Bude, Cornwall
Buglawton Trout Club
B T Fisher
4 Alcester Close
Tunstall, Stoke-on-Trent ST6 6QB
Bungay Cherry Tree Angling Club
I Gosling
37 St Mary's Terrace
Bungay, Suffolk
Waveney
Burford Angling Club
K Wilkes
1 South Mere
Brize Norton
Oxford OX8 3PX
Burgess Hill Angling Society
R Shakeshaft
23 Holmesdale Road
Burgess Hill, Sussex
Arun. Tickets
Burnley Angling Society
J H Walttin
23 St James Row
Burnley, Lancashire
Reservoir. Tickets to local residents only
Burneside Angling Association
P Hockenhull
43 Horncop Lane
Kendal
Cumbria LA9 3SR
Kent. Tickets

Fishing Clubs

When you appoint a new secretary, do not forget to give us details of the change. Write to the publishers (address at front of the book). Thank you!

Burslem Suburban Angling Club
F W Newbold
115 Bank Hall Road
Burslem, Stoke-on-Trent
Burton-on-Trent Mutual Angling
Association
D J Clark
7 Denton Rise
Burton-on-Trent,
Staffordshire DE13 0QB
Bury Angling Assocation
N Bruton
Newport Pagnell
Bucks MK16 0DS
Tel: 0284 761774
Bury and District Angling Society
F Booth
142 Bury Road
Tottington, Bury
Lancashire
Ponds, reservoirs. Tickets
Bury St Edmunds Angling Association
N J Bruton
Sarafand
Tut Hill
Fornham All Saints
Bury St Edmunds, Suffolk
Buxton Fly-Fishers' Club
M Plimmer
8 Glenmoor Road
Buxton, Derbyshire
By Brook Fly-Fishers' Club
M V M Clube
Hilton Lodge
20 Downleaze
Bristol 9
Trout. Members only
Byfleet Angling Association
T R Notley
20 Godley Road
Byfleet
Weybridge,
Surrey KT14 7EW
Wey. Dt.
Caldy Anglers
J J Hopper
2 Raeburn Avenue
West Kirby, Wirral
Merseyside LA8 5JE
Calder Angling Association
A W Rigg
Allona
Calderbridge, Seascale
Cumbria
Calf Heath Anglers
I D R Miller
4 Deanery Close
Shareshill
Wolverhampton WV10 7JW

Calne Angling Association
Miss J M Knowler
123A London Road
Calne, Wiltshire SN11 0AQ
Camborne Angling Association
S Hosking
18 Cooliford Crescent
Camborne, Cornwall
Cambridge Albion Angling Society
D Turpin
79 Kings Hedges Road
Cambridge CB4 23D
Cambridge Fish Preservation and
Angling Society
G W Tweed
27A Villa Road
Impington, Camb
Cambridge Izaak Walton Society
T J Sawyer
6 Pump Lane
Hardwick
Cambs CB3 7QW
Cambridge Trout Club
J Dillon-Robinson
Sammy's, Widdington
near Saffron Walden, Essex
Cambridgeshire and Isle of Ely
Federation of Anglers
Roy Page
1 Fen Road
Milton, Cambridgeshire
24 affiliated clubs
Canterbury and District Angling
Association
N Stringer
Riversdale
Mill Road
Sturry, Kent
Carlisle Angling Association
T Graham
23 Orton Road
Carlisle, Cumbria CA2 7HA
Eden. Tickets
Carlton Angling Club
H Park
18 Court Gardens
Snaith, Goole
DN14 9JP
Carnforth and District Allglers'
Association
A McCartney
3 Ullswater Crescent
Carnforth, Lancashire LA5 9AY
Keer. Tickets
Castleford and District of Society Anglers
Clubs
P France
35 Amber Street
Castleford, West Yorks

Nidd, Ouse, Wharfe, Rye, Derwent, Pickering Beck, etc. Some tickets

Central Association of London and Provincial Angling Clubs
Mr J Henry, Fisheries Officer
3 Kings Road
Belmont, Sutton
Surrey SM2 6DG
or
A J Jenkinson
68 Taynton Drive
Merstham, Surrey
RH1 3PT

Chapeltown and District Angling Association
J W Rowlinson
8 Brook Rd
High Green
Sheffield S30 4GG

Chard Angling Association
B Netherway
45 Millers Way
Honiton, Devon EX14 8JB

Charing and District Angling Club
E R Bennet
Rosary
Warren Street Road
Charing, Kent

Chatton Angling Association
A Jarvis
New Road, Chatton
Alnwick

Cheadle Angling Club
R F Heakin
Police House, Barnfields Lane
Kingsley, near Cheadle
Staffordshire

Cheddar Angling Association
A T Lane
1 Orchard Close
Cheddar,
Somerset

Chelmsford Angling Association
J Hopkins
Secretary
45 Bruce Grove
Chelmsford
or
Mrs R Lewis
Membership Secretary
60 Delamere Road
Chelmsford,
Essex
Chelmer. Tickets

Cheltenham Angling Club
E Cortijo
88 Chosen Way
Hucclecote
Gloucestershire

Chepstow and District Angling Club
A J Black
51 Severn Avenue
Tutshill, Chepstow, Gwent

Cherry Hinton and District Angling Club
C Frost
14 St Marys, Earith
Cambs

Cheshire Anglers' Association
George Brassington
12 Highfield Drive
Nantwich, Cheshire
Severn, Dane, canal. Members only

Cheshunt Angling Club
See Kings Arms

Cheshunt Carp Club
A T Davies
28 Pollards Close
Waltham Cross
Hertfordshire

Chester-le-Street and District Angling Club
T Wright
156 Sedgeletch Road
Houghton le Spring
Tyne and Wear

Chester-le-Street Angling Club
G Curry
62 Newcastle Road
Chester-le-Street
Co Durham DH3 3UF
Wear. Day ticket

Chew Fly-Fishing Club
Dr R R Fells
17 Mortimer Road
Clifton,
Bristol 8
Chew. Members and guests only

Chichester and District Angling Society
Mrs Loffman
3 Birdham Close
Bognor Regis
or
Mrs E Few
c/o Fishermen's Den
Canada Grove
Bognor Regis

Chichester Canal Angling Association
J Cooper
Jaspers
Coney Road
East Wittering
Nr Chichester,
W Sussex
Tickets

Chippenham Angling Club
P Collins
2 Northwood, Chippenham
Wiltshire

Chipping Norton Angling Society
R Jarvis
7 Wards Road
Chipping Norton
Oxon OX7 5BU

Christchurch Angling Club
R Andrews
4 Marley Close
New Milton
Hants BH25 5LL

Churchfield Tavern Angling Club
J A Dangerfield
29 Westminster Road
Stone Cross
West Bromwich B71 2JJ

Cinque Ports Angling Society
Mrs R M Harris
Broom Villa
West Hythe Road
West Hythe, Kent
CT21 4NT

Cinque Ports, Sea Angling Society
G Colley
8 Wingate Road
Folkestone, Kent

City of Bristol Angling Association
M G Haskins
27 Hill Lawn
Brislington,
Bristol BS4 4LF

Civil Service Angling Society
Mr A P Hughes
17 Chester Road
Northwood
Middx HA6 1BG
Thames, Medway, Kennet, lakes, reservoirs. No tickets

Civil Service Flyfishers' Society
J Ford
304 Knightsfield
Welwyn Garden City
Hertfordshire AL8 7NQ

Clacton Sea Angling Club
M Wenham
21 Wratting Road
Haverhill
Suffolk CB9 6)A
or
D Snell
Little Oak
Chisbon Heath
Clacton-on-Sea CO16 9BX

Clanfield Angling Club
F Baston
47 Mill Lane, Clanfield
Oxon

Clevedon and District Angling Club
Mr Newton
64 Clevedon Road, Tickenham
Clevedon, Somerset

Clevedon and District Freshwater Angling Club
D A Harper
5 Kingsley Road
Clevedon, Avon BS21 6NT

Clitheroe Angling Association
B McNulty
16 Mitton Road
Whalley, Lancs
BB6 9RX
Ribble, Hodder and Lune
Limited tickets through members only

Clive Vale Angling Club
B Towner
9 Lewis Road
St Leonards-on-Sea
Sussex TN38 9EJ
Reservoirs. Period tickets

Cockermouth and District Angling Association
K Simpson
Moor Road
Great Broughton
Cockermouth, Cumbria
Cocker. Season tickets only

Cobham and District Angling Association
K Sherlock
13 Berrylands
Surbiton
Surrey KT5 8JT

Colchester Angling Preservation Society
M K Turner
29 Lodge Road
Braintree, Essex CM7 7JA
Colne, Stour and gravel pits. No tickets

Colchester Piscatorial Society
N Browning
3 Greenstead Court
Colchester,
Essex
Colne. No tickets

Collingham Angling Association
Mrs J Wilson
93 Braemar Road

Fishing Clubs

When you appoint a new secretary, do not forget to give us details of the change. Write to the publishers (address at front of the book). Thank you!

Collingham
Nottinghamshire NG23 7PN
Colne (Lancs) Angling Association
B Dean
282 Gisburn Road
Blacko, Nelson, Lancashire
Brownhills Reservoir. Members only
Colnes' Angling Society
K Murrells
1 Hillie Bunnies
Earls Colne, Colchester, Essex
Suffolk Stour
Colt Crag Angling Association
F L Brogdon
The Bungalow
Hexham, Northumberland
Compleat Angler Fishing Club
V W Honeyball
12 Bodmin Close
Longlands Road
Eastbourne, E Sussex BN20 8HZ
Cuckmere and Pevensey Levels Tickets
Comrades Angling Club
L J Wickham
1 Hollands Lane
Henfield, Sussex
Congleton Angling Society
N J Bours
8 Norfolk Road
Congleton, Cheshire
**Coniston and Torver Anglers'
Association**
D E Lancaster
Wetherlam, Mount Pleasant
Greenodd, Nr Ulverston
Cumbria LA12 7RF
Coquet Angling Club
J Engles
80 Castle Terrace
Ashington, Northumberland
Corbridge Riverside Sports Club
M J Broadey
5 Greencroft Avenue
Corbridge
Northumberland NE4 55DW
Tyne. Tickets for members' guests
Cotmanhay Angling Club
D H Plackett
164 Hassock Lane South
Shipley, Nr Heanor
Derbys DE7 7JH
Cotterstock Angling Association
Mrs Joan E Popplewell
40 North Street
Oundle, Peterborough PE8 4AL
Tel: 0832 273671.
Cove Angling Society
M Mills
4 Chestnut Close

Blackwater
Camberley, Surrey
Loddon, Hart, Whitewater, Fleet Pond.
No tickets
**Coventry and District Angling
Association**
A J Hyde
1 Oak Tree Avenue
Green Lane
Coventry CV3 6DG
Avon, Anker, Vyrnwy, Nene, Cherwell
canals, reservoirs, etc
Crawley Angling Society
Mr Kichols
24 Rillside
Furness Green
Crawley, Sussex
Lakes, streams. Some tickets
Crawley and District Sea Anglers
C R Woolger
70 Wakehurst Drive
Southgate, Crawley, Sussex
**Crayford Kingfishers Angling
Preservation Society**
E G Costen
4 Ravensbourne Road
Crayford, Kent
Cray and lake. Season tickets
Crediton Fly Fishing Club
R E Knowles
Meadow End Cottage
Sandford
Crediton, Devon
7m of trout fishing on Yeo and Creedy;
tickets
Crewe Amalgamated Anglers
T Kelly
9 Beech Street
Crewe, Cheshire
Crewe Pioneers
W J Hart
83 Underwood Lane
Crewe CW1 3JT
Croft Angling Club
L H Dent
11 High Street
Skegness, Lincolnshire
Steeping. Permits
Cromford Fly-Fishers Club
F W Cooper
Wishingstone Cottage
Bull Lane, Matlock
Derbyshire DE4 5LX
Cromwell Sea Angling Club
B Fukes
39 Daubney Street
Cleethorpes, S Humberside DN35 7BB
Cross Keys Fishing Club
P S Holloway

12 Oxford Avenue
Sneyd Green
Stoke-on-Trent,
Staffs ST1 6DJ
Crown Angling Club
A C Caton
12 Southwell Estate
Eccleshall, Staffs ST21 6EB
Croydon Angling Society
G Hobbs
69 Woodmere Avenue
Shirley, Croydon, Surrey
Use of water on Arun, Mole and Medway
Danby Angling Club
F Farrow
11 Dale End, Danby
Whitby, N Yorkshire Y021 2JF
Darent Valley Trout Fishers
R F Cobbett
15 Birchwood Drive
Wilmington, Kent DA2 7NE
Darent. No tickets
Darley Dale Fly-Fishing Club
A L Carter
Holly Mead
Kempton
Craven Arms, Salop
Darlington Anglers Club
I Ablott
58 Swaledale Avenue
Darlington DL3 9AL
Darlington and District Angling Club
D McMasters
2 The Firs
Darlington DL1 3PH
**Darlington Brown Trout Angling
Association**
G Coulson
5 Grange Avenue, Hurworth Place
Darlington
Darlington Fly Fishers Club
W D Holmes
39 Barrett Road
Darlington DL3 8LA
**Dartford and District Angling and
Preservation Society**
Lake House
2 Walnut Tree Avenue
Wilmington, Kent DA11 1LJ
Dart Angling Association
S J F Lovegrove
Moorlands House
Churscombe Road
Marldon Cross
Paignton, Devon
Dart. Some tickets
**Dartmouth and District Angling
Association**
L Berry, Chairman

c/o Club HQ
5 Oxford Street
Dartmouth,
Devon
Darwen Anglers' Association
F W Kendall
45 Holden Fold
Darwen, Lancashire
Reservoirs. Limited day tickets
Davenham Angling Club
A Cook
41 Fairfield Road, Leftwich
Northwich CW9 8DG
Daventry and District Angling Society
B G Pullan
8 Cameron Close
Cherry Orchard
Daventry NN11 5HX
Dawley Angling Society
Mrs Ellen Rogers
68 Coronation Crescent
Madeley, Telford
Shropshire TF7 5EH
Dawlish Sea Angling Club
L Loram
82 Churchill Avenue
Dawlish, Devon
Deal 1919 Angling Club
R Tunnicliff
8 Bulwark Road
Deal, Kent CT14 6PE
Deal and Walmer Angling Association
Mr P Short
58 Park Avenue
Deal, Kent
Dean Clough Angling Society
G Crabtree
5 Peabody Street
Lee Mount, Halifax
W Yorks HX3 5EG
Deanshanger Angling Association
Eric Longhurst
Puxley, Potterspury,
Towcester, Northamptonshire
Great Ouse. Members only
**Deanshanger and The Stratfords Angling
Club**
T R Valentine
34 Malletts Close
Wolverton, Bucks MK11 1DQ
Debden Angling Society
Hon Secretary
15 Cleland Road
Loughton,
Essex
Roding. Tickets
Deeping St James Angling Club
D L Bailey
11 Lime Tree Avenue

Towngate West
Market Deeping
Peterborough
Lincs PE6 8DQ

Derby Angling Association
B Sharratt
64 Haig Street
Alvaston
Derby

Derbyshire Angling Federation
S W Clifton
14 Highfield Road
Little Eaton
Derby DE2 5AG

Derbyshire County Angling Club
O W Handley
Osprey House, Ogston
Higham, Derby DE55 6EL

Dereham and District Angling Club
S R Allison
Pound Cottage
Cemetery Road
East Dereham, Norfolk NR19 2E
Wensum. Tickets

Derwent (Durham) Angling Association
J Hope
16 Sandford Rd, Bridgehill
Consett, Co Durham
Derwent (Tyne). Members only

Derwent (Yorks) Anglers' Club
I V Brett, F.R.I.C.S
North House
Wykeham YO12 0BR
Derwent. Tickets

Derwent Flyfishing Club
Dennis North
Green Farm, Curbar
Via Sheffield

Devizes Angling Association
T W Fell
21 Cornwall Crescent
Devizes,
Wiltshire SN10 5HG
Kennet and Avon Canal. Tickets

Dewsbury Angling Club
Mr T Butler
12 Selso Road
Dewsbury WF12 7LU

Dingle Fly Fishing Club
W Ashton
2 The Crescent
Westhoughton, Bolton

Dinnington Angling Association
R Arkle
36 Sycamore Avenue
Dinnington
Newcastle Upon Tyne NE13 7JY

Diss and District Angling Club
R Johnson
4 Copeman Road
Roydon, Diss
Norfolk

Ditherington Angling Society
G Moss
4 Morville Road
Heath Farm Estate, Shrewsbury

The Dog Angling Club
E D Roberts
The Cottage
Oak Lane
Calf Heath, Nr Wolverhampton

Doncaster and District Angling Association
D T Ward
9 Cemetery Road
Hatfield
Doncaster DN7 6LT

Dorchester (Dorset) Angling Society
J Parkes
5 Malta Close
Dorchester, Dorset DT1 1QT
Stour, Frome, ponds; coarse fishing
Members and friends only

Dorchester (Dorset) Fishing Club
J J Fisher
Rew Hollow, Godmanstone
Nr Dorchester, Dorset DT2 7AH
Frome (Dorset). No tickets

Dordon Angling Club
W Coggins
167 Long Street, Dordon
Tamworth, Staffordshire

Dorking and District Angling Society
P Knight
28 Falkland Road
Dorking, Surrey
Mole. Tickets

Douglas (IOM) and District Angling Club
Mrs S McCoubrey
47 Hildesley Road
Douglas, Isle of Man

Dover Sea Angling Association
14 Priory Road

Fishing Clubs

When you appoint a new secretary, do not forget to give us details of the change. Write to the publishers (address at front of the book). Thank you!

Dover, Kent CT17 9RG

Downtown Angling Association
B Hayward
37 Bridge Street
Fordingbridge
Hampshire
Avon, lakes

Dreadnought Sea Angling Society
E F Joslin
61 Sherrick Green Road
Willesden, London NW1O

Drawbridge Angling Club
D J Leesing
5 Webster Close
Kimberworth
Rotherham, South Yorks

Draycott Angling Club
D Pollard
44 Fairfield Crescent
Old Sawley
Long Eaton, Nottinghamshire
NG10 3AH

Driffield Anglers
S Madden
Brimley
Molescroft, Beverley
HU17 7EN

Droitwich and District (Talbot) Angling Society
c/o Talbot Hotel, High Street
Droitwich, Worcestershire
Severn. Tickets

Dudley Angling Club
A R Dalwood
4 Warrens Road
Dudley
West Midlands

Dudley Angling Federation
D Hendry
210 Standhills Road
Kingswinford
West Midlands

Duke of Gloucester Angling Society
Barry Neville
21 Lincoln Close
Woodside Green, London SE25
Medway. Members only

Dunmow and District Piscatorial Society
E G Gilbey
11 Market Place
Dunmow, Essex

Durham City Angling Club
G Hedley
3 Hawthorne Crescent
Durham DH1 1ED

Durham Ox Angling Club
S Owen
39 Powtrell Place
Ilkeston

Derbys DE7 5SW

Durweston Angling Society
J H Thatchell
Methody, Durweston
Near Blandford,
Dorset DT11 0QA

Earl of Harrington Angling Club
J Callaghan
3 Calvin Close
Alvaston, Derby DE2 0HX

Earls Barton Angling Club
B F Hager
113 Station Road
Earls Barton
NN6 0NX

East Anglian Piscatorial Society
J March
Clarence Harbour
Clarence Road, Norwich

Eastbourne Angling Association
The Club House
Royal Parade
Eastbourne, Sussex

East Hastings Sea Angling Club
19 Upper Glen Road
St Leonards-on-Sea
East Sussex

Eastleigh District Angling Club
325 Market Street
Eastleigh, Hants

East Cowes Angling Society
G Wood
19 York Street
Cowes IoW

Eastern Rother Angling Club
Mrs V Smithers
'North Bank'
June Lane
Midhurst, Sussex

East Grinstead Angling Society
W Ford
20 Greenstede Avenue
East Grinstead, Sussex

East Hastings Sea Anglers' Association
C F Thomas
17 Rymill Road
St Leonards-on-Sea,
Sussex

Eastleigh District Angling Club
J Remington
121 Desborough Road
Eastborough
Hants SO5 5NP

Ecclesbourne Flyfishers' Club
W Smith
Wayside, Longfield Lane
Ilkeston,
Derbyshire
Ecclesbourne. Strictly private

Eden Vale Angling Association
A A B Williams
26 Springbank Road
Littledown
Bournemouth
Dorset

Egremont Angling Association
C Fisher
69 North Road
Egremont, Cumbria
Ehen. wt.

Elan Valley Angling Association
Honorary Secretary
2 Glangrafon, Elan Valley
Rhayader, Powys

Elite Angling Club
B Fitzpatrick
17 Birch Close
Birchmore
Tamworth, Staffs

Ellen Angling Association
G Howard
36 Main Street, Ellenborough
Maryport, Cumbria
Ellen. Permits

Elm Park, Hornchurch and District Angling Society
P W Darling
40 Rosslyn Avenue
Harold Wood, Essex
Roding

Ellesmere Angling Club
Mrs B Roger
Newton Cottages
Ellesmere, Shropshire
Vyrnwy, lake and canal. Some tickets

Elmore (Sea) Angling Club
L A Woods
12 Beacon Way
Park Gate, Southampton

Ely Beet Sports and Social Club
R J Oakham
15 Berry Close
Stretham, Cambs

Ennerdale Lake Fisheries
D Crellin
3 Parklands Drive
Egremont, Cumbria

Entwistle Fly Fishers
Geoff Thirkell
87 Higher Ainsworth Road
Radcliffe
Manchester M26 0JJ

Epsom Angling Society
J C J Wood
19 West Hill Avenue
Epsom,
Surrey KT19 8LE
Mole. No tickets

Esk Fishery Association
K Bristow
2 The Shallows
The Square
Stamford Bridge
York YO4 1AF
Yorkshire Esk. Tickets

Essex Fly-Fishers' Club
D A L Birrell (Chairman)
High Hedges, Little Waltham
Chelmsford, Essex
Reservoir. Trout. Members only

Evode Angling Club
R J Edgerton
c/o 25 Underwood Close
Parkside
Stafford ST16 1TB

Exeter and District Angling Association
D Cornish
9 Denmark Road
Exeter EX1 1SL
Exe. Culm, canals, ponds, etc. Tickets

Exmouth Deep Sea Fishing Club
J H R Lethbridge
6 Lower King's Avenue
Exeter

Fakenham Angling Club
G Parsons
26 St Peter's Road
Fakenham, Norfolk

Falmouth Shark and Big-Game Angling Club
W Lane
4 Railway Cottages
Falmouth, Cornwall

Farmoor Fly Fishing Club
R Foreman
27 Manor Road
Ducklington
Near Witney
Oxfordshire OX8 7YD

Farnborough Angling Society
D Rance
Orchard Bungalow
Henley Park, Normandy
Guildford, Surrey GU3 2AB

Farnham Angling Society
R T Frost
70 Prince Charles Crescent
Farnborough
Hants GU3 2AB

Faversham Angling Club
A P Baldock
5 Kennedy Close
Faversham, Kent
Pits. Tickets

Featherstone and District Angling Association
M Daley

70 Huntwick Crescent
Featherstone
Pontefract WF7 5JH

Federated Anglers (Preston Centre)
R Mayor
258 Brownedge Road
Bamber Bridge
Preston, Lancs
Ribble & tributaries. Canals. Tickets

Felixstowe Sea Angling Association
P G Borley
2 Oak Close
Felixstowe, Suffolk

Felling Fly Fishing Club
A S Hunt
4 Fell Close, Albany
Washington NE37 1AX
Tyne and Wear

Fenland Association of Anglers
Colin Clare
1 Mount Pleasant Road
Wisbech
Cambridgeshire PE13 3NF

Fenton and District Angling Society
C Yates
The Puzzels
5 Gatley Grove
Meir Park
Stoke-on-Trent, Staffs

Ferryhill and District Angling Club
Barry Hignett
Tel: 091 388 3557

Ferry Pickering Angling Club
Mrs M R Shilton
34 Holt Road
Burbage, Hinckley
Leics LE10 2QA

Fife Street Angling Club
D Cartwright
18 Dorset Close
Nuneaton
CV10 8EN

Filey Brigg Angling Society
K C Carpenter
18 Ash Grove
Filey YO14 9LZ, N Yorks

Foston Fishing Club
E Hirst
Mereside
Garton on the Wolds
Driffield YO25 0ES
Yorkshire
Foston Beck. Members only

Fowey Angling Club
D Johnson
c/o Club Headquarters
Safe Harbour, Fowey, Cornwall

**Frampton and District Angling
   Association**

G Blewett
The Post Office
Frampton-on-Severn
Gloucester

Frome and District Angling Association
R J Lee
Marvic, Keyford Terrace
Frome, Somerset
Frome. Tickets conditional

Frome Vale Angling Club
L Fullbrook
15a Elmleigh
Mangotsfield
Bristol BS17 3EX

Frosterley Angling Club
S Crampsie
Glen Brae, Front Street
Frosterley, Co Durham

Fry's Angling Club
M Parslow
32 Aldwick Avenue
Hartcliffe, Bristol
River Avon

Furness Fishing Association
D Thompson
205 Rating Lane
Barrow-in-Furness

Galgate Angling Association
I Shaw
16 Rose Grove
Galgate, Lancashire
Condor. No tickets

Galleon Angling Club
P Hamilton
35 Silicon Court
Shenley Lodge
MK5 7DJ

Gamefishers Club
J H Andrews
Meadow View, Dinedore
Hereford HR2 6LQ
Fly-fishing on streams in Worcestershire
and Welsh border. Guest permits only

**Garstang and District Angling
   Association**
F C Moreland
6 Pringle Court
Garstang, Lancashire
PR3 1LN
Wyre. Some wt for resident holiday visi-
tors

Gate Inn (Amington) Angling Club
V R Garbett
c/o 75 Collett
Glascote
Tamworth, Staffordshire

**Gillingham and District Angling
   Association**
J R K Stone

Ferndale
Ham
Gillingham, Dorset SP8 4LL
Stour. Tickets
Gipping Angling Preservation Society
George Alderson
19 Clover Close
Chantry, Ipswich, Suffolk
Gipping. Tickets
Gipping Valley Angling Club
D Bishop
17 Brettenham Road
Buxhall, Stowmarket
Suffolk
Glaston Manor Angling Association
J Ogden
10 Dovecote Close
Farm Lane
Street, Somerset
Brue, South Drain
Glebe Angling Club
C J Broom
2 Crockett Close
Links View
Northampton NN2 2LL
Glendale Angling Club
R P Lane
33 Ridley Road
London NW10
Globe Angling Society
R Eaton
80 Caversham Avenue
Palmers Green, London N13 4LN
Gloucester United Anglers' Association
J Gibby
70 Robert Raikes Avenue
Lower Tuffley
Gloucester GL4 0HJ
Glyme Valley Fly Fishers
Derek Weston
Crown Cottage
Wootton
Woodstock, Oxon
Members only
Goathland Angling Club
P H Skelton
Darnholme, Goathland
Whitby, Yorkshire
Godalming Angling Society
M Richardson
87 Summers Road
Farncombe, Godalming, Surrey
Godalming and District Angling Society
A G Johnson
86 Peper Harow Road
Godalming, Surrey
Wey and lake. Tickets
**Godmanchester Angling and Fish
  Preservation Society**

Mrs L Christian
33 London Road
Godmanchester
Huntingdon, Cambs
Great Ouse
Golden Hill Club
A O Harland
61 Main Street
Skidby, Cottingham
N Humberside HU16 5TZ
No tickets
Golden Valley Fishing Club
S Hooper
155a High Street
Bitton, Near Bristol
Boyd Brook, Frome, Avon, Axe, ponds
Tickets to members' guests only
Goole and District Angling Association
L Rogers
29 Westfield Square
Goole
North Humberside DN15 6QR
Derwent. Some tickets
Gorleston Sea Anglers
G Baker
7 Pier Walk, Gorleston
Great Yarmouth, Norfolk
Gosforth Anglers' Club
11 fell View, Gosforth
Seascale, Cumbria
Grafton Angling Association
M Webster
12 Vernon Street
Worksop, Notts S80 2JX
Grantham Angling Association
W J C Hutchins
28 Cottesmore Close
Grantham, Lincolnshire NG31 9JL
**Great Yarmouth Gorleston and District
Amalgamated Angling Association**
W Platten
1 Audley Street
Great Yarmouth, Norfolk
Greenwich Angling Society
A Cole
1 Bexhill Road
London SE4
Greyshott Angling Club
Mr Metcalfe
Merrow
Bridle Close, Greyshott
Hindhead,
Surrey GU26 6EA
Grimsby and District Society of Anglers
J M Marshall
62 Caistor Drive
Nunsthorpe, Grimsby
Lincolnshire
Pond at Cleethorpes. Tickets

Grizedale Angling Association
N W Holliday
c/o Forestry Commission
Grizedale, Hawkshead
Ambleside, Cumbria
Grizedale Beck. Tickets

Groe Park and Irfon Angling Club
H G Lloyd
Dolrhedyn
Irfon Road
Bulith Wells, Powys LD2 3DE
Irfon. Tickets

Guernsey 30-Fathom Club
T W Rowe
Carantec, Rue du Marnis
Vale, Guernsey, Channel Islands

Hadleigh and District Angling Society
J S Hill
18 Highlands Road
Hadleigh, Ipswich, Suffolk
Brett. No tickets

Hailsham Angling Association
Alan Dean
5 Garfield Road
Hailsham, Sussex BN27 2BD
Cuckmere. Tickets

Halifax and District Angling Club
M Bottomley
23 The Grove
Hipperholme
Halifax
Yorkshire

Halifax Fly-Fishers' Club
L Stott
6 Craven Court
Hopwood Lane
Halifax, Yorkshire

Halstead-Hedingham Angling Club
M Hardy
13 Tryon Court
Halstead CO9 3NZ, Colne
Some tickets only

**Haltwhistle and District Angling
Association**
Chris Wilson
Melkridge House, Melkridge
Haltwhistle, Northumberland
NE49 0LT

**Hampshire and Sussex Alliance (inc
Portsmouth, Bognor Regis, Petworth
and Petersfield clubs)**
D J Robinson
17 Crowsbury Close, Emsworth
Portsmouth PO10 7TS
Rivers, canal, lakes. Weekly ticket and
some daily tickets

**Harleston, Wortwell and District Angling
Club**
N Poll

27 School Lane
Harleston, Norfolk
Pits. Tickets

Harlow Angling Society
W J Pegram
Burnside, 5 The Hill
Harlow, Essex
Stort. Tickets

Harlow Fishing Association
Recreation & Entertainment Manager
Harlow Council
1 Adams House, The High
Harlow, Essex CM20 1BE

Harrogate Angling Association
W Walker
22 Mercia Way
Leeds LS15 8UA

**Harrogate and Claro Conservative
Angling Association**
M G Cooke
1 Kirkham Road,
Bilton
Harrogate, Yorkshire
Ure. Tickets

Harrogate Flyfishers' Club
Alan H Heaton
5 Westminster Crescent
Harrogate, N Yorks
HG3 1LX

Harthill Angling Association
H R King
8 Carver Close
Harthill, Sheffield S31 8XA

**Hartlepool and District Angling
Association**
J Hartland
7 Chillingham Court
Billingham, Cleveland

Hartlepool and District Sea Angling Club
W Colling
6 Wilson Street
West Hartlepool, Co Durham

Harwich Angling Club
S Dye
28 Main Rd
Harwich CO12 3LU

**Hastings and St Leonards Sea Angling
Society**
G Wall
3 Marine Parade
Hastings, Sussex

**Hastings, Bexhill and District Freshwater
Angling Association**
P T Maclean
37 Colliers Road
Hastings TN34 3JR
Tickets from
T Barton
51 Helen's Park Road

Hastings
Hastings Flyfishers' Club Ltd
D E Tack
23 Wealden Way
Little Common
Nr Bexhill-on-Sea
E. Sussex TN39 4NZ
Trout fishing in reservoirs. Waiting list
for membership. Daily ticket at reservoirs
Hatfield and District Angling Society
E F Denchfield
44 Stockbreach Road
Hatfield, Hertfordshire
Hatfield Colliery Angling Club
R Daines
28 The Crescent
Dunscroft
Doncaster DN7 4EW
Hawes Angling Association
Beech House
Cowan Bridge, Via Carnforth
Lancs LA6 2HS
**Hawes and High Abbotside Angling
Association**
A H Barnes
Beech House
Cowan Bridge
Kirkby Lonsdale
Via Carnforth LA6 2HS
Yore. Tickets
Hawkesbury Angling Society
K Bull
138 Aldermans Green Road
Coventry, West Midlands CV2 1PP
Hawkridge Fly Fishing Club
D Salter
3 Dunster Close
Taunton, Somerset
Hay-on-Wye Fishermans' Association
B Wigington
The Flat
4 High Town
Hay-on-Wye, Herefords.
**Haywards Heath and District Angling
Society**
J Kenward
60 Franklynn Road
Haywards Heath, W Sussex
RH16 4DH
Hazeldine Anglers Association
J W Hazeldine
8 Dudley Road
Sedgley
Dudley, Staffs DY3 1SX
Heathfield Angling Club
A P Hopkinson
23 Arkwright Walk
The Meadows
Nottingham NG2 2HW

Hebden Bridge Angling Society
N Pickles
17 Underbank Avenue
Hebden Bridge HX7 6PP
Todmorden, W Yorks
Helperby and Brafferton Angling Club
F Marrison
Gardeners Cottage
Helperby, York
North Yorkshire
Henfield and District Angling Society
Mrs Jean Crawford
6 Lower Faircox
Henfield, West Sussex BN5 9UT
**Hereford and District Angling
Association**
J Astley
The Lindens
Bishopstone, Hereford
Wye and Lugg. Tickets
Herne Bay Angling Association
Honorary Secretary
c/o HQ, 59 Central Parade
Herne Bay, Kent
Heron Angling Society (Herne Bay)
Red Shelter
Spa Esplanade
Herne Bay, Kent
or
Mrs P Bushby
85a Bennells Avenue
Whitstable
Kent CT5 2HR
**Hertfordshire Anglers' Consultative
Association**
E F Banfield
14 Catham Close
St Albans, Hertfordshire
Herts-Chiltern Anglers
Peter Frost
28 Garden Road
Dunstable, Bedfordshire
Hexham Angling Syndicate
W Glendinning
42 Hencotes
Hexham, Northumberland
Tyne. No tickets
Higham Ferrers Angling Club
M Haynes
Elmhurst, Roland Way
Higham Ferrers
Northamptonshire
Highbridge Angling Association
J Underhill
215 Berrow Rd
Burnham-on-Sea
Somerset
Highflyer Fishing Club
H R Page

35 Old School Lane
Milton, Cambridgeshire

High Wycombe Thames Angling Club
N L Charik
1 Orchard Close
Hughenden
High Wycombe
Bucks HP14 4PR

Highworth Angling Club
M Mills
58 Croft Road
Swindon, Wilts
Thames at Buscot

Hinckley and District Angling Association
P Donnachie
5 Farm Road, Burbage
Hinckley, Leicestershire LE10 2PL
Soar, Sence, Thames and Avon, canals, lakes and reservoirs. Permits

Histon and District Angling Club
Colin Dodd
11 Rockmill End
Willingham, Cambs
Old West River, Members only

Holbeach and District Angling Clubs
S H Bowell
67 Battlefields Lane
Holbeach, Lincolnshire

Holland Anglers' Society
G S Mankelow
51 Warren Lane
Holland, Oxted
Surrey
Eden (Kent). Members only

Holmesdale Angling Society
S Banks
58 Chevening Road
Chipstead
Sevenoaks, Kent
Lake at Sevenoaks

Holmesfield Angling Club
C D Hodson
202 Jayshaw Avenue
Great Barr
Birmingham B43 5RH

Holme Valley Piscatorial Association
P Budd
39 Derwent Road
Honley, Huddersfield
Netherton, Huddersfield
Yorkshire

Holme Valley Sea Angling Club
Victoria Inn
Woodhead Road
Holmfirth, W Yorks

Hooke Piscatorial Society
Springhead
Kingcombe Road
Beaminster
Dorset DT8 3PD

Horse and Jockey Angling Club
N Billan
16 Nursery Grove
Ecclesfield, Sheffield

Horse and Jockey (Lichfield) Angling Club
M R Bennett
38 Ponesfield Road
Lichfield, Staffs WS13 7NL

Horley Piscatorial Society
J Davies
32 Lechford Road
Horley, Surrey
RH6 7BN

Horsham and District Angling Association
G R and L T Kempson
11 Clarence Road
Horsham, Sussex

Houghton and Wyton and Hemingfords Angling Society
A Rout
The Haven, Fenstanton
Huntingdonshire
Great Ouse. Daily ticket

Houghton Bridge and District Angling Society
W G Charman
27 South Lane
Houghton, Sussex

Houghton Fishing Club
P K George
The Old Parsonage
Shorne, Gravesend, Kent
Test. No tickets

Hove Deep Sea Anglers
R Robinson
Club House, Western Esplanade
Hove, Sussex

Huddersfield Angling Association
C A Clough
38 Holly Bank Avenue
Upper Cumberworth

Fishing Clubs

When you appoint a new secretary, do not forget to give us details of the change. Write to the publishers (address at front of the book). Thank you!

Huddersfield, Yorkshire HD8 8NY
Water on reservoirs
Hull and District Angling Association
P O Box 188
Hull HU9 1AN
Humber Sea Angling Club
A S Burman
134 Penshurst Road
Cleethorpes
S Humberside DN35 9EN
Hungerford Canal Angling Association
A A Chandler
27 Bockhampton Road
Lambourn, Newbury
Berkshire
Hungerford and K and A Canals. Tickets
**Huntingdon Angling and Fish
Preservation Society**
Mrs A Wallis
8 Claytons Way
Huntingdon
Cambridgeshire
Great Ouse. Tickets
Hutton Ambo Angling Club
Paul Thompson
Firby Hall
Firby, Yorks
Hutton Rudby Angling Association
J D Gifford
23 Linden Close
Hutton Rudby
Yarm-on-Tees, Yorkshire
Tees, Leven Limited st.
**Ilchester and District Angling
Association**
B Bushell
1 Friars Close
Ilchester
Yeo, Somerset
**Ilfracombe and District Anglers'
Association**
George Bond
21 Burnside Rd
Ilfracombe
N Devon EX34 8LX
Ilkley and District Angling Association
J A Cockerill
31 Grange Estate
Valley Drive
Ilkley, Yorkshire
Wharfe. Tickets
**Ilminster and District Angling
Association**
P Lonton
Mashala, Cottage Corner
Ilton, Ilminster
Somerset
Ingatestone and Fryerning Angling Club
J Anderson

57 Tor Bryan
Ingatestone, Essex
Ingleton Angling Association
N W Capstick
Bower Cottage,
Uppergate, Ingleton
via Carnforth, Lancashire
Greta (Lune). Tickets
Ipswich Sea Angling Association
H D Ellwood
105 Wallace Road
Ipswich,
Suffolk
Irby Angling Club
51 Barnston Road
Thingwal, Wirral
Merseyside
**Irthlingborough, Raunds and District
Angling Club**
C E Crawley
20 Palmer Avenue
Irthlingborough
Northamptonshire
Isfield and District Angling Club
Mrs H Wickham
33 Stonedene Close
Forest Row
Sussex
Uck, Ouse and lakes
Isis Angling Club
Peter Gilbert
Peter Gilbert Cameras
Havelock Street
Swindon, Wilts
or
K D Sykes
53 Arnolds Way
Cirencester, Glos
Avon, Marden, Thames, lakes.
No tickets
Isle of Man Angling Association
K A Walmsley
13 Berkley Street
Douglas, Isle of Man
or
W Ashton
Treasurer
58 Laurel Avenue
Birch Hill
Onchan, Isle of Man
Isle of Wight Angling Society
D Yerbury
5 Maple Drive
Newport, IoW
**Isle of Wight Freshwater Angling
Association**
M J Steed
6 Priors Walk
Newport, IoW

Isle of Wight Freshwater Fishing
Ian de Gruchy
8 Black Pan Close
Lake,
Isle of Wight
Ivel Protection Association
R Hitchcock
10 The Crescent, Beeston,
Sandy, Bedfordshire
Ivel. No tickets
Izaak Walton AA, see Aylesbury and Stafford
Izaak Walton AC, see Cambridge
Izaac Walton AS, see Walsall
Jersey Sea Fishing Club
HQ, 16 Broad Street
St Helier, Jersey, CI
Jolly Anglers
R Dell OBE
Brookside, Winterbrook
Wallingford, Berkshire
Thames. Tickets
Keighley Angling Club
Dennis Freeman
62 Eelholme View Street
Keighley, W Yorks
or
c/o Willis Walker Sports Shop
109 Cavendis Street
Keighley
Kelvedon and District Angling Association
M Murton
189 High Street
Kelvedon, Essex
Blackwater, pits. Dt for pits only
Kempston Angling Club
N Birdsall
66 Hastings Road
Kempstone, Beds
Kendal and District Angling Club
Mrs J Singleton
109 Milnthorpe Road
Kendal, Cumbria
Kent Anglers Consultative Association
B J Turner
17 Mill Lane
Sevenoaks
Kent
Kent, Bela, Winster, Leven and Duddon Fisheries Association
O R Bagot
Levens Hall, nr Kendal
Cumbria
Advisory body
Kent (Westmorland) Angling Association
P D Bayliss
The Hyena
9 Fountain Brow

Kendal, Cumbria LA9 4NW
Kent, Mint, Sprint and reservoir,
Tickets
Keswick Angling Association
W Ashcroft
Spring Haven, How Lane
Portinscale, Keswick, Cumbria
Greta (Cumberland) and Derwentwater
Tickets
Kettering, Thrapston and District Angling Association
L R Garrett
10 Naseby Road
Kettering, Northamptonshire
Nene. Tickets
Keynsham Angling Association
G A Edwards
10 Clyde Avenue
Keynsham, Bristol
Avon BS18 1PZ
Chew, Avon. Tickets
Kibworth and District Angling Society
H Taberer
11 Weir Road,
Kibworth-Beauchamp
Leicestershire
Canal. Tickets
Kidderminster and District Angling Association
M Millinchip
246 Marpol Lane,
Kidderminster
Worcestershire
Severn. Members and associates only
Kidlington Angling Society
S J Hewlett
141 Blakes Avenue
Kidlington
Oxford
Kidsgrove and District Angling Association
S J Walker
16 Nalor Street
Pitshill, Tunstall
Stoke on Trent ST6 6LS
Kilnsey Angling Club
E N Wood
Moorside Cottage
Ogden, Halifax
HX2 8XP
Kingfisher Youth Angling Club
A & J Hatfield
2 Langstone Drive
Exmouth
Devon EX8 4HU
King of French Angling Club
W E West
31 Listowel Crescent
Clifton, Nottingham

Trent. No tickets

Kings Arms & Cheshunt Angling Club
J Connor
Tel: 0992 762414
Cheshunt North Reservoir

Kings Langley Angling Society
E Howell
38 Lonsdale
Highfield, Hemel Hempstead
HP2 5TR

King's Lynn Angling Association
M R Grief
67 Peckover Way
South Woorrow
King's Lynn PE30 3UE

Kingswood Disabled Angling Club
G Thompson
1 Honey Hill Road
Kingswood, Bristol

Kintbury Angling Association
Brian Culley
Bray Cottage
Kintbury, Berkshire
No tickets

Kirkby Fleetham Angling Club
S Schofield
1 Colstan Road
Northallerton, Yorkshire
DL6 1AZ

Kirkby Lonsdale and District Angling Association
G Clough
Keepers Cottage
Burrow via Carnforth LA6 2RN
Lune. Tickets

Kirkby Stephen and District Angling Association
W A S Kilvington
Market Square, Kirkby Stephen
Cumbria CA17 4QT
Eden. Members only

Kirkham and District Fly Fishers' Club
R Eglon
8 Selby Road
Kirkham
Preston PR4 2JT
Reservoir. Tickets

Knaresborough Anglers' Club
C J Lister
7 Dragon Avenue
Harrogate, Yorkshire

Knaresborough Piscatorials
P Davies
26 Kendal Road
Harrogate HG1 4SH
Nidd. Tickets

Knowle (Bristol) Angling Association
S J Wall
57 Church Road

Hanham, Bristol

Ladykirk and Norham AA
J Blythe
14 St Cuthbert's Square
Norham, Berwick-upon-Tweed

Lamb Angling Club
G S Ghent
Hopleys
Ingram Pit Lane
Amington
Tamworth, Staffs

Lancashire Fly-Fishing Association
J Winnard
Manor House, Grunsagill Tosside
Skipton
N Yorks
Ribble, Hodder, Lune, Wenning, Dean
Clough Reservoir. Day ticket for members' guests only

Lancaster and District Angling Association
V C Price
5 Burnside Close
Morecombe, Lancs

Lancing Anglers
Gilbert A Ramsey
Elinor Lodge, East Street
Lancing, Sussex

Langley Park Angling Association
T Huscroft
1 Garden Avenue
Langley Park, Durham

Langport and District Angling Association
J B Phillips
4 Brooklands Road
Huish Episcopi
Langport

Langney Angling Club
Tickets from
Tony's Tackle
Eastbourne
Langney Haven and ponds

Lanhydrock Angling Association
The National Trust Estate Office
Lanhydrock Park
Bodmin, Cornwall. Fowey

Lansil Angling Association
J E N Barnes
88 West End Road
Morecambe, Lancashire Water on Lune.
Tickets

Lark Angling Preservation Society
E T West
8 Arrowhead Drive
Lakenheath, Suffolk IP27 9JN

Lavington Angling Club
M D Gilbert
Gable Cottage

24 High Street
Erlestoke, nr Devizes, Wilts
Semington Brook
Lawford Angling Society
R W Nunn
Mistley Hall Cottage
Clacton Road, Mistley
Manningtree, Essex
Leamington Spa Angling Association
E G Archer
9 Southway
Leamington Spa,
Warwickshire
Avon and canal. Some tickets
Leatherhead and District Angling Society
R J Boychuk
22 Poplar Avenue
Leatherhead, Surrey
Mole, ponds. Private
**Ledbury and District Angling
Association**
C F Davies
The Wren, Banit Crescent
Ledbury, Herefordshire
**Leeds and District Amalgamated Society
of Anglers**
D Fulthorpe
46 Roxholme Terrace
Leeds LS7 4JH
Ouse and tributaries Tickets
Leek Fishing Club
R Birch-Machin
53 Novi Lane
Leek, Staffs ST13 6NX
Leek and Morlands Fishing Club
H Emery
20 Osbourne Street
Leek, Staffs
Churnet, canal
**Lee Valley Anglers Consultative
Association**
T Mansbridge
7 Warren Road
Chingford
London E4 6QR
Leicester Angling Club
V D Coles
60 Chadwell Road
Leicester
Grand Union Canal. Tickets
Leicester Angling Society
M Forrest
23 Needham Avenue
Glen Parva
Leicester LE2 9JL
Soar, Grand Union Canal. Tickets
**Leicester and District Amalgamated
Society of Anglers**
R T Bent Fossey

431 Gleneagles Avenue
Rushey Mead,
Leicester
Wreake, Nene, Eye, Soar, Grantham and
Grand Union Canals. Tickets
Leigh and District Association of Anglers
Thomas Kelly
70 Diamond Street
Leigh, Lancs WN7 4JG
Leintwardine Fishing Club
2 Nacklestone Bungalows
Craven Arms, Leintwardine
Shropshire SY7 0LZ
**Len Valley Angling and Preservation
Society**
Mrs J Baldwin
10 Mallaras Way, Bearstead
Maidstone, Kent ME15 8XH
Letchworth Angling Club
C Pell-Walpole
12 Burwell Road
Shepwell, Stevenage
Herts
Leven Angling Association
D A While
Birkdault, Haverthwaite
Ulveston, Cumbria LA12 8LY
Lewisham Piscatorials Association
D J Head
75 Riverview Park
Catford
London SE6 4PL
**Licensed Victuallers' Deep Sea Angling
Club (South-Eastern)**
E D Goodwin
15 Greenhill Bridge Road
Herne Bay, Kent
London and South:
E E Doree
1 Norfolk Court
Rustington, Sussex
Lichfield Marina Angling Society
C H Turner
Streethsay Basin
Burton Road
Lichfield, Staffs
Lincoln and District Angling Association
J Walvers
74 Edgehill, Brant Road
Lincoln LN5 9TZ
Lake. Tickets
Lincolnshire Anglers' Federation
J D McGuire
6 Churchill Drive
Boston,
Lincolnshire
**Lincolnshire Rivers Anglers'
Consultative Association**
J D McGuire, as above

Linesmen Angling Club
Andrew Wilson
30 Baker Street
London W1
Fisheries in eight counties

Linton, Threshfield and Grassington Angling Club
J A Birdsall M A
River End, School Cottages
Wood Lane, Grassington
Skipton, Yorkshire
BD23 5LU

Liskeard and District Angling Club
O G Gilbert
11 Richmond Road
Pelynt Nr Looe, Cornwall
Fowey, Camel, Lynher, Seaton,
Looe,Inny. Tickets

Littleborough Angling Society
H Ingham
86 Whalley Avenue, Littleborough
Rochdale, Lancashire
Canal. No tickets

Littlehampton and District Angling Club
Fisherman's Quay
Littlehampton

Littleport Angling Club
John W Shelsher
20 New River Bank
Littleport, Cambs CB7 4TA
Great Ouse, tickets

Liverpool and District Anglers' Association
J Johnson
97 Liverpool Road North
Maghull, nr Liverpool
Lancashire River Dee. Tickets

Llandrindod Wells Angling Association
B D Price
The Cedars
Llanyre
Llandrindod Wells, Powys Ithon. Tickets

Llanfair Fishing Club
Honorary Secretary
Llanfair-Caereinion
Powys
Banwy. Some tickets

Llanidloes Angling Society
I J Dallas Davies
Dresden House
Great Oak Street
Llanidloes,
Powys
Severn, Clywedog, Dulus. Tickets

London Anglers' Association
Mrs P Ellis
Isaak Walton House
2A Hervey Park Road
Walthamstow,

London E17 6LJ
(LAA offices) Thames, Lee and tributaries; Hampshire Avon, Arun, Great Ouse
Suffolk Stour, canals, lakes, etc, day tickets for some waters

London Brick Co (Angling Section)
R Peake
Phorpres Club
London Road, Fetton
Peterborough
Brick pits; members only

London Catchers Club
Dave Lawrence
57 Knightsbridge,
London, SW1
Offers service to anglers. Tickets for many waters

Long Buckby Angling Club
M Hill
33 South Close
Long Buckby
Northants NN6 7PX

Long Eaton and District Angling Federation
W Parker
75 College Street
Long Eaton, Notts
Soar, Trent, Erewash Canal, Radcliffe
Deeps

Long Eaton Victoria Angling Society
D L Kent
2 Edge Hill Court
Fields Farm
Long Eaton
Notts, NG10 1PQ
Trent. Tickets

Long Preston Angling Club
J Bowker
Pendle View, Long Preston
Skipton,
N Yorks
Ribble. Tickets

Lonsdale Angling Club
G Foote
9 Beaufort Road
Morecambe, Lancs

Looe and District Sea Angling Association
c/o Cotton's Tackle Shop
The Quay, E Looe, Cornwall
PL13 1AQ

Lostwithiel Fishing Association
J H Hooper
4 Reeds Park
Lostwithiel, Cornwall
Water on Fowey. Tickets

Loughborough Soar Angling Society
M Downs
16 Durham Road

Loughborough
Leicestershire
Soar and canal. Tickets

Louth Cawacs Angling Association
G Allison
15 Florence Wright Avenue
Louth, Lincolnshire

Lower Frankton Angling Club
C Ellis
Bridge Cottage
Lower Frankton
Nr Oswestry, Shropshire

Lower Teign Fishing Association
P M Knibbs
Morningside
Long Lane, Sheldon
Teignmouth, Devon
Teign. Tickets

Lowestoft Freshwater Angling Club
David Shreeve
52 Highland Way
Lowestoft, Suffolk

Lowestoft (South Pier) Angling Club
G Hooks
132 Bevan Street
Lowestoft, Suffolk

Ludlow Angling Club
C Jones
Mitre House, Lower Corve Street
Ludlow, Shropshire

Lune and Wyre Fishery Association
R A Challenor
6 Main Street
Kirkby Lonsdale

Luton and District Anglers' Association
S R Branch
3 Holmbrook Ave
Luton, Bedfordshire

Luton Angling Club
G J Buss
179 Tithe Farm Road
Houghton Regis
Beds LU5 5JF
or
D Edwards
Tel: 0582 28114
Rivers, canal, pits, day tickets

Lutterworth and District Anglers
R Makepiece
3 New Street
Lutterworth, Leics LE17 4PJ

Lychnobite Angling Society
E S Bourne
63 Handsworth Avenue
Highams Park
London E4 9PG

Lymington and District Sea Fishing Club
B Greenwood
2 Boldre Lane
Lymington, Hampshire

Lymm Angling Club
S Griffiths
18 Manor Way
Lymm WA13 0AY
Lake. Tickets

Lyttelton Angling Association
F M Rowley
2A Red House Road
Astley Cross
Stourport
Worcestershire DY13 0NW
Severn. Tickets

Mablethorpe, Sutton-on-Sea and District
   Angling Club
V A Hardy
33 Alford Road
Sutton-on-Sea, Mablethorpe
Lincolnshire
Great Eau

Macclesfield and District Amalgamated
   Society of Anglers
C Sparkes
High Lodge, Upton
Macclesfield, Cheshire

Macclesfield Flyfishers' Club
W F Williams
1 Westwood Drive
Brooklands, Sale
Cheshire M33 3QW
Dane and Clough, lakes. No tickets

Macclesfield Victoria Angling Society
A Jackson
8 Barton Street
Macclesfield, Cheshire
Canal. Tickets

Macclesfield Waltonian Angling Society
Michael E Bowyer
7 Ullswater
Macclesfield
Cheshire SK11 7YN

Maidenhead and District Angling
   Association
G W Rance
Ivydean, Forlease Road
Maidenhead, Berks

Maldon Angling Society
P Revill
Furzeland Farm
Maypole Road, Langford
Maldon. Essex CM9 7SZ
Blackwater. No tickets

Malton and Norton Angling Club
M Foggin
Westwood
123 Welham Road, Norton
Malton,
Yorkshire
Derwent. Tickets

Manchester Anglers' Association
F Fletcher
7 Alderbank Close
Kearsley
Bolton
Lancs, BL4 8JQ
Ribble and Lune. No tickets

Manchester Federation of Anglers
C McDonough
38 Solway Road
Crossacres
Wythenshawe, Manchester

Mansfield and District Angling Association
A Quick
158 Huthwaite Road
Sutton-in-Ashfield
Nottinghamshire NG17 2GX
River Devon, pits. Members only

Mannin Angling Club
A Pennington
10 Lhag Beg
Port Erin, I.O.M.

Manor Angling Club
D Cartwright
18 Dorset Close
Nuneaton, Warwickshire CV10 8EN

Manx Game Fishing Club
A W J Cottle
24 Queen Street
Castletown, Isle of Man

Marazion Angling Club
B Trevitt
6 Chyandaunce Close
Gulval, Penzance

March and District Federation of Anglers
J Abbott
17 North Street
March, Cambridgeshire
Fen waters. Tickets

March Working Men's Angling Club
H Davis
North Drive, March
Cambridgeshire
Twenty Foot. Permits

Marconi Angling Society
Honorary Secretary
Marconi Athletic Social Club
Beehive Lane, Chelmsford, Essex Canal.
Tickets

Mardon Angling Club
C G Austin

70 Whiteway Road
St George, Bristol
River Avon

Margate Fishing Club
F Lamberton
2 Chilham Avenue
Westgate-on-Sea, Kent

Market Drayton Angling Club
C Booth
The Willows
Ashbourne Drive
Prospect Road
Market Drayton, Shropshire TF9 3EA

Market Harborough and District Society of Anglers
R Haycock
16 Maurice Road
Market Harborough
Leicestershire
Canal. Tickets

Market Weighton Angling Club
T Brown
19 Glenfield Avenue
Market Weighton
Yorkshire

Marlborough and District Angling Association
M Ellis
Failte, Elcot Close
Marlborough, Wiltshire
Kennet and Avon Canal. Tickets limited

Marlow and District Angling Association
G W Hoing
15 Greenlands
Flackwell Heath, High Wycombe

Marsden Star Angling Society
D H G Brown
36 Western Avenue
Riddlesden
Keighley, Yorks BD20 5DJ

Martham and District Angling Club
M L Goodwin
34 Yarmouth Road
Ormesby, Great Yarmouth
Norfolk

Masham Angling Club
Peter W L Proud
Thorn Hill, Fearby Road
Masham, Ripon
N Yorks HG4 4ES

Mawgan Angling Club
T J Trevenna

Fishing Clubs

When you appoint a new secretary, do not forget to give us details of the change. Write to the publishers (address at front of the book). Thank you!

Lanvean House
St Mawgan, Newquay
Cornwall
Measham Fishing Club
J Wainwright
6 The Square
Oakthorpe
Burton-on-Trent DE12 7QS
**Medway Victory Angling and Medway
 Preservation Society**
J Perkins
33 Hackney Road
Maidstone, Kent
Medway. Tickets
**Melksham and District Angling
 Association**
D Branton
16 Ingram Road
Melksham
River Avon
Melton Mowbray Society of Anglers
R W Benskin
24 Chetwynd Drive
Melton Mowbray, Leicestershire
Eye and Wreake (Trent). Tickets
Mere Angling Club (Derwent Sector)
W H Smith
1 Cecil Court, Ryndleside
Scarborough, Yorkshire
No tickets
Mevagissey Sea Angling Club
The Ship Inn
Pentowan
Cornwall
**Michelmersh and Timsbury Angling
 Society**
A Ware
Embley Brook
Embley Park
Romsey, Hants
Middlesbrough Angling Club
R Thompson
25 Endsleigh Drive
Acklam, Middlesbrough
Cleveland TS5 4RG
Middlewich Angling Society
C Bratt
43 Elm Road
Middlewich, Cheshire
Midland Angling Society
J Bradbury
19 Ethel Avenue, Lindby
Hucknall, Notts NG15 8D8
Trent
Midland Flyfishers
A R Collins
Pearl Assurance House
4 Temple Row
Birmingham B2 5HG

Onny, Welsh Dee. Tickets
**Mid-Northants Trout Fishers'
 Association**
T Broughton
52 Bush Hill
Northampton
Mildenhall Angling Club
M Hampshire
63 Downing Close
Mildenhall, Suffolk
IP28 7PB
Millhouse Beck Fishing Club
D J Broady
Ings Lane, Dunswell
Hull, Yorkshire
Beck. Members only
Millom and District Angling Association
D Dixon
1 Churchill Drive
Millom, Cumbria
Members only
Milnthorpe Angling Association
A R Park
Hawkshead House, Priest Hutton
Carnforth, Cumbria LA6 1JP
Bela. No tickets
Milton Keynes Angling Association
P Oxley
23 Breton
Fairfield Estate
Stony Stratford
Milton Keynes, Bucks
Monmouth and District Angling Society
A Doolan
2 Elm Drive
Monmouth
Monnow
Montgomeryshire Angling Association
P Hulme
306 Heol-y-Coleg
Vaynor Estate, Newtown
Powys SY16 1RA
Moor Hall and Belhus Angling Society
M Tilbrook
46 Mill Road
Aveley, Essex
Stour, Ham River, pits. No tickets
Morecambe Bay Angling Club
J Smith
17 Barnes Road
Morecambe, Lancashire
Moss Side Social Angling Society
A Jones
10 Purley Avenue
Northenden, Manchester 22
Dee. Members only. Bosley Reservoir
Tickets
Mounts Bay Angling Society
D Cains

29 Treassowe Road
Penzance, Cornwall
Myddelton Angling Club
J B Harland
Barradene, 57 Grove Road
Ilkley, Yorkshire
Wharfe. Tickets
Nantwich Angling Society
Mrs B M Sutton
91 Waverley Court
Crewe, Cheshire CW2 7BH
Weaver. No dt
NETA Angling Society
F Rye
42 Northfield Road
Laleham, Middlesex
**Newark and District Piscatorial
Federation**
J N Garland
58 Riverside Road
Newark, Notts NG24 4RJ
Newark Dyke. Tickets
**Newbrough and Fourstones Angling
Association**
C Telford
Howlett Hurst
Fourstones
Hexham, Northumberland.
S Tyne
Newbury Angling Association
D Buckwell
37 Pegasus Road
Oxford 0X4 5DS
Kennet, canal. No tickets
Newhaven Deep Sea, Anglers' Club
D F Wood
Lakri, 56 Slindon Avenue
Peacehaven, Sussex
Newland Angling Club
19 Fettiplace Road
Whitney, Oxon
Newport (Gwent) Angling Association
P Climo
2 Darwin Drive
Newport, Gwent
Newport Pagnell Fishing Association
R D Dorrill
Sunnyside
7 Bury Street
Newport Pagnell
Buckinghamshire MK16 0D5
Great Ouse, gravel pits. Tickets
New Studio Angling Society
W Dexter
62 Battersby Road
London SE6
Medway. Members only
Newton Abbot Fishing Association
D Horder

22 Mount Pleasant Road
Newton Abbot
Devon
Lakes. St only
Nidderdale Angling Club
Miss R Breckon
Jobadach
Greenwood Avenue
Pateley Bridge, nr Harrogate
Nidd. Tickets
Norfolk and Suffolk Flyfishers Club
T Riches
Farthings, Church Road
Tasburgh, Norfolk
Norfolk Flyfishers Club
R Gibbons
Mirema, Welbourne Road
Mattishall
Dereham, Norfolk
Northallerton and District Angling Club
G Easby
24 Quaker Lane
Northallerton, Yorkshire
Swale. Tickets
Northampton Britannia Angling Club
C W Gray
61 Bouverie Walk
Northampton NN1 5SN
Northampton Castle Angling Association
T R Rodhouse
12 Somerville Road
Daventry
Northants
Northampton Nene Angling Club
J Ringer
Haddon House, Guilsborough Road
Ravensthorpe
Northampton NN6 8EW
Ouse, Nene. Tickets
North Buckinghamshire Angling
N Clutton
95 Lakes Lane
Newport Pagnel
Buckinghamshire
North Country Anglers
I G Whale
17 Watling Terrace
Willington
Crook,
County Durham DL15 0HL
Northern Anglers' Association
A G R Brown
10 Dale Road
Golborne, Wigan
Ribble, Dee, canals, etc.
North Oxford Angling Society
L Ballard
70 Blackbird Leys Road
Cowley

Oxford 0X4 5HR
Water north of Oxford. No tickets
North Romford Angling Society
Mrs Partridge
Tel: 0708 24461
Bedfords Park Lake
North Somerset and West Wilts Federation of Anglers
R J Lee
Marvic
Keyford Terrace
Frome, Somerset
North Somerset Association of Anglers (Embracing Cheddar, Highbridge, Clevedon and Weston-super-Mare clubs)
R Newton
64 Clevedon Road
Tickenham
Cleveden, Avon BS21 6RD
Northumbrian Anglers' Federation
P A Hall
25 Ridley Place
Newcastle upon Tyne
Northumberland NE1 8LF
Salmon and trout water on Coquet, Tyne Tickets
North-West Durham Angling Club
Gordon Byers
78 Castledean Road
Delves Lane, Consett
Co Durham
Northwich Anglers Association
J Clithero
P O Box 18
Northwich, Cheshire
Weaver. Tickets
North Yorkshire and South Durham Federation of Angling Clubs
D McMasters
2 The Firs, Darlington
Co Durham DH1 3PH
Norwich and District Angling Association
C E Wigg
3 Coppice Avenue
Norwich NR6 5RB
Thurne, Bure, Broads. Tickets
Norwich Sea Anglers
D Mundford
68 Heath Road
Norwich
Nottingham Anglers' Association
224 Radford Road
Nottingham
Trent. Tickets
Nottingham and District Anglers' Joint Council
N A Cade
82 Broxtowe Lane

Nottingham NG8 5NJ
Nottingham and District Federation of Angling Societies
W Belshaw
17 Spring Green
Clifton Estate, Nottingham
For matches contact Mrs M Whitmore
47 Criftin Road, Nottingham
Trent. Tickets
Nottingham Fly Fishers' Club
P J Ardwinckle
34 Renal Way
Calverton, Nottingham
Lakes and river. No tickets
Oakham Angling Society
R Taylor
8 Beech Road
Oakham,
Rutland
Welland, Glen canal and ponds. No tickets
Offord and Buckden Fishing Society
A Plumb
75 High Street
Gt Paxton
Huntingdon, Cambs
Great Ouse, Limited tickets
Oldham United Anglers' Society
J K Lees
18 Chichester Crescent
Chadderton
Oldham
Reservoirs. Tickets
Olditch Angling Club
D Elks
43 Whitfield Avenue
Newcastle
Staffs ST5 2JQ
Old Windsor Angling Club
D A Meakes
51 Bulkeley Avenue
Windsor, Berks SL4 3NG
Thames. Tickets
Olton Mere Club
J E Cox
Mere Cottages
Warwick Road
Olton, Solihull
Orpington and District Angling Association
R Bright
133 The Drive
Bexley, Kent
Lakes. No tickets
Ossett and District Angling Club
182 Kingsway
Ossett WF5 8DW
Oswestry Angling Club
Les Allen

30 Brookfields
Weston Rhyn, Oswestry
Otley Angling Club (Trout Preserves)
D M Lane
Braeburn, Cherin Avenue
Menston, Ilkley,
W Yorks, LS29 6PR
Wharfe. Members only
Ottermouth Trout Association
W K H Coxe
Council Chambers
Budleigh Salterton, Devon
Oulton Broad Piscatorial Society
O Lay
205 Victoria Road
Oulton Broad
near Lowestoft, Suffolk
Oundle Angling Association
D Laxton
31 St Peters Road
Oundle, Northamptonshire
Nene. Members only
Ouse Angling Preservation Society
E W McLening
Old Barn Cottage
Peak Lane
East Preston
W Sussex BN16 1RN
Wessex Ouse. Limited season tickets
Over and Swaveley Angling Society
M D Cook
c/o Happy Eater
Red Lodge
Nr Newmarket
Suffolk
Oxford and District Anglers' Association
R Disley
14 Briar Way
Blackbird Leys
Oxford OX4 5SE
Oxford Canal Alliance
W J Moore
9 Cotswold Drive
Linslade
Leighton Buzzard, Beds
Paignton Sea Anglers' Association
C Holman
50 Hayes Road
Paignton, Devon TQ4 5PL
**Pangbourne and Whitchurch District
Fishing Club**
S R Cox
49 Bath Road, Calcot Row
Reading Berks RG3 5QH
Park Angling Club
M Kelly
14 Sycamore Close
Wellington, Telford
Salop TF1 3NH

Peak Forest Angling Club (Derbyshire)
C Gardiner
10 Leyfield Road
Dore, Sheffield
Peel Angling Club
G Black
17 Friary Park
Ballabeg
Arbory, Isle of Man
Penkridge Anglers
W J Robins
Tight Lines
Market Street
Penkridge, Staffs ST19 5DH
Penrith Angling Association
J Smith
3 Barco Avenue
Penrith, Cumbria CA11 8LU
Eden, Eamont, Petterill (Eden) and Low-
ther. Tickets
Penshurst Angling Society
M Mills
3 Montgomery Road
Tunbridge Wells, Kent
Medway and Eden (Kent). No tickets
Peper Harow Flyfishers' Club
c/o Littlehurst
1 Flitwick Grange
Milford, Godalming
Surrey GU8 5DS
**Peterborough and District Angling
Association**
W Yates
75 Lawn Avenue
Dogsthorpe, Peterborough
Nene .
Peterborough Jolly Anglers' Society
C Graves
8 Saxon Road
Peterborough
Petersfield and District Angling Club
A P Wigley
Tel: 0730 67592
Heath Pond. Tickets
Petworth Angling Club
G J Mason
Tel: 0798 42172
Rother and Arun
**Petworth, Bognor and Chichester
Amalgamated Anglers**
A W Pascoe
53 Wesley Lane
Copnor, Portsmouth
Western Rother. Tickets
Pewsey and District Angling Club
Mrs M Draper
14 Haines Terrace
Pewsey,
Wiltshire SN9 5DXK

Phoenix Angling Club
J A Mobley
155 Greenhill Road
Halesowen
West Midlands B62 8EZ
Pickering Fishery Association
C Norton
School House, Swainsea Lane
Pickering, Yorkshire
YO18 8NG
Pike Anglers' Club of Great Britain
23 Theocs Close
Tewkesbury Park
Tewkesbury
Glos GL20 5TX
Pirelli Angling Club
P R Woolley
80 Meadow Lane
Newhall,
Burton-on-Trent
Staffs DE11 0UW
Piscatorial Society
J H S Hunt
76 High Street
Market Lavington
Devizes, Wilts SN10 4AG
**Plymouth and District Freshwater
Angling Association**
D L Owen
39 Burnett Road
Crownhill
Plymouth PL6 5BH
Plym. Members only
Plymouth Federation Sea Angling Clubs
B Lavis
47 Rigdale Close
Eggbuckland
Plymouth
Plymouth Sea Angling Club
Sea Angling Centre
Vauxhall Quay,
Plymouth,
Devon
Polruan Sea Angling Club
R Libby
9 Greenbank
Polruan, Fowey
Cornwall PL23
Portsmouth and District Angling Society
R Snook
86 Caernarvon Road
Portsmouth

**Portsmouth Services Fly Fishing
Association**
Captain F Hefford OBE, DSC, AFC, RN
(Retired)
20 Stoatley Rise
Haslemere,
Surrey GU27 1AF
Rivers Meon and Itchen
**Potter Heigham and District Angling
Club**
W Platten
1 Audley Street
Great Yarmouth, Norfolk
Potteries Angling Club
D Heath
180 Broadway
Meir, Stoke-on-Trent
Preesall Angling Club
C Rowe
24 Sandy Lane
Preesall, Lancashire
Wyre. Members only
Preston Federation of Anglers
Roy Mayor
27 Shirley Lane
Longton, Preston PR4 5WJ
Prestwood and District Angling Club
B H Poynter
56 Perry Street
Wendover
Bucks HP22 6DJ
Halton Reservoir
Pride of Derby Angling Association
A Miller
16 Mercia Drive
Willington, Derby
Trent. Members only. Waiting list
Prince Albert Angling Society
J T Lovatt
63 Beggerman's Lane
Knutsford
Cheshire WA16 9BB
or
Queens Hotel
Waters Green
Macclesfield
Rivers, streams, lakes, pools
Pulborough Angling Society
M Booth
5 South Lane
Houghton
Arundel, W Sussex

Fishing Clubs

When you appoint a new secretary, do not forget to give us details of the change. Write to the publishers (address at front of the book). Thank you!

Arun
Quorn Angling Society
W Boyd
28 Beaumont Road
Barrow-on-Soar, Leicestershire
Soar, canal. Tickets
Radcot Angling and Preservation Club
C R Neville
Clanville House, Bampton Road
Clanfield, Oxfordshire
Thames. Tickets
Raleigh Fishing Club
110 Cantrell Road
Bulwell
Nottingham NG6 9HJ
Ramsey Angling Club
K Bragg
c/o Onchan District Commissioners
Office
Main Road
Onchan,
Isle of Man
Raven Angling Club
E G Mears
16 Broomshouse Road
Fulham, London SW6 3QX
Reading and District Angling Association
W Brown Lee
47 Calbourne Drive
The Orchard, Calcot
Reading RG3 7DB
Tbe Red Admiral Angling Club
G Thorne
15 Yately Avenue
Great Barr,
Birmingham B42 1JW
**Redditch and District Federation of
Anglers**
S Mousley
Tel: 0527 854160
Red Spinner Angling Society
L J Halliday
28 Cranfield Crescent
Cuffley Hertfordshire EN6 4EH
Evenlode, Stour (Dorset) Ebble, Hamp-
shire Avon Cheshunt Reservoir Bear-
wood Lake. Members only
Remenham Angling Society
W A Hickman
Bell Cottage
Beverlay Gardens
Wargrave
Reading, Berks
Thames. Tickets
Retford and District Angling Association
H Wells
31 Ainsdale Green
Ordsall, Retford
Nottinghamshire DN22 7NQ

Chesterfield Canal. Tickets
Rhayader Angling Association
G H Roberts
Belmullet
Rhayader, Powys
LD6 5BY
Ribble and Wyre Fisheries Association
S A Gray
18 Lord Street, Wigan
Lancs WN1 3BN
Ribblesdale Angling Association
J N Bailey
56 Moorland Crescent
Clitheroe, Lancs BB7 4PY
**Richmond (Yorks) and District Angling
Society**
D Hutchinson
28 Cross Lanes
Richmond, N Yorkshire
Swale. Tickets
Ridgeway Angling Association
R Walker
30 Ingleston Road
Wickwar, Wooton-under-Edge
Glos GL12 8NH
**Ringwood and District Anglers'
Association**
R Smith
1 Avon Castle Drive
Matchams Lane
Ringwood, Hampshire
Ripley and District Angling Club
R Turner
2a Argyll Road
Ripley, Derbyshire
Amber, reservoirs. Tickets
Ripon Piscatorial Association
S Looney
Corner Stones
2 Hellwath Grove
Redwell Heath
HG4 2JT
Yore, Laver, Skell, reservoir.Tickets
Ripponden Fly-Fishers
H Hamer
The Hollies, Greetland
Halifax, Yorkshire
Reservoir
River Glaven Fishery Association
T G Bird
Newgate Green
Cley, Holt, Norfolk
Trout fishing in Glaven
Riverside Angling Club
R A Jones
71 Hertford Road
Alcester,
Warks
River Alne

Robin Hood Angling Club
G Smith
Robin Hood Inn
High Street, Rookery
Kidsgrove, Stoke-on-Trent ST7 4RL
Rochdale Walton Angling Society
D R Gent
59 Crofthead Drive
Milnrow, Rochdale 0L16 30Z
Roche Angling Club (St Austell)
R Brooke
5 Creed Lane, Grampound
Truro, Cornwall TR2 4SH
Romsey and District Angling Society
E Hoskins
40 Aldermoor Avenue
Aldermoor,
Southampton
Ross-on-Wye Angling Club
T Gibson
10 Redwood Close
Ross-on-Wye. Wye
Tickets
Rothbury and Thropton Angling Club
C Bell
1 Silverdale Cottages
Snitter, Thropton
Northumberland NE65 7EL
Rother Angling Club
A G Imwood
2 Poplar Way, Midhurst
Sussex GU29 9JP
or
D Merritt
Membership Secretary
Tel: 0730 816365
Western Rother. Tickets
Rother Fishery Association
S Crowley
9 Haydens Close
Orpington, Kent
Rotherham and District Limited Anglers'
Federation
H Howarth
4 Scarborough Road
Wickersley
Rotherham, Yorkshire
Rowley and District Angling Society
R Woodhouse
52 St Brades Close
Landsdowne Heights
Trividale, Warley
W Midlands B69 1NX
Severn. No tickets
Royal Exchange Angling Society
R Brindley
24 Scotia Road
Cannock,
Staffs

Royal Leamington Spa Angling
Association
E G Archer
9 Southway
Leamington Spa, Warwickshire
Royal Ramsgate Invicta Angling
Association
B A Kirkaldie
67 Boundary Road
Ramsgate, Kent
Royal Tunbridge Wells Angling Society
Clifford C Lupini
25 The Drive
Hedge Barton, Fordcombe
Kent
Rother, Teise, Medway.
No tickets except to members
Royston and District Angling Club
D N Hellier
60 Heathfield
Royston, Herts
Rubery Owen Angling Club
Tony Harrison
73 Talbot Street
Whitchurch
Shropshire SY1 3PJ
Rudgewick Angling Society
D Taylor
Holmhurst, Church Street
Rudgewick
Sussex RH12 3ET
Rugby Federation of Anglers
G Lawrence
53 Manor Road
Rugby CV21 2TG
Avon, canals. Permits
Rugeley and Brereton Angling Society
J T Connolly
36 Ravenslea Road
Brereton, Staffs WS15 1AF
Rushden and Higham Ferrers &
Irchester Angling Association
D Parkins
3 Mountfield Road
Irthlingborough
Northants NN9 55Y
Anglers Depot
26 Church Street
Rushden, Northants
or
A Ireson (Chairman)
3 Abbey Way, Rushden
NN10 9YT
Ryedale Anglers' Club
J A W Leech
Northfield House
Hovingham,
Yorks YO6 4LG
Rye. Members only

Saddington Angling Society
J Mason
8 Honiton Close
Wigston, Leicestershire
Saddleworth and District Angling Club
Charles T Johnson
3 Birch Road
Uppermill
Nr Oldham,
Lancs OL3 6JN
St Helens Angling Association
L Bromilow
4 Bassenthwaite Ave
Moss Bank, St Helens
Merseyside WA11 7AB
Welsh Dee, canal, lakes. Limited weekly
tickets
**St Ives and District Fish Preservation and
Angling Society**
H Pace
48 Fairfields
St Ives, Cambs
Great Ouse. Tickets
St Leonards Sea Anglers
HQ, 16 Grand Parade
St Leonards, Sussex
St Mawgan Angling Club
T J Trevenna
Lanvean House
St Mawgan, Newquay, Cornwall
River Menalhyl
**St Neots and District Angling and Fish
Preservation Society**
Ms D Linger
Skewbridge Cottage
Paxton Hill
St Neots, Cambs
Great Ouse. Tickets
**Salcombe and District Sea Anglers'
Association**
Headquarters
Victoria Inn
Fore Street
Salcombe, Devon TQ8 8BT
Salisbury and District Angling Club
R W Hillier
Inverleith
29 New Zealand Avenue
Salisbury
Wiltshire SP2 7JX
Saltaire Angling Association
William M Troman
7 Hall Royd
Shipley, Yorkshire BD18 3ED
Wharfe and Aire. Tickets
Salt Hill Angling Society
H W Mayo
16 Old Way Lane
Chippenham, Slough

Thames at Windsor and Eton
Sandgate Sea Angling Society
R J Piddock
Kerry Vale
West Street
New Romney, Kent
Sandown and Lake Angling Society
A D Wilson
56 Silver Trees
Shanklin
Isle of Wight PO37 7ND
**Sandwich and District Angling
Association**
D Daniels
48 Hazelwood Meadows
Sandwich CT13 0AR
Sawbridgeworth Angling Socieiy
C Guiver
19 Hedgerows, Sawbridgeworth
Hertfordshire
Scarborough Boat Angling Club
J A Martin
26 Ling Hill
Newby,
Scarborough
Scarborough Mere Angling Club
J Millward
3 Dale Edge, Eastfield
Scarborough, Yorkshire
Scarborough Rock Anglers
H Dobson
1 Uplands Avenue
East Ayton, near Scarborough Yorkshire
Sceptre Angling Club
D T Hobbs
77 The Gossamers
Garston
Watford, Herts
**Scunthorpe and District Angling
Association**
J R Walker
11 Waddington Drive
Bottesford
Scunthorpe, Yorks DN17 2TL
Seabrook Sea Anglers' Association
R Perrin
74 Horn Street
Hythe, Kent
Seaford Angling Club
G Martin
4 South Road
Newhaven, E Sussex BN9 9QJ
**Sedbergh and District Angling
Association**
G Bainbridge
El Kantara, Frostrow
Sedbergh
Cumbria LA10 5JL
Trout water on Lune. Tickets

Selby District and Miners Welfare Angling Club
A Smales
6 Cherry Tree Close
Selby YO8 9HF

Selsey Tope Fishers Specimen Club
R G Horrod
28 Beach Road
Selsey,
Sussex

Services Dry Fly Fishing Association (Salisbury Plain)
Colonel D A N C Miers
HQ SPTA
Bulford Camp
Salisbury SP4 9PA
Avon. Private

Settle Anglers' Association
T McMahon
10 Hurrs Road
Skipton, N Yorks BD23 2JX
Ribble. Tickets

Seven Angling Club
Mrs Betty J Stansfield
Sun Seven
Sinnington, Yorkshire
Seven. Members only

Seven Stars Angling Club
B Chambers
12 Mason Close
Headless Cross, Redditch B97 5DF

Severnside Angling Club
Michael J Thomas
253 Measyrhandir
Newtown, Powys SY16 1LB

Shackerstone and District Angling Association
Mrs B M Andrews
6 Church Road
Shackerstone
Nuneaton CV13 6NN

Shanklin Angling Society
M Kingswell
52 North Road
Shanklin, Isle of Wight

Sheffield Amalgamated Anglers' Society
A D Baynes
39 Sparken Hill, Worsop
Notts S80 1AZ
HQ Lord Nelson
166/8 Arundel Street
Sheffield
Trent and tributaries, canals, etc. Permits

Sheffield and District Anglers' Association
F E Turner
142/4 Princess Street
Sheffield S4 7UW
Trent and tributaries, canals, etc. Permits

Sheffield Piscatorial Society
Mr Dawson
20 St Michaels Crescent
Sheffield S13 8AN

Shefford and District Angling Association
C Rose
120 High Street
Stotfold
Hitchin
Herts SG9 4LH

Shiplake and Binfield Heath Fishing Club
M R Alder
11 Littlestead Close
Caversham Park
Reading, Berks RG4 0UA
Thames. Members only

Shipston-on-Stour and District Angling Club
E Draper
37 Station Road
Shipston-on-Stour, Warwickshire

Shrewsbury Angling Society
D Clarke
5 Albert Street, Castlefields
Shrewsbury, Salop

Shropshire Anglers Federation
D Skinner
17 West Place, Gobowen
Oswestry SY11 3NR

Shuttington and Alvecote Angling Club
M H Taylor
39 Alvecote Cottages
Alvecote
Nr Tamworth, Staffordshire B79 0DJ

Sidmouth Sea Angling Club
A C Thorne
25 Coleridge Road
Ottery St Mary, Devon

Silver Dace Angling Association
J Cox
21 Ingleside Road
Kingswood, Bristol BS15 1HJ
Avon, Frome, Chew

Sittingbourne Angling Club
W Adcock
8 Brisbane Avenue
Sittingbourne, Kent
Pits. Dt (restricted).

Skegness Angling Association
L H Dent
11 High Street
Skegness, Lincolnshire

Skegness Sea Angling Club
S Kinning
20 West End
Burgh-le-Marsh
Skegness,
Lincs PE24 5EY

Skerton and Morecambe Angling Society
C Boswell
16 Slyne Road
Skerton,
Lancashire
Skipton Angling Association
J W Preston
Hill Crest, Beech Hill Road
Carleton, Skipton
Yorkshire BD23 3EN
Aire. Tickets
Slaithwaite and District Angling Club
S K Makin
11 Mountfield Avenue
Waterloo
Huddersfield
Yorkshire HD7 8RD
Soho Loop Anglers Association
M T Holt
26 Worcester Road
Oldbury
Warley, West Midlands
Somerfords Fishing Association
D Hitchings
Woodlands, Cleeve Wood Road
Downend, Bristol
Frome, Loddon. Tickets to members'
guests
South Cerney Angling Club
H J Franklin
Tel: 0285 830362
South Cerney Pits
South Coast Sea Angling Association
R G Horrod
28 Beach Road
Selsey, Sussex
South Molton Angling Club
I T S Binding
40 Parklands
South Molton, Devon
EX34 4EW
Tickets for Taw, Mole.
Southampton Piscatorial Society
P J Dowse
33 Arnheim Road
Lordswood, Southampton
Southampton Sea Angling Club
P Thomas
28 Laundry Road
Shirley, Southampton SO1 6AN
Southend Amateur Angling Society
G Kirby

25 The Meads, Vange
Pitsea, Essex
Southern (IOM) Angling Club
D Corkish
88 Ballamaddrell
Port Erin, Isle of Man
Southern Anglers
T Irons
7 Nelson Crescent
Horndean, Portsmouth PO8 9LZ
Southern Counties Angling Federation
(31 member clubs)
Douglas Richardson
117-121 Rose Green Road,
Rose Green
Bognor Regis, Sussex
Southern Essex Group Angling Bodies
Consultative Committee
R Smith
46 Shortcrofts Road
Dagenham, Essex
Essex lakes
Southgate and District Angling Society
D G Hodgkins
18 Cedar House
Winkfield Road
Wood Green,
London N22
South Manchester Angling Club
D Crookall
12 Winscombe Street
Rusholme, Manchester M14 7PJ
Southport and District Angling
Association
M M Bannister
7 Sunny Road
Southport PR9 7LU
Southsea Sea Angling Club
T Stewart
2 King John Avenue
Portchester, Fareham
Hampshire PO16 9AP
South Tyne Angling Association
G Liddle
North Bank
Haydon Bridge, Hexham
Northumberland
S Tyne. Tickets to local residents only
Spenborough and District Angling Club
c/o Commercial Hotel
Cleckheaton,
W Yorks

Fishing Clubs

When you appoint a new secretary, do not forget to give us details of the change. Write
to the publishers (address at front of the book). Thank you!

Spilsby Angling Association
G Matthews
57 Ancaster Avenue
Spilsby, Lincolnshire
Stafford Izaak Walton Anglers'
Association
T H Babbs
4 Fieldside
Wildwood, Stafford
Sowe. Penk and canal
Stainford and Keadby Joint Angling
Committee
J Cunliffe
13 Wesley Road
Kiveton Park
Sheffield
Stalbridge Angling Association
Diana Fletcher
Corner Cottage
High Street, Stalbridge
Dorset DT10 2LH
Stalybridge Fox Angling Society
Jack Brooks
6 Robinson Street
Stalybridge
Cheshire SKl5 1UN
Stamford Welland Amalgamated Anglers
Association
G E Bates
16a Austin Street
Stamford, Lincs PE9 2QP
Stanhope Angling Association
J J Lee
1 Eastcroft, Stanhope
Co Durham
Wear. Tickets
Stapleton Angling Association
A Harrison
18 The Chippings
Southside
Stapleton, Bristol
Avon, Chew, Frome
Star Angling Club
A G Jones
6 Blandford Gardens
Burntwood
Nr Walsall, Staffordshire
Staveley and District Angling Association
D A Taylor
18 Rawes Garth, Staveley
Cumbria, Kent
Gowan, lake. Tickets
Stevenage Angling Society
W J Lewis
54 Stonycroft
Stevenage, Hertfordshire
No water
Stirrup Cup Angling Club
N Davies

26 Orchard Rise
Sheldon
Birmingham B26 IQT
Stockton Angling Association
G Cruickshank
29 The Green, High Coniscliffe
Darlington, Co Durham
No tickets
Stoke City and District Anglers'
Association
P Johansen
31 East Crescent, Sneyd Green
Stoke-on-Trent ST1 6ES
Stoke-on-Trent Angling Society
Albert Perkins
Muirshearlich
Fowlers Lane
Light Oaks
Stoke-on-trent, Staffs ST2 7NB
Stoke-sub-Hamdon Angling Association
D Goad
2 Windsor Lane
Stoke-sub-Hamdon, Somerset
Parrot. Members only
Stone and District Angling Society
Mrs C A Bond
21 Princes Street
Stone
Staffs ST15 8HY
Stonehaven and District Angling
Association
D C M MacDonald
Clachaig
93 Forest Park
Stonehaven AB3 2GF
Stour Fishery Association
L G Holtom
Barton Mill
Canterbury
Kentish Stour. No tickets
Stowe Angling Club
J Freedstone
2 Hazel Close
Brackley
Northamptonshire
Stowmarket and District Angling
Association
J Eade
37 Windermere Road
Stowmarket, Suffolk
Stratford-upon-Avon Angling
Association
D Evason
School House, Ullenhall
Solihull B95 5PA
Stroud and District Angling Club
Mr Price
94 Matthews Way
Pagenhil, Stroud

Glos GL5 4DU
Sturminster Angling Association
L J Warren
16 Honeysuckle Gardens
Shillingstone, Blandford
Dorset DT11 0TJ
Sudbury and District Angling Society
T R Fairless
39 Pot Kiln Road
Gt Cornard
Sudbury, Suffolk
Stour. Tickets
Suffolk Fly Fishers' Club
J Bird
27 Norbury Road
Ipswich, Suffolk
Sunmead Angling Society
P Tanner
24 Ryebrook Road
Leatherhead
Surrey KT22 7QG
Sussex Anglers Consultative Association
Dr B Lindsey
3 St Anne's Crescent
Lewes, E Sussex
Sussex County Angling Association
Miss S Colquhorn
38 Limes Avenue
Horley, Sussex
Sussex Piscatorial Society
Dr P Ashdown
Slindon College
Slindon, Arundel
W Sussex BN18 0RH
Ponds and lakes. Tickets for members'
guests only
**Swadlincote and District Anglers'
Association**
P Woolrich
27 Chapel Street
Smisby
Nr Ashby-de-la-Zouch
Leics LE6 5TJ
Swaffham Angling Club
Honorary Secretary
30 Kings Street
Swaffham, Norfolk
Trout lake. St.
Swan Angling Club
J Stanhope
4 High Road
Lane Head
Willenhall, West Midlands
Swanage and District Angling Club
Peveril Slipway
Swanage, Dorset
Secretary
W Brooks
72 D'Urberville Drive

Swanage, Dorset
**Swindon Golden Carp Angling
Association**
K Hale
11 Elmina Road
Swindon, Wiltshire
K and A Canal. Tickets
Swindon Isis Angling Club
K D Sykes
53 Arnolds Way
Cirencester, Glos GL7 1TA
Avon, Sutton Benger
**Tadcaster Angling and Preservation
Association**
S Barker
4 Westfield Square
Tadcaster, N Yorks
Wharfe. Tickets
Talbot Angling Society
R W Griffin
11 St Richards Gardens
Droitwich Spa, Worcestershire
Severn. Tickets
Tameside Federation of Anglers
Mrs B Smart
20 Kingston Gardens
Hyde, Cheshire SK14 2DB
Tamworth Working Men's Club
B F Shaw
7 Elizabeth Drive
Leyfields Tamworth
Staffordshire B79 8DE
Tanfield Angling Club
J Whitfield
7 King Street, Mirfield
W Yorks WF14 8AP
Tickets to guests of members only
Tarporley Angling Club
R W Cross
25 Burton Avenue
Tarporley, Cheshire
Oulton Mill Pool. Tickets
Taunton Angling Association
H King
145 Henson Park
Chard, Somerset TA20 1NL
Tone, Taunton Canal, Drains
Taunton Fly-Fishing Club
J Greene
2 Old Vicarage
Bradford on Tone
Taunton TA4 1HG
Tavy, Walkham and Plym Fishing Club
Ian H Parker
Marina Cottage, Marina Terrace
Mutley, Plymouth
Devon
Taw Fishing Club
J C C Jourdan

Bush House
Spreyton
Crediton, Devon
Taw. Restricted tickets

Tawe Disabled Fishers Association
R G Waters
23 Verig Street
Manselton, Swansea SA5 9NQ

Tawe & Tributaries Angling Association
M Matthews
32 Farm Road
Cwrt Sart, Briton Ferry
Neath, West Glamorgan

Tebay and District Angling Club
H Riley
White Cross House
Tebay, via Penrith
Cumbria
Lune. Tickets

Teignmouth Sea Angling Society
Mrs L Hexter
1 Headway Rise
Teignmouth
Devon TQ14 9UL

Teise Anglers' and Owners' Association
Dr N Goddard
Chickenden Farmhouse
Staplehurst
Kent
Teise. Tickets

Tenbury Fishing Association
Mrs L M Rickett
The Post House
Berrington Road
Tenbury Wells, Worcestershire
WR15 8EN

Tenterden and District Angling Club
J Whitehead
37 Shrubcote
Tenterden
Kent TN30 7BP

Test and Itchen Association Ltd
Jim Glasspool
West Haye, Itchen Abbas
Winchester SO21 1AX

Tewin Fly-Fishing Club
K F Atkins
9 Warren Way, Digswell
Welwyn, Hertfordshire
Mimram. Members only

Tewkesbury Popular Angling Association
R Smith
10 Tretawn Gardens
Newtown, Tewkesbury
Gloucestershire
Severn. Tickets

Thames Angling Preservation Society
A E Hodges
The Pines

32 Tile Kiln Lane
Bexley, Kent
(Crayford 25575). Voluntary body concerned with fishery improvement

Thameside Works Angling Society
c/o 200 Rochester Road
Gravesend
Kent DA12 4TY

Thatcham Angling Association
K G Roberts
12 Malham Road
Thatcham Farm
Thatcham, Berkshire
Kennet. No tickets

Thirsk Angling Club
R W Stephenson
76 New Estate, Norby
Thirsk, Yorkshire
Cod Beck, Thirsk and Swale. Tickets

Thornaby Angling Association
D Speight
10 Stainsby Gate
Thornaby
Cleveland
Tees, Eden, Swale, Ure. Members only

Thorne Coronation Angling Club
P Bingley
11 Birchwood Close
Thorne, Doncaster
S Yorks DN8 4HR

Thurrock Angling Club
D Nutt
94 Eriff Drive
South Ockendon, Essex
Lakes. No tickets

Tinsley and District Angling Clubs Association
D M Dearman
2 Trentham Close
Brinsworth
Rotherham, South Yorks S60 5LS

Tisbury Angling Club
H J Haskell
The Forge, Fovant
Salisbury
Wilts SP3 5JA

Tiverton and District Angling Club
R Retallick
21 Alstone Road
Canal Hill, Tiverton
Devon
Exe

Tiverton Fly Fishing Club
M J Ford
9 William Street
Tiverton, Devon
Exe. Limited tickets

Todmorden Angling Society
R Barber

12 Grisedale Drive
Burnley, Lancs
BB12 8AR
**Tonbridge Angling and Fish Preservation
Society**
R Keywood
1 Meadow Road
Tonbridge TN9 2SX
Torridge Fly Fishing Club
G Petschelt
Oak Cottage
Main Road, Bickington
Barnstaple, Devon EX31 2LT
Reservoirs
**Towcester and District Angling
Association**
J Buxton
9 Church View
Greens Norton
Northampton
Trent and Mersey Canal Angling Society
R Hankey, see Northwich AA
Trimpley Angling Association
10 College Road
Kidderminster
Worcestershire DY10 1LU
The Tring Anglers
P Welling
PO Box 1947
Tring, Herts HP23 5IZ
Grand Union Canal. Tickets
Tunbridge Wells Angling Association
A R Woodhams
19 Park Street
Tunbridge Wells
Kent.
Twickenham Piscatorial Society
L C Pallett
37 Stuart Way
Windsor, Berks
Kennet, Thame, pits. Tickets
Two Mills Flyfishers' Club
R Bricknell
Tallangatta
The Ley Box
Corsham, Wiltshire SN14 9LZ
By Brook. No tickets
Twyford Angling Club
G L Addy
16a Woods Road
Caversham, Reading,
Berkshire
Thames. No tickets
**Tyne Fishery District Riperian Owners
Association**
T Forster
Ravernsbourne
Bellingham, Hexham
Northumberland

Ulverston Angling Association
H B Whittam
29 Lyndhurst Road
Ulverston, Cumbria
Lakes, becks and canal. Tickets
Unity Angling Club
E K Mann
19 Busfield Street
Bradford, Yorks BD4 7QX
Upper Alde and Ore Angling Club
R C Foster
Maltings Farm, Aldham
Ipswich, Suffolk
Alde. Trout tickets
Upper Coquetdale Angling Club
C F Ranken
Clifton House
28 East Street, Whitburn
Tyne & Wear SR6 7BX
Upper Tamar Fishing Club
M Summers
Carey View, Tower Hill
St Giles on the Heath
Devon
Upper Tanat Fishing Club
George Lewis
c/o Crampton Pym and Lewis
The Poplars, Willow Street
Oswestry, Shropshire
Tanat. No tickets
Upper Teign Fishing Association
J Getliff
22 The Square
Chagford, Devon
Teign. Tickets
Upper Weardale Angling Association
H C Lee
School View
Wearhead, Bishop Auckland
Co Durham DL13 1BP
Wear. Tickets
Upton Angling Association
A Page
Severn View, Ripple
Nr Tewkesbury, Glos
Upton Angling Club
Anthony M Ankers
28 Queens Crescent
Upton-by-Chester
Cheshire CH2 1RG
Uttoxeter Angling Association
I E Davies
Three Oaks
Hollington Lane
Stramshall
Uttoxeter, Staffordshire
ST14 5AJ
Vauxhall Angling Club
R W Poulton

20 Leeches Way
Cheddington
Beds LU7 0SJ

Vectis Boating and Fishing Club
M T Sawyer
27 Salters Road
Ryde, Isle of Wight

Ventnor Angling Club
R Gibbons
43 Dudley Road
Ventnor, Isle of Wight

Victoria Angling Club
R Clive Hutter
The Victoria
King Street
Newcastle-under-Lyme
Stoke-on-Trent ST5 1HX

Victoria and Biddulph Angling Society
P Moston
73 Mayfield Road
Biddulph, Staffs ST8 7BX

Victoria Institute Angling Club, Arundel
S Worth
Tel: 0903 723569
River Arun

Wadebridge Angling Association
A Gill
Jasmine Cottage
Kelly Park
St Mabyn
Bodmin, Cornwall, PL30 3BL

Wakefield Angling Club
B D Harper
29 Victorian Crescent
Horsforth
Leeds

Waltham Abbey Angling Consortium
P King
32 Ashdown Crescent
Cheshunt, Herts EN8 0RS
Cornmill Stream

Walsall Izaak Walton Angling Society
38 Lichfield Road
Bloxwich, Walsall
W Mids WS3 3LY

Walton Sea Angling Club
Mr K L Brown
South View
1 Cliff Way
Frinton-on-Sea CO13 9NL
30 Naze Park Road
Walton-on-the-Naze, Essex

Walton-on-Thames Angling Society
A Finalyson
14 Harrow Road
West Belfont
Feltham,
Middlesex
Mole, lake. No tickets

Wansbeck Angling Association
A K Lowes
30 Stanton Drive
Pegswood
Morpeth,
Northumberland
Wansbeck. Members only

Wansford, Yarwell, Nassington and District Angling Club
C W J Howes
43 Elton Road, Stibbington
Wansford, Peterborough

Wantsum Angling Club
Mr East
18 Goodwin Road
Ramsgate, Kent CT11 0LP

Ware Angling Club
D Bridgeman
30 Musley Lane
Ware, Herts SG12 7EW

Wareham and District Angling Society
P Dominy
Tel: 0929 625337

Warmington Angling Club
I G W Brudenell
10 Church Street
Warmington
Peterborough PE8 1TE
No tickets.

Warminster and District Angling Club
D M M Vickers
113 Westleigh
Warminster
Wilts BA12 8NJ

Warrington Anglers' Association
F Lythgoe
PO Box 71
Warrington WA1 1LR
Lancashire
Dee, Severn and tributaries, Ribble, Dane, canal, lakes, etc. Members only

Warwick and District Angling Association
L C Sargeant
218 Warwick Road
Warwick CV8 1FD

Watchet Fishing Club
c/o The Gardeners Arms
Bishops Lydeard
Taunton, Somerset

Waterbeach Angling Club
H Reynolds
3 Crosskeys Court
Cottenham, Cambs

Waterside Angling Association
A Chivers
57 Specklemead, Paulton
Near Bristol
Cam Brook

**Wath Brow and Ennerdale Angling
  Association**
D F Whelan
11 Crossing Close
Cleator Moor, Cumberland
Ehen. Tickets
Watford Piscators
N F Brandon
25 Leaford Crescent
Watford,
Hertfordshire
Gade, canal, lakes
Wear and Tees Fishery Association
C H Noble
30 The Green
Hurworth on Tees
Darlington, Co Durham
**Wellingborough and District Nene
  Angling Club**
K J Billington
22 Hillary Road
Rushden NN10 9NZ
**Wellington (Somerset) Angling
  Association**
M Cave
1 Chitterwell Cottage
Sampford Arundell
Wellington, Somerset
Tone. Tickets
Wellworthy Angling Club
I H Dibble
28 Longstone Avenue
Bridgwater
Welshpool Angling Association
F Eakins
Westwood Park Hotel
Salop Road
Welshpool, Powys
Severn, Mule, Rhiew and Banwy. Some
permits
Wem Angling Club
N T Mansfield
38 Bowens Field
Wem, Shropshire
Lake. Tickets
Wensleydale Angling Association
Mr Scarr
Cravenholme Farm
Bainbridge
Leyburn DL8 3EG
Yore. Tickets
Wessex Federation of Angling Clubs
J J Mathrick
Perham Farmhouse
Wick, Langport
Somerset TA10 0NN
Parret, Isle; affiliated clubs share rights
West Bay Sea Angling Club
Mr D George

4 Kingfisher Court
West Bay
Bridport, Dorset
DT6 4HQ
West Country Fly Fishers
J W Hamilton Roberts
64 Hampton Park
Redland, Bristol BS6 6LJ
West End Anglers
Malcolm Young
Carson House
2 Battlehouse Road
Stocksfield NE43 7QZ
The West End Angling Club
77 Travers Road
Sandiacre, Notts
The West End Angling Club
D J Abbotts
229 Corbridge Road
Hamley
Stoke-on-Trent ST1 5JP
Western Wight Angling Club
Mrs R A Pearson
The Quarn
Moortown Lane
Brighstone, IoW
West Ham Angling Society
M J Groman
46 Cobden Road
Leytonstone E11
Lee. Some tickets
West Hampstead Angling Society
E Baker
38 Townholme Crescent
Hanwell
London W7 2NA
Westminster Angling Society
N Patterson
118 Hall Place
London W2 1NF
Club fishes Paddington Basin
**Weston-super-Mare and District Angling
  Association**
K Tucker
26 Coniston Crescent
Weston-super-Mare, Avon
Westwater Angling
3 Crossways
East Bolton
Tyne & Wear NE36 0LP
Wellington Angling Association
M Cave
1 Chitterwell Cottage
Sampford Arundell
Wellington
Somerset
Weswater Angling Club
The Clubhouse
Hallington Reservoirs

Colwell, Hexham
Northumberland
Wetherby and District Angling Club
F H Atkinson
Quarry Farm
Kirk Deighton
Wetherby, Yorkshire
Wharfe. Tickets
Weybridge Angling Club
P Daymon
61 Byron Road, Addlestone
Weybridge, Surrey
Wey Navigation Angling Amalgamation
Secretary
c/o Village Hall
Byfleet
Surrey
Weymouth Angling Society
L Thomas
Angling HQ
Commercial Road
Weymouth, Dorset
Wheatsheaf Angling Club
J P Jeffrey
73 Springfield Road
Sherburn-in-Elmet
Leeds LS25 6DF
Wheelock Angling Society
A Darlington
Overland House, Moss Lane
Elsworth
Sandbach,
Cheshire
Whitbread Angling Club
J Stokes
326 Longford Lane
Longford, Gloucester GL2 9BX
Whitchurch Angling Association
Alan Smout
34 Alkington Gardens
Whitchurch, Shropshire
SY13 1TQ
White Eagle Anglers
F A Edensor
24 Lichfield Road
Stafford ST17 4LL
White Hart Dagenham Angling Society
D Brown
100 Crescent Road
Dagenham, Essex
White Swan Piscatorial Society
C E Clarke

186 Walford Road
Birmingham B11 1GE
Whitmore Reans Const. Angling Association
R H Hughes
Star Chamber
Princes Square
Wolverhampton
West Midlands
Whitstable and District Angling Society
Mr Foyle
48 Albert Street
Whitstable, Kent
Whitstable Sea Fishing Association
H S Noel
34 Grimshill Road
Whitstable, Kent
Whittlesey Angling Association
J Canham
12 Aliwal Road
Whittlesey
Peterborough PE7 2AY
Nene, Twenty Foot, Cock Bank, pits
Tickets
Wigan and District Angling Association
G Wilson
11 Guildford Avenue
Chorley,
Lancashire
PR6 8TG
Ribble, Wyre, Winster, Lake Windermere, reservoirs, flashes, ponds. Tickets
Wigston Angling Society
P A Hebborn
87 Hillcrest Avenue
Kibworth Beauchamp,
Leics LE8 0NH
Canal tickets
Willington and District Angling Club
R Lumb
18 Shipley Terrace
West View Estate
Crook, County Durham
Wear; dt
Wilmslow and District Angling Association
P H Curbishley
16 Alderdale Grove
Wilmslow,
Cheshire
No tickets

Fishing Clubs

When you appoint a new secretary, do not forget to give us details of the change. Write to the publishers (address at front of the book). Thank you!

Wilton Fly-Fishing Club
J D Mcgill
Hillside Cottages
60 Church Rd
Sundridge
Sevenoaks
Kent TN14 6EA
Wylye. Limited membership

Wimbleball Fly Fishers Club
A D Ridgeway
13 Glen Drive
Taunton, Somerset
TA2 7RG

Wimborne and District Angling Club
Tim Powell
25 Kirkway
Broadstone, Dorset
BH18 8ED

Winkworth Fly Fishers
M Richardson
87 Summers Road
Farncombe
Godalming, Surrey

Windermere, Ambleside and District Angling Association
Martin Lazenby
Low Ghyll
Smithy Lane
Bowness on Windemere
Cumbria LA23 3AR
Rothay, Troutbeck and Rydal Water Tickets

Windmill Angling Association
N Gooding
11 Chilkwell Street
Glastonbury
Somerset
Butleigh Wootton Lake

Windsor Angling Society
G E Johncey
2 Bradshaw Close
Windsor, Berkshire
Thames

Winsford and District Angling Association
J Stewart Bailey
22 Plover Avenue
Winsford CW7 1LA

Wiremill Angling Club
M Aldous
4 Ward Lane,
Warlingham
Surrey

Wirrall Game Fishing Club
Derek Jones
31 Meadway
Upton, Wirral

Wisbech and District Angling Association
B Lakey

The Cot
Leverington Common
Wisbech, Cambridgeshire

Witham and Dist Joint Anglers Federation
R Hobley
30 Gunby Avenue,
Lincoln LN6 0AW

Witham Sea Anglers Club
Leonard Harding
65 Chelmer Road
Witham,
Essex

Witney Angling Society
M V S Mann
86 Early Road
Witney 0X8 6EU
Members only

Woking and District Angling Association
D Powell
Maymont
Guildford Road, Knaphill
Woking, Surrey
Wey. Tickets

Wolsingham Angling Association
D J Peart
37 West End
Wolsingham
Co Durham DL13 3AS

Woodbridge and District Angling Club
T Pryke
12 Bredford Road
Woodbridge, Suffolk

Woodford Angling Society
Honorary Secretary
22 Evanrigg Terrace
Woodford Green, Essex
Roding. Members only

Wooler and Doddington Angling Association
T Ehitlock
6 Cottage Road
Wooler, Northumberland
NE1 6AA

Wootton Bassett Angling Club
T Strange
15 Shakespeare Road
Wootton Bassett
Swindon, Wiltshire
Lake, Brinkworth Brook. Members only

Worcester Angling Club
R Bullock
406 Ombersley Road
Worcester

Worcester and District United Anglers' Association
Barbourne Ex Service Men's Club
The Moors,
Worcester

Workington Angling Association
Dr A B Culdicott
51 St Andrews Road
Stainburn
Workington, Cumbria
Worksop and District Amalgamated Anglers Association
G Williams
9 Edwards Street
Worksop, Notts
Canals and Trent. Tickets
Wormleighton Fishing Club
J Roe
47 Northumberland Road
Coventry CV1 3AP
Worthing and District Piscatorial Society (Freshwater)
Tickets from
Ken Denman Ltd
2 Marine Place
Worthing
Rivers Arun and Adur
Worthing Sea Anglers' Association
M Kempster
Flat 1, 8 Navarino Road
Worthing, Sussex
Headquarters. Worthing Pier, Worthing, Sussex
Wroxham Angling Club
B Westgate
31 The Paddocks
Norwich NR6 7HF
Wyche Anglers Club
F McGarry
91 London Road
Nantwich
Cheshire CW5 6LH
Wylye Fly-Fishing Club
Commander P D Hoare, RN (Retd)
Monks Farm House
Corsham,
Wiltshire
Members and guests only

Wymondham Angling Club
T Binks
25 Rosemary Road
Sprowston,
Norwich NR7 8ER
Yarm Angling Association
A W Allen
4 Blenavon Court
Yarm
Stockton-on-Tees,
Cleveland
Tees. Tickets
Yeovil-Sherborne Angling Association
N Garrett
18 Springfield Road
Yeovil,
Somerset
Trout and coarse fish on Yeo and tributaries; two ponds
York Angling Association
39 Lowfields Drive
Acomb
York YO2 3DQ
Derwent, Pocklington Canal. Tickets and match bookings
York Fly Fishers' Club
J Rowbottom
35 Huntington Road
York YO3 7RL
Trout lakes. No tickets
York Tradesmen's Angling Association
J R May
1 Neville Drive
Bishopthorpe,
York
Various becks. Members only
Yorkshire Flyfishers' Club
Honorary Secretary
2 Devonshire Crescent
Leeds LS8 1EP
Yorkshire Eden, Eamont, Lyvennet, Ribble and Yore. No tickets

---

Fishing Clubs

WELSH FISHING STATIONS

In the pages that follow, the catchment area of Wales, are given in alphabetical order, being interspersed with the streams and the lakes of the Principality under headings such as 'Powys (streams)'; 'Gwynedd (lakes)', etc. The rivers of each catchment area are arranged in the manner described under the heading 'English Fishing Stations', on p.21 and the other notes given there apply equally to Wales. The whole of the Wye and the Severn, it should be remembered, are included in the section on England, while the whole of the Dee is listed among the Welsh rivers.

Note: *Sea trout are commonly referred to as 'sewin' in Wales although some associations define sewin as immature sea trout returning to the river for the first time.*

AERON

(For close seasons, licences, etc, see Welsh Region NRA, see p18)

Rises in Llyn Eiddwen, 7m north-west of Tregaron, and flows about 17m to sea at Aberaeron. Excellent run of sewin from June onwards with smaller salmon run. Brown trout plentiful but small.

Aberaeron (Dyfed). Salmon, sea trout and brown trout. Aberaeron Town AC has a 2½m stretch on R Aeron; 3m on **Arth**, a stream to the north, which holds fine brown trout and has an excellent run of sea trout; and 3 stretches on **Teifi,** north of Lampeter. Permits from Ceilee Sports, Bridge St. Tackle shop: F K Moulton & Son, Aeron Sports & Fishing Tackle, 6 Water St.

Talsarn (Dyfed). Salmon, sea trout, carp, tench and rudd. Fishing on ½m stretch of Aeron; one coarse pond; and one trout pool. Day permits from Mr A R Parkin, Cilbwn, Talsarn, Lampeter.

ANGLESEY (streams)

(For close seasons, licences, etc, see Welsh Region NRA, p.18)

ALAW: Rises above Cors y Bol bog and flows some 7m to sea beyond **Llanfachraeth,** opposite Holyhead. Fishes well (trout) for first three months of season and again in September when good run of small sea trout expected; usually too low in summer. Permission of farmers.

BRAINT: Small stream which flows almost whole width of the island, parallel with Menai Straits, to sea at Aber Menai, beyond **Llangeinwen.** Trout, some sea trout, but usually fishable only first three months of season. Permission of farmers.

CEFNI: Rises above Llangwyllog, flows through Llyn Frogwy, on to **Llangefni** and Cefni Reservoir, and then to sea in 6m. Lower reaches canalised. Only fairsized river in island. Brown trout and chance of late salmon or sea trout. Permission of farmers.

CEINT: Small stream entering sea at Red Wharf Bay; some trout; permission of farmers; summer conditions difficult. Fishing station: **Pentraeth.**

FFRAW or GWNA: Under the name of Gwna rises 4m above **Bodorgan** and waters Llyn Coron just below village. Stream then takes name of Ffraw and runs to sea at **Aberffraw** in 2m. Little more than brook. One or two pools fishable early on, but overgrown June onwards. Trout, some sea trout.

WYGYR: Small stream falling into sea at Cemaes Bay. Trout; restocked.

Cemaes (Gwynedd). Wygyr FA has about 2m (both banks); permits from Treasurer. Good sea fishing in bay. Hotel: Harbour, Cemaes Bay; Cefn Glas Inn, Llanfechell.

ANGLESEY (lakes)

Llyn Alaw. Llanerchymedd (Gwynedd). Situated in open lowland countryside this productive 777 acre reservoir offers fly fishing, spinning and worming, for brown and rainbow trout. Season 20 March - 17 Oct for brown. 14 March - 31 Oct for rainbow. Dt £8, evening £7.50, st £300, from Visitor Centre at reservoir (dt and evening from machine in car park). Concessions to OAPs, juniors and disabled.

Boat for disabled available at no extra charge. Further information available from Llyn Alaw Visitor Centre, Llantrisant, Holyhead, Anglesey, Gwynedd LL65 4TW (tel: 0407 730762). **Parc Newydd Trout Fisheries**, 5 acre, manmade lake; stocked with trout. Accommodation also available in self-catering cottages. For further information contact Mrs Edna Evans, Parc Newydd, Nr Llanerchymedd LL71 7BT.

Bodafon Lake. Llanallgo (Gwynedd). Rudd and tench; contact Trescawen Estate, Anglesey, Gwynedd.

Cefni Reservoir. Llangefni (Gwynedd). 172 acres. Brown and rainbow trout; fly only; good wading; boats. Leased by Welsh Water plc to Cefni AA. Permits from D G Evans (Treasurer), Wenllys, Capel Coen, Llangefni; dt and wt from Ken Johnson, Tackle and Guns, Devon House, Water St, Menai Bridge and D Rowe, Jewellers, Llangefni. Hotels: Nant yr Odyn Country; Tre Ysgawen Hall.

Llyn Coron. Bodorgan (Gwynedd). Trout, sea trout; fly only. St £90, wt £30, dt £6 and evening tickets £5. St and NRA licences from Bodorgan Estate Office, Gwynedd LL62 5LP; other tickets available at lake.

Ty Hen Lake. Rhosneigr (Gwynedd). 1½ acres of natural spring water (Ph 7.8, nitrate 0.01) for specimen carp, tench, roach and rudd. Dt £5 available at lake.

All fish to be returned to water. Cottage and caravan self-catering family holidays with fishing, and information available from Mr Bernard Summerfield, Ty Hen Farm, Station Road, LL64 5QZ (tel: 0407 810331 or mobile: 0831 535583). Tackle shop: Tackle Bar, William St, Holyhead. Hotel: Maelog. Accommodation: Mrs Williams, Bodwina Farm, Gwalchmai, Anglesey LL65 4RL (tel. 0407 720233).

Llywenan Lake. Bodedern (Gwynedd). Brown trout. Apply to H T Radcliffe, Bryn Adfed, Bodedern.

Llyn Maelog. Rhosneigr (Gwynedd). Roach, perch, rudd, bream, brown trout. Permission to fish from various landowners. Information, licences and tackle (not bait) from K D Highfield, 7 Marine Terrace, Rhosneigr. Hotels: Maelog Lake, Cefn Dref, and Glan Neigr.

Llyn y Gors. Llandegfan (Gwynedd). 5 acres coarse fishery, two lakes. Mixed lake with carp, tench, roach, rudd and perch ; and carp lake with carp to 25lb. Permits, tackle and bait available on site. Self-catering cottages available. Further information from Llyn y Gors, Llandegfan, Menai Bridge, Anglesey, LL59 5PN (tel: 0248 713410, fax: 0248 716324). Trout fishing on **Llyn Jane**; 3 small, man-made lakes including pool for juniors. Contact Dewi & Linda Owen, Bryngwyn, Llandegfan.

CLEDDAU (Eastern and Western)
(For close seasons, licences, etc, see Welsh Region NRA, p18)

East Cleddau rises on the east side of Prescelly Mountains and flows 15m south-west, partly along old Carmarthenshire border, to north branch of Milford Haven. West Cleddau rises in the hills and valleys south-west of Mathry and flows east towards Castle Morris. It is joined by streams such as the Afon Cleddau and Nant-y-Bugail and then flows south-east to Wolf's Castle. Here it is joined by the Afon Anghof and Afon Glan Rhyd. It then flows south to Haverfordwest and on to join the E Cleddau in a creek in the Haven. Fishing for sewin and trout is mainly in June, July and August; for salmon in August.

WESTERN CLEDDAU: Salmon, sewin and trout.

Haverfordwest (Dyfed). Pembrokeshire AA has 15m stretch from Wolf's Castle to Haverfordwest; salmon, sea trout, brown trout; st £34, wt £34, dt £6; permits from County Sports, 3 Old Bridge; facilities for disabled in field at Nan-y-Coy. Further information from hon sec. Hamdden Ltd manages 2 reservoirs in the area on behalf of Welsh Water plc. **Llysyfran Reservoir** (212 acres), rainbow trout reared on in cages within the reser-

voir and brown trout. Season Mar - 31 Oct; winter fishing at weekends only until mid Dec; catch limit 6 fish (evening 3 fish); size limit 10"; boats available; permits and tackle from Visitor Centre Shop. **Rosebush Reservoir** (33 acres) brown trout fishery in Prescelly Hills. Now operated by local syndicate but bank and boat rods available from Llysyfran Reservoir; advanced booking advisable. For further information contact T Davies, Visitors Centre, Llysyfran Reservoir, Clarbeston Road, Nr Haverfordwest,

Disabled anglers go afloat on Llys-y-Fran Reservoir, Dyfed, for an international competition. *Photo: Al Mogridge.*

Dyfed SA63 4RR (tel: 0437 532273/532694). **Hayscastle Trout Fishery**, 3 acre, stocked trout lake; fly only. Booking advisable. Permits from Hayscastle Trout Fishery, Upper Hayscastle Farm, Hayscastle, Dyfed (tel. 0348 840393). Riparian owners may give permission elsewhere. Sewin fishing good June to August. Rosemoor Country Cottages, Walwyns Castle, accommodation and fly fishing in 5 acre lake on a trout stream which is stocked annually; tuition available. Hotels: Mariners.
EASTERN CLEDDAU. Trout in all rivers and tributaries in E Cleddau area but little angling activity; stocks mostly small fish under 7½". Trout, sewin and salmon in **Syfynwy**, a tributary of E Cleddau.

Llandissilio (Dyfed). Fishing in E Cleddau controlled by individual syndicates as far as the ford at Llandissilio; day tickets are sold at Langwm Farm, Llandissilio. Upstream seek farmers permission. Downstream it is difficult and expensive to join syndicates. Glancleddau Farm, Felinfach and Landre Egremont have holiday caravan parks where visitors enjoy some of the best fishing in the area. NRA rod licences from Post Office, Felinfach.

CLWYD

(For close seasons, licences, etc, see Welsh Region NRA, p18)

A celebrated sea trout and salmon river which has its source in the high ground to the north of Corwen and runs down through Ruthin, passes Denbigh, St Asaph and Rhuddlan and finally enters the Irish Sea at Rhyl.

Best fished for sea trout from June onwards as these fish tend to run during latter part of the month. The native brown trout population is composed of small fish, though stocking of larger specimens is undertaken annually by most of the angling clubs. There are no coarse fish species in this area.

Rhyl (Clwyd). Salmon, sea trout, brown trout. No permits needed for stretch from sea to railway bridge, however, no holding pools therefore salmon and sea trout tend to run straight through; for salmon, trout and eels, NRA licence needed; close season 30 Sept-31 May. Rhyl and District AA has excellent fishing on **Elwy** and **Clwyd**. Approx 10m, 4 beats on Clwyd and 6 beats on Elwy. Members only. St £70 + £100 joining fee; apply to hon sec. Waiting list approx 1 year. No day tickets. Concessions for juveniles. **Llyn Aled Isaf** is a Chester AA water; assn also has private fishing on **Rough Hill Farm Lake**; st £9 (jun £3). **Tan-y-Mynydd Lake**, rainbow, brown and brook trout from 1½ to 10lb; purpose-built trout lakes, total 4 acres. Permits from A Jones, Moelfre, Abergele, Clwyd. Self-catering cottages also available. Tackle shops: Wm Roberts Ltd, 131 High St; Harry's Fishing Tackle, 20 Queens Market Hall, Sussex St.

St Asaph (Clwyd). Salmon, sea trout and brown trout. St Asaph AA has excellent and various fishing: 6 beats on Clwyd; 2 beats on **Elwy**, 4m in St Asaph area and 1m double bank at Llanfair Talhaiarn; a beat on **Aled**, 1½m double bank at **Llansannan**; and an excellent beat on **Conwy** at Bettws-y-Coed. St £47 (OAP £31, jun £16, parent + juniors £63) + £45 joining fee. Day permits available for Elwy; dt £3 on Llanfair Talhaiarn beat (unlimited rods), from Black Lion Hotel and Foxon's Tackle; and dt £6 on Gypsy Lane beat (limited rods), from Foxon's Tackle. Tackle shop: Foxon's Tackle, Penrhewl Post Office, St Asaph (tel: 0745 583583). Hotel: Oriel House.

Denbigh (Clwyd). Clwyd, 2m E; salmon,

Check before you go

While every effort has been made to ensure that the information given in **Where to Fish** *is correct, the position is continually changing, and anglers are urged, in their own interests, to make enquiries before travelling to selected venues. This is especially important with reference to prices quoted. Anglers attention is also drawn to the fact that hotels mentioned under the various fishing stations do not necessarily have water of their own. Any amendments or further data for inclusion in subsequent editions, and any criticism, will be welcome.*

sea trout, brown trout. Denbigh & Clwyd AC has extensive water on Clwyd, **Ystrad, Elwy, Wheeler,** and also on small stocked trout lake; members only, waiting list. Tickets from hon sec or Treasurer, Barclays Bank. **Llyn Brenig** and **Alwen Reservoirs,** 11m SW; trout. **Llyn Aled,** 11m SW; coarse. Permits for Llyn Brenig, Alwen and Llyn Aled; from machines at Visitor Centre, Llyn Brenig.

Coarse fishing at **Lleweni Parc,** Mold Road, Denbigh. Tackle shop: Toys & Tackle, 9 Henllan St. Hotel: Fron Haul.

Ruthin (Clwyd). Trout, salmon, sea trout. Denbigh & Clwyd AC has water on Clwyd and on **River Clywedog;** members only. NRA licences from G H Smith, Llais-yr-Afon, Bontuchel, Ruthin. Hotel: Ruthin Castle.

Tributaries of the Clwyd

ELWY: Brown trout, sea trout (June onwards), salmon. No coarse fish.

St Asaph (Clwyd). St Asaph AA has Gypsy Lane Waters: dt £6 from Foxon's Tackle, St Asaph. Capenhurst AC has water; salmon, trout and grayling; member only. **Felin-y-Gors Fisheries,** brown and rainbow trout; 4 lakes; fly only. Fish caught are weighed, cleaned and packed, or smoked, free of charge (filleting of fish, if required, will incur a small charge per fish). Tuition and accommodation also available. Bookings in advance from Robert Monshin, St Asaph Road, Bodelwyddan, Clwyd LL18 5UY (tel: 0745 584044).

Llanfair Talhaiarn (Clwyd). St Asaph AA has water: dt £3; from Black Lion Hotel, Llanfair-Talhaiarn.

Llansannan (Clwyd). St Asaph AA has 1½m double bank on Aled. **Dolwen** and **Plas Uchaf Reservoirs** a few miles SW of St Asaph; well stocked with brown and rainbow trout; fly, spinning and worming; 6 fish limit. Season 14 Mar - 31 Oct. Dt £6.50 (evening £5.50); from D & J Davies, Newsagents, 12 Church View, Bodelwyddan, St Asaph (tel: 0745 582206). Booking advised as rods limited to 16. Concession OAP and jun.

WHEELER: Trout.

Afonwen (Clwyd). Denbigh & Clwyd AC has 2m; some fly only. Mold Trout A has 1¼m. Mold Kingfishers AC has fishing on Wheeler and on lake at Afonwen.

CLYWEDOG: Salmon and sea trout (very late), trout. All water strictly preserved.

Ruthin (Clwyd). Denbigh & Clwyd AC has stretch from confluence with Clwyd to Rhewl; and has water in Bontuchel and Llanrhaeadr areas; member only. Capenhurst AC has stretch at Bontuchel; salmon, sea trout and trout; members only. Members children (under 18) may fish free of charge, but must be accompanied by adult.

CONWY

(For close seasons, licences, etc, see Welsh Region NRA, p18)

Rises on Migneint, in Gwynedd and flows between the old Caernarvonshire and Denbighshire boundaries for much of its course, emptying into the Irish Sea near Conwy. The upper part of its valley is noted for its beauty. Spate river with salmon runs throughout season (May and June usually best); grilse early July; sea trout late June to September.

Conwy (Gwynedd). Tidal; sea fishing only. Codling, dabs, plaice, bass and mullet above and below suspension bridge. Boats available. Salmon and sea trout; Prince Albert AS has ½m on Conwy, 6m from Conwy. **Llyn Gwern Engan,** a small lake on Sychnant Pass Common; rudd, tench, carp, gudgeon; free fishing available, contact Snowdonia National Park Committee, Penrhydeudraeth, Gwynedd. **Clobryn Pool,** Clobryn Rd, Colwyn Bay; tench, crucian carp, roach, rudd, perch. **Llyn Nant-y-Cerrig,** Brynymaen, 1½ acres, bream, carp, roach, rudd, tench. **Glas Coed Pools;** Bodelwyddan, set in grounds of

Keep the banks clean

Several clubs have stopped issuing tickets to visitors because of the state of the banks after they have left. Spend a few moments clearing up.

Bodelwyddan Castle, carp, tench, roach, rudd. Permits for Clobrin Pool, Llyn Nant-y-Cerrig and Glas Coed Pools from The Tackle Box, 17 Greenfield Rd, Colwyn Bay LL29 8EL (tel. 0492 531104); the shop offers a full list of trout, coarse and specialist waters in the area and the proprietor (a previous Welsh bass champion) can also advise on all aspects of local sea fishing.

Dolgarrog (Gwynedd). Salmon, sea trout and brown trout; deep tidal pools. Dolgarrog FC has tidal water. Club also has rainbow and brown trout fishing on **Llyn Coedty**; and trout fishing on **Llyn Eigiau**. Permits from hon sec. **Llyn Melynllyn**, 5m E; **Llyn Dulyn**, 6m E; **Llyn Cowlyd** (5m W Llanwrst); all trout reservoirs belonging to Welsh Water plc; free to licence holders. Enquiries to Dwr Cymru, Conwy Unit Office, Cefndy Road, Rhyl, Clwyd LL18 2HG.

Llanrwst (Gwynedd). Salmon and good sea trout; brown trout poor. Llanrwst AC has 1¼m, both banks. Limited wt £45 (to 12 Sept only) from hon sec and The Old Library Tackle Shop, Bridge St. Sunday fishing allowed. Permits from Forestry Commission, Gwydyr Uchaf, for left bank of **Machno** from junction with Conwy and portion of right bank. Dt 60p, from P Haveland, Manchester House, Penmachno. Tackle shop: Gwen Booth, The Square. Hotels: Maenan Abbey, Vic-

toria (both have salmon and trout).
Betws-y-Coed (Gwynedd). Salmon, sea trout, brown trout. Betws-y-Coed AC has 4½m of salmon, sea trout and brown trout fishing on Conwy and **Llygwy**; on the Conwy, from the Waterloo Bridge (left bank) downstream to the confluence of the **Llygwy**. The club also three trout lakes: **Elsi Lake**, stocked with American brook trout and brown trout; **Llyn Goddionduon**, stocked with brown trout; and **Llyn Bychan**. St £105 from hon sec; wt (Mon-Fri) £40 and dt £15 (river) and £10 (lake) from Mr G Parry, Tan Lan Café (nr Post Office). No wt or dt after end of August and no weekend river tickets for visitors. Concessions jun. St Asaph AA has ¾m stretch. Gwydyr Hotel has 8m of salmon and sea trout fishing; season 20 Mar - 17 Oct; tickets for residents only. For further information contact Owen Wainwright, Gwydyr Hotel, Bangor Road, Betws-y-Coed LL24 0AB (tel: 0690 710777). Tackle available at hotel. Bryn Trych Hotel has salmon, trout and sea trout fishing on Conwy, tributaries and lakes. Other hotels: Craig-y-Dderwen Country House; Waterloo.
Ysbyty Ifan (Gwynedd). Brown trout. National Trust has stretch at Ysbyty Ifan and Dinas Water on upper Conwy; fly only. Permits from National Trust, Trinity Square, Llandudno, Gwynedd; and R Ellis, Bryn Ryffud, Padog, Betws-y-Coed.

Tributaries of the Conwy

ROE: Trout.
Rowen (Gwynedd). Fly fishing impossible on lower reaches. **Conwyn Valley Fisheries**, 2 acre, spring fed lake, rainbow trout, fly only, all year round. Tackle is available for hire and fly fishing lessons can be arranged. Shop stocks flies and accessories. Accommodation available at Glyn Isa in 4 self-contained cottages with free fishing on Conwy Valley Fisheries. Contact Conwyn Valley Fisheries, Glyn Isa, Rowen, Nr Conwy LL32 8PT (tel. 0492 650063).
DDU: Trout.
Pont Dolgarrog (Gwynedd). Trout. Ddu enters Conwy ½m below village; drains Llyn Cowlyd. **Llyn Cowlyd**, brown trout and Artic char; fly only; free permits from Welsh Water plc, Conwy Unit Office, Cefndy Road, Rhyl, Clwyd LL18 2HG (tel. 0244 550015).
CRAFNANT: Trout.

Trefriw (Gwynedd). Trout and coarse fishing on Llyn Crafnant, one of the most beautiful lakes in Wales, 60 acres, stocked rainbow trout supplementing wild brown trout. Sunday fishing. Day tickets, rod licences, boats and information from Mr & Mrs J Collins, Lakeside Café, Llyn Crafnant, Trefriw, LL27 0JZ (tel: 0492 640818). Hotel: Princes Arms.
LLEDR: Trout, sewin, salmon.
Dolwyddelan (Gwynedd). Plas Hall Hotel has stretch, salmon and sea trout; available to residents and limited number of day tickets. Permits from Plas Hall Hotel, Pont-y-Pant, Dolwyddelan LL25 0PJ. Dolwyddelan FA has salmon, sea trout and brown trout fishing; most of both banks from village to Pont-y-Pant. Permits from Post Office or hon sec. Prince Albert AS has stretch here; enquire hon sec. Llynnau Diwaunedd (two) 3m W; trout; preserved.

LLYGWY: Salmon, sea trout, brown trout. **Betws-y-Coed** (Gwynedd). Betws-y-Coed AC has stretch from Swallow Falls downstream to the confluence of Conwy on right bank and to railway bridge on left bank. Permits from Tan Lan Café, Betws-y-Coed. **MACHNO:** Trout. **Penmachno** (Gwynedd). National Trust has water on Machno; brown trout; fly only. Permits from National Trust, Trinity Sq, Llandudno, Gwynedd; and R Ellis, Bryn Ryffud, Padog, Betws-y-Coed. **NUG:** Trout. **Pentrefoelas** (Gwynedd). Now private, advance applications may be considered, apply to Cooke Wood & Caird, 154 High Street, Bangor LL57 1NU.

DEE (Welsh)

(For close seasons, licences, etc, see Welsh Region NRA, p18)

Usually has a spring run of fish up to 30lb. Grilse enter in June and there is a run of grilse and summer fish until the end of the season as a rule. In spring most fish are taken from Bangor to Corwen. Trout from Bangor upstream and grayling above Llangollen. Coarse fish predominate downstream of Bangor. River holds good bream, roach, dace, perch and pike.

Holywell (Clwyd). Holywell A has fishing on **Llyn Helyg;** carp, tench, pike, roach, rudd; members only. Rainbow and brown trout fishing at **Forest Hill Trout Farm,** Mostyn, Nr Holywell, CH8 9EQ (tel. 0745 560151); 2 shaded peaceful lakes fed by spring water, stocked with home reared rainbow and brown trout, fly or bait. **Seven Springs Trout Farm and Fishery,** Caerwys, Nr Holywell, CH7 5AT (tel. 0352 720511); 4 pools containing rainbow trout and 2 pools containing rainbow trout, bream, tench and carp; fishing tackle hire and tuition. Coarse fishing at **Gym Castle Fishery,** Llanasa, Nr Holywell CH8 9BG (tel. 0352 853500), 3 acre lake stocked with carp, rudd and tench; barbless hooks only. Fishermen's hut with tea and coffee-making facilities. Dt £12.50; only 5 permits per day allowed. Permits from Mr & Mrs Ellis, Gym Castle Estate, South Lodge, Glan-yr-Afon (tel. 0745 561677). Greenfield Valley Trust AC issue permits for **Flour Mill Pool;** 4 acre fishery situated in Greenfield Valley Heritage Park; stocked with roach, rudd and carp. Delyn Borough Council issue a free guide to angling in Delyn, contact Delyn Borough Council, Civic Offices Holywell, Clwyd CH8 7LX.

Connah's Quay (Clwyd). Connah's Quay and Dist AC has 2m trout fishing at **Wepre Brook;** 2½m trout and coarse fishing on **River Alyn;** no dt. Club also has coarse fishing at **Wepre Pool, Swan Lake** and **Cymau Pools;** st and dt from Deeside Tackle & Sport, Chester Road, Shotton, Deeside. Tackle shop: Mrs I M Williams, 316 High Street, Connah's Quay.

Chester (Cheshire). Coarse fish. Little permit-free fishing. No licence for coarse fishing in tidal waters. Most fishing on River Dee controlled by Chester AA. Assn also has fishing on **River Vyrnwy, River Severn, Llyn Aled Isaf** and **Rough Hill Farm Lake** at Marlston-cum-Lache. Regular matches for juniors with free entry and reduced membership. St £9 (OAP and jun £3) for trout and coarse fishing only from hon sec or Chester area tackle shops. Free fishing is available Mon to Fri, on Eaton Estate from public footpath that adjoins river; beat can be booked through V Hedley, 6 Percy Rd, Handbridge, Chester. **River Gowy,** which runs into Mersey, passing by Mickle Trafford about 3m from Chester; Warrington AA has water. **Meadow Fishery,** Mickle Trafford, rainbow trout; 5 acres; st and dt. Tel: 024 300 236. Tackle shops: Henry Monk (Gunmaker), 8 Queen Street; David Gibson, Upper Northgate St; Jones Fishing Tackle & Pet Foods, 39 Vernon Rd; Hoole Angling Centre, 17 Hoole Rd, Hoole.

Holt (Clwyd). Salmon, trout, pike, bream. Holt and Farndon AA has stretch at Holt; bream, dace, roach, perch; st and dt from hon sec. Dee AA rent approx 10m of Dee from Chester AA in the Farndon and Sutton Green area. Maps can be obtained from hon sec, price 30p plus SAE. Assn issues salmon permits (limited) for Sutton Green stretch; separate trout and coarse fish permits. Permits from local tackle shops and B W Roberts, 23 Alpraham Crescent, Upton, Chester. Maghull and Lydiate AC has stretch on Dee at Lower Hall; roach, bream, chub, perch, sea trout, salmon, trout and gudgeon;

members only. Membership £20 and £10 (junior, OAP and disabled). Instruction for juniors and competitive events for all members. Grosvenor AA has stretch at Shocklach; member only, limited number. Warrington AA has Shocklach Water and stretch at Almere; members only, but visiting anglers accommodated, providing they supply date of visit in advance. Lavister AC, which affiliated to Chester AA and North Wales Federation of Coarse Anglers, has stretch at Almere; bream, dace, roach, perch; members only, number limited. Kirkdale AA has 2m at Holt; members only. Cheshire AA has 1m on Dee upstream of Farndon Bridge, south bank.

Bangor-on-Dee (Clwyd). Salmon, trout, coarse fish. Bangor-on-Dee AA has stretch downstream. Permits from hon sec. Northern A has stretches on **Dee** and **Worthenbury Brook;** club also has fishing on **Shropshire Union Canal** and **River Alyn;** members only. Warrington AA has water on Worthenbury Brook.

Overton (Clwyd). Salmon, sea trout, trout, coarse fish; Bryn-y-Pys AA has approx 7m between Overton Bridge and Bangor-on-Dee; no salmon fishing; pike fishing allowed in salmon pools from 16 Oct to 25 Jan using live bait only. St £24 plus £10. Dt £7. Permits from Deggy's Fishing Tackle, 2 Ruabon Road, Wrexham. Boat Inn, Erbistock, has salmon and trout beat. **Trench Fisheries** have 2 pools with brook, brown and rainbow trout fishing; 1½ acres; contact A Huntloch, Trench Farm, Red Hall Lane, Penley, Nr Wrexham (tel: Overton-on-Dee 233).

Cefn Mawr (Clwyd). Trout, salmon, coarse fish (including pike and grayling). Maelor AA has water. Coarse fishing good September onwards. Tickets from hon sec. Newbridge AA has Wynnstay Estate Waters from Newbridge Old Bridge downstream on wooded bank, approx 3m; salmon, trout, grayling, dace and pike fishing; members only, except for salmon rods on top beat; members to reside within local radius of 5m. Salmon

permits from hon sec. Tackle shop: Derek's Fishing Tackle, London House, Well St. Hotel: Wynnstay Arms, Ruabon.

Llangollen (Clwyd). Salmon, sea trout, brown trout, grayling, pike. The stretches from Llangollen to Bangor are predominantly privately owned and contain some of the best spring fish salmon pools on the Dee. Llangollen AA has about 12m of bank fishing in and around the town. All waters above Chain Bridge Hotel are strictly fly only for trout and grayling; below Chain Bridge Hotel worm fishing for trout, grayling, coarse fish and eels; no maggots, spinning or other baits allowed. St £68 + £30 joining fee (S) and £28 + £10 joining fee (T), wt £30 (S) and £15 (T), dt £10 (S) and £3 (T); from D M Southern, Newsagents, 12 Chapel Street, LL20 8NN (tel: 0978 860155). Concessions for jun. Salmon membership, long waiting list with preference given to trout members. Salmon tickets issued from 26 Jan - 30 Sept; trout tickets issued from 3 Mar - 30 Sept. **Abbey Fishery**, a trout farm 2½m from Llangollen; 2 bait ponds, 1 fly pond and ½m of river. Accommodation available in log cabins. Contact D Penman & Sons, Abbey Fishery, Abbey Cottage, Nr Llangollen (tel. 0978 860266). Northern A has stretch on **Shropshire Union Canal** from Hurleston Junction to Llantysilio; members only. Hand Hotel (tel: Llangollen 860303) own stretch of water below the bridge on right bank, which is open to hotel residents. Liverpool & Dist AA has salmon and trout fishing at Chain Bridge; st and dt. Hotels: Hand; Royal; Bryn Howell.

Glyndyfrdwy (Clwyd). Salmon, trout and grayling. Berwyn Arms Hotel has 2m private fishing on R Dee at rear of hotel. Special terms for mini breaks. Apply to Paul Gallagher, The Manager (tel: 049083 210). Mold Fly Fishers has 2 tickets on Thursdays for Berwyn Arms Hotel stretch. Midland Flyfishers has 4m stretch from Groeslwyd to Glyndyfrdwy; fly fishing for trout and grayling only. Salmon fishing is prohibited except to

---

POLLUTION

Anglers are united in deploring pollution. To combat it, urgent action may be called for at any time from any one of us. If numbers of fish are found dead, dying, or seriously distressed, take samples of both fish and water and contact the officer responsible for pollution at the appropriate National Rivers Authority.

full members. Season permits are limited; apply to T J P Lea, Keepers Cottage, Hill Lane, Elmlea Castle, Nr Pershore, Worcs WR0 3JA. Dt £3, available from Post Office, Glyndyfrdwy; Berwyn Arms Hotel, Llangollen; and Neil Elborn, Newsagent, Llangollen.

Corwen (Clwyd). Corwen and Dist AC has **Rhug Estate Water**, approx 4m mostly double bank, trout and grayling, fly only except winter grayling; ¼m stretch at **Cynwyd** including large holding pool, salmon, trout and grayling; ¾m stretch at **Carrog**, 3 named pools and runs, salmon, trout and grayling. Club also has several miles of water on **Rivers Alwen** and **Ceirw** at Bettws Gwerfil Goch and Maerdy; salmon and sea trout, mid to late season; and good trout early and late. No dt; members only. Application for membership welcome with concessions for juniors and OAPs. Capenhurst AC has stretch downstream of Carrog Bridge, Carrog; salmon, sea trout and trout; members only. **Gwyddelwern Pool**, Corwen, ¾ acre lake, stocked with brown and rainbow trout; bag limit 4 (charge per lb made for each fish retained); permits from D M Lewis (tel: Corwen 2151). NRA licences from A Roberts, 5 Bridge St. Hotel: Owain Glyndwr; Crown.

Cynwyd (Clwyd). Trout, grayling, salmon. Corwen and Dist AC has stretch on Dee from Gascoed to Cynwyd Bridge; and trout fishing on **Cynwyd Reservoir;** Sunday fishing, fly only. Members only.

Llandrillo (Clwyd). Salmon, trout, grayling, perch and pike. Strictly preserved by executors of Duke of Westminster's Pale Estate. Tyddyn Llan Country Hotel arranges fishing for guests; tuition and equipment available. NRA licences available from Tyddyn Llan Country House Hotel & Restaurant.

Llandderfel (Gwynedd). Salmon, trout, grayling. Pale Hall Hotel, LL23 7PS, has prime salmon and trout fishing during game season. Excellent grayling fishing provides ideal winter sport with specimens reaching 3lbs. Fishing is based on 6m of **River Dee** with access to brown trout in mountain lake. Coarse fishing on **Bala Lake** included in permit.

Bala (Gwynedd). Salmon, trout, perch, pike and grayling. Bala AA has water, including from confluence with Tryweryn to Bala Lake; and fishing on Bala Lake (members only). Assn also has water on Rivers**Tryweryn, Lliw,** and **Llafar** (dt); **Cwm Prysor Lake** (trout. fly only, dt); **Llyn Celyn** (brown trout). Sunday fishing allowed. St £40, wt £25 and dt £7; concessions for juniors. Instruction and competitions for juniors. Permits from tackle shop and J A Jones, Post Office, Frongoch, Nr Bala. **Bala Lake** (Llyn Tegid); trout, roach, perch, pike, grayling, eel; owned by County Council. Permits from tackle shops and Lake Warden, Warden's Office, 24, Ffordd Pensarn, Bala (tel: Bala 520626). Tackle shop: D Evans, Yr Eryr Sports & Tackle, 31-33 High Street, Bala LL23 7AF. Hotels and accommodation: White Lion Royal; Plas Coch; Mrs Shirley Pugh, 4 Castle St; Mr Glyn Jones, Fron Dderw, Bala; Penbryn Farm Guesthouse, Sarnau (coarse fishing available).

Llanuwchllyn (Gwynedd). Trout and grayling. Prince Albert AS has trout and grayling fishing on Little Dee, Twrch and Lliw; members only; waiting list. Hendre Mawr Farm Caravan Park has fishing; tuition and equipment available.

Tributaries of the Dee

ALYN: Trout. Drains hills to west of Clwydian Range, runs past Mold towards Wrexham and finally opens into lower part of Dee on Cheshire Plains near Farndon at Almere.

Rossett (Clwyd). Trout. Rossett and Gresford FF has ¾m stretch between Rossett and Gresford (both banks); and stretch at Cefn-y-Bedd. Fly only; bag limit. St £25 (£5 junior) from hon sec. Warrington AA have water lower down and stretch on Dee, at Almere.

Gresford (Clwyd). Trout. Llay AA has **Gresford Flash;** roach, mirror, carp,

bream, rudd, perch, pike, crucian carp, tench; members only. Griffin AC has three stretches; members only.

Wrexham (Clwyd). Wrexham and Dist AA has water on Alyn; trout fishing, fly only. Permits issued to guests of members only. Other clubs in area: Caergwrle AC; Bradley AC (members only); Llay AA; Griffin AC; Rossett and Gresford FFC. Wrexham & East Denbighshire Water Co, Packsaddle, Wrexham Rd, Rhostyllen, Wrexham LL14 4DS, manage 3 local reservoirs: **Ty Mawr Reservoir** (20 acres), **Penycae Upper**

Reservoir (7 acres) and **Penycae Lower Reservoir** (5 acres). Brown and rainbow trout; fly fishing only; stocked. St £210, dt £15-£9.50 (Penycae) and £14.50-£9 (Ty Mawr). At least 12 hrs notice must be given in order to reserve a rod. Number of rods limited. Contact the bailiff (tel. 0978 840116). Ponciau AS has **Ponciau Pool**, 2½m from Wrexham; roach, bream, tench, carp; members only. Rhostyllen AC has coarse fishing at pool near Sontley; club also has access to extensive game and coarse fisheries on **Dee, Vyrnwy** and **Shropshire Union Canal.** Tackle shops: Deggy's Fishing Tackle, 2 Ruabon Rd; Caldwells, Unit 5, South Mall, Chester St, LL13 8BA; Pearson's Tackle Shop, York St.

Llay (Clwyd). Llay AA has good coarse fishing on **Llay Reservoir** (tench, carp, rudd, perch, pike) and **Cymau Pool** (carp, rudd, tench, perch, roach, crucian carp and gudgeon). Members only. St £8.50 (jun £3.50 and OAP £1) from hon sec, local shops or bailiff on bank.

Hope (Clwyd). Wrexham and Dist AA has trout fishing from Llong railway bridge to Pont y Delyn; fly only; permits issued

Where
can you advertise
for *so many*
months at a price
many would charge
for *one month?*
in
Where to Fish

Get in touch!
(The Publishers' address is at the front of the book)

to members' guests only. Caergwrle AC has 3m; stocked regularly with brown and rainbow trout; wet and dry fly and worming; spinning prohibited. Permits available from hon sec; dt from June 1 only. Brown and rainbow trout fishing available at **Tree Tops Fly Fishery**; ten lakes - nine lakes stocked with rainbow trout and tenth with brown trout. Rods to hire and basic tuition by arrangement. Cafe and tackle shop. Accommodation also available. For further details contact Joy & Peter Price, Tree Tops Fly Fishery, Llanfynydd, Nr Wrexham, Clwyd LL11 5HR (tel. 0352 770648).

Mold (Clwyd). Mold TA has 5m on Alyn and 2m on **R Wheeler;** and fishing on **New Lake,** Rhydymwyn. All fisheries stocked with brown and rainbow trout. Permits from Grovenor Pet and Garden Centre, Grosvenor St (tel. 0352 754264). Mold Fly Fishers has trout fishing on **Pistyll Pool** at Newcwys, 1½ acres, stocked brown and rainbow; and 1¾m salmon, trout and grayling fishing on **River Dee** (Thursdays only); members only; day tickets available if accompanied by member. St £55 plus £35 joining fee. Concessions for juniors. Mold Kingfishers AC has stretch on **R Wheeler** and lake at Afonwen; also coarse fishing at **Hendre Tilcon Quarry Pool** and **Lloyds Gravel Quarries.** Northern A has stretch near Llanferres; members only. Buckley AA has **Trap Pool**, a good mixed fishery; permits from Hope & Anchor Inn, Ewloe Pl, Buckley; Lionels Tackle Shop, Ashgrove, Pentre Lane, Buckley; Grovenor Pets, Grovenor St, Mold; Ken Johnson, Tackle Shop, rear of 63 Wrexham Rd, Mold. Alltami AC has coarse fishing on **Alltami Clay Pits**; carp, tench, bream, roach; no dt. Accommodation: Old Mill Guest House.

Cilcain (Clwyd). Cilcain FFA has four trout reservoirs nearby; stocked with rainbow trout; fly only. Permits from H Williams, Treasurer, 20 Maes Cilan (tel: 0352 740924). **Nant-y-Gain Fishery** (tel. 0352 740936), 2 pools stocked with brown and rainbow trout, fly only. Access and facilities for disabled anglers.

Nannerch (Clwyd). **Sam Mill Fishery**, Sam Mill (tel. 0352 720323), 5 pools; one pool wild brown trout; 2 pools stocked with brown trout and rainbow trout; 2 pools stocked with brown trout, rainbow trout, roach, rudd, tench and carp. Bait for sale, fishing tackle for hire and camp site for tents and caravans. **Wal Goch Fly Fishing**, Wal Goch Farm, CH7 5RP (tel. 0352 741378); 2 pools stocked with brown and rainbow trout.

CEIRIOG: Trout.

Chirk (Clwyd). Good coarse fishing on **Shropshire Union Canal.** Chirk Fishery Co Ltd. has hatchery here. Chirk AA has water on Ceiriog and **Dee;** trout, fly only; day permits only.

Glyn Ceiriog (Clwyd). Farmers sometimes give permission. Hotel: Golden Pheasant, Glyn Ceirog LL20 7BB.

Llanarmon Dyffryn Ceiriog (Clwyd). Ceiriog, 2½m, brown trout. West Arms Hotel has 1½m (both banks) trout fishing; shallow clear water with some deep pools. Free to hotel residents; dt available for non-residents. Limit 2 rods per day; fly only. Hand Hotel has trout and coarse fishing for guests (both hotels issue NRA licences).

ALWEN: Flows out of large reservoir (trout, perch) on Denbigh Moors and enters Dee near Corwen. Very good trout fishing and some salmon.

Cerrig-y-Drudion (Clywd). Cerrig-y-Drudion AA has river fishing on Alwen and on **R Ceirw,** parallel with A5 road; members only. Membership from hon sec. Crown Inn, Llanfihangel Glyn Myfyr, has trout fishing; fly and worm; permits available (free to hotel residents). Tel: 049 082 209. Welsh Water plc manage three reservoirs north of town. **Llyn Brenig**, 919-acre reservoir amid heather moorland and forest. Fly only, brown and rainbow trout. Llyn Brenig was the venue for 1990 World Fly Fishing Championship and 1993 Home Fly Fishing International. St £300, dt £9, evening £7.50, boats £17 per day. Season: 20 Mar - 30 Oct. Concessions OAP & jun; block bookings offered. Tickets from machine at Visitor Centre at reservoir. **Alwen Reservoir** (368 acre), moorland reservoir stocked with rainbow and brown trout, although also natural population of brown trout and perch; dt £6.50. Fly fishing, spinning and worming permitted; catch limit 6 trout. Season 20 Mar - 30 Oct. **Llyn Aled Reservoir** (110 acres), holds large numbers of roach, perch and pike and is a good match venue; occasional wild brown trout. Season 16 Jun - 14 Mar (coarse fish). Dt £2.50. Concessions OAP and jun. Permits and further information from Visitor Centre, Llyn Brenig, Cerrig-y-Drudion LL21 9TT (tel. 0490 420463). Coarse fishing at **Tyddyn Farm Field Centre**, Cefn Brith, Cerrig-y-Drudion, Corwen LL21 9TS. Trout fishing at **Dragonfly Fisheries,** Pant Dewdwydd, Cerrig-y-Drudion; dt available.

TRYWERYN: Joins Dee below Lake Bala. Good trout fishing.

Bala (Gwynedd). Bala AA has 2 stretches on Tryweryn, **Llyn Celyn** and mountain lake **Cwm Prysor.** Tickets from E W Evans, Sports & Tackle Shop, 31-33 High St, LL23 7AF.

DYFI (DOVEY)

(For close seasons, licences, etc, see Welsh Region NRA, p18)

Rises on east side of Aran Fawddwy and flows 30m south and south-west to Cardigan Bay at Aberdovey. Has long estuary and provides splendid sport with sewin (sea trout) and salmon. Many large sea trout taken. Salmon run in small numbers from May to October; sea trout from May on. Best months: July, August, September. Small tributaries hold some little trout, and leave can generally be obtained from owners.

Aberdyfi (Gwynedd). At estuary mouth; surf and estuary fishing. Free trout fishing in Happy Valley on permission of farmers; stream; trout small.

Machynlleth (Powys). Sea trout and salmon. New Dovey Fishery Association controls 15m (both banks) of river between Llyfnant stream and Nant Ty-Mawr and left bank, from opposite Llyfnant mouth to Abergwybedyn brook.

Fishing available?

*If you own, manage, or know of first-class fishing available to the public which should be considered for inclusion in **Where to Fish** please apply to the publishers (address in the front of the book) for a form for submission, on completion, to the Editor. (Inclusion is at the sole discretion of the Editor).*

Limited number of weekly permits. There is an allocation of dt £9 to fish a portion of assn water marked by notice boards. These are available from Service Garage, Cemmaes Road and Mrs E Jones, PO, Cemmaes. Other enq to hon sec (tel. Machynlleth 702721). Permission from farmers for **Pennal Stream;** rapid water; trout small. Corris AC controls 3m of **N Dulas;** and **Glanmerin Lake,** 5 acres, brown trout. Permits from hon sec and tackle shop. Llugwy Hotel, Pennal, has half-mile on **S Dulas** free to guests. Hotels: Wynnstay Arms, White Lion, Dolguog Hall.

Cemmaes (Powys). Trout, sea trout, salmon. New Dovey Fishery Association water.

Llanbrynmair (Powys). On **River Twymyn,** a tributary of **Dyfi;** sewin, salmon. Llanbrynmair and Dist AC has water on Twymyn from village to confluence with Dyfi (apart from one stretch held by Prince Albert AS). Permits from hon sec at Service Garage, Cemmaes Road and Mrs Lewis, Cegin Dyfi. Prince Albert AS control 3m of Twymyn; enquiries to hon sec. Hotel: Star Inn & Trekking Centre, Dylife, Nr Staylittle, Llanbrynmair (tuition and equipment available).

Dinas Mawddwy (Gwynedd). Sewin, salmon, trout; fishing good. Brigands Inn, Mallwyd, has some of the best pools on upper reaches and stretch on **Cleifion;** day tickets for guests only. Buckley Arms Hotel has water from the Cowarch down to hotel, for residents only. Sea trout runs (water permitting) May, July, Sept; best July to October. **Twrch,** 8m E; good trout fishing. Prince Albert AS has 2½m stretch of Dyfi at Gwastad Coed, Gwerhefin. Other hotel: Dolbrawmaeth Hall (½m on Dyfi; dt issued); Buckley Pines (salmon and sea trout on hotel water).

DWYRYD

(For close seasons, licences, etc, see Welsh Region NRA, p18)

Rises in small, nameless pool 3m above Tanygrisiau and flows into Cardigan Bay through estuary north of Harlech. Holds trout, sewin and salmon. Salmon and sea trout run up as far as the falls on the main river and its tributaries, Teigl and Cynfal. Late June to Oct best months for sea trout and salmon.

Maentwrog (Gwynedd). Dwyryd Anglers Ltd has fishing for salmon, sewin and brown trout (north bank only) at **Tanybwlch Fishery** on River Dwryrd, 1¾m downstream from Maentwrog Bridge. June to Oct best. St £30 (limited), wt £15 and dt £6. Concessions available. Permits from Gareth Price, Tackle Shop, Hafan, Ffestiniog (tel. 076676 2451). Dwyryd Anglers Ltd also has 4m of private water on Dwyryd (salmon and sewin); some beats may become available, contact G. Price for information.

Blaenau Ffestiniog (Gwynedd). Principal trout lakes controlled by Cambrian AA as follows: **Dubach,** well stocked with brown trout; **Manod,** fishing rather rough due to rocky shore conditions, holds plenty of fish; **Morwynion,** most easily accessible, average weight 12ozs; **Cwmorthin,** well stocked with brown trout 8 to 9ozs. Other Cambrian AA lakes, **Llagi, Cwm Foel, Llyn-yr-Adar, Corsiog, Conglog, Ffridd** and **Gamallt.** Visitors tickets: st £20, wt £10, dt £5; from local tackle shop. Concession for juniors. **Tanygrisiau Reservoir** (2m NW), 95 acres, stocked with brown and rainbow trout; controlled by local syndicate. St £125, dt £6, evening £4.50 from local tackle shop. Spinning and bait fishing allowed. Tackle shop: F W Roberts, 32 Church Street. Hotels: Pengwern Arms, Ffestiniog.

Tributaries of the Dwyryd

PRYSOR:

Trawsfynydd (Gwynedd). Prysor AA manage **Trawsfynydd Lake,** 1200 acres; brown and rainbow trout (average 1½lb), also perch and rudd. Season: rainbow trout 1 Feb - 31 Dec; brown trout 1 Mar - 30 Sept; coarse fish 1 Feb - 31 Dec. Fly fishing, bottom fishing and spinning. St £80, wt £40, dt £7.50. Boats with motors per day £28 (pair) and £20 (single). Concessions for OAP. Fly only from boats. Regular trout stocking. Assn also control 5m on **Prysor River;** provides good trout fishing especially towards the end of the season when the lake brownies run up. Also 3m on upper **Eden:** salmon and sea trout July onwards. Membership and permit enquiries to Secretary, Trawsfynydd Lake Management Committee, Prysor Hatchery, Trawsfynydd (tel. 076687 313), or to Permit Agent, M P Atherton, Newsagent, Manchester House, Trawsfynydd (tel. 076687 234). Hotels: Cross Foxes and White Lion, Trawsfynydd; Grapes and Oakely Arms, Maentwrog; Abbey Arms and Pengwern Arms, Ffestiniog. Accommodation also available at Fron Oleu Farm, Trawsfynydd and in self catering chalets at Trawsfynydd Holiday Village.

DYFED (streams)

(For close seasons, licences, etc, see Welsh Region NRA, p18)

ALUN. St David's (Dyfed). 6m long; 4m suitable for fishing, mostly on private property on owners permission; trout good quality but small. Trout fishing at **Llanferran Fishpool**, 1 acre; bookings through Mr Chapman's Fishing Tackle Shop, 25 Nun St, St Davids (tel 0437 720301). NRA licences available from Post Office, 13 New Dew St.

BRAWDY BROOK. Brawdy (Dyfed). Small trout. Brook, 7m long, is mostly on private property. Licences can be purchased at Angling Shop, Haverfordwest; and Post Office, 13 New Dew St, St David's.

CARNE. Loveston (Dyfed). Carne rises 1½m W of Templeton, runs 3m to Loveston, and 1m down is joined on left bank by **Langden Brook**. Little or no rod fishing interest; fishing wiped out in 1993 with agricultural pollution; although an important spawning area for salmon and sea trout. Possible sea trout late in season if adequate flows and no pollution. From confluence of Carne and Langden Brook into Cresswell, fishing controlled by Cresselly Estate. Coarse Fishing Reservoir at **Roadside Farm**. Day, week and year permits available. Caravan and camping club. Contact D A & S C Crowley, Roadside Farm, Templeton (tel. 0834 891283).

CAREW BROOK. Carew (Dyfed). This river, which rises by Redberth, is 4m long, joining sea water at Carèw which is an inlet from Milford Haven. Although there is an element of rod fishing effort put into this river and its tributaries, the controlling interest is the farmer and the catchment is prone to agricultural pollution. The river does support a very small number of sea trout which only seem to appear in the close season. **Rainponds Fishery** drains into this catchment. The pond is owned by Mr John who stocks it with carp, tench, roach and perch; fishermen simply start fishing and pay Mr John when he visits the pond.

CLARACH. Good numbers of sea trout can be found in the river late July onwards. **Aberystwyth** (Dyfed). Enters sea 1m N of Aberystwyth. Holds trout, sewin and occasional salmon; preserved. Permission from farmers.

CYWYN. Sarnau (Dyfed). Sea trout, occasional salmon. Only worth fishing June onwards. Permission from farmers.

DISSILIO. Llandissilio (Dyfed). Dissilio is 6m long. 1m W runs Tydi, 6m long. Small trout. NRA licences available from Mr Philips, Old Post, Llandissilio, Nr Clynderwen.

GWAUN. Fishguard (Dyfed). This 8-9m trout stream rises on lower slopes of Prescelly Mountains, and runs through a beautiful wooded valley. Trout not large but provide excellent sport with fly, and sewin also caught in season. A few salmon. **Yet-y-Gors Trout Fishery** has two adjoining lakes covering 3 acres, well stocked with rainbow trout; fly only; tuition available. Further information from Yet-y-Gors Trout Fishery, Manorowen, Fishguard SA65 9RE (tel. 0348 873497). Tackle shops: Thomas and Howells, Dyfed Sports, 21 West St (issue NRA licences). Hotel: Glanmoy Country House.

GWENDRAETH FACH. Kidwelly (Dyfed). Carmarthen and Dist AC has 5m; very good trout fishing; occasional sea trout in lower reaches. Llangennech AC has 4m stretch from Llandyfaelog to Llangendeirne, brown trout and sea trout. **Gwendraeth Fawr** runs 1m E from Kidwelly; trouting fair. Hotel: White Lion; Pen-y-Bac Farm (river fishing for trout, sewin and salmon; tuition and equipment available). NRA licences available from Lyric Sports, King St, Carmarthen.

KILRELGY BROOK. Begelly (Dyfed). This stream, 5m long, has no fishing interest as it suffers low-level agricultural pollution, although a possible spawning area.

LLANDILO BROOK. Maenclochog

(Dyfed). Small trout. Electro-fishing surveys show very few fish of takeable size. No angling clubs. Seek permission from farmers to fish.

LLETHI. Llanarth (Dyfed). Llethi Gido rises 3m above Llanarth, and 2m down is joined on left bank by brook 4m long. Llethi runs to Llanina and sea. One mile NE runs Drowy to sea, 4m long. Small trout. **Nine Oaks Fishery**, fly and coarse fishing, 2m inland between Newquay and Aberaeron; rainbow and brown trout in four pools; rainbow trout in learner pool; carp, tench and bream in coarse fishing lake. Tackle hire, beginners tuition and accommodation available. Permits from Tony Evans, Nine Oaks Trout and Coarse Fishery, Oakford, Nr Aberaeron, SA47 0RW (tel. 0545 580 482).

MARLAIS. Narberth (Dyfed). Gwaithnoak, 2m. Eastern Cleddau, 2m. Taf, 5m. Small trout. NRA licences available from: Salmon & Son, Narberth Ltd, 28 High St; S H Davies, 1 St James St.

MULLOCK BROOK. St Ishmael's (Dyfed). Small trout, 6m long, joining the sea at Dale Road.

NEVERN: Rises near Crymmych and flows to sea at **Nevern** (Dyfed). Fast-flowing, densely wooded, deep holding pools. Nevern AA has salmon, sea trout and brown trout fishing. 4½m on **Nevern**, central point Trewern Arms, Nevern; 1¼m on **Teifi**, 1m north of Llechryd. St £30 plus joining fee £25 from hon sec. Wt £20 and dt £10 from Trewern Arms; The Bookshop, Newport; and The Reel Thing, Market Stall, Cardigan. Concessions for juniors. There are also club outings and fly tying lessons. Hotels: Trewern Arms; Cnappan, Newport.

PERIS. Llanon (Dyfed). Peris is 6m long. Llanon, 4m long, runs ½m. Small trout.

Hotel: Plas Morfa.

RHEIDOL. Aberystwyth (Dyfed). Salmon, sea trout. Hydro-electric scheme governs flow. River almost entirely Aberystwyth AA water. Assn also share a stretch in the lower reaches of **River Ystwyth** with Llanilar AA; and trout fishing on eight lakes. Permits from Aber Fishing Tackle and Gun Shop, 3 Terrace Road; Mrs Lee, Erwyd Garage, Ponterwyd, Aberystwyth; Tea Rooms, Cwm Rheidol; and Post Office, Blaenplwyf. Assn has 2-berth caravans at **Frongoch Lake**; weekly charges from £90 which includes weekly fishing permit and use of boat. Coarse fishing at **Cwm Nant Nursery**; 2½ acre pond; carp, roach and tench. Permits from Mr W Evans, Cwm Nant Nursery, Capel Bangor, Aberystwyth SY23 3LL. Coarse fishing also available at **Tair Llyn Coarse Fishery**; privately owned 9 acre lake; carp, bream, roach, tench, rudd and perch. Permits from Mrs Ruth Jones, Tair Llyn, Cwm Rheidol, Aberystwyth. Hotels: Conrah; Chancery; Bay; Belle Vue Royal.

WYRE. Llanrhystyd (Dyfed). Trout (small), some salmon and sometimes good for sewin. Fishing controlled by a number of riparian owners.

YSTWYTH. Aberystwyth (Dyfed). Llanilar AA has 15m sea trout and salmon fishing on stretch of Ystwyth from Aberystwyth to Pontrhydygroes. Best fishing is by fly at night, spinning in high water and with quill minnow as water clears; fly is also effective during the day when there is a touch of colour in the water. St £46, wt £30, dt £10. Concessions for OAP and junior. Permits from hon sec; Leather Shop, 3 Terrace Rd, Aberystwyth; Post Office, Crosswood; The Garage, Llanilar; The Shop, Blaen Plwyf.

DYFED (lakes)

Lake Berwyn. Tregaron (Dyfed), 4m SE. Liming has taken place and as a result it holds excellent brown trout up to 1 - 2lbs. Stocked periodically. Tregaron AA hold fishing rights; st £40 (£23 OAP and £7 junior), dt £6 (£2 OAP) from Medical Hall, Tregaron; Post Office, Pontrhydfendigaid; W Rees, London House, Llanddewi Brefi; Post Office, Llanfair Clydogau; and Alan Williams, Bridge St, Lampeter.

Devil's Bridge (Dyfed). Aberystwyth AA has the Penrhyncoch lakes in the hills between Devil's Bridge and Nant-y-Moch Reservoir (**Llyn Craig-y-Pistyll, Llyn Rhosgoch, Llyn Blaenmelindwr** and **Llyn Pendam**); the Trisant lakes 2m SW of Devil's Bridge (**Llyn Frongoch and Llyn Rhosrhydd**); and part ownership of **Bray's Pool** and **Llyn Glandwgan.** Some are stocked, others self-stocking. Several contain trout up to 2lb. Fly only on Rhosgoch, Frongoch and Rhosrhydd; spinning and fly only on Craig-y-Pistyll. Permits from Aber Fishing Tackle and Gun Shop, 3 Terrace

Road; and Erwyd Garage, Ponterwyd, Aberystwyth. Hotel: Hafod Arms.

Nant-y-Moch and **Dinas Reservoirs. Ponterwyd** (Dyfed). PowerGen waters in hills about 12m E of Aberystwyth. Dinas, 38 acres, stocked weekly with brown and rainbow trout; fly, spinning and worming. Dt £7 and £4 (OAP, jun and evening). Season 1 April to 31 Oct. Nant-y-Moch, 600 acres, native brown trout, fly only. St £20, dt £2.55. Season 1 April to 30 Sept. Permits from Mrs Dee, Erwyd Garage, Ponterwyd; Aberystwyth Sports Centre, North Parade, Aberystwyth; Aber Fishing Tackle & Gun Shop, 3 Terrace Road, Aberystwyth; Mr Hubbard, Compton Tackle Shop, Borth; Sundorne Fishing Tackle & Leisure, Shrewsbury.

Pembroke (Dyfed). Pembroke Town Mill Pool; mullet, bass, flatfish; also trout and sewin higher up. **West Orielton Lake,** 3m; coarse fish, no pike; permission sometimes obtainable; enquire at West Orielton Farm. **Bosherston Lily Ponds,** Stackpole (6m). Pike, perch, tench, roach. Pembroke and Dist AC. Permits

from Donovan Sports, 61 Bush Street, Pembroke Dock. Hotel: Milton Manor.

Talybont (Dyfed). Talybont AA has exclusive rights on **Llyn Conach, Llyn Dwfn, Llyn Nantycagal** and **Llyn Penrhaeadr.** Lakes some 7-9m into hills from village; 3 lakes stocked with brook trout and some rainbow trout; native wild brown in Penrhaeadr. Fly only on all lakes. Boat available on Conach and Dwfn for holders of season tickets. Assn also has fishing on Forestry Commission land; 1m, both banks, on **River Leri** from Talybont to Dolybont; and both banks on **River Einion** from Eglwysfach to source at Llyn Conach. NRA has recently put some 15,000-20,000 small fry into Leri which contains trout, sea trout and salmon. Day and season tickets from: Spar Store, Talybont; White and Black Lion Hotels, Talybont; Hubbard's Gift Shop, Borth; Leather Shop, Aberystwyth; and Flymail Tackle Shop, Aberystwyth.

Teifi Lakes. Pontrhydfendigaid (Dyfed). Lakes at headwaters of Teifi. Permits from Post Office, Pontrhydfendigaid.

DYSYNNI

(For close seasons, licences, etc, see Welsh Region NRA, p18)

Rises in Llyn Cau, on steep southern side of Cader Idris, then falls rather rapidly via Dol-y-Cau. Falls into Talyllyn Valley about half a mile above well known Talyllyn Lake. Emerging from lake, flows westwards as typical upland stream to Abergynolwyn where, joined by the Gwernol, it turns north through narrow valley until it enters upper end of broad Dysynni Valley. At Peniarth it becomes deep and sluggish and finally enters Cardigan Bay 1½m north of Tywyn. Trout along whole length and tributaries, and sea trout (sewin) and salmon travel beyond Talyllyn Lake and up to Dolgoch on Afon Fathew. In lower reaches good sport may be had, early and late in season, with trout and sewin; August generally best. Also excellent grey mullet and bass in estuary.

Tywyn (Gwynedd). Salmon, sewin, trout, eels, with grey mullet in tidal pans and excellent bass fishing at mouth and from adjacent beaches. NRA licence only needed for fishing on estuary. The Sports Shop issues permits for several beats on River Dysynni: Penowern Water, ½m left bank from confluence with Afon Fathew; Peniarth Estate, Llanegryn, has 4 beats, permits available for 2 beats (st £37, wt £12.50, dt £5.50); and Estimaner AA water at Abergynolwyn. Permission from farmers for **Afon Fathew.** Prince Albert AA has one beat on Dysynni; members only. **Peniarth Uchaf Fishery,** 2½m both banks, held by Hamdden Ltd; permits from Tynycornel Hotel, Talyllyn. Tackle shop: The Sports Shop, 6 College

Green, LL36 9BS.

Abergynolwyn (Gwynedd). Salmon, sea trout, brown trout. Estimaner AA has 3m on Dysynni; stocking at intervals during seasons. Membership only available to local residents. Visitors permits: st £25, wt £12, dt £5 (concessions for jun). Tickets from The Post Office; Railway Inn; The Sports Shop, 6 College Green, Tywyn.

Talyllyn (Gwynedd). Salmon, sea trout, brown trout. Tynycornel Hotel issues permits for **River Dysynni,** 3½m of mostly double bank fishing; **Talyllyn Lake,** 220 acre; and **Llyn Bugeilyn,** 45 acres. Brown trout fishing second to none. Tackle shop, gillie service, fishing tuition, boat hire (with engine) and tackle

Members of the Corris Angling Club plant out sea trout smolts in the River Dulais, a tributary of the Dovey. With the help and co-operation of the proprietor of the Dyfi Hatchery, this stocking was a do-it-yourself initiative on the part of the club. *Photo: Moc Morgan.*

hire. Boat hire priority given to hotel residents but day tickets for boat and bank fishing invariably available. Permits from The Fishery Manager, Tynycornel

Hotel, Talyllyn, Tywyn, Gwynedd LL36 9AJ. Phone 0654 782282 (hotel) or 0654 782663 (tackle shop) for permit availability.

GLAMORGAN (West, Mid and South)

(For close seasons, licences, etc, see Welsh Region NRA, p18)

AFAN. Aberavon (West Glamorgan). Small trout stream (with sewin on lower reaches) on which Afan Valley AC has water from Aberavon to Cymmer. Assn has improved sport; 3 salmon caught in 1991 season; tremendous runs of sewin in last few years; regular stocking. Fly only in March; worming allowed rest of season; spinning July-Sept at certain water levels. Permits, NRA licences and tackle from Selwyn Jenkins Sports, 45 Station Road, Port Talbot. **River Nedd** 4m away; trout, sewin. Hotels: The Twelve Knights; Grand Hotel, Beach.

CADOXTON STREAM. Fishing station: **Cadoxton.** Cadoxton Stream rises 6½m from Cardiff and enters the sea 2m below Cadoxton. Small trout; permission from farmers (Glamorgan RD).

Eglwys Nunydd Reservoir. Margam (West Glamorgan). British Steel plc (Port Talbot) reservoir. Excellent trout fishing, brown and rainbow. Season: 3 Mar - 31 Oct. Very high stocking levels. Special terms for working and retired employees, and families. 3 boats for members or visitors. St £85 and dt £8. Motor boats £13 per day plus day ticket. Fishing lodge available for anglers. Apply Sports Club, British Steel plc, Groes, Margam, Port Talbot. (Port Talbot 871111 Ext 3368 during day).

NEATH. Rises in the Brecon Beacons and flows 27m to sea. Salmon, sewin, brown trout. Tributaries of the Neath are **Dulais** and **Pyrddin.**

Neath (West Glamorgan). Neath and Dulais AA has fishing on **Rivers Neath** and **Dulais**, brown trout, sea trout and salmon; and on **Neath Canal,** which holds a head of coarse fish and is stocked with brown trout. Regular restocking with 8-10 inches trout. St 35 + £20 joining fee, wt £20 and dt £8; from hon sec. Concessions for juniors. Tackle shop: Tackle and Bait, Stockhomes Corner.

Glynneath (West Glamorgan). Glynneath and Dist AA has salmon, sewin and brown trout waters on Neath and its tributaries, **Pyrddin, Nedd Fach** and **Mellte** and two stillwaters on Aberpergwn Estate

at Pontneathvaughan and Ynyscymmer Farm. Fly, worm and spinning from June only. Junior (under 12s) competition in June. St £25, wt £12 and dt £6 (concessions for OAP, disabled and juniors). Daily and weekly permits available from Dave Pittman, Hairdresser; H Griffiths, Bazaar, 38 High St; and White Horse Inn, Pontneddfechan. Pyrddin AS (10m from Neath) has water; trout, salmon, sea trout; permits from hon sec. In headwaters of the Neath is Ystradfellte Reservoir. Tackle shops: Bazaar, 38 High St. Glynneath. Hotel: White Horse Inn at Pontneddfechan, nr Glynneath.

OGMORE.

Porthcawl (Mid Glamorgan). Porthcawl SAA has coarse fishing on **Wilderness Lake** and **Pwll-y-Waem Lake.** Membership £18 for year or £2.50 for day. Dt £2.50. Permits from Porthcawl Angling, Dock St; and Ewenny Tackle Shop, Bridgend. Hotel: Brentwood, St Mary St.

Bridgend (Mid Glamorgan). Ogmore AA has 15m of Ogmore and tributaries **Ewenny, Llynfi** and **Garw**; salmon, sea trout and brown trout. Membership is restricted but weekly tickets are available from secretary at £25. Concessions for juniors. Competitions for juniors; and fly tying and casting lessons. Ogwr Borough AA has water on Ogmore and Garw. Membership restricted to residents but weekly tickets available to visitors. St £25 and wt £15. Concessions for juniors and OAPs. Tackle shops: Ewenny Angling, Bridgend; Keens Tackle & Guns, 119 Bridgend Rd, Aberkenfig. Hotel: Heronstone.

Maesteg (Mid Glamorgan). **River Llynfi,** a tributary of Ogmore. Llynfi Valley AA has 8m excellent trout fishing and coarse fish pond; permits from hon sec. Tackle shop (and licence distributor): C Gow, Sports Shop, 19 Commercial Street, Maesteg; Murphy's Tackle and Bait, 44 Commercial St (tel. 0656 735702).

RHYMNEY. Rhymney (Mid Glam). About 30m long, rises above town. Polluted in lower reaches, but some trout fishing higher up. Bute AS has coarse fishing on a stretch of Rhymney near Cardiff; members only. Rhymney and Dist AS has rights on two reservoirs: **Butetown** and **Rhos-Las.** Both well stocked with coarse fish of all usual species; pike in Rhos-las. All coarse fish, except pike, to be returned to water. Matches run most Saturdays Jun-Aug, plus aggregate awards. St £10 first year then £8 (jun £3.50), dt £2 (jun £1) for both reservoirs from hon sec; PO, Middle Row, Butetown, Rhymney (opp Butetown Reservoir); Cal White, The Square, Pontlottyn; H Green, Tackle Shop, Pontllanfraith, Gwent; T Draper, Tackle Shop, Tredegar, Gwent.

TAWE. Lower tidal reach now impounded by a barrage. Salmon and sewin runs have increased in recent years and they can be caught from Abercraf to Morriston. Upper reaches noted for scenery. Fishing controlled by clubs in all but tidal reaches.

Swansea (West Glamorgan). Swansea Amateur AA has salmon and sea trout fishing on **Cothi** and **Towy.** St £80 and dt £5. Permits for members and guests only. Swansea AC has coarse fishing at Gower on **Fairwood Lake**, pike, bream, carp, perch, tench, roach, rudd, eels; and **Werganrows**, bream, carp, perch, tench, roach, rudd, eels. Members only. No day tickets. St £25 plus £10 joining fee. Concessions for juniors; also junior matches and match league coaching. Swansea City Council has coarse fishing on 4 lakes. **Brynmill Lake**, Brynmill Park, 2 acres; carp, tench, bream, roach, rudd, perch, crucian crap. **Singleton Boating Lake**, Singleton Park, 2 acres; carp, tench, rudd, perch, crucian carp, eels; angling permitted when boats not in use. **Clyne Valley Pond**, small, very deep lake; perch, rudd, eels, trout. **Pluck Pond**, Lower Swansea Valley, 1 acres; perch, rudd. Further information from Leisure Services Dept, The Guildhall, Swansea (tel. 0792 302411). **Felindre Trout Fishery**, Blaen-Nant Ddu, Felindre, Swansea SA5 7ND (tel. 0792 796584); fly only. Riverside Caravan Park has stretch on Tawe; bungalow accommodation and touring caravan park with all facilities. For further information contact Riverside Caravan Park, Ynysforgan Farm, Morriston, Swansea SA6 6QL. Coarse fishing at **Ladbrokes,** a large water situated in **Morriston,** just outside Swansea; acquired in 1990 by council; fairly good head of fish from carp up to 16lb and bream up to 7lb; an added bonus is wonderful surroundings. Permits from P E Mainwaring, Fishing Tackle. Tackle shops: P E Mainwaring, Fishing Tackle, 9 Dillwyn Road, Sketty (tel. 0792 202245); Capstan House, Unit 16, Beaufort Rd, Plasmarl (tel. 0792 310311); Dave's Angling Centre, 74a Brynymor Rd (tel. 0792 648635); Hook, Line & Sinker, Viking Way, Enterprise Park, Winchwen (tel. 0792 701190).

Pontardawe (West Glamorgan). From Pontardawe to Morriston about 6m, is largely Pontardawe and Dist AS water; good trout fishing. Trout fishing on **Cray Reservoir,** near Trecastle, Powys. Apply Glamorgan RD, 86 Kingsway, Swansea SA1 5JL, or reservoir keeper. Llangyfelach and Dist AA has water on **River Llan;** sewin, brown trout; permits:T Day, 27 Vicarage Rd, Morriston, Swansea.

Ystradgynlais (Mid Glamorgan). Tawe and Tributaries AA has 25m on **Tawe** and tributaries **Twrch**, **Gwys**, **Llynfell**, **Giedd**, **Lech**, **Gurlais** and **Cwn Du**, above Pontardawe. Membership restricted to local residents but permits available to non members. St £36 and dt £10. Concessions for juniors and OAPS. Junior river competition held annually. Tackle shops: J G Davies, 3-7 Station Road; Pet, Garden and Sports Centre (tel. 0639 843194). Hotel: Copper Beech Hotel, Abercrave.

Check before you go

While every effort has been made to ensure that the information given in **Where to Fish** *is correct, the position is continually changing, and anglers are urged, in their own interests, to make preliminary enquiries before travelling to selected venues. This is especially important with reference to prices quoted. Inevitably the rate of inflation is affecting stability in this quarter. Anglers' attention is also drawn to the fact that the hotels mentioned under the various fishing stations do not necessarily have water of their own. Any amendments or further data for inclusion in subsequent editions, and any criticism, will be welcome.*

GLASLYN

(For close seasons, licences, etc, see Welsh Region NRA, p18)

Rises in Llyn Glaslyn, 3m south-west of Pen-y-Gwyrd, and flows through three lakes to Beddgelert then along Pass of Aberglaslyn to lower reaches and Porthmadog, where it enters the sea. Noted sea trout river and efforts are being made to increase salmon run. Best trout fishing in upper reaches, mountain lakes and tributaries. Best spots for salmon and sewin are: Glaslyn Hotel Bridge; Verlas; and above the pass.

Porthmadog (Gwynedd), Sea trout and salmon. Glaslyn AA has 7½m stretch on Glaslyn from Beddgelert to Porthmadog (both banks, except two private stretches); assn also has bank fishing on **Llyn Dinas**. Best months are: April and May for trout; April to Oct for salmon; May to Oct for sewin. St £50, wt £25, dt £10. Concessions for OAP and jun. Permits from tackle shops; and Aberglaslyn House, Beddgelert. **Llyn Cwmystradllyn**, Caernarfon Rd, wild brown trout fishery, 95 acres, dt £5, 6 bag limit. **Llyn Glan Morfa Mawr**, Morfa Bychan, 8 acre lake, rainbow trout, 6 bag limit, dt £8. Permits from Angling and Gun Centre. Tackle shops: Angling & Gun Centre,

Madog St, LL49 9LR (tel. 0766 512464); Pen Guns, Penrhyndeudraeth. Hotels: Royal Sportsman, High St; Madog, Tremadog.

Beddgelert (Gwynedd). Sea trout and salmon. Best for sea trout mid-May to early Sept; salmon May-Oct. Glaslyn AA has Glaslyn from Beddgelert to Porthmadog; and **Llyn Dinas**, 2m NE, sea trout and salmon. St £50, dt £10 (Mon to Fri); left bank (only) on Llyn Dinas, no boats, one day. Concessions jun & OAP. Permits from Aberglaslyn Bridge Café. Further information from R T Gauler, Bridge House, Aberglaslyn, Beddgelert LL55 4YF (tel. 076686 229).

GWYNEDD (streams)

(For close seasons, licences, etc, see Welsh Region NRA, p18)

ABER. Aber, nr **Llanfairfechan** (Gwynedd). Aber rises in Llyn Anafon, runs to Aber and sea in 2m. Trout (average 7-8 in). Now a Nature Reserve. No fishing.

ARTRO. Rises in Llyn Cwm Bychan, 6m E of Harlech, and enters sea 1m below **Llanbedr**. Good bass fishing in tidal waters. Noted for night fishing for sea trout. Good fly pools below village and above Dol-y-Bebin.

Llanbedr (Gwynedd). Artro and Talsarnau FA has salmon and sea trout fishing on Artro. Assn also has water on **River Nantcol**, brown trout; **Cooke's Dam**, rainbow trout; **Llyn Tecwyn Uchaf** and **Llyn Tecwyn Isaf** at Talsarnau, brown trout; **River Glyn** at Talsarnau, sea trout and salmon; and **Llyn Fedw** at Harlech, brown trout. St £40, wt £15, dt £6. Concessions for OAP and junior. Permits from Newsagent, Llanbedr; Post Office, Talsarnau; and tackle shops in Barmouth, Harlech, Penrhyndeudraeth and Porthmadog. Hotels: Victoria; Ty-Mawr.

DARON. Aberdaron (Gwynedd). Daron and Cyll-y-Felin run down two valleys and join at Aberdaron; restocked and hold good sized trout. Sea fishing for mackerel, pollack, lobsters, crab, etc, from

rocks or boat. Tackle and licences from R G Jones, Eleri Stores, Aberdaron LL53 8BG.

DWYFAWR. Best part of river lies 1m W of Criccieth, where there is length of 12m unobstructed and good for fly fishing. Salmon fishing has greatly improved owing to restrictions on netting. Sewin very good; late June to Oct; night fishing best.

Criccieth (Gwynedd). Sea trout and salmon. Criccieth, Llanystumdwy and Dist AA controls about 10m both banks. Assn also has about 2m on **Dwyfach**; shorter river than Dwyfawr (about 10m) and rather heavily wooded. Improved catches of sea trout in 1993, many fish over 4lb. NRA licences and assn permits from R T Pritchard, Sheffield House, High Street, LL52 0EY (tel. 0766 522116). Coarse fishing at **Gloddfa Lake**, rudd; permits from G Hamilton, Criccieth, Llanystumdwy and Dist AA. Good sea fishing in this area. Hotels: Glyn y Coed; Lion; Marine.

ERCH. Pwllheli (Gwynedd). Pwllheli and Dist AA has brown trout, sea trout and salmon fishing on **Rivers Erch** and **Rhydhir. Assn also has brown trout fishing on Llyn Cwmystradllyn;** approx

10m NW; 95 acre lake holding wild and stocked brown trout; an upland fishery, situated in the heart of the rugged foothills of Snowdonia. Bag limit 6 brown trout per day. St £17 (local) and £35 (visitor). Weekly and daily tickets available. Concessions for juniors and OAPs. Permits from D & E Hughes, Walsall Stores, 24 Penlan St, LL53 5DE (tel. 0758 613291).

GEIRCH. Nefyn (Gwynedd). Geirch, 2m W, 5m long; good sea fishing at Morfa Nefyn. Tackle shop: Bryn Raur Sports Shop, Morfa Nefyn.

GWYRFAI. Issues from Llyn Cwellyn, near Snowdon, and flows into Menai Strait through Betws Garmon and Llanwnda. Salmon, sea trout, trout.

Betws Garmon (Gwynedd). Seiont, Gwyrfai and Llyfni AS controls much of Gwyrfai, salmon, sea trout and brown trout. Wt £42, dt £12. Permits from Post Office, Betws Garmon; Post Bach, Pool St, Caernarfon. Castell Cidwm Hotel water; permits which include use of boat, from Mr & Mrs D Roberts, Castell Cidwm Hotel, Betws Garmon, Nr Caernarfon. Preference given to hotel guests. **Bontnewydd Fishery**, salmon, sea and brown trout; dt from G J M Wills, Bryn Mafon, Caethro, Caernarfon.

Rhyd-Ddu (Gwynedd). Seiont, Gwyrfai and Llyfni AS offers boat and bank fishing on **Llyn Gadair**, brown trout; **Llyn Cwellyn**, brown trout, char, salmon and sea trout; **Llyn-y-Dywarchen**, regularly restocked with rainbow trout, fly only, bag limit 4. Wt £42, dt £12 (Llyn Cwellyn £5 and Llyn-y-Dywarchen £7). Permits from Cwellyn Arms.

LLYFNI. Penygroes (Gwynedd). Rises in Drws y Coed, 4m E of town and runs through Nantlle Lake; salmon, sea trout (good), trout. Seiont, Gwyrfai and Llyfni AS controls most of river. Wt £42, dt £12. Permits from A D Griffiths, Newsagent, Snowdon St.

SOCH. Llangian (Gwynedd). Trout and rudd; an early stream; dry fly useful; weeds troublesome later; some sewin, late; plenty of sea fishing, bass, pollack, whiting, flatfish, at Abersoch, from which this stream can be fished. Hotel: Rhydolion (Soch runs on boundary of farm, equipment available); Coed-y-Llyn, Sarn Bach Rd, Abersoch.

YSGETHIN. River rises in **Llyn Bodlyn.** Brown trout, Artic char.

Tal-y-bont (Gwynedd). Llyn Bodlyn, apply to The Hall, Llyn Bodlyn, Tal-y-bont, Nr Barmouth.

GWYNEDD (lakes)

(For close seasons, licences, etc, see Welsh Region NRA, p18)

Bala Lake or Llyn Tegid. **Bala** (Gwynedd). Owned by Gwynedd County Council, Caernarfon. Permits from Lake Warden, Warden's Office, 24 Ffordd Pensarn, Bala (tel: Bala 520626) and tackle shop. Salmon may sometimes be taken and trout early in season. Pike, perch, roach, grayling, eels. Bala is largest natural lake in Wales, 4m long, 1m wide. Here, too, is found that rare and interesting fish called the gwyniad, a land-locked whitefish. Coarse fishermen will find all their wants more than provided for; pike up to 25lb; perch and good roach. NRA licence required. Tackle shop: Eryr Sports & Tackle, 31 High St (tel: Bala 520370).

Llyn Celyn. Bala (Gwynedd). Situated in the Snowdonia National Park at the foot of the Arenig Mountains; rainbow trout are stocked to supplement wild brown trout. Reservoir managed under licence by Bala AA; permits from D Evans, Tackle Shop, 31-33 High Street. Concessions for jun and OAP. Sunday fishing.

Hafod-y-Llyn. Llanbedr (Gwynedd). Roach, perch, eels. Permits from Lewis Bros, Tyddyn Ddu, Llanfair, Nr Harlech.

Cwm Bychan Lake. Llanbedr (Gwynedd). Trout and sewin; good fishing. For permission to fish, apply to Farm Manager, Cwm Bychan Farm, Cwn Bychan. For **Gloywlyn Lake** apply Cwmrafon Farm. **Llyn Perfeddau**, trout, good fishing; free.

Maentwrog (Gwynedd). **Y-Garnedd**, 1m N (trout) and **Hafod-y-llyn**, 1m NW (pike, coarse fish) are both private. Cambrian AA lakes in area: **Morwynion, Cwmorthin, Manod, Barlwyd, Dubach, Dubach-y-bont, Llagi, Cwm Foel, Llyn-yr-Adar, Corsiog, Conglog, Ffridd, Gamallt**. Permits from F W Roberts, 32 Church St, Blaenau Ffestiniog.

Talsarnau (Gwynedd). Artro and Talsarnau FA has water on **Llyn Tecwyn Uchaf** and **Llyn Tecwyn Isaf**, brown trout; and on **River Glyn**, sea trout and salmon. St £40, wt £15, dt £6. Permits from Post

Office. Hotels: Ship Aground; Motel.

LLWCHWR (or LOUGHOR)

(For close seasons, licences, etc, see Welsh Region NRA, p18)

Rises some 3m east of Llandybie on Taircarn Mountain and flows 15m south-west through Ammanford and Pontardulais to Burry Inlet, north of Gower Peninsula. Fishing very good for sewin, and some brown trout and salmon (Apr-July; Aug-Oct best). Salmon and sewin runs reported to be increasing. Most fishing controlled by clubs, from whom tickets are available.

Llanelli (Dyfed). Llanelli Borough Council controls fishing on **Upper** and **Lower Lliedi Reservoirs**; season 20 Mar - 30 Oct; both reservoirs stocked with brown and rainbow trout. Fly only on Upper Lliedi. Boat available to members on Upper Lleidi; £6 per day. Permits from Thomas Bros, 10 Thomas St; and S Bassett, Anglers Corner, 80 Station Rd (tel. 0554 773981). For further information, contact The Director of Public Services, Ty Elwyn, Llanelli.

Llangennech (Dyfed). Llangennech AC has 2m on **River Morlais**, a tributary of R Loughor, and 4m on **River Gwendraeth Fach**; mainly brown trout with good runs of sea trout in both rivers. Bag limit 6 fish. St £16 plus £15 joining fee. Concessions for juniors, OAPs and disabled. Season members only, application forms from hon sec or Anglers Corner, Station Rd, Llanelli (tel. 0554 773981).

Club offers fresh water and some sea fishing competitions; and, during the close season, runs fly tying classes.

Pontardulais (Glamorgan). Trout and a run of sea trout; some salmon. Pontardulais and Dist AA has 6m good fishing; permits from Bridge Café. Concessions for OAP and jun. Llangyfelach AA also has water. **Whitesprings Fishery** at Pentrebach; for further information Whitesprings Fishery , Garnswllt Rd, Pentrebach, Pontardulais.

Ammanford (Dyfed). Ammanford & Dist AA has water on middle and upper reaches of Llwchwr and tributaries. Boat available for club members at **Llys-y-Fran Reservoir**, much improved sea trout run, biggest fish 16½lb. Permits from Dyfed Rod & Guns, 72 Wind St (tel. 0269 592380). Hotels: Gwyn; Penrhiw Guest House, Ammanford; Wernolau Hotel, Pontamman.

Tributaries of the Llwchwr

AMMAN. Trout, sewin, few salmon. Very fast running; fishes well in spate.

Ammanford (Dyfed). Ammanford & Dist AA has water on **Llwchwr**, 5m; **Amman**, 3m; **Lash**, 3m; **Marlais**, 3m; **Cennen**, ½m; **Gwili**, 1½m. Sea trout run from May onwards. St £25 + £25 joining fee, wt £20, dt £5 (day and weekly tickets available for bona fide visitors). Concessions for juniors, youth and ladies. In-

struction available, fly-tying classes and competitions. Permits from Dyfed Rod and Gun, 72 Wind Street. Accommodation: The Mill, West End Guest House, Pen-Rhiw Guest House.

MARLAIS BROOK. Llandybie (Dyfed). Sewin, July onwards. **Llwchwr**, 3m. **Gwendraeth Fawr**, 5m W. **Llyn Lechowen**, 5m W.

MAWDDACH

(For close seasons, licences, etc, see Welsh Region NRA, p18)

Rises in hills between Bala and Trawsfynydd Lakes and flows 10m south to confluence with Wnion, 2m below Dolgellau, and thence through long estuary to sea at Barmouth. River

---

Fishing available?

If you own, manage, or know of first-class fishing available to the public which should be considered for inclusion in **Where to Fish** *please apply to the publishers (address in the front of the book) for a form for submission, on completion, to the Editor. (Inclusion is at the sole discretion of the Editor).*

holds salmon, sea trout and brown trout and is all preserved, although permits can be had for some stretches. Successful stocking with locally hatched salmon fry. Salmon and sea trout may be taken up to Pistyll Mawddach.

Barmouth (Gwynedd). Rivers Mawddach and **Wnion;** trout, sea trout and salmon. Run of sea trout and salmon is from beginning of June to end of season. Trout fishing on **Cregennan Lakes** at Arthog; 2 natural lakes owned by the National Trust, situated on northern slopes of Cader Idris overlooking beautiful Mawddach Estuary. Large lake with island, 27 acres, wild brown trout only, fly spin or worm; dt £5 and evening £3. Small lake, 13 acres, regularly stocked with rainbows, plus a good head of wild brown trout, fly only; dt £10 and evening £5. Boat available but booking advisable. Permits from Emlyn Lloyd, Fridd Boedel Farm, Arthog, Nr Fairbourne (tel. 0341 250468).

Penmaenpool (Gwynedd). Salmon, sea trout. George III Hotel, LL40 1YD (tel. 0341 422 525) issues permits for over 12m of river and lake fishing on Rivers Mawddach and **Wnion**, and **Llyn Cynach Lake**; with free permits for hotel guests.

Ganllwyd (Gwynedd). Salmon, sea trout. Dolgellau AA has left bank of upper beat from Ganllwyd to Tyn-y-Groes Pool. Hotels: Tyn-y-Groes, Ganllwyd, (1½m salmon and sea trout fishing on river); Dolmelynllyn Hall, Ganllwyd (1¼m salmon and sea trout fishing on Mawddach, priority given to guests).

Tributaries of Mawddach.

WNION: Salmon, sewin, sea trout.
Dolgellau (Gwynedd). Salmon and sea trout. Wnion and Mawddach rivers. Wnion runs by Dolgellau and joins Mawddach 2m below town. Best months for salmon and sea trout: May-Oct. Sewin

fishing Jul-Oct. Dolgellau AA owns fishing rights on 12-13m of Mawddach and Wnion. Stocked with salmon and sea trout from Mawddach Trust Hatchery. St £50, wt £26, dt £9. Assn also has wild brown trout and rainbow trout fishing on

Llyn Cynwch; dt £7. Permits available from Fishing Gear, Eldon Sq (tel. 0341 422730); Seafarer, Church St, Barmouth (tel. 0341 280978). Hotels: Dolmelynllyn Hall, Ganllwyd, Dolgellau; Dolserau Hall, Dolgellau; and George III Hotel, Penmaenpool, Dolgellau. These hotels can arrange fishing holidays for residents on all Dolgellau AA waters.

OGWEN

(For close seasons, licences, etc, see Welsh Region NRA, p18)

Rises in Ogwen Lake, halfway between Bethesda and Capel Curig, with tributaries running in from Ffynnon Lloer and Bochlwyd Lakes, and runs from lake to outlet at Menai Straits, near Bangor, about 10m in all. Excellent trout fishing; leased by Ogwen Valley AA from Penrhyn Estate. Extensive restocking programme, with trout, sea trout (sewin) and salmon. Catches improving. Autumn good for salmon.

Bangor (Gwynedd). **Ogwen**, 2m E; salmon, sewin, trout. Sea trout run starts about mid-June. Salmon best Aug-Oct. Parts of river leased by Ogwen Valley AA. Hotels: Waverly, British, Castle, Railway.

Bethesda (Gwynedd). Ogwen Valley AA has water. Assn also has lake fishing on four trout lakes: **Ogwen, Idwal, Ffynon Lloer** and **Bochlwyd**. Wt £25, dt £9; from Ron Edwards, Fishing Tackle, High St, Bethesda.

POWYS (lakes)

Llyn Clywedog. Llanidloes (Powys). NW 3m; 615 acres; Llanidloes and Dist AA. Reservoir shared with sailing club; western half is fishery area, but fishing also permitted in much of eastern half by arrangement with sailing club. Well stocked with brown and rainbow trout averaging $1\frac{3}{4}$lb. Fly only. Boat hire available. Dt £6 (evening £3.50), st £60 (concessions for jun and OAP) from hon sec and Mrs Gough, Traveller Rest Restaurant, Longbridge Street, Llanidloes (tel. 0686 412329). NRA licence required. Tackle shop: Maesbury Casuals, Great Oak St. Hotels: Mount Inn; Unicorn; Lloyds; Trewythen Arms.

Llangorse Lake. Llangorse (Powys). Holds good pike, good bream, perch, roach, eels. Close season: 14 Mar - 16 Jun. Fishing from boats only; can be hired. Permit needed to launch privately owned boats. Caravans for hire from Apr-Oct. Permits, tuition and equipment available from Ray Davies, Lakeside Caravan and Camping Park, LD3 7TR (tel. 0874 84226). Accommodation and fishing available at Trewalter Farm, LD3 0PS; equipment available at extra cost. Llynfi runs from lake to Wye at Glasbury and holds a few trout; overgrown in places; requires short rod. Hotel: Red Lion.

Talybont Reservoir. Brecon (Powys). Reservoir in Brecon Beacons National Park, 318 acres, good wild brown trout fishery. Season 20 Mar - 17 Oct; fly only; catch limit 6 fish; size limit 9 inches. Dt £4.50 from machine at treatment works below dam. Further information from C Hatch, Area Manager, Hamdden Ltd, Pentwyn Road, Nelson, Treharris, Mid Glamorgan.

Lake Vyrnwy. Llanwddyn (Powys). 1,100 acre lake stocked with rainbow and brown trout. Annual catch 3,000 to 3,500 averaging 1lb. Fly only. Ghillies and instructors can be arranged together with hire of rods. Apply to Lake Vyrnwy Hotel, Llanwddyn, via Oswestry, Shropshire SY10 0LY. (Tel: 069 173 692).

SEIONT

(For close seasons, licences, etc, see Welsh Region NRA, p18)

Rises in two tarns in Cwm-glas, under crest of Snowdon, and runs to Llanberis, 3m, where it enters the Llanberis Lakes, Llyn Peris and Llyn Padarn. Flows thence to Menai Straits to

---

Keep the banks clean

Several clubs have stopped issuing tickets to visitors because of the state of the banks after they have left. Spend a few moments clearing up.

Caernarfon. Attractive river with long flats, nice runs and excellent pools holding salmon (May onwards), sea trout (June onwards), and brown trout. Trout rather small, but in faster water can give good account of themselves.

Caernarfon (Gwynedd). Salmon, sea trout, trout. Seiont, Gwyrfai and Llyfni AS has 40 miles of salmon, sea trout and brown trout fishing on Rivers **Seiont, Gwyrfai** and **Llyfni**. Assn also has boat and bank fishing on **Llyn Padarn**, brown trout, char, salmon, sea trout; **Llyn Cwellyn**, brown trout, char, salmon, sea trout; **Llyn Gadair**, brown trout; **Llyn-y-Dwarchen**, 35 acres, rainbow trout and brown trout, fly only. Season ticket on application only. Wt £42, dt £12 (£5 Llyn Padarn and Llyn Cwellyn; £7 Llyn-y-Dywarchen), from Post Bach, Pool St; A D Griffiths, Newsagent, Penygroes; Pet Shop, Llanberis; Cwellyn Arms, Rhyd-Ddu; Post

Office, Betws Garmon. Maps and information from hon sec. Seiont Manor Hotel at Llanrug, has fishing for guests on society waters. Hotels: Royal; Black Boy Inn; Minffordd Guest House, Bethel, Caernarfon.

Llanberis (Gwynedd). Brown trout, Artic char, salmon, sea trout. Seiont, Gwyrfai and Llyfai AS has bank and boat fishing on almost the whole of **Llyn Padarn**; dt £5 available from A C Philips at Boat Hire Jetty on lake (special rates for boats for fishing). Permits and tackle available from Pet Shop. Hotels: Lake View; Victoria.

TAF

(For close seasons, licences, etc, see Welsh Region NRA, p18)

Rises on Prescelly Mountains and flows about 25m south-west and south-east to Carmarthen Bay at mouth of Towy. Has good runs of salmon most years. Brown trout fishing excellent upstream of Whitland. Sewin can be caught most seasons from late March onwards.

St Clears (Dyfed). Salmon, sewin, brown trout fair. April, May, Sept best for salmon. Sewin mid-June onwards. Some open waters. Camarthen and Dist AC have water on Taf and stretch on **Dewi Fawr**. St Clears and District AA has good water on Taf. Assn also has trout and sewin fishing on **R Gynin**, 2m; R Dewi Fawr, 1m; **R Cowin**, 3m. Permits from hon sec; Taf Tackle; and The Pharmacy. Other waters on these rivers available by permission of farmers. Tackle shop: Taf Tackle, Crown Cottage, High St, SA33 4DZ. Hotels: Black Lion; Garde House; Corporation Arms, Laugharne. Caravan

sites at St Clears and Laugharne.

Whitland (Dyfed). Salmon, sea trout, brown trout. Whitland AA has 6m of fishing. St £50, wt £25 and dt £6 from Ithel Parri-Roberts, Swyddfa'r Post Office, Hendygwyn-ar-daf; and Iorry Griffiths, ESSO Garage, Market Street (tel: 0994 240753). Fly fishing at **White House Mill Trout Fishery**; fly-tying and fly casting instruction available. Contact White House Mill, Whitland. Coarse fishing on **Llyn Carfan**; stocked with carp, tench, roach and rudd. Rods and tackle for hire. Contact Llan Carfan, Whitland SA34 0ND.

TAFF and ELY

(For close seasons, licences, etc, see Welsh Region NRA, p18)

Taff has its source in two headstreams on the Brecon Beacons and flows about 40m south-east to enter the Severn Estuary at Cardiff. A short and steep river, heavily polluted since the 19th century by local iron, coal and steel industries. However, by the early 1980's there had been major improvements in the water quality due to economic recession and improved pollution control; and sea trout and some salmon were again entering lower reaches of river. Since then, the Welsh Water Authority, and subsequently the National Rivers Authority, have been successfully carrying out a strategy for rehabilitating salmon in the Taff; through pollution control, building fish passes, transporting adult fish upstream, artificial propagation and control of exploitation. Ely joins mouth of Taff at Penarth.

Cardiff (Glamorgan). Brown trout (stocked) and run of sea trout and salmon. Glamorgan AC (membership 500) has about 6m on **Trothy** at Dingestow and

Mitchel Troy (trout); 5m on Ely, at Llantrisant (trout); 8m on Taff (salmon, trout, coarse), stretches from Canton Bridge, Cardiff, to Radyr station. Club also holds rights on freshwater reservoir at Barry Docks and on the **St-y-Nyll Ponds** at St Brides. Tickets from hon sec, but no dt for trout issued from May 1 to Aug 1 inclusive. Trout season March 1 to Oct 1. Bute AA has fishing at **Marshfield Reens;** good carp, tench, etc. St from hon sec. Also coarse fishing on **Wye** and **Usk**. Bute AS and Birchgrove (Cardiff) AS have fishing on R Taff in city limits; coarse (chub, roach, dace, gudgeon with barbel introduced recently); and game (salmon, sewin and brown trout) under auspices of combined Cardiff clubs known as Taff Fisheries. Day tickets available from Gary Evans, 105 Whitchurch Rd, Heath, Cardiff, and A E Bales & Son, Frederick St, Cardiff. Bute AS also has coarse fishing on **Rivers Rhymney, Ely** and **Wye;** members only. Birchgrove AS also has coarse fishing on **R Ely** and through kindness of riparian owners, fishing on prime stretches on **R Wye** between Glasbury and Builth. **Roath Park Lake** (Cardiff Corporation) holds rudd, roach, carp, tench. **Llanishen** (59 acres) and **Lisvane** (19 acres) **Reservoirs**, located within Cardiff City boundary, approach via B4562 road; leased to Cardiff Fly Fishing Club; day tickets available at reservoirs. **Hendre Lake** controlled by Cardiff Nomads; permits, bait and NRA licences from Garry Evans, Fishing Tackle, 105 Whitchurch Rd, CF4 3JQ (tel. 0222 619828). Tackle shop: A Bale & Son, 3 Frederick Street (information, bait, licences); Gary Evans, 105 Whitchurch Road, Heath; Anglers Supplies, Penarth Rd; Tackle Shop, Cowbridge Rd, Ely Bridge. Hotels: Angel; Cardiff International; Clare Court; Glenmor.

Merthyr Tydfil (Glamorgan). Merthyr Tydfil AA offers a large variety of waters from wild brown trout fishing on the Up-

per Neuadd Reservoir in the heart of the Brecon Beacons to salmon fishing on the Usk, with ponds and reservoirs for the coarse fishing enthusiast. The assn has 17m on **Taff** and **Taf Fechan** at Merthyr Tydfil from Pontsticill Reservoir to Quaker's Yard, brown trout, regularly stocked, size limit 10", bag limit 6 fish; **Upper Neuadd Reservoir,** wild brown trout, very lightly stocked, fly only; **Taf Fechan Reservoirs,** trout (20 Mar - 17 Oct) and coarse (16 Jun - 17 Mar), no pike or other coarse fish to be removed; **Penywern Ponds,** coarse fish including carp in excess of 10lb, dt available. Permits from Cefn Coed Tackle, High St, Cefn Coed (tel. 0685 379309); G Gulliford, 46 Hawthorn Avenue, Gurnos Estate; A Rees, 13 Alexandra Avenue (tel. 0685 723520); N Morgan, 20 James St, Twynyroddyn. Assn also has 2 stretches of salmon and trout fishing on **Usk** at **Mardy Fishery,** 1¼m, dt from PM Tackle, Monk Street, Abergavenny; and **Kemeys Commander Fishery,** ¾m, dt from Sweet's Fishing Tackle, 14 Porthycarne St, Usk. Reservoirs in Taf Fawr Valley managed by Hamdden Ltd: **Beacons Reservoir** (52 acres) brown trout, fly only; **Cantref Reservoir** (42 acres) rainbow and brown trout, fly only; **Llwyn-Onn Reservoir** (150 acres) rainbow and brown trout, fly, worm and spinner. All located in Brecon Beacons National Park adjacent to A470 (T) road, 3m north of Merthyr Tydfil and 15m south of Brecon. Dt from machine at Llwyn-Onn water treatment works. For further information contact C Hatch, Hamdden Ltd, Pentwyn Road, Nelson, Treharris, Mid Glamorgan CF46 6LY. Tackle shops: Cefn Coed Tackle, High St, Cefn Coed; AC's Tackle, The Square, Troedyrhiw.

Tributaries of Taff

RHONDDA FAWR and RHONDDA FACH:

Pontypridd (Mid Glamorgan). At Junction of Rhondda Fawr and Fach, and Taff.

Tonypandy (Mid Glamorgan). Glyncornel AA has trout fishing on Rhondda; restocked annually with brown and rainbow trout. St £19 and wt £6. Concessions for juniors. Competitions for adults and juniors. Permits from Army Stores; Four Seasons; Valley Sports, Treorchy. Club

also holds rights on coarse fishing at **Darran Lake,** Ferndale. Hotel: Village Inn, Trehafod, Pontypridd.

Ferndale (Glamorgan). Maerdy and Ferndale AC has water on River Rhondda Fach and 2 reservoirs at Maerdy; st £35 plus £10 joining fee and dt £5. Permits from J Thomas, 21 Maerdy Rd, Maerdy, Rhondda. Concessions for jun. Tackle shop: Top Line Angling, 7 Cemertary Rd, Porth, Rhondda.

ELY:

Peterston (Glamorgan). Trout, Glamorgan AC has coarse fishing in **St-y-Nyll Ponds** at St Brides.

Llantrisant (Glamorgan). Trout. Glamorgan AC has 5m (not continuous), beginning at Miskin Weir (upstream limit of Taff and Ely water) and total length of **Clun Brook**. Trout fishing at **Otters Brook Trout Pool**, Brynsadler, Nr Pontyclun (tel. 0443 227786); and at **Seven Oaks Trout Fishery**, Ystradown, Nr Cowbridge (tel. 0446 775474).

TEIFI

(For close seasons, licences, etc, see Welsh Region NRA, p18)

Rises in Llyn Teifi, near Strata Florida, in NE Dyfed, flows south-west and then west, entering Cardigan Bay below Cardigan Town. Association water provides salmon, sea trout (sewin) and brown trout fishing. April and May are the best months of spring salmon; summer salmon fishing depends on floods. Sea trout run from May onwards. Coracle and draft nets come off 1st September.

Cardigan (Dyfed). Salmon, sewin, trout. Bass, mullet and flounders below bridge to sea, 2m; boats available. Teifi Trout Assn has 16m of Lower Teifi from Llandyfriog, nr Newcastle Emlyn, to Llechryd, nr Cardigan, including fishing at Cenarth. Surcharge on Cenarth waters. St £125 plus £20 joining fee (surcharge £40) from Edgar George, Membership Secretary, Romalyn, 14 Bryngwyn, Cardigan SA43 3DS (tel. 0239 612438). Wt £35 (surcharge £20) and dt £10 (surcharge £10) from Mrs Shaw, The Reel Thing, Market Tackle Shop; Thomas Sports Shop. Concessions for OAPs, invalids and juniors. Other tackle shops: James Fishing Tackle, 1 College Row; Cardigan Sports, 9 High St.

Llechryd (Dyfed). Salmon, sea trout. Castle Malgwyn Hotel has 1m, one bank; best time for salmon July and Aug; special rates for parties. Llwyndyris Mansion Hotel has 650 yards; wt issued. Nevern AA has 1¼m stretch. Teifi Trout Assn water.

Cenarth (Dyfed). Salmon, sewin, trout. Famous falls; last site of historical coracle fishing for salmon. Teifi Trout Assn water; surcharge for Cenarth Fishery. Permits from The Salmon Leap; Cenarth Caravan Park. West Wales School of Fly Fishing, Ffoshelyg, Llancych, Boncath, SA37 0LJ (tel. 023977 678); runs courses for beginners and for those keen to improve their skills. Two small trout lakes, one stocked with brown trout and one with rainbow; and 2m of river fishing, brown trout, sea trout and salmon. Free fishing to participants on courses. Day tickets available outside courses dates. Free fly casting and fly fishing lessons for school children on Fridays during summer holidays. Contact Pat O'Reilly, Senior Instructor, West Wales School of Fly Fishing, Ffoshelyg, Llancych, Boncath, SA37 0LJ (tel. 023977 678). The Three Horseshoes Inn and Cenarth Caravan Park specialise in accommodation and meals for fishermen.

Newcastle Emlyn (Dyfed). Salmon and sea trout. Good centre for Teifi; Teifi Trout Assn has water. Pensarnau Arms Hotel has salmon, sewin and trout fishing; tuition available in fly, spinning and worm fishing; tackle hire. Hotels: Emlyn Arms; Cawdor; Dolhaiadd Isaf (game fishing available on ¾m of Teifi). NRA rod licences from Chwaraeon Andrew Sports, 7 Sycamore St; and Dr D Rowe, Dol-Haidd Isaf.

Llandysul (Dyfed). Salmon, sewin, brown trout. Popular centre; fishing good. Best April-May and Aug-Sept for salmon; sewin July onwards. Llandysul AA has 28m of Middle Teifi. Members only; day tickets are available. Permits from Gwilym Jones, The Alma Sports Store, Llandysul (tel. 055936 3322) and Alan Williams, Lampeter Angling, 57 Bridge St, Lampeter (tel. 0570 422985). Free instruction by qualified instructors from the West Wales School of Fly Fishing available every Fri through Aug, including for non-members. Cerdin Twelli; trout (good). Clettwr, 2m; trout (good). Bargoed, 5m. Hotels: Kings Arms; Castle Howell; Henllan Falls, Henllan, Llandysul; Porth and County Gate, Llanfihangel-ar-Arth, Pencader.

Llanybydder (Dyfed). Salmon, sewin, brown trout. Llanybydder AA has approx 5m of Middle Teifi. St £42, wt £31.50 and £36.50, dt £8.50 and £12.50. Concessions for jun. Full membership is restricted to

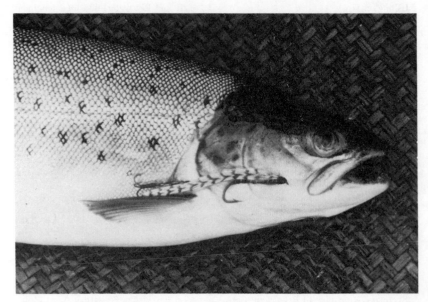

Importance is attached by Welsh sea trout fishers to the fly having a 'life'. This one appears to have possessed that attribute. *Photo: Moc Morgan.*

those residing within 15m of Llany-bydder, however, long-stay holiday visitors may apply for membership. Permits from hon sec and David Morgan, Siop-y-Bont, Llanybydder. Hotels: Crosshands; Black Lion; Grannell, Llanwnnen.

Lampeter (Dyfed). Salmon, April onwards; sewin, late June, July, August onwards; brown trout, both dry and wet fly. Both Llandysul AA and Tregaron AA have water on Teifi around Lampeter. **Hendre Pools,** rainbow trout; permits from O G Thomas, Hendre, Cilcennin, Nr Lampeter SA48 8RF. **Troed-y-Bryn Fisheries,** rainbow and brown trout, privately owned lakes, 3½ acres, fly only; permits from Mrs E E Edwards, Troed-y-Bryn,

Cribyn, Lampeter. NRA licences from A Williams, Alan's Gent's Hairdressers, 57 Bridge St.

Tregaron (Dyfed). Good fly fishing for brown trout. Salmon fishing also good when conditions right. Tregaron AA has 14m of Teifi from Lampeter to Pontrhydfendigaid. St £35-£40. Concessions for jun & OAP. Permits from Post Office, Pontrhydfendigaid; W Rees, London House, Llanddewi Brefi; Post Office, Llanfair Clydogau; and Alan Williams, 57 Bridge St, Lampeter. Permits for **Teifi Pools** from Post Office, Pontrhydfendigaid. Other good fishing on Aeron, 6m. Hotel: Talbot. Accommodation: Brynawel and Aberdwr Guest Houses.

TOWY (or TYWI)

(For close seasons, licences, etc, see Welsh Region NRA, p18)

Rises in the Cambrians, near source of Teifi, and enters seaward end of Bristol Channel by small estuary. Lower reaches near Carmarthen are tidal holding trout, salmon and sewin in season (May, June and July best); association waters. Above this Towy mostly preserved, but some fishing by leave, ticket or from hotels. Salmon average 12lb and sea trout up to 8lb are taken; brown trout generally small.

Carmarthen (Dyfed). Salmon, sewin, trout. April and May usually good for

large sewin. Tidal up to Carmarthen and 3m above. Carmarthen Amateur AA has fishing on **Towy** at Cwm, Palace, Bwlch, Penlan Cystanog, Tycastell. Rwyth, Plasnewydd, Glanyrynys, Glantowylan, Capel Dewi and Tyllwyd. Assn also has fishing on Rivers **Cothi, Gwili** and **Cynin**. Competitions and fly fishing instruction for juniors. Permits from Lyric Sports, King Street. Carmarthen and Dist AC has useful waters within 2 or 3m of town and extending for 2m of Towy. These cover tidal reaches, which give sport with salmon, sewin and trout. Club has water also on Cothi, Gwili; sea trout, trout, some salmon; **Gwendraeth Fach** (6m to 8m away; sea trout lower, trout only upper); **Taf** (10m away) and **Dewi Fawr.** Trout only (average ¼lb) in **Gwendraeth Fach** and Dewi Fawr. Permits and NRA licences from Jones-Davies, King St, Carmarthen; Towy Sport, 9 King St, Llandeilo; R Thomas, Stepney St, Llanelli; and PO, Nantgaredig. Brynderwen Hotel, Llangunnor has salmon, sea trout and trout fishing on Rivers Towy, Cothi and Gwili; coarse fishing on farm ponds. Hotel: Pontercothi Hotel, Pontercothi, Carmarthen.

Nantgaredig (Dyfed). Salmon, trout, sewin; fishing private. Cothi; salmon, sewin. Carmarthen Amateur AA has water on **Cothi** and **Gwili**. NRA licences available from Post Office Dolgoed, Station Rd. Tackle shop: The Armourers Shop, Ye Olde Post Office, Felingwm Uchaf.

Llandeilo (Dyfed). Salmon, sea trout, brown trout. Llandeilo AA preserves 8½m on Towy, about 1½m on **Lower Dulais** and about 3m on **Lower Cennen.**

St £50 + joining fee £100, members only (waiting list), from hon sec; wt £50, dt £12.50 from hon sec and Towy Sport, 9 King St. Concessions for jun. Fishing good when water in condition. Black Lion Inn, Llansawel, has 2½m on Towy; rods also available on **Teifi** and **Cothi. Cennen** good trout stream. Hotels: King's Head; Cawdor Arms; Castle; Edwinsford Arms; Plough Inn; White Hart; Cottage Inn; Ty-Isaf Fishing Lodge and Country Cottages, Trapp, Llandeilo (game fishing on rivers and reservoirs; tuition available).

Llangadog (Dyfed). Salmon, sewin, trout. Llangadog AA have water. Wt, dt and limited night-fishing tickets issued.

Llanwrda (Dyfed). Salmon and sea trout. Swansea Amateur AA rents 1m (both banks), on an annual basis; access south of railway station; fly only. Members and guests only. St £80 and dt £5. Concessions for juniors. Glanrannell Park Country House Hotel, Crugybar, Llanwrda, SA19 8SA (tel. 0558 685230), has fishing available to guests on various private and club waters on **Rivers Cothi, Towy** and **Teifi**. Almost all on day ticket basis and hotel can obtain all tickets in advance if required.

Llandovery (Dyfed). Salmon, sewin (best June-Sept), trout. Day and weekly tickets for visitors on Llandovery AA waters; 2m on **Gwydderig,** 3m on **Bran** and 10½m on **Towy,** clubs best water. Tackle shop: Llandovery Sports, 28 Store St, SA20 0JP. Hotels: Glenrannell Park Country House, Crugbar, Llanwrda, Nr Llandovery.

Tributaries of the Towy

GWILI. Small river of 12ft to 16ft in width which joins Towy 1m north of Carmarthen. Sea trout (sewin), fish running from early June onwards, averaging 2lb and attaining 6lb. Brown trout fishing poor. A few salmon caught on Gwili, especially at the end of year.

Llanpumsaint (Dyfed). Sewin, trout, occasional salmon. Carmarthen Amateur AA and Carmarthen and Dist AC both have stretches on Gwili. Hotel: Fferm-y-Felin (18th century farmhouse with 15 acres of countryside for fishing and bird watching, tuition and equipment available).

COTHI. Larger river than Gwili, but rocky and difficult to fish in some areas. Excellent sport with sewin (June onwards);

salmon very good. Some fly water middle and upper reaches. Worm most popular, but spinning also much used.

Carmarthen (Dyfed). Carmarthen Amateur AA and Carmarthen & Dist AC both have stretches on Cothi. Cothi Bridge Hotel, Pontarcothi, has a short stretch of salmon fishing and has arrangements for guests to fish on other private and club waters. Tackle shops: Lyric Sports, King St; M Lewis, Fishing & Shooting Supplies, 33 King St.

Brechfa (Dyfed). Salmon and sea trout. Swansea Amateur AA has 2m (both banks), between Abergorlech and Brechfa. Members and guests only. St £80 and dt £5. Hotels: Ty Mawr.

Pumpsaint (Dyfed). **Cothi** and **Twrch.**
Trout, sea trout (June onwards); salmon
from early July. Dolaucothi Arms has 4½m
stretch running through National Trust
property; fishing reserved for guests; limited permits available if guests not fishing. Glanrannell Park Hotel, Crugybar
has trout fishing on **Glanrannell Brook**
and salmon, sea trout and trout fishing on

Teifi, Cothi and Twrch.
SAWDDE. Llanddeusant (Dyfed). Trout.
Accommodation and fishing available at
Cross Inn and Black Mountain Caravan
and Camping Park, Llanddeusant, Nr
Llangadog SA19 9YG; rainbow and
brown trout fishing on **Usk Reservoir**
(3m), also on Sawdde (3m) and Towy
(6m).

USK and EBBW

(For close seasons, licences, etc, see Welsh Region NRA, p18)

The River Usk is a good salmon river and first rate for trout. Geological formation is red
sandstone, merging into limestone in lower reaches. Trout average from about ¾lb in the
lower reaches to ¼lb towards the source. Some tributaries also afford good trout fishing:
Afon Llwyd, Honddu, Grwyne, Yscir and Bran. Salmon fishing mostly private, but several
opportunities for trout. The River Ebbw flows into the Severn Estuary between the mouths
of the River Rhymney and the River Usk. The Ebbw has recently experienced great improvements in water quality which has been reflected in the fishery improvements, with very good
trout and reports of sea trout. The Sirhowy, a tributary of Ebbw, also has good trout fishing.

Newport (Gwent). Newport AA has stretch
of **Monmouthshire and Brecon Canal,
Woodstock Pool, Morgans Pool** and
Liswerry Pond; all providing good
coarse fishing, including carp and tench.
Assn also has ½m (left bank) trout and
coarse fishing on **R Ebbw;** and 1½m
salmon and coarse fishing on **R Wye** be-
tween Goodrich and Symonds Yat (mem-
bers only and no day tickets for Wye).
Permits from Newport tackle shops. Isl-
wyn & Dist AC have trout fishing on
Ebbw, **Sirhowy** and **Penyfan Pond.**
Membership from Mrs J Meller, Membership Secretary, 7 Penllwyn Street,
Cwmfelinfach. Day tickets from
Pontllanfraith Leisure Centre. Tackle
shops: Garry Evans, 29 Redland St; Pill
Angling Centre, 160 Commercial Rd;
Dave Richards, 73 Church Road. Hotels:
King's Head, Queen's, Westgate, Tredegar Arms.
Pontypool (Gwent). Usk private. Tributary
Afon Llwyd, good trout fishing and regularly stocked by local clubs. Subject to
periodic pollution but soon recovers due
to exceptionally fast flow. Pontypool AA
and Cwmbran AA have stretches. Pontypool AA also has **Olway Brook,** nr Usk,
trout, dace and chub: **Pontypool Park
Lake,** not yet fully developed: and restricted fishing on Llandetty stretch of
River Usk (1 Oct-16 Jan). St £16, dt £4;
available from Pill Angling. **Llandegfedd Reservoir** (429 acres) owned by
Welsh Water plc is a major boat fishery;
well stocked with brown and rainbow

trout; season 20 Mar-31 Oct (rainbow),
20 Mar-17 Oct (brown). Fly only; catch
limit 6 fish (part day, 4 fish). St £300, dt
£9 (morning £7 and evening £6.50); from
Sluvad Treatment Works, Llandegfedd
Reservoir, Panteg, Pontypool (tel: 0495
755122); and vending machines on site.
Forty boats available, pre-booking is recommended. Cwmbran AA has coarse
fishing on **Monmouthshire & Brecon
Canal;** average depth 4ft; stocked with
bream, tench, crucian carp, roach, perch,
good eels in parts; strict control on litter.
Assn also has coarse fishing at **Llantarnam Industrial Estates Ponds** (2 ponds
opened as fisheries in 1986 and stocked
with roach, perch and dace and one
stocked with rudd and bream opened in
1989): and excellent mixed fishing on
River Monnow, trout, grayling, bream
(recently stocked), roach, perch, dace,
chub and carp. Night fishing on canal and
Monnow. Permits available from
Cwmbran Pet Stores and Angling Supplies, Commercial St, Old Cwmbran. No
day tickets on Llantarnam Ponds; members only.
Usk (Gwent). Usk Town Water Fishery Association holds about 2m mostly above
Usk Bridge. Trout fishing only. NRA licence required. Wading advisable. Merthyr Tydfil AA has water at **Kemeys
Commander.** Permits, tackle and licences from Sweet's Fishing Tackle, 14
Porthycarne Street, NP5 1RY (tel. 0291
672552). Hotels: Three Salmons; Castle;
Cross Keys; Glen-yr-Avon; Kings Head;

Chain Bridge, Nr Usk; Bridge Inn.
Abergavenny (Gwent). Salmon, trout. Monmouth D.C. holds town waters, both banks from Llanfoist Bridge to Sewer Bridge. Tickets from Bridge Inn, Llanfoist and PM Fishing Tackle. Crucorney Trout Farm, on **River Honddu;** small river fishing with lots of cover; stocked with 1-2lb rainbows, wild browns; fly only; permits from farm shop. Advance booking essential. Tel: 0873 890545. Merthyr Tydfil AA has rights to **Mardy Fishery,** 1¼m above town. Tickets for various waters from PM Fishing Tackle. Tackle shops: PM Fishing Tackle, 12 Monk Street; Fussells Sports, 53 Cross Street, both Abergavenny; Brutens, Market Street, Ebbw Vale. Hotel: Wenallt; Penpergwm House.
Glangrwyney (Powys). Salmon, sea trout, brown trout. Bell Hotel has water here and issues tickets to residents and non-residents for salmon and trout fishing. Hotel stocks Usk flies.
Crickhowell (Powys). Salmon, sea trout, wild brown trout. Gliffaes Country House Hotel, NP8 1RH (tel. 0874 730371) *(see advt)* has 1m on Usk adjacent to hotel and a further 1½m upstream. Excellent wild

brown trout water; salmon improving and some sea trout. Primarily hotel guests but outside rods if space available. Dt (S) £17 and (T) £12. Bridge End Inn has short length below bridge. **Trecastle** and **Talybont Reservoirs** are within reach. Hotel: Stables.
Brecon (Powys). Brecon AS has water on Usk; stretches on Upper, Middle and Lower Newton; and Newton Wier. Trout fishing only on Usk from boathouse to Llanfaes Bridge. Season tickets - members only. Dt £3 from Mrs Lindsey Wilding, Post Office, Llanfaes, Brecon (tel. 0874 622739); and H.M. Supplies Ltd, Watton, Brecon (tel. 0874 622148). Brecon Borough Council has stretch on Usk from boathouse to promenade Watton. Salmon and trout fishing on Wye and Usk in the Brecon and Builth Wells area; day tickets are available from Woosnam & Taylor (Chartered Surveyors & Land Agents), Dolgarreg, North Road, Builth Wells, Powys LD2 3DD (tel. 0982 553248). Brecon FA has 1m both banks below Llanfaes Bridge; trout; fly only. Permits and rod licences, also coarse fishing permits for pools at Darew Farm, Llyswen. Anglers visiting the farm pools

The River Usk enjoys distinction as both a salmon and a brown trout river. Here an angler fishes the fly for the former from the rapid above a pool. *Photo: Eric Chalker.*

are advised to bring their bait with them. 6m from Brecon, **Llangorse Lake;** pike, perch, roach and bream; no permits required only NRA licence. Boats and caravans from Mr Davies at Waterside. Hotels: Griffin Inn, Llyswen, Brecon; Castle of Brecon; Nythfa, Uskview GH.

Sennybridge (Powys). Rods available on **Crai Reservoir** (100 acres) owned by Cnewr Estate Ltd, Sennybridge, Brecon LD3 8SP (tel. 0874 636207). Wild trout; fly fishing from bank only. Dt £7 from reservoir keeper (£4 OAP & jun). Self-catering accommodation is usually available with the fishing. Hotels: Tir y Graig Uchaf.

Trecastle (Powys). **Usk Reservoir** (280 acres), one of the best trout fisheries in Wales, well stocked with rainbow and brown trout supplementing natural production. Fly fishing, spinning and worming. Catch limit 6 fish; size limit 9 inches.

Anglers are permitted to use their own boats by prior arrangement. Dt £7.50 from machine on site. For further information contact C Hatch, Area Manager, Hamdden, Pentwyn Rd, Nelson, Treharris, Mid Glamorgan. Hotel: Castle.

Ebbw Vale (Gwent). Ebbw Vale Welfare AC has coarse fishing on **River** Wye at Foy, nr Ross-on-Wye, 2½m (chub, dace, roach and barbel); **Monmouthshire & Brecon Canal**, nr Crickhowell, ½m (roach, perch, bream); **Machine Pond** at Brynmawr, 5 acres (carp, roach, perch); and 10 ponds in the Ebbw Vale area (carp, pike, roach, perch and gudgeon). Members only. Membership open to all; available from hon sec and local pet shop. Contact hon sec for season tickets for people on holiday (£10 and £3 for ponds only). Concessions for juniors. Tackle shops: J Williams & Son, Bethcar St; Petsville, Bethcar St.

WELSH SEA FISHING STATIONS

Those given in the following list are arranged from south to north. Sea fishing is available at other places also, but those mentioned are included because they cater specially for the sea angler. Further information may be had from the tackle shops and club secretaries (whose addresses will be found in the club list). When writing, please enclose stamped addressed envelope for reply. Local authorities will help with accommodation.

Swansea (West Glamorgan). Bass, flatfish from beaches and rocks (Worm's Head). Fish baits cast from Llanmadoc take conger, tope, thornbacks and monkfish. Mackerel caught in warmer months. Bass, mullet and flounders in estuary at Loughor Bridge. Excellent boat fishing in Carmarthen Bay and off Worm's Head. Welsh Tope, Skate and Conger Club charters boats leaving Swansea riverside quays and fishing the bay and Pwlldu. All booking for boats and bait (which is difficult) can be obtained by P E Mainwaring, Specialists in Fishing Equipment, 9 Dillwyn Road, Sketty, Swansea (tel: Swansea 202245). Club membership made through qualifying fish. HQ: Rock and Fountain Inn, Skewen. Small bass, mullet, flatfish and mackerel off Mumbles Pier; no night fishing. Docks permit required for Queens Dock breakwater; good for cod in winter. Bait can be dug in Swansea Bay and estuary; squid, herring, sprats and mackerel from Swansea Market. For details of charter-boats, apply to Derek Jones, 24 Cilonen Road, Three Crosses. Tackle shops: Mainwarings, Sketty; Capstan House, Unit 16, Beaufort Rd, Plasmarl; Dave's Angling Centre, 74a Brynymor Rd: Hook, Line & Sinker, Fishing Tackle Shop, Viking Way, Enterprise Park, Winchwen: Mumbles Sea Angling Centre, Knab Rock, Mumbles Rd, Mumbles; The Pilot House, Marina Maritime Quarter, Pilots Wharf; Sea Angling Centre, Pilot House Wharf, Maritime Quarter; Linnard Sports, 25 High St; Marine Centre, 1 Fishmarket Quay, Marina.

Tenby (Dyfed). Good sport from Old Pier; whiting, pollack, bass, codling and grey mullet; good bass fishing from south and north sandy beaches, and spinning from rocks. Fine mackerel fishing most seasons, and tope off Caldey Island. For boats enquire tackle shop. Shark trips also arranged. Tackle shop: Morris Bros, Troy House, St Julian Street.

Milford Haven and **Pembroke** (Dyfed). Fine surf-fishing and spinning from rocks for bass from Freshwater West and Broad Haven (Bosherton); best late summer and autumn. Kilpaison good for bass, flatfish early on; also codling and coalfish. Stone piers and jetties inside Haven provide deep water sport for pollack, skate, rays, whiting, codling, dogfish and coalfish. Hobbs Point (Pembroke Dock) excellent for conger and skate. Mackerel from rocks and boats (Stackpole Quay good). Tope from boats in Barafundle Bay and mackerel and bass from rocks. Other useful venues are Nab Head, Martins Haven and Angle Bay, Thorn, Rat and Sheep Islands and Harbour Rock. Mackerel from boats at harbour entrance. Lugworm and razor fish may be dug in several places, esp mud-flats at Kilpaison and Angle Bay. Pennar Gut and Pembroke River. Brindley John Ayers, "Antique Fishing Tackle", 8 Bay View Drive, Hakin, Milford Haven SA73 3RJ (tel 0646 698359) is a mail orders business that collects and specialises in used high quality fishing tackle; visitors are welcome; and bed and breakfast is available. Tackle shops: Sports and Leisure, Main Street; Donovan Sports, 61 Bush Street, Pembroke; Penfro Fishing Tackle, Pembroke Dock.

Fishguard (Dyfed). Main captures from shore and breakwaters are flatfish, codling, conger, pouting, mackerel, bass, pollack, whiting and some tope. Sea trout and mullet near mouth of Gwaun. Tope, mackerel, conger, skate, etc. from boats. Boats from Fishguard Yacht & Boat Co, Main Street, Goodwick. Tel Fishguard 873377 and Brooks, Lower Town. Tackle shop: Thomas and Howells, Dyfed Sports, 21 West Street. Hotel: Beach House, Fishguard Bay, Goodwick, Dyfed SA64 0DH (sea fishing trips and packed lunches plus freezer for keeping catch).

Aberystwyth (Dyfed). From the shore, May to November, bass (especially on soft crab bait), pollack, painted ray, mullet, huss, conger, wrasse. From October to January, whiting; July to September,

Porbeagle sharks of 140 lbs. and 145 lbs. caught off Aberystwyth. *Photo: Vic Haigh.*

mackerel. Dogfish, dabs and flounder throughout the year. Fish caught off the rocks, off storm beaches, from the harbour and stone jetty. Borth beach and Leri estuary specially good for flounders; Tan-y-bwlch beach particularly good for whiting. Bull huss and thornback ray form the backbone of the boat fishing, but dogfish, dabs, gurnard, pollack, tope, bream, turbot, monkfish and porbeagle shark are taken in their seasons. Boat trips are run from the harbour ranging from 2 hour sessions for mackerel to 12 hours out at sea. There are many well-equipped boats commanded by highly experienced skippers. Endeavour Deep Sea Angling Club, May to October, two 36ft Scoresby offshore sport-fishing vessels, have established or broken 30 Welsh and 2 British records. Full SOLAS survival equipment. GPS navigator and plotter precision on unfished wrecks. Individual membership and club affiliations invited to enjoy low cost angling. Tuition available, April to October. Further information from hon sec (tel. 0970 84474). Tackle shops: Aber Fishing Tackle & Gun Shop, 13 Terrace Road. Accommodation: Shoreline Guest House, 6 South Marine Terrace.

Barmouth (Gwynedd). Bass (large), flatfish, mullet in Mawddach estuary and from nearby beaches; also codling, mackerel, flatfish, and even tope and skate from boats. Ynys y Brawd island good for bass and flounders from shore and boats.

Porthmadog (Gwynedd). Mackerel and deep sea fishing trips available; 2hr, 4hr and 8hr; bookings from Angling and Gun Centre, Madog St, LL49 9LR (tel. 0766 512464).

Pwllheli and **Criccieth** (Gwynedd). Improved bass fishing April-October with new size limit to protect small bass; dogfish, dabs, plaice, skate, pollack and a few sole the year round; mackerel, tope and monkfish from June to September and black bream now on the increase (2 fish of over 4lb taken in 1991). October to January; whiting and coalfish. Boats and bait available. Tackle shops: D & E Hughes, Walsall Stores, 24 Penlan Street, Pwllheli LL53 5DE; R T Pritchard & Son, Sheffield House, High Street, Criccieth LL52 0EY.

Bangor (Gwynedd). Centre for Menai Straits and Anglesey. Excellent bass and plaice in Menai Straits. Best beaches on Anglesey. Good rock marks abound for wrasse, pollack, thornback, smooth hound, mackerel, herring and bull huss. Good cod fishing in winter. Boats, for parties and clubs, apply A J Regan, 106 Orme Road (tel: 0248 364590). Tackle shops: BASS Fishing Tackle, Unit 2, Plaza Buildings, High St.

Deganwy (Gwynedd). Wide variety of fish taken from boats in Gt Orme, Menai Straits and Puffin Island areas. Bass in estuary and off Benarth, Bodlondeb and Deganwy Points and Beacon Light. Wreck fishing. Bait from shore and estuary. Sea fishing trips (wreck fishing a speciality); and tackle for sale or hire; from Meurig Davies, Pen-y-Berllan, Pentywyn Road, Deganwy LL31 9TL (tel: 0492 581983). Club: Bangor City Angling Club.

Llandudno (Gwynedd). Skate, cod, codling, pollack, bass, mackerel, plaice, whiting, conger, coalfish, etc. Rocky beach at corner of Little Orme good for bass; so is west shore, especially Black Rocks area. Bait plentiful. Fishing from pier, beach, rocks and boats. Tope and mackerel taken by boat fishers. Tackle shop: Llandudno Fishing Tackle, 41a Victoria St, Craig-y-Don. Hotel: Epperstone (fishing can be organised from hotel).

Colwyn Bay (Clwyd). Bass off Rhos Point and Penmaenhead. Whiting, codling in winter from beach. Dabs, whiting, some plaice from pier (dt available all year). Tope and skate from boats. For sea fishing contact Rhos-on-Sea Fishing, Rhos-on-Sea Harbour, Rhos-on-Sea, Colwyn Bay (tel. 0492 544 829). Tackle shops: Duttons, 52 Sea View Road (bait); R D Pickering, 60 Abergele Road; Pet Stores, Market Hall. Hotel: Ashmount Hotel, College Avenue, Rhos-on-Sea , Colwyn Bay LL28 4NT (a variety of activities available including sea fishing trips); Stanton House, Rhos-on-Sea (sea fishing organised by hotel).

Rhyl (Clwyd). Skate, dabs, codling, whiting, plaice, gurnard, dog-fish, tope. From Foryd Harbour at Rhyl, east towards Dee Estuary at Prestayn, no licence or permit to fish is required, providing tackle and bait used are for sea fishing and not game fishing. Several boats, fully licensed to take fishing parties and charter booking, are available at Foryd Harbour from Blue Shark Fishing Trips, The Harbour, Quay

---

Check before you go

Street (tel: 0745 350267). Tackle shops: Wm Roberts Ltd, 131 High Street.

ANGLESEY

Holyhead and **Holy Island.** Fishing off Holyhead Breakwater, $1\frac{3}{4}$m long, good on any tide; summer and winter fishing, many species caught. Very good fishing also on Stanley Embankment, at Cymyran, Rhoscolyn, Trearddur Bay, Porthdafarch and Holyhead Mountain. Bull huss, dogfish, pollack, wrasse, mullet, cod, plaice, dab, flounder, conger, whiting, codling, thornback ray and bass all taken in season from the various shore-marks. Boat-fishing, possible in all but the worst of weather, yields also shark, tope, ling and smoothhound. Bait readily available. Excellent boat fishing; thornbacks, tope, etc. Bait in harbour or from tackle shops: Dorset Stores, Kingsland; R P Owen; Thos Owen, 19/20 Cybi Street; Holyhead (J's) Sports, 2 Boston Street, which acts as an agency for charter-boat hire. Sells fresh and frozen seabait, provides instruction, and repairs rods and reels on the premises. Boat hire at Cymyran Bay from John Crouch, tel: 0407 740019. Hotels: Alma Lodge; Bull.

Amlwch (Gwynedd). Tope taken to 40lb, skate, conger, herring, mackerel, etc, from boats; obtainable at Amlwch and at Bull Bay ($1\frac{1}{2}$m). Tackle shop: Pilot Stores and Fishing Tackle, 66-68 Machine St, Amlwch Port. Hotel: Bryn Ednyfyd, Amlwch Port. Hotels: Lastra Farm, Trees.

Beaumaris (Anglesey). Big bass, tope, pollack, mullet and mackerel opposite Beaumaris and along the Straits. Between Menai and The Tubular Bridge fair-sized bass and conger are caught. For boat fishing contact Stan Zalot, Starida Boats, Little Bryn, off Rosemary Lane (tel: 0248 810251), and Dave Jones, Beaumaris Marine Services, The Anchorage, Rosemary Lane (tel: 0248 810746). Tackle shop: Anglesey Boat Co, The Shop, Gallows Point (tel. 0248 810359); Ken Johnson, Menai Bridge (tel. 0248 714508). Hotels: Ye Olde Bulls Head Inn; Bulkeley; Bishopsgate.

FISHING CLUBS & ASSOCIATIONS IN WALES

Included in this list of fishing clubs and associations in Wales are some organisations which have their water on the upper reaches of the Wye or Severn, details of which are contained in the English section of **Where to Fish**. Further information can usually be had from the Secretaries and a courtesy which is appreciated is the inclusion of a stamped addressed envelope with postal inquiries. Please advise the publishers (address at the front of the book) of any changed details for the next edition.

NATIONAL BODIES

Wales Tourist Board
Brunel House
2 Fitzalan Road
Cardiff
South Glamorgan CF2 1UY
Tel: 0222 499909
Welsh Federation of Coarse Anglers
Mrs A Mayers
6 Biddulph Rise
Tupsley
Hereford HR1 1RA
Welsh Federation of Sea Anglers
G H Jones
8 Moreton Road

Holyhead
Gwynedd LL65 2BG
Tel 0407 763821
Welsh Salmon and Trout Association
M J Morgan
Swyn Teifi
Pontrhydfendigaid
Ystrad
Meurig, Dyfed SY25 6EF
Welsh Tope, Skate and Conger Club
Colin Delfosse
25 Mill Place
Ely, Cardiff CF5 4AJ

CLUBS

Aberaeron Town Angling Club
D S Rees
10 North Road
Aberaeron, Dyfed SA46 0JF
Aberaeron Angling Club
Nigel R Davies
Wenallt
16 Belle Vue Terrace
Aberaeron
Dyfed SA46 0HB
Abergwili Angling Club
Eric Thomas
60 Abergwili Road
Carmarthen, Dyfed
Aberystwyth Angling Association
Peredur W Eklund
42 Erwgoch
Waunfawr
Aberystwyth

Dyfed SY23 3AZ
Tel. 0970 623021
Afan Valley Angling Club
M Reynolds
8 Newlands
Baglan
Port Talbot
W Glamorgan
Alltami Angling Club
J Joyce
27 Moel View Rd
Buckley, Clwyd
Ammanford and District Angling Association
Ron Woodland
2 Pontarddulais Road
Llangennech
Nr Llanelli
Dyfed SA14 8YF

Fishing Clubs

When you appoint a new secretary, do not forget to give us details of the change. Write to the publishers (address at front of the book). Thank you!

Tel. 0554 820477
Artro and Talsarnau Fishing Association
P G Cozens
Awelfryn
Llanbedr
Gwynedd LL45 2HL
Bala and District Angling Association
David Gumbley
Llwyn Ffynnon
17 Mawnog Fach
Bala
Gwynedd LL23 7YY
Bangor City Angling Club
Mrs Pat Thomas
21 Lon-y-Glyder
Bangor
Gwynedd
Bangor-on-Dee Salmon Angling
Association
S L Adams
Hendy
High Street
Bangor-on-Dee, Wrexham
Clwyd LL13 0BB
Betws-y-Coed Anglers' Club
Melfyn Hughes
Cae Garw
Betws-y-Coed
Gwynedd LL24 0BY
Tel. 0690 710618
Birchgrove (Cardiff) Angling Association
J S Wilmot
4 Clydesmuir Rd
Tremorfa, Cardiff CF2 2QA
Bodelwyddan Angling Society
I C Hall
Tel. 0745 856239
Bradley Angling Club
Graham Hughes
11 Cedar Close
Bradley
Nr Wrexham, Clwyd
Brecon Angling Society
Mr Denzil Harris
66 Coryton Close
Brecon, Powys
Tel. 0874 625552
Brynmill Angling Club
T J East
52 Cnap Illwyd Road
Morriston
Swansea
Bryn-y-Pys Angling Association
Mrs A Phillips
2 Ruabon Road
Wrexham, Clwyd LL13 7BB
Buckley Angling Association
R W Jones
Cresta

35 Bryn Awelon
Mold, Clwyd CH7 1LT
Bute Angling Society
S G Allen
37 Aberporth Road
Gabalfa, Cardiff CF4 2RX
Tel. 0222 618579
Caergwrle Angling Club
Mrs E Lewis
Bronwlfa
Hawarden Road
Caergwrle
Nr Wrexham, Clwyd LL12 9BB
Cambrian Angling Association
K I Williams
11 Dorfil St
Blaenau Ffestiniog
Gwynedd LL41 3UY
Capenhurst Angling Club
A T Howdon
24 Saughall Hey
Saughall
Chester, Cheshire CH1 6EJ
Carmarthen Amateur Angling
Association
Ron Ratti
Rhydal Mount
The Parade
Carmarthen
Dyfed SA31 1LZ
Camarthen and District Angling Club
L R Thomas
71 Caeglas
Cross Hands
Llanelli, Dyfed
Carmarthen Fishermens Federation
Garth Roberts
Talrhyn
Tresaith Road
Aberporth
Dyfed SA43 2EB
Tel. 0239 810515
Cefni Angling Association
G R Williams
Tyn Lon, Gaerwen
Pentre Berw
Anglesey
Cerrig-y-Drudion Angling Association
W M Roberts
4 Cae Lwydd
Cerrig-y-Drudion
Clwyd
Cheshire Anglers Association
G Brassington
12 Highfield Drive
Nantwich,
Cheshire
Chester Association of Anglers
B W Roberts

23 Alpraham Crescent
Upton Cross
Chester, Cheshire
Tel. 0244 381193
Chirk Angling Association
J L Davies
76 Longfield, Chirk
Nr Wrexham, Clwyd
Cilcain Fly Fishing Association
A E Williams
Gwynfryn
Caerwys Hill
Caerwys, Mold
Clwyd
Tel. 0352 720554
Connah's Quay and District Angling Club
H Messham
45 Lyndon Avenue
Connah's Quay, Clwyd
Corris and District Angling Association
Denis Woodvine
Ty Isaf
Ceinws, Machynlleth
Powys
Corwen and District Angling Club
Gordon H Smith
Llais-yr-Afon
Bontuchel
Ruthin
Clwyd LL15 2DE
Tel. 08246 609
Criccieth, Llanystumdwy and District Angling Association
Gordon Hamilton
Morawel
Llanystumdwy
Criccieth, Gwynedd LL52
Crickhowell Angling Club
Tom Probert
Crickhowell
Powys
Cross Hands and District Angling Association
L R Thomas
71 Caeglas
Cross Hands
Llanelli, Dyfed
Cwmbran Angling Association
P M Gulliford
305 Llantarnam Rd
Cwmbran, Gwent NP44 3BJ
Tel. 0633 874472
Cwmcelyn Angling Club
P Hunt
East Pentwyn Farm
Blaina, Gwent NP3 3HX
Cwmllynfell Fly Fishing Club
D Lloyd

73 Bryn Road
Bryn Villas
Cwmllynfell
West Glamorgan
Dee Anglers Association
B J Green
189a Saughall Road
Blacon
Chester, Cheshire
Denbigh and Clwyd Angling Club
C P Harness
8 Llwyn Menlli
Ruthin, Clwyd LL15 1RG
Dolgarrog Fishing Club
Peter Jones
12 Hillside Cottages
Dolgarrog
Gwynedd LL32
Dolgellau Angling Association
E M Davies
Maescaled, Dolgellau
Gwynedd LL40 1UF
Tel. 0341 422706
Dolwyddelan Fishing Association
J Lloyd Price
Bryn Melyn
Dolwyddelan
Gwynedd LL25 0EJ
Dwyryd Anglers Ltd
Gareth Ffestin Price
Hafan
Ffordd Peniel
Ffestiniog
Gwynedd LL41 4LP
Tel. 076676 2451
Ebbw Vale Welfare Angling Club
R Satterley
8 Pen-y-lan
Ebbw Vale
Gwent NP3 5LS
Elan Valley Angling Club
Noel Hughes
25 Brynheulog
Rhayader
Powys LD6 5EF
Endeavour Deep Sea Angling Club
B Haigh
Ty Llyn
Cwmrheidol
Aberystwyth
Dyfed SY23 3NB
Estimaner Angling Association
J Baxter
11 Tan y Fedw
Abergynolwyn, Tywyn
Gwynedd LL36 9YU
Tel. 0654 782632
Felindre Angling Club
M Randall

77 Water Street
Kidwelly, Dyfed
Gilwern and District Angling Club
H R Lewis
27 Brynglas, Gilwern
Nr Abergavenny
Gwent NP7 0BP
Glamorgan Anglers' Club
D Rees
54 Pentrbane Road
Fairwater
Cardiff CF5 3R3
Glaslyn Angling Association
Alan Pritchard
Dolafon, Maes-y-Garth
Minffordd, Penrhyndeudraeth
Gwynedd LL48 6EE
Tel. 0766 770025
Glyncornel Angling Association
J M Evans
126 Ystrad Road
Ystrad, Rhondda
Mid Glamorgan CF41 7PS
Tel. 0443 439961
**Glynneath and District Angling
Association**
Kevin Siddley
21 Bethania St
Glynneath, Neath
West Glamorgan
Tel. 0639 722590
Clwb Godre Mynydd Du
203 Cwmamman Road
Glanamman
Dyfed
Greenfield Valley Trust Angling Club
Basingwerk House
Greenfield Valley Heritage Park
Greenfield
Nr Holywell
Clwyd CH8 7BQ
Tel. 0352 715159
Griffin Angling Club
D C Cope
22 Meadow View
Marford
Nr Wrexham, Clwyd
Gro Park and Irfon Angling Club
Dolshedyn
15 Irfon Road
Builth Wells
Powys LD2 3DE

Tel. 0982 552262
Grosvenor Angling Association
D E Whitehouse
Stretton
School Lane
Guilden Sutton
Chester, Cheshire
Gwaun-Cae-Gurwen Angling Association
P E Edwards
32 Heol Cae, Gurwen
Gwaun-Cae-Gurwen
Amman Valley
West Glamorgan
Gwent Avengers
R Dalling
3 The Spinney
Malpas Park
Newport, Gwent
Holt and Farndon Angling Association
R Williams
4 The Cross
Holt, Wrexham
Clywd
Holywell Anglers
B Brushett
27 Long Ceiriog
Prestayn, Clwyd
Isca Angling Club
P Facey
357 Pilton Vale
Newport
Gwent NP9 6LU
Islwyn and District Anglers
Mrs J Meller
7 Penllwyn Street
Cwmfelinfach, Gwent NP1 7HE
Kingfishers Angling Club
M Howells
97 Bwllfa Road
Cwmdas, Aberdare
Mid Glamorgan
Kirkdale Angling Association
A C Hoer
61 Baythorne Road
Liverpool L4 9TJ
Lavister Angling Club
G Watkins
Rathgillan
Lache Hall Crescent
Lache Lane
Chester, Cheshire

Fishing Clubs

When you appoint a new secretary, do not forget to give us details of the change. Write
to the publishers (address at front of the book). Thank you!

Llanbrynmair and District Angling Club
Tony Marsh
Plas Llysyn
Carno,
Powys
Llandeilo Angling Association
J M Walters
Gwynfan
21 Alan Road
Llandeilo, Dyfed SA19 6HU
Tel. 0558 823682
Llandovery Angling Association
M Davies
Cwmrhudden Lodge
Llangadog
Llandovery, Dyfed
Llandybie Angling Association
R Jones
9 Margaret Rd
Llandybie
Dyfed SA18 3YB
Llandysul Angling Association
Artie Jones
Glas-y-Dorlan
Llynyfran Road
Llandysul, Dyfed SA44 4JN
Llanelli Angling Association
D Watkins
60 Llwyn Hendy
Llanelli, Dyfed
Llangadog Angling Association
E Jones
15 Bryniago
Llangadog, Dyfed SA19 9LL
Llangennech Angling Club
D A Owen
99 Hendre Road
Llangennech
Llanelli
Dyfed SA14 8TH
Tel. 0554 820948
Llangollen Angling Association
W N Elbourn
Bwthyn Bach
2 Green Lane
Llangollen, Clwyd LL20 8TB
Llangyfelach and District Angling Association
R L Griffiths
Cefn Cottage
Cilibion
Llanrhidian
Swansea SA3 1ED
Llangynidr Service Station Angling Club
T B Williams
Llangynidr Service Station
Llangynidr
Crickhowell, Powys NP8 1LU

Llanidloes and District Angling Association
J Dallas Davies.
Dresden House
Great Oak Street
Llanidloes, Powys SY18 6BU
Llanilar Angling Association
John H Astill
Dryslwyn, Llanafan
Aberystwyth, Dyfed SY23 4AX
Tel. 09743 237
Llanrwst Anglers' Club
David W P Hughes
36 Station Road
Llanrwst, Gwynedd
Llanybydder Angling Association
William Wilkins
Maes-y-fedw
Llanybydder
Dyfed SA40 9UG
Tel. 0570 480038
Llay Angling Association
John Preston
20 Mold Road Estate
Gwersyllt, Wrexham
Clwyd LL11 4AA
Tel. 0978 758178
Llynfi Valley Angling Association
A Lewis
19 Pit Street
Garth, Maesteg
Mid Glamorgan
Llysyfran Angling Club
P J Eaton
18 Mount Pleasant Way
Milford Haven
Pembrokeshire SA73 1AB
Maelor Angling Association
K Bathers
Sunnyside, Hill Street
Cefn Mawr, Wrexham
Clwyd
Maerdy and Ferndale Angling Club
T Pain
16 Highfield
Ferndale, Rhondda
Mid Glamorgan CF43 4TA
Maghull and Lydiate Angling Club
J Johnson
97 Liverpool Rd (North)
Maghull
Merseyside L31 2HG
Tel. 051 526 4083
Merthyr Tydfil Angling Association
Nigel Morgan
20 James Street
Twynyrodyn
Merthyr Tydfil
Mid Glamorgan

Tel. 0685 377848
Midland Flyfishers
Anthony R Collins
Pearl Assurance House
4 Temple Row
Birmingham B2 5HG
Mold Fly Fishers
A T Allcock
3 Highfield Avenue
Mynydd Isa
Mold, Clwyd CH7 6XY
Tel. 0244 548319
Mold Kingfishers Angling Club
R W Ambrose
25 Pinewood Avenue
Connah's Quay, Clwyd
Mold Trout Anglers
Alun Powell
Makuti
Sunny Ridge
Mold, Clwyd CH7 1RU
Tel. 0352 752468
Montgomeryshire Angling Association (including Llanfair Caereinion FC, Newtown FC, Welshpool AC)
P Hulme
306 Heol-y-Coleg
Vaynar Estate
Newtown, Powys SY16 1RA
Neath and Dulais Angling Association
I J Jones
5 Bryndulais Row
Seven Sisters
Neath
West Glamorgan SA10 9EB
Tel. 0639 701187
Nevern Angling Association
Nica Pritchard
Spring Gardens
Parrog Road
Newport, Pembs
Dyfed SA42 0RJ
Tel. 0239 820671
Newbridge Angling Association
Kerry F R Clutton
28 Worseley Avenue
Johnstown
Nr Wrexham
Clwyd
LL14 2TD
Tel. 0978 840377
New Dovey Fishery Association (1929) Ltd
Glyn Thomas
Plas,
Machynlleth
Powys SY20 8ES
Tel. 0654 702721

Newport Angling Association
L J Clarke
14 Allt-yr-yn Ave
Newport
Gwent NP9 5DB
Newport District Sea Anglers
Joe Guscott
51 Monnow Walk
Bettws
Newport
Gwent NP9 6SS
Newport Reservoir Fly Fishing Association
Jack Stone
13 Hawke Close
Royal Oak
Newport, Gwent
New Quay Angling Club
H Davies
Min-yr-Afon
Abergorlech
Dyfed SA32 7SN
Northern Anglers Association
B Davies
51 Brennard St
Burnley, Lancs
North Wales Angling Association
Paul M Litson
Penmaes Villa
High Street
Dyserth, Clwyd LL18 6AA
Ogmore Angling Association
W A Protheroe
Henllan
Coychurch Road
Pencoed, Bridgend
Mid Glamorgan CF35 5LY
Tel. 0656 861139
Ogwen Valley Angling Association
Bryn Evans
31 Erw Las
Bethesda,
Gwynedd
Ogwr Borough Angling Association
T J Hughes
20 Heol Glannant
Bettws, Bridgend
Mid Glamorgan CF32 8SP
Pembroke and District Angling Club
Mrs T Lustig
10 Deer Park
Stackpole
Pembrokeshire
Pembrokeshire Anglers Association
Mrs B Summers
72 City Road
Haverfordwest
Pembrokeshire
Dyfed SA61 2RR

Tel. 0437 763216
Pembrokeshire Fly Fishers
Captain & Mrs Oliver
Red House
Llawhaden
Narberth
Pembrokeshire
Pencoed and District Angling Club
Dr G M Gwilliam
5 Velindre Road
Pencoed, Bridgend
Mid Glamorgan
Penllwyn Lodges Angling Club
Derek Thomas Field
Penllwyn
Garthmyl
Powys SY15 6SB
Picton Waters Angling Club
I Richards
North Pines
Wiston
Haverfordwest, Dyfed
Ponciau Angling Society
D K Valentine
Bryn Yr Owen
Ponciau
Wrexham, Clwyd
**Pontardawe and District Angling
Association**
R H Lockyer
8 Bwllfa Road
Ynystawe
Swansea
**Pontardulais and District Angling
Association**
J Gabe
20 James Street
Pontardulais, Swansea
West Glamorgan SA4 1HY
Pontypool Angling Association
B J Jones
79 Robertson Way
Woodlands
Malpas, Newport
Gwent NP9 6QQ
Porthcawl Sea Angling Association
(Freshwater Section)
J Lock
67 West Road
Nottage
Porthcawl, Mid Glamorgan

Prince Albert Angling Society
Queen's Hotel
Albert Place
Waters Green
Macclesfield, Cheshire
Prysor Angling Association
David Griffith Williams
Bryn Gwyn
Trawsfynydd
Gwynedd LL41 4UW
Tel. 0766 87310
Pwllheli and District Angling Association
R G Jones
18 Lleyn Street
Pwllheli
Gwynedd
Tel. 0758 613551 (evenings)
Pyrddin Angling Society
Robert Browning
91 Main Road
Duffryn Cellwen
Nr Neath, West Glamorgan
Pysgotwyr Maesnant
D P Higgins
90 Maesceinion
Waunfawr
Aberystwyth SY23 3QQ
Ridgeway Angling Club
R Martin
Hillcroft
Bethlehem
Cardigan Road
Haverfordwest, Dyfed
Rhayader Angling Association
G H Roberts
Belmullet, Rhayader
Powys LD6 5BY
Rhostyllen Angling Club
J R Williams
57 West Grove
Rhostyllen
Wrexham, Clwyd
Rhyl and District Angling Association
Martin Fowell
Bon Amie
28 Ffordd Tanrallt
Meliden
Prestatyn
Clwyd LL19 8PS
Tel. 0745 854390
Rhymney and District Angling Society
G H Roper

Fishing Clubs

When you appoint a new secretary, do not forget to give us details of the change. Write to the publishers (address at front of the book). Thank you!

72 Penybryn Avenue
Cefn Fforest
Blackwood, Gwent NP2 1LH
Tel. 0443 821099
Rossett and Gresford Fly Fishers
L Roberts
Roselea
Clapper Lane
Gresford, Clywd LL12 8RW
Tel. 0978 854829
St Asaph Angling Association
W J P Staines
Delamere
Coed Esgob Lane
St Asaph
Clwyd LL17 0LH
Tel. 0745 583926
St Clears Angling Association
David J Bryan
Madras Cottage
Laugharne
Carmarthen, Dyfed SA33 4NU
**Seiont, Gwyrfai and Llyfni Anglers'
Society**
H P Hughes
Llugwy, Ystad Eryri
Bethel, Caernarfon
Gwynedd LL55 1BX
Tel. 0248 670666
Sevenside Angling Club
Michael John Thomas
253 Measyrhandir
Newtown, Powys SY16 1LB
Skewen Angling Club
M W Doyle
58 The Highlands
Skewen, Neath
West Glamorgan
**Swansea Amateur Angling Association
Ltd**
Peter Bowen-Simpkins
38 Walter Road
Swansea SA1 5NW
Tel. 0792 655600
Swansea Angling Club
Paul Cannin
9 Heol Ceri
Waunarlwydd
Swansea SA5 4QU
Tel. 0792 872123
**Talsarnau and District Angling
Association**
I Owen
Eryri Llanfair
Harlech
Gwynedd
Talybont Angling Association
Ithel Jones
Wern

Talybont, Dyfed SY24 5ER
Tel. 0970 86363
**Tawe and Tributaries Angling
Association**
Michael Matthews
32 Farm Road
Briton Ferry
Neath
West Glamorgan SA11 2TA
Tel 0639 632070
Tawe Disabled Fishers' Association
R W Hale
Willow Bank
Ilston
Swansea SA2 7LD
Teifi Trout Association
Brian Gore
Cwm Broch, Trelledyn
Bridell
Cardigan, Dyfed
Tel. 0239 841332
Tenby and District Angling Club
Mr Bird
Primrose Villa
Narbeth Road
Tenby
Pembrokeshire
Trawscoed Angling Club
C Evans
A D A S
Trawscoed
Aberystwyth, Dyfed
Tregaron Angling Association
M J Morgan
Swyn Teifi
Pontrhydfendigaid
Dyfed
Warrington Angling Association
Frank Lythgoe, Secretary
P O Box 71
Warrington WA1 1LR
Headquarters
52 Parker Street
Warrington
(Open every Friday 7pm - 9.30pm)
**Wentwood Reservoir Fly Fishing
Assocaition**
D G P Jones
123 Castle Lea
Caldicot, Gwent
Whitland Angling Association
Ithel Parri-Roberts
Swyddfa'r Post Office
Hendygwyn-ar-Daf
Whitland
Dyfed SA34 0AA
Wirral Game Fishing Club
P Liddiard
13 Kingswalk

West Kirby
Wirral L48
**Wrexham and District Angling
Association**
J E Tattum
Llys Athro, King Street
Leeswood, Mold
Clwyd CH7 4SB

Wygyr Fishing Association
J M Fraser (Treasurer)
Crug Mor Farm
Rhydwyn
Llanfaethlu
Anglesey

Jonathon Hughes with a 20 lb. pollack and a 22 pdr. The larger fish became a Welsh record for the species in 1993. The fish were caught over the wreck of a ship sunk in the Irish Sea in 1917. *Photo: Vic Haigh.*

FISHING IN SCOTLAND

District Boards and Close Season for Salmon and Trout

Fishing in Scotland is under the general jurisdiction of the Scottish Office, Agriculture and Fisheries Department, Pentland House, 47 Robb's Loan, Edinburgh, EH14 1TW.

The annual close season for **trout** in Scotland extends from October 7 to March 14, both days included. Trout may not be sold between the end of August and the beginning of April, nor at any time if the fish are less than 8 in long.

Visiting anglers are reminded that on Scottish rivers and lochs the owner of the fishing is the riparian proprietor, whose permission to fish should be obtained. The only public right of fishing for brown trout is in those portions of the rivers which are both tidal and navigable, but the right must not be exercised so as to interfere with salmon or sea-trout fishing and can be exercised only where there is a right of access to the water from a boat or from the banks.

Salmon. Provision is made in the Salmon Act, 1986, for the formation and amalgamation of District Boards, composed of representatives of proprietors of salmon fisheries in each district. These boards, the addresses of which are given on pages below, are responsible for the administration and protection of the salmon fisheries in their districts, and boards have been formed for practically all the important salmon rivers. In districts in which boards have not been formed, the salmon fisheries, of which sea-trout fisheries are legally part, are under the direct control of the proprietors.

In the following list, the days fixing the start and finish of the annual close time for net fishing and for rod fishing respectively are in all cases inclusive, and, as in the case of the Add, the first river in the list, the first pair of dates are the limits of the net season and the second pair apply to rod fishing.

Add. Annual close time for net-fishing: From Sept 1 to Feb 15, both dates inclusive. Annual close time for rod-fishing: From Nov 1 to Feb 15, both days inclusive.

Ailort. Aug 27 to Feb 10; Nov 1 to Feb 10.

Aline. Aug 27 to Feb 10; Nov 1 to Feb 10.

Alness. Aug 27 to Feb 10; Nov 1 to Feb 10.

Annan. Sept 10 to Feb 24; Nov 16 to Feb 24.

Applecross. Aug 27 to Feb 10; Nov 1 to Feb 10.

Arnisdale. Aug 27 to Feb 10; Nov 1 to Feb 10.

Awe. Aug 27 to Feb 10; Oct 16 to Feb 10.

Ayr. Aug 27 to Feb 10; Nov 1 to Feb 10.

Baa and Goladoir. Aug 27 to Feb 10; Nov 1 to Feb 10.

Badachro and Kerry. Aug 27 to Feb 10; Nov 1 to Feb 10.

Balgay and Shieldaig. Aug 27 to Feb 10; Nov 1 to Feb 10.

Beauly. Aug 27 to Feb 10; Oct 16 to Feb 10.

Berriedale. Aug 27 to Feb 10; Nov 1 to Feb 10.

Bervie. Sept 10 to Feb 24; Nov 1 to Feb 24.

Bladnoch. Aug 27 to Feb 10; Nov 1 to Feb 10.

Broom. Aug 27 to Feb 10; Nov 1 to Feb 10.

Brora. Aug 27 to Feb 10; Oct 16 to Jan 31.

Carradale. Sept 10 to Feb 24; Nov 1 to Feb 24.

Carron. Aug 27 to Feb 10; Nov 1 to Feb 10.

Clayburn. Sept 10 to Feb 24; Nov 1 to Feb 24.

Clyde and Leven. Aug 27 to Feb 10; Nov 1 to Feb 10.

Conon. Aug 27 to Feb 10; Oct 1 to Jan 25.

Cowie. Aug 27 to Feb 10; Nov 1 to Feb 10.

Cree. Sept 14 to Feb 28; Oct 15 to Feb 28.

Creran (Loch Creran). Aug 27 to Feb 10; Nov 1 to Feb 10.

Crowe and Shiel (Loch Duich). Aug 27 to Feb 10; Nov 1 to Feb 10.

Dee (Aberdeenshire). Aug 27 to Feb 10; Oct 1 to Jan 31.

Fishing available?

If you own, manage, or know of first-class fishing available to the public which should be considered for inclusion in **Where to Fish** *please apply to the publishers (address in the front of the book) for a form for submission, on completion, to the Editor. (Inclusion is at the sole discretion of the Editor).*

Dee (Kirkcudbrightshire). Aug 27 to Feb 10; Nov 1 to Feb 10.

Deveron. Aug 27 to Feb 10; Nov 1 to Feb 10.

Don. Aug 27 to Feb 10; Nov 1 to Feb 10.

Doon. Aug 27 to Feb 10; Nov 1 to Feb 10.

Drummachloy (Bute). Sept 1 to Feb 15; Oct 16 to Feb 15.

Dunbeath. Aug 27 to Feb 10; Oct 16 to Feb 10.

Earn. Aug 21 to Feb 4; Nov 1 to Jan 31.

Eachaig. Sept 1 to Feb 15; Nov 1 to Feb 15.

East Lewis. Aug 27 to Feb 10; Oct 17 to Feb 10.

Eden. Aug 21 to Feb 4; Nov 1 to Feb 4.

Esk, North. Sept 1 to Feb 15; Nov 1 to Feb 15.

Esk, South. Sept 1 to Feb 15; Nov 1 to Feb 15.

Ewe. Aug 27 to Feb 10; Nov 1 to Feb 10.

Fincastle. Sept 10 to Feb 24; Nov 1 to Feb 24.

Findhorn. Aug 27 to Feb 10; Oct 7 to Feb 10.

Fleet (Kirkcudbrightshire). Sept 10 to Feb 24; Nov 1 to Feb 24.

Fleet (Sutherlandshire). Sept 10 to Feb 24; Nov 1 to Feb 24.

Forss. Aug 27 to Feb 10; Nov 1 to Feb 10.

Forth. Aug 27 to Feb 10; Nov 1 to Jan 31.

Fyne, Shira and Aray. Sept 1 to Feb 15; Nov 1 to Feb 15.

Garnock. Sept 10 to Feb 24; Nov 1 to Feb 24.

Girvan. Sept 10 to Feb 24; Nov 1 to Feb 24.

Glenelg. Aug 27 to Feb 10; Nov 1 to Feb 10.

Gour. Aug 27 to Feb 10; Nov 1 to Feb 10.

Grudie or **Dionard.** Aug 27 to Feb 10; Nov 1 to Feb 10.

Gruinard and Little Gruinard. Aug 27 to Feb 10; Nov 1 to Feb 10.

Halladale. Aug 27 to Feb 10; Oct 1 to Jan 11.

Helmsdale. Aug 27 to Feb 10; Oct 1 to Jan 10.

Hope and Polla. Aug 27 to Feb 10; Oct 1 to Jan 11.

Howmore. Sept 10 to Feb 24; Nov 1 to Feb 24.

Inchard. Aug 27 to Feb 10; Nov 1 to Feb 10.

Inner (Jura). Sept 10 to Feb 24; Nov 1 to Feb 24.

Inver. Aug 27 to Feb 10; Nov 1 to Feb 10.

Iorsa (Arran). Sept 10 to Feb 24; Nov 1 to Feb 24.

Irvine. Sept 10 to Feb 24; Nov 16 to Feb 24.

Kannaird. Aug 27 to Feb 10; Nov 1 to Feb 10.

Kilchoan. (Loch Nevis). Aug 27 to Feb 10; Nov 1 to Feb 10.

Kinloch (Kyle of Tongue). Aug 27 to Feb 10; Nov 1 to Feb 10.

Kirkaig. Aug 27 to Feb 10; Nov 1 to Feb 10.

Kishorn. Aug 27 to Feb 10; Nov 1 to Feb 10.

Kyle of Sutherland. Aug 27 to Feb 10; Oct 1 to Jan 10.

Laggan and **Sorn** (Islay). Sept 10 to Feb 24; Nov 1 to Feb 24.

Laxford. Aug 27 to Feb 10; Nov 1 to Feb 10.

Leven. Aug 27 to Feb 10; Nov 1 to Feb 10.

Little Loch Broom. Aug 27 to Feb 10; Nov 1 to Feb 10.

Loch Long. Aug 27 to Feb 10; Nov 1 to Feb 10.

Loch Roag. Aug 27 to Feb 10; Oct 17 to Feb 10.

Loch Sunart. Aug 27 to Feb 10; Nov 1 to Feb 10.

Lochy. Aug 27 to Feb 10; Nov 1 to Feb 10.

Lossie. Aug 27 to Feb 24; Nov 1 to Feb 24.

Luce. Sept 10 to Feb 24; Nov 1 to Feb 24.

Lussa (Mull). Aug 27 to Feb 10; Nov 1 to Feb 10.

Moidart. Aug 27 to Feb 10; Nov 1 to Feb 10.

Morar. Aug 27 to Feb 10; Nov 1 to Feb 10.

Mullanageren. (North Uist). Sept 10 to Feb 24; Nov 1 to Feb 24.

Nairn. Aug 27 to Feb 10; Oct 8 to Feb 10.

Naver and **Borgie.** Aug 27 to Feb 10; Oct 1 to Jan 11.

Nell, Feochan and **Euchar.** Aug 27 to Feb 10; Nov 1 to Feb 10.

Ness. Aug 27 to Feb 10; Oct 16 to Jan 14.

Nith. Sept 10 to Feb 24; Dec 1 to Feb 24.

Orkney Islands. Sept 10 to Feb 24; Nov 1 to Feb 24.

Ormsary. Aug 27 to Feb 10; Nov 1 to Feb 10.

Pennygowan and **Aros** (Mull). Aug 27 to Feb 10; Nov 1 to Feb 10.

Resort. Aug 27 to Feb 10; Nov 1 to Feb 10.

Ruel. Sept 1 to Feb 15; Nov 1 to Feb 15.

Sanda. Aug 27 to Feb 10; Nov 1 to Feb 10.

Scaddle. Aug 27 to Feb 10; Nov 1 to Feb 10.

Shetland Islands. Sept 10 to Feb 24; Nov 1 to Feb 24.

Shiel (Loch Shiel). Aug 27 to Feb 10; Nov 1 to Feb 10.

Sligachan (Skye). Aug 27 to Feb 10; Nov 1 to Feb 10.

Snizort (Skye). Aug 27 to Feb 10; Nov 1 to Feb 10.

Spey. Aug 27 to Feb 10; Oct 1 to Feb 10.
Stinchar. Sept 10 to Feb 24; Nov 1 to Feb 24.
Strathy. Aug 27 to Feb 10; Oct 1 to Jan 11.
Tay. Aug 21 to Feb 4; Oct 16 to Jan 14.
Thurso. Aug 27 to Feb 10; Oct 6 to Jan 10.
Torridon. Aug 27 to Feb 10; Nov 1 to Feb 10.

Tweed. Sept 15 to Feb 14; Dec 1 to Jan 31.
Ugie. Sept 10 to Feb 24; Nov 1 to Feb 9.
Ullapool (Loch Broom). Aug 27 to Feb 10; Nov 1 to Feb 10.
Urr. Sept 10 to Feb 24; Dec 1 to Feb 24.
Wick. Aug 27 to Feb 10; Nov 1 to Feb 10.
Ythan. Sept 10 to Feb 24; Nov 1 to Feb 10.

DISTRICT SALMON FISHERY BOARDS

The names, addresses and telephone numbers of the clerks of the various salmon district fishery boards in Scotland are as follows: Please note that their duties are purely to operate the Acts and that they do not have fishing to let.

Alness District Salmon Fishery Board. J H S Stewart, Messrs Munro and Noble, 26 Church Street, Inverness IV1 1HX (Tel. 0463 221727)

Annan District Salmon Fishery Board. Ms C A K Rafferty, Messrs McJerrow and Stevenson, Solicitors, 55 High Street, Lockerbie, Dumfriesshire DG11 2JJ (Tel. 05762 202123/4).

Awe District Salmon Fishery Board. T C McNair, Messrs MacArthur, Stewart & Co, Solicitors, Boswell House, Argyll Square, Oban, Argyllshire PA34 4BD (Tel. 0631 62215).

Ayr District Salmon Fishery Board. G Hay, D & J Dunlop, 2 Barns Street, Ayr KA7 1XD (Tel. 0292 264091).

Beauly District Salmon Fishery Board. J Wotherspoon, MacAndrew & Jenkins WS, Solicitors and Estate Agents, 5 Drummond Street, Inverness, IV1 1QF (Tel. 0463 233001)

Bladnoch District Salmon Fishery Board. Peter M Murray, Messrs A B & A Matthews, Bank of Scotland Buildings, Newton Stewart, Wigtownshire DG8 6EG (Tel. 0671 3013).

Broom District Salmon Fishery Board. Messrs Middleton, Ross and Arnot, Solicitors, PO Box 8, Mansfield House, Dingwall, Ross-shire IV15 9HJ (Tel. 0349 62214).

Brora District Salmon Fishery Board. C J Whealing, Sutherland Estates Office, Duke Street, Golspie, Sutherland, KW10 6RR (Tel. 0408 633268).

Caithness District Salmon Fishery Board. P J W Blackwood, Estate Office, Thurso East, Thurso, Caithness KW14 8HW (Tel. 0847 63134).

Conon District Salmon Fishery Board. Miles Larby, Finlayson Hughes, 45 Church Street, Inverness IV1 1DR (Tel. 0463 224343).

Cree District Salmon Fishery Board. Peter M Murray, Messrs A B & A Matthews, Solicitors, Bank of Scotland Buildings, Newton Stewart, Wigtownshire DG8 6EG (Tel. 0671 3013).

Creran District Salmon Fishery Board. Lady Stewart, Salachail, Appin, Argyll.

Crowe and Shiel (Loch Duich) Salmon Fishery Board. Lord Burton (Chairman), Dochfour Estate Office, Dochgarroch, Inverness IV3 6JP.

Dee (Aberdeen) District Salmon Fishery Board. George Alpine, Messrs Paull & Williamson, Solicitors, Investment House, 6 Union Row, Aberdeen AB9 8DQ (Tel. 0224 621621).

Dee (Kirkcudbrightshire) District Salmon Fishery Board. J W Campbell, New Cottages, St Mary's Isle, Kirkcudbrightshire DG6 4XB (Tel. 0557 30242).

Deveron District Salmon Fishery Board. John A Christie, Murdoch, McMath and Mitchell, Solicitors, 27-29 Duke Street, Huntly AB54 5DP (Tel. 0466 792291).

Don Distinct Board. George Alpine, Messrs Paull & Williamson, Solicitors, Investment House, 6 Union Row, Aberdeen AB9 8DQ (Tel. 0224 621621).

Doon District Salmon Fishery Board. Hew S Campbell, Messrs R & J A MacCallum, Solicitors, 8 Alloway Place, Ayr KA7 2AF (Tel. 0292 269131).

Eachaig District Salmon Fishery Board, Robert C G Teasdale, Quarry Cottage, Rashfield, By Dunoon, Argyll PA23 8QT (Tel. 0369 84510)

East Lewis District Salmon Fishery Board. George H MacDonald, Estate Office, 20 Cromwell Street, Stornoway, Isle of Lewis PA87 2DD (Tel. 0851 2002).

Esk District Salmon Fishery Board. John Alexander Scott, Messrs Campbell, Middleton, Burness & Dickson, Clydesdale Bank Chambers, 112 High Street, Montrose, Angus DD10 8JH (Tel. 06747 2929).

Ewe District Salmon Fishery Board. G C Muirden, Messrs Middleton, Ross and Arnot, Solicitors, PO Box 8, Mansfield House, Dingwall, Ross-shire IV15 9HJ (Tel. 0349 62214).

Findhorn District Salmon Fishery Board. A J McCartan, Messrs Mackenzie & Grant, Solicitor, 100 High Street, Forres, Morayshire IV36 0NX (Tel. 0309 672126).

Fleet (Kirkcudbrightshire) District Salmon Fishery Board. C R Graves, Pinnacle, Gatehouse of Fleet, Castle Douglas DG7 2HH (Tel. 0557 814 610).

Forth District Salmon Fishery Board. Mrs J Duff, Lochfield Farm, Doune, Stirling FK16 6AX (Tel. 0786 841082).

Girvan District Salmon Fishery Board. S B Sheddon, Messrs James Smith & Valentine, Solicitors and Estate Agents, 16 Hamilton Street, Girvan, Ayrshire KA26 9EY (Tel. 0465 3476)

Gruide or **Dionard District Salmon Fishery Board.** A MacKenzie, Redwood, 19 Culduthel Road, Inverness IV2 4AA (Tel. 0463 235353).

Gruinard District Salmon Fishery Board. Messrs. Middleton, Ross and Arnot, Solicitors, P O Box 8, Mansfield House, Dingwall, Ross-shire IV15 9HJ (Tel. 0349 62214).

Halladale District Salmon Fishery Board. Mrs J Atkinson, 8 Sinclair Street, Thurso, Caithness KW14 7AJ (Tel. 0847 63291).

Harris District Salmon Fishery Board. A Scherr, Borve Cottage, Borve Lodge Estate, Isle of Harris PA85 3HT (Tel. 085985 202).

Helmsdale District Salmon Fishery Board. John Douglas-Menzies, Mounteagle, Fearn, Ross-shire IV20 1RP (Tel 086 283 2213).

Hope and Polla District Salmon Fishery Board. Messrs Middleton, Ross and Arnot, Solicitors, PO Box 8, Mansfield House, Dingwall, Ross-shire IV15 9HJ (Tel. 0349 62214).

Iorsa (Arran) District Salmon Fishery Board. D T Brambles, High Feorline, Shiskine, Isle of Arran (Tel. 0770 86491).

Inver District Salmon Fishery Board. D L Laird, Thornton Oliver WS, Solicitors and Estate Agents, 53 East High Street, Forfar, Angus DD8 2EL (Tel. 0307 66886).

Kirkaig District Salmon Fishery Board. D L Laird, Thornton Oliver WS, Solicitors, 53 East High Street, Forfar, Angus DD8 2EL (Tel 0307 66886).

Kinloch District Salmon Fishery Board. A Sykes, Messrs Brodies WS, 15 Atholl Crescent, Edinburgh EH3 8HA (Tel. 031 228 4111).

Kyle of Sutherland District Salmon Fishery Board. G C Muirden, Messrs Middleton, Ross and Arnot, Solicitors, PO Box 8, Mansfield House, Dingwall, Ross-shire IV15 9HJ (Tel. 0349 62214).

Laggan & Sorn District Salmon Fishery Board, R I G Ferguson, Messrs Stewart, Balfour & Sutherland, 2 Castlehill, Campeltown, Argyll PA28 6AW (Tel. 0586 552871).

Laxford District Salmon Fishery Board. A R Whitefield, The Estate Office, Achfary, by Lairg, Sutherland IV27 4PQ (Tel. 0971 500221).

Leven District Salmon Fishery Board. Alister M Sutherland, Burness WS, Solicitors, 242 West George Street, Glasgow G2 4QY (Tel. 041 248 4933).

Loch Fyne District Salmon Fishery Board. Robert N Macpherson, Messrs Stewart & Bennet, Solicitors, 82 Argyll Street, Dunoon, PA23 7NE.

Loch Inchard District Salmon Fishery Board. N W Buchanan, Messrs J & F Anderson, Solicitors, 48 Castle Street, Edinburgh, EH2 3LX (Tel. 031 225 3912)

Loch Roag District Salmon Fishery Board. George H MacDonald, Stornoway Trust, Estate Office, 20 Cromwell Street, Stornoway, Isle of Lewis PA87 2DD (Tel. 0851 702002).

Loch Shiel District Salmon Fishery Board. E T Cameron Kennedy, Robertson, Neilson & Co, 95 Bothwell Street, Glasgow G2 7JH (Tel. 041 204 1231).

Lochy District Salmon Fishery Board. H MacColl, Primrose Cottage, Torlundy, Fort William, Inverness-shire (Tel. 0397 702 547).

Lossie District Salmon Fishery Board. A J McCartan, Messrs MacKenzie & Grant, Solicitors, 100 High Street, Forres, Moray IV36 0NX (Tel. 0309 672 126).

Luce District Salmon Fishery Board. E A Fleming-Smith, Stair Estates, Estate Office, Rephad, Stranraer, Wigtownshire DG9 8BX (Tel. 0776 2024).

Morar District Salmon Fishery Board. M H Spence, 2 Gray's Inn Square, Gray's Inn, London WC1R 5JH (Tel. 071 242 4986).

Mullanagearan District Salmon Fishery Board. The Clerk, Estate Office, Lochmaddy, Isle of North Uist (Tel. 0876 3324).

Nairn District Salmon Fishery Board. S Newbould, Silver Glade, Tornagrain Road, Can-try, Inverness IV1 1AA (Tel. 06678 324).

Naver and Borgie District Salmon Fishery Board. J A Douglas-Menzies, Mounteagle, Fearn, Ross-shire IV20 1RC (Tel. 086 283 2213).

Ness District Salmon Fishery Board. F Kelly, Messrs Anderson, Shaw & Gilbert, Solicitors, York House, 20 Church Street, Inverness IV1 1ED (Tel. 0463 236123).

Nith District Salmon Fishery Board. R Styles, Walker and Sharp, Solicitors, 37 George Street, Dumfries DG1 1EB (Tel. 0387 67222).

Skye District Salmon Fishery Board. Capt D E P George, Mossbank, By Portree, Isle of Skye IV51 9NF (Tel. 0478 612110).

Spey District Salmon Fishery Board. C D R Whittle, Messrs R & R Urquhart, 121 High Street, Forres, Morayshire IV36 0AB (Tel. 0309 72216).

Stinchar District Salmon Fishery Board. Mrs A McGinnis, West View Cottage, Barr, Nr Girvan, Ayrshire KA26 9TX (Tel. 0465 86259).

Tay District Salmon Fishery Board. R P J Blake, Messrs Condies, Solicitors, 2 Tay Street, Perth PH1 5LJ (Tel. 0738 33171).

Tweed Commissioners. J H Leeming, River Tweed Commissioners, Dock Road, Tweedmouth, Berwick upon Tweed, TD15 2BE (Tel. 0289 330474).

Ugie District Salmon Fishery Board. B Milton, Masson & Glennie, Solicitors, Broad House, Broad Street, Peterhead AB42 6JA (Tel. 0779 74271).

Ythan District Salmon Fishery Board. M H T Andrew, Estate Office, Mains of Haddo, Tarves, Ellon, Aberdeenshire AB41 0LD (Tel. 0651 851664).

Note. Anglers visiting Scotland to fish for coarse fish should note that it is not, in certain districts, lawful to fish with two or more rods simultaneously. The rule is one rod only.

A typical scene on the River Alness, Ross & Cromarty. *Photo: Eric Chalker.*

SCOTTISH FISHING STATIONS

The nature of Scotland with its many rivers and lochs, especially on the west coast, makes it impracticable in some cases to deal with each river's catchment area separately. Thus some fisheries on the west coast, north of the Firth of Clyde are group under the heading 'West Coast Rivers and Lochs'.

The need again arises to decide whether a river should be included in England or Scotland. The Border Esk is dealt with in the English section, together with the Kirtle and the Sark, which happen to fall within the Esk's catchment area on the map. The Tweed and *all* its tributaries are included in this Scottish section. All the Scottish Islands, including Shetland and Orkney, are considered as within one watershed, viz, 'The Islands', in which, for convenience, Kintyre is included. The exact position in the book of any river or fishing station can, of course, readily be found by reference to the index.

ALNESS and GLASS

Alness drains **Loch Morie**, then flows 12 miles to enter Cromarty Firth at Alness. Glass drains Loch Glass then flows into Cromarty Firth near Evanton.

Alness (Ross-shire). Salmon, sea trout, grilse and brown trout. Alness AC has water on R Alness, salmon, sea trout, brown trout; and on Loch Morie, brown trout and Artic char. Good bank fishing on Loch Morie; worm or fly only. Permits from hon sec. Novar Estate, Evanton, also issues permits for fishing on R Alness; salmon, sea trout, grilse and brown trout.

Evanton (Ross-shire). Brown trout fishing on R Glass and **Loch Glass**; bank fishing on loch. Permits from Factor, Novar Estates Office (tel: 0349 830208). Salmon, sea trout and brown trout fishing on Rivers Glass and **Skiach**; and brown trout fishing on Loch Glass. Permits from Alcock, Newsagent, 16 Balconie St (tel: 0349 830672).

ANNAN

Rises in Moffat Hills and flows about 30 miles to Solway Firth. Strong tidal river. Several good pools on river NE of Annan. Good spring salmon, sea trout in May and June. Good herling in July and August, and salmon in late autumn; brown trout.

Annan (Dumfriesshire). Warmanbie Hotel has stretch; salmon, sea trout and brown trout. Hotel also has access to other waters, including on **Rivers Nith** and **Eden**, plus access to Sunday trout fishing. Rod and tackle hire, tuition and ghillie can be arranged. Hotel also stocks a range of tackle for sale. For further information contact Warmanbie Hotel, Annan DG12 5LL (tel: 0461 204015). Tackle shop: Annan Anglers, High St.

Ecclefechan (Dumfries & Galloway). Annan, 2m SW; salmon, herling (late July onwards), brown trout. Hoddom & Kinmount Estates, Estate Office, Hoddom, Lockerbie DG11 1BE (tel. 0576 300244), have Hoddom Castle Water, over 2m stretch on Annan. Salmon; grilse late July onwards; sea trout, May-Aug. Dt £8-£14; limited to 15 rods per day. Fly only, except when river height is above white line on Hoddom Bridge when spinning is permitted. Hoddom & Kinmount Estates also have trout fishing on **Purdomstone Res-**

ervoir; and coarse fishing on **Kelhead Water**, **Castle Loch** and **Ashyard**. Purdomstone Reservoir, brown trout; 2 boats; 2 rods per boat; dt £8 per boat. Kelhead Water; brown and rainbow trout, perch, roach, bream, carp, pike, tench, eels; dt £3.50; suitable for disabled. Permits for Hoddom Castle Water and Purdomstone Reservoir may be booked from Water Bailiff, Bridge Cottage, Hoddom, Lockerbie (tel: 057 300488); and for Kelhead Water from Water Bailiff, Kelhead Bungalow, Cummertrees (tel: 04617 344). Hotel: Ecclefechan.

Lockerbie (Dumfriesshire). R Annan 1½m W; salmon, sea trout, brown trout. Castle Milk Estate has beats on R Annan and a beat on **River Milk**. Castle Milk Water; salmon and sea trout; 2m, left bank; fly only. Dt £15 (early season) and £28 (late season). Royal Four Towns Water; salmon, sea trout, brown trout, herling, chub, grilse; 3¾m, both banks. Dt £10 (early season) and £12 (late season).

River Milk at Scroggs Bridge; sea trout and brown trout; fly only. Permits from Anthony Steel, Kirkwood, Lockerbie (tel. 057 65 200). **Halleaths Water**, west bank of Annan, near Lockerbie and Lochmaben; salmon and trout, fly only. Three tickets per week available in the season, 25 Feb - 15 Nov. Permits from McJerrow and Stevenson, Solicitors, 55 High St, Lockerbie DG11 2JJ. **Black Esk Reservoir**: bank fishing; fly and spinner only. Salmon and sea trout fishing on **River White Esk**, 6m, both banks, with a number of named pools, 12m from Langholm. Salmon and sea trout run from late July. For permits for Black Esk Reservoir and R White Esk, apply John D Medcalf, Hart Manor Hotel, Eskdalemuir, By Langholm, Dumfriesshire DG13 0QQ (tel. 0387 373217). Upper Annandale AA has salmon, trout fishing on Applegarth Estate, this includes stretches on R Annan, **Kinnel Water** and **Dryfe Water**. Grayling and chubb, which are also caught on this beat, may only be fished in salmon season. Permits from Video Sports, 48 High St; J Graham, Agricultural Contractor, Millhousebridge.

Lochmaben (Dumfries & Galloway). Salmon, sea trout, trout, chub (good). Royal Four Towns Water, Hightae.

Salmon season, Feb 25 to Nov 15; trout, March 15 to Oct 6. No Sunday fishing. Permits from Clerk, Mrs Kathleen Ratcliffe, Jay-Ar, Preston House Road, Hightae, Lockerbie DG11 1JR (tel: 0387 810 220). From Sept-Nov advance booking advisable. Brown trout fishing on **Water of Ae** in Forest of Ae; fly only. Permits from Forest Enterprise, Ae Village, Dumfries DG1 1QB. Coarse fishing on **Castle Loch**; permits from Warden, Lochfield, Lochmaben. **Hightae Mill Loch**, bream, carp, perch, tench, rudd, chub and roach; boat fishing only. Permits from J Wildman, Annandale Cottage, Greenhill, Lockerbie. Hotels: Balcastle; Royal Four Town, Hightae.

Wamphray (Dumfriesshire). 4m of R Annan controlled by Upper Annandale AA. Permits from Red House Hotel; and General Store, Johnstonebridge.

Beattock (Dumfriesshire). Upper Annandale AA water on river; permits from Beattock House Hotel.

Moffat (Dumfries & Galloway). Upper Annandale AA has 4m on **Upper Annan** and 1m on **Moffat Water**; salmon, brown trout, sea trout, herling. Wt £16-£32, dt £6. No day tickets after 15 Sept. Permits from Helen Smith, Hairdressers, Well St; Esso Petrol Station, Moffat.

AWE and LOCH AWE and LOCH ETIVE

A short river, but one of best-known salmon streams of west coast. Connects Loch Awe to sea by way of Loch Etive, which it enters at Bonawe. River fishes best from July onwards.

Taynuilt (Argyll). Salmon, sea trout, trout. Inverawe Fisheries, Taynuilt, Argyll PA35 1HU (tel: 08662 446), has ½m on River Awe, salmon and sea trout; and three lochs stocked daily with rainbow trout. Fly only. Wt and dt, with half-day and father/son concessions. Tuition, tackle for hire and refreshments available. Salmon and trout fishing also available from A R Nelson, Muckairn, Taynuilt, who has a stretch on R Awe. Loch Etive, brown, sea, rainbow trout and sea fish; no permit required. Hotel: Polfearn Hotel.

LOCH AWE. Salmon, sea trout, brown trout, char, rainbow trout, perch and pike. Free fishing for entire length of loch. There is a road right round loch. Salmon are most often caught by trolling. Sea trout are rarely caught and only at north end. Trout can be caught anywhere and average just under ½lb; best months Apr, May, Jun and Sep. Char are caught on a

very deep sunk line. Pike and perch can be taken on a spun lure but are rarely fished for.

Lochawe (Argyll). Loch Awe Improvement Association is a club open to all but whose members are those who buy season tickets rather than daily permits. Assn has trout and pike fishing on Loch Awe, **River Avich** and **Loch Avich**. St £30, wt £10 and dt £2. Concessions for OAPs and juniors. Permits available from Nigel Bower, Drishaig, Lochawe; Sonachan House, Portsonachan; Ardanaiseig Hotel, Kilchrenan; Jonathan Brown, Hayfield, Kilchrenan; and many other sales points including tackle shops in Glasgow and Edinburgh (a full list is available from Assn).

Kilchrenan (Argyll). Taychreggan Hotel, on lochside, has pike, trout and salmon fishing on Loch Awe. Fish run to good size. 2 boat with outboard engines. Ghillie can be arranged. Fishing also available on River Awe (salmon), **River Orchy** (salmon) and Loch Etive (sea trout). Good sea fishing. Hotel has own jetty and it is possible to arrive by seaplane from Glasgow. Permits and further information from Annie Coutts Paul, Taychreggan Hotel, Kilchrenean, By Talnuilt, Argyll PA35 1HQ (tel. 08663 211). Cuilna-Sithe Hotel has boats on Loch Awe; free to weekly residents. Brown trout fishing on **L Nant** (two mile walk); Oban & Lorn AC permits available from Trading Post.

Portsonachan (Argyll). Portsonachan Hotel on shore of Loch Awe has fishing in loch; trout, salmon, sea trout, perch pike. Boats available to hotel guests. Salmon fishing and fishing on hill lochs also arranged. Sonachan House, also on shore of Loch Awe, issues permits for boat fishing on Loch Awe. Self-catering accommodation in flats, chalets and caravans for anglers. Rods and tackle for hire, and lures for sale. Apply to Jonathan and Jane Soar, Sonachan House, Portsonachan, By Dalmally, Cargyll PA33 1BN (tel. 08663 240).

Dalavich (Argyll). Forestry Commission has fishing on Loch Awe (brown trout, rainbow trout, char, perch, pike), **Loch Avich** (brown trout) and **River Avich** (salmon and brown trout). Dt £2. Permits, boat hire and rod hire, from N D Clarke, 11 Dalavich, By Taynuilt (tel: 08664 209).

Ford (Argyll). **Cam** and other hill lochs: brown trout, bank fishing, dt £3. Permits for hill lochs and also for Loch Awe (dt 2.50) available from D Murray, Ford Hotel.

Tributaries of the Awe

ORCHY: Good salmon.

Dalmally (Argyll). River flows into Loch Awe here, excellent salmon fishing in May, June, Sept and Oct. Permits for several beats on Orchy, **Loch Awe** and **Loch Avich**, available from Alan Church, Croggan Crafts (tel: 0838 200 201), who can also supply fishing tackle for sale or hire. Hotels: Glenorchy Lodge; Orchy Bank; Craic Villa.

Bridge of Orchy (Argyll). Inveroran Hotel has 2m stretch on **Orchy** and also brown trout fishing on **Loch Tulla**, fly only. Permits available from Inveroran Hotel, Black Mount, Bridge of Orchy (tel: Tyndrum 220); and Alan Church, Croggan Crafts, Dalmally.

AYR

Rises in Glenbuck and flows into Firth of Clyde through town of Ayr opposite south end of Isle of Arran. Good brown trout river (av ½lb) with fair runs of salmon and sea trout.

Ayr (Ayrshire). Mostly preserved, but tickets can be had for ¾m water at Ayr from the Director of Leisure Services, Kyle and Carrick District Council, 30 Miller Rd, Ayr, and from tackle shops. Ayr AC has stretch on River Ayr at Ayr and near Annbank (salmon, sea trout, brown trout); and on **Loch Shankston** and **Loch Spallander** (rainbow and brown trout). Members only. Wading essential for good sport. Water restocked with brown trout. Membership from Gamesport of Ayr, 60 Sandgate. Prestwick AC has fishing on **Raith Waters**, rainbow trout. St £18 and dt £6. Concession for juniors and OAPs. Competitions for juniors. Permits from Rankin, Ayr; Gamesport of Ayr, Ayr; Newall's Newsagent, Monkton; Wheatsheaf Inn, Monkton; Wallace's Shoe Repairer, Prestwick. Hotel: Manor Park, Monkton. **Belston Loch** at **Sinclairston**, a small rainbow trout fishery, 6m from Ayr; for further information contact Gamesport of Ayr. Tackle shops: Gamesport of Ayr, 60 Sandgate, Ayr, and James Kirk, 5 Union Arcade, Ayr, from whom tickets for town and other waters on Rivers Ayr and **Doon** can be obtained, and for coarse fish lochs.

Mauchline (Ayrshire). Salmon, sea trout and brown trout fishing on Rivers **Ayr**, **Cessock** and **Lugar**; and brown and rainbow trout fishing on **Loch Belston** at Sinclairston. Boats available on Loch Belston. Permits available from Linwood & Johnstone, Newsagent, The Cross.

Muirkirk (Ayrshire). Fish pass has been built at Catrine Dam, allowing fish to run to headwaters at Muirkirk. Muirkirk AA has approx 6m on River Ayr, both banks; salmon, sea trout, brown trout, grayling. Assn also has fishing on **Greenock Water**; trout only. Brown trout restocking program. Season tickets sold but membership full in 1993. Dt £5, Mon-Fri, limited to 6 per day. Apply to Mr Scott Davidson, President, 3 Lapraik Avenue, Muirkirk (tel. 0290 61800). Concessions for juveniles and 3 competitions per year for juveniles. Hotel: Black Bull.

Tributaries of the Ayr

COYLE. Sea trout, trout, grayling, few salmon.

Drongan (Ayrshire). Drongan Youth Group AC issues permits for **River Coyle** and **Snipe Loch;** brown and rainbow trout stocked weekly; fish up to 11lb are being caught. Permits from H Lees, 2 Reid Place, and Snipe Loch.

BEAULY

Beauly proper is about 9m long, being formed by junction of Glass and Farrar. Flows into Beauly Firth and thence into Moray Firth. Good salmon and sea trout, April to October.

Beauly (Inverness-shire). Salmon, sea trout, brown trout. Beauly AA has water below Lovat Bridge. Fly only. Permits for assn water and for sea trout fishing on Beauly Firth from Morison's, Ironmonger, High Street, Beauly. Sea trout fishing on Beauly Firth at Clachnaharry and North Kessock; permits from Grahams, 37 Castle St, Inverness; M Jamieson, Fishing Tackle, 58 Church St, Inverness; Kessock PO, North Kessock. Good sea trout from the beginning of the season. **Loch Aigas**, brown trout and stocked rainbow trout (up to 6lb). Fly only. Permits from Office, Aigas House and Field Centre, By Beauly.

Tributaries of the Beauly.

FARRAR and GLASS:

Struy (Inverness-shire). Lovat Estate, Beauly, has fishing on R Glass; st available. Permits from Mr & Mrs E R Venn, Kerrow House, Cannich, Strathglass, Inverness-shire IV4 7NA (tel. 0456 415 243), for 3½m of brown trout fishing on River Glass (fly only). Fly fishing on **R Farrar** and **Glass**. Dt £15 -£35 (salmon) and £10 (trout); from F Spencer-Nairn, Culligran House, Glen Strathfarrar, Struy, Nr Beauly (tel: 046 376 285). Priority given to guests of Culligran Cottages (self-catering), brochure available. Hotels: Cnoc; Chisholm Stone House.

Tomich (Inverness-shire). Tomich Hotel, Tomich, Strathglass, By Beauly IV4 7LY, has fishing in **Guisachan Hill Lochs;** brown and rainbow trout. Season: 1 May - 6 Oct.

CANNICH.

Tributary of the Glass.

Cannich (Inverness-shire). At confluence of Cannich and Glass. Glen Affric Hotel issues permits for brown trout fishing on **River Cannich, Loch Benevean, Loch Monar, Loch Beannacharan, Loch Mullardoch, Loch A-Bhana** and **Knockfin Forestry Hill Lochs.** Also salmon fishing on 1½m of **River Glass.** Permits for Loch Benevean, Loch Mullardoch and Knockfin Hill Lochs only available if not required by hotel guests. Pike and eel fishing can also be arranged after 15 Oct. Reservations direct to Glen Affric Hotel, Cannich, by Beauly (tel: 0456 415 214). Fishing from boat. Fly only. No Sunday fishing. Glen Affric Hotel, in conjunction with Caledonian Hotel, Beauly, offers a special trout fishing package; seven nights DBB, boat on a different loch every day (including engine and petrol), £295 per person subject to 2 persons sharing a boat.

Check before you go

While every effort has been made to ensure that the information given in **Where to Fish** *is correct, the position is continually changing, and anglers are urged, in their own interests, to make enquiries before travelling to selected venues. This is especially important with reference to prices quoted. Anglers attention is also drawn to the fact that hotels mentioned under the various fishing stations do not necessarily have water of their own. Any amendments or further data for inclusion in subsequent editions, and any criticism, will be welcome.*

BERVIE

Rises on Glen Farquhar Estate and flows 14m to North Sea near Inverbervie. Essentially an autumn river for finnock, sea trout and salmon although also good for brown trout.

Inverbervie (Kincardineshire). Finnock, sea trout, salmon (best Sept-Oct). Free tickets for foreshore for fortnightly periods (restricted; advance booking advised), bookable from Joseph Johnstone & Sons, 3 America Street, Montrose DD10 8DR (tel. 0674 72666). For fishing upstream from Donald's Hole; dt £2 from Kincardine & Deeside District Council, Area Officer, Church St, Inverbervie, Montrose DD10 0RU.

BRORA

After being joined by tributaries Blackwater and Skinsdale, Brora flows through Loch Brora and into sea at Brora.

Brora (Sutherland). **Loch Brora**; salmon, sea trout and brown trout. Permits and boats on Loch Brora can be hired from Rob Wilson's Tackle Shop, Fountain Square (tel: Brora 621373). Hotel: Royal Marine.

CARRON (Grampian)

Rises in Glenbervie and flows about 9m to the North Sea at Stonehaven. Trout.

Stonehaven (Kincardineshire). About 2½m brown trout fishing available to visitors from Stonehaven and Dist AA. Permits also issued for **River Cowie** (about 1¼m), sea trout, salmon and brown trout. Best July, August and Sept. Permits available from David's Sports Shop, 31 Market Sq. Good sea fishing. Hotels: Eldergrove, Arduthie House.

CLYDE

Rises near watershed of Tweed and Annan, and flows about 50m to the Atlantic by way of Glasgow. Once a famous salmon river, but long since spoiled by pollution. Trout and grayling fishing passable, especially in higher reaches. The Clyde's most famous tributary, the Leven, which connects with Loch Lomond, still has run of salmon and sea trout. In north-west corner of Renfrewshire is Loch Thom, linked by water spill with Loch Compensation, which, when water is high, drains into River Kip in Shielhill Burn. United Clyde Angling Protective Association Ltd, controls much of Clyde and tributaries. Association has hatchery and rearing pond, and restocks annually. Avon AC, Stonehouse, Lanarkshire, controls leases on Avon.

Greenock (Strathclyde). On the estuary of Clyde. Greenock & Dist AC preserves **Loch Thom** (365 acres, trout - three to the pound). Also rights on **Compensation Reservoir**, 38 acres, trout; **Yetts, No. 8 and No. 6** (Spring Dam), good trout. Permits from hon sec; Brian Peterson, The Fishing Shop; John M Clark, Cornalees Farm; Jean Caskie, Garvocks Farm; Jimmy Rankin, Waterside Cottage, Loch Thom. Club membership restricted to persons resident in Greenock and district, but permits available to visitors; Sunday fishing; no parties. Fly only. Bank fishing only. Good sea fishing - cod, skate, dogfish, conger, haddock and plaice. Tackle shop: The Fishing Shop, 12 Kelly St.

Glasgow (Strathclyde). Glasgow has excellent trout, sea trout and salmon fishing within a radius of 60m. Lochs Lomond, Dochart, Awe, Tay, Ard, Leven, Lubnaig, Venachar, Lake of Menteith, etc, and Rivers Annan, Goil, Cur (head of Loch Eck), Clyde (trout and grayling only), Teith, Tweed, Allan, Dochart, Leven, Kinglass etc, all accessible from here. Coarse fishing on whole of **Forth**

Keep the banks clean

Several clubs have stopped issuing tickets to visitors because of the state of the banks after they have left. Spend a few moments clearing up.

and Clyde Canal; pike, perch, roach, tench, rudd and bream. No close season. Canal is leased by K-Mac AC; dt £1. Permits from J B Angling, Kirkintilloch. For further details apply to British Waterways, Rosebank House, Main St, Camelon, Falkirk FK1 4DS. Free coarse fishing in 5m radius of Glasgow at **Auchenstarry Pond**, Kilsyth (tench, roach, perch and rudd); **Kilmadinny Loch**, Bearsden; **Bardowie Loch**, Balmore; **Mugdock Park Pond**, Milgavie; **Tench Pool**, Milgavie; **Carp Pond**, Seafar; and **Hogganfield Loch**, Glasgow. For further information contact Milton Coarse AC. United Clyde Angling Protective Association, issues season tickets for stretches on Clyde and **R Douglas** near Motherwell, Lanark, Carstairs, Robertson and Thankerton; brown trout and grayling fishing. Permits from hon sec or tackle shops. Tackle shops: Cafaro Bros, Queen's; Tackle & Guns, 918 Pollokshaws Rd; Anglers Rendezvous, 74-78 Saltmarket; William Robertson & Co Ltd, 61 Miller St; J B Angling, Kirkintilloch.

Coatbridge (Lanarkshire). **Lochend Loch** is Monklands Dist water; pike, perch, brown and rainbow trout. Permits from waterside. Monklands District Coarse AC now manages **Monklands Canal**; skimmer bream, perch, gudgeon, common and mirror carp, dace and tench. St £11 and dt £1. Day tickets available on bank, fishing is allowed during close season, all anglers are welcome. Junior summer and winter league, as well as annual Monklands Junior Open. Hotel: Coatbridge.

Airdrie (Lanarkshire). Airdrie AC has **Hillend Reservoir**; brown and rainbow trout. All legal methods. Bag limit 6 fish. Boat and bank fishing. No ground bait. Permits from hon sec. Clarkston Independent AC has **Lilly Loch** at Calderdruix; rainbow and brown trout. Season 15 Mar - 6 Oct. Any legal method (fly only from boats). Dt £3 (£2 OAPs & juniors). Tickets from bailiffs on site. Hotel: Old Truff Inn, Caldercruix, By Airdrie.

Motherwell (Lanarkshire). United Clyde APA has water on **Clyde** and **Douglas**; brown trout and grayling. Permits from local tackle shops. Coarse fishing on **Strathclyde Country Park Loch** and adjacent R Clyde; carp, bream, roach, pike, perch and dace. No close season. No fly fishing. Lead free weights recommended. Also trout and grayling fishing; 15 Mar-29 Sept. Permits from Booking Office, Strathclyde Country Park, 366 Hamilton Rd, Motherwell. Tackle shop: Macleod's Tackle Shop, 176 High St, Newarthill, Motherwell.

Strathaven (Lanarkshire). Avon and Clyde; trout and grayling. United Clyde Angling Protective Assn has water on Clyde; permits available from tackle shops in Glasgow and Lanarkshire. Avon AC controls 14m on **Avon** from Stonehouse to Strathaven; brown trout and grayling; well stocked. Permits from Sportsman Emporium, Hamilton; Country Lines, 29 Main St; The Village, East Kilbride. Concessions OAP & jun.

Lanark (Lanarkshire). Trout and grayling. United Clyde APA water on Clyde and **Douglas**; permits from local tackle shops. Coarse fishing on **Lanark Loch**; carp and tench. No close season. Hotel: Cartland Bridge.

Carstairs (Strathclyde). Trout and grayling. United Clyde APA water on Clyde and **Douglas**; permits from local tackle shops.

Thankerton (Strathclyde). Lamington AIA has 9m of water from Thankerton to Roberton; trout and grayling. St £17, wt £10, dt £4. Grayling season, 7 Oct - 14 Mar; st £5 and dt £2. Permits from hon sec, bailiffs or Bryden Newsagent, Biggar. Concessions for OAP and junior. No Sunday fishing. United Clyde APA water below Thankerton.

Biggar (Lanarkshire). 1½m to Clyde; tickets from Lamington AIA. Other Assn water at **Lamington, Symington and Roberton**. Hotels: Hartree Country House; Shieldhill. Tackle shop: Bryden, Newsagent, High Street.

Abington (Lanarkshire). Trout and grayling; UCAPA water. Other assn water at **Crawford** and **Elvanford**. Hotel: Abington.

Tributaries of the Clyde

LEVEN AND **LOCH LOMOND**: Salmon, trout, pike and perch.

Loch Lomond (Strathclyde). Good trout, sea trout and salmon fishing (also perch and pike) can be had from various centres on loch. Under control of Loch Lomond Angling Improvement Assn, c/o R A Clements & Co, 29 St Vincent Place, Glasgow G1 2DT (tel: 041 221 0068). Fishing reserved for full members only on **Fruin**, **Blane**, **Falloch** and some stretches of **Endrick**. Dt are issued for Leven and Loch Lomond at all local centres. St and children's permits also obtainable for Leven. No Sunday fishing. Annual membership £210, juniors £60 plus £25.54 entrance fee, wt £27 for Loch Lomond, dt £9 for Loch Lomond and dt £12.50 for River Leven. Permits from tackle shops, boat hirers and hotels. Late April and May earliest for fly on Loch Lomond (sea trout and salmon). Tackle shops: I & A Gibson, The Tackle Box, Bank St, Alexandria; McFarlane & Son, The Boatyard, Balmaha (boats also available); and Balloch Tourist Information Centre, Balloch.

Rowardennan, By Drymen (Stirlingshire). Convenient for Loch Lomond; permits and boats. Hotel: Rowardennan.

Balloch (Dunbartonshire). Trout, good sea trout and salmon fishing on River Leven and Loch Lomond; large perch and pike in loch; fishing controlled by Loch Lomond AIA. Vale of Leven & Dist AC issues permits for brown trout fishing on **Loch Sloy**. Fly only. Dt £2.50. Apply to hon sec. Ghillie service for Loch Lomond available from D McKenzie, Mossburn Avenue. Hotel: Balloch, Tullichewan. Also Tullichewan Caravan Park.

FRUIN: (tributary of Loch Lomond).

Helensburgh (Strathclyde). Salmon, sea trout and brown trout. Fly only. Permits issued by Loch Lomond AIA. Full members only.

Ardlui (Dunbartonshire). Trout, sea trout and salmon fishing in Loch Lomond. Hotel: Ardlui.

ENDRICK: (tributary of Loch Lomond).

Killearn (Stirling). Good trout, sea trout and salmon fishing. Loch Lomond AIA has water. No worm fishing; spinning restricted. No Sunday fishing. Accommodation arranged. Ghillie and boat hire available. Full members only.

GRYFE (or GRYFFE): Brown trout, salmon, sea trout.

Bridge of Weir (Strathclyde). Bridge of Weir River AC has 3m of water. Trout: 15 Mar - 6 Oct. Salmon: 15 Mar - 31 Oct. St £25 (locals only) from hon sec. Day tickets from Duncan's Paper Shop, Main St; Mon-Fri only.

Kilmacolm (Strathclyde). Strathgryfe AA has water on R Gryfe, **Green Water**, **Black Water** and **Burnbank Water**; approx. 25m in all. St £11 plus £10 entrance fee, dt £2.25-£3.25. Concessions for jun. Permits from Membership Sec, J Orr, 18 Myerton Ave. Day permits also available from Cross Caff, Kilmacolm. No day tickets on a Sunday.

CALDER and BLACK CART:

Lochwinnoch (Strathclyde). St Winnoch AC has stretch of Calder (brown trout); and **Castle Semple Loch**, pike, perch, roach and eels. St £6 and dt £1-£3. Concessions for juniors. Permits from hon sec or A&G (Leisure) Ltd, 48 McDowall St, Johnstone. Also from Rangers Centre at loch.

CONON (including Blackwater)

Drains Loch Luichart and is joined by Orrin and Blackwater before entering the Moray Firth and North Sea by way of Cromarty Firth. Spring fishing has declined and main salmon runs now take place from July to September. Sport then among best in Highlands.

Dingwall (Ross-shire). Salmon, sea trout and brown trout. Dingwall & District AC has lower beat on R Conon. Fly only, for salmon, sea trout and brown trout. Thigh waders only. Season: Jan 26 to Sept 30, best months May, Aug and Sept. Also fishing for brown trout, pike, perch and char on **Loch Luichart**. Season March 15 to Oct 6. Dt £10 from H C Furlong, Sports & Model Shop, Tulloch Street, Dingwall.

Permit also covers **Loch Chuilin** and **Loch Achanalt**. Brown trout fishing on 3 beats of **R Conon**; and on **Brahan**, a stocked, brown trout pond. Coarse fishing on **Loch Ussie**, pike and perch. Permits from Seaforth Highland Estates, Brahan, by Dingwall (tel: 0349 61150). Contact Sports & Model Shop for information (tel: 0349 62346). Other tackle shop: Maclean Sport, High St. Hotels:

Conon at Conon Bridge; Craigdarroch and Coul House, both Contin.

Strathpeffer (Ross-shire). **R Conon**, above Loch Achonachie, salmon and brown trout; fly or spinning. **River Blackwater** above Rogie Falls, salmon, brown trout and pike. **Loch Achonachie**, brown trout, perch and occasional salmon; bank and boat fishing; use of a boat produce best results; fly or spinning. **Loch Meig**, brown trout; boat and bank fishing; fly only. Permits from John MacMillan, Newsagent, The Square (tel: 0997 21346); and East Lodge Hotel, Strathconon (tel: 09977 222). East Lodge Hotel also issues permits for brown trout fishing on **Loch Beannacharain** and 6 hill lochs. Fishing is restricted on hill lochs during deer stalking season. Coul House Hotel issues permits for beats on Rivers Conon, **Blackwater** and **Beauly** (salmon, sea trout, brown trout); and for **Lochs**

Tarvie (rainbow trout), **Achonachie** (brown trout) and **Meig** (brown trout). Apply to Coul House Hotel, Contin, by Strathpeffer IV14 9EY (tel: 0997 421487). Hotel provides full angling service, including rod racks, rod and reel hire, small tackle shop, guest freezer, drying room and fish-smoking arranged.

Garve (Ross-shire). Garve Hotel (tel. 0997 414205) has excellent fishing on **Loch Garve**, which holds large trout (fish up to 12lb taken) also pike to 30lb and perch; and brown trout fishing on $1\frac{1}{2}$m of **River Blackwater** within hotel grounds. Free fishing for hotel patrons. **Loch an Eich Bhain (The Tarvie Loch)**, 25 acres; stocked with rainbow trout to 8lbs and brown trout to 4lbs; fly only. Fishing almost exclusively by boat, bank access being very limited. **Loch Ruith a Phuill**, 12 acres; wild brown trout; coarse and fly fishing tackle allowed. Permits from

A salmon well hooked on the Boat Pool, Upper Fairburn beat, River Conon. *Photo: Eric Chalker.*

Tarvie Lochs Trout Fishery, Tarvie, by Strathpeffer; Morison, Ironmonger, Beauly; Sports & Model Shop, Tulloch St, Dingwall; and Mike Jamieson, Church St, Inverness. **Loch Glascarnoch**, brown trout, pike and perch; fly only. Contact Aultguish Inn, by Garve (tel: 09975 254).

CREE and BLADNOCH

Cree drains Loch Moan and flows about 25m to sea at Wigtown Bay. Runs of salmon and sea trout in summer and early autumn. **Minnoch**, tributary of Cree, is also a salmon river, joining Cree about six miles from Newton Stewart. Bladnoch, a strong tidal river, flows into Cree Estuary at Wigtown. Salmon and sea trout in season. Good pools.

Newton Stewart (Wigtownshire). Salmon, sea trout; best early in season. Newton Stewart AA has fishing on Cree, salmon and sea trout; **Bladnoch**, salmon; and **Bruntis Loch,** brown and rainbow trout, bank fishing only; **Kirriereoch Loch,** brown trout, bank fishing, fly only. Permits from A J Dickinson, Galloway Guns & Tackle, 36a Arthur St, Newton Stewart DG3 6DE (tel. 0671 3404), who supply all game, coarse and sea fishing tackle together with frozen and live bait. Forestry Commission has fishing on **R Palnure**, salmon, sea trout, brown trout; **R Minnoch**, brown trout (Mar-Jun) and salmon (Jul-Oct); **Black Loch,** brown trout, stocked, fly only until 1 July; **Loch of Lowes**, brown trout, fly only; **Lilies Loch**, brown trout; **Lochs Spectacle** and **Garwachie**, pike, perch, tench, roach, rudd; **Loch Eldrig**, pike, perch, roach. Permits from Forestry Commission Office, Creebridge, Newton Stewart (tel: 0671 2420); and Galloway Wildlife Museum. Creebridge House Hotel, Newton Stewart DG8 6NP, offers fishing on **R Bladnoch**, good spring run of grilse, Feb-Oct, 2m for up to 4 rods: **R Minnoch**, a tributary of Cree fed by Glentrool Loch, 4m for up to 6 rods, spawning pools: **Upper Cree**, at Bargrennan, 2m salmon fishing: also assn water on stretch of Cree which runs through town to estuary mouth. Hotel has excellent food and accommodation, and can accommodate rods in a lockable room and has freezer and drying facilities. Corsemalzie House Hotel, Port William, DG8 9RL, has salmon and trout fishing on **Bladnoch** and **Tarf**, 5m on each, dt £18, wt £80; trout fishing on **Malzie Burn**; and coarse fishing in nearby lochs. Ghillie available. Salmon, brown trout and pike fishing on Tarf; pike and perch fishing on **Whitefield Loch;** and trout and coarse fish on **Torwood Lochs**. Permits from David Canning, Torwood House Hotel, Glenluce, Newton Stewart. Trout fishing on **Black Loch**, and mixed coarse and pike fishing on **Lochs Heron** and **Ronald**; permit and boat hire available from A Brown, Three Lochs Caravan Park, Nr Kirkcowan, Newton Stewart DG8 0EP (tel. 067183 304). Castlewigg Hotel, nr Whithorn, 19m S of Wigtown, can arrange salmon and trout fishing in local lochs and rivers; and sea angling from Port Patrick and Isle of Whithorn. Tel: 098 85-213. Permits for salmon and trout fishing on River Bladnoch from Bladnoch Inn, Wigtown (tel. 098 842200).

Barrhill (Ayrshire). Drumlamford Estate Fisheries comprising 1m of salmon and trout fishing on **River Cree**; three stocked trout lochs; and **Loch Dornal**, a coarse fish loch. Boats available. Permits from keeper, Colin Hastings, The Lodge. (046 582 256).

CROSS WATER OF LUCE

Dependent on flood water for good salmon fishing, but very good for sea trout after dark. Best July onwards.

Stranraer (Wigtownshire). Excellent centre for river, loch and sea fishing. Stranraer & Dist AA has **Soulseat Loch**, rainbow and brown trout, fly and bait; **Dindinnie Reservoir**, brown trout, fly only; **Knockquassan Reservoir**, brown trout, fly only; and **Penwhirn Reservoir**, brown trout, fly only. Permits from The Sports Shop, 90 George St; and Rogersports, Charlotte St. Cross Water of Luce

administered by J V Greenhill, Leswalt, Stranraer. Torwood House Hotel issues permits for **Torwood Lochs,** trout, bream, tench, carp, roach, rudd, perch; and **Whitefield Loch**, pike and perch. Apply to D Canning, Torwood House Hotel, Glenluce (tel: 05813 469). Sea fishing in **Loch Ryan**, Irish Sea and Luce Bay. Charter boats and bait available locally. Hotel: Ruddicot.

DEE (Aberdeenshire)

Second most famous salmon river of Scotland; for fly fishing probably the best. Also holds sea trout and brown trout. Rises in Cairngorms and flows into North Sea at Aberdeen. Best months for salmon: February to mid-June. Best for finnock (small sea trout) mid-August to end of September.

Aberdeen. Salmon, sea trout, brown trout; sea fishing. Many owners let for whole or part of season, but some good stretches held by hotels. Some hotel waters free to guests during summer. Lower reaches give good finnock fishing. Sea fishing is good in vicinity of Aberdeen. Hotels: Bucksburn Moat House; Cults; Dee Motel.

Banchory (Kincardineshire). Salmon and sea trout. Banchory Lodge Hotel by river can arrange salmon and trout fishing on Dee for five rods, bait fishing to April 15, fly only after; at rates ranging from £25 period per day to £300 per week, according to date. Ghillies and tuition available. Apply to Mr & Mrs Dugald Jaffray, Banchory Lodge Hotel, Banchory AB31 3HS (tel. 033 082 2625). Feughside Inn, Strachan, by Banchory, issues Aberdeen Dist AA permits for 1½m on **River Feugh**, salmon and sea trout, dt £30. Salmon and sea trout fishing on Dee at Blairs; apply to Salar Properties UK Ltd, 60 Castle St, Edinburgh EH2 3NA. Other hotels: Invery House, Raemoir Lodge.

Aboyne (Aberdeenshire). Dee, salmon and sea trout; and **Loch Aboyne**, rainbow trout, stocked. Fly only. No Sunday fishing on Dee. Permits from Brooks House, Glen Tanar (tel: 03398 86451). Coarse fishing on Loch Aboyne; pike and perch;

permits from The Warden, Loch Aboyne, Holiday Park. **Tillypronie Loch**, brown trout, fly only. Permits hourly or daily, tel: 03398 81332. Hotels: Birse Lodge; Huntly Arms.

Ballater (Aberdeenshire). Balmoral, Mar, Glenmuick and Invercauld Estates preserve most of Upper River Dee salmon fishings. **River Gairn**, brown trout, fly only. St £9, wt £5, dt £1.50; from tackle shop. Ballater AA has fishing on **Loch Vrotichan**, brown trout, fly only. Permits from hon sec and tackle shop. Tackle shop: Countrywear, 15 & 35 Bridge St, Ballater (tel: 03397 55453). Hotels: Gairnshiel Lodge.

Braemar (Aberdeenshire). Salmon fishing: Invercauld Estate lets Crathie, Lower Invercauld and Monaltrie beats, 20m in all, details from The Factor, Invercauld Estates Office, Braemar, By Ballater AB3 5XQ (tel: 03397 41224). Brown trout fishing on **Rivers Gairn** and **Clunie**. Permits from Invercauld Estates Office; Tourist Office, Braemar; and Countrywear, Tackle Shop, Bridge St, Ballater. **Lochs Bainnie** and **Nan Ean,** brown trout, fly only; permits from Invercauld Estates Office and the keeper, Mr R Hepburn (tel: Glenshee 206). Hotels: Invercauld Arms; Braemar Lodge.

Keep the banks clean

Several clubs have stopped issuing tickets to visitors because of the state of the banks after they have left. Spend a few moments clearing up.

DEE (Kirkcudbrightshire), (including Lochs Dee and Ken)

Flows through Loch Ken about 16m to Solway. Salmon, sea trout and brown trout. Netting reduced and river stocked with salmon fry. An area in which acidification problems have been reported. Some lochs affected.

Castle Douglas (Kirkcudbrightshire). Forestry Commission has fishing on **R Dee**, trout; and **Stroan Loch**, mainly pike but also perch, roach and trout. Dt £1, from dispenser at Raider's Road entrance. **Woodhall Loch**, best known as pike water but also roach, perch and large trout; good winter venue with big pike catches, including 20lb plus fish. Dt £1.50 from Mossdale Shop. Castle Douglas AA has 7m stretch on **River Urr**; salmon, sea trout and brown trout; re-stocked annually; good runs of sea trout and grilse starting in June. Dt £5 and £15 (Sept, Oct, Nov). Assn also has brown and rainbow trout fishing on **Loch Roan**; 4 boats. Dt £15 per boat for 2 rods. Permits from Tommy's Sports, 178 King Street. **Loch Ken**, pike and perch; open all year for coarse fish. Permits from Galloway View, Balmaclellan, Castle Douglas; and local hotels. Brown trout fishing on **Lairdmannoch Loch** at Twynholm; boat fishing only. Permits from G M Thompson & Co Ltd, 27 King St; self-catering accommodation also available. Other tackle shop: McGowan's, King St. Hotels: Douglas Arms; Imperial; Urr Valley Country House.

Crossmichael (Kirkcudbrightshire). Boats for **Loch Ken** available from Crossmichael Marina, which has been recently upgraded and re-equipped, boats available all year round. Loch Ken, pike, perch, roach, brown trout, rainbow trout, sea trout, salmon, some bream, eels. Hotel: Culgruff House Hotel.

New Galloway (Kirkcudbrightshire). Dee private. **Loch Dee**, stocked brown trout; **Lillies Loch**, brown trout (ideal for beginners); and **Stroan Loch**, pike, perch, trout and very occasional salmon. No bag limit. Permits from Forest Enterprise, 21 King St, Castle Douglas DG7 1AA (tel. 0556 3626); and Clatteringshaws Forest Wildlife Centre, New Galloway DG7 3SQ (tel. 06442 285). New Galloway AA controls stretch of **River Ken**, brown trout, salmon, pike, roach, perch; stretch of **Loch Ken**, brown trout, pike, perch, and salmon run through loch during season; **Blackwater of Dee** (N bank only), brown trout, salmon, pike; **Mossdale Loch,** native brown trout and stocked rainbow trout, fly only; and **Clatteringshaws Reservoir**, brown trout, pike, perch, roach. Fishing on Clatteringshaws Reservoir shared with Newton Stewart AA. Visitors permits, for all except Loch Ken and Mossdale Loch, £2 per rod per day or £10 per week; Loch Ken, dt £2 plus 50p surcharge if permit bought from bailiffs; Mossdale Loch, dt £10 per boat (1 rod) per day. Permits from hotels in town; Ken Bridge Hotel; G & J Brown, Grocer, High St; Mr Hopkins, Grocer, High St; Post Office, Mossdale; Deer Museum, Clatteringshaws; and Kenmore Hotel. Concession for jun. Ken Bridge Hotel has own stretch on R Ken (wt £10, dt £2), both this hotel and Cross Keys can arrange fishing on rivers and lochs. **Barscobe Loch;** brown trout; dt (incl boat) £5 from Sir Hugh Wontner, Barscobe, Balmaclellan, By Castle Douglas. Tackle shop: Gun & Tackle.

Dalry (Kirkcudbrightshire). Dalry AA has fishing on **River Ken** from Dalry to Boatknowe, left bank; good stocks of brown trout and occasional salmon; fly only to 1 June. Assn also has water on **Carsfad Loch**, stocked annually with brown trout, bank fishing (west bank). Coarse fish must not be returned. No Sunday fishing. No keep nets or ground baiting of any description. Visitors tickets available from 15 Mar - 30 Sept. Permits from Clachan Inn; Post Office, Carsphairn; Ken Bridge Hotel, New Galloway. Milton Park Hotel (Tel Dalry 286), rainbow and brown trout fishing on **Lochs Moss**, **Roddick**, **Brack** and **Barscobe**, boats available. Hotel also has fishing on **Loch Earlstoun** at rear of hotel, with boat. All waters stocked with trout. Tickets for non-residents but guests have priority. Lochinvar Hotel can arrange fishing in rivers, lochs and reservoirs (salmon, trout, pike and perch). Permits available from Duchrae Farm for **Lochinvar Loch;** wild brown trout, no shore fishing, fly only. Hotel: De Croft.

DEVERON

Rises in Cabrach and flows some 45m into the Moray Firth at Banff. A salmon river, but has a reputation for its brown trout fishing. There are also some large sea trout, many of 8-10lb. Sea trout run June to September; finnock mid-July to end of October.

Banff (Banffshire). Salmon, sea trout, brown trout. Fife Lodge Hotel, Banff Springs and County Hotel can sometimes arrange fishings. Early bookings advisable as best beats are heavily booked. Best months: salmon, March to Oct; sea trout June to Aug; brown trout, April, May and Sept. Sea trout improving. Banff and Macduff AA has about 1m, left bank only, of tidal. St £10 restricted to residents within 5m of Banff; wt £10 and dt £4, Mon-Fri fishing only, from Jay-Tee Sports, Low Street, Banff. Sea trout fishing (July onwards) in **Boyne Burn**, 6m away. Tickets from Seafield Estate, Cullen (no charge, but limited).

Turriff (Aberdeenshire). Turriff AA has salmon, sea trout and brown trout fishing on Deveron. Wt £50-£80, Mon-Fri, for resident visitors only. No day tickets ex-

cept Feb-April when £5 per day; 6 rods per day limit. Permits from tackle shop. Fly only when level falls below 6in on gauge. Best months July, August and Sept; also a fishery on opposite bank, dt £5. Bognie, Mountblairy and Frendraught Group, has salmon, grilse, sea trout and brown trout fishing on R Deveron. 11 Feb to 31 Oct. Wt £50-£250 depending on time of year. Fishing is available to anyone, usually on a weekly basis along with holiday cottages. Day permits are only available up until May. Permits from BMF Group, Estate Office, Frendraught House, Forgue, by Huntly AB54 6EB (tel: 046 47 331). Enquiries to Bell Ingram, 7 Walker Street, Edinburgh for **Beldorney Castle Water**. £55 per rod per week. Tackle shop: Ian Masson, Fishing Tackle, 6 Castle St. Hotels: Union; White Heather. Bed and breakfast accommodation suitable for anglers, from Fiona Angus, Bridgend Farm House, Turrif AB53 8AA; and Jenny Rae, Silverwells, St Mary's Well, Turrif AB53 8BS.

Huntly (Aberdeenshire). Salmon, sea trout, brown trout. Permits for **Deveron**, **Bogie** and **Isla**; st £50, mt £40, wt £30, dt £15 from Clerk, Huntly Fishings Committee, 27 Duke Street, Huntly AB54 5DP. Only 10 day tickets per day and none on Saturdays or Public Holidays. Castle Hotel *(see advt)* has Castle Beat from meeting of Deveron and Bogie downstream; both banks. An extensive improvement scheme carried out in early 1991 has improved and restored a number of croys to form new lies and pools. Wt £80 - £180. Hotel can also arrange for other good private fishing. Forbes Arms Hotel at Rotheimay issue permits for Deveron; salmon, sea trout and brown trout; fly fishing and spinning. The Old Manse of Marnoch Hotel, on the banks of the Deveron, caters for anglers with ample freezer and drying space; although the hotel does not sell permits these are available locally on a daily and weekly basis. Apply to Patrick and Keren Carter, The Old Manse of Marnoch, Bridge of Marnoch, By Huntly, Aberdeenshire AB54 5RS.

DIGHTY

Drains some small lochs and falls into the Firth of Tay not far from Dundee. Banks built up on lower reaches. Now clear of pollution. Trout, odd sea trout and salmon. Badly weeded and difficult to fish in summer.

Dundee (Angus). Trout with occasional sea trout; free. **Monikie** and **Crombie Reservoirs** leased to Monikie AC. Reservations via the bailiff (tel: Newbiggings 300). **Lintrathen Reservoir** leased to Lintrathen AC. Good trout fishing; boats available; catch limit 15 fish (over 10")

per boat. Club bookings from Dr Parratt, 91 Strathern Road, Broughty Ferry, Dundee, tel: 0382 77305. **Loch Fitty** near Dunfermline also with in easy reach. Tackle shop: Shotcast Ltd, 8 Whitehall Crescent. Hotel: Northern.

DON (Aberdeenshire)

Rises near Ben Avon and flows for nearly 80m to North Sea at Aberdeen. Good salmon river which is also noted as a dry-fly trout water. Spring salmon fishing falling off but autumn fishing and grilse runs improving. Some sea trout.

Kintore (Aberdeenshire). Salmon and trout fishing on both banks of River Don; 2½m on right bank and 3½m on left bank. Permits from Sloans of Inverurie, 125-129 High St, Inverurie AB51 3QJ (tel: 0467 625181). No Sunday fishing.

Inverurie (Aberdeenshire). **River Don** (2½ miles) and **River Urie** (3½ miles) salmon, brown trout and occasional sea trout. No Sunday fishing on Don. Salmon best March, April, May and Sept-Oct. Permits from Sloans of Inverurie, 125-129 High St, Inverurie AB51 3QJ (tel: 0467 625181).

Kemnay (Aberdeenshire). Salmon, sea

trout, brown trout. Mrs F J Milton, Kemnay House, AB51 9LH (tel. 0467 642220), issues limited permits for two beats on Don at Kemnay; wt £70, dt £15 and £6 (trout). Booking essential. Hotel: Parkhill Lodge.

Alford (Aberdeenshire). 25m from Aberdeen. Salmon, brown trout and some sea trout. Forbes Arms Hotel, Bridge of Alford AB33 8QJ (tel. 09755 62108), has 3¼m of Don for guests and also issues permits. Wt £45-£85, dt £8-£17. Preference given to guests. Some good trout burns (free) in vicinity.

Kildrummy (Aberdeenshire). Kildrummy

Tailing a salmon from the Canary Pool, Middle Blackhall beat. *Photo: Eric Chalker.*

Castle Hotel has good stretch of salmon and brown trout fishing. Trout best early, salmon late.

Glenkindie (Aberdeenshire). Glenkindie Arms Hotel issue permits for salmon and trout fishing. No Sunday fishing; 4 rod limit.

Strathdon (Aberdeenshire). Colquhonnie Hotel has 3m salmon water, 9m of trout fishing. Permits for salmon fishing also available from Glenkindie Arms Hotel; and Kildrummy Castle Hotel, Kildrummy.

DOON

Drains Loch Doon on the Solway Firth's watershed and flows right through the old County of Ayr to the Firth of Clyde, near Ayr Town. Good salmon, sea trout and brown trout water.

Ayr (Ayrshire). On Rivers Doon and Ayr. Salmon and sea trout July onwards. Burns Monument Hotel, Alloway, has water on Doon. Salmon and sea trout fishing on Skeldon Estate stretch of Doon available from Mrs Campbell (tel. 0292 56656). District Council issues permits for **Ayr**. Club membership and permits for various club waters issued by Gamesport of Ayr, 60 Sandgate, Ayr KA7 1BX (tel. 0292 263822). Hotel: Parson's Lodge, 15 Main St, Patna.

Dalmellington (Ayrshire). Good salmon and sea trout (July onwards). **Loch Doon**, 6m; plenty of small brown trout and occasional salmon and char; fishing free; boats for hire. Craigengillan Estate has both banks of River Doon from Loch Doon to the Straiton Road Bridge. Tickets from keeper. Brown trout and occasional salmon and sea trout. Apply Farm, Craigengillan (Tel: Dalmellington 550 366).

EDEN (Fife)

Rises in Ochil Hills not far from Loch Leven and falls into North Sea in St Andrews Bay. Provides some very fair trout fishing. Slow-flowing stream suitable for dry-fly fishing. Some sea trout below Cupar.

St Andrews (Fife). **Cameron Reservoir**, brown trout; stocked by St Andrews AC (trout av 1¼lb). Fly only. Sunday fishing. Boat and bank fishing. Boat hire (3 rods per boat) £21 per session. Bank permit £7 per session. Permits sold at reservoir. Tackle shop: J Wilson & Son, 169-171 South St, St Andrews KY16 9EE (tel: 0334 72477). Hotels: Homelea; Rufflets Country House; Sporting Laird.

Cupar (Fife). Salmon, sea trout and brown trout fishing on Eden; permits from J Caldwell, Newsagent & Fishing Tackle,

Main St, Methihill, Fife. Clatto and Stratheden AA has brown trout fishing on **Clatto Reservoir**. Dt £5, evening £6; from Waterman's Cottage at reservoir. Boats available, £4.

Ladybank (Fife). Fine dry-fly fishing; trout. Some free, but mostly preserved. **Lindores Loch**, near **Newburgh** (7m NW), holds brown and rainbow trout; fly only; no bank fishing. Permits available from F G A Hamilton, The Byre, Kindrochet, St Fillans, Perthshire PH6 2JZ (tel: 0764 685 337).

Check before you go

While every effort has been made to ensure that the information given in **Where to Fish** *is correct, the position is continually changing, and anglers are urged, in their own interests, to make preliminary enquiries before travelling to selected venues. This is especially important with reference to prices quoted. Inevitably the rate of inflation is affecting stability in this quarter. Anglers' attention is also drawn to the fact that the hotels mentioned under the various fishing stations do not necessarily have water of their own. Any amendments or further data for inclusion in subsequent editions, and any criticism, will be welcome.*

ESK (North)

Formed by junction of Lee and Mark, near Lochlee, and flows for nearly 30m to North Sea near Montrose. Good river for salmon and sea trout.

Montrose (Angus). Sea trout, finnock (whitling) and brown trout. Joseph Johnston & Sons Ltd, 3 America Street, Montrose DD10 8DR, issue permits for salmon fishing on the Gallery and Canterland beats, charges varying from £6 to £50, according to time of year. Spring and Autumn best fishing. Local club: Montrose AA. Other tackle shops: D Rollston, High St; The Gun Shop, 122 High Street; Cobb, Castle Place. Hotels: Carlton, George, Hillside.

Edzell (Angus). Salmon and sea trout. Dal-

housie Estates, Brechin DD9 6EL, has boats to hire for trout fishing on **Loch Lee** in Glen Esk; no bank fishing, and fly only. Permits from Mrs Taylor (tel: 03567 208); also salmon beats to let by the week on North Esk at Edzell, dt available when no weekly lets, details from Dalhousie Estates. Panmure Arms Hotel has 1m of fishing on **West Water** (trout, sea trout and occasional salmon); and can arrange fishing on North Esk and Loch Lee.

ESK (South)

Rises in Glen Clova and flows some 49m to North Sea near Montrose. Good salmon river with plentiful runs of sea trout. Best months for salmon are February, March and April. Good autumn river (mid-September onwards).

Brechin (Angus). Good centre for North and South Esk. Salmon and sea trout; fishing good, but mostly reserved. South Esk Estates Office, Brechin, let beats on 2½m, usually by the week or longer periods, but limited dt £13 (Feb-Aug) and £19 (Sept-Oct) available. Brechin AC has fishing on **Loch Saugh** near Fettercairn, brown trout, fly only; and **River West Water**, brown trout, salmon and sea trout. Permits for **L Saugh** from Ramsay Arms Hotel, Fettercairn; Drumtochty Arms Hotel, Auchenblae; and Bridgend Bar, Brechin. Bridgend Bar issues limited

dt for West Water, after 11am. Tackle shop: Sports Shop, High St. Hotel: Northern.

Kirriemuir (Angus). Kirriemuir AC has approx 7m on South Esk. Salmon, sea trout, a few brown trout. Permits from hon sec (tel: 0575 73456). Some fly only water, but much of it unrestricted. Concessions to jun. No Sunday fishing and no permits on Saturdays. Strathmore AIA has rights on lower **Isla** and **Dean**; permits from tackle shops in Dundee, Blairgowrie and Forfar.

EWE

This river has good runs of salmon (best May onwards) and sea trout (end June onwards) up to Loch Maree. Fishing again excellent, after problems caused by disease.

Aultbea (Ross-shire). Bank fishing for wild brown trout on **Aultbea Hill Lochs**. Permits from Bridgend Stores; Woodcraft Shop, Birchburn, Aultbea; Post Office, Laide. Bridgend Stores, as well as issuing permits, has a comprehensive range of tackle; contact Bridgend Stores, Aultbea, Achnasheen, Ross-shire IV22 2JA (tel. 0445 731204). Hotels: Aultbea; Drum-

chork Lodge; Ocean View, Laide.

Poolewe (Ross-shire). Salmon, sea trout, brown trout. The National Trust for Scotland, Inverewe Estate, Visitors' Centre (tel. 044 586 299), has trout fishing on three lochs. Dt £4.50, boat £3. No Sunday fishing. Reduction for members. Permits and tackle available from Norvana Gift Shop.

Fishing available?

If you own, manage, or know of first-class fishing available to the public which should be considered for inclusion in **Where to Fish** *please apply to the publishers (address in the front of the book) for a form for submission, on completion, to the Editor. (Inclusion is at the sole discretion of the Editor).*

A calm day on Loch Maree. A better 'dapping' breeze would be found beyond the headland.
Photo: C. Hancock.

LOCH MAREE (Ross & Cromarty). Spring salmon fishing from April until June. Sea trout from June until Oct. Also brown trout fishing.

Talladale (Ross-shire). Salmon, sea trout, brown trout. Loch Maree Hotel has fishing. Heavy demand for sea-trout season so early booking advised. Hotel owned by anglers' syndicate which provides excellent facilities. Boat fishing only; 8 boats available; 2 persons with ghillie. Dt £38 (Apr-Jun), £48 (Jul-Aug) and £43 (Sept-Oct); price includes ghillie. Apply to Loch Maree Hotel, Talladale, By Achnasheen, Wester Ross IV22 2HL. Gairloch Anglers also have fishing in many hill lochs, apply to hotel.

Kinlochewe (Ross-shire). Salmon and sea trout fishing on loch. Boats available. Permits from Kinlochewe Hotel (tel: 044584 253) and Kinlochewe Holiday Chalets (tel: 044584 234). Brown trout and sea trout fishing on **Loch Bharranch**; and brown trout, pike and perch fishing on **Loch a'Chroisg**. Permits and boat bookings from Glendocherty Craft Shop. **Loch Rosque**, ¼m from village; pike, perch, brown trout; permits available from Ledgowan Lodge Hotel, Achnasheen, Ross-shire IV22 2EJ (tel. 044 588 252).

FINDHORN

Rises in Monadhliath Mountains and flows over 60m to Moray Firth. Good salmon river with many rock pools, mostly preserved by owners. Also sea trout and brown trout. Best months: July and August. An area in which acidification problems have been reported: some lochs affected.

Forres (Moray). Salmon fishing on Findhorn, 4 beats with 2 rods per beat; and trout fishing on **Clunas Reservoir** (brown and rainbow) and **Loch of Boath** (brown); from The Factor, Cawdor Estate Office, Cawdor, Nairn IV12 5RE (tel. 066 77 666). Good trout fishing on nearby lochs; **Loch of Blairs, Loch Lochindorb**; permits from J Mitchell, Tackle Shop, 96D High St.

FLEET (Kirkcudbrightshire)

Formed by junction of Big and Little Water, empties into the Solway Firth at Gatehouse. Good sea trout and herling, and few grilse and salmon; best months July and August.

Gatehouse-of-Fleet (Dumfries and Galloway). Murray Arms Hotel, Gatehouse-of-Fleet DG7 2HY (tel. 0557 814207), issue permits for Rusko and Cally Estate waters on River Fleet. Sea trout and herling with some grilse and salmon. No sunday fishing. Gatehouse and Kirkcudbright AA has **Loch Whinyeon**, 120 acres, 3½m from town, brown trout, stocked and wild; fly only. Two boats available; bank or boat fishing. Assn also controls **Loch Lochenbreck**, 40 acres, 3m from Lauriston, rainbow and brown trout. Fly only. Bank or boat fishing. Permits from Watson McKinnel, 15 St Cuthbert St, Kirkcudbright. Hotels: Angel; Selkirk Arms, Kirkcudbright.

FORTH (including Loch Leven and Water of Leith)

Formed from junction of Avendhu and Duchray not far from Aberfoyle, and thence flows about 80m to its firth at Alloa, opening into North Sea. Principal tributaries, Teith and Allan, flow above Stirling. A large salmon river, which at times, and especially on upper reaches, provides some good sport. Good run in lower reaches during February and March, as a rule. This river and Teith, Balvaig, Leny Water and Allan Water being extensively restocked with salmon and sea trout by Forth District Salmon Fishery Board. (Howietown and Northern Fisheries Co, Stirling, providing hatchery facilities). Trouting in upper reaches and tributaries, particularly in lochs, where salmon also taken.

Dunfermline (Fife). **Loch Fitty**, good trout water. Bank and boat fishing, 30 boats, tackle shop and restaurant to which visitors are most welcome. Boats, including outboard motor, for 3 anglers, day (10am-5pm) £29; evening (5.30pm-dark) £32 with reductions during Apr, Aug, Sept; bank permits £11.30 per session. Reduced boat charges for single anglers, and 'father and son/daughter'. Apply to The Lodge, Loch Fitty, Kingseat, by Dunfermline, Fife (tel. 0383 620666).

Halfway House Hotel by Loch Fitty welcomes anglers and can arrange fishing for guests. Apply to Ann Witheyman or Vic Pegg, Halfway House Hotel, Kingseat, Dunfermline KY12 0TJ (tel. 0383 731661). Civil Service SA has brown trout fishing on **Loch Glow** in Cleish Hills near Kelty; fly, bait and spinning. Regularly stocked. Permits from Mr Balfour, Lochornie Cottage, Kelty; and tackle shops in Dunfermline, Cowdenbeath, Kelty and Kinross. Tackle shops: D W Black, The Hobby and Model Shop, 10-12 New Row; Gamesport, St Andrews St, Dunfermline; S & A MacKenzie, 225 Main St, Kelty; Fife Tackle Centre, 56 High St, Cowdenbeath; Alex Constable, 39a High St, Kirkcaldy; Aladin's Cave, 259 High St, Leslie. Hotels: Abbey Park House, Auld Toll Tavern, King Malcolm Thistle.

Stirling (Stirlingshire). Forth, **Allan** and **Teith** may be fished from here. Herling in Forth in spring and autumn. Salmon fishing from Lands of Hood to mouth of Teith (7½m) including Cruive Dykes is controlled by District Council. Good run in lower reaches, March and Aug-Sept. Permits for Forth and Teith; salmon, sea trout and brown trout; from D Crockart & Son, 47 King St, Stirling FK8 1AY (tel. 0786 473443). **North Third Trout Reservoir**, rainbow and brown trout; fly only; boat and bank fishing. Advanced booking advisable. Permits from North Third Trout Fishery, Greathill, Cambushbarron, Stirling.

Aberfoyle (Perthshire). Trout; a few salmon taken. Aberfoyle APA has brown trout fishing on **Loch Ard**; fly only; stocked with young brown trout. Dt £2.50. Boats are available; £10 per day. Boats and permits from Addison's, Newsagent, Main St; Altskeith Hotel, Kinlochard; and Forest Hills Hotel, Kinlochard. Free fishing for residents of Altskeith and Inverard Hotels; apply to hotels for details of package. Brown trout fishing on **Loch Arklet**, **Loch Katrine** and **Glen Finglas**; fly fishing from boats only. Dt £14 per boat. Permits from Strathclyde Water, 419 Balmore Rd, Glasgow G22 6NU (tel. 041 355 5333). Brown trout, pike and perch fishing on **Loch Chon** and **Loch Drunkie**. Fly only on Loch Chon. Bank fishing only on Loch Drunkie. Permits from Forestry Commission, Aberfoyle; and Queen Elizabeth Forest Park Visitor Centre (open Easter to Oct). Access to Loch Drunkie via Forest Drive; no vehicle access after Oct. Among other accessible waters are **Lake of Menteith**, brown and rainbow trout, fly only. Permits from Lake Menteith Fisheries Ltd, Port of Menteith (tel: 08775 664). Tackle shop: D Crockart & Son, King St, Stirling. Hotel: Inverard.

Tributaries of Forth

ALMOND. West of Edinburgh the river flows into the Firth of Forth at Cramond.

Cramond (West Lothian). Cramond AC has fishing on River Almond and tributaries. Salmon, sea trout and brown trout. Permits from Post Office, Cramond; Country Life, Balgreen Rd, Edinburgh; Hook, Line and Sinker, Morningside Rd, Edinburgh. Members' day tickets from Shooting Lines, Roseburn Terrace, Edinburgh.

Livingston (West Lothian). River Almond AA has 20m of Almond; salmon, sea trout and brown trout. Permits from hon sec, Mr Craig Campbell, 2 Canmore St, South Queensferry; Livingston Sports, Almondvale Centre; Country Life, Balgreen Rd, Edinburgh; Shooting Lines, Roseburn Terrace & Hope Park Terrace, Edinburgh. **Crosswood Reservoir**, 30 acres; stocked brown trout. Fly only. 3 boats. No bank fishing. Bag limit: 6 trout.

Permits from Lothian Regional Council, Dept of Water and Drainage, Lomond House, Beveridge Square, Livingston (tel: Livingston 414004). **Morton Fishery**, brown and rainbow trout; fly only; bag limits 3-6 fish. Advanced bookings. Permits from Morton Fishery, Morton Reservoir, Mid Calder, West Lothian.

NORTH ESK and **SOUTH ESK**. These two rivers are fed by Lothian regional reservoirs and join near Dalkeith to form the River Esk. The Esk flows a short way down to enter the Firth of Forth at Inveresk.

Musselburgh (East Lothian). Musselburgh and District AA has salmon, sea trout and brown trout fishing on Esk; permits from Givan Shop, 67 Eskside West; Musselburgh Pet Centre, High St; Mike's Tackle, High St, Portobello. No Sunday fishing.

Penicuik (Midlothian). Esk Valley AIA has

rainbow and brown trout fishing on North and South Esk; fly rod and reel only to be used. Permits from hon sec. Lothian Regional Council manages three reservoirs in **Pentland Hills Regional Park**, which feed North Esk: **Glengorse**, **Clubbiedean** and **Bonaly Reservoirs**; and one in local nature reserve, which feeds South Esk: **Gladhouse Reservoir**. Brown and rainbow trout; fly only; boat only. Platform for disabled at Clubbiedean and boat for disabled at Gladhouse. Permits from Lothian Regional Council, Dept of Water and Drainage, Comiston Springs, 55 Buckstone Terrace, Edinburgh EH10 6XH (tel: 031 445 4141). No permits required for Bonaly. **Rosebery Reservoir**, is also managed by Lothian Regional Council; 52 acres; brown and rainbow trout, pike, perch. Fly only (Apr-Jun). Spinning and worm fishing (Jul-Sep). 3 boats and bank fishing. Bag limit: 6 trout. Permits from Reservoir Keeper, Watermans Cottage.

West Linton (Peeblesshire). Brown trout fishing on **West Water Reservoir**; 93 acres; fly only. 2 boats. No bank fishing. Permits from Lothian Regional Council, Dept of Water and Drainage, Comiston

Springs, 55 Buckstone Terrace, Edinburgh EH10 6XH (tel: 031 445 4141); and Slipperfield Estate, c/o Romano Inn, Romano Bridge, Peeblesshire (tel: 0968 60781).

DEVON: Fair brown trout stream; sea trout and salmon lower down.

Alloa (Clackmannanshire). Devon AA has salmon, sea trout and brown trout fishing on Devon; fly only until 1 May. Assn also has brown trout fishing on **Glenquey Reservoir**, near Muckhart; fly only, no spinning; bank fishing only. No Sunday fishing. Season tickets for sea trout and salmon are only available from hon sec (postal application only). Permits for brown trout fishing from Scobbie Sports, 2-4 Primrose St; W Orr, Tron Sports, Tron Court, Tullibody; D Crockart & Son, 47 King St, Stirling; Hobby & Model Shop, 10 New Row, Dunfermline; McCutcheons Newsagents, Bridge St, Dollar; and A Shearer, The Inn, Crook of Devon; Muckhart PO; A B Waugh, Main St, Menstrie; and Mrs Small, Rackmill Caravan Site, Dollar. **Gartmorn Dam Fishery**, brown trout; bank and boat fishing. Permits from D Crockart & Son, 47 King St, Stirling; Gartmorn Dam Country

Park, by Sauchie; and Clackmannan District Council, Leisure Services Dept. Fife Regional Council control **Upper** and **Lower Glendevon Reservoirs,** and **Castlehill Reservoir**; brown trout; fly only. No Sunday fishing on **Glendevon Reservoirs.** Permits from Fife Regional Council, Craig Mitchell House, Flemington Rd, Glenrothes; and from The Boathouse, Castlehill Reservoir, Muckhart. Fife Regional Council also lease out a number of reservoirs to local clubs; **Cameron Reservoir** to St Andrews AC; **Clatto Reservoir** to Crawford Priory Estate; **Craigluscar Reservoirs** to Dunfermline Artisan AC; **Glenquey Reservoir** to Devon AA; **Harperleas Reservoir** to Fife Technical Teachers' Assn; **Lochmill Reservoir** to Newburgh AC; **Stenhouse Reservoir** to Burntisland AC; **Upper Carriston Reservoir** to Methilhaven & District AC (0592 713008). Hotels: Castle Campbell, Dollar; Castle Craig, Tillicoultry; Tormaukin, Glendevon.

Gleneagles (Perthshire). The Gleneagles Hotel, Auchterarder PH3 1NF, has access to Lower Scone and Almondmouth beats on **River Tay**; salmon, grilse and sea trout. Trout fishing on **Fordoun Loch**; and also on **Laich Loch**, in hotel grounds, free to guests from mid-Jan to late Oct. Apply to Country Club, The Gleneagles Hotel (tel: 0764 662231).

AVON: Flows 18m to estuary of Forth near Grangemouth. Lower reaches polluted; good brown trout elsewhere (av ½lb with few around 2lb). River fishes best in late June, July and Aug.

Linlithgow (West Lothian). **Bowden Springs**, Carribber, Nr Linlithgow, small rainbow and brown trout fishery. Two lochs of 2 and 5 acres; fly only; boat and bank fishing; min size 1lb. Ghillies available. For further details contact Will Martin, tel: 0506 847269. **Linlithgow Loch**, close to Linlithgow Palace, is stocked with trout by Forth Area Federation of Anglers; limited dt for bank and boat fishing; fly only. Permits from Lothian Sports, Regent Centre. **Beecraigs Reservoir**, a chalk spring loch stocked with rainbow trout, and the occasional brown and brook trout. Open 7 days a week. 6 boats available for hire; 2 rods per boat, extra charge for 3 fishing. Permits from The Park, Beecraigs Country Park, Nr Linlithgow, West Lothian EH49 6PL. Advanced booking recommended. **Union**

Canal from Edinburgh to Falkirk; pike, perch, roach, carp and tench; no close season. Permits from Tourist Office, Linlithgow.

Slamannan (Stirlingshire). Slamannan Angling and Protective Assn controls 5-6m of water; no permits. Long waiting list for membership.

CARRON

Larbert (West Lothian). Larbert & Stenhousemuir AC issue permits for **Loch Coulter**, near Carronbridge; brown and rainbow trout. Fly only. No Sunday fishing. Permits: Mrs Shaw, Sauchie Filters.

Denny (Stirlings). Central Regional Council controls **Carron Valley Reservoir**, brown trout. No bank fishing. Fly only. Advance booking essential; apply Director of Finance, Central Regional Council, Viewforth, Stirling.

TEITH: Noted salmon and brown trout fishery, with good sea trout in summer.

Callander (Perthshire). Stirling District Council controls part of Teith, in which excellent salmon, sea trout and brown trout. Brown trout average ¾lb. Fishing open to visitors; st £46.50, dt £13. Concessions for residents, OAP & jun. **Loch Venachar** controlled by the Town Council; good salmon, sea trout and brown trout fishing: trout average 1lb; fishing from bank permitted on parts of loch; st £35, dt £5.50, with concessions to OAP & juniors; boats available. Permits for Teith and Loch Venachar, and boats on Loch Venachar obtainable from James Bayne, Fishing Tackle, 76 Main St. Permits for **Loch Drunkie** (brown trout), **Loch Achray** (brown trout, perch, pike) and **Lochan Reoidhte** (brown trout, fly only). Boat hire available on Lochan Reoidhte. Permits from Queen Elizabeth Forest Park Visitors' Centre, Aberfoyle; and James Bayne, Tackle Shop.

BALVAIG and CALAIR (Tributaries of Teith): salmon and brown trout.

Balquhidder (Perthshire). Salmon and brown trout fishing on **R Balvaig, Loch Voil** and **Loch Doine**; available from Kings House Hotel, Balquidder, Perthshire FK19 8NY (tel. 0877 384646). Boat hire and ghillie can be arranged. Rod and tackle hire, and tuition from hotel or Craigruie Sporting Estate, Balquidder, Perthshire FK19 8PQ (tel. 0877 384262).

Strathyre (Perthshire). Salmon and brown trout fishing available from Munro Hotel. Season 1 Feb-1 Oct. No boats.

Loch Leven

Famous Kinross-shire loch which produces quick-growing trout. Loch is nowhere deep so feed is good, and practically whole area is fishing water. Under efficient management, this has become one of the most notable trout fishing lochs of Scotland.

Kinross (Kinross-shire). Loch Leven Fisheries is a predominantly brown trout loch which boasts the famous Loch Leven trout. These average over 1lb pound with many specimen of 3-4lbs being taken. It is also stocked each year with high quality rainbow trout. Fly fishing by boat only. The pier is ¼m out of Kinross. Boats are bookable by letter or phone. For full information on charges and booking conditions, apply to the Manageress, The Pier, Kinross, Tayside KY13 7UF (tel: 0577 863407). Tackle can be bought at the pier. Top quality trout fishing on **Heatheryford**; brown and rainbow trout; bank fishing. Permits from office on site (tel: 0577 64212). Tackle shop: James Philip, 102 High St. Hotel: Green.

Ballingry (Fife). Rainbow and brown trout fishing on **Loch Ore**; bank and boat. Permits from Lochore Meadows Country Park, Crosshill, Balligry, Fife KY5 8BA (tel. 0592 860086).

Glenrothes (Fife). Permits may be had from Fife Regional Council for reservoir trout fishing on **Holl, Castlehill, Glenfarg, Upper Glendevon** and **Lower Glendevon Reservoirs**. Morning and evening sessions. Boats (2 rods) £10. Bank (Lower Glendevon and Castlehill only) £3. Concessions for jun. Permits from Glendevon Treatment Works; Glenfarg Treatment Works; and Fife Regional Council, Water Division, Craig Mitchell House, Flemington Road, Glenrothes.

Water of Leith

Local people who know river well get fair numbers of trout.

Edinburgh (West Lothian). Lothian Regional Council manage Water of Leith and thirteen water supply reservoirs in the area. Water of Leith, running through the city, is stocked annually with brown trout. Permits issued free of charge from Regional HQ, George IV Bridge, Edinburgh. Permits for trout, boat fishing at **Gladhouse, Glencorse, Clubbiedean, Bonaly, Harperrig** and **Crosswood**, and **West Water Reservoirs** from Dept of Water & Drainage, Comiston Springs, 55 Buckstone Terrace, Edinburgh (031 445 4141). Bank permits for Harperrig from ticket machine on site. Brown trout fishing on **Megget Reservoir**; permits from Tibbie Shiels Inn, St Mary's Loch (tel: 0750 42231). **Rosebery Reservoir**, brown and rainbow trout, pike, perch; permits from Reservoir Keeper, Watermans Cottage (tel: 8300 353). **Talla** and **Fruid Reservoirs**, brown trout; permits from Reservoir Superintendent, Victoria Lodge (tel: 08997 209). Permits for **Whiteadder Reservoir** from Mrs Kerr, Waterkeeper's House, Hungrey Snout, Whiteadder Reservoir (03617 362). Permits for **Hopes Reservoir** from Lothian Regional Council, Dept of Water & Drainage, Alderston House, Haddington (062 082 4131). For details of all above waters contact Director of Planning, Lothian Council, 12 Giles Street, Edinburgh EH1 1PT. Coarse fishing on **Doddington Loch**; carp and perch. Loch situated in a bird sanctuary, therefore a restricted area. Bank fishing. No lead weights. No close season. Permits from Historic Monuments & Buildings, 20 Brandon St, Edinburgh. **Union Canal** from Edinburgh to Falkirk; pike, perch, roach, carp and tench; no close season. Permits from Tourist Office, Linlithgow. Tackle shops: John Dickson & Son, 21 Frederick Street; Shooting Lines Ltd, 18 Hope Park Terrace and 23 Roseburn Terrace; F & D Simpson, 28 West Preston Street; Countrylife, 299 Balgreen Rd; Mike's Tackle Shop, 48 Portobello High St.

Balerno (Mid Lothian). Trout fishing on Water of Leith; permits from Balerno PO, 36 Main St; and Colinton PO. Brown and rainbow trout fishing on **Threipmuir** and **Harlaw Reservoirs**. Fly fishing only. Bank fishing only. Season tickets are balloted for, contact The Factor, Dalmeny Estate Office, Dalmeny Estate, South Queensferry, West Lothian EH3O 9TQ (031 331 4804). Day tickets from Flemings Grocery Shop, 42 Main Street, Balerno (tel. 031 449 3833). Concessions for OAP and jun. Cobbinshaw AA has fishing on Top Loch, **Cobbinshaw Reservoir**, leased from BWT. Permits from keeper at reservoir. **Harperrig Reservoir**, 237 acres; brown trout. Fly only. 4 boats and bank fishing. Boat fishing permits from Lothian Regional Council,

Dept of Water and Drainage, 55 Buckstone Terrace, Edinburgh EH10 6XH (tel: 031-445 4141). Bank permits from machine at reservoir (50p pieces).

GIRVAN

Drains small loch called Girvan Eye and thence runs 25m to the Atlantic at Girvan. Good salmon and sea trout; fair brown trout. Salmon run March onwards; sea trout from July.

Girvan (Ayrshire). Salmon, sea trout, brown trout. Carrick AC issues permits, available from Mrs Campbell, Girvan Chandlers, 4 Knochcushan St, Girvan KA26 9AG (tel. 0465 2897). **Penwhapple Reservoir**, near Barr, stocked with brown trout; Penwhapple AC water. Fly only. Dt £6 and evenings £4; boats £5 (9-5) and £3 (5-10), apply Mrs Stewart, Lane Farm, Barr (½m beyond reservoir). Hotels: King's Arms, Ailsa Craig.

Straiton (Ayrshire). Salmon (late), sea trout, brown trout. Blairquhan Estate

water, fly only. Permits from D Galbraith, The Kennels, Blairquhan Estate, Straiton. Forestry Commission controls fishing in Galloway Forest Park. Brown trout fishing on **Lochs Bradan, Skelloch, Brecbowie** and **Dhu Loch**; Lochs Bradan and Skelloch stocked regularly throughout season. Pike fishing on **Linfern Loch.** Permits from Robin Heaney, Tallaminnoch, Straiton (tel: 06557 617); and Forestry Commission Office, Straiton (tel: 06557 637).

HALLADALE

Rises on north slope of Helmsdale watershed and empties into sea at Melvich Bay. Early salmon March onwards, 10-16lbs. Grilse run from June, 5-7lbs.

Melvich (Sutherland). Melvich Hotel, Melvich, By Thurso, Sutherland KW14 7YJ (tel. 06413 206), 18m from Thurso, offers trout fishing on several lochs, one of which has a boat. Fly only. Dt £7.50 for bank fishing and £15 for boat fishing.

Forsinard (Sutherland). Salmon sport good, especially after freshets. For salmon beats on Halladale from Forsinard to Melvich Bay: contact Mrs J Atkinson, Factor, 8 Sinclair Street, Thurso,

Caithness (tel. 0847 63291). Accommodation; self catering in Lodge. Forsinard Hotel has salmon fishing on River Halladale, 2½m stretch from Forsinain bridge to junction with River Dyke; and on **River Strathy**; both fly only. Hotel also has trout fishing on 6 lochs exclusively for guests and on 14 lochs open to non-residents. Apply to Forsinard Hotel, Forsinard KW13 6YT (tel. 06417 221).

HELMSDALE RIVER

Formed by two headstreams near Kinbrace, this river flows 20m southeast through Strathullie to sea. Excellent salmon river, where there is now no netting.

Helmsdale (Sutherland). Salmon and sea   trout. Salmon beat lettings from Roxton

---

Check before you go

While every effort has been made to ensure that the information given in 'Where to Fish' is correct, the position is continually changing, and anglers are urged, in their own interests, to make preliminary inquiries before travelling to selected venues. This is especially important with reference to prices quoted. Inevitably the rate of inflation is affecting stability in this quarter. Anglers' attention is also drawn to the fact that the hotels mentioned under the various fishing stations do not necessarily have water of their own. Any amendments or further data for inclusion in subsequent editions, and any criticism, will be welcome.

SCOTLAND FOR FISHING 1994

In Association with the Scottish Tourist Board
Gazetteer of Where to Fish
Articles by Leading Anglers
Records & Regulations – Fishing Clubs
Where to Stay? – Maps

ON SALE IN
EVERY GOOD BOOKSHOP – TACKLE SHOP – SPORTS SHOP
or
Cut out the Coupon & send Cheque or Postal Order for
£4.20, inc. P. & P.

to
**Pastime Publications, 32/34 Heriot Hill Terrace,
Edinburgh EH7 4DY**

Send to: **NAME**..

ADDRESS ....

....

.... **POST CODE** ....

I enclose Cheque/Postal Order for £ ....

LURES AND SALMON FLIES

TANDEM MUDDLER

WHITE MARABOU

BLACK MARABOU

MUDDLER MINNOW

YELLOW MUDDLER

ABBOT

NAILER

WHISKY FLY

ELIZABETH OF GLAMIS

LEPRECHAUN

SWEENY TODD

BOWLER HAT

BEARDED DOLL

BABY DOLL

PINK DOLL

ORANGE DOLL

LIME DOLL

MUNRO KILLI

STOATS TA

ORANGE SHRIM

MACKENZIE GREE

TEAL, BLUE, & SILVE

BOURACH

GENERAL PRACTITION

ELIZABETH OF GLA

'Spring' fishing for salmon on the River Helmsdale. *Photo: Eric Chalker.*

The River Helmsdale in a different mood. *Photo: Eric Chalker.*

Bailey Robinson, Fishing Agents, 25 High St, Hungerford, Berks RG17 0NF (0488 683222). Lower Helmsdale only: permits from Strathullie Crafts, Dunrobin St (tel: 04312 343). Information from J A Douglas Menzies, Mounteagle, Fearn, Ross-shire. Navidale House Hotel arranges fishing for brown trout on six lochs, fly only on all but one. Other hotel: Bridge.

INVER (including Kirkaig and Loch Assynt)

Draining Loch Assynt, this river flows into a sea loch on the west coast of Sutherland known as Lochinver (village and loch having the same name), a little north of the old Ross-shire border. Holds salmon and sea trout but fishing is hard to come by.

Lochinver (Sutherland). The Inver, running out of Loch Assynt (6m) is private. Inver Lodge Hotel has salmon fishing on **River Kirkaig**, 3½m S of Lochinver; and brown and rainbow trout fishing on **Loch Culag**, **Fionn Loch** and numerous hill lochs. Apply to Inver Lodge Hotel, Lochinver IV27 4LU (tel: 05714 496).

Assynt AC controls numerous lochs, with a run of salmon and sea trout. Permits from Tourist Office, Lochinver. Kylesku Hotel, Kylesku, By Lairg, has brown trout fishing for guests.

Ledmore (Sutherland). The Alt Bar and Motel, 20m N of Ullapool, has brown trout and char fishing on **Loch Borralan**.

Boat £15 and bank £3 per day. Also, 12m of double bank salmon and sea trout fishing from Rosehall to Bonar Bridge on the Kyle of Sutherland at £15 per day. Bed and breakfast, and self-catering accom-

modation available. Further information from Bruce and Albe Ward, The Alt Bar and Motel, The Altnacealgach, Nr Ledmore Junction, By Lairg, Sutherland IV27 4HF (tel: 085 486 220).

Loch Assynt

Inchnadamph (Sutherland). Salmon fishing (fair) from June on upper end of Loch Assynt. Permits from Inchnadamph Hotel for celebrated **Gillaroo Loch, Loch Assynt** and **Loch Awe** (£3.50 per rod plus £7.50 for boat). Season from May 1

till Oct 10. Best months for trout, mid-May to mid-July, and Sept; for salmon, mid-June to mid-July, and Sept. Hotel: Inchnadamph; fishing free to guests on loch. Ten boats available.

IRVINE (including Annick, Garnock and Lugton)

Rises near Loudonhill and flows about 20m to Firth of Clyde at Irvine Town. Main tributaries are Cessnock Water, Kilmarnock Water and Annick. Fishing controlled largely by clubs. Salmon and sea trout July onwards; brown trout average ½lb; early season best.

Irvine (Ayrshire). Salmon, sea trout, trout; Irvine and Dist AA issues permits for 2m on Irvine and 3m Annick (no dt Saturdays). Irvine Water runs from estuary to Red Bridge, Dreghorn, on north bank and to Bogie Bridge on south bank. Annick Water is from confluence with Irvine to northern boundary of Annick Lodge Estate, except for one private stretch.

Dreghorn (Ayrshire). Salmon, sea trout, trout; Dreghorn AC issues wt and dt for 12m water on both banks of Irvine and Annick; apply hon sec or R W Gillespie, 16 Marble Ave or Alyson's Flowers, 10 Bank St, Irvine. Applications for new associate membership must be made in writing to hon sec. July to Sept best for salmon and sea trout. Brown trout average ½lb.

Kilmarnock (Ayrshire). Salmon, sea trout, trout. Permits for stretches on Irvine at Hurlford and Crookedholm from P & R Torbet, 15 Strand St.

Galston (Ayrshire). Good sport with salmon and brown trout. Aug to Oct for salmon. Galston AC has salmon and trout fishing on Irvine and **Cessnock**. Permits from hon sec; W & E Pattison, Wallace St; P & R Torbet, 15 Strand St, Kilmarnock.

GARNOCK: Trout, sea trout, salmon.

Kilwinning (Ayrshire). Garnock and Irvine join in tidal water and have common

mouth. Salmon, sea trout, brown trout. Kilwinning Eglinton AC has 9m on Garnock and **River Lugton**. No Saturday or Sunday fishing. Permits from Craft Shop, 42 Main St.

Kilbirnie (Ayrshire). Kilbirnie AC has water on river Garnock and **Kilbirnie Loch** (brown and rainbow trout) and two reservoirs. Yearly stocking of brown trout; monthly stocking of rainbow trout. Kilbirnie Loch best trout: brown 9lb 2oz. Kilbirnie Loch, any legal method. St £15; wt £7, dt £5. Club has excellent brown trout fishing on **Camphill Reservoir**; fly and boat only. Season holders £5 per boat per day and non-holders £12 per boat per day. Permits from hon sec; R T Cycles, Glengarnock; and Glengarnock PO. Tackle from R T Cycles.

ANNICK: Brown trout; small runs of salmon and sea trout Sept-Oct.

Irvine (Ayrshire). Dreghorn AC issues permits for 12m of water on Irvine and Annick. Permits from hon sec.

Kilmaurs (Ayrshire). Kilmaurs AC has fishing on Annick and **Glazert**; sea trout and brown trout, with salmon in autumn. Permits from T C McCabe, 8 East Park Crescent; McGregors Paper Shop.

Stewarton (Ayrshire). Stewarton AC has water on Annick and tributaries, and **White Loch**; permits from hon sec and John Gordon Sports, High Street.

Fishing Clubs

When you appoint a new secretary, do not forget to give us details of the change. Write to the publishers (address at front of the book). Thank you!

THE ISLANDS

The term 'The Islands' includes the Inner and Outer Hebrides, the Orkney and Shetland Islands and, for convenience, Kintyre.

ARRAN: In the rivers, brown trout are generally small, although brown trout up to 1lb have been recorded. In Aug, Sept and Oct there is often a good run of sea trout, especially in post spate conditions, along with good salmon catches, particularly in **Sliddery**, **Kilmory**, **Sannox** and **Cloy**. **Benlister** and **Monamore** are also worth fishing under spate conditions. The Tourist Office at Brodick pier provides a free Information Sheet detailing all the main freshwater fishing opportunities on Arran, with charges. It also issues day and 6-day permits for various Arran AA waters. These include Kilmory (from above the bridge at Lagg Hotel), Cloy, Benlister, Monamore, Sannox, **Ashdale**, Sliddery Water and **Loch Garbad** (stocked with brown trout).

Machrie. Machrie Fishings consistently record excellent sea trout and salmon returns. Rods are limited and enquiries should be made to Mrs M Wilson, Former Balnaguard Inn, Balnaguard, By Pitlochry, Perthshire PH9 0PY (tel. 0796 482256), or to the Water Bailiff, Riverside Cottage, Machrie. No Sunday fishing.

Dougarie. The **Iorsa River** and **Loch** has also recorded excellent sport with sea trout and the occasional salmon, and permit enquiries should be directed to The Estate Office, Dougarie, Isle of Arran (tel: 0770 84259).

Blackwaterfoot. **Blackwater** offers good sea trout catches and also salmon under suitable conditions; permits are obtainable from the General Store, Blackwaterfoot.

Brodick. The **Rosaburn** often has an early run of finnock, as well as a good sporting run of sea trout and salmon in Aug, Sept and Oct. There are also brown trout but these are small. Permits from The Factor, Sannox Estate, Arran Estate Office, Brodick, Isle of Arran KA27 8EJ; and Brodick Tourist Information Centre. As all the rivers are 'short run', spate and post spate conditions offer particularly good sport. Fishing ceases at end of October.

BARRA: Island in Outer Hebrides below South Uist.

Castlebay. Brown trout. Clachan Beag Hotel has bank fishing on 4 lochs. Contact D MacNeil (tel: 08714 279).

BENBECULA: Lies between N and S Uist. Numerous lochs, giving good sea and brown trout fishing.

Balivanich. South Uist AC has brown trout fishing on many lochs in South Uist and Benbecula. Bank and boat fishing. Permits from Colin Campbell Sports. Creagorry Hotel, Creagorry, has fishing for guests on several lochs and three sea pools; boats available on some waters; waders useful; trout to 1lb; farthest water 5m; June to Sept best for brown trout and August and Sept for sea trout. Sea trout up to 8lb in sea pools.

BUTE: 5m from Ayrshire coast; 16m long and 3-5m wide. Trout and coarse fish.

Rothesay. **Loch Ascog**, 1½m pike, perch and roach. **Loch Quien**, 5m first-class trout fly fishing (fish averaging 1lb). Fishes best early and late in season for brown trout. Applications to Bute Estate Office, Rothesay (Tel 502627). **Loch Fad**, 175 acres, rainbow and brown trout fishing. Boat and bank fishing. 23 boats;

booking advisable. Permits available from bailiff's hut at Loch (tel. 0700 504871). Further information from Isle of Bute Trout Co Ltd, Ardmaleish, Isle of Bute PA20 0QJ (tel. 0700 502451). Permits for Loch Fad and accommodation available from Carleol Enterprises Angling Holidays, 3 Alma Terrace, Rothesay. Sea fishing from rocky shore popular and good: by boat regularly from Rothesay pier.

Tighnabruaich. Kyles of Bute AC has fishing on Loch Ascog, brown and rainbow trout, fly only; on **Powderworks Reservoir**, brown and rainbow trout, fly and bait only; and on **Tighnabruaich Reservoir**, brown trout. Permits from several shops in Kames and Tighnabruaich.

COLONSAY: Reached by car ferry from Oban. Colonsay Fly Fishing Association has been formed to protect the Colonsay loch fishing. In recent years the fishing has been abused by the use of coarse fishing methods, bubble floats and even nets; fishing has continued late into the season and affected breeding fish, and a large number of fish (many undersized) have been taken from the island.

Scalasaig. Colonsay FFA control most of the loch fishing on the island, including brown trout fishing on **Lochs West Fada, Mid Fada, East Fada** and **Turamin**. Best months, May, June and Sept; fish average 10-16oz; fly only. Boats available. Permits from Isle of Colonsay Hotel and shop at Scalasaig. Further information from Kevin Byrne, Isle of Colonsay Hotel, Argyll PA61 7YP (tel 09512 316).

CUMBRAE: Small islands lying between Bute and Ayr coast. Largs is nearest mainland town, approx 30m from Glasgow.

Millport. Cumbrae AC has trout fishing on two reservoirs, **Top Dam** and **Bottom Dam**. Club restricted to 30 members only. Juveniles must be accompanied by an adult and be over 12 years; dams are too steep and could be dangerous. Wt £25 and dt £7.50; from Tobacconist, Stuart Street, Millport. Sea fishing good from shore or boats. Tackle shops: Mapes; Masties, Main St, Largs. Hotel: Royal George.

HARRIS: Southern part of the island of Lewis and Harris, Outer Hebrides.

Tarbert. Salmon and sea trout fishing on **Lacasdale Lochs**. Boat and bank fishing. Fly only. Fishing on 3 lochs in rotation. Ghillies can be arranged with advance notice. Self-catering accommodation may be available. Further information from S MacLeod, The Anchorage, Ardhasaig, Isle of Harris, Western Isles (tel. 0859 2009). Alternative accommodation available a few miles from lochs at The Harris Hotel, the headquarters of Harris Fresh Water AC. Borve Lodge, Scarista, has fishing on sea trout lochs. Dt sometimes available. Enquire Tony Scherr, Factor, Borve Lodge Estates, Isle of Harris (0859 85202). Horsacleit Lodge let furnished for six guests with fishing for salmon and sea trout on river and on 5 lochs; for brown trout on **Loch Drinishader**. Bookings to Mr C J Lucas, Warnham Park, Horsham, Sussex RH12 3RU.

ISLAY: Most southern island of Inner Hebrides. Lies on west side of Sound of Islay, in Argyllshire. Greatest length is 25m and greatest breadth 19m. Sport with salmon, sea trout and trout. Hotel: Harris

Bridgend. Salmon and sea trout fishing on **Rivers Sorn, Laggan** and **Grey River**; all within 2m of Bridgend; fly only. Brown trout fishing on **Lochs Gorm, Finlaggan** and **Skerrolo**; boats available. Also trout fishing on numerous hill lochs without boats. Permits and self-catering accommodation available from B. Wiles, Headkeeper, Head Gamekeeper's House, Islay House Square, Bridgend, Isle of Islay, Argyll PA44 7NZ (tel: 049 681 293). Bridgend Hotel has trout fishing in five good lochs, six boats.

Port Askaig. By staying at Port Askaig Hotel, trouting can be had in **Lochs Lossit**, **Ballygrant** and **Allan**. Dt (boat) from Post Office. Sport on other lochs by arrangement. Salmon fishing in **River Laggan** available. Best months: May, June and Sept.

Port Ellen. Machrie Hotel has salmon and sea trout fishing on **R Machrie**. Apply to Machrie Hotel, Port Ellen, Isle of Islay, Argyll PA42 7AN.

KINTYRE: This peninsula is part of Argyll and lies between Islay and Arran.

Campbeltown (Argyll). Brown trout fishing on **Loch Lussa**; fly only; permits from tackle shop. Carradale AC has fishing on **Tangy Loch**, 60 acres, trout to 2lb. Access road to waters edge. Permits from tackle shop. Sea fishing in harbour and **Firth of Clyde**. Tackle shop: A P McGrory, 16-20 Main Street. Hotel: White Hart.

Carradale (Argyll). Excellent salmon and sea-trout fishing may be had on **Carradale Water**, a small spate river. Carradale Estate lease the water to Carradale AC. Bait and spinner under certain conditions, otherwise fly only. Assn also has brown trout fishing on **Tangy Loch**. St £30, ft £21, wt £16, dt £5. Apply hon sec; J Semple, The Garage; D Oman & Co, The Pier; A P McGrory, Fishing Tackle, Main St, Campbeltown. Hotel: Carradale.

Crinan (Argyll). Near west end of Crinan Canal. Brown trout lochs controlled by Lochgilphead Dist AC. Canal (trout).

Lochgilphead (Argyll). At east end of Crinan Canal. Lochgilphead and Dist AC has rights on eleven hill lochs; good brown trout; wt £15, dt £4 from The Sports Shop, 39 Lochnell Street. Forestry Commission has leased fishing on **Lochs Coille Bhar** and **Barnluasgan** to Lochgilphead AC; brown trout. Boat hire and permits from A MacVicar, Gartnagrenach, Achnamara (tel: 85210). Forestry Commission also has brown trout fishing on **Lochs Glashan**, **Blackmill** and **Bealach Ghearran**; fly only. Boat hire and permits from Forest District Office, Whitegate, Lochgilphead; and R Hardie, No 1 Nursery Cottages, Birdfield, Mi-

nard, Argyll. Stag Hotel can arrange fishing on **River Add** and various lochs. Salmon and sea trout in river, brown trout in lochs. River Add, permits are available from Robin Malcolm, Duntrune Castle, Kilmartin, Argyll. Tackle shop: Sports Shop, 39 Lochnell St.

LEWIS: Some salmon, much trout fishing on lochs.

Stornoway. Little salmon fishing for visitors. For salmon and sea trout fishing in **River Creed** and **Loch Clachan** enquire of the Factor, Stornoway Trust, Estate Offices, 20 Cromwell St, Stornoway. Stornoway AC has brown trout fishing on 9 lochs. Bank fishing, mt £4. Boat on 3 lochs, dt £10. From July sea trout fishing on one loch. Permits from Sportsworld, 1-3 Francis St (tel. 0851 70 5464). Soval AA has brown trout fishing on several lochs within easy distance of Stornoway. Wt £5 if staying in Soval area and £10 if not, dt £2, from hon sec; and J M MacLeod, Treasurer, 15 Balallan (tel. 0851 83255). **Loch Keose**, a beautiful 90 acre loch with plentiful wild brown trout. Permits from Murdo Morrison, Handa; Sportsworld; Western Isles Tourist Board. Accommodation, boats and equipment available. For further information apply to Murdo Morrison, Handa, 18 Keose Glebe, (Coes) Lochs, Isle of Lewis PA86 9JX (tel: 0851 83334). Hotels: Caberfeidh, Caledonian.

Garynahine. The **Grimersta** belongs to Grimersta Estate Ltd, who occasionally have salmon, sea trout and brown trout fishing available for individuals or small parties in April, May and early June. Accommodation available at the estate.

Uig. Salmon, sea trout and brown trout fishing on Scaliscro and North Eishen Estates including **Loch Langavat**. Bank and boat fishing. Also sea angling trips in **West Loch Roag**. Permits, boat and tackle hire, and ghillies; apply to Estate Office, Scaliscro Lodge, Uig, Isle of Lewis PA86 9ER (tel: 0851 75 325).

Kintarvie. The Aline Estate, on the march of Lewis and North Harris, has two salmon and sea trout systems: **Kintarvie River** and **Loch Tiorsdam**; and part of **Loch Langavat**, 9m loch that forms the head water of Grimersta River, very prolific salmon (July onwards) and above average wild brown trout. The estate also has numerous brown trout lochs. Kintarvie system reserved for lodge guests. Loch Langavat, dt £5 (bank fishing) and sometimes boat and ghillie available. If four or more anglers, transport (Landrover) provided to Langavat at £20 extra. Brown trout loch fishing, dt £5. Contact Head Game Keeper, Mr J McGarrity (tel: 0859 2006).

MULL:

Tobermory. Salmon and sea trout fishing on **Rivers Aros, Bellart** and **Forsa**. No Sunday fishing on Bellart and Forsa. Salmon, sea trout and brown trout fishing on **Loch Squabain**; boat fishing only. Fishing on **Torr Loch**, sea trout, wild brown trout and some rainbow trout; no Sunday fishing; 2 boats; banks clear. Permits from Tackle & Books, 10 Main St. Tobermory AA has fishing on **Mishnish Lochs**, brown trout only, 3 boats for hire on daily basis; and **Aros Loch**, brown and rainbow trout, open all year for rainbow. Dt £6 and wt £18. Boat hire: £5 for 4 hrs and £10 all day. Permits from A Brown & Son, Tackle Shop, 21 Main Street. Fishing on **Loch Frisa**, good brown trout, some salmon and sea trout; and River Lussa. Apply to Forest Enterprise, Mull Office, Aros (tel. 0680 300346). Hotels: Mishnish, Macdonald Arms, Western Isles, Strongarbh, Tobermory, Ulva House, Harbour House.

Bunessan. Argyll Arms Hotel has good salmon, sea trout and brown trout fishing on **Loch Assapol**. Fly and spinner only. No Sunday fishing.

RAASAY:

The Isle of Raasay is near Skye. Free trout fishing in lochs and streams; spare tackle and waders should be taken.

RUM:

The fishing in the streams and lochs of the Isle of Rum is all preserved by the Nature Conservancy.

NORTH UIST: Island in Outer Hebrides, 17m long and 3-13m broad. More water than land with over 400 named lochs and lochans, and many more unnamed, some probably unfished. Plenty of lochs by road-side for elderly or infirm anglers.

Lochmaddy. North Uist AC members may fish all waters on North Uist with the exception of sea trout and salmon systems where permission must be obtained from the Factor of the North Uist Estate

first. The club sells tickets for the Newton Estate fishing, previously controlled by the Dept of Agriculture and Fisheries. St £35, wt £15 and dt £4. No charge for under 16's. Tickets available from Lochmaddy Hotel *(see advt)*. Boat on 3 lochs, book through hon sec, who also runs a small tackle shop. Visitors are invited to any of the club outings during their stay.

SOUTH UIST:

Bornish. South Uist AC has trout fishing on many lochs in South Uist and **Benbecula**. Bank and boat fishing; boats on 12 lochs. Permits from Mrs Kennedy, Bornish Stores.

Lochboisdale. Lochboisdale Hotel issues permits for brown trout fishing on many lochs; sea trout and salmon fishing may also be available. Boats on several lochs. Fly only. Contact John Kennedy, Lochboisdale Hotel (tel: 087 84 332).

Keep the banks clean

Several clubs have stopped issuing tickets to visitors because of the state of the banks after they have left. Spend a few moments clearing up.

ORKNEY

While sea fishing for skate, ling, halibut (British record), haddock, cod, etc, is general in waters about Orkney, and good fun may be had in the evenings with saithe comparatively close to the shore anywhere, good quality trout fishing is confined to the mainland and Rousay for both brown and sea trout, but in the latter island the lochs are private, in contrast to the mainland, where all but one (Loch of Skaill) of the best lochs are "open" water. Sea trout, for which the east shores of the island of Hoy also have a good reputation, may be found at any point where fresh water enters the sea as well as in the Lochs of Stenness and Harray in March and April and from July to the end of October, and may be taken from a boat in the lochs. Wading trousers are useful in the estuaries.

Principal fishing lochs on the mainland are **Loch of Stenness**, 12m from **Kirkwall** and 3m from **Stromness**, which yields brown and sea trout, from March to October, the average weight being nearly 1lb. The best part of the season for this loch is probably June to August. **Loch of Harray**, 11m from Kirkwall and 4m from Stromness, is connected to Loch of Stenness and fishes well from April to end of September, the average being about 1lb. The **Lochs of Swannay**, **Boardhouse** and **Hundland** are in close proximity to each other in the north of the mainland, about 20m from Kirkwall, and fish well, particularly Swannay, which yields good brown trout of more than 1lb average weight. All three lochs are fairly early in form and good sport may be had from April until the end of September. Boats are available for hire on all of these lochs, in most cases without boatmen, though in certain cases this may be arranged. Fishing is also available on the Lochs of Wasdale, Kirbister and Bosquoy.

Orkney Trout Fishing Association is a non-profit making, voluntary body dedicated to the preservation and enhancement of game-fishing throughout the islands of Orkney. Assn operates a trout hatchery. Restocking has yielded excellent results, notably in the Loch of Swannay. Membership £12, visitors season £10, OAP & jun season £6, invalid season £3. Membership entitles anglers to use assn facilities, which include access to fishing on **Loch of Skaill**. Subscription accepted at **Orkney Tourist Board Office, Kirkwall;** Barony Hotel, Birsay; J I Harcus, Bridge St, Kirkwall; Merkister Hotel, Harray; The Longship, Broad St, Kirkwall; W S Sinclair, Tackle Shop, Stromness; E Kemp, Bridge St, Kirkwall. Information from hon sec. Accommodation is available in Kirkwall at several hotels including the Kirkwall Hotel, and there are taxi services to fishing waters. Anglers might prefer to stay closer to the waters they want to fish, however. All details available in Stan Headley's A Trout Fishing Guide to Orkney; price £1.95 plus postage from Headley Chaddock, St Michael's Manse, Harray, Orkney. Merkister Hotel, Harray, is close to Loch of Harray (now the best of the Orkney Lochs) and affords excellent loch fishing: boats, outboards, ghillies; tel: (085 677) 366. The Standing Stones Hotel, Stenness (fully licensed and under new management; boats, outboards, ghillies) stands on the shores of Loch of Stenness and is also convenient for Loch Harray, while Smithfield Hotel (Dounby) and The Barony (Birsay), are convenient for the Lochs of Boardhouse, Hundland and Swannay. Keldroseed Guest House, Sandwick, By Stromness, overlooks Loch Stenness.

SHETLAND

The following notes have been compiled mainly with the aid of Manson's Shetland Guide but help has also been sought from a booklet written by James Coutts and published by The Highlands and Islands Development Board. They should be read in the light of the fact that reports from our local correspondent now underline the fears expressed by conservationists on the bearing oil-related development would have on the famous Shetland sea trout fishings. Now, it is suggested, visitors might do better to think in terms of loch fishing for brown trout.

The sea trout fishing season in Shetland extends from February 25 to October 31, and that for the brown trout fishing from March 15 to October 6. Nearly all mainland waters are controlled by The Shetland Anglers' Association (Hon sec Andrew Miller, 3 Gladstone Terrace, Lerwick) and remainder are usually available. St for association waters £10. There are monthly, weekly, and daily permits. Juniors are free. Season tickets are available from hon sec, hon treasurer, tackle shops and the Tourist Office, Commercial Street. Association waters now include **Spiggie Loch**, the largest loch in the islands and a famous sea trout fishery.

Where the sea trout fishing so far remains unaffected, late March to early May, and

September and October are the prime months. As regards size, fish up to 3lbs are not uncommon; fish up to 7lbs are not altogether rare; but the general runs of sea trout average between 1lb and 2lbs. The larger fish are grilse returning from the sea for the first time.

Sea trout fishing, like all branches of this sport, cannot be made the subject of hard and fast rules, and both the methods and equipment used are entirely a matter for personal choice. It is not essential to have any special equipment apart from the ordinary outfit of a trout fisher, except perhaps such safeguards as are necessary against the corrosive effects of the salt water on certain types of aluminium reels and fitments of that nature. The sea trout takes a fly in salt water as readily as a brown trout takes it in the waters of a loch; and any of the standard types of sea-trout flies will, in favourable conditions, produce results until such time as the fisher develops those faiths and fancies to which all anglers are prone. He may then swear by his teal and red, or his blae and black, as his personal experience will no doubt have taught him to swear; or he may have become a disciple of the lure, which is often used to good effect, especially in weather which does not permit easy control of a lighter fly. He may even have recourse to bait-fishing to discover that the use of worm or strips of mackerel are not unproductive of good baskets.

There are two methods of fishing with mackerel. The easiest and most popular is to mount a strip of it on one of the hooks of any spoon or lure. The second approach is to use a rod of at least 12 feet, with fly-line and long tapered cast, and to attach a piece of mackerel strip to the hooks of Stewart or Pennel tackle. Fished in tidal water, allowing the current to work the bait as in salmon fishing, mackerel strip is the nearest thing to a live sand-eel.

The brown trout are more or less native to the freshwater lochs, of which literally thousands are populated by brown trout, most of them underfished. Generally speaking, they average about ½lb to ¾lb. There are bigger fish - in fact, there are individual lochs which occasionally produce exceptionally big ones; but most of the many lochs which have fish in any quantity rarely produce a higher average weight, and often a lower one, a re-stocking programme is in progress. Only in exceptional cases is a boat available for fishing the lochs; but almost in every case fishing can be done from the bank or shore, by wading. It is often desirable to wade, rather than to fish from the bank, in order to clear heather slopes which can so effectively wreck a light fly cast. The Anglers' Association now has 5 boats situated on the most favoured lochs. A boat key common to all boats may be obtained from hon sec at a fee of £10.

The failure of a fishing holiday in Shetland at the proper time of year can scarcely ever be attributed to lack of fish. Occasionally, as in all places, there are spells of weather which result in poor baskets; but as the Shetland weather is rather noted for its changeability, the day for the angler is usually not long to wait. At a time when trout fishing is becoming increasingly difficult to procure, Shetland has a hundred spots to offer the angler where he is more or less free to fish at will, and a hundred more when these are exhausted. It is true there is a growing tendency among landowners to regard these fishings as a possible source of revenue, but, with the habits of sea trout what they are, there will always remain in the islands the possibility of fishing untrammelled by the restrictions which have placed so many of Scotland's rivers beyond the reach of the average fisherman. Shetland regards her trout fishings as an attraction which will result in visitors discovering the islands for themselves, and the measure of freedom she has to offer in an age of increasing restriction may well be the measure of her future prosperity.

Sea fishing off the Shetlands is excellent - large skate, also ling, tusk, cod, haddock, pollack, etc. The fishing is done invariably by boat, and the rock fishing, popular at some places on the mainland of Scotland, is practised only occasionally in the capture of young saithe (called "pilticks") which can be taken on fly from the shore. Boats and equipment are easy to obtain and comparatively inexpensive. The fish caught consist mainly of haddock and whiting, while at certain places the catch may include rock-cod, ling, flounder - in fact, a general assortment of fish which makes very interesting fishing indeed.

Generally speaking, the fishing grounds lie beyond the limits of the voes, but during July and August, in certain of the larger voes, good fishing can be had without going farther afield. Fishing is by rod or hand-line at a depth between 20-50 fathoms; and, when the fish are plentiful, big catches, numbering scores, are taken. Also generalizing, early and late months provide the best fishing. Tackle shops on the island are J A Manson, Commercial Street,

Lerwick; and Rod & Line, Market St, Lerwick.

NOTE: Anglers are recommended to bring their own cars, owing to the lack of public transport. Ferry services from Aberdeen. Shetland Tourist Organisation, Market Cross, Lerwick, will help with accommodation and other details. The association also issues a leaflet on angling and a booklet with extensive information, cost £1.50. Shetland AA reports a disturbing decline in sport with sea trout and grilse following the advent of commercial fishing and fish processing. Association conducting vigorous campaign against netting.

Unst. Balta Sound Hotel, most northerly in British Isles, offers sea and trout fishing to guests.

Bressay. Loch and foreshore fishing leased from Garth Estate by Shetland AA; fishing by permit from hon sec; brown trout in Loch of Brough and Loch of Setter.

Delting. Lerwick 20m. Brown trout fishing on Mill Loch, Loch of Glen, Saewater, Loch of Voe. Sea trout at Dales Voe and Collafirth. Good sea trout fishing also at Garths Voe, Orka Voe, Voxter, Scatsta, Toft, Firth and Swinister Voes.

Dunrossness. Sea trout fishing at Spiggie, St Ninian's Isle, Channerwick, Cunningsburgh; also in Loch Spiggie during the fall fishing. Hotel: Spiggie.

Laxo. Laxo Voe, one of the finest grilse and sea trout waters in the islands, now under the supervision of the Shetland AA.

Lerwick. The Shetland AA controls most of loch and sea trout fishing in Shetland (including Bressay). Best brown trout lochs (six in number) are located in valley of Tingwall. Tingwall is about 6m from Lerwick and 1 to 2m from Scalloway. Sea trout run into two of the above-mentioned lochs in season. Sea trout also obtained in nearby voes. Following voes (with distances from Lerwick) all contain sea trout. Full body waders are recommended. Laxo Voe (20m), Laxfirth (6m), Wadbister (8m). Information regarding other fishing readily given to visiting anglers by hon sec. Shetland AA and the Tourist Office issue permits: wt £10 and dt £2. Boats have been placed on the 5 most popular lochs: **Spiggie** (fly only), **Tingwall**, **Bonston**, **Clousta** and **Eela Water**. Boat permits cost £10 and can be obtained from The Tourist Office, Commercial St. Juveniles (under 16) free. All competitions open to visitors. Tuition in fly fishing and fly tying available. Tackle shops: J A Manson & Son, Commercial Street; The Tackle Shop, Market St. Hotels: Shetland, Grand, Queen's Hotel, Lerwick Hotel, both Lerwick; Royal Hotel, Scalloway Hotel, both Scalloway.

Northmavine. Good brown trout fishing in **Eela Water**, near Ollaberry and Bardister, and in many neighbouring lochs. In Pundswater, S of Hillswick, fish run larger. Good fishing and shooting over Lochend Estate. Sea trout in all lochs and numerous burns. Fishing and shooting can be rented (contact A P Cromarty, Lochend House, Lochend). Sea trout also at Queyfirth, Ronas Voe, Ollaberry, Bardister, Sullom, Mangaster, Hillswick. Also at Hamar Voe, Gunnister and Nibon. Good brown trout in numerous lochs between Nibon and Mangaster (Busta Estate). Car advised. Close to Busta Estate brown and sea-trout fishing.

Sandness, Bridge of Walls, etc. Brown trout and sea trout in lochs and voes.

Scalloway. Numerous lochs and voes. Hotel: Scalloway (excellent fishing in lochs and voes).

Scousburgh. Famous Loch of Spiggie holds good brown trout and sea trout in

Spinning the Sligachan River, Skye, with the Cuillins in the background. *Photo: Eric Chalker.*

season. Fishing by assn season ticket. Best months: brown trout, May and June; sea trout, late Aug and Sept.

Weisdale. John White, Kergord (Weisdale 6) gives permission to holders of assn permits to fish the Burn of Sandwater reputed one of the best in the islands and four lochs, including Sandwater, when the fishing is not required by himself or his guests. Sea trout run through burn to reach **Sandwater**, 3m inland. Mr White or the manager at the Kergord Estate Salmon Hatchery (Weisdale 305) should also be approached for permission to fish Weisdale Burn and the Burn of Strom.

SKYE

Trout and salmon fishing generally preserved, but some good free fishing for hotel guests. Sea trout especially good in places. Excellent sea fishing.

Dunvegan. Numerous streams in area can be very good for sea trout in May and June. Hotels: Atholl House; Misty Isle.

Sleat. Brown trout and sea trout fishing on a number of small rivers and lochs in the South of Skye. Permits from Fearran Eilean Iarmain, Eilean Iarmain, An t-Eilean, Sgitheanach (tel: 0478 2197).

Portree. Lochs Fada and **Leathan** have good brown trout (average 1lb, occasionally 5lb). **Storr Lochs** are 4m away. Bank fishing; 10 boats. Mid-May to mid-June and early Sept best. Permits for Storr Lochs and other hill lochs from Anderson, MacArthur & Co, Somerled Sq. There is also salmon fishing in **Staffin, Lealt** and **Kilmuluag** rivers. Sea trout in **Brogaig** and numerous small brown trout lochs in the north of the island. St and dt for these fishings. Enquiries to hon sec Portree AA. Also sea fishing, for pollack and saithe in harbour. Sea trips from Portree daily, apply Tourist Office. Tackle shop: Jansport, Somerled Square. Hotel: Cuillin Hills.

Skeabost. Skeabost House Hotel has salmon and sea trout fishing on **River Snizort** and trout fishing; discounts for residents. Further information from Skeabost House Hotel, Skeabost Bridge, Isle of Skye IV51 9NP (tel. 047 032 202).

Sligachan. Sligachan Hotel has salmon and sea trout fishing in 2m **Sligachan River** and brown trout fishing in **Loch na-Caiplaich** free for guests; salmon few, sea trout quite plentiful; best months, mid-July to end Sept. Brown trout fishing by arrangement in Storr Lochs (15m); boats available; season, May to end Sept.

Staffin. Salmon, sea trout, brown trout. Portree AA hold the fishing rights. Tickets from D Burd, College of Agriculture, Portree.

Struan. Ullinish Lodge has salmon, sea trout and brown trout fishing in three lochs and on **Rivers Ose** and **Snizort**. Special rates for residents of hotel; trout free, salmon fishing charges adjusted according to water conditions.

Uig. Uig Hotel can arrange fishing on north bank **River Hinnisdale** and **Storr Lochs:** also on various hill lochs on which Portree AA has rights. River Hinnisdale is run by angling club.

LOCHY (including Nevis and Coe)

Drains Loch Lochy and, after joining the Spean at Mucomir, flows about 8m to salt water in Loch Linnhe close to Fort William. Very good salmon and sea trout river but affected by hydro works at Falls of Mucomir. Best months: July, August and Sept. Whole river is on weekly lets only. Further information from River Lochy Association, c/o Mr J A Douglas-Menzies, Mounteagle, Fearn, Ross-shire.

Tributaries of the Lochy

SPEAN: Flows from Loch Laggan. A rocky river with good holding pools. Good fishing for salmon and sea trout from May to October. For lettings and permits enquire at Rod & Gun Shop, 18 High Street, Fort William.

Spean Bridge (Inverness-shire). Beats available on dt for left bank only, also for **Lochs Arkaig** and **Lochy**. Enquire at Spean Bridge Hotel.

ROY (tributary of Spean): Salmon. A spate river; fishes best July onwards.

Roy Bridge (Inverness-shire). Lower half let to Roy Bridge AC; and Glenspean Lodge. Permits from Roy Bridge Hotel and Stronlossit Hotel. Upper half owned by Roy Fisheries; permits from Finlayson Hughes, 29 Barossa Pl, Perth (tel: 0738 30926) and keeper, Braeroy Estate. Roy Bridge AC has fishing on **Loch na Turk**; stocked rainbow trout; apply to hon sec.

NEVIS: A short river flowing around south side of Ben Nevis and entering Loch Linnhe at Fort William, not far from mouth of Lochy. Very good salmon and sea trout fishing.

Fort William (Inverness-shire). River Nevis; salmon, grilse, sea trout. Fort William AA has about 6m; dt from tackle shop after 9am on day required. No spinning; best June onwards. Good brown trout fishing on **Loch Lundavra** 6m from town. Dt £12.50, boat and £3, bank; from Mrs A MacCallum, Lundavra Farm, Fort William PH33 6SZ (0397 702582). For **Loch Arkaig** and **Loch Lochy**, sea trout and brown trout; bank fishing only. Permits from West Highland Estates Office, 33 High St. Tackle shop: Rod & Gun Shop, 18 High St (licences and permits for town beat on River Lochy). Hotels: Imperial, Grand, Alexandra, West End, Milton.

COE. River flows through Glen Coe to enter **Loch Leven** and from there into **Loch Linnhe**. Salmon, sea trout and brown trout.

Glencoe (Argyll). Salmon and sea trout fishing on 1½m stretch; May until Oct; fly, spinning and worm permitted. Apply to H S J MacColl (tel: 08552 256). Brown trout and salmon fishing on Coe; permits from National Trust Visitor's Centre, Glencoe. Further information from The National Trust for Scotland, Glencoe Visitor's Centre, Glencoe, Argyll PA39 4HX (tel. 085 52 729). Brown and rainbow trout fishing on **Loch Achtriochtan**. Forestry Commission has brown and rainbow trout fishing on **Hospital Loch**; fly only. Permits from J Alabater, Scorrybreac Guest House. Hotels: Clachaig Inn; Mamore Lodge, Kinlochleven.

LOSSIE

Drains Loch Trevie and flows about 25m to the Moray Firth at Lossiemouth. A good trout stream; salmon runs improving, July onwards. Provides good sport with sea trout from June onwards, especially near estuary.

Lossiemouth (Moray). Salmon, sea trout. Elgin and Dist AA, has water; estuary and sea; salmon, sea trout and finnock. Permits and information on other fishings available from hon sec and tackle shops in Elgin and Lossiemouth. Hotels: Stotfield, Huntly House.

Elgin (Moray). Elgin AA has water on Lossie at Elgin (salmon, sea trout and brown trout) and **Loch Park** fishings (brown trout). Permits available from The Angling Centre, Moss St (tel. 0343 547615); and The Tackle Shop, 188 High St (tel. 0343 543129). For membership apply to Membership Secretary, A F Garrow, 8 School Walk, New Elgin, Elgin, Moray (tel. 0343 546168), enclosing £1 to cover administrative costs. Trout fishing can be had on the Town Council's Millbuies Estate: **Glen Latterich Reservoir**, brown trout; and **Millbuies Loch**, brown and rainbow trout. permits from Moray District Council, Dept of Recreation, 30-32 High St; and the warden at Millbuies. Hotels: Braelossie; Mansefield House; Mansion House.

LUNAN

Rises near Forfar and flows about 13m to North Sea between Arbroath and Montrose. Some good trout, dry fly good. Sea trout and finnock in autumn. A protection order now in force requiring all anglers to be in possession of proper permits.

Arbroath (Angus). Lunan and its tributary, the **Vinney**, about 8m of water, leased to Arbroath AC by riparian owners; restocked each year, holds good head of brown trout, also sea trout and occasional salmon. Bag limit 6 fish. River mouth, sea trout and salmon. Upstream, st £15 and dt £3; river mouth, dt £3. Concession for OAPs and juniors. Permits from Arbroath Cycle & Tackle Centre, 274 High Street, Arbroath DD11 1JE (tel: 0241 73467). Good sea fishing. Local sea angling trips daily.

Forfar (Angus). **Rescobie Loch**, 3m E of Forfar; fly fishing for large trout (brown and rainbow). Bank and boat fishing; st £70, dt £7 and boat £6 (electric outboard motors £3) from Mr J Yule, South Lodge, Reswallie, Forfar. Tel: 030781 384. Special rates for all disabled anglers. Canmore AC (members of Strathmore Angling Improvement Association) has trout fishing on **River Dean**, fly only; **Cruick Water; R Kerbet**, fly only; R Lunan; **R Lemno; R Airneyfoul;** Rescobie Loch; **Den of Ogil Reservoir**, fly only, no Sunday fishing; **R Isla**; and **For-far Loch**. Permits for Lunan and Isla

from C Kerr, 1 West High St. For other permits contact hon sec.

NAIRN

Rises in Monadhliath Hills and flows about 36m to Moray Firth at Nairn. Salmon, sea trout, finnock and yellow trout.

Nairn (Nairn). Tickets for the lower reaches (estuary to Cantray Bridge 8m) can be had from Nairn AA; salmon and sea trout. Best months: July to September for salmon. Tuition for club juniors. Wt £37 and dt £11. Permits from Pat Fraser, Radio, TV and Sports Shop, 41 High Street. Clava Lodge Holiday Homes, Culloden Moor, By Inverness, also issues permits for a stretch on Nairn. McDer-

mott's AC has water at Clunas Dam, near Nairn; rainbow and brown trout; permits from Mrs Jackson, Harbour St; General Stores, 19 Harbour St. **Lochs Lochindorb, Allan**, and **Loch-an-Tutach** privately owned; brown trout; dt and boat. Other tackle shop: Sportscene, Harbour St. Other hotels: Meallmore Lodge, Daviot (private stretch of river); Newton (river and loch fishing by arrangement).

NAVER (including Borgie and Loch Hope)

Drains Loch Naver and flows about 24m to north coast at Naver Bay. The Borgie, which also debouches into Naver Bay, drains Loch Laighal and has course of about 7m. Both are good salmon and sea trout rivers; all preserved, but beats can be arranged, usually for weekly periods.

Altnaharra (Sutherland). Altnaharra Hotel, By Larg, Sutherland IV27 4UE (tel. 054 981 222), which specializes in catering for fishermen, provides salmon fishing in **Loch Naver** and **River Mudale**; sea trout fishing in **Loch Hope** and brown trout fishing in a number of lochs; all lochs have boats and are close to the road. Some are open to non-residents. Dt £12 to £30. Excellent sea trout water; also holds salmon. No bank fishing; fly only. Hotel has fully stocked tackle shop; and provides outboard motors, tuition and accommodation.

Tongue (Sutherland). Limited day tickets available for quality salmon fishing on River Naver from Bettyhill TIC. Salmon and sea trout fishing on **Loch Hope**; ap-

prox £100 per week. Early booking advisable. Contact Ian MacDonald, Keeper (tel: 084756 272). Tongue Dist AA (HQ at Ben Loyal Hotel) has brown trout fishing on 14 lochs; fly only. Boats available on **Lochs Loyal, Cormach**, and **Craggie**, and **Lochan Hakel**. Ghillie by arrangement. St £20, wt £12 and dt £3; from hotel. Drying room and freezer space available at hotel. Kyle of Tongue estuary also assn water; excellent sea trout when shoals are running; fly or spinner. **R Borgie**, stretch from Borgie Hotel to sea; permits from David Crichton, Water Bailiff (tel: 06412 255). Private beats on Borgie; Apt-Sept; fly only; contact Jamie & Partners, Rectory Pl, Loughborough, Leics (tel: 0509 233433).

NESS

Drains Loch Ness and flows to North Sea close to Inverness. Notable salmon and sea trout river. Best July to October.

Inverness (Inverness-shire). Salmon, sea trout, brown trout. Inverness AC has stretch from estuary upstream for about 3¾m, both banks. No day tickets on Saturdays; no Sunday fishing. Permits from tackle shops; the River Watcher; and Tourist Board, Bridge St. **Loch Ruthven**, brown trout; fly only; boat only; permits from J Graham & Co; and R Humfrey, Balvoulin, Aberarder. Sunday fishing permitted. **Loch Choire**, brown trout; fly only; permits from R Humfrey, Balvoulin, Aberarder. Sea trout fishing on North Kessock sea shore; permits from North Kessock PO; and J Graham & Co. Tackle shops: J Graham & Co, 37-39 Castle St (0463 233178); Frasers, Market Arcade; Ormiston & Co, 20 Market Brae Steps. Hotels: Glen Mhor; Loch Ness House; Haughdale.

LOCH NESS: Sea trout at Dochfour and Aldourie; salmon, especially out from Fort Augustus and where **Rivers Moriston, Enrick** and **Foyers** enter the loch. Brown trout all round the margins. Boats and boatmen from hotels at Fort Augustus, Drumnadrochit, Foyers, Lewiston and Whitbridge.

Dochgarroch (Inverness-shire). Dochfour Estate has brown trout fishing on **Loch Ness** and **Loch Dochfour**; north bank only. No Sunday fishing. Permits from Dochfour Estate Office, Dochgarroch, Inverness IV3 6JP (tel: 0463 86 218).

Drumnadrochit (Inverness). Salmon and brown trout. **River Enrick**, which enters loch here; best months, April, May, June. **Loch Meiklie**, brown trout; fly only. Permits for Enrick and Loch Meiklie from Mrs Taylor, Kilmartin Hall, Glenurquhart.

Foyers (Inverness). Foyers Hotel has salmon and brown trout fishing on Loch Ness. Boats and ghillie available. Several other lochs may also be fished, including **Lochs Bran, Garth, Farraline** and **Killin.**

Invermoriston (Inverness). **River Moriston** enters Loch Ness here. Permits for River Moriston; trout fishing on hill lochs on Glenmoriston Lodge Estate; and salmon fishing by boat on **Loch Ness**; from Headkeeper, Levishie House, Glenmoriston (tel: 0320 51219).

Fort Augustus (Inverness). Salmon and brown trout. Salmon season opens Jan 15. Trout season, March 15. Dt for **River Oich** (S) £15, (T) £2.20, from A D McDonald, Craigphadric, Fort Augustus (tel: 0320 6230). Permits for brown trout fishing on **River Tarff, Invervigar Burn** and **Loch A'Mhuilinn**; and brown and rainbow trout fishing on **Loch Unagan**; from Macaskills, Canal Side (tel: Fort Augustus 6207). Brown trout fishing on **Loch Quoich**; permits and boats from Lovat Arms Hotel. Rod hire and tackle from Thorps Store. Hotels: Lovat Arms, Caledonian, Brae, Inchnacardoch.

Tributaries of Loch Ness

FOYERS. Free brown trout fishing.
Foyers (Inverness-shire). **Loch Mhor**, 18m from Inverness, is 4m long by ½m broad, and contains trout averaging ½lb. Outlet from loch enters Loch Ness via River Foyers. Accommodation ½m from loch at the Old Manse Guest House, Gorthleck and 2½m from loch at Whitebridge Hotel, Whitebridge, Inverness IV1 2UN (tel. 0456 486226). Tackle for purchase or hire, and boats (£12 per day); available from Whitebridge Hotel. **Loch Ruthven** can be fished, also **Loch Bran** and **River Fechlin.**

Whitebridge (Inverness). Whitebridge Hotel has boats for use of guests on **Loch Knockie** and **Loch Bran**; brown trout; fly only. Arrangements also made for guests wishing to troll on Loch Ness. River and burns dried out in course of hydro-electric development. Other hotel: Knockie Lodge.

MORISTON: Salmon, brown trout.
Glenmoriston (Inverness-shire). Glenmoriston Lodge Estate, Invermoriston, IV3 3YA, has fishing rights on Loch Ness, salmon and brown trout; R Moriston, salmon and brown trout; and **Glenmoris-**

Keep the banks clean

Several clubs have stopped issuing tickets to visitors because of the state of the banks after they have left. Spend a few moments clearing up.

ton hill lochs, brown trout. Permits from Headkeeper, Levishie House (tel: 0320 51219). **Loch Cluanie**, brown trout. No Sunday fishing. Permits and boats from Colin Campbell, Stalker, Cluanie Lodge, Glenmoriston.

OICH and GARRY. Garry rises in loch SW of Loch Quoich and runs into that loch at western end, thence to Lochs Poulary, Inchlaggan and Garry. Good salmon and trout river. Outlet to Loch Garry dammed by North of Scotland Hydro-Electric Board. At Loch Poulary are fish traps; at Invergarry, a hatchery.

Invergarry (Inverness). Glen Garry FC controls fishing on the whole of Upper Garry (both banks), **Lochs Quoich, Poulary, Inchlaggan** and **Garry**. Loch Quoich holds brown trout record and Loch Garry holds Artic charr record; both lochs hold charr. Salmon only good July onwards, closing mid-Oct. Boats available on all lochs and some of pools of Upper Garry. Permits from Tomdoun Ho-

tel (tel: 08092 218) and Garry Gualach, Glengarry (tel: 08092 230). Garry Gualach also issues permits for Loch Inchlaggan; fly only. Tomdoun Hotel issues permits for **Lochs Quoich, Poulary, Inchlaggan, Garry** and **Loyne**, and Upper River Garry; trout, salmon, char and pike (no salmon in Quoich and Loyne, and no pike in Quoich). Upper Garry reserved for hotel guests. Boat fishing only on Quoich. Bank fishing only on Loyne. Boats available from hotel for all waters except Loyne. Apply to G F Heath, Tomdoun Hotel, Invergarry, Inverness-shire PH35 4HS (tel. 08092 218/244). Bed and breakfast accommodation plus a self-catering chalet available from Mrs P A Buswell, who can arrange fishing holidays and operates a small mini bus to collect and transport clients who have no transport. Apply to Mrs P A Buswell, Nursery Cottages, Invergarry, Inverness-shire PH35 4HL (tel. 0809 501 297).

NITH

Rises on south side of Ayr watershed and flows south and east to Solway, which it enters by an estuary with Dumfries at its head. Is the largest and best known river in the Dumfries and Galloway region and has established a reputation for the quality of its salmon and sea trout which continue to improve. Carries a good head of small trout.

New Abbey (Kirkcudbrightshire). New Abbey AA has 2m on a small tributary of Nith; occasional salmon, good sea trout and herling, and stocked with brown trout and rainbow trout. Visitor's st £12 and dt £3. Concession for jun. Permits from hon sec; The Shop, The Square; and Criffel Inn, The Square. Hotels: Abbey Arms; Criffel Inn.

Dumfries (Dumfries & Galloway). Dumfries Common Good Fishing, 3m on Nith, 1½m on **Cairn** (tributary); salmon, sea trout, brown trout and grayling; best, March-May and Sept-Nov. St £170, wt £75, dt £30 (cheaper dt and wt prior to 30 June). Juveniles half price. Permits from Director of Finance, Nithsdale DC, Municipal Chambers, Buccleuch St, Dumfries DG1 2AD (tel. 0387 53166 - ext 230). Dumfries and Galloway AA has 3m on Nith and 16m on Cairn; salmon, sea trout and brown trout. Fly fishing anytime; spinning and bait fishing restricted to water level. Daily and weekly tickets available; no daily tickets on Saturday. Concessions for juniors. Permits from D McMillan, Fishing Tackle Specialists. **Glenkiln Reservoir** (trout) controlled by

Dumfries and Galloway Regional Council, Director of Water and Sewage, Marchmount House, Marchmount, Dumfries DG1 1PW. St £20, wt £10, dt (bank) £2.75. Boats available. Bank fishing free to OAP and disabled residents. **Jericho Loch,** rainbow and brown trout; fly only; bank fishing only. Permits from Mousewald Caravan Park, Mousewald, By Dumfries; Thistle Stores, Locharbriggs, Dumfries. **Barony College Sports Fishery** has rainbow and brown trout fishing, contact Barony College, Parkgate (tel: 0387 86251). Tackle shops: D McMillan, 6 Friar's Vennel (tel. 0387 52075); Malcolm Pattie, 109 Queensberry Street.

Thornhill (Dumfriesshire). Mid Nithsdale AA has 3½m on Nith and tributary **Scaur;** salmon, sea trout and brown trout. No permits on Saturdays. Assn also has brown and rainbow trout fishing on **Kettleton Loch** 4m NE of Thornhill, 40 acres. Advanced booking for autumn fishing. Permits from hon sec. Drumlanrig Castle Fishing on the Queensberry Estate offers salmon and sea trout fishing on River Nith, 7m, both banks, 4 beats; **Morton Castle Loch** and **Starburn Loch,**

rainbow and brown trout; and **Morton Pond** and **Dabton Loch**, coarse fish. Accommodation available in Auchenknight Cottage on estate. Apply to The Factor, The Buccleuch Estates Ltd, Drumlanrig Mains, Thornhill, Dumfriesshire DG3 4AG (tel: 08486 283). Barjarg Estate has stretch on Nith; salmon, grilse, coarse fish, brown trout and grayling. Daily or weekly permits until end August; normally weekly from Sept to end Nov. Self-catering accommodation also available. Apply to Andrew Hunter-Arundel, Newhall, Auldgirth, Dumfriesshire DG2 0TN (0848 331342). **Loch Ettrick** near Closeburn, rainbow and brown trout; apply to Gilchristland Estate Office, Closeburn, Thornhill DG3 5HN (tel: 0848 30827). Hotels: Buccleuch, George, Elmarglen.

Sanquhar (Dumfries & Galloway). Upper Nithsdale AC has approx 11m of Nith; and stretches on tributaries **Kello**, **Crawick**, **Euchan** and **Mennock**.

Salmon, sea trout, brown trout and grayling. No Sunday fishing. No Saturday day tickets. Reduced membership charge for resident juveniles; and Forsyth Shield presented each year in Jan to resident boy for heaviest fish caught. Permits from K McLean Esq, Solicitor, 61 High Street, Sanquhar (tel. 0659 50241). Day tickets for grayling fishing, Jan and Feb, from W Laidlow, Water Bailiff, 22 Renwick Place. Tackle shop: Alex Stenhouse, Ironmongers, High St. Hotels: Nithsdale; Glendyne; Mennockfoot Lodge; Blackaddie House.

New Cumnock (Ayrshire). New Cumnock AA has brown trout fishing on River Nith, **Afton Water** and **Afton Reservoir**; and on parts of **Rivers Deugh** and **Ken**, and **Carsphairn Lane Burn**. Club also has grayling fishing on River Nith and rainbow trout fishing on **Creoch Loch**. Creoch Loch open all year. Permits from hon sec; and Stanleys and Lapwing. Hotels: Lochside House, Crown.

OYKEL (including Carron, Cassley, Shin and Loch Ailsh)

Rises at Benmore Assynt, flows through Loch Ailsh and thence 14m to enter the Kyle of Sutherland at Rosehall. Excellent salmon and sea trout fishing. The Lower Oykel has produced an average catch of over 780 salmon in recent years.

Oykel Bridge (Ross-shire). Lower reaches fish very well for salmon early on and good grilse and sea trout run usually begins in the latter half of June. Loch Ailsh. Good sea and brown trout fishing with occasional salmon. Best months **Lower Oykel**, March to September. **Upper Oykel** and **Loch Ailsh**, mid-June to September. Inver Lodge Hotel has salmon and trout fishing on Oykel. Contact Inver Lodge Hotel, Lochinver IV27 4LU.

CASSLEY: Some 10m long, river is divided at Rosehall into upper and lower Cassley by Achness Falls. Below falls fishing starts early. Upper Cassley fishes well from May to Sept. Sea trout July and Aug.

Rosehall (Sutherland). Rods let by week (av £200) on both banks. Sole agents: Bell Ingram, Estate Office, Bonar Bridge, Sutherland IV24 3AE. Hotel: Achness House.

SHIN (Loch Shin and Kyle of Sutherland): Loch Shin is largest fresh water loch in Sutherland, 16m long. Brown trout in loch av ½lb, but very large fish taken early in season. Outlet from Loch Shin controlled by hydro-electric works. River flows about 7m and empties into

Kyle of Sutherland at Invershin. Salmon fishing privately let.

Lairg (Sutherland). Lairg AC has trout fishing in Loch Shin and hill lochs, including a new water, **Loch Beannach** (brown trout, 5m from Lairg, 1m walk). Loch Shin, brown trout including ferox up to 12lbs. Competitions held on Loch Shin throughout the season - details from club hut at loch side. St £10 from hon sec; wt £10 and dt £3 from local tackle shop. Concessions for juveniles. Boats available. Bookings from hon sec (tel: 0549 2010). Best mid-May to end of July. No Sunday fishing. Sutherland Arms Hotel, Lairg, IV27 4AT, can arrange salmon fishing on River Shin; and trout fishing on Loch Shin and hill lochs (tel: 0549 2291). Overscaig Hotel, on shore of **Loch Shin**, has boats on loch and others on **Lochs A' Ghriama** and **Merkland** with many hill lochs within walking distance. Facilities usually available for sea trout and salmon fishing on **Lochs Stack** and **More**. Hotel ghillies, advice and instruction. Large brown trout caught on hotel waters in recent years. Fishing free to residents. Boats with ob motors. For further information contact Overscaig

Lochside Hotel, Loch Shin, by Lairg IV27 4NY. Tackle shop: Messrs R Ross (prop. D Keniston), New Buildings, Main St.

DORNOCH FIRTH:

Dornoch (Sutherland). At entrance to Firth. Permits from Dornoch AA for sea trout at **Little Ferry**; wt £6, dt £2 and brown trout on **Lochs Lannsaidh**, **Buidhe**, **Laoigh**, **Lagain**, **Laro** and **Cracail Mor**, boat,

£12 per day and bank on Buidhe, Laoigh and Lagain £5. Assn has recently acquired salmon, sea trout and brown trout fishing on **Loch Brora**; boat only, £15 per day. Fly only on lochs. Spinning allowed on Little Ferry. No Sunday fishing. Permits from W A MacDonald, Hardware Store, Castle St. Hotels: Burghfield House; Castle.

KYLE OF DURNESS

Durness (Sutherland). Cape Wrath Hotel at Keoldale has good salmon and sea trout fishing on **Rivers Dionard**, **Grudie** and **Dall**, and the Kyle of Durness. Best for salmon and sea trout mid-June to mid Sept. Big brown trout in **Lochs Calladale**, **Crosspool**, **Lanlish**, and **Bor-**

ralaidh - well-conditioned fish of 8lbs in weight have been taken - and there are several lochs, three with boats. Lochs and rivers stocked with salmon, sea trout, brown trout fry. Hotel open throughout year. Enquiries to Cape Wrath Hotel, Keoldale, by Lairg, Sutherland.

SCOURIE (including Laxford River and Lochs Stack and More)

Scourie (Sutherland). Excellent centre for sea trout, brown trout and salmon fishing. About 200 trout lochs. Scourie Hotel has extensive fishing rights on over 100; four with salmon and sea trout. Boats avail-

able on many. Ghillies may also be employed. Dt varies between £15 and £40, depending on season. Days on **Loch Stack** and **Loch More** (by permission of Duchess of Westminster) available to

Preparing for a day on Loch Insh. *Photo: Fisher Photos.*

guests during July, Aug and Sept. Salmon, sea trout (good), brown trout. For further information apply to Ian A S Hay, Scourie Hotel, Scourie, By Lairg IV27 4SX (tel. 0971 502396). Laxford River is preserved. Scourie & Dist AC has rights on 33 lochs to N of village and 2 lochs S; trout around ½lb mark, but some larger fish. Wt £12 and dt £4 (boat £3 extra) from D Ross, Post Office. Tackle available for hire.

SHIEL (Argyll/Inverness-shire) (including Moidart and Loch Shiel)

Short but good salmon river, only about 3m long, draining Loch Shiel. Moidart is a good spate river with excellent holding pools. Loch Shiel is fed by four major rivers, **Slatach**, **Finnan**, **Callop** and **Alladale**, which all tend to spate rivers. The Loch is best for salmon from April 1 until end May or early June. The sea trout run from July onwards and fishing closes at the end of October.

Acharacle (Argyll). River preserved. **Loch Shiel**, 17m long, holds salmon and sea trout, and a few brown trout; best mid-May to end of October; good late run. No bank fishing. Boats and permits for Loch Shiel from D Macaulay, Dalilea Farm (tel: 096 785 253); Fergie MacDonald, Clanranald Hotel; and Loch Shiel Hotel. Also apply to Fergie MacDonald, Clanranald Hotel, for salmon and sea trout fishing on **Rivers Carnoch**, **Strontian** and **Moidart**; boats available. Fly fishing on the Ardnamurchan Peninsular in **Lochs Mudle** and **Mhadaidh**; wild brown trout, sea trout and the occasional salmon. Permits from Nick Peake, Sithean Mor, Achnaha, Nr Kilchoan, By Acharacle, Argyll PH36 4LW (tel. 0972 501 212). Fly fishing tuition, tackle and boat hire, accommodation, sea fishing, and hill walking also available from Nick Peake. Permits for fresh water fishing also available from Kilchoan Post Office; and Natural History and Visitors Centre, Glenmore. Some tackle can be bought at the Post Office.

Glenfinnan (Inverness-shire). The Stage House, Glenfinnan, Inverness-shire PH37 4LT (0397 722 246) has 4 boats on **Loch Shiel**; salmon, sea trout and brown trout. Boat fishing only. Dt £5. Boat plus outboard £15 per day. Family run hotel with fishing package holidays. Glenfinnan House Hotel also issues permits. The record 36lb salmon caught on Loch Shiel can be seen at Rod and Gun Shop, Fort William.

SPEY

Rises mile or two above Loch Spey and flows NE about 100m to North Sea, emptying between Banff and Elgin. Historically, one of the great salmon rivers, but spring run much diminished of late. Well organised facilities for visitors though, including tuition. Good sea trout and brown trout in places.

Fochabers (Morayshire). Salmon fishing leased by Gordon Castle Estate; all beats privately let. Fochabers AA lease a stretch (1¾m) from May 16 to Aug 31; resident members only; four visitor permits on a daily basis. Permits from Fochabers Tackle & Guns, 91 High St, Fochabers, Moray IV32 7DH (tel. 0343 820327); and Mrs McLennon, No 2 Cottage, Bogmuir. Best months, July and Aug. Gordon Arms Hotel issue permits for salmon fishing on Spey. Mill House Hotel, Tynet, By Buckie, Banffshire AB56 2HJ, cater for fishermen and fishing parties.

Craigellachie (Banffshire). Salmon, sea trout, trout. Craigellachie Hotel, Craigellachie, Speyside, Banffshire AB38 9SR (tel. 03940 881204), arranges salmon fishing on Spey and brown trout fishing on local lochs for residents.

Aberlour (Banffshire). Salmon, sea trout. Aberlour Association water. Six tickets per day on first-come-first-served basis. Hotels Dowans and Aberlour have 3 bookable tickets for residents. Dt £15 and wt £75. No day tickets issued on Saturdays. Permits from J A J Munro, Fishing Tackle, 93-95 High St, Aberlour, Banffshire AB38 9PB (tel. 0340 871428). Season 11 Feb - 30 Sept. Best season usually March till June but can be very good in July and August too. J A J Munro also issues weekly permits for private fishings on **River Findhorn**; and is a specialist supplier of hand-tied salmon flies.

Grantown-on-Spey (Moray). Salmon and
sea trout. Strathspey Angling Improvement Association has 7m on **Spey**, and
12m on **Dulnain**; salmon, sea trout and
brown trout. Permits available to visitors
resident in Grantown, Cromdale, Duthill,
Carrbridge, Dulnain Bridge and Nethy
Bridge areas. Permits from tackle shop.
Trout fishing on **Avielochan**, bank fishing only; **Loch Dallas**, fly only; **Loch
Mor**, fly only; and **Loch Vaa**, boat fishing only. Permits from tackle shop. Arthur Oglesby runs occasional game
angling courses at the Seafield Lodge Hotel; for dates and information apply to
Alasdair Buchanan, The Seafield Lodge
Hotel, PH26 3JN (tel. 0479 2152). *(see
advt)* Tackle shop: Mortimer's, High St.

Nethy Bridge (Inverness-shire). Salmon,
trout. Best months, May, June, July. Per-
mits for Abernethy AIA water on River
Spey and **River Nethy** from Allen's
Tackle Shop, Boat of Garten. Hotels:
Nethy Bridge.

Boat of Garten (Inverness-shire). Salmon,
sea trout, brown trout. Abernethy Angling Improvement Assn issues tickets
for Abernethy Beat, 6¾ mile stretch of

Spey, both banks (owned by Barratts
Timeshare); and Broomhill Pool. No Sunday fishing. Certain stretches restricted to
fly only when river below certain level,
otherwise spinning and worming allowed; no prawn or shrimp allowed at any
time. Brown trout fishing - fly only at all
times. Permit only available for those
staying locally, 6-day ticket £75, dt £25;
from A J Allen, Allen's, Tackle Shop,
Deshar Rd, Boat of Garten PH24 3BN
(tel. 047 983 372). Hotels: The Boat;
Craigard; Nethy Bridge, Nethy Bridge.

Aviemore (Inverness-shire). The principal
Spey Valley tourist centre. Kinara Estate
has salmon and trout fishing on Spey;
apply to Kinara Estate Office, Aviemore.
Trout and pike fishing on Rothiemurchus
Estate; apply to Rothiemurchus Fish
Farm, Aviemore PH22 1QH. Trout fishing on **Loch Morlich** at Glenmore. Permits from Warden's Office, Glenmore
Forest Camping and Caravan Park, Glenmore, by Aviemore.

Kingussie (Inverness-shire). Alvie Estate
has fishing on Spey, salmon and trout;
Loch Alvie, brown trout and pike; and
Loch Insh, salmon, sea trout, brown trout
and char. Fly fishing or spinning. Apply
to Alvie Estate Office, Kincraig, by Kingussie; and Dalraddy Caravan Park,
Aviemore. Badenoch AC has fishing on
River Spey, 3 beats; **River Calder**,
brown trout only; **River Tromie**, left
bank only from Tromie Bridge down;
Spey Dam, fly only, 6 fish limit; **Loch
Ericht**, fishing on Sundays only after 31
Aug, limit 40 rods; **Loch Laggan**, no
weekday fishing after 31 Aug, limit 30
rods. Permits from Spey Tackle; The Paper Shop; Laggan Stores, Laggan; Ashdown Stores, Newtonmore. Assn also has
fishing on **River Trium** for local season
ticket holders only; permits must be obtained in advance from Sandy Bennett,
Water Bailiff, Kingussie. Loch Insh Sailing School also has fishing on **Loch Insh**;
boats available. Apply to Loch Insh Sailing School, Kincraig, By Kingussie. Ossian Hotel has private fishing; salmon
and brown trout. Permits from Ossian
Hotel, Kincraig, By Kingussie PH21
1NA (tel. 0540 651 242). Tuition available from Jock Dallas, Castwell, Fishing
Instruction School, Kingussie.

Newtonmore (Inverness-shire). Badenach
AA has trout fishing on Upper Spey,
Loch Laggan, Loch Quoich and **Spey
Dam**. Boat and permits: Mains Hotel.

Tributaries of the Spey

AVON: Main tributary of Spey.

Ballindalloch (Banffshire). Ballindalloch Estate owns 5m stretch on Avon from junction with Spey; salmon and sea trout. Weekly and daily permits. Special rates for guests staying at Delnashaugh Inn. Permits from The Estate Office, Ballindalloch, Banffshire AB37 9BS (tel. 0807 500 205). Hotel: Seafield Lodge Hotel

(see Grantown-on-Spey).

Tomintoul (Banffshire). Sea trout, grilse and salmon. Richmond Arms has 6m of fishing on Avon and 2½m on **Livet** for guests. Gordon Arms Hotel guests can fish 2m of Avon and 1m of Livet. Price varies depending on duration of stay. Fishing only available to residents of hotel.

STINCHAR

One of west coast streams, rising on western slope of Doon watershed and flowing about 30m to Atlantic at Ballantrae. Has a very late run of salmon, lasting till middle of October. Also good sea trout and brown trout.

Colmonell (Ayrshire). River rises and falls rapidly after rain. Salmon and sea trout. Permits for Stinchar available from Boars

Head Hotel and Queen's Hotel. Permits for Knockdolian from Estate Office, Colmonell, Ballantrae (tel: 046588 237).

TAY

A prestigious salmon river. Tay proper runs out of Loch Tay, but its feeder, the Dochart, at head of loch, takes its head water from slopes of Ben More. River fished mainly from boats, but certain beats provide also spinning and fly fishing from banks. Notable in particular for run of spring fish, though autumn fishing often gives good results. After a course of some 120m it empties into North Sea by a long firth. Netting extends as far as Stanley, some miles above Perth. At least half a dozen of its tributaries are salmon rivers of little less repute than main stream. An excellent run of sea trout, big brown trout (less often fished for), grayling, and coarse fish (scarcely ever fished for).

Perth (Perthshire). Stormont AC has salmon fishing on Tay, 3 beats; and on **R Almond**, 2 beats. Members only (c. 550). Assn also has brown trout and coarse fishing on Tay and Almond. Permits for 3 beats available to public from Estates Office, Scone Palace; and MG Guns & Tackle. Perth & Dist AA has various leases for brown trout and salmon fishing on Tay. Assn also has fishing on **Black Loch**, rainbow trout; **Loch Horn**, rainbow and brown trout; and **Balthatock Loch**, brown trout. All game fishing members only. Brown trout on Tay permits from P D Malloch. Permits for Perth Town Water; salmon, trout, grilse and also coarse fish; from Perth and Kinross District Council, Leisure & Recreation Dept, 3 High St, Perth PH1 5JU; and Tourist Information Centre, 45 High St, Perth PH1 5TJ. Advisable to book in advance; only 20 permits per day and only 2 permits in advance by any one person. Tackle shops: P D Malloch, 259 Old High St; and PFS, 13 Charlotte St. Hotels: Royal George; Tayside (*see advt*), Stanley.

Stanley (Perthshire). Stanley & Dist AC

has brown trout and grayling fishing on several beats of Tay. During salmon season, fly only; from 16 Oct-14 Jan, any legal means may be used to fish for grayling. Dt £1. Permits from Stanley PO (Mon-Fri); and Tayside Hotel (Sat-Sun). Other Hotel: Stanley.

Dunkeld (Perthshire). Dunkeld & Birnam AA and Perth & Dist AA have trout fishing on **Tay**. Wt £10 and £5; dt £2 and £1, respectively. Permits are also issued for grayling, mostly in the trout close season. Coarse fishing on **Loch Clunie**; dt £2. Concessions for OAP & jun. Permits from Kettles of Dunkeld, Atholl St, Dunkeld PH8 0AR (tel: 03502 727 556). Dunkeld & Birnam AA also has brown trout fishing on **River Braan**; and **Loch Freuchie** at Amulree, bank fishing only. Permits for R Braan from Kettles and for L Freuchie from Amulree PO. Stakis Dunkeld House Hotel has salmon and trout fishing on Tay; 2 boats with 2 rods; 8 bank rods; experienced ghillies; no salmon fishing on Sundays. **Butterstone Loch**, rainbow and brown trout; fly only. Boats available. Permits from The Bailiff, Lochend Cottage, Butterstone, by Dunkeld.

Grandtully (Perthshire). Permits for Tay from Grandtully Hotel; salmon, brown trout and grayling; fly, bait or spinning. Boat and ghillie available. Booking advisable.

Aberfeldy (Perthshire). Salmon, brown trout and grayling fishing on Tay. Permits from Jamiesons Sports Shop, 41 Dunkeld St. Weem Hotel has trout and salmon fishing available to guests on River Tay, salmon, trout sea trout; Loch Tay, salmon, and trout; and various hill lochs, including coarse fish and wild brown trout. Permits also issued to non-resi-

dents. Special fishing breaks available with accommodation either serviced or self-catering. Full ghillie service, tuition and tackle hire on request. Apply to The Weem, Weem, By Aberfeldy, Perthshire PH15 2LD (tel. 0887 820 381).

Kenmore (Perthshire). Tay leaves **Loch Tay** at Kenmore. Salmon and trout fishing on river and loch for guests at The Kenmore Hotel, Kenmore PH15 2NU (tel. 0887 830 205: boats available. Permits for non-residents from hotel or Post Office.

Killin (Perthshire). Killin & Breadalbane AC has fishing on **Loch Tay, River Dochart** and **River Lochay**, all in immediate area of Killin; salmon, brown trout, rainbow trout, perch, pike and char. Regular stocking policy which includes stocking with mature brown trout throughout year. Club has its own hatchery which supplies some 70,000 hatchlings for stocking local streams. Salmon of up to 30lbs are caught regularly; rainbows of 5-6lbs. An excellent venue for visiting anglers who are made very welcome. Rods for hire. Permits from J Lewis, Newsagent & Tackle Shop, Main St. J Lewis also issues permits for **Lochan-an-Laraig** (brown trout).

Crianlarich (Perthshire). Crianlarich AA has trout fishing on **Loch Dochart** (good early in the season), **Loch Iubhair** and **River Fillan**, a tributary of Tay. In summer, salmon find their way into loch and up Fillan and tributaries. Best months: May, June, July and Sept. St £15, wt £7, dt £3. Day tickets for River Fillan from Ben More Lodge Hotel, Crianlarich FK20 8QS (tel. 0838 300 210). Permits for Loch Dochart from Portnellan Lodge House (tel: 08383 284). Boats, tackle, engines and ghillies available.

Tributaries of the Tay

EARN: Salmon, sea trout, brown trout (av ½lb) and excellent grayling.

Bridge of Earn (Perthshire). Rainbow trout fishing on **Sandyknowes Fishery**, 8 acres; fly only; bank fishing only. Bag limit 4 trout. Permits from E C Christie, The Fishery Office, Sandyknowes, Bridge of Earn (tel. 0738 813033).

Crieff (Perthshire). Crieff AC has stretch; brown, sea trout, salmon, rainbow trout and grayling. No bait fishing before 1 May. Season 1 Feb-15 Oct; no Saturdays in Oct. Permits from Crieff Tourist Of-

fice. Brown and rainbow trout fishing on **Monzievaird**; fly only; boat fishing only. Permits from J D Groot, Ochtertyre House, by Crieff. Brown trout fishing on **Loch Turret**; fly only; boats available. Permits from Director of Finance, Central Scotland Water Board, 30 George St, Glasgow; and A Boyd, King St, Crieff. Hotels: Drummond Arms; and Drummond Arms, Muthill.

St Fillans (Perthshire). Trout fishing for visitors in **Loch Earn**. Whole of loch controlled by St Fillans & Lochearn AA.

Permits from Post Office (also tackle) and Drummond Arms Hotel.

Lochearnhead (Perthshire). Loch Earn, brown trout ($\frac{1}{2}$-$\frac{3}{4}$lb). St Fillans & Lochearn AA water. Permits from Post Office; Clachan Hotel; and Sturrock's Garage.

ISLA: Trout (av $\frac{1}{2}$lb and up to 3lb) and grayling. Pike also in lower reaches.

Dundee (Angus). Permits for brown trout and grayling fishing from Strathmore AIA; and local tackle shops. Assn also issues permits for **Dean Water**, tributary of Isla; brown trout. Tackle shop: John R Gow Ltd, 12 Union St, Dundee DD1 4BH.

ALYTH (tributary of Isla):

Alyth (Perthshire). Several streams in neighbourhood. Isla contains trout and grayling in lower reaches. Above Reekie Linn trout very numerous but small. Alyth Hotel can arrange salmon and trout fishing on River Tay and a number of its tributaries; also trout fishing on a selection of lochs. Both day fishermen and coach parties are catered for. Apply to Graham Marshall, The Alyth Hotel, Alyth, Perthshire PH11 8AF (tel. 08283 2447).

ERICHT (tributary of Isla):

Blairgowrie (Perthshire). Salmon and brown trout. Blairgowrie, Rattray and Dist AC has fishing on **Rivers Ardle** and **Blackwater**, tributaries of Ericht, Ericht and Isla and on numerous trout lochs. St £40; dt £12 (S) and £2 (T); from local tackle shops and Tourist Information Centre. Salmon fishing for non-club members on Mon, Wed and Fri. Loch fishing in area; many lochs hold pike and perch. **Loch Marlee** best, permits from Marlee Hotel, by Blairgowrie; bank fishing only. At **Kirkmichael** (13m NW), Log Cabin Hotel issues permits for **Ardle River**. Tackle shop: Kate Fleming, Shooting and Fishing, 26 Allan St, Blairgowrie PH10 6AD (tel: 0250 3990); James Crockart & Son, 28 Allan St, Blairgowrie PH10 6AD. Other hotels: Bridge of Cally.

Blacklunans (Perthshire). Dalrulzion Hotel, Glenshee, PH10 7LJ (tel. 0250 882222), has salmon and trout fishing on **River Blackwater** from hotel grounds. Free to guests. Day permits available to non-residents. Other fishings available.

BRAAN:

Dunkeld (Perthshire). Forestry Commission, National Trust and riparian owners have leased water on R Braan and **Tay** to Dunkeld and Birnam AA. Brown trout and grayling. Permits from Kettles of Dunkeld, Atholl St. Amulree Hotel, Amulree, by Dunkeld, has private trout fishing on R Braan for hotel residents; fly only.

TUMMEL: Salmon, trout and grayling.

Pitlochry (Perthshire). Pitlochry AC has salmon fishing on R Tummel from marker post below Pitlochry Dam to bottom of Milton of Fonab Caravan Site; south bank only. Spinning, bait or fly. Dt £6-£30; 3 anglers per day. Advance booking recommended, particularly for Apr-Jun. Contact Ross Gardiner (tel: Pitlochry 472157). Club also has fishing on **R Tummel**, brown trout and grayling; and on **Lochs Bhac** and **Kinardochy**, brown trout. Bank and boat fishing on Bhac; boat only on Kinardochy. Fly only. Permits from Mitchell's of Pitlochry. Permits for trout fishing on R Tummel also available from Tourist Office, Atholl Rd; Fonab Caravan Site; Ballinluig PO; and Ballinluig Service Station. General advice (by phone, evenings) from Ron Harriman (472484) or Ross Gardiner (472157). **Loch Faskally**; salmon, brown trout, pike, perch; any legal lure for salmon. Permits from D McLaren, Boathouse, Loch Faskally, Pitlochry. Tackle shops: Mitchell's of Pitlochry, 23 Atholl Rd; Atholl Sports, Atholl Rd.

GARRY: Good river for about 6m.

Blair Atholl (Perthshire). Blair Atholl has trout fishing on R Garry and **Tilt** (approx 4m); and a stocked rainbow trout loch. Permits from Highland Guns & Tackle. The Highland Shop, Blair Atholl, Perthshire PH18 5SG (tel: 0796 481 303). Private salmon fishing on **R Tilt** (3m); and trout and pike fishing on **Errochty Dam**; tickets from Highland Gun & Tackle.

Dalwhinnie (Inverness-shire). Fishing on **Loch Ericht** (22m long) and rivers; st £15, wt £10, dt £2.50. Permits from Loch Ericht Hotel, Dalwhinnie, Inverness-shire PH14 1AF (tel. 052 82 257).

LOCH RANNOCH: Trout, some large but averaging 9lbs; best May to October.

Kinloch Rannoch (Perthshire). Loch Rannoch Conservation Assn has fishing on Loch Rannoch; brown trout, pike and char. Permits from hon sec, and local shops and hotels. For **Dunalastair Loch** contact Lassintullich Fisheries (tel: 08822 238); brown trout, 5 boats, no bank

The Ardeonaig Hotel
Loch Tay

Salmon and Trout fishing on Loch Tay. River fishing can be arranged on several local rivers. For brochure contact us on (Killin) 0567 820 400 (Fax: 0567 820 282)

fishing, fly only. Moor of Rannoch Hotel, Rannoch Station PH17 2QA, has trout fishing on **L Laidon, R Gaur** and **Dubh Lochan**, which is stocked with brown trout. Rannoch & District AC has fishing on **Loch Eigheach**, Rannoch Station; brown trout and perch. Fly fishing only. Bank fishing only. June best month. St £15, wt £8, dt £3, from J Brown, The Square, Kinloch Rannoch; and Moor of Rannoch Hotel, Rannoch Station. Tackle shop: Country Store. Hotel: Dunalastair.

LYON (near Loch Tay): Good salmon and trout river in lovely valley.

Aberfeldy (Perthshire). Salmon and brown trout fishing on **Lyon**; max 4 rods; no bait fishing. Permits from Coshieville Hotel, by Aberfeldy PH15 2NE. Rods and ghillies available for hire.

Fortingall (Perthshire). Fortingall Hotel has 3m on Lyon; dt £20 (salmon) and £5 (trout). Also **River Tay** and **Loch Tay** by arrangement from £20 per day. Special rates for guests. Apply to Alan Schofield,

Fortingall Hotel, By Aberfeldy, Perthshire PH15 2NQ (tel. 0887 830 367).

DOCHART (feeds Loch Tay):

Killin (Perthshire). At confluence of Dochart and Lochay, near head of Loch Tay. Salmon fishing best in July, Aug and Sept. Trout numerous and run to a fair size. Water is very deep and sluggish from Luib to Bovain, but above and as far as Loch Dochart there are some capital streams and pools. Auchlyne & Suie Estate Water; trout and salmon. Permits issued by G D Coyne, Keeper's Cottage, Auchlyne, Killin FK21 8RG; Luib Hotel; and Glendochart Caravan Park. Trout fishing best April-May, good run of autumn salmon. Ardeonaig Hotel *(see advt)*, South Lochtayside, Perthshire FK21 8SU, has own harbour with 4 boats on **Loch Tay**; salmon, trout and char. Hotel fishing for residents only. Loch Tay Highland Lodges, Milton Morenish, by Killin, have salmon and trout fishing on Loch Tay; boats available.

Check before you go

While every effort has been made to ensure that the information given in **Where to Fish** *is correct, the position is continually changing, and anglers are urged, in their own interests, to make preliminary enquiries before travelling to selected venues.*

THURSO

A noted salmon river and one of the earliest in Scotland. However, the spring run has not been so good in recent times. Water level is regulated by a weir at Loch More on the upper reaches. The river is entirely preserved.

Thurso (Caithness). Salmon fishing (fly only) can be arranged through Thurso Fisheries Ltd, Thurso East, Thurso KW14 8HW (tel: 0847 63134). Bookings usually by week, fortnight or month, but day lets arranged. Weekly charges, including accommodation, range from £515 to £900, according to date. Fishing improves progressively from opening on Jan 11 to close on Oct 5. First-class loch, burn and river fishing for trout. Thurso AA has one beat; members only, but possibility of permit if no members fishing. Royal Hotel has rights on **Loch Calder**; free to guests; trout. Pentland Hotel has rights on **Lochs Watten, St John's** and **Stemster**, and can arrange fishing on **Loch Calder**; boats available; trout. St Clair Arms Hotel, Castletown, has rights on all these lochs and **Loch Hielan**. Tackle shops: Harper's Fly Fishing, Drill Hall, Sinclair Street; Pentland Sports Emporium. 14 Olrig St.

Halkirk (Caithness). The Ulbster Arms Hotel has fishing on **Loch Calder** and many other hill lochs; excellent accommodation and fishing, £410-£900 per week. Salmon fishing on **Thurso River.** Information from Secretary, Thurso Fisheries Ltd, Thurso East, Thurso, Caithness KW14 8HW.

Dunnet (Caithness). House of the Northern Gate, Dunnet Estate. 7 Estate Lochs for good brown trout. £100 per day inclusive (inc. drinks). Fishing for residents only. Fishing and boats on St Johns Loch. Sea

fishing from Estate boat. Contact Michael Draper (084 785 622) *(see advt)*. St John's Loch AA has fishing on **St John's Loch**; bank and boat fishing. Permits from Northern Sands Hotel. Hotel can arrange fishing on other lochs; also some river fishing for salmon and sea trout.

TWEED

Rises in corner formed by watersheds of Clyde and Annan, and flows over 100m to North Sea at Berwick-upon-Tweed, forming, for much of its course, boundary between England and Scotland. Tweed is second only to Tay in its fame as a Scottish salmon river. It contains over 300 named casts and its salmon harvest is considerable. Sport more affected by height of the water than most rivers. Tweed produces strain of sea trout which are remarkable both for size and distance they are known to travel in sea. Formerly called bull trout, they rise badly to fly. Excellent brown trout in main river and tributaries, and grayling. 'Tweedline' is a service for fishermen provided by the Tweed Foundation, a charitable trust established by the River Tweed Commissioners to promote the development of salmon and trout stocks in the Tweed river system.

'Tweedline' provides information on: fishing catches and prospects, tel: 0898 666 410 (T Hunter, Anglers Choice Tackle Shop, Melrose, Roxburghshire); river levels, tel: 0898 666 411 (The Tweed River Purification Board, Mossilee Road, Galashiels, Selkirkshire); and last minute fishing lets, tel: 0898 666 412 (J H Leeming, Letting Agents, Stichill House, Kelso, Roxburghshire TD5 7TB). For further information write to Tweed Foundation, Dock Rd, Tweedmouth, Berwick-upon-Tweed TD15 1HE.

Berwick-upon-Tweed (Northumberland). Salmon, sea trout, trout, grayling, coarse fish. Tidal Tweed gives free fishing for roach and grayling. Salmon fishing on Tweed available from J H Leeming, Letting Agents, Stichill House, Kelso, Roxburghshire TD5 7TB; 11 beats between Tweedhill, near Berwick, and Peebles; £25-£500 per rod per day; early booking advisable. Berwick and Dist AA has brown trout fishing on 8m of **River Whiteadder**, which joins Tweed 1m from Berwick. St £25 (OAP & jun £10), wt £10, dt £4. Permits from Game Fair, Marygate; Jobsons, Marygate; Allanton Inn, Main St, Allanton; Canty's Brig, Cantys, Nr Berwick; and Hoolets Nest, Paxton. **Till** enters Tweed 2½m above Norham, 9m from Berwick. **Coldingham Loch**, near Great North Road, Ayton. Brown and rainbow trout, 4 boats, bank fishing for 4 rods. Permits from Dr E J Wise, West Loch House, Coldingham, Berwickshire (tel: 08907 71270), who has chalets and cottages to let. Booking essential. Coldingham is noted for the quality and size of the trout caught there. Tackle shops: Game Fair, 12 Marygate; and Jobsons, Marygate. Hotels: Castle; Kings Arms; Chirnside Hall, Chirnside; Hay Farmhouse, Cornhill-on-Tweed; Coach House, Crookham, Cornhill-on-Tweed. The owner of Wallace Guest House is prepared to arrange early starts and late returns for fishermen and has private parking; apply to J Hoggan, Wallace Guest House, Wallace Green, Berwick upon Tweed (tel. 0289 306539). **Horncliffe** (Northumberland). Tidal. Salmon, trout, grayling, roach, dace and eel. No permits required for trout and coarse fishing. Salmon fishing on Tweedhill Beat; 3m single bank; 6 rods; 2 ghillies; 2 huts. Available from J H Leeming, Letting Agent, Kelso.
Norham (Northumberland). Salmon, trout. Salmon fishing on Ladykirk and Pedwell Beats available from J H Leeming, Letting Agent, Kelso. Ladykirk, 3½m single bank, 4 huts, 5 boats and up to 1-5 ghillies, 6-10 rods; over 3 years average catch 195; also good sea trout water. Pedwell, 1½m single bank for 2 rods with hut, boat and ghillie; Fri and Sat only. Ladykirk & Norham AIA has much water in the district - brown trout, grayling and coarse fish. Reputed to be one of the best waters along border. St £20, wt £12 and dt £3. Permits from Mace Shop; Masons Arms Hotel; and Victoria Hotel.

Coldstream (Berwickshire). Tweed; salmon, sea trout. Salmon fishing on The Lees and West Learmouth Beats available from J H Leeming, Letting Agent, Kelso. The Lees is a prime quality spring and autumn beat including the well known Temple Pool; 2m, 4 rods, 2-3 ghillies, 2 huts, 4 boats. West Learmouth is a good spring and autumn beat for 2 rods opposite The Lees; ⅔m of single bank with boat and ghillie. Tillmouth Park Hotel has salmon, sea trout and brown trout fishing; boats and ghillies available. Special terms for residents. Facilities for anglers include rod hire, freezing, tackle shop and drying room. Contact Tillmouth Park Hotel, Cornhill-on-Tweed, Northumberland TD12 4UU (tel. 0890 882255). Hotels: Collingwood Arms; Purves Hall.
Kelso (Roxburghshire). Salmon and sea trout preserved, trout and grayling. Salmon and sea trout fishing can be obtained daily during summer months on some of the best beats of the Tweed, for further information contact James H Leeming, Stichill House, Stichill, By Kelso (tel: 0573 470 280). Kelso AA has about 8m of Tweed and **Teviot**, and short stretch on **River Eden**; brown trout and grayling. No Sunday fishing; size limit 10in; restrictions on spinning; trout sea-

son, April 1 to Sept 30. Trout fishing good. St £15, wt £8, dt £4. Concessions for OAPs and juniors. Permits from local tackle shops. Brown and rainbow trout fishing on **Wooden Loch** at Eckford. Boat available. No bank fishing. Advance booking necessary. Apply A H Graham, Gamekeeper's House, Eckford, Kelso. Tackle shops: Forrest & Son, 35 The Square; Intersport, 43 The Square; Tweedside Tackle, 36 Bridge St. Hotels: Cross Keys; Ednam House; Sunlaws House, Heiton, By Kelso.

St Boswells (Roxburghshire). St Boswells & Newtown District AA rent miscellaneous stretches on River Tweed between Ravenswood and Mertown; brown trout; rod limits on 4 stretches. Permits from Agnes Laing, Newsagent; Christine Grant, Newsagent, Newtown St Boswells; Railway Hotel, Newtown St Boswells; and Anglers Choice, Melrose. Assn also has rainbow trout fishing on **Eildon Hall Pond**, nr Newtown St Boswells. Permits from Langlands Garage, Newtown St Boswells. Hotel: Buccleuch Arms; Railway, Newtown St Boswells; Dryburgh Abbey, Dryburgh.

Melrose (Roxburghshire). Salmon fishing on Bemersyde Beat, prime beat superbly set in beautiful wooded gorge; 1m with 6 rods, 1-2 ghillies, 4 boats. Apply to J H Leeming, Letting Agent, Kelso. Melrose and Dist AA has several stretches open to visitors for trout and grayling fishing. No Sunday fishing; no spinning or use of natural minnow or maggot permitted. Tickets from Anglers' Choice, The Square. Hotels: Burts.

Earlston (Berwickshire). A good centre for Leader and Tweed trout fishing. Earlston AA controls about 5m of **Leader** adjacent to Earlston, with the exception of two small private stretches. St £5 (OAP & jun £1), dt £1, from local hotels and shops; and Anglers Choice, Melrose. No Sunday fishing and Saturday fishing for st holders only. 2 day permits available at £1 each on River Tweed at Gledswood Estate for st holders. Other portions of Tweed are reserved. No salmon or sea-trout fishing is available on trouting portions of Tweed. Hotel: Red Lion.

Galashiels (Selkirkshire). Salmon fishing on Fairnlee Beat, good varied autumn beat in lovely scenery; 3m of single bank, 20 small pools; 9 rods; ghillie, huts and full facilities. Available from J H Leeming, Letting Agent, Kelso. Gala AA has trout fishing on 10-12m of Tweed; st £15,

wt £10, dt £5 (no Sunday tickets; no spinning). Tickets from J & A Turnbull, Tackle Shop, 30 Bank St; and Anglers' Choice, Market Square, Melrose. April to Sept provides best daytime sport; Mid-June to Aug best evenings. **Gala Water** is included in permit. The School of Casting, Salmon and Trout Fishing, offer weekly salmon and trout fly fishing courses throughout the season, mainly based at the Tweed Valley Hotel, Walkerburn, Peeblesshire, but also for the '94 season 3 weeks of courses during the summer from the Glen Affric Hotel, Cannich, By Beauly, Inverness-shire. Further information from Michael Waller or Margaret Cockburn, The School of Casting, Salmon and Trout Fishing, Station House, Clovenfords, Galashiels, Selkirkshire TD1 3LU (tel. 089685 293).

Selkirk (Selkirkshire). Salmon fishing preserved. Good centre for Tweed, **Yarrow** and **Ettrick**, covering 80m of trout fishing. Selkirk and Dist AA has water on Ettrick and Yarrow; restocks annually from own hatchery; size limit 10". Permits from hon sec; Gordon Arms; Bridge End PO; Honey Cottage Caravan Site; P & E Scott, High St. Trout average four to the pound and go up to 3lb. No spinning allowed. Hotels: Glen, Heatherlie House, Woodburn, Philipburn House.

Walkerburn (Peeblesshire). Salmon, trout. Tweed Valley Hotel, EH43 6AA, has salmon fishing on hotel's private beat. Peak season spring and autumn. Hotel also has river and loch, trout and grayling fishing on private and Peeblesshire Trout FA water; available all season. Hotel offers fishing courses at £97.50 one week adult. Tackle hire available. Season: salmon, 1 Feb-30 Nov.

Innerleithen (Borders). Salmon, trout. Salmon fishing on Traquair Beat, good late autumn beat in grounds of Scotland's oldest inhabited historic house; 3m of easy casting and access for 10 rods; ghillie. Available from J H Leeming, Letting Agent, Kelso. Peeblesshire Trout FA has trout and grayling fishing on Tweed; tickets are available at Sonny Sports, 29 High St; and Traquair Arms Hotel.

Peebles (Borders). Salmon fishing on approx 1½ miles of River Tweed. Season Feb 21 to Nov 30. Fly fishing only. Tickets (limited in number) issued by Peeblesshire Salmon FA. St £130, apply by Jan 31, to Blackwood & Smith WS, 39 High St, Peebles EH45 8AH. Dt £25 and £35 - 15 Oct to 30 Nov only. Permits from

Well-known Scottish angler and angling writer, Bill Currie, with a small but shapely Autumn fish from the Tweed.

Tweeddale Tackle Centre, 1 Bridgegate, Peebles EH45 8RZ (tel. 0721 720979). Salmon and trout fishing on Town Water and Crown Water. Permits: £44 per 3 day, 16 Sept - 30 Nov; £11 per week, 21 Feb - 14 Sept. Apply to Tweeddale District Council, Rosetta Road, Peebles. Peeblesshire Trout FA has approx 23m on Tweed and 5m on **Lyne**; trout and grayling. Season April 1 to Sept 30. No spinning or float fishing. Fly only April and Sept and all season on upper reaches. Fish under 9" must be returned. Waders desirable. Good trout April/May on wet fly then dry best. St £24 (per beat), wt £18, dt £6. Permits from hon sec (tel: 0721 720131); Tweeddale Tackle Centre; Green Tree Hotel; Peebles Hotel Hydro; and Rosetta Caravan Park. Tweeddale Tackle Centre, besides issuing permits on the waters above, will arrange fishing on private beats for salmon, sea trout and trout; and also arrange casting tuition by qualified specialists in all fly fishing techniques. Kingsmuir Hotel, Springhill Rd, Peebles EH45 9EP (tel. 0721 720151), can arrange salmon and trout fishing on Rivers Tweed, Lyne and tributaries.

Tweedsmuir (Peeblesshire). Crook Inn issues permits for Peeblesshire Trout FA water on Tweed. **Talla Reservoir** (300 acres) and **Fruid Reservoir** (293 acres); wild brown trouts. Talla: fly only. Fruid: fly fishing, spinning and worm fishing. 2 boats and bank fishing on each reservoir. Permits from Reservoir Superintendent, Victoria Lodge, Tweedsmuir (tel: 08997 209). **Megget Reservoir**, brown trout; permits from Tibbie Shiels Inn, St Mary's Loch. Hotels: Kingsmuir; Park.

Tributaries of the Tweed

WHITEADDER: Runs from junction with Tweed via Cantys Bridge and Allanton Bridge to source. A good trout stream. Upper waters, from Blanerne Bridge to source, including tributaries, are largely controlled by Whiteadder AA; st £10, dt £2.50 from bailiffs, hotels and public houses. Tickets must be obtained before fishing begins. Concessions to OAP, ladies and juniors. Assn has restocked water with brown trout. Trout av ½lb. Best months June-August. Many burns.

Allanton (Berwickshire). Blackadder joins river here. Fishing reported good. Whiteadder AA has from above Blanerne Bridge to source. 1¼m Berwick and Dist AA water from ½m above Allanton Bridge to Cantys Bridge; trout; visitors living outside 15m radius; wt and dt. St and dt for water above Blanerne Bridge obtainable locally. Hotel: Red Lion.

Chirnside (Berwickshire). Trout. Chirnside is good centre for Whiteadder. From here to source, except for stretches at Ninewells, Abbey St Bathans Estate, Chirnside Paper Mills and Cumledge Bridge, river is controlled by Whiteadder AA, including all tributaries entering above Chirnside, except **Monynut** above Bankend; **Fasney** above Fasney Bridge; and certain stretches of the **Dye**. Tickets from bailiffs, hotels and public houses. **River Eye**, runs parallel to Whiteadder a few miles to N, entering sea at Eyemouth. Eye Water AC has water on River Eye and **Ale**

Water; river stocked annually with brown trout. Tickets from McMurchies, High Street, Eyemouth. Hotels: Mitchells; Red Lion; Waterloo Arms; Ship, Whale, Home Arms, Dolphin, all in Eyemouth; Red Lion, Ayton.

Duns (Berwickshire). Trout. The following streams are within easy reach: **Blackadder, Whiteadder, Fasney, Bothwell, Dye, Blacksmill, Monynut** and **Watch**. These, except Blackadder, are, with main stream, largely controlled by Whiteadder AA. Riparian owners may grant permission. Tackle shop: R Welsh, 28 Castle Street. Hotels: Bungalow, Blanerne, White Swan, Barnikin, Plough, Black Bull, Whip & Saddle.

Longformacus (Borders). Some 7m from Duns. On Dye, Watch and Blacksmill burns. Whiteadder runs near Rathburne Hotel. Permits for Whiteadder AA fisheries are available at Todlee Cottage, Ellemford, 3m from Longformacus. Brown and rainbow trout fishing on **Watch Reservoir**; fly only. Permits from W F Renton, The Watch Fly Reservoir.

Cranshaws (Borders). Lothian Regional Council manage **Whiteadder Reservoir**; 193 acres, brown trout. Fly only. Bag limit 10 trout. 3 boats and bank fishing (from 1 Jun). Permits from Mrs Kerr, Waterkeeper's House, Hungry Snout, Whiteadder Reservoir (tel: 036 17 362).

BLACKADDER (tributary of Whiteadder): Very good for brown trout early in season.

Greenlaw (Borders). About 12m held by Greenlaw AC. Season from 1 April to 6 Oct. St £5 and dt £2; from Doigs Store, Post Office, The Cafe, and all hotels. Concessions for OAP and jun. Hotel: Blackadder; Castle.

TILL and BREAMISH: Trout, sea trout, salmon, good grayling, some pike and perch.

Milfield (Northumberland). Local beats on River Till all have good seasonal runs of salmon and sea trout with resident stocks of brown trout and grayling. No Sunday fishing. Ford Public Water, 3m stretch; daily, weekly and seasonal tickets available from Post Office, Milfield; and Post Office, Ford. Redscar Beat, 1m stretch; let by day or week, max 3 rods. Tindlehouse Beat, 2m stretch; let by day or week, max 4 rods. Bookings for Redscar and Tindlehouse Beats from Brian R Thompson, River Keeper, Redscar Cottage, Milfield, Wooler, Northumberland NE71 6JQ (tel. 06686 223).

Wooler (Northumberland). Good centre for Till (2m N) and **Glen**, which join below Wooler, running through Milfield Plain into Tweed, and are open for sea trout and salmon angling from Feb to Nov. Whitling early summer if conditions right; later on large fish numerous. Wooler and Doddington AA preserves 2m of the Till and 1m of **Wooler Water**; limited dt £6 issued to visitors staying locally, but not for Sundays; fixed-spool reels prohibited; no maggot fishing; fly only, Feb-April inclusive and from Sept 14 to Nov 30. Tickets from hon sec. Some miles from Wooler, at Bewick Bridge, Breamish becomes Till. Wading in Till dangerous. White Swan Inn, Yetholm,

A nice one comes ashore at Tweedswood. *Photo: Eric Chalker.*

can give details of fishing on **Bowmont** and **Kale Waters.** Trout (small), grayling, with good sea trout in wet season.

Chatton (Northumberland). Trout, grayling; and some fine roach: preserved by Chatton AA for 6½m. Limited number of associated members' tickets, waiting list 5 years; st apply by Jan 1 to hon sec; dt from hotel.

EDEN: Trout

Ednam (Borders). No salmon fishing available to general public. Kelso AA has trout fishing. Permits from Kelso tackle shops.

Gordon (Berwickshire). Permits for brown trout fishing from J H Fairgrieve, Burnbrae, Gordon. No spinning. No Sunday fishing.

TEVIOT: First class for trout and grayling.

Roxburgh (Roxburghshire). Kelso AA controls some miles of brown trout fishing on Teviot and Tweed. Visitors tickets from Kelso tackle shops.

Eckford (Borders). Eckford AA issues dt for Teviot; salmon and trout. The Buccleuch Estate has Eckford Beat, 1m: 1½m on **Kale Water:** and **Wooden Loch.** Tickets from Waterkeeper, Keeper's Cottage, Eckford (tel: 08355 255). Morebattle & Dist AA has brown trout fishing on Kale Water, **Bowmont Water** and **Oxnam Water.** Permits from hon sec; the Garage; and Templehall Hotel.

Hawick (Roxburghshire). Hawick AC has fishing on River Teviot and tributaries **Slitrig, Borthwick** and **Ale;** salmon, sea trout, brown trout and grayling. Club also has fishing on Lochs **Alemoor,** pike, perch and brown trout; **Hellmoor,** brown trout, perch and pike; **Acremoor,** brown trout and perch; **Williestruther,** rainbow trout and brown trout; **Acreknowe,** rainbow trout and brown trout; **Synton Mossend,** rainbow trout and brown trout. Permits from hon sec; The Pet Store, 1 Union Street; and Country Sports, Jedburgh. Hotels: Elm House.

Jedburgh (Roxburghshire). Jedforest AA has water on Teviot, salmon, trout and grayling; **River Jed,** trout; **River Oxnam,** trout; and **Hass Loch,** rainbow trout. Concessions for OAP & jun. Visitors permits for salmon from hon sec; for Hass Loch from W Renwick, Broombaulks, Camptown; for trout from Sanford's Game and Country Enterprises, 6/8 Canongate and W Shaw, Canongate. Jedforest Hotel has stretch of Jed Water,

which runs by hotel (brown trout). Royal Hotel can arrange fishing in Jed Water and Teviot.

LEADER: Trout (4 to lb).

Lauder (Borders). Lauderdale AA controls 6m of Leader and 20m of tributaries upwards from Whitslaid Bridge to Carfraemill with the exception of waters in Thirlestane Castle policies. St £4, wt £3, dt £2 from hon sec, shops, hotels and Post Office. Earlston AA has water. Hotels: Tower, Oxton; Carfrae Mill (4m from Lauder); Lauderdale; Black Bull.

Oxton (Borders). Lauderdale AA has Leader Water from Carfraemill and tributaries.

GALA WATER: Popular trout water; fish average about 5 to lb.

Stow (Borders). Salmon and trout fishing on Gala Water. No permit required for local trout fishing. Royal Hotel stands on banks of Gala; apply to The Royal Hotel, Townfoot, Stow, Nr Galashiels TD1 2SG (tel. 0578 730 226).

ETTRICK and YARROW: Salmon.

Bowhill (Selkirkshire). The Buccleuch Estates has 4½m on River Ettrick; salmon and trout; fly only. Dt £20-35. Estate also has brown and rainbow trout fishing on **Bowhill Upper Loch;** fly only; 2 rods per boat and limit of 8 fish per boat. Dt £35 per boat. Permits from Estate Office, Bowhill, Selkirk TD7 5ES (tel: 0750 20753). All trout fishing in Ettrick and Yarrow by ticket; water being restocked with brown trout by Selkirk AA. Permits from hon sec; Gordon Arms, Selkirk; Bridge End PO; Honey Cottage Caravan Site, Selkirk; P & E Scott, High St, Selkirk.

Ettrick Bridge (Selkirkshire). Ettrickshaws Hotel issues permits for salmon and brown trout fishing on Ettrick.

St Mary's Loch (Selkirkshire). Lothian Regional Council manage **Megget Reservoir;** 640 acres; stocked brown trout. Fly only. 6 boats and bank fishing. Bag limit: 6 trout. Permits from Tibbie Shiels Inn (tel: 0750 42231). St Mary's Loch AC has fishing on **St Mary's Loch** (500 acres) and **Loch o' The Lowes** (100 acres); brown trout, pike and perch. Boat and bank fishing; fly and spinning; no private boats allowed. Boats available from Keeper; outboard motors are really essential for boats on St Mary's Loch, but they must be supplied by the angler as none are available for hire. Permits from Mr Brown, Keeper, Henderland East Cottage, Cappercleuch (tel: 0750 42243); Tibbie Shiels Inn; The Glen Cafe, Cappercleuch; Gordon Arms Hotel, Yarrow; Anglers' Choice, Melrose; Sonny's Sport Shop, Innerleithen; Tweeddale Tackle Centre, Peebles.

TYNE (Lothian)

Rises on north slopes of Lammermuir Hills and flows about 25m to North Sea a little south of Whitberry Ness, known best as brown trout stream.

Haddington (East Lothian). Trout. East Lothian AA controls most of water in county. St £6 and dt £2.50 from Main & Son, 87 High Street, and L Walker, 3 Bridge Street, East Linton; also river watchers. No Sunday fishing; no spinning. Concessions OAP & jun. **Maltings Fishery** near Dunbar; brown and rainbow trout; fly only. All year for rainbow. Permits from Dunbar Trout Farm, West Barn, Dunbar, East Lothian (tel: 0368 63244). North Berwick AC has no club water but organises 15 outings per year on various waters, for example, Loch Leven, Loch Fitty and North Third Fishery. **Hopes Reservoir**, near Gifford; 35 acre; brown trout. Fly only. Bag limit 10 trout. 2 boats. No bank fishing. Permits from Lothian Regional Council, Dept of Water and Drainage, Alderston House, Haddington (tel: 062 082 4131). Edinburgh Coarse Anglers have fishing on **Danskine Loch**, also near Gifford; roach, perch, carp, crucian, carp. Season 1 Mar - 20 Oct. Strictly members only. Membership £15 plus £10 joining fee. Apply to hon sec.

UGIE

A small river entering the sea at Peterhead. Salmon, good sea trout, some brown trout. Salmon and sea trout best from July to October; good run of finnock in February and March.

Peterhead (Aberdeenshire). Permits available for approx 13m of fishing leased by Ugie AA. St £80, wt £30, dt £15 from Robertson Sports, 1 Kirk Street, Peterhead (tel. 0779 72584); and Dick's Sports, 54 Broad Street, Fraserburgh. Concessions OAP & jun. **Crimonmogate Fisheries**, 9m N of Peterhead; fly fishing on two trout lakes. Crimonmogate Lake, 6 acres, wild brown trout and stocked with rainbow. Season 1 Apr-30 Sep. Limit 5 fish. **Loch Logie**, newly formed, 5 acres, stocked rainbow trout and wild brown trout. Open all year. Limit 4 fish. Tuition for beginners and tackle hire available. Permits issued on bank. For bookings and enquiries contact Crimonmogate Estate Office, Lonmay, by Fraserburgh, Aberdeenshire AB43 4UE (tel: 0346 32203). Hotels: Albert, Waterside Inn.

Tributaries of the Ugie

STRICHEN (or North Ugie):
Strichen (Aberdeenshire). Free trout fishing (subject to permission of riparian owners). Salmon fishing strictly preserved.

URR

Drains Loch Urr and flows to Solway. Late run of salmon; also sea trout, herling and brown trout.

Dalbeattie (Kirkcudbrightshire). Dalbeattie AA has 3½m both banks; salmon, grilse, sea trout, herling and brown trout. Assn has rainbow trout fishing on **Dalbeattie Reservoir**; fly only; stocked with brown and rainbow trout. Permits from M

Fishing available?

If you own, manage, or know of first-class fishing available to the public which should be considered for inclusion in **Where to Fish** *please apply to the publishers (address in the front of the book) for a form for submission, on completion, to the Editor. (Inclusion is at the sole discretion of the Editor).*

BLACK PT NYMPH

TOBACCO PT NYMPH

DAMSEL NYMPH

GOLDEN OLIVE
MIDGE PUPA.

TANDEM MARABOU MUDDLERS.

WET FLIES AND NYMPHS

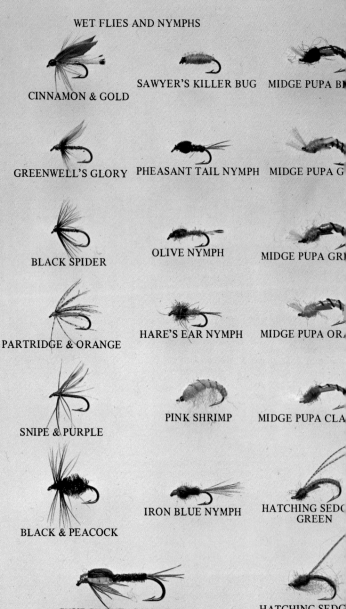

PETER ROSS

CINNAMON & GOLD

SAWYER'S KILLER BUG

MIDGE PUPA B

BUTCHER

GREENWELL'S GLORY

PHEASANT TAIL NYMPH

MIDGE PUPA G

MARCH BROWN

BLACK SPIDER

OLIVE NYMPH

MIDGE PUPA GR

BLUE ZULU

PARTRIDGE & ORANGE

HARE'S EAR NYMPH

MIDGE PUPA OR

SOLDIER PALMER

SNIPE & PURPLE

PINK SHRIMP

MIDGE PUPA CLA

INVICTA

BLACK & PEACOCK

IRON BLUE NYMPH

HATCHING SEDG
GREEN

BLACK PENNELL

CHURCH PHEASANT TAIL
LIME GREEN

HATCHING SEDG
BROWN

MALLARD & CLARET

CHURCH PHEASANT TAIL
ORANGE

MAYFLY NYMPH

McCowan & Son, 43 High Street. Castle Douglas AA has about 5m of Urr; brown trout, sea trout and salmon. Assn also has fishing on **Loch Roan**, 60 acres, no bank fishing, 8 fish limit. Permits from

Tommy's Sports Goods, 178 King St, Castle Douglas. Rainbow trout fishing on **Barend Loch**; fly only. By the hour. Rods for hire. Permits from Barend Chalet Park, Sandyhills, By Dalbeattie.

WEST COAST STREAMS AND LOCHS

Some complex fisheries and one or two smaller - though not necessarily less sporting - streams are grouped here for convenience. Other west coast waters will be found in the main alphabetical list.

AILORT

A short but good sea trout river which drains Loch Eilt and enters sea through saltwater Loch Ailort. One of the few rivers where run of genuine spring sea trout takes place.

Lochailort (Inverness-shire). Salmon and sea trout fishing on **Loch Eilt** and River Ailort; loch is renowned for some of largest sea trout caught in Britain. Fly only. Permits from Lochailort Inn. **Loch Morar**, a few miles north; good brown trout and occasional salmon and sea trout. Fly, spinning and trolling allowed. Fishing from banks free. Boats available from A G MacLeod, Morar Hotel, Morar, Mallaig, when not wanted by guests.

LOCH BROOM (including Rivers Broom, Dundonnell, Garvie, Oscaig and Ullapool)

Achiltibuie (Ross-shire). Sea trout, brown trout and sea fishing. Summer Isles Hotel has much fishing for guests on rivers and lochs in the vicinity. Sea trout and brown trout: **Lochs Oscaig** and **Lurgain**. Boat on Oscaig £24.50 (electric outboard £6); no boats on Lurgain. Brown trout lochs, dt £5. Ghillies can be arranged £20 per day extra. Own boats for sea fishing. Apply to Robert Mark Irvine, Summer Isles Hotel, Achiltibuie, By Ullapool, Ross-shire IV26 2YG (tel: 085 482 282). For salmon, sea trout and brown trout fishing on River Garvie, **Polly Lochs, Loch Sionascaig** and **Loch Bad a'Ghaill**. Dt £3 (bank), £12 (boat), £8 (outboard). Also brown trout fishing on **Black Loch** and **Stac Loch**. Apply to Inverpolly Estate Office, Inverpolly (tel: 0854 82 452).
Ullapool (Ross-shire). **Ullapool River**, sea trout, brown trout and salmon; dt £15 (upper beat) and £5 (lower beat). **Loch Achall**, salmon, sea and brown trout; dt £12 (boat) and £5 (bank). Permits from Ullasports. Salmon and sea trout fishing on **River Kaniard** at Strathkanaird; prices according to time in season. Full details from Ullasport. Ullapool AC has brown trout fishing on Strathkanaird hill

lochs: **Lochs Dubh** (brown trout), **Beinn Dearg** (brown and rainbow trout) and **na Moille** (brown trout and salmon). Membership for residents in area. 3 rainbow limit, 3 salmon limit, no brown trout limit. All lochs fly only except Loch na Moille where under 15's may spin or bait fish. Local annual pike fishing competition on third Sunday in October. Day tickets £10. Permits from Ullasport. Tackle shops: Ullasport, West Argyle St (tel: 0854 612621), who have large range of fly rods, reels and flies; and Lochbroom Hardware, Shore Street (tel: 0854 612356). Hotel: Argyle; Arch Inn.
Leckmelm (Ross-shire). Brown trout fishing on Leckmelm Estate lochs; excellent fish up to 4lb. Permits from Leckmelm Holiday Cottages (tel: 0854 612471).
Inverbroom (Ross-shire). **River Broom** is a spate river sometimes suitable for fly-spinning. Inverlael Lodge has approx 1½m, single bank, including 10 pools. The bottom pool is tidal. Inverlael Lodge also has fishing on **River Lael** and on some hill lochs. Apply to Inverlael Lodge, Loch Broom, by Ullapool (tel: 0854 612471).
Dundonnell (Ross-shire). **Dundonnell River;** salmon and sea trout.

LOCH DUICH (including Shiel and Croe)

Glenshiel, by Kyle of Lochalsh (Ross-shire). Salmon and sea trout. Fishing

available on **River Croe**, a spate-river with late runs. Dt £8-£10 from National

Trust for Scotland, Morvich Farm House, Inverinate, by Kyle IV40 8HQ. Reduc-

tions for members. Sea fishing on Loch Duich.

EACHAIG (including Loch Eck)

Drains Loch Eck and flows about 5m into Atlantic by way of Holy Loch and Firth of Clyde. Salmon and sea trout.

Kilmun (Argyll). On Holy Loch and Firth of Clyde. Eachaig enters sea here. Salmon, sea trout in Loch Eck (5m), where Whistlefield Inn, Loch Eck, has boats for guests: fly best at head of loch where **River Cur** enters. Other hotel: Coylet, Eachaie.

Dunoon (Argyll). Salmon and sea trout; limited weekly lets available on River Eachaig from R C G Teasdale, Fishing Agent, Quarry Cottage, Rashfield, Nr Dunoon, Argyll PA23 8QT (tel. 0369 84 510). Coylet Hotel and Whistlefield Inn have salmon (mainly trolling), sea trout and brown trout fishing on **Loch Eck** for guests (preferential terms for residents); st £40, wt £15 and dt £3; boats available at hotels. Loch Eck is about 7m long. No

good for salmon until early June; best in August, Sept. Apply to Whistlefield Inn, Loch Eck, By Dunoon PA23 8SG (tel: 036 986 440). Dunoon & Dist AC has **Rivers Cur, Finnart** and **Massan,** salmon and sea trout, any legal lure; **Lochs Tarsan** and **Loskin,** brown trout, fly only; and **Dunoon Reservoir,** rainbow trout, fly only. Permits from Purdies of Argyll, 112 Argyll Street (tel: 0369 3232). Permits for River Finnart; sea trout, and occasional salmon; from S Share, Keeper's Cottage, Ardentinny, Argyll PA23 8TS. Glendaruel Hotel at **Glendaruel** (18m) has salmon, sea trout and trout fishing on **River Ruel** (best July to Sept). Permits £1 day. Hotel: Clifton.

LOCH FYNE (including Rivers Douglas, Fyne, Kinglas, Shira and Garron, and Dubh Loch)

Large sea loch on west coast of Argyll, which provides good sea fishing and first-class salmon and sea trout in streams. These are spate rivers; best from June to September.

Inveraray (Argyll). Argyll Estates have fishing on Rivers **Aray,** Shira, Douglas and Garron, Dubh Loch, and hill lochs. Weekly lets inclusive of accommodation, available. No Sunday fishing. Apply to

The Factor, Argyll Estates Office, Cherry Park, Inveraray PA32 8XE (tel: 0499 2203). Salmon and sea trout fishing on R Douglas; fly only. Permits available from Argyll Caravan Park.

GAIRLOCH

A sea loch on the west coast of Ross.

Gairloch (Ross-shire). Gairloch AA manages more than 30 trout lochs to W of Gairloch, some easily accessible, but the best involve a good walk. Permits from Wild Cat Stores; and Mr K Gunn, Strath, Gairloch. Permits for **Fionn Loch** also from Mr K Gunn. Gairloch Hotel has sea

angling; and trout fishing in hotel's own hill lochs. Permits for **Loch na h-Oidhche** from Mr H Davis, Creag Beag, Gairloch; fishing from mid-June. Salmon and sea trout fishing in **River Kerry,** a spate river; easily accessible; season May-Oct; best Aug-Oct. Permits from

---

Check before you go

While every effort has been made to ensure that the information given in **Where to Fish** *is correct, the position is continually changing, and anglers are urged, in their own interests, to make preliminary enquiries before travelling to selected venues. This is especially important with reference to prices quoted. Inevitably the rate of inflation is affecting stability in this quarter. Anglers' attention is also drawn to the fact that the hotels mentioned under the various fishing stations do not necessarily have water of their own. Any amendments or further data for inclusion in subsequent editions, and any criticism, will be welcome.*

Creag Mor Hotel. Shieldaig Lodge Hotel, by Gairloch, has salmon and trout fishing on **Badachro River** and trout fishing on hill lochs. Casting instruction for salmon

and trout, rod repairs and special fly tying service available from D W Roxborough, The Old Police Station.

GLENELG

Rises in Glen More and flows about 10m to the sea at **Glenelg**. Salmon and sea-trout fishing preserved by owner of Scallasaig Lodge. Rod occasionally let for the day at owner's discretion.

LOCH LONG (including Rivers Finnart and Goil)

A sea loch opening into the Firth of Clyde. Good sea trout, some salmon in streams. Finnart good in spates. Forestry Commission intend to lease Rivers Finnart and Goil to local angling clubs but arrangements have not yet been finalized.

Ardentinny (Argyll). River Finnart enters Loch Long at Ardentinny. Dunoon and District AC lease **River Finnart** from Forestry Commission on condition that river is kept open to the public at a low cost. Grilse and sea trout, season July to mid-October. Small brown trout in plenty; wild stock and healthy. Catch and return policy advised for late coloured spawning fish. Spate and high rivers due to wet Argyll climate makes all parts of river fishable - not many permits. Fishing peaceful and enjoyable. Permits for River Finnart and advice on local fishing from S Share, River Warden, Keeper's Cottage, Ardentinny, Argyll PA23 8TS (tel. 036 981 228).

Arrochar (Dunbartonshire). Cobbler Hotel (tel 03012 238) overlooks Loch Long,

where good sea fishing obtainable. Hotel has trout fishing in **Loch Lomond** (1½m).

Carrick (Argyll). Carrick Castle Hotel has salmon, sea trout and brown trout on River and **Loch Goil**, free to guests. Boat on loch.

Lochgoilhead (Argyll). River Goil Angling Club has 15 years lease on **River Goil** fishings, and has bought the salmon netting stations on **Loch Goil** with the intention of closing them for good. Club also has plans to stock the river over the next few season. River Goil - salmon and sea trout. Loch Goil (sea fishing) - mackerel, dabs and cod. Permits, boat hire and accommodation from J Lomont, Shore House Inn (tel. 03013 340). A tackle shop in village and at Carrick Castle.

FIRTH OF LORN (including Loch Nell)

Forming the strait between Mull and the mainland on the west coast. Lochs Linnhe and Etive open into it. Good sea trout and a few salmon.

Oban (Argyll). Oban & Lorn AC has trout fishing on **Oude Reservoir** and on numerous lochs in the Lorn district. Oude Reservoir, stocked with brown trout; club boat often located on this loch; bank fishing can be difficult because of fluctuating water level. **Loch Nell**, salmon, sea trout, brown trout and char; salmon best in summer; sea trout all through season. Brown trout fishing on 25 lochs, including **Lochs Nant** and **Avich**. No bait fishing and fishing with more than one rod is illegal. Except for Loch Nell and Oude Reservoir, where spinning, bubble and fly are permitted, all lochs are fly only. There is a junior section which has separate outings and competitions; and juniors are given instruction, etc. Annual membership £12, wt £25, dt £5 and boat

£5. Permits from tackle shops in Oban; and Cuilfail Hotel, Kilmelford. Forestry Commission has brown and rainbow trout fishing on **Glen Dubh Reservoir**; fly only. Permits J Lyon, Appin View, Barcaldine, Argyll. Brown trout fishing on **Loch Gleann a'Bhearraidh** at Lerags; one boat available. Permits from Cologin Homes Ltd, Lerags, by Oban; and The Barn Bar, Lerags, by Oban. Tackle shops: Anglers Corner, John St, Oban PA34 5NS (tel. 0631 66374); David Graham's, 9-15 Combie St, Oban PA34 4HN (tel. 0631 62069). Hotel: Ayres; Columba; Manor House.

Kilninver (Argyll). On **Euchar** estuary (10m south of Oban on A816). Good salmon, sea trout and some brown trout fishing may be had from Mrs Mary

McCorkindale, Glenann, Kilninver, By Oban (tel: 08526 282). Boat + 2 rods on **Loch Scammadale** £10 per day. Bank and river fishing dt £2. As the Euchar is a spate river, bookings are not accepted more than a week in advance. Price concession for full week booking. Permits for Euchar also from Lt Col P S Sandilands, Lagganmore, Kilninver; salmon, sea trout and brown trout; fly only; 3 rods per day only; no Sunday fishing. **Knipoch**, by Oban (Argyll). **Dubh Loch** (Loch Leven and brown trout) and **Loch Seil**, (sea trout and brown trout); dt £5 with boat. **River Euchar**, salmon and sea trout; dt £5. **Loch Tralaig**, near Kilmelford; trout; bank fishing only. Permits from Mrs J Mellor, Barndromin Farm (tel: 085 26 273).

LOCH MELFORT

A sea loch opening into the Firth of Lorn south of Oban. Sea trout, mackerel, flounders, etc.

Kilmelford (Argyll) 15m from Oban. Cuilfail Hotel, Kilmelford, Argyll PA34 4UZ, can arrange fishing on **Lochs nan Drimnean** (10 min walk, trout; March-May, Aug-Sept best; fly only; 10in limit), **a'Phearsain** (15 min walk; trout, char; fly only; April-June, Aug-Sept best), **Avich** (5m by road; trout; May-Oct best), **na Sreinge** (8m by road and 35 min walk; trout; May-Oct best), **Scammadale** (8m by road; sea trout, salmon; end June-Sept), Melfort (10 min walk; sea trout, mackerel, flounders, skate, etc; June-Aug best), and five hill lochs (hour's walk and climb; trout; June-Oct). Wt £25, dt £5. Membership would be with Oban & Lorn AC. Season: March 15 to Oct 15.

MORVERN

Lochaline (Argyll). Salmon and sea trout fishing on both **River Aline** and **Loch Arienas**. Native brown trout in over 16 hill lochs. River fishing £33 per day for 2 rods; loch fishing dt £4. Boats available. Contact Ardtornish Estate Co Ltd, Morven, By Oban, Argyll PA34 5XA (tel: 0967 421 288). Fishing tackle available from Estate Information Centre and Shop; and self-catering accommodation available in estate cottages and flats.

LOCH TORRIDON

River Torridon, small salmon and sea trout river, flows into Upper Loch Torridon. Outer Loch Torridon offers excellent sea angling for a wide variety of species.

Torridon (Ross-shire). Torridon Hotel at Torridon Loch, has fishing on **Rivers Torridon**, and **Thrail**, on **Lochs an Iascaigh** and **Damph**, and hill lochs. Apply to Torridon Hotel, Torridon, By Achnasheen, Wester Ross, IV22 2EY (tel: 044 587 242). Hotel can also arrange sea angling on Outer Loch Torridon with local fishermen; minimum number 5 persons; weather permitting. Salmon and sea trout fishing on **River Balgy**, which drains Loch Damph into southern shore of Upper Loch Torridon. Permits available on Tue, Thu and Sat; from Tigh an Eilean Hotel, Shieldaig. Hotel guests have priority.

WICK

Salmon, sea trout and brown trout fishing on Wick. Spate river with good holding pools. River controlled by Wick AA. Famous Loch Watten (trout) is 7m from Wick.

Wick (Caithness). Wick AA has fishing on River Wick; salmon, sea trout and brown trout. River well stocked from association's own hatchery. Fly and worm fish-

---

Keep the banks clean

Several clubs have stopped issuing tickets to visitors because of the state of the banks after they have left. Spend a few moments clearing up.

ing. Assn also has fishing on **Lochs Watten**, **St Johns** and **Calder**; wild brown trout. Fly only on Watten and St Johns; all legal methods on Calder. Permits, boats and tackle hire from Hugo Ross, Fishing Tackle Specialist, 16 Breadalbane Cres (tel. 0955 4200).

Lybster (Caithness). Lybster is 12m S of Wick at mouth of Reisgill Burn. Portland Arms Hotel can usually arrange salmon fishing on **Berriedale River,** also by arrangement on **River Thurso**. Trout fishing on several hill lochs by arrangement, also on **Lochs Watten** and **Calder**. Hotel has a boat on **Sarclet**.

YTHAN

Rises in 'Wells of Ythan' and runs some 35m to North Sea at Newburgh. Late salmon river which used to fish best in autumn. River of no great account for brown trout, but noted for sea trout and finnock, which run up from June through to September, with some fish in October. Ythan has very large estuary for so small a river and is markedly tidal for the lower five miles or so of its course.

Newburgh (Aberdeenshire). Sea trout and finnock and salmon. Fishing on the large estuary controlled by Ythan Fisheries. Sea trout average $2-2\frac{1}{2}$lb run up to 12lb; finnock May onwards with large ones in September. Fly fishing and spinning only; spoons. Ythan Terrors, devons and Sutherland Specials fished on a 7-8ft spinning rod with 8-12lb line as most usual tackle. Worm, maggot, bubble float and other bait not allowed. Lead core lines, sinking lines not allowed. Floating line with sinking tip allowed. Much fishing from bank, but boats available. Best months June to September. Limited fishing available from 1 June to 30 Sept. Prices on application to Mr E I Forbes, Fishing Manager, Ythan Fisheries, 3 Lea Cottages, 130 Main Street, Newburgh, Ellon, Aberdeenshire AB41 0BN. (Tel: 0358 789 297), who also stocks tackle.

Ellon (Aberdeenshire). Buchan Hotel (tel. Ellon 720208) issues permits for Ellon Water on River Ythan.

Methlick (Aberdeenshire). Some spring fish, but main run Sept to Oct. Good early run of finnock; a second, smaller run in the autumn. Sea trout; June-Oct. Fishing on Haddo Estate water; now leased to Haddo House AA. Dt £6-£15. Permits from S French & Son, Methlick. Hotel: Ythanview.

Fyvie (Aberdeenshire). Brown trout, sea trout and salmon. Sept and Oct best

months for salmon. Fyvie AA has approx 3m on upper River Ythan, single bank. St £20 and dt £5-£7; obtainable from Vale Hotel; Sheiling Tor Café; Spar Grocer; Clydesdale Bank.

October on the Garry. *Photo: John Marchington.*

SEA FISHING STATIONS IN SCOTLAND

It is only in recent years that the full sea angling potential of the Scottish coast, indented by innumerable rocky bays and sea lochs, has come to be appreciated. Working in conjunction, tourist organisations and local sea angling clubs smooth the path for the visiting angler. He is well supplied in matters of boats and bait, natural stocks of the latter remaining relatively undepleted in many areas.

Note: The local name for coalfish is 'saithe' and for pollack 'lythe'.

Stranraer (Dumfries & Galloway). Loch Ryan, the W coast of Wigtownshire and Luce Bay offer first-class sea fishing, boat and shore. Loch Ryan: codling, whiting, plaice, flounders, dabs, skate, conger, tope and dogfish. Other species found in Luce Bay and off Irish Sea coast include pollack, bass, wrasse, mackerel and tope. Tackle shop supply blast frozen sea baits, ammodytes and starmers. Tackle shop: Sports Shop, George St, Stranraer.

Girvan (Ayrshire). Mostly saithe, haddock, cod, pollack and mackerel, which run quite heavy towards Ailsa Craig; July onwards best. Shore fishing and boats from harbour; inquire of Harbourmaster. The Rachel Clare, a fully-equipped, charter boat for wreck-fishing, is for hire from Girvan Harbour (tel. 0294 833 724). Tackle shop: Mrs Campbell, Girvan Chandlers. Hotel: Mansefield

Ayr (Ayrshire). Saithe, whiting, cod, mackerel, conger, eels, flounders; from pier, shore. Good mackerel fishing (trolling) in July and August. Tackle shops: James Kirk, 5 Union Arcade; Game-sport, 60 Sandgate; J A Newbiggin, 19 Aitken St, Largs.

Saltcoats and **Ardrossan** (Ayrshire). Cod, haddock, conger, saithe, flatfish. Good beach fishing in Irvine Bay and small bay between Saltcoats and Ardrossan. Boatmen include: A Gibson, 1 Fleck Avenue, Saltcoats. Tackle shop: Leisure Time, 42 Hamilton Street. Clubs: Saltcoats SAA and Ardrossan and District SAC.

Brodick and **Lamlash** (Isle of Arran). Brodick: cod, haddock and flatfish. Boats available from Brodick Boat Hire, The Beach, Brodick. Lamlash is a growing centre with an Angling Festival at Whitsun. Horseshoe Bay very popular. Cod, haddock, whiting and flatfish. Boats and bait available at Old Pier, Lamlash. Boats also available from Jim Ritchie at Whiting Bay. N C Mclean, Torlin Villa. Kilmory, will answer sea angling enquiries. Tackle shop: Johnston Marine, Lamlash.

Campbeltown (Argyll). Good sport with cod, haddock, flatfish, etc, in Kildalloig Bay and from The Winkie, causeway between Davaar Island and mainland. Some boats; trips arranged. Further details from the Tourist Information Office. Tackle shop: A P MacGrory & Co, Main Street.

Oban (Argyll). Accessible beaches overfished, but good sport in Firth of Lorne and tidal waters near Kerrera Island with saithe, pollack, mackerel, huss, conger and flatfish. Sea fishing for whiting, mackerel, common skate, conger, ling and cod available in Sound of Mull. Fishing trips available in Oban and surrounding district. Tackle shop: Simmonds, Tackle and Tack, 19 Combie St, Oban PA34 4HN (tel: 0631 62223).

Mallaig (Inverness-shire). Good centre in beautiful area. Excellent sea fishing can be found, mainly from the shore. Flatfish, pollack, conger, mackerel, coalfish in bay and from rocks and new piers. Boats from John Henderson & Son. Around coastline of Lochaber area, there are many sea lochs where good fishing can be found. No permits are required for most of these lochs but fishing the mouths of the salmon rivers is not allowed. In Loch Linnhe good shore and boat fishing for mackerel, cod, coalfish, dogfish and flounders. Tackle shops: Johnston Bros; Mallaig Bookshop. Hotel: West Highland.

Shieldaig (Ross-shire). Skate, cod, conger, saithe, ling, huss, dabs, sole and mackerel. Fishing in sea lochs of Shieldaig, Torridon and Upper Torridon; sheltered water nearly always. Outside lochs conditions can be dangerous. D N Cameron, 'Hillcroft', takes boat parties out; boat charter £125 per day, suitable for 10 rods.

Gairloch (Ross-shire). Cod, haddock, mackerel, whiting, pollack, saithe and flatfish in sea loch here, especially around Longa Island. Boats for sea angling available from West Highland Marine Ltd, Badachro, by Gairloch (tel:044583 291); and Gairloch Cruises, Pier Rd. Tackle shops: West Highland & Marine Ltd, Shop and Booking Office, Pier Rd. Further information from Ross & Cromarty Tourist Board, Gairloch IV21 2DN (tel: 0445 2130).

Ullapool and **Summer Isles** (Ross-shire). Noted for large skate, fish over 100lb have been landed from boats. Also haddock, whiting, codling, pollack, coalfish, mackerel, gurnard, flatfish, thornback ray, conger, dogfish, turbot and wrasse. Excellent inshore sport from dinghies and in charter boats around the Summer Isles. Good shore fishing at Morefield, Rhu and Achiltibuie. Charter boats from I McLeod, Achiltibuie. Boats and fishing tackle for hire, from Ardmair Point Caravan Site and Boat Centre (tel: 0854 612054). Tackle shop: Lochbroom Hardware, Shore Street, Ullapool.

Lochinver (Sutherland). Cod, halibut, skate, tope, saithe, codling, lythe, mackerel. Badnaban Cruises offer sea angling (rods for hire); max 8 passengers. Apply to Badnaban Cruises, Suilven, Badnaban (tel. 05714 358). Hotel: Lochinver.

Portree (Isle of Skye). Good sport in harbour, loch and shore, with great variety of fish. Boats available. Most hotels will arrange facilities.

Stornoway (Isle of Lewis). Cod, haddock, whiting, saithe, skate, etc. Fast-growing centre with local club, Stornoway Sea AC, South Beach Quay, whose secretary will gladly help visiting anglers, offers seasonal membership £10. Club organises Western Isles Open Boat Championships in July/August. Sea angling trips from Stornoway harbour, contact Alex Murray, 18 Seaforth Rd (tel: 0851 703263). Tackle shop: Sports World, 1-3 Francis St; and C Morrison and Son, Point Street. Hotels: County, Caledonian, Royal. At Lochs, Isle of Lewis, sea angling charter vessel available from Hebrides Holidays, 11A Habost; and sea angling trips and fishing gear for hire from M J MacDonald, 10 Ranish. For sea angling on other Outer Hebridian Islands, contact Harris Sea AC which organises occasional sea angling trips and competitions; and Uist Sea AC which organises the popular Uist Boat Championships. Harris Sea AC fish in East Loch Tarbet and approaches, including Shiant Islands,

and as far south as Scadabay; fish caught include lythe, sillock, mackerel, cod and coalfish. Club is based at Tarbert Pier and MacLeod's Motel. Accommodation on Harris at MacLeod's Motel, Harris Hotel and numerous B&Bs.

Kirkwall (Orkney). Sheltered waters in Scapa Flow hold variety of fish (record skate; halibut over 150lb). Boats available. Orkney Tourist Board, Broad Street, Kirkwall KW15 1NX, will supply further details. Tackle shops: E Kemp, 31-33 Bridge St; W.S. Sinclair, 27 John St, Stromness. Hotels: Stromness; Royal Hotel, Stromness.

Lerwick (Shetland). Superb skate fishing: Nearly 200 skate over 100lb taken. Also excellent mixed fishing for ling, cod, tusk, haddock, pollack, etc, and chance of halibut. Area holds British records for tusk, homelyn ray, grey gurnard and Norway haddock. Also Scottish hake record. Tackle shops: J A Mason, Commercial St; The Tackle Shop, Harbour St. Hotels: Lerwick, Shetland; and Busta House, Brae.

Wick (Caithness). Mainly rock fishing for conger, pollack, saithe, cod, haddock, mackerel and flatfish. Good points are: Longberry, Broadhaven, Sandigoe and Helman Head. Excellent cod fishing off Noss Head. Best months: June to Sept. Tackle Shop: Hugo Ross, Fishing Tackle Shop, 16 Breadalbane Crescent, Wick. Hotels: Nethercliffe, Mackay's, Mercury Motor Inn, Queen's. Caithness Tourist Board, Whitechapel Road.

Portmahomack (Ross-shire). The fishing off the Easter Ross coast gives the serious angler and tourist, alike, ample opportunity to catch substantial numbers of cod, ling, pollack, etc. The best of the season runs from April to October, probably peaking in August and September. Good reef and limited wreck fishing. Two charter vessel for parties of up to 20; boats charged at £25 per hour or £150 per day including roads and bait. Accommodation can be arranged. Contact John R MacKenzie, Carn Bhren, Portmahomack, By Tain (tel: 0862 87 257). Tackle shop: R McLeod, Tackle Shop, Lamington St (wide and comprehensive stock including bait). Hotels: Caledonian; Castle; Oyster-catcher; and Balintore, Balintore.

Lossiemouth (Moray). Notable centre for sea-trout fishing off east and west beaches; spinning into breakers provides splendid sport. Also mackerel, saithe, flatfish from beach, pier and boats. Tackle shops: Angling Centre, Moss St, Elgin; The Tackle Shop, High St, Elgin.

Aberdeen (Aberdeenshire). Excellent rock fishing for codling, saithe, mackerel, whiting, haddock and flatfish. Few boats. Hotels: Caledonian, Imperial, Royal.

Stonehaven (Kincardineshire). Rock fishing for haddock, flounder and mackerel very good. Cod, haddock, ling, etc, from boats; available from A Troup (tel: 0569 62892), A Mackenzie (tel: 0569 63511), W Lawson (tel: 0569 63565) and J Lobban (tel: 0569 65323). Bait may be ordered from the above. Tackle shops: Davids, Market Square. Hotel: Arduthie House.

Nairn (Nairn). Sea angling on Moray Firth. Most fishing is done from two piers at the entrance to the harbour which is tidal. Boats: one or two privately owned will often take a passenger out. Enquiries should be made at the harbour. Lugworm available on the beach at low water. MacAulay Charters offer sea angling trips for up to 12 anglers; times depend on tides. Tackle shops: Pat Fraser, Radio, TV and Sports shop, 41 High St. Hotels: Altonburn; and Greenlawns Guest House.

Dundee (Angus). Fishing from rocks, pier and boats at Broughty Ferry, Easthaven and Carnoustie for mackerel, cod, saithe, lythe and flatfish. Fishing from boats at Arbroath; for bookings apply to Doug Masson, 12 Union St (0382 25427). Tackle shop: John R Gow Ltd, 12 Union Street.

Dunbar (Lothian). Excellent rock, pier and boat fishing. Saithe, cod (up to 10lb), codling, dabs, plaice, flounders, eels and, at times, small whiting, gurnard and mackerel can be caught.

Rosehall Bridge on the River Cassley. *Photo: Eric Chalker.*

FISHING CLUBS & ASSOCIATIONS IN SCOTLAND

Included in the list of fishing clubs and associations in Scotland are those organisations which are in England, but which have water on the Tweed and its tributaries or on the Border Esk. Further information can usually be had from the Secretaries and a courtesy which is appreciated is the inclusion of a stamped addressed envelope with postal inquiries. Please advise the publishers (address at the front of the book) of any changed details for the next edition.

NATIONAL BODIES

Anglers' Co-operative Association
Iain J MacKenzie
46 Ormidale Terrace
Edinburgh EH12 6EF
The body that fights against pollution

Committee for the Promotion of Angling for the Disabled
Scottish Sports Association for the Disabled
Fife Sports Institute
Viewfield Road
Glenrothes
Fife KY6 2RA
Tel. 0592 771700

Forestry Commission
Inverness Forest District
Smithton
Inverness
Tel: 0463 791575

Forestry Enterprise
Lorne Forest District
Mull Ofiice
Aros
Isle of Mull
Tel: 0680 300346

Salmon and Trout Association
Burgh House
7/9 King Street
Aberdeen
Tel: 0224 626300

Scottish Anglers' National Association
Caledonia House
South Gyle
Edinburgh EH12 9DQ

Scottish Federation of Sea Anglers
Caledonia House
South Glyde

Edinburgh EH12 9DQ
Tel: 031 317 7192

Scottish Lame Duck (Disabled) Angling Club
K Foster
13 Gordon Terrace
Dunfermline, Fife KY11 3BH
Tel. 0383 727824

The Scottish Office Agriculture and Fisheries Department
Marine Laboratory
PO Box 101
Victoria Road
Aberdeen AB9 8DB
Tel. 0224 876544

The Scottish Office Agriculture and Fisheries Department
Freshwater Fisheries Laboratory
Faskally
Pitlochry
Perthshire PH16 5LB
Tel. 0796 472060

The Scottish Office Agriculture and Fisheries Department
Pentland House
47 Robb's Loan
Edinburgh EH14 1TW
Tel. 031 244 6230

Scottish Record Fish Committee (Saltwater)
G T Morris
8 Burt Avenue
Kinghorn,
Fife
Tel: 0592 890055
Aims as for British Record Fish Committee

Fishing Clubs

When you appoint a new secretary, do not forget to give us details of the change. Write to the publishers (address at front of book). Thank you!

Scottish River Purifaction Boards
Association
Robert L Cowan
1 South Street
Perth PH2 8NJ
Tel. 0738 27989

Scottish Tourist Board
23 Ravelston Terrace
Edinburgh EH4 3EU
Tel: 031-332 2433
Gives information on fishing holidays in
Scotland

CLUBS

Aberfeldy Angling Club
G MacDougall
60 Moness Crescent
Aberfeldy
Perthshire PH15
Aberfoyle Angling Protection Association
P A Joynson
Laraich
Aberfoyle, By Stirling
Perthshire FK8 3TQ
Tel. 08772 232
Abernethy Angling Improvement
Association
D Nicholson
Revack Lodge
Grantown-on-Spey
Inverness-shire
Airdrie and District Angling Club
Roy Burgess
21 Elswick Drive
Caldercruix
Airdrie
Lanarkshire ML6 7QW
Alness Angling Club
J B Paterson
33-35 High Street
Alness, Ross-shire
Annan and District Anglers' Club
S Begg
63 High Street
Annan
Dumfriesshire DG12 6AD
Tel. 0461 202616
Arbroath Angling Club
c/o Arbroath Cycle and Tackle Centre
274 High Street
Arbroath
Angus DD11 1JE
Tel. 0241 73467
Arran Angling Association
Dave Freeman
26 Murray Estate
Lamlash
Isle of Arran
Arran Sea Angling Association
Mrs S Allison
7 Braithwick Place
Brodick
Isle of Arran

Assynt Angling Club
S McClelland
Baddidarroch, Lochinver
Sutherland
Avon Angling Club
P Brooks
3 The Neuk
Stonehouse
Lanarkshire ML9 3HP
Ayr Angling Club
Irvine Chapman
19B Glendale Crescent
Ayr KA7 3SE
Badenoch Angling Association
A Bennett
113 High St
Kingussie, Inverness-shire
Ballater Angling Association
Martin Holroyd
59 Golf Road
Ballater
Aberdeenshire
Banff and Macduff Angling Association
D A Galloway
26 Thomson Road
Banff
Banffshire AB4 1BT
Beauly Angling Club
Morison's, Ironmongers
High Street
Beauly
Inverness-shire
Berwick and District Angling Association
David Cowan
3 Church Street
Berwick-upon-Tweed
Northumberland TD15 1EE
Blairgowrie, Rattray and District
Angling Association
Walter Matthew
4 Mitchell Square
Blairgowrie, Perthshire
Tel. 0250 873679
Brechin Angling Club
D E Smith
3 Friendly Park
Brechin, Angus
Bridge of Weir River Angling Club
J V Gibson

46 Mimosa Road
Bridge of Weir
Renfrewshire
Canmore Angling Club
E Mann
44 Sheriff Park Gardens
Forfar,
Angus
Carradale Angling Club
Donald Paterson
21 Tormhor
Carradale
Argyll
Tel. 05833 334
Carrick Angling Club
Peter Noble
50 The Avenue
Girvan, Ayrshire
Tel. 0465 3069
Castle Douglas and District Angling Association
Stanley Kaye
2 Cairnsmore Road
Castle Douglas, Galloway DG7 1BN
Tel. 0556 2695
Chatton Angling Association
A Jarvis
7 New Road
Chatton Alnwick
Northumberland NE66 5PU
Civil Service Sports Association (Rosyth)
John Mill
12 Kingseat Road
Dunfermline
Fife KY12 0DB
Tel. 0383 722128
Clarkston Independent Angling Club
Peter Gunn
6 Poplar Street
Airdrie
Lanarkshire ML6 8JZ
Clatto and Stratheden Angling Club
J Paisley
Eathall Farm
Cupar
Fife
Cobbinshaw Angling Association
Malcolm W Thomson
21 Heriot Row
Edinburgh EH3 6EN
Coldstream and District Angling Association
Brian Turnbull
Binning Cottage
Duns Road
Coldstream
Berwickshire TD12 4DR
Crianlarich Angling Association
David Taylor

180 Cedar Road
Abronhill
Cumbernauld
Glasgow G67 3BJ
Cramond Angling Club
Thomas Lithgow
11 Ochiltree Crescent
Mid-Calder
West Lothian
Tel. 0506 882269
Crieff Angling Club
Colin Duncan
Dunsinane
The Wynd
Muthill
Perthshire
Cumbrae Angling Club
John Pace
12 Bute Terrace
Millport
Isle of Cumbrae KA28 0BA
Dalbeattie Angling Association
G W Garroch
7 The Meadows
Dalbeattie
Kirkcudbrightshire DG5 4AS
Tel. 0556 611859
Dalry Angling Association
W J Sale
12 St John's Way
St John's Town of Dalry
Castle Douglas
Kirkcudbrightshire DG7 3UQ
Devon Angling Association
R Breingan
33 Redwell Place
Alloa
Clackmannanshire FK10 2BT
Dingwall and District Angling Club
Cliff Furlong
The Sports and Model Shop
Tulloch Street
Dingwall,
Ross-shire IV15 9JZ
Dornoch and District Angling Association
Michael A Banks
Kaitness
Poles Road
Dornoch
Sutherland IV25 3HP
Tel. 0862 810589
Dreghorn Angling Club
Mr Wallace
14 Lismore Way
Dreghorn, Ayrshire
Drongan Youth Group Angling Club
J Hunter
76 Coyle Avenue

Drongan
Ayrshire KA6 7DW

Dunfermline Artisan Angling Club
J Mitchell
5 William Street
Dunfermline

Dumfries and Galloway Angling Association
David Byers
4 Bloomfield
Edinburgh Road
Dumfries DG1 1SG
Tel. 0387 53850

Dunkeld and Birnam Angling Association
K L Scott
Mandaya
Highfield Place
Bankfoot
Perthshire PH1 4AX
Tel. 0738 87448

Dunoon and District Angling Club
A H Young
Ashgrove
28 Royal Crescent
Dunoon, Argyll PA23 7AH

Earlston Angling Association
P Hessett
2 Arnot Place
Earlston, Berwickshire TD4 6DP
Tel. 089684 577

East Kilbride and District Disabled Anglers Association
A S Meikle
3 Malov Court
Whitehills
East Kilbride
Glasgow G75 0DY

East Loch Tay Angling Club
George Gartshore
4 Aberfeldy Road
Kenmore
Perthshire PH15 2HQ

East Lothian Angling Association
John Crombie
10 St Lawrence
Haddington
East Lothian EH41 3RL

Easter Ross Sea Angling Club
David Meek
Newfield
Balintore, Tain
Ross-shire
Tel. 0862 832429

Eckford Angling Association
R B Anderson, WS
Royal Bank Buildings
Jedburgh, Roxburghshire

Edinburgh Angling Club
Ron Woods

23 Terragles
Pencuik, Midlothian

Edinburgh Coarse Anglers
R Woods
23 Terregles
Penicuik, Midlothian

Edinburgh Walton Angling Club
Robert Brough
108 Whitehouse Road
Edinburgh EH4 6LB

Elgin and District Angling Association
W E Mulholland
9 Conon Crescent
Elgin, Moray IV30 1SZ
Tel. 0343 544032

Esk and Liddle Fisheries Association
R J B Hill
Bank of Scotland Buildings
Langholm,
Dumfriesshire DG13 0AD

Esk Valley Angling Improvement Association
Kevin Burns
53 Fernieside Crescent
Edinburgh

Eye Water Angling Club
William S Gillie
2 Tod's Court
Eyemouth
Berwickshire TD14 5HR

Fort Augustus and District Angling Club
C Sidley
Taorluidh
The Riggs
Fort Augustus
Inverness-shire

Fort William Angling Association
c/o Rod and Gun Shop
High Street
Fort William,
Inverness-shire

Forth and Clyde Coarse Angling Club
P Morrisey
18 Daiglen
Tillicoultry
Clackmannanshire

Fyvie Angling Association
J D Pirie
Prenton
South Road
Oldmeldrum, Inverurie
Aberdeenshire AB51 0AB
Tel. 0651 872229

Gairloch Anglers
D Roxbourgh
The Old Police Station
Gairloch, Ross-shire

Gala Angling Association
S Grzybowski

3 St Andrews Street
Galashiels, Selkirkshire TD1 1EA
Tel. 0896 55712
Galston Angling Club
J Steven
12 Millands Road
Galston, Ayrshire
Gatehouse and Kirkcudbright Angling Association
E J Farrer
32 Boreland Rd
Kirkcudbright DG6 4JB
Tel. 0557 30303
Glasgow Deaf Angling Club
158 West Reget Street
Glasgow
Glasgow Match Angling Club
F Hetherington
4 Rosebery Place
Eliburn
Livingston, West Lothian
Glendale Graying Club
N J Price
Copperbeeches
Tenter Hill
Wooler, Northumberland
Glenurquhart Sea Angling Club
R MacGregor
Bernera
Lewiston
Drumnadrochit
Inverness-shire
Gordon Fishing Club
Mrs M Forsyth
47 Main Street
Gordon, Berwickshire
Greenlaw Angling Association
J Purves
9 Wester Row
Greenlaw, Berwickshire
Greenock and District Angling Club
J McMurthie
68 Cawder Crescent
Greenock, Renfrewshire
Haddo House Angling Association
J French
Kirkton
Methlick
Ellon, Aberdeenshire
Harris Fresh Water Angling Club
The Harris Hotel
Isle of Harris
Western Isles PA85 3LD
Tel. 0859 2154
Harris Sea Angling Club
J A MacDermid
Bunavoneader
Harris
Isle of Harris PA85 3AL

Hawick Angling Club
Ronald A Sutherland
20 Longhope Drive
Hawick
Roxburghshire TD9 9DW
Tel. 0450 75150
Inverness District Angling Club
c/o Graeme Peterson
14 Caulfield Place
Inverness
Irvine and District Angling Club
A Sim
51 Rubie Crescent
Irvine, Ayrshire
Jedforest Angling Association
J T Renilson
72 Howdenburn Court
Jedburgh, Roxburghshire
Kelso Angling Association
Euan M Robson
Elmbank
33 Tweedsyde Park
Kelso
Roxburghshire TD5 7RF
Tel. 0573 225279
Kilbirnie Angling Club
Ian Johnstone
12 Grahamston Avenue
Glengarnock,
Kilbirnie, Ayrshire KA14 3AF
Killin and Breadalbane Angling Club
D Allan
12 Ballechroisk
Killin
Perthshire
Kilmaurs Angling Club
J Watson
7 Four Acres Drive
Kilmaurs, Ayrshire
Kintyre Fish Protection and Angling Club
F W Neate
Kilmoray Place
High Street
Campbeltown,
Argyll
Kirkintilloch Angling Club
J Brown
13 Boghead Road
Kirikintilloch, Nr Glasgow
Kirriemuir Angling Club
H F Burness
13 Clova Road
Kirriemuir, Angus DD8 5AS
Kyles of Bute Angling Club
R Newton
Viewfield Cottage
Tighnabruaich,
Argyll

Ladykirk and Norham Angling Improvement Association
R G Wharton
8 St Cuthberts Square
Norham
Berwick-on-Tweed
Northumberland TD15 2LE

Lairg Angling Club
J M Ross
St Murie
Church Hill Road
Lairg, Sutherland IV27 4BL

Lamington and District Angling Improvement Association
B Dexter
Red Lees
18 Boghall Park
Biggar, Lanarkshire ML12 6EY

Larbert and Stenhousemuir Angling Club
A Paterson
6 Wheatlands Avenue
Bonnybridge
Stirlingshire

Lauderdale Angling Association
Donald M Mulligan
Gifford Cottage
Main Street, Gifford
Haddington
East Lothian EH41 4QH
Tel. 062 081 301

Lintrathen Angling Club
Lintrathen Loch
Glenisla
Dundee, Angus

Linlithgow Angling Club
E Gilbert
12 Claredon Road
Linlithgow, West Lothian

Loch Achonachie Angling Association
George Cameron
33 Wrightfield Prk
Maryburgh
Ross-shire IV7 8ER

Loch Awe Improvement Association
T C Macnair
Macarthur Stewart
Boswell House
Argyll Square
Oban, Argyll PA34 4BD

Lochgilphead and District Angling Club
D MacDougall
23 High Bank Park
Lochgilphead, Argyll
Tel. 0546 602104

Loch Keose and Associated Waters
M Morrison
Handa
18 Keose Glebe

Lochs
Isle of Lewis

Loch Lomond Angling Improvement Association
R A Clement & Co,
Chartered Accountants
29 St Vincent Place
Glasgow G1 2DT
Tel. 041 221 0068

Loch Rannoch Conservation Association
Mrs Anita Steffen
Cuilmore Cottage
Kinloch Rannoch
Perthshire PH16 5QB
Tel. 0882 632 218

MacDermott's Angling Club
Mrs M Taylor
13 Sandwood Drive
Tradespark
Nairn

Melrose and District Angling Association
T McLeish
Planetree Cottage
Newstead
Melrose, Roxburghshire

Mid-Nithsdale Angling Association
I R Milligan
37 Drumlanrig St
Thornhill, Dumfriesshire DG3 5LS

Milton Coarse Angling Club
D Morrison
112 Scaraway Street
Milton, Glasgow G22 7JF
Tel. 041 762 3645

Monklands District Coarse Angling Club
John McShane
5 Crinian Crescent
Townhead
Coatbridge
Lanarkshire ML5 2LG

Montrose Angling Association
2 Meridan Street
Montrose, Angus

Morebattle Angling Club
H Fox
Orchard Cottage
Morebattle
Kelso
Roxburghshire

Muirkirk Angling Association
Robert K Wilson
20 Wellwood Street
Muirkirk
Ayrshire KA18 3RR
Tel. 0290 61367

Murthly and Glendelvine Trout Angling Club
A M Allan
Drummond Hall

Murthly, Perthshire

Musselburgh and District Angling Association
c/o 36c Inverek Road
Musselburgh
East Lothian EH21 7BH
Tel. 031 653 2787

Nairn Angling Association
Graeme Symon
The Little House
Thurlow Road
Nairn
Inverness IV12 4HJ

New Abbey Angling Association
I D Cooper
West Shambellie
New Abbey
Dumfries DG2 8HG
Tel. 038 785 280

New Cumnock Anglers Association
T Basford
Burnbrae Cottage
1 Pathhead
New Cumnock
Ayrshire KA18 4DS

New Galloway Angling Association
Allan Cairnie
4 Carsons Knowe
New Galloway
Castle Douglas
Kirkcudbrightshire DG7 3RY
Tel. 06442 760

Newton Stewart Angling Association
Bertie Marr
1 St Coans Place
Newtown Stewart
Wigtownshire

North Berwick Angling Club
George B Woodburn
29 Craigleith Avenue
North Berwick
East Lothian EH39 4EN

North Uist Angling Club
Albert Thompson
Sea Swallow Cottage
Loch Maddy
North Uist
Outer Hebrides PA82 5AA

Oban and Lorn Angling Club
Brian Kupris
Greenbank
Glenmore Road

Oban, Argyll PA34 4NB

Orkney Sea Angling Association
Secretary
Quarryfield
Orphir
Orkney
KW17 2RF
Tel. 0856 81 311

Orkney Trout Fishing Association
Malcolm A Russell
Caolica
Heddle Road
Finstown, Orkney Isles

Peeblesshire Salmon Fishing Association
Messrs Blackwood & Smith, W.S.
39 High Street
Peebles, Peeblesshire EH45 8AH

Peeblesshire Trout Fishing Association
David G Fyfe
Blackwood and Smith, W.S.
39 High Street
Peebles, Peeblesshire EH45 8AH

Perth and District Anglers' Association
Alan Fraser
4 Fairhill Avenue
Oakbank
Perth PH1 1RP
Tel. 0738 32881

Pitlochry Angling Club
R Harriman
Sunnyknowe
Nursing Home Brae
Pitlochry, Perthshire

Portree Angling Association
Hillcroft
Treaslane
By Portree
Isle of Skye IV51 9NX

Prestwick Angling Club
C Hendrie
12 Glen Park Avenue
Prestwick
Ayrshire KA9 2EE
Tel. 0292 70203

Rannoch and District Angling Club
John Brown
The Square
Kinloch Rannoch
Perthshire PH16 5PN
Tel. 0882 632 268

River Almond Angling Association
H Meikle

Fishing Clubs

When you appoint a new secretary, do not forget to give us details of the change. Write to the publishers (address at front of the book). Thank you!

23 Glen Terrace
Deans, Livingston
West Lothian
River Goil Angling Club
I Given
Bonny Rigg
35 Churchill Drive
Bishopton, Renfrewshire
Royal Four Towns' Fishings
Commissioners of
Kathleen Ratcliffe
Jay-Ar
Hightae, Lockerbie
Dumfriesshire DG11 1JR
St Andrew's Angling Club
Peter F Malcolm
54 St Nicholas Street
St Andrews
Fife KY16 8BQ
Tel. 0334 76347
**St Boswells and Newtown District
Angling Association**
I M Horn
6 Grantsfield
Maxton
Melrose
Roxburghshire TD6 0RR
Tel. 0835 22559
**St Fillans' and Loch Earn Angling
Association**
Mrs W Henry
Tullichettle Lodge
Comrie, Crieff
Perthshire PH6 2HU
Tel. 0764 670323
St John's Loch Anglers' Association
Adam Black
Headwalk
Braugh
By Thurso,
Caithness
St Mary's Loch Angling Club
John Miller
25 Abbottsford Court
Colinton Road
Edinburgh EH10 5EH
Tel. 031 447 4187
St Winnoch Angling Club
J Blane
Burnside
Gates Road
Lochwinnoch
Renfrewshire PA12 4HF
Tel. 0505 843098
Scourie and District Angling Club
Derek Smith
Scouriebeag Cottage
Scourie,
By Lairg

Sutherland IV27 4SX
Selkirk and District Angling Association
A Murray
40 Raeburn Meadow
Selkirk
Shetland Anglers' Association
Andrew Miller
3 Gladstone Terrace
Lerwick
Shetland Isles ZE1 0EG
Tel: 0595 3729
Sorn Angling Club
J Gray
62 Glenshamrock Drive
Auchinleck, Ayrshire
Soval Angling Association
Edward Young
Stile Park
Willowglen Road
Stornoway
Isle of Lewis PA87 2EW
Tel. 0851 703248
South Uist Angling Club
Colin Campbell Sports
Balivanich
Isle of Benbecula
Stanley and District Angling Club
S Grant
7 Murray Place
Stanley,
Perth
Tel. 0738 828179
Stewarton Angling Club
S T Lynch
Hollybank
2 Standalane
Stewarton
Ayrshire
**Stonehaven and District Angling
Association**
David McDonald
Clachaig
93 Forest Park
Stonehaven
Stormont Angling Club
The Factor
Estates Office
Scone Palace
Perth PH2 6BD
Stornoway Angling Club
Hamish Fraser
5 Laxdale
Stornoway
Isle of Lewis
Tel. 0851 70 3990
Stornoway Sea Angling Association
Beach Quay
Stornoway
Isle of Lewis

Strathclyde Angling Club
Jim Byers
16 Jade Terrace
Bellshill,
Lanarkshire
**Stranraer and District Angling
Association**
John Nimmo
Inchparks School House
Stranraer
Wigtownshire DG9 8RR
Strathgryfe Angling Association
C Browning
7 Hillside Avenue
Kilmacolm
Renfrewshire PA13 4QL
**Strathmore Angling Improvement
Association**
Mrs Henderson
364 Blackness Road
Dundee,
Angus DD2 1SF
Tel. 0382 68062
Thurso Angling Association
Hon. Secretary
Horndean
Glengolly
By Turso
Caithness KW14 7XP
Tobermory Angling Club
Mrs Olive Brown
Stronsaule
Tobermory
Isle of Mull PA75 6PR
Tel. 0688 2020
Tongue and District Angling Association
c/o Ben Loyal Hotel
Tongue,
by Lairg
Sutherland
Turriff Angling Association
W Smith
23 Hillcrest Road
Turriff,
Aberdeenshire
Ugie Angling Association
I B Robertson
20 Kirkburn Drive
Peterhead
Aberdeenshire
Uist Sea Angling
The Secretary,
RAR Sea Angling Club
RA Range

Balivanich
Isle of Benbecula
Ullapool Angling Club
T McDougall
25 Morefield Place
Ullapool
Ross-shire IV26 2TS
Tel. 0854 612 655
**United Clyde Angling Protective
Association**
Joseph Quigley
39 Hillfoot Avenue
Wishaw,
Lanarkshire
Upper Annandale Angling Association
A Dickson
Woodfoot
Beattock
Moffat
Dumfriesshire DG10 9PL
Tel. 06833 592
Upper Nithsdale Angling Club
Kenneth McLean
61 High Street
Sanquhar
Dumfriesshire DG4 6DT
Vale of Leven and District Angling Club
George McKenzie
11 Hardie Street
Alexandria
Dunbartonshire
Tel. 0389 57843
Wick Anglers' Association
Per Hugo Ross, Fishing Tackle Specialist
16 Breadalbane Crescent
Wick
Caithness KW1 5AS
Tel. 0955 4200
Wiggins Teape Anglers' Club
The Mill
Corpach
Fort William
Inverness-shire
Whiteadder Angling Association
R Baker
Millburn House
Duns,Berwickshire TD11 3TN
**Wooler and Doddington Angling
Association**
A Nicholson
8 Broomy Road
Wooler,
Northumberland NE71 6NZ

FISHING IN NORTHERN IRELAND

Boards of Conservators, Close Seasons, etc.

For game fisher and coarse fisher alike, Northern Ireland is still largely undiscovered country. There is a wealth of lakes, large and small; miles of quiet unpolluted river, plentifully stocked with large, healthy fish, anything but well-educated to anglers and their methods. By the standards of most other parts of Britain, all of it is underfished. In recent years, coarse fishermen have begun to find out what Northern Ireland has to offer, and there is much, too, for the game fisherman. The visitor as yet unfamiliar with the province is recommended to concentrate on the waters owned and managed by the Department of Agriculture, possibly the largest single fishery proprietor in Northern Ireland. They include some of the very best.

The Dept of Agriculture (Fisheries Division, Hut 5, Castle Grounds, Stormont, Belfast BT4 3PW, tel: 0232 523434) is the ultimate authority for fisheries in Northern Ireland. In addition to the Department, and working in co-operation with it, there are two Conservancy Authorities, The Foyle Fisheries Commission; and The Fisheries Conservancy Board for Northern Ireland. They operate in separate areas.

The Department publishes an Angling Guide to the waters under its control, available from Fisheries Division at the above address, and from many tackle shops.

The Foyle Fisheries Commission (8 Victoria Road, Londonderry BT47 2AB, Tel: 0504 42100) act as conservator and issues rod licences in the Foyle area: i.e. the North-Western parts of the province drained by the Foyle/Mourne/Camowen river systems and the rivers Faughan and Roe. The Foyle Fisheries Commission is controlled jointly by the Governments of Northern Ireland and The Republic of Ireland, including in the total area the former Moville District in the Republic and the former Londonderry District in N.I.

The Fisheries Conservancy Board for Northern Ireland (1 Mahon Road, Portadown, Co Armagh BT62 3EE, Tel: Portadown 334666). This board acts as conservator and issues licences for the remainder of the province.

The Northern Ireland Tourist Board (St Anne's Court, 59 North Street, Belfast BT1 1NB, (Tel: 0232 31221) is also involved in angling, concerning itself with development and promotion, and issues literature on travel and accommodation.

Under the provisions of The Fisheries Act (N.I.) 1966, **The Fisheries Conservancy Board** and **The Foyle Fisheries Commission** co-operate with the **Dept of Agriculture** in the development and improvement of fisheries. As a result, there has been in recent years a dramatic improvement in the quantity and quality of angling, game and coarse, available to visitors. The department's Watercourse Management Division is also actively engaged in the improvement of fisheries in watercourses under its control. Works include the construction of fishery weirs, groynes and deflectors; restoration of gravel, landscaping of altered watercourses and comprehensive schemes of tree-planting.

Rod Licences. With the following exceptions, anglers are required to take out a rod licence. 1. Anglers under 18 years of age are not required to take out a licence in the Conservancy Board area. 2. Rod licences do not have to be taken out in the Foyle area by *any* angler fishing exclusively for coarse fish. Rod licences are issued by The Foyle Fisheries Commission and The Fisheries Conservancy Board in their respective areas. The holder of a licence in one area *may obtain on payment an endorsement to cover the other area.* (Charge included in the details below.)

A **Game Fishing Rod Licence** in **The Fisheries Conservancy Board** area is valid for both game and coarse fishing, *but a coarse fishing rod licence is valid for coarse fishing only on designated coarse fishing waters.* A list of these is obtainable from the Board. Licences may be obtained directly from the Authorities, or from tackle dealers.

Fisheries Conservancy Board rod licence charges
Game Fishing
Season game fishing rod licence £17

8-day fishing rod licence £8.50
Endorsement to Foyle Fisheries Commission game fishing rod licence £13.55
Joint licence/Department of Agriculture permit (8 days) £20.50
Coarse Fishing
Season coarse fishing rod licence £6.50
8-day coarse fishing licence £3.25
Joint licence/Department of Agriculture permit (8 days) £8.25
Joint licence/Department of Agriculture permit (3 days) £4.85

Foyle Fisheries Commission rod licence charges
Game Fishing
Season game fishing rod licence £16
14-day game fishing rod licence £10.50
Under 18-years of age game fishing rod licence £8
Endorsement to Fisheries Conservancy Board season game fishing rod licence £12.70

Department of Agriculture permits to fish on DANI waters

GAME FISHING	Cost Ex VAT £	Cost Inc VAT £
Under 18 years old		
Juvenile Season Game Permit	5.79	6.80
18 Years old and over		
Fishing all season on any DANI Public Water		
General Season Game Permit	36.38	42.75
Fishing all season on a number of specified DANI Public Waters (see list of local areas)		
Local Season Game Permit	22.98	27
Fishing during 8 consecutive days on any DANI Public Water		
8-day General Game Permit	10.21	12
Fishing for one day on any DANI Public Water		
Daily General Game Permit	6.34	7.45
Fishing for disabled anglers on		
any DANI Public Water, all season	17.02	20

(available only from Fisheries Division) (Ask distributor for application form)

COARSE FISHING
Under 18 Years Old - no permit required for one rod
Otherwise

Annual Coarse Fishing permit	12.77	15

The Department of Agriculture provides Local Game Fishing Permits for anglers who wish to confine their sport to a local area. These are annual permits which only cover game waters in the area named on the permit. However, in addition to these waters, holders may fish on all Department of Agriculture coarse fisheries in the Province. The following list shows the game and mixed fisheries which are available under each local permit.

Name of Local Permit and Waters Covered
East Antrim:
Upper South Woodburn, Lower South Woodburn, Middle South Woodburn, North Woodburn, Lough Mourne, Copeland (Marshallstown)
North Antrim:
Killylane, Dungonnell and Altnahinch Reservoirs, River Bush (unrestricted stretch), Margy, Carey and Glenshesk Rivers.
South Antrim/North Down:
Stonyford, Leathemstown and Portavoe Reservoirs, Hillsborough Lake and Ballykeel Lougherne.
Armagh/Tyrone:
Craigavon City Park South Lake, Brantry Lough, Lough Brickland, White Lough and River Blackwater.
South Down:
Lough Brickland, Castlewellan Lake, Spelga Reservoir, Quoile Basin and Shimna River.

With two like that on the bank, why change the fly? A change in light or temperature, perhaps. *Photo: Eric Chalker*

East Fermanagh:
Corranny and Corry Loughs, Upper and Lower Lough Erne, Mill Lough (Bellanaleck), Colebrook River.
Mid Fermanagh:
Mill Lough (Bellanaleck), Upper and Lower Lough Erne, Ballinamallard River (Riversdale) and River Erne.
West Fermanagh:
Lough Melvin, Lough Keenaghan, Navar Forest Lakes (Achork, Meenameen and Glencreawan), River Erne.
Londonderry/Tyrone:
Binevenagh Lake, Loughs Ash, Moor, Braden and Lee and River Roe.

Disabled Anglers' Permit
The Disabled Anglers' Permit is valid for all Department of Agriculture Game Fishing Water. Those in receipt of one of the following benefits may apply for this permit, using an application form which may be obtained from distributors or the Department of Agriculture: Disability Living Allowance if aged 65 or under; Attendance Allowance if aged over 65; War Disablement Pension; Severe Disablement Allowance.
In addition it is, like other Local Permits, valid for all the Department's Coarse Fishing Waters.
Seasons. There are no statutory close seasons for coarse fish in Northern Ireland, nor for rainbow trout in designated trout waters in the **Conservancy Board** area. (List of such waters from Board, and displayed by licensed sellers). For salmon, sea trout and brown trout, the OPEN seasons are: **Foyle area;** in general, rivers; April 1 to Oct 20; lakes: March 1 to Oct 20. **FCB area: Lough Melvin:** Feb 1 to Sept 30. **Lough Erne** system: March 1 to Sept 30.

Bush: March 1 to Oct 20. **Other waters,** in general, March 1 to Oct 31, but late openings and early closings introduced in some stocked trout lakes. The season on the following loughs has been extended to Oct 31: Corrany, Corry, Mill Lough, Navar Forest Lakes.

As an amendment to general information about Department's free fishing, anglers may require owners' permission on the following waters: Rivers Finn, at Newtownbutler; Cam, Sillies, Colebrook; Loughs Annashanco, Drumnacrittan, Derryallen, Corracosh, Barry, Accrussel, Laragh, Drumcullion, Derryhowlaght, Sand, Friars, Doo, Clonmin, Cargin, Killmacbrack, Carran, Unshinagh, Aleen; Moorlough, Lisnaskea; Ur Calliagh.

Check before you go

While every effort has been made to ensure that the information given in **Where to Fish** *is correct, the position is continually changing, and anglers are urged, in their own interests, to make preliminary enquiries before travelling to selected venues. This is especially important with reference to prices quoted. Inevitably the rate of inflation is affecting stability in this quarter. Anglers' attention is also drawn to the fact that the hotels mentioned under the various fishing stations do not necessarily have water of their own. Any amendments or further data for inclusion in subsequent editions, and any criticism, will be welcome.*

FISHING STATIONS IN NORTHERN IRELAND

As in other sections, principal catchment areas are dealt with in alphabetical order, and details of close seasons, licences, etc, will be found on preceding page. Anglers wanting further details of accommodation, etc, should write to the Northern Ireland Tourist Board, St Anne's Court, 59 North Street, Belfast, BT1 2NB, or 11 Berkeley Street, London (071-493 0601).

BANN (Lower)

(For close seasons, licences, see under Boards)

A mainly sluggish river running approx 30m from where it leaves Lough Neagh to where it enters the sea below Coleraine. River is canalised at upper end. Good coarse fish population; sea trout fishing in the tideway. Salmon stretches are mostly in private hands but some days, on some beats, are available to visitors.

Coleraine (Co Derry). River tidal below Cutts. Good game and coarse fishing above tidal stretches. Bann Systems Ltd, Dundarave, Bushmills, Co Antrim BT57 8ST, has beats which are available to certain clubs on Fri, Sat and Sun; and also has salmon fishing available to tourists on **River Bush;** dt £25-£50, depending on season. Coleraine AA allow dt fishing on R Bann at ford nr Coleraine, R Ree, and Ballyinreese Reservoir, obtainable from E Kee, 3 Kings Rd, Coleraine. Agivey AA has 12m stretch on R Agivey plus stretch on **Wee Agivey,** nr **Garvagh.** Permits (£10, £5) from Mrs J McCann, 162 Agivey Rd, Aghadowey. **Ballyrashane Trout Lake,** Creamery Rd: fly only, stocked r trout, dt £10, 4 fish limit. Contact Council Offices, Coleraine, tel: 52181. Tackle shops: Smyth's, 1 Park St. Atkins, 67 Coleraine Rd, Garvagh. Hotels: Lodge; Bohill Auto Inn.

Kilrea (Co Derry). Pike and perch in local canals and loughs. Salmon and trout day tickets on Kilrea & Dist AC waters, from Sean Donagh, Kilrea. Flood gate operation has marred local angling.

Portglenone (Co Antrim). **Clady River** joins Bann below town. Brown trout, late salmon and dollaghan. Dt £5 (1 Mar-30 Sept), £10 (Oct), from Clady & Dist AC, who control whole river and tributaries. Obtainable from Weirs, Clady Rd, or M Cushanan, Main St, both Portglenone. Tackle shop: McGall's, Main St. Accommodation: Bannside Farmhouse, 268 Gortgole Road.

Toomebridge (Co Antrim). Here, the Lower Bann leaves L Neagh. Dept of Ag controls **Lower Bann Navigational Canal** at **Toome, Portna** and **Movanagher.** Tickets from tackle shops. **Lough Neagh,** with an area of 153 sq miles, is the largest sheet of inland water in the British Isles. It supports an immense commercial eel fishery, but apart from that, its potential is as yet largely untapped. The bottom-feeding habits of Lough Neagh trout and the exposed conditions on this enormous stretch of water have so far discouraged anglers from trying to exploit it. A principal problem is the absence of sheltered bays.

BANN (Upper)

Flows west and north from its source in the Mourne Mountains to enter Lough Neagh near the middle of its southern shore at a point north of Portadown.

Portadown (Co Armagh). Pike, perch, roach, bream and trout. Dept of Ag has 10m stretch from Portadown to Lough Neagh; a designated coarse fishery which is one of the best in Europe. Permits from Fisheries Conservancy Board, 1 Mahon Rd. Moy AC has fishing here; tickets from The Field and Stream, Moy. Tackle shop: Tetford's Sport, 28 West St (tel: 0762 338555). Hotels: Carngrove; Seagoe.

Banbridge (Co Down). Late salmon, brown trout and coarse fish for 15 miles from **Rathfriland** to **Moyallen;** controlled by Rathfriland AC u/s from **Katesbridge.** Banbridge AC fishes from Katesbridge to **Lenaderg,** and has 76 acre **Corbet Lough,** rainbow trout. Dt £4.50 lake,

£3.50 river, conc. Gilford AC fishes from Lenaderg to Moyallen, plus **Kernan Lake**. **Lough Brickland,** 62 acres, Dept of Ag, fly only, b and r trout. **Altnadue Lake,** b trout, licence only required. Coarse fishing: **Newry Canal** (roach, bream, rudd, perch, pike); **Lough Shark;** Lakes **Drummillar, Drumaran, Drumnavaddy; Skillycolban** (Mill Dam, perch, pike, eels); Lakes **Ballyroney, Hunshigo, Ballyward, Ballymagreehan,** pike, perch, F C B coarse licence required. Tackle, licences and permits from Coburns Ltd, 32 Scarva St, Banbridge, tel: 08206 62207. Hotels: Belmont, Banville, Downshire. Wright Lines, 08206 62126, offers two day Angling Breaks for £43. Mrs J Fleming, 08206 22348, has accom. close to Corbet Lough, above. Mrs M Maginn, 08206 38090, has accom. half mile from R Bann.

Hilltown (Co Down). Dept of Ag have four good trout lakes, totalling more than 350 acres in the area: **Spelga, Castlewellan, Hillsborough, Lough Brickland**. Castlewellan and Annsborough AC fish **Ballylough, Annsborough,** a few miles north east. Brown and rainbow trout, fly only. Day tickets £8, available from Cheshunt Inn, Lower Square, Castlewellan. Shimna AC has **Altnadue Lough,** stocked with rainbows. Dt £5 from The Four Seasons, Newcastle. Tackle shops: J Coburn, 32 Scarva Street Banbridge; W McCammon, Main St, Castlewellan; W R Timble, 25 Downpatrick St, Rathfriland. Hotels: Downshire Arms and Belmont, Banbridge. Chestnut Inn, Castlewellan, 03967 78247, offers trout fishing weekends and mid-week breaks on Ballylough.

BLACKWATER

(For close seasons, licences, see under Boards)

The largest of the rivers flowing into L Neagh, rising in S Tyrone to enter the lough at its SW corner. Coarse fish and trout.

Blackwatertown (Co Armagh). Dept of Ag has 1½m, mainly coarse fishing but short stretch of good game fishing. Permits from K Cahoon, 2 Irish St, Dungannon. Ulster Coarse Fishing Federation has water from Bond's Bridge to end of Argory Estate, a mixed fishery with excellent match weights. Individuals may fish free on F C B licence. Three trout lakes near **Dungannon**: Dungannon Park, 12 acres, tel: 08687 27327; **Aughadarragh,** tel: 06625 48320, r trout; **Altmore Fishery,** 5 acres, tel: 08687 58977. Charlemont House Hotel, 4 The Square, Dungannon has fishing on Tyrone bank for guests. Tel: 08687 84895. Two other hotels in Dugannon area have fishing holidays: Inn on the Park, Moy Rd, 08687 25151; Glengannon, Ballygawley Rd, 08687 27311. Nr Dugannon close to B45, **Ballysaggart Lough**: bream, eels, perch, pike, roach, rudd, tench. No permit needed. Contact 08678 22231.

Moy (Co Tyrone). Moy AC has coarse fishing on Blackwater at Moy, tickets available from tackle shop The Field and Stream, Killyman St, Moy. Hotels: Charlemont House; Tomneys Licenced Inn (08687 84895).

Benburb (Co Tyrone). Trout for 2½m downstream. Armagh & Dist AC leases or owns stretch on river, and seven lakes. Dep of Ag has **Brantry Lough** (brown trout); and **Loughs Creeve** (pike to 35lb) and **Enagh** (pike, perch, bream). Permits from Hamilton's, 14/16 James St, Cookstown. Dept of Ag also has coarse fishing on **Clay Lake,** nr **Keady** (Co Armagh);

Check before you go

While every effort has been made to ensure that the information given in **Where to Fish** *is correct, the position is continually changing, and anglers are urged, in their own interests, to make preliminary enquiries before travelling to selected venues. This is especially important with reference to prices quoted. Inevitably the rate of inflation is affecting stability in this quarter. Anglers' attention is also drawn to the fact that the hotels mentioned under the various fishing stations do not necessarily have water of their own. Any amendments or further data for inclusion in subsequent editions, and any criticism, will be welcome.*

120 acres, pike rudd and perch, open all year; permits from J McKeever, Hardware Shop, Bridge St, Keady. Hotel, Salmon Leap View offers private fishing on riverbank, at £10 B & B, plus £1.50 fishing.

Clogher, Augher and **Aughnacloy.** (Co Tyrone). Local stretch of river is undergoing fishery rehabilitation following a major drainage scheme of the Blackwater River. Permits from Aughnacloy AC, Clogher & Dist AC, Augher Dist & Upper Blackwater AC and landowners. Permission from landowners for tributaries. **Callan, Oona** and **Torrent.** Dept of Ag has rainbow trout fishing on **White Lough.** 4 fish per day, min. size 10 ins. Fly only from boats, otherwise, spinning and worming permitted. Permits from R Morrow, 48 Rehaghey Road, Aughnacloy. Accommodation: Mrs K Hillen, 48 Moore St, Aughnacloy.

Armagh (Co Armagh). Beside **River Callan,** centre for Blackwater and its tributaries, with many fishing lakes in district. Six of these are controlled by Armagh AC, who offer day tickets on three, with brown and rainbow trout. Fly only on **Shaws Lake** and **Seagahan Reservoir,** all legal methods on **Aughnagorgan Lake.** Tackle shop: Armagh Garden and Sports Centre, 48 Dobbin St. Carnwood Lodge Hotel, 61 Castleblaney Rd, Keady (0861 538935), is close to **Keady Trout Lakes,** and caters for anglers.

SMALLER RIVERS EMPTYING INTO LOUGH NEAGH

MAINE (Co Antrim): Flows 25m from source in Glarryford Bogs to enter lough south of Randalstown, Co Antrim. With tribs **Kellswater, Braid, Clough** and **Glenwherry** provides good fishing for salmon, trout and dollaghan. Gracehill, Galgorm and Dist AC has 3m stretch at **Ballymeda,** brown trout with salmon from July. Dt available from Galgorm P O. 6 fish limit. Randalstown AC controls Maine from **Randalstown** Road Bridge to Andraid Ford. Trout, with salmon and dollaghan in season. Dt £3 from C Spence, 32 New Street, Randalstown. Membership £20 p.a, juv £3. Kells and Connor AC has dt £3 or £1 for fishing on Kells and Glenwherry. B and r trout and late salmon run. Available from Duncan's Filling Station, Kells. Dept of Ag has brown trout fishing on **Dungonnell** and **Killylane Reservoirs,** 70 and 50 acres. Limit 4 fish. Maine AC issues 12 day tickets (£3) on 4 miles of river from above **Cullybackey** to Dunminning Bridge; brown trout and salmon. From Simpsons, Main St, Cullybackey. Tackle shops: D Matthews, 72 Ballymoney St; McGroggans, 34 Broughshane St, both Ballymena. Hotels: Adair Arms; Leighinmore House and Tullyglass House, Ballymena.

SIXMILEWATER: Flows 15m from Ballyclare to enter lough at Antrim, at its NE corner. A heavily-fished but highly productive trout water. Antrim & Dist AC issues £3 and £2 permits for water between **Ballycare** and **Antrim;** brown trout, salmon from August; available from The Bridge Tackle Shop, High St, Antrim, or Templepatrick Supermarket. Mrs Marigold Allen, The Beeches Guest House, 10 Dunadry Rd, Muckamore (08494 33161) has accom. with 2 day permits for Sixmilewater between Antrim and **Doagh.** Dunadry Inn, 08494 32474, has fishing for guests on Sixmilewater. Ballynure AC issues £2 dt for water between Doagh and **Ballynure,** available from Craigs Hardware, Main st, Ballyclare. Dept of Ag has trout fishing on **Woodburn Reservoirs, nr Carrickfergus.** Upper South, 65 acres, Middle South 64 acres, Lower South 22 acres, North, 18 acres. Lough Mourne, 127 acres, Copeland (Marshallstown) 24 acres. North Woodburn, Rainbow, others, rainbow and brown. Limit 4 fish. Fishing at trout farm nr **Ballycarry:** Mr J Caldwell, 73 Bridgend Rd, Ballycarry, tel: 09603 72209. Permits from Sport & Leisure, 31 High St; J. Hill, 4 West St, both Carrigfergus. Hotel: Deer Park, Antrim. Tackle shop: B Graig, 79 Main St, Ballyclare.

CRUMLIN AND GLENAVY (Co Antrim): small rivers which flow west through these villages to enter lough. Trout fishing near their mouths. Centre: Crumlin. Tackle shop: Fur, Feather and Fin, 3a West Terrace, Mill Rd (tel: 084 94 53648). Accommodation: Hillvale Farm, 11 Largy Road.

BALLINDERRY: Flows east for approx 30m, through Cookstown, to enter lough about midway along west shore. Good fishing for brown trout and dollaghan for 20m up from the mouth. Permission from

Where to Fish

Cookstown AC and landowners. Moy AC has stretch at Coagh. Tickets from The Field and Stream, Moy. Hotels: Glenavon House 06487 64949 (Angling Breaks - fishing on local river); Greenvale, both Cookstown, Co Tyrone.

MOYOLA (Co Londonderry): Flows east and south from its source in S Derry to enter lough at NW corner. Some brown trout in lower reaches and a reasonably good run of salmon from July. Fishing rights held by Castledawson AC, Chairman Mr W Evans, Hillhead Rd, Moyola; and Moyola and Dist AC, dt from G Ewings Confectionary, 41 Main St, Castle Dawson and tackle shop H Hueston, 55 Main St, Castledawson. Accommodation: Moyola Lodge, 9 Brough Road.

BUSH

(For close seasons, licences, see under Boards)

The Bush flows 30m west and north through Bushmills, Co Antrim, to enter the sea near Portballintrae. The fishing rights of the entire catchment (except the stretch from the sea to Bushmills) have been acquired by the Dept of Agriculture primarily as an experimental river for studies into the biology and management of salmon. Within the terms of this programme, salmon angling is maintained at the highest possible level. Trout in the Bush and its tributaries are small but plentiful: there is a modest run of spring salmon and a grilse run for which the river is best known which begins in June or July, according to flow. It is important to report catches of fin-clipped fish. Bush season has been extended to 20 October.

For angling management, the river is divided into the following sections: the *Town Stretch* about 200 yds downstream of the Project Centre at Bushmills; the *Leap Stretch* upstream (approx 600 yds of water); the *New Stretch* (500 yds); and the *Unrestricted Stretch*, the remaining 24m of fishing water. The *Walk Mills* stretch (700 yds), from the top of the salmon leap to Ballyclogh Burn is now available for day tickets. Special daily permits, bookable in advance, are required for the Town, Leap and New stretches, as shown under 'Licences, permits and close seasons.' Weekend or Bank Holiday angling must be booked and paid for by 1400 hours on the preceding Friday or normal working day. Half day tickets are available on the Town and Leap stretches from 1 June to 20 Oct. Tributary: **River Dervock**, flowing through the village of that name, offers 2m of good trout fishing. *(For details of permit charges see under Boards).*

Bushmills (Co Antrim). Salmon, sea trout and brown trout. Bann System Ltd, Dundarave, Bushmills BT57 8ST, has excellent salmon fishing stretch from Bushmills to the sea. Dt £25 and £50. Fishing lodge also available. Dept of Ag has short stretches (Town, New, Leap and Walk Mill) near Bushmills. Dt from The Hatchery, and should be booked in advance. M C McKeever, Bushmills (02657 31577) has accom. with R Bush fishing. Dept of Ag has 24m stretch (unrestricted). Bank fishing only. Permits from The Hatchery and A Truss, 79 Main St; R Bell, 38/40 Ann St, Ballycastle; Smyths Tackle, 17 Enagh Rd, Bally-

money. Other Bushmills tackle dealer: Angling Supplies, 39 Main St. Hotels: Bushmills Inn; Antrim Arms, Ballycastle.

Ballymoney (Co Antrim). **Bush River** may be fished for brown trout, as can the Ballymoney Burn. Good coarse fishing on **Movanagher Canal** and **R Bann.** Brown and rainbow trout fishing on **Altnahinch Reservoir,** at head of R Bush. Dept of Ag water, 44 acres, bag limit 4 fish, bank fishing only. Permits from Smyth's Tackle, 17 Enagh Rd; Pollocks Filling Station, Rodeing Foot, also E J Cassell, 43/45 Main St, all Ballymoney.

Fishing available?

*If you own, manage, or know of first-class fishing available to the public which should be considered for inclusion in **Where to Fish** please apply to the publishers (address in the front of the book) for a form for submission, on completion, to the Editor. (Inclusion is at the sole discretion of the Editor).*

LOUGH ERNE (Upper and Lower)

(For close seasons, licences, under Boards)

Upper and Lower Lough Erne, with the R Erne and tributaries feeding the loughs, comprise 37,800 acres of mixed game and coarse fishing owned and annually restocked by the Dept of Agriculture and offering some of the best sport in Europe. The flow is in a NW direction, through the beautiful and largely unspoilt Fermanagh countryside, via Belleek, to where the R Erne reaches the sea at Ballyshannon. Infinitely varied fishing in the lakes, with innumerable secluded bays, inlets and small islands. Rich, unpolluted waters teeming with fish-life, the Erne system is truly an angler's paradise. Centres: Belleek; Kesh; Enniskillen; Bellanaleck; Lisnaskea; Newtownbutler.

RIVER ERNE. River heavily populated with large bream and roach, pike of record-breaking proportions. Good salmon runs in late summer and autumn. **Belleek,** Co Fermanagh, is a good centre for fishing river and Lower Lough. Dept of Ag has 3¾ miles with brown trout and salmon. Limit, 6 fish; also b and r trout on **Lough Keenaghan,** 38 acres. **Scolban Lough** (171 acres) has pike to 20lb as main quarry. Permits from The Carlton, Belleek. Carlton Cottages, Belleek, 036565 8181, offers fishing breaks with boat and engine, rod hire, etc.

LOWER LOUGH ERNE. The trout fishing areas, in which the fish may run very large, are in the north and west of the lake. Recommended areas are from Roscor Bridge up to the Heron Island, and across to the **Garvary River.** South and east of a dividing line, the lake may be fished on coarse fishing licence and permit only.

TRIBUTARIES FEEDING LOWER LOUGH: Ballinamallard River flows south through the village of Ballinamallard, to enter the lake near St Angelo Airport. Dept of Ag controls 1 mile nr Ballinamallard; brown trout. **Colebrook** and **Tempo** enter lake from the West. 2 miles of Colebrook is Dept of Ag Designated Coarse fishery, nr Lisnaskea: roach, bream, perch, rudd, eels, the occasional pike, trout and salmon. Tackle shop: J A Knaggs, Main St, Ballinamallard.

UPPER LOUGH ERNE: Principally coarse fish: pike, eel, perch, rudd, bream, roach, occasional salmon and sea trout. Centres: **Lisnaskea; Newtown Butler; Enniskillen.** The Crom Estate has fishing on Inisherk and Derryvore Islands. Dt £2.50 from Gate Lodge, Crom Estate, Newtownbutler, Fermanagh. Boats can be hired at various locations, including the following: Mrs R A Graham, Manville House, Aughablaney, Letter; Carry-

bridge Angling Centre, Lisbellaw; Lough Erne Hotel, Kesh; Stella Marina, Castle Archdale. Ely Island Chalets, 0365 89777, and Killyhevlin Chalets, 0365 323481 both have coarse fishing breaks on offer. **Mill Lough, Bellanaleck:** 100 acres Dept of Ag r and b trout fishery 4 miles from Enniskillen, 4 fish limit. At Castle Coole, **Lough Coole,** National Trust Fishery. B and r trout to 5lbs. ½ dt (boat) £3. Boats for hire: A Burrell, tel: 0365 322882. **Killyfole Lough,** 56 acres, nr Lisnaskea, had a variety of coarse fish, incl perch and pike. Permits from S Dowler, Main St, Lisnascia. Tackle shops: J E Richardson, East Bridge Street, Enniskillen (tickets for local fishing); Erne Tackle, Main Street, Lisnaskea; Lakeland Tackle and Guns Shop, Sligo Road, Enniskillen, Co Fermanagh. Hotels: Killyhevlin; Manor House; Railway; all Enniskillen; and Ortine, Lisnaskea. Ely Island Chalets (036589 777) offer self-catering accom. with boats and tackle available, also private trout lake, with breeding rainbows. Riverside Farm, Gortadrehid, Enniskillen (0365 322725) has accom. with boats and bait supplied. Derryad Cottages, Lisnaskea (081 5674487): fishing holidays with motor boats supplied. J & S Reihill (03657 21360), accom. with fishing on 80 acre **Inniscorkin Island** shoreline. Killyhevlin Hotel, Enniskillen, has chalets on banks of Erne, with fishing stages. Tel: 0365 323481. Other accom. at Lough Erne Cottages, Bolusty, c/o J E Richardson, see above. Boats and engines available.

TRIBUTARIES FEEDING UPPER LOUGH ERNE: Swalinbar River flows north from Co Cavan to enter the lough midway on the S side. Coarse fish in lower reaches, trout in upper. Permission from landowners. The **Silies River** flows from above Derrygonelly to enter the lough between Enniskillen and Lisgoole

Abbey. Excellent coarse fishing, some trout. **Arney River** flows from Lower Lough Macnean to Upper Lough Erne (large trout and exceptional pike fishing) to enter Upper L Erne near **Bellanaleck.** Good mixed fishing all the way to **Lough Macnean.** Upper and Lower L Macnean both have coarse fishing available on them, notably pike. Permits from P Catterall, Corralea Forest Lodge, Belcoo, or tackle shops in Bellanaleck and Enniskillen, Also ten Dept trout lakes of various sizes in the area (5 acres to 100 acres), including the famous **Navar Forest Lakes,** and **Mill Lough** at Bellanaleck which holds trout to 5lb. Dept of Ag permits for Mill Lough from G A Cathcart, Bellanaleck Post Office; and for Navar Forest Lakes from Carlton Park Information and Fishing Centre, Belleek.

FOYLE

(For close seasons, licences, see under Boards)

The Foyle system is half in Northern Ireland, half in the Republic. It is formed by the **Derg** (draining Lough Derg) and the **Strule,** constituting the **Mourne,** which unites with the **Finn** at Strabane to become the Foyle proper, which enters the sea at Londonderry. That part of the system in Northern Ireland, including the **Faughan** and **Roe,** is the largest salmon and trout fishery in the country. It drains the north and west slopes of the Sperrin Mountains and most of Co Tyrone.

Londonderry. River tidal here, with fishing for salmon in tidal pools from July. Also a run of sea trout. Permits from Foyle Commission. Tackle shops: Rod and Line, 1 Clarendon St (tel: 0504 262877); P McCrystal, Spencer Rd; Fitzpatrick Sports, Spencer Rd; Hills (Derry Ltd), Spencer Rd, all Waterside, Londonderry. Hotels: White Horse Inn, Everglades, Broomhill House.

Strabane (Co Tyrone). Here **Mourne** and **Strule** unite to form Foyle. Salmon and sea trout. Permits from Foyle Commission. Dept of Ag has five lakes in the area. Fir Trees Hotel, Melmount Rd, tel: 0504 382382, offers weekend fishing breaks, £99. Tackle shop: T Glackin, 10 Bridge Street. Hotel: Fir Trees Lodge.

Tributaries of the Foyle

MOURNE: Excellent fishing in the 10m between Strabane and Newtownstewart, but largely private and unavailable to visitors.

Sion Mills (Co Tyrone), Dept of Ag has 4m stretch managed by Sion Mills AC, salmon, brown and sea trout; 10 dts from T Kee, Mourne Bar, Victoria Bridge; 20 dts from M Gough, 6 New St, Sion Mills. Tackle shop: N M Tackle, 9 Alexandra Place.

Newtownstewart (Co Tyrone). The **Owenkillow** and **Glenelly** enter here, offering 30m of ideal game fishing waters noted for their sea trout and salmon. Owenkillen is spate river, only worth fishing in Jun/Oct. Fori **Gortin** fishing on Owenkillow and Owenrea, contact G Treanor, 06626 48543. Blakiston-Houston Estate has fishing on 6m stretch of **Owenkillen** and 3m stretch of **Owenrea**; salmon and sea trout; dt from Gabriel Treanor, 56 Main St, Gortin 06626 48534/48824, or K Fleming, 51 Gorticashel Rd, Gortin. Omagh AA holds most of fishing rights on Mourne, Strule and Owenkillow around this area, (some 28 miles) and offers dt £12. These, also Gaff AC dt (£5) on **Glenelly River** from tackle shop: Campbell's Mourne Valley Tackle, 50 Main St, Newtonstewart (tel: 06626 61543), who offer accommodation and private fishing on Rivers **Mourne** and **Glenelly.** Baronscourt Cottages, tel: 06626 61013, has pike fishing for guests. Weekend break, £54, mid-week, £46.50.

STRULE: Very good trout fishing from Omagh to Newtownstewart.

Omagh (Co Tyrone). Dept of Ag controls the coarse fishing on a stretch of R Strule

Keep the banks clean

Several clubs have stopped issuing tickets to visitors because of the state of the banks after they have left. Spend a few moments clearing up.

by arrangement with Omagh AA. Roach and eels. Assc also controls stretches of **Camowen, Owenkillen** and **Drumragh Rivers.** More good fishing upstream of Omagh, to Camowen, but fish smaller. Salmon in season. **Owenragh, Quiggery/Fintona** and **Drumragh** enter near **Omagh.** Dept stillwaters, **Loughs Bradan** and **Lee,** 60 and 37 acres, 5 miles from **Castlederg;** Brown trout fishing, 4 fish limit, per day, min. size 10 ins. Tackle and Permits for Strule from C A Anderson, 64 Market St, Omagh. Omagh hotels: Royal Arms; Silverbirch.

FAIRYWATER: Flows E from Drumquin (trout) to enter **Strule** below Omagh. Remarkably good roach fishing in lower reaches. No permit required. Small brown trout and salmon in season in **Burndennett.**

DERG: flows E from Donegal for 50m to enter **Mourne** N of **Newtownstewart.** Good trout water for 15m to above Castlederg, Co Tyrone. Permission from Castlederg AA, Mournebeg & Derg AA. Tackle shop: Campbell's Mourne Valley Tackle, 30 Main St, Newtownstewart, tel: 06626 61543.

FAUGHAN and ROE

(For close seasons, licences, see under Boards)

The Faughan flows N for 20m to enter the Foyle area E of Londonderry city; the Roe flows the same distance in the same general direction to enter the Foyle Estuary N of Limavady, Co Londonderry. Salmon, sea trout and brown trout in Faughan; principally sea trout in Roe, but also salmon from July.

FAUGHAN: River Faughan AA leases the fishing rights of the river, a 30 mile stretch of water divided into two sections, approx 2m tidal and 28m freshwater, situated between Londonderry and Claudy. Both sections are productive of sea trout and salmon. Visitors weekly and daily (24 hr) permits and licences are available from Club Office, 26A Carlisle Rd, Londonderry.

ROE:

Limavady (Co Londonderry). Good fishing for 15m from Limavady to Dungiven. Dept of Ag has 1¼m at **O'Cahan's Rock,** S of Limavady, with salmon and sea trout. Roe AA offers 12 day tickets for most of a 34 mile stretch, both banks, from source to river mouth, available from Limavady tackle shops. Dungiven AC controls 6m between Ross' Mill and Bovevagh Bridge, salmon, sea trout, best Sept/Oct. Dt £5 available from P McGuigan, 24 Station Rd, Dungiven, and Bovevagh P O. Tackle shops: R Douglas & Son, Rod & Gun, 6 Irish St, Limvaday; S J Mitchell, 29 Main St, Limavady, who displays map of all local fishings, issues permits and is a reliable source of local information. Hotels: Gorteen House, Limavady; Alexander Arms; many guest houses.

GLENS OF ANTRIM RIVERS

(For close seasons, licences, see under Boards)

GLENARM: Short privately-owned spate river. Salmon and sea trout. No permits.

GLENARIFF: Small sea trout river which flows into Red Bay at Glenariff. Permission from Glens AC.

GLENDUN: enters sea at **Cushendun.** Fair run of late salmon and sea trout. Dt £4 for Glens AC water on Dun, Glenariffe and Dall Rivers, from Mrs M McFettridge, 116 Tromara Rd, Castle Green, Cushendun. Fly, spinning, worm permitted, but no bait digging allowed.

MARGY/CAREY/GLENSHESK: a system of small rivers entering the sea at **Ballycastle.** Sea trout, brown trout and salmon. Dept of Ag waters. Tickets from R Bell, 38/40 Ann St, Ballycastle. Hotels: Antrim Arms, Ballycastle; Thornlea, Cushendun. Tackle shop: R Bell, 40 Ann St, Ballycastle.

Fishing Clubs

When you appoint a new secretary, do not forget to give us details of the change. Write to the publishers (address at front of the book). Thank you!

LAGAN
(For close seasons, licences, see under Boards)

A productive river which flows into the **Belfast Lough.** Trout fishing upstream from Magheralin, Co Down, for 12m.

Belfast (Co Antrim). Dept of Ag has 2¼m of coarse fishing on R Lagan. Permits from: Tight Lines, 120 Templemore Avenue; J Braddell, 11 Lower North St; J Dowds, 173 Victoria St; H D Wolsey, 60 Upper Newtownards Rd; G McGlade, Sports Equipment, 114 Royal Avenue.

Lisburn (Co Antrim). Iveagh AC has stretch of 7 miles from Thornyford Bridge, Dromore, to Spencer's Bridge, Flatford. 10 free dt for holders of Dept. of Ag annual game season permit. Tickets from Premier Angling, 17 Queen St, Lurgan. Lisburn & Dist AC fish on 7 miles of **Lagan** between Lisburn and Maira, containing a fair head of b trout, roach, bream; also a stretch of a small tributary, the **Ravarnette,** with b trout to 3lb not uncommon, also roach and bream. This fishing is open to general public with no charge. Club membership is £12 p.a. Dept of Ag has brown and/or rainbow trout lakes, totalling more than 700 acres, in the Lagan Valley area. Near to Belfast, these waters are fished more heavily than most in N Ireland. They include: **Stoneyford** and **Leathemstown Reservoirs,** 160 and 28 acres, b and r trout, fly, spinning and worm, 4 fish limit, no boat angling; **Ballykeel Loughherne,** 53 acres, b and r trout, fly only. Abundant coarse fishing on canals and loughs **Henney, Begney, Aghery, Beg, Neagh.** All with pike, perch, etc. Tackle shops: McBride's Sports, 4 Haslem's Lane; Gun and Tackle, Smithfield Sq; Lisburn Sports, 9 Smithfield Square. Hotels: Greenan Lodge, Conway, both Dunmurry.

Lurgan (Co Armagh). Dept of Ag water: **Craigavon City Park Lakes,** 168 acres, South Lake, r trout, fly, spinning, worming, 4 fish limit. North Lake, coarse fishery with pike and roach. Permits from F C Computers & Tackle, 28 High St; Premier Angling, 17 Queen St.

Dromore (Co Down). Dromore AC has 2 miles of river below, and 5 miles above Dromore: good trout water, for wet and dry fly. Season starts 1 March. Dt £3.50, juv £1, available from J McCracken's Confectionary, Gallows St, Dromore. 5 miles away at **Hillsborough,** 40 acres r trout fishery, Dept of Ag water, season 1 Feb-31 Dec. Accom. at Win Staff B+B, Banbridge Rd; Mrs Rhoda Marks, B+B, Milebush Rd, both Dromore.

LOUGH MELVIN
(For close seasons, licences, see under Boards)

A 5,000 acre natural lake, approximately one fifth of which lies in Northern Ireland, (Co Fermanagh). A good spring run of salmon starts in February and a grilse run in June, but the lake is famous chiefly for the quality of its native brown trout. In addition to fish of orthodox appearance, there are dark 'sonaghan' caught over the deeper water and the yellow-bellied 'gillaroo', found in the shallows near to shore. Regarded as the Dept of Agriculture's best game fishery. No coarse fishing. **Garrison,** Co Fermanagh is the centre for fishing the lough and **Lough Macnean,** Upper and Lower, also in the vicinity. (Pike, large trout, general coarse fishing.) Small trout in **L Lattone** may be caught from the roadside between Belcoo and Garrison. Boats for hire: Carlton Park Information and Fishing Centre, Belleek; M Gilroy, Melvin Bar, Garrison; Peter Cox, tel: 036565 685. Accommodation: Lough Melvin Holiday Centre and Heathergrove Guest House, Garrison, who offer boats and gillies. Clarke & McGrath, Belleek (036565 8181), have accom. with gillie, boat and instruction, if needed.

NEWRY RIVER
(For close seasons, licences, see under Boards)

A small system flowing into the head of **Carlingford Lough** at **Newry,** Co Down. 3m of fair brown trout water above Carnbane Industrial Estate. Newry & Dist AC issues dt £4 for **Clanrye River, Grinan Lake,** stocked with brown and rainbow trout and **McCourt's Lake, Poyntzpass,** brown trout, fly only. Available from Mrs E McAlinden, 12 Lisgullion Park, Armagh Rd, Newry. 3m from town, Cooper's Lake, fly fishing for brown trout. Two Dept of Agriculture trout lakes in area: **Lough Brickland** and **Glassdrumman.** Tackle shop: J C

Smith, 7 and 9 Kildare Street, Newry.

NEWRY SHIP CANAL

The first ship canal in British Isles, ceased operation in 1976. The fishable section which runs from Newry to sea locks on Omeath road, 3½m apprx, has produced match weights of over 50lb. Summer algae improves roach and bream catches, while large pike are to be caught in winter. Most winter fishing is in Albert Basin. There is free fishing for licence holders.

QUOILE

(For close seasons, licences, see under Boards)

Flows into top of **Strangford Lough** at **Downpatrick,** Co Down. Coarse fish and some trout in lower reaches; fair trout waters between Annacloy Bridge and Kilmore. Dept of Ag has fishing rights on **Quoile Basin** (100 acres) and 7m of Quoile River from Downpatrick to Kilmore; pike, perch, rudd, eels and brown trout; south bank fishing only. No fishing on nature reserve d/s of Steamboat Quay. No wading. Other Dept of Ag fisheries, **Portavoe Reservoir,** nr Donaghadee and Bangor, 31 acres b and r trout, fly only, 20 rods per day, 4 fish limit; **Lough Money,** 53 acre coarse fishery with pike, perch, eels, nr **Downpatrick.** Downpatrick & Dist AA hold fishing rights to **Laughinisland Lake** and **Magheraleggan Lake;** guests only when accompanied by a member. 2m north of Downpatrick is **Finnebrogue Fishery**, 30 acre lake trout fishery. Tel: 0396 616969. A new fishery for disabled anglers has been opened at **Marybrook Mill**, nr Ballynahinch. Rainbow trout and coarse fish. Tel: 0396 830173. 2 miles north of **Portaferry, Lough Cowey,** 70 acres, trout and salmon, now managed by Ards District Fly Fishing Club. Dt plus boat hire, £10 (4 hours), £25 (8 hours, 4 salmon and trout per boat); contact J Crothers, c/o Fishery, Lough Cowey Rd, 02477 28946. Tackle shops: H W Kelly & Son, Market Street, Downpatrick; Dairy Fishery, 179 Belfast Rd, Ballynahinch. Hotel: Portaferry, 02477 28231, offers fishing breaks on Lough Cowey.

SHIMNA

(For close seasons, licences, see under Boards)

Small attractive river with deep rocky pools flowing from E slope of Mournes to enter sea at **Newcastle,** Co Down. Sea trout and salmon from July. Dept of Agriculture fishery in forest areas. Bag limit 2 fish. No Sunday fishing. Permits from Forest Office at Tolleymore Forest Park and the Forest Ranger. The rest of the river is controlled by Shimna AC. Wt £25 and dt £7 available, from Four Season, see below. Fishing is by all legal methods. Dept stillwaters: **Spelga Reservoir,** 148 acres, b trout; **Castlewellan Lake,** 4 miles from Newcastle, 103 acres, b and r trout, 4 fish limit. Fly, spinning and worming. Tackle shop: The Four Seasons, 47 Main Street, Newcastle. Hotels: Slieve Donard; Enniskeen.

WHITEWATER

(For close seasons, licences, see under Boards)

Small attractive sea trout water flowing into sea W of **Kilkeel,** Co Down, 3m of good fishing. Kilkeel AC offers dt £2 for Kilkeel and Whitewater system, available from Nicholson's Hardware, The Square, Kilkeen, or tackle shops: J Graham, 66 Greencastle St; McConnell & Hanna, 19 Newcastle St, both Kilkeen. Hotel: Kilmorey Arms, Kilkeel.

POLLUTION

Anglers are united in deploring pollution. To combat it, urgent action may be called for at any time from any one of us. If numbers of fish are found dead, dying, or seriously distressed, take samples of both fish and water and contact the officer responsible for pollution at the appropriate National Rivers Authority.

The tailer in use on the Blackwater in Ireland. Generally speaking, a much-underemployed item of landing equipment. *Photo: S. J. Newman.*

SEA FISHING STATIONS IN NORTHERN IRELAND

The popularity of sea fishing in N Ireland has grown immensely in recent years, leading to the discovery of new and exciting possibilities. 300 miles of unpolluted coastline offers fishing for a variety of species from rock and beach alike. Sheltered inlets of which Strangford and Belfast Loughs are the largest and best known, offer protection to the boat angler when the open sea may be unfishable due to adverse weather. Twenty-four species of sea fish are caught regularly, including blue shark, skate, tope, cod, bass and flatfish.

Magilligan (Antrim). From point, surf fishing for dogfish, flounder, occasional bass. From strand, where lug and ragworm can be dug, beach fishing for flounder. Other venues are: Benone Strand, Downhill Strand, **Castlerock** beach and breakwater, **Barmouth** pier (spinning for mackerel) and beach; flatfish, coalfish, whiting, occasional mullet and bass.

Portrush (Antrim) and **Portstewart** (Derry). Near mouths of Lough Foyle and River Bann. Rock, pier and beach fishing for pollack, mackerel, wrasse, dogfish, coalfish, flounder, plaice, conger and bass. Conger fishing in Portrush harbour. Rock fishing from Ramore Head east and west, Blue Pool rocks, and **Dunseverick.** Skerries, 2m off Portrush produce good catches of turbot, plaice, dogfish, dab. Causeway bank off **Giants Causeway** good rock fishing for wrasse, coalfish, pollack, plaice, turbot. Many boats available for hire: B Black, tel: Portstewart 4840; M Collins, 4651; G Farrow, 026583 3633; R Cardwell, 0265 822359; J McLean, 0265 52124, and others. Tackle shop: Joe Mullan, 74 Main Street, Portrush. Hotels: Northern Counties; Magherabuoy House, Eglington, Kilnan-Oge; all Portrush (and many more).

Ballycastle (Co Antrim). Rock fishing for wrasse, pollack, coalfish, mackerel from Ballintoy. At Ballycastle strand, codling, plaice, small coalfish and whiting. Best in autumn, on evening tides. Spinning or float fishing for cod and pollack. **Rathlin Island**, just off the coast opposite Ballycastle, has wreck fishing for conger in Church Bay; and cod, coalfish, dogfish, plaice, pollack, turbot, haddock, ling, herring, conger eel, spurdog and skate off Bull point. Boats available from C McCaughan, 45 Ann St, tel: 02657 62074, and others. Tackle shop: R Bell, 40 Ann St. Hotel: Antrim Arms. Marcus Jameson (02657 62385) has accom. with sea fishing trips arranged.

Larne (Antrim). No fishing from harbour, but bottom fishing at nearby beach for coalfish, cod, dogfish, wrasse. Lugworm can be dug at Larne, **Glynn** and **Magheramorne** strands or bought at McCluskey's. Local venues are: Glenarm, popular night fishing mark for codling, flatfish; **Murlough Bay,** spinning from rocks for coalfish, mackerel, pollack; Garron point, codling, wrasse, pollack, coalfish, dogfish. Boats available from W Mann, 0574 74547. Tackle shops: Foster Sports, 60 Main St (tel: 0574 60883); S McCluskey, 47 Coastguard Rd (tel: 0574 63128). Hotels which cater for anglers: Magheramorne House, Curran Court, Halfway House, Kilwaughter House.

Whitehead and **Carrickfergus** (Antrim). Opposite Bangor at entrance to Belfast Lough (Belfast 16m). Pollack, mackerel, coalfish, cod, whiting, from rocks, beach and boats. Wrecks off Blackhead for cod, pollack, coalfish. Local venues are Whitehead Promenade, Carrickfergus Harbour and East pier, Ballycarry Causeway, nr **Islandmagee.** Below Blackhead lighthouse, conger, wrasse, cod, mackerel. Boat trips from Marina, Rogers Quay, tel: 09603 66666, as well as Sailing Club, The Harbour, tel: 09603 51402. Clubs: Woodburn AC and Greenisland AC. Hotels: Dobbins Inn; Coast Road, both Carrickfergus.

Bangor (Down). Bangor is on Belfast Lough, 12m from capital. Cod, plaice, turbot, whiting. Lugworm can be dug on beaches at Bangor, ragworm at Kinnegar. Smelt Mill Bay and Orlock point are good summer venues for wrasse, codling, coalfish, dogfish, mackerel. Bangor and **Donaghadee** piers for mackerel, coalfich, flatfish. Boats available from B Meharg, 25 Holborn Avenue (tel: 0247 455321); Nelson's, 0247 883403. Also three 2½ hr boat trips per day from North pier, with tackle on board: Tackle shops:

Field and Tackle, 22 Dromore St; Trap & Tackle, 6 Seacliff Rd (tel: 2047 458515).

Donaghadee (Down). Fishing from pier or rocks for pollack, codling and mackerel. Rigg sandbar (3m off Donaghadee) for cod, whiting, gurnard, coalfish, flatfish, mackerel, rays, dogfish, plaice, pollack. Back of Sandbar for big huss. Boats available from B Lennon, 4A The Parade, 0247 888653, and Q Nelson, 146 Killaughey Rd, 0247 883403. Tackle shop: Kennedy's, 1 The Parade.

Strangford Lough (Down). Good boat fishing in estuaries and inlets around the lough. Big skate (Aug-Oct), spurdog, huss, thornback. Skate and tope are protected species in lough, and must be returned to the water alive. Codling, turbot, whiting, haddock, mackerel, spurdog and wrasse at deep-water entrance to lough. Best fishing in slack water. Lugworm is plentiful at Island Hill nr Comber and shore at Kircubbin. Wreck fishing for big ling and conger outside lough. Boats in

Portaferry: P Wright, 0247 813457; D Rogers, 0247 728297. Tackle and bait from Hillview Service Station, 91 High St, Portaferry; Scott's Service Station, 34 Catherine St, Killyleagh; Hook, Line and Sinker, 43 South Street; Counrty Sports, 48a Regent St, both Newtownards.

Kilkeel (Down). Harbour fishing for coalfish and mackerel; West strand for flatfish, dogfish. Black Rock, **Ballymartin,** produces mackerel and codling; **Carlingford Lough,** flatfish, dogfish, thornback, a few bass. Good points are Cranfield and Greencastle. Lugworm can be dug in **Newcastle** harbour and **Greencastle,** rag and lug at **Warrenpoint** beach. Boats are available at Newcastle, phone Newcastle Centre, 03967 22222, or Harbourmaster, 03967 22106/22804. Boats are also for hire at Greencastle (06937 62422) and Warrenpoint (72682 or 73776). Tackle shops: J Graham, 47 Greencastle St, McConnell & Hanna, 19 Newcastle St; Four Seasons, 47 Main St, Newcastle.

Check before you go

While every effort has been made to ensure that the information given in **Where to Fish** *is correct, the position is continually changing, and anglers are urged, in their own interests, to make preliminary enquiries before travelling to selected venues. This is especially important with reference to prices quoted. Inevitably the rate of inflation is affecting stability in this quarter. Anglers' attention is also drawn to the fact that the hotels mentioned under the various fishing stations do not necessarily have water of their own. Any amendments or further data for inclusion in subsequent editions, and any criticism, will be welcome.*

FISHING CLUBS ETC. IN NORTHERN IRELAND

The following is an alphabetical list of fishing clubs and associations in Northern Ireland. Particulars of the waters held by many will be found by reference to the Index, in the section headed 'Fishing Stations in Northern Ireland', and information about the others, which may not have their own water, could be had from the Secretaries. A courtesy they appreciate is the inclusion of a stamped addressed envelope with postal inquiries. Please advise the publishers (address at the front of the book) of any changed details for the next edition.

NATIONAL BODIES

Ulster Coarse Fishing Federation
Robert Buick, Chairman
7 Knockvale Grove
Belfast BT5 6HL
Fisheries Conservancy Board for
Northern Ireland
1 Mahon Road

Portadown,
Craigavon
Co Armagh BT62 3EE
Fisheries Office
Riversdale
Ballinamallard
Co Fermanagh

CLUBS

Agivey Anglers Association
J P McCusker
27 Drumeil Road
Aghadowey
Co Londonderry
BT51 4BB
Antrim and District Angling Association
T Wilson
6 Alder Park
Greystone Road, Co Antrim
Ards Fly Fishing Club
James Crothers
c/o Lough Cowey Fishery
Lough Cowey Road
Co Down
Armagh and District Angling Club
Contact
Amagh District Council
The Palace Demesne
Armagh BT60 4EL
Ballymoney and District Angling Club
J McKay
15 Pharis Road
Ballymoney
Ballynure Angling Club
J Arneill

15 Grange Park
Ballyclare
Co Antrim
Banbridge Angling club
J Curran
2 Ballydown Road
Banbridge, Co Down
Bangor Sea Anglers
Seacliffe Road
Bangor
Belfast Anglers' Association
John A Collinson
7 Hawthorne Drive
Belfast BT4 2HG
Belfast Shore Anglers Club
c/o Cherryhill Avenue
Dundonald BT16 0JD
Blue Circle Angling Club
N Hutchinson
c/o Blue Circle
Sandholes Road
Cookstown
British Legion Angling Club
C McFetridge
c/o British Legion
Burn Road

Fishing Clubs

When you appoint a new secretary, do not forget to give us details of the change. Write to the publishers (address at front of the book). Thank you!

Cookstown
Co Tyrone
Castlederg Angling Association
S P Mannion
Mount Bernard
Castlederg, Co Tyrone
Castlewellan and Annsborough Angling Club
S P Harrison
Garden Cottage
Forest Park
Castlewellan
Clady and District Angling Club
H Doherty
95 Clady Road
Portglenone
Co Antrim BT44 8LB
Dromore Angling Club
R Russell
49 Ravenscroft Avenue
Belfast
Dundonald Angling Club
c/o 139 Ardenleen Avenue
Belfast BT6 OAE
Dundonald Sea Angling Club
c/o 24 Tara Crescent
Newtownards BT23 3DF
Dungiven Anglers Club
Now amalgamated with Roe AA
Enler Fishing Club
Comber
Co Down
Faughan Anglers Association
26A Carlisle Road
Londonderry
Gaff Angling Club
c/o Campbell's Mourne Valley Tackle
50 Main Street
Newtownstewart
Co Tyrone
Galgorm and District Angling Club
N Anderson
56 Ballykennedy Road
Gracehill
Gilford Angling Club
M Magee
Station Road
Scarva Craigavon
Glenravel & Clough Angling Club
D Anderson
6 Old Cushendun Road
Newtowncrommelin
Co Antrim
Glens Angling Club
Robert Sharpe
Titruhan
Glenariffe Road
Glenariffe
Ballymena,

Co Antrim
Gracehill, Galgorm and District Angling Club
Norman Anderson
50a Ballykennedy Rd
Gracehill, Co Antrim
Greenisland Angling Club
W Hinton
18 Glenkeen Drive
Greenisland
Carrickfergus
Holywood Flydressers Guild
A J Kennedy
6 Demesne Park
Holywood BT18 9NE
Holywood Fly Fishing Club
C F Kyle
2 Seymour Park
Crawfordsburn Road
Bangor
Kells and Connor Angling Club
N Wilson
35 Templemoyle
Kells, Ballymena
Co Antrim
Kilkeen Angling Club
A Kilgore
4 Mill Street
Annalong
Kilrea and District Angling Club
J Templeton
Main Street
Garvagh,
Co Londonderry
Kingfisher Angling Centre
24A Hiltonstown Road
Portglenone
Co Antrim
Kings Road Game Angling Club
c/o 8 Kirn Park
Dundonald, BT5 7GA
Lisburn and District Anglers' Club
D Croot
109 Benson Street
Lisburn, Co Antrim
BT28 2AF
Lower Bann Coarse Angling Association
John Saville
Broughshane
Ballymoney
Maine Angling Club
Eddie Hopkins
5 Lenaghan Avenue
Belfast
Maine System Game Angling Association
David Henry
142 Queen Street
Ballymena
Co Antrim

Mid-Antrim Angling Club
R Topping
24 Cameron Park
Ballymena
Co Antrim

Mid-Ulster Angling Club
D Boner
57 Molesworth Road
Cookstown
Co Tyrone

Moy Angling Club
D Tomney
10 The Square
Moy, Dungannon
Co Tyrone

Newry and District Angling Club
D Kidd
8 Cloneden
Dallan Road
Warrenpoint
Co Down

Omagh Angling Association
J Fergy
4 Strahulter Rd
Grange
Newtownstewart
Co Tyrone

Randalstown Angling Club
J Goodrich
41 Clonkeen Road
Randalstown
BT41 3JZ

Rathfriland and District Angling Association
D A Crory
5 Castlewellan Road
Rathfriland, Co Down

River Faughan Anglers' Association
Lance Thompson
c/o Club Office
26A Carlisle Road
Londonderry
Co Londonderry

Roe Angling Association
S Maxwell
51 Scroggy Road
Limavady, Co Derry

Sea Ramblers Angling Club
c/o Oberon Street
Belfast
BT6 8NZ

Shimna Angling Club
P Mornin
84 Bryansford Road
Newcastle, Co Down
BJ33 0LE

Sion Mills Angling Club
Eddie McCrea
35 Main Street
Sion Mills
Co Tyrone

Warrenpoint, Rostrevor and District Angling Club
John O'Crey
Springfield Road
Warrenpoint
Co Down

Woodburn Angling Club
W Moore
544 Upper Road
Woodburn
Carrickfergus

Fishing Clubs

When you appoint a new secretary, do not forget to give us details of the change. Write to the publishers (address at front of the book). Thank you!

FISHING IN IRELAND

The Irish Republic is world famous for the quality of its fisheries. Salmon, sea trout, brown trout, pike and other coarse fish, are to be found there at their best. The seas around Ireland contain very good quantities of many varieties of fish which provide excellent sport for visiting and native sea anglers. Where to fish in Ireland is virtually everywhere. Fisheries are administered by a Central Fisheries Board and by seven Regional Fisheries Boards answering to the Central Board. The function of each Regional Board is to conserve, protect and develop every aspect of the inland fisheries (salmon, trout, coarse fish, eels), including sea angling, within the Board's fisheries region.

Rod/Line Licences:

Salmon/Sea Trout - Season (All districts) £25
Salmon/Sea Trout (Single District Only) £12
Salmon/Sea Trout Juvenile £8
Salmon/Sea Trout 21-Day £10
Salmon/Sea Trout 1 Day £3
Foyle Area Extension £17

Central/Regional Fisheries Board Permits

Ordinary (Season) £5. Day £2
Pensioner/Juvenile (Season) £2, (Day) £0.50

South Western Board Permits
Annual £20. Three week £10. Day £3.

The modified close seasons now in force for salmon, sea trout and brown trout differ not only as between regions, but also within regions, in a formulation too complex for reproduction here in detail. The general pattern is that seasons for migratory fish tend to open early and close early, while that for brown trout opens early in many places (Feb 15) and does not close until a date in October. There are, however, important exceptions and anglers proposing to visit the Republic, especially early or late in the year, should make careful enquiries with the appropriate Regional Board before making firm plans, whether the intention be to fish for salmon, migratory or brown trout.

There is no annual close season for angling for coarse fish or for sea fish.

Overall responsibility for the country's fisheries rests with the Department of the Marine, Leeson Lane, Dublin 2, tel: 01 6785444.

The Central Fisheries Board consists of the Chairman of the seven Regional Boards and from four to six members nominated by the Minister for Fisheries and Forestry. The functions of the Central Board are prescribed in the Fisheries Act 1980 and include such things as co-ordination and, where necessary, direction of the regional boards in the performance of their functions; management of any fishery, hatchery or fish farm possessed by the Central Board; etc.

The Central Fisheries Board owns and operates an important commercial and rod salmon fishery on the River Corrib at Galway, Co Galway (inquiries to the Manager, The Fishery, Nun's Island, Galway, Co Galway, tel: 091 62388), and the famous Erriff Fishery in Co Galway. Enquiries for fishing and accommodation here - at Aasleagh Lodge or Cottage - to the Manager, R Erriff Fishery, Aasleagh Lodge, Leenane, Co Galway (tel: 095 42252).

The Electricity Supply Board also holds extensive fishing rights: principal salmon waters are the River Mulcair and the Shannon at Parteen, above Limerick, and at Castleconnell, Co Limerick. The Board preserves and develops the fisheries under its control. Inquiries to Electricity Supply Board, Fisheries Division, Ardnacrusha, Co Clare (tel: 061 345588).

Inquiries about accommodation and general tourist angling information (e.g. leaflets, brochures about local angling resources and amenities throughout the country) should be

Picture opposite: Almost as much fun as the actual fishing. Catching live mayflies for dapping is a common sight on an Irish lough shore - in this case, Lough Arrow.

addressed to **Bord Failte, Baggot Street Bridge, Dublin 2, tel: 01 765871,** or **The Irish Tourist Board, 150 New Bond Street, London.**

THE REGIONAL BOARDS

The Eastern Regional Fisheries Board. Covers all lakes and river systems entering the sea including coastal waters between Carlingford Lough, Co Louth and Kiln Bay, Co Wexford. Inquiries to: Regional Manager, Balnagowan House, Mobhi Boreen, Glasnevin, Dublin 9 (tel: 01 379209).

The Southern Regional Fisheries Board. Covers all lakes and river systems entering the sea, including coastal waters, between Kiln Bay, Co Wexford and Ballycotton Pier, Co Cork. Inquiries to the Board's Regional Fisheries Manager, Anglesea St, Clonmel, Co Tipperary (tel: 052 23624).

The South Western Regional Fisheries Board. Covers all lakes and river systems entering the sea, including coastal waters, between Ballycotton Pier, Co Cork and Kerry Head, Co Kerry. Inquiries to the Board's Regional Fisheries Manager, Nevilles Terrace, Massey Town, Macroom, Co Cork (tel: 026 41221/2; fax 026 41223).

The Shannon Regional Fisheries Board. Covers all lakes and rivers entering the sea, including coastal waters, between Kerry Head, Co Kerry and Hag's Head, Co Clare. Inquiries to the Board's Regional Fisheries Manager, Thomond Weir, Limerick, Co Limerick (tel: 061 455171).

The Western Regional Fisheries Board. Covers all lakes and rivers entering the sea, including coastal waters, between Hag's Head, Co Clare and Pigeon Point, near Westport, Co Mayo. Inquiries to The Board's Regional Fisheries Manager, The Weir Lodge, Earl's Island, Galway (tel: 091 63118).

The North Western Regional Fisheries Board. Covers all lakes and rivers entering the sea, including coastal waters, between Pigeon Point, near Westport, Co Mayo, and Carrickgarve, Co Sligo. Inquiries to the Board's Regional Fisheries Manager, Ardnaree House, Abbey St, Ballina, Co Mayo (tel: 096 22788; fax: 096 70543).

The Northern Regional Fisheries Board. Covers all lakes and rivers entering the sea, including coastal waters, between Carrickgarve, Co Sligo and Malin Head, Co Donegal. Inquiries to the Board's Regional Fisheries Manager, Station Road, Ballyshannon, Co Donegal (tel: 072 51435/ 52053; fax: 072 51816).

POLLUTION

Anglers are united in deploring pollution. To combat it, urgent action may be called for at any time from any one of us. If numbers of fish are found dead, dying, or seriously distressed, take samples of both fish and water and contact the officer responsible for pollution at the appropriate Regional Fisheries Board.

FISHING STATIONS IN IRELAND

Details of close seasons, licences, etc, for Irish rivers and loughs listed alphabetically here will be found in pages on the previous pages. Anglers wanting further details of accommodation should write to **Bord Failte (Irish Tourist Board), Baggot Street Bridge, Dublin, 2.** Anglers in the **Western Fisheries Region** should note the fact that the killing of sea trout is is now illegal. **All sea trout must be returned alive to the water.**

BALLYSODARE and LOUGH ARROW

(For close seasons, licences, etc, see The Regional Fisheries Board).

River Ballysodare formed by junction of three rivers, **Unshin** or **Arrow, Owenmore** (not to be confused with Owenmore River, Co Mayo), and **Owenbeg**, near Collooney, flows into Ballysodare Bay. Near mouth of river, at Ballysodare Falls, is earliest salmon ladder erected in Ireland (1852). Salmon, trout, very few sea trout. R Arrow, which runs out of Lough Arrow, contains small stock of brown trout for which fishing is free. The Owenmore has good coarse fishing, especially bream, at Ballymote. Lough Arrow is a rich limestone water of 3,123 acres on the border of Sligo and Roscommon. It is about 5m long and varies in width from ½m to 1½m. The lough is almost entirely spring-fed and has a place of honour among Ireland's best known mayfly lakes. Nowhere else is the hatch of fly so prolific or the rise so exciting. Three and four-pounders are common. Trout rise to mayfly from late May to mid-June and sport is varied at this time by dapping, wet-fly and dry-fly fishing with green drake and the spent gnat. This is followed soon after (mid-July to mid-Aug) by a late evening rise to big sedge called the Murrough and Green Peter which may give the lucky angler as much fun as mayfly. The marked improvement in fishing at Lough Arrow can be attributed to the removal of coarse fish from these waters by the Central Fisheries Board and regular stocking with trout. Boats and gillies may be hired at all times and at many centres on lake shore.

Collooney (Co Sligo). Dt at times from Collooney and Dist AA. Best season, May to July. Fishing dependent on sufficient rain. Leave for sea and brown trout sometimes obtainable. Good dry fly. River contains sizeable pike; permission from riparian owners. **Lough Bo** fished from here.

Castlebaldwin via **Boyle** (Co Sligo). Trout fishing on L Arrow, free. Season 1 March-30 Sept. Bank fishing not recommended. Boats can be hired on lakeshore from Dodd Boats, Ballindoon. L Arrow FPS fishes in Loughs **Arrow** and **Augh** (pike, perch, b trout in L Arrow). **Lough Bo,** in hills provides good shore fishing for brown trout. Fly only. Season 1 April-30 Sept. **Lake na Leibe** has rainbow trout stocked by Central Fisheries Board. Season 1 April-30 Sept. Fishing from shore or boat. Good stock of brown trout in **Lough Feenagh;** boats available. River fishing on **R Unshin** and **R Feorrish**

(above Ballyfarnon); trout. Coarse fishing on **Templehouse Lake** and **Cloonacleigha Lake;** good pike fishing; boats available. Coarse and trout fishing on **Lough Key**, 3m east of Arrow. Contact sec of L Arrow FPS. Hotels: Cromleach Lodge, Rock View.

Boyle (Co Roscommon). L Arrow, trout, free; contact Fishery Inspector (tel: 079 66033) for information. **River Boyle,** a tributary of R Shannon, connects **Loughs Gara** and **Key.** Boat hire from F Dodd, 071 65162; R Acheson, 079 66181. Tackle shops: Abbey Marine, Carrick Rd; Christy Wynne, Main St, who supplies live and ground bait. Michael Rogers, Ballymote. Hotel: Royal. Accom for anglers: Arrow Angling Accommodation, 079 66181/66050; Mrs Kelly, Forest Park, 079 62227; Mrs Mitchell, Abbey House, 079 62385; Arrow Lakeside Accom, 01035731 65065.

BANDON

(For close seasons, licences, etc, see The South Western Regional Fisheries Board)

Salmon fishing extends all the way from **Inishannon** u/s to **Togher Castle,** depending on conditions. An estimated 1,300 salmon are caught each season; about 300 of these are spring fish. Grilse run at end of June. Big run of sea trout from early July, and good stocks of browns. Good stretches are: from Innishannon u/s to **Desert Bridge,** excellent; from Desert Bridge u/s to **Enniskeane Bridge,** fair. Good from Carbery Factory to **Manch Bridge.** Some contacts for private fishing are: Mr C Good, Inishannon, 021 75261; Ms A Blanchfield, Ballinhassig, 021 885167; D Lamb, Enniskeane, 023 47279.

Bandon (Co Cork). About 6m river controlled by River Bandon Salmon and Trout AA. Tickets from M J O'Regan, Oliver Plunkett St, Bandon.

Ballineen (Co Cork). The 4m stretch of river to about 1m above Ballineen Bridge is controlled by Ballineen and Enniskeane AA; salmon and trout. St and dt from Tom Fehilly, Bridge Street, Ballineen.

Dunmanway (Co Cork). Above Manch Bridge is Dunmanway Salmon and Trout AA water. Tickets from P MacCarthy, Yew Tree Bar, Dunmanway. River fishable for about 8m. Many small trout loughs in region, incl **Cullenagh** (4½m west), **Coolkeelure** (2¼m north west), **Ballynacarriga, Atarriff, Chapel Lake;**

free fishing, small browns; for **Curraghalickey Lake,** contact P MacCarthy, *see above.*

CAHA RIVER. Joins Bandon 3m north of Dunmanway. Holds good stock of trout to 14 oz, for 3m up from confluence. Free fishing, best in early season, because of weed. Free fishing on **Neaskin Lough,** 3¼m north of Dunmanway. Difficult access, but plenty of 6oz browns.

Clonakilty (Co Cork). **River Argideen,** flowing into **Courtmacsherry Harbour,** has salmon and sea trout. Permit from Fishery Office, Inchy Bridge. Tickets for **Sheperton Lakes, Skibbereen** (stocked with b and r trout), £3 from N Connolly, 028 33328. Hotels: Emmet, Inchydoney, O'Donovans, Imperial.

BARROW (including Suir and Nore)

(For close seasons, licences, etc, see The Southern Regional Fisheries Board)

Rises well up in the centre of Ireland on the eastern slopes of the Shannon watershed and flows over 120m southerly to the sea at Waterford Harbour, entering by a long estuary. Limited salmon fishing available in main channel. Good brown trout river suitable for dry fly. Plentiful stocks of coarse fish, including bream, rudd, eels, pike, and tench fishing around **Goresbridge.**

Waterford (Co Waterford). Reservoirs, **Knockaderry** and **Ballyshunnock:** both 70 acres at normal level, with wild brown and stocked rainbow, 6 fish limit. Boats (£4) on Knockderry, fly only, book in advance, 051 84107. All legal methods on Ballyshunnock, bank only, no maggot. Dt £1.50 on both, st £20. Available at Carrolls Cross Inn, 051 94328. **Mahon River** (15m) holds sea trout and salmon, and mackerel, bass and pollack abound along the coast. Dunmore Deep Sea AC, Co Waterford, welcomes visitors. Tackle shop: Morgans, 22 Ballybricken, Waterford.

Graighuenamanagh (Co Carlow). Good coarse fishing, with pike and large bream. Local venues are Tinnehinch Lower Weir and Bahanna. Contact J Butler, Tinnahinch, Graighuenamagh.

Carlow (Co Carlow). Bream, rudd, pike. Trout fishing on **Rivers Lerr, Greese, Douglas** and **Burren,** which fish well wet or dry, controlled by Barrow AC and re-stocked yearly (membership £2 from local tackle shops). Club: Carlow AA. Annual membership £2. Permits for Mil-

ford Weir to canal mouth d/s of Milford Bridge from Lock House, **Milford.** Tackle shops: John Boyd, 3 Castle Hill; Tully's Sports, Tullow St, Carlow; Byrne & Dawson, Main Street, Tullow. Accom: Royal Hotel; Mrs Quinn, Milford, 010 353 503 46261.

Athy (Co Kildare). Trout, bream, rudd, pike. Several tributaries within easy reach. **R Greese,** from Colbinstown Bridge to Barbers Bridge fishable on permit from Greese AC. Bream to 8lb are regularly caught in Barrow, as well as pike, perch, rudd and game fish. **Grand Canal** holds good head of tench, pike, perch, rudd and bream. There is some good free dry-fly water on left bank d/s of Athy, known as the Barrow Track, owned by Office of Public Works. Kilberry & Cloney AC fish 5m **Boherbaun River** from Milltown Bridge to Forth of Dunrally Bridge (natural browns, 1-4lb); st available, £5, from tackle shops. Athy & Dis AC fishes Barrow from Dunrally Bridge to Maganey Lock. In Sept 1992 club released 20,000 brown trout into Barrow as part of a general improvement program. There are no fishing rights on Barrow, but a club card allows access from landowners. Membership £5 p.a. from tackle shops: The Sports Shop, Emely Sq; Griffin Hawe, Duke St. Accommodation: Mr Jim Crean, Milltown Cottage, 010 353 502 25189.

Portarlington (Co Laois). River at town is easily accessible, and holds some salmon from March. Portarlington AC has approx 6 miles of good trout fishing on **Upper Barrow**. Best mid-May to mid-Sept. Tickets, £1, £5, are available from treasurer Mr Hargrove, Barrowbank, Portarlington; Mick Finlay, publican, Bracklone St. Monasterevin AC has approx 6 miles of very good trout and coarse fishing d/s of town, and some free coarse fishing on parts of the **Figile River,** a tributary of the Barrow. Another tributary, the **Cushina River,** north of **Monasterevin** is fished by Cushina AC: tickets available from P Dunne, Clonsast,

Rathangan. For general information about local fishing, and tickets, contact Kieran Cullen, Gun and Tackle, Monasterevin, 045 25902/25329.

GRAND CANAL (Co Kildare). Much free fishing. Canal runs through **Prosperous** and **Robertston** where it contains bream, rudd, tench, hybrids and some pike. Prosperous Coarse AC fishes on a length of some 20m. For information contact Ned O'Farrell, 045 68092. At **Edenderry,** Co Offaly, canal has bream, perch and pike. Contact Padraic Kelly, 48 Murphy St, Edenderry.

GRAND CANAL, BARROW BRANCH (Co Kildare). Fishing for bream, rudd and pike at **Rathangan.** Information from M J Conway, Kildare Rd, Rathangan. At **Monasterevin** canal has pike, perch and bream. Contact Pat Cullen, Tackle Shop. At **Vicarstown,** Co Laois, fishing for bream, tench, pike and rudd. Contact Jim Crean, Vicarstown Inn.

SUIR

(For close seasons, licences, etc, see The Southern Regional Fisheries Board)

A fairly shallow river with deep glides, which drains large areas of limestone. Runs into the same estuary as Nore and Barrow, and is much better salmon river. Noted also for its trout fishing. Record salmon for Ireland, 57lb, was caught in Suir, in 1874. Salmon fishing opens on 1 Feb, and in good years large 'springers' up to 25lb are caught. Grilse runs usually begins in late May and continues to end of Sept. Late August and Sept often bring bigger fish, over 10lb. Dry and wet fly fishing for trout is available from late April onwards.

Carrick-on-Suir (Co Tipperary). Start of tidal water. **Duffcastle** to Carrick-on-Suir is last freshwater section, well stocked with trout. Carrick-on-Suir AA has north bank from Carrick-on-Suir westward to Duffcastle, also **Coolnamuck Fisheries,** 3 miles south bank, fishing for salmon, trout, twait shad. Tickets and gillies are available though J O'Keeffe, *see below.* Free trout fishing on tributary **Lingaun River,** which runs from north into tidal water east of Carrick-on-Suir; landowners consent reqd. Up river there is good trout fishing and occasional sea trout; free for 400m on left bank d/s of **Kilsheelin.** 1½m south bank is available from Mrs Maura Long, Glencastle, Kilnasheelin, 052 33287; salmon and trout, £15, £5. About 4m to south mountain loughs, largest of which are **Coumshingaun** and **Crotty's,** provide very good fishing as also does **Clodiagh River,** which springs from loughs and is close to road for part of way. Angler in search of good salmon and trout fishing

would be advised to seek it anywhere from Carrick to Cashel. Most of river preserved for salmon, but some owners give permission to fish for trout. Tackle shop: O'Keeffe, OK Sports, New St, 051 40626. Hotel: Orchard House.

Clonmel (Co Tipperary). Free fishing between the bridges in town. Clonmel and Dist AC controls water from **Knocklofty Bridge** d/s one mile on south bank, also from Clonmel New Bridge to **Anner River.** Tickets from John Carroll, 3 New Quay. Clonmel Salmon AA also has water, stretch above Knocklofty Bridge, and both banks at **Kilsheenan;** apply to treasurer, J Kavanagh, *see below.* **Nire** and **Tar** trout streams are within easy reach. Nire Valley Angling Holidays has 4m, plus 2m on Suir and 2m on Tar. Contact Mrs E Ryan, Clonanvan Farmhouse, 052 36141. Nire Valley AC has 6m of **Nire,** st £5 from Mrs Wall, Hanoras Cottage, Ballymacarbry. Mountain loughs can also be reached from this centre. Tackle shop: Kavanagh's Sports Shop,

O'Connell St. Hotels: Clonmel Arms; Hotel Minella.

Ardfinnan (Co Tipperary). Ardfinnan AC has much trout fishing in locality, d/s of Rochestown to Corabella. Permits from John Maher, Green View, Ardfinnan.

Cahir (Co Tipperary). Cahir and Dist AA, controls Suir above Quillane slip nr Golden, to weir in Cahir Town, Swiss Cottage area d/s to **Ballybrada; Carrightahan** to the small stream. Salmon dt £5 and tackle from Mrs B Morrissey, Castle St; Other tackle shop: Suirtackle, The Square, Cahir. Hotels: Cahir House, Galtee and Kilcoran Lodge; 8m salmon and trout water. Licences from D K Kavanagh, West Gate. Clonmel. Salmon and brown trout flies from E Heavey, Cahir Park, and R J Watkins, Castle Street. Hotels: Castle Court, Kilcoran Lodge.

Cashel (Co Tipperary). Brown trout and salmon. Cashel, Golden and Tipperary AA issues visitors' permits for **Suir** from Camas Bridge south to **Ballycarron Bridge,** fly only, dt £5 from Mrs Ryan, Friar St. Dundrum Dist AA fly fishes on **Marl Lake, Dundrum.** Permits from Dundrum House Hotel. Other hotels: Cashel Place; Ardmayle House; Baileys, Cashel, Ryans, and others.

Thurles (Co Tipperary). Good centre for upper river. Thurles, Holycross and Ballycamas AA has water from **Holycross** to Kileen Flats both banks, fly only. Dt £5 from Hayes Hotel. Club also fishes **R Clodiagh** and **R Drish**. Good stocks of trout to 3lb. U/s from Drish Bridge weeded in summer; d/s fishable throughout season, usually. Accom: Cappamurra House, Dundrum, 062 71127.

Templemore (Co Tipperary). Templemore AA water; visitors' dt for Suir (trout only, av ½lb).

BLACKWATER RIVER (Co Kilkenny). This tributary joins the Suir about 2 miles upstream of Waterford City. It is tidal as far as the weir below **Kilmacow,** and holds good stocks of small trout between Kimacow and **Mullinavat.** Some fishing is available with landowners consent. Enquire at local tackle shops.

PORTLAW CLODIAGH (Co Waterford). Tributary, which joins **Suir** east of Portlaw. Moderate trout stocks. Fishing rights on entire river owned by the Marquis of Waterford, but fishing is freely available u/s of **Lowrys Bridge** and d/s of **Portlaw.**

ARA/AHERLOW (Co Tipperary). Tributary joins Suir north of Cahir, flowing from a westerly direction. Ara AA has trout fishing from **Tipperary Town** to **Kilmyler Bridge,** where R Ara meets R

Spinning on the Suir. *Photo: Borde Failte.*

Aherlow; fly, spinning or worming, wt   £5, from J Evans, Main St, Tipperary.

NORE

(For close seasons, licences, etc, see The Southern Regional Fisheries Board)

Lies between Barrow and Suir, and runs into same estuary. Salmon fishing now mainly preserved and overnetting has lowered stocks. Spring fish are heavy; big grilse run from June onwards. Trout fishing good (regularly restocked), fish average $\frac{1}{2}$-$\frac{3}{4}$lb. Tributaries also have been restocked and sport excellent.

Thomastown (Co Kilkenny), Thomastown AA has excellent salmon and trout stretch of Nore and issues temporary cards to visitors, st £50 to dt £7 or £3. Available from Synott's Shop, The Quay, Thomastown. Trout fishing is fly or worm only. Inistioge AC offers permits (available at Castle Inn, Inistioge) for $\frac{3}{4}$m both banks at **Inistioge.**

Kilkenny (Co Kilkenny). Kilkenny AA has some excellent salmon and trout fishing on **Nore,** left bank from **Dinin R** to **Greenville** weir, and from **Maddockstown** to 1m u/s of **Bennetsbridge;** also **Dinin R,** Dinin Bridge to Nore. Assc issues permits to visitors, available from P Campion, Tackle Shop, Kilkenny. Durrow & Dist AC fishes from **Watercastle Bridge** to **Owveg** confluence, and **Erkina R** from **Durrow Castle** to R Nore. Dt from Bill Lawlor, Foodmarket, The Square, Durrow. Rathdowney AC fishes **Erkina R** from **Coneyburrow Bridge** to **Boston Bridge,** early season best, dt available from M White, Moorville, Rathdowney. **Kings River;** good brown trout. Tackle shops: M McGrath, 3 Lower Patrick Street, Kilkenny; Kilkenny Sports Scene, 1 Irishtown, Kilkenny. Hotels: Newpark,

Flannery's.

Abbeyleix (Co Laois). Abbeyleix & Dist AC fishes from **Shanahoe Bridge** to **Waterloo Bridge,** dt available from V Bowell, Sandymount, Abbeyleix. Guest houses with fishing: Mrs S Pratt, Dealgrove; Mrs H M Seale, The Glebe, Attanagh, Portlaoise. Fishing much deteriorated due to pollution and drainage works.

Mountrath (Co Laois). Nore; brown trout, pike, perch. Mountrath & Dist AC stocks and fishes Nore mainchannel from Nore/**Delour** confluence to New Bridge at **Donore,** and **Whitehorse River,** also Ballyfin Lake (pike). Permits from Tom Watkins, 0502 32540. Tackle from Mrs Kelly, Main St. Accom: Mrs Geraldine Guilfoyle, Redcastle, 0502 32277; Mrs Fiona Wallis, Coote Terrace, 0502 32756.

KINGS RIVER (Co Kilkenny). Tributary which joins Nore above Thomastown. Callan & Dist AA fishes from Metal Bridge, $2\frac{1}{2}$m u/s of Callan to Newton Bridge, $2\frac{1}{2}$m d/s. Dt from Chris Vaughan, Green St, Callan. Kells AC also has water: permits available, enquire locally.

BLACKWATER

(For close seasons, licences, etc, see The Southern Regional Fisheries Board)

Perhaps most famous salmon river in Southern Ireland. Rises west of Killarney Mountains and flows eastwards about 70m until it reaches town of Cappoquin, where it becomes tidal and turns sharply south, entering sea by estuary 15m long at Youghal Bay. Salmon (best stretches mainly between Mallow and Lismore), sea trout, brown trout, but large quantities of dace, bream, perch and pike in some parts. Best fishing strictly preserved. Big runs of spring salmon from Feb to April; grilse June to Sept; and often good run of autumn salmon during Aug and Sept. Sea trout in Blackwater and Bride, June onwards.

Youghal (Co Cork). Youghal Sea AC has fishing on main river and tributaries. All arrangements through secretary. At **Castlemartyr** on Cork/Youghal road is **Lough Aderry,** rainbow trout fishery, 6 fish limit, fly, worm and spinning.

Cappoquin (Co Waterford). The freshwater here is backed up by the tide and fishing is best when the water is either rising or falling. Salmon and trout, good coarse fishing for roach and dace throughout year but best autumn and spring. Cappoquin Salmon & Trout AC have many miles of water. Tickets from 'The Toby Jug'. Good bream fishing at **Dromana Lake,** south of Cappoquin. Trout fishing

Truly wild fish. The class of trout for which anglers from all over Europe visit Ireland. *Photo: Trout and Salmon.*

on **Rivers Owenshed** and **Finisk** and on R Blackwater downstream of **Lismore Bridge**; permits from Lismore Estate Office *(see advt)*: Tackle shop: Mary Fives Tackle & Gift Shop, Main St. Hotel: Richmond House. Anglers accom: 'The Toby Jug'; Flynn's River View Guesthouse, 010 353 58 54073.

Ballyduff and **Upper Ballyduff** (Co Waterford). Ballyduff Trout FAA has approx 3m east of bridge and 3m west, both banks. Visitors may apply to Eamon Bolger, Post Office. Private salmon fishing at **Blackwater Lodge Hotel** (tel: 058 60235, fax: 058 60162). *(see advt)* 17 beats covering 30 miles of river. Dt £30, self-catering accom, tackle, smokery and gillies available from Hotel. Tackle shop: Bolger's, Ballyduff. Guesthouses: Elgin Cottage, 058 60255; Hillside, 058 60297.

Conna (Co Cork). Salmon fishing at **Dempster Fishery;** 7m stretch of single and double bank fishing on some of best sections of R Blackwater. All beats include good fly waters. Grilse run commences in late May, best month usually Sept. Average catch, 1988-92: 344 salmon and grilse. Dt £20-£33; rods numbers are kept down, advance booking necessary. Gillies available. Permits, tackle and details of fishing accommodation from Peter Dempster Ltd, Carrigeen Hill, Conna, Co Cork (tel: 35358 56248).

Fermoy (Co Cork). Salmon, brown trout, dace, roach, perch, gudgeon and pike. Four coarse fishing beats are available by courtesy of Fermoy Salmon AA, best being Barnane Walk, Jones Field and Hospital bank. Permits from Toomey's, *see below.* Salmon fishing on R Blackwater at **Careysville Fishery**, 1¾m stretch, both banks with well defined pools. One of the most prolific salmon fisheries in the country. Grilse run in June. Fishing peaks on the lower beats in June and on the rest of river in July. Max 2 to 4 rods per day depending on month. Gillie price included in fishing charges. Permits from Brian Murphy, Careyville (tel: 025 31094). Stretches near town which hold roach and dace; waters accessible and banks well kept. For information on coarse fishing contact Hon Sec, Fermoy Coarse AC (tel: 025 32074); and Jack O'Sullivan, Tackle Shop, 4 Patrick St (tel: 025 31110), who also stocks bait. U/s of Fermoy is **Ballyhooley Castle Fishery;** contact Merrie Green, Ballyvolane House, Castlelyons. **Araglin** holds brown trout; good dry fly. **Funshion** runs in near Careysville on north bank; trout, dace, rudd. Other tackle shop: Brian Toomey, Sports and Leisure, MacCurtain St, Fermoy, 025 31101. Hotels; Grand, Avonmore Country House. B & B information from Jack O'Sullivan.

Mallow (Co Cork). Salmon fishing from 1 Feb to end of Sept; trout 15 Feb to end of Sept. Mallow Game & Coarse AC has 4m both banks, salmon, trout, dace and roach. Dt available, coarse fishing free. Information from the Bridge House Bar. Tackle shop: Pat Hughes, the Spa, Mallow. Hotels; Hibernian; Central.

BRIDE. This tributary of the Blackwater holds salmon and sea trout as well as brown trout; also dace.

Tallow (Co Waterford). River is 500 yds from town. Tallow & Dist AC have 4½m fishing from Mogeely Bridge to Bride Valley Fruit Farm. Brown trout, sea trout; salmon and peal from June onwards. Fly only between Mogeely and Tallow Bridges, otherwise, maggot, worm, etc. There is also coarse fishing for big dace and roach. Visiting anglers welcome. St (£7) and dt (£4) available from Bride View Bar, or tackle shops: John Forde; Dan Delaney, both Main St; Peter Dempster, Conna. Hotels: Bride View Bar; Devonshire Arms.

AWBEG. Tributary which runs into the Blackwater midway between Mallow and Fermoy. A very good trout stream, especially for dry fly.

BOYNE

(For close seasons, licences, etc, see The Eastern Regional Fisheries Board)

Rises near Edenderry and flows for about 70m, entering the sea near Drogheda north of Dublin. One of Ireland's premier game fisheries, in main channel and tributaries. Good salmon fishing between Navan and Drogheda. Excellent run of sea trout as far up river as Slane Bridge. Superb stocks of brown trout in Boyne and tributaries. Virtually no free fishing, but permits are available on many club waters. Contact Joint Council of Boyne Anglers, Mrs T Healy, Little Grange, Drogheda, tel: 041 24829. Fishable tributaries include **Rivers Trimblestown** (small browns), **Kells Blackwater** (trout, u/s of Headford Bridge), **Borora** (7m good trout fishing from Corlat d/s to Carlanstown), **Martry** (small stream, trout to 1lb), **Stoneyford** (excellent trout water, Rathkenna Bridge to Shanco Bridge), **Deel** (a few salmon at Riverdale, trout), **Little Boyne** (spring trout fishery, club based at Edenberry), **Nanny** (sea trout up to Julianstown, browns to Balrath Bridge).

Drogheda (Co Louth). Drogheda and District AC has game and coarse fishing on Boyne and **Nanny;** and also **Reservoirs Killineer** and **Barnattin** which are stocked with brown and rainbow. Permits from Military Connection, Laurence St. Lower parts of Boyne and Mattock preserved. Tickets for Slane and Robin Anglers fishing from Teresa Healy, Littlegrange, Drogheda. Brown trout in two reservoirs; St from Drogheda Corporation. Hotels: Central, White Horse, Boyne Valley, Rosnaree, Cooper Hill House (Julianstown).

Navan (Co Meath). Salmon and sea trout. Navan Angler's Fishery consists approx 10m of single and double bank fishing on R Boyne and 1m on R Blackwater. Hotels: Central and Russell Arms.

Slane (Co Meath). Fishing good, but preserved. Hotel: Conyngham Arms.

Trim (Co Meath). Good trout in main river and tributaries. Trim, Athboy and Dist AA preserves and restocks **Athboy River** and some stretches on Boyne itself; st £16; dt £5. Concessions to jun and OAP, from sec. Deel and Boyne AA has trout and salmon water on tributary **Deel.** Longwood Anglers also have salmon and trout fishing on Boyne. Hotel: Wellington Court; Brogans Guest Accommodation.

Kells (Co Meath). Good trout fishing on **River Blackwater,** a tributary of R Boyne, dry fly. Mayfly fishing good. 15m preserved and restocked by Kells AA; st £10 and dt £3. Permits from Tom Murray, Farrell St. Trout up to 7lb may be had in the river, also large pike and salmon, 1½m of free fishing from source. Hotel: Headford Arms. Tackle shop: Tom Murray, Shooting & Fishing, Farrell St.

Virginia (Co Cavan). On headwaters of R Blackwater. Lough Ramor gives good trout fishing and excellent fishing for bream, roach, perch and pike; boats available, two tributaries. Ten lakes and four rivers within 5m; trout and coarse fish. Virginia and Dist AC has fishing on **Lough Ramor** and **Lisgrea Lake** (all species); and **Rampart River** (roach, perch and bream). **Mullagh Lake** is a popular pike fishery. For further information contact Pat McCabe, Rahardrum (tel: 049 47649); Nattie Dogherty, Salmon Lodge, Main St; and Edward Toben, Mullagh Rd. Accommodation: Mrs McHugh, White House, 010 353 49 47515; P & M

Geraghty, Knocknagarton, 010 353 49 47638, both Virginia. To north east, **Bailieboro** is another good centre for coarse fishing, with several lakes within easy reach, incl **Castle, Parker's, Galbolie, Drumkeery.**

BUNDROWES RIVER AND LOUGH MELVIN

(For close seasons, licences, etc, see The Northern Regional Fisheries Board)

About 4m south of Erne, the Bundrowes River carries water of Lough Melvin to sea in Donegal Bay. The entire 6 mile river is open to anglers except for private stretch from Lareen Bay to the Four Masters Bridge. For accommodation and information, contact T Gallagher.*(see below under Kinlough entry.)* The lough is 8m by 2m, approx 5,000 acres; part of it is free and part under private ownership. It is renowned for its three different species of trout, these being sonnaghan, gilaroo and ferrox. Good run of big spring salmon in Feb and March; smaller fish arrive in April and May; grilse in late May and run right through to June. Best time for fly fishing for salmon late April to end June. Trolling baits, where permitted, takes place from early Feb.

Bundoran (Co Donegal). Salmon, trout. Bundrowes R, 1½m, and west end L Melvin, 3m. Salmon season 1 Jan-30 Sept (Bundrowes); 1 Feb-30 Sept (Melvin). **Bunduff River,** 3½m from Bundoran, flows 8m to enter Donegal Bay near Castlegal; salmon, brown trout. Best salmon, June to Aug. Brown trout in upper reaches. Bunduff Angling Syndicate has water; dt £8 from Mrs Alice McGloin, The Shop, Bunduff Bridge, Co Leitrim. Also Kinlough Anglers, c/o John Fahy, Kinlough. Tackle shops: Alice McGloin (above); Pat Barrett, Main St; Rogans, Bridgend, Ballyshannon, Co Donegal. Hotels: Allingham; Foxes Lair.

Kinlough (Co Leitrim). Salmon, grilse, trout. Season for spring salmon, Jan to Apr; grilse, sea trout, May to Sept. Boats and tickets for **Bundrowes** fishing from Thomas Gallagher, Glenaun, Edenville, Kinlough (tel: 072 41208); Thomas Kelly (tel: 072 41497). Tackle shop: The Fishery Office, Lareen Park.

Rossinver (Co Leitrim). Salmon, grilse, sonaghan and gillaroo trout. Rossinver Bay, fly only. Gillies available. Dt £7, boat, engine and 2 rods £28, from Peter Bradley, Rossinver Fishery, Eden Quay (tel: 072 54201). Part of Lough Melvin is in Northern Ireland and is served by village of Garrison (Co Fermanagh).

CLARE

Flows into **Lough Corrib,** near Galway, and was considered one of best spawning streams for Galway River fish. Best season: Spring salmon, mid-April to mid-May; grilse, third week June to third week July; brown trout, April to June. Holds large trout and suitable for dry fly.

Galway (Co Galway). For lower reaches. 25m W of Galway on coast road is Carraroe Hotel; sea and lake fishing. Permits from WRFB, 091 63112; Mr S Martin, Esso Station, Galway Rd, Tuam, 093 24151; P Balfe, Corofin, 093 41715.
Tuam (Co Galway). For upper waters.

Tuam and Dist Trout AA caters for visitors, and has recently acquired eastern half of **R Clare** at Kilgevrin Tuam. A private club (Corofin Association) has salmon and dry-fly trout water on river; particulars from hon sec. **Castlegrove Lake;** pike, perch, bream, rudd.

Check before you go

While every effort has been made to ensure that the information given in **Where to Fish** *is correct, the position is continually changing, and anglers are urged, in their own interests, to make enquiries before travelling to selected venues. This is especially important with reference to prices quoted. Anglers attention is also drawn to the fact that hotels mentioned under the various fishing stations do not necessarily have water of their own. Any amendments or further data for inclusion in subsequent editions, and any criticism, will be welcome.*

Co. CLARE (streams and loughs)

A number of salmon and sea trout rivers and streams run from Co Clare to the Shannon estuary or to the west coast. Most of them offer free fishing, with landowners permission. Trout and coarse fishing lakes abound in the East Clare 'lakeland' and in the south west. The rivers are listed here in their geographical order, westwards from Limerick.

BUNRATTY. Enters Shannon at Bunratty Castle, and holds a small stock of ½lb brown trout; modest grilse and sea trout run, best in June/July, from tide to D'Esterres Bridge, 3m. Free fishing. At source, **Doon Lough** nr Broadford, is a fine coarse fishery with large bream and other species; boats available locally. Several other coarse fishing Loughs in region: **Rosroe** and **Fin**, nr Kilmurry: pike over 20lb, from boat; **Cullaun**, 400 acres, 2m from **Kilkishen**, specimen pike and large bream, best from boat; just south, **Stones Lough**: big tench. As well as these, there are other less accessible lakes for the angler to explore. Further north east is another notable group of coarse fishing loughs: **Kilgory**, nr **O'Callaghan's Mills**, with large bream; **Bridget** (Silvergrove), 50 acres, with tench to 6lb; by **Scarriff, O'Grady (Canny's Lough)**, shallow water, difficult access, but good bream fishing, with pike, tench and big rudd; and **Keel Lough**, inaccessible and unfished, with large tench, bream and rudd. On the **Scarriff River**, shoals of good bream and pike, easily accessible. On **R Graney** is **Lough Graney, Caher**, a big lake with abundant perch, boat essential, available at Caher. North of Tulla are **Loughs Clondanagh** and **Clondoorney**, easily accessible fishing for rudd, with pike and perch.

RINE (QUIN RIVER). Runs from the lakes of East Clare to the estuary of the **Fergus**. Fishing similar to Bunratty; about 5m fishing from Latoon Bridge u/s to Quin. Permission to fish **Dromoland Castle** water from Rec. Manager, 061 71144. Castle also has 20 acre lough in grounds, stocked trout fishery. Rest of fishing free.

FERGUS. This is a limestone river with several loughs along its course. It holds good stocks of brown trout, av ¾lb, with fish to 3½lb. Good dry fly water. Approx 200 spring salmon and grilse each year, salmon Feb-March, grilse June-Sept. Free with landowners permission. **Loughs Dromore** and **Ballyline.** 6m east of Ballyline; limestone waters with trout to 5lb. Best March-May and Sept. Free

fishing, boat hire, contact M Cleary, corofin, 065 27675. **Ballyteige Lough:** 100 acre limestone fishery, trout to 7lb. Best in March/Apr, at dusk in June/July. Boat necessary; contact M Cleary. **Inchiquin Lough,** 260 acres: excellent stock of wild browns, av 1¼lb. Fishes well in early season, and Sept. Boats from Burkes Shop, Main St, Corofin, 065 37677. **Lough Cullaun** (Monanagh Lake): limited stock of big trout; also a good pike fishery. Trolling popular method. **Muckanagh Lough (Tullymacken Lough):** 180 acre shallow lake with good trout and pike. Boat necessary. Boats through M Cleary for both these loughs. **Lough Atedaun,** 1m from Corofin, has excellent fishing for large pike, tench and rudd. Best fished from boat. **Lough Ballycullinan,** 1½m from Corofin, has good stocks of large pike, perch, some bream and hybrids. Boat essential. Contact Burke's, Corofin, tel: 065 37677.

CLOON. This small river enters north east corner of Clonderalaw Bay. It gets a sea trout run in June/July, and is fishable for 2m d/s of new bridge on secondary road. Free fishing. Nearby trout loughs are **Knockerra,** 50 acres, **Gortglass,** 80 acres, and **Cloonsneaghta,** 30 acres. Boat hire on Gortglass (M Cleary, tel: 065 27675), free fishing on all, with permission.

DOONBEG. A better known salmon and sea trout river, rising in Lissycasy, flowing west to the sea at Doonbeg. Small spring salmon run, fair grilse and sea trout from June. Overgrown in places; best fishing on middle and upper reaches. Free with permission. For **Knockerra Lough,** *see Kilrush, under Shannon.*

CREEGH. Small spate river, running to west coast north of the Doonbeg, on which 150 to 200 grilse are taken each season. Small brown trout, and sea trout under the right conditions. Free fishing. Near Kilmihil is **Knockalough,** with good stock of small browns. Boat is helpful; dapping with daddylonglegs in Aug/Sept. Free fishing.

ANNAGEERAGH. Runs into **Lough Donnell.** Sea trout fishing at dusk for about

1m u/s of lough in June/July. Sea trout fishing and a few grilse in rest of river. **Doo Lough,** 220 acres, a little north west of Glenmore, holds good stock of small browns.

KILDEEMEA. A small spate river which enters sea 2m south west of **Miltown Malbay.** Excellent sea trout, to 3lb. Best June/July, fishable over ½m stretch on south bank from Ballaclugga Bridge u/s. Fly and spinner, fly best at night. Free fishing.

CULLENAGH (INAGH). This river is a good coarse fishery for 8m from Inagh towards sea. Open banks for pike and rudd fishing, easily accessible. Near village, **Inagh Loughs** contain good numbers of small brown trout. Free fishing. 2m west of Inagh, **Lough Caum,** 45 acres, stocked trout fishery, 4 fish limit,

boat fishing only, boats for hire. Permission from James Allard, Breechpark, Ennis, 065 24367.

DEALAGH. Joins sea from north east at Liscannor. Spate river with sea trout and grilse in June/July. Sea trout best at night, between first and fourth bridges u/s from tidal water. Free, with permission. **Lickeen Lough,** 200 acres, 2m south of **Kilfenora,** contains small wild browns and stocked rainbows to 2lb. Boat available. Contact John Vaughan, sec of Lickeen Trout AA, 065 71069.

AILLE. Small spate river running from **Lisdoonvarna** to **Doolin.** Stock of 14" browns, moderate grilse and sea trout. Best between Roadford and Lisdoonvarna; access difficult, banks overgrown. Free fishing.

CORK South West (rivers and loughs)

ARGIDEEN. Runs from west, above Clonakilty, and enters sea at **Timoleague.** A sea trout river, most of which is jointly managed by Argideen AA and SWRFB. Best methods are single worm by day, or fly at night. Tickets from P Wolstenholme, 023 46239, or SWRFB, 026 41222. To west of river, **Lough Atariff,** permission from P McCarthy, Dunmanway salmon & Trout AC, Yew Tree Bar, Dunmanway; and **Curraghalicky Lake,** free fishing. Both with good stock of small wild brown trout.

ILEN. A medium sized Spate river about 21 miles long, rising on watershed of Bantry district and flowing into sea through long estuary, at Skibbereen. Spring salmon from late March. Main salmon runs in Apr-Jun. Average size 8-10lb. Sea trout begin in March, and average 2lb in Apr-June. Fly, spinning and worming are practiced. Prawn and shrimp not permitted.

Skibbereen (Co Cork). R Ilen AC has 4m fishing on river, as far as **Caheragh Bridge,** with salmon and sea trout. Tickets (dt £8, wt £30) available from Fallons. Other fishing, with permission, as far as **Inchengeragh Bridge.** Trout fishing on **Shepperton Lakes,** dt from bailiff. **Ballin Lough** is stocked by Ballin L. AC. Boats and tickets at lough. Information from sec Jim Maxwell, 028 33266. 3m south west of Dunmanway is **Garranes Lake,** 25 acres, Stocked rainbows and wild browns. Jointly run by SWRFB and

Dunmanway & Drinagh AA. Dt and boats from G Carolan, Filling Station, Garranes, Drimoleague. 3m south of **Leap, Lough Cluhir,** free fishing on small lough for wild brown trout, good av size, and taken at 4lb. Tench to 5lb. Tackle shop: Fallon's Sports Shop, 20 North Street, Skibbereen. Hotel: West Cork, Eldon, Illenside.

Bantry (Co Cork). Bantry Salmon & Trout AC fishes **Lough-Bo-Finne,** or **Bofinne,** 3m east of Bantry, 25 acres, first class rainbow and brown trout fishery, stocked weekly by Fisheries Board. Tickets (st £20, dt £3) from Sports Shop or from Mrs P Spillane, The Bungalow, Lough-Bo-Finne. Tackle shops; Vickery's Store; Keehans Saddlers; Sports Shop, all Main St, Bantry. Hotels; West Lodge; Vickry's; Bantry Bay Hotel.

MEALAGH. 1m north of Bantry, salmon and sea trout. Free except for bottom pool below falls.

OUVANE and **COOMHOLA.** Small spate rivers which run into north east Bantry Bay. Salmon and sea trout, the latter declined in Ouvane, better in **Coomhola R.** Ouvane has four good pools in first mile, and three more below Carriganass Falls. Coomhola Anglers, O'Brien's Shop, Coomhola Bridge, Bantry, offer permits to fish some 20 pools on Coomhola R.

GLENGARRIFF. This small river flows into Bantry Bay at north east end, and has good salmon and trout fishing. Rights are held by Glengarriff AA, who offer dt £5.

Tackle shops: Shamrock Stores and Maureens, Glengarriff. Hotels incl Eccles, Golf Links, Mountain View, Caseys.

BEARA PENINSULAR. (Co Cork). **Adrigole River** runs into Bantry Bay on north side: 6m long spate river with grilse and sea trout, controlled by Kenmare AA. Contact J O'Hare, 21 Main St, Kenmare, 064 41499. Beara AA has tickets available for local lough fishing. Craigies Hotel, Castletownbere, has tickets for salmon and trout fishing. **Upper** and **Lower Loughs Avaul** contain wild

brown tout. Tickets from Glengarriff AA, c/o B Harrington, Publican, Glengarriff. High in the Caha Mountains, south west of Glengarriff, free fishing on **Loughs Eekenohoolikeaghaun** and **Derreenadovodia,** and **Barley Lake,** 100 acres: small wild brown trout. Other small loughs in area with similar stock: **Glenkeel, Moredoolig, Begboolig, Shanoge** (larger fish, many over 1lb). Best in April/May and Sept. South of **Ardgroom** is **Glenbeg Lough,** leased by Berehaven AA. Big stock of small browns; tickets from Harrington, *see above.*

CORRIB SYSTEM

(For close seasons, licences, etc, see The Western Regional Fisheries Board)

River Corrib drains Lough Corrib and runs 5½m to Galway Bay passing virtually through the city of Galway. Salmon, trout. Salmon fishing very good. For particulars as to present conditions and rods apply Central Fishery Board, Nuns Island, Galway. Best fishing for springers early in season; grilse, May-June. Rods let by the day or by week.

Galway (Co Galway). Salmon fishing at Galway Fishery, situated in City of Galway, less than 1m from sea. Applications to The Manager, Galway Fishery, Nun's Island, Galway, 091 62388. Dt £25 to £12, depending on season. The flow of the river is controlled by a regulating

weir and the short stretch down stream of the weir is the salmon angling water. **Kilcolgan River** (10m E) part tidal, salmon and sea trout. WRFB controls 645 yards of north bank in townland of Stradbally East. Dt £3, from WRFB, 091 63118. Tackle shops: Freeney's, 19 High St.

LOUGH CORRIB

This, the largest sheet of water in Republic (41,617 acres, 68 sq m), is dotted with islands, around which are shallows which make for good fishing. Specially noted for large brown trout. Trout fishing opens on Feb 15 and is mainly by trolling until April. Wet fly good in April and early May, but lough best known for dapping with mayfly (beginning last week in May) and daddy-longlegs (mid-July to end of season). Good dry-fly fishing on summer evenings. Salmon taken mainly by trolling, and in June on wet fly in many of the bays. Also big pike and other coarse fish in Corrib, so that angling of some kind is available all year. Fishing free, but salmon licence required. Many hotels issue licences. Boats and boatmen at Portacarron, Oughterard, Baurisheen, Derrymoyle, Glan Shore, Cong, Greenfield, Doorus, Carrick, Salthouse, Carey's and Inishmacatreer.

Oughterard (Co Galway). Best fishing is from April to early June. **Owenriff River** flows through Oughterard; good in high water late summer. Local club is Oughterard Anglers Assc. There is additional good fishing for bream and roach on **Moycullen Lakes,** Moycullen, on Galway/Oughterard Rd. Tackle shops: Tucks, Main Street; M Keogh. Galway tackle shops: Freeney's, 19 High St and Murt Folan, Wood Quay. Hotels: Currarevagh House (tel: 09182 313) provides boats, gillies, outboard motors with fuel and tackle if necessary for a charge of £30 per day, also has boat on top lake of **Screebe** sea trout fishery. Oughterard House (free fishing on Corrib; Private

water within 12m; salmon and sea trout); Corrib, Angler's and Egan's Lake. Also new motel: Connemara Gateway (Reservations: Tel: 01-567 3444) and Ross Lake Hotel, Rosscahill (boats and boatmen).

Clonbur (Co Galway). Good centre for **Loughs Corrib** and **Mask.** Clonbur AC fishes these waters, **Loughs Coolin, Nafooey** (pike over 36lb) and others, and is affiliated with Corrib Federation. Annual sub. £10. Tackle shop: Ann Kynes, Clonbur, 092 49197. Accom: Fair Hill Guest House, Clonbur, 092 46197; Noreen Kyne, 092 46169; Ann Lambe, Ballykine House, 092 46150. Self-catering with boats, J O'Donnell, 092 46157.

Headford (Co Galway). Convenient for the

The class of trout - the sort which used to be termed 'ferox' - which has been drawing anglers to the West of Ireland for generations. This one, taken from L. Mask on a trolled copper and silver spoon in 1983, weighed $17^3/_4$ lb. Shown with it is a typical $1^3/_4$ lb specimen taken on a fly. *Photo: Bord Failte.*

east side of Lough Corrib. **Black River** (limestone stream) provides excellent if somewhat difficult dry fly water. Affected by drainage work. Best near village of **Shrule**. A £3 dt is available from WRFB, Weir Lodge, Galway, 091 63118. Tackle shop: Kevin Duffy. Accommodation at Angler's Rest Hotel and guest houses.

Greenfields, nr Headford (Co Galway). Trout, salmon and coarse fish. Situated on shore of **L Corrib.** Boatmen available. Accommodation and apartments, tackle, boats, apply to M Walshe, Ower House, Greenfields, Headford, Co Galway (tel: 093 35446).

Cong (Co Mayo), Good for **Lough Mask,** also, Hotels: Ashford Castle which provides boats and gillies £30 per day. Boats also available from Michael Ryan, River Lodge (tel: 092 46057); boats and accom. from M Holion, Bayview Boats and Guesthouse, The Derries Cross, Nr Cong (tel: 092 46385). Tackle shops: O'Connors, Cong; T Cheevers. Northgate Street, Athenry.

LOUGH MASK

Limestone lake of 20,496 acres connected by underground channel with Lough Corrib holding large brown trout, pike, eels, perch and a few char. Trout to 15lb are taken by trolling and on dap (5-6lb not uncommon). Mayfly, May, June, and July; daddy-long legs and grasshopper, late June to Sept; wet fly, Mar-April and July-Sept. Ballinrobe, **Cong, Clonbur** and **Tourmakeady** are good centres. At Cong is Cong AA; (st £5), at Ballinrobe is Ballinrobe and Dist AA (st £5) and at Tourmakeady is Tourmakeady AC. All are open to visitor-membership. Tackle shops: Fred O'Connor, Cong; D O'Connor, Main Street, Ballinrobe; Mayo Flycraft, Rathbawn Dr; J J O'Connor, 15 Spencer St, Castlebar. Boats for hire at Cushlough Pier, Bay of Islands Park, Rosshill Park, Caher Pier. Good accommodation at Tourmakeady Lodge, recently converted into guest house and which caters especially for fishermen. Also Mask Lodge and Mask Villa on lake shore. River fishing on **Finney** and canal joining Mask and Corrib. At Tourmakeady are some good spate rivers, and mountain lake fishing can be had in **Dirk Lakes;** brown trout. Connected to Mask are **Lough Carra** (4,003 acres, limestone, brown trout run large; boats from Mrs J Flannery, Keel Bridge, Partry, 092 41706; Mr P Roberts, Kilkeeran, Partry, 092 43046; Mr R O'Grady, Chapel St, Ballinrobe, 092 41142) and **Lough Nafooey** (good coarse fish). Good trout, perch, pike in three tributaries of Mask: Robe, **Finney, Bulkaun.**

NORTH DONEGAL (streams)

(For close seasons, licences, etc, see The Northern Regional Fisheries Board)

Donegal is mostly salmon and sea trout country. Its waters are generally acid; rocky or stoney streams and small lakes in which the brown trout run small - though there are one or two fisheries where they may be taken up to 2lb and more.

LENNON. Rises in Glendowan Mountains and flows through **Garton Lough** and **Lough Fern** before entering **Lough Swilly** at Ramelton. Historically is one of the best salmon rivers in Donegal. It is best known as a spring river and its most famous pool, The Ramelton Pool is privately owned. The rest of the river is a 'free fishery' and only a state licence is required. Season 1 Jan-30 Sept. May to Sept for grilse. Trout fishing equally good on upper and lower reaches; best April to July.

Ramelton (Co Donegal). Salmon fishing on lower portion of river at Ramelton owned and fished privately by Ramelton Fishery Ltd. **Lough Fern** is best fished from a boat and produces mostly grilse. Licences available from Hugh Whoriskey, Bridgend; Anglers Haven Hotel, Kilmacrennan, Co Donegal.

SWILLY. Flows into Lough Swilly. Much free salmon and trout fishing of good quality in region. Recently, the river has

---

Keep the banks clean

Several clubs have stopped issuing tickets to visitors because of the state of the banks after they have left. Spend a few moments clearing up.

undergone major development with work being carried out by the Northern Regional Fisheries Board and the Letterkenny and District AA.

Letterkenny (Co Donegal). Letterkenny AA has salmon, sea trout and brown trout fishing on Rivers **Swilly, Lennon, Owencarrow,** and more than 25 lakes; trout av ½lb. Salmon run into Lakes **Glen, Gartan** and **Lough Fern.** Boats on Glen Lake: J Doherty, tel 38057; on Lough Keel: P Cullen, 39015 or W Gallagher, 39233. Membership and permits from tackle shop: Joe Nash, Donegal Brew at Home & Fishing Tackle Shop, 65 Upper Main St; A McGrath, Port Rd. Hotels: Mount Errigal, Gallagher's.

Churchill (Co Donegal). **Lough Beagh** situated in the heart of the **Glenveagh National Park;** 4m long by ½m wide; salmon, sea trout and brown trout. Best known for quality of sea trout fishing in August and Sept. Boat fishing only; 2 boats available for hire. Anglers are requested to respect the birdlife on this lake, as there are some rare and interesting species residing. Season 1 Jan-30 Sept. Dt £20, from The Superintendent, Glenveagh National Park (tel: 074 37090).

CRANA. Enters **Lough Swilly** at Buncrana. Primarily a spate river which gets a good run of grilse and sea trout. Access to fishing is excellent.

Bucrana (Co Donegal). Salmon and sea trout. Buncrana AA issues permits. For first week £25 and for each subsequent week £10; from Bertie O'Neill, Bridgend; Mr McLoughlin, Lower Main St; Seamus Gill, 077 61064. Other waters: **Mill River;** brown trout to ½lb numerous; free. **Lough Inch** (6m): good sea trout; free. **Dunree River** (6m) free; brown trout, occasional salmon and sea trout. **Clonmany River** (5m); salmon sea trout and brown trout fishing; fair sport in good water; best June onwards. Loughrin Estate, Clonmany. Hotel: Lake of Shadows.

WEST DONEGAL (streams)

(For close seasons, licences, etc, see The Northern Regional Fisheries Board)

EANY and **ESKE.** Eany is a spate river which flows for 10m SW from Blue Stack Mountains and enters sea in Inver Bay close to Inver village. Good run of salmon and sea trout and has resident population of small brown trout. The Eany has undergone extensive development in 1992/3 and is now in the ownership of the Regional Fisheries Board. Salmon runs in 1993 were excellent. Salmon 20 April-30 Sept. Trout 20 April-9 Oct. **Eske River** drains **Lough Eske** (900 acres) then runs SW for about 5m to join sea at Donegal Bay. The system gets a good run of salmon and a fair run of sea trout; and has a resident stock of brown trout and char. Salmon 1 March-30 Sept. Trout 1 March-30 Sept. Most fishing is on the lake from boats and the river has a number of good pools. In recent years the system has been getting a declining run of fish but this may be temporary.

Donegal (Co Donegal). Donegal Town & Dist AC controls fishing on Eany and Eske rivers and part of Lough Eske. Dt £6 from Charlie Doherty, Tackle Shop, Main St. Hotels: Central; Abbey; Ernan Park, St Ernan's; Island.

GLEN. Flows S for 8m from Slievetooe to enter sea at Teelin Bay beside the town of Carrick. A spate river but has a number of good holding pools. Salmon and sea trout. Fishes best in summer after a flood.

Carrick (Co Donegal). Salmon and trout. Private fishing. Tackle shop: Hugh Cunningham.

FINN. Flows from Lough Finn in an easterly direction until it joins Foyle below Strabane. At **Ballyboffen,** Cloghan Lodge has good salmon and trout fishing facilities.

OWENEA AND OWENTOCKER. Short rivers running into head of Loughrosmore Bay near Ardara. Owenea is primarily a spate river with a run of spring fish, grilse, sea trout, and has a resident stock of small brown trout. It has a number of good pools about halfway between Glenties and Ardara, and when in condition is one of the best in the country for salmon. Season 1 Mar-30 Sept.

Ardara and **Glenties** (Co Donegal). Fishing controlled by Northern Regional Fishery Board, Glenties, Co Donegal (tel: 075 51141). Fishery has been upgraded and there are additional facilities for anglers. Dt £10; st £20 for Glenties and Ardara Angling Clubs members. Permits from Glenties Hatchery and Mary Kennedy, both Glenties; John McGill, Tackle

Shop, Main St, Ardara. Free salmon and
sea trout fishing on Rivers Brackey and
Doug. Many lakes also free. Hotels: Nesbitt Arms, Ardara; Highlands, Glenties.

GWEEBARRA. Drains **Lough Barra** and
flows south-west about 7m to Doochary
Bridge, where it becomes tidal and flows
hence through long estuary between high
hills a further 6m to the Atlantic.

Doochary (Co Donegal). Bridge here marks
end of tidal water; several trout lakes in
vicinity. Salmon, sea trout. Best season:
Spring salmon, Feb-May; grilse and sea
trout, end of June to Sept. Fishing belongs to riparian owners, leave obtainable. Salmon and sea trout run into Lough
Barra in large numbers and into tributaries.

THE ROSSES. The Rosses Fishery is made
up of five salmon and sea trout rivers,
including **River Dungloe**, and one hundred and thirty lakes, some of which contain salmon and sea trout, all of which
contain brown trout.

Dungloe (Co Donegal). Salmon and sea
trout. Rosses Fishery controlled by Rosses AA. **Loughs Meeala, Dungloe,
Craghy,** stocked with browns and rainbows. Season 2 Feb-12 Oct. Fly only on
all lakes. Prices are: wt £5, boat £10 for
two per day; with gillie, £25. River prices
vary for season on **Crolly River** and
Clady River. Permits from Charles Bonner, Tackle Shop, Bridge End (tel: 075
21163); Bill McGarvey, Main St, Dungloe. Hotels: Sweeneys; Ostan na
Rosann.

EAST COASTAL STREAMS

(For close seasons, licences, etc, see The Eastern Regional Fisheries Board)

AVONMORE RIVER. Runs through Rathdrum, Co Wicklow, from **Loughs Tay**
and **Dan,** approx 8m north. It joins **River
Avonbeg,** runs into the **Avoca** and
reaches sea at Arklow. Big stocks of
small brown trout. Two clubs have
salmon and trout fishing: Rathdrum Trout
Anglers, Aughrim Anglers, Vartry Anglers, have fishing for salmon, sea trout,
brown and rainbows. Tickets (£2) available from Geoghagans, or Tourist Office,
Rathdrum.

BROADMEADOW RIVER. Dublin District; trout. Drainage scheme has affected
sport. Broadmeadow AC fishes river and
Tonelgee Reservoir. Contact K Rundle,
01 438178.

DARGLE RIVER. Short river which
reaches sea at Bray. Salmon, sea trout.
Dargle AC has fishing. Contact Michael
Keenan, 01 515540. Tackle from Dargle
Tackle, U5 Everett Cntr, Castle St, Bray.

DELVIN RIVER. In Drogheda District.
Fair brown trout stream entering sea at
Gormanstown; Holds few sea trout. Gormanstown and Dist AA has water. River
being stocked and developed with cooperation of landowners and members. Balbriggan is convenient centre. (Hotel:
Grand).

DODDER. Dublin District; brown trout (av
9oz, but fish to 2lbs caught), with some
sea trout fishing in tidal portion. Dodder
AC controls all fishing; contact R O'Hanlon, 82 Braemor Rd, Dublin 14, tel: 01
982112. Fishing on Dublin Corporation's
Bohernabreena and **Roundwood Reservoirs** (10m from Dublin); by st £10, wt
£4, dt £1.50 from Dublin Corporation,
Block 1, Floor 3, Civic Offices, Fishamble St, Dublin 8. No boats available.
Conc for OAP. Members of these clubs
are entitled to reduced rates: Dublin
Trout AA; Wicklow AA; Dodder AC.

GLENCREE RIVER. In Dublin District. Enniskerry is a centre; small brown trout. Mostly free.

NANNY RIVER. In Drogheda District. River enters sea at Laytown, Co Meath. Fair brown trout fishing; some sea trout in lower reaches. Drogheda and Dist AC has water and issues permits at small charge.

TOLKA RIVER. In Dublin District. A once excellent trout stream which has suffered from pollution. Best fishing is from Finglas Bridge to Abbotstown Bridge. For fishing information contact secretary, Tolka AC, tel: 01 361730.

VARTRY. Small river which drains **Roundwood (Vartry) Reservoir** and flows into sea near Wicklow, with sea trout from late August, and small brown trout. Vartry AC controls river and Co Wicklow AA controls Roundwood Reservoir, the latter on lease from Dublin Corporation. Tickets available. Fishing station: Rathnew (Co Wicklow). Hotels: Hunter's, Tinakilly House.

ERNE

(For close seasons, licences, etc, see The Northern Regional Fisheries Board)

A large hydro-electric scheme has turned the River Erne into two large dams. Sea trout fishing in estuary from June to Sept. Coarse fishing excellent; bream, rudd and perch abundant and roach multiplying following their introduction in recent years.

Ballyshannon (Co Donegal). **Assaroe Lake** is a man-made lake resulting from the Erne Hydro-Electric Generating Scheme. Located above Kathleen Falls Power Station, it acts as a reservoir. Trout fishing is available, controlled by ESB: st £10, wt £5, from ESB Station, Ballyshannon; Jim McWeeney, Rossnowlagh Road, Ballyshannon. Other ESB waters are Gweedore Fishery: **Nacung** and **Dunlewy Loughs,** free trout fishing, permits from Generation Manager, Hydro Group, Ardnacrusha; Rivers **Clady** and **Crolly,** dt £5 from same address. Tackle shops; E McAloon, Newsagent; Pat Barrett's, Main St and Jack Phillips, West End, both Bundoran. Hotels: Creevy Pier, Dorians Imperial.

Belturbet (Co Cavan). Good centre for **Rivers Erne** and **Woodford,** and some thirty seven lakes, with most coarse fish and some trout. **Putighan** and **Derryhoo Lakes** are popular venues, tench to 5lb in L Bunn, to 3lb in L Carn. New developments at Loughs Grilly, Killybandrick, Bunn, Drumlaney, Greenville, Round. Bait, boats and tackle from J McMahon, Bridge St, tel: 049 22400. Anglers accom. includes Kilduff House, 2m from Belturbet and Fortview House, Cloverhill.

Cavan (Co Cavan). All lakes and rivers in the area hold coarse fish except **Annagh Lake** (100 acres) which holds brown and rainbow trout; fly only, no bank fishing, 6 fish limit. Trout season 1 March-30 Sept. **Lough Oughter,** a maze of lakes fed by **R Erne** and **R Annalee,** holds a wealth of coarse fish; bream, rudd, roach, pike perch, tench. Further details from The Secretary, Cavan Tourist Assn. Tackle shop: Magnet Sports Store, Town Hall. Accom. catering for anglers: Mrs Myles, Halcyon, Cavan Town; Lakevilla, Blenacup, and Forest Chalets, both Killykeen.

Lough Gowna (Co Cavan). Coarse fishing on Lough Gowna, the source of R Erne. Information is available from Lough Gowna Tourist Assc. Anglers accom. can be found at Kilbracken Arms Hotel, Greenville House, both Carrigallen; Lakeview House, Lough Gowna; Mr & Mrs Barry, Farrangarve, Co Cavan.

Check before you go

While every effort has been made to ensure that the information given in **Where to Fish** *is correct, the position is continually changing, and anglers are urged, in their own interests, to make preliminary enquiries before travelling to selected venues. This is especially important with reference to prices quoted. Inevitably the rate of inflation is affecting stability in this quarter. Anglers' attention is also drawn to the fact that the hotels mentioned under the various fishing stations do not necessarily have water of their own. Any amendments or further data for inclusion in subsequent editions, and any criticism, will be welcome.*

Cootehill (Co Cavan). Numerous lakes with coarse fish, and **Rivers Dromore** and **Annalee:** bream, rudd, tench, roach, perch. Fishing free. Local clubs are Cootehill AC, Moyduff AC and Bunnoe AC. Anglers accom: Riverside House, Cabragh Farmhouse, Hillview House, Cootehill. Cootehill Tourist Assc is at Riverside House, Cootehill.

Clones (Co Monaghan). Coarse fishing. **River Finn,** a sluggish tributary of Upper Lough Erne, good for bream. Six lakes within 5m of town: pike, perch, rudd, bream. A Few miles north of **Monaghan** is **Emy Lake Fishery,** Emyvale, 136 acres trout fishing, fly only, 6 fish limit. Tackle shop: T J Hanberry, 3/4 Fermanagh St, Clones. Hotels: Creighton, Lennard Arms.

WOODFORD RIVER. Ballinamore (Co Leitrim) is close to river, which produces large catches of Bream av 2½lb, roach, tench, pike and other coarse fish. River runs into **L Garadice,** one of 28 lakes in this area. McAllister's Hotel caters for anglers, also Jackie's Hotel, and Riversdale Farm; Kennedy, Glenview, 010353 78 44157; Price, Ardrum Lodge, 010 353 78 44278, all Ballinamore.

FANE (including Glyde and Dee)

(For close seasons, licences, etc, see The Eastern Regional Fisheries Board)

Rises in **Lough Muckno** at Castleblaney and flows SE to enter sea at Blackrock, 4m S of Dundalk. Good run of salmon, and greater numbers of sea trout as a result of improvements made to river.

Dundalk (Co Louth). Waters from Knockbridge to border, plus all **Castletown** and **Ballymascanlon** Rivers and tributaries controlled by Dundalk & Dist Brown Trout AA. Assn stocks each year with browns, and there is a good run of sea trout and salmon (Aug-Oct best). St £10, dt £3, from tackle shops and tourist office. Tackle shops: Island Tackle, 58 Park St; Mac's Sports, 3 Demense, Dundalk. Hotels: Ballymascanlon, Derryhale.

Inniskeen (Co Monaghan). Waters in Inniskeen area controlled by Inniskeen AC. Trout, fly only. Salmon, fly, spinning, lure or shrimp. Membership from A Campbell, Monvallet, Louth, Co Louth. Dt £5 from Ruddys Filling Station, Dundalk.

Castleblayney (Co Monaghan). Several coarse fishing loughs in area; **Lough Muckno,** large expanse of water with pike, perch, roach, bream, and other species; good fishing from several islands in lough; **Lough Egish** (5m), pike, perch and eel. **Dick's Lake,** large roach; **Smith's Lake,** good tench fishing, also bream, roach, perch; **Loughs Na Glack** and **Monalty,** big bream. Castleblayney Trout AA has trout fishing on **Milltown Lough** (3m); stocked annually with 3,000 brown trout; dt from hon sec. Tackle shop: J Flanagan, Main Street. Hotels: Glencarn, Central. Fishing accom. at Hillside, 010 353 42 40385, and Hazelwood, 010 353 43 46009.

Ballybay (Co Monaghan). Excellent coarse fishing centre for **Dromore River** and loughs, of which there are a large number; some, it is claimed, have never been fished. There is much free coarse fishing for visiting anglers. £3 dt for trout, £4 for salmon, is available. Details from hon sec, Ballybay AA. Town holds annual coarse angling festival. Tackle from Marlin O'Kane. Accom: Lakelands House, Ballybay, 010353 4241356; Ardmore House, Ballybay, 010353 4241088, and others.

GLYDE: Rises near Kingscourt in Co Cavan and flows E for 35m to join River Dee before entering the sea at Annagassan. Flows through some prime coarse fisheries in upper reaches, notably **Rahans** and **Ballyhoe Lakes.** Small run of spring salmon and fair run of grilse in late summer depending on water levels. Good stock of brown trout. Excellent Mayfly hatch. Due to drainage works some years ago, there are some steep banks on which care should be taken. Good centre for anglers is **Carrickmacross,** with several fine coarse lakes near to hand, incl **Lisaniske, Capragh** and **Monalty** Lakes, **Lough Na Glack,** and fishing accommodation: Mrs Haworth, Rose-Linn Lodge, Carrickmacross, 010353 42 61035; Mrs Campbell, Glencoe, 010 353 42 67316; Mrs Tinnelly, Corglass, 010 353 42 67492, both Kingscourt.

Castlebellingham (Co Louth). Salmon, sea trout, brown trout. Season 1 Feb-30 Sept. Dee & Glyde AC protect and fish river. St

£7 and dt £2 from Moonan's Fishing Tackle, Ardee. Hotel: Bellingham Castle.

DEE: Rises above **Whitewood Lake,** near Kilmainham Wood. Flow E for 38m, joining **River Glyde** at **Annagassan.** Fair runs of spring salmon, some grilse and good runs of sea trout to 5lb (May). Lower reaches below **Ardee** and **Drumcar** yield most salmon and sea trout. Brown trout water above Ardee. Due to drainage works some years ago, many banks are steep and dangerous. Weeds can be a problem during dry summers, rendering fishing useless in many sections. Season 1 Feb-30 Sept.

Dunleer (Co Louth). Salmon, sea trout. Drumcar Fishery has water. St £10 and dt £3, from The Reception, St Mary's, Drumcar House. Permits available 9am-5pm only. Sea trout fishing allowed after dark.

Ardee (Co Louth). Dee & Glyde AC has water on Rivers Dee and Glyde. St £7 and dt £2, from Moonan's Tackle Shop. Other tackle shop: Ardee Sports Co, John St. Hotel: The Gables.

Drumconrath (Co Meath). Drumconrath AC issues permits. Dt from Callans, Main St. **Ballyhoe Lakes,** tench fishing, plus bream, roach, perch, pike; coarse fishing in **Lough Mentrim,** (specimen bream and tench), **Lake Balrath,** Corstown. Fishing accom. at Inis Fail, 010 353 41 54161, and Ballyhoe, 010 353 41 54400/54104.

Nobber (Co Meath). Nobber AC has stretch from **Whitewood Lake** to Yellow-Ford Bridge. Mainly brown trout, occasional salmon in late autumn, usually during flood water. Weeds can be a problem during low water. St £10 and dt £2, from Bert Onions, Nobber; Callans, Main St, Drumcanrath.

MULLAGHDUFF: Tributary which enters Lough Muckno. A good trout stream, wet fly fishing best from April onwards, dry fly late in season.

FRANKFORT: Short river which connects Milltown Lough with Lough Muckno, stocked by local assoc. Trout to 3lb. Best in May-July.

FEALE

(For close seasons, licences, etc, see The Shannon Regional Fisheries Board)

Rises on north-west slopes of Blackwater watershed and runs into Atlantic near extreme end of Shannon estuary on south shore. Salmon, sea trout, brown trout (small). Spate river, with season from March to mid/late September.

Abbeyfeale (Co Limerick). Best centre for Feale. Waders essential. Abbeyfeale AA has water 5m d/s of town, with salmon and sea trout; st £20, plus £25 joining fee and dt £10 from Ryan's, New Street, Abbeyfeale. Brosna AA has 6m upstream; trout permit from S Quinlan, Kilmanahan, Abbeyfeale. Hotel: Leen's. Tackle shops: P Ryan, New Street; Mary Roche, Bridge Street; Lane (manufacture of the famous 'Lane' artificial minnow) New Street.

Listowel (Co Kerry). North Kerry AA has 7m on R Feale and 3m (single bank) on **River Smearlagh,** a tributary of Feale; salmon and sea trout; wt £20, and dt £5, from hon sec or tackle shop. Tralee AA has 2m, both banks; dt issued. Fly fishing for salmon quite good from mid-Aug. Salmon licences from Tom Walsh, Tackle, Church Street. Landers Leisure Lines, Courthouse Lane, Tralee. Hotels: Stack's, Listowel Arms.

GALWAY and MAYO (streams and smaller loughs)

(For close seasons, licences, etc, see The Western Regional Fisheries Board)

BALLYNAHINCH

An extensive system of lakes, tributaries and connecting rivers draining into Bertaghboy Bay. One of the most important salmon and sea trout fisheries in the west of Ireland.

Ballinafad (Co Galway). Salmon and sea trout. The famous **Ballynahinch Castle Fishery** consists of **Ballynahinch River**

($2\frac{1}{2}$m) and **Ballynahinch Lake;** situated at bottom of 25m long system of river and lakes. Salmon best June to Sept. Sea trout best July to Oct. Fly fishing (shrimp fishing for salmon for 2 hrs each day). Dt £30-£60. Max 28 rods. Gillies £25 per day. Permits available for non-residents from The Manager, Ballynahinch Castle Hotel (tel: 095 31006). Fishing permits for **Lakes Aleen** and **Tombeola,** from Mrs L Hill, Angler's Rest (tel: 095 31091). Tackle shops: Ballynahinch Castle Hotel; Percy Stanley and Paddy Price, both Clifden, Co Galway.

Recess (Co Galway). Salmon and sea trout. Lough Inagh Lodge Hotel, Recess, 095 31006, is central to the **Lough Inagh Fishery,** seven beats including two outstanding loughs, **Inagh** and **Derryclare,** and associated rivers; situated at top of Ballynahinch system in heart of Connemara. Dt, boats and Gillies available. Permits from John O'Connor. Lough Inagh Lodge (tel: 095 34706); Della MacAuley, Inagh Valley Inn (tel: 095 34608). Tackle for sale or hire at fishery office. **Athry Fishery** comprises five loughs on Upper Ballynahinch, including **Lough Athry.** Lower loughs get run of sea trout and occasional salmon, and upper loughs sea trout only. Season mid-July to 12 Oct. Dt £25 (boat and 2 or 3 rods). Max 9 rods. Gillies £25 per day. Permits from John Prendergast, The Zetland Hotel, Cashel (tel: 095 31111). For fishing on **Bealnacarra River** and **Glendollagh Lake,** apply to W Holling and B Gilmore, Recess House.

Maam Cross (Co Galway). Salmon and sea trout. Top Waters Ballynahinch Fishery comprises six lakes and part of **Owentooey** and **Recess Rivers. Lough Oord,** at top of system, is 2m W of Maam Cross with **Loughs Shannakeela, Derryneen** and **Cappahoosh** forming a chain westward. Season mid-June to 12 Oct. Wt (boat) £100, dt (boat) £18 and (bank) £10. Permits and accommodation from Mr L Lyon and Mrs Iris Lyons-Joyce, Tullaboy House (tel: 091 82305).

CARROWNISKY: rises in Sheefry Hills and flows 6m to sea beyond Louisburgh. Spate river, overgrown by trees in parts, making fishing difficult. Lower reaches characterised by long flat stretches. Runs of salmon and sea trout from June. Roonagh Lough, into which river runs, offers fishing for both, either by fly or dapping.

Louisburgh (Co Mayo). Permits for Carrowinsky fishing from Charles Gaffney's Pub, tel: 098 66150; st £50, dt £10. Salmon and trout in **Altair Lake.** Good shore fishing for bass, pollack, etc; boats available at Roonagh and Old Head. **Bunowen River:** spate river with some deep pools. Sea trout and salmon, best from mid-June. Season: 1 Apr to 30 Sept. Permits £10, for river and **Lough Namucka** from Charles Gaffney's Pub, as above. Hotels: Old Head, Durkans. For sea fishing Bay View Hotel, Clare Island, recommended; boats available.

CASHLA: drains a complex system of lakes then flows into Cashla Bay at Costelloe. Fair run of salmon, mostly grilse but it is as sea trout fishery that it really excels.

Costelloe (Co Galway). Sea trout, salmon. Costelloe and Fermoyle Fishery: Lower fishery includes R Cashla and **Lough Glenicmurrin,** and holds excellent sea trout and good salmon; Upper fishery includes **R Fermoyle, Lough Fermoyle** and **R Clohir,** and holds excellent sea trout. Dt £10-£15. Boat and boatman £40-£50. Max 30 rods. Permits and tackle from Tim Moore, Bridge Cottage, Costelloe (tel: 091 72196); accom. may be booked through fishery. Tackle shops: Freeney's, 19 High St; Murt Folan, Fishing Tackle, Wood Quay; Hugh Duffy, Mainguard St, all Galway, Co Galway.

DAWROS: drains Kylemore Lakes then flows 5m before entering Ballinakill Harbour. Run of spring salmon, grilse, sea trout. Best July to Sept (sea trout); Aug (salmon).

Renvyle (Co Galway). Salmon, grilse, sea trout. Renvyle House Hotel has water. Dt £12 on river; £20 per boat. Gillies available. Apply Renvyle House Hotel (tel: 095 43511). Tackle shops: Percy Stanley, Clifden, Co Galway; Hamilton's, Leenane, Co Galway.

DOOHULLA: drains a number of lakes, then runs $\frac{1}{4}$m to Ballyconneely Bay. Holds some summer salmon and excellent sea trout. Best sea trout July to Sept.

Fishing available?

If you own, manage, or know of first-class fishing available to the public which should be considered for inclusion in **Where to Fish** *please apply to the publishers (address in the front of the book) for a form for submission, on completion, to the Editor. (Inclusion is at the sole discretion of the Editor).*

Best salmon June to Aug.

Ballyconneely (Co Galway). Between Roundstone and Ballyconneely lies the Doohulla Fishery, consisting of The Pool at Callow Bridge, **Doohulla River,** and **Loughs Maumeen, Emlaghkeeragh** and others. Salmon, sea trout, browns. Dt £10 (The Pool) and £5. Hire of boats £20. Gillie available. Permits from N D Tinne, Emlaghmore (tel: 095 23529). Clifden tackle shops: Pryce; Stanley.

ERRIFF AND BUNDORRAGHA:good salmon and sea trout rivers lying short distance north of Ballynahinch country and flowing into Killary Harbour.

Leenane (Co Galway). **Erriff Fishery** consists of River Erriff (8m) and **Tawnyard Lough.** River noted for salmon and sea trout; and lough for sea trout. Fishery acquired by Central Fisheries Board in 1982. Dt £13 (April-mid-June), £25 (mid-June-Sep 30). Three boats on Tawnyard Lough (sea trout), July 1-Sep 30, boat for 2 rods, £25. River season April-Sept, on lough, July 1-Sept 30. Accommodation at Aasleagh Lodge. Enquiries to Erriff Fishery Office, Aasleagh Lodge, Leenane, Co Galway (tel: 095 42252). **Delphi Fishery,** six miles away, has the following waters: **Bundorragha River,** 3 rods, sea trout June to Aug, salmon all season, salmon and sea trout on **Loughs Glencullin, Doolough, Finlough, Tawnyard,** and **Cunnel.** Fly only, but limited trolling on Doolough. Boats on all loughs except Cunnel. Dt with boat £50. Gillies available, £30. Apply to Peter Mantle, Delphi Lodge, Leenane, Co Galway (tel: 095 42211, fax: 095 42296). Accommodation available at Delphi Lodge and 4 fishing cottages. Tackle shops: The Fishery Office, Delphi Fishery; Hamilton's.

NEWPORT: drains Lough Beltra and runs into Clew Bay, at Newport. River over 7m long and usually fished from banks. Good for salmon and very good sea trout. There are about 20 pools, some for both day and night fishing. Fly only. River known for length of season 20 March-30 Sept.

Newport (Co Mayo). Salmon and sea trout. Newport House Hotel has fishing on **Newport River, Lough Beltra** (fine run of spring fish) and 4m on **River Skerdagh,** a tributary. Dt £23, £76 for 2 rods with boat and gillie, from The Fishery Manager, Newport House *(see advt)* (tel: 098 41222). Newport AC, whose

members are free to fish Newport River by concession of Newport House, issue permits for salmon and sea trout fishing (June to Sept) on **Owengarve,** a small spate river near **Mulrany.** Various small trout loughs around Newport. Hotel also issues tickets to non-members, when available. A few miles from Newport, boat fishing for salmon and sea trout at **Burrishoole Fishery** which consists of **Loughs Feeagh** and **Furnace** with short tidal stretch of river. Fishery owned and administered by Salmon Research Agency of Ireland; fishing season effectively mid-June to end September. Boats available with or without boatmen, package holidays arranged by request incorporating local accommodation of varying grades. Full details from SRTI, Newport, Co Mayo. Tel (098) 41107. Agency also controls **Ballinlough Fishery,** 54 acres, 2m north west of Westport: stocked rainbow and brown trout, limit 6 fish.

OWENDUFF: Good for salmon from end of Mar. Grilse and sea trout, mid-June to end of Sept. Provides excellent all-round fishing when water right.

Ballycroy (Co Mayo). Salmon, sea trout. Upper reaches privately owned by Rock Estates (Newport) Ltd, Ballycroy (tel: 098 49137), together with **R Bellaveeny** and **L Gall** fishing. For dt apply to John Campbell, tel: 098 49116. Middle reaches owned by Craigie Bros, Finglass, Co Dublin (no lettings). Lagduff Lodge (lower beat). All privately held, but occasional lettings by lodges named. Lower down, a small beat is owned by Mr Justice Barra O'Brien of Enniskerry, Co Wicklow. Good accommodation, Shranamanragh Lodge, let with fishing and shooting by the month. Good for salmon (April/May), grilse and sea trout (July onwards).

OWENGARVE: Spate river. Salmon, grilse and sea trout, early June to early Oct.

Mulrany (Co Mayo). Most of river controlled by Newport AC, which has mutual agreement with Dr J Healey, Rosturk Castle, Rosturk, Westport, Co Mayo, whereby whole river can be fished. Daily (£2), weekly and monthly rods available from club hon sec or from Rosturk Castle.

ACHILL ISLAND: Off Mayo coast, has become famous in recent years for its sea fishing *(see Sea Fishing section).* Excellent sea trout. Good brown trout fishing on four lakes, fish plentiful but small. St

£20, wt £10, dt £2 from J O'Malley, Island Sports, Keel PO (tel: 098 43125). Club: Achill Sporting Club. Hotel: Achill Head, Keel. Accom at Achill Sound, 098 45245, or 45272.

OWENGOWLA and INVERMORE:two short rivers, each draining a complex of lakes. Owengowla flows into Bertraghboy Bay and Invermore flows into Kilkieran Bay. Both are excellent sea trout fisheries.

Cashel (Co Galway). Sea trout. **Gowla Fishery** consists of **R Owengowla,** with holding pools, and about 14 loughs, of which available from Fishery Office. **Invermore Fishery** has ten sea trout lakes and an additional brown trout lake. Upper lakes are remote, but accessible by path. Lower lakes fish from mid-June; upper lakes governed by summer rainfall. There are 10 boats on the fishery, and accommodation. Dt (boat) £25 from Mrs Margaret McDonagh, Glenview (095 31054). Gillies available at both fisheries.

OWENMORE: 20m long and principally spate river from Bellacorick Bridge, rises near Ballycastle and flows into Blacksod Bay. Principal tributary is **Oweniny** (Crossmolina AA). River divided among number of owners. Good for spring salmon from April 1, given really high water; good grilse and sea trout from mid-June to end of Sept, if water is right. To the south of river are a number of small loughs with brown trout. Some of these have free fishing, including **Loughs Brack, Nambrock,** and **Nalagan.** They are remote, but worth exploring.

Bangor Erris (Co Mayo). Upper and middle reaches owned by syndicate. Information from Dr I R Moore, 20 Temple Gardens, Dublin 6, and Michael Varian, Glasthule Lodge, Adelaide Road, Glengeary, Co Dublin. Lodges and fishings let by the fortnight when syndicate-members are not fishing. Part of fishery let to Bangor Erris FC. Dt from hon sec. Enquiries respecting **Carrowmore Lough,** salmon, sea trout and brown trout, plus 4m of **Owenmore** and **Glenamoy** Rivers, to Seamus Henry, West End Bar, Bangor Erris, Ballina, 097 83487. For lower reaches inquire of Mr W J Sweeney, Bridge House, Achill, Westport. Tackle shops: O'Connor, Main Street, Ballycastle.

SCREEBE: drains a group of lakes, including Lakes **Ardery, Shindilla, Loughan-free, Ahalia** and **Screebe,** then flows into

Camus Bay at Screebe. Gets good run of grilse and sea trout, and some summer salmon.

Screebe (Co Galway). Salmon and brown trout. Screebe Estate Fishery is professionally managed and includes Screebe River and numerous lakes. It also has its own hatchery. Fly fishing only. Permits from The Manager, Screebe Estates, Camus (tel: 091 74110). Hotel: Currarevagh House Hotel, Oughterard, Co Galway (tel: 35391 82312/3), good centre for local fishing, caters for anglers. Tackle shops: Tommy Tuck (Oughterard AA); M Keogh, both Oughterard, Co Galway.

MAYO North (streams)

Several small sea trout rivers run to the coast in north west of county. **Glenamoy** and **Muingnabo** both empty into a sea lough at **Broad Haven Bay,** and have salmon and sea trout. Fishing on the **Muingnabo R.** is free. Near **Ballycastle** are **Glencullin** and **Ballinglen Rivers,** both with sea trout, late run on Glencullin, a few salmon in Ballinglen. Free fishing on both. The **Cloonaghmore River** runs into **Killala Bay,** west of the **Moy.** It has both salmon and sea trout. Free fishing with permission of local assc.

GARAVOGUE and LOUGH GILL

(For close seasons, licences, etc, see The North-Western Regional Fisheries Board)

Garavogue River connects Lough Gill with sea, which it enters in Sligo Bay to south of Donegal Bay and Erne. Salmon, trout, coarse fish. Lough Gill is a fine coarse fishery, with excellent stock of bream at Hazelwood, Doonee, Kilmore and Armagh

Sligo (Co Sligo). Salmon, trout. **Lough Gill,** a large lake 5m long. Good run of spring salmon; best Feb to March. Northern and eastern shores controlled by Sligo AA. St £8, from Barton Smith, Tackle Dealer, Hyde Bridge. Fishing on the rest of the lake is free. Boats £10 per day, from Blue Lagoon, Public House (tel: 071 42530); Frank Armstrong, 14 Riverside (also tackle hire and gillie service). Sligo AA also has fishing on **Glencar Lake,** 7m; salmon (grilse), sea and brown trout; boat available. **Lough Colga,** 4m; brown trout; free. Permits from Barton Smith, Tackle Shop, Hyde Bridge (tel: 071 42356).

Dromahair (Co Leitrim). **River Bonet** feeds Lough Gill; salmon, trout. Best for salmon in summer. Dromahair AA fishes locally. Permits available from McGoldricks Mace Foodmarket. Abbey Hotel has free, all-round fishing for guests. Manorhamilton AA also preserve some water on river and **Glencar Lake.** St £12, dt £5, from A Flynn, Post Office. Manorhamilton (tel: 072 55001). Also abundance of coarse fishing in river and **Loughs Belhavel, Glenade** and **Corrigeencor;** all free, with pike and perch. Tackle from Spar, Main St.

Co. KERRY (streams and loughs)

(For close seasons, licences, etc, see The South Western Regional Fisheries Board)

KENMARE BAY. Several small salmon rivers empty into this bay, which provides excellent sea fishing (large skate, tope, etc). Best season, May to August.

Kenmare (Co Kerry). Kenmare Salmon Angling Ltd owns part of **Roughty** at Ardtully Castle, 5 miles from Kenmare-Cork Road. Spring salmon, March to June; good grilse runs, June to Aug; fly, spinning, prawning and worming permitted; fish average 9lb. Permits are available (dt £10, wt £30) for visitors staying locally, from John O'Hare, 21 Main St, Kenmare, 064 41499. No Sunday fishing

---

Fishing available?

If you own, manage, or know of first-class fishing available to the public which should be considered for inclusion in **Where to Fish** *please apply to the publishers (address in the front of the book) for a form for submission, on completion, to the Editor. (Inclusion is at the sole discretion of the Editor).*

for visitors. **Sheen River** runs in on south shore and is preserved by owner. It produces approx 1,000 salmon and grilse every season. Contact the Manager, Sheen Falls Lodge, Kenmare, 064 41600. Tributary **Comeen** is worth fishing. Contact Lodge. **Finnihy River** is overgrown and requires determination, but has grilse run: free fishing. **Lough Barfinnihy** 35 acres, is $6\frac{1}{2}$m from Kenmare, off Killarney Rd. Good brown and stocked rainbows. Permits for this and for **Uragh Lough** from J O'Hare, *see above*. **Cloonee Loughs**, on the south shore, have excellent game fishing. Permission and boats from May O'Shea, Lakehouse, Cloonee, 064 84205. Contact Kenmare Estate Office, 064 41341, for **Lough Inchiquin:** char, sea trout, salmon, browns. One boat available. For fishermen with taste for mountain climbing there are at least 40 lakes holding brown trout on plateau of **Caha Mountains,** all easily fished from Kenmare. *See also 'South West Cork'.* **Kerry Blackwater** drains **Lough Brin** and is preserved, but permission can be obtained from Mr Keith Johnston, Estate Office, Kenmare. Blackwater is excellent salmon river, and

Glencar House

GLENCAR, COUNTY KERRY, IRELAND
TEL: 066-60102   FAX: 066-60167

Glencar house offers excellent Salmon fishing in private waters of Upper Caragh River.

7 Beats, 1 rod per beat, available weekly.

10 years average catch 310 salmon.

Also lakes Cloon, Acosse with boats and engines available daily.

Comfortable accommodation with a friendly homely atmosphere. Restaurant, Bar, and TV lounge.

also holds good stock of sea trout from June onwards. Best fishing is up about 4m from sea. Estate also has fishing on **Lough Brin,** 10m north west, trout to 1lb, and sea trout from August. **Sneem River,** farther west, is let with holiday cottage: H Cowper, Sneem. run of grilse and sea trout July/August. Hotels: Park Hotel, Kenmare Bay, Riversdale, Dunkeron Lodge.

WATERVILLE (or Currane) and INNY: Waterville River, short river joining **Lough Currane.** Popular with visitors. Salmon, sea trout, brown trout. All migratory fish running to Lough Currane go through this river, which also has spring run of large sea trout. There is a commercial fishery, traps of which are lifted on July 15. Lough Currane (excellent trout and salmon fishing) free to licence-holders. Boats available. Inny is a grilse river with sea trout; best season mid-June to Oct.

Waterville (Co Kerry). Waterville House, 0667 4244, lets occasional rods on **Waterville** and **Inny,** for 4 hour periods. Spinning allowed in spring, thereafter, fly only. Several other owners have fishing to let on Inny, incl Butler Arms Hotel, Waterville, 0667 4156; J O'Connell, Foildrenagh, Mastergeehy, Killarney; J O'Shea, Killenleigh, Mastergeehy; M J O'Sullivan, 0667 4255. Tackle shops: Coomaciste Crafts; Sean O'Shea. Other hotels: Silver Sands, White House.

CARHAN and FERTA: small spate rivers which enter Valentia Harbour. Small run of grilse and sea trout. Carhan is overgrown and worm is the best method. **Kells Lough** is between **Glenbeigh** and **Caherciveen.** Plentiful stock of small browns.

CARAGH: river runs through **Caragh Lake** to sea at Dingle Bay. Salmon, sea trout, trout. Salmon best from May, sea trout late, good fishing at night. Bass and mullet in estuary. Immediately to the east of Caragh Lake is a large group of small loughs, incl **L Nakirka,** 20 acres. For permit contact D Foley, Killorglin, 066 61193.

Glenbeigh (Co Kerry). For lower water; wt £26 and dt £6, from Towers Hotel. Hotel also issues permits for 6m of **Laune** (single bank only), $8\frac{1}{2}$m of **Feale,** 3m of **Flesk, Behy** and **Loughs Caragh** and **Currane.** To south west of Glenbeigh is a group of small trout loughs drained by **R Behy,** incl **Coomnacronia** and

Looking over Lough Arrow towards Hargadon's Point.

Coomaglaslaw: free fishing on all of them.

Glencar (Co Kerry) Glencar House Hotel *(see advt)* has 7 beats, one rod per beat, reserved for guests only; salmon; best months, Feb to end of June; grilse June onwards; sea trout. Average salmon catch over 10 years, 310 per annum. The hotel also has fishing on **Loughs Cloon, Acoose** and **Reagh.** Many smaller rivers and lakes holding brown trout. Gillies and boats available. Tackle and licences at hotel, tel: 066 60102.

MACGILLYCUDDY'S REEKS (Co Kerry). In the Gap of Dunloe, a line of three small lakes drain into **Laune** at Beaufort Bridge: **Black Lake, Cushvalley** and **Auger.** Free fishing for plentiful small brown trout that fight extremely well. Very small fly recommended. At head of Black Valley are **Cummeenduff**

Loughs and **Lough Reagh,** which are approached via Gap of Dunloe. Free fishing with spring salmon and good grilse run. Boats from J O'Donoghue, Black, Valley, Killarney.

DINGLE PENINSULAR (Co Kerry). Several small rivers and loughs are fishable in this area; **Rivers Milltown** and **Owenascaul** on south side, free fishing with some sea trout; **Owencashla, Glennahoo, Scarid, Owenmore** on north side: some migratory fish in spate, worth fishing. Mostly free, permission for Owenmore from G Connor, 066 38244 and B Brosnan, 066 26753. Owencashla overgrown. Loughs incl **Anascaul,** with sea trout in Aug/Sept; **Gill,** west of **Castlegregory:** free, for small browns; **Adoon,** with sea trout from August, free; and many others worth exploring.

LAUNE and MAINE (including Killarney Lakes)

(For close seasons, licences, etc, see The South-Western Regional Fisheries Board)

LAUNE: Drains Killarney Lakes and flows 14m NW to Dingle Bay. Salmon, sea trout. Best months March-May and Sept. There is fishing available at the following: **Muckross Fishery,** permits from Knockrear Estate Office, Killarney, 064 31246, information from SWRFB; Land Commission Fishery at **Meanus, Tubrid** and **Mweelcara** townlands, enquiries to SWRFB; Laune Salmon AA, c/o T O'Riordan, 50 Oak Park Demesne, Tralee, tel 066 24690; J Mangan, 066 61393.

Beaufort (Co Kerry). For upper reaches. Permits and light tackle from O'Sullivans, Beaufort Bridge, Killarney, 064 44397. Self-catering house on banks.

MAINE: Maine and tributaries **Little Maine** and **Brown Flesk** hold salmon, sea trout and brown trout. Salmon fishing fair, after drainage setbacks in 1950s, and Brown Flesk has at least 35 holding pools; over 200 salmon per season, sea and brown trout fishing often good. River is late. Best at medium to low water; good grilse from end of June, sea trout in July. Little Maine has seven or eight salmon pools and good fishing for small browns. Sea trout best at night. Part of this system is free fishing: check with SWRFB.

KILLARNEY LAKES: Consist of three lakes: **Upper Lake, Muckross Lake** (middle), **Lough Leane,** or **Lein** (lower), last being much the largest, connected with sea by **R Laune.** Salmon and trout fishing good; free. Best season for salmon: Lough Leane, Feb to July; Muckross and Upper, Jan 17 to April or May. Mayfly hatch in June. **R Flesk** feeds **Lough Leane.** Spinning best for salmon. Many small mountain lakes; free trout fishing. **Kilbrean Lake** is well stocked with brown trout, fishing by permit only.

Killarney (Co Kerry). Salmon fishing best in May/June. Sea trout fishing poor, brown trout excellent, best June, and Sept to mid-Oct. Fishing on R Flesk is available for £5 per week from Lough Lein AA. **Lough Leane** (4500 acres), largest of Killarney lakes; famous for beauty of scenery; estimated that local fishermen get hundreds of salmon and grilse by trolling baits every season. Free fishing; max rods 40-50. Boats available from Harry Clifden, Ross Castle (tel: 064 32252); and Alfie Doyle (tel: 064 33652). Tackle shops: O'Neill's, 6 Plunkett St; The Handy Stores, Main St. Many hotels and guest houses.

LEE

(For close seasons, licences, etc, see The South-Western Regional Fisheries Board)

Draining **Gougane Barra Lake** and flowing 53m to Cork Harbour, Lee was formerly notable early salmon river (Feb to May) but fishing spoilt by hydro-electric schemes; salmon sport restricted to lower 6m. Experimental trout stocking programme is planned. Trout are more plentiful from Leemount Bridge to below Inniscarra Dam. SWRFB **Inniscarra Fishery** is a ¾m double bank salmon fishery, below hydro-electric station. Fishable from March, peaks in April-May, mid-June for grilse. Tel: 026 41221.

Cork (Co Cork). Salmon fishing on lower R Lee at Inniscarra Dam and below Millbro; season Feb 1 to Sept 30. Fishing is privately owned or leased and controlled mainly by Lee Salmon A and Cork Salmon A (dt £10, from sec). Salmon fishing licence is required, obtainable from tackle shops. Trout fishing on **R Shournagh, Martin, Bridge** and **Dripsey;** small streams with brown trout; fishing mostly free. For information contact Cork Trout AA, Blarney AA and tackle shops. Lough in Cork City, 10 acres, has large carp (Irish record 22lb) and eels, 2lb to 6lb. Tackle shops: T W Murray & Co, 87 Patrick St; The Tackle Shop, 6 Lavitts Quay. Hotels: Jurys, Gabriel House, Imperial.

Macroom (Co Cork). Stocked brown trout fishing on **Inniscarra Reservoir;** contact SW Fisheries Board, Macroom, 026 41222. **Carrigohid Reservoir** is good pike fishery, with perch shoals. Other venues for pike are lower **Sullane River, Middle Lee, Lough Allua.** Middle Lee, Rivers Sullane, Laney and Foherish, and **Gougane Barra** lake are good fisheries for small trout. Hotels: Castle, Victoria.

Keep the banks clean

Several clubs have stopped issuing tickets to visitors because of the state of the banks after they have left. Spend a few moments clearing up.

LIFFEY

(For close seasons, licences, etc, see The Eastern Regional Fisheries Board)

Winding river with two reservoirs along its course, rises some 13m SW of Dublin but flows over 80m before entering sea at Islandbridge, Dublin. Subject to hydro-electric floods, it has salmon, brown trout and some sea trout in lower reaches. Recorded salmon run about 3000 pa with rod catch of 500-800. Mayfly hatch end of May. Best trout fishing from Lucan upstream. Best salmon between Straffan and Islandbridge.

Dublin (Co Dublin). Most water controlled by clubs. Dublin & Dist Salmon AA: Liffey at Islandbridge, Lucan, and below Leixlip Bridge; Dublin Trout AA: about 6m on Upper and Lower Liffey at Ballyward Bridge, Clane, Straffan/Celbridge, **Leixlip, Blessington** and **Upper** and **Lower Bohernabreena Reservoirs**; mainly trout fishing, some salmon in Liffey, and pike, also. Dt £5-£2, depending on water. Clane Trout and Salmon AA: apprx 4m of excellent brown trout water, best from early May, with moderate salmon after July. Dt £5 (from M Casey, Blackhall, Clane, 045 68995), fly, bait fishing discouraged, no coarse; North Kildare Trout & Salmon AA: Millicent Bridge to Kilcullen Bridge; Kilcullen Trout and Salmon AA: Kilcullen u/s to Harristown; Ballymore Eustace Salmon and Trout AA, Ballymore Eustace to Harristown; Kilbride AC: Ballyfoyle to Ballysmutton; Lucan AC fishes Lucan stretch and Chapelizod AC also has water. Broadmeadow AC fishes **Broadmeadow R** and **Tonelgee Reservoir.** Tickets from tackle shops. Dt £2 for Dublin Trout AA waters from Dan O'Brien, New Rd, Blackhall, Clane, Co Kildare and Sy Gallagher, Reeves, Straffan, Co Kildare. Dublin Corporation controls fishing on **Roundwood Reservoir** (20m) and on **Bohernabreena Reservoir** (8m); the former leased to Co Wicklow AA; fly only; bank fishing; st and dt. **Grand Canal,** which runs alongside Liffey for some distance, holds brown trout, bream, rudd, perch and pike. Coarse fishing also in **Royal Canal,** similar species. Tackle shops: P Cleere & Son, 5 Bedford Row; Nolan's, 80 North Strand; Rory's, 17a Temple Bar, Dublin 2.

Naas (Kildare). Ballymore Eustace Trout & Salmon AA has fishing on Liffey from **Ballymore Eustace** to **Harristown,** and also **Golden Falls Lake.** St and dt are available from Michael Murphy, Publican, The Square, Ballymore Eustace. Kilcullen & Dist Trout and Salmon AA fishes Liffey at Kilcullen, u/s to Harristown. Prosperous Coarse AC fishes 20m of **Grand Canal,** *see 'Grand Canal.'* Tackle shops: Cahills Sports; J Prescott, Pachelli Rd, both Naas; bait from Prescott. Hotel; Ardenode, Ballymore Eustace. Several guest houses, incl Cassidy, 045 68173; Dempsey, 045 69146; Duff, 045 68314; Hanlow, 045 68698.

MOY

(For close seasons, licences, etc, see The North Western Regional Fisheries Board)

Flowing 63m from its source in the Ox Mountains to enter Killala Bay at Ballina, its tributaries drain an area of some 800 square miles. One of Ireland's premier salmon rivers, particularly famous for its grilse and summer salmon. Stretches to suit all forms of angling from fly fishing to spinning to worm fishing. Spring run starts in early Feb; main grilse run starts in May and peaks in June.

Ballina (Co Mayo). Salmon fishing on three beats owned by **Moy Fishery,** May to end of Sept. Beat 1, £10 per day, rods limited; beat 2, ghillie and boat of two rods, £65; beat 3, £8 per day, st £20. Apply to Moy Fishery, Bridge Pool Rd, Ballina (tel: 096 21332). Moy Fishery can also arrange boats and engines for **Lough Conn** fishing. Ballina Salmon AA issues permits for a stretch downstream of Ridge Pool, apply to Billy Egan, Barret St, Ballina. Mount Falcon Castle Hotel has 7½m between Ballina and **Foxford,** including famous Wall Pool. Wt £50, dt £10. Apply to Mrs Aldridge, Mount Falcon Castle (tel; 096 21172). Alpine Hotel has fishing on left bank, contact J Byrne, Alpine Hotel, Enniscrone, Co Sligo (tel: 096 36144). Armstrong Fishery has adjoining left bank stretch of about 1m. Contact George Armstrong at fishery, tel: 094 5680. For the next mile up river, left bank, contact Gannons, Post Office, Foxford, 094 56101. Tackle shops: John Walkin, Tone

St; Vincent Doherty, Bridge St; M Swartz, Ballina Angling Centre, Dillon Terrace. Hotels: Balleek Castle, The Imperial, Downside.

Foxford (Co Mayo). Pontoon Bridge Hotel offers salmon and trout fishing on 4m of water, including renowned salmon pool at Pontoon Bridge, and on **Lakes Conn** and **Cullin.** Tuition from May to Oct, and school of landscape painting for non-fishing partner! Boats on lake, with or without motor and gillie £12-£30 per day from hotel or tackle shop; tackle also available (tel: 094 56120). Other local fisheries on **R Moy** are Foxford Salmon Anglers, both banks above Foxford, tel 094 56238; **Leckee Fishery,** r bank, dt from Post Office, *see above;* dt £10 from Clongee Fishery, l bank above and below Lough Cullin, r bank near Foxford: dt £10 from Michael Ruane, Clongee (tel: 094 56634); East Mayo AA, two separate beats above Foxford, dt £12: contact Mrs Wills, Ballylahan Bridge, 094 51149. Free fishing on Loughs Conn and Cullin,

and on a short stretch of R Moy downstream of Foxford Bridge. Healys Hotel at **Pontoon** has boats at southern end of Lough Conn and at Lough Cullin. Also M McCormack, Foxford.

Tackle shop: J J Connor, Spencer St, Castlebar, Co Mayo.

Crossmolina (Co Mayo). Salmon, grilse, trout. Free fishing on **Lough Conn.** Boats available from J Moffat, Kilmurry House (tel: 096 31227); L NcNeely, 096 31202; Mrs Mary Higgins, Cloghans, Ballina, who is secretary of Lough Conn AC and can also provide accommodation (tel: 096 31227). Tackle shop: Joseph Munnelly, Main St (tel: 096 31314). Hotel Dolphin.

Swinford (Co Mayo). Spring salmon best from mid-March, grilse June onwards. Swinford AA issues permits, apply to Mrs Wills, Ballylahon Bridge (tel: 094 56221); Seamus Boland, Bridge St. **Lough Talt** is good brown trout lake, free.

Tributaries of the Moy

GWEESTION. Glore River and **Trimoge River** join to become **Gweestion,** flowing from south easterly direction. Both have a large stock of small brown trout, with free fishing.

MULLAGHANOE and OWENGARVE. These two rivers flow from the **Charlestown** area westwards. They contain a good stock of browns to 1½lb. Fishing free, excellent on Owengarve d/s of Curry Village.

EINAGH. Joins main river from **Lough Talt** near **Aclare.** Brown trout to 3lb, but average at 10oz. Sea trout run; free fishing in river and lough (browns, av ½lb).

LOUGH CONN SYSTEM. Lough Conn, 12,000 acres, together with L Cullin, has free fishing for salmon, main run from end of March through April, brown trout

(excellent stock, av 1lb), and char. A long mayfly season from late May until end of June. A good late season for trout in August. Several rivers run into **Loughs Conn** and **Cullin** which offer free fishing for game and coarse fish. From north west, **Deel River:** salmon in spring and summer, brown trout u/s of Deel Bridge. From the south, **Clydagh** and **Manulla Rivers,** and the outflow from **Castlebar Lakes** all join a few miles above lough. On Clydagh free salmon fishing; on Manulla free trout fishing between **Moyhenna** and **Ballyvary** bridges. Some free fishing for wild browns on location in **Islandeady Bilberry Lough. Upper** and **Lower Lough Lannagh** and **Lough Mallard,** nr **Castlebar,** have been developed as free trout fisheries.

Check before you go

While every effort has been made to ensure that the information given in **Where to Fish** *is correct, the position is continually changing, and anglers are urged, in their own interests, to make preliminary enquiries before travelling to selected venues. This is especially important with reference to prices quoted. Inevitably the rate of inflation is affecting stability in this quarter. Anglers' attention is also drawn to the fact that the hotels mentioned under the various fishing stations do not necessarily have water of their own. Any amendments or further data for inclusion in subsequent editions, and any criticism, will be welcome.*

SHANNON

(For close seasons, licences, etc, see The Shannon Regional Fisheries Board)

Largest river in British Isles, 160m long with catchment area covering greater part of central Ireland. Enters Atlantic on west coast through long estuary. A typical limestone river, rich in weed and fish food, of slow current for most part, and though some its sources rise in peat, acidity counteracted by limestone reaches. Many of the adverse effects of hydro-electric scheme introduced 45 years ago now overcome by re-stocking and other forms of fishery management. With exception of famous Castleconnell Fisheries, Shannon mostly sluggish. Salmon run from March to May, grilse from end of May to September. Primary sea trout waters are **Feale** and **Doonbeg**. Permits are available from local tackle shops. Trout fishing is a feature of Shannon and tributaries, Mulcair, **Newport, Nenagh, Brosna, Little Brosna, Fergus**; and **Maigue**. there is a mayfly rise, when excellent sport can be enjoyed, free of charge, in **Loughs Derg** and **Ree** at Athlone. Trolling is the usual method, otherwise; trout grow large. River has well-deserved reputation for its coarse fishing. Excellent fisheries for tench, perch, rudd, shoals of bream and roach, at Plassey, O'Brien's Bridge, u/s of Portumna, Banagher, Shannonbridge. The three main pike fisheries of the system are R Shannon itself, Lough Derg, R Fergus. There is a limit on the killing of pike: one per angler per day, max size, 3kgs. Coarse fishing may also be had in Derg and Ree. **Lough Allen,** northernmost lake of Shannon, specially good for pike. Eel fishing is growing more popular in Shannon region, which has sluggish stretches ideal for the species, large catches coming from Shannon, **R Fergus, L Derg** and **East Clare Lakes;** Mouth of Suck at Shannonbridge and mouth of Brosna are good spots to try. The Lower Shannon Trout & Coarse Fisheries Development Society are a co-operative existing to raise funds for the improvement of trout and coarse fishing. Share certificates are sold, from £3 for three days, to £12 per annum. Contact Secretary, J Guilfoyle, 16 Cusack Lawn, Cloughleigh Rd, Ennis, Co Clare, tel: 065 40116.

Kilrush (Co Clare). West Clare AA has fishing in this corner of Co Clare, on Lakes **Knockerra** (50 acres), **Knockalough, Doolough, Kilkee Reservoir,** all fly and worm only. The trout fishing is free, but anglers accept voluntary subs for development of fishing in area. Tackle shop: M L O'Sullivan, Moore St. Hotels: Inis Cathaig; Victoria, Halpins, both Kilkee.

Limerick (Co Limerick). On tidal Shannon. Clancy's Strand is the lowest bottom fishery on Shannon, mainly trout fishing, which can be very good, on fly, worm, dead minnow or spinner. ESB permit required. On outskirts of city is the Long Shore Fishery: wide, deep tidal water with spring salmon run; it can be fished from both banks. Boat hire with gillie through Jim Robinson, *see below.* Good spring salmon fishing at **Plassey** (2m); 500 yds salmon fishing which peaks in May, and trout. ESB permit reqd. Limerick tackle shops: J Robinson, Thomond Shopping Centre; McMahon, Roches Street; Nestor Bros, O'Connell Street and Limerick Sports Stores, 10 William Street.

Castleconnell (Co Limerick). Principal centre for salmon angling on Shannon and within 3m of **Mulcair River.** Traditional big fish water; catches improved recently. Fishing on six Castleconnell beats controlled by Regional Manager, Hydro Generation Region, Ardnacrusha, Nr Limerick, who will book beats and provide information. Permits £10 to £25 available from Head Warden, M Murtagh, O'Briens Bridge, 061 377289. Advance booking advisable, from ESB, 061 345588. Best beats to book are nos. 8, 7 and 4. Best months for spring salmon, April to mid-May, grilse mid-May to end June. Fly, spinning and worm. Trout fishing free. The best coarse fishing in Limerick area is located just below Castleconnell salmon fishery. This is free fishing. Hotel: Castle Oaks House. Accom. at Stradbally, 010 353 61 377397; J Moloney, Riverside, O'Brien's Bridge, 010 353 61 377303.

Killaloe (Co Clare). At outlet from Lough Derg, good centre for trout and coarse fishing on lake. Trout angling can be very good in May and autumn; fish average 3-4lb. Boats available. **Doon Lough,** 8m west, is a fine coarse fishery, with a good stock of bream to 3lb, also boat fishing for large pike. Boats for hire. Good bream fishing at caravan park on west shore. Tackle shop: McKeogh's, Ballina. Hotel: Lakeside.

Scariff Bay (Co Clare). From Aughinish Point into bay there is good fishing for specimen pike, also stocks of bream, tench, perch and rudd. Boat essential. Further west shore centres for coarse fishing are **Mountshannon/Whitegate:** Church Bay contains large tench, pike, bream and rudd; **Williamstown Harbour:** big tench from boat, quay fishing for pike, perch and bream; **Rossmore** pier: good place for same species, and a nice spot for camping. Boats and gillies are available for hire.

Dromineer (Co Tipperary). Best centre for middle sections of **Lough Derg.** Large trout taken spinning or trolling; also good centre for dry fly and dapping; trout up to 10lb caught. Mayfly starts about first week in May. Coarse fishing very good at **Youghal Bay,** Dromineer, **Kilgarvan** and **Terryglass** from quays, harbour walls and shore; Carrigahorig Bay has shoals of big bream and large pike: boat essential; fishing free. Eight fishing clubs on lake are represented by Lough Derg AA. **River Nenagh** flows into R Shannon at Dromineer; a major trout fishery with small number of salmon; in wider stretches trout can reach 2lb, about ½lb in narrows. No coarse fish except between Ballyartella Weir and mouth of river (1m); 22m of fishable water. Fly fishing best Mar-May, wet and dry fly. Rivers Nenagh and tributary **Ollatrim** (trout fishery only, no maggot fishing) are controlled by Ormond AA; st £5 from Whelan's Tackle Shop, Summerhill, Nenagh, Co Tipperary. Hotels; Waterside; Ormond, Nenagh.

Portumna (Co Galway). At northern inlet end of **Lough Derg.** Some good dapping bays within reach. Bream and rudd fishing in Shannon. Best pike months are March to May, and Oct. Good perch fishing in summer months. Local club membership £5 from tackle shop. Tackle shop: Garry Kenny, Palmerstown Stores, 0509 41071. Hotels: Westpark; Portland House. Many guest houses.

Lough Rea (Co Galway). 19m NW of Portumna; fairly large limestone lake with trout, pike and perch. Fishing on lough and river open to members of Loughrea AA, which has improved and restocked water; trout average 2lb, pike run to over 30lb; for dt and boats contact Sweeney Travel, Loughrea, 091 41552. Loughrea tackle shop: Beatty's, Church St. Hotel: O'Deas.

Banagher (Co Offaly). Brown trout, coarse fishing good: bream, rudd, hybrids, pike, perch, eels. River is wide at **Meelick,** with islands, pools and weirs. There is some east bank fishing for salmon, mainly from boat. Access to west bank is from **Kilnaborris:** bank fishing possible, in fast water. Occasional spring salmon, mainly grilse. **Brosna** and **Little Brosna River** and small tributary **Camcor River,** nr **Birr,** controlled by Central Fisheries Board; brown trout; a licence to fish required. Coarse fishing on **Grand Canal.** Shannon Regional Fisheries Board stock **Pallas Lake** (18m E) with rainbow and brown trout. Season 1 May-12 Oct. Bank fishing. Fly only. 6 fish limit. Permits from Jim Griffin, Tackle Shop, Rahan, Co Offaly; Al Conroy, Tackle Shop, Kilbride St and Joe Finlay, 15 William St, both Tullamore, Co Offaly. Hotels: Brosna Lodge; Shannon.

Shannonbridge (Co Offaly). Junction of Shannon and **Suck** is a fine centre for coarse fishing; long stretches of bank ideal for bream, hybrids, tench and rudd. Hot water from the Power Station attracts tench. Eel fishing also, is good here. Tackle shop: Dermot Killeen, Main St, 0905 74112.

Athlone (Co Westmeath). Athlone AA has water within 20m radius; restocked with trout. Some salmon. Shannon and Lough Ree abound with trout (good rise to mayfly, late May to late June), pike, roach and bream; bank or boat. Tench plentiful on **Lough Ree. Lough Garnafailagh,** which has produced remarkable catches of tench and bream, may be fished from here. Tackle shops: Foy's, 33 Church Street, Denis Connell, Dublin Gate Street

---

Fishing available?

If you own, manage, or know of first-class fishing available to the public which should be considered for inclusion in **Where to Fish** *please apply to the publishers (address in the front of the book) for a form for submission, on completion, to the Editor. (Inclusion is at the sole discretion of the Editor).*

and Sean Egan, 59 Connaught Street. Anglers accom: Mrs Denby, Shelmalier, 010353 902 72245; Mrs Duggan, Villa St John, 010 353 902 92490.

Lanesborough (Co Longford). Bream, rudd, rudd-bream hybrids, perch, pike, eels. Coarse fishing on **R Shannon, Lough Ree** and **Feorish River.** Good stock of big fish early in season on hot water stretch of Shannon below Power Station, from July these move out into lake. Baits from M Healey, Lakeside Stores. Tackle from Finns, Main St, Roscommon. Accom. for anglers at Mrs watts, Dunamase, 010 353 43 21201; Mrs Keenan, Tarmonbarry, 010 353 43 26052/26098; Abbey Hotel, Roscommon, tel: 0903 26250/26015.

Strokestown (Co Roscommon). Convenient centre for Shannon and **Lough Lea,** a chain of small lakes with rudd, perch, bream, pike and tench. **Cloonfree Lake,** one mile from town, is another good coarse fishery, especially for rudd. **Kilglass Lake,** a five-mile long chain, is 4 miles out on Dumsa Rd: plentiful bream and rudd. Local club, Strokestown AC. Several guest houses and self-catering units, incl Anne Kelly, Drinane; Mr & Mrs P Tighe, Clooncullane, D Colley, Strokestown; Mrs Cox, Church View, Strokestown, 078 33047.

Rooskey (Co Leitrim). Centre for coarse fishing on Rivers Shannon, **Rinn** or **Rynn,** and many small lakes in the area. Bream, tench, rudd, perch, pike, roach. Some brown trout in Shannon. Good catches in **Drumdad Lake** near **Mohill.** Mohill is also a good centre for **Loughs MacHugh, Erril, Lakes Cloonboniagh** and **Creenagh:** fine waters for tench and bream, with pike. Bait from J Moloney, Glebe House, Mohill. Tackle shops: Roosky Quay Enterprises; Lakeland Bait,

Knocknacrory. Accommodation catering for anglers: Lakeland House; Avondale; Kelly's of Mohill; Mrs Davis, Avondale, 010353 78 38095; Mrs Duffy, Killianiker, 010 353 78 38016.

Carrick-on-Shannon (Co Leitrim). Centre for **Shannon, Boyle, Loughs Key, Allen, Corry, Drumharlow** and many others. Trout and coarse fish. Boyle carries heavy head of roach. Good venues are: **Hartley Bridge, Drumsna, Carrick, Albert Lock.** Heavy catches are consistent. Tackle shops: The Creel, Main St; Tranquility Tackle, Kilclare. Many guest houses and hotels offer special anglers accommodation, including Weir House, with 200m Shannon and 41 lakes within 6 miles; **Lough Bran,** with boats for hire; Aisleigh House; Ard-na-Greine House.

Drumshanbo (Co Leitrim). R Shannon rises in Cuilcagh Mountains a short distance N of here. Free coarse fishing on R Shannon, **Lough Allen** and twelve small lakes, incl. **Acres, Derrynahoo, Carrickport** and **Scur.** Trout fishing on Shannon, esp. below **Bellantra Bridge,** in fast water. Lough Allen Conservation Assc has stocked L Allen with over 100,000 trout in past five years. Lough also has a good stock of coarse fish, including specimen pike over 30lb and some big trout. However, as lough acts as a reservoir for the power station near Limerick and has sluice gates at lower end, the waters fluctuate considerably and at low water there are many hazardous rocks; and also there can be sudden strong winds. Local club is Lough Allen AC, visitors welcome, membership £10. Anglers accom: The Thatch, 078 41128, Woodside Guesthouse, 078 41106; Mrs Costello, Forest View, 078 41243; McGuires Rent a Cottage, 078 41033.

Principal Tributaries of the Shannon

DEEL. Enters estuary near Askeaton some miles below Limerick. Fishing stations; **Rathkeale** (Limerick), and **Askeaton** (Limerick), (best Feb-May), white trout (on summer floods), a few salmon and good brown trout (best mid-Mar to Sept). Parts of river preserved by Mrs R Hunt, Inchirourke, Askeaton, and Altaville Estate. Hotels at Rathkeale; Central, Madigan's. Deel AA issues st £5 for 15m at Rathkeale. nearest tackle shop at Limerick.

MAIGUE. Enters estuary between mouth of Deel and Limerick. Brown trout; a few salmon.

Adare (Co Limerick). Adare Manor Hotel has 2m stretch available to guests. Dunraven Arms Hotel has 1¼m fishing free to guests. Some free tidal water below town.

Croom (Co Limerick). Maigue AA has brown trout fishing. Season 1 March-30 Sept. Fly only. Bag limit 6 fish. Trout ¾lb-3lb. St £25, mt £17, wt £10, dt £5, from hon sec. Preserved water below town, free above to Bruree and beyond. Tributaries Camogue, Loobagh and Morningstar mostly free and very good for trout.

Kilmallock (Co Limerick). Kilmallock & Dist AC has brown trout fishing near town on **R Loobagh,** from Riversfield Bridge to Garrouse Bridge, fly only. River is recovering from drainage scheme, and fish average small. Tickets available from club members.

MULCAIR. Enters Shannon 4 miles east of Limerick, and is joined by **Slievenohera River,** which is a confluence of the Newport and Annagh Rivers. Mulcair River has mainly grilse, salmon from March, small brown trout. The Slievenhera system gets spate runs of grilse from late June. St, wt and dt from Regional Manager, Hydro Generation Region, Ardnacrusha, Nr Limerick.

FERGUS. Limestone stream with gin-clear water, trout fishing good; few salmon in spring. Fishing free. *See also Co Clare Streams and Loughs.*

Ennis (Co Clare). Good centre for fishing principal waters of Co Clare, including several coarse fish lakes and rivers (tench, pike, perch, rudd). Good brown trout fishing in Fergus and lakes it drains. **Knockerra Lake** has rainbow trout to 8lb. Tackle shop in Ennis: M F Tierney, Fishing & Cycle Centre, 17 Abbey St, 065 29433. Accommodation: Auburn Lodge, Old Ground, Queen's, West Country Inn; G & J Finn, Druimin, 065 24183.

Corofin (Co Clare). Numerous lakes very good for trout, others for perch, rudd and tench, and all for pike. Accommodation at number of family guest houses. Lakes Inchiquin, Atedaun and Ballycullinan and R Fergus close by; boats.

Tulla (Co Clare). Area is noted for its excellent bream fishing; also roach, tench and pike; fishing free in about 20 lakes within 10m radius (Ennis 10m).

SUCK. Joins Shannon at Shannonbridge, between Banagheer and Athlone. Trout and coarse. Pike, bream, rudd and perch fishing very good. Tench to 6lb at Shan-

nonbridge Power Station. Specimen rudd in L Ree. Good fishing in Coreen Ford area, nr Ballinasloe.

Ballinasloe (Co Galway). Suck and tributaries, including **Lough O'Flyn, Ballinlough,** 600 acres trout fishery, controlled by CFB. **Bunowen** and **Shiven** hold excellent stock of trout, especially good early in season. **Lough Acalla,** 8m from town; rainbow trout up to 5lbs, good for wet fly in June (CFB). St from Keller Brothers. Hayden's Hotel offers anglers accommodation with salmon and coarse fishing in Rivers Shannon and Suck.

Ballygar (Co Galway). For middle R Suck and also tributaries, **Rivers Bunowen** and **Shiven.** Excellent coarse fishing. St £5 from Tom Kenny, Public House, The Square. Tackle from Hanley's Tackle Shop.

Roscommon (Co Roscommon). Coarse fishing on R Suck and **Lough Ree.** River is good for trout in mayfly season. Irish record rudd (3lb 1oz) caught in nearby **Kilglass Lake.** Roscommon Gun and Rod Club has Hind River; trout; dry-fly water. Hotels: Grelly's, Royal, O'Gara's, Abbey.

Castlerea (Co Roscommon). For upper R Suck reaches which hold trout in some areas. **Lough O'Flynn** now has excellent trout fishing, thanks to CFB improvement work. Trout and coarse fish in **Lough Glinn** and **Errit Lakes.** Hotels: Don Arms, Tully's.

INNY. A slow-flowing river densely populated with roach, large bream and large tench. Trout between Abbeyshrule and Shrule Bridge.

Mullingar (Co Westmeath). Inny AA controls much fishing. Many coarse loughs in area, including **Kinale** (roach, pike), **Iron, Patrick** (tench), **Sheever, Ballinafid** (bream), **Doolin** (carp), **Derravaragh** (coarse and trout). Trout fishing on famous limestone lakes, **Lough Ennell** (3,200 acres) and **Lough Owel** (2,500 acres); and also on Mount Dalton Lake, a small lake stocked with brown trout. Season 1 March-12 Oct (Ennell and Owel); 1 May-12 Oct (Mt Dal-

---

Keep the banks clean

Several clubs have stopped issuing tickets to visitors because of the state of the banks after they have left. Spend a few moments clearing up.

ton). Size limit 30cm. Bag limit 6 fish. Fly only on **Mt Dalton Lake**. St £5 and dt £2, from Shannon Regional Fisheries Board, Tudenham, Mullingar (tel: 044 48769); David O'Malley, *see below*. Local assc: L Owel Trout PA, membership £5 p.a. Boats available from Myles Hope, 044 40807; and for L Ennell; Jack Doolan, Levington, Mullingar (tel: 044 42085) for L Owel; Mrs C Gibson Brabazon, Mt Dalton, Rathconrath, Mullingar, (tel: 044 55102) for Mt Dalton Lake. Tackle shop: David O'Malley, 33 Dominick St (tel: 044 48300); Mullingar Tackle Shop, 8 Woodlands Ave. Hotels: Bloomfield House, Greville Arms. Lakeside accom: Mrs S T Kelly, Beechwood, 044 71108; Mrs A Ginell, Lough Owel Lodge, 044 48714; Mrs A Smyth, WHitehall Farm House, 044 61140.

Castlepollard (Co Westmeath). Trout and coarse fish. **Lough Derravaragh** (2,700 acres), a limestone lake once famous for trout but in recent years trout stocks have decreased to be replaced by a large population of roach. **Lough Glore** (86 acres) holds excellent stock of wild brown trout; boat fishing only. **White Lake** (80 acres) is stocked annually with rainbow trout and some brown trout. Lakes controlled by Shannon Regional Fisheries Board. Season 1 March-12 Oct (Derravaragh and Glore); 1 May-12 Oct (White Lake). Bag limit 6 fish. St £9.50, dt £2; from Thomas Murphy, Hardware, The Square (tel: 044 61137). Boats from Mrs Nancy McKenna, Fore (tel: 044 611781) for White Lake; Fergus Dunne, Oldcastle Rd, for L Glore.

Kilnaleck (Co Cavan). Brown trout fishing on **Lough Sheelin** (4,654 acres); rich limestone lough with capacity to produce and maintain a large stock of big brown trout. There has been a eutrophication problem due mainly to local intensive farming practices. Season 1 March-12 Oct. Mayfly from about mid-May to early June. Bag limit 6 fish. Coarse fishing is prohibited. No live bait fishing. Suitable flies and dt £5 from Kilnahard Pier, Mountnugent, L Sheelin; dt also present from Central Fisheries Board. Local assc: Lough Sheelin Trout PA. Hotels: Sheelin Shamrock; Crover House, both Mountnugent. Boats available from both hotels.

SLANEY

(For close seasons, licences, etc, see The Eastern Regional Fisheries Board)

Rises in corner between Barrow and Liffey watersheds and flows south 73m to Wexford Harbour. During most of course has rocky beds, rapids alternating with deep pools. Good spring salmon river, especially in Tullow-Bunclody reaches (Mar, April, May best; no autumn run) but of little account for brown trout save in upper reaches and in some tributaries. Good sea trout lower down and in tributaries Urrin and Boro. Best sea trout fishing in lower reaches, late June to August. Most salmon fishing private, but certain parts let from season to season and no permission needed to fish for salmon or sea trout from Enniscorthy Bridge to Ferrycarrig (Feb 26 to Sept 15). Fly fishing only, from 1 Apr to 31 Aug.

Wexford (Co Wexford). Garman AC has made efforts to restock. **Owenduff;** good white trout fishing in June, July and Aug. **Sow River** near Castlebridge good for brown trout and sea trout; permits from angling club. Fishing for brown trout on **Wexford Reservoir**. Sea fishing (inc. sea trout, bass and mullet) in estuary. Tackle shop: Bridges of Selskar, North Main Street. Hotels: Talbot, White's, County.

Enniscorthy (Co Wexford). Sea trout good; brown trout poor; free fishing downstream of bridge. Tackle shops: Paddy Lennon, 26 Main Street; Nolan, 3 Wafer Street, and C L Cullen, 14 Templeshannon. Hotels: Portsmouth Arms, Slaney Valley.

Bunclody (Co Wexford). Salmon and sea trout, browns and rainbows, coarse fishing for eels. Much fishing in area on Slaney, Clody and Derry, either free or for nominal fee. Bunclody Trout AC has fishing for visitors. Tackle shop (licences): John Nolan's Sports Shop, Ryland Rd. Accom: P Kinsella, Meadowside, 054 77459.

Tullow (Co Carlow). Tullow Salmon and Trout AA have water on Slaney; st £8 (T), wt £5 (T), dt £12 (S), from hotel and O'Neills Garage, Carlow Rd. Trout and salmon fishing is free on Slaney from Rathvilly to Baltinglass, and also on **River Derreen** with permission from landowners. Hotel: Slaney.

SEA FISHING STATIONS IN IRELAND

As elsewhere, the sea fishing in the Irish Republic has been growing in popularity. The inshore potential of these waters is now widely appreciated. Bass are much sought after along the south and west coasts, and pollack are abundant off the rocks. Deep-sea boats land specimen skate, conger, halibut, turbot and so on. Fishing facilities are improving all the time. Space will not permit more than a few centres to be listed, but club secretaries and local tackle shops will be pleased to give further information and to help visitors.

Dundalk (Co Louth). Bay is shallow for the most part, but contains spurdog, ray and flatfish for boat anglers off north shore. Quay fishing from **Gyles Quay** at high water for flatfish and dogfish; the quay on **Castletown River** south bank, mullet in summer. 8m south at **Glyde** and **Dee** junction, spinning from southern breakwater for bass, mackerel, occasional sea trout. Good fishing rocks north of **Drogheda** at **Clogher Head:** pollack, coalfish, codling and mackerel. Club is North Louth Sea AC. Town also has two game angling clubs. Tackle shops: Macs Sports, Demesne Shopping Centre; Island Fishing Tackle, Park St (permits and licences); Military Connection, 8 Laurence St, Drogheda. Hotels: Ballymascanion, Imperial and others.

Dublin and **Dun Laoghaire** (Co Dublin). To north, **Howth Harbour** is popular venue: from piers, whiting, pollack, coalfish and codling; from rocks, mackerel, flatfish and others. Good boat fishing for large spurdog. Howth club holds annual festival. Estuary at **Sutton** is a good place to dig lugworm and clam. Ragworm can also be found. In Dublin Bay good points are: Dollymount Strand, (some large bass, flounder, eels, codling, good in autumn at evening); sea wall running south, (pollack, codling, whiting, bass and flounder); Liffey between Ringstead Basin and Pidgeon House Power Station (mullet and bass in large numbers); spinning below Poolbeg Lighthouse (bass, mackerel); Sandymount Strand, a large beach with gullies and pools, with bass, mullet, big flounder. This beach can be dangerous at flood tide. Ferryport at **Dun Laoghaire** provides pier fishing from West Pier: dabs and conger in summer; whiting, codling, pouting, coalfish in autumn/winter; also Coal Quay, for mullet fishing. Dublin has over thirty sea angling clubs affiliated to the Leinster Council of the IFSA. Several Dublin Tackle shops, and Dun Laoghaire Angling, George's St, Dun Laoghaire.

Arklow (Co Wexford). Local boats offer deep sea angling over inshore banks for dogfish, ray, codling, whiting, bull huss, plaice, flounder, and tope. Bass can be numerous; codling and dabs may be fished for from Roadstone Pier. Good beach fishing on Clones Strand: codling, bass, flounders. Mullet fishing is very good at **Courtown Harbour.** The are more than two dozen good shore venues between Arklow and **Wexford.** Tackle from Bolands, Pat Kelly, both Main St. Hotel: Arklow Bay.

Rosslare (Wexford). Good pier fishing for conger, occasional bass and flatfish. Access is difficult because of shipping. Fishing from shore at St Helens for bass, flatfish, mackerel and other species. Rock and surf fishing for bass and tope between Rosslare and **Kilmore Bay. Ballyteigue Lough** is a fine venue for flounders, and beach fishing is very good at **Cullenstown,** for bass and flounders. Ballytrent beach is good for flatfish by night. Boats can reach Splaugh Rock, a massive reef, and Tuskar Rock: mainly cod fishing. Two boats operate from **Carne:** contact D Duggan at Carne Lodge.

Kilmore Quay (Wexford). Record Irish Pouting taken in 1983, and large coalfish taken recently. Fishing at high tide from pier produces flounder and occasional bass. Mullet may sometimes be taken by ground baiting. **St Patrick's Bridge,** reef of rocks to east of harbour, is boat mark for good bass fishing. Excellent pollack, bass and tope around **Saltee Islands.** Surf fishing for bass and tope at **Ballyteigne Bay.** Mullet and flatfish abound. Lugworm from harbour. **Burrow** shore is popular beach for competitions, best at night. Club: Kilmore Quay SAC. Tackle shops in Rosslare, Wexford and Kilmore Quay.:

Fethard Bay (Co Wexford). Bottom fishing for flounder, bass, plaice, best at night. Hook Head has spinning at high tide for pollack, coalfish, mackerel, bottom fishing for conger and other species. Along shore at Cummins Quay, **Ballyhack**, conger fishing.

Dungarvan Bay (Waterford). From **Ballinacourty** pier, bass, flatfish and dogfish, half flood to early ebb. Abbeyside and Barnawee; spinning for bass, bottom fishing for flounder. Fishing at Dungarvan for bass and flatfish. A number of large bass, 6lb to 9½lb have been caught in 1991, but mackerel have been scarce. Pier at **Helvick** provides good sport with congers; distance casting catches ray. Mullet taken in Helvick Harbour. Fewer blue shark than there were. Conger, mackerel, pollack, wrasse (specimen taken) off Helvick Head. Crab and lugworm on foreshore. Local clubs are Abbeyside Shore AC (Pat Buckley, Leigh, Ring, Co Waterford) and Dungarvan SAC, which concentrates on boat competitions. Boats from Dungarvan Sea Angling & Diving Service Ltd, 42 Lower Main St (plus information on all types of fishing), Dungarvan Charter Angling, or Gone Fishin', Lower Main St, 058 43514. £18 per angler daily, wreck, shark, or bottom fishing. Daily boat charter, £80 to £180.

Ardmore and **Youghal** (Cork). Several venues around Ardmore and Ram Head, incl surf fishing from Ballyquin Strand for bass and flatfish (flounder to 3½lb), Ardmore beach and pier, bass, flatfish; Goat Island and Whiting Bay, similar species. Fishing from Mangans Cove through Youghal, to Knockadoon Head and pier offers more than a dozen venues. Species caught include flounder, plaice (to 5lb), codling, ray, turbot, bass, dogfish, conger (to 41lb), ling (to 38lb), cod (to 28lb 12oz), pollack, coalfish, gurnard, whiting, wrasse, blue shark (135lb) and most deep sea species. Youghal Sea AC also has freshwater fishing on Blackwater and tributaries. Charter-boats: B O'Keeffe, tel: 024 92820, 6/8 anglers: £80, rods for hire; 'Shark Hunter', 31 ft, tel: 024 92699. Tackle shop: Arcade Stores, North Main St. Hotels: Hilltop, Devonshire Arms, Avonmore Roseville and Green Lawn Guest Houses.

Ballycotton (Cork). One of the best-known of Irish sea fishing centres; large catches of prime fish and excellent facilities. Many specimen caught, including skate, blue shark, turbot, ling, pollack, coalfish, bass, hake, spur and spotted dog. Big cod in winter months. Fishing from pier at

Ballycotton and **Knockadoon,** rocks from Knockadoon Head, Ballinwilling Reef and other marks, or boat; surf fishing at **Ballymona;** bass, flounder and codling. Good mullet in harbour. Lugworm may be dug at Ballycrenane and Ardnahinch. Boat hire: Ballycotton Angling Centre (£80 per boat min, 10.30 to 17.30) tel: 021 646773; Dietmar Scharf, Kullderrig, Cloyne, 021 646056, £70 daily. Monthy competitions May to Oct. Another local body is East Cork Angling, Loughcarrig House, Midleton, 021 631952, specialists in wreck, reef, and shark fishing, also freshwater angling on Blackwater. Local club: Ballycotton Deep Sea AC, c/o Sheila Egan, Main St. Tackle shops: T H Sports, Main St, Midleton. Hotels: Bayview, Garryvoe; Mrs B Murray, 021 646713; Mrs M Tattan, 021 646177. Many hotels around Midleton.

Cobh (Cork). Cobh Sea AC runs an international sea angling festival each year in first week of September. Species caught include skate, bass, pollack, coalfish, tope, l s dogfish. Conger 44lb 12oz has been weighed in. For deep sea fishing there is a fleet of well equipped 11m boats suitable for 8 to 10 rods, £16 per angler. Tackle shop: Cobh Tackle Shop, Town Centre. Hotel: Commodore. Guest houses: M O'Driscoll, Upper Park; I Browne, Ringville, and others.

Cork (Cork). Fishing both inside and outside Harbour offers the following species: dogfish, codling, conger, pollack, turbot, plaice, ray, wrasse. 144lb blue shark caught in Harbour, and record angler fish. Charter boats operate from Cork Harbour and **Crosshaven,** for shark, wreck and bottom fishing. Local club is Bishopstown & Dist SAC, Bill Emery, c/o Lee's, below. Cork Harbour Boats Ltd, 021 841348/841633; Charles Robinson, 021 372896; Barry Twomey, Crosshaven, 021 831843, fax 021 831448. Daily charges, £90 to £95. Tackle for hire. Tackle shops: Lee's, 40B Popes Quay; R Day & Son, 2 Bowling Green St, The Tackle Shop, Lavitts Quay.

Kinsale (Cork). Old Head Sea AC holds closed competitions. Best-known centre on the south coast for deep-sea fishing, especially for shark, ling, conger, dogfish, ray, pollack, coalfish, red bream and wrasse. Well-equipped boats and experienced skippers. £15 to £25 per angler daily; £90-£110 boat charter; from Kinsale Marine Services, 021 772611; Kinsale Angling Centre, 021 778054; M & P Gannon, Courtmacsherry Pier, 023 46427 (£70 to £120, £18 per angler). All operators offer rod and tackle hire. Kinsale Sea AC run many competitions during season. Hotels: Trident, Actons, Perryville House; Atlantic, Garretstown.

Rosscarbery (Cork). Noted for surf fishing for flatfish, mackerel, occasional bass; three fine beaches. Bass and mullet also taken in small harbour, and from mouth of estuary. Mackerel spinning from pier. Lugworm and ragworm in estuary, sandeel from beach. Boats for shark, wreck and bottom fishing from Patrick Houlihan, Clonkilty, 023 33654, £12 per angler daily, £45 to £90 charter. Club: Rosscarbery SAC.

Baltimore (Cork). Shark (very good, July-Oct), skate, conger, tope, ling, cod, pollack and mackerel from boats; pollack, bass and mackerel from shore. Best June-Oct. Deep sea boat charter: T Brown, Baltimore Harbour Cottages, Tel 028 20319; M Walsh, Marine Services, 028 20145/20352, £120 to £150, £20 per angler. Skibbereen boat hire; M Cotter, 028 38203, £15 per angler, £120 charter. Tackle shop: Kieran Cotter Ltd, Baltimore.

Mizen Peninsula (Co Cork). Fishing in harbours, rocks, coves, for pollack, mackerel, coalfish, flatflash, etc. Schull Pier offers bottom fishing for flounder, float fishing for mullet. Wreck fishing within easy reach. Schull boat operators may be contacted at Black Sheep Inn, Main St, Schull, 028 28203, or N Dent, 028 37287. Crookhaven boat operator: Bear Havinga, Main St, Crookhaven, 028 35240, for Rocks of Mizen fishing, excellent pollack. Tackle from Barnett's, Main St, Schull.

Bantry (Co Cork). Town is convenient centre for Bantry Bay deep sea fishing. Large conger are caught, ling, pouting, whiting, bull huss, l s d. Shore fishing best on south side of bay: thornback, dogfish, flatfish, wrasse, pollack. Boats operated by Bill O'Donnell, Anchor Bar, 027 50012, John Minehan, West End Bar, 027 50318. Tackle from O'Mahony's and Cuhane's, both Main St.

Castletownbere (Cork). Fine harbour for sheltered fishing in Berehaven and offshore at marks in Bantry Bay. Shark, pollack, ling, conger, tope, ray, skate, pouting, bass, bream, wrasse, spurdog,

gurnard, flounder, plaice, grey mullet, whiting and mackerel. Boats are always available. Shore fishing at harbour pier, Muccaragh, Seal Harbour and Zetland Pier. Tackle shop and tourist agent: C Moriarty, The Square. Hotel: Cametrignane House.

Derrynane (Kerry). Surf fishing for flatfish and occasional bass. Deep sea angling for bull huss, ling, conger, monkfish, spur dogfish, pollack. Charter boats: S O'Shea, 064 45187, shark and bottom fishing, £100, tackle for hire; A McAuliffe, 0667 74519, shark and bottom fishing, £15 per angler, £90 charter, tackle available.

Cahirciveen (Kerry). For **Valentia Island.** Catches include conger (up to 72lb), turbot (to 26lb), red bream (to 9lb), bass (to 16lb). Also large gurnard, mackerel, garfish, tope, ling, puting, whiting, cod and blue shark. Boat fishing most popular, but good sport also from shore. International Deep Sea Festival at Cahirciveen in Aug. Club: Cahirciveen Sea & Shore AC. At Valencia, M O'Sullivan operates GRP Starcraft, shark and bottom fishing, £20 per rod, £120 charter. Tel: 066 74255. Tackle from Anchor Bar & Tackle Shop.

Dingle Peninsula (Kerry). Rock fishing for pollack, wrasse, conger. Inshore fishing for ray; offshore for pollack, coalfish, bream, conger, ling, tope, cod, whiting, huss, spurdog, gurnard, pouting and shark. Club: Dingle SAC. Charter boats operate from Valentia (M O'Sullivan, 066 74255, D McCrohan, 0667 76142), Dingle (G Burgum, 066 51337, N O'Connor, 066 59947) and Fenit (M Moriarty, 066 36303); £75 to £150. Tackle shops: Walter Sheeny's, Dingle; Tim Landers, Tranlee.

Shannon Estuary. Following the coast of Co Limerick in an easterly direction, points for shore fishing are: **Beal Point** and **Littor Strand,** bottom fishing for dogfish, flatfish, and bull huss; several marks around **Carrig Island** and **Saleen Quay,** where good bottom fishing is to be had from rocks and quay: ballan wrasse, dogfish, bull huss, some tope. **Tarbert** and **Glin** piers are best at high tide for flatfish, conger at night; **Foynes** piers produce conger, thornback ray, codling, whiting and flounder. Best baits, crab, lugworm, mackerel. North side of estuary has pier fishing available at **Kildysart** (flounder, crab bait essential), and **In-**

nishmurray (bull huss, thornback, conger, freshwater eels), Kilrush, *(see below)*, and **Carrigaholt** (bottom fishing for dab and flounder, spinning for pollack and wrasse). Beach fishing at **Shannakea** and **Killimer** for thornback, conger, dogfish and bull huss, and rock fishing at **Aylvaroo Point** for similar species, plus codling and whiting in winter, are among several other venues. Plenty of opportunities for bait digging. Boats for estuary, T Conway, 068 34455, £25 per angler, daily.

Kilrush (Co Clare). Pier fishing from **Cappagh** pier, conger, dogfish on flood tide. Several towns on the coast of Co Clare have charter boats available for shark, wreck and bottom fishing, 35 ft average, tackle for hire. At Kilrush, Atlantic Adventures, 065 52133, fax 065 51720, £20 per angler, £200 charter, 8 to 10 capacity. **Liscannor:** M Lynch, 065 28421. £300 daily charter, 12 persons. **Doolin**: K O'Driscoll, 065 76112, £250 £250 charter.

Galway Bay (Co Galway). **R Spiddal** enters on north side, with skate, tope, ray, huss, dogfish, monkfish, cod, ling, conger, flatfish. Boats and gillies available. Deep sea charter boats operate from the following bases: **Spiddal**, T Curran, 091 83535, 33 ft, shark, bottom and wreck fishing, £300 charter; R Ellis, 40 ft, £30, £300 daily charter, 12 anglers, tackle available from both operators.

Clifden (Co Galway). First-class boat and shore angling in sheltered conditions. Blue shark, tope, coalfish, pollack, skate, ray, ling, cod, turbot, brill and plaice. Good marks include: Slyne Head; Barrister wreck off **Inishark;** Inishbofin; Inishturk and Fosteries Shoals. Other good bays are Mannin, Ballinakill, Killary, Roundstone, Cleggan and Bunowen. Tackle shops: E Sullivan, Main Street, and P Stanley, Market Street. Deep sea charter boats: J Brittain, 095 21073; J Ryan, 095 21069. Charges, £25, £160 charter, tackle available. Sea trout and brown trout fishing available *(see freshwater section)*. Club: Clifden Sea AC. Hotels: Clifden Bay, Alcock & Brown, Abbeyglen, Clifden House, Atlantic Coast and Celtic. Boats available at Bunowen and Roundstone.

Westport (Mayo). Good boat and shore fishing in shallow water. Local clubs run sea angling competitions in the area each year. Fish caught include: the record monkfish (69lb), skate (up to 167½lb), tope and conger (to 40lb and more), cod, codling, pollack, flounders, plaice, gurnard, coalfish, bass, wrasse, turbot, dog fish, white skate (146lb), blue shark, and porbeagle shark. Good marks include Tower in Inner Bay, off Lighthouse, Pigeon Point, Cloghormack Buoy. Sheltered sport in **Clew Bay.** 36 ft Boat available from Reg Roynan, 098 26514, £120 charter, 6 rods shark, 12 rods bottom fishing. Tackle shop: Hewetson's, Dyar's Bridge Street. Clubs: Westport Sea AC and Westport AC, which has trout fishing on Ballinlough, by Westport-Newport Rd: dt £10, incl boat. Hotels: Clew Bay; Grand Central; both offer good terms to anglers.

Achill Island (Mayo). Excellent boat fishing; pollack, conger, ling, ray, cod, etc; fish run large. Noted area for blue shark and porbeagle. Holds records for heaviest fish caught in Irish waters for both men and women: 365lb (man), 362lb (woman), plus blue shark record, 206lb. Pollack and wrasse fishing off rock produces specimens in 15lb class. Good marks are Carrick Mor, Gubalennaun, Alennaun Beag, Dooega and Dugort. Flatfish from **Tullaghan Bay** on north side of island. Good shore fishing at Keel Strand and Keem Bay; Mackerel and pollack fishing from **Cloughmore Pier.** Sea trout late June to early Aug (plentiful and good size); mackerel; plaice etc. Boats from **Purteen Harbour** at following numbers (tel: 098) 43265; 43301; 43112. Tackle shops: Sweeney and Son, Achill Sound (tel: 098 45211); Island Sports Shop, Keel PO (tel: 098 43125). Hotel: Achill Head, Keel; Atlantic, Dooagh Achill Sound; Lavelle's, Dooega; Strand, Dugort.

Newport (Mayo). One of Eire's finest sea fishing centres. Large mackerel, tope, skate, conger, dogfish, monkfish, whiting, coalfish, pollack, gurnard may be taken in Clew Bay. Boats from SAC, st £3. Boats for 8 anglers, £80 per day, three boats available. Contact Tom Moran, 098 41712. Tackle from Hewetson's, Bridge St, Westport. Hotels: Black Oak Inn, Newport House.

Belmullet (Mayo). Rapidly rising in popularity as sea-fishing centre. Sheltered water. 38 species and many specimen caught to date, incl present Irish record red gurnard and halibut; turbot, bream and pollack especially good. Belmullet

Sea AC (097 81076) has been active in improving sea fishing in the area. Deepsea charter boat (29 ft) from **Blacksod Bay:** M Lavelle, 097 85669, £15 £80 charter, 8 rods. Sheeran Charters (097 81105), operate out of Belmullet. Well organized annual festival in August. At Porturlin Pier, **Ballina,** P O'Donnell (097 88982) operates 26 ft boat for tope and bottom fishing, 8 rod charter, £80, £10 per angler. Tackle from M J Nallen, Main St. Hotel: Western Strands.

Donegal Bay (Donegal). There are more than twenty good shore fishing points around bay, from **Darbys Hole** in south through **Erne Estuary** (flounder), **Donegal Quays** (float fishing for mullet with ground bait), rocks at Heelin Port, spinning from St John's Point, **Killybegs Harbour** (mackerel, etc from East Pier), beach fishing at Nun's Cove for flatfish, mackerel from **Muckross Pier** and Head, **Teelin Pier** (specimen conger, mackerel, flatfish) and White Strand (flatfish from beach plus mackerel). Deep sea charter boat operates from **Mount Charles.** M O'Boyle, 073 35257, 26 ft 'Martin Og', 8 rods. Tope or bottom fishing charter, £50 to £80, £10 per angler. At Killybegs, E O'Callaghan, 073 31288: 36 ft charter boat for shark or bottom fishing, 6 rods shark, 10 rods bottom. £15, £85 charter; P O'Callaghan, 073 31569: 36 ft 'Fine Girl', 8 rods shark, 10 rods bottom fishing. £20, £45 to £85 charter. At **Teelin,** Smith Campbell, 073 39079. At **Mountcharles,** M O'Boyle, 073 35257. Species caught include pollock, ling, congor (10lbs av), cod (5lb), mackerel, coalfish, wrasse, flatfish and others.

Rosapenna (Donegal). Boat fishing for

tope. For deep-sea bookings apply Mrs C O'Donnell, 'The Fleets Inn', Downings (Tel: 21). Other information from Donegal Deep Sea Angling Ltd, 1 Mount Southwell, Letterkenny. Tackle shop: Co-operative Stores.

Lough Swilly (Donegal). Good fishing to be had locally, with haddock in June and July, and shark in Aug/Sept. There is an annual sea angling festival of Glengad-Malin at end of Aug. 1st Class wreck fishing in early morning, sea trout in estuaries. Shark and bottom fishing charter boat, 30 ft 'Charlie Girl', operates at **Letterkenny** and **Port-na-Blagh.** 5 rods shark, 7 rods bottom. £15, £85 to £90 charter, contact John McClean, tel: 074 22443. Also Pat Robinson, 074 36290. Species caught: cod, haddock, tope, charr, whiting, dogfish, ling, etc. At **Rathmullan Pier,** 'Pegasus II', 33 ft, takes 8 rods shark fishing or 10 rods bottom fishing. £10, £70 to £100 charter. Tel: 074 58282, M Bowden. Tackle available from both.

Malin Head (Donegal). Charter boats operate from Bunagee and Culduff, species caught are whiting, haddock, cod, conger, ling, gurnard, pollock. Contact Inishowen Boating, J McLaughlin, 077 70605. Hotels: Malin, McGrory Guest House, Mrs Ann Lynch, Culdaff and others.

Moville (Donegal). Tope, pollack, cod, gurnard, whiting, wrasse, flatfish and others. Foyle Sea AC arranges Lough Foyle Festival of Sea Angling, an annual 8-day festival in August. Club owns boat and can arrange wreck fishing. Plenty of boats (20ft-30ft) and bait. Tackle from Pat Harkin, Malin Rd. Hotels: McNamara's, Foyle, Redcastle.

Check before you go

While every effort has been made to ensure that the information given in **Where to Fish** *is correct, the position is continually changing, and anglers are urged, in their own interests, to make preliminary enquiries before travelling to selected venues. This is especially important with reference to prices quoted. Inevitably the rate of inflation is affecting stability in this quarter. Anglers' attention is also drawn to the fact that the hotels mentioned under the various fishing stations do not necessarily have water of their own. Any amendments or further data for inclusion in subsequent editions, and any criticism, will be welcome.*

FISHING CLUBS ETC. IN IRELAND

The following is an alphabetical list of angling clubs and associations in the Ireland. Particulars of the waters held by many will be found, by reference to the Index, in the section headed 'Fishing Stations in Ireland', and the information about the others, which may not have their own water, could be had from the Secretaries, whose addresses are given. An addressed envelope should be enclosed with inquiries. Please advise the publishers (address at the front of the book) of any changed details for the next edition.

NATIONAL BODIES

Bord Fáilte (Irish Tourist Board)
Baggot Street Bridge
Dublin 2
Tel: Dublin 765871
Central Fisherles Board
Balnagowan House
Mobhi Boreen, Glasnevin,
Dublin 9
Tel: 379206/7/8
Fax: 01 360060
Department of Tourism, Fisheries and Forestry
Leeson Lane
Leeson Street
Dublin 2
Tel: 01 210111
International Fly Fishing Association
R W Newport
'Nairn'
Glenvar Park
Blackrock, Co Dublin
Tel: Dublin 2881712
Irish Federation of Sea Anglers
Hon. Sec.
67 Windsor Drive
Monkstown
Co Dublin
Tel: 01 806873/806901

Irish Match Angling and Surfcasting Association
Hon. Sec.
36 Ralapine, Ballybrack
Co Dublin
Tel: 01 854159
Irish Specimen Fish Committee
Balnagowan House
Mohbi Boreen
Glasnevin, Dublin 9
Tel: 01 379206
I.S.A.A.C.
Loughcarrig House
Midleton
Co Cork
Tel: 021 631952
Charter boats and
accommodation for sea anglers
National Coarse Fishing Federation of Ireland
Brendan Coulter
Blaithin, Dublin Road
Cavan
Tel: (049) 32367
Trout Angling Federation of Ireland
Stephen Monaghan
Abbeylands, Navan
Co Meath
Tel: 046 21479

CLUBS

Abbeyfeale Anglers' Association
Pat O'Callaghan
Ballybethy
Abbeyfeale,
Co Limerick

Abbeyleix Angling Club
Permits from
V Bowell
Sandymount, Abbeyleix
Co Laois

Fishing Clubs

When you appoint a new secretary, do not forget to give us details of the change. Write to the publishers (address at front of the book). Thank you!

Achill Sporting Club
John O'Malley
Island Sports
Keel PO
Achill, Co Mayo
Tel: (098) 43125

Ara Anglers Association
John Evans
Main Street
Tipperary
Co Tipperary

Ardfinnan Angling Association
J Maher
Greenview
Ardfinnan
Clonmel, Co Tipperary

Arklow Sea Anglers Club
Pat Byrne
4 St Patricks Terrace
Arklow
Co Wicklow

Athy Angling Association
Denis Whelan
29 Graysland, Carlow Road
Athy, Co Kildare
0507 38537

Ballybay Anglers Association
Talbot Duffy
4 Lake View Terrace
Ballybay,
Co Monaghan

Ballycotton Deep Sea Anglers
Mrs Sheila Egan
Main Street
Ballycotton
Co Cork
021 646786

Ballyduff Trout Fly Angling Association
Eamon Bolger
Post Office
Ballyduff, Co Waterford
058 60201

Ballymore Eustace Trout and Salmon Angling Association
Tom Deegan
928 Briencan
Ballymore Eustace
Co Kildare

Bandon River Angling Association
G P Baines
Riversdale
Bandon, Co Cork

Bantry Salmon and Trout Anglers Club
Arthur L Corbridge
c/o Mobile Home Park
Drumleigh
Bantry,
Co Cork
010 35327 51621

Beara Anglers Association
R Craigie
Craigies Hotel
Castletownbere
Co Cork

Belmullet Sea Angling Club
Gerard Murphy
Belmullet
Co Mayo

Bray Sea Angling Club
L Cullen
3 South Summer Street
Dublin 8

Brittas Angling Club
J Scanlon
Dowrey
Manor Kilbride
Co Wicklow

Broadmeadow Angling Club
K Rundle
119 Orlynn Park
Lusk, Co Dublin
01 438178

Cahir and District Angling Association
John Purtill
86 Woodview, Cahir
Co Tipperary

Callan Angling Association
Permits from C Vaughan
Green Street
Callan,
Co Kilkenny

Cappoquin Salmon and Trout Angling Club
Maurice J Noonan, Vice Chairman
'The Toby Jug'
Cappoquin, Co Waterford
Tel: 010 353 5854317/5854044.

Carrick-on-Suir and District Anglers' Association
James Houlhan
Sir John Terrace
Carrick-on-Suir
Co Tipperary

Cashel, Golden and Tipperary Angling Club
Frank Burke
Lowergate, Cashel
Co Tipperary
Tel: 062 61133

Castletown Trout Anglers' Club
D Twomey
Castletownbere
Co Cork

Chapelizod Anglers Club
T McMahon
Martin's Row
Chapelizod
Dublin 20

Clane Angling Association
A McDonnell
96 Ryevale Lawns
Leixlip, Co Kildare
Clonakilty Angling Association
David Spiller
41 Pearse Street
Clonakilty, Co Cork
Clonbur Angling Club
Eoin Burke
Clonbur
Co Galway
Tel: 092 46175
Clondalkin Anglers Association
G O'Connor
2 Millview
Nangor Road
Clonalkin
Dublin 22
Clonmel and District Anglers Club
J Carroll
Skinner & Co
New Quay, Clonmel
Co Tipperary
Tel: 052 21123
Clonmel and District Salmon and Trout Anglers' Association
J Kavanagh, Treasurer
O'Connell Street
Clonmel, Co Tipperary
Cobh Sea Angling Club
Mrs Mary Geary
Sycamore House
Cobh, Co Cork
Cork and District Pike Anglers
J Keating
Tel: 021 961175
Cork Salmon Anglers' Association
John Buckley
Raheen House
Carrigrohane
Co Cork
Tel: 021 872137
Cork Trout Anglers' Association
J A O'Connell, President
87 Patrick Street, Cork
or
J Riordan, Secretary
Jalna
Bishopstown Avenue West
Cork
021 543623

Co Wicklow Anglers
D W Browne
Inchagoill, Red Lane
Kilmacanogue, Co Wicklow
01 876920
Cushina Angling Club
Permits, Peter Dunne
Clonsast
Rathangan, Co Kildare
Dee and Glyde Angling Association
Mrs Moore
Castle Street
Ardee, Co Louth
Dingle Sea Angling Club
G Burgum
Ocean Lodge
Beenbawn
Dingle
Co Kerry
Dodder Angling Club
R O'Hanlon
82 Braemor Road
Dublin 14
01 982112
Drogheda and District Anglers' Club
Gerard Kelly
Saint Endas
North Road
Drogheda, Co Louth
Dromahair Anglers' Association
Sean Ward
Drumlease
Dromahair
Co Leitrim
Dublin and District Salmon Anglers' Association
Pat O'Molloy
1B Whitehall Cross
Terenure, Dublin 6
01 558594
Dublin Trout Anglers' Association
J R Miley
4 Dodder Park Road
Rathfarnham, Dublin 14
Dundalk and District Salmon Anglers' Association
Sean Garvey
289 Greenacres
Dundalk, Co Louth
Dundalk and District Brown Trout Anglers' Club
John Dollard

Fishing Clubs

When you appoint a new secretary, do not forget to give us details of the change. Write to the publishers (address at front of the book). Thank you!

Parnell Road
Dundalk, Co Louth

Dundrum District Anglers Association
Gerry Ryan
Deerpark, Dundrum
Co Tipperary
Tel: 062 71274

Dungarvan Sea Angling Club
Tel: 058 41395

Dun Laoghaire Sea Anglers' Association
K Bolster
136 Beaumont Road
Beaumont, Dublin 9

Durrow and District Anglers Club
M Walsh
18 Erkina Drive
Durrow, Co Laois

Fermoy and District Trout Anglers' Association
Gerry Lane
27 Liam McGearailt Place
Fermoy, Co Cork
025 32063

Foyle Sea Anglers Club
G V Sona
Droim a' Mhaoir
Moville
Co Donegal

Glengariff Anglers' Association
B Harrington, Treasurer
Glengariff, Co Cork
027 63021
or
J D'Arcy
The Village, Glengariff
027 63194

Greese Anglers Club
Permits from P Leigh
Woodhill, Narraghmore
Ballitore
Co Kildare

Howth Sea Angling Club
Peter Gaffey
227 Howth Road
Killester
Dublin 5

Inistioge Anglers Club
Permits from
Castle Inn
The Square
Inistioge, Co Kilkenny

Kenmare Salmon Angling Ltd
Lt Col M Harrington
Killowen Road
Kenmare, Co Kerry

Kenmare Trout Anglers
John O'Hara
21 Main Street
Kenmare

Co Kerry

Kilberry and Cloney Anglers Club
Permits from
L Foy
553 Kilberry
Athy, Co Kildare

Kilbride Anglers' Club
Des Johnston
54 Avondale Park
Raheny, Dublin 5
01 318786

Kilcullen and District Trout and Salmon Anglers Association
E Delahunt
22 Bishop Rogan Park
Kilcullen
Co Kildare
045 81498

Kilkenny Anglers' Association
Permits from
Sports Shop
Kilkenny, Co Kilkenny

Kilmallock and District Angling Club
Eamon O'Riordan
Ballinhown
Kilmallock, Co Limerick
Tel; 063 98687

Kilmore Quay Sea Angling Club
W McLoughlin
Spencerstown, Clearistown
Co Wexford
053 39169

Laragh and Glendalough Anglers
J Doyle
Bracken, Annamoe
Co Wicklow
0404 5300

Lee Trout Restocking Committee
C Healey
32 Meadow Park Avenue
Ballyvolane
Co Cork

Lee Salmon Anglers
Padraig Lucey
5 Perrott Avenue
Cork, Co Cork

Leinster Council of the IFSA
Jean Shanahan
209 Brandon Road
Drimnagh, Dublin 12
01 501612

Letterkenny and District Anglers' Association
Permits from
Arthur McGrath
50 Port Road
Letterkenny, Co Donegal

Lickeen Trout Anglers Association
J Vaughan

Lickeen, Kilforna
Co Clare
065 71069
Lough Allen Angling Club
Mrs Pauline Charles
Church Street
Drumshanbo
Co Leitrim
Lough Arrow Fish Preservation
Association
R Acheson
Andresna House
Corrigeenroe
Boyle
Lough Derg Anglers' Association
B Chadwick
22 St Patricks Terrace
Nenagh
Co Tipperary
Lough Gowna Angling Club
Lough Gowna
Co Cavan
Lough Lein Anglers' Association
Paddy O'Donovan
High Street
Killarney, Co Kerry
Tel: 064 31082
Lough Owel Trout Preservation
Association
P J Isdell
The Crest
Lough Owel
Mullingar, Co Westmeath
Tel: 044 40240
Loughrea Anglers' Association
M Sweeney
Athernry Road
Loughrea, Co Galway
Lough Sheelin Trout Protection
Association
Michael Callaghan
Virginia Road
Ballyjamesduff, Co Cavan
Malahide Sea Angling Club
K Friel
10 Texas Lane
Malahide
Co Dublin
Mallow Game and Coarse Anglers' Club
M Willis
5 Pearse Avenue
Mallow, Co Cork

022 42339
Monasterevin Angling Club
Jim Rosney
Cowpasture
Monasterevin
Co Kildare
Mountrath Anglers Club
Permits from T Watkins
6 St Fintan's Terrace
Mountrath
Co Laois
Newport Sea Angling Club
Alex Latto
5 Quay Road
Westport
Co Mayo
New Ross and District Sea Angling Club
Michael Browne
9 Chapel Lane
New Ross, Co Wexford
Nire Valley Angling Club
Paddy Halpin
Clogheen, Ballymacarbry
Co Tipperary
North Clare Anglers' Association
Kevin Duffy
Ennistymon, Co Clare
North Kerry Salmon Anglers'
Association
J Sheehan
23 Church Street
Listowel, Co Kerry
North Kildare Trout and Salmon
Anglers' Association
Patrick Byrne
21 College Park
Newbridge, Co Kildare
Tel: 045 31991
North Louth Sea Anglers Club
J O'Malley
Annies, Kilcurry
Dundalk, Co Louth
Old Head Sea Angling Club
Vincent McOwyer
Aghadoe, Carrigmore
Carrigaline, Co Cork
021 372631
Ormonde Angling Association
Joe O'Donoghue
Cameron
Gortlandroe
Nenagh, Co Tipperary

Fishing Clubs

When you appoint a new secretary, do not forget to give us details of the change. Write to the publishers (address at front of the book). Thank you!

Oughterard Angling Association
Paul Lydon
The Square
Oughterard, Co Galway
Tel: 091 82249

Portarlington Angling Club
Patsy Farrell
White Hart Lane
Kilmalogue, Portarlington
Co Laois

Prosperous Coarse Anging Club
E O'Farrell
Prosperous
Naas
Co Kildare
045 68092

Rathdrum Anglers
James B Kelly
Church View
Lower Street
Rathdrum
Co Wicklow

River Ilen Anglers' Club
A Taylor
Cois Abhann
Coolnagarrane
Skibbereen
Co Cork

Rosses Anglers' Association
Charles Boyle
Iniscrone
Carnmore Road
Dungloe, Co Donegal
075 21107

Strokestown Angling Club
D Colley
Elphin Street
Strokestown, Co Roscommon
Tel: 078 33317

Tallow Anglers' Association
T McCarthy
Lisfiney Cottage
Tallow, Co Waterford

Thomastown Anglers
John J Dunphy
25 Dangan Terrace
Thomastown, Co Kilkenny

Thurles, Holycross and Ballycamas Anglers' Association
M L Mockler
Ballycahill
Thurles, Co Tipperary
Tel: 0504 22493

Tolka Angling Club
T Foley
34 Virginia Park
Finglas
Dublin 11

Trim, Athboy and District Anglers' Association
G Lee
Loman Street
Trim, Co Meath

Tuam Angling Club
Thomas Casserly
Clare Tuam
Tuam, Co Galway

Tulla and District Coarse Angling Association
Brian A Culloo
Tulla, Co Clare

Vartry Angling Club
Ray Dineen
Tara House, Redcross
Co Wicklow
0404 74485

West Clare Angling Association
F Meaney
Francis Street
Kilrush, Co Clare

Westport and District Anglers' Club
John T Gibbons
Fair Green
Westport, Co Mayo

Wexford and District Sea Angling Club
Sean Furlong
117 The Faythe, Wexford

Youghal Sea Anglers' Club
Myles Clancy
13 Strand Street
Youghal, Co Cork
Tel: 024 92699

Fishing Clubs

When you appoint a new secretary, do not forget to give us details of the change. Write to the publishers (address at front of the book). Thank you!

FISHING ABROAD

T he primary purpose of this section is to give the angler contemplating visiting, or even, in the case of Commonwealth countries, emigrating to, one of the countries listed a brief description of the fishing to be had. It is neither necessary nor practicable to enter into such detail as in the British sections, but the addresses of various authorities from whom further information can be obtained are given, together with that of the appropriate London tourist or Government information office, at the end of each description.

CENTRAL AFRICA

ZAMBIA. Most rivers and lakes carry good stocks of fish, giving very reasonable sport. But the angler must be prepared to travel long distances over rough roads, carrying his own camp equipment and finally making his camp beside the river he intends to fish. There are very few hotels off the main roads, and fewer still in fishing areas, though the Tourist Board is conducting a successful drive for more hotels and rest houses, particularly the lodges in the national wildlife parks, where good fishing is to be had on the rivers. For parties who appreciate camping holidays in the bush, some delightful trips can be planned, particularly in August and September, when there is little fear of rain and the nights are warm enough to make camping pleasant. Most of the rivers are either heavily wooded right down to the water or are swamp-edged, so the addition of a boat and outboard motor to the camp equipment is a sound policy. On the other hand, canoes and paddlers can be hired, and the latter are usually good guides to the best fishing grounds. Youths are also very helpful as camp attendants, and little trouble is normally experienced in hiring one or two to take care of the heavy work of the camp. The visiting fisherman must remember that the hippopotamus and crocodile are found in nearly all Zambian waters. Wading in rivers can be a dangerous pastime, and hippos, especially with calves, should be given a wide berth. An insecticide spray against tsetse fly and a malarial prophylactic are recommended.

Indigenous species. These include tiger-fish, which probably provide the best sport, and goliath tiger fish, a separate species running up to 80lb or more; fish of the Nile perch variety and their close relatives, giant perch (top weight around 200lb); giant vundu (sampa); large-mouthed, small-mouthed and humped bream; catfish; barbels; local pike; lake salmon; labeo; and nkupi. There are two species of fish which are referred to as nkupi, one is found in Lake Tanganika and is a cichlid, it is also called a giant yellow belly; and the other is a citharinid found in the middle Zambesi including Lake Kariba.

The great **Zambezi** and its large tributary, the **Kafue,** are outstanding among the rivers. A good centre for the Zambezi is **Livingstone,** though there is small, comfortable hotel Mongu, in Western Province. Another town which has become a tourist centre is Siavonga on Lake Kariba. There is an all weather road from Lusaka (capital of Zambia) to Siavonga, which can be reached within a two-hour drive. The centre has several modern lodges, some of which are air-conditioned. Sport fishing including angling and spearing are very important here. Good fishing centres on the Karfue are at Itezhi-tezhi, Lochinvar and the Lower Kafue, near Chirundu. At Itezhi-tezhi, the angler will come across the famous small yellow belly and the Kafue pike. At Lochinvar, bream are important sport fish and at Lower Kafue, vundu. All three centres are served by good lodges: Musungwa (at Itezhi-tezhi), Lochinvar (at Lochinvar near Monze), and Gwabi (at Lower Kafue near Chirundu).

Lake Tanganyika is another anglers' mecca and a good centre is **Kasaba Bay,** where there are three small lodges. A launch service is operated by the Zambia Travel and Touring Co Ltd. The lake holds giant perch, tiger-fish, yellow belly and vundu among a wide variety of sporting fish.

Apart from Nile perch and sampa, which call for heavy tackle, most of the fish mentioned can be landed with a spinning rod. Steel traces are necessary for tiger-fish, nkupi and pike. A light bait-casting rod will usually cover other species. Fishing is free as a rule and can take place all the year round, but most rivers are in spate during the rainy season from December to April.

Exotic species. Zambia is unlikely to prove to be a land in which trout will thrive, owing both to the high temperature range and the lack of suitable highlands, but an exception may be provided by the picturesque **Nyika Plateau,** north of **Chipata** on the Malawi border, where an experimental stocking with rainbow trout in the headwaters of the **Shire River** is being carried out.

Useful addresses are: **Ministry of Agriculture, Food and Fisheries, Mulungushi House, PO Box 50197, 15100 Ridgeway, Lusaka** (tel: 228244/58); **Department of Fisheries, Kafue Road, PO Box 350100, Chilanga** (tel: 260 1 278418); **Zambia Information Services, Block 26, Independence Avenue, PO Box RW 50020, Lusaka**. Tel: 217254; **Zambian National Tourist Board, 2 Palace Gate, Kensington, London W8 5NG**. Tel: 071 589 6343; fax: 071 581 1353.

ZIMBABWE. Zimbabwe offers some of the best fishing to be found in central Africa. The angler has scope to pit his skills against a diversity of species, ranging from the fighting tiger-fish of the **Zambezi** and **Save** river systems, to introduced species like the rainbow and brown trout in the mountain streams and dams of the Eastern Highlands.

Much of centre of the country acts as a watershed, with the streams forming rivers which flow north to the Zambezi river system, on which lies the huge expanse of Lake Kariba; south to the Limpopo; southeast to the Save and Runde; and east into the Pungwe system of Mozambique. Many dams exist on all of the rivers feeding the various systems. Not all of the 117 species of fish found here are of interest to the angler, but he will certainly find more than enough to suit his tastes. There is an excellent road, rail and air network ensuring that chosen fishing locations are readily accessible.

The main area of interest to fishermen is the Zambezi River, with **Lake Kariba** (250km in length with a surface area of some 5,250 square kilometres) and the **Victoria Falls** forming the chief focal points. Tourist facilities in both these locations are excellent, the visitor being able to choose from a varied list of accommodation ranging from basic camping and National Parks sites to luxury houseboats, lodges and hotels.

Tigerfish are most commonly taken using trolling or spinning methods, but they may sometimes be tempted with a fly. They are lightening-fast, fighting fiercely after the first vigorous take. The average size is between 2lb and 6lb, but double figure fish are common, especially in the legendary stretch above Victoria Falls. The current Zimbabwean and world record for this species stands at 34lbs 3oz.

Another freshwater fish which is proving popular with British anglers is the mighty vundu. The vundu is a giant catfish, in Africa, second only in size to the Nile perch. This species, although not often fished for by local anglers, is a formidable opponent, growing to well over 100lbs. Prospective fishermen would do best to try Lake Kariba first, using a sturdy boat rod and multiplier type outfit (capable of withstanding powerful runs often exceeding 100yds) plus the services of a guide.

The other most commonly sought after species are members of the tilapia and serranchromis families, known to local fishermen as bream. Besides being a popular table fish, the various species give an excellent account of themselves on light tackle and may be caught using a variety of methods ranging from conventional coarse fishing techniques to the use of spinners and flies.

Other indigenous species include the Cornish Jack, bottlenose, chessa, nkupe, hunyani salmon, purple labeo and the sharptooth catfish. Introduced species include the largemouth bass, a fine fighting fish introduced from USA several years ago and now widespread in Zimbabwean waters; rainbow, brown and brook trout, well stocked in the rivers and lakes of the Nyanga and Chimaniamni mountain ranges (a picturesque

region often likened to Scotland); and carp, which are stocked is selected waters such as the **Mazowe Dam** near Harare and fish in excess of 50lbs have been caught.

The fishing season is any month with an 'R' in it and so ideally suits European anglers, who will, moreover, find that the high cost of the international airfare is pleasantly offset by the excellent value for money once there.

For more fishing information, contact the following operators specialising in fishing trips to Zimbabwe: **Bewick Sporting Agency, PO Box 50, Stirling FK7 9YB, Scotland**; and **Hunt Travel Ltd, Worth Corner, Turners Hill Road, Pound Hill, Crawley, West Sussex RH10 4SL** (tel. 0293 882609, fax 0293 886982).

For further general information contact the **Zimbabwe Tourist Office, 429 The Strand, London WC2R 0SA** (tel. 071 836 7755).

MALAWI. Excellent sport with rainbow trout may be enjoyed in the bracing climate of the **Zomba, Mulanje** and **Nyika Plateaux** as a result of consistent restocking of rivers and streams by the Government. **Lake Malawi** holds over 400 species; including varieties of catfish, perch and carp. Most of these are found in the **Shire River** above **Livingstone Falls,** but below the falls the main species are related to those found in the **Zambezi.** They include the famous tiger-fish. Further information may be obtained from the **Angling Society of Malawi, PO Box 744, Blantyre, Malawi.**

EAST AFRICA

KENYA. Kenya is well-developed for the sporting tourist and offers a variety of fishing off the coast, in its rivers and in the lakes or the **Great Rift Valley.** Licence fees: are modest; accommodation of some variety is established at or near virtually all main centres.

The coast. Black, blue and striped marlin, broadbill swordfish, sailfish, yellow fin tuna, wahoo, barracuda, cobia, dorado, mako shark. Centres at **Mombassa, Shimoni** (for the famous **Pemba Channel** fishing), **Kilifi, Watamu, Lamu** and **Malindi,** the latter the largest. Accommodation at club premises or hotels. Charter boats. Good fishing almost all the year round, peaking Oct-April: at least attractive May-June.

The mountain rivers. Stocked early in the century with brown trout, later with rainbows. Camps with rondavel accommodation at **Thiba, Thego, Kimakia, Koiwa.** Rest house at **Kaibabich;** lodges at **Ngobit** and **Kiandorogo.** A dozen or more specially recommended hotels and clubs. Camp accommodation may be primitive; nothing should be taken for granted. There are limits on size, method and bags, but wholesale poaching is an ever-present problem despite sincere governmental efforts to curb it.

The **lakes. Naivasha** is famous for black bass, but the angler in pursuit of them should forget any preconceptions he might have. Smallish coppery-tinted bar-spoons are the most successful lure and the bigger fish are found not so much in the shallows as in pockets of deeper water inshore, where they shelter in the papyrus. In **Lake Turkana** (formerly Rudolph) the principal quarry are Nile perch and tiger-fish, the former growing to more than 250lb. Also in Turkana, the rare and beautiful golden perch, which may weigh 150lb. **Lake Baringo,** well off the beaten track, is noted for its tilapia fishing; also for its wildlife watching potential, but that is a bonus attaching to much of the Kenya fishing. Sport-fishing is now developing in **Lake Victoria** and the **Sasamua Dam.** Accommodation at all centres, but the extreme variety of types calls for detailed investigation in advance. The **Pemba Channel Fishing Club** address is **PO Box 86952, Mombasa**, tel: 313749; fax: 316875. The **Kenya Tourist Office** is at **25 Brook's Mews, London W1Y 1LG**. Tel: 071-355 3144. Fax: 071-495 8656.

TANZANIA. Tanzania can provide some of the finest big-game fishing in the world.

Big-game fishing: From October to March there is first-class sport with sailfish, shark, tunny, marlin, wahoo, horse mackerel and dolphin, particularly off **Dar es Salaam,** around **Latham Island** and **Mafia Island,** and also in the **Pemba Channel** off **Tanga.** Mafia offers some of the finest sport in the world in quantity, variety and excitement, and here particularly, and in addition to those already mentioned, can be found king fish, barracuda, red snapper and rock cod. There is a lodge on Mafia Island, with 30 air-conditioned rooms. Boats and equipment can be hired from the Seafaris Company. Flights to Mafia Island from the mainland (about 30 minutes run) are operated daily in each direction by Air Tanzania Corporation and air charter services from Dar es Salaam, also.

Lake fishing: the great **Lakes Victoria, Nyasa** and **Tanganyika** provide the best sport fishing where, from **Kigoma, Mwanza** and **Itungi,** it is possible to catch Nile perch, tiger fish and tilapia, which provide excellent sport. The **Great Ruaha River** is another inland fishing ground.

Trout fishing: At the moment, less organised than other branches of the sport, but can be arranged on request.

Further information (licences etc) may be obtained from the **Tanzania Tourist Corporation, PO Box 2485, IPS Building, Maktaba Street, Dar es Salaam**, and **PO Box 694, Arusha** (for Mt Meru fishing).

SOUTH AFRICA

CAPE PROVINCE. Since the establishment of large-mouthed and small-mouthed black bass, the inland fisheries of the Cape area have been greatly extended; but this development has not been at the expense of the rainbow trout fisheries, which are as flourishing as ever. A few rivers hold brown trout, and brown trout were also introduced to upland waters some time ago. All the inland waters fall under the laws of the Cape Provincial Administration. In proclaimed trout rivers no fishing may be done at all except with the artificial fly and during the open season for trout, which extends from the beginning of September to the end of May. Trout licences are required but the charges are extremely moderate. In addition, however, the permission of riparian owners will be needed and sometimes a fee is payable.

Most of the rivers in the Western Cape are within a day's motoring of **Cape Town** on tarred roads, and some of the best waters are on State Forest Reserves, to which anglers have access on permit. This area has a winter rainfall and the best months are September, October and November, late April and early May. **Steenbras Reservoir** holds a rare hybrid known as 'tiger trout' which is a cross between brown trout and the American eastern brook trout.

The **Olifants River** in the **Citrusdal** and **Clanwilliam** districts provide excellent fishing for small-mouthed bass and the indigenous yellowfish, *Barbus capensis.* The latter takes artificial lures, is very game and runs as large as 20lb. Further afield, the mountainous area of **East Griqualand,** adjoining the **Transkei,** have rivers which provide boundless opportunities for the trout fisherman.

Sea fishing along the **Cape Province's** coastline is very good indeed, with hundreds of species to be caught. Cape Town has emerged as the world's leading Broadbill Swordfish fishing venue. The big-game potential is only beginning to be realised, and remarkable catches of yellowfin and longfin tuna have been taken. Tuna catches predominate throughout spring, summer and autumn; snoek in the winter months. Skiboat fishing is an interesting and highly successful technique for taking many varieties of off-shore fish. Every type of tackle is available and accommodation is plentiful and comfortable.

NATAL. The streams originating in the **Natal Drakensberg** mountains, which rise to 11,000 ft, form several river systems before emptying into the Indian Ocean. Although the sources are in general too steeply graded to support fish life in any quantity, below the torrent source each river enters a series of pools and rapids suitable for trout and other fish. Moreover, the construction of numerous dams in the Natal Midlands has been the means of providing many extra fishable waters.

Only waters at an altitude of about 4,000 ft and more have, in general, been stocked with trout. Below this level most rivers are too warm and silt-laden for the species to thrive. Black bass and carp have been established in a number of these midland dams with tilapia species inhabiting the warmer areas. However, other species to be caught are the indigenous 'scaly' (yellowfish), catfish, and eels. The State dams administered by the Natal Parks, Game and Fish Preservation Board (Albert Falls, Midmar, Wagendrift, Spioenkop, Chelmsford, Hazelmere and Craigie Burn) not only provide abundant angling for many types of fish, including those mentioned above, but also provide a wide range of other recreational facilities and comfortable accommodation.

Rainbow and brown trout are the most important sporting fish of the Drakensberg area (midlands) and warmwater angling (carp, black bass, catfish, scaly, eels and tilapia) of the lower inland areas. The open season for trout streams is from September 1 to June 1, but dams are open throughout the year. The best fishing is usually obtained at the beginning and end of the season. From November to February the heavy summer rains and thunderstorms are apt to discolour the lower waters and render fly fishing difficult. It is almost always feasible, however, to obtain fishing on the headwaters or on artificial lakes and dams. The average size of Natal trout runs from about ½lb to 2lb, but on the larger waters, especially dams, much heavier fish can be expected and each season a few trout of more than 5lb are taken. The Natal record for a rainbow trout is 5.54kg (12lb 12oz) caught in the Swartberg district in May 1958.

Public waters and the Provincial nature reserves (where accommodation is available close to fishing areas) are controlled by the Natal Parks, Game and Fish Preservation Board; all queries regarding licences, accommodation etc should be directed to the **Natal Parks Board Pietermaritzburg**, who will supply full information to visitors and handle reservations. Natal Parks Board rangers are stationed at the more important public fishing areas to assist visitors and enforce regulations for the protection of trout, black bass, carp and indigenous fish.

Sea fishing. The majority of salt water anglers fish in the surf, casting their baits and lures from sandy beaches or from rocky promontories. Estuaries offer sport, while the open sea attracts those who have access to suitable craft. A wide variety of fish may be caught in the surf, ranging from sharks to small members of the bream family. Tackle varies accordingly, but a light fibre-glass rod of about 10-13ft together with a fixed-spool or multiplying reel gives a chance of catching many of the inshore species. Visitors should acquaint themselves with size restrictions and open seasons which apply to certain species of fish. Full details are obtainable from The Natal Parks Board.

In June and July the annual migration of 'sardines' may attract game fish such as king mackerel into the surf and sport is likely to be fast and furious. The best estuarine fishing is **Lake St Lucia,** a nature reserve-controlled by the Natal Parks Board; large numbers of grunter and kob enter the estuary leading to the main lake in spring and autumn. Deep sea angling takes place from ski-boats (small, speedy, flat-bottomed craft) as well as from the larger types of vessel. Advice on the organisation of deep sea trips will be provided by the Natal Parks Board. Tackle for every branch of angling is obtainable. Innumerable hotels, holiday cottages, holiday flats and rest camps provide accommodation for visitors to the Natal or Zululand coastal resorts (Zululand offers marlin, sailfish and tiger fishing).

TRANSVAAL. Rainbow trout can be caught in a number of fine mountain streams in the Eastern Transvaal at altitudes varying from 4,000 to 6,000ft. **Magoebaskloof, Sabie, Pilgrim's Rest, Lydenburg, Machadodorp, Belfast, Dullstroom** and **Waterval Boven** are the principal trout fishing centres. Some waters contain only fish over 3lb in weight. There is no closed season for trout fishing although fishing conditions are at their best in October and April. The rule is fly only, with dry and wet flies being used. Most waters are privately owned and, except where angling clubs have fishing rights, the permission of the riparian owner must be obtained. Good bass fishing is to be found in a large number of public, club and private waters. Large-mouth bass are widely distributed but some of the best waters are in the **White River** area of the Eastern Transvaal: dams in that region, such as **Longmere, Klipkoppies, Witklip, Stanford** and **Dagama** have produced excellent fishing in recent times. Tiger-fish may be caught in the **Komati River** at **Komatipoort** and in the **Limpopo.** Minimum takeable size, 12in, daily bag limit, 6. Tiger-fish are best caught in September and October.

Yellowfish abound in the waters of the **Transvaal.** There are four species, all belonging to the genus *Barbus*. In the **Vaal River** they grow to 30lb in weight and can be caught on mealiemeal dough, earthworms, grasshoppers or crabs. The two species of the east-flowing rivers grow to 15lb and take crab, earthworms, mealiemeal dough and spinners.

Tilapia, commonly known as 'kurper', is a very popular fish. There are two species, both being restricted to warmer waters. They can be caught on earthworms, mealiemeal dough (a paste bait) and spinners, with a light trout rod. They average about $1\frac{1}{4}$lb, but specimens of $4\frac{1}{2}$lb are commonly caught. The best waters for this species are the **Hartebeestpoort, Rust der Winter, Roodeplaat, Loskop** and **Njelele dams,** also those in the White River area - although they may be caught in almost any lowveld water.

Not just the Transvaal, but the whole of the Republic of South Africa is a carp angler's paradise, with the fish attaining exceptional weights in very short periods, due to the nature of South Africa's waters. The record caught on rod and line is 48lb 10oz, although much larger specimens have been caught but not recorded, and the heaviest known fish was a monster of $83\frac{1}{4}$lb which was trapped in an irrigation furrow near **Bon Accord Dam** north of Pretoria. Carp are found throughout South Africa in many public and private dams. No bag or size limits apply to these fish.

It is also possible to stay in and fish within some of South Africa's game reserves, including Loskop and Willem Pretorius.

General Information: Licences relative to the particular province can be obtained from Receivers of Revenue, magistrates' offices and reputable tackle stores throughout the Republic.

For further information contact the **South African Tourism Board, 5/6 Alt Grove, Wimbledon, London SW19 4DZ**, tel: 081-944 6646; telex: 298946; fax: 081 944 6705.

Some time between May and July every year sardines in vast numbers migrate from east to west along the south coast of Natal, followed by large schools of shad, barracuda, shark and other predatory species of great interest to the angler. In certain conditions of wind and tide, sardines are washed ashore by the shoal to provide pickings for all present as in the picture.

FISHING IN AUSTRALASIA; INDIA; SRI LANKA AND MALAYSIA

AUSTRALIA

As a result of acclimatization and planned research in Australia, many of the lakes and rivers in the State of Tasmania, New South Wales, Western Australia and Victoria are well stocked with trout, which sometimes reach a large size. The island State of **Tasmania** is world-famous as a trout fishing centre, and continues to attract anglers from all parts of the Commonwealth each year.

Many rivers are still subject to flooding despite hydro schemes and this imposes a standstill on angling, so that the tendency is to reduce close seasons. The angler is strongly advised to check on river levels before going to fish. Before water temperatures have warmed up will be found to be the best times - midsummer is generally worst for trout fishing.

Freshwater Murray cod, perch and blackfish are found in good number in Australia. The **Murray River,** which forms the boundary of the eastern States of **Victoria** and **New South Wales,** and its many tributaries provide good sport for thousands of anglers, including trout in the upper reaches, Murray cod may weigh up to 150lb; another Murray River fish, the callop or golden perch, grows to over 50lb. Macquairie perch (to 11lb) and silver perch or grunter (to 6lb) are also taken. Another perch, or Australian bass, is taken in coastal streams and estuaries.

Australia was said by the late Zane Grey, noted big game authority, to possess the finest big game fishing grounds in the world. Centre of interest for sportsmen is **Montague Island,** off the coast of New South Wales, where there are marlin, tuna, shark and other big fish. The island is 14m from **Bermagui,** a safe harbour that can be used in all weathers. The tropical waters of the **Great Barrier Reef,** which extends for about a thousand miles along the east coast of Queensland, form Australia's most fascinating grounds; there are many unusual varieties of fish. There is good beach and rock fishing almost everywhere.

The principal fishing organisation is the **Game Fishing Association of Australia, Birkenhead Point, Drummoyne, NSW 2047.**

For further information contact **The Australian Tourism Commission**, Gemini House, 10-18 Putney Hill, Putney, London SW15 6AA, tel. 081 780 1424.

NEW SOUTH WALES. The streams near **Sydney** are mostly too small to support a large trout population, but good sport may be had in parts of the Blue Mountains area. Easily best from the fishing point of view, however, is the **Snowy Mountains** area. Very large reservoirs constructed as part of the hydro-electric scheme in the Southern Alps are now ranked equal to any in the world for brown and rainbow trout. The scenic beauty of the streams and these lakes is outstanding. **Lake Eucumbene** is the largest of the dams and in recent years has become the mecca of Australian trout anglers, but there are many other fine fisheries. Good accommodation and camping sites are available and many fine fishing waters are reached easily over good roads. Another good area for trout fishing is the **New England Tableland,** north of Sydney. Centred on the University Town of **Armidale,** the area's many streams and high altitude provide excellent fishing.

Apart from these new waters, one of the most renowned centres is **Cooma,** which has produced many of the heavier fish caught in the state. The **Murrumbidgee** and its tributaries near **Kiandra** are well worth fishing at the right time.

With the exception of a number of small spawning creeks, which have extended close seasons, and the larger impoundments, which are open all the year round, the trout streams are open to fishing from the mid-October to the end of June. Other inland waters are open the whole year. The most popular times for trout fishing are in the cooler months of the open season; that is October, November, March, April and May.

Anglers do not need a licence to fish in New South Wales. There are many attractive native species inhabiting the freshwater streams. Murray cod being perhaps the most popular, and the taking of fish up to 50lb is not uncommon; these fish do, in fact, run much larger. There are size and bag limits for trout and native fish and there is a closed season for Murray cod during September, October and November. Further information is available by writing to **NSW Fisheries, Locked Bag 9, Pyrmont 2009**.

The State is noted for its attractive coastal lagoons and estuary fisheries. At many excellent resorts bream, flathead, whiting, black fish, etc, give good sport, while big game fish like tuna, marlin and shark abound in waters off the coast. Tourist information can be had from the **NSW Government Travel Centre, 19 Castlereagh Street, Sydney**.

QUEENSLAND. There are no trout fishing centres, no licence fees and no close season except for Barramundi Angling (Nov 1 to Jan 31). Golden perch or 'yellow-belly' are found in the freshwater rivers of the south-west and as far north as the upper river of the **Dawson**. Murray cod are also caught in the south-western rivers, and freshwater perch or grunters (several species) are found in most inland streams. Barramundi are taken from all inland rivers of eastern Queensland north of and including the Dawson River. Nile perch have been introduced into a number of waters.

Off the coast are the **Greater Barrier coral** reefs (1,230 miles long), which abound in fish life. Big game fish are plentiful along the whole coastline, and the following species are commonly caught: Marlin, spearfish, tuna, bonito, Spanish mackerel, sharks (white pointer, mako, tiger, whalers, etc), amberjacks, emperor, trevally, etc.

Cairns and Far North Queensland are known world wide as a big game area for the big black marlin in the last quarter of the year. Large marlin are regularly landed.

The area off **Brisbane** provides one of the best light tackle game fish grounds in the world in the first half of the year particularly for tuna and sailfish.

The mainland coast provides excellent estuary beach and rock fishing for bream, whiting, flathead, tailor, trevally, giant perch, grunter, jew fish, and so on.

Further information can be had from the **Queensland Tourist and Travel Corporation, 392 Strand, London WC2R 0LZ.** Tel: 071-836 7242. Fax: 071-836 5881.

SOUTH AUSTRALIA. South Australia has very few freshwater streams if the **River Murray** is excluded. Relatively little trout fishing is available except in some streams near capital city of Adelaide and in farm dams. There is no closed season on trout fishing but there is a legal minimum length of 28cm.

The River Murray, which flows through the State to the sea, supports both commercial and recreational fisheries for native freshwater species, callop, silver perch and catfish and yabbies. Introduced golden carp, common carp (up to 30lb), English perch, redfin and tench are also caught. Murray crayfish and Murray cod are fully protected in South Australia.

Very enjoyable and profitable sea fishing can be had along most of the coast of South Australia with rod and line or hand line. Amateur anglers do not require licences.

South Australia's premier saltwater table fish is the King George whiting and these are accessible to boat anglers in most waters of the State, including waters adjacent to Adelaide. Snapper up to 30lb or more and sweet tasting garfish are also by boat anglers in the relatively sheltered waters of **Gulf St Vincent** and **Spencer Gulf**. A large number of piers along the South Australian coast allow good fishing for a variety of species. Excellent sport fishing for Australian salmon, sharks and large mulloway is available to shore anglers along the surf beaches of the more exposed parts of the coast.

Anglers do not require a licence to fish with a rod or hand line, but must observe legal minimum lengths of fish, bag limits, and closed areas, and must not take protected species. Fishing is not permitted in most Aquatic Reserves.

Tourist information can be had from the **South Australian Tourism Commission, Travel Centre, 1 King William Street, Adelaide**, and further information on fishery matters from the **Primary Industries (Fisheries), 135 Pirie Street, Adelaide, 5000,** and the **Honorary Secretary, South Australian Fly Fishers Association Inc, Box 489, PO North Adelaide, SA 5006.**

TASMANIA. Tasmania, not without justification, describes itself as Australia's 'Fisher-men's Mecca'. A multitude of lakes and rivers are generously stocked with introduced brown, rainbow and brook trout, species which have achieved growth-rates on the island second to none. The size-bracket in which the angler expects his captures to fall spans 2-10lb, with even larger trout an ever-present possibility. Most of the waters are within motoring distance or of air-services from **Hobart** and **Launceston**. Mobile campers are widely employed. Guides are available, and can arrange, where necessary, flies, lures, boats and camp services.

Popular waters include **Great Lake** (situated in the central plateau of the island at an altitude of 3,372ft, 83 miles from Hobart, the capital, and about the same distance from

Launceston, second largest city in the island, situated in the north), **Lake King William, Lake St Clair, Lake Echo, Little Pine Lagoon, Brady's Lake, Dee Lagoon, Arthurs Lake, Lake Rowallan** and **Lake Pedder.** Other popular fishing waters are **Lake Leake** and **Tooms Lake** on the east coast, and **Lakes Sorell** and **Crescent** in the central midlands.

The northern part of the island is more richly endowed with trout streams than the south, having the **South Esk, North Esk, Macquarie** and **Brumby.** The north-west has the **Mersey, Forth, Leven, Blyth, Duck** and **Inglis.** In the south are the **Derwent,** and **Huon.**

Angling licences, full season, 14 days, 3 days and 1 day are available from most sports stores, police stations and Tasmanian travel centres or the Inland Fisheries Commission. The principal angling associations are the Southern Tasmanian Licensed Anglers Association, the Northern Tasmanian Fisheries Association, and the North-Western Fisheries Association.

Further information can be obtained from **The Tasmanian Travel Centre, 80 Elizabeth Street, Hobart** and **The Inland Fisheries Commission, 127 Davey Street, Hobart 7000.**

VICTORIA. Although Victoria may be known for its Yarra River at Melbourne, the State has many other excellent opportunities for both freshwater, sea and estuary fishing. Anglers are able to use bait, lures or flies in Victoria's public waters.

Freshwater Fishing. The **Yarra,** just one of Victoria's many rivers, passes through Melbourne, the capital of Victoria. It is known for its discolouration, caused by readily dispersable soils being washed into it. However, the Yarra River has edible fish throughout its length, from the headwaters of the forested catchment to Melbourne, where it enters Port Phillip Bay. The clear headwaters (about 2 hours drive from Melbourne) have trout and blackfish, whereas about halfway down the river near **Wonga Park** there are Macquarie perch, and further downstream at **Eltham** there is are Murray cod. Other angling fish in the lower sections of the river include: redfin, roach and carp. Brown trout are sometimes stocked into the lower part of the river by the Victoria Fisheries. Common fish in the estuary include bream and yellow-eyed mullet, which can be caught from the banks within the city. Eels are present throughout the catchment, as they are in most of the streams that enter the sea from the southern half of Victoria. There are other streams near Melbourne, such as the **Maribyrnong** and the **Werribee Rivers,** which have trout in the headwaters, coarse fish in the middle sections, and estuary fish in the lower sections. Apart from the far north west of the state where it is very dry, there are streams, reservoirs and lakes suitable for angling throughout Victoria. Many streams have a number of self-supporting fish populations. These include some of the following species: brown trout, rainbow trout, blackfish, golden perch, Macquarie perch, Murray cod, silver perch, eel-tailed catfish, eels, redfin, carp, roach, tench and goldfish. Some streams and many lakes are stocked with brown trout and rainbow trout, and two lakes, **Bullen Merri** and **Purrumbete,** receive chinook salmon. More streams and lakes are now being stocked with Australian native fish (golden perch, Murray cod and Macquarie perch). Trout fishing is popular in the north east, south east and south west of the state, and in central Victoria along the **Goulburn River** which includes the **Eildon Reservoir** and its tributaries. Blackfish exist over most of the state, and other freshwater native fish are sought over the northern half, in the river catchments draining north into the **Murray,** a New South Wales river forming the border between the states. It has numerous native fish including Australia's largest freshwater fish, the Murray cod, which can weigh over 220lb. New South Wales regulations apply to fishing in the Murray River.

Saltwater Fishing. Melbourne and its suburbs are situated around **Port Phillip Bay,** and it is only an hours drive south east to **Westernport Bay.** These bays (about 25 and 15 miles across respectively) are very popular with boat and shore anglers for a variety of fish including flathead, whiting, snapper, mullet, bream, garfish, trevally and Australian salmon. Most snappers are caught from October to March when they enter Port Phillip Bay to spawn. Snapper have been taken weighing up to 29lb. Further to the east and west of Melbourne there are estuaries, inlets, saltwater lakes, surf beaches and rocky shorelines that are very popular with saltwater anglers, who fish from the shore, jetties, rocks, beach and boats. Probably the most popular area for saltwater angling is the **Gippsland Lakes** at Lakes Entrance, where a series of very large lakes provide extensive marine fishing opportunities, with the 90 mile surf beach nearby. Many of Victoria's river estuaries, inlets, saltwater lakes and coastal zones are popular holiday resorts for anglers. Some of these fishing venues are amongst National Parks which provide an attractive scenic environment. The commonly sought saltwater fish are bream, mullet, luderick, estuary perch, flathead and bass in the estuaries and saltwater lakes; salmon, mullet, sharks and tailor in the surf and various fish such as sweep, leatherjackets and parrot fish from rocky shorelines.

There are too many popular angling spots around Victoria to mention individually. However, tackle stores and newsagents provide numerous publications and video tapes about where and how to catch fish in the State. A most useful book for freshwater anglers, sold by the Victoria Government is *A Guide to the Inland Angling Waters of Victoria*, 4th Edition 1991, Tunbridge, B. R., Rogan, P.L., & Barnham, C.A.: Fisheries Management Division, Department of Conservation & Environment; which provides excellent information about features and locations of Victoria's main angling streams and freshwater lakes, the fish present, and advice about fish sizes and abundance.

Anglers (unless exempted such as those under the age of 16) require an Amateur Fishing Licence to fish in inland waters, but do not require a licence to fish in bays and coastal waters. 'Inland Waters' generally includes the river or estuary down to the coast, but exceptions for some estuaries, inlets and lakes are stated in the regulations, and outlined in the Victoria Recreational Fishing Guide (VRFG). Licences valid for 28 days ($A10), 1 year ($A20), or 3 years ($A60) may be purchased from offices of the Victorian Department of Conservation & Natural Resources and many retail fishing tackle outlets. The VRFG lists exemptions from licence requirements and summarises such regulations as minimum legal lengths, closed seasons, bag limits, closed waters and other restrictions. The VRFG is issued with Amateur Fishing Licences, and may also be obtained from the Department of Conservation & Natural Resources, or from Tourism Victoria.

Fishing advice may be obtained from **Victorian Fisheries Department of Conservation & Natural Resources, 240 Victoria Parade, East Melbourne, Victoria, Australia 3002**. Tourist information is available from **Tourism Victoria, 13th Floor, 55 Swanston St, Melbourne, Victoria, Australia 3000**. The address of the **Victoria Government Office** in London is **Victoria House, Melbourne Place, Strand, London WC2B 4LG** (tel. 071 836 2656).

WESTERN AUSTRALIA. Stretching from the tropical north to the cool southern oceans, the vast coastal waters of Western Australia provide superb ocean sports fishing. Some of the best angling in the world can be found on the doorstep of Western Australia's major cities.

Around 300,000 West Australians go fishing at least once a year, and the state attracts many visiting anglers

Principal centres for ocean fishing are: **Exmouth, Shark Bay, Carnarvon, Kalbarri, Broome Dampier Geraldton, Fremantle, Perth, Rottnest Island, Mandurah, Bunbury, Busselton, Augusta, Albany** and **Esperance.** Main species to be caught include: mulloway, whiting, tailor, Australian salmon, snapper, jewfish, and Spanish mackerel. Annual game-fishing classics are held in the tropical waters of **Exmouth** and **Broome** where marlin and other gamefish are target species. In the **Swan River,** on Perth's doorstep, locals hand-trawl for prawns. World famous western rock lobsters can be taken from the reefs around many mid-west coastal centres.

A Recreational Fishing Licence must be held for the taking of lobster, maroon, abalone or to use a gill net, and is available from Fisheries Department offices. Bag limits apply to all species of fish.

The **Fisheries Department** located at **108 Adelaide Terrace, East Perth 6004**, and the address of the **Western Australian Division** of the **Australian Anglers' Association is PO Box 375, Subiaco, WA 6008.** The address of the **Western Australian Tourist Commission** is **Albert Facey House, Forrest Place (cnr Wellington Street), Perth**. The address of the **Western Australian Government Office** in London is: **115 Strand, London WC2R 0AJ** (071-240 2881).

NEW ZEALAND

(Notes compiled by George Aitken)

Fishing in New Zealand can be compared in some ways to Caesar's Gaul, in that it divides into three parts - Trout, Salmon and Big Game angling.

Trout, both brown and rainbow, were introduced about 100 years ago and have long been fully distributed on both islands. Rainbow predominate in the North Island, and browns in the South, but many waters have a mixture of the two in varying proportions.

The main areas in the North are centred on **Lake Taupo** and the **Rotorua** district with its group of important lakes. The rivers flowing into and out of these lakes are also noted fisheries, particularly late in the season when the main runs commence. The **Tongariro, Waitahanui, Tauranga-Taupo** and others flow into Lake Taupo, while in the Rotorua area there are the **Kaituna, Ohau Channel,** and **Ngongotaha** to name a few.

The South Island has thousands of miles of rivers and streams, and numerous lakes of all sizes. It was once calculated, at the turn of the century, that there are 17,000 miles of river fishing in New Zealand, and of course it is all open to the public, subject only to right of access and to reasonable accessibility.

Good trout fishing is widely available, and large trout can still be caught within an hour's drive of the main cities, but obviously many of the best waters are more remote and some are seldom fished, although helicopter or floatplane services are readily available out of the towns of **Queenstown, Wanaka** and **Te Anau** to reach places like **Lakes Alabaster** and **McKerrow,** or the **Pyke** and **Hollyford** rivers for example.

The main, and also the lesser, rivers of **Southland** and **Otago** provinces offer excellent dry fly and nymph fishing for brown trout, and fish of from 12 to 15 pounds are caught each season, but a good average would be from 3 to 4 pounds. Guide services are again widely available, although obviously concentrated somewhat in the more popular areas. An Angling Guides Association was formed some time ago, all professional guides are licensed, and are fully supported with 4-wheel drive vehicles and boats as necessary for their local areas.

In general, the open season is from Oct 1 until the end of April (North Island - 1 Oct to end of June) but some waters open early to take advantage of the runs of whitebait which provide feed for sea-run trout, while others, principally in the Taupo and Rotorua areas, stay open all the year, particularly the lower reaches of the larger streams feeding Lake Taupo, Rotorua and Wakatiou themselves.

Salmon, the Pacific Quinnat or King Salmon, introduced to the main **Canterbury** rivers, are fished for in about eight of them, the main ones being the **Waimakariri, Rakaia, Ashburton, Rangitata** and **Waitaki.** The fishing is mainly heavy spinning, with spoons most favoured as lures, in the lower rivers, estuaries and even in the surf at the mouths. A certain amount of fly fishing, using very large lures or flies, is done upriver, notably in the **Rakaia Gorge** area. In all the salmon rivers the fish are mostly in the 12 to 20 pound class, but larger are quite frequent. The rivers are often unfishable for many days at a time due to cloudy glacial melt water, and trips undertaken with salmon exclusively in mind are not to be recommended.

Big Game Fishing, made famous by Zane Grey, continues its excellent tradition. The main bases for this are **Russell, Paihia** and **Whangerei** in the **Bay of Islands,** and also out from **Tauranga** to the **Mayor Island** area. There are ample charter boats, with professional skippers and hands, based in these places, catering for parties of up to four anglers. The tackle, bait and so on are all provided in the charter. Sailfish, marlin and shark are caught at no great distance from the shore. The southern part of the West Coast of the South Island, known as 'Fiordland', is now assuming increased importance for big game fishing. Boats are now based there, at Milford Sound and elsewhere.

Big Game angling is mainly from January to the end of April, with the period from mid-February on offering fine sport.

Licences are needed for trout and salmon fishing. There is a special Tourist Licence which covers the whole country and is only available from the Tourism Rotorua Information Office in Rotorua. Alternatively licences may be purchased from other districts which allow the visitor to fish in any district with the exception of Rotorua and Taupo, separate licences being needed for these two districts.

For further information and advice on angling in New Zealand, contact **New Zealand Professional Fishing Guides Association, PO Box 16, Motu, Gisbourne,** or **New Zealand Tourist Office, New Zealand House, Haymarket, London SW1Y 4TQ.** Telephone 071-973 0360.

INDIA

One of the big attractions for the fisherman in India - in more senses than one - is the mighty mahseer. This renowned sporting quarry is found in the upper reaches of the large rivers where the water is cold and the river-bed strewn with boulders and pebbles. It lies in

A 62 lb black mahseer caught by an English visitor, John Wilson, from the Bangalore Club water on the Cauvery River in 1989. Not the biggest fish of the trip (a golden mahseer weighing 87 lbs) this one was hooked on a spoon in a fifteen knot current and had to be followed 300 yards downstream before its captor triumphed. *Photo: A T Davision.*

pools above or below the rapids and preys on small fish.

The mahseer can be taken on a spoon, but strong tackle is essential. It not only runs large - the biggest caught on rod and line weighed 119lb (Cauvery River, South India, 1919) - but is a splendid fighter. The sport has, in fact, been compared most favourably with salmon fishing.

Mahseer abound in the upper reaches of the **Brahmaputra** and its many tributaries in Assam, and the beautiful **Titsa** river valley in **North Bengal** is good just before and after the rainy season (June to September). Large fish may also be taken in the **Bombay** area - in the **Rivers Kalu, Bhima** and **Mula.** One of the best centres in the **Punjab** is **Tajewala,** on the **River Jamuna.** A catch of 80lb of mahseer a few years ago is recorded in the visitors' book at the Rest House there. The **River Jhelum** in Kashmir also holds mahseer - fish of more than 90lb have been taken - but the fishing is not now so good as it was some years ago.

Kashmir is renowned for sport with brown and rainbow trout, which have thrived since they were introduced at the turn of the century. The many streams in the area are regularly stocked from two large hatcheries and are divided into 'beats' of about two miles. Great variety is available, the rivers ranging from foaming torrents, when spinning is permitted, to gentle streams suitable for dry fly. There are 'fly only' beats. The most suitable flies are those usually included in every angler's selection, but in Kashmir they are usually dressed on hook sizes between No. 9 and No. 5 (old sizes). The season lasts from May to September.

India's rivers contain numerous other species. The **Jamuna** at **Okhla,** in **Delhi,** for instance, holds no fewer than eight species, including heavy catfish, the silund - a predator running up to 50lb, which can be taken on a spinner - and a humpbacked fish called the cheetul or moh, which will be seen constantly rising to the surface and turning over broadside. There is also plenty of huge carp in the slow-flowing rivers and the lakes and tanks. The sea fishing can be excellent, too, but is dependent upon seasonal migrations and the weather. A considerable body of angling literature has now been published by the **Bombay Natural History Society, 114 Apollo Street.**

While the tourist-angler should not expect to find luxurious cabins on his expeditions, numerous camping-sites and comfortable rest-houses have been provided, often in the most beautiful surroundings and at **Corbett,** the call of the tiger and the trumpeting of wild elephants may sometimes be heard.

So far as tackle is concerned, the trout or mahseer fisherman will be specially well catered for at **Srinagar,** capital of Kashmir, where he may obtain first-class gear, but rates are rising due to restricted imports, and it is preferable to take one's own equipment.

Further information from the **India Government Tourist Office, 7 Cork Street, London W1X 2AB** (Tel 071-437 3677).

SRI LANKA (CEYLON)

Nuwara Eliya is the best centre for trout fishing. As it is above the 6,000ft level, the climate is temperate. Good hotel accommodation is available. The fishing is, with few exceptions, restricted to fly only and most common patterns of wet fly are successful. Dry fly is rarely used, there being little natural fly. There is no statutory close season, though the club imposes one in parts following restocking. Size limits vary from 8in to 15in.

The main waters are: **Nuwara Eliya** stream (flows through the golf course and park); **Ambawela** stream (8m from Nuwara Eliya; jungle and grassland); **Bulu Ella** stream (2½m jungle); **Portswood Dam** (4m; tea estate); **Agra Oya** and **Gorge Valley** rivers (10-15m; tea estates), and the magnificently spectacular **Horton Plains** stream (30m; jungle and grassland, Nature reserve). Motor transport can be hired. On any of these waters it is possible to maintain an average of 1lb and several fish over 3lb are caught.

Trout fishing is now controlled by the Nuwara Eliya District Fishing Club. Stocking has so far been carried out in Portswood Dam, the Horton Plains, Agra Oya and Gorge Valley. For licences application should be made to the **Honorary Secretary, Nuwara Eliya District Fishing Club, Court Lodge Estate, Kandapola.** Visitors are advised to bring their tackle as fly tackle is scarce in Sri Lanka.

The two main species of indigenous sporting fish in Sri Lanka are the mahseer and the walaya (freshwater shark), found in the jungle rivers of the Low Country, particularly the **Mahawehi,** the upper reaches of the **Kelani** and the **Amban Ganga.** Ceylon mahseer, though small compared with those in some Indian rivers, provide good sport, but fishing for them can be somewhat difficult. Fishing for indigenous sporting fish in Sri Lanka is free. With a shoreline of 1,140 miles and a continental shelf of 10,000 square miles, the seas around Ceylon have an unlimited fishing potential hardly exploited.

The outfalls of 103 major river basins and hundreds of other estuaries, lagoons and coastal lakes all round the island are the most popular spots frequented by local surf casters as well as bait fishermen. Many varieties of game fish of the Carangid family, locally called paraw and know elsewhere as trevally, horse mackerel, etc, are taken. These swift and powerful carnivorous fish attain a length of 5ft and a weight of 150lb. The schooling habits of the caranx, their keen eyesight and some built-in sensory mechanism make them congregate in estuaries immediately after monsoons and rains.

Next in popularity among surf-casters come the barracuda and Spanish mackerel. Both these species of voracious predatory fish attain lengths of 6ft as do other species known locally as 'giant perch', 'threadfins' and 'tassel fish' which frequent the estuaries.

Trolling over the continental shelf yields catches of tuna ranging from the 2-3ft skipjack to the 6ft yellowfin and bluefin, the acrobatic dolphin, swordfish and marlin which attain a size to provide a challenge to the best big game fishermen of any country. The broadbill swordfish found in deeper waters reach a length of 15ft and a weight of well over 1,000lb. Though reaching only 10ft and 250lb, the sailfish compensate for their smaller size by their remarkable agility.

The monsoons regulate the fishing in Sri Lanka Seas. The western and southern coasts are favoured during the North-East monsoon (from October to April) and the east coast during the South-West monsoon (from May to September).

Further information can be obtained from **London Director, Sri Lanka Tourist Board, 13 Hyde Park Gardens, London W2 2LU,** tel: 071-262 5009/1841; telex: 25844; fax: 071-262 7970.

MALAYSIA

Some good sport is available in the jungle-covered highlands where fast-flowing, clean streams will delight the eye. These are well stocked with cyprinids or members of the carp family, which include the well-known mahseer of India, known locally as kelah. This group of which the most common species are kelah (up to 20lb), sebarau (up to 12lb), and kejor or tengas (up to 8lb), are sporting fish which fight well when hooked. Kelah and tengas are good to eat. They are best when curried and provide a good change or diet in the jungle when living on operational 24-hour pack rations.

All these fish will take an artificial bait; the most popular being a 1in or 1½in silver or silver/copper spoon. A normal salmon spinning outfit is ideal. For those who prefer it, a fixed-spool reel can be used provided it will hold sufficient line. Owing to the crushing power of the jaws of the kelah, extra strong treble or large single hooks should be used and some people recommend the use of a 2ft wire trace.

Taman Negara, on the borders of **Kelantan, Trengganu** and **Pahang,** provides the best fishing, and a visit to the HQ at **Kuala Tahan** is well worth the journey. It may be reached by rail to **Kuala Tembeling** and thence by water, in long, narrow, locally-built boats fitted with 40hp outboard motors which can do the journey up the **Sungaï Tembeling** in three to four hours depending on the condition of the river. At Kuala Tahan there are bungalows and a rest-house providing full board. A number of visitors' lodges and halting bungalows have been built throughout the park so the fishermen can stay near the river they are fishing.

From Kuala Tahan all onward movement is by smaller boats with lower-powered engines to negotiate the shallower rivers, such as the Tahan itself. There are many large pools well stocked with fish in the lower reaches, and above the **Lata Berkoh** barrier many pools and rapids, all excellent fishing water. Malay and Aborigine boatmen are happy to act as guides and are delightful companions.

It is easier and pleasanter to cast from the bank, but this will necessitate some wading where the bank is steep and overhung by the jungle. The water is pleasantly warm and waders would be far too hot to wear. Those with a good sense of balance can try fishing from a slowly paddled perahu, but as this is only a shell at the most 2ft wide, it is liable to be something of a circus act.

Most reliable times to fish are the months February/March and July/August, because in other months fishing will be spasmodic owing to the heavy rainfall. Spates and floodwater so colour the rivers that fishing is a waste of time.

In **Terengganu State** is the massive **Kenyir Lake,** a well known attraction to visiting anglers, where baung, toman, sebarau, kelah, kelisa and arowana can be caught, and houseboat holidays are available: for information contact Jabatan Perhutanan, **Kuala Brang, Hulu Terengganu,** tel: 09 811259 for **Sekayu** area, or **Kenyir Lake Resort, Kenyir Dam, Hulu Terengganu,** tel: 09 950609, for **Kenyir Dam** area.

Apart from the fishing there is always the chance of seeing the wild animals of Malaysia at the many salt licks. There are usually monkeys, monitor lizard, snakes and flying foxes to be seen, as well as many varieties of birds such as hornbill eagle and kingfishers.

Intending visitors should write well before the date of their visit, giving as much information as possible on their special interests to the **Director-General, Dept of Wildlife and National Parks, Km10, Jalan Cheras, Kuala Lumpur, Malaysia,** so as to enable the Dept of Wildlife and National Parks to plan their itineraries.

FISHING IN NORTH AMERICA

CANADA

On the Atlantic side of the Dominion there are plenty of salmon rivers in **Quebec** and **New Brunswick**, and a good deal of fishing is available to the non-resident who takes out the appropriate provincial licence. There is a great deal of splendid trout fishing in many of the inland lakes and rivers, while in the **Great Lakes** region there are big muskellunge, and fine black bass fishing in various waters. The land-locked salmon is found in Quebec, both in the tributaries and discharge of **Lac St John**, and in some lakes in **Nova Scotia**, such as **Grand Lake** and **Beaver Bank Lake**. The 'trout' of this side of Canada are char *(Salvelinus fontinalis)*, while some of them are migratory and become 'sea trout'. In the lakes are 'grey trout', some of which reach a great size. There are also char *(Salvelinus namaycush)* in the Arctic.

On the other side of Canada, British Columbia offers splendid opportunities of sport with Pacific salmon, steelhead and rainbow trout. Fishing for Pacific salmon has until recently been considered of necessity a matter for tidal waters. The **Campbell River, Vancouver Island,** has been the most favoured, and there quinnat (now known locally as tyee) up to 70lb have been caught on the troll. At **Prince Rupert** a 93lb quinnat was caught on a spoon in 1929 by Mr O P Smith, a professional fisherman. An 82lb tyee was caught in August, 1951, at **Rivers Inlet.** The coho has been caught on fly, also in tidal waters. Of late years it has become clear that quinnat will take in fresh water in certain conditions. To the far north there are evident possibilities of sport in **Yukon** and NW Territories.

So far as tackle is concerned, the trend is towards lighter outfits. Brook trout, for instance, are almost universally taken on a nine-foot, five-ounce fly rod, and many anglers use the same rod for steelhead or Kamloops trout, although this is probably foolhardy. Tackle should always be carefully geared to the area and quarry, and on-the-spot advice is desirable.

Much work is done by the Federal and Provincial hatcheries, and waters in various parts of Canada are supplied with fry of species suitable to their needs, chiefly salmonidae, but also bass and other kinds of the best big game fishing so far discovered anywhere.

Note: The Canadian Tourist Office holds literature relevant to fishing in the country. This includes holiday brochures in addition to provincial brochures. For further information please contact **The Canadian Tourist Office, Canada House, Trafalgar Square, London SW1Y 5BJ,** tel: 071 258 6346.

ALBERTA. Alberta is fortunate in having more than 4,000 miles of good fishing streams and more than 1,000 lakes found in the mountains, foothills and prairies, as well as the more northern region of the boreal forests.

There are 15 species of sportfish in Alberta of which there are 9 cold water and 6 warm water sportfish. The cold water sportfish include brook, brown, cutthroat, golden, rainbow, and lake trout, bull trout, Arctic grayling and mountain whitefish. These fish are generally found in the lakes and streams in the foothills and mountain areas in the west of the province.

The warm water sportfish include lake whitefish, walleye, perch, pike, goldeye, and lake sturgeon. These fish are generally found in rivers and lakes throughout the south east and northern areas of the province.

Hatchery production of five million trout are stocked annually throughout the province into lakes that do not conain native fsh and which are readily accessible to the public.

Further information may be obtained by writing to **The Director, Fisheries Management Division, Alberta Fish and Wildlife Services, Main Floor, North Tower, Petroleum Plaza, 9945-108 Street, Edmonton, Alberta, Canada T5K 2C9.**

BRITISH COLUMBIA. The game fish of British Columbia comprise five species of salmon: sockeye, chum, the chinook or spring (large specimens often referred to as 'Tyee'), the pink (tidal waters only), and the coho, which may be taken with the fly, but are more easily caught by trolling; all varieties of Pacific Coast trout, particularly the steelhead, the rainbow, and the cut-throat; Arctic grayling; two species of char, of which the commoner is the Dolly Varden; and the Eastern brook trout which has been introduced. The province has a coastline of 7,000 miles and is drained by innumerable rivers and freshwater lakes.

Some of the most important fishing areas are **Kootenay District, Okanagan District** (including **Beaver, Bear, Dee, Ideal, Mabel, Sugar, South** and **Woods Lakes), Kamloops**

District (including **Adams, East Barriere, Murtle, Shuswap** and **Nicola Lakes**), **Cariboo District** (including **Quesnel, Horsefly** and **Canim Lakes,** and **Fraser** and **Thompson Rivers**), and **Merrit District,** which abounds with small productive, accessible lakes, such as **Chataway, Dot, Gypsum, Antler, Corbett, Peter Hope** and **Roche Lakes.** Most of the southern lakes and rivers are easily accessible, especially by car, and yield excellent fishing. Flying in to the less accessible waters is now a common practice. Lodges, cabins and boats are widely available.

The **Skeena Region** of northwest **British Columbia** has a wide variety of attractive fisheries. The **Burns Lake** area boasts a number of great trout fishing lakes, and **Terrace** is the centre of exceptional sport fishing for steelhead trout and chinook and coho salmon. Some restrictions apply on certain steelhead waters as conservation of this species poses particularly difficult problems. Information may be obtained from the Victoria address below.

Vancouver Island offers excellent cut-throat and steelhead trout fishing. The important waters are **Cowichan, Cameron, Sproat Lakes, Alberni** and **Qualicum Districts** and the **Campbell River** area. Steelhead trout are in **Sproat, Somass, Ash** and **Stamp Rivers,** to name but a few. Quinnat (or spring) salmon and coho are found in good quantities in all of the main streams, bays and tributaries of the mainland draining into the Pacific Ocean. On Vancouver Island there is splendid salmon fishing to be had at **Brentwood Bay, Finlayson Arm, Cowichan Bay, Comox Bay, Port Alberni, Beecher Bay, Victoria,** and **Campbell Bay** and river. Campbell River is famous on account of the large Tyee chinook caught there.

Further information (including details of licence charges and open seasons) can be had from the **Fisheries Branch, Ministry of Environment, Parliament Buildings, Victoria, BC V8V 1X5** and **Department of Fisheries and Oceans, Suite 400, 555 W. Hastings St, Vancouver, B.C. V6B 5G3.** For travel information, write to **Ministry of Development, Trade and Tourism, Parliament Buildings, Victoria B.C., V8V 1X4.**

MANITOBA. Manitoba is at the centre of a country more than 4,500 miles wide, from **St John's, Newfoundland** on the east to **Victoria, British Columbia** on the west.

The province is enormous by British standards, covering 250,000 square miles and measuring 735 air miles from north to south. Lake Winnipeg, 40 miles north of the capital city of **Winnipeg,** is the seventh largest inland body of water in North America. The northern three-fifths of the province is laced with innumerable streams and rivers, and someone claims to have counted more than 90,000 lakes, although many are too small to even appear on a map.

As the trout waters in the wilderness areas of this province become better known, they are acquiring the reputation of providing some of the finest trout fishing in North America. In particular, the **Knife** and **Gods Rivers** in north-eastern Manitoba is famous for trophy-sized brook and lake trout, northern pike and walleye. Lake trout *(Cristivomer namaycush)* are widely distributed from the south-eastern area of the province through to the northern boundaries in the deep, cold-water lakes of the Pre-Cambrian shield. Specimens over 35lbs are taken each year.

The Arctic grayling *(Thymallus arcticus)* is common along the north-western coast of Hudson Bay and its tributary streams, which include the **North Knife, Seal, Little Seal** and **Wolverine** rivers. With its spectacular beauty, it is the delight of those fly-fishermen who are able to travel to the Churchill area or the fly-in area of Nueltin Lake in the far North.

Other fish. In the smaller lakes and streams in the southern part of the province, walleye, northern pike and yellow perch are plentiful. In **Lake Winnipeg** and the tributary **Red River,** carp and channel catfish to 30lbs are taken in large numbers at certain seasons. **Winnipeg River** is the locale for large walleye, and great northern pike, together with an abundance of small-mouth bass, which provide excellent sport.

Further information (including details of licence charges and open seasons) can be had from **Travel Manitoba, Department 4310, 7th Floor, 155 Carlton Street, Winnipeg, Manitoba R3C 3H8.**

NEW BRUNSWICK. Atlantic salmon in the **Restigouche, Upsalquitch, Kedgwick, Patapedia, Jacquet, Nepisiquit, Tabusintac, North-West Miramichi, South-West Miramichi, Little South-West Miramichi, Sevogle, Renous, Dungarvon, Cains, Rocky Brook, Clearwater Brook, St John River, Nashwaak, Tobique, Serpentine** and **Salmon** rivers. Parts of some of these streams are leased, some are Crown reserve waters and some are privately owned, but there are open stretches on all except the **Kedgwick, Patapedia, Rocky Brook, Clearwater** and **Serpentine,** and non-residents who take out the appropriate provincial licence can fish a good deal of water. To avoid confusion and to make the most efficient use of valuable angling time, purchase of the services of a licensed outfitter is suggested. Since 1984, salmon larger than 63cm must be released immediately after capture. Grilse only may be retained by the angler.

In addition to salmon fishing, there is good brook trout fishing in many of the lakes and streams of New Brunswick. Small-mouth bass and landlocked salmon are caught in some waters in the south-west of the province and a few striped bass in the **St John River** and **Bathurst Harbour.**

Non-resident licences must be obtained from a Forest Service Office in the province. These must be carried by the holder at all times, but do not convey right of fishing on Crown-reserve waters or any private fishery without the consent of the lessee or owner. Every non-resident when angling on designated Atlantic salmon rivers, requires a licensed guide. One guide is required per angler when fishing from a boat, or one guide for up to three anglers when wading or fishing from shore. There is now a strictly enforced tagging programme in operation for Atlantic salmon. Further information, including details of licences and open seasons, can be had from the **Department of Natural Resources and Energy, Fish and Wildlife Branch, PO Box 6000, Fredericton E3B 5H1,** and **New Brunswick Dept of Tourism, PO Box 12345, Fredericton E3B 5C3.**

NEWFOUNDLAND and LABRADOR. Newfoundland has probably some of the best game-fishing in North America. Almost a quarter of the island's area is water, and its many fine salmon rivers, some of them practically unfished, flow through unspoiled forest and hill country. During 1988 season a total of 45,364 grilse and 710 large salmon were angled in Newfoundland and in Labrador. Ouananiche (land-locked salmon) are common in Newfoundland waters. Several kinds of trout - speckled, brown, rainbow and lake (char). Sea-run brown trout streams in the province are mainly concentrated along a 100-kilometre coastal area immediately south of St. John's; 15lb fish have been taken. Scheduled (licensed) rainbow trout waters comprise a small group of streams and ponds immediately north of St. John's; rainbows are also frequently caught in unscheduled water throughout the province. All the trout except the brown are at least as plentiful (and on average significantly larger) in Labrador as on the island; most Labrador angling waters are of much more difficult access, however. Tuna fishing was relatively good a decade or more ago, but in recent years only a handful are caught annually (e.g.- four in 1987, seven in 1988).

The salmon season varies among groups of rivers and from year to year, ranging from about June 1 to September 15, with most rivers open from mid-June to the first week in September. Scheduled rainbow trout waters are open from late May-early June to mid-September. The province has scheduled salmon rivers on the Island of Newfoundland and in Labrador, and scheduled rainbow trout streams.

Fishing in all inland waters in the province is restricted to rod, hook, and line, with a variety of baits and lures permissable in most waters; angling in scheduled salmon rivers is further restricted to fly fishing only.

Licence-fees for non-residents are as follows. Salmon: $50; trout $20. Special licenses are required to fish inland waters within the boundaries of National Parks. Anglers should consult with park officials regarding their fishing regulations. Licences are obtainable Wildlife Divisional Regional Offices, in most tackle and hardware shops and from **Department of Development and Tourism, Tourism Branch, PO Box 2016, St John's, Newfoundland, Canada A1C 5R7.**

The bag limit for salmon is two retained per day; and four hooked and released per day: when one or other of these limits has been reached, the angler must cease fishing for the day. There is a season limit of 10 retained, when this has been reached the angler must cease fishing for the season. The bag-limit for lake trout and arctic char is four per day: of other trout and northern pike, 24 per day.

Booklets on angling holidays, accommodation and other information, including licence charges and names and addresses of 'operators' and guides can be had from the Department of Development and Tourism (address above).

Further information can be obtained from the **Department of Fisheries & Oceans, Communications Division, PO Box 5667, St Johns, Newfoundland.** Tel: 709 772 4421.

NOVA SCOTIA (including **Cape Breton Island**). Atlantic salmon in **St Mary's, La Have, Medway, Margaree, Stewiacke, Moser, Musquodoboit, Gold, North**, and **Liscomb** rivers; some 30 additional rivers have substantial runs of salmon but water levels and conditions are a major factor in the annual take. There are 13 rivers scheduled and posted for fly fishing only, but it should be noted Atlantic salmon may only be taken by fly; brook trout are common in streams and lakes, many of which are accessible from woods roads known as roads to resources; sea trout (brook and brown) in most tidal streams in the Northern and Eastern part of the province; salt water charter boats are available for ground fishing in all areas except the upper reaches of the **Bay of Fundy**. Tuna charter boats are available in the **St George's Bay** and Halifax areas.

The Department of Tourism and Culture publishes and distributes several brochures on outdoor sports activities. For further information please contact the **Department of Tourism and Culture, PO Box 456, Halifax, Nova Scotia B3J 2R5.**

ONTARIO. Brook trout are widely distributed in eastern Canada. In Ontario this excellent game-fish occurs from the **Great Lakes** northward to streams entering **Hudson Bay** and **James Bay.** Included in the eastern part of this area west of the **Québec** boundary are **Algonquin Park,** tributaries of the **Upper Ottawa River,** North Bay, Temagami Metachewan, the Porcupine, Matheson-Abitibi and Cochrane areas, the Moosonee and the Goose country.

The western and northern area includes waters draining into **Lake Superior** west of **Sault Ste Marie** to **Nipigon Bay, Nipigon River** (where the world record brook trout 14½lbs was caught, in 1916), **Lake Nipigon Forest Reserve,** the Lakehead District and the **Lake St Joseph** and the Albany wilderness. The numerous tributary waters of the **Albany River** offer some of the finest trout fishing to be found in Ontario.

In southern **Ontario,** west of the eastern area, the brook trout waters include the **Muskoka lakes,** the **Haliburton** and **Hastings** highlands and the **Magnetawan** area. Farther south and west, trout are available in some streams tributary to **Lakes Huron, Erie, Ontario** and **Georgian Bay.** Lying between the eastern and western areas of northern Ontario there are numerous brook trout waters, among which are the **Sudbury, Manitoulin, Sault, Michipicoten, Mississauga, Gogama, Chapleau, Missinabi-White River-Franz, Elsas, Oba, Hornepayne, Hearst, Kapuskasing, Nakina** and **Albany** River areas.

The range of bass fishing, small-mouth and large-mouth, in Ontario extends from the **Ottawa** and **St Lawrence** rivers and Lake Ontario and Lake Erie to Temagami and the north channel of Georgian Bay. Included in this range are the following areas: **Long Point Bay** (Lake Erie), **Rideau lakes, Haliburton Lake District, Kawartha lakes, Muskoka lakes, Lake Nipissing,** the **French** and **Pickerel rivers,** and the Georgian Bay District areas. In the north-west section of Ontario bass are found in **Quetico Provincial Park.**

The muskellunge range in Ontario includes the Ottawa and St Lawrence rivers, Lake Erie, Lake St Clair and Georgian Bay, Kawartha Lake, Lake Nipissing, French and Pickerel rivers and tributary waters. The best fishing is in the mouth of the **Moon River** and the **Lake of the Woods** district in the north-western section of the province, an extensive area some 150m wide east to west, and 160m from the international boundary north. This district has hundreds of lakes, and large muskies are taken here every year. Lake trout, lake whitefish, yellow pickerel (walleye) and Gt Northern pike are fairly plentiful throughout the province. Rainbow and brown trout (neither is native to the province) have been stocked in limited areas. Rainbow trout fishing is booming in southern Georgian Bay, especially in the **Owen Sound-Collingwood** area. The rainbow fishing peaks in the spring and in the fall. In recent years rainbow trout fishing has also become popular in Lake Ontario in the **Port Hope** area.

Splake, a cross between lake trout and brook trout (speckled trout), have been introduced into some waters for a number of years now and are doing quite well. There exists now some good splake fishing at **Owen Sound, Parry Sound** and at **Providence Bay** on **Manitoulin Island.** Fishing for Pacific salmon, introduced into the Great Lakes, has escalated, especially in Lake Ontario where anglers flock to the **Port Credit-Niagara** area each year in late summer and early fall to catch large coho and chinook salmon. In the North Channel of Lake Huron and in Lake Superior pink salmon attract many anglers in early fall.

There are nearly 500 fish and game associations in the province, many of which are federated with the **Ontario Federation of Anglers and Hunters (Executive Vice President, Box 28, Peterborough, Ontario, K9J 6Y5).**

A Quebec lake trout that reached double figures before meeting an honourable and pain-free death. Respect for the quarry is at the heart of angling.

Apply to the **Natural Resources Information Centre, Room M1-73, Macdonald Block, 900 Bay Street, Toronto, Ontario M7A 2C1, Canada,** for Non-residents Fishing Licences and the Sport Fishing Regulations booklet published by the Ministry of Natural Resources.

PRINCE EDWARD ISLAND. This island, which lies in the Gulf of St Lawrence off the north coast of **Nova Scotia,** has an enviable reputation for its speckled trout fishing. The streams and rivers are spring fed, and the whole province may be considered a natural hatchery for trout and salmon. The salmon fishing, however, is not first class, and the best runs, with the exception of an early run on the **Morell River,** do not begin until towards the end of the season. Both non-migratory and migratory trout are to be caught. Fishing for rainbow trout can be had in **Glenfinnan,** and **O'Keefe's lakes.** Noted trout streams are the **West, Morell** and **Dunk** rivers, and large freshwater dams also afford good sport. Mackerel fishing is becoming popular (late July to September) in coastal waters.

Further information may be obtained from the **Prince Edward Island Visitor Services Division, PO Box 940,** and **Dept of Environmental Resources, Fish and Wildlife Unit, PO Box 2000,** both **Charlottetown, PE1.** Post codes **C1A 7M5** and **C1A 7N8** respectively.

QUÉBEC. Québec is lavishly laced with countless lakes and rivers where a variety of fishing keeps anglers smiling. Over the last few years, the entire Québec population has enjoyed equal access to the wildlife resources. More than 1,200 private clubs have been replaced by a network of some 73 ZECs, (Zones where Exploitation is Controlled) which are managed by non-profit organizations authorized by the Government. The present network offers clients some 65 territories, well populated by a rich variety of wildlife species on a land area covering 44,000km, and eight salmon fishing territories spread along a course of 568km of river.

Fishing and many other activities may be enjoyed in Québec Parks and Wildlife Reserves. Fishing may be engaged in by a variety of options: by the day or with stayover; on a lake from a boat or by wading in some streams. The Québec fishing licence is mandatory in all parks and wildlife reserves.

Some private enterprises also offer anglers and hunters a number of accompanying services, including accommodation - these are outfitter establishments. Some outfitter establishments hold exclusive fishing, hunting and trapping rights. Those who want to practise any one of these activities within the boundaries of an outfitter's establishment, must engage the services of the establishment concerned.

Québec's Ministère du Loisir, de la Chasse et de la Pêche, (Recreation, Fish and Game department), provides opening and closing dates on fishing, hunting and trapping seasons, wildlife species, licences, rates, regulations, among others. Available free of charge is the booklet 'Parks and Wildlife Reserves'.

These publications may be obtained by written request or by telephone. The mailing address is: **Ministère du Loisir, de la Chasse et de la Pêche, 150, Boul. Rene Levesque est, Québec, QC, G1R 4Y1.** Telephone: (418) 643-3127.

SASKATCHEWAN. Pike, perch and walleye are found throughout the province and represent the largest portion of the sport catch. Lake trout and arctic grayling are plentiful in the northern areas. Rainbow, brook, brown and splake trout are stocked in streams and lakes throughout the province.

Further information (including details of limits, accommodations, outfitters, guides and licence charges) is available from **Tourism Saskatchewan, Economic Development, 1919 Saskatchewan Drive, Regina, Saskatchewan S4P 3V7,** tel: 1 306 787 2300, fax: 1 306 787 5744.

THE UNITED STATES OF AMERICA

The United States of America covers an enormous area of land and water space, offering everything between the near-Arctic conditions met in winter near the 49th parallel and the semi-tropical climate of Florida, Louisiana and Arizona, providing almost every conceivable environmental opportunity for freshwater or saltwater fish-species to exploit to their full advantage. This creates a great swathe of corresponding angling opportunities on such a scale that holidays spent fishing and camping in the backwoods have long been a commonplace of the American way of life as holidays on the coast - and, more recently, on the shores of the Mediterranean - have been of the British.

Such a demand compels a supply: and there is nowhere in the world where so sophisticated a blend of modern comfort and primitive atmosphere can be found at the waterside, made, as it were, to measure. And signs reading 'Keep out: fishing private' are not readily to be found in America. Apart from small lakes on private land immediately adjacent to private homes, the water and its inhabitants are the property of the community, managed expertly for the good of all by the community's public agencies. Fishing may not literally be 'free', but it is available to all with a few dollars to invest in recreation. The US population is four times Britain's; but the space available for it is ten times greater.

Because of the way in which, traditionally, exchange-rates and living costs have related, the USA has never in the past figured as a place where the adventurous British angler was likely to take a fishing holiday. All that, though, has now changed and it makes just as much sense, financially and otherwise, for an Englishman to holiday in **Tennessee,** fishing for large-mouth bass, or in **Minnesota** in search of *Esox masquinongy,* as for a Texan to come to Scotland to catch a Spey salmon. Going out from the **Florida Keys** in pursuit of marlin, sailfish or tarpon has for many years been a branch of the sport attracting a trickle of wealthy Britishers, but fishing American freshwaters has been a practice confined to angling writers and such, out to broaden their professional education.

Since it is the state geographically nearest to Britain, let us begin our review of the northern tier of states and their fishing with **Maine,** whose beaches offer the classical opportunity to contact the greatest of all saltwater sporting fish to be angled feasibly from the shore anywhere, the striped bass. Though scarcer now than in years gone by, unfortunately, there are still fine specimens to be taken by the persistent specialist surf-caster. Offshore, there are cod and pollack, the bluefin tuna, some of these registering on the beam-scale weights of more than 500lb.

Inland, there is a multitude of wilderness lakes and streams offering sport with smallmouth bass, brown and rainbow trout and the unique native of Eastern North America, the brook trout, actually a fine handsome member of the char family. Atlantic salmon which ran Maine's rivers by the ten thousand a hundred years ago suffered near-extermination, but are now being nursed back by conservation technology.

Moving west to the **Great Lakes,** thoughts turn back to another char, the 'lake trout', a fish which grows to great size in deep and cold water throughout this latitude and in Canada. One fishes for them in hopes of a 40-pounder. An attempt to pass over without comment the damage done to some waters, the Great Lakes included, by the consequences of unthinking industrialisation would be dishonest, but remedy is now the order of the day. None has been more spectacular in its success than the stocking of **Lake Michigan** with coho salmon from the Pacific shore. Here, a new and tremendously exciting sport-fishery has been created, as it were, out of nothing, based on a food-supply left uncropped by lake trout no longer present in sufficient numbers to preserve a natural balance. Most see that as a net gain. The coho gives better sport than the 'Mackinaw', as it is sometimes named farther north.

On to a state where water-area challenges land-space: **Minnesota,** as the North American Indian dialect-name implies, and the cream of the fishing for great northern pike (our pike), walleyes (resembling our zander) and the greatest lantern-jaw of them all, *Esox masquinongy,* the muskellunge or 'muskie'. While these predators are distributed throughout the region, Minnesota is the heartland. Muskies there may grow to 80lb weight and leap like trout when hooked.

Passing through a varied landscape, some of it watered by trout streams, we arrive eventually among the foothills of the **Rockies,** where the brilliantly-coloured dolly varden and cut-throat trout (the former another char, to be pedantic) and representatives of the five sub-species of the so-called 'golden' trout join the ranks awaiting the angler's thinning, not to mention the sea-going rainbow trout, the steelhead. It was in the Rocky Mountain watershed that the rainbow, sedentary and sea-going, was first encountered and employed to provide the bloodstock for the eventual artificial populating of the entire temperate world with this enormously successful species.

Over the mountains: the ocean: and the feeding grounds of the Pacific salmon, five species, of which two, the king or 'Tyee' and the coho, are of sporting significance.

Going back East and starting again farther south, we traverse a band of warmer states, less favourable to the cold-water salmonids, but affording an ideal environment for pickerel (another pike-species) and for the small-mouth and large-mouth bass, the fish on which the romance of North American angling is largely founded. These big athletic cousins of the

European perch (called there, incidentally, the 'yellow perch') hit surface flies and lures with astonishing ferocity, fight like tigers when hooked and lie habitually in the shade and cover of the water-plant zone where only the most expert of tackle-handlers can present the offering and cope with the ensuing seizure without disaster. As the cooler uplands are again reached, the typical population of the upland waters is met again, and the pattern replicates.

Repeat the journey starting in **Georgia**, and one covers territory with a yet warmer climate, swamplands, and then an area of low rainfall. Traditionally, what fishing there was did not enjoy sporting prestige. The image was one of a poor coloured man employing crude tackle to harvest cheap protein; a typical quarry, the Mississippi catfish. One is south of that section of the lowland region where water temperature falls low enough to permit salmonids to spawn successfully in natural waters.

But the water-demand for growing population growing also in affluence has necessitated the construction of chains of dams in the drier states; vast new sheets of deep water offering environments novel in their setting, with a variety of temperature regimes encouraging the successful introduction of some of the great sporting species found naturally to the north and west. Even **Arizona** - the 'dry county' itself - now provides fine fishing for sport, and offers it in hot sunshine, a combination of pleasures not frequently encountered by the proverbially frozen-fingered angler acquiring lumbago from his water-logged nether end.

We have discussed none but the prime sporting species. They, however, are not the last word. US waters are inhabited also by others; carp, blue-gill sunfish, crappies and what-have-you, fish present in higher population densities and easier to catch, fish whose presence has traditionally ensured that the less expert members of the specialist angler's family on holiday may take their share of the pleasures and the triumphs. The travel business had now started international operations in this field and British anglers can expect a rapid growth in attractive opportunities.

MEXICO

Freshwater fishing: river trout fishing has been spoilt by local netting, but during the past few years black-bass fishing has become popular in Mexico, with exaggerated claims of 100 to 200 bass per day. For information about **Vicente Guerrero Dam**, near Ciudad Victoria, (fishing license 10 dollars per week), write to Sunbelt Hunting and Travel Inc., Box 3009, Brownsville, Texas 78520. For **Diaz Ordaz Dam**, contact Roberto Balderrama, Santa Anita Hotel, Los Mochis, Sinaloa. 8lb bass are common here, and at the San Lorenzo Dam, near Xicotencatl. Sea fishing: popular spots are Acapulco, Puerto Valarta, Manzanillo, Mazatlan, Guaymas, Loreto, La Paz, Cancun, Cozumel, Tampico, Veracruz, Cabo San Lucas and Jose del Cabo, with improved facilities. Good charter boats are available, with expert crews. Amongst coastal species are Pargo, yellowtail, rock bass, grouper, barracuda, totoava, snook, giant sea bass. Pelagic species include blue and striped marlin, yellowfin tuna, black marlin, bonito, sailfish, swordfish and mackerel. These are usually found a good distance from the shore. For more information contact Mexican Fishing Federation, Londres 250, Mexico D.F. Bonefishing is a sport practised by U.S. anglers in Quintana Roo, near Cancum. Write to *Turismo Boca Paila S.A. de C.V.*, Apartado Postal 59, Cozumel, Quintana Roo, Mexico 77600.

The **Mexican Ministry of Tourism** has an office at **60/61 Trafalgar Square, London WC2N 5DS** (tel 071-734 1058) from which more detailed information can be obtained.

THE CARIBBEAN

Forty years ago, so little was the Caribbean exploited by the indigenous peoples dwelling on its islands and about its shores that the United Nations Food & Agriculture Organisation gave a priority to the encouragement of commercial fishing there. What little fish was eaten in Central America had come traditionally in the form of salted fillets imported from countries - Norway and North America particularly - which had well-established cold water fisheries for cod in the prolific waters of the North Atlantic and the Arctic.

Various geophysical features were thought at that time to inhibit the Caribbean from ever becoming a region rich in exploitable fish populations. That, in one sense, may have been correct, but there are more ways than one of exploiting a resource, a fact already known by that time to charter-boat proprietors operating out of Florida resorts to crop the wonderful harvest of American anglers in search of sport more dramatic than the salmon or the

An exciting addition to the sport - fly fishing for 'bill-fish' (marlin, swordfish, sailfish) in the Caribbean. The sailfish above weighed 120 lbs. After photography it was returned unharmed to the water in compliance with the conservationist policies of the Costa Rican Government. The fishing party was out from Bahia Paz Vela. *Photo: Evelyn Letfuss.*

muskellunge could offer in freshwater.

Thus the possibilities of the **Gulf of Mexico** and the seas around the **Bahamas** became known - marlin, swordfish, sawfish, sailfish, barracuda, tarpon and tuna the quarry, individual fish which took angling statistics from measurement by the pound to measurement by the hundredweight. The same geophysical conditions which had led to doubts as to the possibility of upgrading national catches of readily marketable fish for human consumption in the region had concentrated the big predators at water-depths where they could be found and profitably angled for.

During these forty years, facilities for Big Game fishing as it soon became known, spread progressively throughout the area and one may now fish for these splendid creatures from bases in **Mexico, Honduras, Nicaragua, Costa Rica, Panama, Colombia, Venezuela** (which was the first country in the region seriously to exploit its fish stocks in the traditional fashion) and the oceanic islands all the way south to **Trinidad.**

Originally, the big fish were angled for with a trolled dead bait and tackle powerful enough to master a bolting horse. Nowadays they are sought for with the fly rod, too, reflecting the fact that official records are maintained not only for maximum species weights, globally speaking, but for tackle categories, too, expressed in terms of line-strength - i.e. IGFA rules.

Astonishingly, billfish - to use the up-to-date term for swordfish and sailfish species grouped together - five feet in length have been brought to the glove in ten minutes from hooking with a conventional fly rod and single-action fly reel.

Tourist offices in London maintained by Mexico and Islands in the West Indies give details on hotels, facilities for boat charter, (with professional help integral to the hire-package) and of what restrictions apply to limits, seasons, and species of fish and other marine quarry which are excluded locally from the angler's activities. These restrictions are not onerous.

ANTIGUA AND BARBUDA

Antigua and **Barbuda** have developed their big game fishing. Marlin, sailfish, tuna, wahoo, snapper, grouper, angel, trigger, margate, amber jack, black jack, and barracuda are all present around the islands, according to the conformation of the sea-bed. There are many reefs and coral formations. Lobster fishing is particularly good around the wrecks off Barbuda, which number more than 50. Anglers should note that use of dynamite is strictly forbidden. Boats are available out of Marora Bay and from Catamaran Hotel, Falmouth, tel: 31036.

For further information contact the **Antigua and Barbuda Tourist Office, Antigua House, 15 Thayer Street, London W1M 5LD** (tel. 071-486 7073/5).

THE BAHAMAS

The Bahamas comprise twelve major groups of islands spaced over 1,000 square miles or more of ocean. **Bimini** is probably the best known of the fishing centres and it was here that the largest Bahamian marlin recorded by an angler - a fish weighing more than 1,000 lbs - was brought into harbour.

But **San Salvador, Exuma, Long Island, Eleuthera, Cat Island, Andros, Nassau, Chub Cay,** the **Abacos, Grand Bahama, Great Harbour Cay** and **Harbour Island** all offer splendid opportunities for sport. Tournaments are held frequently throughout the islands: hotels catering specially for anglers abound. Charter rates vary with duration of fishing trips and species sought.

One can buy two day's fishing for bonefish for $604, including three nights luxury accommodation, bait, packed lunches and a professional guide, or pay $600 a day for the fishing alone.

The **Bahamas Tourist Office at 10 Chesterfield Street, London W1X 8AH** (tel. 071-491 9311) supplies brochures giving details of many alternative programmes, fully costed.

BERMUDA

Licences are not required: twenty-six species, including billfish and five species of tuna, are there to be caught in Bermudian waters. Charter boats are available the year round, supply and demand peaking from May to November. Seventeen operators are named in the information given by the **Bermuda Tourist Office at 1 Battersea Church Road, London SW11 3LY** (tel. 071-734 8813). The majority are operated under the auspices of the **Bermuda Sport Fishing Association, Creek View House, 8 Tulo Lane, Pembroke HM O2** (10 boats); **Charter Fishing Boat Association, PO Box SB 145, Sandys SB BX** (2 boats); and **St. George's Game Fishing and Cruising Association, PO Box GE 107, St. George's GE**

BX. The remainder are operated by independent charter fishermen. Hotel facilities are excellent.

LESSER ANTILLES
South of Puerto Rico is the chain of small islands known as the **Lesser Antilles** - the **Leeward** and **Windward** groups.

PUERTO RICO
Puerto Rico also offers developed facilities for big game fishing. There is an office of the **Commonwealth of Puerto Rico Tourism Co. at 67 Whitfield Street, London W1P 5RL** (tel. 071-636 6558).

TRINIDAD AND TOBAGO
Finally, **Trinidad** & **Tobago,** the large islands which lie just off the coast of Venezuela and terminate the chain. Their waters, too, are abundantly supplied with billfish species, tuna, tarpon, barracuda and many other species of interest to the angler, if offering rather less dramatic sport than the 'stars' on the angler's stage. The tourist office, **8A Hammersmith Broadway, London, W6 7AL** (tel 081-741 4466) supplies names and addresses of charter-boat operators in both islands.

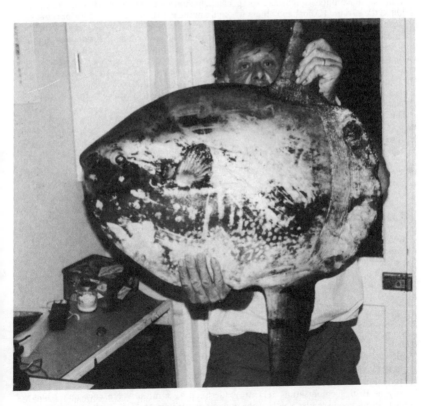

44lb sunfish caught off West Bay, Dorset by David Choldcroft. Only a tiddler by international standards, sunfish in favourable conditions grow to 13ft in length and more than 3000lbs in weight.

SOUTH AMERICA

BRAZIL. This is a vast country in the same league as China, Canada, Australia and the United States of America. With the world's biggest river draining it, it lacks neither water nor fish.

Anglers from the USA have already explored its possibilities with exciting results, but little of the country has yet been opened to international angling and it is in the southern half of the sub-continent that the sport has been energetically developed.

ARGENTINA. Here, although the South Atlantic is probably now the world's most productive fishing zone, the emphasis in terms of sport shifts back to freshwater fishing. Salmonids were introduced from the northern hemisphere many years ago - land-locked salmon *(Salmo salar sebago)* the brown trout (in both its sedentary and migratory forms) and the brook trout *(Salvelinus fortinalis)*. The home of these species is in the Andean lake district. Specimen brook trout up to 10lbs, have been caught; in the case of the other species named, specimens topping 30lbs.

In the river-catchments of the lower-lying regions of the country, especially those of the **Parana** and **Plata,** there are two fine native species of fish, the dorado *(Salminus maxillosus)* and the perch *(Percicathys trucha)* which are rated as highly or higher than salmonids. The perch grows to weights approaching 20lbs, while the dorado reaches a weight of 50lbs.

In the same habitats are found other species which grow to be enormous - the mangururu (200lbs) the surubi (120lbs) and others which do not reach such spectacular weights but still offer splendid sport.

Spinning from a boat piloted by a guide is the usual method of fishing for dorado, but they will also take a fly (not exactly a blue winged olive!) and in an Argentinean torrent quite a challenge to the fly rod, also the fish it naturally feeds on, offered as either a live or a dead bait. This splendid sporting fish is found throughout the catchments of the rivers Plata and Parana. Centres specially recommended for the quality of the fishing guides, boats and accommodation are **Paso de la Patria** (Corrientes), **Isla del Carrito** (Chaco) and **Posadas** (Misiones).

The best fishing is in the summer - August to March. Annual competitions are held early in the season. Five vast National Parks offer the best of the fishing for salmonids, all of them on the west side of the country, in the uplands bordering Chile.

From **Punta Piedras** in the north to **Tierra del Fuego** in the extreme south, Argentina has more than 2,200 miles of Atlantic coastline. The water so far south is too cold for tuna, billfish and tarpon, but their place is taken for the big game angler by all the Atlantic species of shark.

For the Argentineans themselves, though, the peak of the sea angling year is when the warm current from Brazil brings down the black corvina, whose shoals provide many specimens of 40lbs, and better. **San Clemente de Tuyu** is the most famous centre for fishing the corvina, where the fish arrive in December. They then work their way down the coast, arriving in **Bahia Blanca** in February. There is plenty of shore fishing, but boats are to be had, though not on quite the sophisticated scale to be met with in the Gulf of Mexico and the Caribbean.

Very good information is provided by the tourist office at the **Consulado General de la Republica Argentina, 5th Floor, 100 Brompton Road, London SW3 1ER** (tel. 071 589 3104).

CHILE. Chile's coastline matches that of the neighbouring Argentine, but the fishing promoted is that for introduced salmonids, especially in Chilean Patagonia. The trout run extremely large; the country in that region is thinly populated and attractively wild, the climate mild. The cities recommended as start-points for the angler are **Temuco, Puerto Montt** and **Coihaque.** All are accessible by air or rail from **Santiago.**

THE FALKLAND ISLANDS. One of the least known tourist attractions in the South Atlantic, but for the angler the best researched and the most promising. How else? - with its history of British colonisation, recently underlined by a military presence and a notable victory. From nowhere else south of the equator has **Where to Fish** received such comprehensive information. The whole development of sea trout fishing in the Falklands has taken place in less than a lifetime. Nature left the Islands with only the Falkland trout - *(aplochiton* *zebra)* which is not a trout or even a char, and a few minor species in its rivers. The first real trout *(Salmo trutta)* were introduced less than forty years ago, but a fast growing migratory strain quickly became established and spread around the islands, giving us today some of the finest sea trout fishing in the world.

Sea trout of five to ten pounds are common, and many fish in excess of ten pounds are taken every season. The best recorded sea trout taken on a fly to date was 22lb 12.5oz, caught on the San Carlos River by Alison Faulkner.

The main sea trout rivers - the **Warrah** and **Chartres** on West Falkland and the **San Carlos** on East Falkland - are ideal for fly fishing, with treeless banks being free of casting obstructions. However a strong wind often blows, so this is no place for a poor caster with mediocre tackle. Farmhouse accommodation at Little Chartres Farm, within walking distance of the River Chartres, is available for very small groups.

Most rivers have fair numbers of resident brown trout, but most are small, dark fish, typical of acid rivers.

Major sea trout rivers where visitor accommodation and guides are available

West Falkland
Warrah River: Can be fished from **Port Howard Settlement,** where accommodation is available. The river is about 12 miles from the settlement. The main tributary, the **Green Hills Stream,** which is crossed on the way to the Warrah, is also worth fishing.

East Falkland
San Carlos River: Administered jointly by the local farmer and the owner of Blue Beach Lodge, the river is accessed through San Carlos settlement. Blue Beach Lodge offers comfortable accommodation, while the permanent San Carlos Fishing Camp offers more basic facilities within walking distance of fresh water where good catches are reported.

Mullet fishing: as a bonus, you will probably come into contact with the Falkland mullet *(Eleginus falklandicus)* if fishing in tidal water. Like the British mullet, the Falkland species follows the tide right into shallow water, where it can be seen swimming just below the surface with a very obvious wake, but there the similarity ends. It is not even related to our mullet and is much larger, with fish recorded up to 20 pounds and mullet of 8 pounds are quite common. The dorsal fin runs virtually from head to tail along a tapering body, and the pectoral fins are huge in relation to the size of the fish.

The Falkland mullet is a powerful fish which makes long runs and would be much valued as a game fish if it existed in Britain. It often takes the sea-trout angler's fly or spinner, but the local method normally used is to suspend a piece of mutton (fresh sheep meat) on a size 4 or 2 hook a couple of feet below a small pike bung. This tackle is cast out wherever there are signs of mullet activity, and the response is rarely long delayed.

Small to medium mullet can be caught virtually on your doorstep at places like **Port Howard.** The really large fish are often found in specific locations, at some distance from the settlements. It is worth considering setting aside a little time for a trip specifically for big mullet.

Flights leave Brize Norton on Mondays and alternate Thursdays. Return flights leave Mount Pleasant in the Falklands on Wednesdays and alternate Saturdays.

Accommodation for fishermen is available at Stanley, Blue Beach, San Carlos Fishing Camp and Little Chartres. There are also lodges in wildlife centres (fishermen may like to take some time off to see the large colonies of penguins, seals and other wildlife).

The **Falkland Islands Tourist Board** office is at **Falkland House, 14 Broadway, Westminster, London, SW1H 0BH.** (Tel 071-222 2542).

NOTE. The tourist board strongly recommend that visitors travel with a recognised tour operator.

FISHING IN EUROPE

AUSTRIA

Austria is understandably popular with anglers from all over the world, with its abundance of streams and lakes, providing first-class sport with brown and rainbow trout, grayling, char, and coarse fish such as pike and pike-perch, huck, sheat-fish and carp. Some of the main centres tend to be overfished, so a car is immensely valuable; many mountain streams of indescribable beauty are easily reached by road. Much of the sport is on the lower reaches of these mountain rivers, but the more venturesome can often find better fishing on the high alpine streams and lakes. Grayling are highly regarded, often more so than trout, the **Traun** and the **Lammer** being two of the best grayling rivers in Europe. **Salza, Traisen, Erlauf** and **Ybbs** are other recommended rivers.

To keep the sport at a high level, the authorities maintain strict conservation measures and a specially close watch is kept on pollution and abstraction. Generally speaking the rule is fly only for trout, grayling and char. Spinning is usually only permitted for larger fish such as lake trout, pike, huck, pike-perch (depending on the local authority) and so on, and natural bait and sheatfish only for coarse fisheries. Many waters are controlled by the two principal fishing associations, the Austrian Fishing Association (ÖFG) and the Association of Austrian Workers' Fishing Clubs (VÖAFV). The former issues temporary permits for several trout preserves as well as daily ones costing up to 600 Austrian schillings. Temporary permission and information can be obtained from the association's office. The same applies to the VÖAFV. There is a provincial fishing association in Upper Austria which issues licences *(see below for addresses)*.

Wherever he fishes, the visitor usually needs two permits, a general licence issued by the State and costing up to 240 Austrian schillings, according to the province - or a temporary fishing permit from the local owner costing up to 120 schillings for up to 4 weeks - and a private permit from the local owner which usually costs from 50-150 schillings a day, but . may be as much as 600.

Accommodation is no problem, as many fine hotels offer anglers first class facilities on the more important lakes and rivers. More information and angling booklets can be obtained from the **Austrian National Tourist Office, 30 St George Street, London W1R 0AL** (071-629 0461). Addresses of the main angling association are **Österreichische Fischereige- sellschaft, 1010 Wien 1, Elisabethstrasse 22; Verband der Österreichischen Arbeiter- Fischerei-Vereine, A-1080, Wien VIII, Lenaugasse, 14**; and **Landesfischereiverein (Provincial Fishing Assn), Postfach 185, A-4021, Linz.**

BELGIUM

Although Belgium has never made a name for itself as a visiting fisherman's country, it has, in fact, in its many canals and rivers, most of the fish which British fishermen know, with sea fishing along its 40 miles of coast.

In general terms the freshwater fishing water can be divided thus: The **Scheldt** basin, with the rivers **Scheldt, Lys, Rupel, Dyle, Demer, Dendre** and **Nèthe** holding bream, roach, perch, pike, smelt, shad and eels; the **Meuse** basin, with the rivers **Meuse, Semois, Lesse, Sambre, Ourthe, Amblève, Warche** and **Vesdre** holding trout, grayling, chub, barbel, perch, roach, bream, pike, carp, tench and eels; and the streams between the Sambre and the Meuse, holding trout, grayling, chub, perch, pike, roach, bream, carp, tench and eels. Many waters of the lowlands and near industrial centres suffer from pollution and overfish- ing.

All Belgian waters fall into one of three categories; closed water, not subject to fishing laws; public, or navigable, water belonging to the State; preserved, or non-navigable water belonging to the landowners. Waters in the last two groups are subject to the fishing laws, and anyone fishing in them must possess a current licence. The cost varies from 30 francs to 500 francs, according to the type of fishing, number of rods used and the number of days' fishing to be done in a week. Trout fishermen should note, for example, that they will need a 500-franc licence to enter the water, in addition to any other permit necessary. Licences may be obtained at post offices. The close seasons are: Coarse fish, from the Monday following the fourth Sunday of March until the second Sunday of June, with certain exceptions; trout, October 1 to fourth Sunday of March. Fly fishing falls off sharply on the Ardennes streams after June.

For visiting trout fishers the greatest attraction probably lies in the streams of the **Ardennes**, where many hotels have private fishing and there is a good deal of association water. These are mostly mixed fisheries on the lines of the Hampshire Avon in England, with trout and grayling predominating in the upper reaches and being increasingly joined by coarse fish on moving downstream. The best fishing will usually be found in the least accessible places. Standard British fly patterns will take fish on the Ardennes streams but the local flies should be tried where possible.

Sea fishing along the sandy, shelving coast is largely for dabs and plaice (Oct-June), flounders (all year) and sole (May-Oct), with piers and breakwaters providing sport with conger (all year), cod (Sept-Mar), and whiting (Oct-Jan). Turbot are occasionally taken (May-Sept) and rays, shad and garfish are also caught (Sept-Oct), **Zeebrugge, Ostend, Niewpoort, Blakenbergh,** and **Knokke-Heist** are good centres.

Belgian fishing legislation is extremely complex and anglers are strongly advised to consult the local tourist centres. For example, **Namur** province publishes a special angling brochure in French. Further detailed information (in English) from the **Belgian National Tourist Office, Premier House, 2 Gayton Road, Harrow, Middlesex HA1 2XU** (081-861 3300) and, in Belgium itself, from the secretary of the **Fédération Sportive des Pêcheurs Francophones de Belgique. N H Balzat, rue de Wynants 33, 1000 Brussels,** tel: 25 11 68 48; and from the secretary of the **Fédération de Pêche en Mer, Parc Leopold 14, 8410 Wenduine,** tel: 50 41 33 92.

DENMARK

Fishing in Denmark is plentiful, varied and easy to come by. A few of the rivers hold salmon, and many of them sea trout, brown trout and grayling, as well as coarse fish, which are found also in many lakes.

In many places visitors can fish by purchasing tickets from the local fishing association. The association tickets are invariably cheap and available through local tourist bureaus.

The principal rivers are all in **Jutland.** They are **Skjern Aa, Store Aa, Varde Aa, Ribe Aa** and **Karup Aa.** All are game-fish waters, most of them the best salmon fishing is probably to be had on the Skjern and the best sea trout fishing on the Karup. The water is generally good for fly fishing, and the flies used are much the same as those used in this country. Spinning is much practised. Added variety is given by the sea trout fishing which can be had from the rocks and from boats off both the mainland and the various Baltic islands.

Denmark has a coastline of 7,500 kilometres, much of it unfished but accessible, with good possibilities for cod, coalfish, flatfish, tope, mackerel, garfish, whiting, ling and pollack, and for turbot, brill, plaice, sole, dab and flounder. One should not fish within 50 metres of a private dwelling place without the owners permission. Anglers are warned about the danger of breakwater fishing from **Jutland** west coast in rough weather.

Salmon and sea trout fishing in fresh water is best from Apr/May to July, and September (salmon), June to Sept, and Oct/Nov, smaller rivers (sea trout).

The coarse fishing potential is considerable and relatively unexplored. Many lakes are hardly ever fished and could hold some surprises, notably for the carp fisherman.

Further information about both fishing and accommodation can be had from the **Danish Tourist Board, Sceptre House, 169-173 Regent Street, London, W1R 8PY** (071-734 2637).

FINLAND

Finland can offer the angler no fewer than 187,888 lakes and rivers, and some 3,000 miles of sea-shore and archipelago. In the north and centre of the country he can catch very big fish on very big, remote waters; conditions which, in Europe at any rate, are becoming increasingly harder to find. The long days of midsummer give plenty of fishing time - the best sport in fact is often enjoyed in the brief twilight which elsewhere is called 'night'. In the South and in the archipelago area the best fishing periods are spring and autumn.

Salmon, sea trout, brown trout and brook trout all run well above the European average, and the size of grayling, too, is often remarkable; four-pounders are not rare. There are also arctic char *(Salvelinus alpinus)* which in the right conditions will take a fly.

The cream of the sport is to be found in **Lapland,** though there are individual waters farther south which can match them in quality. Some of the best game fishing in Europe is to be found in the region north of **Lake Inari,** and especially the rivers emptying into the lake. A very good possibility is the lake itself, holding taimen, very big grayling and brown trout to 20lb and more. Best fished for during their migratory runs up the tributaries in late summer.

The salmon fishing, however, is not what it was. Hydro-electric schemes have ruined the runs in many famous waterways. Salmon rivers are, however, recovering and several of them can be offered for salmon and sea trout fishing - the **Kiiminki,** the **Simo,** the **Lesti,** and the **Tornio** which Finland shares with Sweden.

There are problems, too, for the fly fisherman. Many rivers are so wide, deep and fastflowing that comfortable fishing from the bank is out of the question; it is often impossible to reach the salmon and sea trout lies, in fact. Hence on great rivers like the **Teno** and **Näätämö** which flow along the frontier with Norway, the fishing is mainly from a boat with an outboard motor from which large flies are cast by short but stout rods over enormous pools and streams - a technique known as 'harling'. Reels carrying 250 yards of line of up to 1mm thick and over 40lb breaking strain are employed.

These rivers, incidentally, are subject to special rules, involving the purchase of a permit from both countries in those parts through which the common national frontier passes. They are heavily poached. The spring fishing is usually best.

Another problem is transport - many of the best waters are 'off the beaten track' and although there are excellent air services between the main centres, after that the angler is on his own and must be prepared for a good deal of foot-slogging and camping. A car, with a fibreglass boat strapped to the roof, is a valid alternative where the roads are not too bad.

The Finnish coast with its large archipelago, not to mention the **Aland Islands,** offers very good prospects for trout, pike, and perch-fishers. Even the immediate surroundings of big cities should not be ignored. As to the catch - the sea area is best.

Some very good coarse fishing is to be found in the south, notably for pike and perch and pike-perch - not, as many believe, a hybrid, but a separate species. Opportunities for the fly fisherman in the south have been extended in recent years by the stocking of ponds with rainbow, brown and brook trout.

The National Board of Forestry administers 85 fisheries, which it manages mainly by restocking. Most of these are in eastern and northern Finland.

Fishing regulations are strict and strictly enforced - there are game wardens even in remote districts. A licence is required. They can be bought at post offices or branches of Postipankki (closed Sat and Sun). Then a fishing permit must be bought from the owners of the local fishing waters.

Close seasons: salmon and trout, Sept 10-Nov 16; pike-perch, June; grayling, April and May. In the Aland Islands shore fishing is banned between 15 Apr and 15 June, in order to protect nesting sea birds

One important accessory for the angler is some form of repellant to ward off mosquito attacks, which can often be unbearable - some Finnish fishermen wear head-nets.

Further information can be obtained from the **Finnish Tourist Board, UK Office, 66/68 Haymarket, London SW1Y 4RF.** Tel: 071-930 5871.

FRANCE

Excellent sport with trout and some salmon fishing are available at reasonable cost in this country. French waterways are divided into the navigable public rivers, where fishing rights are owned by the State, and private rivers, where they belong to the riparian owner, fishing association or local authority. Even on the public rivers, however, anglers must belong to an angling and fish-breeding association and pay a tax based on the method of fishing adopted. Most rivers of this type provide coarse fishing only. Trout and salmon rights will nearly always be privately held, but the visitor should have little difficulty in obtaining a permit. Information should be sought from the local club or tackle dealer.

Close seasons vary a great deal according to the locality, especially for salmon, and it is best to make local inquiries. A rough guide, however, would be: salmon, Oct 1 to Jan 10; trout and char, from last Tuesday in Sept to third Friday in Feb; coarse fish, from Tuesday following April 15 to Friday following June 15.

Perhaps the best salmon fishing in France is to be found on a small number of fast flowing

Anglers from Britain often visit France these days for the excellent carp fishing found in its kindlier climate. Dr. Bruno Broughton, organiser of the tackle trade's Angling Foundation, displays a fine specimen from a reservoir on the R. Lot. *Photo by the angler.*

streams in the **Western Pyrenees.** The noted **Gave d'Oloron** is in this area. **Oloron, Sauveterre** and **Navarrenx** are good centres for this river. The **Gave d'Aspe,** which joins it at Oloron, and its tributary, the **Lourdios,** have provided good sport in recent years. They may be fished from **Lurbe.** At **Peyrehorade** the Gave d'Oloron is joined by the **Gave de Pau,** on which sport has also been improving, and Pau itself makes a fine place to stay. Salmon also run up the **Gaves d'Ossau** and **de Nive.**

Because of melting snow, the season begins later here than elsewhere in France, but it extends later, too. For the Oloron area the best months are from June to the end of August.

Brittany, too, provides some opportunities for the salmon fisherman, though the fish are on the small side, especially on the **River Aulne,** which flows into the sea near **Brest.** Try the **Châteaulinn** area until April and **Chateauneuf-du-Faou** later on. Châteaulinn is also a good centre for the **Ell'le** and from **Landerneau** and **Landivisiau** the **Ellorn** may be fished. Other productive streams are the **Blavet, Laita** and **Odet,** which flow into the Atlantic; the **Trieux** and its tributary the **Leff,** with **Guingamp** a suitable venue.

Flowing northwards through picturesque countryside to feed the **Loire,** the **Allier** offers the best opportunities for salmon fishermen in **Auvergne.** This is a region comparatively unknown to British anglers. The place to make for is **Brioude,** on the upper reaches of the river. The **Bajace dam,** where salmon congregate before taking the leap, is half a mile away. **Vichy, Pont-du-Château, Veyre** and **Issoire** are other centres. The upper reaches of the Loire itself can provide good sport. **Roanne** is a suitable place to stay.

Some of the **Normandy** rivers have good runs of fish, but the best of the fishing is hard to come by, being largely in the hands of syndicates. The visitor may find opportunities, however, on the **Orne** and **Vire,** the **Sée,** the **Sienne** and the **Sélune; Pontfarcy, Quetteville, Avranches** and **Ducey** are suggested centres.

France is a splendid country for the trout fisherman, with an abundance of well-stocked streams flowing through glorious scenery. He may find solitude and beauty not very far from Paris - in fact, on the upper reaches of the **Seine** and its tributary, the **Ource.** A little farther south lies **Avallon,** from which the **Cure** and its tributaries may be fished.

But the visitor will find the **Pyrenees** very hard to beat for trout. The **Gave d'Ossau** is one of the best of the many first-class streams in this area, offering particularly fine sport at the **Fabrège dam.** From **Lurbe** the **Gave d'Aspe** and its tributary, the **Lourdios,** may be fished, and excellent sport is available on the **Gave d'Oloron** above **Pont-de-Dognen,** the **Nive** above **Itxassou,** and the **Gave de Pau** upstream of **Pont-de-Lescar.**

In the fascinating and comparatively unexplored regions of **Creuse, Haute-Vienne, Corrèze** and **Lot,** are innumerable streams with torrential upper reaches holding fine trout. Downstream they become less tumultuous and wider until, in the **Dordogne,** they harbour a variety of coarse fish. Figeac is a good centre for the trout. Farther east lies the wild, mountainous region of **Lozère,** where grand and beautiful rivers like the **Lot** and its tributary, the **Colagne,** may be fished. The **Bès** and **Truyère** should also be tried.

Wherever one turns in France, it seems, there are trout to be caught. In the **Savoy Alps** are innumerable streams of quality, like the **Isère** and **Doron,** near **Albertville,** and the **Sierroz, Tillet** and **Chéron** near **Chatelard-en-Bauges,** the **Arvan** and **Arc,** near **Saint-Jean-de-Maurienne.** Auvergne and the **Dauphiny Alps** are ideal for the explorer with a fly rod. **Grenoble** commands a number of valleys through which flow some noted trout streams.

Normandy has some trout fisheries of high repute, like Risle, Eure, Charenton and Andelles, but they are strictly preserved for the most part. Fishing on the streams of Brittany is more easily obtainable. **Quimper** is an excellent centre for the large fish of the **Odet** and its tributaries. Trout abound throughout **Finistère,** notably in the Aulne tributaries.

The lake fisherman is also well catered for in France, with some splendid opportunities in the Pyrenees, especially near **Luz-Saint-Sauveur,** and in the Alps. **Lakes Leman, Annecy** and, farther south, **Lauvitel** and **Beason** are good for trout.

One cautionary note for the fly fisherman - many French rivers are so torrential and boulder-strewn that they cannot be fished with fly. It is as well to check with a club or tackle dealer in the area to avoid disappointment. Best months of the fly are generally May, June and Sept in the north and before April and in Sept in the south. British patterns do well in the north, but are not so good in the south.

Further details from the **French Tourist Office, 178 Piccadilly, London W1V 0AL,** who will supply literature, including their *Angling in France* brochure, on receipt of 80p in stamps.

GERMANY

Bavaria and the **Black Forest** offer the best prospects for the trout fisherman. Although pollution and over-fishing are producing a decline in sport, Bavarian waters like the **Wiesent, Pegnitz, Loisach, Isar, Ammer, Saalach** and **Salzach,** to name only a few, still offer fishing of high quality amid beautiful surroundings. Brown and rainbow trout, as well as grayling, are widely distributed.

For anglers who like to fly-fish for trout and char from a boat, the **Hintersee** at **Berchtesgaden** is highly recommended - the char in particular are good, reaching weights of 6lb and more.

In the Black Forest, streams like the **Kinzig, Murg, Obere Wolf, Nagold** and **Bernbach** provide good sport with trout and grayling. The best waters are usually fly-only.

The **Harz** mountain area, south-east of **Hanover,** is also well worth exploring - the **Radau,** fished from **Bad Harzburg,** is good. Trout are found, too, in some of the streams and lakes of the **Rhineland-Palatinate,** especially in the Eifel district, and in some parts of **North Rhine-Westphalia** and **Lower Saxony.**

Elsewhere there is good coarse fishing. In **Baden-Wuerttemberg** (apart from the Black Forest) carp, bream, tench, whitebait, roach, barbel, pike, eels and trout can be had in the **Neckar Valley,** the Hohenloe district, the **Swabian Forest** area and elsewhere, including trout, pike and barbel fishing in the **Danube.** Other coarse-fishing areas are the Rhineland Palatinate (Moselle, Ahr, Lahn), and most of Lower Saxony.

The angler will need a licence from the Landrats or Ordnungsamt (rural district council) or from the local police (Dm10 to Dm20) and a permit from the owner or lessee of the fishing. Many Hotels and clubs also have fishing rights. The principal seasons are as follows: river trout, Mar 2-Oct 9; sea trout, March 2-Oct 9; lake trout, Jan 1-Sept 30; river char, Jan 11-Oct 9; lake char, Jan 1-Oct 31; pike, May 1-Dec 31; pike-perch, July 1-Mar 31; huck, May 1 to last day of Feb. (The seasons vary slightly in the different Federal states).

Further information about fishing can be had from the **German Anglers' Association, Venusberg 36, 20459 Hamburg,** and the **Verband Deutscher Sportfischer, Siemenstrasse 11-13, 63071 Offenbach/Main,** and general tourist information from the **German National Tourist Office, 65 Curzon Street, London W1Y 7PE** (071-495 3990).

A memorable 4 lb. brown trout taken on a black wet fly from a tributary of the Danube. Stomach contents included a 6" rainbow trout and a half digested mole. *Photo: Cori Gebhart.*

HOLLAND

Fishing has become one of the biggest forms of outdoor recreation in Holland. There are about 150,000 acres of fishing waters which hold eel, carp, pike, perch, pike-perch (*Stizostedion lucioperca*), roach, bream. To fish one must have a sportvisakte or national fishing document, which is inexpensive and can be obtained from any Dutch post office, angling club or tackle shop. It is valid for a year, from 1st January to 31st December. One also needs the right licence, and this is usually obtainable by joining one of the fishing clubs affiliated to the national angling organisation NVVS.

For information on Dutch angling clubs contact **Nederlandse Vereniging van Sportvissersfederaties, Afd. Voorlichting, Postbus 288, 3800 AG Amersfoort, Holland.** Tel: 033 634924.

For general tourist information and details on accommodation, please contact the **Netherlands Board of Tourism, PO Box 523, London SW1E 6NT.** Tel: 0891 200 277.

ICELAND

There are five species of fish which are found naturally in fresh water: salmon, trout, char, common eel and stickleback. Rainbow trout were imported from Denmark about twenty years ago. Iceland has a large number of rivers, and salmon run up nearly sixty, while trout run up still more. The Icelandic salmon is usually 4-12 pounds in weight and between 55-85 cm in length, but each year a few fish of up to 30lb are caught. Sea trout average between 1-4lb, occasionally caught to 20lb, and char, normally 1-2lb, although sometimes as much as 12lb. The salmon river fishing season is short, from May 20 to Sept 20. Sea trout fishing is permitted between Apr 1 and Sept 20.

The best salmon rivers are in the southwest section, and two thirds of the Icelandic salmon are caught near **Reykjavik**, on the outskirts of which flows the most well-known salmon river in Iceland, the **Ellioaar**. In the northwest section of the country there are some quite good salmon rivers, the best of these being the **Miofjaroara**, the **Vioidalsa**, the **Vatnsdalsa**, the **Laxa** and the **Blanda**. Sea trout are fished in rivers all over the country, especially the southeast and southwest. These are caught to 20lb in the **Skafta**, to the west of the Vatnajokull glacier.

There are fewer than 100 lakes in the country of more than one sq km, and the largest of these is **Thingvallavatn**, 25 miles east of Reykjavik, surface area 82.6 sq km. The commonest fish caught there is the lake char, as well as brown trout of up to 26lb. Fishing for char of 1-6lb is available on **Medalfellsvatn**, Kjosarsysla, half and hour away from Reykjavik. Open from May 1 to Sept 20. Icelandair, 172 Tottenham Court Rd, London W1P 9LG, tel: 071 388 5599, issues a pamphlet on this and other lake fisheries in the vicinity, as well as information about salmon fishing holidays in Laxa/Kjos from £625 per day. An excellent 90 page fishing guide called *Veidiflakkarinn* is published by the Icelandic Farm Holidays Association, Baendahollin v/Hagatorg, 107 Reykjavik, which gives full details of a large number of lake and river fishings.

Daily air services are operated by Icelandair. Travel within Iceland is mostly by air and bus services. Further tourist information may be obtained from the **Iceland Tourist Information Bureau, 172 Tottenham Court Road, London W1P 9LG.**

ITALY

Fishing can be had in many parts of Italy, in rivers, mountain torrents and lakes, for trout, pike, perch, carp and several local varieties. Generally speaking, the trout fishing is in waters above the 1,800 ft contour, the close season being Oct 15 to Jan 15. Sport is often good though pollution has caused a sharp decline on many of the lowland lakes. A government rod-fishing licence issued by the Provincial Administration is required. It costs about £1.50 and is valid for a year. Ninety per cent of Italian waters are managed by the Italian Sport Fishing Federation (FIPS). Membership costs £2 and is valid for a year. The **Bolzano** and **Trentino** districts and the Dolomites are good.

Sea fishing is first class. Deep-sea sport with tuna, albacore and swordfish has become increasingly popular, and so has underwater fishing. Underwater fishing with aqualungs in all Italian waters is not permitted, though their use is allowed for other purposes. Sea sport fishing may be practised both from the shore and from a boat. Only in some ports a special permit issued by the Harbourmaster's Office is required.

Only those over sixteen are allowed to use underwater guns and such equipment. When submerged, an underwater fisherman is required to indicate the fact with a float bearing a red flag with a yellow diagonal stripe, and must operate with a radius of 50m of the support barge or the float bearing the flag. Fishing is prohibited: at under 500m from a beach used by bathers; 50m from fishing installations and ships at anchor.

The most suitable coasts for underwater fishing are those of **Sardegna, Sicilia, Aeolian Islands, Pontine Islands, Tremiti** Islands and the rocky shores of **Liguria, Tuscany, Latium, Campania, Calabria, Basilicata** and **Puglie.**

Further information can be had from the **Italian State Tourist Board in London, 1 Princes Street, London W1** (071-408 1254), from the **Federazione Italiana Pesca Sportiva e Attivita' Subaquee, Viale Tiziano 70, 00196 Roma,** or from the provincial tourist boards (their addresses may be obtained from the Tourist Board in London).

LUXEMBOURG

Most of the rivers of Luxembourg are mixed fisheries holding trout, grayling and coarse fish, including pike, barbel, chub, roach, carp and tench. Much of the water is private, although visitors can obtain sport on various hotel lengths or on private water with the owner's permission. There is a fine reservoir at the head of the Sûre, heavily stocked with lake trout, char and roach, and carrying a good head of pike, some of them very large.

A licence is required in order to fish in the Grand Duchy. The legislation regulating the practice of fishing is very complex and visitors are advised to contact the **Administration des Eaux et Forêts, PO Box 411, L-2014 Luxembourg,** for up-to-date information.

Tackle can be purchased, and local information gained, from **Maison Tony van der Molen, 16 rue de la Montagne, L-6470 Echternach, Grand Duchy of Luxembourg.** Further information, including details of hotels with fishing, from the **Luxembourg National Tourist Office, 36/37 Piccadilly, London, W1,** tel: 071-434 2800; fax: 071 734 1205.

NORWAY

Norway has acquired a world-wide reputation for its salmon and sea trout, which can be fished for in a superb setting of mountains and fjords, spectacular waterfalls and peaceful valleys. Beats on such renowned waters as the **Tana, Alta, Laerdal, Driva** and **Surna,** fetch very high prices and are in the hands of specialised agencies (inquire Hardy's of London and Sporting Services International). Excellent sport at more modest charges may be had from the many hotels with private stretches, especially in the north. The salmon season is from late May to Sept 5 (best in June and July) and the best sea trout fishing is to be had in August, although the season extends into Sept, the actual date varying in different districts.

Floating line fishing is becoming more widely practised, but it is more usual on the big rivers to employ heavy, fast-sinking lines and large flies, from size 3/0 upwards. Streamers and bucktails are popular for salmon, and sea-trout are often fished dry fly or nymph - in the clear waters the fish can often be seen and cast to.

Less well known, and much less expensive, is fishing for brown trout and char, which can be very good indeed. Countless streams and lakes well stocked with trout lie within easy reach of **Oslo,** while anglers prepared to travel further afield will be amply rewarded. Trout of 25lb and over have been caught in the lake **Steinsfjorden,** near **Vikersund,** and the **Randselven,** near **Kistefoss,** and **Lake Mjösa,** near **Gjövik.** Several fish of around this weight have fallen to fly.

Arctic char are mostly found in the deep and cold mountain lakes, where they can provide thrilling sport, though this is a difficult art. There are taxi flights to the lakes from the big towns. The brown trout season varies with altitude, the extremes being late May until mid-Sept. As several rivers have rather swift currents, strong tackle is recommended. Most fishing rights are owned privately, but there are vast areas of Crown land where good fishing may be enjoyed at no great cost. Any fisherman in Norway, in addition to the application fee, is required to take out a licence available from post offices. It covers the entire country for a year, and prices vary. Many hotels in the country have their own rivers and lakes for brown trout fishing, making no charge to guests.

Dry-fly fishing is very popular, especially in smaller lakes and tarns or slow rivers. Most suitable gear is a fly-rod of 9½ft to 10½ft, with a No.7 line, which may be used anywhere

Leading salmon angler Arthur Oglesby with a 50 pdr. from Norway's Vosson River. Spinning slow and deep accounted for this exceptional fish - as it has accounted for many others in powerful Norwegian rivers.

at any time. Best flies are those in douce colours, such as March brown and Greenwell's Glory etc. For red char fishing, use stronger colours such as Red Cardinal, Butcher or Coachman, etc. The best all-round spinning lures are those with slow movements and in golden or red colours. For hooking, use Devon or Phantom lures, or artificial minnows. No gaff is required, but a large landing-net is desirable. Rubber boots or waders come in handy, practically everywhere.

Fishing regulations. Anyone over 16 fishing for salmon, sea trout, sea char or freshwater fish in waters on common land, has to pay an annual fee, 'fisketrygdavgift', of NOK 80. This can be done at any post office. The normal local fishing licence must then be purchased in addition. The cost of this varies from place to place. Licences are sold at sports suppliers, kiosks, tourist offices, hotels, and campsites etc. A licence generally covers the waters in a certain area, whilst some are valid for one lake or part of one only. A licence can be purchased for a day, a week, a month, or a whole season. Restrictions are normally stated on the licence. As a rule, a separate licence is needed for net or otter fishing.

Nets and crayfish tackle which have been used outside Norway, may not be utilised there: The same applies to gear used in waters found to be diseased, unless this gear has been disinfected. Crayfish tackle used in Norway has to be disinfected before it is employed again in the new season.

Live bait is forbidden in Norway. Also, to protect trout, char and salmon stocks, fish must not be transferred from one body of water to another. New restrictions have been introduced to protect stocks of anadromous salmonid fish.

For further details, contact the **Norwegian Tourist Board, Charles House, 5 Lower Regent Street, London SW1,** tel: 071-839 6255. The Norwegian Tourist Board publishes a comprehensive guide to fishing in Norway entitled *Angling in Norway,* which is available from **Scandinavian Books and Maps, 21 Sheen Court Road, Richmond, Surrey TW10 5OG.**

PORTUGAL

Salmon and trout are found mostly in the **River Minho** and its tributaries in the far north, but the lack of controls has diminished sport. Very good sea trout fishing may be enjoyed in the Minho estuary near **Moledo** and on the **Lima** near **Viana do Castelo.** The fish are usually taken on bait or spinner, but fly fishing should prove productive. The coarse fisherman, too, can find sport. All Portuguese rivers hold barbel, while those in the centre and south of the country hold good carp and black bass.

The close season for salmon and trout fishing is from Aug 1 to end Feb and for other species from March 15 to end May. Licences for visitors are not as a rule required.

The sea fishing is excellent, partly owing to the structure of the continental shelf, and the narrow strip of 50 to 100 miles shallower water. More than 200 different species are taken. Among these are many of the fish known to British fishermen in home waters, but in the south it includes game species such as swordfish, blue and white marlin, tunny, bonito and amberjack, as well as blue porbeagle, thresher and mako sharks. School tunny and meagre (the so-called salmon-bass) are also taken.

Many of the fish known to British fishermen reach heavier weights in Portuguese waters. Bass of around 20lb are reported to be taken inshore from boats, for instance, and smaller fish of 10lb-14lb from the shore. Large shoals of mackerel up to 6lb were found by a British team fishing off Peniche in 1956. Good shore fishing for bass can be had more or less everywhere. Other fish regularly caught include: mullet (to 5lb), conger and dogfish, various types of bream, some running up to 25lb; pollack, cod, turbot, rock gurnard, wrasse, John Dory, tope and several others. Meagre attain weights up to 90lb, amberjack to 18lb, and school tunny to 80lb. The comparatively recent discovery of this vast potential has led to a rapid development of a number of small fishing ports. Boats and boatmen are available at most of them, and hotel accommodation is reported to be good. Most important of the new-found fishing centres is perhaps **Sesimbra,** south of **Lisbon.** Others are **Praia da Rocha** (near **Portimao**) and **Faro** in the south, **Cascais** (near **Estoril**), **Nazaré,** and **Ericeira** (all to the north-west of Lisbon) and **Sines** (south of Sesimbra). Apart from the fishing, most of these places have good beach and rock casting, and are good holiday and tourist centres. Boats are available at many places, including **Albufeira, Lagos** and **Monte Gordo.**

Visiting anglers will be made welcome at such clubs as the 'Clube dos Amadores de Pesca de Portugal', Rua do Salitre 175R/CD, Lisbon Tel: 684805 (for all kinds of angling, especially big game fishing), 'Clube Invicta de Pesca Desportiva' at Rua 31 de Janeiro 85-10, Tel: 321557, and the 'Amadores de Pesca Reunidos', at Largo dos Lojas 79 (second floor), Tel: 324501, both **Oporto,** where information on local fishing may be obtained and where all visitors will be treated as honorary members. In the **Algarve,** several hotels provide or can arrange sea fishing parties. They include the Hotels Praia, Algarve and Baleeira. The best centres in this region are in the **Sagres** and **Cabo Carroeiro** areas where large mackerel are frequently taken. Details can be had from the **Portuguese National Tourist Office, 1/5 New Bond Street, London W1Y 0NP.** Tel: 071-493 3873.

RUSSIA

The Kola Peninsula

Over the last few years the Kola Peninsula has built up a reputation for some of the most consistent Atlantic salmon and sea trout fishing available anywhere in the world. Situated in north-western Russia, jutting into the White Sea, from its border with north-eastern Norway, the peninsula is approximately the same size as Scotland, with as many rivers supporting salmon and sea trout runs.

With few roads, a very small population, and lying mainly above the Arctic Circle, the peninsula is true remote wilderness, and it has taken some years to overcome the logistical problems this incurs. Although western fishermen have only fished the Kola since 1989 in recent times, its rivers were a topic of great interest in the *Fishing Gazette* as long ago as 1925, a few englishmen having fished there shortly after the turn of the century.

Hard work by a few western specialist organisations over the last few years has now made it possible to fish the Kola relatively easily. They have all combined their experiences of fishing with Russian local knowledge to build camps on the most prolific and consistent rivers. Remoteness and the logistics mean that it is still not possible to fish there except through these organisations. To get to the rivers one must fly via Moscow, St Petersburg or Helsinki to the peninsula and then onward to the rivers by helicopter.

The season runs from the beginning of June, the winter snow having melted in May, until late September, when the approach of the severe Arctic winter prohibits access. The rivers can be divided into those which flow north into the Barents Sea, and those which flow east and south into the White Sea.

The southern of these were the first to be organised with the main salmon run in June and July, and a smaller run in September. Sea trout run throughout the season, perhaps not starting until July on some rivers. Large catches can be expected, with salmon of 5lb to 20lb being normal. The main salmon run in the northern rivers, which have only been fished seriously since 1991, is from mid-June to mid-July, although it does go on into August. To date, fish from these rivers have averaged 15lb to 20lb, with many in the 30lb to 40lb range. The 1993 season saw a fish of well over 60lb caught.

The majority of fishing is on floating, intermediate or sink tip lines using traditional salmon flies. A sink line may be necessary on the northern rivers. A large number of fish are surprisingly taken on dry flies, usually fished 'on the hitch' downstream. The majority of the rivers require chest waders and wading staffs.

The rivers vary greatly in character. The **Panoi**, flowing east into the White Sea, is large, with prolific runs of salmon. Running South is the **Varzuga** system, including the **Pana** and **Kitsa**, which perhaps has the largest salmon runs anywhere and, in parts, is compared to the Aberdeenshire Dee. The **Polanga**, **Babia**, **Likhodyevka** and **Pyalitsa**, fished together, are probably the prettiest rivers on the peninsula requiring little wading and are similar to the Scottish Carron, Oykel and Cassley; their salmon run is not quite as prolific, but is boosted by large runs of sea trout. The **Kharlovka**, **Eastern Litsa**, **Varzina** and **Yokanga** in the north all have runs of large salmon, but can be, in places, very rocky and steep, with fast water and difficult wading.

Fishing is fly only, except in a few cases, and all rivers operate a policy of catch and release for salmon, allowing rods one or two fish a week for the table.

For further information contact **Nimrod Safaris Ltd, Water Eaton, Cricklade, Wiltshire SN6 6JU.** Tel: 0285 810132.

SPAIN

Spain is a well-endowed country, offering the most southerly fishing for Atlantic salmon in Europe; brown and rainbow trout, coarse fish including large carp and barbel, both in rivers, and shore fishing for sea bass, mackerel, mullet, conger and other species. Black bass, pike and Danube salmon are among comparatively recent introductions.

Twenty-six rivers draining the Cantabrian range and the Galician Coast are entered by salmon. The **Deva-Cares, Navia, Sella, Narcea,** and **Asón** provide the best sport. Arrangements for licences and permits for visitors are not uniform and the British angler contemplating salmon fishing in Spain is advised to contact the **Spanish Tourist Office, 57 St James Street, London SW1A 1LD** (tel: 071-499 0901). Much the same is to be said of the trout fishing, applying equally to seasons and permitted methods. In some areas, trout grow impressively large. Spain has not yet become as notable for high-grade coarse fishing as it may at some future date, but few who have connected with large carp or barbel in a deep, fast-flowing Spanish river do not cherish ambitions to renew the experience.

The tourist office publishes an interesting full-colour map on fishing in the country.

SWEDEN

Sweden cannot be compared with Norway for salmon, but there are splendid opportunities for sea trout, fish of well over 20lb having been caught on the rod. The country is rich in brown trout waters and well supplied with char and grayling.

The game fisherman will be advised to go north for his sport, where swift and powerful waterways hold some really heavy trout and up which migratory fish run in fair numbers from mid-July onwards; rivers like the **Torneälv, Kalixälv** and **Vindelälven**, so far untouched by hydro-electric schemes which have marred sport in so many other Swedish waters.

For the fly fisherman, however, such awe-inspiring torrents present special difficulties. They are too wide, deep and fast-flowing to be fished effectively from the bank, except perhaps for sea trout which swim closer to the shore than salmon but which are not too plentiful in these northern parts. The most productive angling technique is harling - casting large flies into vast pools from a boat equipped with an outboard motor. Quite a few salmon, however, taken on spinning lures, especially where rock ledges can be found to command the pools.

Many once-famous salmon rivers are hardly worth fishing nowadays, notably the **Mörrum** in Blekinge Province, where the National Board of Crown Forests and Lands (Domänverket) still issues permits for fishing over a 3m stretch. This used to be the best salmon river in the country, but the spring fishing is now chiefly for sea trout kelts and there are relatively few fresh-run fish later on. The **Em, Ätran** and **Örekil** are other salmon streams which provide somewhat indifferent sport, though the Em is good for sea trout.

Farther north, in central Sweden, the position on the **Dalälven** is not much better, but the river still has a fair run of large fish from midsummer to late autumn; harling is again the most effective way of taking them.

If the present situation in regard to salmon fishing is far from favourable, the outlook is somewhat brighter. The Swedes are engaged in a massive restocking programme with smolts which is already bringing results, and a determined drive against pollution has resulted in salmon once again being caught in the centre of **Stockholm.**

Most of the fishing for sea trout is with the dry fly, as the wet fly will rarely take fish by day. Hackled coch-y-bondhu patterns are commonly employed. Of course in the north 'night' fishing is something of a misnomer as it never really gets dark during summer.

There are some very big trout to be caught in the large rivers and lakes of the north - fish of 20lb and more - and trout also run to a respectable size in the lowland streams. The grayling, too, are not to be despised. It will interest anglers to learn that they can be caught in the sea along the Baltic coast, using small dry flies and keeping well out of sight as grayling in the sea tend to be shy. Sport with arctic char is confined mainly to the deep cold lakes. It can be exciting at times, but nearly always difficult. Char are best taken on wet fly from the shallows where a stream enters a lake.

Many of the best fishing areas are away from roads and habitation, but the angler who takes a tent with him and is used to mountainous terrain has every chance of success.

There is no stream fishing in the Stockholm region but there is an increasing amount of sport with rainbow, brown and brook trout in artificially stocked lakes.

Pike, perch and carp abound in these lowland lakes and the City of Stockholm issues a card at a modest charge which is valid for several places in **Lake Mälaren** and in the archipelago.

For salmon and trout fishing, licence charges vary considerably; charges for trout fishing in stocked lakes and ponds are somewhat higher than for natural waters. No charge is made to fish for grayling in the sea.

Close seasons vary widely. For salmon and sea trout it usually runs from Sept 1 to Jan 1, though fishing is prohibited in some waters after Aug 15.

Further and more detailed information can be had from the year book published by **Sportfiskarna** (The Swedish National Sportfishing Association), **Box 2, S-163 21 Spanåga**, which lists about 1,800 fishing waters. The association cannot, however, answer detailed inquiries from abroad. These should be directed to the **Swedish National Tourist Office, 3 Cork Street, London W1X 1HA** (tel: 071-437 5816) or to **The Fishery Board, Box 423, S-401 26 Göteborg** , or **Doman Turist AB, Box 521, S-18215 Danderyd.**

SWITZERLAND

There is no shortage of water in Switzerland - 20,000 miles of rivers and streams, and 520 square miles of lakes within a small area - and as most of these waters hold trout, the country is a fly-fisherman's dream.

Unfortunately, the dream is often of brief duration, as the streams at appreciable altitudes are in snow spate often until July. But in the lower valleys there is sport to be had from May to the end of the summer. Lake fishing consists mainly in trolling at great depth. Swiss waters may be classed as follows:

The **Lakes.** Most of the lakes contain trout and char, pike, perch and other coarse fish. The trout and char (Ombre chevalier) run to a great size, but they lie at such depths that fly fishing or trolling with a rod is practically useless. Most of the lakes in the central plain are now suffering to some degree from pollution, but they still provide sport. Best results are obtained by spinning with light tackle.

The **Great Rivers.** Both the **Rhine** and **Rhône** hold very big trout. Spinning with a 2¼in silver Devon is the best method, though a small silver-bodied salmon fly will sometimes give good results. The Rhône, above the lake of **Geneva,** is fishable only till the middle of April.

In summer months it is thick with snow water. Many Swiss rivers contain good stocks of coarse fish, including barbel, carp and pike.

Plain and Lower Valley Streams. Trout in these streams run from ¼lb to 2½lb or more. There is always a good hatch of fly, and the Mayfly is up on most of them from May to July. Wading is not as a rule necessary. Fine tackle is essential. Carry a couple of small silver Devons for thick water.

The Hill Torrents. Trout run four or five to the pound in the best of the hill torrents, rather smaller in the others. As the hatch of fly is usually poor, the upstream worm pays best. The coch-y-bondhu is sometimes useful, while in July and Aug the 'daddy-longlegs' is deadly. Wading is usually an advantage. Watch for the spate that often occurs towards midday owing to melting snow.

It should be said that Switzerland, in common with most European countries, is experiencing a growth of angling pressures, but the authorities, concerned to ensure that sport remains at a high level, release at least 100 million fish, mostly trout, from hatcheries every year.

The close season for trout runs most commonly from Oct 1 to Mar 15, and for grayling from Mar 1 to April 30.

Fishing regulations vary. Generally speaking the angler will require a canton licence and may also need a permit for private waters. Further information is obtainable from the local Tourist Offices in the area to be visited or from **Schweizer Sportfischer-Verband, Dorfstrasse 16, 4657 Dulliken, Switzerland.** General tourist information can be had from the **Swiss National Tourist Office, Swiss Centre, Swiss Court, London W1V 8EE,** tel: 071-734 1921; fax: 071 437 4577.

YUGOSLAVIA

This text is retained from the previous edition. Obviously, the political situation in Yugoslavia while this edition is in preparation does not encourage the hopeful angler to set off, rod in hand, for a pleasant trip to Dubrovnik or certain other venues. It is to be hoped that the country's conflict soon finds a peaceful resolution.

The country, under normal circumstances, is well worth exploring by the angler. The rivers are often difficult to reach, but offer sport of the highest quality. Even the more accessible places, sport with trout (brook and rainbow) and grayling is often very good indeed.

Some streams are too torrential for the fly, but many rivers and lakes provide excellent fly fishing. Sport is carefully supervised. Each province, or people's republic, has its own federation of fishing societies which encourages fishing as a sport and protects and restocks the waters.

Mostly the rivers are clear and fast-flowing direct or indirect tributaries of the **Danube.** There are 25 species of game fish out of a total of 198 all told in Yugoslav waters. Besides brook and rainbow trout there are large river char and marble trout. Among coarse fish, the pike-perch of the Danube basin is a big attraction. In the lakes trout run large and some lakes contain pike, carp and eels. Fishing throughout the country is by district licence, annual, weekly and daily, obtainable from fishery controllers, tourist offices and many of the hotels. There are also restrictions on methods and bags, varying in some instances from district to district. In **Croatia** visitors staying in **Dubrovnik** can easily make one-day fishing expeditions, reaching the river after a drive of only thirty minutes. In **Zagreb** the Croatian Federation can provide expert guides, linguists as well as fishermen, and tackle. **Bosnia** and **Herzogovina,** however, probably form the most interesting fishing region, the best season for brook trout being May and June and from late Sept to the first frosts, while rainbows give best sport then onwards to Feb. The **Drina** river and tributaries form a splendid and extensive fishery, containing large huck, trout and grayling. **Slovenia** also affords good sport likely to appeal to British fishermen. There the season is May 1 to Sept 15.

Further detailed information can be had from **Sport Fishing Federation of Yugoslavia, Slobodana Penezia Krcuna 35/V, 11000 Belgrade,** or through the **Yugoslav National Tourist Office, 143 Regent Street, London W1R 8AE** (071-734 5243), who issue an excellent English language booklet containing all the necessary detailed information and a directory of suitable hotels.

Spring salmon fishing on the Spey at Craigellachie, by the old bridge. *Photo: Eric Chalker.*

NOTABLE BRITISH AND IRISH FISH, INCLUDING THE OFFICIAL RECORDS

Until the British Record (Rod Caught) Fish Committee was set up in 1957, there was no recognised method of establishing a list of record fish. Such lists as did exist were based largely on data culled from books, the angling press and so on. Clearly, many of the claims were suspect, as the committee found when it examined the lists it had inherited and, as a result, discarded many so-called 'records'. Some have been discarded and replaced since the previous edition of **Where to Fish** was published.

Fisherman catching fish equal to or greater in weight than the established record should claim recognition of the fish through the Secretary of the appropriate governing body: National Federation of Anglers (coarse fish claims); National Federation of Sea Anglers (saltwater fish); The Salmon and Trout Association (game fish claims). The addresses appear in the preamble material to 'Fishing Clubs and Associations in England'. National claims for fish caught in Scotland, N Ireland or Wales will be processed by these officers. Some change in the arrangements is possible during the life of this edition of **Where to Fish** but if so the officers referred to will be in a position to advise. A claim should be made soon as possible after the capture of the fish, preferably by telegram or telephone and a confirmatory letter should give full details of the catch (date, time, tackle etc) and the names and addresses of two independent and reliable witnesses capable of identifying the fish, which should be retained for inspection, dead or alive, by the committee or its representative. Fish should not be weighed on spring balances, but on a steel-yard or scales which can be tested if necessary.

The committee is always pleased to receive similar details of any unusual catches. Only fish in the coastal waters of England (including the Channel Islands and the Isle of Man), Scotland, Wales and Northern Ireland are eligible. Fish caught in the Irish Republic should be reported to the Secretary, Irish Specimen Fish Committee, Balnagowan, Mobhi Boreen, Glasnevin, Dublin 9.

Fish marked * as records in the following lists are those recognised by the BRFC after very careful examination of all the relevant factors, as the official record for the species.

Irish records, that is, those recognised by the Irish Specimen Fish Committee - are indicated thus † in the following lists. Note: The Irish keep separate records for rivers and lakes in respect of pike and brown trout.

For some years, there has been concern about British records awarded for trout, brown and rainbow alike, reared in conditions of semi-captivity. This dilemma has now been resolved by awarding seperate records for genuinely wild fish ("natural" - *) and the others now classed as 'cultivated' and marked in these lists with a double asterisk - "**".

The other notable catches recorded here - ie those apart from the establised records - are included for interest only and, because they have not been subjected to such rigorous scrutiny, should not be viewed as beyond question. Further data any of these fish would be welcome.

Official British Records are as updated at the meeting of the Committee 29/9/93.

FRESHWATER FISH

BARBEL (*Barbus barbuss*, Linn)
16lb 1oz C H Cassey, while spinning for salmon in the Hampshire Avon at Ibsley on March 6, 1960. Fish was foulhooked and therefore disallowed as a record.
15lb 7oz* R Morris, River Medway, Jan 1993.
14lb 11oz D Taylor, River Medway, Nov 1992.
14lb 8oz D Taylor, River Medway, Nov 1992.
14lb 6oz D Williams, River Avon, Sept 1992.
14lb 6oz D Williams, River Medway, Sept 1992
14lb 6oz T Wheeler, Thames at Molesey in 1888.
14lb 6oz* H D Tryon, Hampshire Avon (Royalty Fishery), Sept, 1934.

14lb 6oz F W Wallis, Royalty Fishery, Sept, 1937. The same angler had another of 14lb 4oz from the Royalty in Sept, 1933.

14lb 4oz R Jones, Thames at Radcot Bridge in 1909.

14lb 2oz P Reading, from a Wessex river, Aug, 1987.

14lb 1oz G Buxton, from a Wessex river, Sept, 1984.

14lb E A Edwards, River Kennet, 1954.

14lb Mr Simmons, Dorset Stour, Sept, 1930.

13lb 14oz C A Taylor, Hampshire Avon, Oct, 1934.

13lb 14oz P Mays, Troop Fishery, Dorset Stour, Oct, 1964.

BLEAK (*Alburnus alburnus*, Linn)
5¼oz Henry Stubbins, Nottingham, at Radcliffe-on-Trent, about 1890. Recorded by H Coxon in his Coarse Fish Angling, 1896.

4¼oz* B Derrington, R, Monnow, Oct, 1982.

4oz 2dm F Brown on Trent at Long Higgin, 1959.

3oz 15dm D Pollard, Staythorpe Pond nr Newark, Aug, 1971.

3oz 8dm N D Sizmur, Thames at Walton, Surrey, 1963.

BREAM (COMMON) (*Abramis bramma*, Linn)
16lb 9oz* M McKeown, from a private water in the South of England, June 1991

16lb 6oz A Bromley, from a Staffordshire mere, Aug, 1986.

15lb 10oz J Knowles, Queensford lagoon, July, 1985.
(Part of a bag including other bream of 14lb 14oz, 13lb 11oz and 13lb 2oz, caught during two days.)

15lb 6oz A Nicholson, Queensford lagoon, Sept, 1984.

13lb 14oz C Dean, Oxford gravel pit, 1983.

13lb 12oz A Smith, Oxford gravel pit, Aug, 1983.

13lb 9oz M C Davison, Beeston Lake, Wroxham, Norfolk, July, 1982.

13lb 8oz A R Heslop, private water, Staffs, 1977.

13lb 8oz E G Costin, Chiddingstone Castle Lake, in Oct, 1945.

13lb R Willis, Duchess Lake, Bristol, Sept, 1949.

12lb 15oz F T Bench, Tring Reservoirs, Oct, 1945.

12lb 14oz G J Harper, Suffolk Stour, July, 1971.

12lb 14oz Caught by one of two brothers (Messrs Pugh), Tring Reservoirs, on July 28, 1933. They had two other bream, 12lb and 10½lb, on same day.

12lb 12½oz A J Fisher, July 30, 1931, Tring Reservoirs (thus beating an Irish fish of 11⅓lb, which had held the record for 49 years). Later that year Lord Rothschild reported a fish of 13lb 10oz found dying at Tring. Several other fish of 12lb and over have been taken from Tring.

11lb 12oz W Gollins, Ellesmere (Salop), 1970.

11lb 12oz† A Pike, River Blackwater (Co Monaghan), 1882.

BREAM (SILVER) (*Blicca bjoernka*, Linn)
4lb 8oz C R Rhind from Tortworth Lake, Gloucestershire, in 1923.

4lb 4oz K Armstrong, lake at Rugeley, Staffs, Jan, 1970.

4lb Two fish of this weight were caught by J Bowater from Yorkshire Derwent in July, 1933.

4lb G Burwash from Thames at Egham in Feb, 1922.

4lb J Bowater, Yorkshire Derwent, July, 1933.

3lb 7½oz A Engers from Plucks Gutter (Stour, Kent), July, 1949.

15oz* D E Flack, Lakenheath, Aug 26, 1988.

CARP (*Cyprinus carpio*, Linn)
51lb 8oz* C Yates, Redmire Pool, Herefordshire, 16/6/80.

45lb 12oz R Macdonald, Yateley, summer 1984.

44lb Richard Walker on Sept 13, 1952, Redmire Pool, Herefordshire. The best of many huge carp from Redmire. "Dick" Walker himself had another of 31lb 4oz in June, 1954.

42lb R Clay, Billing Aquadrome, Sept, 1966.

40lb 8oz E G Price, Redmire Pool, Sept 27, 1959. King carp.

40lb 0½oz R Groombridge from a lake at Hemel Hempstead, July, 1956.

38lb 8½oz R Bowskill, Redmire Pool, Sept, 1966.

37lb 8oz J Sims, Wyver Pool at Belper, Derbys, July, 1968.

37lb 4oz D Stanley, W Sedgemoor Drain, Oct, 1986.
36lb 4oz W Quinlan, Redmire Pool, Oct, 1970.
35lb J Hilton, Redmire Pool, Oct, 1967.
34lb 8oz J Ward, pond near Wokingham, Berkshire, July 28, 1959.
34lb 4oz W Beta, Electricity Cut, River Nene at Peterborough, June, 1965. Thought to be the
   record river carp. The Electricity Cut has produced several big carp - one of 33lb 12oz was
   taken by P Harvey in Jan, 1965.
34lb P Chillingworth, Billing Aquadrome, June, 1970.
Fish of over 30lb (some of them more than 40lbs) have also come from the Ashlea Pool,
   Gloucester (two), Waveney Valley Lakes, the Layer Pits, near Colchester and from lakes
   and ponds in the home counties. Biggest catch of carp is thought to have been taken by
   Bob Reynolds from Billing Aquadrome. In August, 1957 he took carp of 26lb 1oz, 27lb
   9oz, 27lb 13oz, and 28lb 4oz, making 109lb 11oz in all. The record Irish carp is a fish of
   18lb 12oz taken by J Roberts from Abbey lake in 1958.

CARP (CRUCIAN) (*Carassius carassius*, Linn)
5lb 10½oz* G Halls, King's Lynn lake, June, 1976.
4lb 15½oz J Johnstone, Johnson's Lake, New Hythe, Kent, June, 1972.
4lb 11oz H C Hinson, Broadwater Lake, Godalming, 1938.
4lb 10oz M Benwell, Notts gravel pit, July, 1971.
4lb 9½oz B Cole, Kent lake, Sept, 1971.
4lb 8oz F J Axten, Bedfont Lake, July, 1964.
4lb 8oz B Burman, Shoebury Park Lake, Sept, 1971.
4lb 7½oz A Palfrey, South Ockendon pit, 1962.
4lb 7½oz F James, Leighton Buzzard pit, June, 1965.
4lb 7½oz A Donison, Guildford lake, Aug, 1968.
4lb 6½oz G Bott, Godalming lake, March, 1966.

CARP, GRASS (*Ctenopharyngodon idella*)
25lb 4oz* D Buck, at Honeycroft Fisheries, Canterbury, Aug 1993.
16lb 1oz J P Buckley, Horton Fishery, Berks, July, 1990
16lb K Crow, from lake near Canterbury, July 1986.
9lb 12oz G A Gwilt, Trawsfynydd Lake, June, 1983.

CHARR (*Salvelinus alpinus*)
8lb*, F Nicholson, L Arkaig, 1992.
7lb 14½oz Roy Broadhead, June, 1991.
4lb 13oz P Savage, Loch Garry, May 1987.
3lb 5oz A Robertson, Loch Earn, 1985.
3lb 4oz S C Rex, Knoydart Dubhlochan, Oct, 1982.
1lb 12oz M C Imperiale, Loch Insh, Inverness, May, 1974.
1lb 11oz B A Richardson, Lake Windermere, April, 1973.
1lb 9oz A Stein, Lake Windermere, March, 1973.

CHUB (*Squalius cephalus*, Linn)
10lb 8oz Dr J A Cameron from the Annan in 1955.
8lb 14oz Caught out of season on the Wissey by J Roberts in May, 1960, while spinning for
   trout.
8lb 12oz J Lewis, River Mole, Oct, 1964.
8lb 8oz D Deeks from Sussex Rother, July, 1951.
8lb 4oz* G F Smith from Avon at Christchurch, Dec, 1913.
8lb C Harmell, Royalty Fishery, Aug, 1964.
7lb 15oz P Minton, Yorkshire Ouse, Oct, 1964.
7lb 14½oz Mrs H M Jones, from Stour at Canford (Dorset) in Sept, 1937.
7lb 10oz* P J Goddard, Bristol Avon, 1987.
7lb 6oz W Warren, Hampshire Avon, 1957.

DACE (*Leuciscus leuciscus*, Linn)
1lb 8¾oz S Horsfield, Derbyshire, Derwent, Jan, 1947.
1lb 8oz R W Humphrey, from tributary of Hampshire Avon, Sept, 1932.
1lb 7¾oz J S Upton, from the Penk, Dec, 1933.

1lb 7½oz F W Arnold, River Mole, Jan, 1934.
1lb 7½oz S Rolfe, Suffolk Stour, Feb, 1962.
1lb 7oz Abe Hibbard, near Sheffield, Feb, 1934.
1lb 5oz 2dm S Wilson, Llynfi, July, 1966.
1lb 5oz R Walker, Cam, July, 1938.
1lb 5oz J Cartwright, Cynon, 1965.
1lb 4½oz* J L Gasson, Little Ouse, Thetford, Feb, 1960.
1lb 2oz† J T Henry, River Blackwater, (Cappoquin), 1966.

EEL (*Anguilla anguilla,* Linn)
11lb 2oz* S Terry, Kingfisher Lake, Hants, 1978.
8lb 10oz A Dart, Hunstrete Lake, July, 1969.
8lb 8oz C Mitchell, Bitterwell Lake in 1922. An eel of equal weight was taken from a trap
  on the Warwickshire Avon in Aug, 1960.
8lb 4oz J McFarlane, River Tees, 1964.
8lb 4oz J Taylor from pond at Arlesey, Bedfordshire, in July, 1958.
8lb R Jones, Monmouthshire lake, May, 1968. Mr Jones had another from the same lake of
  7lb 8oz.
8lb M Bowles, Weirwood Reservoir, June 1986.
7lb 15oz P Climo, Monmouthshire lake, May, 1969.
7lb 13oz, M Hill, Arlesey Lake, Beds, Aug, 1970.
7lb 5¼oz B Young, Pluck Pond, Swansea, Aug, 1970.
7lb 1oz D Holwill, River Wallington, Fareham, Oct, 1968.
7lb W F Simmons from Dorset Stour at Christchurch in 1931.
An interesting catch was made by R Smith (13) and W Bush (14) from Hollows Pond, Whipps
  Cross, London, in Sept, 1958, when an eel weighing 6lb 8oz took both boys' baits.

GOLDEN ORFE (*Leusiscus idus*)
6lb 2oz*, P Corley, at Lymm Vale, Cheshire, Sept 1993.
5lb 15oz G Sherwin, Lymm Vale, Cheshire, Oct 1990.
5lb 6oz M Foot, River Slea, Hants, 1978.
4lb 12oz J Moran, Burton Towers, N Wales, June 1986.
4lb 3½oz D R Charles, River Kennet, Aug, 1983.
4lb 3oz B T Mills, R Test, Jan, 1976.

GRAYLING (*Thymallus thymallus,* Linn)
7lb 2oz From River Melgum by J Stewart, July, 1949. The fish is believed to be somewhat
  legendary and was eliminated as a record by the British Record Fish Committee in 1968.
  4lb 8oz Dr T Sanctuary on the Wylye at Bemerton in 1885. A fish of 4lb 12oz was netted
  from the Avon at Longford by G S Marryat and Dr Sanctuary in the same year and returned
  to the water.
4lb 4oz G Bryant on the Itchen.
4lb 3oz* S R Lanigan (16 years old) Dorset Frome, Jan. 8, 1989.
4lb Three a fraction over this weight caught by H J Mordaunt and M Headlam on the Test
  (Oakley Stream) at Mottisfont on Boxing Day, 1905.
4lb E Chambers, Chess, near Chorley Wood, Jan, 1955. Mr Chambers had another of 3lb
  13oz on the same outing, making a remarkable brace.
3lb 14oz E J Stanton, Driffield Canal, Sept, 1967.
3lb 12oz J Wigram on the Test near Stockbridge, in 1873.
3lb 12oz J W Gieve from the Test in 1917.
3lb 12oz M T Hooper, Loudsmill, Dorchester, 1988.
3lb 10oz I White, River Allen, Dorset, Aug, 1983.
2lb 13oz P B Goldsmith, R Test, 1981.
2lb 9¼oz D Hauxvell, R Teviot, Jan 12, 1980.

GUDGEON (*Gobio gobio,* Linn)
5oz* D H Hull, R Nadder, Jan 1990.
4¼oz M J Bowen, pond at Ebbw Vale, Gwent, 1977.
4¼oz Geo Cedric from the Thames at Datchet in Aug, 1933.
4¼oz W R Bostock from Hogg's Pond, Shipley, near Derby, in Oct, 1935.
4¼oz J D Lewin from the Soar in 1950.

4oz 1dm Caught at Sudbury by O S Hurkett, Mar, 1950.

PERCH (*Perca fluviatilis,* Linn)
5lb 15oz 6dm P Clark, Suffolk Stour, 1949.
5lb 14½oz D Florey from Farlows Lake, Dec, 1953.
5lb 12oz E V Hodd from Diana Pond, Hampton Court, in Aug, 1957.
5lb 9oz* J Shayler from a private lake in Kent, 1985.
5lb 8oz† S Drum from Lough Erne, 1946.
5lb 4½oz H Green from Stradsett Lake, Norfolk, on Nov 9, 1936.
5lb 4oz Caught at Sandford Mill, Woodley, Berks, by Wm Leach in 1873.
5lb 4oz K Gardner from a lake in Norfolk, July, 1970. Other fish of over 5lb were reported from lakes in Worcester and Suffolk, and a pit in Colchester.
4lb 12oz S F Baker, Oulton Broad, 1962.

PIKE (*Esox lucius,* Linn)
53lb Lough Conn in July, 1920, by John Garvin. This fish is entitled to rank as the premier pike landed in Great Britain and Ireland. Mr Garvin caught a 30-pounder on the same day. Bigger pike than this have been reported, including a fish of 72lb from Loch Ken in 1774 and one of 60lb found dying at Dowdeswell. One approaching the weight Mr Garvin's fish 52lb is said to have been recovered when Whittlesey Mere, Cambs, was drained in 1851.
48lb Reported from Lough Corrib in 1905.
47lb 11oz T Morgan from Loch Lomond in July, 1945.
46lb 13oz* R Lewis, Llandegfed Reservoir, S Wales, Oct, 1992.
45lb 6oz Gareth Edwards, Llandegfedd Reservoir, Gwent, 1990.
44lb 14oz M G Linton, Ardleigh Reservoir, Jan, 1987.
42lb D Amies, River Thurne, Aug, 1985.
42lb M Watkins, River Barrow (spoon), 1964, Irish river record.
41lb 8oz From Foxborough, Tulsk, Ireland, by P J Mannion in June, 1922.
41lb Mr Cawley from Lough Conn in Mar, 1918.
40lb From Lough Arrow. The fish was sent to The Fishing Gazette in 1900, together with another of 35lb. These fish were caught on "set lines".
40lb E Oulton from Lough Ramor in Nov, 1950.
40lb Lough Erne by John H Thompson in 1922. Hooked while the angler was playing another and smaller pike.
40lb P Hancock, Horsey Mere, Feb, 1967.
39lb C Loveland, Knipton Reservoir, 1967.
38lb 4oz P Emmings, Cheshunt pit, Dec, 1969.
38lb H Mumford Smith, Lough Conn, June 8, 1929.
38lb H A Robinson on Lough Mask in 1905. Various fish from this weight up to 40lb or more have been reported from Irish lakes, and there is little doubt that most of them have been authentic.
38lb† P Earl, Lough Ree (minnow), 1967 (Irish lake record).
37lb 8oz C Warwick, Avon at Fordingbridge, Oct, 1944.

PIKE PERCH (Walleye) (*Stizostedion vitrium*)
11lb 12oz F Adams, The Delph, 1934.

PIKEPERCH (Zander) (*Stizostedion lucioperca*)
18lb 10oz* R Armstrong, River Severn, March 1993.
18lb 8oz R N Meadows, Cambridge stillwater, 1988.
17lb 4oz D Ditton, Gt Ouse Relief Channel, 1977.
16lb 6oz S Smith, Cut-off Channel, Oct, 1976.
15lb 5oz W G Chillingworth, Gt Ouse Relief Channel, February 1971. This angler had another of 12lb 13oz from the Relief Channel, Feb, 1971.
12lb 12oz Neville Fickling, Relief Channel, October, 1979. (This angler had another of 12lb 6½oz.) He had another of 12lb 7½oz from the same water the previous August.
12lb 5oz Dr R B Rickards, Relief Channel, Feb, 1970.

ROACH (*Rutilus rutilus,* Linn)
4lb 3oz* R N Clarke, Dorset Stour, Oct, 1990.
4lb 1oz R G Jones, Gravel Pits, Notts, 1975.

3lb 14oz W Penny, Metropolitan Water Board's Lambeth Reservoir at Molesey, Sept 6, 1938 (118½in, g12⅝in).

3lb 14oz A Brown, Oakham gravel pit near Stamford, Lincs, 1964.

3lb 14oz Caught out of season on fly by F I Hodgson while fishing for trout in a spring-fed Lancashire pond in May, 1960.

3lb 10oz W Cutting, Hornsea Mere, Yorkshire, in 1917. On the same day he had another 3-pounder.

3lb 10oz A Whittock from the Hampshire Avon, Jan, 1953.

3lb 9¾oz T G Player from the Thames at Sonning in June, 1949.

3lb 9oz J Osborn, River Thurne, July, 1962.

Staines Reservoir produced three roach, each weighing 3lb 6oz in the autumn of 1962 and 1964.

RUDD (*Scardinius erythrophthalmus*, Linn)

4lb 8oz* The Rev E C Alston on a mere near Thetford, July, 1933. He had another of 3lb 15oz during the month.

4lb 4oz Caught at Blackheath by J F Green, 1888.

3lb 15oz W Clews, Moor Lane Fisheries (Staines), 1957.

3lb 13oz A Oldfield from a mill pool in Cheshire, 1960.

3lb 13oz W Tucker, from the Thames at Chertsey, Jan, 1962.

3lb 12oz D A Fisher, pond at Stanmore, July, 1959.

3lb 12oz L Lindsay, Landbeach Lake, 1962.

3lb 12oz K Palfrey, Bridgwater and Taunton Canal, 1963.

3lb 10½oz E G Costin, Home Pond, Swanley, Oct, 1954.

3lb 10oz A Brogan, The Delph at Wisbech, July, 1935.

3lb 10oz Master D Denham, pit at Shepperton, July, 1954.

3lb 1oz† A E Biddlecombe, Kilglass Lake, on worm, 1963.

SALMON (*Salmo salar*, Linn)

69lb 12oz By the Earl of Home on Tweed about 1730. The "record" rod-caught salmon for the British Isles. This fish has been described as "somewhat legendary". In 1935, however, the Earl of Home sent a note giving evidence that the fish indeed existed.

67lb On the Nith at Barjarg by Jock Wallace in 1812. Wallace, a well-known poacher, is said to have played the fish from 8am to 6pm.

64lb* On the Tay (Glendelvine water) by Miss G W Ballantine on Oct 7, 1922. Hooked in the Boat Pool at 6.15pm and landed half a mile below at 8.5pm. The fish took a spinning bait, a dace. The biggest salmon caught by a lady. Length 54in, girth 28½in. A cast of the fish was made and is at Glendelvine.

61lb 8oz On the Tay below Perth by T Stewart on the last day of the season, 1907, with a worm. It took an hour to land.

61lb J Haggart on the Tay in 1870.

61lb Mrs Morison on the Deverton on 1¼in fly (the weight probably was more as the fish was not weighed until 24 hours after capture), Oct 21, 1924.

60lb On the Eden by Lowther Bridge in 1888. Length 54in, girth 27in. Exhibited in the British Museum. It appears to be the biggest fish caught on fly in English rivers.

59lb 8oz On the Wye at Lower Winforton by Miss Doreen Dovey on Mar 12, 1923. This appears to be not only the record fish for the Wye, but also the biggest spring fish so far caught on a rod in Great Britain.

59lb On the South Esk by J K Somerville in Oct, 1922. Length 53in, girth 28in.

58lb Reported from the Shannon in 1872.

57lb 8oz On the Tweed (Floors water) in 1886 by Mr Pryor. This is usually accounted the biggest Tweed fish.

57lb† From the Suir by M Maher in 1874. The record fish for Ireland.

57lb On the Awe by Major A W Huntingdon on July 8, 1921. Length 52½in, girth 27½in.

56lb From the Deveron on Oct 31, 1920, by Col A E Scott. The fish took a 1in fly. Length 50in, girth 29in.

56lb On the Dee, Ardoe Pool, by J Gordon in 1886.

56lb From the Eden at Warwick Hall by G Mackenzie in 1892.

56lb On the Awe (Pol Verie) on June 12, 1923, By H G Thornton. Took a 5/0 fly and fought from 1pm till 3.30pm.

SEA TROUT (*Salmo trutta,* Linn)
25lb 5$\frac{1}{4}$oz*, J Farrant, River Test Estuary, Sept 1992.
22lb 8oz S Burgoyne, R Leven, Strathclyde, July 22, 1989.
22lb 8oz S R Dwight, Dorset Frome, at 11am, above the hatches at Bindon Mill, May 18, 1946.
21lb The Rev A H Upcher, Bothie Pool on the Awe on June 30, 1908. The "record" Scottish sea trout.
21lb Dorset Frome at Bindon in Mar, 1918, by R C Hardy, Corfe.
20lb 2oz* V R Townsend, River Esk, Yorks, Sep, 1986.
20lb 2oz T Williams, the Dovey, in June, 1935. The "record" Welsh sea trout.
20lb G Leavy, River Tweed, Nov, 1983.
16lb 12oz T J McManus, Shimna River, Co. Down, N Ireland, Oct, 1983.

TENCH (*Tinca tinca,* Linn)
14lb 7oz* G Beavan, from a private gravel pit, Sept 1993.
14lb 3oz P A Gooriah, Wraysbury No One, June 1987.
12lb 8$\frac{3}{4}$oz A Wilson from Wilstone Reservoir, Tring, 1985.
10lb 2oz E Edwards, undisclosed private water, 1983.
10lb 1$\frac{1}{4}$oz A J Chester, Wilstone Reservoir, Herts, 1981.
10lb 1oz L W Brown, Peterborough Brick Pit, Aug, 1975.
9lb 1oz J Salisbury, gravel pit at Hemingford Grey, Hunts, 1963.
9lb G Young, Berkshire pond, Oct, 1964.
8lb 14oz K Baldock, Staplehurst pit, Aug, 1970.
8lb 12oz P Pilley, Middx lake, June, 1970.
8lb 9oz F Bailey, Lincolnshire drain, Aug, 1970.
8lb 8oz M Foode, Leicester Canal, Aug, 1950.
8lb 6oz K Morris, Cheshunt pit, Aug, 1964.
8lb 6oz J Brooksbank, Farningham pit, Dec, 1964.
8lb 4oz J Marshall, Grantham lake, 1961.
8lb 4oz R Hill, Bucks lake, Aug, 1970.
8lb 2oz A Lowe, Wraysbury pit (date unknown).
7lb 13$\frac{1}{4}$oz† Raymond Webb, River Shannon, Lanesboro, 1971 (bread flake).
Tench of 11lb and 9lb 9oz 12dm were caught from a pit at Wraysbury, Middlesex, in July, 1959. The larger fish was returned to the water; the smaller one was sent to the London Zoo where it subsequently died. An autopsy showed it to be diseased and to contain 1lb 12oz of fluid. The larger fish was probably also diseased and neither could be allowed as a new record. Garnafailagh Lough, Westmeath, has produced a remarkable series of big tench in recent years, many over 7lb.

TROUT (BROWN) (*Salmo trutta,* Linn)
39lb 8oz On Loch Awe by W Muir in 1866. It was foul-hooked on a trout fly and took two and a half hours to land. It was set up, but the case was unfortunately lost in a fire.
30lb 8oz J W Pepper on spoon bait, Lough Derg, 1861. The Irish Times gave credence to this fish in 1903. The same angler claimed to have caught one of 24lb from Lough Corrib about the same period.
29lb On Loch Stenness in 1889 on a hand line. A "slob" or estuarine trout. A cast of this fish is in the Flyfishers' Club.
27lb 8oz Colonel Dobiggin on the Tay at Murthly in 1842; length 39$\frac{1}{2}$in. Recorded by the late Duke of Rutland in his book on The Trout.
27lb 4oz Dr H H Almond, of Loretto, on the Inver about 1870. Said to have take a small salmon fly. Probably a fish from Loch Assynt.
26lb 2oz† From Lough Ennel by W Meares on July 28, 1894, on a spoon bait. (Irish lake record).
22lb From Loch Rannock by F Twist in 1867.
21$\frac{1}{2}$lb Lough Derg by James Lucas, keeper at Derry Castle. The fish was preserved. Date of capture uncertain. (There was also a case containing a brace of trout, 16lb, 13lb, caught at the same time by trolling).
21lb Loch Rannock by Miss Kate Kirby in July, 1904. Probably the biggest trout ever caught by a lady.
21lb 3$\frac{1}{2}$oz** S Collyer, Dever Springs Trout Fishery, July, 1993.

20lb† From the Shannon in February, 1957, by Major H Place on a trolled silver Devon. (Irish river record.)
19lb 10¼oz* A Thorne, from L Awe, April 1993.
19lb 9¼oz J A F Jackson, Loch Quoich, Invernesshire, 1978.
19lb 4½oz From Lower Lough Erne, Co Fermanagh, NI, by T Chartres, April 6, 1974.
19lb 2oz F Smith from Lough Corrib on spoon, Aug, 1971.
18lb 2oz K J Grant, Loch Garry, Tomdoun, on a Black Pennel fly, in July, 1965.
Note: Lt Col G F McDonald, proprietor of Strathgarve Lodge Hotel, Garve, Ross-shire, has a trout of 26lb in a glass case reported taken in Loch Garve on September 17, 1892, by Wm Ogilvy Dalgeish. Among notable Thames trout is a fish of 14lb taken by A Pearson (Shepperton) on fly in August, 1962.

TROUT (RAINBOW) *(Salmo gairdnerii)*
30lb 1¼oz* P Carlton, Dever Springs Trout Fishery, July, 1993.
24lb 2¾oz J Moore, Pennine Fishery, Littleborough, Sept 15, 1989.
22lb 15oz† V Raymond, Dever Springs, Andover, July 4, 1989.
22lb 6oz B Hamilton, Pennine Fishery, Littleborough, Nov 19, 1988.
21lb 4oz* D Graham, Loch Awe, Oct, 1986.
20lb 7oz P Cockwill, Avington, Sept, 1986.
19lb 8oz* A Pearson, Avington Fisheries, Hants, 1977.
19lb 2oz R W Hopkins, Avington Fisheries, Hants, April, 1977.
18lb† Richard Walker, Avington Fisheries, Hants, 1976.
18lb A Pearson, Avington Fisheries, Hants, June, 1976.
14lb 4oz J L Farmer, Avington Fisheries, Hants, July, 1975.
13lb 2oz Dr W J Drummond, Downton Tannery Stream (tributary of W Avon) Sept 28, 1974.
10lb ¼oz M Parker from a private lake in King's Lynn, July, 1970.
8lb 14oz Brian Jones, Packington Fisheries, May, 1970 (taken out of Trent RA season).
8lb 10oz C F Robinson, River Test at Stockbridge, Aug, 1970.
8lb 8oz From Blagdon in Sept, 1924, by Lieut-Colonel J Creagh Scott.
8lb 7oz† On Lough Eyes, Co Fermanagh, by Dr J P C Purdon on fly, in March, 1968. Irish record; Fish was just over 4 years of age.

TROUT (AMERICAN BROOK) *(Salvelinus fontinalis)*
5lb 13½oz* A Pearson, Avington Fisheries, Hants, 1981.
5lb 6oz A Pearson, Avington Fisheries, Hants, 1979.

WELS (Catfish) *(Silurus glanis)*
49lb 14oz* S Poyntz, from Homersfield Lake, Norfolk, Sept 1993.
43lb 8oz R J Bray, Tring, 1970.

WHITEFISHES *(Coregonidae)*
These fishes are confined in the British Isles to a limited number of large, deep lakes where they are known under a variety of local names: Schelly (Haweswater, Ullswater) gwyniad (Bala) powan (Loch Lomond, Loch Eck) vendace (Derwentwater, Bassenthwaite Lake, Loch Maben) and pollan (Loughs Erne, Rea, Derg and Neagh). Although closely related to the salmonids, they do not grow large, nor have they attracted much attention by anglers. Although there is some confusion as to how many of the local names distinguish separate species rather than isolated populations of a single species, since March 18th 1988 no whitefish may be angled for lawfully in the United Kingdom of Gt. Britain and N. Ireland. At that date they were added under the nomenclatures *Coregonus albul* and *Coregonus lavaretus* to Schedule 5 of the Wildlife & Countryside Act 1981. The following records have been retained in these lists purely for their historical interest.
2lb 1½oz* S M Barrie, Haweswater, 1986.
1lb 10oz W Wainwright, Ullswater, 1976.
1lb 7oz J M Ryder, Loch Lomond, 1972.
1lb 4oz J R Williams, Lake Bala, 1965.

SEA FISH:

ANGLER (*Lophius piscatorius*, Linn)

94lb 12¼oz*	S M A Neill	Belfast Lough	Nov 1985
82lb 12oz	K Ponsford	Mevagissey	April, 1977
74lb 8oz	J J McVicar	Eddystone	Aug, 1972
71lb 8oz†	M Fitzgerald	Cork (Cobh)	July, 1964
68lb 2oz	H G Legerton	Canvey Island	1967

BASS (*Morone Labrax*, Linn)

19lb*	D L Bourne	Dover	Sept 3, 1988
18lb 6oz	R Slater	off the Eddystone	Aug, 1975
18lb 2oz	F C Borley	Felixstowe Beach	Nov, 1943
17lb 8oz	W G Byron (caught with a Gig-gan bait), l 12¼in, g 32½in	Castlerock, Derry	Oct 22, 1935
17lb 4oz	J Drysdale	Kinsale	Aug, 1943
16lb 6oz	T Browne	Bangor	July, 1935
16lb†	Major Windham. Reported taken with a fly on a trout rod	Waterville	1909

A fish of 18½lb was reported caught in the Teifi estuary by a salmon fisher in 1956.

BLACK-FISH (*Centrolophus niger*)

4lb 9oz*	H G Lunt	Moggs Eye, Lincs	Nov 25, 1988
3lb 10½oz	J Semple	off Heads of Ayr	1972

BLUEMOUTH (*Helicolenus dactylopterus*)

3lb 2½oz*	Anne Lyngholm	L Shell, S'way	1976

BOGUE (*Boops boops*)

1lb 15¼oz*	S G Torode	Guernsey CI	1978

BREAM (BLACK) (*Spondyliosoma cantharus*, Gonelin)

6lb 14¼oz*	J A Garlick	from wreck off Devon coast	1977
6lb 7¾oz	J L D Atkins	E Blackstone Rocks, Devon	Aug 1973
6lb 5oz	M Brown, jnr	Menai Straits	Oct, 1935
6lb 1oz	F W Richards	Skerries Bank	Sept, 1969
4lb 14oz	A Procter	Looe	Aug, 1953
4lb 12½oz	H Pavey	Littlehampton	1963

BREAM (GILTHEAD) (*Sparus aurata*)

9lb 15¼oz*	C Bradford	Salcombe	1991
9lb 8 oz*†	R Simcox	off Salcombe	July 16, 1989
8lb 2oz	A Marquand	Guernsey	Sept, 1983
5lb 3oz	P King	Salcombe	July, 1983
5lb	A H Stratton-Knott	St. Mawes	1978

BREAM, RAY'S (*Brama brama*)

7lb 15¾oz*	G Walker	Hartlepool	1967

BREAM (RED) (*Pagellus centrodontus*, De La Roche)

9lb 8¾oz*	B H Reynolds	off Mevagissey	July, 1974
9lb 6oz†	P Maguire	Valentia	Aug, 1963
7lb 8oz	A F Bell	Fowey	July, 1925
6lb 3oz	Brig J A L Caunter	Nine miles of Looe	June, 1939
5lb 12½oz	Brig J A L Caunter	Looe	1954

BRILL (*Scopthalmus rhombus,* Linn)

16lb*	A H Fisher	Derby Haven, Isle of Man	1950
13lb 10oz	J L Williams	Brighton	1933

BULL HUSS (*Scyliorinus stellaris*)

22lb 4oz*	M L Hall	Minehead	1986
21lb 3oz	J Holmes	Hat Rock, Looe	1955
21lb	F C Hales	Poole, Dorset	Aug, 1936
21lb	H Jupp	Brighton	Oct, 1953
20lb	F Matthews	Newhaven	Sept, 1954
19lb 14oz†	G Ebbs	Pwllheli	May, 1992
19lb 12oz†	M Courage	Bray	1969

CATFISH (*Anarhichas lupus*)

26lb 4oz*	S P Ward	off Whitby	1989
24lb 3oz	N Trevelyan	Whitby	1980
15lb 12oz	E Fisher	off Filey, Yorkshire	1973
12lb 12½oz	G M Taylor	Stonehaven, Scotland	1978

COALFISH, or **Saithe** (*Gadus virens,* Linn)

37lb 5oz*	D Brown	S of Eddystone	1986
35lb 4oz	T Neatby	50m off Whitby	July, 1983
33lb 10oz	W H Saunders	off Dartmouth, Devon	Jan, 1983
33lb 7oz	L M Saunders	Start Point, Devon	1980
30lb 12oz	A F Harris	S of Eddystone	Feb, 1973
29lb 2½oz	R Phillips	SE of Eddystone	Jan, 1973
27lb 12½oz	J J McVicar	Eddystone	Jan, 1972
26lb 2oz	T J Trust	Start Point, Devon	1971
24lb 7oz†	J E Hornibrook	Kinsale	1967
23lb 8oz	Capt Hugo Millais	Land's End (Carnbase)	1921

COD (*Gadus callarias,* Linn)

58lb* 6oz	N Cook	Off Whitby	Aug, 1992
53lb	G Martin	Start Point, Devon	June, 1972
46lb 0½oz	R Baird	Firth of Clyde	Feb, 1970
45lb 14oz	D D Dinnie	Gourock	Jan, 1970
44lb 8oz	Brandon Jones	Barry (Glam)	Mar, 1966
42lb†	Ian L Stewart	Ballycotton	1921
34lb	The late R Blair	Ballycotton	1916
33lb 8oz	John E Timmins	Kinsale	Sept, 1962

A cod of 140lb landed at Hull Fish Dock in July, 1927, is worth adding to the record as a remarkable specimen, though it was not, of course, an angling trophy.

COMBER (*Serrana cabrilla*)

1lb 13oz*	Master B Phillips	off Mounts Bay	1977

CONGER (*Conger conger,* Linn)

112lb 8oz*		Over a wreck SE of Plymouth	July, 1992
110lb 11oz	H C Glausen	off Plymouth	1991
109lb 6oz	R W Potter	SE of Eddystone	Sept, 1976
102lb 8oz	R B Thomson	off Mevagissey	June, 1974
95lb 11oz	W K Oaten	Berry Head, S Devon	July, 1973
92lb 13oz	P H Ascott	Torquay	June, 1970
85lb	C E Chapman	Hythe (Hants)	June, 1970
84lb	H A Kelly	Dungeness	July, 1933

On the same day this angler had four more congers, 70lb, 33½lb, 21½lb, 15½lb.

80lb 8oz	H J West	Brixham	July, 1966
74lb	Mrs H Eathorne	Looe	1954
72lb†	James Green	Valentia	June, 1914

66lb   W H Pryce .... Coverack .... June, 1941
63lb 3oz   Miss B Klean .... Hastings 1922

DAB (*Limanda limanda,* Linn)
2lb 12¼oz*   R Islip .... Gairloch .... Aug, 1975
2lb 10¾oz   A B Hare.................. Skerries Bank .... April, 1968
2lb 9½oz   M L Watts................ Morfa Beach, Port Talbot........ July, 1936
2lb 8½oz   L White.................. Netley Pier, Southampton .... Nov, 1937
2lb 5½oz   C Stone .... Ryde, IoW .... Dec, 1934
2lb 4¼oz   N Coleman .... Hastings .... Jan, 1951
2lb 4oz   P A Heale .... Southsea..................... Dec, 1933
1lb 12½oz†   I V Kerr .... Kinsale 1963

DOGFISH, BLACK-MOUTHED (*Galeus melastomus*)
2lb 13½oz*   J H Anderson .... L Fyne 1977

DOGFISH (LESSER SPOTTED), or **Rough Head** (*Scyliorhinus caniculus,* Linn)
4lb 15oz†*   S Ramsey .... Abbey Burnfoot, Kirkudbrights Aug 10, 1988
4lb 8oz   J Beattie .... Ayr Pier 1969
4lb 2oz   B J Solomon.............. Newquay .... Oct, 1976
3lb 15oz†   unknown.................. S Ireland...................... 1980
3lb 12½oz   A Gibson.................. Firth of Clyde .... July, 1967

FLOUNDER (*Platichthys flesus,* Linn)
5lb 11½oz*   A G L Cobbledick .... Fowey...................... 1956
5lb 5½oz   D Clark .... Littlesea .... Mar, 1957
4lb 13oz   R Hitchman .... Exmouth...................... 1949
4lb 5oz   E F J Plumridge .... Fowey Estuary.............. April,1938
4lb 3oz†   J L McMonagle .... Killala Bay...................... 1963

FORKBEARD, GREATER (*Phycis blennoides*)
4lb 11¼oz*   Miss M Woodgate .... Falmouth 1969

GARFISH (*Belone belone,* Linn)
3lb 10¼oz†   E G Bazzard.............. Kinsale .... Sept, 1967
3lb 8oz   Hanson Horsey............ Kinsale .... Oct, 1969
3lb*   J Nardini.................. Penzance 1981
2lb 14oz   K C Ettle................. Kinsale .... Aug, 1968
2lb 14oz   D O'Donovan............. Kinsale .... Aug, 1968
2lb 13oz
14dm   Stephen Claeskens.......... Newton Ferrers .... Aug, 1971
2lb 12oz   K C Ettle................. Kinsale .... Aug, 1968
2lb 12oz   M L Walsh .... Ballycotton................... June, 1967
2lb 11¾oz   Dennis Collins .... Kinsale 1966
2lb 10½oz   J O'Sullivan .... Courtmacsherry, Co Cork .... Aug, 1971
2lb 10oz   Mrs Sandra Parker......... Kinsale .... Sept, 1969
2lb 9oz 2dm   A W Bodfield............. Dartmouth 1963
2lb 9oz   F T Goffin .... Coverack .... July, 1935

GREATER WEEVER (*Trachinus draco*)
2lb 4oz   P Ainslie .... Brighton......................... 1927
Record declared open at qualifying weight of 1lb 4oz.

GURNARD (GREY) (*Eutrigla gurnardus*)
3lb 1oz†   B Walsh .... Rosslare Bay 1967
2lb 7oz*   D Swinbanks .... Caliach Point, Isle of Mull....... July, 1976
2lb 2oz   D H Taylor............... Off Portrush, NI .... July, 1973

1lb 10oz   D Cameron-McIntosh .... Isle of Arran...................... 1971
1lb 6oz   K R Manson .... Bressay, Shetland 1971

GURNARD (RED) (*Aspitrigla cuculus*)
5lb   D B Critchley (captor aged 9) off Rhyl...................... July, 1973
4lb 9½oz   C Butler.................. off Anglesey.................. June, 1973
4lb 4¾oz   W R Shaw................ Conway.................... June, 1973
2lb 8½oz*   D Relton .... 22m NW of Tobermory, I. O. Mull July, 1985

GURNARD, STREAKED (*Trigloporus lastoviza*)
1lb 6½oz*   H Livingstone Smith .... L Goil, Firth of Clyde.............. 1971

GURNARD, YELLOW, or **Tub Fish,** (*Trigela lucerna,* Linn)
12lb 3oz*   G J Reynolds .... Langland Bay, Wales 1976
11lb 7¼oz   C W King .... Wallasey...................... 1952
10lb 8oz†   C Gammon .... Belmullet 1970
10lb 2¼oz   E Sederholm.............. Belmullet .... May, 1969
9½lb   W Adams .... Isle of Man.................... 1907

HADDOCK (*Gadus aegifinus,* Linn)
13lb 11¼oz* G Bones.................. off Falmouth.................... 1978
12lb 10oz   Sub-Lieut K P White .... Manacles, Falmouth Bay .... Jan, 1975
10lb 13½oz† F A E Bull................ Kinsale, Co Cork.............. July, 1964
10lb 12oz   A H Hill................. Looe .... July, 1972
10lb 0½oz   David Hare .... Valentia 1971
9lb 14½oz   J O'Gilvie .... Valentia .... Aug, 1969
9lb 8¾oz   L A Derby................ Kinsale .... June, 1965
9lb 4½oz   Mrs M Morley .... Mevagissey.................... 1969
9lb 2¼oz   Eric Smith................ Kinsale .... July, 1963

HADDOCK, NORWAY (*Sebastes viviparus*)
1lb 13½oz*   T Barrett .... off Southend-on-Sea.............. 1975

HAKE (*Merluccius merluccius,* Linn)
25lb 5½oz*† H W Steele .... Belfast Lough................. 1962
20lb   Frank Vinnicombe.......... Falmouth.................... Aug, 1960
17½lb   Mrs J T Ashby .... Penzance........................ 1911

HALIBUT (*Hippoglossus hippoglossus*)
234lb*   C Booth.................. off Dunnet Head, Scotland.......... 1979
212lb 4oz   J A Hewitt................ off Dunnet Head .... Aug, 1975
196lb   J T Newman .... off Dunnet Head, Caithness ..... April, 1974
161lb 12oz   W E Knight............... Orkney .... Aug, 1968
152¾lb†   E C Henning.............. Valentia 1926
He also had two, 128¾lb, 120½lb on another day in 1926.
135lb   J N Hearn .... Ballycotton.................... 1912
A Halibut weighing 500lb was landed by a commercial fishing boat at Grimsby in October 1957.

HERRING (*Clupea haringus*)
1lb 11oz*   B Barden................. off Bexhill-on-Sea.................. 1973

JOHN DORY (*Zeus Faber,* Linn)
11lb 14oz*   J Johnson................ off Newhaven.................... 1977
10lb 12oz   B L Perry................ Porthallow, Cornwall 1963
8lb 8oz   J F Vallin .... Mevagissey.................... 1922
8lb 4oz   R Brown, Dreadnought SAS.. Fowey .... July, 1932

LING (*Molva molva*, Linn)

59lb 8oz*	J Webster	off Bridlington	July 10, 1989
57lb 8oz	I Duncan	off Stonehaven	May, 1982
57lb 2½oz	H Solomons	off Mevagissey	1975
57lb 8oz	B M Coppen	off Eddystone	Mar, 1974
46lb 8oz†	A J C Bull	Kinsale	July, 1965
46lb	T D Walker	off Plymouth	Mar, 1974
45lb	H C Nicholl	Penzance	1912

LUMPSUCKER (*Cyclopterus lumpus*)

20lb 9¾oz*	A J Perry	Weymouth pier	1987
14lb 3oz	W J Burgess	Felixstowe Beach	1970

MACKEREL (*Scomber scombrus*, Linn)

6lb 2½oz*	W J Chapple	1½ miles off Penberth Cove, Cornwall	1984
5lb 6½oz	S Beasley	Eddystone Lighthouse	1969
4lb 11oz	L A Seward	Flamborough Head	1963
4lb 0½oz	F/Lt P Porter	Peel, Isle of Man	June 9, 1952
3lb 10oz	A Cave	Peel, Isle of Man	Aug, 1953
3lb 8oz	W Adams	-	1906
3lb 6oz†	J O'Connell	Valentia	1969

A fish of 4½lb was caught at Looe in June, 1935, by W C Butters on a handline.

MEGRIM (*Lepidohumbus wiffiagonis*)

3lb 12½oz*	Master P Christie	Gairloch	Aug, 1973

MONKFISH (*Squatina Squatina*, Linn)

69lb†	Monsieur Fuchs	Westport	July, 1958
66lb*	C G Chalk	Shoreham	1965
62lb	S Morris	Littlehampton	1919
62lb	A E Beckett	Porthcawl	1960

A fish of 68lb was reported from Beaulieu in August, 1953.

MULLET (GOLDEN GREY) (*Liza aurata*)

2lb 13¼oz*	C Fletcher	Rocquaine, Guernsey	1990
2lb 12¾oz	J Reeves	Alderney, CI	Sep 2, 1989
2lb 11½oz	D M Bohan	Fort Doyle, Alderney CI	1984
2lb 10¼oz	F Odoire	Alderney	Nov, 1983
2lb 10oz	R J Hopkins	Burry Port	1976

MULLET (GREY, THICKED-LIPPED) (*Chelon Labrosus*)

14lb 2¾oz*	R S Gifford	Aberthaw, S Wales	1979
10lb 1oz	P/O P C Libby	Portland	1952
8lb 12oz	W E Wallis	Portland	1921
8lb 7oz	F V Daunou	Margate	About 1903

MULLET (GREY, THIN-LIPPED) (*Liza ramada*)

7lb*	N Mableson	Oulton Broad	1991
6lb 4oz	H E Mephan	Kentish Rother	1981
3lb 7oz	D Davenport	Christchurch Estuary	Aug, 1983
3lb 2oz	J Corner	Christchurch Harbour	July, 1983

MULLET (RED) (*Mullus surmuletus*)

3lb 10oz*	J E Martel	Guernsey	Oct, 1967
2lb 1oz 3dm	T F Cleal	Guernsey	Oct, 1967

OPAH (*Lampris guttatus*)

128lb*	A R Blewitt	Mounts Bay, Penzance	1973

PELAMID (BONITO) (*Sarda sarda*)
8lb 13¼oz* J Parnell .... Torbay.......................... 1969

PERCH, DUSKY (*Epinephelus guaza*)
28lb*   D Cope .... off Durlston Head, Dorset 1973

PLAICE (*Pleuronectes platessa*, Linn)
10lb 3½oz* Master H Gardiner......... Longa Sound .... Oct, 1974
8lb 7oz   R Moore .... Southbourne................ June 18, 1989
7lb 15oz   Ian Brodie................ Salcombe .... Oct, 1964
7lb 13oz 1dm W F Parker .... Teignmouth 1961
7lb 6oz   D Brown .... Dartmouth (Skerries) .... June, 1963
7lb 6oz   J P Wright.............. Dartmouth................... May, 1960
7lb 5oz 6dm C Riggs .... Teign Estuary.................... 1949
7lb†   E Yemen .... Portrush 1964

POLLACK, or **Lythe** (*Gadus pollachius*, Linn)
29lb 4oz* W S Mayes .... Dungeness 1987
27lb 6oz   R S Milkins................ Salcombe 1986
26lb 7oz   R C Perry .... 31 miles S of Salcombe 1984
25lb   R J Hosking .... Eddystone...................... 1972
23lb 8oz   G Bartholomew .... Newquay........................ 1957
22lb 8oz   W Digby .... Looe 1955
21lb   Capt Hugo Millais .... Land's End (Carnbase)............. 1921
Capt Millais had others of 17lb and 18lb at the same place
20lb 8oz   Mrs Hugo Millais.......... Land's End (Carnbase)............. 1921
Mrs Millais also had a specimen of 19½lb
20lb 8oz   J H Layton .... Lochinver...................... 1920

POUTING (*Gadus luscus*, Linn)
5lb 8oz*   R S Armstrong .... Berry Head...................... 1969
4lb 10oz   H B Dare................ Coverack.................... Sept, 1935
4lb 10oz† W G Pales................ Ballycotton.................... 1937
4lb 9oz   E Burton .... Belfast Lough............... April, 1968

PUFFER FISH (*Lagocephalus lagocephalus*)
6lb 9¼oz* S Atkinson .... Chesil Beach .... Oct, 1975

RAY (BLOND) (*Raia brachyura*, Lafont)
37lb 12oz* H T Pout .... Salcombe .... Oct, 1973
36lb 8oz† D Minchin................ Cork (Cobh)................. Sept, 1964
35lb 9oz   A J Pearce.............. Portland .... May, 1970
34lb 8oz   T Hutchinson .... Cobh .... Sept, 1967

RAY (BOTTLE-NOSED) (*Raja alba*)
76lb*   R Bulpitt................ off The Needles, IoW 1970

RAY (CUCKOO) (*Raio naevus*)
5lb 11oz* V Morrison............... off Causeway Coast, NI 1975
5lb 6oz†   K Derbyshire .... Causeway Coast, Co Antrim ..... Aug, 1971
5lb 3oz   P J Rankin................ off Causeway Coast, NI 1974
5lb   N C McLean.............. Lamlash Bay, Isle of Arran ..... June, 1968

RAY (EAGLE) (*Myliobatis aquila*)
61lb 8oz* M Drew.................... off IoW.................... Aug 28, 1989
52lb 8oz   R J Smith................ off Nab Tower, IoW 1972

RAY (ELECTRIC) (*Torpedo nobiliana*)
96lb 1oz* N J Cowley............... off Dodman Point, Cornwall ..... July, 1975
47lb 8oz   R J F Pearce .... Long Quarry, Torquay .... Aug, 1971

RAY (MARBLED ELECTRIC) (*Torpedo marinurata*)
13lb 15¾oz   M E Porter .... off Jersey 1990
5lb 8¼oz   M A Shales.............. Jersey CI .... Aug 31, 1988
2lb 8½oz   B T Maguire.............. St Aubin, Jersey .... July, 1983

RAY (SMALL-EYED) (*Raia microcellata*)
16lb 6½oz*   J B Lush .... off Minehead................ April, 1982
16lb 4oz   H T Pout................. Salcombe .... Sept, 1973
14lb 8oz   T Pooley................. nr Stoke Point, Devon .... May 25, 1989
13lb 11½oz   H T Pout................. Bolt Tail, Devon 1971
13lb 8oz   Mrs T Whippy .... Pevensey Bay .... Aug, 1969
12lb 1½oz   A T Scoones.............. Littlehampton .... July, 1969

RAY (SPOTTED) (*Raia montagui*)
16lb 3oz   E Lockwood.............. Lerwick, Shetland.................. 1970
14lb 3oz   W C Furnish.............. St Anne's Head, Pembroke 1970
8lb 4oz*   G Brownlie............... IoWhithorn, Galloway June15, 1989
7lb 12oz   J Cochrane .... off Causeway Coast, NI........ Aug, 1982
6lb 14oz   H A Jamieson............. Causeway Coast, NI................ 1978

RAY (STING) (*Trigon pastinaca*, Linn)
65lb 8oz*   J K Rawle................ off Bradwell-on-Sea................ 1990
61lb 8oz*   V W Roberts.............. off Pwllheli 1979
59lb   J M Buckley.............. Clacton-on-Sea 1952
52lb 8oz   T E Stone .... Lymington River mouth............. 1938
52lb   J Manser .... Brighton......................June, 1954
51lb 8oz   P J Hill .... Hastings .... Oct, 1956

RAY (THORNBACK) (*Raia clavata*, Linn)
57lb   S G Lugger.............. Exmouth.................... July, 1951
38lb   J Patterson, Jnr.......... Rustington Beach .... May, 1935
37lb†   M J Fitzgerald .... Kinsale .... May, 1961
31lb 7oz*†   J Wright .... Liverpool Bay .... July, 1981

RAY (UNDULATE) (*Raja undulata*)
21lb 4½oz*   S Titt................... off Swanage...................... 1987
21lb 4oz   K Skinner .... St Catherine's Lghtho, Jersey, CI . Sept, 1983
20lb 12¼oz   F J Casado .... off Corbierre, Jersey, CI .... May, 1982
19lb 7oz   L R LePage.............. Herm, CI 1970

ROCKLING (THREE-BEARDED) (*Onos tricirratus*, Block)
3lb 4¼oz*   G Hurst.................. off I.O.Wight...................... 1992
3lb 2½oz   Mrs G Haves .... off Dartmouth 1990
2lb 14¼oz   S F Bealing.............. Poole Bay..................... Oct, 1972
2lb 13oz 2dm K Westaway.............. Portland Harbour.............. June, 1966

SCAD, or **Horse Mackerel** (*Trachurus trachurus*, Linn)
3lb 5¼oz*   M A Atkins.............. Torbay 1978
3lb 4½oz   D O Cooke .... Mewstone, Plymouth 1971
3lb 3oz   J B Thorton............. Deal.......................... July, 1934

SHAD (ALLIS) (*Alosa alosa*)
4lb 12½oz*   P B Gerrard .... Chesil Beach, Dorset 1977
3lb 4½oz   B H Sloane .... Princess Pier, Torquay 1964

SHAD (TWAITE) (*Alosa finta*, Cuvier)
3lb 2oz   T Hayward .... Deal......................... Nov, 1949

| 3lb 2oz | S Jenkins | Torbay | 1954 |
| 2lb | S Gower | Poole Harbour | Oct, 1984 |

SHARK (BLUE) (*Carcharinus glaucus*, Linn)

218lb*	N Sutcliffe	Looe	July, 1959
206lb†	J L McGonagle	Achill	Oct, 1959
184lb	T Robinson	Looe	1960
180lb	H Widdett	Looe	1955
180lb	F A Mitton	Looe	1960

SHARK (MAKO) (*Isurus oxyrhinchus*, Raf

500lb*	Mrs J M Yallop	Eddystone Light	1971
498lb 8oz	K Burgess	Looe	July, 1966
476lb	W J Rogers	Falmouth	July, 1964
435lb	S G Miller	Looe	June, 1964
428lb 8oz	J E Sefton	Looe	1961

It was not until 1956 that the mako shark was positively identified as a British species, and it is probable that some of the fish listed earlier as porbeagles were, in fact, makos.

SHARK (PORBEAGLE) (*Lamna cornubica*, Gonetin)

507lb*	C Bennett	off Dunnet Head, Caithness	March, 1993
465lb	J Potier	off Padstow, Cornwall	July, 1976
430lb	D Bougourd	South of Jersey	1969
367lb	B D Phillipps	Jersey, CI	June, 1960
365lb†	Dr O'Donnel Browne	Keem Bay, Co Mayo	1932
324lb	T Paince	Nab Tower	Aug, 1968
311lb	K C Wilson	Looe	1961
300lb††	J Eathorne	Looe	1951

The identification of the mako shark in British waters has thrown some doubt on the authenticity of this list. Dr O'Donnel Browne's fish was certainly a porbeagle, but the one marked †† is now thought probably to have been a mako. Fish caught since 1956 are definitely porbeagles.

SHARK, SIX-GILLED (*Hexanchus priseus*)

| 154lb† | A Bull | off Kinsale | Aug 28, 1968 |
| 9lb 8oz* | F E Beeston | off Plymouth | 1976 |

SHARK (THRESHER) (*Alopias vulpes*, Gonetin)

323lb*	S Mills	Nab Tower, off Portsmouth	July, 1982
295lb	H J Aris	Dunose Head, IoW	1978
280lb	H A Kelly	Dungeness	1933
149lb	R Romilly Lunge	Christchurch	July, 1937

SKATE (COMMON) (*Raia batis*, Linn)

336lb	Captor unknown	Beer	1934
227lb*	P Banks	off Tobermory	1986
226lb 8oz	R S Macpherson	Shetland	Aug, 1970
221lb†	T Tucker	Ballycotton	1913
218lb 8oz	E C Henning	Valentia	1927
214lb	J A E Olsson	Scapa Flow	July, 1968
211lb	Dr C Ayton Marrett	Ballycotton	1912
208lb	Leonard F Hopkins	Clare Island, Co Mayo	Aug, 1971
205	A W Bowie	Kinsale	Aug, 1956

SMOOTHOUND (*Mustelus mustelus*)

| 28lb* | A T Chilvers | Heacham | 1969 |

SMOOTHOUND (STARRY) (*Mustelus asterias*)

| 28lb* | R Grady | Maplin Sands, Essex | 1980 |
| 23lb 2oz | D Carpenter | Bradwell on Sea | 1972 |

SOLE (*Solea solea,* Linn)

6lb 8½oz	N V Guilmoto	S Coast Boulders, Alderney	1991
6lb 2oz	J Bartram	Nr Braye, Alderney, CI	1984
5lb 7oz	L Dixon	Alderney, CI	1980
4lb 8oz	H C L Pike	Alderney, CI	1978
4lb 3½oz	R Wells	Redcliffe Beach	Mar, 1974
4lb 1oz 14dm	R A Austin	Guernsey	Dec, 1967
4lb 1¾oz*	M Eppelein	off Channel Islands	June, 1993
4lb	M Stinton	Clevedon Pier	Sept, 1943
3lb 4oz	S Hayman	Weymouth	Nov, 1956

SOLE (LEMON) (*Microstumus Kitt*)

2lb 7¾oz*	W N Callister	Douglas, Isle of Man	1980
2lb 3oz	D R Duke	Douglas, Isle of Man	1971

SPANISH MACKEREL (*Scomber japonicus*)

1lb ½oz*	P Jones	off Guernsey CI	1972

SPURDOG (*Squalus acanthias,* Linn)

21lb 3½oz*	P R Barnett	off Porthleven	1977
20lb 3oz	J Newman	Needles	May, 1972
17lb 1oz	S Bates	Deal	1971
16lb 12½oz	R Legg	Chesil Beach	1964
16lb 4oz†	C McIvor	Strangford Lough	June, 1969
15lb 12oz	John Rowe	Killala Bay, Sligo	Aug, 1967
15lb 5oz	J S W Fisher	Strangford Lough	Oct, 1971
15lb	W Hamilton	Strangford Lough	July, 1969
14lb 6oz	J C Nott	Clare Island	June, 1969
14lb 1oz	D R Angiolini	Valentia	Sept, 1968
14lb	R Wickens	Kinsale	Oct, 1962

SUNFISH (*Mola mola*)

108lb*	T F Sisson	Saundersfoot	Aug, 1976
49lb 4oz	M G H Merry	Cornwall	Aug, 1976

TADPOLE FISH (*Raniceps raninus*)

1lb 13¾oz*	D A Higgins	Whitley Bay	1977

TOPE (*Eugaleus galeus,* Linn)

82lb 8oz*	R Chatfield	off Bradwell-on-Sea	1991
79lb 12oz	P J Richards	Bradwell-on-Sea	1986
74lb 11oz	A B Harries	Caldy Island	July, 1964
73lb 3oz (female)	L Andrews	Hayling Island	1949
65lb	Lt-Col R I P Earle	Studland	1956
64lb 8oz	J H Swan	Camel Estuary, Padstow	July, 1963
62lb 11oz	A J Drew	Herne Bay	1911
62lb 8oz (female)	R J Weston	Eastbourne	June, 1955
62lb 2oz (female)	A B Fitt	Herne Bay	June, 1951
62lb (male)	D S Southcombe	Weymouth	1946
61lb 8oz (female)	G T Northover	Herne Bay	June, 1936
60lb 12oz†	C McIver	Strangford Lough	1968

TORSK (*Brosme brosme*)

15lb 7oz*	D J MacKay	Pentland Firth	July, 1982

12lb 1oz   D Pottinger .... Shetland 1968

TRIGGER FISH (*Balistes carolinensis*)
5lb 5¹⁄₄oz*   D H Bush .... Poole Quay...................... 1990
4lb 9¹⁄₄oz   E Montacute .... Weymouth Bay 1975
4lb 6³⁄₄oz   E Bainbridge.............. Chesil Beach .... Aug 31, 1989
4lb 6³⁄₄oz   A Kershaw .... Chesil Beach .... Sep 10, 1989

TUNA, BIG-EYE*(*Thunnus obesus*)
66lb 12oz*   S Atkinson .... Newlyn Harbour .... Oct 1985

TUNA BLUE-FIN (Tunny) (*Thunnus thynnus*)
The fish given in the following list were all caught in the North Sea tunny fishing grounds off Scarborough and Whitby:
851lb*   L Mitchell-Henry, ... 1933
764lb   H W Holgate, ... 1934
812lb   Colonel E T Peel, ... 1934
763lb   G Baker, ... 1933
798lb   H G Smith, ... 1934
762lb   M W Holgate, ... 1935
798lb   Colonel E T Peel, ... 1932
749lb   S Cohen, ... 1949
785lb   Major R T Laughton, ... 1947
747lb   H E Weatherley,... 1952
660lb   H E Weatherley,... 1954

TUNA (LONG-FINNED) (*Thunnus alalunga*)
4lb 12oz*   B Cater, Salcombe... 1990

TURBOT (*Scophthalmus maximus*, Linn)
33lb 12oz*   R Simcox.................. Salcombe, Devon.................. 1980
32lb 8oz†   Unknown.................. S Ireland 1980
32lb 3oz   D Dyer................... off Plymouth .... May, 1976
31lb 4oz   Paul Hutchings (11)......... Eddystone Light............... July, 1972
29lb   G M W Garnsey............ The Manacles.................. Aug, 1964
28lb 0¹⁄₂oz   T Tolchard .... Dartmouth...................... 1961
27lb 14oz   F·S Stenning............. Salcombe 1907
26lb 8oz   J F Eldridge .... Valentia 1915
25lb 8oz   Mat Kearney.............. Cork Harbour................... Aug, 1971
25lb 4oz   R Tolchard (age 12)......... off Dartmouth .... June, 1958

WHITING (*Gadus merlangus*, Linn)
6lb 12oz*   N R Croft .... Falmouth....................... 1981
6lb 4oz   S Dearman Bridport......... April, 1977
6lb 3oz 3dm   Mrs R Barrett .... Rame Head, Cornwall............. 1971
6lb   E H Tame .... Shieldaig.................. Mar, 1940
5lb 2oz   H C Nicoll............... Penzance...................... 1912
5lb 1oz   H W Antenbring........... Shieldaig.................. June, 1938

WITCH (*Glyptocephalus cynoglossus*)
1lb 2³⁄₄oz*   T J Barathey .... Colwyn Bay 1967

WRASSE (BALLAN) (*Labrus bergylta*, Ascanius)
12lb 1oz   F A Mitchell-Hedges........ Looe 1912
12lb   F A Mitchell-Hedges........ Looe 1912
11lb 8oz   F A Mitchell-Hedges........ Looe 1912
10lb 12oz   F A Mitchell-Hedges........ Looe 1912
9lb 6oz   M Goodacre .... Eddystone gully................... 1981
8lb 10³⁄₄oz*   J le Noury .... St Peter's Port Harbour, C.I. ... March 1993

7lb 13½oz   D R Gabe .... off Start Point, Devon................ 1978
7lb 10oz
  15dm   B K Lawrence .... Trevose Head, Cornwall............. 1970
7lb 6oz†   A J King .... Killybegs 1964

WRASSE (CUCKOO) (*Labrus mixtus*)
2lb 3.12oz* A B Welch Lymm Bay, 1990
2lb 2½oz*   D Davies.................. off Plymouth .... Dec 3, 1989
2lb 0½oz   A M Foley .... Plymouth .... Nov, 1973
1lb 14¾oz   R G Berry................. Sennen, Cornwall .... Sept, 1973
1lb 12½oz   L C Le Cras .... Guernsey .... Aug, 1972
1lb 10oz 8dm B Perry .... Torquay .... Sept, 1971

WRECKFISH (*Polyprion americanus*)
10lb 10oz*   B McNamara .... off Eddystone 1980
7lb 10oz   Cdr E StJ Holt .... Looe, Cornwall 1974

A 69 lb. tope and six turbot. Not a bad reward for a day's pleasure! *Photo: Vic Haigh.*

THE SALMON AND TROUT ASSOCIATION

This association is the only body which exists solely to protect the interests of game fish, fisheries and fishermen in the United Kingdom.

Director: Christopher Poupard, Fishmongers Hall, London EC4R 9EL. Tel: 071-283 5838 Fax: 071-929 1389.

Field Secretary - England and Wales:
Bill Davies, 29 Neale Close, Harbury, Warwicks CV33 9JQ. 0926 612661.

The Association is organised into Regions which correspond with those of the National Rivers Authority.

ENGLAND
NORTH WEST REGION
James Carr (Regional Representative), Moorhouse Hall, Warwick-on-Eden, Carlisle CA4 8PA
North & West Cumbria:
James Carr (Branch Chairman), Moorhouse Hall, Warwick-on-Eden, Carlisle CA4 8PA (0228) 561993
T L Atkinson (Branch Secretary), Cairnhill House, Springkell, Eaglesfield, Lockerbie, Dumfriesshire DG11 3AG. (0228) 26292 (Business), 0461 6263 (Home)
South Cumbria & North Lancashire:
J Cleaver (Branch Treasurer), Lowick Mill Cottage, Lowick Bridge, Ulverston, Cumbria LA2 8EF
Lancashire:
Mr J J B Rawkins (Branch Chairman), Alston Cottage Farm, Alston Lane, Alston, Longridge, Preston (0772) 784049
J M Croft (Branch Organiser & Secretary), Moss Side Farm, Thornley, Preston PR3 2ND (0772) 782223
Mr R Horsfall (Recruitment Officer), Sowerby Hall, St Michaels, Preston PR3 0TU
Dr R B Broughton (Water Resources Officer), 10 Park Road, Salford, Lancashire M6 8HL
Cheshire & Manchester:
Mr D R Green (Secretary & Treasurer), Orchard Piece, Marbury Road, Comberbach Northwich, Cheshire CW9 6AU (0606) 891654
Mr K Crosbie (Branch Organiser), Brookfield, Free Green Lane, Over Peover, Knutsford, Cheshire WA16 TQY
Merseyside:
S Newton (Branch Chairman), 13 Mount Pleasant, Oxton, Birkenhead, Merseyside 051 652 6242

NORTUMBERLAND REGION
G Curry (Regional Stillwater Fisheries Officer), 62 Newcastle Road, Chester-Le-Street, Co Durham
J G Ellison (Regional Chairman & Secretary, Regional Water Resources Officer & Representative), 3 Burnside Court, Hartburn Avenue, Stockton-on-Tees, Cleveland TSl8 4EU
P S Jackson (Regional Vice Chairman), 14 Sudburn Avenue, Staindrop, Darlington DL2 3TY
C H Noble (Regional Abstraction Officer & Representative), 30 The Green, Hurworth-on-Tees, Darlington Co. Durham, (0325) 720450 (home), (0325) 381381 (work)
J E D Brown (Regional Migratory Fish Officer), Baydale Farm, Coniscliffe Road, Darlington, Co Durham, (0325) 487999
Dr D J Alcock (Regional Pollution Officer), 35 Castle View, Witton-le-Wear, Bishop Auckland, Co. Durham DL14 0DH
J Winter (Regional Stock & Welfare of Migratory Fish Officer), 7 Royal Grove, Crook, Co. Durham
P Dawson (Regional Sports Officer), 15 Preston Lane, Stockton-on-Tees, Cleveland Tel: (0642) 781187
Mrs Annette Taylor, 29 Darlington Lane, Norton, Stockton-on-Tees, Cleveland TS20 1EP Tel: (0642) 559226
Northumbria:
C H Noble (Branch Chairman & Organiser) 30 The Green, Hurworth-on-Tees, Darlington, Co. Durham DL2 2AA (0325) 720450 (home), (0325) 381381 (work)
J E D Brown (Branch Organiser), Baydale Farm, Coniscliffe Road, Darlington, Co. Durham (0325) 487999
Cleveland
Mr Jeremy W Spooner (Branch Chairman), 29 Darlington Lane, Norton, Stockton-on-Tees, Cleveland TS20 1EP Tel: (0642) 559226
Mrs Annette Taylor (Branch Organiser), 29

Darlington Lane, Norton, Stockton-on-Tees, Cleveland TS20 1EP Tel: (0642) 559226

Peter Dawson (Events Organiser (Fishing), Tel: (0642) 781187

SEVERN-TRENT REGION

P Buckland-Large (Regional Representative), Crudwell House, Holmfield Avenue, Stoneygate, Leicester, LE12 2BG (0533) 707607

Shropshire & Montgomery:

Mr H M Milnes (Branch President), Marnwood, Buildwas, Shropshire TF8 7BJ (095245) 2211

T Williams (Branch Chairman), The Old Pound, Loppington, Shropshire SY4 5SR

Peter Stacy, The Orchard, Homer, Much Wenlock, Shropshire (Water Abstraction)

Mr Roy Owen (Branch Organiser), 11 Portmans Way, Bridgnorth, Shropshire WV16 5AT (07462) 762500

Nottinghamshire & Derbyshire:

Dr G Owen (Branch Chairman), The Firs, 66A Dore Road, Dore, Sheffield S17 3NE (0742) 363791

C E B Frost (Branch Organiser), Green Meadows, Cross Lane, Monyash, Bakewell, Derbyshire DE4 1JN (0629) 813813

Janice Jackson (Secretary), 8 Bradley Close, Birchover, Matlock, Derbyshire

C J Stokes (Branch Treasurer), Broadhay Farm, Highlow, Hathersage, New Sheffield (0433) 50263

C Lee (Abatement & Pollution Officer), Piscatoria, Hebden Court, Bakewell, Derbyshire

P Wilson (Publicity & Recruitment), Splash Cottage, Bagshall Hill, Bakewell, Derbyshire (0629) 813557

Staffordshire:

Alan Smith (Branch Chairman), Ravensoak, Stone Road, Hill Chorlton, Whitmore, Newcastle-under-Lyme

J M Bevan BA (Branch Organiser), 66 Sneyd Avenue, Westlands, Newcastle-under-Lyme, Staffs (0782) 616848 (home), (0782) 613918 (office)

R Hawley (Water Abstraction Officer), Wellington House, Stone, Staffs

D Airie (Treasurer), 8 Shropland, Badgers Brow, Loggerheads, Nr Market Drayton, Shropshire

West Midlands & Warwickshire:

Lord Guernsey (Branch Chairman), Packington Hall, Meriden, Nr Coventry, West Midlands CV7 7HF (0676) 22754

J P Hickman (Branch Secretary/Treasurer), 25 Charlesworth Avenue, Shirley, Solihull, West Midlands B90 4SE

Leicestershire:

P Buckland-Large (Branch Chairman), Crudwell House, Holmfield Avenue, Stoneygate, Leicester LE12 2BG (0533) 707607

I Kilgour (Branch Organiser), 3 Hall Farm Road, Thurcaston, Leicestershire LE7 7JF

N Everson (Branch Treasurer), 6 Meadowcourt Road, Leicester LE2 2PB

Peter Smith (Water Resources Officer), Wychwood, 17 The Fairway, Oadby, Leicestershire LE2 2PB

Worcestershire:

D Malpass (Branch Organiser), 82 Oak Crescent, Malvern, Worcestershire

Birmingham City Branch:

Mr J Fazakerley (Branch Organiser), 30 Rosafield Avenue, Halesowen, West Midlands B62 9BU (021 422) 3173 (home), (021 200) 3111 (work), (021 233) 9615 (fax)

YORKSHIRE REGION

Yorkshire Region (including North Humberside):

The Rt Hon The Lord Mason of Barnsley (President), The House of Lords, Westminster, London SW1A 0PW

Lt Col H S le Messurier (Deputy President, North), Thornton Grange, Thorton Steward, Ripon HG2 2BQ

Mr G R Stocks (Deputy President, South), 6 School Walk, Old Edlington, Doncaster DN12 1PU

Mr Ian Davis (Chairman), Oxton Close, Ouston Lane, Tadcaster LS24 8DF

Michael E Stewart (Deputy Chairman), Thornhill, Clint, Harrogate, HG3 3DS

M J Needham FRICS FCIArb (Regional Secretary), 30 Leadhall Road, Harrogate HG2 9PE, (0423) 64163 or (0423) 872339

Mrs Jean Whitehead (Regional Treasurer), 7 Forster Close, Burley in Wharfedale, Ilkley LS28 7HE

G R Stocks (Regional Abstraction Officer), 6 School Walk, Old Edlington, Doncaster, South Yorkshire, DN1 1PU (0709) 862497

R J Hodgson (Regional Auditor), Oakridge, Summerbridge, Harrogate HG3 2JJ (0423) 780458

M J Thompson (Regional Planning Officer), 32 The Balk, Walton, Wakefield WF2 6JU

Mr Ian Rae (Trout Interest Officer), 316

Ringinglow Road, Sheffield S11 7PY

Dr Hugh Evans (Education and Training), 8 Park Edge, Harrogate HG2 8JU

North & East Yorkshire:

Richard Benwell (Branch Chairman), The Gardens, Kilnwick, Driffield, North Humberside YO25 9JG (0377) 70216

Keith Coupland (Branch Organiser), 2 White Cottages, South Cliffe, Hotham, York YO4 3UX (0430) 827308

Mr Jonathan Storrs-Fox (Branch Treasurer), 22 Station Road, South Cave, Brough, East Yorkshire HU15 2AA

Nidderdale:

Mr Donald C G Walker (Chairman), Weir House, Nidd Bank, Knaresborough, North Yorkshire HG5 9BX (0423) 862588

Mr Michael E Stewart (Vice Chairman), Thornhill, Clint, Harrogate HG3 3DS (0423) 771722

Mr William S Harrison (Branch Secretary & Organiser), 12 Park Edge, Harrogate HG2 8JU (0423) 883476

Mr J Breckton (Social Secretary), Jobadach, Pateley Road, Harrogate

Mr P Stevenson (Social Secretary), Orchard View, Low Laithe, Harrogate HG3 4DD

Dr Hugh D Evans (Tuition Officer), 8 Park Edge, Harrogate HG2 8JU

Mr Jerry Wastling (Pollution & Water Resources Officer), 2 Leadhall Gardens, Harrogate HG3 4DD

York & District:

Mr Ian Davies (Branch Chairman), Oxton Close, Ouston Lane, Tadcaster LS24 8DF

Mr John Lazenby (Vice Chairman), Maugerhay, Main Street, Askham, Bryan, York YO2 3QS

Mrs Susan Keech (Secretary/Organiser), 21 Meadlands, York YO3 ONU

A A Keech (Treasurer), 21 Meadlands, York Y03 ONU

South Yorkshire:

G R Stocks (President & Abstraction Officer), 6 School Walk, Old Edlington, Doncaster, South Yorkshire DN12 1PU (0709) 862497

Mrs S Murray (Branch Chairman), 3 Belgrave Drive, Sheffield S10 3LQ (0742) 302123

S Crofts (Branch Organiser), 4 Stottercliffe Road, Penistone, Sheffield S30 6EB (0226) 766940

Mr D Calvert (Treasurer), The Long Barn, Overacre, Oughterbridge, Sheffield S30 3HJ

P Towers (River Don Secretary), 19 Richard Road, Darton, Barnsley, South York-shire

Mr A Davis (Social Secretary), 64 Airedale Avenue, Tickhill, Donncaster (0302) 750760

Mr I Rae (Stillwater Officer), 316 Ringinglow Road, Sheffield S11 7PY

Mr B Marsh (Minutes Secretary), 23 Spoonhill Road, Sheffield S6 5PA

Swaledale & Wensleydale:

Lt Col H S le Messurier (Branch President), Thornton Grange, Thornton Steward, Ripon HG2 2BQ (0677) 50351

Mr Peter Knox (Branch Chairman), 58 Silver Street, Barton, Richmond DL10 6JN (0325) 77258

B H Belshaw (Vice Chairman), Tan House, Borrowby, Thirsk YO7 4QL (0845) 537245

J W Gormley (Branch Organiser), The Old Vicarage, Pickhill, Thirsk, York YO7 4JG (0845) 567240 (home), (0845) 522770 (work)

Mrs Jennie Baker (Branch Membership Secretary), Bridge View Cottage, Bainbridge, North Yorkshire (0969) 50478

R Hawkins (Branch Treasurer), Meadow Croft, Cross Lane, Ingleby Arncliffe, Northallerton DL6 3ND (0609) 776056

G S Grimsditch (Press Officer), Thymallus, Hazel Grove, Grewelthorpe, Ripon (0765) 83741

Dr D Hoyle (Stillwater Officer), The Surgery, Aysgarth, Leyburn DL8 3AA (0969) 3222

Lt Col P A Macgillivray (Water Abstraction Officer), 8 Bridge Street, Richmond DL10 4RW (0748) 823565 (home), (0748) 832521 ext 2017 (work)

Mrs D E Porter (Events Secretary), 3 Church View, Hornby, Bedale D18 3NH (0748) 818951

West Yorkshire:

D P H Hield (Branch Chairman)(Personal), Hield Brothers Ltd, Brigella Mills, Bradford, West Yorkshire BD5 0AQ (0423) 74538 (0274) 571181

P A Ormondroyd (Branch Organiser & Secretary), 8 Nidderdale Walk, Baildon, Shipley, West Yorkshire BD17 6TW (0274) 593741

Mrs J Whitehead (Branch Treasurer), 7 Forster Close, Burley in Wharfedale, Ilkley L28 7HE (0943) 862673

ANGLIAN REGION

A J Cony (Regional Representative), Lavendon Mill, Olney, Bucks MK46 4HJ

Northamptonshire, North Buckinghamshire, Cambridgeshire & Bedford-

shire:

Chris Fleming Jones (Branch Chairman), Elfleda House, 581 Newmarket Road, Cambridge CB5 8PA (0223) 214115

Don Valentine (Branch Organiser), 5 Church Street, St Ives, Huntingdon, Cambridgeshire PE17 4DG

J Goodey (Branch Treasurer), 34 London Street, Whittlesea, Cambridgeshire PE7 1TB

Mr M Heckler (Water Resources Officer), Blunham Court, Blunham, Bedford

Norfolk:

Lt Commander L D Temple-Richards (Branch Chairman), Vale Farm, Stibbard, Fakenham, Norfolk NR21 0EQ (032 8788) 217

Mr P G Pledger (Branch Organiser), Drishaig, Letton Green, Thetford, Norfolk IP25 7PT (0362) 820677 (home), (0362) 820296 (work), Fax: (0362) 820952

Mr R J Deteding (Water Resources Officer), Kelling Hall, Holt, Norfolk NR25 7EW

Lincolnshire & South Humberside:

Dr R W Wallis (Branch Chairman), Hamilton House, Bowl Alley Lane, Horncastle, Lincolnshire LN9 5EQ (0507) 522266

Sqn/Ldr G G Bevan (Branch Organiser), Midthorpe, West Ashby, Lincoln LN9 5PZ (0507 52) 3503

The Rev R G Spaight (Publicity Officer), The Vicarage, Station Road, Langworth, Lincoln LN3 5BB (0522) 754233

Mr David Lang (Treasurer), 4 The Avenue, Healing, Grimsby DN37 7NG (0472) 886109

Hertfordshire:

Dr Ivor S Moss (President), 2 Meadow Banks, Barnet Road, Arkley, Barnet, Herts EN5 3LF

Paul Sansom-Timms (Chairman), Croxley Hall Trout Fishery, Croxley Hall Farm, Rickmansworth, Hertfordshire WD3 3BQ (0923) 778290

Suffolk:

Mr Peter Smith (Chairman), Model Cottage, Brockford Green, Stowmarket, Suffolk IP14 5NL (0449) 767761

Mr C P Forrest, Little Shambles, Swilland, Nr Ipswich, Suffolk IP6 9LT

Essex:

Col J C Carter (Chairman), Round Hill House, Boxted, Colchester, Essex CO4 5ST (0206) 272392

Mr Philip Edge (Secretary), 2 Rye Mill Lane, Feering, Colchester CO5 9SA (0376) 570159

Mr Arthur Preou (Treasurer), 24 Heath Drive, Gidea Park, Romford, Essex RM2 5QJ (0708) 755055

Mr Robert Cracknell (Events Organiser), 83 Hawkswood Road, Sible Hedingham, Halstead, Essex CO9 3JS (0787) 60546

Mr Brian Pugh (Water Resources), Rainbows End, Mayes Lane, Sandon, Chelmsford, Essex CM2 7RW (0245) 223574

THAMES REGION

C W M Glover (Regional Representative), 2 The High Street, Streatley, Berkshire (0491) 872224 (home), 071 377 9242 (work)

Chilterns:

J F Reid (Chairman), 5 Courtlands Drive, Watford, Hertfordshire WD1 3HF

Mr J H Harris (Organiser/Secretary), Vine Cottage, Shabbington, Aylesbury, Buckinghamshire HP18 9HE (0844) 201553

Berkshire:

C W M Glover (Chairman/Organiser), 2 The High Street, Streatley, Berkshire RG8 9JA (0491) 872224 (home), 071 377 9242 (work)

Barry John (Branch Secretary), Ferndown, Spray Road, Ham, Nr Marlborough, Wiltshire SN8 3QR (0488) 668341

R W G Hornsby (Treasurer), The Cruck, 39 The Causeway, Steventon, Oxfordshire OX13 6SE (0235) 831431 (home), (0993) 703041 (work)

Dennis A Boreham MBE (Water Resources Representative), 114 City Road, Tilehurst, Reading, Berkshire RG3 5SD (0734) 421186 (home), (0734) 535354 (office)

Andre Sobczak (P R Representative), 57 Addington Road, Reading, Berkshire RG1 5PZ (0734) 669181

M Metcalfe, Walnut Tree Cottage, Sulham, Pangbourne, Berkshire RG8 8EA (0734) 842494

J A G Coates CBE DFC, 3 The Forge, Bridge Street, Hungerford, Berkshire RG17 0EG (0488) 683694

Jack Hatt, Fox Covert, Goring Heath, Reading, Berkshire (0491) 680424

London:

Mrs A Mallett (Chairman), 23 The Gateways, Chelsea, London SW3 3HX, 071 581 2815

D Chalk (Branch Organiser), 24 Walpole Road, Strawberry Hill, Twickenham, Middlesex TW2 5SN 071 353 9961 (office)

Melville Trimble Esq (Treasurer), 22 Rylett

Road, London W12 9SS, 071 581 2828 (office)

Brian Fratel (Committee Member), 127a Fullwell Avenue Barkingside, Essex IT6 2JG

Surrey:

C L T Jenkins (Branch Chairman), Little Lodge, Fairmile Lane, Cobham, Surrey K11 2DG (0932) 863137 (home), 071 638 4831 (office)

Mr D Bradley (Branch Vice-Chairman and Organiser), 75 Crutchfield Lane, Walton on Thames, Surrey KT12 2QY (0932) 226095(home), 081 568 6884 (office)

Mr P C Radley (Branch Treasurer), 73 Brancaster Lane, Purley, Surrey CR2 1HL 081 660 6614 (office), (0622) 763958 (home)

Mr R Meier (Secretary), Hawkesworth, Childs Hall Road, Bookham, Leatherhead, Surrey KT23 3QG (0372) 457407

SOUTHERN REGION

C B P Duffey, 68 St Cross Road, Winchester, Hampshire SO23 9PS

Hampshire:

C B P Duffey (Chairman), 68 St Cross Road, Winchester, Hampshire SO23 9PS (0420) 82421 (daytime), (0962) 852620 (home)

Mrs D Lewis (Show Organiser), Northbourne, Greywell, Basingstoke

W M Baron (Water Resources), Brandymount House, Alresford, Hampshire SO24 9EG

Dr T Woodcock (Stillwater Liaison), 31 Hiltingbury Road, Chandlers Ford, Hampshire

M Ferguson (Water Resources), Brook House, Wonston, Sutton Scotney, Hampshire

East Sussex

P L McArthur, MC, TD, (Branch Chairman), Pear Tree Cottage, Buckham Hill, Isfield, East Sussex TN22 5XZ (0825) 762552

Lt Cdr Robert Hales (Branch Secretary), 87 Tongdean Lane, Brighton, East Sussex BN1 5JE (0273) 507832

R Osbon (Branch Treasurer), 1 Ashdean Cottages, Rocks Lane, High Hurstwood, Uckfield, East Sussex TN22 6BN (0825) 813629

Dr J Thomas (Water Resources Officer), 1 Lockitt Way, Kingston, Lewes, East Sussex BN7 3LG (0273) 473997

West Sussex:

R M Kohlor (Chairman), Nuthurst, Copse Lane, Walberton, Arundel, West Sussex BN18 0QH

Garry Branningan (Branch Organiser & Secretary), Keeper's Cottage, East Mascalls Lane, Lindfield, West Sussex RH16 2QJ (0444) 484759

Kent:

Colin North (Chairman), 2 Reigate Road, Downham, Bromley, Kent

John Smith (Treasurer), The Cottage, Egerton, Nr Ashford, Kent

Geoffrey Bucknall (Branch Secretary & Organiser), 26 Burnt Ash Lane, Bromley, Kent BR1 4DH, 081 460 9334

Col J Hatherell (Water Resources Officer), 15 Frant Road, Tunbridge Wells, Kent TN2 5SD (0892) 527407

Philip Sharnock (Fishing for Fun Organiser), 34 Shirley Gardens, Rustall, Tunbridge Wells, Kent

WESSEX REGION

D Gifford (Regional Representative), 18 Stanshalls Lane, Felton, Bristol, Avon BS18 7UG (0275) 474495

Wiltshire:

David Maggs (Chairman), 6 The Ridge, Blunsdon, Swindon, Wiltshire (0793) 721429

R Winning (Branch Organiser), Stonecroft, 14 Brewery Street, Highworth, Wiltshire SN6 7AJ (0793) 762836

Gloucestershire, Avon & Somerset:

The Lord Darling (Branch President), Puckpits, Limpley Stoke, Bath, Avon BA3 6JH (0225) 60824

D Gifford (Branch Chairman), 18 Stanshalls Lane, Felton, Bristol, Avon BS18 7UG (0275) 474495

C A Klee (Branch Secretary), Bristol Waterworks Company, P O Box 218, Bridgwater Road, Bristol BS99 7AU (0272) 665881

Dorset:

Christopher R Rothwell (Branch Chairman), The Grey House, East Lulworth, Wareham, Dorset (092 941) 359 (home), (092 941) 352 (work)

R Slocock (Branch Organiser and Water Resources), Wessex Flyfishing, Lawrence's Farm, Southover, Tolpuddle, Nr Dorchester, Dorset DT2 7HF (0305) 848460

SOUTH WEST REGION

Devon & Cornwall:

Mrs Rowan Crichton (Regional Representative), Lapfordwood House, Lapford, Crediton, Devon EX17 6QU Tel: (0363) 83231

North Devon:
Maj Gen T S C Streatfield (Branch Chairman), Toatley Farm, Chawleigh, Chulmleigh, Devon EX18 7HW

T J C Pearkes (Branch Secretary and Organiser), Preston House, Bow, Crediton, Devon EX17 6EZ (0363) 82887

Mr A R Chappell (Branch Treasurer), Silver House, East Street, Chulmleigh, Devon EX18 7DD (0769) 80766

Mr R F J Parrington (Water Resources Officer), Bakers Elstone, Elstone, Chulmleigh, North Devon

South & East Devon & Tamar:
J Hern (Branch Secretary), Watercress Farm, Nr Newton Abbot, Devon Tel: (0626) 852168

Cornwall:
T E F Mutton (Branch Chairman), Lamorran, Old Falmouth Road, Truro, Cornwall TR1 2HN (0872) 73858

S Gardiner (Branch Organiser/Acting Treasurer/ Membership Secretary), 68 Trefusis Road, Flushing, Falmouth, Cornwall TR11 5TY (0326) 377177 (24 hours), Fax: (0326) 372595

A Hawken (Meetings Secretary), 5 Meadow Close, St Stephen, St Austell, Cornwall PL26 7PE (0726) 822343

Gary Champion (Stillwaters Officer), Draycote, 1 Higher Terrace, Ponsanooth, Cornwall TR3 7EW (0872) 863551

Tyson Jackson (Branch Water Res. Officer), Butterwell, Nanstallan, Nr Bodmin, Cornwall PR30 5LQ (0208) 831515

P Boggia (Abstraction & Discharge Applications Officer), 28 Daniell Street, Truro, Cornwall (0872) 72739 (work), (0872) 41389 (home)

Howard Tonkin (Casting Demonstrations), 42 Statham Road, Bodmin, Cornwall (0208) 73219

Ray Burrows (Branch Events Organiser), 26 Meadow Place, Bodmin, Cornwall (0208) 75513

WALES
WELSH REGION (which includes the Wye catchment area)
NORTH WALES
Regional Representative: Mr N Closs Parry, Bryn Ceres, Carmel, Holywell CH8 7DD
SOUTH WALES
Regional Representative: Dr D A T Thomas 29 Lakeside Drive, Cardiff, South Glamorgan CF2 6DD (0222) 689064

Herefordshire:
P Wood (Branch Chairman), 46 The Rugg, Leominster, Herefordshire HR6 8TE

(0568) 614137
Mr N Craddock (Branch Secretary), 8 South Street, Leominster, Herefordshire HR6 8JB (0568) 616999

S Finnegan (Branch Treasurer), Old School House, Brimfield, Ludlow, Shropshire SY18 4MZ (0568) 611479 (work), (058472) 202 (home)

I Watson (Water Resources Officer), Little Hundred, Hundred Lane, Middleton-on-the-Hill, Leominster HR6 6HZ (0584) 72411

S Greatorex-Davies (Public Relations Officer), Ravenshott, Wellington, Hereford HR4 8AT (0432) 71218

Clwyd:
Posts vacant

Gwynedd:
B J Crichton (Branch Chairman), Plas Trefor, Llansadwrn, Isle of Anglesey LL59 5SP

Tom Morgan Jones (Branch Secretary), Tan-y-Waen, Waenfawr, Caernarvon, Gwynedd

Glamorgan:
D Nehemiah (Branch Chairman & Organiser), 13 East Cliff, Pennard, Swansea SA3 2AS (044 128) 2174

R Denner (Assistant Branch Secretary), Broadmead, 24 Oldway, Bishopston, Swansea, West Glamorgan SA3 3DE

Dyfed:
G Roberts (Branch Organiser), Talrhyn, Tresaith Road, Aberporth, Cardigan, Dyfed SA43 2EB (0239) 810515

Powys (South) & Gwent:
A L Carter (Chairman), Old Pengoyffordd, Llanfilo, Brecon, Powys LD3 0RN

C E Brain (Branch Organiser), 24 Porthycarne Street, Usk, Gwent NP5 1RY (02913) 3580 (home), (0633) 214441 (work)

Major S Jones (Treasurer), 52 Edward VII Avenue, Newport, Gwent NP7 4NH

Dr M T P Holloway (Water Resources Officer), 1 Warleton, Duffryn, Cardiff, South Glamorgan CF5 6SW

Cardiff Branch:
Col G C A Greenwood (President), Harpers, 14 Cyncoed Avenue, Cardiff CF2 6SU

Dr T Thomas (Branch Chairman), 29 Lakeside Drive, Cardiff

Mr Tom Hunt (Treasurer), Copperfield, Llancarfan, Barry, South Glamorgan CF6 9AD

Mr S Brown (Secretary & Branch Organiser), 73 Nant Talwg Way, Barry, South Glamorgan CF6 8LZ (0446) 720703

Mr Paul Lillicoe (Water Resources Officer), Top Flat, 31A Coity Road, Bridgend, Mid Glamorgan CF31 1LT (0656) 667522

SCOTLAND
Council Representatives
Mr D M Bythell, vacant (alternate)
Mr J B B Stewart, Mr J B Neill (alternate)

SCOTLAND
The Hon Lord Marnoch (Chairman), 17 Wester Coates Terrace, Edinburgh EH12 5LR

D H Bythell (Vice-Chairman), East Kirkland, Newton Stewart, Wigtownshire D68 9TA

G Bentinck (Treasurer), Messrs Peterkins, Burgh House, 7/9 King Street, Aberdeen AB2 3AA (0224) 626300

Secretarial Office:
Mrs Mary Brown, Kidsons Impey, 23 Queen Street, Edinburgh EH2 1JX. 031 225 2417

Members of the Scottish Council
Honorary Vice Presidents:
Hon Lord Hunter VRD, Little Ruchlaw, Stenton, Dunbar, East Lothian

A D Tennant, Muiresk House, Turriff, Aberdeenshire AB53 7HD

The Hon Lord Marnoch (Chairman), 17 Wester Coates Terrace, Edinburgh EH12 5LR 031-337-5883

Mr Gerald W S Barry, Forge Cottage, Humbie, East Lothian. 087-553-277 (home)

Mr David H Bythell, East Kirkland, Newton Stewart, Wigtownshire DG8 9TA. 09884 2266

Lt Col Robert A Campbell, Altries, Maryculter, Aberdeen AB1 0RD. 0224 733258

The Hon Mrs Jean Cormack, 2 Fethen View, Glen Estate, Innerleithen, Peebleshire EH44 6PX. 0896 830322

Mr Roger Dowling, East Hillocks House, Tullynessle, Alford, Aberdeenshire AB33 8QR

Colin W Innes, 8 Eton Terrace, Edinburgh EH14 1QD. 031-33-2742

Gavin A Hepburn, 22 Mansion House Road, Edinburgh EH9 2OD 031-667-7767 (home), 031-220-3388 (work)

Mrs Mary A H Hunter, 8 Buckingham Terrace, Edinburgh EH4 3AA. 031-332-9028 (home), 031-226-4006 (work), 031-654-2606 (Fax)

Mr John Neill, 10 Oswald Road, Edinburgh EH9 2HF. 031-667-8443 (home), 031-226-4006 (work), 031-654-2606 (fax).

Mr Michael C Smith, Burnside, Dalguise,

By Dunkeld, Tayside PH8 0JL 0350-727593

Mr J B B Stewart, 18 Hope Terrace, Edinburgh EH9 2AR. 031-447-1626

Michael I Wigan, Borrobol, Kinbrace, Sutherland KW11 6UB Fax/Tel 043-13-264

Mr Duncan R Wilson, 152 South Anderson Drive, Aberdeen (0224) 313440

Co-opted Members
Colin Carnie, Messrs Crouch Hogg Waterman, 35 Baird Street, Glasgow G4 0BB. 041 552 2000, 050 587 3144 (home)

Peter C MacDonald, Colzuim Farm, Kirknewton, Midlothian EH27 8DH Tel/Fax 0506 880607

Christopher Robinson, Messrs Roxton Bailey Robinson, 25 High Street, Hungerford, Berkshire RG17 0NF (0488) 683222 (work), (0488) 682977 (fax)

Bruce Sandison, Hysbackie, Tongue, Sutherland. 0847 55274-Tel, 0847 55262 -Fax

Dr Alastair Stephen, 18 Main Street, Kirkcowan, Newton Stewart, Dumfries DG8 0HG. 0671 83322 (work)

Ronald J Stewart, 4 Murthly Terrace, Birnam, Dunkeld PH8 0EG. 0350 727 628

Alan R Whitfield, Laxford House, Laxford Bridge, By Lairg, Sutherland. 059 986 340 and 0971 2300, 0971 84221 (work)

Dr John Pirie, Prenton, South Road, Old Meldrum, Aberdeenshire AB51 0AB (0651) 872229

NORTHERN IRELAND
W Ross MP, Turmel, Dungiven, Co Londonderry, Northern Ireland

Northern Ireland:
T Morrison (Chairman), 55 Shankbridge Road, Kells, Ballymena, Co Antrim (0266) 891512 (home), (08494) 68666

Sir Patrick Macnaghten (Vice-Chairman), 20 Dundarave, Bushmills, Co Antrim (02657) 31215

Mr John Todd (Secretary), 7 Cooleen Park, Jordanstown, Newtownabbey, Co Antrim (0232) 862419

Mr Kenneth E McCracken (Treasurer), 67 Carricknakielt Road, Maghera, Co Londonderry. (0648) 43722 (home), (0648) 68611/68211 (work)

Committee:
Miss E Hamilton, 51 Rathmore Road, Antrim, Co Antrim BT41 2HG (0762) 334666

Neil McWhirter, 36 Woodgreen Road, Shankbridge, Kells, Co Antrim (0232) 322657 (work), (0266) 8916406 (home)

Index

INDEX OF ADVERTISERS